Wimbledon Compendium 2015

Alan Little
Honorary Librarian
Wimbledon Lawn Tennis Museum

The All England Lawn Tennis and Croquet Club
Wimbledon, London

WIMBLEDON COMPENDIUM 2015
Twenty Fifth Year of Publication

Published by
The All England Lawn Tennis and Croquet Club,
Church Road, Wimbledon,
London, SW19 5AE

ISBN 978 1 899039 43 2

Front Cover: The 2014 Singles Champions – Novak Djokovic (Serbia) and
Petra Kvitova (Czech Republic)

Abbreviations of countries

AHO	Netherlands Antillies	GER	Germany (including	POL	Poland
ARG	Argentina		the Federal Republic	PUR	Puerto Rico
AUS	Australia		of Germany,	RHO	Rhodesia
AUT	Austria		1946–1990)	ROM	Romania
BAH	Bahamas	GRE	Greece	RUS	Russia
BEL	Belgium	HAI	Haiti	SCG	Serbia and Montenegro
BLR	Belarus	HKG	Hong Kong	SLO	Slovenia
BOM	Bohemia Moravia	HUN	Hungary	SMR	San Marino
BRA	Brazil	IND	India	SRB	Serbia
BRI	British Isles	INA	Indonesia	SRH	Southern Rhodesia
BUL	Bulgaria	IRL	Ireland	SVK	Slovak Republic
CAN	Canada	ISR	Israel	RSA	South Africa
CEY	Ceylon	ITA	Italy	ESP	Spain
CMR	Cameroon	JAM	Jamaica	STA	Stateless
CHI	Chile	JPN	Japan	SWE	Sweden
CHN	China, People's	KAZ	Kazakhstan	SUI	Switzerland
	Republic of	KEN	Kenya	TCH	Czechoslovakia
CIS	Commonwealth of	KOR	Korea, Republic	THA	Thailand
	Independent States		of (South)	TPE	Chinese Taipei
COL	Colombia	LAT	Latvia	TUN	Tunisia
CRO	Croatia	LEB	Lebanon	UKR	Ukraine
CUB	Cuba	LTU	Lithuania	URS	Union of Soviet
CYP	Cyprus	LUX	Luxembourg		Socialist Republics
CZE	Czech Republic	MAR	Morocco	URU	Uruguay
DEN	Denmark	MEX	Mexico	USA	United States of
ECU	Ecuador	MKD	Macedonia		America
EGY	Egypt	NED	Netherlands	UZB	Uzbekistan
ESA	El Salvador	NZL	New Zealand	VEN	Venezuela
FIN	Finland	NOR	Norway	YUG	Yugoslavia
FRA	France	PAR	Paraguay	ZIM	Zimbabwe
GBR	Great Britain	PER	Peru		
GEO	Georgia	PHI	Philippines		

Contents

8

Champions, Finals and Semi-finals – Scores, Seeding and Duration

The following record shows the concluding matches which have decided the five Championships over the years. From 1878 to 1921 the holder of the Gentlemen's Singles title did not compete until the Challenge Round, when he met the winner of the All Comers' Singles to decide The Championship. When the holder did not defend his title the winner of the All Comers' Singles automatically became champion and the years when this occurred are indicated by an asterisk. The same system applied to the Ladies' Singles and Gentlemen's Doubles from 1886 to 1921, but not the Ladies' Doubles and Mixed Doubles, which both commenced in 1913. In 1922 the Challenge Round was abolished and subsequently all competitors played through.

The duration of the matches, where known, are shown in the last column.

At the end of the section can be found the Ladies listed under different names.

Gentlemen's Singles Championship

CHALLENGE ROUND

Year	Champion	Loser	Score	Mins
1877	S.W. Gore (BRI)			
1878	P.F. Hadow (BRI)	S.W. Gore (BRI)	7-5 6-1 9-7	–
1879*	J.T. Hartley (BRI)		w.o.	
1880	J.T. Hartley (BRI)	H.F. Lawford (BRI)	6-3 6-2 2-6 6-3	–
1881	W.C. Renshaw (BRI)	J.T. Hartley (BRI)	6-0 6-1 6-1	37
1882	W.C. Renshaw (BRI)	J.E. Renshaw (BRI)	6-1 2-6 4-6 6-2 6-2	85
1883	W.C. Renshaw (BRI)	J.E. Renshaw (BRI)	2-6 6-3 6-3 4-6 6-3	89
1884	W.C. Renshaw (BRI)	H.F. Lawford (BRI)	6-0 6-4 9-7	69
1885	W.C. Renshaw (BRI)	H.F. Lawford (BRI)	7-5 6-2 4-6 7-5	122

ALL COMERS' FINAL

Winner	Runner-up	Score	Mins
Gore	W.C. Marshall (BRI)	6-1 6-2 6-4	48
Hadow	L.R. Erskine (BRI)	6-4 6-4 6-4	–
Hartley	V.T.St.L. Goold (BRI)	6-2 6-4 6-2	–
Lawford	O.E. Woodhouse (BRI)	7-5 6-4 6-0	–
Renshaw	R.T. Richardson (BRI)	6-4 6-2 6-3	–
Renshaw	R.T. Richardson (BRI)	7-5 6-3 2-6 6-3	–
Renshaw	D.C. Stewart (BRI)	0-6 6-3 6-0 6-2	48
Lawford	C.W. Grinstead (BRI)	7-5 2-6 6-2 9-7	–
Lawford	J.E. Renshaw (BRI)	5-7 6-1 0-6 6-2 6-4	–

Year	Champion	Loser	Score	Mins	Winner	Runner-up	Score	Mins
1886	W.C. Renshaw (BRI)	H.F. Lawford (BRI)	6-0 5-7 6-3 6-4	96	Lawford	E.W. Lewis (BRI)	6-2 6-3 2-6 4-6 6-4	–
1887*	H.F. Lawford (BRI)		w.o.		Lawford	J.E. Renshaw (BRI)	1-6 6-3 3-6 6-4 6-4	120
1888	J.E. Renshaw (BRI)	H.F. Lawford (BRI)	6-3 7-5 6-0	51	Renshaw	E.W. Lewis (BRI)	7-9 6-1 8-6 6-4	113
1889	W.C. Renshaw (BRI)	J.E. Renshaw (BRI)	6-4 6-1 3-6 6-0	63	Renshaw	H.S. Barlow (BRI)	3-6 5-7 8-6 10-8 8-6	–
1890	W.J. Hamilton (BRI)	W.C. Renshaw (BRI)	6-8 6-2 3-6 6-1 6-1	96	Hamilton	H.S. Barlow (BRI)	2-6 6-4 6-4 4-6 7-5	–
1891*	W. Baddeley (BRI)		w.o.		Baddeley	J. Pim (BRI)	6-4 1-6 7-5 6-0	–
1892	W. Baddeley (BRI)	J. Pim (BRI)	4-6 6-3 6-3 6-2	75	Pim	E.W. Lewis (BRI)	2-6 5-7 9-7 6-3 6-2	110
1893	J. Pim (BRI)	W. Baddeley (BRI)	3-6 6-1 6-3 6-2	65	Pim	H.S. Mahony (BRI)	9-7 6-3 6-0	–
1894	J. Pim (BRI)	W. Baddeley (BRI)	10-8 6-2 8-6	117	Baddeley	E.W. Lewis (BRI)	6-0 6-1 6-0	–
1895*	W. Baddeley (BRI)		w.o.		Baddeley	W.V. Eaves (BRI)	4-6 2-6 8-6 6-2 6-3	95
1896	H.S. Mahony (BRI)	W. Baddeley (BRI)	6-2 6-8 5-7 8-6 6-3	120	Mahony	W.V. Eaves (BRI)	6-2 6-2 11-9	–
1897	R.F. Doherty (BRI)	H.S. Mahony (BRI)	6-4 6-4 6-3	67	Doherty	W.V. Eaves (BRI)	6-3 7-5 2-0 ret'd	–
1898	R.F. Doherty (BRI)	H.L. Doherty (BRI)	6-3 6-3 2-6 5-7 6-1	55	Doherty	H.S. Mahony (BRI)	6-1 6-2 4-6 2-6 14-12	140
1899	R.F. Doherty (BRI)	A.W. Gore (BRI)	1-6 4-6 6-3 6-3 6-3	–	Gore	S.H. Smith	3-6 6-2 6-1 6-4	–
1900	R.F. Doherty (BRI)	S.H. Smith (BRI)	6-8 6-3 6-1 6-2	72	Smith	A.W. Gore (BRI)	6-4 4-6 6-2 6-1	–
1901	A.W. Gore (BRI)	R.F. Doherty (BRI)	4-6 7-5 6-4 6-4	95	Gore	C.P. Dixon (BRI)	6-4 6-0 6-3	–
1902	H.L. Doherty (BRI)	A.W. Gore (BRI)	6-4 6-3 3-6 6-0	84	Doherty	M.J.G. Ritchie (BRI)	8-6 6-3 7-5	–
1903	H.L. Doherty (BRI)	F.L. Riseley (BRI)	7-5 6-3 6-0	–	Riseley	M.J.G. Ritchie (BRI)	1-6 6-3 8-6 13-11	–
1904	H.L. Doherty (BRI)	F.L. Riseley (BRI)	6-1 7-5 8-6		Riseley	M.J.G. Ritchie (BRI)	6-0 6-1 6-2	35
1905	H.L. Doherty (BRI)	N.E. Brookes (AUS)	8-6 6-2 6-4	65	Brookes	S.H. Smith (BRI)	1-6 6-4 6-1 1-6 7-5	–
1906	H.L. Doherty (BRI)	F.L. Riseley (BRI)	6-4 4-6 6-2 6-3	74	Riseley	A.W. Gore (BRI)	6-3 6-3 6-4	–
1907*	N.E. Brookes (AUS)		w.o.		Brookes	A.W. Gore (BRI)	6-4 6-2 6-2	–
1908*	A.W. Gore (BRI)		w.o.		Gore	H.R. Barrett (BRI)	6-3 6-2 4-6 3-6 6-4	–
1909	A.W. Gore (BRI)	M.J.G. Ritchie (BRI)	6-8 1-6 6-2 6-2 6-2	95	Ritchie	H.R. Barrett (BRI)	6-2 6-3 4-6 6-4	88
1910	A.F. Wilding (NZL)	A.W. Gore (BRI)	6-4 7-5 4-6 6-2	–	Wilding	B.C. Wright (USA)	4-6 4-6 6-3 6-2 6-3	–
1911	A.F. Wilding (NZL)	H.R. Barrett (BRI)	6-4 4-6 2-6 6-2 retd	–	Barrett	C.P. Dixon (BRI)	5-7 4-6 6-4 6-3 6-1	–
1912	A.F. Wilding (NZL)	A.W. Gore (BRI)	6-4 6-4 4-6 6-4	–	Gore	A.H. Gobert (FRA)	9-7 2-6 7-5 6-1	–
1913	A.F. Wilding (NZL)	M.E. McLoughlin (USA)	8-6 6-3 10-8	–	McLoughlin	S.N. Doust (AUS)	6-3 6-4 7-5	–
1914	N.E. Brookes (AUS)	A.F. Wilding (NZL)	6-4 6-4 7-5	–	Brookes	O. Froitzheim (GER)	6-2 6-1 5-7 4-6 8-6	–
1919	G.L. Patterson (AUS)	N.E Brookes (AUS)	6-3 7-5 6-2	–	Patterson	A.R.F. Kingscote (BRI)	6-2 6-1 6-3	–
1920	W.T. Tilden (USA)	G.L. Patterson (AUS)	2-6 6-3 6-2 6-4	–	Tilden	Z. Shimidzu (JPN)	6-4 6-4 13-11	–
1921	W.T. Tilden (USA)	B.I.C. Norton (RSA)	4-6 2-6 6-1 6-0 7-5	–	Norton	M. Alonso (ESP)	5-7 4-6 7-5 6-3 6-3	–

Challenge Round abolished.

FINAL

Year	Champion	Seeded	Runner-up	Seeded	Score	Mins
1922	G.L. Patterson (AUS)		R. Lycett (BRI)		6-3 6-4 6-2	–
1923	W.M. Johnston (USA)		F.T. Hunter (USA)		6-0 6-3 6-1	46
1924	J.R. Borotra (FRA)		J.R. Lacoste (FRA)		6-1 3-6 6-1 3-6 6-4	80
1925	J.R. Lacoste (FRA)		J.R. Borotra (FRA)		6-3 6-3 4-6 8-6	–
1926	J.R. Borotra (FRA)		H.O. Kinsey (USA)		8-6 6-1 6-3	65
1927	H.J. Cochet (FRA)	4	J.R. Borotra (FRA)	3	4-6 4-6 6-3 6-4 7-5	–
1928	J.R. Lacoste (FRA)	2	H.J. Cochet (FRA)	1	6-1 4-6 6-4 6-2	–
1929	H.J. Cochet (FRA)	1	J.R. Borotra (FRA)	2	6-4 6-3 6-4	60
1930	W.T. Tilden (USA)	U	W.L. Allison (USA)	2	6-3 9-7 6-4	70
1931	S.B.B. Wood (USA)	7	F.X. Shields (USA)	3	w.o.	
1932	H.E. Vines (USA)	2	H.W. Austin (GBR)	6	6-4 6-2 6-0	50
1933	J.H. Crawford (AUS)	2	H.E. Vines (USA)	1	4-6 11-9 6-2 2-6 6-4	120
1934	F.J. Perry (GBR)	1	J.H. Crawford (AUS)	1	6-3 6-0 7-5	72
1935	F.J. Perry (GBR)	1	G. von Cramm (GER)	2	6-2 6-4 6-4	80
1936	F.J. Perry (GBR)	1	G. von Cramm (GER)	2	6-1 6-1 6-0	40
1937	J.D. Budge (USA)	1	G. von Cramm (GER)	2	6-3 6-4 6-2	65

SEMI-FINAL

Winner	Loser	Seeded	Score	Mins
Patterson	J.O. Anderson (AUS)		6-1 3-6 7-9 6-1 6-3	–
Lycett	J.B. Gilbert (BRI)		8-6 9-7 6-3	–
Johnston	B.I.C. Norton (RSA)		6-4 6-2 6-4	–
Hunter	F.G. Lowe (GBR)		6-3 7-5 6-4	–
Borotra	L.B. Raymond (RSA)		6-2 6-4 7-5	–
Lacoste	R.N. Williams (USA)		6-1 3-6 6-2 6-3	–
Lacoste	J.O. Anderson (AUS)		6-4 7-5 7-1	–
Borotra	H.J. Cochet (FRA)		5-7 8-6 6-4 6-1	–
Borotra	H.J. Cochet (FRA)		2-6 7-5 2-6 6-3 7-5	–
Kinsey	J. Brugnon (FRA)		6-4 4-6 6-3 3-6 9-7	120
Cochet	W.T. Tilden (USA)	2	2-6 4-6 7-5 6-4 6-3	105
Borotra	J.R. Lacoste (FRA)	1	6-4 6-3 1-6 1-6 6-2	–
Lacoste	W.T. Tilden (USA)	3	2-6 6-4 2-6 6-4 6-3	105
Cochet	J.C. Boussus (FRA)	U	11-9 3-6 6-2 6-3	–
Cochet	W.T. Tilden (USA)	3	6-4 6-1 7-5	63
Borotra	H.W. Austin (GBR)	U	6-1 10-8 5-7 6-1	–
Tilden	J.R. Borotra (FRA)	3	0-6 4-6 6-0 7-5	–
Allison	J.T.G.H. Doeg (USA)	4	6-3 4-6 8-6 3-6 7-5	–
Wood	F.J. Perry (GBR)	5	4-6 6-2 6-4 6-2	–
Shields	J.R. Borotra (FRA)	1	7-5 3-6 6-4 6-4	–
Vines	J.H. Crawford (AUS)	8	6-2 6-1 6-3	40
Austin	J. Satoh (JAP)	U	7-5 6-2 6-1	52
Crawford	H.J. Cochet (FRA)	7	6-3 6-4 2-6 6-4	–
Vines	J. Satoh (JAP)	3	6-2 8-6 3-6 6-1	–
Perry	S.B.B. Wood (USA)	7	6-3 3-6 7-5 5-7 6-3	105
Crawford	F.X. Shields (USA)	5	2-6 4-6 6-4 6-3 6-4	125
Perry	J.H. Crawford (USA)	3	6-2 3-6 6-4 6-4	95
von Cramm	J.D. Budge (USA)	U	4-6 6-4 6-3 6-2	90
Perry	J.D. Budge (USA)	5	5-7 6-4 6-3 6-4	94
von Cramm	H.W. Austin (GBR)	7	8-6 6-3 2-6 6-3	105
Budge	F.A. Parker (USA)	8	2-6 6-4 6-4 6-1	90
von Cramm	H.W. Austin (GBR)	4	8-6 6-3 12-14 6-1	140

The Final

Year	Champion	Seeded	Runner-up	Seeded	Score	Mins
1938	J.D. Budge (USA)	1	H.W. Austin (GBR)	2	6-1 6-0 6-3	59
1939	R.L. Riggs (USA)	2	E.T. Cooke (USA)	6	2-6 8-6 3-6 6-3 6-2	135
1946	Y.F.M. Petra (FRA)	5	G.E. Brown (AUS)	3	6-2 6-4 7-9 5-7 6-4	–
1947	J.A. Kramer (USA)	1	T.P. Brown (USA)	3	6-1 6-3 6-2	45
1948	R. Falkenburg (USA)	7	J.E. Bromwich (AUS)	2	7-5 0-6 6-2 3-6 7-5	125
1949	F.R. Schroeder (USA)	1	J. Drobny (TCH)	6	3-6 6-0 6-3 4-6 6-4	100
1950	J.E. Patty (USA)	5	F.A. Sedgman (AUS)	1	6-1 8-10 6-2 6-3	120
1951	R. Savitt (USA)	6	K.B. McGregor (AUS)	7	6-4 6-4 6-4	62
1952	F.A. Sedgman (AUS)	1	J. Drobny (EGY)	2	4-6 6-2 6-3 6-2	80
1953	E.V. Seixas (USA)	2	K. Nielsen (DEN)	U	9-7 6-3 6-4	80
1954	J. Drobny (EGY)	11	K.R. Rosewall (AUS)	3	13-11 4-6 6-2 9-7	157
1955	M.A. Trabert (USA)	1	K. Nielsen (DEN)	U	6-3 7-5 6-1	73
1956	L.A. Hoad (AUS)	1	K.R. Rosewall (AUS)	2	6-2 4-6 7-5 6-4	117
1957	L.A. Hoad (AUS)	1	A.J. Cooper (AUS)	2	6-2 6-1 6-2	57
1958	A.J. Cooper (AUS)	1	N.A. Fraser (AUS)	4	3-6 6-3 6-4 13-11	130
1959	A.R. Olmedo (USA)	1	R.G. Laver (AUS)	U	6-4 6-3 6-4	71
1960	N.A. Fraser (AUS)	1	R.G. Laver (AUS)	3	6-4 3-6 9-7 7-5	130

Semi-Finals

Winner	Loser	Seeded	Score	Mins
Budge	F.A. Puncec (YUG)	5	6-2 6-1 6-4	60
Austin	H.E.O. Henkel (GER)	4	6-2 6-4 6-0	58
Riggs	F.A. Puncec (YUG)	4	6-2 6-3 6-4	65
Cooke	H.E.O. Henkel (GER)	5	6-3 4-6 6-4 6-4	100
Petra	T.P. Brown (USA)	U	4-6 4-6 6-3 7-5 8-6	–
Brown	J. Drobny (TCH)	U	6-4 7-5 6-2	–
Kramer	J.E. Patty (USA)	U	6-3 6-3 6-3	–
Brown	D.R. Pails (AUS)	4	6-1 3-6 6-1 6-0	–
Falkenburg	G.P. Mulloy (USA)	3	6-4 6-4 8-6	–
Bromwich	J. Asboth (HUN)	U	6-2 14-12 6-2	–
Schroeder	E.W. Sturgess (RSA)	7	3-6 7-5 5-7 6-1 6-2	61
Drobny	J.E. Bromwich (AUS)	5	6-1 6-3 6-2	95
Patty	E.V. Seixas (USA)	12	6-3 5-7 6-2 7-5	120
Sedgman	J. Drobny (EGY)	3	3-6 3-6 6-3 7-5 6-2	120
Savitt	H. Flam (USA)	5	1-6 15-13 6-3 6-2	85
McGregor	E.W. Sturgess (RSA)	8	6-4 3-6 6-3 7-5	70
Sedgman	M.G. Rose (AUS)	8	6-4 6-4 7-5	147
Drobny	H. Flam (USA)	6	6-2 6-4 0-6 8-10 6-4	158
Seixas	M.G. Rose (AUS)	3	6-4 10-12 9-11 6-4 6-3	60
Nielsen	J. Drobny (EGY)	4	6-4 6-3 6-2	105
Drobny	J.E. Patty (USA)	7	6-2 6-4 4-6 9-7	115
Rosewall	M.A. Trabert (USA)	1	3-6 6-3 4-6 6-1 6-1	86
Trabert	J.E. Patty (USA)	7	8-6 6-2 6-2	124
Nielsen	K.R. Rosewall (AUS)	2	11-9 6-2 2-6 6-4	93
Hoad	H.F. Richardson (USA)	6	3-6 6-4 6-2 6-4	144
Rosewall	E.V. Seixas (USA)	8	6-3 3-6 6-8 6-3 7-5	86
Hoad	S.V. Davidson (SWE)	4	6-4 6-4 7-5	135
Cooper	N.A. Fraser (AUS)	5	1-6 14-12 6-3 8-6	83
Cooper	M.G. Rose (AUS)	3	7-9 6-2 6-3	170
Fraser	K. Nielsen (DEN)	6	6-4 6-4 17-19 6-4	58
Olmedo	R.S. Emerson (AUS)	8	6-4 6-0 6-4	225
Laver	B.B. MacKay (USA)	5	11-13 11-9 10-8 7-9 6-3	68
Fraser	R. Krishnan (IND)	7	6-3 6-2 6-2	117
Laver	N. Pietrangeli (ITA)	5	4-6 6-3 8-10 6-2 6-4	

Year	Champion	Seeded	Runner-up	Seeded	Score	Mins
1961	R.G. Laver (AUS)	2	C.R. McKinley (USA)	8	6-3 6-1 6-4	55
1962	R.G. Laver (AUS)	1	M.F. Mulligan (AUS)	U	6-2 6-2 6-1	51
1963	C.R. McKinley (USA)	4	F.S. Stolle (AUS)	U	9-7 6-1 6-4	78
1964	R.S. Emerson (AUS)	1	F.S. Stolle (AUS)	6	6-4 12-10 4-6 6-3	127
1965	R.S. Emerson (AUS)	1	F.S. Stolle (AUS)	2	6-2 6-4 6-4	67
1966	M.M. Santana (ESP)	4	R.D. Ralston (USA)	6	6-4 11-9 6-4	104
1967	J.D. Newcombe (AUS)	3	W.P. Bungert (GER)	U	6-3 6-1 6-1	71
1968	R.G. Laver (AUS)	1	A.D. Roche (AUS)	15	6-3 6-4 6-2	60
1969	R.G. Laver (AUS)	1	J.D. Newcombe (AUS)	6	6-4 5-7 6-4 6-4	136
1970	J.D. Newcombe (AUS)	2	K.R. Rosewall (AUS)	5	5-7 6-3 6-2 3-6 6-1	163
1971	J.D. Newcombe (AUS)	2	S.R. Smith (USA)	4	6-3 5-7 2-6 6-4 6-4	170
1972	S.R. Smith (USA)	1	I. Nastase (ROM)	2	4-6 6-3 6-3 4-6 7-5	161
1973	J. Kodes (TCH)	2	A.I. Metreveli (URS)	4	6-1 9-8 (7-5) 6-3	110
1974	J.S. Connors (USA)	3	K.R. Rosewall (AUS)	9	6-1 6-1 6-4	93
1975	A.R. Ashe (USA)	6	J.S. Connors (USA)	1	6-1 6-1 5-7 6-4	125
1976	B.R. Borg (SWE)	4	I. Nastase (ROM)	3	6-4 6-2 9-7	110
1977	B.R. Borg (SWE)	2	J.S. Connors (USA)	1	3-6 6-2 6-1 5-7 6-4	194
1978	B.R. Borg (SWE)	1	J.S. Connors (USA)	2	6-2 6-2 6-3	108

Winner	Loser	Seeded	Score	Mins
Laver	R. Krishnan (IND)	7	6-2 8-6 6-2	58
McKinley	M.J. Sangster (GBR)	U	6-4 6-4 8-6	80
Laver	N.A. Fraser (AUS)	3	10-8 6-1 7-5	89
Mulligan	J.G. Fraser (AUS)	U	6-3 6-2 6-2	60
McKinley	W.P. Bungert (GER)	U	6-2 6-4 8-6	71
Stolle	M.M. Santana (ESP)	2	8-6 6-1 7-5	90
Emerson	W.P. Bungert (GER)	U	6-3 15-13 6-0	107
Stolle	C.R. McKinley (USA)	2	4-6 10-8 9-7 6-4	142
Emerson	R.D. Ralston (USA)	4	6-1 6-2 7-9 6-1	105
Stolle	E.C. Drysdale (RSA)	U	6-3 6-4 7-5	–
Santana	O.K. Davidson (AUS)	U	6-2 4-6 9-7 3-6 7-5	170
Ralston	E.C. Drysdale (RSA)	7	6-8 8-6 3-6 7-5 6-3	170
Newcombe	N. Pilic (YUG)	U	9-7 4-6 6-3 6-4	145
Bungert	R. Taylor (GBR)	U	6-4 6-8 2-6 6-4 6-4	130
Laver	A.R. Ashe (USA)	13	7-5 6-2 6-4	–
Roche	C.E. Graebner (USA)	S	9-7 8-10 6-4 8-6	150
Laver	A.R. Ashe (USA) .	S	2-6 6-2 9-7 6-0	92
Newcombe	A.D. Roche (AUS)	2	3-6 6-1 14-12 6-4	162
Newcombe	A. Gimeno (ESP)	14	6-3 8-6 6-0	75
Rosewall	R. Taylor (GBR)	16	6-3 4-6 6-3 6-3	112
Newcombe	K.R. Rosewall (AUS)	3	6-1 6-1 6-3	85
Smith	T.W. Gorman (USA)	U	6-3 8-6 6-2	82
Smith	J. Kodes (TCH)	5	3-6 6-4 6-1 7-5	130
Nastase	M. Orantes (ESP)	3	6-3 6-4 6-4	74
Kodes	R. Taylor (GBR)	3	8-9 (7-9) 9-7 5-7 6-4 7-5	216
Metreveli	A. Mayer (USA)	U	6-3 3-6 6-3 6-4	102
Connors	R.L. Stockton (USA)	U	4-6 6-2 6-3 6-4	–
Rosewall	S.R. Smith (USA)	4	6-8 4-6 9-8 (8-6) 6-1 6-3	188
Ashe	A.D Roche (AUS)	14	5-7 6-4 7-5 8-9 (4-7) 6-4	171
Connors	R.L. Tanner (USA)	11	6-4 6-1 6-4	78
Borg	R.L. Tanner (USA)	7	6-4 9-8 (7-2) 6-4	–
Nastase	R.C. Ramirez (MEX)	8	6-2 9-7 6-3	112
Borg	V.K. Gerulaitis (USA)	8	6-4 3-6 6-3 3-6 8-6	180
Connors	J.P. McEnroe (USA)	U	6-3 6-3 4-6 6-4	157
Borg	T.S. Okker (NED)	U	6-4 6-4 6-4	–
Connors	V.K. Gerulaitis (USA)	3	9-7 6-2 6-1	121

The Final

Year	Champion	Seeded	Runner-up	Seeded	Score	Mins
1979	B.R. Borg (SWE)	1	L.R. Tanner (USA)	5	6-7 (4-7) 6-1 3-6 6-3 6-4	169
1980	B.R. Borg (SWE)	1	J.P. McEnroe (USA)	2	1-6 7-5 6-3 6-7 (16-18) 8-6	233
1981	J.P. McEnroe (USA)	2	B.R. Borg (SWE)	1	4-6 7-6 (7-1) 6-4	202
1982	J.S. Connors (USA)	2	J.P. McEnroe (USA)	1	3-6 6-3 6-7 (2-7) 7-6 (7-5) 6-4	256
1983	J.P. McEnroe (USA)	2	C.J. Lewis (NZL)	U	6-2 6-2 6-2	85
1984	J.P. McEnroe (USA)	1	J.S. Connors (USA)	3	6-1 6-1 6-2	80
1985	B.F. Becker (GER)	U	K.M. Curren (USA)	8	6-3 6-7 (4-7) 7-6 (7-3) 6-4	198
1986	B.F. Becker (GER)	4	I. Lendl (TCH)	1	6-4 6-3 7-5	122
1987	P.H. Cash (AUS)	11	I. Lendl (TCH)	2	7-6 (7-5) 6-2 7-5	165
1988	S.B. Edberg (SWE)	3	B.F. Becker (GER)	6	4-6 7-6 (7-2) 6-4 6-2	170
1989	B.F. Becker (GER)	3	S.B. Edberg (SWE)	2	6-0 7-6 (7-1) 6-4	132
1990	S.B. Edberg (SWE)	3	B.F. Becker (GER)	2	6-2 6-2 3-6 3-6 6-4	178
1991	M.D. Stich (GER)	6	B.F. Becker (GER)	2	6-4 7-6 (7-4) 6-4	153
1992	A.K. Agassi (USA)	12	G.S. Ivanisevic (CRO)	8	6-7 (8-10) 6-4 6-4 1-6 6-4	170
1993	P. Sampras (USA)	1	J.S. Courier (USA)	3	7-6 (7-3) 7-6 (8-6) 3-6 6-3	178
1994	P. Sampras (USA)	1	G.S. Ivanisevic (CRO)	4	7-6 (7-2) 7-6 (7-5) 6-0	115
1995	P. Sampras (USA)	2	B.F. Becker (GER)	3	6-7 (5-7) 6-2 6-4 6-2	149

The Semi-Finals

Year	Winner	Loser	Seeded	Score	Mins
1979	Borg	J.S. Connors (USA)	3	6-2 6-3 6-2	106
1979	Tanner	P. Dupre (USA)	U	6-3 7-6 (7-3) 6-3	–
1980	Borg	B.E. Gottfried (USA)	U	6-2 4-6 6-2 6-0	118
1980	McEnroe	J.S. Connors (USA)	3	6-3 6-3 6-4	–
1981	McEnroe	R.J. Frawley (AUS)	U	7-6 (7-2) 6-4 7-5	182
1981	Borg	J.S. Connors (USA)	3	0-6 4-6 6-3 6-0 6-4	199
1982	Connors	M.R. Edmondson (AUS)	12	6-4 6-3 6-1	99
1982	McEnroe	T.S. Mayotte (AUS)	U	6-3 6-1 6-2	117
1983	McEnroe	I. Lendl (TCH)	3	7-6 (7-5) 6-4 6-4	111
1983	Lewis	K.M.Curren (RSA)	12	6-7 (3-7) 6-4 7-6 (7-4) 6-7 (3-7) 8-6	224
1984	McEnroe	P.H. Cash (AUS)	U	6-3 7-6 (7-5) 6-4	128
1984	Connors	I. Lendl (TCH)	2	6-7 (4-7) 6-3 7-5 6-1	177
1985	Becker	A.P. Jarryd (SWE)	5	2-6 7-6 (7-3) 6-3 6-3	166
1985	Curren	J.S. Connors (USA)	5	6-2 6-2 6-1	92
1986	Becker	H. Leconte (FRA)	3	6-2 6-4 6-7 (4-7) 6-3	144
1986	Lendl	S. Zivojinovic (YUG)	7	6-2 6-7 (5-7) 6-3 6-7 (1-7) 6-4	210
1987	Cash	J.S. Connors (USA)	U	6-4 6-4 6-1	115
1987	Lendl	S.B. Edberg (SWE)	7	3-6 6-4 7-6 (10-8) 6-4	183
1988	Edberg	M. Mecir (TCH)	4	4-6 2-6 6-3 6-4	190
1988	Becker	I. Lendl (TCH)	9	6-4 6-3 6-7 (8-10) 6-4	229
1989	Becker	I. Lendl (TCH)	1	7-5 6-7 (2-7) 2-6 6-4 6-3	241
1989	Edberg	J.P. McEnroe (USA)	1	7-5 7-6 (7-2) 7-6 (7-5)	193
1990	Edberg	I. Lendl (TCH)	5	6-1 7-6 (7-2) 6-3	108
1990	Becker	G. Ivanisevic (YUG)	1	4-6 7-6 (7-4) 6-0 7-6 (7-5)	148
1991	Stich	S.B. Edberg (SWE)	1	4-6 7-6 (7-5) 7-6 (7-5) 7-6 (7-2)	188
1991	Becker	D. Wheaton (USA)	U	6-4 7-6 (7-4) 7-5	165
1992	Agassi	J.P. McEnroe (USA)	U	6-4 6-2 6-3	111
1992	Ivanisevic	P. Sampras (USA)	5	6-7 (4-7) 7-6 (7-5)	132
1993	Sampras	B.F. Becker (GER)	4	6-4 6-2	134
1993	Courier	S.B. Edberg (SWE)	2	7-6 (7-5) 6-4 6-4	160
1994	Sampras	T. Martin (USA)	6	4-6 4-6 6-2 6-4	154
1994	Ivanisevic	B.F. Becker (GER)	7	6-4 3-6 6-3	114
1995	Sampras	G.S. Ivanisevic (CRO)	2	6-2 7-6 (8-6) 6-4	153
1995	Becker	A.K. Agassi (USA)	1	2-6 7-6 (7-1) 6-4 7-6 (7-1)	175

Finals

Year	Champion	Seeded	Runner-up	Seeded	Score	Mins
1996	R.P.S. Krajicek (NED)	S	M.O. Washington (USA)	U	6-3 6-4 6-3	94
1997	P. Sampras (USA)	1	C.A. Pioline (FRA)	U	6-4 6-2 6-4	94
1998	P. Sampras (USA)	1	G.S. Ivanisevic (CRO)	14	6-7 (2-7) 7-6 (11-9) 6-4 3-6 6-2	172
1999	P. Sampras (USA)	1	A.K. Agassi (USA)	4	6-3 6-4 7-5	115
2000	P. Sampras (USA)	1	P.M. Rafter (AUS)	12	6-7 (10-12) 7-6 (7-5) 6-4 6-2	182
2001	G.S. Ivanisevic (CRO)	U	P.M. Rafter (AUS)	3	6-3 3-6 6-3 2-6 9-7	182
2002	L.G. Hewitt (AUS)	1	D.P. Nalbandian (ARG)	28	6-1 6-3 6-2	116
2003	R. Federer (SUI)	4	M.A. Philippoussis (AUS)	U	7-6 (7-5) 6-2 7-6 (7-3)	119
2004	R. Federer (SUI)	1	A.S. Roddick (USA)	2	4-6 7-5 7-6 (7-3) 6-4	151
2005	R. Federer (SUI)	1	A.S. Roddick (USA)	2	6-2 7-6 (7-2) 6-4	101
2006	R. Federer (SUI)	1	R. Nadal (ESP)	2	6-0 7-6 (7-5) 6-7 (2-7) 6-3	178
2007	R. Federer (SUI)	1	R. Nadal (ESP)	2	7-6 (9-7) 4-6 7-6 (7-3) 2-6 6-2	225
2008	R. Nadal (ESP)	2	R. Federer (SUI)	1	6-4 6-4 6-7 (5-7) 6-7 (8-10) 9-7	288
2009	R. Federer (SUI)	2	A.S. Roddick (USA)	6	5-7 7-6 (8-6) 7-6 (7-5) 3-6 16-14	258
2010	R. Nadal (ESP)	2	T. Berdych (CZE)	12	6-3 7-5 6-4	133
2011	N. Djokovic (SRB)	2	R. Nadal (ESP)	1	6-4 6-1 1-6 6-3	149
2012	R. Federer (SUI)	3	A.B. Murray (GBR)	4	4-6 7-5 6-3 6-4	204
2013	A.B. Murray (GBR)	2	N. Djokovic (SRB)	1	6-4 7-5 6-4	190
2014	N. Djokovic (SRB)	1	R. Federer (SUI)	4	6-7 (7-9) 6-4 7-6 (7-4) 5-7 6-4	238

Semi-finals

Winner	Loser	Seeded	Score	Mins
Krajicek	J.R. Stoltenberg (AUS)	U	7-5 6-2 6-1	100
Washington	T.C. Martin (USA)	13	5-7 6-4 6-7 (6-8) 6-3 10-8	229
Sampras	T.A. Woodbridge (AUS)	U	6-2 6-1 7-6 (7-3)	104
Pioline	M.D. Stich (GER)	U	6-7 (2-7) 6-2 6-1 5-7 6-4	180
Sampras	T.H. Henman (GBR)	12	6-3 4-6 7-5 6-3	144
Ivanisevic	R.P.S. Krajicek (NED)	9	6-3 6-4 5-7 6-7 (5-7) 15-13	202
Sampras	T.H. Henman (GBR)	6	3-6 6-4 6-3 6-4	168
Agassi	P.M. Rafter (AUS)	2	7-5 7-6 (7-5) 6-2	124
Sampras	V. Voltchkov (BLR)	U	7-6 (7-4) 6-2 6-4	99
Rafter	A.K. Agassi (USA)	2	7-5 4-6 7-5 4-6 6-3	198
Ivanisevic	T.H. Henman (GBR)	6	7-5 6-7 (6-8) 0-6 7-6 (7-5) 6-3	198
Rafter	A.K. Agassi (USA)	2	2-6 6-3 3-6 6-2 8-6	180
Hewitt	T.H. Henman (GBR)	4	7-5 6-1 7-5	139
Nalbandian	X. Malisse (BEL)	27	7-6 (6-2) 6-4 1-6 2-6 6-2	198
Federer	A.S. Roddick (USA)	5	7-6 (8-6) 6-3 6-3	104
Philippoussis	S.R. Grosjean (FRA)	13	7-6 (7-3) 6-3 6-3	116
Federer	S.R. Grosjean (FRA)	10	6-2 6-3 7-6 (8-6)	120
Roddick	M. Ancic (CRO)	U	6-4 4-6 7-5 7-5	171
Federer	L.G. Hewitt (AUS)	3	6-3 6-4 7-6 (7-4)	128
Roddick	T.J. Johansson (SWE)	12	6-7 (6-8) 6-2 7-6 (12-10)	179
Federer	J.L. Bjorkman (SWE)	U	6-2 6-0 6-2	77
Nadal	M. Baghdatis (CYP)	18	6-1 7-5 6-3	148
Federer	R. Gasquet (FRA)	12	7-5 6-3 6-4	105
Nadal	N. Djokovic (SRB)	4	3-6 6-1 4-1 retd	101
Nadal	R. Schuettler (GER)	U	6-1 7-6 (7-3) 6-4	122
Federer	M. Safin (RUS)	U	6-3 7-6 (7-3) 6-4	102
Federer	T. Haas (GER)	24	7-6 (7-3) 7-5 6-3	123
Roddick	A.B. Murray (GBR)	3	6-4 4-6 7-6 (9-7) 7-6 (7-5)	187
Berdych	N. Djokovic (SRB)	3	6-3 7-6 (11-9) 6-3	138
Nadal	A.B. Murray (GBR)	4	6-4 7-6 (8-6) 6-4	141
Nadal	A.B. Murray (GBR)	4	5-7 6-2 6-2 6-4	179
Djokovic	J-W. Tsonga (FRA)	12	7-6 (7-4) 6-2 6-7 (9-11) 6-3	187
Federer	N. Djokovic (SRB)	1	6-3 3-6 6-4 6-3	140
Murray	J-W. E Tsonga (FRA)	5	6-3 6-4 3-6 7-5	168
Djokovic	J.M. Del Porro (ARG)	8	7-5 4-6 7-6 (7-2) 6-7 (8-6) 6-3	284
Murray	J. Janowicz (POL)	24	6-7 (2-7) 6-4 6-4 6-3	172
Djokovic	G. Dimitrov (BUL)	11	6-4 3-6 7-6 (7-2) 7-6 (9-7)	182
Federer	M. Raonic (CAN)	8	6-4 6-4 6-4	102

Gentlemen's Doubles Championship

CHALLENGE ROUND

Year	Champions	Losers	Score	Mins
1884	J.E. Renshaw and W.C. Renshaw (BRI)			-
1885	J.E. Renshaw and W.C. Renshaw (BRI)			-
1886	J.E. Renshaw and W.C. Renshaw (BRI)	C.E. Farrer and A.J. Stanley (BRI)	6-3 6-3 4-6 7-5	-
1887*	P.B. Lyon and H.W.W. Wilberforce (BRI)		w.o.	-
1888	J.E. Renshaw and W.C. Renshaw (BRI)	P.B. Lyon and H.W.W. Wilberforce (BRI)	2-6 1-6 6-3 6-4 6-3	-
1889	J.E. Renshaw and W.C. Renshaw (BRI)	G.W. Hillyard and E.W. Lewis (BRI)	6-4 6-4 3-6 0-6 6-1	-
1890*	J. Pim and F.O. Stoker (BRI)		w.o.	-
1891	H. Baddeley and W. Baddeley (BRI)	J. Pim and F.O. Stoker (BRI)	6-1 6-3 1-6 6-2	-
1892	H.S. Barlow and E.W. Lewis (BRI)	H. Baddeley and W. Baddeley (BRI)	4-6 6-2 8-6 6-4	72
1893	J. Pim and F.O. Stoker (BRI)	H.S. Barlow and E.W. Lewis (BRI)	4-6 6-3 6-1 2-6 6-0	140
1894*	H. Baddeley and W. Baddeley (BRI)		w.o.	-
1895	H. Baddeley and W. Baddeley (BRI)	W.V. Eaves and E.W. Lewis (BRI)	8-6 5-7 6-4 6-3	-
1896	H. Baddeley and W. Baddeley (BRI)	R.F. Doherty and H.A. Nisbet (BRI)	1-6 3-6 6-4 6-2 6-1	-
1897	H.L. Doherty and R.F. Doherty (BRI)	H. Baddeley and W. Baddeley (BRI)	6-4 4-6 8-6 6-4	90
1898	H.L. Doherty and R.F. Doherty (BRI)	C. Hobart and H.A. Nisbet (BRI)	6-4 6-4 6-2	-
1899	H.L. Doherty and R.F. Doherty (BRI)	C. Hobart and H.A. Nisbet (BRI)	7-5 6-0 6-2	-

ALL COMERS' FINAL

Winners	Runners-up	Score	Mins
Renshaw and Renshaw	E.W. Lewis and E.L. Williams (BRI)	6-3 6-1 1-6 6-4	-
Renshaw and Renshaw	C.E. Farrer and A.J. Stanley (BRI)	6-3 6-3 10-8	-
Farrer and Stanley	P. Bowes-Lyon and H.W. Wilberforce (BRI)	7-5 6-3 6-1	-
Bowes-Lyon and Wilberforce	E. Barratt-Smith and J.H. Crispe (BRI)	7-5 6-3 6-2	-
Renshaw and Renshaw	E.G. Meers and A.G. Ziffo (BRI)	6-3 6-2 6-2	-
Hillyard and Lewis	A.W. Gore and G.R. Mewburn (BRI)	6-2 6-1 6-3	44
Pim and Stoker	G.W. Hillyard and E.W. Lewis (BRI)	6-0 7-5 6-4	-
Baddeley and Baddeley	H.S. Barlow and J.E. Renshaw (BRI)	4-6 6-4 7-5 0-6 6-2	-
Barlow and Lewis	H.S. Mahony and J. Pim (BRI)	8-10 6-3 5-7 11-9 6-1	120
Pim and Stoker	H. Baddeley and W. Baddeley (BRI)	6-2 4-6 6-3 5-7 6-2	-
Baddeley and Baddeley	H.S. Barlow and C.H. Martin (BRI)	5-7 7-5 4-6 6-3 8-6	-
Eaves and Lewis	W.G. Bailey and C.F. Simond (BRI)	6-4 6-4 6-3	-
Doherty and Nisbet	C.G. Allen and E.R. Allen (BRI)	3-6 7-5 6-4 6-1	-
Doherty and Doherty	C.H.L. Cazalet and S.H. Smith (BRI)	6-2 7-5 2-6 6-2	-
Hobart and Nisbet	G.W. Hillyard and S.H. Smith (BRI)	2-6 6-2 6-2 6-3	-
Hobart and Nisbet	H.R. Barrett and A.W. Gore (BRI)	6-4 6-1 8-6	-

Year	Champions	Losers	Score	Mins	Winners	Runners-up	Score	Mins
1900	H.L. Doherty and R.F. Doherty (BRI)	H.R. Barrett and H.A. Nisbet (BRI)	9-7 7-5 4-6 3-6 6-3	-	Barrett and Nisbet	F.L. Riseley and S.H. Smith (BRI)	6-2 2-6 6-8 8-6 6-2	-
1901	H.L. Doherty and R.F. Doherty (BRI)	D.F. Davis and H. Ward (USA)	4-6 6-2 6-3 9-7	97	Davis and Ward	H.R. Barrett and G.M. Simond (BRI)	7-5 6-4 6-4	-
	(The match had started the day before but was abandoned due to rain with the score at 4-6 6-0 9-9.)							
1902	F.L. Riseley and S.H. Smith (BRI)	H.L. Doherty and R.F. Doherty (BRI)	4-6 8-6 6-3 4-6 11-9	-	Riseley and Smith	C.H.L. Cazalet and G.W. Hillyard (BRI)	7-5 2-6 6-8 6-3 6-1	-
1903	H.L. Doherty and R.F. Doherty (BRI)	F.L. Riseley and S.H. Smith (BRI)	6-4 6-4 6-4	-	Doherty and Doherty	H.S. Mahony and M.J.G. Ritchie (BRI)	8-6 6-2 6-2	-
1904	H.L. Doherty and R.F. Doherty (BRI)	F.L. Riseley and S.H. Smith (BRI)	6-1 6-2 6-4	-	Riseley and Smith	G.A. Caridia and A.W. Gore (BRI)	6-3 6-4 6-3	-
1905	H.L. Doherty and R.F. Doherty (BRI)	F.L. Riseley and S.H. Smith (BRI)	6-2 6-4 6-8 6-3	-	Riseley and Smith	N.E. Brookes and A.W. Dunlop (AUS)	6-2 1-6 6-2 6-3	-
1906	F.L. Riseley and S.H. Smith (BRI)	H.L. Doherty and R.F. Doherty (BRI)	6-8 6-4 5-7 6-3 6-3	-	Riseley and Smith	C.H.L. Cazalet and G.M. Simond (BRI)	6-2 6-2 5-7 6-4	-
1907*	N.E. Brookes (AUS) and A.F. Wilding (NZL)		w.o.		Brookes and Wilding	K. Behr and B.C. Wright (USA)	6-4 4-6-2	-
1908*	M.J.G. Ritchie (BRI) and A.F. Wilding (NZL)		w.o.		Ritchie and Wilding	H.R. Barrett and A.W. Gore (BRI)	6-1 6-2 1-6 9-7	-
1909*	H.R. Barrett and A.W. Gore (BRI)		w.o.		Barrett and Gore	S.N. Doust (AUS) and H.A. Parker (NZL)	6-2 6-1 6-4	-
1910	M.J.G. Ritchie (BRI) and A.F. Wilding (NZL)	H.R. Barrett and A.W. Gore (BRI)	6-1 6-1 6-2	-	Ritchie and Wilding	K. Powell (BRI) and R.B. Powell (CAN)	9-7 6-0 6-4	-
1911	M.O. Decugis and A.H. Gobert (FRA)	M.J.G. Ritchie (BRI) and A.F. Wilding (NZL)	9-7 5-7 6-3 2-6 6-2	-	Decugis and Gobert	S.P. Hardy (USA) and J.C. Parke (BRI)	6-2 6-1 6-2	-
1912	H.R. Barrett and C.P. Dixon (BRI)	M.O. Decugis and A.H. Gobert (FRA)	3-6 6-3 6-4 7-5	-	Barrett and Dixon	A.E. Beamish and J.C. Parke (BRI)	6-8 6-4 3-6 6-3 6-4	-
1913	H.R. Barrett and C.P. Dixon (BRI)	H. Kleinschroth and F.W. Rahe (GER)	6-2 6-4 4-6 6-2	-	Kleinschroth and Rahe	A.E. Beamish and J.C. Parke (BRI)	6-3 6-2 6-4	-
1914	N.E. Brookes (AUS) and A.F. Wilding (NZL)	H.R. Barrett and C.P. Dixon (BRI)	6-1 6-1 5-7 8-6	-	Brookes and Wilding	A.H. Lowe and F.G. Lowe (BRI)	6-2 8-6 6-1	-
1919*	R.V. Thomas and H. O'Hara Wood (AUS)		w.o.		Thomas and Wood	R.W. Heath (AUS) and R. Lycett (BRI)	6-4 6-2 4-6 6-2	-
1920*	C.S. Garland and R.N. Williams (USA)		w.o.		Garland and Williams	A.R.F. Kingscote and J.C. Parke (BRI)	4-6 6-4 7-5 6-2	-
1921*	R. Lycett and M. Woosnam (BRI)		w.o.		Lycett and Woosnam	A.H. Lowe and F.G. Lowe (BRI)	6-3 6-0 7-5	-

Challenge Round abolished

FINAL

Year	Champions	Seeded	Runners-up	Seeded	Score	Mins
1922	J.O. Anderson (AUS) and R. Lycett (BRI)		G.L. Patterson and P.O. Wood (AUS)		3-6 7-9 6-4 6-3 11-9	-
1923	L.A. Godfree and R. Lycett (GBR)		E. Flaquer and Count M. de Gomar (ESP)		6-3 6-4 3-6 6-3	-
1924	F.T. Hunter and V. Richards (USA)		W.M. Washburn and R.N. Williams (USA)		6-3 3-6 8-10 8-6 6-3	-
1925	J.R. Borotra and J.R. Lacoste (FRA)		R.J. Casey and J.F. Hennessey (USA)		6-4 11-9 4-6 1-6 6-3	-
1926	J. Brugnon and H.J. Cochet (FRA)		H.O. Kinsey and V. Richards (USA)		7-5 4-6 6-3 6-2	-
1927	F.T. Hunter and W.T. Tilden (USA)	3	J. Brugnon and H.J. Cochet (FRA)	1	1-6 4-6 8-6 6-3 6-4	-
1928	J. Brugnon and H.J. Cochet (FRA)	2	J.B. Hawkes and G.L. Patterson (AUS)	4	13-11 6-4 6-4	-
1929	W.L. Allison and J.W. Van Ryn (USA)	U	I.G. Collins and J.C. Gregory (GBR)	4	6-4 5-7 6-3 10-12 6-4	-
1930	W.L. Allison and J.W. Van Ryn (USA)	2	J.T.G.H. Doeg and G.M. Lott (USA)	1	6-3 6-3 6-2	-

SEMI-FINAL

Winners	Losers	Seeded	Score	Mins
Anderson and Lycett	G.C. Caner and D. Mathey (USA)		6-2 6-3 6-2	-
Patterson and Wood	H.R. Barrett (BRI) and B.I.C. Norton (RSA)		6-1 3-6 5-7 6-3 15-13	-
Godfree and Lycett	L.S. Deane and A.H. Fyzee (IND)		8-6 6-4 6-3	-
Flaquer and de Gomar	J.R. Borotra and J.R. Lacoste (FRA)		11-9 4-6 6-4 3-6 7-5	-
Hunter and Richards	L.B. Raymond and P.D.B. Spence (RSA)		6-4 6-4 6-2	-
Washburn and Williams	L.A. Godfree and R. Lycett (GBR)		4-6 12-10 6-3 7-7 retd	-
Borotra and Lacoste	U.L. de Morpurgo (ITA) and B. von Kehrling (HUN)		11-9 7-9 6-1 6-1	-
Casey and Hennessey	J. Brugnon and H.J. Cochet (FRA)		7-5 5-7 9-7 6-4	-
Brugnon and Cochet	B. von Kehrling (HUN) and C.E. van Lennep (NED)		9-7 6-4 6-2	-
Kinsey and Richards	H.W. Austin and R. Lycett (GBR)		7-5 6-4 6-4	-
Hunter and Tilden	H.W. Austin and R. Lycett (GBR)	U	6-0 10-8 6-4	-
Brugnon and Cochet	J.J. Condon and J.B. Raymond (RSA)	4	6-1 6-2 7-5	-
Brugnon and Cochet	J.F. Hennessey and G.M. Lott (USA)	3	11-9 6-4 3-6 7-5	-
Hawkes and Patterson	F.T. Hunter and W.T. Tilden (USA)	1	7-9 7-9 6-4 6-4 10-8	-
Allison and van Ryn	F.T. Hunter and W.T. Tilden (USA)	3	6-3 12-10 6-3	160
Collins and Gregory	J.F. Hennessey and G.M. Lott (USA)	2	4-6 7-5 6-1 4-6 7-5	-
Allison and van Ryn	I.C. Collins and J.C. Gregory (GBR)	4	4-6 7-5 6-3 6-3	-
Doeg and Lott	J. Brugnon and H.J. Cochet (FRA)	3	8-6 3-6 6-3 6-1	-

Year	Champions	Seeded	Runners-up	Seeded	Score	Mins	Winners	Losers	Seeded	Score	Mins
1931	G.M. Lott and J.W. Van Ryn (USA)	1	J. Brugnon and H.J. Cochet (FRA)	2	6-2 10-8 9-11 3-6 6-3	-	Lott and van Ryn Brugnon and Cochet	G.P. Hughes and F.J. Perry (GBR) F.X. Shields and S.B.B. Wood (USA)	3 U	6-4 11-9 8-6 6-4 7-5 6-2	-
1932	J.R. Borotra and J. Brugnon (FRA)	4	G.P. Hughes and F.J. Perry (GBR)	3	6-0 4-6 3-6 7-5 7-5	-	Borotra and Brugnon Hughes and Perry	W.L. Allison and J.W. van Ryn (USA) J.C. Boussus and A. Merlin (FRA)	1 U	6-3 6-2 6-4 8-6 6-1 6-3	-
1933	J.R. Borotra and J. Brugnon (FRA)	1	R. Nunoi and J. Satoh (JPN)	U	4-6 6-3 6-3 7-5	-	Borotra and Brugnon Nunoi and Satoh	N.G. Farquharson and V.G. Kirby (RSA) W.O.E. Nouney and G. von Cramm (GER)	4 U	5-7 3-6 6-4 6-3 6-4 7-5 3-6 6-4 6-1	-
1934	G.M. Lott and L.R. Stoefen (USA)	2	J.R. Borotra and J. Brugnon (FRA)	1	6-2 6-3 6-4	-	Lott and Stoefen Borotra and Brugnon	H.C. Hopman (AUS) and D.D. Prenn (GER) I.G. Collins and F.H.D. Wilde (GBR)	U U	6-4 4-6 6-3 8-6 7-5 3-6 6-2 6-4	-
1935	J.H. Crawford and A.K. Quist (AUS)	2	W.L. Allison and J.W. Van Ryn (USA)	1	6-3 5-7 6-2 5-7 7-5	-	Crawford and Quist Allison and van Ryn	J.D. Budge and C.G. Mako (USA) G.P. Hughes and C.R.D.Tuckey (GBR)	3 U	6-2 13-11 6-3 4-6 6-4 6-2 6-2	-
1936	G.P. Hughes and C.R.D. Tuckey (GBR)	4	C.E. Hare and F.H.D. Wilde (GBR)	U	6-4 3-6 7-9 6-1 6-4	-	Hughes and Tuckey Hare and Wilde	W.L. Allison and J.W. van Ryn (USA) J.R. Borotra and J. Brugnon (FRA)	2 U	7-5 6-4 3-6 11-9 6-1 4-6 6-1 6-4	-
1937	J.D. Budge and C.G. Mako (USA)	2	G.P. Hughes and C.R.D. Tuckey (GBR)	1	6-0 6-4 6-8 6-1	-	Budge and Mako Hughes and Tuckey	H.E.O Henkel and G. von Cramm (GER) L. Hecht and R. Menzel (TCH)	3 U	4-6 4-6 6-2 6-4 6-3 6-2 6-2 6-4	-
1938	J.D. Budge and C.G. Mako (USA)	1	H.E.O. Henkel and G. von Metaxa (GER)	4	6-4 3-6 6-3 8-6	-	Budge and Mako Henkel and von Metaxa	G.P. Hughes and F.H.D. Wilde (GBR) F. Kukuljevic and J. Palada (YUG)	U U	6-2 6-4 12-10 7-5 6-2 6-4	-
1939	E.T. Cooke and R.L. Riggs (USA)	2	C.E. Hare and F.H.D. Wilde (GBR)	4	6-3 3-6 6-3 9-7	-	Cooke and Riggs Hare and Wilde	J.R. Borotra and J. Brugnon (FRA) J.S. Olliff and R.A. Shayes (GBR)	3 U	6-4 3-6 6-2 6-3 6-2 6-4 6-4	-
1946	T.P. Brown and J.A. Kramer (USA)	1	G.E. Brown and D.R. Pails (AUS)	2	6-4 6-4 6-2	-	Brown and Kramer Brown and Pails	J.E. Patty (USA) and F. Segura (ECU) D. Mitic and J. Palada (YUG)	U 3	6-3 6-3 6-2 6-4 6-3	-

Year	Champions	Seeded	Runners-up	Seeded	Score	Mins	Winners	Losers	Seeded	Score	Mins
1947	R. Falkenburg and J.A. Kramer (USA)	1	A.J. Mottram (GBR) and O.W.T. Sidwell (AUS)	U	8-6 6-3 6-3	-	Falkenburg and Kramer	G.E. Brown and C.F. Long (AUS)	3	10-8 6-4 6-4	-
							Mottram and Sidwell	J.E. Bromwich and D.R. Pails (AUS)	2	6-3 6-3 7-5	-
1948	J.E. Bromwich and F.A. Sedgman (AUS)	3	T.P. Brown and G.P. Mulloy (USA)	2	5-7 7-5 7-5 9-7	120	Bromwich and Sedgman	R. Falkenburg and F.A. Parker (USA)	1	6-2 6-8 4-6 6-4 6-1	-
							Brown and Mulloy	L. Bergelin (SWE) and J.E. Harper (AUS)	U	1-6 6-3 4-6 6-4 8-6	-
1949	R.A. Gonzales and F.A. Parker (USA)	1	G.P. Mulloy and F.R. Schroeder (USA)	3	6-4 6-4 6-2	-	Gonzales and Parker	J.E. Patty (USA) and E.W. Sturgess (RSA)	U	6-3 6-1 3-6 5-7 7-5	-
							Mulloy and Schroeder	G.E. Brown and O.W.T. Sidwell (AUS)	U	6-4 3-6 6-8 6-3 9-7	-
1950	J.E. Bromwich and A.K. Quist (AUS)	2	G.E. Brown and O.W.T. Sidwell (AUS)	4	7-5 3-6 6-3 3-6 6-2	120	Bromwich and Quist	J. Drobny (EGY) and E.W. Sturgess (RSA)	3	6-4 3-6 6-3 6-4	-
							Brown and Sidwell	J.E. Patty and M.A. Trabert (USA)	U	6-4 6-4 6-3	-
1951	K.B. McGregor and F.A. Sedgman (AUS)	1	J. Drobny (EGY) and E.W. Sturgess (RSA)	4	3-6 6-2 6-3 3-6 6-3	-	McGregor and Sedgman	J.E. Patty and H.F. Richardson (USA)	U	6-4 2 6-3	-
							Drobny and Sturgess	G.P. Mulloy and R. Savitt (USA)	2	4-6 6-4 6-3 6-4	-
1952	K.B. McGregor and F.A. Sedgman (AUS)	1	E.V. Seixas (USA) and E.W. Sturgess (RSA)	4	6-3 7-5 6-4	56	McGregor and Sedgman	J. Drobny (EGY) and J.E. Patty (USA)	3	6-3 6-4 7-9 6-4	-
							Seixas and Sturgess	L.A. Hoad and K.R. Rosewall (AUS)	U	6-4 8-6 6-8 7-5	-
1953	L.A. Hoad and K.R. Rosewall (AUS)	1	R.N. Hartwig and M.G. Rose (AUS)	3	6-4 7-5 4-6 7-5	-	Hoad and Rosewall	J. Brichant and P. Washer (BEL)	U	4-6 6-0 6-4 3-6 6-1	-
							Hartwig and Rose	G.P. Mulloy and E.V. Seixas (USA)	2	14-16 6-3 6-3 6-4	-
1954	R.N. Hartwig and M.G. Rose (AUS)	1	E.V. Seixas and M.A. Trabert (USA)	2	6-4 6-4 3-6 6-4	-	Hartwig and Rose	G.P. Mulloy and J.E. Patty (USA)	4	4-6 6-4 6-2 6-1	-
							Seixas and Trabert	L.A. Hoad and K.R. Rosewall (AUS)	3	6-3 7-5 3-6 4-6 8-6	-
1955	R.N. Hartwig and L.A. Hoad (AUS)	3	N.A. Fraser and K.R. Rosewall (AUS)	2	7-5 6-4 6-3	-	Hartwig and Hoad	M.G. Rose and G.A. Worthington (AUS)	U	7-9 6-4 6-4 2-6 6-1	-
							Fraser and Rosewall	E.V. Seixas and M.A. Trabert (USA)	1	6-2 1-6 6-1 4-6 6-3	-
1956	L.A. Hoad and K.R. Rosewall (AUS)	1	N. Pietrangeli and O. Sirola (ITA)	U	7-5 6-2 6-1	-	Hoad and Rosewall	R.N. Howe (AUS) and A.D. Larsen (USA)	U	4-6 2 7-5 6-3	-
							Pietrangeli and Sirola	A.J. Cooper and N.A. Fraser (AUS)	U	6-4 6-4 8-6	-

Year	Champions	Seeded	Runners-up	Seeded	Score	Mins	Winners	Losers	Seeded	Score	Mins
1957	G.P. Mulloy and J.E. Patty (USA)	U	N.A. Fraser and L.A. Hoad (AUS)	1	8-10 6-4 6-4 6-4	-	Mulloy and Patty	R. Becker (GBR) R.N. Howe (AUS)	U	9-7 7-5 6-3	-
							Fraser and Hoad	N. Pietrangeli and O. Sirola (ITA)	4	14-12 1-6 8-6 6-3	-
1958	S.V. Davidson and U.C.J. Schmidt (SWE)	U	A.J. Cooper and N.A. Fraser (AUS)	1	6-4 6-4 8-6	-	Davidson and Schmidt	N. Pietrangeli and O. Sirola (ITA)	U	8-6 3-6 6-3 7-5	-
							Cooper and Fraser	B.B. MacKay (USA) and M.G. Rose (AUS)	3	3-6 8-6 7-5 7-5	-
1959	R.S. Emerson and N.A. Fraser (AUS)	1	R.G. Laver and R. Mark (AUS)	4	8-6 6-3 14-16 9-7	172	Emerson and Fraser	L.Legenstein (STA) and T. Ulrich (DEN)	U	6-3 6-2 6-2	-
							Laver and Mark	N. Pietrangeli and 0. Sirola (ITA)	2	6-4 6-4 6-3	-
1960	R.H. Osuna (MEX) and R.D. Ralston (USA)	U	M.G. Davies and R.K. Wilson (GBR)	U	7-5 6-3 10-8	80	Osuna and Ralston	R.G. Laver and R. Mark (AUS)	2	4-6 10-8 15-13 4-6 11-9	185
							Davies and Wilson	R.A.J. Hewitt and M.F. Mulligan (AUS)	U	3-6 6-3 6-2 6-4	-
1961	R.S. Emerson and N.A. Fraser (AUS)	1	R.A.J. Hewitt and F.S. Stolle (AUS)	U	6-4 6-8 6-4 6-8 8-6	165	Emerson and Fraser	K.N. Fletcher and J.D. Newcombe (AUS)	U	10-8 11-9 6-1	-
							Hewitt and Stolle	R.G. Laver and R. Mark (AUS)	2	4-6 10-8 6-3 6-4	-
1962	R.A.J. Hewitt and F.S. Stolle (AUS)	2	B. Jovanovic and N. Pilic (YUG)	U	6-2 5-7 6-2 6-4	-	Hewitt and Stolle	J.G. Fraser and R.G. Laver (AUS)	3	8-6 5-7 7-5 6-2	-
							Jovanovic and Pilic	R.S. Emerson and N.A. Fraser (AUS)	1	4-6 6-3 6-4 6-4	-
1963	R.H. Osuna and A. Palafox (MEX)	U	J.C. Barclay and P. Darmon (FRA)	U	4-6 6-2 6-2 6-2	-	Osuna and Palafox	G.L. Forbes and A.A. Segal (RSA)	U	6-3 5-7 6-4 6-4	-
							Barclay and Darmon	R.S. Emerson (AUS) and M.M. Santana (ESP)	2	6-2 7-5 3-6 6-3	-
1964	R.A.J. Hewitt and F.S. Stolle (AUS)	4	R.S. Emerson and K.N. Fletcher (AUS)	3	7-5 11-9 6-4	114	Hewitt and Stolle	R.H. Osuna and A. Palafox (MEX)	2	6-2 6-2 6-3	-
							Emerson and Fletcher	I.S. Crookenden and L.A. Gerrard (NZL)	U	14-12 6-2 6-1	-
1965	J.D. Newcombe and A.D. Roche (AUS)	2	K.N. Fletcher and R.A.J. Hewitt (AUS)	4	7-5 6-3 6-4	-	Newcombe and Roche	R.D. Ralston and H.F. Richardson (USA)	3	5-7 14-12 6-4 1-6 6-2	-
							Fletcher and Hewitt	C.E. Graebner and M.C. Riessen (USA)	U	7-5 6-4 6-4	-
1966	K.N. Fletcher and J.D. Newcombe (AUS)	U	W.W. Bowrey and O.K. Davidson (AUS)	4	6-3 6-4 3-6 6-3	-	Fletcher and Newcombe	C.E. Graebner and M.C. Riessen (USA)	3	6-3 7-5 6-1	-
							Bowrey and Davidson	M. Cox and A.R. Mills (GBR)	U	6-2 6-4 9-7	-

Year	Champions	Seeded	Runners-up	Seeded	Score	Mins
1967	R.A.J. Hewitt and F.D. McMillan (RSA)	2	R.S. Emerson and K.N. Fletcher (AUS)	4	6-2 6-3 6-4	65
1968	J.D. Newcombe and A.D. Roche (AUS)	4	K.R. Rosewall and F.S. Stolle (AUS)	2	3-6 8-6 5-7 14-12 6-3	180
1969	J.D. Newcombe and A.D. Roche (AUS)	1	T.S. Okker (NED) and M.C. Riessen (USA)	6	7-5 11-9 6-3	-
1970	J.D. Newcombe and A.D. Roche (AUS)	1	K.R. Rosewall and F.S. Stolle (AUS)	6	10-8 6-3 6-1	-
1971	R.S. Emerson and R.G. Laver (AUS)	U	A.R. Ashe and R.D. Ralston (USA)	U	4-6 9-7 6-8 6-4 6-4	150
1972	R.A.J. Hewitt and F.D. McMillan (RSA)	1	S.R. Smith and E.J. van Dillen (USA)	2	6-2 6-2 9-7	-
1973	J.S. Connors (USA) and I. Nastase (ROM)	1	J.R. Cooper and N.A. Fraser (AUS)	2	3-6 6-3 6-4 8-9 (3-7) 6-1	-
1974	J.D. Newcombe and A.D. Roche (AUS)	4	R.C. Lutz and S.R. Smith (USA)	3	8-6 6-4 6-4	-
1975	V.K. Gerulaitis and A. Mayer (USA)	U	C. Dowdeswell (RHO) and A.J. Stone (AUS)	U	7-5 8-6 6-4	-
1976	B.E. Gottfried (USA) and R.C. Ramirez (MEX)	1	R.L. Case and G. Masters (AUS)	U	3-6 6-3 8-6 2-6 7-5	165

Winners	Losers	Seeded	Score	Mins
Hewitt and McMillan	W.W. Bowrey and O.K. Davidson (AUS)	3	6-2 10-8 6-2	-
Emerson and Fletcher	P.W. Curtis and G.R. Stilwell (GBR)	U	6-4 8-6 4-6 5-7 9-7	-
Newcombe and Roche	R.S. Emerson and R.G. Laver (AUS)	1	6-3 8-6 2-6 7-5	-
Rosewall and Stolle	R.A.J.Hewitt and F.D. McMillan (RSA)	6	6-2 6-3 6-4	-
Newcombe and Roche	R.A.J.Hewitt and F.D. McMillan (RSA)	5	3-6 6-3 14-12 6-2	-
Okker and Riessen	R.S. Emerson and R.G. Laver (AUS)	2	6-3 3-6 6-3 6-4	-
Newcombe and Roche	R.A.J. Hewitt and F.D. McMillan (RSA)	4	7-5 8-6 5-7 5-7 6-4	-
Rosewall and Stolle	I. Nastase and I. Tiriac (ROM)	U	6-4 3-6 10-8 0-6 6-3	-
Emerson and Laver	J.G. Alexander and P.C. Dent (AUS)	U	6-4 3-6 6-3 6-4	-
Ashe and Ralston	C.E. Graebner (USA) and T. Koch (BRA)	U	8-9 () 6-3 8-6 6-4	-
Hewitt and McMillan	J.R. Cooper and N.A. Fraser (AUS)	U	8-6 4-6 9-8 (7-4) 6-2, 9-7 6-1 6-4	-
Smith and van Dillen	P.S. Cornejo and J.J. Fillol (CHI)	U		-
Connors and Nastase	J. Fassbender and K. Meiler (GER)	U	9-7 3-6 6-4 6-3	-
Cooper and Fraser	D.A. Lloyd and J.G. Paish (GBR)	U	3-6 6-3 6-2 6-4	-
Newcombe and Roche	J.S. Connors (USA) and I. Nastase (ROM)	1	3-6 4-6 6-3 6-2 6-4	-
Lutz and Smith	E.C. Drysdale (RSA) and T.S. Okker (NED)	7	3-6 6-1 7-5 9-7	-
Gerulaitis and Mayer	J. Fassbender and H.J. Pohmann (GER)	U	8-9 () 3-6 6-3 6-3	-
Dowdeswell and Stone	R.D. Crealy (AUS) and N. Pilic (YUG)	U	9-8 () 3-6 4-6 9-8 () 6-3	-
Gottfried and Ramirez	An. Armitraj and V. Armitraj (IND)	U	6-3 7-5 8-6	-
Case and Masters	R.C. Lutz and S.R. Smith (USA)	5	6-4 6-3 6-4	-

Year	Champions	Seeded	Runners-up	Seeded	Score	Mins
1977	R.L. Case and G. Masters (AUS)	7	J.G. Alexander and P.C. Dent (AUS)	U	6-3 6-4 3-6 8-9 (4-7) 6-4	165
1978	R.A.J. Hewitt and F.D. McMillan (RSA)	1	P.B. Fleming and J.P. McEnroe (USA)	U	6-1 6-4 6-2	80
1979	P.B. Fleming and J.P. McEnroe (USA)	1	B.E. Gottfried (USA) and R.C. Ramirez (MEX)	7	4-6 6-4 6-2 6-2	130
1980	P.B. McNamara and P.F. McNamee (AUS)	7	R.C. Lutz and S.R. Smith (USA)	4	7-6 (7-5) 6-3 6-7 (4-7) 6-4	149
1981	P.B. Fleming and J.P. McEnroe (USA)	1	R.C. Lutz and S.R. Smith (USA)	3	6-4 6-4 6-4	103
1982	P.B. McNamara and P.F. McNamee (AUS)	3	P.B. Fleming and J.P. McEnroe (USA)	1	6-3 6-2	49
1983	P.B. Fleming and J.P. McEnroe (USA)	1	T.E. Gullikson and T.R. Gullikson (USA)	7	6-4 6-3 6-4	108
1984	P.B. Fleming and J.P. McEnroe (USA)	1	P.H. Cash and P.F. McNamee (AUS)	5	6-2 5-7 6-2 3-6 6-3	142
1985	H.P. Guenthardt (SUI) and B. Taroczy (HUN)	8	P.H. Cash and J.B. Fitzgerald (AUS)	5	6-4 6-3 4-6 6-3	118
1986	J.K. Nystrom and M.A.O. Wilander (SWE)	7	G.W. Donnelly and P.B. Fleming (USA)	12	7-6 (7-4) 6-3 6-3	98

Winners	Losers	Seeded	Score	Mins
Case and Masters	M. Cox (GBR) and E.C. Drysdale (RSA)	U	6-1 6-4 6-1	-
Alexander and Dent	R.J. Carmichael (AUS) and B.D. Teacher (USA)	U	8-9 ( ) 6-1 9-7 3-6 6-4	-
Hewitt and McMillan	J.G. Alexander and P.C. Dent (AUS)	4	9-7 7-5 6-4	-
Fleming and McEnroe	W. Fibak (POL) and T.S. Okker (NED)	2	1-6 6-3 9-7 6-4	-
Fleming and McEnroe	R.A.J. Hewitt and F.D. McMillan (RSA)	4	6-3 7-6 ( ) 6-1	-
Gottfried and Ramirez	J. Sadri and T. Wilkison (USA)	U	6-4 2-6 7-5 3-6 6-3	180
McNamara and McNamee	P.B. Fleming and J.P. McEnroe (USA)	1	6-3 6-2 6-3	-
Lutz and Smith	A. Mayer and E. Mayer (USA)	U	6-4 6-4 2-6 1-6 8-6	-
Fleming and McEnroe	T.S. Okker (NED) and R.L. Stockton (USA)	U	6-3 6-2 6-4	84
Lutz and Smith	P.B. McNamara and P.F. McNamee (AUS)	2	6-4 2-6 4-6 7-6 (7-5) 6-4	176
McNamara and McNamee	S.E. Stewart and F. Taygan (USA)	2	4-6 6-4 6-7 (1-7) 7-6 (7-5) 6-4	183
Fleming and McEnroe	K.M. Curren (RSA) and S.B. Denton (USA)	4	6-2 6-4 2-6 6-3	-
Fleming and McEnroe	A.P. Jarryd and H.K.I. Simonsson (SWE)	6	6-2 6-2 6-4	97
Gullikson and Gullikson	K.M. Curren (RSA) and S.B. Denton (USA)	2	7-6 (7-5) 6-7 (6-8) 7-6 (7-5) 6-3	161
Fleming and McEnroe	A. Mayer and F. Taygan (USA)	7	7-6 ( ) 7-6 ( ) 6-4	-
Cash and McNamee	P. Doohan and M.T. Fancutt (AUS)	U	6-1 3-6 6-3 6-7 (1-7) 7-5	179
Guenthardt and Taroczy	P.B. McNamara and P.F. McNamee (AUS)	1	6-7 (3-7) 6-1 6-2 6-4	132
Cash and Fitzgerald	P.B. Fleming and J.P. McEnroe (USA)	6	7-6 (13-11) 2-6 6-1 6-4	-
Nystrom and Wilander	P.T. Annacone and C.J. van Rensburg (USA)	16	4-6 6-3 7-6 (9-7) 6-3	153
Donnelly and Fleming	J. Hlasek (SUI) and P. Slozil (CZE)		6-4 7-5 3-6 6-4	148

Year	Champions	Seeded	Runners-up	Seeded	Score	Mins	Winners	Losers	Seeded	Score	Mins
1987	K.E. Flach and R.A. Seguso (USA)	7	S. Casal and E. Sanchez (ESP)	8	3-6 6-7 (6-8) 7-6 (7-3) 6-1 6-4	171	Flach and Seguso / Casal and Sanchez	A. Gomez (ECU) and S. Zvojinovic (YUG) / S.B. Edberg and A.P. Jarryd (SWE)	3 / 4	7-6 (8-6) 2-6 7-6 (7-5) 6-4 / 6-3 7-5 6-2	- / -
1988	K.E. Flach and R.A. Seguso (USA)	1	J.B. Fitzgerald (AUS) and A.P. Jarryd (SWE)	2	6-4 2-6 6-4 7-6 (7-3)	156	Flach and Seguso / Fitzgerald and Jarryd	E. Edwards and G.R. Muller (RSA / P. Doohan (AUS) and J.F. Grabb (USA)	U / U	6-4 6-4 7-6 (14-12) / 7-6 (7-5) 6-2 1-6 7-6 (7-3)	111 / 161
1989	J.B. Fitzgerald (AUS) and A.P. Jarryd (SWE)	3	R.D. Leach and J.R. Pugh (USA)	1	3-6 7-6 (7-4) 6-4 7-6 (7-4)	175	Fitzgerald and Jarryd / Leach and Pugh	K.E. Flach and R.A. Seguso (USA) / J.A. Frana (ARG) and L. Lavalle (MEX)	2 / U	4-6 6-2 6-2 6-3 / 6-3 6-3 6-4	142 / 96
1990	R.D. Leach and J.R. Pugh (USA)	1	P. Aldrich and D.T. Visser (RSA)	2	7-6 (7-5) 7-6 (7-4) 7-6 (7-5)	139	Leach and Pugh / Aldrich and Visser	S. Kruger (RSA) and G.S. van Emburgh (USA) / J.A. Frana (ARG) and L. Lavalle (MEX)	U / U	4-6 6-4 7-6 (7-2) 6-3 / 6-4 6-3 6-2	142 / 89
1991	J.B. Fitzgerald (AUS) and A.P. Jarryd (SWE)	2	J.A. Frana (ARG) and L. Lavalle (MEX)	U	6-3 6-4 6-7 (7-9) 6-1	143	Fitzgerald and Jarryd / Frana and Lavalle	G.D. Connell and G. Michibata (CAN) / W.R. Ferreira and P. Norval (RSA)	4 / 15	6-2 6-7 (4-7) 7-6 (7-5) 6-4 / 6-2 6-4 7-6 (7-4)	160 / 97
1992	J.P. McEnroe (USA) and M.D. Stich (GER)	U	J.F. Grabb and R.A. Reneberg (USA)	4	5-7 7-6 (7-5) 3-6 7-6 (7-5) 19-17	301	McEnroe and Stich / Grabb and Reneberg	G. Forget (FRA) and J. Hlasek (SUI) / M.R. Woodforde (AUS)	13 / 2	7-6 (7-4) 6-3 7-6 (7-4) / 7-6 (7-3) 4-6 4-6 7-6 (7-4) 6-4	151 / 207
1993	T.A. Woodbridge and M.R. Woodforde (AUS)	1	G.D. Connell (CAN) and P.J. Galbraith (USA)	5	7-5 6-3 7-6 (7-4)	120	Woodbridge and Woodforde / Connell and Galbraith	P.K. Kuhnen (GER) and G.R. Muller (RSA) / R.H. Bergh (SWE) and B.D. Talbot (RSA)	U / U	6-4 6-4 6-4 / 6-3 6-4 6-4	102 / 85
1994	T.A. Woodbridge and M.R. Woodforde (AUS)	5	G.D. Connell (CAN) and P.J. Galbraith (USA)	2	7-6 (7-3) 6-3 6-1	115	Woodbridge and Woodforde / Connell and Galbraith	W.R. Ferreira (RSA) and M.D. Stich (GER) / M-K.P. Goellner (GER) and Y.A. Kafelnikov (RUS)	16 / 14	6-2 7-6 (7-5) 6-2 / 4-6 6-3 6-4 6-2	100 / 111
1995	T.A. Woodbridge and M.R. Woodforde (AUS)	2	R.D. Leach and D.S. Melville (USA)	U	7-5 7-6 (10-8) 7-6 (7-5)	143	Woodbridge and Woodforde / Leach and Melville	M.S. Knowles (BAH) and D.M. Nestor (CAN) / M-K.P. Goellner (GER) and Y.A. Kafelnikov (RUS)	11 / 14	6-3 6-3 6-3 / 3-6 7-6 (14-12) 6-7 (2-7) 7-6 (7-3) 6-3	90 / 203
1996	T.A. Woodbridge and M.R. Woodforde (AUS)	1	B.H. Black (ZIM) and G.D. Connell (CAN)	3	4-6 6-1 6-3 6-2	127	Woodbridge and Woodforde / Black and Connell	M.A. Philippoussis and P.M. Rafter (AUS) / E.R. Ferreira (RSA) and J.M. Siemerink (NED)	11 / 8	6-3 7-6 (12-10) 7-6 (7-2) / 6-4 6-2 7-6 (74)	140 / 92

Finals

Year	Champions	Seeded	Runners-up	Seeded	Score	Mins
1997	T.A. Woodbridge and M.R. Woodforde (AUS)	1	J.F. Eltingh and P.V.N. Haarhuis (NED)	2	7-6 (6-4) 7-6 (9-7) 5-7 6-3	172
1998	J.F. Eltingh and P.V.N. Haarhuis (NED)	1	T.A. Woodbridge and M.R. Woodforde (AUS)	2	2-6 6-4 7-6 (7-3) 5-7 10-8	245
1999	M.S. Bhupathi and L.A. Paes (IND)	1	P.V.N. Haarhuis (NED) and J.E. Palmer (USA)	8	6-7 (12-10) 6-3 6-4 7-6 (7-4)	161
2000	T.A. Woodbridge and M.R. Woodforde (AUS)	1	P.V.N. Haarhuis (NED) and S.F. Stolle (AUS)	2	6-3 6-4 6-1	97
2001	D.J. Johnson and J.E. Palmer (USA)	4	J. Novak and D. Rikl (CZE)	3	6-4 4-6 6-3 7-6 (8-6)	167
2002	J.L. Bjorkman (SWE) and T.A. Woodbridge (AUS)	5	M.S. Knowles (BAH) and D.M. Nestor (CAN)	2	6-1 6-2 6-7 (7-9) 7-5	155
2003	J.L. Bjorkman (SWE) and T.A. Woodbridge (AUS)	4	M.S. Bhupathi (IND) and M.N. Mirnyi (BLR)	1	3-6 6-3 7-6 (7-4) 6-3	160
2004	J.L. Bjorkman (SWE) and T.A. Woodbridge (AUS)	1	J. Knowle (AUT) and N. Zimonjic (SCG)	16	6-1 6-4 4-6 6-4	137
2005	S.W.I. Huss (AUS) and W.A. Moodie (RSA)	U	M.C. Bryan and R.C. Bryan (USA)	2	7-6 (7-4) 6-3 6-7 (2-7) 6-3	141
2006	M.C. Bryan and R.C. Bryan (USA)	1	F.V. Santoro (FRA) and N. Zimonjic (SCG)	6	6-3 4-6 6-4 6-2	117

Semi-finals

Winners	Losers	Seeded	Score	Mins
Woodbridge and Woodforde	W.H. Black (ZIM) and J.F. Grabb (USA)	U	7-6 (6-3) 6-4 3-6 6-3	159
Eltingh and Haarhuis	M. Damm and P. Vizner (CZE)	13	6-2 6-2 6-4	88
Eltingh and Haarhuis	W.H. Black (ZIM) and S.D. Lareau (CAN)	12	6-4 6-4 7-5	100
Woodbridge and Woodforde	J.L. Bjorkman (SWE) and P.M. Rafter (AUS)	5	6-4 1-6 6-2 7-5	131
Bhupathi and Paes	O.N.H. Delaitre and F.V. Santoro (FRA)	5	2-6 6-3 7-6 (7-5) 4-6 7-5	200
Haarhuis and Palmer	M.S. Knowles (BAH) and D.M. Nestor (CAN)	6	3-6 7-5 7-6 (7-4) 4-6 8-6	213
Woodbridge and Woodforde	L.J.N. Kulti and M. Tillstrom (SWE)	11	6-4 7-6 (7-2) 6-2	122
Haarhuis and Stolle	D.D. Adams and J-L. De Jager (RSA)	6	6-4 7-6 (7-5) 6-7 (4-7) 6-4	153
Johnson and Palmer	M.N. Mirnyi and V. Voltchkov (BLR)	U	7-6 (7-3) 4-6 7-5 6-3	152
Novak and Rikl	M.C. Bryan R.C. Bryan USA	15	6-4 7-6 (7-1) 4-6 6-1	123
Bjorkman and Woodbridge	D.J. Johnson and J.E. Palmer (USA)	1	7-5 4-6 6-7 (3-7) 7-5 6-2	210
Knowles and Nestor	M.C. Bryan and R.C. Bryan (USA)	6	7-6 (7-4) 7-6 (7-5) 7-6 (7-4)	187
Bjorkman and Woodbridge	J.D. Erlich and A. Ram (ISR)	U	6-2 4-6 6-2 6-1	121
Bhupathi and Mirnyi	L.A. Paes (IND) and D. Rikl (CZE)	5	6-7 (6-8) 6-4 7-6 (9-7) 6-3	166
Bjorkman and Woodbridge	W.S. Arthurs and P.J. Hanley (AUS)	7	7-5 7-5 7-6 (7-4)	139
Knowle and Zimonjic	M.S. Knowles (BAH) and D.M. Nestor (CAN)	5	6-2 3-6 6-3 6-7 (7-9) 6-3	179
Huss and Moodie	J.L. Bjorkman (SWE) and M. Mirnyi (BLR)	1	2-6 6-2 6-4 7-6 (7-4)	154
Bryan and Bryan	W.H. Black and K.R. Ullyett (ZIM)	4	4-6 6-3 6-4 6-4	127
Bryan and Bryan	M.S. Knowles (BAH) and D.M. Nestor (CAN)	3	6-4 6-7 (3-7) 7-6 (7-3) 6-1	143
Santoro and Zimonjic	M. Damm (CZE) and L.A. Paes (IND)	7	6-2 6-1 7-5	97

Final

Year	Champions	Seeded	Runners-up	Seeded	Score	Mins
2007	A. Clement and M. Llodra (FRA)	10	M.C. Bryan and R.C. Bryan (USA)	1	6-7 (5-7) 6-3 6-4 6-4	151
2008	D.M. Nestor (CAN) and N. Zimonjic (SRB)	2	J.L. Bjorkman (SWE) and K.R. Ullyett (ZIM)	8	7-6 (14-12) 6-7 (3-7) 6-3 6-3	160
2009	D.M. Nestor (CAN) and N. Zimonjic (SRB)	2	M.C. Bryan and R.C. Bryan (USA)	1	7-6 (9-7) 6-7 (3-7) 6-3	160
2010	J. Melzer (AUT) and P. Petzschner (GER)	U	R.J. Lindstedt (SWE) and H.V. Tecau (ROM)	16	6-1 7-5 7-5	117
2011	M.C. Bryan and R.C. Bryan (USA)	1	R.J. Lindstedt (SWE) and H.V. Tecau (ROM)	8	6-3 6-4 7-6 (7-2)	103
2012	J.F. Marray (GBR) and F.L. Nielsen (DEN)	U	R.J. Lindstedt (SWE) and H.V. Tecau (ROM)	5	4-6 6-4 7-6 (7-5) 6-7 (5-7) 6-3	163
2013	M.C. Bryan and R.C. Bryan (USA)	1	I. Dodig (CRO) and M.P.D. Melo (BRA)	12	3-6 6-3 6-3 6-4	163
2014	V. Pospisil (CAN) and J.E. Sock (USA)	U	M.C. Bryan and R.C. Bryan (USA)	1	7-6 (7-5) 6-7 (3-7) 6-4 3-6 7-5	186

Semi-finals

Winners	Losers	Seeded	Score	Mins
Clement and Llodra	M.P.D. Melo and A.R. Sa	U	7-6 6-3 6-3	118
Bryan and Bryan	F. Santoro (FRA) and N. Zimonjic (SRB)	4	7-6 6-4 7-6	120
Nestor and Zimonjic	L. Dlouhy (CZE) and L.A. Paes (IND)	9	7-6 (7-4) 4-6 6-1 4-6 8-6	197
Bjorkman and Ullyett	M.C. Bryan and R.C. Bryan (USA)	1	7-6 (7-3) 5-7 7-6 (11-9)	182
Nestor and Zimonjic	J.R Blake and M. Fish (USA)	U	5-7 3-6 6-2 7-6 (7-3) 10-8	209
Bryan and Bryan	W.A. Moodie (AUS) and D. Norman (BEL)	9	7-6 (7-4) 7-6 (7-3) 6-4	123
Melzer and Petzschner	W.A. Moodie (AUS) and D. Norman (BEL)	7	7-6 (7-3) 6-3 3-6 5-7 6-3	194
Lindstedt and Tecau	J.L. Chela and E.J. Schwank (ARG)	16	6-4 7-5 6-2	101
Bryan and Bryan	M. Llodra (FRA) and N. Zimonjic (SRB)	6	6-4 6-4 6-7 (8-10) 6-7 (4-7) 9-7	218
Lindstedt and Tecau	C. Kas (GER) and A. Peya (AUT)	U	6-3 7-6 (7-3) 6-2	135
Marray and Nielsen	M.C. Bryan and R.C. Bryan (USA)	2	6-4 7-6 (11-9) 6-7 (4-7) 7-6 (7-5)	155
Lindstedt and Tecau	J. Melzer (AUT) and P. Petzschner (GER)	10	6-4 6-7 (10-12) 6-4 6-3	158
Bryan and Bryan	R. Bopanna (IND) and E.C. Roger-Vasselin (FRA)	14	6-7 (4-7) 6-4 6-3 5-7 6-3	168
Dodig and Melo	L.A. Paes (IND) and R. Stepanek (CZE)	4	3-6 6-4 6-1 3-6 6-3	176
Bryan and Bryan	M. Llodva and N. Mahut (FRA)	12	7-6 (7-4) 6-3 6-2	107
Pospisil and Sock	L.A. Paes (IND) and R. Stepanek (CZE)	5	7-6 (7-5) 6-3 6-4	142

Ladies' Singles Championship

CHALLENGE ROUND / ALL COMERS' FINAL

Year	Champion	Loser	Score	Mins	Winner	Runner-up	Score	Mins
1884	Miss M.E.E. Watson (BRI)				Watson	Miss L.M. Watson (BRI)	6-8 6-3 6-3	-
1885	Miss M.E.E. Watson (BRI)				Watson	Miss B. Bingley (BRI)	6-1 7-5	-
1886	Miss B. Bingley (BRI)	Miss M.E.E. Watson (BRI)	6-3 6-3	34	Bingley	Miss A. Tabor (BRI)	6-2 6-0	-
1887	Miss C. Dod (BRI)	Miss B. Bingley (BRI)	6-2 6-0	-	Dod	Mrs. C.J. Cole (BRI)	6-2 6-3	-
1888	Miss C. Dod (BRI)	Mrs. G.W. Hillyard (BRI)	6-3 6-3	-	Dod	Miss Howes (BRI)	6-1 6-2	-
1889*	Mrs. G.W. Hillyard (BRI)		w.o.		Hillyard	Miss H.G.B. Rice (BRI)	4-6 8-6 6-4	-
1890*	Miss H.G.B. Rice (BRI)		w.o.		Hillyard	Miss M. Jacks (BRI)	6-4 6-1	-
1891*	Miss C. Dod (BRI)		w.o.		Rice	Mrs. G.W. Hillyard (BRI)	6-2 6-1	-
1892	Miss C. Dod (BRI)	Mrs. G.W. Hillyard (BRI)	6-1 6-1	-	Dod	Miss E.M. Shackle (BRI)	6-1 6-4	-
1893	Miss C. Dod (BRI)	Mrs. G.W. Hillyard (BRI)	6-8 6-1 6-4	-	Hillyard	Miss E.M. Shackle (BRI)	6-3 6-2	-
1894*	Mrs. G.W. Hillyard (BRI)		w.o.		Hillyard	Miss E.L. Austin (BRI)	6-1 6-1	-
1895*	Miss C.R. Cooper (BRI)		w.o.		Hillyard	Miss H. Jackson (BRI)	7-5 8-6	-
1896	Miss C.R. Cooper (BRI)	Mrs. W.H. Pickering (BRI)	6-2 6-3	-	Cooper	Miss E.L. Austin (BRI)	4-6 6-3 6-3	-
1897	Mrs. G.W. Hillyard (BRI)	Miss C.R. Cooper (BRI)	5-7 7-5 6-2	-	Pickering	Mrs. W.H. Pickering (BRI)	6-2 7-5	-
1898*	Miss C.R. Cooper (BRI)		w.o.		Cooper	Miss M.L. Martin (BRI)	6-4 6-4	-
1899	Mrs. G.W. Hillyard (BRI)	Miss C.R. Cooper (BRI)	6-2 6-3	-	Hillyard	Mrs. N.J. Durlacher (BRI)	7-5 6-8 6-1	-
1900	Mrs. G.W. Hillyard (BRI)	Miss C.R. Cooper (BRI)	4-6 6-4 6-4	-	Cooper	Miss M.L. Martin (BRI)	8-6 5-7 6-1	-
1901	Mrs. A. Sterry (BRI)	Mrs. G.W. Hillyard (BRI)	6-2 6-2	-	Sterry	Miss M.L. Martin (BRI)	6-3 6-1	-
1902	Miss M.E. Robb (BRI)	Mrs. A. Sterry (BRI)	7-5 6-1	-	Robb	Miss A.M. Morton (BRI)	6-2 6-4	-

(The match had started the day before but was abandoned due to rain with the score at 4-6 13-11.)

Year	Champion	Loser	Score	Mins	Winner	Runner-up	Score	Mins
1903*	Miss D.K. Douglass (BRI)		w.o.		Douglass	Miss E.W. Thomson (BRI)	4-6 6-4 6-2	-
1904	Miss D.K. Douglass (BRI)	Mrs. A. Sterry (BRI)	6-0 6-3	-	Sterry	Miss A.M. Morton (BRI)	6-3 6-3	-
1905	Miss M.G. Sutton (USA)	Miss D.K. Douglass (BRI)	6-3 6-4	-	Sutton	Miss C.M. Wilson (BRI)	6-3 8-6	-
1906	Miss D.K. Douglass (BRI)	Miss M.G. Sutton (USA)	6-3 9-7	57	Douglass	Mrs. A. Sterry (BRI)	6-2 6-2	-
1907	Miss M.G. Sutton (USA)	Mrs. R.L. Chambers (BRI)	6-1 6-4	-	Sutton	Miss C.M. Wilson (BRI)	6-4 6-2	-
1908*	Mrs. A. Sterry (BRI)		w.o.		Sterry	Miss A.M. Morton (BRI)	6-4 6-4	-
1909*	Miss P.D.H. Boothby (BRI)		w.o.		Boothby	Miss A.M. Morton (BRI)	6-4 4-6 8-6	-
1910	Mrs. R.L. Chambers (BRI)	Miss P.D.H. Boothby (BRI)	6-2 6-2	-	Chambers	Miss E.G. Johnson (BRI)	6-4 6-2	-
1911	Mrs. R.L. Chambers (BRI)	Miss P.D.H. Boothby (BRI)	6-0 6-0	25	Boothby	Mrs. F.J. Hannan (BRI)	6-2 7-5	-
1912*	Mrs. D.T.R. Larcombe (BRI)		w.o.		Larcombe	Mrs. A.Sterry (BRI)	6-3 6-1	-
1913*	Mrs. R.L. Chambers (BRI)		w.o.		Chambers	Mrs. R.J. McNair (USA)	6-0 6-4	-
1914	Mrs. R.L. Chambers (BRI)	Mrs. D.T.R. Larcombe (BRI)	7-5 6-4	-	Larcombe	Miss E.M. Ryan (USA)	6-3 6-2	-
1919	Miss S.R.F. Lenglen (FRA)	Mrs. R.L. Chambers (BRI)	10-8 4-6 9-7	125	Lenglen	Mrs. C.R. Satterthwaite (BRI)	6-1 6-1	-
1920	Miss S.R.F. Lenglen (FRA)	Mrs. R.L. Chambers (BRI)	6-3 6-0	-	Chambers	Miss E.M. Ryan (USA)	6-2 6-1	-
1921	Miss S.R.F. Lenglen (FRA)	Miss E.M. Ryan (USA)	6-2 6-0	-	Ryan	Mrs. C.R. Satterthwaite (BRI)	6-1 6-0	-

Challenge Round abolished

FINAL

Year	Champion	Seeded	Runner-up	Seeded	Score	Mins
1922	Miss S.R.F. Lenglen (FRA)		Mrs. F.I. Mallory (USA)		6-2 6-0	23
1923	Miss S.R.F. Lenglen (FRA)		Miss K. McKane (GBR)		6-2 6-2	-
1924	Miss K. McKane (GBR)		Miss H.N. Wills (USA)		4-6 6-4 6-4	75
1925	Miss S.R.F. Lenglen (FRA)		Miss J.C. Fry (GBR)		6-2 6-0	25
1926	Mrs. L.A. Godfree (GBR)		Miss E.M. de Alvarez (ESP)		6-2 4-6 6-3	60
1927	Miss H.N. Wills (USA)	1	Miss E.M. de Alvarez (ESP)	4	6-2 6-4	-
1928	Miss H.N. Wills (USA)	1	Miss E.M. de Alvarez (ESP)	2	6-2 6-3	-
1929	Miss H.N. Wills (USA)	1	Miss H.H. Jacobs (USA)	5	6-1 6-2	-
1930	Mrs. F.S. Moody (USA)	1	Miss E.M Ryan (USA)	8	6-2 6-2	-
1931	Miss C. Aussem (GER)	1	Miss H. Krahwinkel (GER)	4	6-2 7-5	-
1932	Mrs. F.S. Moody (USA)	1	Miss H.H. Jacobs (USA)	5	6-3 6-1	50
1933	Mrs. F.S. Moody (USA)	1	Miss D.E. Round (GBR)	2	6-4 6-8 6-3	120
1934	Miss D.E. Round (GBR)	2	Miss H.H. Jacobs (USA)	1	6-2 5-7 6-3	-
1935	Mrs. F.S. Moody (USA)	4	Miss H.H. Jacobs (USA)	3	6-3 3-6 7-5	100
1936	Miss H.H. Jacobs (USA)	2	Mrs. S. Sperling (GER)	5	6-2 4-6 7-5	101
1937	Miss D.E. Round (GBR)	7	Miss J. Jedrzejowska (POL)	4	6-2 2-6 7-5	60
1938	Mrs. F.S. Moody (USA)	1	Miss H.H. Jacobs (USA)	U	6-4 6-0	-
1939	Miss A. Marble (USA)	1	Miss K.E. Stammers (GBR)	6	6-2 6-0	30
1946	Miss P.M. Betz (USA)	1	Miss A.L. Brough (USA)	3	6-2 6-4	-

SEMI-FINAL

Winner	Loser	Seeded	Score	Mins
Lenglen	Mrs. G.E. Peacock (RSA)		6-4 6-1	-
Mallory	Mrs. A.E. Beamish (GBR)		6-2 6-2	-
Lenglen	Mrs. A.E. Beamish (GBR)		6-0 6-0	-
McKane	Miss E.M. Ryan (USA)		1-6 6-2 6-4	-
McKane	Miss S.R.F. Lenglen (FRA)		w.o.	-
Wills	Mrs. C.R. Satterthwaite (GBR)		6-2 6-1	-
Lenglen	Miss K. McKane (GBR)		6-0 6-0	30
Fry	Mrs J. Billout (FRA)		6-2 4-6 6-3	-
Godfree	Miss J.P. Vlasto (FRA)		6-4 6-0	-
de Alvarez	Mrs. F.I. Mallory (USA)		6-2 6-2	-
Wills	Miss J.C. Fry (GBR)	U	6-3 6-1	-
de Alvarez	Miss E.M. Ryan (USA)	5	2-6 6-0 6-4	105
Wills	Miss E.M. Ryan (USA)	4	6-1 6-2	25
de Alvarez	Miss D.J. Akhurst (AUS)	U	6-3 6-0	70
Wills	Miss E.A. Goldsack (GBR)	U	6-2 6-2	51
Jacobs	Miss J.C. Ridley (GBR)	5	6-2 6-2	115
Moody	Mrs. R. Mathieu (FRA)	5	6-2 6-2	-
Ryan	Miss C. Aussem (GER)	6	6-3 0-6 4-4retd	-
Aussem	Mrs. R. Mathieu (FRA)	3	6-0 2-6 6-3	-
Krahwinkel	Mrs G.M. Heeley (GBR)	6	10-8 0-6 6-4	105
Moody	Mrs R. Mathieu (FRA)	U	6-2 6-0	25
Jacobs	Mrs R. Mathieu (FRA)	2	7-5 6-1	70
Moody	Miss H. Krahwinkel (GER)	6	6-4 6-3	51
Round	Miss H. Krahwinkel (GER)	5	4-6 6-2	115
Round	Miss R. Mathieu (FRA)	8	6-4 5-7 6-2	-
Jacobs	Miss J.M. Hartigan (AUS)	U	6-2 6-2	40
Moody	Miss J.M. Hartigan (AUS)	8	6-3 6-3	42
Jacobs	Mrs. S. Sperling (GER)	2	6-3 6-0	48
Sperling	Miss J. Jedrzejowska (POL)	7	6-4 6-2	-
Round	Mrs. R. Mathieu (FRA)	6	6-3 6-2	60
Jedrzejowska	Mrs. R. Mathieu (FRA)	6	6-4 6-0	-
Moody	Miss A. Marble (USA)	5	8-6 6-2	-
Jacobs	Mrs. S. Sperling (GER)	4	12-10 6-4	110
Marble	Miss A. Marble (USA)	2	6-4 6-4	60
Stammers	Miss S. Sperling (GER)	8	6-0 6-0	19
Betz	Mrs. M. Fabyan (USA)	8	7-5 2-6 6-3	105
Brough	Miss D.M. Bundy (USA)	5	6-2 6-3	60
	Miss M.E. Osborne (USA)	2	8-6 7-5	-

Year	Champion	Seeded	Runner-up	Seeded	Score	Mins	Winner	Loser	Seeded	Score	Mins
1947	Miss M.E. Osborne (USA)	1	Miss D.J. Hart (USA)	3	6-2 6-4	-	Osborne	Mrs. R.A. Summers (RSA)	7	6-1 6-2	27
							Hart	Miss A.L. Brough (USA)	2	2-6 8-6 6-4	87
1948	Miss A.L. Brough (USA)	2	Miss D.J. Hart (USA)	4	6-3 8-6	76	Brough	Miss R.B. Todd (USA)	3	6-3 7-5	-
							Hart	Mrs. W. DuPont (USA)	2	6-4 2-6 6-3	-
1949	Miss A.L. Brough (USA)	1	Mrs. W. duPont (USA)	2	10-8 1-6 10-8	120	Brough	Miss R.B. Todd (USA)	U	6-3 6-0	-
							DuPont	Miss E.H. Rihbany (USA)	3	6-2 6-2	-
1950	Miss A.L. Brough (USA)	1	Mrs. W. duPont (USA)	2	6-1 3-6 6-1	62	Brough	Miss D.J. Hart (USA)	4	8-6 4-6 8-6	-
							DuPont	Miss R.B. Todd (USA)	5	6-3 6-1	45
1951	Miss D.J. Hart (USA)	3	Miss S.J. Fry (USA)	4	6-1 6-0	35	Hart	Miss B.J. Baker (USA)	1	6-4 6-3	-
							Fry	Miss A.L. Brough (USA)	3	6-3 3-6 6-1	-
1952	Miss M.C. Connolly (USA)	2	Miss A.L. Brough (USA)	4	7-5 6-3	65	Connolly	Miss S.J. Fry (USA)	5	6-1 6-1	32
							Brough	Miss R.B. Todd (USA)	3	6-2 6-2	35
1953	Miss M.C. Connolly (USA)	1	Miss D.J. Hart (USA)	2	8-6 7-5	67	Connolly	Miss S.J. Fry (USA)	4	6-1 6-1	33
							Hart	Mrs. D.P. Knode (USA)	8	2-6 6-3 6-3	-
1954	Miss M.C. Connolly (USA)	1	Miss A.L. Brough (USA)	4	6-2 7-5	50	Connolly	Miss E.C.S. Pratt (USA)	2	6-3 8-6	80
							Brough	Miss D.J. Hart (USA)	6	6-3 6-0	40
1955	Miss A.L. Brough (USA)	2	Mrs. J.G. Fleitz (USA)	3	7-5 8-6	90	Brough	Miss D.R. Hard (USA)	1	6-4 4-6 6-3	90
							Fleitz	Miss D.J. Hart (USA)	U	6-1 6-4	46
1956	Miss S.J. Fry (USA)	5	Miss A. Buxton (GBR)	6	6-3 6-1	50	Fry	Miss A.L. Brough (USA)		6-1 6-1	41
							Buxton	Miss P.E. Ward (GBR)		6-2 6-3	43
1957	Miss A. Gibson	1	Miss D.R. Hard (USA)	5	6-3 6-2	50	Gibson	Miss C.C. Truman (GBR)			
							Hard	Mrs. D.P. Knode (USA)			
1958	Miss A. Gibson	1	Miss F.A.M. Mortimer (GBR)	U	8-6 6-2	62	Gibson	Miss A.S. Haydon (GBR)	4	6-2 6-0	31
							Mortimer	Mrs. Z. Kormoczy (HUN)	U	6-0 6-1	31
1959	Miss M.E.A. Bueno (BRA)	6	Miss D.R. Hard (USA)	4	6-4 6-3	43	Bueno	Miss S.M. Moore (USA)	6	6-2 6-4	45
							Hard	Miss S. Reynolds (RSA)	7	6-4 6-4	48
1960	Miss M.E.A. Bueno (BRA)	1	Miss S. Reynolds (RSA)	8	8-6 6-0	59	Bueno	Miss C.C. Truman (GBR)	5	6-0 5-7 6-1	58
							Reynolds	Miss A.S. Haydon (GBR)	3	6-3 2-6 6-4	77
1961	Miss F.A.M. Mortimer (GBR)	7	Miss C.C. Truman (GBR)	6	4-6 6-4 7-5	96	Mortimer	Miss S. Reynolds (RSA)	4	11-9 6-3	90
							Truman	Miss R. Schuurman (RSA)	1	6-4 6-4	38
1962	Mrs. J.R. Susman (USA)	8	Mrs. C. Sukova (TCH)	U	6-4 6-4	57	Susman	Miss A.S. Haydon (GBR)	U	8-6 6-1	62
							Sukova	Miss M.E.A. Bueno (BRA)	5	6-4 6-3	46
1963	Miss M. Smith (AUS)	1	Miss B.J. Moffitt (USA)	U	6-3 6-4	51	Smith	Miss D.R. Hard (USA)	3	6-3 6-3	55
							Moffitt	Miss P.F. Jones (GBR)	4	6-4 6-4	62
1964	Miss M.E.A. Bueno (BRA)	2	Miss M. Smith (AUS)	1	6-4 7-9 6-3	90	Bueno	Miss L.R. Turner (AUS)	4	3-6 6-4 6-4	98
							Smith	Miss B.J. Moffitt (USA)	4	6-3 6-4	43
1965	Miss M. Smith (AUS)	2	Miss M.E.A. Bueno (BRA)	1	6-4 7-5	56	Smith	Miss C.C. Truman (GBR)	3	6-4 6-0	36
							Bueno	Miss B.J. Moffitt (USA)	5	6-4 5-7 6-3	90
1966	Mrs. L.W. King (USA)	4	Miss M.E.A. Bueno (BRA)	2	6-3 3-6 6-1	68	King	Miss M. Smith (AUS)	1	6-3 6-3	45
							Bueno	Mrs. P.F. Jones (GBR)	3	6-3 9-11 7-5	110

Year	Champion	Seeded	Runner-up	Seeded	Score	Mins
1967	Mrs. L.W. King (USA)	1	Mrs. P.F. Jones (GBR)	3	6-3 6-4	60
1968	Mrs. L.W. King (USA)	1	Miss J.A.M. Tegart (AUS)	7	9-7 7-5	69
1969	Mrs. P.F. Jones (GBR)	4	Mrs. L.W. King (USA)	2	3-6 6-3 6-2	71
1970	Mrs. B.M. Court (AUS)	1	Mrs. L.W. King (USA)	2	14-12 11-9	148
1971	Miss E.F. Goolagong (AUS)	3	Mrs. B.M. Court (AUS)	1	6-4 6-1	62
1972	Mrs. L.W. King (USA)	1	Miss E.F. Goolagong (AUS)	2	6-3 6-3	50
1973	Mrs. L.W. King (USA)	2	Miss C.M. Evert (USA)	4	6-0 7-5	53
1974	Miss C.M. Evert (USA)	2	Miss O.V. Morozova (URS)	8	6-0 6-4	59
1975	Mrs. L.W. King (USA)	3	Mrs. R.A. Cawley (AUS)	4	6-0 6-1	38
1976	Miss C.M. Evert (USA)	1	Mrs. R.A. Cawley (AUS)	2	6-3 4-6 8-6	120
1977	Miss S.V. Wade (GBR)	3	Miss B.F. Stove (NED)	7	4-6 6-3 6-1	98
1978	Miss M. Navratilova (USA)	2	Miss C.M. Evert (USA)	1	2-6 6-4 7-5	102
1979	Miss M. Navratilova (USA)	1	Mrs. J.M. Lloyd (USA)	2	6-4 6-4	60
1980	Mrs. R.A. Cawley (AUS)	4	Mrs. J.M. Lloyd (USA)	3	6-1 7-6 (7-4)	93
1981	Mrs. J.M. Lloyd (USA)	1	Miss H. Mandlikova (TCH)	2	6-2 6-2	60
1982	Miss M. Navratilova (USA)	1	Mrs. J.M. Lloyd (USA)	2	6-1 3-6 6-2	87
1983	Miss M. Navratilova (USA)	1	Miss A. Jaeger (USA)	3	6-0 6-3	54
1984	Miss M. Navratilova (USA)	1	Mrs. J.M. Lloyd (USA)	2	7-6 (7-5) 6-2	84
1985	Miss M. Navratilova (USA)	1	Mrs. J.M. Lloyd (USA)	1	4-6 6-3 6-2	107
1986	Miss M. Navratilova (USA)	1	Miss H. Mandlikova (TCH)	3	7-6 (7-1) 6-3	72

Winner	Loser	Seeded	Score	Mins
King	Miss K.M. Harter (USA)	U	6-0 6-3	37
Jones	Miss R. Casals (USA)	U	2-6 6-3 7-5	67
King	Miss P.F. Jones (GBR)	4	4-6 7-5 6-2	-
Tegart	Mrs. N.A. Richey (USA)	3	6-3 6-1	39
Jones	Mrs. B.M. Court (AUS)	1	10-12 6-3 6-2	123
King	Miss R. Casals (USA)	U	6-1 6-0	28
Court	Miss R. Casals (USA)	5	6-4 6-1	50
King	Miss F.G. Durr (FRA)	6	6-3 7-5	67
Goolagong	Mrs. L.W. King (USA)	2	6-4 6-4	55
Court	Mrs. D.E. Dalton (AUS)	U	4-6 6-1 6-0	67
King	Miss R. Casals (USA)	6	6-2 6-4	51
Goolagong	Miss C.M. Evert (USA)	4	4-6 6-3 6-4	95
King	Miss E.F. Goolagong (AUS)	3	6-3 5-7 6-3	97
Evert	Mrs. B.M. Court (AUS)	1	6-1 1-6 6-1	77
Evert	Miss K.A. Melville (AUS)	6	6-2 6-3	47
Morozova	Miss S.V. Wade (GBR)	5	1-6 7-5 6-4	85
King	Miss C.M. Evert (USA)	1	2-6 6-2 6-3	96
Cawley	Mrs. B.M. Court (AUS)	5	6-4 6-4	66
Evert	Miss M. Navratilova (USA)	4	6-3 4-6 6-4	90
Cawley	Miss S.V. Wade (GBR)	3	6-1 6-2	48
Wade	Miss C.M. Evert (USA)	1	6-2 4-6 6-1	114
Stove	Miss S.D. Barker (GBR)	4	6-4 2-6 6-4	104
Navratilova	Mrs. R.A. Cawley (AUS)	3	2-6 6-4 6-4	85
Evert	Miss S.V. Wade (GBR)	4	8-6 6-2	96
Navratilova	Miss T.A. Austin (USA)	4	7-5 6-1	75
Lloyd	Mrs. R.A. Cawley (AUS)	3	6-3 6-2	62
Cawley	Miss T.A. Austin (USA)	2	6-3 0-6 6-4	107
Lloyd	Miss M. Navratilova (USA)	2	4-6 6-4 6-2	99
Lloyd	Miss P.H. Shriver (USA)	7	6-3 6-1	65
Mandlikova	Miss M. Navratilova (USA)	4	7-5 4-6 6-1	87
Navratilova	Miss B. Bunge (GER)	11	6-2 6-2	53
Lloyd	Mrs. L.W. King (USA)	12	7-6 (7-4) 2-6 6-3	123
Navratilova	Miss Y. Vermaak (RSA)	U	6-1 6-1	42
Jaeger	Mrs. L.W. King (USA)	10	6-1 6-1	46
Navratilova	Miss K. Jordan (USA)	6	6-3 6-4	68
Lloyd	Miss H. Mandlikova (TCH)	3	6-1 6-2	46
Navratilova	Miss Z.L. Garrison (USA)	8	6-4 7-6 (7-3)	87
Lloyd	Miss K.S. Rinaldi (USA)	16	6-2 6-0	67
Navratilova	Miss G.B. Sabatini (ARG)	10	6-2 6-2	54
Mandlikova	Mrs. J.M. Lloyd (USA)	2	7-6 (7-5) 7-5	100

Year	Champion	Seeded	Runner-up	Seeded	Score	Mins	Winner	Loser	Seeded	Score	Mins
1987	Miss M. Navratilova (USA)	1	Miss S.M. Graf (GER)	2	7-5 6-3	69	Navratilova	Miss C.M. Evert (USA)	3	6-2 5-7 6-4	123
							Graf	Miss P.H. Shriver (USA)	5	6-0 6-2	51
1988	Miss S.M. Graf (GER)	1	Miss M. Navratilova (USA)	2	5-7 6-2 6-1	93	Graf	Miss P.H. Shriver (USA)	3	6-1 6-2	59
							Navratilova	Miss C.M. Evert (USA)	4	6-1 4-6 7-5	129
1989	Miss S.M. Graf (GER)	1	Miss M. Navratilova (USA)	2	6-2 6-7 (1-7) 6-1	92	Graf	Miss C.M. Evert (USA)	4	6-2 6-1	68
							Navratilova	Miss C. Lindqvist (SWE)	U	7-6 (7-5) 6-2	64
1990	Miss M. Navratilova (USA)	2	Miss Z.L. Garrison (USA)	5	6-4 6-1	75	Navratilova	Miss G.B. Sabatini (ARG)	4	6-3 6-4	78
							Garrison	Miss S.M. Graf (GER)	1	6-3 3-6 6-4	125
1991	Miss S.M. Graf (GER)	1	Miss G.B. Sabatini (ARG)	2	6-4 3-6 8-6	127	Graf	Miss M.J. Fernandez (USA)	5	6-2 6-4	81
							Sabatini	Miss J.M. Capriati (USA)	9	6-2 6-4	95
1992	Miss S.M. Graf (GER)	2	Miss M. Seles (YUG)	1	6-2 6-1	58	Graf	Miss G.B. Sabatini (ARG)	3	6-3 6-3	74
							Seles	Miss M. Navratilova (USA)	4	6-2 6-7 (3-7) 6-4	115
1993	Miss S.M. Graf (GER)	1	Miss J. Novotna (CZE)	8	7-6 (8-6) 1-6 6-4	134	Graf	Miss I.C. Martinez (ESP)	6	7-6 (7-0) 6-3	78
							Novotna	Miss M. Navratilova (USA)	2	6-4 6-4	83
1994	Miss I.C. Martinez (ESP)	3	Miss M. Navratilova (USA)	4	6-4 3-6 6-3	119	Martinez	Miss L.M. McNeil (USA)	U	3-6 6-2 10-8	155
							Navratilova	Miss B.C. Fernandez (USA)	U	6-4 7-6 (8-6)	91
1995	Miss S.M. Graf (GER)	1	Miss A.I.M. Sanchez Vicario (ESP)	2	4-6 6-1 7-5	122	Graf	Miss J. Novotna (CZE)	4	5-7 6-4 6-2	130
							Sanchez Vicario	Miss I.C. Martinez (ESP)	3	6-3 6-7 (5-7) 6-1	131
1996	Miss S.M. Graf (GER)	1	Miss A.I.M. Sanchez Vicario (ESP)	1	6-3 7-5	88	Graf	Miss K. Date (JPN)	12	6-2 2-6 6-3	100
							Sanchez Vicario	Miss J. McGrath (USA)	U	6-3 6-2	64
1997	Miss M. Hingis (SUI)	1	Miss J. Novotna (CZE)	1	2-6 6-3 6-3	110	Hingis	Miss A.S. Kournikova (RUS)	U	6-3 6-2	62
							Novotna	Miss A.I.M. Sanchez Vicario (ESP)	8	6-4 6-2	67
1998	Miss J. Novotna (CZE)	3	Miss N. Tauziat (FRA)	16	6-4 7-6 (7-2)	94	Novotna	Miss M. Hingis (SUI)	1	6-4 6-4	83
							Tauziat	Miss N.M. Zvereva (BLR)	U	1-6 7-6 (7-1) 6-3	111
1999	Miss L.A. Davenport (USA)	3	Miss S.M. Graf (GER)	2	6-4 7-5	75	Davenport	Miss A.W. Stevenson (USA)	U	6-1 6-1	48
							Graf	Miss M. Lucic (CRO)	U	6-7 (3-7) 6-4 6-3	111
2000	Miss V.E.S. Williams (USA)	5	Miss L.A. Davenport (USA)	2	6-3 7-6 (7-3)	84	Williams	Miss S.J. Williams (USA)	8	6-2 7-6 (7-3)	87
							Davenport	Miss J. Dokic (AUS)	U	6-4 6-2	51
2001	Miss V.E.S. Williams (USA)	2	Miss J. Henin (BEL)	8	6-1 3-6 6-0	69	Williams	Miss L.A. Davenport (USA)	3	6-2 6-7 (1-7) 6-1	102
							Henin	Miss J.M. Capriati (USA)	4	2-6 6-4 6-2	88
2002	Miss S.J. Williams (USA)	2	Miss V.E.S. Williams (USA)	1	7-6 (7-4) 6-3	78	S.J. Williams	Miss A. Mauresmo (FRA)	9	6-2 6-1	55
							V.E.S. Williams	Miss J. Henin (BEL)	6	6-3 6-2	77
2003	Miss S.J. Williams (USA)	1	Miss V.E.S. Williams (USA)	4	4-6 6-4 6-2	123	S.J. Williams	Mrs P.Y. Henin-Hardenne (BEL)	3	4-6 6-3 6-1	70
							V.E.S. Williams	Miss K. Clijsters (BEL)	2	4-6 6-3 6-1	100
2004	Miss M Sharapova (RUS)	13	Miss S.J. Williams (USA)	1	6-1 6-4	74	Sharapova	Miss L.A. Davenport (USA)	5	2-6 7-6 (7-5) 6-1	114
							S.J. Williams	Miss A. Mauresmo (FRA)	4	6-7 (4-7) 7-5 6-4	147
2005	Miss V.E.S. Williams (USA)	14	Miss L.A. Davenport (USA)	1	4-6 7-6 (7-4) 9-7	166	V.E.S. Williams	Miss M. Sharapova (RUS)	2	7-6 (7-2) 6-1	102
							Davenport	Miss A. Mauresmo (FRA)	3	6-7 (5-7) 7-6 (7-4) 6-4	136

Year	Champion	Seeded	Runner-up	Seeded	Score	Mins
2006	Miss A. Mauresmo (FRA)	1	Mrs P-Y Hardenne (BEL)	3	2-6 6-3 6-4	123
2007	Miss V.E.S. Williams (USA)	23	Miss M.S. Bartoli (FRA)	18	6-4 6-1	90
2008	Miss V.E.S Williams (USA)	7	Miss S.J. Williams (USA)	6	7-5 6-4	111
2009	Miss S.J. Williams (USA)	2	Miss V.E.S Williams (USA)	3	7-6 (7-3) 6-2	86
2010	Miss S.J. Williams (USA)	1	Miss V. Zvonareva (RUS)	21	6-3 6-2	67
2011	Miss P. Kvitova (CZE)	8	Miss M. Sharapova (RUS)	5	6-3 6-4	86
2012	Miss S.J.Williams (USA)	6	Miss A.R. Radwanska (POL)	3	6-1 5-7 6-2	121
2013	Miss M.S.Bartoli (FRA)	15	Miss S.K. Lisicki (GER)	23	6-1 6-4	81
2014	Miss P. Kvitova (CZE)	6	Miss E.C.M. Bouchard (CAN)	13	6-3 6-0	55

Winner	Loser	Seeded	Score	Mins
Mauresmo	Miss M. Sharapova (RUS)	4	6-3 3-6 6-2	133
Hardenne	Miss K. Clijsters (BEL)	2	6-4 7-6 (7-4)	91
Williams	Miss A. Ivanovic (SBR)	6	6-2 6-4	86
Bartoli	Miss J. Henin (BEL)	1	1-6 7-5 6-1	116
V.E.S. Williams	Mis E.F. Dementieva (RUS)	5	6-1 7-6 (7-3)	102
S.J. Williams	Miss J. Zheng (CHN)	U	6-2 7-6 (7-5)	85
V.E.S. Williams	Miss E.F. Dementieva (RUS)	4	6-7 (4-7) 7-5 8-6	170
S.J. Williams	Miss D. Safina (RUS)	1	6-1 6-0	52
S.J. Williams	Miss P. Kvitova (CZE)	U	7-6 (7-5) 6-2	93
Zvonareva	Miss T.K. Pironkova (BUL)	U	3-6 6-3 6-2	107
Kvitova	Miss V.F. Azarenka (BLR)	4	6-1 3-6 6-2	104
Sharapova	Miss S.K. Lisicki (GER)	U	6-4 6-3	88
Radwanska	Miss A. Kerber (GER)	(8)	6-3 6-4	70
S.J. Williams	Miss V.F. Azarenko (BLR)	(2)	6-3 7-6 (8-6)	96
Lisicki	Miss A. Radwanska (POL)	4	6-4 2-6 9-7	139
Bartoli	Miss K. Flipkens (NED)	20	6-1 6-2	63
Bouchard	Miss S. Halep (ROM)	3	7-6 (7-5) 6-2	95
Kvitova	Miss L. Safarova (CZE)	23	7-6 (8-6) 6-1	80

Ladies' Doubles Championship

FINAL

Year	Champions	Seeded	Runners-up	Seeded	Score	Mins
1913	Miss P.D.H. Boothby and Mrs. R.J. McNair (BRI)		Mrs. R.L. Chambers and Mrs. A. Sterry (BRI)		4-6 2-4 ret'd	–
1914	Miss A.M. Morton (BRI) and Miss E.M. Ryan (USA)		Mrs. F.J. Hannam and Mrs. D.T.R. Larcombe (BRI)		6-1 6-3	–
1919	Miss S.R.F. Lenglen (FRA) and Miss E.M. Ryan (USA)		Mrs. R.L. Chambers and Mrs. D.T.R. Larcombe (BRI)		4-6 7-5 6-3	–
1920	Miss S.R.F. Lenglen (FRA) and Miss E.M. Ryan (USA)		Mrs. R.L. Chambers and Mrs. D.T.R. Larcombe (BRI)		6-4 6-0	–
1921	Miss S.R.F. Lenglen (FRA) and Miss E.M. Ryan (USA)		Mrs. A.E. Beamish (BRI) and Mrs. G.E. Peacock (RSA)		6-1 6-2	–
1922	Miss S.R.F. Lenglen (FRA) and Miss E.M. Ryan (USA)		Miss K. McKane and Mrs. A.D. Stocks (BRI)		6-0 6-4	–
1923	Miss S.R.F. Lenglen (FRA) and Miss E.M. Ryan (USA)		Miss J.W. Austin and Miss E.L. Colyer (GBR)		6-3 6-1	–
1924	Mrs. G. Wightman and Miss H.N. Wills (USA)		Mrs. B.C. Covell and Miss K. McKane (GBR)		6-4 6-4	–
1925	Miss S.R.F. Lenglen (FRA) and Miss E.M. Ryan (USA)		Mrs. A.V. Bridge and Mrs. C.G. McIlquham (GBR)		6-2 6-2	–

SEMI-FINAL

Winners	Losers	Seeded	Score	Mins
Boothby and McNair	Mrs. D.T.R. Larcombe and Mrs. E.G. Parton (BRI)		6-3 6-4	–
Chambers and Sterry	Mrs. B.R. Armstrong and Miss O.B. Manser (BRI)		6-3 2-6 6-3	–
Morton and Ryan	Mrs. R.L. Chambers and Mrs. A. Sterry (BRI)		6-4 6-1	–
Hannam and Larcombe	Miss M. Broquedis (FRA) and Miss V.M. Pinckney (BRI)		6-2 6-0	–
Lenglen and Ryan	Mrs. R.J. McNair and Mrs. E.G. Parton (BRI)		6-2 6-1	–
Chambers and Larcombe	Mrs. A.A. Hall and Miss E.D. Holman (BRI)		6-1 6-2	–
Lenglen and Ryan	Mrs. B.R. Armstrong and Miss O.B.Manser (BRI)		6-1 6-0	–
Chambers and Larcombe	Mrs. A.E. Beamish and Miss H. Hogarth (BRI)		6-1 6-1	–
Lenglen and Ryan	Miss P.L. Howkins and Miss D.C. Shepherd (BRI)		6-2 6-0	–
Beamish and Peacock	Mrs. A.C. Craddock and Miss M. McKane (BRI)		6-2 6-1	–
Lenglen and Ryan	Mrs. A.C. Geen and Mrs. R.J. McNair (BRI)		6-0 6-1	–
McKane and Stocks	Mrs. E.D. Holman and Mrs J.L. Leisk (BRI)		w.o.	–
Lenglen and Ryan	Mrs R.L. Chambers and Miss K. McKane (GBR)		6-1 6-2	–
Austin and Colyer	Miss E.F. Rose and Miss J.S. Youle (GBR)		8-6 6-4	–
Wightman and Wills	Miss E.A. Goss and Miss J.B. Jessop (USA)		8-6 6-4	–
Covell and McKane	Mrs R.L. Chambers and Mrs W.P. Barron (GBR)		6-4 3-6 6-4	–
Lenglen and Ryan	Mrs A.E. Beamish and Miss E.R. Clarke (GBR)		6-0 6-2	–
Bridge and McIlquham	Mrs R.L. Chambers and Miss E.H. Harvey (GBR)		6-1 2-6 6-4	–

Final

Year	Champions	Seeded	Runners-up	Seeded	Score	Mins
1926	Miss M.K. Browne and Miss E.M. Ryan (USA)		Miss E.L. Colyer and Mrs. L.A. Godfree (GBR)		6-1 6-1	-
1927	Miss E.M. Ryan and Miss H.N. Wills (USA)	2	Miss E.A.L. Heine and Mrs. G.E. Peacock (RSA)	1	6-3 6-2	-
1928	Miss M.A. Saunders and Mrs. M.R. Watson (GBR)	3	Miss E.V. Bennett and Miss E.H. Harvey (GBR)	2	6-2 6-3	-
1929	Mrs. M.R. Watson and Mrs. L.R.C. Michell (GBR)	2	Mrs. B.C. Covell and Mrs. W.P. Barron (GBR)	3	6-4 8-6	-
1930	Mrs. F.S. Moody and Miss E.M. Ryan (USA)	1	Miss E.A. Cross and Miss S.H. Palfrey (USA)	4	6-2 9-7	-
1931	Mrs. W.P. Barron and Miss P.E. Mudford (GBR)	U	Miss D.E. Metaxa (FRA) and Miss J. Sigart (BEL)	4	3-6 6-3 6-4	-
1932	Miss D.E. Metaxa (FRA) and Miss J. Sigart (BEL)	4	Miss H.H. Jacobs and Miss E.M. Ryan (USA)	2	6-4 6-3	-
1933	Mrs. R. Mathieu (FRA) and Miss E.M. Ryan	1	Miss W.A. James and Miss A.M. Yorke (GBR)	U	6-2 9-11 6-4	-
1934	Mrs. R. Mathieu (FRA) and Miss E.M. Ryan (USA)	1	Mrs. D.B. Andrus (USA) and Mrs. C.F.. Henrotin (FRA)	U	6-3 6-3	-
1935	Miss W.A. James and Miss K.E. Stammers (GBR)	3	Mrs. R. Mathieu (FRA) and Mrs. S. Sperling (GER)	2	6-1 6-4	-

Semi-finals

Winners	Losers	Seeded	Score	Mins
Browne and Ryan	Mrs A.E. Beamish and Miss E.R. Clarke (GBR)		6-2 6-3	-
Colyer and Godfree	Mrs. H.J. Feilden and Miss N. Welch (GBR)		6-2 6-3	-
Ryan and Wills	Miss L.A. Godfree and Miss B.M. Nuthall (GBR)	3	6-2 6-2	-
Heine and Peacock	Miss E.H. Harvey and Mrs. C.G. McIlquham (GBR)	4	5-7 6-2 6-1	-
Saunders and Watson	Mrs. R. Lycett (GBR) and Miss E.M. Ryan (USA)	1	6-3 6-1	-
Bennett and Harvey	Miss D.J. Akhurst and Miss E.F. Boyd (AUS)	U	6-8 6-3 6-2	-
Michell and Watson	Miss E.H. Harvey and Mrs. C.G. McIlquham (GBR)	U	6-4 5-7 6-2	-
Barron and Covell	Miss B.M. Nuthall (GBR) and Miss E.M. Ryan (USA)	1	6-4 3-6 9-7	-
Moody and Ryan	Mrs. C.F. Henrotin (FRA) and Miss J. Sigart (BEL)	U and U	6-2 6-0	-
Cross and Palfrey	Miss M.H.B. Feltham and Miss G.M. Heeley (GBR)	U	8-6 6-2	-
Barron and Mudford	Miss L.A. Godfree and Miss D.E. Round (GBR)	U	7-5 3-6 6-3	-
Metaxa and Sigart	Miss B.M. Nuthall and Mrs. E.O.F. Whittingstall (GBR)	1	4-6 8-6 6-4	-
Metaxa and Sigart	Miss E.H. Harvey and Mrs. M.R. Watson (GBR)	U	7-5 6-2	-
Jacobs and Ryan	Miss L. Payot (SUI) and Miss M.A. Thomas (GBR)	U	6-1 6-2	-
Mathieu and Ryan	Miss J.B. Pittman and Miss J.C. Ridley (GBR)	U	6-1 4-6 6-4	-
James and Yorke	Miss L.A. Godfree and Mrs. L.R.C. Michell (GBR)	U	5-7 6-0 6-4	-
Mathieu and Ryan	Miss L. Payor (SUI) and Miss M.A. Thomas (GBR)	U	7-5 6-0	-
Andrus and Henrotin	Mrs. L.A. Godfree and Miss M.C. Scriven (GBR)	U	6-3 12-10	-
James and Stammers	Mrs. R.E. Haylock and Mrs. J.S. Kirk (GBR)		6-3 6-0	-
Mathieu and Sperling	Mrs. J. deMeulemeester (BEL) and Mrs. P.D. Howard (FRA)	U	6-4 8-6	-

Year	Champions	Seeded	Runners-up	Seeded	Score	Mins	Winners	Losers	Seeded	Score	Mins
1936	Miss W.A. James and Miss K.E. Stammers (GBR)	1	Mrs. M. Fabyan and Miss H.H. Jacobs (USA)	2	6-2 6-1	-	James and Stammers Fabyan and Jacobs	Mrs. D.B. Andrus (USA) and Mrs. C.F. Henrotin (FRA) Miss J.M. Ingram and Mrs. M.R. King (GBR)	U 	6-0 6-4 6-4 6-3	- -
1937	Mrs. R. Mathieu (FRA) and Miss A.M. Yorke (GBR)	2	Mrs. M.R. King and Mrs. J.B. Pitman (GBR)	U	6-3 6-3	-	Mathieu and Yorke King and Pittman	Miss E.M. Dearman and Mrs. J.M. Ingram (GBR) Mrs. D.B. Andrus (USA) and Mrs. C.F. Henrotin (FRA)	4 U	7-5 6-3 6-3 6-4	- -
1938	Mrs. M. Fabyan and Miss A. Marble (USA)	2	Mrs. R. Mathieu (FRA) and Miss A.M. Yorke (GBR)	1	6-2 6-3	-	Fabyan and Marble Mathieu and Yorke	Mrs. J.H.K. Miller and Miss M. Morphew (RSA) Mrs. D.B. Andrus (USA) and Mrs. C.F. Henrotin (FRA)	4 U	7-5 6-4 3-6 6-3 6-4	- -
1939	Mrs. M. Fabyan and Miss A. Marble (USA)	1	Miss H.H. Jacobs (USA) and Miss A.M. Yorke (GBR)	2	6-1 6-0	-	Fabyan and Marble Jacobs and Yorke	Mrs. S.H. Hammersley and Miss K.E. Stammers (GBR) Miss J.A.B. Nicoll and Miss B.M. Nuthall (UBR)	U 4	8-6 6-3 5-7 6-4 11-9	- -
1946	Miss A.L. Brough and Miss M.E. Osborne (USA)	1	Miss P.M. Betz and Miss D.J. Hart (USA)	2	6-3 2-6 6-3	-	Brough and Osborne Betz and Hart	Miss D.M. Bundy and Mrs. R.B. Todd (USA) Mrs. E.W.A. Bostock and Mrs M. Menzies (GBR)	4 3	6-4 6-2 3-6 6-3 64	- -
1947	Miss D.J. Hart and Mrs. R.B. Todd (USA)	2	Miss A.L. Brough and Miss M.E. Osborne (USA)	1	3-6 6-4 7-5	-	Hart and Todd Brough and Osborne	Mrs. E.W.A. Bostock and Mrs. R. Hilton (GBR) Mrs. N.W. Blair and Mrs. M. Menzies (GBR)	3 U	6-0 6-1 6-2 6-1	- -
1948	Miss A.L. Brough and Mrs. W. duPont (USA)	1	Miss D.J. Hart and Mrs. R.B. Todd (USA)	2	6-3 3-6 6-3	-	Brough and duPont Hart and Todd	Mrs. E.H. Rihbany and Miss B.V. Schofield (USA) Mrs. N.W. Blair and Mrs. E.W.A. Bostock (GBR)	U 3	7-5 6-0 6-4 8-6	- -
1949	Miss A.L. Brough and Mrs. W. duPont (USA)	1	Miss G.A. Moran and Mrs. R.B. Todd (USA)	2	8-6 7-5	-	Brough and duPont Moran and Todd	Miss J.I. Gannon and Miss R. Hilton (GBR) Miss S.J. Fry and Mrs. E.H. Rihbany (USA)	4 U	6-2 6-2 6-0 7-5	- -
1950	Miss A.L. Brough and Mrs. W. duPont (USA)	1	Miss S.J. Fry and Miss D.J. Hart (USA)	2	6-4 5-7 6-1	60	Brough and duPont Fry and Hart	Miss R.A. Buck and Miss N.A. Chaffee (USA) Mrs. N.M. Long (AUS) and Miss A.J. Mottram (GBR)	U U	6-1 6-3 6-0 6-2	- -
1951	Miss S.J. Fry and Miss D.J. Hart (USA)	2	Miss A.L. Brough and Mrs. W. duPont (USA)	1	6-3 13-11	85	Fry and Hart Brough and du Pont	Miss B.J. Baker and Miss N.A. Chaffee (USA) Mrs. G.C. Davidson and Miss B.R. Rosenquest (USA)	4 3	6-0 6-2 6-1 6-3	- -

Year	Champions	Seeded	Runners-up	Seeded	Score	Mins	Winners	Losers	Seeded	Score	Mins
1952	Miss S.J. Fry and Miss D.J. Hart (USA)	1	Miss A.L. Brough and Miss M.C. Connolly (USA)	2	8-6 6-3	-	Fry and Hart	Miss J.S.V. Partridge and Mrs I.F. Rinkel (GBR)	4	7-5 6-3	-
							Brough and Connolly	Mrs. M.N. Long (AUS) and Mrs. R.B. Todd (USA)	3	5-7 6-1 6-4	-
1953	Miss S.J. Fry and Miss D.J. Hart (USA)	1	Miss M.C. Connolly and Miss J.A. Sampson (USA)	2	6-0 6-0	-	Fry and Hart	Miss H.M. Fletcher and Mrs. I.F. Rinkel (GBR)	3	6-0 6-0	-
							Connolly and Sampson	Miss F.A.M. Mortimer and Miss J.A. Shilcock (GBR)	U	6-2 6-3	-
1954	Miss A.L. Brough and Mrs. W. duPont (USA)	2	Miss S.J. Fry and Miss D.J. Hart (USA)	1	4-6 9-7 6-3	-	Brough and du Pont	Mrs. W. Brewer (BER) and Miss K.M. Hubbell (USA)	U	6-1 6-1	-
							Fry and Hart	Miss F.A.M. Mortimer and Miss J.A. Shilcock (GBR)	3	6-2 6-1	-
1955	Miss F.A.M. Mortimer and Miss J.A. Shilcock (GBR)	4	Miss S.J. Bloomer and Miss P.E. Ward (GBR)	3	7-5 6-1	-	Mortimer and Shilcock	Miss E.F. Muller and Mrs. L.A. Hoad (AUS)	U	6-2 6-1	-
							Bloomer and Ward	Mrs. J.G. Fleitz and Miss D.R. Hard (USA)	2	6-3 9-7	-
1956	Miss A. Buxton (GBR) and Miss A. Gibson (USA)	3	Miss E.F. Muller and Miss D.G. Seeney (AUS)	U	6-1 8-6	-	Buxton and Gibson	Miss A.L. Brough and Miss S.J. Fry (USA)	1	7-5 6-4	-
							Muller and Seeney	Miss F.A.M. Mortimer and Miss J.A. Shilcock (GBR)	2	6-4 6-2	-
1957	Miss A. Gibson and Miss D.R. Hard (USA)	1	Mrs. K.E. Hawton and Mrs. M.N. Long (AUS)	2	6-1 6-2	-	Gibson and Hard	Miss S. Reynolds and Miss R. Schuurman (RSA)	U	6-2 6-2	-
							Hawton and Long	Miss Y. Ramirez and Mrs R.M.D. Reyes (MEX)	4	7-5 6-2	-
1958	Miss M.E.A. Bueno (BRA) and Miss A. Gibson (USA)	1	Mrs. W. duPont and Miss M. Varner (USA)	U	6-3 7-5	-	Bueno and Gibson	Mrs K.E. Hawton and Mrs M.N. Long (AUS)	3	6-3 6-2	-
							duPont and Varner	Miss Y. Ramirez and Miss R.M.D. Reyes (MEX)	4	6-2 6-3	-
1959	Miss J. Arth and Miss D.R. Hard (USA)	1	Mrs. J.G. Fleitz (USA) and Miss C.C. Truman (GBR)	3	2-6 6-2 6-3	-	Arth and Hard	Miss S. Reynolds and Miss R. Schuurman (RSA)	4	6-0 6-2	-
							Fleitz and Truman	Miss Y. Ramirez and Miss R.M.D. Reyes (MEX)	2	8-6 6-1	-
1960	Miss M.E.A. Bueno (BRA) and Miss D.R. Hard (USA)	1	Miss S. Reynolds and Miss R. Schuurman (RSA)	4	6-4 6-0	-	Bueno and Hard	Miss K.J. Hantze and Miss J.S. Hopps (USA)	3	3-6 6-1 6-4	-
							Reynolds and Schuurman	Mrs. K.E. Hawton and Miss J.P. Lehane (AUS)	U	7-5 6-1	-
1961	Miss K.J. Hantze and Miss B.J. Moffitt (USA)	U	Miss J.P. Lehane and Miss M. Smith (AUS)	3	6-3 6-4	-	Hantze and Moffitt	Miss S.M. Moore (USA) and Miss L.R. Turner (AUS)	4	6-3 6-0	-
							Lehane and Smith	Miss M.L. Hunt and Miss L.M. Hutchings (RSA)	U	6-1 6-1	-

Year	Champions	Seeded	Runners-up	Seeded	Score	Mins	Winners	Losers	Seeded	Score	Mins
1962	Miss B.J. Moffitt and Mrs. J.R. Susman (USA)	2	Mrs. L.E.G. Price and Miss R. Schuurman (RSA)	4	5-7 6-3 7-5	-	Moffitt and Susman Price and Schuurman	Miss J.C. Bricka (USA) and Miss M. Smith (AUS) Miss M.E.A. Bueno (BRA) and Miss D.R. Hard (USA)	3 1	6-3 6-4 6-3 6-3	-
1963	Miss M.E.A. Bueno (BRA) and Miss D.R. Hard (USA)	2	Miss R.A. Ebbern and Miss M. Smith (AUS)	1	8-6 9-7	-	Bueno and Hard Ebbern and Smith	Miss A.V. Dmitrieva (URS) and Miss J.A.M. Tegart (AUS) Mrs. P.F. Jones (GBR) and Miss R. Schuurman (RSA)	U 4	6-4 9-7 7-5 3-6 6-3	-
1964	Miss M. Smith and Miss L.R. Turner (AUS)	1	Miss B.J. Moffitt and Mrs. J.R. Susman (USA)	2	7-5 6-2	-	Smith and Turner Moffitt and Susman	Mrs. P. Haygarth (RSA) and Mrs. P.F. Jones (GBR) Miss M.E.A. Bueno (BRA) and Miss R.A. Ebbern (AUS)	4 3	6-3 6-2 4-6 6-2 6-3	-
1965	Miss M.E.A. Bueno (BRA) and Miss B.J. Moffitt (USA)	2	Miss F.G. Durr and Miss J.P. Lieffrig (FRA)	U	6-2 7-5	-	Bueno and Moffitt Durr and Lieffrig	Mrs. C.E. Graebner and Miss N.A. Richey (USA) Miss E. Buding and Miss H. Schultze (GER)	3 U	6-4 6-2 6-4 7-5	-
1966	Miss M.E.A. Bueno (BRA) and Miss N.A. Richey (USA)	2	Miss M. Smith and Miss J.A.M. Tegart (AUS)	1	6-3 4-6 6-4	-	Bueno and Richey Smith and Tegart	Miss K.M. Krantzcke and Miss K.A. Melville (AUS) Mrs. P.F. Jones and Miss S.V. Wade (GBR)	U 4	6-2 6-3 10-8 6-4	-
1967	Miss R. Casals and Mrs. L.W. King (USA)	3	Miss M.E.A. Bueno (BRA) and Miss N.A. Richey (USA)	1	9-11 6-4 6-2	-	Casals and King Bueno and Richey	Mrs. P.F. Jones and Miss S.V. Wade (GBR) Miss J.A.M. Tegart and Miss L.R. Turner (AUS)	2 4	6-1 6-4 4-6 6-4 6-4	-
1968	Miss R. Casals and Mrs. L.W. King (USA)	1	Miss F.G. Durr (FRA) and Mrs. P.F. Jones (GBR)	3	3-6 6-4 7-5	-	Casals and King Durr and Jones	Mrs W.W. Bowrey and Miss J.A.M. Tegart (AUS) Mrs. J.A.G. Lloyd and Miss F.V.M. MacLennan (GBR)	4 U	1-6 6-1 10-8 6-1 6-0	-
1969	Mrs. B.M. Court and Miss J.A.M. Tegart (AUS)	1	Miss P.S.A. Hogan and Miss M. Michel (USA)	U	9-7 6-2	-	Court and Tegart Hogan and Michel	Mrs. P.W. Curtis and Miss V.J. Ziegenfuss (USA) Miss K.M. Krantzcke and Miss K.A. Melville (AUS)	U U	6-4 6-4 4-6 6-2 7-5	-
1970	Miss R. Casals and Mrs. L.W. King (USA)	2	Miss F.G. Durr (FRA) and Miss S.V. Wade (GBR)	4	6-2 6-3	-	Casals and King Durr and Wade	Miss K.M. Krantzcke and Miss K.A. Melville (AUS) Miss H.F. Gourlay (AUS) and Miss P.M. Walkden (RSA)	3 U	6-2 8-6 6-4 0-6 6-3	-
1971	Miss R. Casals and Mrs. L.W. King (USA)	1	Mrs. B.M. Court and Miss E.F. Goolagong (AUS)	2	6-3 6-2	-	Court and King Court and Goolagong	Mrs. J.B. Chantreau and Miss F.G. Durr (FRA) Mrs. P.W. Curtis and Miss V.J. Ziegenfuss (USA)	4 U	4-6 6-4 6-4 6-2 6-4	-

Year	Champions	Seeded	Runners-up	Seeded	Score	Mins	Winners	Losers	Seeded	Score	Mins
1972	Mrs. L.W. King (USA) and Miss B.F. Stove (NED)	1	Mrs. D.E. Dalton (AUS) and Miss F.G. Durr (FRA)	3	6-2 4-6 6-3	-	King and Stove	Miss W.M. Shaw and Mrs. G.M. Williams (GBR)	U	7-5 3-6 6-3	-
							Dalton and Durr	Miss R. Casals (USA) and Miss S.V. Wade (GBR)	2	6-4 6-1	-
1973	Miss R. Casals and Mrs. L.W. King (USA)	1	Miss F.G. Durr (FRA) and Miss B.F. Stove (NED)	3	6-1 4-6 7-5	-	Casals and King	Miss E.F. Goolagong and Miss J.A. Young (AUS)	U	7-5 7-5	-
							Durr and Stove	Miss F.M. Bonicelli (URU) and Miss I. Fernandez (COL)	U	7-5 8-6	-
1974	Miss E.F. Goolagong (AUS) and Miss M. Michel (USA)	U	Miss H.F. Gourlay and Miss K.M. Krantzcke (AUS)	U	2-6 6-4 6-3	-	Goolagong and Michel	Miss C.M. Evert (USA) and Miss O.V. Morozova (URS)	3	7-5 6-2	-
							Gourlay and Krantzcke	Miss J.K. Anthony and Miss R.A. Schallau (USA)	U	9-8 ( ) 6-2	-
1975	Miss A.K. Kiyomura (USA) and Miss K. Sawamatsu (JPN)	U	Miss F. G. Durr (FRA) and Miss B.F. Stove (NED)	U	7-5 1-6 7-5	-	Kiyomura and Sawamatsu	Mrs. J.B. Chanfreau (FRA) and Miss H.F. Gourlay (AUS)	U	8-6 6-8 6-2	-
							Durr and Stove	Miss R. Casals and Mrs. L.W. King (USA)	2	2-6 8-6 6-2	-
1976	Miss C.M. Evert (USA) and Miss M. Navratilova (TCH)	2	Mrs. L.W. King (USA) and Miss B.F. Stove (NED)	1	6-1 3-6 7-5	-	Evert and Navratilova	Miss D.A. Boshoff and Miss I.S. Kloss (RSA)	U	8-6 8-6	-
							King and Stove	Miss L.J. Charles and Miss S. Mappin (GBR)	U	6-4 6-3	-
1977	Mrs. R.L. Cawley (AUS) and Miss J.C. Russell (USA)	U	Miss M. Navratilova (USA) and Miss B.F. Stove (NED)	1	6-3 6-3	55	Cawley and Russell	Miss L.J. Charles and Miss S. Mappin (GBR)	7	6-3 6-4	-
							Navratilova and Stove	Miss F. G. Durr (FRA) and Miss S.V. Wade (GBR)	4	6-8 6-2 6-2	-
1978	Mrs. G.E. Reid and Miss W.M. Turnbull (AUS)	4	Miss M. Jausovec (YUG) and Miss V. Ruzici (ROM)	7	4-6 9-8 (10-8) 6-3	-	Reid and Turnbull	Miss S.D. Barker (GBR) and Mrs. T.E. Guerrant (USA)	6	6-3 6-2	-
							Jausovec and Ruzici	Miss F.G. Durr (FRA) and Miss S.V. Wade (GBR)	3	6-4 6-4	-
1979	Mrs. L.W. King and Miss M. Navratilova (USA)	1	Miss B.F. Stove (NED) and Miss W.M. Turnbull (AUS)	2	5-7 6-3 6-2	-	King and Navratilova	Miss F.G. Durr (FRA) and Miss S.V. Wade (GBR)	3	6-2 6-4	-
							Stove and Turnbull	Miss M. Jausovec (YUG) and Miss V. Ruzici (ROM)	6	6-1 7-5	-
1980	Miss K. Jordan and Miss A.E. Smith (USA)	4	Miss R. Casals (USA) and Miss W.M. Turnbull (AUS)	2	4-6 7-5 6-1	-	Jordan and Smith	Mrs. L.W. King and Miss M. Navratilova (USA)	1	6-2 4-6 6-4	-
							Casals and Turnbull	Miss C.S. Reynolds and Miss P.G. Smith (USA)	U	6-7 ( ) 7-6 ( ) 6-0	-
1981	Miss M. Navratilova and Miss P.H. Shriver (USA)	2	Miss K. Jordan and Miss A.E. Smith (USA)	1	6-3 7-6 (8-6)	80	Navratilova and Shriver	Miss S.D. Barker (GBR) and Miss A.K. Kiyomura (USA)	4	6-3 6-7 ( ) 6-2	-
							Jordan and Smith	Miss R.D. Fairbank and Miss T.J. Harford (RSA)	7	6-1 6-2	50

Year	Champions	Seeded	Runners-up	Seeded	Score	Mins	Winners	Losers	Seeded	Score	Mins
1982	Miss M. Navratilova and Miss P.H. Shriver (USA)	1	Miss K. Jordan and Miss A.E. Smith (USA)	2	6-4 6-1	52	Navratilova and Shriver	Miss B. Bunge and Miss C.G. Kohde (GER)	U	6-3 6-4	55
							Jordan and Smith	Miss R. Casals (USA) and Miss W.M. Turnbull (AUS)	3	6-2 2-6 6-4	88
1983	Miss M. Navratilova and Miss P.H. Shriver (USA)	1	Miss R. Casals (USA) and Miss W.M. Turnbull (AUS)	6	6-2 6-2	49	Navratilova and Shriver	Miss J.M. Durie and Miss A.E. Hobbs (GBR)	3	7-6 (7-4) 6-4	75
							Casals and Turnbull	Miss B.C. Potter and Miss S.A. Walsh (USA)	7	6-1 6-7 (2-7) 6-4	87
1984	Miss M. Navratilova and Miss P.H. Shriver (USA)	1	Miss K. Jordan and Miss A.E. Smith (USA)	7	6-3 6-4	54	Navratilova and Shriver	Miss J.M. Durie (GBR) and Mrs. D. Hayashi (JPN)	6	6-3 6-4	67
							Jordan and Smith	Miss B.C. Potter and Miss S.A. Walsh (USA)	4	3-6 6-3 6-2	93
1985	Miss K. Jordan (USA) and Mrs. P.D. Smylie (AUS)	3	Miss M. Navratilova and Miss P.M. Shriver (USA)	1	5-7 6-3 6-4	97	Jordan and Smylie	Miss C.G. Kohde-Kilsch (GER) and Miss H. Sukova (TCH)	2	5-7 6-1 6-4	-
							Navratilova and Shriver	Miss H. Mandlikova (TCH) and Miss W.M. Turnbull (AUS)	4	6-4 6-2	62
1986	Miss M. Navratilova and Miss P.H. Shriver (USA)	1	Miss H. Mandlikova (TCH) and Miss W.M. Turnbull (AUS)	3	6-1 6-3	42	Navratilova and Shriver	Miss E.M. Burgin (USA) and Miss R.D. Fairbank (RSA)	8	6-4 6-3	71
							Mandlikova and Turnbull	Miss P.A. Fendick (USA) and Miss J.M. Hetherington (CAN)	U	6-3 6-7 (4-7) 6-3	108
1987	Miss C.G. Kohde-Kilsch (GER) and Miss H. Sukova (TCH)	3	Miss H.E. Nagelsen (USA) and Mrs. P.D. Smylie (AUS)	5	7-5 7-5	85	Kohde-Kilsch and Sukova	Mrs A. Parkhomenko and Miss L.I. Savchenko (URS)	6	1-6 6-4 7-5	-
							Nagelsen and Smylie	Miss L.M. McNeil and Miss R.M. White (USA)	7	6-4 6-7 (4-7) 6-4	-
1988	Miss S.M. Graf (GER) and Miss G.B. Sabatini (ARG)	3	Miss L.I. Savchenko and Miss N.M. Zvereva (URS)	11	6-3 1-6 12-10	169	Graf and Sabatini	Miss C.M. Evert (USA) and Miss W.M. Turnbull (AUS)	13	6-3 6-4	57
							Savchenko and Zvereva	Miss K.M. Adams and Miss Z.L. Garrison (USA)	8	6-3 6-3	59
1989	Miss J. Novotna and Miss H. Sukova (TCH)	2	Miss L.I. Savchenko and Miss N.M. Zvereva (URS)	2	6-1 6-2	50	Novotna and Sukova	Miss M. Navratilova and Miss P.H. Shriver (USA)	1	7-6 (7-4) 7-5	-
							Savchenko and Zvereva	Miss N.A-L. Provis (AUS) and Miss E. Reinach (RSA)	U	6-2 6-2	54
1990	Miss J. Novotna and Miss H. Sukova (TCH)	1	Miss K. Jordan (USA) and Mrs. P.D. Smylie (AUS)	6	6-3 6-4	58	Novotna and Sukova	Miss P.A. Fendick and Miss Z.L. Garrison (USA)	10	7-6 (7-1) 6-4	102
							Jordan and Smylie	Miss L.I. Savchenko and Miss N.M. Zvereva (URS)	3	6-2 7-6 (7-3)	73
1991	Miss L.I. Savchenko and Miss N.M. Zvereva (URS)	2	Miss B.C. Fernandez (PUR) and Miss J. Novotna (TCH)	1	6-4 3-6 6-4	112	Savchenko and Zvereva	Miss M. Navratilova and Miss P.H. Shriver (USA)	8	2-6 6-2 6-4	105
							Fernandez and Novotna	Miss M.J. Fernandez and Miss Z.L. Garrison (USA)	4	7-5 6-2	94

Year	Champions	Seeded	Runners-up	Seeded	Score	Mins	Winners	Losers	Seeded	Score	Mins
1992	Miss B.C. Fernandez (USA) and Miss N.M. Zvereva (CIS)	2	Mrs. A. Neiland (LAT) and Miss J. Novotna (TCH)	1	6-4 6-1	74	Fernandez and Zvereva	Miss A.I.M. Sanchez Vicario (ESP) and Miss H. Sukova (TCH)	3	6-1 6-7 (2-7) 7-5	118
							Neiland and Novotna	Miss M. Navratilova and Miss P.H. Shriver (USA)	4	7-5 6-7 (3-7) 6-3	118
1993	Miss B.C. Fernandez (USA) and Miss N.M. Zvereva (BLR)	1	Mrs. A. Neiland (LAT) and Miss J. Novotna (CZE)	2	6-4 6-7 (4-7) 6-4	127	Fernandez and Zvereva	Miss M.J. Fernandez and Miss Z.L. Garrison (USA)	5	3-6 6-1 10-8	155
							Neiland and Novotna	Miss P.H. Shriver (USA) and Mrs. P.D. Smylie (AUS)	6	6-2 6-2	60
1994	Miss B.C. Fernandez (USA) and Miss N.M. Zvereva (BLR)	1	Miss J. Novotna (CZE) and Miss A.I.M. Sanchez Vicario (ESP)	2	6-4 6-1	60	Fernandez and Zvereva	Miss M.M. Bollegraf (NED) and Miss M. Navratilova (USA)	4	6-4 6-4	71
							Novotna and Sanchez Vicario	Miss N.J. Arendt (USA) and Miss K.L. Radford (AUS)	U	4-6 7-5 6-3	118
1995	Miss J. Novotna (CZE) and Miss A.I.M. Sanchez Vicario (ESP)	2	Miss B.C. Fernandez (USA) and Miss N.M. Zvereva (BLR)	1	5-7 7-5 6-4	125	Novotna and Sanchez Vicario	Miss G.B. Sabatini (ARG) and Miss A. Neiland (LAT)	9	7-6 (7-5) 6-7 (4-7) 6-4	148
							Fernandez and Zvereva	Mrs S. McCarthy (NED) and Miss M.J. McGrath (USA)	5	7-6 (7-5) 6-7 (7-9) 6-2	123
1996	Miss M. Hingis (SUI) and Miss H. Sukova (CZE)	8	Miss M.J. McGrath (USA) and Mrs. A. Neiland (LAT)	4	5-7 7-5 6-1	104	Hingis and Sukova	Mrs P.D. Smylie (AUS) and Miss L.M. Wild (USA)	15	6-4 4-6 6-4	118
							McGrath and Neiland	Miss B.C. Fernandez (USA) and Miss N.M. Zvereva (BLR)	2	6-4 3-6 11-9	158
1997	Miss B.C. Fernandez (USA) and Miss N.M. Zvereva (BLR)	1	Miss N.J. Arendt (USA) and Miss M.M. Bollegraf (NED)	6	7-6 (6-4) 6-4	76	Fernandez and Zvereva	Miss S. Appelmans and Miss M.J.M.M. Oremans (NED)	12	6-1 6-2	46
							Arendt and Bollegraf	Mrs. A. Neiland (LAT) and Miss H. Sukova (CZE)	4	6-2 3-6 6-1	78
1998	Miss M. Hingis (SUI) and Miss J. Novotna (CZE)	1	Miss L.A. Davenport (USA) and Miss N.M. Zvereva (BLR)	2	6-3 3-6 8-6	112	Hingis and Novotna	Miss L.M. Raymond (USA) and Miss R.P. Stubbs (AUS)	7	6-2 6-3	60
							Davenport and Zvereva	Miss M. deSwardt (RSA) and Miss D.A. Graham (USA)	17	6-3 6-0	58
1999	Miss L.A. Davenport and Miss C.M. Morariu (USA)	7	Miss M. de Swardt (RSA) and Miss E.V. Tatarkova (UKR)	9	6-4 6-4	82	Davenport and Morariu	Miss L. Horn (RSA) and Miss K. Srebotnik (SLO)	U	7-6 (7-0) 6-3	84
							deSwardt and Tatarkova	Miss J. Novotna (CZE) and Miss N.M. Zvereva (BLR)	1	6-4 2-6 7-5	119
2000	Miss S.J. Williams and Miss V.E.S. Williams (USA)	8	Mrs. A. Decugis (FRA) and Miss A. Sugiyama (JPN)	4	6-3 6-2	71	Williams and Williams	Miss A.S. Kournikova (RUS) and Miss N.M. Zvereva (BLR)	5	6-3 7-6 (7-4)	85
							Decugis and Sugiyama	Miss L.M. Raymond (USA) and Miss R.P. Stubbs (AUS)	1	3-6 7-5 6-2	102
2001	Miss L.M. Raymond (USA) and Miss R.P. Stubbs (AUS)	1	Miss K. Clijsters (BEL) and Miss A. Sugiyama (JPN)	9	6-4 6-3	54	Raymond and Stubbs	Mrs O.G.H-P Messerli (USA) and Miss N. Tauziat (FRA)	5	6-3 7-5	72
							Clijsters and Sugiyama	Miss V. Ruano Pascual (ESP) and Miss P.L. Suarez (ARG)	2	6-4 6-4	75

Year	Champions	Seeded	Runners-up	Seeded	Score	Mins	Winners	Losers	Seeded	Score	Mins
2002	Miss S.J. Williams and Miss V.E.S. Williams (USA)	3	Miss V. Ruano Pascual (ESP) and Miss P.L. Suarez (ARG)	2	6-2 7-5	80	Williams and Williams	Miss A.S. Kournikova (RUS) and Miss C.R. Rubin (USA)	U	6-7 (3-7) 6-0 6-3	86
							Ruano Pascual and Suarez	Miss C.C. Black (ZIM) and Miss E. Likhovtseva (RUS)	4	6-3 6-4	106
2003	Miss K. Clijsters (BEL) and Miss A. Sugiyama (JPN)	2	Miss V. Ruano Pascual (ESP) and Miss P.L. Suarez (ARG)	1	6-4 6-4	76	Clijsters and Sugiyama	Miss L.A. Davenport and L.M. Raymond (USA)	4	6-1 0-6 6-4	78
							Ruano Pascual and Suarez	Miss E.F. Dementieva and Miss L. Krasnoroutskaya (RUS)	15	3-6 6-1 6-2	87
2004	Miss C.C. Black (ZIM) and Miss R.P. Stubbs (AUS)	6	Mrs A. Huber (RSA) and Miss A. Sugiyama (JPN)	5	6-3 7-6 (7-5)	80	Black and Stubbs	Miss V. Ruano Pascual (ESP) and Miss P.L. Suarez(ARG)	1	7-6 (9-7) 4-6 6-4	125
							Huber and Sugiyama	Miss M. Navratilova and Miss L.M. Raymond (USA)	3	7-6 (7-4) 7-5	99
2005	Miss C.C. Black (ZIM) and Mrs A. Huber (RSA)	2	Miss S. Kuznetsova (RUS) and Miss A. Mauresmo (FRA)	U	6-2 6-1	63	Black and Huber	Miss B.M. Stewart and Miss S.J. Stosur (AUS)	11	6-0 6-2	49
							Kuznetsova and Mauresmo	Miss A-L Groenefeld (GER) and Miss M Navratilova (USA)	8	6-4 6-4	68
2006	Miss Z. Yan and Miss J. Zheng (CHN)	4	Miss Y. Ruano Pascual (ESP) and Miss P.L. Suarez (ARG)	U	6-3 3-6 6-2	129	Yan and Zheng	Miss C.C. Black (ZIM) and Miss R.P. Stubbs (AUS)	2	6-2 7-6 (7-3)	83
							Ruano Pascual and Suarez	Miss Y.L. Fedak and Miss T. Perebiynis (UKR)	U	6-4 6-3	78
2007	Miss C.C. Black (ZIM) and Mrs A. Huber (RSA)	2	Miss K. Srebotnik (SLO) and Miss A. Sugiyama (JPN)	4	3-6 6-3 6-2	120	Black and Huber	Miss A.H. Molik (AUS) and Miss M. Santangelo (ITA)	6	6-4 4-6 6-1	110
							Huber and Srebotnik	Miss L.M. Raymond (USA) and Miss S.J. Stosur (AUS)	1	1-6 3-6 6-2	93
2008	Miss S.J. Williams and Miss V.E.S. Williams (USA)	11	Miss L.M. Raymond (USA) and Miss S.J. Stosur (AUS)	16	6-2 6-2	59	Williams and Williams	Miss N. Dechy (FRA) and Miss C. Dellacqua (AUS)	U	6-3 6-3	63
							Raymond and Stosur	Miss C.C. Black (ZIM) and Miss A. Huber (USA)	1	6-3 6-3	75
2009	Miss S.J. Williams and Miss V.E.S. Williams (USA)	4	Miss S.J. Stosur and Miss R.P Stubbs (AUS)	3	7-6 (7-4) 6-4	95	Williams and Williams	Miss C.C. Black (ZIM) and Mrs A. Huber (USA)	1	6-1 6-2	62
							Stosur and Stubbs	Miss A. Medina Garrigues and Miss V. Ruano Pascual (ESP)	2	6-7 (3-7) 6-4 6-2	127
2010	Miss V. King (USA) and Miss Y.V. Shvedova (KAZ)	U	Miss E.S. Vesnina and Miss V. Zvonareva (RUS)		7-6 (8-6) 6-2	94	King and Shvedova	Mrs A Huber and Mrs B.L. Sands (USA)	5	6-4 6-4	87
							Vesnina and Zvonareva	Miss G.A. Dulko (ARG) and Miss F. Pennetta (ITA)	4	6-3 6-1	67

Year	Champions	Seeded	Runners-up	Seeded	Score	Mins
2011	Mrs. T. Peschke (CZE) and Miss K. Srebotnik (SLO)	4	Miss S. Lisicki (GER) Miss S. Stosur (AUS)	U	6-3 6-1	71
2012	Miss S.J. Williams and Miss V.E.S. Williams (USA)	U	Miss A. Hlavackova and Miss L. Hrdecka (CZE)	6	7-5 6-4	78
2013	Miss S-W. Hsieh (TPE) and Miss S. Peng (CHN)	8	Miss A.Barry and Miss C. Dellacqua (AUS)	12	7-6 (7-1) 6-1	96
2014	Miss T. Babos (HUN) and Miss K. Mladenovic (FRA)	2	Miss S. Errani and Miss R. Vinci (ITA)	14	6-1 6-3	56

Winners	Losers	Seeded	Score	Mins
Lisicki and Stosur	Miss M. Erakovic (NZL) and Miss T. Tanasugarn (THA)	U	6-3 4-6 8-6	153
Peschke and Srebotnik	Miss S. Mirza (IND) and Miss E. Vesnina (RUS)	4	6-3 6-1	66
Williams and Williams	Mrs. A. Huber and Miss L.M. Raymond (USA)	1	2-6 6-1 6-2	97
Hlavackova Hradecka	Miss F.L. Pennetta and Miss F. Schiavone (ITA)	U	2-6 6-3 6-4	127
Hsieh and Peng	Miss S. Aoyama (JPN) and Miss C. Scheepers (RSA)	U	6-4 6-3	70
Barry and Dellacqua	Miss A-L.Groenfeld (GER) and Mrs T. Peschke (CZE)	(7)	7-6 (8-6) 6-3	78
Errani and Vinci	Miss A. Hlavackova (CZE) and Miss J. Zheng (CHN)	9	6-3 6-2	68
Babos Mladenovic	Miss A. Petkovic (GER) and Miss M. Rybarikova (SLO)	U	6-1 6-3	58

Mixed Doubles Championship

FINAL

Year	Champions	Seeded	Runners-up	Seeded	Score	Mins
1913	H. Crisp and Mrs. C.O. Tuckey (BRI)		J.C. Parke and Mrs. D.T.R. Larcombe (BRI)		3-6 5-3 retd	-
1914	J.C. Parke and Mrs. D.T.R. Larcombe (BRI)		A.F. Wilding (NZL) and Miss M. Broquedis (FRA)		4-6 6-4 6-2	-
1919	R. Lycett (BRI) and Miss E.M. Ryan (USA)		A.D. Prebble and Mrs. R.L. Chambers (BRI)		6-0 6-0	-
1920	G.L. Patterson (AUS) and Miss S.R.F. Lenglen (FRA)		R. Lycett (BRI) and Miss E.M. Ryan (USA)		7-5 6-3	-
1921	R. Lycett (BRI) and Miss E.M. Ryan (USA)		M. Woosnam and Miss P.L. Howkins (BRI)		6-3 6-1	-
1922	P.O. Wood (AUS) and Miss S.R.F. Lenglen (FRA)		R. Lycett (BRI) and Miss E.M. Ryan (USA)		6-4 6-3	-
1923	R. Lycett (GBR) and Miss E.M. Ryan (USA)		L.S. Deane (IND) and Mrs. W.P. Barron (GBR)		6-4 7-5	-
1924	J.B. Gilbert and Miss K. McKane (GBR)		L.A. Godfree and Mrs. W.P. Barron (GBR)		6-3 3-6 6-3	-
1925	J.R. Borotra and Miss S.R.F. Lenglen (FRA)		U.L. de Morpurgo (ITA) and Miss E.M. Ryan (USA)		6-3 6-3	-

SEMI-FINAL

Winners	Losers	Seeded	Score	Mins
Crisp and Tuckey	N.S.B. Kidson and Mrs. E.A. O'Neill (BRI)		6-2 6-3	-
Parke and Larcombe	T.M. Mavrogordato and Mrs. E.G. Parton (BRI)		6-3 6-4	-
Parke and Larcombe	H. Crisp and Mrs. C.O. Tuckey (BRI)		4-6 6-2 6-2	-
Wilding and Broquedis	H.I.P. Aitken and Mrs. F.J. Hannam (BRI)		6-3 4-6 6-3	-
Lycett and Ryan	R.V. Thomas (AUS) and Mrs. D.T.R. Larcombe (BRI)		6-2 6-3	-
Prebble and Chambers	M.O. Decugis (FRA) and Miss M.L. Addison (BRI)		6-1 6-0	-
Patterson and Lenglen	A.E. Beamish and Mrs. A.E. Beamish (BRI)		6-1 6-4	-
Lycett and Ryan	B.I.C. Norton (RSA) and Mrs. D.T.R. Larcombe (BRI)		6-3 6-4	-
Lycett and Ryan	A.E. Beamish and Mrs. D.T.R. Larcombe (BRI)		6-4 6-1	-
Woosnam and Howkins	M. Alonso (ESP) and Mrs. R.J. McNair (BRI)		6-1 6-4	-
Wood and Lenglen	C.J.T. Green and Mrs. J.S. Youle (BRI)		6-2 6-2	-
Lycett and Ryan	J.B. Gilbert and Mrs. R.J. McNair (BRI)		6-2 6-1	-
Lycett and Ryan	J. Washer (BEL) and Miss S.R.F. Lenglen (FRA)		7-5 6-3	-
Deane and Barron	V. Richards and Mrs. F.I. Mallory (USA)		5-7 6-3 6-4	-
Gilbert and McKane	E.T.T. Lamb and Miss E.H. Harvey (GBR)		6-2 6-4	-
Godfree and Barron	M. Woosnam and Mrs. B.C. Covell (GBR)		6-4 6-4	-
Borotra and Lenglen	R. Lycett and Mrs. R. Lycett (GBR)		6-4 5-7 6-3	-
Morpurgo and Ryan	J.D.P. Wheatley and Mrs. R.L. Chambers (GBR)		9-7 6-4	-

Year	Champions	Seeded	Runners-up	Seeded	Score	Mins	Winners	Losers	Seeded	Score	Mins
1926	L.A. Godfree and Mrs. L.A. Godfree (GBR)		H.O. Kinsey and Miss M.K. Browne (USA)		6-3 6-4	-	Godfree and Godfree	V. Richards and Miss E.M. Ryan (USA)		7-5 6-4	-
							Kinsey and Browne	R.A. Berger and Mrs. F.M. Strawson (GBR)		5-7 6-4 6-0	-
1927	F.T. Hunter and Miss E.M. Ryan (USA)	3	L.A. Godfree and Mrs. L.A. Godfree (GBR)	1	8-6 6-0	-	Hunter and Ryan	L.B. Raymond and Miss E.L. Heine (RSA)	U	6-3 6-4	-
							Godfree and Godfree	D.M. Greig and Mrs. M.R. Watson (GBR)	U	6-3 6-4	-
1928	P.D.B. Spence (RSA) and Miss E.M. Ryan (USA)	2	J.H. Crawford and Miss D.J. Akhurst (AUS)	U	7-5 6-4	-	Spence and Ryan	F.T. Hunter and Miss H.N. Wills (USA)	3	4-6 6-4 6-3	-
							Crawford and Akhurst	G.R.O. Crole-Rees and Mrs. M.R. Watson (GBR)	4	6-3 7-5	-
1929	F.T. Hunter and Miss H.N. Wills (USA)	2	I.G. Collins and Miss J.C. Fry (GBR)	U	6-1 6-4	-	Hunter and Wills	N.G. Farquharson and Miss E.L. Heine (RSA)	U	6-8 6-2 6-3	-
							Collins and Fry	J.C. Gregory (GBR) and Miss E.M. Ryan (USA)	3	6-2 6-3	-
1930	J.H. Crawford (AUS) and Miss E.M. Ryan (USA)	2	D.D. Prenn and Miss H. Krahwinkel (GER)	U	6-1 6-3	-	Crawford and Ryan	H.J. Cochet (FRA) and Mrs. E.O.F. Whittingstall (GBR)	3	6-3 7-9 6-4	-
							Prenn and Krahwinkel	G.R.O. Crole-Rees and Miss P.E. Mudford (GBR)	U	4-6 6-3 6-3	-
1931	G.M. Lott and Mrs. L.A. Harper (USA)	U	I.G. Collins and Miss J.C. Ridley (GBR)	U	6-3 1-6 6-1	-	Lott and Harper	F.J. Perry and Miss G.M. Heeley (GBR)	U	1-6 3-4 retd	-
							Collins and Ridley	P.D.B. Spence (RSA) and Miss B.M. Nuthall (GBR)	2	4-6 6-4 6-4	-
1932	E.G. Maier (ESP) and Miss E.M. Ryan (USA)	4	H.C. Hopman (AUS) and Miss J. Sigart (BEL)	6	7-5 6-2	-	Maier and Ryan	H.J. Cochet (FRA) and Mrs. E.O.F. Whittingstall (GBR)	2	7-5 3-6 6-1	-
							Hopman and Sigart	J. Brugnon and Miss R. Mathieu (FRA)	3	6-4 6-4	-
1933	G. von Cramm and Miss H. Krahwinkel (GER)	U	N.G. Farquharson (RSA) and Miss G.M. Heeley (GBR)	4	7-5 8-6	-	von Cramm and Krahwinkel	C.H. Kingsley and Mrs. L.A. Godfree (GBR)	U	6-3 8-6	-
							Farquharson and Heeley	J.R. Borotra (FRA) and Miss B.M. Nuthall (GBR)	2	8-6 11-9	-
1934	R. Miki (JPN) and Miss D.E. Round (GBR)	U	H.W. Austin and Mrs. W.P. Barron (GBR)	U	3-6 6-4 6-0	-	Miki and Round	H.G.N. Lee and Miss W.A. James (GBR)	U	6-3 6-2	-
							Austin and Barron	J.S. Olliff and Miss J.M. Ingram (GBR)		6-4 6-1	-
1935	F.J. Perry and Miss D.E. Round (GBR)	3	H.C. Hopman and Mrs. H.C. Hopman (AUS)	U	7-5 4-6 6-2	-	Perry and Round	A.K. Quist (AUS) and Miss J. Jedrzejowska (POL)	U	6-1 6-3	-
							Hopman and Hopman	G. von Cramm and Mrs. S. Sperling (GER)	1	6-4 6-4	-

Year	Champions	Seeded	Runners-up	Seeded	Score	Mins	Winners	Losers	Seeded	Score	Mins
1936	F.J. Perry and Miss D.E. Round (GBR)	1	J.D. Budge and Mrs. M. Fabyan (USA)	2	7-9 7-5 6-4	-	Perry and Round	F.H.D. Wilde and Miss M.E. Whitmarsh (GBR)	U	6-4 1-6 6-3	-
							Budge and Fabyan	C.E. Malfroy (NZL) and Mrs. S. Sperling (GER)	4	6-4 6-3	-
1937	J.D. Budge and Miss A. Marble (USA)	1	Y.F.M. Petra and Mrs. R. Mathieu (FRA)	2	6-4 6-1	-	Budge and Marble	C.G. Mako (USA) and Miss J. Jedrzejowska (POL)	U	6-3 6-2	-
							Petra and Mathieu	D.D. Prenn (STA) and Miss E.M. Dearman (GBR)	U	6-2 6-4	-
1938	J.D. Budge and Miss A. Marble (USA)	1	H.E.O. Henkel (GER) and Mrs. M. Fabyan (USA)	2	6-1 6-4	-	Budge and Marble	R.A. Shayes and Miss J.D. Saunders (GBR)	U	6-4 6-2	-
							Henkel and Fabyan	A.D. Russell (ARG) and Miss W.A. James (GBR)	U	6-3 1-6 6-3	-
1939	R.L. Riggs and Miss A. Marble (USA)	2	F.H.D. Wilde and Miss N.B. Brown (GBR)	U	9-7 6-1	-	Riggs and Marble	C.E. Malfroy (NZL) and Miss B.M. Nuthall (GBR)	3	3-6 6-2 6-4	-
							Wilde and Brown	E.T. Cooke and Mrs. M. Fabyan (USA)	1	6-3 7-5	-
1946	T.P. Brown and Miss A.L. Brough (USA)	3	G.E. Brown (AUS) and Miss D.M. Bundy (USA)	2	6-4 6-4	-	Brown and Brough	H.C. Hopman (AUS) and Miss M.E. Osborne (USA)	1	6-3 6-3	-
							Brown and Bundy	J.E. Patty and Miss P.M. Betz (USA)	U	12-10 6-2	-
1947	J.E. Bromwich (AUS) and Miss A.L. Brough (USA)	1	C.F. Long and Mrs. G.F. Bolton (AUS)	3	1-6 6-4 6-2	-	Bromwich and Brough	L. Bergelin (SWE) and Miss D.J. Hart (USA)	4	6-4 6-2	-
							Long and Bolton	T.P. Brown and Miss M.E. Osborne (USA)	2	7-5 6-2	-
1948	J.E. Bromwich (AUS) and Miss A.L. Brough (USA)	1	F.A. Sedgman (AUS) and Miss D.J. Hart (USA)	4	6-2 3-6 6-3	-	Bromwich and Brough	J. Drobny (TCH) and Mrs. R.B. Todd (USA)	3	5-7 6-1 8-6	-
							Sedgman and Hart	T.P. Brown and Mrs. W. duPont (USA)	2	6-4 3-6 6-3	-
1949	E.W. Sturgess and Mrs. R.A. Summers (RSA)	4	J.E. Bromwich (AUS) and Miss A.L. Brough (USA)	1	9-7 9-11 7-5	-	Sturgess and Summers	O.W.T. Sidwell (AUS) and Mrs. W. duPont (USA)	2	6-4 7-9 6-3	-
							Bromwich and Brough	G.A. Worthington and Mrs. M.N. Long (AUS)	U	6-1 6-2	-
1950	E.W. Sturgess (RSA) and Miss A.L. Brough (USA)	1	G.E. Brown (AUS) and Mrs. R.B. Todd (USA)	4	11-9 1-6 6-4	85	Sturgess and Brough	F.A. Sedgman (AUS) and Miss D.J. Hart (USA)	3	6-2 9-7	-
							Brown and Todd	G.A. Worthington and Mrs. M.N. Long (AUS)	U	9-7 6-4	-
1951	F.A. Sedgman (AUS) and Miss D.J. Hart (USA)	2	M.G. Rose and Mrs. G.F. Bolton (AUS)	U	7-5 6-2	-	Sedgman and Hart	K.B. McGregor (AUS) and Mrs. W. duPont (USA)	3	6-2 4-6 6-3	-
							Rose and Bolton	E.W. Sturgess (RSA) and Miss A.L. Brough (USA)	1	7-5 6-2	-

Year	Champions	Seeded	Runners-up	Seeded	Score	Mins	Winners	Losers	Seeded	Score	Mins
1952	F.A. Sedgman (AUS) and Miss D.J. Hart (USA)	1	E.J. Morea (ARG) and Mrs. M.N. Long (AUS)	U	4-6 6-3 6-4	-	Sedgman and Hart	D.W. Candy (AUS) and Mrs. R.B. Todd (USA)	4	6-2 6-3	-
							Morea and Long	K.B. McGregor (AUS) and Miss A.L. Brough (USA)	2	6-3 7-5	-
1953	E.V. Seixas and Miss D.J. Hart (USA)	1	E.J. Morea (ARG) and Miss S.J. Fry (USA)	4	9-7 7-5	-	Seixas and Hart	L.A. Hoad (AUS) and Miss J.A. Sampson (USA)	U	6-3 7-5	-
							Morea and Fry	G.A. Worthington (AUS) and Miss P.E. Ward (GBR)	U	6-2 6-2	-
1954	E.V. Seixas and Miss D.J. Hart (USA)	1	K.R. Rosewall (AUS) and Mrs. W. duPont (USA)	3	5-7 6-4 6-3	-	Seixas and Hart	M.A. Orway and Miss J.F. Burke (NZL)	U	6-4 6-1	-
							Rosewall and duPont	L.A. Hoad (AUS) and Miss M.C. Connolly (USA)	2	6-8 6-4 6-4	-
1955	E.V. Seixas and Miss D.J. Hart (USA)	1	E.J. Morea (ARG) and Miss A.L. Brough (USA)	2	8-6 2-6 6-3	-	Seixas and Hart	L.A. Hoad and Mrs. L.A. Hoad (AUS)	4	6-3 9-7	-
							Morea and Brough	N.A. Fraser and Miss B.E.J. Penrose (AUS)	U	7-9 6-4 6-4	-
1956	E.V. Seixas and Miss S.J. Fry (USA)	1	G.P. Mulloy and Miss A. Gibson (USA)	3	2-6 6-2 7-5	-	Seixas and Fry	R.N. Howe (AUS) and Miss D.R. Hard (USA)	4	6-3 7-5	-
							Mulloy and Gibson	T.T. Fancutt (RSA) and Miss D.G. Seeney (AUS)	U	6-4 6-4	-
1957	M.G. Rose (AUS) and Miss D.R. Hard (USA)	4	N.A. Fraser (AUS) and Miss A. Gibson (USA)	2	6-4 7-5	-	Rose and Hard	L.A. Ayala (CHI) and Mrs. M.N. Long (AUS)	U	3-6 6-3 6-2	-
							Fraser and Gibson	R.S. Emerson and Miss M.B. Hellyer (AUS)	U	6-4 6-4	-
1958	R.N. Howe and Miss L.G. Coghlan (AUS)	4	K. Nielsen (DEN) and Miss A. Gibson (USA)	2	6-3 13-11	-	Howe and Coghlan	F. Contreras and Miss R.M.D. Reyes (MEX)	U	6-4 6-4	-
							Nielsen and Gibson	W.A. Knight and Miss S.J. Bloomer (GBR)	U	7-5 6-3	-
1959	R.G. Laver (AUS) and Miss D.R. Hard (USA)	3	N.A. Fraser (AUS) and Miss M.E.A. Bueno (BRA)	2	6-4 6-3	-	Laver and Hard	W.A. Knight (GBR) and Miss Y. Ramirez (MEX)	1	6-2 5-7 6-2	-
							Fraser and Bueno	R. Mark (AUS) and Miss J. Arth (USA)	U	6-3 6-2	-
1960	R.G. Laver (AUS) and Miss D.R. Hard (USA)	1	R.N. Howe (AUS) and Miss M.E.A. Bueno (BRA)	2	13-11 3-6 8-6	-	Laver and Hard	R. Mark (AUS) and Miss J.S. Hopps (USA)	U	4-6 6-1 6-2	-
							Howe and Bueno	J. Javorsky and Miss V. Puzejova (TCH)	U	6-1 2-6 6-4	-
1961	F.S. Stolle and Miss L.R. Turner (AUS)	1	R.N. Howe (AUS) and Miss E. Buding (GER)	4	11-9 6-2	-	Stolle and Turner	J. Javorsky and Mrs. C. Sukova (TCH)	3	7-5 6-3	-
							Howe and Buding	E.J. Morea (ARG) and Miss M. Smith (AUS)	2	6-3 6-2	-

Year	Champions	Seeded	Runners-up	Seeded	Score	Mins	Winners	Losers	Seeded	Score	Mins
1962	N.A. Fraser (AUS) and Mrs. W. duPont (USA)	3	R.D. Ralston (USA) and Miss A.S. Haydon (GBR)	U	2-6 6-3 13-11	-	Fraser and duPont	F.S. Stolle and Miss L.R. Turner (AUS)	1	4-6 6-3 6-4	-
							Ralston and Haydon	R.N. Howe (AUS) and Miss M.E.A. Bueno (BRA)	2	6-3 8-10 6-4	-
1963	K.N. Fletcher and Miss M. Smith (AUS)	2	R.A.J. Hewitt (AUS) and Miss D.R. Hard (USA)	U	11-9 6-4	-	Fletcher and Smith	R.D. Ralston (USA) and Mrs. P.F. Jones (GBR)	3	6-1 7-5	-
							Hewitt and Hard	F.S. Stolle and Miss L.R. Turner (AUS)	1	5-7 6-2 6-2	-
1964	F.S. Stolle and Miss L.R. Turner (AUS)	1	K.N. Fletcher and Miss M. Smith (AUS)	2	6-4 6-4	-	Stolle and Turner	T.S. Okker and Miss G.J. Groenman (NED)	U	2-6 6-2 6-3	-
							Fletcher and Smith	F.A. Froehling and Miss J.C. Bricka (USA)	U	7-5 6-3	-
1965	K.N. Fletcher and Miss M. Smith (AUS)	2	A.D. Roche and Miss J.A.M. Tegart (AUS)	U	12-10 6-3	-	Fletcher and Smith	R.D. Ralston (USA) and Miss M.E.A. Bueno (BRA)	3	7-5 6-4	-
							Roche and Tegart	F.S. Stolle and Miss L.R. Turner (AUS)	1	6-3 11-9	-
1966	K.N. Fletcher and Miss M. Smith (AUS)	1	R.D. Ralston and Mrs. L.W. King (USA)	3	4-6 6-3 6-3	-	Fletcher and Smith	F.S. Stolle (AUS) and Miss F.G. Durr (FRA)	4	6-1 7-5	-
							Ralston and King	F.D. McMillan and Miss A.M. van Zyl (RSA)	U	6-4 6-4	-
1967	O.K. Davidson (AUS) and Mrs. L.W. King (USA)	1	K.N. Fletcher (AUS) and Miss M.E.A. Bueno (BRA)	2	7-5 6-2	-	Davidson and King	F.D. McMillan and Miss A.M. van Zyl (RSA)	4	6-3 3-6 6-1	-
							Fletcher and Bueno	R.O. Ruffels and Miss K.M. Krantzcke (AUS)	U	6-3 6-1	-
1968	K.N. Fletcher and Mrs. B.M. Court (AUS)	4	A.I. Metreveli and Miss O.V. Morozova (URS)	U	6-1 14-12	-	Fletcher and Court	O.K. Davidson (AUS) and Mrs. L.W. King (USA)	1	6-4 9-7	-
							Metreveli and Morozova	F.S. Stolle (AUS) and Mrs. P.F. Jones (GBR)	3	6-3 12-10	-
1969	F.S. Stolle (AUS) and Mrs. P.F. Jones (GBR)	4	A.D. Roche and Miss J.A.M. Tegart (AUS)	3	6-2 6-3	-	Stolle and Jones	K.N. Fletcher and Mrs. B.M. Court (AUS)	1	11-9 11-9	-
							Roche and Tegart	R.O. Ruffels and Miss K.M. Krantzcke (AUS)	U	6-4 7-5	-
1970	I. Nastase (ROM) and Miss R. Casals (USA)	U	A.I. Metreveli and Miss O.V. Morozova (URS)	U	6-3 4-6 9-7	-	Nastase and Casals	F.D. McMillan (RSA) and Mrs D.E. Dalton (AUS)	3	5-7 6-2 6-4	-
							Metreveli and Morozova	D. Irvine (RHO) and Miss H.F. Gourlay (AUS)	U	9-11 6-3 6-4	-
1971	O.K. Davidson (AUS) and Mrs. L.W. King (USA)	3	M.C. Riessen (USA) and Mrs. B.M. Court (AUS)	1	3-6 6-2 15-13	150	Davidson and King	I. Nastase (ROM) and Miss R. Casals (USA)	2	6-4 6-1	-
							Riessen and Court	F.D. McMillan (RSA) and Mrs. D.E. Dalton (AUS)	4	7-5 6-3	-

Year	Champions	Seeded	Runners-up	Seeded	Score	Mins	Winners	Losers	Seeded	Score	Mins
1972	I. Nastase (ROM) and Miss R. Casals (USA)	2	K.G. Warwick and Miss E.F. Goolagong (AUS)	1	6-4 6-4	–	Nastase and Casals	C.E. Graebner and Mrs. L.W. King (USA)	3	9-8 (7-4) 7-5	–
							Warwick and Goolagong	P.J. Cramer and Mrs. Q.C. Pretorius (RSA)	U	6-4 6-3	–
1973	O.K. Davidson (AUS) and Mrs. L.W. King (USA)	2	R.C. Ramirez (MEX) and Miss J.S. Newberry (USA)	U	6-3 6-2	–	Davidson and King	A. Metreveli and Miss O.V. Morozova (URS)	3	5-7 7-5 6-1	–
							Ramirez and Newberry	J.R. Cooper and Miss K.M. Krantzcke (AUS)	U	6-1 6-4	–
1974	O.K. Davidson (AUS) and Mrs. L.W. King (USA)	1	M.J. Farrell and Miss L.J. Charles (GBR)	U	6-3 9-7	–	Davidson and King	A.D. Roche (AUS) and Miss F.G. Durr (FRA)	U	3-6 6-3 6-4	–
							Farrell and Charles	N.A. Fraser and Miss H.F. Gourlay (AUS)	U	7-9 8-6 6-2	–
1975	M.C. Riessen (USA) and Mrs. B.M. Court (AUS)	1	A.J. Stone (AUS) and Miss B.F. Stove (NED)	U	6-4 7-5	–	Riessen and Court	J. Kodes and Miss M. Navratilova (TCH)	3	5-7 6-3 6-2	–
							Stone and Stove	A. Metreveli and Miss O.V. Morozova (URS)	4	2-6 6-4 6-4	–
1976	A.D. Roche (AUS) and Miss F.G. Durr (FRA)	U	R.L. Stockton and Miss R. Casals (USA)	U	6-3 2-6 7-5	–	Roche and Durr	F.D. McMillan (RSA) and Miss B.F. Stove (NED)	2	6-3 6-3	–
							Stockton and Casals	R.A. J. Hewitt and Miss G.R. Stevens (RSA)	U	6-3 9-8 ( )	–
1977	R.A.J. Hewitt and Miss G.R. Stevens (RSA)	1	F.D. McMillan (RSA) and Miss B.F. Stove (NED)	1	3-6 7-5 6-4	–	Hewitt and Stevens	P.C. Dent (AUS) and Mrs. L.W. King (USA)	2	5-7 6-4 7-5	–
							McMillan and Stove	R.D. Ralston and Miss M. Navratilova (USA)	4	5-7 6-4 12-10	–
1978	F.D. McMillan (RSA) and Miss B.F. Stove (NED)	2	R.O. Ruffels (AUS) and Mrs. L.W. King (USA)	2	6-2 6-2	–	McMillan and Stove	A.D. Roche (AUS) and Miss F.G. Durr (FRA)	4	7-5 6-3	–
							Ruffels and King	A.J. Stone and Miss D.L. Fromholtz (AUS)	U	6-3 6-4	–
1979	R.A.J. Hewitt and Miss G.R. Stevens (RSA)	2	F.D. McMillan (RSA) and Miss B.F. Stove (NED)	1	7-5 7-6 (9-7)	82	Hewitt and Stevens	J.D. Newcombe and Mrs. R.A. Cawley (AUS)	4	6-7 ( ) 6-4 6-4	–
							McMillan and Stove	K.G. Warwick (AUS) and Miss H.E. Nagelsen (USA)	U	6-2 2-6 6-2	–
1980	J.R. Austin and Miss T.A. Austin (USA)	U	M.R. Edmondson and Miss D.L. Fromholtz (AUS)	6	4-6 7-6 (8-6) 6-3	–	Austin and Austin	F.D. McMillan (RSA) and Miss B.F. Stove (NED)	1	6-4 6-2	75
							Edmondson and Fromholtz	R.L. Case and Miss W.M. Turnbull (AUS)	4	7-6 ( ) 6-4	–
1981	F.D. McMillan (RSA) and Miss B.F. Stove (NED)	2	J.R. Austin and Miss T.A. Austin (USA)	1	4-6 7-6 (7-2) 6-3	–	McMillan and Stove	L.C. Leeds and Miss S.L. Acker (USA)	U	4-6 6-1 6-2	–
							Austin and Austin	A.D. Roche (AUS) and Miss B. Bunge (GER)	U	6-2 7-6 ( )	–

Year	Champions	Seeded	Runners-up	Seeded	Score	Mins	Winners	Losers	Seeded	Score	Mins
1982	K.M. Curren (RSA) and Miss A.E. Smith (USA)	4	J.M. Lloyd (GBR) and Miss W.M. Turnbull (AUS)	3	2-6 6-3 7-5	–	Curren and Smith	C.D. Strode (USA) and Miss A. Temesvari (HUN)	U	6-4 7-5	75
							Lloyd and Turnbull	C.M. Johnstone and Miss P.J. Whytcross (AUS)	U	6-4 6-0	52
1983	J.M. Lloyd (GBR) and Miss W.M. Turnbull (AUS)	2	S.B. Denton and Mrs. L.W. King (USA)	1	6-7 (5-7) 7-6 (7-5) 7-5	100	Lloyd and Turnbull	F.S. Stolle (AUS) and Miss P.H. Shriver (USA)	4	6-7 (4-7) 6-3 6-4	101
							Denton and King	C.D. Strode (USA) and Miss A. Temesvari (HUN)	U	6-4 6-3	56
1984	J.M. Lloyd (GBR) and Miss W.M. Turnbull (AUS)	1	S.B. Denton and Miss K. Jordan (USA)	2	6-3 6-3	56	Lloyd and Turnbull	S.E. Stewart (USA) and Miss E.M. Sayers (AUS)	7	6-1 5-7 6-2	77
							Denton and Jordan	A. Giammalva and Miss S.A. Walsh (USA)	U	7-5 7-5	81
1985	P.F. McNamee (AUS) and Miss M. Navratilova (USA)	2	J.B. Fitzgerald and Mrs. P.D. Smylie (AUS)	7	7-5 4-6 6-2	93	McNamee and Navratilova	S.E. Davis and Miss H.E. Nagelsen (USA)	8	6-7 (4-7) 7-5 23-21	201
							Fitzgerald and Smylie	M.R. Edmondson (AUS) and Miss K. Jordan (USA)	6	7-6 (7-5) 7-5	84
1986	K.E. Flach and Miss K. Jordan (USA)	1	H.P. Guenthardt (SUI) and Miss M. Navratilova (USA)	3	6-3 7-6 (9-7)	74	Flach and Jordan	M. Robertson and Miss E. Reinach (RSA)	U	7-5 6-4	67
							Guenthardt and Navratilova	E. Sanchez (ESP) and Miss B. Bunge (GER)	9	7-6 (7-0) 6-3	65
1987	M.J. Bates and Miss J.M. Durie (GBR)	U	D.A. Cahill and Miss N.A-L. Provis (AUS)	U	7-6 (12-10) 6-3	71	Bates and Durie	D.T. Visser and Miss R.D. Fairbank (RSA)	7	7-6 (7-4) 6-3	-
							Cahill and Provis	A.S. Kohlberg and Miss P.A. Fendick (USA)	13	6-3 7-6 (7-5)	-
1988	S.E. Stewart and Miss Z.L. Garrison (USA)	14	K.L. Jones and Mrs. S.W. Magers (USA)	U	6-1 7-6 (7-3)	69	Stewart and Garrison	J.B. Fitzgerald and Mrs. P.D. Smylie (AUS)	2	6-4 6-7 (10-12) 6-3	110
							Jones and Magers	R.D. Leach and Miss P.A. Fendick (USA)	10	7-6 (7-1) 5-7 6-4	131
1989	J.R. Pugh (USA) and Miss J. Novotna (TCH)	1	M. Kratzmann and Miss J.M. Byrne (AUS)	14	6-4 5-7 6-4	100	Pugh and Novotna	R.A. Seguso and Miss L.M. McNeil (USA)	4	6-1 5-7 6-4	85
							Kratzman and Byrne	R.D. Leach and Miss H.E. Nagelsen (USA)	3	6-4 7-6 (7-2)	61
1990	R.D. Leach and Miss Z.L. Garrison (USA)	3	J.B. Fitzgerald and Mrs P.D. Smylie (AUS)	4	7-5 6-2	73	Leach and Garrison	J.R. Pugh (USA) and Miss J. Novotna (TCH)	1	7-6 (12-10) 7-6 (7-4)	104
							Fitzgerald and Smylie	T. Nelson and Mrs. S.W. Magers (USA)	U	7-6 (10-8) 7-5	83
1991	J.B. Fitzgerald and Mrs. P.D. Smylie (AUS)	2	J.R. Pugh (USA) and Miss N.M. Zvereva (URS)	1	7-6 (7-4) 6-2	71	Fitzgerald and Smylie	C.J. van Rensburg and Miss E. Reinach (RSA)	U	7-5 3-6 7-5	126.
							Pugh and Zvereva	G.D. Connell (CAN) and Miss K.S. Rinaldi (USA)	8	7-5 6-2	66

Year	Champions	Seeded	Runners-up	Seeded	Score	Mins	Winners	Losers	Seeded	Score	Mins
1992	C. Suk (TCH) and Mrs. A. Neiland (LAT)	3	J.F. Eltingh and Miss M.J.M.M. Oremans (NED)	U	7-6(7-2) 6-2	73	Suk and Neiland / Eltingh and Oremans	B.C. Shelton and Miss L.M. McNeil (USA) / T.J.C.M. Nijssen and Miss M.M. Bollegraf (NED)	U / 8	7-6(7-5) 6-4 / 5-7 7-6(7-3) 6-1	90 / 101
1993	M.R. Woodforde (AUS) and Miss M. Navratilova (USA)	12	T.J.C.M. Nijssen and Miss M.M. Bollegraf (NED)	3	6-3 6-4	66	Woodforde and Navratilova / Nijssen and Bollegraf	M. Kratzmann (AUS) and Miss N.M. Zvereva (BLR) / T.A. Woodbridge (AUS) and Miss A.I.M. Sanchez Vicario (ESP)	2 / 1	4-6 6-3 6-4 / 5-7 7-5 6-4	87 / 141
1994	T.A. Woodbridge (AUS) and Miss H. Sukova (CZE)	4	T.J. Middleton and Miss L.M. McNeil (USA)	U	3-6 7-5 6-3	121	Woodbridge and Sukova / Middleton and McNeil	G.D. Connell (CAN) and Miss L.A. Davenport (USA) / B.H. Black (ZIM) and Miss P.H. Shriver (USA)	6 / 2	6-3 6-4 / 6-3 7-6 (10-8)	59 / 102
1995	J.A. Stark and Miss M. Navratilova (USA)	3	C. Suk (CZE) and Miss B.C. Fernandez (USA)	4	6-4 6-4	59	Stark and Navratilova / Suk and Fernandez	M.R. Woodforde (AUS) and Mrs. A. Neiland (LAT) / G.D. Connell (CAN) and Miss L.A. Davenport (USA)	1 / 2	3-6 6-4 6-4 / 7-6(7-4) 6-2	100 / 65
1996	C. Suk and Miss H. Sukova (CZE)	7	M.R. Woodforde (AUS) and Mrs. A. Neiland (LAT)	1	1-6 6-3 6-2	85	Suk and Sukova / Woodforde and Neiland	G.D. Connell (CAN) and Miss L.A. Davenport (USA) / C.J. van Rensburg (RSA) and Miss L. Golarsa (ITA)	2 / U	6-4 6-2 / 6-3 3-6 6-2	53 / 97
1997	C. Suk and Miss H. Sukova (CZE)	4	A. Olhovskiy (RUS) and Mrs. A. Neiland (LAT)	3	4-6 6-3 6-4	97	Suk and Sukova / Olhovskiy and Neiland	G.D. Connell (CAN) and Miss L.A. Davenport (USA) / N.P. Broad (GBR) and Miss M. de Swardt (RSA)	1 / U	3-6 6-2 6-3 / 7-6(9-7) 4-6 6-3	83 / 100
1998	M.N. Mirnyi (BLR) and Miss S.J. Williams (USA)	U	M.S. Bhupathi (IND) and Miss M. Lucic (CRO)	5	6-4 6-4	75	Mirnyi and Williams / Bhupathi and Lucic	P.V.N. Haarhuis and Miss C.M. Vis (NED) / J.J. Gimelstob and Miss V.E.S. Williams (USA)	2 / U	4-6 6-4 7-5 / 6-4 7-5	106 / 81
1999	L.A. Paes (IND) and Miss L.M. Raymond (USA)	1	J.L. Bjorkman (SWE) and Miss A.S. Kournikova (RUS)	3	6-4 3-6 6-3	93	Paes and Raymond / Bjorkman and Kournikova	M.S. Knowles (BAH) and Miss E. Likhovtseva (RUS) / J.P. McEnroe (USA) and Miss S.M. Graf (GER)	4 / 9	6-2 6-4 / w.o.	71 /
2000	D.J. Johnson and Miss K.Y. Po (USA)	8	L.G. Hewitt (AUS) and Miss K. Clijsters (BEL)	U	6-4 7-6(7-3)	75	Johnson and Po / Hewitt and Clijsters	N.A. Lapentti (ECU) and Miss B. Schett (AUT) / J.A. Eagle (AUS) and Miss A. Huber (GER)	U / U	6-3 6-4 / 6-4 7-5	76 / 92
2001	L. Friedl (CZE) and Miss D. Hantuchova (SVK)	U	M.C. Bryan (USA) and Mrs. A. Huber (RSA)	U	4-6 6-3 6-2	85	Friedl and Hantuchova / Bryan and Huber	D. Rikl (CZE) and Miss K. Habsudova (SVK) / M.S. Bhupathi (IND) and Miss E. Likhovtseva (RUS)	15 / 4	6-2 5-7 6-3 / 6-2 6-2	104 / 60

Year	Champions	Seeded	Runners-up	Seeded	Score	Mins
2002	M.S. Bhupathi (IND) and Miss E.A. Likhovtseva (RUS)	3	K.R. Ullyett (ZIM) and Miss D. Hantuchova (SVK)	4	6-4 1-6 6-1	84
2003	L.A. Paes (IND) and Miss M. Navratilova (USA)	5	A. Ram (ISR) and Miss A. Rodionova (RUS)	U	6-3 6-3	61
2004	W.H. Black and Miss C.C. Black (ZIM)	6	T.A. Woodbridge and Miss A.H. Molik (AUS)	8	3-6 7-6 (10-8) 6-4	127
2005	M.S. Bhupathi (IND) and Miss M.C. Pierce (FRA)	U	P.J.Hanley (AUS) and Miss T. Perebiynis (UKR)	U	6-4 6-2	55
2006	A. Ram (ISR) and Miss V. Zvonareva (RUS)	9	R.C. Bryan and Miss V.E.S. Williams (USA)	U	6-3 6-2	56
2007	J.R. Murray (GBR) and Miss J. Jankovic (SRB)	U	J.L. Bjorkman (SWE) and Miss A.H. Molik (AUS)	5	6-4 3-6 6-1	99
2008	R.C. Bryan (USA) and Miss S.J. Stosur (AUS)	U	M.C. Bryan (USA) and Miss K. Srebotnik (SLO)	1	7-5 6-4	63
2009	M.S. Knowles (BAH) and Miss A-L Groenefeld (BAH)	9	L.A. Paes (IND) and Miss C.C. Black (ZIM)	1	7-5 6-3	88
2010	L.A. Paes (IND) and Miss C.C. Black (ZIM)	2	W.A. Moodie (RSA) and Miss L.M. Raymond (USA)	11	6-4 7-6 (7-5)	97
2011	J.Melzer (AUT) and Miss I. Benesova (CZE)	9	M.S. Bhupathi (IND) and Miss E Vesnina (RUS)	4	6-3 6-2	51

Winners	Seeded	Score	Losers	Mins
Bhupathi and Likhovtseva	2	6-4 1-6 6-3	D.J. Johnson and Mrs. O.G.H-P. Messerli (USA)	73
Ullyett and Hantuchova	16	6-3 3-6 6-2	R.L. Koenig (RSA) and Miss E.S.H. Callens (BEL)	93
Paes and Navratilova	10	7-5 6-4	L. Friedl (CZE) and Mrs A. Huber (RSA)	89
Ram and Rodionova	U	6-2 6-3	J.S.H. Kerr (AUS) and Miss M. Sequera (VEN)	61
Black and Black	7	7-5 7-5	R.C. Bryan and Miss L.A. Davenport (USA)	64
Woodbridge and Molik	5	6-4 7-6 (7-3)	P.J. Hanley (Aus) and Miss A. Sugiyama (JPN)	79
Bhupathi and Pierce	3	7-5 6-1	J.L. Bjorkman (SWE) and Miss L.M. Raymond (USA)	65
Hanley and Perebiynis	4	6-3 6-4	K.R. Ullyett (ZIM) and Mrs A. Huber (RSA)	77
Ram and Zvonareva	3	6-7 (4-7) 6-4 11-9	W.H. Black and Miss C.C. Black (ZIM)	98
Bryan and Williams	2	7-5 7-5	M.N. Mirnyi (BLR) and Miss J. Zheng (CHN)	85
Murray and Jankovic	11	6-4 4-6 6-4	D.M. Nestor (CAN) and Miss E. Likhovtseva (RUS)	107
Bjorkman and Molik	U	6-3 3-6 6-3	F. Santoro and Miss E. Bremond (FRA)	99
R.C. Bryan and Stosur	12	2-6 7-6 (7-1) 6-4	J.R. Murray (GBR) and Miss A. Huber (USA)	111
M.C. Bryan and Srebotnik	U	6-4 6-2	L. Andreev and Miss M. Kirilenko (RUS)	74
Knowles and Groenefeld	U	6-2 7-5	J. Murray (GBR) and Mrs. A. Huber (USA)	80
Paes and Black	12	6-4 6-4	S.W.I. Huss (AUS) and V. Ruano Pascual (ESP)	72
Paes and Black	9	6-3 6-3	L. Dlouhy and Miss I. Benesova (CZE)	68
Moodie and Raymond	10	6-4 6-4	M. Melo (BRA) and Miss R.P. Stubbs (AUS)	74
Melzer and Benesova	8	6-4 6-4	D. Nestor (CAN) and Miss Y-J. Chan (TPE)	66
Bhupathiand Vesnina	U	6-2 3-6 7-5	P. Hanley (AUS) and Miss S-W. Hsieh (TPE)	112

Year	Champions	Seeded	Runners-up	Seeded	Score	Mins
2012	M.C. Bryan and Miss L.M. Raymond (USA)	2	L.A. Paes (IND) and Miss E. Vesina (RUS)	4	6-3 5-7 6-4	124
2013	D.M. Nestor (CAN) and Miss K. Mladenovic (FRA)	8	B. Soares (BRA) and Miss L.M. Raymond (USA)	1	5-7 6-2 8-6	124
2014	N. Zimonjic (SRB) and Miss S. Stosur (AUS)	15	M. Mirnyi (BLR) and Miss H-C Chan (TPE)	14	6-4 6-2	56

Winners	Losers	Seeded	Score	Mins
M.C. Bryan and Raymond	N. Zimonjic (SRB) and Miss K. Srebotnik (SLO)	3	6-3 6-4	56
Paes and Vesina	R.C. Bryan and Mrs. A. Huber (USA)	1	7-5 3-6 6-3	112
Soares and Raymond	J-J. Rojer (NED) and Miss V. Dushevina (RUS)	U	6-4 6-4	80
Nestor and Mladenovic	N. Zimonjic (SRB) and Miss K. Srebotnik (SLO)	3	6-2 6-7 (4-7) 11-9	151
Zimonjic and Stosur	A. Qureshi (PAK) and Miss V. Dushevina (RUS)	16	7-5 6-2	68
Mirnyi and Chan	D.M. Nestor (CAN) and Miss K. Mladenovic (FRA)	5	7-6 (7-4) 7-5	90

Ladies listed under different names

Miss B.J. Baker – Mrs. J.G. Fleitz	Miss L. Horn – Mrs. A. Huber	Miss M.A. Saunders – Mrs. L.R.C. Michell
Miss E.V. Bennett – Mrs E.D.F. Whittingstall	Miss P.L. Howkins – Mrs. B.C. Covell	Miss L.I. Savchenko – Mrs. A. Neiland
Miss B. Bingley – Mrs. G.W. Hillyard	Miss A.K. Kiyomura – Mrs. D. Hayashi	Miss E.M. Sayers – Mrs. P.D. Smylie
Miss P.D.H. Boothby – Mrs. A.C. Green	Miss H. Krahwinkel – Mrs. S. Sperling	Miss R.A. Schallau – Mrs. T.E. Guerrant
Miss M. Broquedis – Mrs. J. Billout	Miss E. Likhovtseva – Mrs. M. Baranov	Miss B.V. Schofield – Mrs. G.C. Davidson
Miss C.R. Cooper – Mrs. A. Sterry	Miss K. McKane – Mrs. L.A. Godfree	Miss R. Schuurman – Mrs. R. Haygarth
Miss D.K. Douglass – Mrs. R.L. Chambers	Miss B.J. Moffitt – Mrs. L.W. King	Miss D.C. Shepherd – Mrs. W.P. Barron
Miss C.M. Evert – Mrs. J.M. Lloyd	Miss P.E. Mudford – Mrs. M.R. King	Miss J. Sigart – Mrs. J. de Meulemeester
Miss J.I. Gannon – Mrs. A.J. Mottram	Miss J.A. Nicoll – Mrs. E.W.A. Bostock	Miss M. Smith – Mrs. B.M. Court
Miss E.F. Goolagong – Mrs. R.A. Cawley	Miss M.E. Osborne – Mrs. W. duPont	Miss K.E. Stammers – Mrs. M. Menzies
Miss H.F. Gourlay – Mrs. R.L. Cawley	Miss S.H. Palfrey – Mrs. M. Fabyan	Miss J.A.M. Tegart – Mrs. D.E. Dalton
Miss K.J. Hantze – Mrs. J.R. Susman	Miss K.Y. Po – Mrs. O.G.H-P Messerli	Miss E.W. Thomson – Mrs. D.T.R. Larcombe
Miss A.S. Haydon – Mrs. P.F. Jones	Miss V. Puzejova – Mrs. C. Sukova	Miss L.R. Turner – Mrs. W.W. Bowrey
Miss E.A. Heine – Mrs. J.H.K. Miller	Miss S. Reynolds – Mrs. L.E.G. Price	Miss P.M. Walkden – Mrs Q.C. Pretorius
Miss J. Henin – Mrs. P.Y. Hardenne	Miss B.R. Rosenquest – Mrs. E.C.S. Pratt	Miss H.N. Wills – Mrs. F.S. Moody

Firsts at Wimbledon

The following is a list of "firsts", which most commonly create interest at The Championships (For further information refer to Wimbledon Year by Year.)

Automobile Association – car parking		1927
Aorangi Park – use during The Championships		1982
Ball Girls		1977
Balls	– Ayres	1879
	– Slazenger	1902
	– yellow	1986
Centre Court retractable Roof		2009
Chairs provided on court		1975
Championships	– all five titles retained	1984
	– at Church Road	1922
	– no player used a wooden racket	1988
	– official artist	2006
Double–handed shots	– gentleman	1911
	– lady	1960
Dress	– gentleman wearing shorts	1930
	– gentleman on Centre Court wearing shorts	1933
	– lady without stockings	1927
	– lady on Centre Court without stockings	1931
	– lady on Centre Court wearing shorts	1934
	– player on Centre Court wearing glasses	1931
	– predominately in white	1963
	– almost entirely in white	1995
Hawk-Eye electronic line-calling system		2007
Honorary Stewards		1927
Junior Events		1947
Last Eight Club		1986
Net Cord monitor		1991
Overseas Competitors	– gentlemen's events	1884
	– ladies' events	1900
Overseas Singles champions	– gentleman	1907
	– lady	1905
Park and Ride		1995
Play	– Gentlemen's Singles	1877
	– Gentlemen's Doubles	1884
	– Ladies' Singles	1884
	– Ladies' Doubles	1913
	– Mixed Doubles	1913
	– on a Sunday	1972
	– scheduled on a Sunday (13 days)	1982
	– on a first Sunday	1991
	– scheduled start at 12.30pm	1983
	– scheduled start at Noon	1992
Prize Money	– first introduced	1968
	– equal, Gentlemen and Ladies	2007
Programme	– card	1877
	– stapled book	1924
	– Programme Publications Ltd. associated with production	1947
	– Player biographies	1977
Public Services	– bank	1930
	– chemist shop	1988
	– newsagents	1994

	–	picnic area	1979
	–	Post Office (mobile)	1939
	–	seat cushions	1924
Qualifying competition			1925
Radio broadcast			1927
Radio Wimbledon			1992
Retractable roof			2009
Royalty	–	British	1907
	–	overseas	1895
	–	Queen Elizabeth	1957
St. John Ambulance			1907
Scoreboards	–	electric	1929
Seeding	–	simple form	1924
	–	full	1927
Service line monitors (Cyclops)			1980
Service personnel			1946
Singles final		– toss of coin (charities)	2000
		– interviewed on court	2000
Suppliers		– Coca Cola	1975
		– Evian	2008
		– G4S	1998
		– Hertz	1995
		– HSBC	2008
		– IBM	1990
		– Jaguar	2015
		– Lanson	2001
		– Lavazza	2011
		– Jacobs Creek	2011
		– Philips	1978
		– Ralph Lauren	2006
		– Robinsons	1934
		– Rolex	1979
		– Slazenger	1902
		– Sony	2011
		– Stella Artois	2014
Television large screen		– Aorangi Park	1990
		– southern end of grounds	2001
Television transmission		– black and white	1937
		– colour	1967
Tickets	–	admission reduction after 5pm	1932
	–	all seated Centre Court	1990
	–	price differential for Centre Court	1979
	–	public ballot for Centre Court	1924
	–	public ballot for Centre Court and No. 1 Court combined	1980
	–	Rain, no play – priority next year	1988
	–	Rain, no play – cash refund	1992
Tie–break scoring	–	8 games all	1971
	–	6 games all	1979
Trophies	–	presentation on Centre Court	1949
	–	replicas	1949
Umpires	–	lady umpiring on No. 1 Court	1979
	–	lady umpiring on Centre Court	1981
	–	lady umpiring final on Centre Court	1984
	–	presented on Centre Court	1962
	–	presented with medals on Centre Court	1995
Wimbledon Lawn Tennis Museum			1977
Women's Royal Voluntary Service		– information desks	1950

Wimbledon Year by Year

WORPLE ROAD

1868

The All England Croquet Club was founded on 23rd July, when six gentlemen, John H. Walsh, (Chairman), Capt. R. F. Dalton, J. Hinde Hale, the Revd. A. Law, S. H. Clarke Maddock and Walter Jones Whitmore met in the offices of Herbert Cox, the publisher of "The Field", at 346 Strand in London. Whitmore was elected as Hon. Secretary and Maddock as Hon. Treasurer.

1869

In October a ground of four acres in Wimbledon between Worple Road and the London and South Western Railway was rented for a period of three years at the annual rental of £50, £75 and £100.

Annual subscriptions were set at £1 1s. for a gentleman or lady or £1 11s. 6d. for a husband and wife. Life subscriptions were £10 10s. for individuals and £15 15s. for a husband and wife.

1870

At a cost of £425 the ground was laid out in three terraces. A pavilion was erected and in June a Croquet Championship was held.

1872

The Secretary, John Walsh, offered his pony roller to the Club and sold them his pony for £10.

1875

Lawn Tennis was first played at the Club, when one lawn was set aside for the purpose. Matches were played in accordance with the Marylebone Cricket Club code of laws, issued earlier in the year.

1877

The Club was re-titled The All England Croquet and Lawn Tennis Club and signalled this change of name by instituting the first Lawn Tennis Championship – a Gentlemen's Singles event. A new code of laws was drawn up for the meeting, which was held on July 9th, 10th, 11th, 12th and 19th.

The rectangular court was 26 yards by 9 yards. The height of the net was 5 feet at the posts and 3 feet, 3 inches at the centre. The service line was 26 feet from the net.

The balls were between 2 and $2\frac{1}{4}$ inches in diameter and between $1\frac{1}{4}$ and $1\frac{1}{2}$ ounces in weight. Tennis scoring was adopted with "sudden death" occurring at five games all. Players changed ends between sets. Posts, balls and nets were supplied by Jefferies & Co. of Woolwich.

Available for play were twelve courts, each on lawns, 40 yards x 30 yards.

An entrance fee of one guinea was paid by the 22 players who entered the event. Spencer Gore became champion and won the first prize, value

12 guineas, plus a Silver Challenge Cup to the value of 25 guineas, presented by the Proprietors of "The Field". The second prize was to the value of seven guineas and the third prize to the value of three guineas.

180 balls were used during the meeting.

200 spectators paid a shilling each to watch the final round. A selected few, about 30 in number, were accommodated with seats in a stand of three tiers, erected for the occasion.

1878

The courts were stated to be in excellent condition following levelling during the winter.

The height of the net was altered to 4 feet 9 inches at the posts and 3 feet at the centre. The service line was changed to 22 feet from the net.

"Over-hand" service was reputedly introduced by A.T. Myers.

700 spectators watched the Challenge Round.

1879

1,100 spectators watched the final round.

Balls supplied by Ayres were used for the first time.

1880

Two movable stands provided by F. H. Ayres were erected for the Centre Court.

The first scoring boards were provided.

Additional dressing rooms were made available by the renting of premises at the rear of the pavilion.

Amendment to the Rules altered the height of the net to 4 feet at the posts. The service line was changed to 21 feet from the net. A service touching the net, but otherwise good, was made a "let", while a player touching the net or volleying the ball before it had crossed the net, lost the point.

1,300 spectators watched the Challenge Round.

1881

Temporary Covered Stands A, B and C were erected on the north-west, south-west and north-east sides of the Centre Court, respectively. (The stands were dismantled and stored in sheds during the winter months.)

The Club purchased the freehold of the ground at a cost of £3,000 – £500 down and the balance spread over 7 years at 4%.

1882

Activity at the Club was almost exclusively confined to lawn tennis and the word "Croquet" was dropped from the title.

The height of the net was again altered to 3 feet 6 inches at the posts.

2,000 spectators watched the Challenge Round.

1883

A new horse and heavy roller were purchased.

2,500 spectators were present at the Challenge Round.

1884

Centre Court Stand A was converted into a permanent covered structure.

The Ladies' Singles and Gentlemen's Doubles Championships were started. Both events were played at the conclusion of the Gentlemen's Singles. 13 players entered the Ladies' Singles, which was won by Miss Maud Watson, who defeated her elder sister, Lilian, in the final, 6-8 6-3 6-3. 10 pairs contested the Gentlemen's Doubles.

Ayres introduced a "screw" post which eliminated the use of the guy ropes.

Advantage sets were played in all events.

James Dwight, Arthur Rives and Richard Sears of the United States became the first overseas competitors.

1885

Centre Court Stands B and C were converted into permanent covered structures.

A modified Bagnall-Wild method of draw, which placed all byes in the first round, was accepted by the Committee.

The first tarpaulin for the Centre Court was hired at the cost of £8.

3,500 spectators watched the Gentlemen's Singles Challenge Round.

1886

Improvements were made to the three Centre Court Covered stands which were joined at two corners to form a continuous erection. A section of Stand B was partitioned off for the stewards and press. On the south-east side of the court five raised tiers were built to provide better viewing for over 500 standing spectators. (This uncovered structure became Stand D). Stop nets, eight feet tall, were placed at the rear of all other courts. Refreshments were served in the Pavilion.

The Challenge Round was introduced for the Gentlemen's Doubles and the Ladies' Singles.

William Renshaw won the Gentlemen's Singles for the sixth consecutive year – an all-time record.

1887

The Gentlemen's Doubles and Ladies' Singles were played concurrently with the Gentlemen's Singles.

At the age of 15 years and 285 days, Miss Lottie Dod of the British Isles won the Ladies' Singles – the youngest player to do so.

1888

Bad weather during the previous week forced the opening of the meeting from the Saturday until the following Tuesday.

New entrance gates to the ground were erected.

The full Bagnall-Wild method of draw was accepted.

Sunday play for members was allowed on ground for first time.

1889

The drainage of the lawns was considerably improved. The appearance of the ground was made more picturesque by the planting of shrubs and the laying out of flower beds. The stands were repainted. The pavilion was redecorated.

William Renshaw won the Gentlemen's Singles for the seventh time – an all-time record.

1890

A new tarpaulin was purchased at a cost of £60.

All three titles were won by Irish players.

1893

The stands were repainted. There was a slight falling off in the sale of stand tickets despite a reduction in the cost.

1894

New baths and showers were installed.

1895

A new Centre Court tarpaulin, much larger than before, was provided. The old cover was used on the outside courts.

Crown Princess Stephanie of Austria was the first royal visitor to Wimbledon.

A loss of £33 was incurred at the meeting.

1896

The All England Plate, a non-championship event for Gentlemen eliminated from the first and second rounds of The Championship Singles, was introduced.

1897

The starting date of the meeting was brought forward from July to June.

To mark Queen Victoria's Jubilee no play took place on the first Tuesday.

1899

A non-championship event for the Ladies' Doubles was added to the programme.

The title of the Club changed to The All England Lawn Tennis and Croquet Club.

A new Steel roller was purchased from Cottis and Son of Epping.

1900

A non-championship Mixed Doubles event was introduced. Miss Marion Jones of the United States became the first overseas competitor in the Ladies' Singles.

1901

A new pavilion was built at a cost of £1,200.

1902

Centre Court Stand B replaced by new structure.

Miss Muriel Robb won the Ladies' Singles, but only after twice playing the Challenge Round. In the first contest Miss Robb was one set all against Mrs. Charlotte Sterry when heavy rain stopped play. On the following day it was decided that the whole match should be replayed. Balls supplied by Slazenger and Sons were used for the first time.

1904

A new uncovered Stand D was built on the south-east side of the Centre Court to hold 600 chairs.

For the first time each outside court was surrounded with green canvas, assisting the players to sight the ball.

On the first Friday the only recorded match decided by the toss of a coin occurred in a fifth round match in which Frank Riseley beat Sydney Smith after being two sets all.

1905

Miss May Sutton of the United States became the first overseas Champion.

1906

A record attendance. The Centre Court Stands were rebuilt and enlarged at a cost of £1,300.

The Grand Duchess Anastasie and Grand Duke Michael of Russia were visitors to the tournament.

1907

British Royalty recognised The Championships for the first time when the Prince and Princess of Wales attended the ground on Saturday, 29th June. The same day, the Prince accepted the Presidency of the Club.

For the first time the St. John Ambulance Brigade attended the meeting, being present on the last six days.

Norman Brookes from Australia became the first overseas winner of the Gentlemen's Singles.

The Ladies' Doubles event was discontinued after the tournament.

1908

Not a drop of rain fell during the meeting.

At the age of 37 years and 282 days, Mrs. Charlotte Sterry of the British Isles won the Ladies' Singles – the oldest player to do so.

The Lawn Tennis competition for the Olympic Games (grass) was held at the Club.

1909

A very wet meeting which necessitated play being extended into a third week, for the first time.

A new Centre Court Stand B, which provided an extra 600 seats, was constructed nine feet nearer the baseline of the court. No. 9 Court was raised five inches and relaid.

The intended order of play was printed on the back of the programme. A clock, lent by Benetfink & Co., was displayed on the Centre Court.

At the age of 41 years and 182 days, Arthur Gore won the Gentlemen's Singles – the oldest player to do so.

New Club colours of dark green and purple were introduced.

1910

An extensive undertaking to pave and concrete paths was carried out.

For the first time two overseas players met in the Gentlemen's Singles All-Comers' final.

1911

Excellent weather during the second week.

The Centre Court was provided with a tent-like cover, which allowed the water to run into drains, especially constructed along each side of the court. All stands were repainted.

The Gentlemen's Singles entry reached over 100 for the first time.

On the second day Harold Bache of the British Isles became the first player at The Championships to hit double-handed shots (backhand).

1912

It rained most days and play was carried over to the third Monday. Only the Centre Court had protective covering.

1913

The meeting took on a new look when the "World's Championships on Grass" was added to the traditional title of "The Championships". The newly created International Lawn Tennis Federation awarded this title to the British Isles in perpetuity for services rendered to the game over the years. The Mixed Doubles and the revived Ladies' Doubles were upgraded into Championship events. Near perfect weather assisted in attracting record crowds, who each day packed the courts to suffocation. Around 10,000 people were present at the ground on the second Friday when tickets for the Gentlemen's Challenge Round changed hands for £7 10s. Due to a suffragette raid on the ground, earlier in the year, visitors carrying bags and parcels underwent close scrutiny by the doormen.

A new Centre Court Stand C was constructed. A special tram service between Wimbledon station and the ground was started.

Injuries to two players prevented three finals being completed. Mrs. Ethel Larcombe was struck in the face by a ball and was forced to retire from the Mixed Doubles, and subsequently was unable to defend her Singles title in the Challenge Round, while Mrs. Charlotte Sterry sustained a leg injury and could not complete the Ladies' Doubles.

1914

A new Centre Court Stand A, with covered passage underneath, was constructed at a cost of £1,800. This stand, which was joined to Stands B and

C, increased the seating capacity of the court from 2,300 to 3,500. Two houses adjacent to the ground (108 and 110 Worple Road) were purchased at a cost of £2,400 and converted into ladies' dressing rooms and the club office, while the gardens of the premises were turned into part of the tea lawn.

The meeting was concluded on the third Monday due to the previous Friday's play being abandoned because of rain.

There was discontent at the price of a cup of tea and a piece of cake being raised from 5d. to 6d.

A captive balloon, which hovered over the ground advertising a Sunday newspaper, became an annoyance to the competitors and was promptly removed.

1915–1918

During the First World War The Championships were suspended. Donations from members and well-wishers enabled the Club to survive.

1919

Because of rain the meeting was extended until the third Tuesday.

A stand was erected at the side of No. 4 Court.

A new form of programme was on sale – printed on paper instead of cardboard, and twice the previous size. The price was raised from 6d. to 1s. Entry to the Gentlemen's Singles was extended to 128. The Committee issued a statement saying that they reserved the right to refuse entries of players whose standard of play did not, in their opinion, justify their inclusion.

For the first time all five Championships were won by overseas players.

King George V and Queen Mary twice visited The Championships.

1920

The proposed new ground at Wimbledon Park Road (Church Road) was purchased after efforts to extend the boundaries of the old ground by buying adjoining properties had failed.

A selection Committee was appointed to reduce the Gentlemen's Singles to 128, from about 150 who submitted entries. Miss Suzanne Lenglen became the first player to win three titles in one year.

1921

The last meeting at Worple Road. Miss Suzanne Lenglen of France struck the last ball on the Centre Court during the Ladies' Doubles Final.

CHURCH ROAD

1922

The new $13\frac{1}{4}$ acre ground at Wimbledon Park Road (later Church Road) was opened at a cost of £140,000. The architecture was in the hands of Capt. Stanley Peach who designed the Centre Court with seating capacity of 9,989 and standing room for 3,600.

The erection of the Centre Court was commenced on 9th September, 1921 and was constructed of reinforced concrete. The stand including the Centre Court covered an area of nearly one acre with the covered portion being 46,500 square feet. Some 3,000 tons of shingle, 1,700 tons of sand and 600 tons of cement were used. Nearly 21 miles of wood slats were used in the making of the three miles of seating. The turf was brought from Cumberland. A disc of white paper the size of a farthing, placed on the turf, could be seen from every seat. The Court was placed so that no shadow could appear until 7 p.m. Space was left on the west side of the Centre Court for a hard court with permanent seating to be constructed. Also a tea-hall to accommodate over 1,000 people was planned. Apart from the Centre Court there were 12 other courts available, numbered 3 to 14. No. 1 and No. 2 Courts were not built. There were parking facilities for 400 cars. Ring and Brymer were appointed caterers.

King George V and Queen Mary were present on the first day, 26th June. Play, scheduled to commence at 2.45 p.m., was delayed because of rain. At 3.30 p.m. the King appeared in the Royal Box, gave three blows on a gong and declared the new grounds open. The tarpaulin was then removed and at 3.45 p.m. Leslie Godfree served the first ball to Algernon Kingscote, who netted the return. Godfree raced forward and pocketed the ball as a memento of the historic occasion. Intermittent rain during the afternoon allowed the completion of one further match – a Gentlemen's Doubles. No play was possible outside the Centre Court. The wet weather, particularly in the second week, forced the tournament to run over until the third Wednesday.

The Challenge Round of the Gentlemen's Singles and Doubles and the Ladies' Singles was abolished.

1923

No. 2 Court was brought into commission. Wood taken from the stands at Worple Road was used in the construction of the stand on the west side of No. 2 Court, providing 900 seats, and the back-to-back stand between No. 2 and No. 3 Courts, making available 1,000 seats in each direction. A Lodge, to accomodate staff, was built just inside the Somerset Road main entrance.

This was the last occasion when the five Championship events were designated "World Championships on Grass".

The draw for the Gentlemen's Singles consisted of a record 133 entries.

Over the entrance to the Centre Court, through which the players pass, was placed a board bearing an inscription of a quotation from Rudyard Kipling's poem 'If':
"If you can meet with triumph and disaster
And treat those two impostors just the same"
This board was presented to the Club, in the autumn by Lord Curzon.

In the autumn the four acre Club ground at Worple Road was sold to the Wimbledon High School for Girls, who are still the owners. The area which included 16 grass courts was disposed of for £4000. The two adjoining premises No. 108 and No. 110 Worple Road were sold to other buyers for £1000 and £900 respectively.

1924

No. 1 Court situated on the west side of the Centre Court, was opened. The stands had a seating capacity of 2,500 with room for approximately 750 standing. A special tarpaulin was provided. Season tickets were issued.

The first match on No. 1 Court on the opening day was between Brian Gilbert and Noel Turnbull of Great Britain. The next day Miss Suzanne Lenglen played Miss Sylvia Lumley-Ellis in the first ladies' match on the court.

A ballot for Centre Court tickets was held for the first time.

A restyled programme, with cover, was on sale. Spectators were able to hire seat cushions for the first time.

A simple form of seeding was introduced, in that up to four representatives of each nation were drawn into four different quarters of the draw.

1925

The meeting was extended to the third Monday, when the final of the Gentlemen's Doubles was played. This match was postponed from the previous Saturday to allow two of the competitors, Jean Borotra and Rene Lacoste of France, to rest following their singles final.

For the first time a Qualifying competition for the five Championship events was necessary and this was held at Roehampton, the previous week. In the singles the last eight survivors qualified and in the doubles the last four pairs.

1926

The Jubilee Championships. Many improvements and alterations were made for the occasion including better tea facilities for officials, players and public. More seats were added under cover to the east side of the Centre Court and a further 27 seats for Press accommodation. The Centre Court surface was completely relaid with turf taken from No. 12 and No. 13 Courts while the sides of the court were relevelled in asphalt to improve drainage. Iron railings were placed in the upper gangway between the Centre Court and No. 1 Court to eliminate, as far as possible, crowd congestion.

More entrances to the ground were provided. A postal telegraph office was installed in the North-West Entrance Hall of the Centre Court.

On the opening day of the meeting a band from the Royal Military School of Music at Kneller Hall entertained the Centre Court crowd from 12.30 p.m. until 2.40 p.m. At 3 p.m. 34 surviving ex-champions of the Gentlemen's Singles and Doubles and Ladies' Singles were presented to King George V and Queen Mary on the Centre Court. Each Champion received a silver commemorative medal.

Following the presentation there was an exhibition Ladies' doubles match between Miss Suzanne Lenglen and Miss Elizabeth Ryan and Mrs. Kathleen Godfree and Miss Kea Bouman.

All competitors at The Championships received a bronze commemorative medal. The Duke of York (later King George VI) competed in the Gentlemen's Doubles event.

1927

One of the wettest meetings ever, with heavy rain on most days and the programme having to be extended to the third Tuesday.

All five Championships were fully seeded for the first time. Play started at 1 p.m. on the first Monday to enable the opening round of the Gentlemen's Singles to be completed within the day.

Over 22,000 spectators were present on the first Saturday which set up a new ground record. Queues started outside the ground at 5 a.m. and over 2,000 people were turned away.

Public address equipment was used from the umpire's chair in the Centre Court for the first time.

For the first time the Automobile Association was responsible for the car parking arrangements at The Championships. The daily charge was 2s. 6d. and a season ticket cost £1 1s.

The first radio broadcast from the Centre Court took place.

For the first time all players in the last eight of the Gentlemen's Singles were from overseas.

American Sidney Wood, aged 15, played on the Centre Court dressed in white plus-fours and golfing stockings. On the first Tuesday on No. 10 Court Miss Ruth Tapscott of South Africa became the first woman to play without wearing stockings.

An additional Qualifying competition was held in the North of England, restricted to entries from Northern counties and Scotland.

1928

Many improvements were evident at this meeting. A staircase was erected from the upper gangway between the Centre Court and No. 1 Court so that spectators on the Centre Court West Stand could enter and leave in more comfort. Screens were put up at both ends of the gangway to prevent spectators of No. 1 Court blocking the entrances to the Centre Court.

A new entrance was made to the Committee box on No. 2 Court. Also the public entrances were widened. A tent-like cover was provided for No. 1 Court. A new Press room was built at the cost of £700 over the South-East Entrance Hall of the Centre Court, overlooking the outside courts and adjacent to the Press Stand. The queue barriers inside the fence in Somerset Road and Church Road were extended by about 50 yards, which enabled the public to form up in the variously priced queues inside the ground.

A tarpaulin was provided for No. 2 Court for the first time.

Adjoining land was purchased for use as Car Park No. 1, No. 2 and No. 3.

1929

Prince George (later Duke of Kent) became President of the Club and so began the long association of the Kent family.

Nearly £5,000 was spent on improvements. Structural alterations were made with a view to increasing facilities rather than making more accommodation available, but even so 500 more spectators watched the play on the Centre Court and over 700 more on No. 1 Court. In the West Open

Stand of No. 1 Court, two additional rows of seats were installed at the back in place of standing room. Behind these seats the promenade was raised to allow 1,200 people to watch the play. A tunnel was constructed underneath to allow a third entrance to the stand.

Two electric scoreboards were installed in the Centre Court and a replica outside over the Referee's Office. Two electric clocks were fitted in the Centre Court and one large clock fitted over the main entrance of the Club. The tea bar next to the referee's office was provided with a roof. Two hard courts were converted into grass No. 15 and No. 16 Courts and this enabled No. 7 Court, after two days play, to be converted into the Members' Tea Lawn. This allowed the main tea lawn to be given over to the public. This practice changed after the 1936 meeting.

For the first time linesmen raised their arm when making a call.

Colin Gregory became the first Englishman to be seeded in the Gentlemen's Singles.

1930

The meeting was extended until the third Monday when the final of the Gentlemen's Doubles was played. This match was postponed from the previous Saturday to allow Wilmer Allison, to rest following his Singles final.

After only one year the electric scoreboards on the Centre Court were replaced with larger items, which also showed previous sets and games. Similar scoreboards were installed on No. 1 Court, together with a third over the Referee's Office.

Martins Bank Ltd. opened a branch in the North Hall of the Centre Court.

Refrigeration equipment was installed on the Centre Court to keep the balls at an even temperature.

A new arrangement was devised whereby Centre Court season tickets were divided into two books, each containing six tickets for alternate days.

Wilmer Allison became the first unseeded player to reach the final of the Gentlemen's Singles. On the first day, Brame Hillyard of Great Britain became the first man to play wearing shorts (No. 10 Court).

Adjoining land was purchased for use as Car Park No. 4.

1931

Two new ladies' dressing rooms were provided, one over the upper portion of the South-West Entrance Hall of the Centre Court and one housed to the right when entering the Club. Every dressing room was equipped with synchronised electric clocks and direct telephone lines to the referee's office.

An enquiry office was established at the main entrance to the Club. The Club offices were reorganised. The ball boys' rest room was established near to the referee's office. The wrought iron Doherty Memorial gates were erected at the South-East entrance to the ground.

On all outside courts new scoreboards were installed, having reels either side of the names containing large figures which were turned round by a handle, sets being on the left and games on the right. For the first time iced drinking water was made available in metal urns on all outside courts.

There was no Gentlemen's Singles final. Sidney Wood became champion when he received a walk-over from fellow-American Frank Shields, who was forced to forfeit owing to an injury sustained in the semi-final.

On the first Tuesday Mrs. Joan Lycett of Great Britain became the first woman to play on the Centre Court without wearing stockings. Her opponent, Miss Lili de Alvarez of Spain, also broke tradition by wearing a trousered frock. Miss Rosie Berthet of France became the first player to wear spectacles on the Centre Court.

1932

On the west side of No. 2 Court, a new stand was constructed, with gentlemen's dressing rooms underneath.

The admission charge to the ground was reduced after 5 p.m.

The ball boys were dressed in a new uniform of grey shirt, long grey trousers and grey felt hat.

1933

Standing accommodation for 300 people was provided behind the reserved seats on the south side of No. 1 Court. On the east side of the Centre Court an additional tea bar was built. New turnstiles were erected at the entrances to the ground.

The car parking facilities were improved to hold 2,000 vehicles.

An interpreter, to assist foreign visitors, was stationed in the Centre Court South-West Entrance Hall.

Players from 27 countries took part at the meeting. The All England Ladies' Plate event was inaugurated.

On the opening day Vivian McGrath of Australia became the second player at The Championships to hit double-handed shots (backhand). On the first Thursday Bunny Austin, of Great Britain, became the first man to play on the Centre Court wearing shorts.

1934

The wooden stand between No. 2 and No. 3 Courts was demolished and replaced by a new concrete structure allowing accommodation to be increased by 200 to 1900. The seats made of teak were detachable and stored under the stand during the winter. A germ, which became known as the "Wimbledon Throat", affected many players who were forced to retire.

On the first Tuesday, Mrs. Eileen Fearnley Whittingstall (née Bennett) of Great Britain became the first lady to play on the Centre Court wearing shorts.

Robinsons Lemon Barley Water was available to competitors on the Centre Court and No. 1 Court.

Fred Perry and Miss Dorothy Round won the Singles titles – the first British double since 1909. Miss Elizabeth Ryan won her 19th Championship.

1935

A competitors' restaurant, lounge and bar were erected above the referee's office and under the South Stand of No. 1 Court.

A balcony extending along the outside of these rooms gave a fine view of the outside courts. A new underground tunnel beneath the east side of the Centre Court gave better access. More seating was added to the West Open Stand of No. 1 Court. Tarpaulins were provided for No. 3 and No. 4 Courts. On 31st May new gates were formally opened at the Worple Road ground in the presence of Club and civic representatives. Also, a fountain was erected just inside the entrance to commemorate the Jubilee of King George V.

1936

A newly designed Lawn Tennis Association flag flew alongside The All England Lawn Tennis Club flag at the entrance to the ground.

J. Lyons & Co. Ltd. replaced Ring and Brymer as caterers to The Championships.

Fred Perry became the first player to win the Gentlemen's Singles three times in succession since the abolition of the Challenge Round. British players carried off four titles – the most by the host nation since 1913.

A tarpaulin was provided for No. 5 Court.

1937

No. 7 Court was converted into a Members' Tea Lawn. The outside courts were renumbered.

Matches were televised for the first time.

Donald Budge became the first man to win three titles in the same year.

On Sunday, 9th May, three days before the Coronation of King George VI, an inter-denominational service of thanksgiving was held on the Centre Court, starting at 6.30 p.m.

1938

Roof supporting pillars in the North Stand of No. 1 Court were removed. Consideration was given to removing the pillars in the Centre Court. Americans won all five titles. Mrs. Helen Moody won the Ladies' Singles for the eighth time. Miss Helen Jacobs became the first unseeded player to reach the Ladies' Singles final. Competitors were provided with a free tea for the first time, and also allowed parking facilities at a reduced rate.

1939

Roof supporting pillars in the South Stand of No. 1 Court were removed. Additional seating was provided in the West Open Stand of No. 1 Court.

A mobile Post Office, situated adjacent to the South-East entrance to the grounds, was available for the first time.

Americans won all titles for the second year running, with Robert Riggs and Miss Alice Marble taking three each.

1940–45

During the Second World War The Championships were suspended.

The Club managed to remain open despite severe curtailment of staff. The premises were used for a variety of civil defence and military functions such as fire and ambulance services, the Home Guard and a decontamination unit. Troops used the main concourse for drilling. There was a small farmyard consisting of pigs, hens, etc.

On the night of Friday 11th October, 1940 a "stick" of five 500 pound bombs straddled the Club grounds. The first demolished the Club's tool house. The second struck the roof of the Centre Court. The third fell in Church Road at the Club's north-east entrance and the last two produced bunkers in the Wimbledon Park Golf course. The damage to the Centre Court resulted in the loss of approximately 1,200 seats at the first three meetings after the War.

A token sign that the Club was returning to normal in the summer of 1945 was the staging in June of several Inter-Dominion Service matches on the outside courts. At the end of the month over 6,000 spectators packed the No. 1 Court to see the U.S.A. defeat the British Empire 4–1. The proceeds went to the Mayor of Wimbledon's Resettlement Fund. Four weeks later the Allied Forces defeated the British Forces 4–1 on No. 1 Court before another capacity crowd in support of Mrs. Winston Churchill's Aid-to-Russia Fund. From 15th to 18th August the grounds were "taken over" by U.S.A. servicemen when the final stages of their European Championships were decided. An entry of 6,000 had been reduced to 36 in singles and 18 pairs in doubles by eliminating tournaments held at seven centres around Europe. The finals were played on the No. 1 Court.

1946
The Championships were resumed against a background of many problems created by the rationing of almost every commodity. The weather was ideal throughout the fortnight. Players from 23 nations competed.

Service personnel were used as stewards for the first time.

The ball boys were provided by Dr. Barnardo's Homes.

London Transport announced that they had carried 176,066 passengers by bus between the ground and Southfields and Wimbledon stations during the meeting, compared with 154,000 in 1939.

No Qualifying competitions were held.

1947
Over 20,000 spectators attended the opening day and 30,000 on the first Saturday – both broke records.

King George VI and Queen Elizabeth attended the meeting on the second Friday and presented the Gentlemen's Singles trophy to Jack Kramer, the first champion to wear shorts.

Competitors from 30 nations took part. Overseas junior champions were invited to watch the second week's play. In the mornings the boys and girls played an American tournament.

Post Office facilities were available in the North Hall of the Centre Court.

Programme Publications Ltd. were first associated with the production of the Wimbledon Programme.

The Northern and Southern Qualifying competitions were revived.

Junior Invitation events for boys and girls were played in the mornings.

1948
New results boards were located on either side of the entrance to the tunnel between No. 2 and No. 3 Courts. The Centre Court seats were repainted.

A mobile Post Office was available.

Over 33,000 people were admitted on the first Saturday – a new daily record.

An information Desk was installed in the South-West Hall of the Centre Court and staffed by stewards.

1949

There were record attendances at what was generally regarded as "the greatest Wimbledon". A record 25,000 attended on the opening day.

With building restrictions having been gradually eased, the Centre Court seating was restored to normal. The Members' Stand was extended to hold more seats. After the third day's play, No. 6 Court was turned into a Members' Tea Lawn. This practice changed after the 1965 meeting. Crowd counting equipment was installed at the entrances to the ground. Ted Schroeder was the first Champion to be presented with his trophy on the Centre Court.

For the first time replica trophies were presented to the Champions.

Miss Louise Brough played 117 games over five hours when competing in three matches on the final day.

Lineswomen officiated on the Centre Court for the first time.

The Junior Invitation events were played in public on the outer grass courts during the second week.

1950

The accommodation of the Centre Court Press Stand was increased. A Left Luggage Office was established on the east side of No. 1 Court.

Information Desks were installed in the North, South-East and South-West Halls of the Centre Court. All the Desks were staffed for the first time by the Women's (Royal) Voluntary Service.

1951

A new fence was built in concrete round the ground. The seating of No. 2 Court was renewed. Soft seats were provided in the Centre Court Members' Stand. Players from 34 nations competed.

1952

Alterations were made to the Royal Box and a television interview room was constructed within the Centre Court.

A system of selling Centre Court Two-day season tickets costing £1. 14s. was introduced. 300 seats were made available.

Rain completely washed out play on the second Thursday.

For the first time eight seeds in the Gentlemen's and Ladies' Singles reached their appointed places.

1953

Coronation Year and the balustrades of the Centre Court were decorated with the crests of the LTA and The All England Lawn Tennis Club. The stadium was floodlit in late evening. All competitors received an ash-tray bearing a medallion commemorating the Coronation.

The No. 1 Court South Stand seating accommodation was enlarged.

On Sunday 14th June over 7,000 spectators were admitted free to the grounds to watch a match played on No. 1 and No. 2 Courts between the Club and a team representing the Queen's Club and the International Club of Great Britain, to commemorate the Coronation. The competitors each received a memento.

1954

Boxes were provided at the exits from the Centre Court and No. 1 Court to enable departing spectators to leave partly unused tickets for resale at 1s. each, in aid of the National Playing Fields Association.

There was no play on the first Friday due to rain.

1955

The sum of £100,000 was spent on maintenance and improvements at the ground. The most spectacular innovation was the extension of the West Open Stand structure of No. 1 Court to the height of 50 feet, which provided a further 900 seats and considerable standing room. Underneath the extension three new restaurants were provided for the use of LTA County Officials, Umpires, Stewards and Club staff. Every seat in the Centre Court was modified by the provision of a curved back rest made of plastic. The wooden sight screens at each end of the Centre Court were rebuilt in concrete.

A balcony, overlooking the grounds, was constructed over the main entrance to the Clubhouse. New scoreboards were provided for the outside courts.

The whole of the Centre Court structure was re-cemented, waterproofed and re-sprayed green. This entailed laying back the Boston Ivy creeper on special scaffolding away from the walls while the work was in progress. Over 3,500 nails were used to secure the creeper.

All roads within the grounds were resurfaced.

New iron gates were installed at the South-West entrance to the ground.

The ball boys wore new style shirts in the Club colours of dark green and purple.

A new procedure in the issue of balls for the matches came into operation. Instead of new balls being provided at the beginning of each set, they were changed after the first seven games and each subsequent nine games.

1956

The concourse outside the main entrance to the Club was widened by moving No. 4 and No. 5 Courts back, touching the second row of courts. Alterations to the west-side staircase to No. 1 Court allowed better access.

Independent Television started transmission from Wimbledon.

1957

Queen Elizabeth II attended The Championships for the first time and presented the Ladies' Singles and the Gentlemen's Doubles trophies on court.

During the Gentlemen's Doubles final, Mrs. Helen Jarvis of Croydon invaded the Centre Court, shouting and waving a banner in her campaign for a new world banking system. The message on the banner began with the words "God Save Our Queen". The intruder was escorted from the court by the Referee and a policeman. The Queen watched the incident from the Royal Box.

The television interview room was enlarged. A new cover for the Centre Court was provided.

Approximately 1,200 seats in the back two rows of the Centre Court were made available on Two-day Season tickets priced at £2 2s.

1958

A very wet fortnight. For the first time the Gentlemen's Singles semi-finals were split between the Centre Court and No. 1 Court.

Approximately one third of the Centre Court roof was renewed and four stanchions on each side of the Covered Stand were removed.

Various improvements were carried out, including the construction of a LTA office, modernisation of the ladies' dressing rooms and the building of the competitors' lounge and writing room.

Centre Court season tickets were made available in three books each containing four tickets.

The ball boys wore shorts instead of long trousers.

In August a new building covering the two hard courts in Car Park No. 3 was opened. The oustanding feature of the design was the roof-dome which was one solid piece of concrete, having a span of 175ft. and covering over 15,000 sq. ft. The dome, supported on columns at the four corners only, was the largest in Britain at the time.

1959

Much work was carried out on the Centre Court. The renovation of the roof was completed. An extra 120 seats were made available by the opening of the North Open Stand, while many of the entrances and exits were reconstructed to allow better freedom of movement.

A permanent book and photographic stall was built and situated in the concourse near the South-West Entrance Hall to the Centre Court.

A strike prevented the daily order of play and results of matches being printed in the programme.

1960

Minor alterations to the West Open Stand of No. 1 Court allowed more seating to be installed. The Club general office was enlarged and modernised.

On the first Saturday Miss Jan Lehane of Australia became the first woman player at The Championships to hit double-handed shots (backhand).

The Club Croquet Championship was revived after a lapse of 56 years.

1961

The 75th Championship Meeting. The occasion was celebrated when the Club entertained 38 past and present Champions to lunch. The distinguished gathering included 10 Gentlemen's Singles Champions and the four living British Ladies' Champions headed by Mrs. Charlotte Sterry who won her first singles title in 1895.

The seating in the South Stand of No. 1 Court was renewed.

For the first time since 1914 two English players competed in the Ladies' Singles final. Miss Angela Mortimer defeated Miss Christine Truman.

1962

Queen Elizabeth attended the tournament on the second Friday and presented the trophy to the Gentlemen's Singles winner on court.

Structural changes were visible in the form of a new Press and television room being provided and the Lost Property Office reconstructed. The seating in the West Open Stand of No. 1 Court was increased and the staircase of the south west side altered.

The practice began whereby the Umpires of the Singles Finals were presented on court after the match.

1963

A meeting which was generally cold, miserable and wet. Rain completely washed out play on the last Saturday and the four finals were delayed until the following Monday.

The turnstiles at the entrances to the ground were renewed. A large scoreboard serving No. 2 and No. 3 Courts was constructed at the south end of the courts.

For the first time regulations laid down that competitors must be dressed predominantly in white throughout.

1964

A fortnight of fine weather with the exception of the second day.

The main concourse was extended further by moving No. 2 and No. 3 Courts and the stand between them, back in line with No. 4 and No. 5 Courts. Over the tunnel entrance to the stands was constructed a huge order-of-play and results board which allowed spectators to pick out the information at a glance. New entrances were provided into the Centre Court standing area. Improvements were made to the ball boys' accommodation. For the first time a military band was engaged from noon onwards to entertain early arrivals to the Centre Court on both Finals days. On this occasion it was the band of Her Majesty's Welsh Guards, resplendent in their scarlet tunics.

A Gentlemen's Veterans Doubles event, consisting of 16 pairs, was added to the programme.

1965

A wet first week gave way to splendid weather after the Saturday. Alterations were made to the South-West staircase to No. 1 Court. The court cover was renewed.

Members of the London Fire Brigade were used as stewards for the first time.

1966

A new Members' Tea Lawn of continental design and featuring rose covered pillars and a fountain, was extended over the area previously occupied by No. 6 Court. The turf from this court was used to make a new No. 15 Court and the other courts were renumbered.

Eugene Scott of the United States and Nikki Pilic of Yugoslavia defeated Cliff Richey of the United States and Torben Ulrich of Denmark in a record first round Gentlemen's Doubles match of 98 games.

On the third day, Australian Miss Gail Sherriff defeated her younger sister Carol in the second round of the Ladies' Singles on No. 14 Court, 8-10 6-3 6-3, to record only the second occasion two sisters had ever met in the event. (See 1884)

After this year the Northern Qualifying competition was amalgamated with the Southern Meeting.

1967

Excellent weather for the fortnight.

A new Debenture Holders' Lounge and restaurant was built along the east side of the Centre Court. The North Stand of the Centre Court was extended eastwards. The ball boys were provided by the Shaftesbury Homes.

The International Box was established alongside the Royal Box.

In February Barkers Sports Ground (later Aorangi Park) was purchased by the All England Lawn Tennis Ground Ltd for £150,000.

The very first colour television transmission in this country took place on the first Saturday, when BBC2 showed a four and a half hour programme from the Centre Court, commencing at 2pm. The first match was Cliff Drysdale (RSA) versus Roger Taylor (GBR). Transmissions in colour were also made each afternoon of the following week, plus a 30 minute highlights programme each evening.

Towards the end of August the Wimbledon World Professional Championships, sponsored by the BBC to mark the introduction of colour television, were staged on the Centre Court over three days. Eight players competed for total prize money of £12,500.

In the autumn the grounds were used to film part of the Rank Organisation picture "Nobody Runs Forever", which starred Rod Taylor, Christopher Plummer and Lili Palmer. There were lengthy scenes featuring the Royal Box and action around the Centre Court gangways.

1968

The first time The Championships were Open to all categories of players. Prize money available totalled £26,150. Only £13,410 was actually paid.

The first week was one of the wettest on record and the backlog of matches so great that play into a third week seemed inevitable. However, a dramatic change in the weather combined with a 1 p.m. start on three days enabled the tournament to finish on time. The attendance was down by 24,000 owing to a rail "go-slow" which worsened as the days passed.

The North Open Stand of the Centre Court was extended westwards.

H.J. FitzGibbon (USA) defeated N. Pilic (YUG) 3-6 7-5 6-3 6-2 in the Gentlemen's Singles first round on the No. 4 Court, to become the first amateur to overcome a professional at the tournament.

Independent Television covered The Championships for the last time.

1969

The Press Writing Room was extended.

The Debenture Holders' Lounge and restaurant at the east side of the Centre Court were extended over part of the public tea lawn.

Ball boys were provided by local schools.

There was no play on the first Monday due to rain.

The second week's play was reorganised so that the finals of the Ladies' Singles and Gentlemen's Doubles were played on the Friday and the finals of the Gentlemen's Singles, Ladies' Doubles and Mixed Doubles were played on the Saturday. This practice continued until Sunday play began in 1982.

Rod Laver of Australia won the Gentlemen's Singles for the fourth time – the first player since 1913. Pancho Gonzales and Charles Pasarell of the United States contested a first round Gentlemen's Singles match of 112 games – an all-time record.

Barclays Bank replaced Martins Bank Ltd.

1970

Several alterations were carried out. The competitors' restaurant was enlarged by taking in the writing room and lounge and rebuilding these facilities above. A new Press restaurant was provided.

New radio commentary boxes were installed on the Centre Court. The LTA offices were enlarged.

The North and South Stands of No. 1 Court were re-roofed. An extension to the West Stand of No. 2 Court provided standing room for 1,000 people.

The Prince of Wales watched play from the Royal Box on the first Tuesday.

1971

The Club entrance hall, staircase and landing were redesigned.

The new first floor referee's office was constructed above the previous one. A police office was established. No. 2 and No. 3 Courts received a general overhaul. No. 11 Court was replaced by a new combined stand overlooking No. 10 and No. 12 Courts. No. 12 to No. 15 Courts were renumbered Nos. 11 to 14.

Six new court covers were provided which enabled all outside courts to be protected.

Centre Court season tickets were made available in six books, each containing two tickets.

The tie-break system was adopted to operate when the score reached 8-all in any set except in the third or fifth set of a three set or five set match, respectively.

WIMBLEDON YEAR BY YEAR

1972

A dispute between the International Lawn Tennis Federation and World Championship Tennis led to the governing body banning a number of "contract" professionals from official tournaments, preventing some leading gentlemen players competing at The Championships.

The first rain of the meeting washed out play on the final Saturday and for the first time the Gentlemen's Singles final and other finals were played on a Sunday. The Centre Court and No. 1 Court were packed with spectators who were admitted free of charge.

Courtesy cars and drivers to transport competitors and officials were provided for the first time.

The Honours Boards in the entrance to the Club were renewed.

At the Qualifying competition, all rounds except the last in the Gentlemen's Singles and Doubles were reduced to three sets.

1973

Another political situation resulted in the meeting being boycotted by 80 gentlemen players, who were instructed to do so by the Association of Tennis Professionals following the ILTF suspension of the Yugoslav Nikki Pilic.

Rain on the second Friday necessitated the Gentlemen's Singles Final and the Ladies' Singles Final being contested on the Saturday and play being extended to the Sunday to conclude the Mixed Doubles Semi-Final and Final.

Alterations were made to the North and North-East Hall of the Centre Court by removing a staircase and so allowing better crowd circulation. The numbering of No. 6 to No. 11 Courts was reversed.

New Radio and Press interview rooms were constructed under the gentlemen's dressing rooms, which were renovated.

The first Post Office Telephone Information Service was started – over 450,000 calls were received.

Because of the players' boycott 32 players qualified in the Gentlemen's Singles competition, contesting all matches over three sets.

1974

Three days of fine weather followed by three very wet days forced the second week's programme to be reorganised so that play commenced at noon on all but one of the six days. The Gentlemen's Singles and Ladies' Singles semi-finals were split between the Centre Court and No. 1 Court.

A new mobile Post Office was installed. A 'Portakabin' structure was used as the ILTF office. New bus lay-bys were constructed in Church Road.

1975

A sunbaked fortnight. A new building on the east side of the Centre Court was constructed above the Debenture Holders' Lounge and restaurant. This was principally built to house a museum in the future. Part of the accommodation was used as an overseas press room and ILTF office. The balcony over the main entrance to the Clubhouse was doubled in width.

The West Hall of the Centre Court was widened. More free standing room was made available on No. 2 Court. The bookstall was re-sited on the public Tea Lawn where, for that meeting only, a bookmakers' tent (William Hill) was erected. The Left Luggage Office was resited adjacent to the Church Road entrance.

Chairs were first provided on court to enable players to rest when changing ends.

The qualification for entering the Plate events was altered to allow players beaten in the first, second and third rounds of the Singles, or taking part in the Doubles only, to enter. The Junior Invitation events were renamed Junior Singles Championships.

1976

Probably the hottest meeting on record with no rain.

Extensive widening of the passage between the north-west side of the Centre Court and No. 1 Court was carried out. A temporary stand holding 1,450 spectators was first erected adjacent to No. 14 Court.

Earlier in the year, on the night of 14th January, vandals broke into the grounds and damaged the Centre Court. In the morning staff found five holes in the turf, the largest about nine inches long, and red and white paint splashed about the court. Other paint had been put on the walls and windows surrounding the court.

The umpires and linejudges appeared for the first time wearing their new uniform of navy blue blazer and grey trousers or skirts.

1977

The Centenary Championships. For the occasion the Clubhouse and Centre Court were repainted and special decorations erected around the ground. The main public tea lawn was extended northwards into Aorangi Park. The Wimbledon Lawn Tennis Museum and the Kenneth Ritchie Wimbledon Library, situated above the Debenture Holders' Restaurant on the east side of the Centre Court, were opened in May by the Duke and Duchess of Kent.

On the opening day of the meeting 41 surviving singles champions paraded on the Centre Court and were presented with silver commemorative medals by the Duke and Duchess of Kent.

Queen Elizabeth, accompanied by the Duke of Edinburgh, attended the meeting on the second Friday and presented the trophy to the winner of the Ladies' Singles on court. The whole of the gate money on that day was donated to the Queen's Silver Jubilee Fund.

A Queen's Silver Jubilee Salver was given to the winner of each Championship event, while all competitors received a commemorative pen and pencil set. The Band of the Welsh Guards played on the Centre Court, prior to the start of play, for five days of the meeting.

There were no interruptions to play due to rain during the fortnight.

A special Centenary Invitation doubles event for Gentlemen was staged.

Ball girls were used for the first time on the outside courts. The Gentlemen's and Ladies' Qualifying competitions were held at different centres.

1978

A dull and wet meeting which resulted in seven days being interrupted by rain, including the first Thursday when play was completely washed out. Because of a backlog of matches play began at noon instead of the traditional 2 p.m. for five days from the first Saturday until the second Thursday.

A veterans' singles event was added to the programme for the year only. The Gentlemen's and Ladies' Qualifying competition reverted to the former practice of being held at the same centre.

Just before the Ladies' Final on the second Friday, the Centre Court was used to film part of the Paramount picture "The Players", which starred Dino Martin and Ali McGraw. Guillermo Vilas of Argentina also took part.

After the meeting the boundary of the ground north of the Centre Court was extended into Aorangi Park to line up with the tea lawn extension. The construction of a new building and four grass courts was commenced within the area.

1979

Extensive building and other alterations were carried out. A new raised building along the north side of the Centre Court housed the Debenture Holders' Lounge and restaurant on the first floor and the L.T.A. and Museum offices and the Kenneth Ritchie Wimbledon Library on the second floor.

The roof of the Centre Court was raised by one metre to provide an additional 1,088 seats making the capacity of the Court 11,739. The public Tea Lawn was completely paved, while the extension housed sponsors' marquees and a new Museum Shop and bookstall, plus an area set aside for picnics. The number of turnstile entrances to the ground was increased from 10 to 20.

New clocks were provided throughout the premises and grounds. The Centre Court and No. 1 Court scoreboards were fitted with digital clocks, which also indicated the duration of each match. (Rolex)

The previous Debenture Holders' Lounge and restaurant, on the east side of the Centre Court, was divided into the County Association restaurant and a players' rest room. The old LTA offices above the South-East Entrance Hall were converted into two Press Writing Rooms. The former Press Writing Room was used as a television monitor room.

For the first time a price differential for Centre Court tickets was introduced.

The tie-break regulations were changed to operate at 6-all in any set except the final set of a match. Umpires were issued with stop watches to ensure players did not exceed the time limit between change of ends.

On the first Tuesday Miss Catherine McTavish became the first woman to umpire on the No. 1 Court.

Mrs. Billie Jean King of the United States won the Ladies' Doubles and so brought her total tally of titles to 20.

For two days in July the Centre Court was used to film part of the Paramount film 'Rough Cut', which starred Burt Reynolds, Lesley-Ann Down and David Niven. Over 600 extras were employed.

1980

One of the wettest meetings on record which necessitated play starting at noon on the last nine days.

The Members' Enclosure was made a permanent building. No. 11 Court was converted into a hard court and used as an extension to the Enclosure during the meeting. No. 12 to 14 Courts were re-numbered 11 to 13. Four new grass courts were brought into commission north of the Centre Court and numbered 14 to 17. A temporary stand, holding 740 spectators, was first erected adjacent to the new No. 14 Court. The stands of No. 2 Court were extended to the sides of the Court, dispensing with the aisles, to allow seating to be increased from 1,650 to 2,020.

For the first time the public ballots for Centre and No. 1 Court tickets were combined and a new price differential for Centre Court tickets was introduced. 300 Centre Court seats, previously made available to the public at the gate on the last three days of the meeting, were added to the ballot.

An electronic service line monitor, (Cyclops), using infra-red rays, was used for singles matches on the Centre Court and No. 1 Court.

Bjorn Borg of Sweden became the first player to win the Gentlemen's Singles five times in succession since the abolition of the Challenge Round.

In Aorangi Park 12 grass courts were made available for practice before and during The Championships.

On Sunday morning, the 13th July, a church service to commemorate the 75th Anniversary of the diocese of Southwark was held on the Centre Court, led by the Bishop, Dr. Stockwood. 11,000 people attended.

The permanent office of the International Tennis Federation was set up at the Club during September.

1981

Six daily records were broken.

The No. 1 Court complex was rebuilt. The South Stand was completely demolished and replaced by a building which provided new accommodation for the Competitors' restaurant, bar and lounge, changing rooms for the ladies, ball boys and girls and offices for the Referee and Umpires. The addition of 750 seats in the South Stand, plus 500 in the North Stand, increased the court capacity to 6,350. The public buffet, formerly situated under the South Stand, was resited, as a temporary measure, on the Tea Lawn extension. The Club offices were extended over the area previously occupied by the Ladies' Dressing Room. Electronic repeater scoreboards, showing the progress of matches on the Centre Court and No. 1 Court, were installed above the main entrance to the Clubhouse and on the wall near the Museum entrance, overlooking the Tea Lawn. Two new electronic scoreboards were installed on the No. 1 Court. The use of electronic service line monitors, (Cyclops), was extended to No. 2 and No. 3 Courts.

A special Wimbledon uniform for umpires and linejudges was introduced – dark green jackets and light green trousers or skirts. On the first Tuesday Miss Catherine McTavish became the first woman to umpire on the Centre Court.

A marquee, situated near the North-East Entrance Hall, sold merchandise made under licence to the Club.

On the second Tuesday the match on the Centre Court between Miss Sue Barker and Miss Ann Kiyomura and Miss JoAnne Russell and Miss Virginia Ruzici was halted at 9.35 p.m. due to bad light with the score at 5-5 in the final set. Amid boos and jeers, cushions, programmes and other objects were thrown on the court.

The Gentlemen's Veterans Doubles event was discontinued.

1982

For the first time The Championships were scheduled to last 13 days and for play to terminate on a Sunday. The meeting was one of the wettest on record with play interrupted by rain on ten days. A noon start on the last eight days, together with a continuing rescheduling of matches, including the Gentlemen's Doubles event being reduced to the best of three sets, apart from two first round matches and the two semi-finals, allowed the programme to be concluded on time, with the exception of the Boys' Doubles final, which was played on the third Monday. The Gentlemen's Singles semi-finals were split between the Centre Court and No. 1 Court.

An Underground strike for the first eight days and a rail strike on the seventh and eighth days considerably reduced the attendance.

Aorangi Park was brought into the perimeter of the Club's grounds to give more room during The Championships. This provided additional catering facilities for the public, including a waitress service restaurant, a larger picnic area, more private marquees, an international merchandising shop, a public services area and a scoreboard showing results, game by game, on each court.

The Centre Court first floor press accommodation was extensively enlarged, with a new Press Buffet established in the area previously occupied by the old Debenture Holders' Lounge. The former Press Buffet was converted into a third writing room, mainly for overseas press. The Clubhouse dining room and lounge were completely refurbished. The L.T.A. offices were resited on the Tea Lawn extension. New seating was installed in the first ten rows of the Centre Court and the No. 2 Court West Stand. Two new electronic scoreboards were installed in the Centre Court. Two new forms of signposting around the grounds were installed. For the first time a public ballot for standing room spaces on the Centre Court for the last four days was introduced.

The All England Plate event was discontinued. A 35 and over Gentlemen's Invitation Singles event was inaugurated. Doubles events were added to the Junior Championships.

In December, Miss Virginia Wade became the first lady to be elected to the Club Committee.

1983

The installation of new seating on the Centre Court was completed. The No. 1 Gentlemen's Dressing room was refurbished. The new signposting around the ground was completed. A new electricity supply for the Club was installed. In Aorangi Park a temporary competitors' complex, with garden, light catering, dressing rooms and a créche was made available. An area was set aside to demonstrate the virtues of Short Tennis.

An electronic device to assist the net cord judge was used on the Centre Court and No. 1 Court.

Play commenced at 12.30 p.m. on the outside courts during the first week. The entry for the Ladies' Singles Championship was raised to 128. A 35 and over Gentlemen's Invitation Doubles event was held for the first time.

Trey Waltke of the United States appeared on court dressed in an old-fashioned outfit of white flannels, with a necktie for a belt and a white button-down long-sleeve shirt.

The Club's staff was restructured when the Secretary became the Chief Executive and the posts of Secretary (Championships) and Secretary (Club) were created.

1984

The Ladies' Championship Centenary. The highlight of the celebrations occurred on the second Monday when 17 past lady champions paraded on the Centre Court and were presented with a specially commissioned piece of Waterford Crystal by the Duke and Duchess of Kent. For the first time a ladies' military band played on the Centre Court on both Finals days.

A very dry fortnight during which nine daily records were broken.

Changes were made to the No. 2 Court. A new North Stand, containing three rows of seats, was erected and the area underneath the cantilever section of the West Stand infilled to provide an enlarged No. 2 Gentlemen's Dressing Room, new Umpires' Rest and Changing Rooms, Lost Property Office, Stewards' Office and a doctor's surgery for the players. The stand between No. 2 and No. 3 Courts was totally refurbished with all benches replaced by individual seats.

The Centre Court East, North and West Open Stands were provided with tip-up seats. Glass screening was erected along the walkway between the Centre Court and No. 1 Court. T.V. commentary boxes at the north end of the Centre Court were refurbished.

Play commenced at 12.30 p.m. on the outside courts during the first week and on the second Monday and Tuesday.

For the first time all five Championship titles were retained.

Mrs. Georgina Clark became the first woman to umpire a final on the Centre Court.

The Fred Perry statue, situated opposite the entrance to the Members' Enclosure, was unveiled to commemorate the 50th Anniversary of his first victory in the Gentlemen's Singles. The gates at the Somerset Road entrance to the ground were also dedicated to this player. The weathervane, situated on the roof of the Members' Enclosure, was presented to the Club by Sir Brian Burnett, to mark his retirement as Chairman.

1985

Rain on the first six days necessitated play starting at noon on all courts from the first Thursday until the second Wednesday. On the second Friday a spectacular storm at 2 p.m. hit the Club with 1½ inches of rain falling in 20 minutes. Despite the poor weather the last eight days had record crowds.

The Centre Court East Building was extended a further 25 feet over the Tea Lawn and a third floor added. This vast operation provided an extra 800 seats, additional media commentary boxes at the top of the stand, substantially increased accommodation and facilities for the Press, spread over three floors, a completely redesigned Museum, having 20% more exhibition area, larger offices for the International Tennis Federation and new accommodation for the administrative staff of The Championships and General Office. The Tea Lawn was redesigned and repaved.

The second phase of glass screening between the Centre Court and No. 1 Court was completed and by re-aligning the gangways, an extra 54 seats were made available. Six additional TV boxes were provided in the No. 1 Court North Stand. Air-conditioning was installed in the Debenture Holders' Lounge and upgraded in the press and television interview rooms.

New manual scoreboards were provided for No. 2, No. 3, No. 13 and No. 14 Courts and the full draw of each of the five Championship events were displayed on the Debenture Holders' Lounge wall, facing No. 15 and No. 16 Courts, and updated as soon as the matches were completed.

Play was scheduled to commence at 12.30 p.m. on the outside courts during the first week and on the second Monday. The whole grounds were opened at 11.30 daily but ticket holders and seat purchasers were allowed into Aorangi Park and the Tea Lawn Extension at 10.30 a.m.

The number of court officials on the Centre Court and No. 1 Court was reduced from 13 to 12 by the elimination of the foot-fault judge. The number of officials on other courts was increased from a minimum of six to eight.

Ball girls were used on the No. 1 Court for the first time.

At the age of 17 years and 227 days, Boris Becker became the youngest player, the first unseeded player and the first German to win the Gentlemen's Singles. Paul McNamee and Miss Martina Navratilova played 117 games in three Mixed Doubles matches on the final day. Miss Anne White of the United States appeared on No. 2 Court wearing a neck to ankle all-white leotard.

The Club's executive staff was restructured with the creation of the posts of Championships Director, Financial Director, Marketing Director and Club Secretary, who were made directly responsible to the Chief Executive.

1986

The 100th Championship Meeting. The occasion was commemorated in a variety of different ways including the design of a special logo, the formation of the Last 8 Club and a Dinner Party held on the second Thursday for invited guests who had made significant contributions to The Championships in the past.

A very warm meeting, marred by rain only on the first and twelfth days. On the first Thursday the highest ever daily figure of 39,813 was attained.

The entrance area of the Media accommodation on the first floor of the Centre Court East Building was improved. In Aorangi Park a new two-storey pavilion was built replacing the old dilapitated wooden structure. This housed competitors' dressing rooms, a dining area and a créche, while a tented octagonal structure, containing public services, replaced the scoreboard.

The use of an electronic line monitor on No. 3 Court and a net cord device on the Centre Court and No. 1 Court was abandoned.

Ball girls were used on the Centre Court for the first time.

The courtesy car administration was moved from the Clubhouse entrance to the No. 3 Car Park, stopping the majority of the cars entering the grounds.

On the first Tuesday, in the Royal Box, Boris Becker of Germany presented the Duchess of Kent with a cheque for DM15,000 towards the World Hunger Fund.

Yellow balls were used for the first time.

Players and officials were asked to undergo drug tests for the first time.

1987

The first week of the meeting was marred by very bad weather with no play possible on the opening day. The second week's tennis was played in warm sunshine and with the assistance of early starts on eight days and the Gentlemen's Doubles event reduced to the best of three sets in the first two rounds, the meeting finished on schedule. Five daily record attendances were broken despite a new policy of restricting the crowd to 28,000, instead of 31,000.

For the first time in many years no major improvements were carried out.

The Clubhouse entrance hall was refurbished.

New masts and hoists were purchased for the Centre Court cover and also a new cover was provided for No. 1 Court.

New Museum wrought-iron gates were erected at Church Road.

In Aorangi Park two more practice courts were made available, bringing the total to 14.

Miss Martina Navratilova of the United States won the Ladies' Singles for the sixth time in succession to equal the all-time record of eight victories.

1988

After a week of sunshine rain interfered on each day of the second week, except one. On the concluding Sunday only five games were possible in the Gentlemen's Singles final, which was postponed until the third Monday. This extra day brought the attendance figure to 411,270.

All gates throughout the grounds were opened at 11 a.m., thereby replacing the two-tier opening of 10.30 a.m. in Aorangi Park and 11.30 a.m. in the remainder of the grounds, introduced in 1985.

A new procedure was introduced whereby if as a result of bad weather there was no play on the Centre Court and No. 1 Court, the ticket holder for that day would be given priority for the following year when applying for a seat.

New Press, Television and Radio Interview rooms were accommodated in the former Ladies' Lower Dressing Room under the Centre Court South-East Entrance Hall. An additional Ladies' Dressing room was provided in the No. 1 Court Building in place of the Ball Boys' and Girls' changing rooms which were rehoused in an extended west side of the building.

A new walkway beside No. 1 Court, linking the main concourse to the North Road was constructed, to greatly improve the pedestrian movement from one end of the grounds to the other.

The capacity of No. 14 Court was increased by constructing a temporary 6-row stand at the north and south ends. Also, a 3-row stand was erected along the east side of the No. 17 Court. The Centre Court covered stand seats were completely re-numbered. The International Box was resited in the Centre Court North Open Stand with the previous Box reallocated to Members of the Last 8 Club.

In Aorangi Park an L.T.A. Associate Members' Marquee was provided and a chemist's shop made available in the Octagon.

For the first time a local youth band entertained the public, in Aorangi Park, prior to play on the second Thursday and Friday.

The Members' Kitchen was enlarged and newly equipped.

The permanent offices of the International Tennis Federation ceased to be housed at the Club and the space in the Centre Court East Building, underneath the Museum, reallocated to a new Ticket Office.

For the first time at The Championships no player used a wooden racket.

During the year the Club completely renovated 15 public tennis courts in Wimbledon Park.

1989

Rain badly interfered with the programme on the last three days of the tournament, forcing the Gentlemen's Singles semi-finals to be played on different days and the Gentlemen's Singles final and Ladies' Singles final both to be contested on the Sunday. In spite of great efforts to finish the meeting the Mixed Doubles final and the concluding rounds of the Boys' and Girls' Doubles were held over until the third Monday, when 3,418 spectators were given free entry to the grounds. The 13 day attendance figure was 400,288 – an all-time record. Three daily records were broken.

A new staircase for the south end of No. 1 Court West Stand was constructed. Temporary 3-row stands were erected along the west side of No. 11 and No. 13 Courts and the east side of No. 14 Court. The replacing of the scoreboards on the outside courts was completed. All scoreboards displayed point by point information. The TV Monitor Room in the Press Centre was refurbished and facilities improved.

Many alterations were carried out to improve the aesthetic quality of the grounds.

A new two-tier pricing system for Centre Court and No. 1 Court seat tickets was adopted, which differentiated between seats having the best views and those towards the back of the stand or having some form of restriction.

The Club appointed a TV Marketing Director.

A new Covered Court complex, opened in January, provided three additional courts (Supreme) to the existing two (Red Velvet).

20 acres of recreational land at Raynes Park was purchased by the All England Lawn Tennis Ground Ltd. from the Inner London Education Authority.

1990

Following the tragedies at the Bradford and Hillsborough football grounds the safety standards at places of sport came under greater scrutiny. The Fire Safety and Safety of Places of Sport Acts laid down that any covered stand accommodating over 500 persons must receive a safety certificate from the Local Authority. It was, therefore, necessary for the Club to receive a certificate for the Centre and No. 1 Court complex. As a result the standing room on the Centre Court was replaced by seating and the Centre Court, No. 1, No. 2, No. 3, No. 13 and No. 14 Courts (apart from No. 2 Court standing room) became all ticketed. Ground passes gave access only to 12 of the outside courts and the Centre Court and No. 1 Court complex was restricted to those holding tickets. The ground capacity was fixed at 28,000 and once this number was reached the only means of entry to the grounds was by the purchase of tickets handed in for re-sale by spectators leaving for the day. Consequently, the attendance figure for the fortnight was greatly reduced to 347,979. The grounds were opened to the public at 10.30 a.m. each day.

The new Centre Court seating capacity was 13,107. On each side of the Court a photographers' pit was constructed. All clear glass in the passageways overlooking the No. 1 Court was replaced so that viewing from these positions was not possible. Smoking was prohibited in the covered stands of the Centre Court and No. 1 Court.

A huge television screen, situated adjacent to the Pavilion in Aorangi Park, showed matches on the Centre Court and other courts, messages and other information. The main "matches on court and results" board, situated on the south concourse, between No. 2 and 3 Courts, was demolished and replaced by a security control building. A new "matches on court" board was erected on the wall of the No. 2 Court East Stand.

On the first Saturday, at approx. 7.30 p.m., the Centre Court was cleared due to a bomb scare. When the "all clear" was given 40 minutes later play on that court was abandoned for the day.

Dry and pleasant weather prevailed during the fortnight, apart from rain on the second Wednesday, which necessitated the Gentlemen's Singles quarter-final matches being reallocated to one on each of the Centre Court, No. 1 Court, No. 2 Court and No. 14 Court.

The All England Ladies' Plate event was discontinued. A 35 and over Ladies' Invitation Doubles event was inaugurated.

Miss Martina Navratilova of the United States won the Ladies' Singles to attain the all-time record of nine victories in the event.

1991

One of the wettest first weeks ever, with Monday rained off and only 52 out of approximately 240 scheduled matches completed in the 9 hours 15 minutes play available by Thursday evening. Faced with the prospect of further bad weather the decision was taken on the Friday evening to play for the first time ever on the first (middle) Sunday. This, together with a succession of 11 a.m. starts, the Gentlemen's Doubles event being reduced to the best of three sets until the quarter-final stage and a vast improvement in the weather over the last five days, allowed the programme to be concluded on time.

The Sunday became a unique day in Wimbledon's history. There was a queue stretching for 1½ miles outside the grounds. When the gates were opened at 10 a.m., 11,000 Centre Court and 7,000 No. 1 Court (seat and standing room) tickets at the flat rate of £10 and 5,000 ground passes at £5 were available, on a first come basis. By the start of play at 12 noon the Centre Court was full of excited spectators who created a carnival atmosphere. A special programme was on sale and a full catering service available. Past champions were invited to the Royal Box.

A relaxation of the regulations imposed the previous year, due to The Fire Safety and Safety of Places of Sport Acts allowed the seating on No. 3, No. 13 and No. 14 Courts to revert to primarily unreserved accommodation and the daily ticket sales and evening gate procedure to be simplified. New measures were introduced to minimise the black market sale of tickets.

The Centre Court North Building was extended northwards, on average 20 feet, to provide greater accommodation, on the first floor for the Debenture Holders' Lounge and Restaurant and on the second floor for Museum offices and stores, the Kenneth Ritchie Wimbledon Library and new Club facilities.

The No. 1 Court West Open Stand and the No. 2 Court East Stand terracing were renewed. On the No. 1 Court better facilities were provided for photographers and TV cameras and on No. 2 Court all seats were fitted with backs. The No. 1 Ladies' Dressing Room was extended and totally refurbished.

At eleven locations around the grounds television monitors displayed game-by-game scores, results and messages. The Repeater scoreboards above the main entrance to the Clubhouse were reinstated. Electronic net-cord monitors were provided on each court but the net cord judge was retained.

A 'speed of service' radar gun was employed on the Centre Court for the first time.

Michiel Schapers and Miss Brenda Schultz of The Netherlands defeated Tom Nijssen of The Netherlands and Miss Andrea Temesvari of Hungary in a first round Mixed Doubles match of 77 games – an all-time record.

Replica Gentlemen's Singles (Challenge Cup) and Ladies' Singles trophies were provided.

Redesigned modern galleries, covering the period 1930s to 1990s, were opened in the Museum. A new kiosk, sited on the Tea Lawn Extension, sold postcards, posters and magazines.

1992

For the first time play was scheduled to start on Nos. 2–17 Courts at Noon. A week of fine weather gave way to much rain during the latter part of the second week, which necessitated play starting early on five days. The second Friday was washed out, forcing the Gentlemen's Singles semi-finals to be split between the Centre Court and No. 1 Court on the following day. The programme was extended to the third Monday, when 7,798 spectators were admitted free to watch the Mixed Doubles final and the conclusion of the Gentlemen's Doubles final and the Boys' and Girls' Doubles events.

New arrangements were introduced for the first Saturday in a desire to recreate the special atmosphere of the previous year's first Sunday. On the day nearly 2,000 unreserved Centre Court Open Stand seats were sold at a reduced price. Tickets for No. 1 and No. 2 Courts and ground admission also cost less. Before start of play on the Centre Court the crowd were entertained by a traditional jazz band.

A new scheme was introduced whereby if there was no play at all on the Centre, No. 1 and No. 2 Courts, certain categories of ticket holders could either have a full refund or be given priority to purchase a similar ticket for The Championships the following year at the relevant price for that year. If there was no play until after 6 p.m., ticket holders could claim half their money back.

The Centre Court roof was completely replaced by a new structure supported by 4 pillars instead of 26. This mammoth operation allowed a perfect, instead of a restricted, view from 3,601 seats. At the Somerset Road entrance to the grounds, new wider gates were installed and the gatehouse was rebuilt on the opposite side of the Concourse.

The No. 1 Gentlemen's Dressing Room was refurbished, including upgrading of the air conditioning and the installation of improved lighting. New toilet facilities were built adjacent to the Water Tower.

The South Concourse was completely resurfaced. A section of the Tea Lawn was newly landscaped including upgrading the brick paving.

The use of Electronic net cord monitors was abandoned. A new No. 1 Court canvas cover was provided.

A special radio station known as "Radio Wimbledon" provided visitors and the local community with up to 14 hours of live programming each day during The Championships and included match reports and results, local information on weather, travel and traffic, the daily order of play, features on players, information for visitors about facilities in the grounds and on the spot interviews with players. The station, which broadcast from the grounds, had a range of up to four miles.

The "Wingfield Cafeteria", situated in Aorangi Park, provided light meals on a self service basis. Drinks and snacks were sold adjacent to No. 13 Court.

A large marquee was erected in the Lodge Garden to provide competitors with a quieter area in which to relax.

The 35 and Over Gentlemen's Invitation Singles event was replaced by a 45 and Over Gentlemen's Invitation Doubles event. The Qualifying competition for the Mixed Doubles was discontinued.

A new telephone system, employing the latest technology, was installed, enabling the Club to process calls more efficiently.

As part of The Championships expanding merchandising programme the Club commissioned a Coat of Arms from the College of Heralds.

The Museum building containing the Chronology Gallery was extended northwards above the staircase leading to Entrance 21 of the Centre Court to house a new special exhibition area. A tea room, situated adjacent to the Museum entrance, was made available for visitors throughout the year.

In the autumn the original Covered Court building was extensively refurbished, including alterations to the side doors, renewal of the lighting and provision of background heating. The Red Velvet court surface was replaced by a Green Set Velvelux carpet laid over a suspended wooden floor.

1993

The 100th Ladies' Championships. A number of commemorative events were held for the occasion. Surviving Ladies' Singles champions were presented with a special gold bracelet, while all lady competitors received a gold bracelet and a commemorative shirt. Banners and drapes were hung on the Members' Balcony and Debenture Holders' Lounge and in Aorangi Park a large flower-bed display depicted a specially commissioned 100th Ladies' Championships logo. A magazine entitled "Centre Court" was published by the Club. A ladies' military band played on the Centre Court on the last two days.

A warm and sunny meeting, during which there were no interruptions for rain, attracted a near-record crowd. The temperature on Centre Court soared to 106° and the ball boys/girls were issued with caps.

A major internal refurbishment of the Competitors' Complex in the No. 1 Court Building included changes to the main players' entrance and adjacent offices, the upgrading and modernising of the first floor restaurant and remodelling of the second floor lounge and office areas. An extension to the front elevation of the No. 1 Ladies' Dressing Room provided six larger cubicles and more space for dressing table facilities. The Physiotherapy Room was also enlarged. A covered walk-way was provided in the Members' Enclosure, which underwent a general refurbishment. The comfort and safety of spectators in the standing enclosure of No. 2 Court was improved. The Gentlemen's toilets in the North-West and South-West Halls of the Centre Court and toilets adjacent to No. 6 Court were refurbished. 60 permanent writing desks were installed for members of the International Press. The stabbing of Miss Monica Seles at Hamburg earlier in the year forced much tighter security around the courts. Security alerts closed the grounds before play commenced on the first Friday and second Saturday.

As in the previous year, efforts were made to create a festive atmosphere on the first Saturday. 2,000 reserved Centre Court seats were sold on the day at a reduced price, while ground admission also cost less. The traditional jazz band was re-engaged to entertain before play started at noon. At 2 p.m. a number of the Royal Box guests were introduced to the public, including the 1933–1936 British Davis Cup team (Raymond Tuckey, Harold Lee, Pat Hughes, "Bunny" Austin and Fred Perry), the Chairman's special guests (all ladies) and other sporting personalities.

In March the Club announced its Long Term Plan to enhance and protect The Championships' pre-eminence in the next Century. In December the All England Lawn Tennis Ground Ltd., purchased the freehold of the neighbouring Wimbledon Park Golf Course (73 acres) from the London Borough of Merton for £5.2 million.

The Club provided floodlighting for St Mary's Church.

1994

With the exception of one day The Championships enjoyed excellent weather and ended with the temperature peaking at 116°F on the Centre Court during the final day. A national rail strike on both Wednesdays affected the attendance only marginally.

In view of the Long Term Plan few improvements were carried out during the year. A new scoreboard mounted on the building, overlooking the South Concourse and the Members' Enclosure, displayed in rotation, the current scores of matches on all courts plus results and messages. On the Centre Court and No. 1 Court, the scoreboards displayed the scores of matches on other courts during the players' changeover periods and for the first time girls assisted in the operation of these scoreboards. A temporary canopy was provided over the rear half of the seating on No. 13 Court. Late in the year No. 10 Court was completely relaid.

The Summer Tea Room was redecorated and new showcases provided to display Club trophies and gifts.

At the Bank of England Ground, Roehampton, venue for the Qualifying Competition, five courts were levelled and re-turfed.

In July the All England Lawn Tennis Ground Ltd. purchased the freehold of the three acre site of Southlands College, at the junction of Bathgate Road and Queensmere Road, from the Roehampton Institute. The contract included the purchase of Queensmere House and Callard House.

On 25th July, work commenced in Aorangi Park on the Long Term Plan.

1995

A fortnight of warm and sunny weather, with no interruptions for rain, attracted the highest daily attendance on the first Tuesday and second Sunday. The first Friday was very hot with the temperature reading 110°F on the Centre Court and with Miss Shirli-Ann Siddall of Great Britain collapsing with heat exhaustion during her match on No. 14 Court.

The first nine rows of the Centre Court covered stands (A–J) were re-asphalted and approximately 5,000 new tip-up seats installed. The combined open stand and seating between No. 6 and No. 7 Courts were completely replaced. The Clubhouse Entrance Hall was completely refurbished, including the strengthening of the main staircase. Besides redecoration and fresh carpeting, a new showcase was provided to house the Club's trophies and all Championship Honours boards were replaced. The original Royal Box chairs, made in a traditional basket weave, were replaced. The fire alarm system throughout the grounds was upgraded.

Because of the Club's Long Term Plan many changes in Aorangi Park were evident during The Championships. The cessation of site construction, some two months before the meeting, permitted normal facilities to be provided on a temporary basis. The new No. 1 Court stadium, having reached the second level, allowed the extensive flat slab areas to be used as a platform for marquees and other public facilities. The basement was fitted out to provide kitchens, stores and service areas to support the hospitality chalets, which were formed within the structure. The location of the new No. 18 and No. 19 Courts was reduced to two levels and covered with tarmac to provide a picnic area and food village. Short tennis was the only usual facility not provided. The development of Aorangi Park considerably reduced the area available in the public Car Park No. 4, which was reserved for the use of coaches, motorcycles and cycles only. To compensate for this, a Park and Ride scheme was introduced to operate from the University of London Sports Ground at Motspur Park to the terminus established in the former Car Park No. 1. The price of car parking was £2.00 with no charge for the bus ride.

All Press desks and commentary boxes were fitted with a television receiver on which the Club's 21 channel aerial system was available. Additional cameras extended coverage to 12 courts, with each channel captioned with the score.

The scheme compensating holders of certain categories of tickets for Centre Court, No. 1 Court and No. 2 Court in the event of no play, due to rain, was modified to allow a full refund of the ticket price and priority for a similar ticket for The Championships on the corresponding day next year at the full price that year.

The rule concerning competitors being dressed predominantly in white throughout was clarified to mean "almost entirely in white".

The number of ball boys/girls was increased to allow the full allocation of six to all courts. For the first time umpires of the Gentlemen's and Ladies' singles finals were presented with medals on the Centre Court. The time allowed between the moment the ball goes out of play at the end of each point, until the time the ball is struck for the first service of the next point, was reduced from a maximum of 25 seconds to 20 seconds.

For the first time the top four seeds in both the Gentlemen's and Ladies' Singles reached the semi-final stage in the same year. Miss Chanda Rubin of the United States and Mrs. Patricia Hy–Boulais of Canada, contested a second round Ladies' Singles match of 58 games – an all-time record.

For the first time a player was disqualified from The Championships, when Tim Henman of Great Britain, hit a ball in anger and struck a ball girl during his first round Gentlemen's Doubles match on the first Wednesday. He was fined $2,000. Two other players were disqualified during the meeting. On the first Saturday Jeff Tarango of the United States was disqualified from his third round Gentlemen's Singles match for three offences and was fined a total of $15,500, and on the second Monday Murphy Jensen of the United States was disqualified from his second round mixed doubles and fined $1,000.

The Club appointed an Information Technology Director.

In March surface water drainage was laid from Aorangi Park, across the Wimbledon Park Golf Course to the lake to connect separately to an existing water system. In the autumn No. 5 Court was completely relaid.

At the Bank of England Ground at Roehampton, venue for the Qualifying Competition, a further six grass courts were levelled and relaid. Four extra covers were also provided. Work continued on the Long Term Plan.

1996

Rain on four days of the second week badly interfered with the programme and despite starting at 11am from the second Tuesday onwards, play was extended to the third Monday to complete the Ladies' Doubles final, the Girls' Doubles final and the Mixed Doubles event. 13,518 spectators were admitted free to the grounds to watch a full day's play on the Centre Court.

The attendance for the meeting over 13 days was down compared to the last few years, possibly due to London Underground strikes on the first Thursday and second Wednesday and the Euro 96 football competition. The daily attendance records for the second Saturday and Sunday were broken. The price of admission on the second Sunday was specially discounted at £1 per head, with all proceeds donated to charity.

At the age of 15 years and 282 days, Miss Martina Hingis of Switzerland became the youngest Champion of all time when she won the Ladies' Doubles. Todd Woodbridge and Mark Woodforde of Australia became the first pair to win the Gentlemen's Doubles four times in succession since the abolition of the Challenge Round. The Gentlemen's semi-finals were split between the Centre Court and No. 1 Court. Just prior to the commencement of the Gentlemen's Singles final a female streaker ran across the court.

During a prolonged spell of rain on the second Wednesday, Sir Cliff Richard entertained the Centre Court spectators by singing many of his old songs.

When work ceased in Aorangi Park on the Club's Long Term Plan, for the period of The Championships, the new No. 1 Court Stadium roof steelwork and covering was complete and a major portion of the final facade of the building was in place. During the meeting many facilities such as the Wingfield Restaurant and Cafeteria, Food Village, International Merchandising Shop, Last 8 Club and LTA Information were housed in their permanent locations, but temporarily fitted out. Spectators were able to view the inside of the stadium and the lawn. The public toilets were completed in their finished condition. The roof slabs of the Broadcasting Centre supported a temporary portakabin village, containing TV production units and studios. A number of hospitality suites were contained within a temporary structure, sited between the new grass courts, No. 18 and No. 19, with television studios on the top level. Both courts were formed and turfed. The re-shaped hillside over the tunnel, linking Church Road and Somerset Road, was partly tarmacked for use as a picnic area and for viewing the large TV screen. Roads and walkways around the Stadium were covered with a temporary tarmacadam surface.

The building for the scoreboards for No. 2 and No. 3 Courts was refurbished.

On the first Wednesday, spectators were allowed until 10pm to watch the Euro 96 football match between England and Germany on the large TV screen.

The latter part of the second week's programme was re-organised so that the finals of the Ladies' Singles, Gentlemen's Doubles and Mixed Doubles were played on the Saturday and the finals of the Gentlemen's Singles and Ladies' Doubles were played on the Sunday but rain prevented the plan being carried out and play continued on the third Monday. On that day Mrs Larisa Neiland of

Latvia played four consecutive matches on the Centre Court, lasting a total of 6hrs 25mins. The format of the 35 and over Ladies' Invitation Doubles was changed to a round robin event consisting of six pairs. Because of the bad weather the Junior Doubles were reduced to 16 pairs.

A new electronic net-cord monitoring device, operated by the Umpire, was in action on all courts. The elimination of the net-cord judge reduced the number of officials on the Centre Court, No. 1 and No. 2 Courts to 11. A new high-visibility ball called "Wimbledon Hi-vis" was introduced.

Ball boys and girls were dressed in a newly designed purple shirt and green shorts/skirts. On the second Wednesday, Mark Hillaby, a member of the ground staff, was injured whilst covering the Centre Court, necessitating hospital treatment.

The charge for car parking, as part of the Park and Ride service, was raised to £5.00 per car.

For the first time the Club commissioned its own theme music, entitled "Purple and Green", to be used primarily by TV and radio broadcasters. during The Championships.

The display galleries of the Museum dealing with the years 1968 to date were completely re-built and re-designed.

In April the Club announced that the 1,000 Debenture issue for the new No. 1 Court covering the 1997–2001 Championships had been taken up. Each Debenture cost a total of £9,900.

In September the last match was played on the No. 1 Court during the Davis Cup tie, Great Britain v Egypt. Later a start was made to demolish the Court.

Work continued on the Club's Long Term Plan.

1997

Probably the wettest first week ever, with time lost on Monday, only two matches completed on Wednesday and play on the first Thursday and Friday completely washed out; causing a large backlog of matches. By the Friday evening only 94 had been completed and all car parks had turned into quagmires. The decision to play on the first (middle) Sunday, together with a succession of early starts from the first Thursday until the end, the Gentlemen's Doubles event being reduced to the best of three sets until the quarter-final stage, the Junior Doubles events scaled down to 16 pairs and a gradual improvement in the weather allowed the tournament to be completed on time.

31,204 spectators attended on the first Sunday, when unreserved seats, 11,000 on Centre Court and 10,000 on No. 1 Court, were made available at £15.00 each. 6,500 ground passes were sold for £5.00 each and a special programme at £1.50. Play started on all courts at 11am.

The attendance for the meeting reached record levels with 405,327 present over the scheduled 13 days and 436,531 over 14 days. The daily attendance records for the first Tuesday and Sunday and the second Thursday, Friday, Saturday and Sunday were broken.

With Stage 1 of the Long Term Plan completed, The Championships took on a new presentation, dominated by the new No. 1 Court Stadium situated north of the Centre Court in Aorangi Park.

The new No. 1 Court was officially opened on Monday 23rd June, when a ceremony, commencing at 1.30pm, took place on the court surrounded by ball boys/girls holding the flags of the 58 nations competing at The Championships, whilst in one corner the Central Band of the Royal Air Force provided the music. The Duke of Kent, President of The All England Lawn Tennis Club, accompanied by Mr. J.A.H. Curry, Chairman, and Sir Geoffrey Cass, President of the Lawn Tennis Association, presented a 10 inch silver salver by Garrard, engraved with an aerial view of the court, to the following ten past champions, who had won the singles title at least three times: Miss Louise Brough (Mrs. Clapp), Rod Laver, Miss Margaret Smith/Mrs. Court, Mrs. Billie Jean King, John Newcombe, Miss Chris Evert/Mrs. Lloyd (Mrs. Mill), Miss Martina Navratilova, John McEnroe, Boris Becker and Pete Sampras.

The Master of Ceremonies was John Barrett who introduced each champion in turn and also later the three British singles champions, Miss Angela Mortimer (Mrs. Barrett), Mrs. Ann Jones and Miss Virginia Wade. With the presentations over the Duke of Kent measured the net and proclaimed "I declare the new No. 1 Court officially opened". The first match on court was between Tim Henman of Great Britain and Daniel Nestor of Canada, with the latter serving the first ball.

Besides the 11,432 seater court, the complex contained many public facilities, spread over four levels: 1–Food Village, Wimbledon Shop, LTA Reception and Chemist: 2–Wingfield Restaurant, Conservatory Buffet, ITF and LTA Offices and facilities for LTA County Representatives, Aorangi Food Court: 3–Debenture Holders' Lounge, LTA Members' Lounge, Aorangi Cafe, Hospitality suites G-L; 4–Hospitality suites A-F: Other facilities provided within the Stadium included several public toilets, two First Aid posts and a Left Luggage office.

In addition to the Stadium, the Broadcast Centre and No. 18 and No. 19 Courts were fully operative, likewise the tunnel linking Church Road and Somerset Road and the water feature, close to the picnic terracing, facing the large TV screen. An Order of Play board was provided in this area. Adjacent to Gate 3 in Church Road, the new Championship Entrance Building, housing 20 turnstiles, terminated two public queues for non-ticket holders, one southwards to Wimbledon and the other northwards to Southfields, thereby eliminating queuing in Somerset Road. A large scoreboard, showing the full draw of each of the five Championships and order of play on all courts, together with a new branch of Barclays Bank and left luggage premises were provided in the entrance area. East of the Stadium, ten Retail and Information Kiosks were made available and a new boundary railing was constructed along part of Church Road.

A new board above the entrance to the Centre Court, bearing an inscription of a quotation frrom Rudyard Kipling's 'If' was installed just before The Championships.

No. 14 and No. 15 Courts, which had been completely removed to construct an underground route linking the No. 1 Court and Centre Court, were reconstructed adjacent to their original position and turfed but were not commissioned.

A 'speed of service' radar gun was employed on the No. 1 Court.

The partial demolition of the old No. 1 Court complex carried out earlier in the year consisting of the North Stand, part of the West Stand and the court surface, allowed the facilities within the remaining stands to be used during the Fortnight. (South Building – Competitors' restaurant and lounge, changing rooms for the ladies and ball boys and girls, and offices for the Referee and Umpires: West Building – Buttery for stewards, umpires, ball boys and girls.)

The grounds south of the Centre Court presented a familiar face with the No. 2–13 Courts, Members' Enclosure and Hospitality Marquees (1-28) situated on the Club's hard courts. New to the area were the Last 8 Club Hospitality Marquee, the 'Cafe Croquet' and a second 'Wimbledon Shop'.

The charge for the Park and Ride Scheme operated from Motspur Park was raised to £6.00 per car.

Wristbands were issued for the first time to people queuing, corresponding to the number of seats available each day.

By winning the Ladies' Singles title, Miss Martina Hingis of Switzerland became the youngest champion this century at the age of 16 years and 278 days. Miss Hingis in partnership with Miss Arantxa Sanchez Vicario of Spain defeated Miss Chanda Rubin of the United States and Mrs. Brenda Schultz-McCarthy of The Netherlands in a third round Ladies' Doubles match of 50 games – an all-time record. Todd Woodbridge and Mark Woodforde of Australia won the Gentlemen's Doubles for the fifth successive year.

In the Royal Box on the second Tuesday, the Duke of Kent, presented a Waterford Crystal Vase to Stefan Edberg of Sweden in recognition of his special role at Wimbledon over the years.

The Qualifying Competition held at the Bank of England Sports Ground at Roehampton, the week before the meeting, was severely interrupted by rain, forcing many matches to be decided indoors at Queen's Club and on the covered courts at the Club. The Gentlemen's Doubles was concluded on grass at The Championships on the opening day.

Early in the year nine rows of the Centre Court covered stands (K-T) were re-asphalted and approximately 4,950 tip-up seats installed.

In April the All England Lawn Tennis Ground Ltd sold Callard and Queensmere House, purchased in 1994. On Sunday afternoon, 1st June, the BBC recorded a 'Songs of Praise' programme from the new No. 1 Court, as a way of celebrating its inauguration, as well as giving the Stadium a test run. Over 9,000 people attended, mainly from local churches. The programme was broadcast on Sunday, 29th June.

During August the Centre Court was completely relaid using mature turf which had been grown in Yorkshire for some two years and the Lodge, situated just inside the Somerset Road main entrance, was demolished.

Work continued on the Club's Long Term Plan.

1998

A very wet first week brought about a backlog of matches, which necessitated a succession of early starts from the first Friday until the second Thursday, a reduction of the Gentlemen's Doubles to the best of three sets until the quarter-final stage, the Junior Doubles being restricted to 16 pairs and a change in the weather from the second Tuesday to the end, to allow the meeting to conclude on time.

The total attendance of 424,998 became a new 13-day record, as were the daily figures for the second Friday, Saturday and Sunday.

The construction area of the Centre Court West Stand Extension and new Facilities Building, on the site of the old No. 1 Court complex, was enclosed by hoarding and made safe. There was no West Walkway. The South Building remained, housing the Competitors' restaurant and lounge, changing rooms for the ladies and ball boys and girls and offices for the Referee and umpires, but the remainder of the West Building was demolished and the Buttery for the stewards, umpires and ball boys and girls relocated in a marquee in Car Park 4, adjacent to Aorangi Pavilion.

Several facilities were re-sited, including the ticket resale kiosk near the top of St. Mary's Walk, the Competitors' Marquee, in the covered courts area opposite Gate 13, and the International Tennis Federation office in the North Hall of the Centre Court.

The programme of new signage in the Aorangi Park area was completed. The southern daily queue was allowed on to the Wimbledon Park Golf Course, along the inside of the Church Road boundary wall. The new boundary railing was extended along Church Road from Gate 4 to 5.

New Rolex clocks were installed around the grounds.

After a year's absence No. 14 and No. 15 Courts were again in use. The relocation of No. 16 and No. 17 Courts was completed with the turf, surrounding pavings, walls and planters in place. The courts were not in use during the meeting.

The Centre Court was provided with a new translucent cover and fans were installed at both ends to assist with the drying of the court. A new portable Centre Court viewing platform, accessible from the Museum, was installed for use outside The Championships.

For the first nine days a jazz band played on the temporary erected bandstand at the north end of the Tea Lawn.

The charge for the Park and Ride service was increased to £8.00. per car.

In addition to the 'red boxes', provided at the exits to the stands to encourage spectators leaving the grounds to deposit their seat tickets for resale, a pilot scheme was introduced at Gate 4, whereby spectators prior to leaving, had their tickets scanned to produce another ticket for resale, allowing the holder to retain the original as a souvenir.

A trial of a handheld computer, to replace the traditional umpire's scorecard, was used for selected matches on No. 4 and No. 18 Courts.

Changes in the conditions governing ticket holders in the event no play taking place due to rain, discontinued the priority for a similar ticket for the following year but allowed all categories of ticket holders, including ground passes, to be eligible for a refund.

On the first Saturday smoke from a fire in an adjacent tower block of flats billowed across Aorangi Park. As a precautionary measure play on No. 18 Court, between Todd Martin and Todd Woodbridge, was suspended for a period.

In the Royal Box on the second Tuesday The Duke of Kent presented a Waterford Crystal Vase to Donald Budge of the United States to mark the 60th anniversary of his Grand Slam in 1938.

For the first time a Qualifying Competition for the Junior Singles Championships was held during the opening week of The Championships at the Bank of England Ground at Roehampton.

Work continued on the Club's Long Term Plan.

1999

Excellent weather during the first week and the latter half of the second, together with the raising of the ground capacity figure to 33,500, attracted the all-time record attendance of 457,069. Daily records were broken for nine of the 13 days.

Rain completely washed out the second Tuesday and with play heavily restricted on the Monday and Thursday the programme was badly affected and only a succession of noon starts from the Wednesday until the end and a vast improvement in the weather allowed the meeting to be rescheduled and all events concluded on time. On the Saturday both Gentlemen's and Ladies' Singles semi-finals were played, split between the Centre Court and No. 1 Court, and on the Sunday all five finals were decided – the first time this had ever occurred on the last day. During the blank Tuesday spectators on the Centre Court were entertained by a small band and interviews with well-known players.

The new Centre Court West Stand extension was in use, enabling the court capacity to be increased by 728 seats to the new figure of 13,813. Under the stand public toilets were installed. Six extra wheelchair spaces were provided at the north end, bringing the total to 12. On the No. 1 Court additional screening behind the back row of seats was provided to increase spectators' protection from the wind. A new translucent cover was provided, while at each end fans were installed to assist with the drying of the court.

No. 16 and No. 17 Courts were again in use, bringing the total number of Championship courts to 20.

The construction area of the new Facilities Building, west of the Centre Court, was enclosed by hoarding and made safe. The South Building of the old No. 1 Court complex continued to house the Competitors' restaurant and lounge, changing rooms for the ladies and ball boys and girls and offices for the Referee and umpires. Still as a temporary measure the Buttery for the stewards, umpires and ball boys and girls was located in a marquee in Car Park 4, adjacent to the Aorangi Pavilion.

For the first time spectators on the Centre Court and No. 1 Court were able to see the speed of players' service, displayed in units installed at ground level at both ends of each court. (A radar gun had been employed on the Centre Court since 1991 and No. 1 Court from 1997, without display.)

The umpires and linejudges wore a new uniform in two combinations:

Gentlemen – green blazer, khaki trousers, shirt and tie or sweater, khaki trousers, shirt and tie. Ladies – green jacket, skirt and blouse, or khaki trousers, blouse and sweater. During the second week experiments continued with the use of the Umpire's hand-held computer, the Phillips Velo, for recording the score.

As part of the celebrations to commemmorate the 100th year of the Davis Cup competition, the Trophy was on display for the fortnight, in a case adjacent to No. 16 Court.

During the tournament new tennis promotions were featured. South of No. 13 Court, "Starter Tennis" for under 10s operated daily, as did the "speed of service" net, available for all to test their ability. A booth for players' interviews and autograph signing sessions was located adjacent to the Aorangi Pavilion. During the middle weekend the "ATP Tour", in association with the LTA, Merton Council and Cartoon Network, conducted "Smash Tennis" for aspiring players in Wimbledon Park.

David Nalbandian (ARG) was disqualified in the semi-final of the Boys' Singles because he arrived late for his match.

During August the old No. 1 Court South Building was demolished to make way for the completion of the new Facilities Building as part of the Club's Long Term Plan. The same month the International Club of G.B. celebrated its 75th anniversary by staging the IC Week, which attracted 30 countries.

2000

The Millennium Championships. A fortnight of generally dull weather with very little sunshine. Stoppages due to rain occurred during both weeks which necessitated play starting early from the second Wednesday. However, frequent periods of rain on the last Sunday forced the programme to be extended to the third Monday to play the Ladies' Doubles Final and the Girls' Doubles Final. The attendance on that day was 8,729, which included over 5,200 people paying £5.00 for admission, with the proceeds of £26,750 going to charity – The Cliff Richard Tennis Foundation's 'Kids on Court' Campaign.

To celebrate the Millennium all Singles' Champions, Doubles Champions four or more times and Singles Finalists at least twice, were invited to The Championships for five days over the middle weekend. The highlight of the occasion was on the first Saturday, when 64 players were presented on the Centre Court with a memento by H.R.H. The Duchess of Gloucester, Honorary President of the L.T.A.

Extensive new facilities were provided for the Competitors, Media, Officials and Members by the opening of the Millennium Building and associated Centre Court west stand extension and Officials Pavilion, linked by high level bridges, which replaced the old No. 1 Court complex, west of the Centre Court. The 'W' shaped Millennium Building was opened by the Duke of Kent on the 20th June.

The *Millennium Building* comprises: Level 1 – Members' Entrance and Reception; Officials' Buttery; Ball Boys/Girls' Changing, Rest and Canteen facilities; Competitors' Courtyard, Mini Gymnasium, Doctors' Surgery and Drug Testing Rooms; Plant areas and extension of Royal and Buggy Routes. Level 2- Members' Garden and Self-Service Restaurant; Press Entrance and Reception,

Writing and Interview Rooms; Photographers' facilities and Press Courtyard. Level 3 – Competitors' Main Entrance and Garden; Members Waitress and Private Party Restaurant and Lido areas; Press Writing, Agency and Photographers' rooms. Level 4 – Competitors' Restaurant, Lounge and Lido areas; Press Writing rooms and Restaurant facilities. Level 5 – Plant areas. The *Centre Court West Stand extension* comprises: Level 1 – Ladies' North and South No. 2 Changing Rooms; Public Toilets. Level 2 – Ladies and Gentlemen's No. 1 Changing Rooms; Public Toilets; Press areas; Radio Wimbledon and First Aid Rooms. Level 3 – Gentlemen's North and South No. 2 Changing Rooms; and bridge to Millennium Building. Level 4 – Commentary positions overlooking Centre Court and southern courts. The *Officials' Pavilion* comprises: Level 1 – Lower Referees, Umpires and Ball Boys/Girls' Offices. Level 2 – Referees' Offices, Meeting Room and bridge to Millennium Building. Level 3 – Press Restaurant and bridge to Millennium Building.

The new complex facilities replaced those previously provided for the Competitors and Officials (South Building of the old No. 1 Court), the Media (Centre Court East Building first and second floors) and the Members (old Members' Enclosure adjacent to main Club entrance in Church Road). The former Media area was left vacant during The Championships, apart from the restaurant, which was used solely for Club staff and a temporary 'Millennium' Office.

St. Mary's Walk was extended between the Centre Court and the Millennium Building to provide a pedestrian thoroughfare to meet the South Concourse. This allowed, on a trial basis, the abolition of the viewing lane and the one-way systems outside the Clubhouse. The underground route between the Centre Court and No. 1 Court was completed. The pathway alongside No. 5 and No. 10 Courts, and the old Members' Enclosure, was widened.

The Wingfield Restaurant, on level 2 of the No. 1 Court building, was renamed the Renshaw Restaurant and made over for the use of Centre and No. 1 Court Debenture Holders. The former Members' Enclosure comprised a new self-service 'Café Pergola' and the waitress service Wingfield Restaurant, in marquee accommodation on Hard Court No. 1.

To improve crowd flow, slatted screening was fitted along the side of No. 18 Court, with sliding doors to the court and stand. Additional fans were provided on No. 2, 3, 13 and 18 Courts to quicken the drying of the court surface after rain.

The Centre Court Competitors' and Press seats were reallocated to the north-west corner of the Court, accessed by staircase 10.

New signage was in place for the Centre Court, the Tea Lawn and other public catering facilities.

The Museum 'Tea Room' was renamed Café Centre Court.

Additional Left Luggage facilities were made available outside the grounds, near the Bus terminal, in Car Park 1, and inside the grounds in a kiosk adjacent to Gate 2.

Competitors' transport was operated directly to and from the Millennium Building via the reinstated Gates 14 and 15 and a new internal road, parallel to

Somerset Road. The transport service marquee adjacent to the covered courts was retained, but reduced in size for VIPs and officials etc.

A 'Kids Zone' was established south of No. 13 Court and featured themed interactive tennis areas to introduce youngsters to tennis in a fun way that inspires and motivates them to play. Included were Centre Court (coaching and hitting exercises), IBM Speed of Service cage, Rapid Reactor Wall, Smash attack rebound wall, Target Zone (accuracy skills), Paparazzi Plaza (photo with real or virtual tennis stars) and tennis computer games.

Available for the second year was the Player Autograph and Interview Island, adjacent to the Aorangi Pavilion, and Smash Tennis promotion held during the middle weekend.

In common with other world tournaments, players changed ends (without sitting down) after the first game of each set followed by a 90 seconds interval after each second game. At the end of each set players were allowed a two minute-break, regardless of the score in that set.

Two innovations were introduced for the Gentleman's and Ladies' Finals. Just prior to play, two youngsters, representing nominated charities, performed the coin tossing ceremony to decide which player served first. Immediately after the match Sue Barker (BBC) interviewed both finalists on court.

Pete Sampras, of the United States won the Gentlemen's Singles, for the seventh time, equalling the record. In the Semi-final of the Ladies' Singles, Miss Venus Williams of the USA defeated her younger sister, Serena, 6-2 7-6 (7-3) to record only the third occasion when two sisters had ever met in the event (see 1884 and 1966). They became the first sisters to win the Ladies' Doubles and the first to win a title as Wild Cards.

Todd Woodbridge and Mark Woodforde of Australia won the Gentlemen's Doubles for the sixth time. Mark Philippoussis of Australia and Sjeng Schalken of the Netherlands contested a third round match lasting 5 hours 5 minutes – the third longest singles match ever and the longest completed in a day. The 38 games was also a record for a fifth set in singles.

On the second Monday a male streaker ran across No. 14 Court during the doubles match between Miss Anna Kournikova of Russia and Miss Natasha Zvereva of Belarus and Miss Amy Frazier and Miss Katie Schlukebir of the United States.

Andriy Dernovskyy of Ukraine was disqualified from the Boys' Doubles after assaulting a fellow competitor, Peter-Jon Nomdo of South Africa, at the official players' residence at the Roehampton Institute.

Changes in the format for the Qualifying Competition increased the Ladies' Singles to 96 competitors, playing down to 12 qualifiers. The two doubles events were limited to 16 pairs, with four pairs qualifying.

For the first time behind-the-scenes tours of the Club's grounds were introduced by the Museum. The tours were led by Blue Badge guides.

During the autumn the Clubhouse was closed while exploration and enabling works were carried out in readiness for the refurbishment planned for after the 2001 Championships. Besides the complete removal of the Boston Ivy, the entire face of the building required grit blasting and the cutting out of defective concrete. There was also a need to undertake internal investigation to the condition of the floors and rake beams within the Club's rooms as well as the installation of a new main drain down the road in front of the Clubhouse. During the closure the Members' facilities and Club offices were transferred to the Millennium Building.

2001

A generally warm and sunny meeting was marred by rain on the second Friday and Saturday, which forced the programme to be extended to the third Monday to play the Gentlemen's Singles final, Mixed Doubles final and Girls' Doubles final.

The change of conditions governing ticket holders (see later) did not allow tickets for the Sunday to be used for the Monday. Consequently 10,000 unreserved seats for the Centre Court to see the Gentlemen's Singles final at £40.00 each and 5,000 ground tickets at £ 10.00 each were available on a first come, first served basis from the main Championships gate in Church Road. (£25,000 from the gate receipts was donated to the Club's charities).

Spectators packed the Centre Court and produced an electric atmosphere, where each point brought forth a roar of deafening support for both players. The chanting was continuous and doubtless the noise was unparalleled in the history of The Championships.

The Ladies' Singles final was contested on the Sunday, following the completion of the Gentlemen's Singles semi-final between Tim Henman and Goran Ivanisevic over three days. The Gentlemen's Doubles final and Mixed Doubles final were played on the No. 1 Court. During the Saturday afternoon, when play was restricted to 50 minutes, spectactors were entertained by personality interviews, including the past President of the United States Bill Clinton, and many lively numbers performed by the Band of the Welsh Guards, positioned in the Press Box.

The attendance for the scheduled 13 day's was 476,711 – an all-time record. The addition of 13,370 on the third Monday raised the total for the 14 day period to 490,081 – another all-time record. On eight days the attendance record was broken, with the first Thursday setting the all-time figure of 41,440. The gates were closed early on nine occasions, despite the ground capacity being raised to 34,500.

For the first time, the scheduled start of play on the Centre Court and No. 1 Court was arranged for 1 pm on the first 11 days with both final days unchanged at 2 pm. As events transpired, start of play for the last two days was amended to 1 pm and Noon respectively.

Electric repeater scoreboards for the Centre Court and No. 1 Court were installed on the wall of the Centre Court West Building and an electronic scoreboard, displaying in turn current scores of matches on all courts, was established on the north wall of the Press Centre. A Match Information Display was positioned on the north wall of No. 2 Court displaying the latest point by point scores of all matches and before play the full schedule of matches.

A new vehicular and pedestrian entrance to Gate 1 was sited to accommodate a new location for a footbridge across Church Road during The Championships.

'Speed of service' radar guns and display units were installed on No. 2 and No. 18 Courts.

As usual, spectators gathered on the Aorangi Park Terrace (the 'hill') in their thousands to watch the large TV screen, particularly matches involving Tim Henman. The popularity of this feature prompted the Club to install a second screen at the south end of the grounds adjacent to No. 11 Court for the last four days. Spectators sat in the stand of No. 13 Court and on benches provided on No. 11 and No. 12 Courts. The screen was shipped from Holland and installed overnight, in time for play on Friday.

On the first Saturday the Club invited 12 young players, aged 10–13, from the LTA's National Futures Programme to demonstrate their tennis skills and exercises on the Centre Court (six boys) and No. 1 Court (six girls) before play began. This activity was part of 'The Road to Wimbledon', an initiative launched by the Club to encourage more young people in Britain to play the sport by capitalising on the prestige of Wimbledon.

Prior to play on the second Saturday, a demonstration of wheelchair tennis was given on No. 14 Court by four of Britain's leading players.

After experimenting for several years at The Championships, Chair Umpires used an electronic scorepad, connected to a central computer, to score matches on all courts for the first time. On No. 18 Court the scoreboard, being electronic, was updated directly from the Chair Umpire's scorepad. The scorepad replaced the traditional hand-written scorecard.

Changes in the conditions, governing ticket holders in the event of no play due to rain were made. Purchasers received a full refund if less than an hour's play took place on the court for which the ticket had been bought and if there was more than one hour's play, but less than two hour's play, refunds were limited to half the amount paid. Tickets for the final Sunday were included in this scheme and were therefore no longer valid for admission on subsequent days. If there was any play on the third Monday and following days, admission was via the turnstiles, on a first come, first served basis. Purchasers of ground passes, except those bought after 5 pm, were also eligible for a refund.

For the first time 32 players were seeded in the Gentlemen's and Ladies' Singles events. These were the top 32 players on the ATP Entry System, Position (ESP) and the WTA Tour ranking but the former list was rearranged on a surface based system to reflect more accurately an individual player's grass court achievement.

Goran Ivanisevic became the first Croatian, the first wild card and second unseeded player to win the Gentlemen's Singles Championship. During the event he served a total of 212 aces – beating his own record set in 1992.

Following the practice of a year earlier, two youngsters, representing nominated charities, performed the coin tossing ceremony to decide which player served first, just prior to the Gentlemen's and Ladies' Singles finals on the Centre Court and Sue Barker (BBC) interviewed both finalists immediately after the match on court.

Companion Ladies' Doubles and Mixed Doubles Championship Trophies were presented by the Club.

The Museum was extended southwards to incorporate a new audiovisual theatre and art gallery. The old theatre was converted into part of a new Club office suite. An extension to the Museum offices allowed accommodation for a full-time Education Officer.

During the months leading up to The Championships enabling works continued in the Clubhouse and repairs to the existing concrete structure and main façade of the Centre Court building were completed.

After The Championships work began on the complete refurbishment of the Clubhouse and the development of the southern area of the grounds, both as part of the Long Term Plan. During the closure of the Clubhouse, the Members' facilities and Club Offices were transferred to the Millennium Building. Also, work started in Car Park 4 to provide two grassed terraces and a gardener's complex, with the lower terrace containing two grass practice courts and the top terrace for use as temporary Championship facilities.

2002

A completely dry and mainly sunny first week gave way to cool and showery conditions during the second week, causing frequent interruptions to the programme, which threatened play to be carried over the third Monday. This was avoided by a succession of early starts from the second Wednesday to Saturday plus an improvement in the weather.

The second highest attendance ever of 469,514 over the scheduled 13 days was achieved and included three days when a record crowd was present, on the first Wednesday and Friday and the second Thursday, the 42,457 figure for the Wednesday being the all time record for the ground. The ground capacity was raised to 35,000 and the gates were closed early on 7 days.

It became necessary to split the Gentlemen's Singles semi-finals between The Centre Court and No. 1 Court and play the Gentlemen's Doubles final on No. 1 Court. For the second time ever two sisters, Serena and Venus Williams, of the United States, contested the Ladies' Singles final (see 1884) and as a pair won the Ladies' Doubles title for the second time as Wild Cards. In the opening round of the Gentlemen's Singles, Olivier Rochus of Belgium defeated his brother Christophe. Todd Woodbridge of Australia won the Gentlemen's Doubles crown for the seventh time.

Ryan Henry of Australia and Clement Morel of France fought a second round Boys' Singles match of 75 games, lasting 4 hours and 15 minutes – an all time record. The third set contained 50 games.

During the Gentlemen's Singles final a male streaker invaded the court.

Work on the complete refurbishment of the Clubhouse, which commenced in the Autumn 2000, was concluded on time and the whole premises were made available during The Championships. The new Main Entrance Hall incorporated twin dog-leg staircases leading to the Members' Restaurant, lounge, Summer tea room and kitchens etc., and linking to new entrances/exits to the Royal Box. Also included was a designated corridor to the Millennium Building. The Balcony overlooking the southern end of the grounds was renewed and extended with bridge links to new side balconies.

On the ground floor the offices of the Chairman and executives and a Boardroom lead from the Entrance Hall, which has glass trophy cabinets on two sides and decorative glass doors leading to the Players' Waiting Room and Centre Court. Above the doors is inscribed the quotation from Rudyard Kipling's poem, 'If'. In the basement a Games Room and storage area were provided.

Extensive alterations were carried out at the southern end of the Stadium, where improvements were made to the Royal Box, commentary boxes and the terraces of the stands.

New Boston Ivy was planted against the front wall of the Centre Court stadium.

At the southern end of the grounds many changes were noticeable as the result of Stage 3 of the Long Term Plan which had commenced last Autumn. No. 11 and No. 12 Courts and the gardener's quarters were demolished and in their place a new No. 11 Court (grass) was constructed using a foundation laid in pallets to speed the process of consolidation. Alongside, to the west, an experimental SoftB court was laid and shale Courts No. 4 and No. 5 moved three metres in a southerly direction. A new boundary wall was constructed in this area.

During The Championships the new No. 11 Court was used for practice only and the area of the SoftB Court was covered and made into an attractive public refreshment facility together with a first aid post. The area between the new No. 11 Court and No. 13 Court was block paved, and for the second year an additional huge television screen was erected during the last four days.

The Last 8 Club was resited to the No. 1 Court stadium, suite H.

A new area for wheelchair users and helpers was created in the Centre Court at the stand level, adjacent to staircase 62.

In Car Park 4, two grassed terraces (each capable of containing two practice courts) and a gardener's complex were newly available, all of which were enclosed within security fencing and hedging. The lower terrace had two courts and the top terrace provided temporary Championship facilities.

Following the practice of the past two years, two youngsters, representing nominated charities, performed the coin tossing ceremony to decide which player served first, just prior to the Gentlemen's and Ladies' Singles finals on the Centre Court. The coins used for the toss were Golden Jubilee £5 pieces, donated by the Royal Mint. Two coins were given to the children, two to the charity and one to the Wimbledon Lawn Tennis Museum. Sue Barker (BBC) interviewed both finalists immediately after the match on court

On the first Saturday, before play, the Club invited 16 young players, aged 10-13, from the LTA's National Futures Programme to demonstrate play on the Centre Court (eight girls) and No. 1 Court (eight boys). At a similar time on No.

14 Court, 18 players from the Club's Junior Tennis Initiative performed a mixture of tennis exercises and general sports skills.

Just after 1 pm on the first Saturday, on the Centre Court, John Barrett introduced to the spectators Mr. Robert Brooke, Chairman of Dunlop Slazenger, who was presented with a piece of Waterford Crystal by the Chairman of the Club, in the Royal Box, to mark the 100th anniversary between Slazenger and the AELTC. John Barrett then introduced to the crowd a number of sporting personalities in the Royal Box.

Prior to play on the second Saturday, a demonstration of wheelchair tennis was given on No. 14 Court by four of the world's leading players.

The engraving design on the silver salvers, which are presented to the runners-up of the five Championship events, was changed to incorporate the two new balconies, recently added to the front of the Clubhouse.

WRVS staffed Information Desks for last time.

Immediately after The Championships, work commenced on the construction of six new practice courts and attendant facilities on the Southlands College triangular area site between Bathgate and Queensmere Roads. Work also started on the replacement of the terracing (rows A-H) within the bowl of the Centre Court, clockwise from the south-west corner to the north-east corner.

Four feet tall, custom-made, high voltage electric fences were installed around the Centre Court and No. 1 Court lawns to prevent foxes damaging the surfaces.

On Saturday 23rd November, the first bus service to run along Church Road was started. This was the No. 493 between Richmond and Tooting.

2003

A mainly dry, warm and sunny week, contrasted to the following week in which ran interrupted play on the first four days, particularly on the Wednesday, when there were many periods of frustration. However, early starts on the Thursday and Friday, together with the return of sunny weather, enabled the programme to be completed on time.

The attendance of 470,802 was the second highest ever over the scheduled 13 days and included record crowds present on the first Tuesday and Thursday of 41,929 and 41,967, respectively. On eight days the gates were closed when the ground reached capacity.

Owing to safety concerns, particularly over the size of the overnight queue for the first Saturday, measures were taken to reduce the numbers, estimated to be around 9,000 – an increase of 6,000 on other days. Since 1992, when the first Saturday became a 'special' day, 2000 Centre Court tickets were sold on the day at a reduced price. Also, tickets for No. 1 and No. 2 Courts and ground admission cost less. Arrangements for entry on the Saturday were the same as the first nine days, whereby the number of Centre Court tickets available was 500, similar to No. 1 and No. 2 Courts, with no discount for on-day sales or admission. The other 1,500 Centre Court tickets were redistributed on a shared basis by public ballot and British Tennis (via the LTA).

The new No. 11 Court was used for the first time. No. 10 Court was not used, but designated as a practice court. Temporary seating for 108 spectators was provided on the east side of No. 5 Court. The Match Information Display, positioned on the north wall of No. 2 Court for the previous two years, was moved to the south-west wall of the Centre Court. An Electronic Match Board, displaying up-to-date match information from all courts, using flip dot technology, was installed between the south ends of No. 11 and No. 13 Courts. All match courts were equipped with two scorecards.

The Club President, the Duke of Kent, requested players not to bow or curtsey to Royalty and the Royal Box, except when the Queen or The Prince of Wales were present.

Junior Championship matches were scheduled to start at 11 a.m. during the second week on the outside courts for the first time.

As a new requirement, a proportion of the Wild Cards allocated to the Gentlemen's and Ladies' Singles Championships were determined by contest.

For the third time ever two sisters, Serena and Venus Williams, of the United States, contested the Ladies' Singles final (see 1884 and 2002). Todd Woodbridge of Australia won the Gentlemen's Doubles title for a record eighth occasion.

In the interests of security, all Left Luggage facilities were provided outside the grounds in Car Park 1, the Golf Course and St. Mary's Church car park and extra searches were carried out at all entry points. New permanent public toilets near Gate 12 were completed.

Following the practice of the past three years, two youngsters, representing nominated charities, performed the coin tossing ceremony to decide which player served first, just prior to the Gentlemen's and Ladies' Singles finals on the Centre Court and Sue Barker (BBC) interviewed both finalists immediately after the match on court.

Before play on the first Saturday, the Club invited twenty-two players, between the ages of 10 and 12, from the LTA National Futures Programme to demonstrate play on the Centre Court (4 boys, 4 girls), No. 1 Court (4 boys, 4 girls) and No. 3 Court (6 girls). At a similar time on No. 14 Court, players from the Club's Junior Tennis Initiative squad of 7-14 year olds performed a mixture of tennis exercises and general sports skills.

Just after 1 p.m. on the first Saturday, on the Centre Court, John Barrett introduced to the spectators a number of outstanding personalities in the Royal Box, including sporting stars, past tennis favourites, adventurers and figures from the world of entertainment.

Prior to play on the second Saturday and Sunday, three wheelchair tennis demonstration matches were played on No. 14 Court. Later on the Saturday afternoon, two world ranked players gave a demonstration against two players from the Gentlemen's Singles at The Championships.

During the fortnight, the Kid's Zone attracted around 5700 children, getting to grips with activities such as Target, Rebound Net and Speed of Serve. the latter raised more than £6,000 for the charity CRY.

Two practice grass courts were made available on the lower terrace of Car Park 4, bringing the total number available on-site to 16. The provision of six new practice grass courts and attendant facilities on the Southlands College site was completed, but not in use this year.

During the Spring, a new high voltage cable supply was brought in Gate 1, along Church Road from Southfields to support the increasing demands on electrical power within the grounds. The replacement of the terracing (rows A-H), within the bowl of Centre Court, clockwise from the south-west corner to the north-east corner, was completed. At Wimbledon Park 10 public artificial grass courts were surfaced at the expense of the Club.

The Club entered into an agreement with the production company, 'Working Title Films' to assist in the making of the film 'Wimbledon', a romantic comedy, starring Kirsten Dunst and Paul Bettany. Scenes were filmed during The Championships, and throughout July and August, extensively on the Centre Court, other principal courts and the Aorangi Park practice courts. The Millennium Building and Café Pergola were also featured.

The Club announced that the BBC will continue to be the host broadcaster and UK rights holder for The Championships from 2005 to 2009 inclusive.

Immediately after the meeting, the Championship Entrance Building (turnstiles) including Barclays Bank, adjacent to Gate 3 and the Wimbledon Lawn Tennis Museum Shop, on the Tea Lawn Extension, were completely demolished as part of the Long Term Plan. the clearing of the site made way for the construction of a new building, (later named New Museum Building) containing Club Offices, Turnstile Entrance, Wimbledon Lawn Tennis Museum and Library, Ticket Office and Bank scheduled for occupation by December 2005.

In the Autumn recognition was given to Herman David, Chairman of the Club, 1959-1974, who did so much to pioneer Open tennis, thanks to his children, Tim, Penny and Carol, who commissioned a splendid table from David Linley. The table is located on the landing of the Clubhouse and has inlaid silhouettes of the champions who won Wimbledon during his term.

2004

A meeting badly affected by rain, with only the first Friday and second Monday and Tuesday free of interruptions. The first Wednesday and Saturday were completely washed out, which necessitated the decision to play on the first (middle) Sunday for the third time ever. However, a succession of early starts from the first Thursday until the end of the meeting, the reduction of the Gentlemen's Doubles to the best of three sets until the semi-final stage and the overall rescheduling of matches, enabled the Programme to be concluded, marginally on time.

The Gentlemen's Singles semi-finals were split between the Centre Court and No. 1 Court and the final of the Gentlemen's Doubles decided on No. 1 Court and the final of the Ladies' Doubles on No. 2 Court.

The attendance over the scheduled 13 days was 429,053, well down compared with the past few years. The bad weather, EURO 2004 (football) and a London Underground 24-hour strike, commencing 6.30 pm on the second Tuesday, no doubt contributed to this deficiency. No daily attendance records were broken and only once, on the first Friday, were the gates closed, when the ground reached capacity.

On the first Sunday 11,000 seats in the Centre Court and 10,000 seats in No. 1 Court were on sale, at £35.00 and £30.00 respectively, on a first come, first served basis at the main turnstile entrance with 7,000 ground tickets available at £15 each. As a very stringent security measure, Church Road was closed to vehicle traffic to allow the setting up of a security barrier across the road leading to the entrance of the ground. The gates were opened at 9 am and play began at 11 am on all courts and within a short space of time the Centre Court was full.

The Aorangi Terrace was packed with spectators, particularly to watch Tim Henman play on the large TV screen. A special Programme was on sale, priced £2.00. There was no Park and Ride service and very limited car parking space available. Catering was also very restricted. The attendance for this day was below that expected at 22,155, making the overall figure for the meeting, 451,208.

Work on the construction of the new Championships Entrance Building (later named New Museum Building) to provide new accommodation for the Club Offices, Turnstile Entrance, Wimbledon Lawn Tennis Museum and Library, Ticket Office and Bank had ceased two or three weeks before the meeting, at ground level. On this concrete base, temporary facilities were provided for the Turnstile Entrance, Museum Shop and Bank during The Championship. Other changes around the ground included resiting the Last 8 Club to the private suite (The Tabernacle) just inside Gate 5 on the left, the discontinuation of the First Aid Post in the Centre Court South East Entrance Hall, the non-provision of full Post Office services, leaving the purchase of postage stamps in the hands of the Newsagents and the absence of the Alexandra Rose Day collectors on the first Tuesday, a feature which had been a tradition at the ground for longer than anyone could remember.

The six new practice courts on the Southlands College site were in use.

The Mixed Doubles was reduced from 64 to 48 pairs. The Pre-Qualifying event was discontinued and amalgamated with the LTA Wild Card Play-Off Competition.

Todd Woodbridge of Australia won the Gentlemen's Doubles for a record ninth time.

During a junior match on No. 19 Court, on the second Thursday, a female streaker invaded the court.

Following the practice of the past four years, two youngsters performed the coin tossing ceremony prior to the Gentlemen's and Ladies' Singles finals on the Centre Court, and Sue Barker (BBC) interviewed both finalists on court. Miss Maria Sharapova at No. 13 became the lowest seeded and third youngest player to win the Ladies' Singles. She created a precedent on court by using a mobile phone to call her mother.

Just before play was scheduled on the Centre Court on the first Saturday, the London Stage of the Athens Olympic Torch relay was launched. In a short ceremony in the Royal Box, John Inverdale (BBC) introduced Craig Reedie

(Chairman of the British Olympic Association), Ms Nicky Garron (Deputy Mayor of London) and Sir Roger Bannister (the first four minute miler), before the torch was lit and passed to Sir Roger who saluted the crowd before walking through the Clubhouse to pass the torch over to Tim Henman. He in turn ran through the grounds to Gate 1, where the flame was given to Virginia Wade, who handed over the torch to the first of a series of runners organised throughout London. Unfortunately the whole launch was marred by heavy drizzle.

The demonstrations of play and exercises by the LTA Junior Squads and the Club's Junior Tennis Squad were cancelled on the first Saturday owing to bad weather. On the second Saturday, demonstrations of wheelchair tennis and deaf tennis were held on No. 14 Court. A further demonstration of wheelchair tennis was held on the same court the following day.

Prior to The Championships five head and shoulder busts, cast in bronze and slightly oversize, were unveiled in front of the Clubhouse on 27th April. This celebrated the victories of the five British Ladies' Singles Champions who had won their titles at the Church Road ground – Kathleen McKane Godfree (1924, 1926), Dorothy Round (1934, 1937), Angela Mortimer (1961), Ann Jones (1969) and Virginia Wade (1977). The sculptor of the busts was Ian Rank-Broadley. Also in the spring, Rolex, celebrating 25 years association with the Club, provided new clocks throughout the premises and grounds.

Immediately after The Championships, work continued on the construction of the new Championships Entrance Building (later named New Museum Building).

In the autumn, four new major projects were undertaken: The diversion of services to the North Road, Tea Lawn and South Road and the installation of new subterranean services for both the Centre Court and the Championship Entrance Building were carried out. Work on the replacement of the terracing in the bowl of the Centre Court continued with a further 12 rows (H-T) being renewed, clockwise from the south-west corner to the north-east corner. The existing panel and post walling between Gate 9 and Gate 11, at the southern end of the grounds, was replaced with a new solid brick wall, similar to that provided in Somerset Road. At the same time the two existing Continental Clay courts (No. 7 and 8) were excavated and relaid with a HAR-Tru type surface. The grass in Car Parks 2 and 3 was removed and a firm hardcore laid down. A new durable grass surface was introduced, enabling the car parks to be used all the year, irrespective of the weather.

2005

An excellent warm and sunny first week contrasted to the later stages when persistent rain interruptions on the second Thursday and Friday threatened to take the meeting into a third week. Fortunately, early starts on the Saturday and Sunday, when the weather was dry, allowed the tournament to finish just on time. Part of the rescheduling caused the Ladies' Singles semi-finals to be split over the Centre Court and No. 1 Court and the Gentlemen's Doubles final to be staged on No. 1 Court. The attendance of 467,188 was the fourth highest over the scheduled 13 days and included record crowds on the first Thursday and second Monday, with 42,228 and 41,386, respectively. The gates were closed on six occasions.

Ground entry security arrangements were again tightened with only one bag per person being allowed and that no larger than 18x12x12 inches. Also, no hard-sided hampers, cool-boxes or briefcases were allowed into the grounds.

Roger Federer of Switzerland won the Gentlemen's Singles title for the third year in succession and Miss Venus Williams of the USA became the lowest seed at No. 14 when she won the Ladies' Singles title for the third time. Stephen Huss and Wesley Moodie, an Australian/South African combination became the first qualifiers to win the Gentlemen's Doubles crown. In the opening round of the Girls' Singles, Miss Alexa Glatch of the USA defeated Miss Alla Kudryavtseva of Russia after 49 games, lasting 3 hours 37 minutes, an all time record. A Wheelchair Gentlemen's Doubles event, for four pairs, was staged on No. 14 and No. 15 Courts over the last Saturday and Sunday, for the first time.

Structural work on the new Museum Building, on the east side of the grounds and adjacent to Gate 3, was completed and installation of the services continued. Available within the building were facilities for the ground entrance turnstiles, a Wimbledon Shop at ground level in the south end and a Bank at basement level one in the north end.

Merchandise was sold in seven locations around the grounds, under the umbrella of the 'Wimbledon Shop' – in the No. 1 Court complex (ground floor), in the new Museum Building (south end), in the Centre Court East Building Museum Shop, near to the LTA 'Play Tennis', south of No. 13 Court, and three kiosks, one opposite the Food Village and two in new locations, positioned nearby the No. 18 Court and Referee's Office in St Mary's Walk.

Hospitality marquees were ercted on the two HAR-TRU courts, newly laid at the southern tip of the grounds. The LTA 'Kid's Zone' area to the south of No. 13 Court was relaunched under the 'Play Tennis' banner in a revised format in one large marquee.

Following the accepted practice, a coin tossing ceremony was performed on the Centre Court prior to the Gentlemen's and Ladies' Singles finals, but on this occasion the duty was carried out by a youngster and a Paralympic gold medalist. Sue Barker (BBC) then interviewed both finalists on court. After the Gentlemen's Singles final, the Duke of Kent presented Alan Mills (Referee) and Christopher Gorringe (Assistant Secretary/Secretary/Chief Executive) with a Waterford Crystal vase in recognition of their retirement after 23 and 33 years respectively.

On the first Saturday many Olympic medalists and other sports personalities were introduced from the Royal Box by John Barrett. They included Mary Peters, Jane Torvill, Tessa Sanderson, Denise Lewis, David Hemery, Colin Jackson, Steve Redgrave, Audley Harrison, Matthew Pinsent, Jonathan Edwards, Leslie Law, Sarah Webb, Chris Hoy, Lawrence Dallaglio, John Terry and Ernie Els.

Rafael Nadal of Spain wore piratas on the Centre Court.

Newly introduced were knee protection pads for use by ballboys/girls, if required.

In Veteran matches a third set tie-break was introduced.

After the Championships until the end of the year, a programme was carried out as part of the Long Term Plan, to evacuate the Centre Court East Side to allow the development of the Centre Court. This would increase the capacity from 13,800 to 15,000, offer better facilities to the public and Debenture Holders and provide a retractable roof.

In July, Café Centre Court was closed and catering facilities transferred to part of the Renshaw Restaurant in the No. 1 Court Stadium. Also, Museum accommodation for the Education and Playing for Success groups was relocated to Suites G, H & J in the same building.

At the end of October, the Wimbledon Lawn Tennis Museum and Library closed and all objects etc. stored in the basement, level 2 of the New Museum Building (Gate 3) in preparation for the opening of the Museum, planned for April 2006. At the same time the new Wimbledon Shop, situated on the ground floor at the south end of the building was opened. Also a temporary Visitor Centre was made available to the public in part of the Renshaw Restaurant.

At the beginning of December, Club Staff moved into the first floor offices of the new Museum Building, with the ticket office personnel occupying the ground floor at the north end. The staff restaurant was closed and catering transferred to the restaurant in the Broadcast Centre.

Also, after The Championships, further enabling works were commenced to facilitate the Centre Court development project. This comprised asbestos survey works, ground irrigation works, piling and foundation works, diversion of existing electrical data and telephone services, water services and drainage. In December, subsequent to the evacuation of the East Side of Centre Court, strip out and demolition works, commenced inside the existing building.

2006

Apart from rain on the opening day and periods towards the end of the second week, the weather was very warm and sunny throughout. The attendance of 447,126 was of the order of 20,000 down over recent years, probably due to World Cup football being staged in Germany during the fortnight. No daily attendance records were broken but the gates were closed on eight occasions, when the ground reached capacity.

Ground entry security arrangements were again at a very high level with airport-style searches on entry to the premises.

Roger Federer of Switzerland won the Gentlemen's Singles title for the fourth time in succession and Miss Amelie Mauresmo became the first French woman to win the Ladies' Singles crown for 81 years. Miss Zi Yan and Miss Jie Zheng became the first Chinese players to capture a Championship title when they won the Ladies' Doubles. Likewise, Andy Ram became the first Israeli to win a title, when he took the Mixed Doubles. The longest match ever played at The Championships occurred on the second Wednesday/Thursday on No. 2 Court, when in the quarter-final of the Gentlemen's Doubles, Mark Knowles (Bahamas) and Daniel Nestor (Canada) beat Simon Aspelin (Sweden) and Todd Perry (Australia), 5-7 6-3 6-7(5-7) 6-3 23-21 in six hours, nine minutes. Overnight, the score was 11 all in the fifth set.

During the Ladies' quarter-final match on the Centre Court on the second Tuesday, between Miss Elena Dementieva (Russia) and Miss Maria Sharapova (Russia) a male streaker invaded the court.

On the first Thursday during the Rafael Nadal (Spain) versus Robert Kendrick (USA) match on the Centre Court, a Line Umpire collapsed.

The new Museum Building, east of the Centre Court, was fully completed and occupied. On the ground floor the 'Wimbledon Shop' was located at the south end and, at the other side of the turnstiles at the north end, the Ticket Office. The first floor was allocated to the Club's office staff. Access to the Museum was through the Wimbledon shop to reach level -1, while the Kenneth Ritchie Wimbledon Library, Conservator's office/workshop and Barclays Bank were, with separate entrances, at the north end, level-1.

The Doherty Memorial Gates, erected at the main Church Road entrance to the grounds (Gate 5) since 1931, were removed to allow the installation of wider gates. The original gates were relocated to the southern end of the grounds.

The number of retail units trading under the umbrella of the 'Wimbledon Shop' was increased to 11. Besides the two major shops – the Museum Shop and No. 1 Court Complex (ground floor) – there were nine other small shops or kiosks located around the grounds – Aorangi Pavilion (Gate 1), east side of No. 1 Court, opposite Museum Shop, Play Tennis area (south of No. 13 Court), piazza between No. 11 and No. 13 Courts, St. Mary's Walk, No. 18 Court, inside the hospitality marquee area and in the Centre Court Debenture Holders' Lounge entrance.

Following the accepted practice, a coin tossing ceremony was performed on the Centre Court prior the Gentlemen's and Ladies' Singles finals and, at the conclusion of each match, Sue Barker (BBC) interviewed the finalists on court. Normally these are the only occasions when players are interviewed on court, but an exception was made on the first Saturday after Rafael Nadal (Spain) had defeated Andre Agassi (USA) on the Centre Court. The American, appearing at The Championships for the last time, was interviewed by Sue Barker and given a nostalgic send off by the crowd.

On the first Saturday, before play started on the Centre Court, many distinguished figures from sport and entertainment were introduced from the Royal Box to the public by John Barrett.

First a welcome was given to the President of the International Olympic Committee, Count Jacques Rogge and five members of his Committee, John Coates, Gunilla Lindberg, Denis Oswald, Sir Craig Reedie and Francesco Ricci Bitti, (President of the ITF), plus Gilbert Felli, the Executive Director of the Olympic Games. There followed the introduction of many sporting personalities, including past and present Olympians, Sir Roger Bannister, Jonathan Edwards, Dame Kelly Holmes, Shelley Rudman and Sir Steve Redgrave and stars from other sports – Alec Stewart, Ernie Els, Sir Clive Woodward and Billy Bonds. Household names from the world of entertainment included Bruce Forsyth, Rolf Harris, Michael Parkinson, Nick Park, Jimmy Tarbuck, Alan Titchmarsh and Des Lynam. Tennis personalities introduced were Ashley Cooper, Stan Smith, Todd Woodbridge and Pam Shriver. Finally, five Wimbledon Ladies' Singles Champions who had between them won 28 titles and in total 202 Grand Slam titles in singles, doubles and mixed – Miss Maria Bueno, Mrs. Margaret Court, Mrs. Billie-Jean King, Miss Martina Navratilova and Miss Steffi Graf were introduced. Each was presented with an inscribed Waterford Crystal Lismore Bowl by The Duchess of Gloucester, Honorary President of the LTA.

A change of procedure in the week prior to The Championships had the Seedings announced on the Wednesday and the Draw made on the Friday.

A new Chair and Line Umpire's uniform was introduced, designed by Polo Ralph Lauren, featuring for men and women a navy blue retro blazer, piped in cream and a navy blue and white striped shirt with white collar. The men wore cream pleated 'Oxford Bags' with turn-ups, while the women chose similar trousers or a cream panelled skirt. The traditional colours of green and purple were used on the men's striped tie and on the blazer badge of crossed rackets. Cream canvas shoes completed the outfit. The ball boys/girls also had a new uniform, designed by Ralph Lauren, in French navy with green trim. These included polo shirts, shorts, 'scooters' for the ball girls, caps and practice fleeces.

A facility was added to allow Chair Umpires on the Centre and No. 1 Court to immediately update the electronic scoreboards on court from the scorepad.

Umpires were given the option of recording the result of the point before calling the score or waiting until after calling the score before updating the point.

During the fortnight the Club and the ITF conducted a series of trials using the 'Hawk-Eye' system on grass, before play commenced on certain days. The BBC continued to use the system as a graphics tool on the Centre Court and No. 1 Court.

The BBC for the first time shot Centre Court and No.1 Court in high definition as part of a 12 month trial.

Photographs of all Singles Champions from 1922 to the present day, together with Doubles information, was displayed on canvas-type banners in the North Road.

For the first time, the Club decided to annually commission an artist to produce a unique record of The Championships. Using a variety of media, each artist is asked to record their interpretation of the fortnight – the competitors, the spectators, the support services and the grounds. Mathew Cook was appointed for 2006.

Prior to The Championships, enabling works continued to facilitate the Centre Court development programme, causing much interruption, particularly to the Tea Lawn area and north of the Court. The Members' kitchen was closed and dining transferred to the Millennium Building.

On 12th April HRH The Duke of Kent opened the new Wimbledon Lawn Tennis Museum and Kenneth Ritchie Wimbledon Library.

Following The Championships, all areas of the Centre Court and Tea Lawn were vacated in preparation for a rapid construction start. The whole of the Stadium became a restricted area. The Members' Clubhouse facilities were moved to the Millennium Building, while accommodation for the Ladies' Dressing Room was relocated to the Covered Courts and the Gentlemen's Dressing Room to the No. 2 Court Building.

Between July and September the roof was completely removed, the North Stand accommodation for the old Museum Offices and Library was demolished and a large section of the East Stand removed. The North Debenture Holders' accommodation was stripped out ready for refurbishment.

The new structural steelwork for the North and West Stand extensions commenced early in September and was followed by the installation of new precast concrete terraces and prefabricated commentary boxes. Groundwork, foundations and reinforced concrete works for the new East Stand recommenced in mid September and the new structural steel and concrete frame started erection in November.

2007

The meeting was marred for most of the first ten days by showers continually interrupting play and forcing matches to be constantly rescheduled. However, a succession of early starts from the first Thursday until the end, and the return of the sunshine for the last three days, enabled the programme to be concluded but with no time to spare. This necessitated the Gentlemen's Singles semi-finals to be split between the Centre Court and No.1 Court, the introduction of the 10 point third set tie-break in the four junior events and the playing of the Gentlemen's and Ladies' Doubles finals on the No. 1 Court. Also, some junior matches were played on the six courts at the Southlands College ground on the second Tuesday.

The total attendance of 444,810 was average over the past few years and included a record crowd of 30,173 on the second Saturday. On four days the gates were closed when the ground reached capacity.

Roger Federer of Switzerland won the Gentlemen's Singles title for the fifth time in succession, while Venus Williams of the United States won the Ladies' Singles crown for the fourth occasion, recording the lowest seeded player to do so at No. 23. In the second round of the Gentlemen's Doubles, Marcelo Melo and Andre Sa of Brazil beat Paul Hanley, Australia and Kevin Ullyett, Zimbabwe, 5-7 7-6(7-4) 4-6 7-6(9-7) 28-26, to record the highest number of games ever played in the event at 102. The match was played over four days (rain) and lasted 5 hours and 58 minutes. The 54 games were the highest ever played in a fifth set at The Championships.

Equal prize money was awarded for the first time to Gentlemen and Ladies in all events. The replica trophies presented to the Gentlemen's and Ladies' singles champions were increased to three-quarter size.

Due to the modernization of the Centre Court, as part of the Club's Long

Term Plan, many of the facilities during The Championships were temporarily relocated.

There was no roof on the Centre Court. The new East Building and the extension to the North Building were not fitted out and the space within unusable, apart from rain shelter and toilets. Although there were six rows of terracing added above the normal seating in the east, north and west sides, only seats in the north were filled. Tickets for these 497 seats were obtained by the public via the Internet from Ticketmaster, every evening for the following day's play throughout the fortnight at the usual daily ticket price, plus a service charge. These seats were used as an experiment to try out two new designs. Above the seating on the three sides, new commentary boxes were in use.

The access and stair/lift locations to the Centre Court were different, including temporary public stairs to Staircases 45 to 64 (no staircase to 44). A new wheelchair area was located in the north-west corner at high level, accessed by lift at the west end of the North Concourse.

New wrought iron gates were erected at the main Church Road entrance to the Club (Gate 5).

The two repeater scoreboards previously mounted on the wall adjacent to the Museum entrance were temporarily mounted on the outside of the Centre Court East Building, facing the Tea Lawn.

The Debenture Holders' Lounge and Restaurant were resited in the area normally occupied by the Wingfield Restaurant and Cafe Pergola, adjacent to No. 5 Court. The marquee on Hard Court 1 was two-storey with the Debenture Holders' Summer Marquee on the first floor with separate entrances. The displaced Restaurant and Cafe were positioned south of the grass courts.

Wimbledon merchandise was sold in two main shops in the grounds, one in the No.1 Court complex (ground floor) and the other in the Museum Building by Gate 3.

In addition, there were a series of kiosks situated around the grounds for spectators to purchase souvenir items. Kiosks were also found by the giant television screen on the Aorangi Terrace, by St. Mary's Walk near Gate 1 in front of the Aorangi Pavilion, in the Piazza between No. 11 and No. 13 Courts and in the south-east corner of the Centre Court Building. There were also two kiosks selling tennis books, postcards and other souvenir items by Gate 3.

Following terrorists' car bomb attacks in London and Glasgow over the middle weekend, extra security safeguards were in operation from the second Monday, including concrete vehicle blockers installed at the main entrances to the grounds.

Following the accepted practice, a coin tossing ceremony was performed on the Centre Court, prior to the Gentlemen's and Ladies' Singles finals and, at the conclusion of each match, Sue Barker (BBC) interviewed the finalists on court.

The Wimbledon Junior Tennis Initiative squads gave a one-hour demonstration on No. 14 Court on the Sunday when Dan Bloxham, the Club coach, provided a running commentary and actively involved all watching the proceedings. A Wheelchair Invitation Doubles event for four pairs was staged on the last Saturday and Sunday.

The Hawk-Eye electronic line-calling system was in full operation on the Centre and No.1 Courts for the first time. In order for the players, officials and spectators to see the replays, large screen video boards were installed. As the Centre Court had no roof, two screens (approx. 20 sq m) were located high above the rear seats on the east and west sides of the Court. The No. 1 Court screens were positioned at ground level. Cyclops was used only on No. 2 and No. 18 Courts.

The three Invitation Doubles events were reorganized so that each had eight pairs competing in two round-robin groups, using the 10-point third set tie-break formula. The contest to determine a proportion of Wild Cards allocated to the singles main draws was discontinued and replaced by a similar contest for places in the Qualifying events.

The total sum raised for charity since the Ticket Resale scheme was inaugurated in 1954, reached £1 million.

A special exhibition, 'Court on Camera' – The Story of Photography at Wimbledon' was featured in the Wimbledon Lawn Tennis Museum Gallery.

Luis Morris was commissioned by the Club to be the official Championships artist for 2007.

At the start of the year, construction activity resumed on all fronts of the Centre Court. On the west side, the exterior cladding over St. Mary's Walk was completed. On the north side, exterior cladding was finished and electrical services commenced. Structural repairs were carried out on the south side, above the Clubhouse roof. On the east side of the Centre Court the building was extended a further 11 yards over the Tea Lawn. The structural steelwork was completed by March and the new precast concrete terraces and poured concrete floor slabs quickly followed. The new commentary boxes were installed at the top concourse level. New masonry walls and electrical services commenced while, at the same time, temporary measures were taken to be ready for The Championships.

After The Championships all areas of the Centre Court and Tea Lawn were quickly vacated in preparation for a rapid start by the need to lift materials into the Centre Court as soon as possible. Inside the bowl, a temporary working platform at roof height was erected and the construction of a significant amount of temporary steelwork supports for the installation of the new fixed roof. At the same time, the four tower cranes were re-erected. In July, Somerset Road was closed to allow the large steel roof sections to be transported across from Car Park 2. Lifting, erection and welding of the structural steel roof started in mid-August and continued through the autumn and into the winter. Inside the East and North Buildings, the temporary works installed for The Championships were removed and permanent fitting out works commenced in August. In Car Park 2 work commenced on the construction of the new electrical switchgear and substation building (which will eventually power the moving roof) and infrastructure works commenced for the future Championships chiller plant area.

Following a quick clearance of the Championships temporary facilities around the southern courts, construction work recommenced to complete the new court surrounds and infrastructure to grass courts No. 3-5, 7-10 by October. Demolition of the Water Tower, maintenance workshops and toilet block and a length of Church Road boundary fencing together with general site clearance commenced in July. The Croquet lawn was cleared early in September. Groundworks and piling for the new No. 2 Court started in August while major earthworks and structural concrete works commenced in September.

2008

Although rain interrupted play on the first Friday and three days towards the end of the second week, the fortnight was generally warm and sunny, which enabled the programme to be completed, just in time.

The attendance of 475,812 was the second highest over the normal 13 day schedule and included a record crowd of 40,876 on the first Saturday and 39,262 on the second Tuesday. The gates were closed for 10 days when the grounds reached capacity.

Rafael Nadal of Spain won the Gentlemen's Singles title by defeating the reigning Champion of five years, Roger Federer of Switzerland. This final was, by common consent, the greatest ever, with the Spaniard winning 6-4 6-4 6-7(5-7) 6-7(8-10) 9-7 on his fourth match point. Because of rain the match started at 2.37pm and with two further breaks concluded in the dark at 9.16pm. There was just time for the presentation and quick interview. This final of 62 games lasted 4 hours and 48 minutes – both all-time records. The Mixed Doubles final was reallocated late in the day to the No.1 Court and finished later at 9.34 pm.

Venus Williams of the United States won the Ladies' Singles Championship for the fifth time, defeating her sister Serena in a well-contested encounter. This was their third meeting in the final since 2002.

Following the accepted practice, a coin tossing ceremony was performed on the Centre Court, prior to the Gentlemen's and Ladies' Singles finals and, at the conclusion of each match, Sue Barker (BBC) interviewed the finalists on court.

The modernization of the Centre Court, as part of the Club's Long Term Plan, was complete apart from the installation of the retractable roof, programmed for 2009. The fixed part of the roof was in place. The new East Building, which extended over the Tea Lawn by a further 10 metres was completely fitted out to an extremely high standard and consisted of Ground floor – Tea Lawn (Public self-service Buffet), First floor – Wingfield Restaurant (Public waitress service), Second floor – Terrace Restaurant (Debenture self-service during The Championships (Museum Cafe and Staff Canteen for other weeks of the year, after 2009), Third floor – Champagne

Gallery (Debentures Bar and Lounge) and eight suites, Fourth floor – The Roof Top (Bar area). At the south end a new public toilet facility and Wimbledon Shop, of 4,500 sq feet, was provided. The refurbished North Building consisted of: First floor – The Courtside Restaurant (Debentures waitress service) and Champagne Bar.

The major catering outlets remained the same in the No.1 Court. In the south was the Renshaw Restaurant (Debenture waitress service) and in the east, the Conservatory Buffet (Public self-service). In the north, the LTA's Advantage Restaurant and County Enclosure were jointly renamed 'British Tennis Membership Suite'. Elsewhere, the Cafe Pergola was extended and relocated back to the area south of Gate 5 and a Court Buffet provided light refreshments and a Pimm's Bar, just south of No. 11 Court.

In the Centre Court, the six extra rows of terracing in the east, north and west sides raised the capacity of the Stadium to over 15,000.

The Hawk-Eye electronic system continued to be used on the Centre and No.1 Courts. In order for the players, officials and spectators to clearly see the calls under review, two 4.48m x 2.68m screens were sited at ground level on both courts. These replaced the normal Scoreboards, situated at each end of the court, and combined the match scores and the Hawk-Eye replays in one location. The new board also allowed videos and selected BBC TV output to be shown. The use of Cyclops was abandoned on all courts.

At the southern end of the grounds the new surrounds for Nos. 7 to No. 10 Courts were completed and the new 4,000 seater No. 2 Court, along the west side boundary wall, was essentially completed, but not in use.

The layout of the Tea Lawn was changed. The Bandstand was centrally placed, with the Champagne Bar adjacent and to the north. Above the Bandstand a large information screen was mounted.

Wimbledon merchandise was sold in a large new Retail Shop opened in the south east corner of the Centre Court East Building. Items were also sold in two other main shops in the grounds, one in the No.1 Court complex (ground floor) and the other in the Museum Building by Gate 3. In addition, there were a series of kiosks situated around the grounds for spectators to purchase souvenir items. These were found near the giant television screen on the Aorangi Terrace, by St. Mary's Walk by Gate 3 in front of the Aorangi Pavilion and near No. 11 Court. There were also two kiosks selling tennis books and postcards and other souvenirs, by Gate 3.

On the first Saturday and last Sunday, Dan Bloxham, the Club coach, conducted a one hour demonstration by the Wimbledon Junior Tennis Initiative squads on No. 14 Court. The Wheelchair Gentlemen's Invitation Doubles was held, as usual, over the last weekend.

Also on the first Saturday, before play started on the Centre Court, many distinguished personalities from sport were introduced from the Royal Box by Sue Barker (BBC). Olympic Gold medalists present were Lord Coe, Sir Matthew Pinsent, Sir Steve Redgrave, Jonathan Edwards, David Hemery, Dame Kelly Holmes, Denise Lewis, plus officials, Jacques Rogge (IOC

President) and Sir Craig Reedie (former BOA Chairman). Other sporting figures introduced were Sir Bobby Charlton, Sir Geoff Hurst, Sir Bobby Robson and Neil Quinn (football), Danny Cipriani (rugby), Alastair Hignell (cricket and rugby) Chemmy Alcott (alpine skiing) and Victoria Pendleton (cycling). Tennis was recognized by the presence of Billie Jean King, Martina Navratilova, Ashley Cooper, Neale Fraser, Todd Woodbridge and Tim Henman. From the world of entertainment, Sir Terry Wogan, Jennifer Saunders and Sally Phillips were introduced.

A new special exhibition, 'Raising the Roof, the Creation of the Centre Court' was opened by the Wimbledon Lawn Tennis Museum.

Mick Davies was commissioned by the Club to be the official Championships artist for 2008.

Immediately following The Championships, construction work began and within two weeks the four tower cranes were in action. The removal of all the seats from the Centre Court bowl allowed the re-erection of the temporary working platform at roof level. By the middle of December the remaining eight roof trusses (each 70 tonnes plus) and ten end-arm units (each 16 tonnes) were lifted into position. Fabric installation proceeded.

Construction work on the new substation building, behind the Covered Courts, was completed. The hight voltage switchgear delivers power to the moving roof and to nine chiller units, plus the air supply for the bowl, when the roof is closed.

Fitting out of the new No. 2 Court basement areas and adjacent first aid and toilet facilities continued. Delivery of the new padded seats for the Centre Court and No. 2 Court commenced in December.

2009

Ideal warm and sunny weather throughout the fortnight, spoilt only by light rain on the second Monday evening, attracted the highest ever attendance at the meeting of 511,043. A contributing factor was the increase of the daily ground capacity figure from 36,500 to 40,000. There were record crowds on nine of the 13 days, from Monday to Monday, 42,811, 45,955, 46,826, 43,370, 41,870, 43,432 and 44,478, respectively, the second Wednesday, 39,483 and the Sunday, 30,867. The first Wednesday total became the all-time record. The gates were closed on eight days when the ground reached capacity.

An outstanding feature of the tournament was the spectacle of the newly provided Centre Court retractable roof, which brought the complete modernisation programme for the stadium to an end. During the fortnight there was only once need to close the roof due to the weather, late in the afternoon of the second Monday, when light rain descended. This forced the stoppage of the Amelie Mauresmo of France v Dinara Safin (Russia) match at 4.35 pm. After the roof was closed, the players returned at 5.10 pm and, following a warm-up, the match resumed at 5.20 pm, with the Frenchwoman serving at 4-6 1-4 15 all. The match eventually concluded at

6.19 pm. Although the weather was sunny, the decision was taken to keep the roof closed for the last match on the court, Andy Murray of Great Britain v Stanislas Wawrinka (Switzerland), which began at 6.42 pm and finished at 10.39 pm. This was by far the latest time play had ever taken place on the Centre Court.

Although during the first week the roof was not closed to facilitate play, on two afternoons part of the roof was closed to provide shade for the Royal Box. On the first Saturday, at the conclusion of play at 7.55 pm, the roof was closed. Consideration was given to transferring the Juan Carlos Ferrero v Fernando Gonzales match from No. 1 Court, which was being played in light rain, but this did not occur.

The capacity of the Centre Court was 14,954. New seats were provided throughout, which were padded and wider than before. The seats were numbered on a 3-digit system.

On the first Monday, the Duke of Kent, accompanied by the Club Chairman, Tim Phillips, formally opened the new No. 2 Court, holding 4,084 of the new wider and padded seats, at the southern end of the grounds. This brief ceremony took place at the outside perimeter of the court, where a plaque was mounted recording details of the event. The Duke then tossed the coin on court prior to the first match, between Laura Robson of Great Britain and Daniela Hantuchova of Slovakia. The Hawk-Eye electronic line calling system was in operation on the court. The introduction of this court necessitated renumbering of the southern courts, with No. 2 to No. 11 Courts becoming No. 3 to No. 12 Courts.

On the second Friday, spectators with ground passes were allowed into the No. 2 Court to watch, both Gentlemen's Singles semi-finals on large TV screens from 1 pm. Similar arrangements were made on the Sunday to watch the Gentlemen's Singles final from 2 pm.

Gatehouses 4 and 5, plus ticket collection and accreditation offices were built and the permanent boundary wall in Church Road, between Gate 5 and Gate 8 was in place.

For the sixth time, Roger Federer (Switzerland) won the Gentlemen's Singles title, defeating Andy Roddick (USA) in an epic final, 5-7 7-6(8-6) 7-6(7-5) 3-6 16-14. To many people this encounter was seen as the greatest final, certainly equivalent or superior to the final a year earlier. The length of the match of 4 hours and 16 minutes, the number of games played totalling 77, plus the dramatic 16-14 final set, overhauled all records for previous finals (Roddick lost only one service - in the last game while Federer hit 50 aces.)

Serena Williams (USA) won her third singles crown, beating her sister Venus in the final 7-6(7-3) 6-2. Later that afternoon they paired to win the doubles title for the fourth time.

Following the accepted practice, a coin tossing ceremony was performed on the Centre Court prior to the Gentlemen's and Ladies' Singles finals and, at the conclusion of each match, Sue Barker (BBC) interviewed the finalists on court.

For the first time the scoreboards showed the forenames of the players instead of initials and, in the case of the ladies, the Mrs and Miss were omitted. The official Wimbledon Programme was also brought into line for all events with this procedure

A Wheelchair Ladies' Invitation Doubles for four pairs was held for the first time over the last weekend on No. 4 and No. 14 Courts. The Gentlemen's Wheelchair Doubles was held at a similar time on No. 4 Court.

On the first Saturday and last Sunday, Dan Bloxham, the Club Coach conducted a one-hour demonstration by the Wimbledon Junior Tennis Initiative squad on No. 14 Court.

Wimbledon merchandise was sold in the three main shops in the grounds, in the south east corner of Centre Court, on the ground floor of the No. 1 Court Complex and in the Museum Building by Gate 3. In addition, there was a series of kiosks situated around the grounds for spectators to purchase souvenir items. Kiosks were found by the giant television screen on the Aorangi Terrace, by St Mary's Walk, by Gate 1, in front of the Aorangi Pavilion and by No. 11 Court. There were also two kiosks selling tennis books and postcards and other souvenir items by Gate 3 and a small merchandising kiosk in the north east corner of the new No. 2 Court.

On the first Saturday, before play began on the Centre Court, many distinguished personalities from the Olympic world seated in the Royal Box were introduced by Sue Barker of the BBC. Among these were nineteen gold medallists from the Beijing Olympics - Tim Brabants (Canoeing), Sir Chris Hoy, Jason Kenny, Paul Manning, Victoria Pendleton, Rebecca Romero, Jamie Staff (Cycling), Andrew Triggs Hodge, Ben Hunt-Davis, Mark Hunter, Tom James, Zac Purchase, Peter Reed, Steve Williams (Rowing), Ben Ainslie, Paul Goodison, Andrew Simpson, Sarah Webb, Pippa Wilson (Sailing). They were later joined by Athletics gold medallist Christine Ohuruogu. Olympic greats Dame Kelly Holmes, Sir Steve Redgrave, Sir Matthew Pinsent and Jonathan Edwards were also introduced, as were tennis stars, Maria Bueno of Brazil (Ladies' Singles 1959,1960,1964) and Martina Navratilova of USA, winner of nine Ladies' Singles titles (1978,1979, 1982-1987,1990). Also present in the Royal Box were 2012 Olympic officials, Lord Moynihan (Chairman BOA), Paul Deighton (Chairman LOCOG) and David Higgins (Chief Executive Olympic Delivery Authority) together with four members of the International Olympic Committee: Denis Oswald, Sir Craig Reedie, Gilbert Felli and Hein Verbruggen.

Following the introductions, an announcement reminded the public that the day was 'Armed Forces Day', which has been established to honour the outstanding contribution made by serving and ex-members of the Armed Forces. At Wimbledon there have been volunteer military Service Stewards since 1946. Many of the current Service Stewards had recently served in Operational Theatres.

A special exhibition was held by the Wimbledon Lawn Tennis Museum,

'Fred Perry Life and Legacy', to commemorate the birth of the player in 1909. Professor Eileen Hogan was commissioned by the Club to be the official Championships Artist for 2009.

During the months leading up to The Championships, much testing and preparation was carried out to ensure that the Centre Court retractable roof was functioning entirely satisfactorily. On Sunday afternoon, 17th May, the Club staged a 'Centre Court Celebration' designed to fully test the roof and management systems. Open to the public, tickets were available at £35.00 to see exhibition matches performed by Andre Agassi, Tim Henman, Kim Clijsters and Steffi Graf, which featured a men's and ladies' singles and a mixed doubles match. The public response was overwhelming and 15,000 spectators were entertained for approximately three hours. There was also interlude entertainment provided by Katherine Jenkins, Faryl Smith and Blake.

After The Championships, there followed a period of two weeks to move out of the No.3 Court (old No. 2) accommodation, including the tunnel areas under the grandstand and to demolish the Groundsmen's cottages and surrounding area, ready to commence the final phase of Stage 3. Demolition of the old buildings and the remaining sections of Somerset Road boundary wall, together with general site clearance were complete by mid-August, followed immediately by the arrival of piling rigs on site. Piling to both sites was completed by late September and construction works started on the new foundations and bowl structure.

2010

Glorious warm and sunny weather reigned throughout the fortnight, with no interruptions due to rain. The total attendance of 489,946 was down some 21,000 on the previous year's record, but this was mainly due to the ground capacity being reduced from 40,000 to 37,500 as a consequence of the new No. 3 and No. 4 Courts not being available until 2011. (The No. 3 Court was fully constructed and will hold 2,000 spectators, while the No. 4 Court had only the foundation laid.) There were record crowds on two days, the first Friday, 41,920, and last Sunday, 32,036, with the gates being closed to the ground on eight days, when the capacity figure was reached.

A temporary stand holding 1,000 spectators was in place on the foundation of No.4 Court, overlooking No. 5 Court. Due to the development of the new No. 3 and No. 4 Courts, the southern courts were re-numbered – old No. 2 Court became No. 3 Court, old No. 3 Court became No. 4 Court etc, up to No. 12 Court. (There was no No. 13 Court). Show courts were: Centre Court, No. 1, No. 2, No. 5, No.12 and No.18 Courts. Electronic scoreboards were installed on No. 14–17 Courts. In the Centre Court new public toilets were available on the top level concourse and a new elevated photographers' position was established.

The No. 1 Court Debenture Holders' Lounge and Renshaw Restaurant (public) were completely refurbished . The Fred Perry statue was relocated by the entrance to the Centre Court Debentures' complex.

The Centre Court retractable roof was not used to counter rain but, on one occasion, the first Monday, closed to allow the Gentlemen's Singles first round match between Novak Djokovic (Serbia) and Olivier Rochus (Belgium) to finish. The roof was closed from 8.45pm (play started at 9.20pm) to 10.59pm. The roof was able to be deployed in a new sunshade role after software installation allowed two sections of the roof to be used from each end.

HM Queen Elizabeth honoured the Club and The Championships with a visit on the first Thursday. The Queen arrived at around 11.30am and was met at the Aorangi Terrace by HRH The Duke of Kent (President), Tim Phillips (Chairman), Philip Brook (Vice-Chairman) and Ian Ritchie (Chief Executive). The Queen proceeded down St Mary's Walk between No. 18 and No. 19 Courts, visiting No. 14 Court to watch the Club's Junior Tennis Initiative and to be introduced to Dan Bloxham, the Club's head coach. The Queen continued down St Mary's Walk to the Members' Lawn to meet a collection of players, defending champions, Roger Federer and Serena Williams, past champions, Martina Navratilova and Billie Jean King, top-seeded players, Venus Williams, Caroline Wozniacki, Jelena Jankovic, Rafael Nadal, Novak Djokovic, Andy Roddick and British players, Laura Robson, Heather Watson, Anne Keothavong and Elena Baltacha. The Queen proceeded to the Clubhouse for lunch and afterwards watched from the Royal Box, play between Andy Murray (Great Britain) and Jarkko Nieminen (Finland). Before leaving the grounds, just after 3pm, the Queen was presented with a memento of her visit – half-size Gentlemen's and Ladies' Singles trophies.

Rafael Nadal (Spain) regained the Gentlemen's Singles title and Serena Williams (USA) retained the Ladies' Singles title, to win the crown for the fourth time. Jurgen Melzer (Austria) and Philipp Petzschner (Germany) won the Gentlemen's Doubles title, unseeded. Undoubtedly the outstanding match of the tournament was the marathon Gentlemen's Singles first round encounter between John Isner (USA) and Nicolas Mahut (France), played on No. 18 Court over three days (from Tuesday to Thursday), which produced a total of 183 games and lasted for 11 hours, 5 minutes. The fifth set of 70–68 games took 8 hours, 10 minutes. Immediately the match was over, Ann Jones and Tim Henman presented both players, on court, with souvenirs – 10 inch Tipperary Crystal Bowl and six Waterford Crystal Wimbledon champagne flutes. The Chair Umpire, Mohamed Lahyani, received a 10 inch Tipperary Crystal Bowl, a Wimbledon tie and Wimbledon silver cufflinks. **This match, in time and number of games, was the all-time record for the game (see page 468)**.

On the first Saturday before play began on the Centre Court, many distinguished personalities from the world of sport were introduced by Sue Barker of the BBC – Tim Brabants (canoeing), Sachin Tedulkar (cricket), Sir Chris Hoy, Victoria Pendleton (cycling), Sir Bobby Charlton, Glen Hoddle (football), Sir Bob Charles (golf), Martin Bayfield, Alastair Hignell, Jason Leonard, Lewis Moody (rugby), Chemmy Alcott (skiing), Mark Foster (swimming), Ashley Cooper, Neale Fraser, Evonne Goolagong-Cawley, Jan Kodes, Ilie Nastase, Martina Navratilova, Budge Patty, Roger Taylor (tennis) and Olympic gold medallists, Dame Kelly Holmes (athletics) and Amy Williams (skeleton athelete). Also present were Francesco Ricci Bitti (President ITF) and Paul Deighton (Chairman, LOCOG). Following the introductions, an announcement reminded the public that the day was 'Armed Forces Day' and 14 service personnel present in the Royal Box were named.

On the second Friday, spectators with ground passes were allowed into the No. 2 Court to watch both Gentlemen's Singles semi-finals on a large TV screen from 1pm. Similar arrangements were made on the Sunday to watch the Gentlemen's Singles final from 2pm.

Wimbledon merchandise was sold in three main shops in the grounds, on the south east corner of Centre Court, on the ground floor of the No. 1 Court Complex and in the Museum Building by Gate 3. In addidtion, there were a series of kiosks situated around the grounds for spectators to purchase souvenir items. Kiosks were to be found by the giant television screen on the Aorangi Terrace, by St Mary's Walk, by Gate 1, in front of the Aorangi Pavilion, opposite No. 5 Court and on the corner of No. 2 Court by Gate 7. There were also two kiosks selling tennis books and postcards and other souvenir items by Gate 3.

Following the accepted practice, a coin tossing ceremony was performed on the Centre Court prior to The Gentlemen's and Ladies' Singles finals, and at the conclusion of each match, Sue Barker (BBC) interviewed the finalists on court.

Wheelchair Gentlemen's and Ladies' Doubles events were held on the last weekend on No. 5, No. 16 and No. 14 Courts.

Matt Harvey was commissioned by the Club to be the official poet.

A special exhibition was held by the Wimbledon Lawn Tennis Museum, devoted to the life and tennis times of Ted Tinling, to celebrate the centenary of his birth.

Soon after The Championships, work continued for the construction and fitting out of the various accommodations (public toilets, lost property, programme distribution office) under the new No. 3 Court Stand and the installation of the 2000 new padded seats in the bowl. Also, the installation proceeded of the palletised new No.4 Court and the construction and fitting out of all the above-ground structures for the new Groundsman's accommodation and workshops. The new boundary walls on Somerset Road and the final section on Church Road between Gates 5 and 6 were also completed.

In addition, in this same period, work was undertaken to create additional dining space for the No.1 Court Debenture Holders. This comprised the construction of two reinforced concrete balconies to infill the 'voids' in the building elevations at the south west and south east corners, to be covered with fabric canopies.

2011

The 125th Championships. To commemorate the occasion each competitor was given a souvenir. The gentlemen received a 'Links of London' black leather washbag, embossed with the 125th Championships logo, while the ladies were given a 'Links of London' silver bracelet, incorporating the 125th Championships logo.

Although the first week was overcast with some rainy periods, there followed dry but generally cloudy weather, enabling the programme to proceed with little interruption. The total attendance for the fortnight was 494,761, the second highest total for the normal 13 days, no doubt partly due to the ground capacity figure being raised from 37,500 to 38,500. There were record crowds on the first Friday and second Monday of 43,145 and 44,494, respectively. The gates were closed on six days when the ground reached capacity.

An outstanding feature of the meeting was the opening of the new No. 3 Court adjacent to Gate 13, which accommodated 1980 spectators with approximately one quarter of the total set aside as unreserved seating in the south west corner. There was also a new No. 4 Court, situated east of No. 3 Court, which seated 170 people on the west side.

At the southern apex, new permanent toilet facilities for marquee guests were available. Nearby, a new building was constructed for the groundstaff, providing an office for the Head Groundsman, a mess room, locker rooms, toilets and showers, with machinery store below.

At the south west and south east corner of the No. 1 Court stadium, new canopy covered balcony terraces were provided as additional reception, dining and bar areas for the No. 1 Court debenture holders.

Other minor improvements were made, with the provision of a Press Photographer's Box at high level at the north end of the Centre Court and the complete refurbishment of the Players' Entrance in the Millennium Building. Also, the asphalt surface of the concourse around the Centre Court, clockwise from the South West Entrance Hall to the North East Entrance Hall was relaid with block paving.

On the first Monday, the Duke of Kent, President of the All England Lawn Tennis Club, accompanied by the Chairman, Philip Brook, opened the new No. 3 Court. A brief ceremony took place at the outside perimeter of the court, where a commemorative plaque was mounted. The first match to be played on the court was Katie O'Brien (Great Britain) versus Kimiko Date Krumm (Japan).

There were two new singles champions, Novak Djokovic (Serbia) and Petra Kvitova (Czech Republic). Following the accepted practice, a coin tossing ceremony was performed on the Centre Court prior to the Gentlemen's and Ladies' Singles finals and, at the conclusion of each match, Sue Barker (BBC) interviewed the finalists on court.

The Gentlemen's Doubles was reduced to the best of three sets in the opening round, owing to rain early in the first week.

On the first Saturday, before play began on the Centre Court, many distinguished personalities from the sportsworld, seated in the Royal Box, were introduced by Sue Barker of the BBC. Sir Roger Bannister, Jonathan Edwards, Dame Kelly Holmes (Athletics), Timothy Brabants (Canoeing) Steven Davis, Sachin Tendulkar (Cricket), Geoff Hurst (Football), Beth Tweddle (Gymnastics), Sir Steve Redgrave, Steve Williams, Mark Hunter, Peter Reed (Rowing), Martin Bayfield, Edward Butler, Ben Foden, Austin Healey, Alistair Hignell, Tom James, Jason Leonard (Rugby), Amy Williams (Skeleton Athletics), Jason Kenny (Cycling), George O'Grady (Golf). Ashley Cooper, Martina Navratilova (Tennis). Following their introduction, an announcement reminded the public that the day was 'Armed Forces Day' and 14 service personnel present in the Royal Box were introduced.

On the second Monday, the newly wed Duke and Duchess of Cambridge visited The Championships.

On the second Friday, Saturday and Sunday spectators with ground passes were allowed in to the No. 2 Court to watch the Gentlemen's Singles semi-finals (1 pm), Ladies' Singles Final (2 pm) and the Gentlemen's Singles Final (2 pm), respectively.

Wimbledon merchandise was sold in three main shops in the grounds, on the south east corner of Centre Court, on the ground floor of the No.1 Court complex and in the Museum Building by Gate 3. In addition there was a series of kiosks situated around the grounds for spectators to purchase souvenir items. Kiosks were situated by the giant television screen on the Aorangi Terrace, by St Mary's Walk, by Gate 1, behind No. 15 Court, in front of the Aorangi Pavilion, opposite No.5 Court and on the corner of No. 2 Court by Gate 7. There were also two kiosks, one of which sold tennis books and postcards and other souvenir items by Gate 3.

Wheelchair Gentlemen's and Ladies' Doubles events were held on the last weekend on No. 7 and No. 14 Courts.

A special exhibition *The Queue: A Long Standing British Tradition* was held by the Wimbledon Lawn Tennis Museum.

On Thursday, 24th August the BBC staged an Antiques Roadshow programme on the south concourse and adjacent paths around the grass courts. The recording for the programmes started at 9.30 am and ended at 7 pm.

The current contract between the Club and the BBC was extended by a further three years from 2015 to 2017 inclusive. This will continue to give audiences access to the tournament for TV, radio, online, red button, mobile and tablet.

A new agreement between the Club and ESPN allowed the company to be exclusive broadcaster of live coverage of Wimbledon in the United States for a 12 year period beginning in 2012.

The Club announced a new project to develop a long term plan for the grounds for the next 10 to 15 years. This project named 'Wimbledon 2020' has two objectives in mind. Firstly to find solutions to a significant number of operational challenges created by the growth of The Championships and secondly to consider the redevelopment of areas of the grounds which were not part of the original Long Term Plan.

2012

A fortnight of generally cloudy weather with occasional sunny spells in the first week, followed by overcast skies and periods of prolonged rain. The total attendance of 484,805 was a little below recent years and did not produce any new daily records. The gates were closed on eight days when the grounds reached capacity, which was set again at 38,500. The Centre Court retractable roof was closed on nine days, including for part of the Gentlemen's Singles final.

A revised starting time of 11.30 am was introduced on Nos.2-12 and 14-19 Courts for main draw matches to ensure the optimum chance of being completed the day they were scheduled. As in previous years the gates opened at 10.30 am. On the second Tuesday play started at Noon on the Centre Court and No. 1 Court, 11.30 am on other show courts and 11.00 am on other courts to enable the programme to keep on schedule.

Roger Federer (Switzerland) won the Gentlemen's Singles title for the seventh time, beating Andy Murray in the final, the first Britain to reach this stage of the event since 1938. Serena Williams (United States) captured the Ladies' Singles title for the fifth time and with her sister, Venus, won the Ladies' Doubles crown for the fifth time. There was a surprise in the Gentlemen's Doubles event when the wild card pair of Jonathan Marray (Great Britain) and Frederik Nielsen (Denmark) won the title. Marray was the first Britain to have won the event since 1936. The runners-up in the event, for the third year, were Robert Lindstedt (Sweden) and Horia Tecau (Romania).

For the first time at The Championships a player won 24 consecutive points to win a set, 6-0. This occurred in the first round of the ladies' singles, when Yaroslava Shvedova of Russia beat Sara Errani of Italy, 6-0.

Following the accepted practice, a coin tossing ceremony was performed on the Centre Court prior to the Gentlemen's and Ladies' Singles finals and at the conclusion of each match, Sue Barker (BBC) interviewed the finalists on court. Shortly after leaving the court, the champions for the first time displayed their trophy from the Clubhouse balcony to the crowd of waiting spectators.

The Prince of Wales, accompanied by the Duchess of Cornwall, made a rare visit to The Championships on the first Wednesday. The only other occasion he was present was in 1970.

Several other members of the Royal Family were present during the fortnight, including the Duke of Kent, President of the Club, on six occasions and the Duke and Duchess of Cambridge.

Wheelchair Gentlemen's and Ladies' Doubles events were held during the last three days on No. 3 and No. 14 Courts.

Wimbledon merchandise was sold in three main shops in the grounds, on the south east corner of the Centre Court, on the ground floor of the No. 1

Court complex and in the Museum Building by Gate 4. In addition there was a series of kiosks situated around the grounds for spectators to purchase souvenir items. Kiosks were located by the giant television screen on the Aorangi Terrace, by St Mary's Walk, by Gate 1, behind No. 15 Court, in front of the Aorangi Pavilion, Gate 13 opposite No. 4 Court and on the corner of No. 2 Court by Gate 7. There were also two kiosks, one selling tennis books and postcards and another, souvenirs, by Gate 3.

On the first Saturday, before play began on the Centre Court, many distinguished personalities from the sporting world, seated in the Royal Box, were introduced to the crowd by Sue Barker:- Dame Kelly Holmes (Athletics), Geoffrey Boycott, Alastair Cook. Chris Cowdrey, Andy Flower, Andrew Strauss, Phil Tufnell, Bob Willis (Cricket), Sir Bobby Charlton. Ryan Giggs (Football), Jack Nicklaus (Golf), Sir Craig Reedie, Sir Keith Mills (Olympics), Martin Bayfield, Matt Dawson, Owen Farrell, Adam Jones (Rugby), Mark Foster (Swimming). Boris Becker, Judy Murray, Ilie Nastase. Martina Navratilova, Mary Pierce, Leon Smith (Tennis), Amy Williams (Skeleton Bob). Following the introductions, an announcement reminded the public that the day was 'Armed Forces Day' and six members of the 'Military Wives' choir and their partners, along with conductor, Gareth Malone were also introduced.

On Monday 23rd July the Olympic Torch Relay passed through the grounds of the Club, the torch being carried by Andy Murray, who handed over to Venus Williams.

For three weeks after The Championships the grounds were closed to the public and Club members, while the London Organising Committee for the Olympic Games organised the tennis event. A very successful meeting took place from 28th July to 5th August and involved a total of 184 players competing in the five events. (See *Other Major Events Staged at Wimbledon*)

2013

The weather for the first week was generally overcast with some drizzle on the Thursday and Friday. The following week continued in the same vein, except for the last three days which were warm and sunny.

The total attendance of 486,898 was an average figure for the past few years and did not produce any daily records. The gates to the grounds were closed on 12 days, when the capacity was again set at 38,500.

The starting time of 11.30 am, introduced the previous meeting, on Court Nos.2-12 and 14-19 for main draw matches was continued. Also, the regular 10.30 am opening of the gates was maintained.

Prize money was a record £22.6 million, an increase of 40% over 2012, with the winners of the Gentlemen's and Ladies' Singles Championship each receiving £1.6 million compared with £1.15 million the year before.

Andy Murray became the first British player to win the Gentlemen's Singles Championship for 77 years when he beat Novak Djokovic of Serbia in the final. The longest ever semi-final took place in this event when Novak Djokovic beat Juan Martin del Potro of Argentina over 4 hours 43 minutes.

The Ladies' Singles Championship was captured by Marion Bartoli, the third French lady to do so, when she beat Sabine Lisicki of Germany in the final.

Bob and Mike Bryan of the United States won the Gentlemen's doubles title for the third time and in so doing became the holders of all four Grand Slam titles and Olympic Gold concurrently.

There were some unpredictable results in the first week. By the Thursday, seven of the top 16 seeds in the Gentlemen's Singles and nine of the top 16 in the Ladies' Singles had been eliminated.

Also unusual was the number of players who withdrew, either before or during a match, due to injury.

Following the accepted practice, a coin tossing ceremony was performed on the Centre Court prior to the Gentlemen's and Ladies' Singles finals and at the conclusion of each match, Sue Barker (BBC) interviewed the finalists on court. Shortly after leaving the court, the champions displayed their trophy from the Clubhouse balcony to the crowd of waiting spectators.

Wheelchair Gentlemen's and Ladies' Doubles events were held during the last three days on No. 12 and No. 14 courts.

Wimbledon merchandise was sold in three main shops in the grounds, on the south east corner of Centre Court, on the ground floor of the No. 1 Court complex and in the Museum Building by Gate 4. In addition, there was a series of kiosks situated around the grounds for spectators to purchase souvenir items. Kiosks were to be found by the giant television screen on the Aorangi Terrace, by St Mary's Walk, by Gate 1, behind No. 15 Court, in front of the Aorangi Pavilion, Gate 13 opposite No.4 Court and on the corner of No.2 Court by Gate 7.

There were also two kiosks, one selling tennis books and postcards and other souvenir items by Gate 3. The shops were open daily during The Championships from ground opening to close of play, except on the final Sunday, when Sunday trading hours applied.

On the first Saturday, before play began on the Centre Court, many 2012 Olympic and Paralympic gold medallists, seated in the Royal Box, were introduced to the crowd by Sue Barker:- Danielle Brown (Archery), Josie Pearson (Athletics), Anthony Joshua (Boxing), Steven Burke, Neil Fachie, Philip Hindes, Sir Chris Hoy, Anthony Kappes, Jason Kenny, Danielle King, Victoria Pendleton, David Stone, Laura Trott (Cycling), Natasha Baker, Peter Charles, Deborah Criddle, Charlotte Dujardin, Carl Hester, Lee Pearson, Laura Tomlinson, Sophie Wells (Dressage), Sophie Christiansen (Equestrian), Katherine Copeland, Helen Glover, Katherine Grainger, Alex Gregory, Sophie Hosking, Tom James, Peter Reed, David smith, Andrew Triggs Hodge, Lily van den Broeke, Anna Watkins (Rowing), Helena Lucas (Sailing), Jessica-Jane Applegate, Jonathan Fox, Oliver Hynd (Swimming) and Andy Murray (Tennis).

At the conclusion of the presentations the public were reminded that the day was 'Armed Forces Day'.

A special exhibition *'On the Riviera: Tennis in France, 1874–1939'* was held by the Wimbledon Lawn Tennis Museum.

After The Championships, work commenced as part of the 'Wimbledon Master Plan', with creation of new underground accommodation beneath No. 14 and No. 15 Courts, a tunnel under Somerset Road from the Club to the Covered Courts area, both in August, also the refurbishment of the Clubhouse in September.

On 1st August the Club duly acquired the LTA's 50% shareholding in the All England Lawn Tennis Ground pic, giving the Club sole ownership of the grounds at Wimbledon.

2014

Overall, warm and sunny weather for the fortnight was marred by rain on the first Thursday and Saturday and second Monday. This interrupted the normal scheduling of matches, forcing a succession of early starts during the second week, including a noon start on the Centre Court on the Wednesday, enabling the programme to conclude comfortably on time.

The total attendance of 491,084 for the meeting was excellent and resulted in the third ever highest figure, although no daily records were broken. The gates to the grounds were closed on 12 days, when the ground capacity was again set at 38,500.

The normal availability of 19 courts was reduced by two to 17, owing to No. 14 and No. 15 Courts being out of commission, as new underground accommodation was being provided. The starting time of play of 11.30am, introduced three years earlier for outside courts continued. Also, the regular 10.30am opening of the gates was maintained.

An extra 198 unreserved seats on No.3 Court were made available to Ground Pass holders.

New wrought iron railings were installed along the Church Road boundary of the Wimbledon Park Golf Club, dramatically enhancing the view of the golf course for the Club's neighbours and visitors coming from Southfields.

A gate was installed in the Centre Court players' box to allow the new Singles Champions easier access from the court to receive congratulations from their family and team.

Umpires' chairs were redesigned to give additional height and therefore better visibility.

Prize money rose to an all-time high with the total for the meeting reaching £25 million, with the winners of the Gentlemen's and Ladies' Singles each receiving £1,760,000.

The winners of the Singles, Novak Djokovic of Serbia and Petra Kvitova of the Czech Republic recaptured the titles they attained in 2011. The Gentlemen's final between Djokovic and Roger Federer of Switzerland was outstanding in quality and excitement right up to the very end of the five-set match. The Ladies' final, by comparison was disappointing in that the contest lasted less than an hour, with the runner-up, Eugenie Bouchard of Canada, failing to produce her promising best.

For the first time the presentation party for the two singles finals on the Centre Court included a lady President of the LTA- Mrs Cathie Sabin.

Canada was also to the fore in the Gentlemen's Doubles event, when Vasek Pospisil from British Columbia paired with Jack Sock of the United States captured the title, being unseeded. A rare feature of the Gentlemen's Singles was that no United States player reached the last 16 – last happened in 1911.

On the second Wednesday, the Duke and Duchess of Cambridge watched play from the Royal Box.

On the first Tuesday, on the Centre Court, before the opening match between Sabine Lisicki of Germany and Julia Glushko of Israel, a coin tossing took place. The ceremony, to celebrate the life of the late Elena Baltacha, was performed by the 2013 champion, Marion Bartoli of France accompanied by 9 year-old Elle Rubos-Miller, a player from the Elena Baltacha Academy of Tennis.

On the second Thursday, an announcement was made on the Centre Court that there would be an interval of 30 minutes between the two Ladies' Singles semi-final matches. This was a new departure.

Following the accepted practice, a coin tossing ceremony was performed on the Centre Court, prior to the Gentlemen's and Ladies' Singles finals and at the conclusion of each match, Sue Barker (BBC) interviewed the finalists on court. Shortly after leaving the court, the champions displayed their trophy from the Clubhouse balcony to the crowd of waiting spectators.

Wheelchair Gentlemen's and Ladies' Doubles event was held during the last three days on Nos. 16 and 17 Courts.

Wimbledon merchandise was sold in three shops in the grounds on the south east corner of Centre Court, on the ground floor of the No. 1 Court complex and in the Museum Building by Gate 4. In addition, there was a series of kiosks situated around the grounds for spectators to purchase souvenir items. Kiosks were to be found by the giant television screen on the Aorangi Terrace, by St Mary's Walk, by Gate 1, behind No.15 Court, in front of the Aorangi Pavilion, Gate 13, opposite No.4 Court and on the corner of No.2 Court by Gate 7. There were also kiosks selling tennis books, postcards and other souvenir items by Gate 3. The shops were open daily during The Championships from ground opening to close of play, except on the final Sunday, when Sunday trading hours applied.

On the first Saturday before play began on the Centre Court, many distinguished personalities from the sporting world, seated in the Royal Box, were introduced to the crowd by Sue Barker of the BBC:-

Nicola Adams, David Haye, Anthony Joshua (Boxing), Stuart Broad, Steven Finn, Andrew Strauss, Sachin Tendulkar, Phil Tufnell (Cricket), Victoria Pendleton, Sir Bradley Wiggins (Cycling), Tom Daley (Diving), David Beckham, Sir Bobby Charlton (Football), Ian Poulter, Matthew Fitzpatrick (Golf), Sir Matthew Pinsent (Rowing), Chris Robshaw (Rugby), Amy Williams, Elizabeth Yarnold (Skeleton Bob), Charlotte Evans, Kelly

Gallagher (Skiing), Laura Massaro (Squash), Mark Foster (Swimming), Judy Murray, Peter Norfolk, Leon Smith (Tennis).

At the conclusion of the presentations, the public were reminded that it was 'Armed Forces Day' and service personnel, seated in the Royal Box with their partners, were introduced.

The shuttle bus service from Southfields during The Championships was suspended on a trial basis. The aim was to reduced traffic congestion. A disability shuttle service was in operation.

For the second Championships running, the Wimbledon Lawn Tennis Museum continued the temporary exhibition *On the Riviera: Tennis in France, 1874-1939'*.

Before The Championships, the Club continued work on the Wimbledon Master Plan. The tunnel under Somerset Road was completed, but not opened, as was the creation of a new space underneath Nos. 14 and 15 Courts. These courts were re-laid for use in 2015. Design work was progressing on the proposed changes to No.1 Court. These include the new fixed and retractable roof, an extra 900 seats and additional permanent hospitality space, also a public plaza in place of No. 19 Court. The proposals are subject to planning approval. The scheduled target completion date for the plan remains 2019.

2015

The Championships will start on Monday, 29th June, a week later than previously. This extends the gap between the French Open and The Championships from two to three weeks, which allows a longer grass court season for the build-up and preparation for the meeting.

The re-introduction of No. 14 and No. 15 Courts brings the total number of courts available during The Championships up to the normal number of 19. Basement accommodation is provided for Ball Boys and Girls, Photographers and an expanded 24- hour Media Restaurant. Consequently, as a result, the space freed up in the Millennium Building will be used to provide much needed stretching areas, medical facilities, massage space and ice baths, as well as a larger lounge for the players.

The Hawk-Eye electronic system has been extended to use on No. 12 and No. 18 Courts.

The 30 minute break between the Ladies' semi-final matches introduced in 2014 will be repeated.

The Aorangi Pavilion has been turned into a dedicated player facility. Improvements include locker rooms doubled in size, a new restaurant, a lift to make the building accessible on both levels, new creche facilities, separate toilets for guests and a new warm-up space at the rear.

In Aorangi Park a long-term temporary building has been constructed and will accommodate the Service Stewards, LSS Cleaners and G4S Security Staff during The Championships. Outside The Championships this area will be used for house staff working on the No.1 Court project.

No.3 Court unreserved seating area has been increased to 682 seats.

Meetings

Dates of Meetings and Finals

From 1877 to 1896 the starting date of The Championships was arbitrarily set by The All England Lawn Tennis Club. From 1897 the starting date has been sanctioned by The Lawn Tennis Association, until 1910 as the nearest Monday to the 22nd June and from 1911 to date as six weeks before the first Monday in August (known to 1964 as August Bank Holiday).

From 2015 the start of The Championships is a week later than previously. This extends the usual two week gap between the end of the French Open and The Championships to three weeks, allowing a longer grass court season for the build-up and preparation to The Championships.

From 1877 to 1914 the length of each meeting varied according to the numbers of entries and, for the period 1884–1891, whether the events were run concurrently. From 1919 to 1981 each meeting was scheduled to last two weeks, i.e. 12 days, Mondays to Saturdays. From 1982 the meeting has been scheduled to last 13 days, Monday to Saturday and Monday to Sunday.

The total number of days on which play has taken place from 1877 to 2014 is 2369. In addition there have been 30 days completely lost due to rain and 29 days not scheduled for play during the course of meetings. Play occurred on the second Sunday in 1972 and 1973 and on the first Sunday in 1991, 1997 and 2004 to counter a backlog of matches due to rain.

Year	Scheduled dates of Meetings	Dates of Gentlemen's Final or Challenge Round	Dates of Gentlemen's Doubles Final or Challenge Round	Dates of Ladies' Final or Challenge Round	Dates of Ladies' Doubles Final	Dates of Mixed Doubles Final	Concluding Date of Meeting
1877 (1)	Mon 9 July–	Thu 19 July	—	—	—	—	Thu 19 July
1878 (1)	Mon 8 July–	Thu 18 July	—	—	—	—	Thu 18 July
1879 (1)	Mon 7 July–	Tue 15 July	—	—	—	—	Wed 16 July
1880 (1)	Mon 5 July–	Thu 15 July	—	—	—	—	Thu 15 July
1881 (1)	Sat 2 July–	Wed 13 July	—	—	—	—	Wed 13 July
1882 (1)	Sat 8 July–	Mon 17 July	—	—	—	—	Mon 17 July
1883 (1)	Sat 7 July–	Mon 16 July	—	—	—	—	Mon 16 July
1884 (2)	Sat 5 July–	Tue 15 July	Sat 19 July	Sat 19 July	—	—	Sat 19 July
1885 (2)	Sat 4 July–	Mon 13 July	Fri 17 July	Fri 17 July	—	—	Fri 17 July
1886 (2)	Sat 3 July–	Tue 13 July	Sat 17 July	Sat 17 July	—	—	Sat 17 July
1887 (3)	Sat 2 July–	Thu 7 July	Wed 6 July	Wed 6 July	—	—	Thu 7 July

(see notes on page 136)

Year	Scheduled dates of Meetings	Dates of Gentlemen's Final or Challenge Round	Dates of Gentlemen's Doubles Final or Challenge Round	Dates of Ladies' Final or Challenge Round	Dates of Ladies' Doubles Final	Dates of Mixed Doubles Final	Concluding Date of Meeting
1888 (2)	Sat 7 July–	Mon 16 July	Mon 23 July	Sat 21 July	—	—	Mon 23 July
1889 (4)	Mon 1 July–	Mon 8 July	Sat 13 July	Sat 6 July	—	—	Sat 13 July
1890 (5)	Mon 30 June–	Mon 7 July	Wed 23 July	Fri 4 July	—	—	(5)
1891 (2)	Mon 29 June–	Sat 4 July	Thu 9 July	Thu 9 July	—	—	Thu 9 July
1892 (6)	Mon 27 June–	Mon 4 July	Thu 7 July	Thu 7 July	—	—	Thu 7 July
1893	Mon 10 July–	Mon 17 July	Thu 20 July	Tue 18 July	—	—	Thu 20 July
1894	Mon 9 July–	Tue 17 July	Wed 18 July	Tue 17 July	—	—	Wed 18 July
1895	Mon 8 July–	Sat 13 July	Mon 15 July	Mon 15 July	—	—	Mon 15 July
1896	Mon 13 July–	Mon 20 July	Tue 21 July	Tue 21 July	—	—	Tue 21 July
1897	Mon 21 June–	Wed 30 June	Thu 1 July	Mon 28 June	—	—	Thu 1 July
1898	Mon 20 June–	Mon 27 June	Tue 28 June	Mon 27 June	—	—	Tue 28 June
1899	Mon 19 June–	Mon 26 June	Tue 27 June	Tue 27 June	—	—	Tue 27 June
1900	Mon 25 June–	Tue 3 July	Wed 4 July	Tue 3 July	—	—	Wed 4 July
1901	Mon 24 June–	Mon 1 July	Tue 2 July/Wed 3 July	Wed 3 July	—	—	Wed 3 July
1902	Mon 23 June–	Mon 30 June	Tue 1 July	Tue 1 July/Wed 2 July	—	—	Wed 2 July
1903	Mon 22 June–	Tue 30 June	Wed 1 July	Tue 30 June	—	—	Wed 1 July
1904	Mon 20 June–	Mon 27 June	Wed 29 June	Tue 28 June	—	—	Wed 29 June
1905	Mon 26 June–	Sat 8 July	Fri 7 July	Sat 8 July	—	—	Sat 8 July
1906	Mon 25 June–	Wed 4 July	Thu 5 July	Thu 5 July	—	—	Thu 5 July
1907	Mon 24 June–	Thu 4 July	Fri 5 July	Fri 5 July	—	—	Fri 5 July
1908	Mon 22 June–	Tue 30 June	Wed 1 July	Tue 30 June	—	—	Wed 1 July
1909	Mon 21 June–	Sat 3 July	Mon 5 July	Fri 2 July	—	—	Mon 5 July
1910	Mon 20 June–	Thu 30 June	Sat 2 July	Wed 29 June	—	—	Sat 2 July
1911	Mon 26 June–	Sat 8 July	Fri 7 July	Fri 5 July	—	—	Sat 8 July
1912	Mon 24 June–	Mon 8 July	Mon 8 July	Fri 5 July	—	—	Mon 8 July
1913	Mon 23 June–	Fri 4 July	Fri 4 July	Thu 3 July	Fri 4 July	Thu 3 July	Fri 4 July
1914	Mon 22 June–	Sat 4 July	Mon 6 July	Sat 4 July	Mon 6 July	Mon 6 July	Mon 6 July
1919	Mon 23 June–Sat 5 July	Mon 7 July	Tue 8 July	Sat 5 July	Tue 8 July	Tue 8 July	Tue 8 July (7)
1920	Mon 21 June–Sat 3 July	Sat 3 July	Sat 3 July	Thu 1 July	Sat 3 July	Sat 3 July	Sat 3 July
1921	Mon 20 June–Sat 2 July	Sat 2 July	Sat 2 July	Fri 1 July	Sat 2 July	Sat 2 July	Sat 2 July
1922	Mon 26 June–Sat 8 July	Mon 10 July	Wed 12 July	Sat 8 July	Wed 12 July	Wed 12 July	Wed 12 July (7)
1923	Mon 25 June–Sat 7 July	Sat 7 July	Sat 7 July	Fri 6 July	Sat 7 July	Sat 7 July	Sat 7 July
1924	Mon 23 June–Sat 5 July	Sat 5 July	Sat 5 July	Fri 4 July	Sat 5 July	Sat 5 July	Sat 5 July

(see notes on page 136)

Year	Scheduled dates of Meetings	Dates of Gentlemen's Final or Challenge Round	Dates of Gentlemen's Doubles Final or Challenge Round	Dates of Ladies' Final or Challenge Round	Dates of Ladies' Doubles Final	Dates of Mixed Doubles Final	Concluding Date of Meeting
1925	Mon 22 June–Sat 4 July	Sat 4 July	Mon 6 July	Fri 3 July	Sat 4 July	Mon 6 July	Mon 6 July (7)
1926	Mon 21 June–Sat 3 July	Fri 2 July	Sat 3 July	Sat 3 July	Fri 2 July	Sat 3 July	Sat 3 July
1927	Mon 20 June–Sat 2 July	Sat 2 July	Mon 4 July	Sat 2 July	Tue 5 July	Tue 5 July	Tue 5 July (7)
1928	Mon 25 June–Sat 7 July	Fri 6 July	Sat 7 July	Sat 7 July	Sat 7 July	Sat 7 July	Sat 7 July
1929	Mon 24 June–Sat 6 July	Sat 6 July	Sat 6 July	Fri 5 July	Sat 6 July	Sat 6 July	Sat 6 July
1930	Mon 23 June–Sat 5 July	Sat 5 July	Mon 7 July	Fri 4 July			Mon 7 July (7)
1931	Mon 22 June–Sat 4 July	(8)	Sat 2 July	Fri 3 July	Sat 5 July	Sat 5 July	Sat 4 July
1932	Mon 20 June–Sat 2 July	Sat 2 July	Sat 2 July	Fri 1 July	Sat 2 July	Sat 2 July	Sat 2 July
1933	Mon 26 June–Sat 8 July	Fri 7 July	Sat 8 July	Sat 8 July	Sat 8 July	Sat 8 July	Sat 8 July
1934	Mon 25 June–Sat 7 July	Fri 6 July	Sat 7 July	Sat 7 July	Sat 7 July	Sat 7 July	Sat 7 July
1935	Mon 24 June–Sat 6 July	Fri 5 July	Sat 6 July	Sat 6 July	Sat 6 July	Sat 6 July	Sat 6 July
1936	Mon 22 June–Sat 4 July	Fri 3 July	Sat 4 July	Sat 4 July	Sat 4 July	Sat 4 July	Sat 4 July
1937	Mon 21 June–Sat 3 July	Fri 2 July	Sat 3 July	Sat 3 July	Sat 3 July	Sat 3 July	Sat 3 July
1938	Mon 20 June–Sat 2 July	Fri 1 July	Sat 2 July	Sat 2 July	Sat 2 July	Sat 2 July	Sat 2 July
1939	Mon 26 June–Sat 8 July	Fri 7 July	Sat 8 July	Sat 8 July	Sat 8 July	Sat 8 July	Sat 8 July
1946	Mon 24 June–Sat 6 July	Fri 5 July	Sat 6 July	Sat 6 July	Sat 6 July	Sat 6 July	Sat 6 July
1947	Mon 23 June–Sat 5 July	Fri 4 July	Sat 5 July	Sat 5 July	Sat 5 July	Sat 5 July	Sat 5 July
1948	Mon 21 June–Sat 3 July	Fri 2 July	Sat 3 July	Sat 3 July	Sat 3 July	Sat 3 July	Sat 3 July
1949	Mon 20 June–Sat 2 July	Fri 1 July	Sat 2 July	Sat 2 July	Sat 2 July	Sat 2 July	Sat 2 July
1950	Mon 26 June–Sat 8 July	Fri 7 July	Sat 8 July	Sat 8 July	Sat 8 July	Sat 8 July	Sat 8 July
1951	Mon 25 June–Sat 7 July	Fri 6 July	Sat 7 July	Sat 7 July	Sat 7 July	Sat 7 July	Sat 7 July
1952	Mon 23 June–Sat 5 July	Fri 4 July	Sat 5 July	Sat 5 July	Sat 5 July	Sat 5 July	Sat 5 July
1953	Mon 22 June–Sat 4 July	Fri 3 July	Sat 4 July	Sat 4 July	Sat 4 July	Sat 4 July	Sat 4 July
1954	Mon 21 June–Sat 3 July	Fri 2 July	Sat 3 July	Sat 3 July	Sat 3 July	Sat 3 July	Sat 3 July
1955	Mon 20 June–Sat 2 July	Fri 1 July	Sat 2 July	Sat 2 July	Sat 2 July	Sat 2 July	Sat 2 July
1956	Mon 25 June–Sat 7 July	Fri 6 July	Sat 7 July	Sat 7 July	Sat 7 July	Sat 7 July	Sat 7 July
1957	Mon 24 June–Sat 6 July	Fri 5 July	Sat 6 July	Sat 6 July	Sat 6 July	Sat 6 July	Sat 6 July
1958	Mon 23 June–Sat 5 July	Fri 4 July	Sat 5 July	Sat 5 July	Sat 5 July	Sat 5 July	Sat 5 July
1959	Mon 22 June–Sat 4 July	Fri 3 July	Sat 4 July	Sat 4 July	Sat 4 July	Sat 4 July	Sat 4 July
1960	Mon 20 June–Sat 2 July	Fri 1 July	Sat 2 July	Sat 2 July	Sat 2 July	Sat 2 July	Sat 2 July
1961	Mon 26 June–Sat 8 July	Fri 7 July	Sat 8 July	Sat 8 July	Sat 8 July	Sat 8 July	Sat 8 July
1962	Mon 25 June–Sat 7 July	Fri 6 July	Sat 7 July	Sat 7 July	Sat 7 July	Sat 7 July	Sat 7 July
1963	Mon 24 June–Sat 6 July	Fri 5 July	Mon 8 July	Mon 8 July	Mon 8 July	Mon 8 July	Mon 8 July (7)
1964	Mon 22 June–Sat 4 July	Fri 3 July	Sat 4 July	Sat 4 July	Sat 4 July	Sat 4 July	Sat 4 July
1965	Mon 21 June–Sat 3 July	Fri 2 July	Sat 3 July	Sat 3 July	Sat 3 July	Sat 3 July	Sat 3 July

(see notes on page 136)

Year	Scheduled dates of Meetings	Dates of Gentlemen's Final or Challenge Round	Dates of Gentlemen's Doubles Final or Challenge Round	Dates of Ladies' Final or Challenge Round	Dates of Ladies' Doubles Final	Dates of Mixed Doubles Final	Concluding Date of Meeting
1966	Mon 20 June–Sat 2 July	Fri 1 July	Sat 2 July	Sat 2 July	Sat 2 July	Sat 2 July	Sat 2 July
1967	Mon 26 June–Sat 8 July	Fri 7 July	Sat 8 July	Sat 8 July	Sat 8 July	Sat 8 July	Sat 8 July
1968	Mon 24 June–Sat 6 July	Fri 5 July	Sat 6 July	Sat 6 July	Sat 6 July	Sat 6 July	Sat 6 July
1969	Mon 23 June–Sat 5 July	Sat 5 July	Fri 4 July	Fri 4 July	Sat 5 July	Sat 5 July	Sat 5 July
1970	Mon 22 June–Sat 4 July	Sat 4 July	Fri 3 July	Fri 3 July	Sat 4 July	Sat 4 July	Sat 4 July
1971	Mon 21 June–Sat 3 July	Sat 3 July	Fri 2 July	Fri 2 July	Sat 3 July	Sat 3 July	Sat 3 July
1972	Mon 26 June–Sat 8 July	Sun 9 July	Fri 7 July	Fri 7 July	Sun 9 July	Sun 9 July	Sun 9 July (7) (9)
1973	Mon 25 June–Sat 7 July	Sat 7 July	Sat 7 July	Sat 7 July	Sat 7 July	Sun 8 July	Sun 8 July (7) (9)
1974	Mon 24 June–Sat 6 July	Sat 6 July	Sat 6 July	Fri 5 July	Sat 6 July	Sat 6 July	Sat 6 July
1975	Mon 23 June–Sat 5 July	Sat 5 July	Fri 4 July	Fri 4 July	Sat 5 July	Sat 5 July	Sat 5 July
1976	Mon 21 June–Sat 3 July	Sat 3 July	Fri 2 July	Fri 2 July	Sat 3 July	Sat 3 July	Sat 3 July
1977	Mon 20 June–Sat 2 July	Sat 2 July	Fri 1 July	Fri 1 July	Sat 2 July	Sat 2 July	Sat 2 July
1978	Mon 26 June–Sat 8 July	Sat 8 July	Sat 8 July	Fri 7 July	Fri 7 July	Sat 8 July	Sat 8 July
1979	Mon 25 June–Sat 7 July	Sat 7 July	Fri 6 July	Fri 6 July	Sat 7 July	Sat 7 July	Sat 7 July
1980	Mon 23 June–Sat 5 July	Sat 5 July	Sat 5 July	Fri 4 July	Sat 5 July	Sat 5 July	Sat 5 July
1981	Mon 22 June–Sat 4 July	Sat 4 July	Fri 3 July	Fri 3 July	Sat 4 July	Sat 4 July	Sat 4 July
1982 (10)	Mon 21 June–Sun 3 July	Sun 4 July	Sun 4 July	Sat 3 July	Sat 3 July	Sun 4 July	Mon 5 July (7)
1983	Mon 20 June–Sun 3 July	Sun 3 July	Sat 2 July	Sat 2 July	Sat 2 July	Sun 3 July	Sun 3 July
1984	Mon 25 June–Sun 8 July	Sun 8 July	Sat 7 July	Sat 7 July	Sat 7 July	Sun 8 July	Sun 8 July
1985	Mon 24 June–Sun 7 July	Sun 7 July	Sat 6 July	Sat 6 July	Sat 6 July	Sun 7 July	Sun 7 July
1986	Mon 23 June–Sun 6 July	Sun 6 July	Sat 5 July/Sun 6 July	Sat 5 July	Sun 6 July	Sun 6 July	Sun 6 July
1987	Mon 22 June–Sun 5 July	Sun 5 July	Sat 4 July	Sat 4 July	Sat 4 July	Sun 5 July	Sun 5 July
1988	Mon 20 June–Sun 3 July	Sun 3 July/Mon 4 July	Sat 2 July/Sun 3 July/Mon 4 July	Sat 2 July	Sun 3 July/Mon 4 July	Mon 4 July	Mon 4 July (7)
1989	Mon 26 June–Sun 9 July	Sun 9 July	Sun 9 July	Sun 9 July	Sun 9 July	Mon 10 July	Mon 10 July (7)
1990	Mon 25 June–Sun 8 July	Sun 8 July	Sat 7 July	Sat 7 July	Sat 7 July	Sun 8 July	Sun 8 July
1991 (11)	Mon 24 June–Sun 7 July	Sun 7 July	Sat 6 July	Sat 6 July	Sat 6 July	Sun 7 July	Sun 7 July
1992	Mon 22 June–Sun 5 July	Sun 5 July	Sun 5 July/Mon 6 July	Sat 4 July	Sun 5 July	Mon 6 July	Mon 6 July (7)
1993	Mon 21 June–Sun 4 July	Sun 4 July	Sat 3 July	Sat 3 July	Sat 3 July	Sun 4 July	Sun 4 July
1994	Mon 20 June–Sun 3 July	Sun 3 July	Sat 2 July	Sat 2 July	Sat 2 July	Sun 3 July	Sun 3 July
1995	Mon 26 June–Sun 9 July	Sun 9 July	Sat 8 July	Sat 8 July	Sat 8 July/Sun 9 July	Sun 9 July	Sun 9 July
1996	Mon 24 June–Sun 7 July	Sun 7 July	Sat 6 July	Sat 6 July	Sun 7 July/Mon 8 July	Mon 8 July	Mon 8 July (7)
1997 (11)	Mon 23 June–Sun 6 July	Sun 6 July	Sun 6 July	Sat 5 July	Sun 6 July	Sun 6 July	Sun 6 July
1998	Mon 22 June–Sun 5 July	Sun 5 July	Sat 4 July	Sat 4 July	Sun 5 July	Sun 5 July	Sun 5 July
1999	Mon 21 June–Sun 4 July	Sun 4 July	Sat 8 July	Sun 4 July	Sun 4 July	Sun 4 July	Sun 4 July
2000	Mon 26 June–Sun 9 July	Sun 9 July	Sat 8 July	Sat 8 July	Mon 10 July	Sun 9 July	Mon 10 July (7)
2001	Mon 25 June–Sun 8 July	Mon 9 July	Sat 7 July/Sun 8 July	Sun 8 July	Sun 8 July	Mon 9 July	Mon 9 July (7)

(see notes on page 136)

Year	Scheduled dates of Meetings	Dates of Gentlemen's Final or Challenge Round	Dates of Gentlemen's Doubles Final or Challenge Round	Dates of Ladies' Final or Challenge Round	Dates of Ladies' Doubles Final	Dates of Mixed Doubles Final	Concluding Date of Meeting
2002	Mon 24 June–Sun 7 July	Sun 7 July	Sun 7 July	Sat 6 July	Sun 7 July	Sun 7 July	Sun 7 July
2003	Mon 23 June–Sun 6 July	Sun 6 July	Sat 5 July	Sat 5 July	Sun 6 July	Sun 6 July	Sun 6 July
2004 (11)	Mon 21 June–Sun 4 July	Sun 4 July	Sun 4 July	Sat 3 July	Sun 4 July	Sun 4 July	Sun 4 July
2005	Mon 20 June–Sun 3 July	Sun 3 July	Sat 2 July	Sat 2 July	Sun 3 July	Sun 3 July	Sun 3 July
2006	Mon 26 June–Sun 9 July	Sun 9 July	Sat 8 July	Sat 8 July	Sun 9 July	Sat 8 July	Sun 9 July
2007	Mon 25 June–Sun 8 July	Sun 8 july	Sun 8 July	Sat 7 July	Sun 8 July	Sun 8 July	Sun 8 July
2008	Mon 23 June–Sun 6 July	Sun 6 July	Sat 5 July	Sat 5 July	Sat 5 July	Sun 6 July	Sun 6 July
2009	Mon 22 June–Sun 5 July	Sun 5 July	Sat 4 July	Sat 4 July	Sat 4 July	Sun 5 July	Sun 5 July
2010	Mon 21 June–Sun 4 July	Sun 4 July	Sat 3 July	Sat 3 July	Sat 3 July	Sun 4 July	Sun 4 July
2011	Mon 20 June–Sun 3 July	Sun 3 July	Sat 2 July	Sat 2 July	Sat 2 July	Sun 3 July	Sun 3 July
2012	Mon 25 June–Sun 8 July	Sun 8 July	Sat 7 July	Sat 7 July	Sat 7 July	Sun 8 July	Sun 8 July
2013	Mon 24 June–Sun 7 July	Sun 7 July	Sat 6 July	Sat 6 July	Sat 6 July	Sun 7 July	Sun 7 July
2014	Mon 23 June–Sun 6 July	Sun 6 July	Sat 5 July	Sat 5 July	Sat 5 July	Sun 6 July	Sun 6 July
2015	Mon 29 June–Sun 12 July						

Notes to pages 131–135:
1. Gentlemen's Singles only.
2. Gentlemen's Singles followed by Ladies' Singles and Gentlemen's Doubles.
3. Gentlemen's Singles, Ladies' Singles and Gentlemen's Doubles played concurrently.
4. Gentlemen's Singles and Ladies' Singles followed by Gentlemen's Doubles.
5. Gentlemen's Singles and Ladies' Singles concluded on Monday 7 July. Gentlemen's Doubles played from Monday 21 July to Wednesday 23 July.
6. From this date all events played concurrently.
7. Meeting extended beyond scheduled programme.
8. Gentlemen's Singles final scheduled for Saturday 4 July not played.
9. Play took place on the second Sunday to enable programme to be completed.
10. Play scheduled on the second Sunday for the first time.
11. Play took place on the first Sunday to counter the backlog of matches.

Meetings extended to complete the programme

From 1919 there have been 18 occasions when the meeting has been extended to complete the programme, 16 due to rain and two due to players' commitments.

Year	Dates	Reason
1919	Mon, Tue 7–8 July	Programme delayed due to rain during second week.
1922	Mon–Wed 10–12 July	Programme delayed due to rain on all days of meeting.
1925	Mon 6 July	To play Gentlemen's Doubles final and Mixed Doubles final which were postponed from previous Saturday, to allow French competitors, J. Borotra and R. Lacoste, to rest following their singles final.
1927	Mon, Tue, 4–5 July	Programme delayed due to rain during second week.
1930	Mon 7 July	To play Gentlemen's Doubles final, which was postponed from previous Saturday to allow the American competitor, W.L. Allison, to rest following his singles final.
1963	Mon 8 July	To play Ladies' Singles and Doubles, Gentlemen's Doubles and Mixed Doubles finals and complete other events. Sat 6 July rained off.
1972	Sun 9 July	To play Gentlemen's Singles and Ladies' Doubles finals and complete Mixed Doubles and other events. Sat 8 July rained off.
1973	Sun 8 July	To complete Mixed Doubles and two other events. Fri 6 July rained off.
1982	Mon 5 July	To play Boys' Doubles final. Programme delayed due to rain on most days of meeting.
1988	Mon 4 July	To complete Gentlemen's Singles and Doubles, Ladies' Doubles and Mixed Doubles finals and other events. Play restricted due to rain on Sun 3 July.
1989	Mon 10 July	To play Mixed Doubles final and complete Boys' and Girls' Doubles events. Play restricted by rain on Fri 7 July, Sat 8 July and Sun 9 July.
1991	Sun 30 June	Programme delayed due to rain during first week.
1992	Mon 6 July	To play Mixed Doubles final and complete Gentlemen's Doubles final and Boys' and Girls' Doubles events. Programme delayed due to rain during second week.
1996	Mon 8 July	To complete Ladies' Doubles final and Mixed Doubles event from quarter-final stage and to play Girls' Doubles final. Programme delayed due to rain on most days during second week.
1997	Sun 29 June	Programme delayed due to rain during first week.
2000	Mon 10 July	To complete Ladies' Doubles final and Girls' Doubles Final. Programme delayed due to rain.
2001	Mon 9 July	To play Gentlemen's Singles final, Mixed Doubles final and Girls' Doubles final. Programme delayed due to rain on second Friday and Saturday.
2004	Sun 27 June	Programme delayed due to rain during first week.

Days which have been completely rained off

1877 Mon 16 July	1893 Wed 19 July	1914 Fri 3 July	1987 Mon 22 June
1883 Thu 12 July	1894 Mon 16 July	1952 Thu 3 July	1991 Mon 24 June
1884 Thu 10 July	1900 Mon 2 July	1954 Fri 25 June	1992 Fri 3 July
1886 Mon 12 July	1903 Mon 22 June	1963 Sat 6 July	1997 Thu 26 June
1888 Sat 7 July	1905 Fri 30 June	1969 Mon 23 June	Fri 27 June
Mon 9 July	1906 Fri 29 June	1972 Sat 8 July	1999 Tue 29 June
Wed 18 July	1909 Thu 24 June	1973 Fri 6 July	2004 Wed 23 June
1892 Tue 5 July	Fri 25 June	1978 Thu 29 June	Sat 26 June

First weeks badly interrupted by rain

From 1971, when all courts had a cover available, the first week's programme has been badly interrupted by rain on five occasions. In an uninterrupted week, approximately 365 matches would be completed.

Matches Completed First Week

Year	Mon	Tue	Wed	Thu	Fri	Sat	TOTALS
1982 (3)	(1) 30 GS	(1) 4 GS 8 LS	(1) 8 GS 15 LS	28 GS 29 LS 1 GD	(1) 7 LS	(1) 10 GS 11 LS 1 GD	80 GS 152 70 LS 2 GD
1985	(1) 1 GS	(1) 4 GS 3 LS	(1) 24 GS 9 LS	33 GS 34 LS	(1) 22 GS 2 LS 2 LD	15 GS 49 LS 11 GD 11 LD	99 GS 97 LS 220 11 GD 13 LD
1991 (4)	(2) NIL	(1) 6 GS 22 LS	(1) 2 GS 16 LS	(1) 5 GS 1 LS	45 GS 26 LS	31 GS 31 LS 18 GD 7 LD	89 GS 96 LS 18 GD 210 7 LD
1997 (4)	(1) 9 GS 7 LS	49 GS 27 LS	(1) 2 LS	(2) NIL	(2) NIL	28 GS 41 LS	86 GS 163 77 LS
2004 (4)	(1) 18 GS 22 LS	(1) 21 GS 23 LS	(2) NIL	(1) 38 GS 34 LS 5 GD 5 LD	23 GS 23 LS 25 GD 25 LD	(2) NIL	100 GS 262 102 LS 30 GD 30 LD

GS – Gentlemen's Singles. GD – Gentlemen's Doubles. LS – Ladies' Singles. LD – Ladies' Doubles. (1) – Rain. (2) – Day completely rained off. (3) – Play took place on third Monday. (4) Play took place on first Sunday.

Reduction of Sets due to rain

Traditionally matches in the Gentlemen's Singles and Doubles have been decided over the best of five sets and in the Ladies' Singles and Doubles and Mixed Doubles, over the best of three sets, except in the following Gentlemen's Doubles, when matches were reduced to the best of three sets, to counter a backlog of matches due to rain:

1982   All matches, including the final, except two first round matches and two semi-finals.
1987   Matches in the first and second rounds.
1991 ⎫
1997 ⎬ Matches in the first, second and third rounds.
1998 ⎭
2004   Matches up to the semi-final
2011   Matches in the first round

Weather

1922
The first meeting at the Church Road ground was plagued by rain each day. With only the Centre Court protected by a tarpaulin the outside courts became a quagmire, especially during the second week when on three consecutive days only 11 matches were played. The tournament was eventually completed on the third Wednesday.

1923
After considerable rain on the first Monday the weather was fine, with some days very hot.

1924
The weather throughout the tournament was gloriously fine apart from a total of two hour's rain.

1925
A sometimes cold first week, which contained a very wet Wednesday, gave way to fine weather.

1926
Exceptionally fine weather prevailed throughout the Jubilee meeting with the exception of a thunderstorm during the first Thursday.

1927
A very wet Championship in which, after the first Monday, there was not a day without heavy rain at some time and in consequence play was extended from 12 to 14 days.

1928
Excellent weather except for rain on the first Tuesday.

1929
Fine weather during the fortnight except one afternoon's play curtailed for a couple of hours due to rain.

1930
Excellent weather.

1931
Very good weather throughout the meeting in a summer which proved to be one of the wettest on record. *No rain during meeting.*

1932
Perfect weather apart from intermittent rain on the second Thursday.

1933
Ideal but rather hot weather.

1934
Perfectly fine weather throughout the tournament.

1935
Glorious weather except for the first Tuesday, when a terrific storm burst over the ground just as play was about to start, transforming the courts into lakes and preventing any play until late afternoon.

1936
After three days of very warm weather rain fell on several days of the meeting, including heavy downpours on the first Friday.

1937
Good weather, with one day's play prematurely halted due to rain.

1938
Following a fine first week the weather broke up, with gusty winds and frequent interruptions by rain on most days.

1939
Much of the fortnight was dogged by wind and rain, particularly on the first Wednesday and second Thursday.

1946
Ideal weather, especially during the second week, apart from the second Friday which was cold and windy.

1947
Mixed weather prevailed during the tournament, with torrential rain on the first Friday, which caused severe flooding of the uncovered courts, and on the Saturday.
1948
After rain had delayed the start of The Championships and a miserable second day, the weather became generally warm and sunny.
1949
Brilliant sunshine during the whole meeting.
1950
Heavy rain until late afternoon on the second Monday spoilt the fortnight's excellent weather.
1951
Good weather except for much rain on the second afternoon.
1952
A sequence of eight days of extreme heat was broken by a slight fall of rain on the Wednesday, followed by a complete washout on the Thursday.
1953
A very hot first week was followed by much cooler weather, including some rain on the second Wednesday.
1954
The first rain of the fortnight completely washed out play on the first Friday. Mixed weather followed.
1955
The only rain of The Championships occurred on the second Wednesday, when a tremendous downpour interrupted play and caused flooding in the tunnels adjacent to the Centre Court. The meeting finished in a blaze of sunshine.
1956
Changeable weather with some rain during the second week, particularly on the Wednesday.
1957
After an opening day of rain and cold weather brilliant sunshine and high temperatures persisted throughout.
1958
One of the wettest first weeks ever, with constant interruptions due to rain, particularly on the first Tuesday and Friday. An improvement in the weather allowed the tournament to finish on time.
1959
Beautiful weather, apart from steady rain on the first Wednesday.
1960
After three days of glorious sunshine many days were interrupted by rain.
1961
A very wet first day gave way to extremely hot weather during the middle of the meeting.
1962
Much dull weather and occasional rain in the second week.
1963
A cold miserable meeting. Rain washed out play on the second Saturday and the tournament was concluded on the following Monday.
1964
A fortnight of warm and sunny weather, with the exception of rain on the first Tuesday and showers on the second Friday.
1965
A wet first week followed by splendid weather.
1966
An unsettled first week with rain on most days preceded a mainly dry period.

1967
After a damp first day excellent weather prevailed throughout the meeting.

1968
The first week was one of the wettest on record, so that play into the third week seemed inevitable. But a dramatic change in the weather, combined with early starts on three days, enabled the tournament to finish on time.

1969
Following the first day, which was completely rained off, the weather was near perfect.

1970
A sunny first week gave way to cold, windswept and rainy weather.

1971
A generally fine fortnight, but at times chilly, with blustery winds.

1972
The first rain of the meeting washed out play on the second Saturday and four finals were played on the Sunday for the first time.

1973
Rain at late stage of second week washed out the Friday and play was extended to the Sunday.

1974
Three days of fine weather, followed by three very wet days, forced early starts on all but one of the following six days.

1975
Apart from a damp opening day and a rather chilly first Saturday, the weather was perfect.

1976
The hottest meeting on record. There was no relief from the scorching heat from start to finish. *No rain during meeting.*

1977
The weather, though cold at first, brought no interruption of any kind. *No rain during meeting.*

1978
Rain interrupted play on seven days including first Thursday which was washed out. Play started early from first Saturday to second Thursday.

1979
Apart from a little rain on the first day there was no disruption.

1980
Much rain during the meeting. Play started early on last nine days.

1981
Generally dry but cold. On the first Wednesday the drizzle allowed only a few matches to be concluded.

1982
A very wet first week. Rain interrupted play on 10 days. Play started early on last eight days.

1983
Wonderful weather with only two hours' delay for rain on first Friday.

1984
Superb weather – just two days briefly marred by rain.

1985
A very wet first week with rain each day. Play started early from first Thursday to second Wednesday. On the second Friday afternoon a spectacular storm hit the Club with $1^{1}/_{2}$ inches of rain falling in 20 minutes.

1986
A very warm meeting. Rain only on the first and twelfth days.

1987
Much wet weather during the first week, including first Monday which was washed out. Play started early from first Wednesday to second Thursday.

1988

After a week of sunshine rain occurred each day of second week except one, and play was extended to the following Monday.

1989

Rain badly interrupted play on last three days. In spite of great efforts to conclude the meeting on time a few events were held over until the Monday

1990

Dry and pleasant weather apart from interruptions by rain on the second Wednesday and Thursday.

1991

Probably the wettest first week ever. After four days only 52 out of approximately 240 scheduled matches were completed in the 9 hours, 15 minutes total play possible. The Monday was entirely washed out. 28 matches were completed in the 4 hours, 25 minutes available on the Tuesday, 18 matches in 2 hours, 50 minutes on the Wednesday and 6 matches in 2 hours on the Thursday. Play took place on the first (middle) Sunday and with a succession of early starts and an improvement in the weather the meeting finished on schedule.

1992

A week of fine weather gave way to much rain during the latter part of the second week. The second Friday was washed out and programme extended to Monday.

1993

Apart from the opening two days, which were sometimes overcast, the weather was warm and sunny throughout. *No rain during meeting.*

1994

Other than a dull opening day, rain during the first Tuesday and a thunderstorm late evening on the first Friday, the meeting enjoyed very warm and sunny weather.

1995

A fortnight of warm and sunny weather with the first Friday being particularly hot. *No rain during meeting.*

1996

Mixed weather during the first week was followed by rain on most days causing the programme to be extended to the third Monday.

1997

A very wet first week, containing two days completely lost to rain. Play on the first (middle) Sunday, a succession of early starts from the first Thursday and a gradual improvement in the weather allowed the tournament to end just on time.

1998

Rain interrupted play on several days during the first week and on the second Monday, but thereafter the weather was mild and dry.

1999

A week of fine and sunny weather was followed by much rain during the early part of the second week, including the Tuesday completely rained off.

2000

A fortnight of generally dull weather with little sunshine. Rain the latter half of the second week forced play to the third Monday.

2001

A generally warm and sunny meeting but marred by rain on the second Friday and Saturday.

2002

A dry sunny week gave way to cool and showery weather during the second week interrupting the programme.

2003

Mostly warm and sunny first week, followed by considerable rain in the middle of the second week.

2004
A meeting affected by bad weather, with two days completely lost due to rain. A backlog of matches necessitate play on the first (middle) Sunday.

2005
A warm and sunny first week contrasted to frequent rain interruptions on the following Thursday and Friday.

2006
Apart from rain restricting play on the opening day to 45 minutes and causing delays on the second Wednesday, Thursday and Friday, the fortnight was very warm and sunny throughout.

2007
Frequent rain interruptions during the first week and the early part of the second week gave way to dry and sunny weather.

2008
Apart from rain interrupting play on the first Friday and three days towards the end, the fortnight was generally warm and sunny.

2009
Ideal warm and sunny conditions every day, with only a short period of light rain on the second Monday, late aftenoon.

2010
A glorious fortnight, with every day warm and sunny. *No rain during meeting.*

2011
The first week was overcast with some rainy periods, followed by dry but generally cloudy weather.

2012
A week of sunny periods, interrupted by showers, was followed by some sunny periods but generally cloudy skies and intermittent drizzle.

2013
The weather for the first week was generally overcast with some drizzle on the Thursday and Friday. The following week continued in the same vein, except for the last three days which were warm and sunny.

2014
Generally warm and sunny weather during the fortnight, marred by rain at the end of the first week, the start of the second and the last Saturday.

Days when play was not scheduled

1877	Fri 13 July (1)	1880	Sat 10 July (1)	1885	Sat 11 July (1)
	Sat 14 July (1)	1881	Thu 7 July (1)	1886	Fri 9 July (1)
	Tue 17 July		Fri 8 July (1)		Sat 10 July (1)
	Wed 18 July		Sat 9 July (1)	1889	Fri 5 July
1878	Fri 12 July (1)	1882	Fri 14 July (1)		Fri 12 July
	Sat 13 July (1)		Sat 15 July (1)	1891	Fri 3 July
	Wed 17 July	1883	Sat 14 July (1)	1892	Fri 1 July
1879	Fri 11 July (1)	1884	Fri 11 July (1)	1894	Mon 16 July (2)
	Sat 12 July (1)		Sat 12 July (1)	1897	Tue 22 June (3)
1880	Fri 9 July (1)	1885	Fri 10 July (1)		

Notes: 1 Eton and Harrow cricket match.   2 Oxford v Yale athletic meeting at Queen's Club.
3 Diamond Jubilee of Queen Victoria.

Scheduled Start of Play

1877–1914	Varied from year to year, and on occasions, day to day.
1919–1982	All Courts–2 p.m.
1983–1988	Centre Court and No. 1 – 2 p.m. No. 2–17 Courts – 12.30 p.m. for the first week and on at least the second Monday, thereafter at 2 p.m.
1989	Centre Court and No. 1 Court – 2 p.m., except the second Monday, Centre Court and No. 1 Court, and the second Friday, Centre Court only – 1 p.m. No. 2–17 Courts – 12.30 p.m., on at least the first eight days and thereafter at 2 p.m.
1990–1991	Centre Court and No. 1 Court – 2 p.m., except the second Monday, Wednesday and Friday – 1 p.m. No. 2–17 Courts – 12.30 p.m., on the first eight days.
1992	Centre Court and No. 1 Court – 2 p.m., except the second Monday, Wednesday and Friday – 1 p.m. No. 2–17 Courts – Noon, on the first eight days.
1993–1995	Centre Court and No. 1 Court – 2 p.m., except the first Saturday – Noon and the second Monday, Wednesday and Friday – 1 p.m. No. 2–17 Courts – Noon, on at least the first eight days.
1996	Centre Court and No. 1 Court – 2 p.m., except the first Saturday, second Monday, Wednesday and Friday – 1 p.m. No. 2–17 Courts – Noon, on at least the first eight days.
1997	Centre Court and No. 1 Court – 2 p.m. except the first Saturday, second Monday, Wednesday and Friday – 1 p.m. No. 2–13, 16–19 Courts – Noon, on at least the first eight days.
1998	Centre Court and No. 1 Court – 2 p.m. except the first Saturday, second Monday, Wednesday and Friday – 1 p.m. No. 2–15, 18, 19 Courts – Noon, on at least the first eight days.
1999–2000	Centre Court and No. 1 Court – 2 p.m., except the first Saturday, second Monday, Wednesday and Friday – 1 p.m. No. 2–19 Courts – Noon, on at least the first eight days.
2001	Centre Court and No. 1 Court – 1 p.m., on first 11 days and 2 p.m. on Finals days. No. 2–19 Courts – Noon, on at least the first eight days.
2002	Centre Court and No. 1 Court – 1p.m., on first 11 days and 2pm on Finals days. No. 2–10, 13–19 Courts – Noon, on at least the first eight days.
2003–2007	Centre Court and No. 1 Court – 1 p.m., on first 11 days and 2 p.m. on Finals days. No. 2–11, 13–19 Courts – Noon, on at least the first eight days.

2008	Centre Court and No. 1 Court – 1 p.m., on first 11 days and 2 p.m. on Finals days. No. 3–11, 14–19 Courts – Noon, on at least the first eight days.
2009	Centre Court and No. 1 Court – 1 p.m., on first 11 days and 2 p.m. on Finals days. No. 2–12, 14–19 Courts – Noon, on at least the first eight days.
2010	Centre Court and No. 1 Court – 1 p.m., on first 11 days and 2 p.m. on Finals days. No. 2, 5–12, 14–19 Courts – Noon, on at least the first eight days.
2011	Centre Court – 1 p.m., on first 11 days and 2 p.m. on Finals days. No. 1 Court – 1 p.m. on all days. No. 2–12, 14–19 Courts – Noon on at least the first eight days.
2012–2013	Centre Court – 1 p.m., on first 11 days and 2 p.m. on Finals days. No. 1 Court – 1 p.m. on all days. No. 2–12, 14–19 Courts – 11.30 a.m. on at least the first eight days.
2014	Centre Court – 1 p.m., on first 11 days and 2 p.m. on Finals days. No. 1 Court – 1 p.m. on all days. No. 2–12, 16–19 Courts – 11.30 a.m. on at least the first eight days.
2015	Centre Court – 1 p.m., on first 11 days and 2 p.m. on Finals days. No. 1 Court – 1 p.m. on all days. No. 2–12, 14–19 Courts – 11.30 a.m. on at least the first eight days.

Scheduled days for finals

1877–1932	Varied each year.	
	Friday	**Saturday**
1933–1939	Gentlemen's Singles	Ladies' Singles
1946–1968		Gentlemen's Doubles
		Ladies' Doubles
		Mixed Doubles
1969–1981	Ladies' Singles	Gentlemen's Singles
	Gentlemen's Doubles	Ladies' Doubles
		Mixed Doubles
	Saturday	**Sunday**
1982–1995	Ladies' Singles	Gentlemen's Singles
	Gentlemen's Doubles	Mixed Doubles
	Ladies' Doubles	
1996–2007	Ladies' Singles	Gentlemen's Singles
	Gentlemen's Doubles	Ladies' Doubles
	Mixed Doubles*	
2008–2015	Ladies' Singles	Gentlemen's Singles
	Gentlemen's Doubles	Mixed Doubles
	Ladies' Doubles	

* Saturday or Sunday on Centre Court or No. 1 Court.

Finals not played on the Centre Court

From 1922 all Championship Finals have been played on the Centre Court, except the following:

Year	Date	Event	Court
1961	Sat 8 July	Mixed Doubles	No. 1 Court
1972	Sun 9 July	Ladies' Doubles	No. 1 Court
1973	Sat 7 July	Gentlemen's Doubles	No. 1 Court
1980	Sat 5 July	Gentlemen's Doubles	No. 1 Court
1982	Sun 4 July	Mixed Doubles	No. 3 Court
1986	Sun 6 July	Gentlemen's Doubles	No. 1 Court
		(Started on Centre Court – Sat 5 July)	
	Sun 6 July	Ladies' Doubles	No. 1 Court

1988	Sun 3 July	Gentlemen's Doubles	No. 1 Court
	Mon 4 July		
		(Started on Centre Court – Sat 2 July)	
	Sun 3 July	Ladies' Doubles	No. 2 Court
	Mon 4 July		
	Mon 4 July	Mixed Doubles	No. 1 Court
1989	Sun 9 July	Gentlemen's Doubles	No. 1 Court
	Sun 9 July	Ladies' Doubles	No. 1 Court
	Mon 10 July	Mixed Doubles	No. 1 Court
1992	Sun 5 July	Gentlemen's Doubles	No. 1 Court
	Mon 6 July		
	Sun 5 July	Ladies' Doubles	No. 1 Court
	Mon 6 July	Mixed Doubles	No. 1 Court
1997	Sun 6 July	Ladies' Doubles	No. 1 Court
	Sun 6 July	Mixed Doubles	No. 1 Court
1998	Sun 5 July	Mixed Doubles	No. 1 Court
1999	Sun 4 July	Gentlemen's Doubles	No. 1 Court
		Ladies' Doubles	No. 1 Court
2000	Sun 9 July	Mixed Doubles	No. 1 Court
2001	Sat 7 July	Gentlemen's Doubles	No. 1 Court
	Sun 8 July		
	Mon 9 July	Mixed Doubles	No. 1 Court
2002	Sun 7 July	Gentlemen's Doubles	No. 1 Court
2004	Sun 4 July	Gentlemen's Doubles	No. 1 Court
		Ladies' Doubles	No. 2 Court
2005	Sat 2 July	Gentlemen's Doubles	No. 1 Court
2007	Sun 8 July	Gentlemen's Doubles	No. 1 Court
		Ladies' Doubles	No. 1 Court
2008	Sun 6 July	Mixed Doubles	No. 1 Court

Singles Semi–finals not played on Centre Court

From 1922 all Championship Singles Semi-finals have been played on the Centre Court except the following which have been played on No. 1 Court.

Gentlemen's Singles

Year	Date	Match
1958	Wed 2 July	N.A Fraser (AUS) v K. Nielsen (DEN)
1974	Fri 5 July	J.S. Connors (USA) v R.L. Stockton (USA)
1982	Sat 3 July	J.P. McEnroe (USA) v T.S. Mayotte(USA)
1992	Sat 4 July	G.S. Ivanisevic (CRO) v P. Sampras (USA)
1996	Sat 6 July	R.P.S. Krajicek (NED) v J.R. Stoltenberg (AUS)
1999	Sat 3 July	A.K. Agassi (USA) v P.M. Rafter (AUS)
2002	Fri 5/Sat 6 July	D.P. Nalbandian (ARG) v X. Malisse (BEL)
2004	Fri 2/Sat 3 July	M. Ancic (CRO) v A.S. Roddick (USA)
2007	Sat 7 July	R. Nadal (ESP) v N. Djokovic (SRB)

Ladies' Singles

Year	Date	Match
1946	Thu 4 July	Miss P.M. Betz (USA) v Miss D.M. Bundy (USA)
1952	Fri 4 July	Miss A.L. Brough (USA) v Mrs. R.B. Todd (USA)
1974	Thu 4 July	Miss K.A. Melville (AUS) v Miss C.M. Evert (USA)
1982	Fri 2 July	Miss B. Bunge (GER) v Miss M. Navratilova (USA)
1999	Sat 3 July	Miss S.M. Graf (GER) v Miss M. Lucic (CRO)
2005	Thu 30 June/	Miss L.A. Davenport (Mrs J. Leach) USA v Miss A. Mauresmo
	Fri 1 July	(FRA)

Attendance & Ground Capacity

WORPLE ROAD

Detailed figures of daily totals and championship aggregates are not available. During the peak years, 1913–1921, the scene at the ground was described as "very congested" when 6,000 people were present. When the figure reached 7,500 the ground was said to be "packed to suffocation".

Estimates for the total attendance at the meetings varied between 60,000 and 70,000.

CHURCH ROAD

Record Daily Totals

	First Week		Second Week		Third Week	
Monday	42,811	2009	44,494	2011	15,257	1988
Tuesday	45,955	2009	39,262	2008		
Wednesday	46,826	2009	39,849	2009		
Thursday	45,370	2009	33,560	2002		
Friday	43,145	2011	32,453	1999		
Saturday	43,432	2009	30,173	2007		
Sunday	31,204	1997	32,036	2010		

Record Aggregates

Figures from the early days are not on record but in 1932 over 219,000 spectators were present at the meeting, The number increased to over 250,000 in 1949 to over 300,000 in 1967 and to over 400,000 in 1986. The 500,000 barrier was reached in 2009, when 511,043 attended over the normal scheduled 13 days.

Attendance

YEAR	Monday	Tuesday	Wednesday	Thursday	Friday	Saturday	Monday	Tuesday	Wednesday	Thursday	Friday	Saturday	Sunday	Total
1949	19,540	18,312	22,681	24,714	22,574	26,785	24,525	20,447	25,227	18,134	17,090	15,381	—	253,410
1951	22,177	17,076	25,083	25,190	26,588	26,543	26,582	22,714	22,460	19,660	17,790	15,577	—	267,440
1955	21,203	23,045	32,120	28,360	26,316	28,163	27,144	23,577	23,934	19,794	17,330	16,376	—	287,362
1956	22,547	23,004	30,715	27,581	24,000	26,750	25,125	21,754	21,774	19,830	17,637	16,144	—	276,861
1957	22,159	20,878	30,503	27,406	26,435	24,239	23,662	22,443	22,343	19,077	17,115	15,865	—	272,125
1958	20,875	21,418	25,922	26,455	19,738	27,015	26,405	21,499	23,682	22,792	18,836	16,382	—	271,019
1959	22,568	22,864	27,555	27,312	27,516	27,592	26,340	24,133	23,258	21,471	17,728	16,528	—	284,865
1960	21,318	21,955	28,643	22,023	22,546	26,629	25,827	25,543	26,110	21,044	18,212	17,031	—	276,881
1961	19,866	23,633	29,359	29,435	26,646	24,549	26,112	22,486	24,680	20,671	18,050	17,050	—	282,537
1962	21,063	22,370	30,069	29,523	29,152	29,834	27,557	25,030	23,959	20,846	18,790	17,927	—	296,120
1963	19,682	19,051	26,268	28,403	23,005	24,548	25,990	24,100	24,356	21,134	18,272	17,058	—	271,867
1964	20,168	19,767	29,234	28,237	28,173	27,204	27,504	23,912	24,228	20,711	17,741	17,257	—	284,136
1965	19,333	19,507	24,262	25,679	24,583	27,627	27,916	25,665	24,504	20,971	17,975	17,218	—	275,240
1966	19,496	20,467	26,961	26,383	26,514	26,692	22,981	25,541	25,770	21,400	18,045	16,955	—	277,205
1967	20,527	23,391	31,716	30,307	30,135	27,520	29,614	26,203	25,953	20,908	18,777	16,845	—	301,896
1968	20,082	19,539	27,286	23,750	23,198	26,331	29,331	27,412	136,134 →→→				—	276,270
1969	16,862(2)	22,175	122,720 →→→				25,641	25,177	24,663	19,534	55,648 →→		—	298,811
1970	21,639	23,001	26,585	30,795	29,090	26,807	26,845	26,055	21,280	20,385	17,344	16,696	—	283,589
1971	21,422	24,241	31,437	32,438	30,225	27,918	27,364	24,891	23,696	20,385	17,427	16,807	—	298,896
1972(3)	22,717	24,758	31,767	31,974	30,912	26,118	27,925	27,075	23,332	20,566	17,657	16,705(2)	—	298,761
1973(4)	22,603	25,754	116,609 →→→				34,161	30,024(1)	45,359 →→		16,936(2)	17,911	—	300,172
1974	24,816	26,906	19,213(1)	27,341(1)	30,360(1)	30,492	31,998	29,946	24,972	21,020(1)	19,162	17,694	—	306,161
1975	24,778(1)	31,415	37,081	36,305	37,290	29,058	27,265	26,748	25,249	20,807	17,671	16,993	—	338,591
1976	24,686	27,841	36,743	33,746	33,730	25,808	31,409	30,169	21,553	20,343	18,008	16,975	—	313,446
1977	23,786	26,738	37,389	36,815	37,002	29,285	30,857	26,944	25,589	23,095	17,711	17,428	—	336,416
1978	29,986(1)	33,693	38,290	29,817(2)	36,211	30,200	30,761	29,781	22,154	20,958	18,300	18,091	—	335,501
1979	29,480	31,698	38,291	37,107	35,820	29,449	30,119	34,681(1)	22,903	21,581	18,056	18,164	—	343,091
1980	26,691(1)	28,103(1)	35,622	34,640(1)	35,693(1)	29,561(1)	34,875	31,345	26,570	24,265	19,254	18,565	—	333,764
1981	32,075	32,516	36,676	37,161	35,559	33,295	25,431(1)		24,917	21,962	18,639	19,230	—	358,250
1982(5)	24,445(1)	20,524(1)	29,282(1)	30,159	27,599(1)	26,917(1)	33,490	25,264(1)	29,672	22,068(1)	21,746(1)	18,360(1)	14,597	316,064
1983	27,381	29,155	36,910	36,358	34,255(1)	31,206	33,490	29,485	25,071	21,978	20,561	19,435	15,157	360,442

(See notes on page 149)

Attendance

YEAR	Monday	Tuesday	Wednesday	Thursday	Friday	Saturday	Monday	Tuesday	Wednesday	Thursday	Friday	Saturday	Sunday	Total
1984	32,288	32,939	36,122	37,341	38,215	32,332	35,331	32,665	30,161	24,737	21,499	20,373	17,670	391,673
1985	29,389(1)	28,165(1)	32,379(1)	36,709	37,121(1)	35,234(1)	37,886	38,577	33,592	25,304	21,837(1)	21,671	20,119	397,983
1986	28,161(1)	31,924	37,618	39,813	38,971	33,300	37,438	32,965	31,498	24,986	22,575(1)	20,976	19,807	400,032
1987	25,915(2)	29,323(1)	36,020	29,228(1)	34,973	34,992	38,255	37,364	35,791	27,847	24,165	20,972	20,978	395,823
1988(6)	29,078	33,431	36,940	38,640	37,351	32,449	36,197(1)	27,741(1)	32,136	25,878(1)	22,879(1)	21,734(1)	21,559(1)	396,013
1989(7)	34,154	33,403	33,525(1)	35,929(1)	36,055	32,387	38,910	35,742	29,242	25,723	22,285(1)	21,110(1)	21,825(1)	400,288
1990	28,923	30,075	30,962	31,065	31,332	28,077	30,818	28,208	23,819(1)	21,952	21,302	20,638	20,808	347,979
1991(8)	26,089(2)	25,381(1)	29,972(1)	27,704(1)	31,858	30,543	31,583	29,528(1)	29,341	27,287	22,944	20,301	20,986	353,517
1992(9)	28,233	31,626	33,498	33,246	33,283	32,257	33,880	28,486(1)	25,977(1)	23,527	19,203(2)	20,948(1)	20,897(1)	365,061
1993	31,463	33,373	33,681	36,103	35,657	33,309	36,542	32,001	29,355	23,703	22,496	21,021	22,056	392,760
1994	30,675	28,711(1)	34,252	35,927	34,579	31,736	34,932	30,459	26,897	24,143	22,511	21,065	22,086	377,973
1995	33,016	34,687	37,183	35,625	32,236	32,396	33,327	29,939	27,432	22,917	22,138	21,060	22,926	384,882
1996(10)	32,545	34,447	33,229	32,597	31,653(1)	31,057	31,575(1)	29,163	24,029(1)	24,123(1)	22,081(1)	21,825	23,200	371,524
1997(11)	33,586(1)	37,871	29,333(1)	29,296(2)	27,014(2)	32,307	35,566	36,618(1)	35,101	31,724	26,516(1)	24,523	25,872	405,327
1998	33,838	33,688(1)	37,423	36,003(1)	34,945(1)	35,008(1)	35,647(1)	33,504	33,019	29,236	28,257	26,338	28,065	424,998
1999	36,471	39,254	39,341	40,312	37,214	37,960	36,884(1)	29,870(2)	36,719	30,223(1)	32,453	29,566	30,802	457,069
2000(12)	35,941	38,884	38,837	38,472	37,898	37,073	38,247	34,083	31,789	29,718	28,303	27,542	29,806(1)	446,593
2001(13)	39,330	41,320	41,146	41,440	40,834	40,043	41,236	38,375	36,969	30,120	28,813	27,770(1)	29,315	476,711
2002	38,561	40,995	42,457	41,410	41,595	39,722	38,764	34,448(1)	36,367(1)	33,560	28,016(1)	27,857	29,762	469,514
2003	38,500	41,929	42,787	41,967	39,833	38,913	39,389	34,696	35,911(1)	30,237(1)	29,872	28,246	30,522	470,802
2004(14)	35,335(1)	34,312(1)	29,156(2)	36,130	39,659	32,746(2)	39,229	34,041	33,703(1)	29,404(1)	28,254(1)	27,956	29,128	429,053
2005	38,228	39,685	42,100	42,228	37,242(1)	38,837	41,386	35,030(1)	35,673	28,744(1)	29,700(1)	28,333	30,002	467,188
2006	32,272(1)	38,611	39,991	40,235	39,821	38,269	40,002	32,022	31,890	29,302	28,444	27,695	26,101	447,126
2007	32,916	39,282	37,018	39,770	38,366	34,169	36,309	39,262	32,636	30,936	31,773	30,173	29,440	444,810
2008	39,035	40,653	40,835	40,881	39,982	40,876	40,952	39,262	35,202(1)	29,615(1)	31,270	28,650	28,599	475,812
2009	42,811	45,955	46,826	45,370	41,870	43,432	44,478	38,682	39,849	30,842	31,078	28,983	30,867	511,043
2010	39,696	41,437	41,547	42,608	41,920	41,696	43,066	36,416	38,927	30,776	31,210	28,611	32,036	489,946
2011	38,617	44,441	40,510	43,357	43,145	42,386	44,494	44,989	39,466	31,638	31,458	29,366	30,894	494,761
2012	41,821	43,917	43,044	44,341	43,073	40,967	39,526	33,109	36,908	31,051	30,324	28,680	28,044	484,805
2013	41,715	43,931	41,143	41,661	39,459	42,697	42,615	36,128	36,795	31,153	31,084	29,496	29,021	486,898
2014	41,325	42,673	43,680	43,401	38,750	39,735	41,201	38,698	40,477	31,935	31,618	28,562	29,029	491,084

(See notes on page 149)

(1)Bad weather. (more than two hours play lost)
(2)Entire day rained off.
(3)Play carried over to second Sunday. No attendance figures available.
(4)Play carried over to second Sunday, when attendance was approximately 3,000.
(5)Play carried over to third Monday, when attendance was approximately 53.
(6)Play carried over to third Monday, when attendance was 15,257. Total for 14 days – 411,270
(7)Play carried over to third Monday, when attendance was 3,418. Total for 14 days – 403,706.
(8)Play took place on first Sunday, when attendance was 24,894. Total for 14 days – 378,411.
(9)Play carried over to third Monday, when attendance was 7,798. Total for 14 days – 372,859.
(10)Play carried over to third Monday, when attendance was 13,518. Total for 14 days – 385,042.
(11)Play took place on first Sunday, when attendance was 31,204. Total for 14 days – 436,531.
(12)Play carried over to third Monday, when attendance was 9,159. Total for 14 days – 455,752.
(13)Play carried over to third Monday, when attendance was 13,370. Total for 14 days – 490,081.
(14)Play took place on first Sunday, when attendance was 22,155. Total for 14 days 451,208

Up to 1981 the meeting was scheduled for 12 days. From 1982 the meeting was scheduled for 13 days.

Ground Capacity and the number of days the gates to the grounds were closed

YEAR	Ground Capacity	Number days gates closed	YEAR	Ground Capacity	Number days gates closed
1975		2	1997		6
1976		0	1998	32,000	3
1977		0	1999		7
1978		3	2000	33,500	7
1979		3	2001	34,500	9
1980		2	2002		7
1981	31,000 – 32,000	3	2003	35,000	8
1982		0	2004		1
1983		0	2005	35,500	6
1984		3	2006		8
1985		4	2007	36,000	4
1986		3	2008	36,500	10
1987		6	2009	40,000	8
1988		5	2010	37,500	8
1989	28,000	4	2011		6
1990		4	2012	38,500	8
1991		6	2013		12
1992		6	2014		12
1993		6	2015	39,000	
1994		5			
1995	28,000 – 29,000	7			
1996		7			

Court Capacity

WORPLE ROAD

Figures showing the capacity of the Centre Court in the early days are not available. The first three permanent covered stands (A, B and C) were erected in 1884 and 1885 and these were considerably enlarged in 1906. In 1909 a new Stand B was constructed, giving an extra 600 seats, followed in 1913 by the provision of a new Stand C. In 1914 a major undertaking replaced Stand A and this increased the seating capacity of the court from 2,300 to 3,500, a figure unchanged when the ground was abandoned in 1921. The uncovered Stand D held approximately 600 spectators. Details of standing accommodation around the Centre Court over the years are not available. In 1919 an open stand was erected along one side of No. 4 Court.

CHURCH ROAD

When the Centre Court was built in 1922 there were 9,989 seats and standing accommodation for 3,600. The number of seats remained fairly constant until 1979 when the roof was raised by one metre to provide an additional 1,088 seats, bringing the capacity up to 11,739. In 1985 the extension of the East Side Building added a further 800 seats to make the total 12,433. The replacement of the standing area by seating in 1990 gave the all-seater stadium a capacity of 13,107. The new roof provided in 1992 allowed the capacity to rise to 13,118. In 1999 the West Stand extension added over 728 seats. While in 2008 the further extension of the East-Side Building and six rows at the top of the stadium raised the capacity to 15,000. The original standing figure of 3,600 had gradually diminished by 1989 to 2,000.

When the old No. 1 Court was opened in 1924 there were 2,500 seats and room for approximately 750 standing. Mainly due to major improvement schemes, which added 700 seats in 1929, 450 in 1939, 900 in 1955 and 1,250 in 1981, the seating capacity of the court increased to 6,508 when finally used in 1996. The present No. 1 Court has a seating capacity of 11,393.

The original No. 3 Court was opened in 1922 and No. 2 Court a year later, when permanent stands held 1,000 and 1,900 seats respectively. In 1971 a permanent stand was constructed between the original No. 6 and No. 7 Courts and in 1997 a permanent stand was constructed beside No. 18 Court. In 2009 the new No. 2 Court provided a capacity of over 4,000 and No. 2–11 Courts were renumbered No. 3–12. In 2011 a new No. 3 Court was opened, accommodating 1980 spectators. There was also a new No. 4 Court, situated east of No. 3 Court, which seated 170 people on the west side.

Seating capacity of courts

Year	Centre	No. 1	No. 2	No. 3	No. 4	No. 5	No. 6	No. 7	No. 8	No. 11	No. 12	No. 13	No. 14	No. 15	No. 16	No. 17	No. 18	No. 19
(1)1971–1975	10,651	5,100	1,650	800			250	250										
1976–1978	10,651	5,100	1,650	800			250	250										
1979	11,739	5,100	1,650	800			250	250										
1980	11,739	5,100	2,020	800			250	250										
1981	11,739	6,350	2,020	800			250	250				1,450	1,450					
1982	11,539	6,286	2,020	800			250	250				1,450	1,450					
1983	11,539	6,286	2,020	800			250	250				1,450	740					
1984	11,539	6,286	2,114	800			250	250				1,450	740					
1985	11,539	6,340	2,226	800			250	250				1,450	740					
1986–1987	12,433	6,340	2,226	800			250	250				1,450	1,000					
1988	12,433	6,340	2,226	800			250	250				1,450	1,000					
1989	12,472	6,507	2,226	800			250	250		207		1,452	1,254					
1990	12,502	6,507	2,226	800			250	250		162		1,452	1,254					
1991	13,107	6,508	2,226	800			250	250		162		1,593	1,826					
1992	13,109	6,508	2,220	800			250	250		162		1,604	1,982					
1993–1995	13,109	6,508	2,220	800			250	250		162		1,604	2,048			180		
1996	13,118	6,508	2,220	800			250	250		162		1,604	1,814			180		
1997	13,120	11,432	2,220	800			250	250		162		1,604	1,816			180	788	305
1998	13,120	11,429	2,220	800			250	250		162		1,604	1,816	318		180	788	305
1999	13,813	11,429	2,220	800			250	250		162		1,541	1,705	318	318	180	788	305
2000	13,812	11,429	2,220	800			250	250		162		1,541	318	318	318	180	788	306
2001	13,806	11,428	2,220	800			250	250		162		1,541	318	318	318	152	788	306
2002	13,813	11,429	2,220	800			250	250		162		1,541	318	318	318	318	788	306
2003	13,810	11,429	2,220	800		108	250	250		394		1,541	318	318	318	318	782	306
2004	13,808	11,429	2,220	800		108	250	250		448		1,541	318	318	318	318	782	306
2005	13,802	11,429	2,192	800		120	250	250		448		1,541	318	318	312	318	782	302
2006	13,798	11,429	2,192	800		120	250	250		448		1,541	318	318	312	318	782	302
2007	14,288	11,429	2,192	800		120	250	250		1,541		1,541	318	318	312	309	782	302
2008	15,214	11,393	2,192	800		120	250	250	250	120		1,541	312	318	312	309	782	302
2009	14,954	11,393	4,084	2,192	800	1,000	250	250	165	120	613		312	318	312	309	782	302
2010	14,971	11,393	4,060	1980	170		120	120	170	120	1,020		312	318	312	309	782	302
2011	14,979	11,393	4,063	1980	170			120	170	120	1,020		312	318	312	309	782	302
2012	14,979	11,393	4,063	1980	170			120	170	120	1,020		312	318	312	309	782	302
2013	14,979	11,393	4,063	1980	170			120	170	108	1,089		312	318	312	309	782	302
2014	14,979	11,393	4,063	1980	170			120	170	108	1,065		312	318	320	318	782	305
2015	14,979	11,393	4,063	1980				120		108	1,065		324	330	320	318	782	305

FOR LOCATION OF COURTS EACH YEAR SEE PAGES 153–155

Notes

1. Initial seating capacity: Centre Court (1922) – 9,989; Old No. 1 Court (1924) – 2,500, No. 2 Court (1923) – 1,900; No. 3 Court (1923) – 1,000. (2)
2. A temporary stand was erected on the west side of No. 3 Court in 1922 – seating capacity not known.
3. The capacity of the Centre Court was increased to 14,288 when extra seats were made available at the top of the North Stand

Standing capacity of courts

Year	Centre	No. 1	No. 2	No. 3
1980–1981	2,750	1,500	1,000	
1982	2,400	1,500	1,000	
1983–1984	2,100	1,500	1,000	
1985–1989	2,000	1,500	1,000	
1990–1991		1,000	1,000	
1992		820	1,000	
1993–1996		820	770	
1997–2008			770	
2009				770
2010				

Initial capacity: Centre Court (1922) – 3,600; Old No. 1 Court (1924) – 750; Old No. 2 Court (1970) – 1,000.

Layout of Championship Courts

WORPLE ROAD

1877–1880 [12]

1881–1921 [10]

CHURCH ROAD

1922 [13]

1923 [14]

1924–1928 [15]

1929–1936 [17]

1937–1965 [16]

1966–1970 [16]

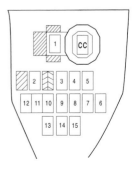

1971–1972 [15]   1973–1979 [15]   1980–1996 [18]

1997   [18]   1998   [18]   1999–2001 [20]

2002   [18]   2003-2007   [19]   2008   [18]

Note: In 1979 the future No. 14 to No. 17 Courts, north of the Centre Court, were laid down but not used. In 1997 replacement No. 14 and No. 15 Courts were laid down but not used. In 1998, replacement No. 16 and No. 17 Courts were laid down but not used. In 2002 replacement No. 11 Court was laid down but not used. In 2008 the new No. 2 Court was built but not used. In 2010 a new No. 3 Court (seating 2,000) was built but not used and a future No. 4 Court foundation laid down, on which was erected a temporary stand overlooking No. 5 Court. In 2014 new No. 14 and No. 15 Courts were laid down but not used.

Nominated Show Courts

1990–1996: Centre, No. 1, 2, 3, 13, 14
1997–2007: Centre, No. 1, 2, 3, 13, 18
2008:   Centre, No. 1, 2, 3, 11, 14, 18
2009:   Centre, No. 1, 2, 3, 4, 18
2010:   Centre, No. 1, 2, 5, 12, 18
2011–2015: Centre, No. 1, 2, 3, 12, 18

Dimensions of Championship Lawns

The dimensions of the Championship lawns are approximately:

Centre Court and No. 1 Court	45yds(41m) x 24yds(22m)
No. 2 and No. 3 Court	40yds(36.5m) x 22yds(20m)
Nos. 4–11 Courts	40yds(36.5m) x 20yds(18m)
Nos. 12, 14–19 Courts	40yds(36.5m) x 22yds(20m)
Earlier Courts	
No. 1 (1924–1996)	43yds(39m) x 21yds(19m)
No. 2 (1923–2008)	40yds(36.5m) x 22yds(20m)
No. 3 (1922–2009)	40yds(36.5m) x 20yds(20m)
Nos. 11 and 12 (1980–2001)	40yds(36.5m) x 20yds(18m)
No. 13 (1980–2007)	40yds(36.5m) x 20yds(18m)
Nos. 14 and 15 (1980–1996)	40yds(36.5m) x 20yds(18m)
Nos. 16 and 17 (1980–1997)	40yds(36.5m) x 20 yds(18m)

The width of the white lines are 2 inches (50mm), except the base lines which are 4 inches (100mm).

Grass Practice Courts

On site

Years	Aorangi Park	Car Park 4	Southlands College Site	Total
1980–1986	12			12
1987–2002	14			14
2003	14	2		16
2004–2015	14	2	6	22

Note: From 2004 all On Site Courts were recognised as being in Aorangi Park and numberd 1-22.

Off site

Years	Grounds	Courts
1965–2000	Queen's Club, Kensington, London W14	6
1979	St. George's Hill Club, Weybridge, Surrey	4
1979–1980	Roehampton Club, London SW15	3
1981–1992	Ealing Club, London W5	8
1993–2009	The Club's ground at Raynes Park, London SW20	6

Seat and Ground Admission Prices

WORPLE ROAD

Centre Court (1880–1921)

| Year | Reserved seat in covered stands | |
	Whole meeting (1)	Daily (2)
1880	7s.6d.	First week – 1s.0d., Second week – 2s.6d.
1881–1890	10s.0d.	—
1891	10s.6d.	—
1892–1894	5s.0d., 7s.6d., and 10s.0d.	From 1s.0d.
1895	7s.6d. and 10s.0d.	From 1s.0d.
1896–1897	7s.6d. and 10s.6d.	From 1s.0d.
1898–1903	7s.6d. and 10s.6d.	1s.0d., 2s.6d., and 5s.0d.
1904	7s.6d.	2s.6d.
1905–1907	17s.6d.	—
1908–1912	£1.1s.0d.	—
1913	£1.1s.0d.	2s.0d. and 3s.0d.
1914	£1.11s.6d.	—
1919–1921	£1.15s.0d.	3s.6d.

Notes: 1. From 1883 to 1904 the price did not include ground admission.
From 1905 to 1921 the price did include ground admission.
2. The price did not include ground admission.

Ground Admission

Year	Whole meeting	Daily
1877–1878	—	1s.0d.
1879–1880	5s.0d.	1s.0d.
1881–1882	7s.6d.	First five days – 1s.0d. After – 2s.6d.
1883	7s.6d.	1s.0d. Last five days –2s.6d.
1884	12s.6d.	1s.0d. Final – 2s.0d.
1885–1886	12s.6d.	First three days – 1s.0d. After – 2s.6d.
1887–1888	7s.6d.	1s.0d. Finals – 2s.6d.
1889–1890	10s.0d.	1s.0d. Finals – 2s.6d.
1891	10s.0d.	1s.0d. Semi-finals and Finals – 2s.6d.
1892–1895	7s.6d.	First three days – 1s.0d. After – 2s.6d.
1896–1904	7s.6d.	First day – 1s.0d. After – 2s.6d.
1905–1908	7s.6d.	2s.6d.
1909–1913	10s.0d.	2s.6d.
1914	15s.0d.	2s.6d.
1919–1921	17s.6d.	3s.6d.

CHURCH ROAD
Centre Court (1922–2015)
Season tickets – Covered Stands

Year	Period	Price	Equivalent Daily Rate
1922–1923	Twelve Days	£3.3s.0d.	5s.3d.
1924–1929	,, ,,	£4.4s.0d.	7s.0d.
1930–1939	Six Days	£3.3s.0d.	10s.6d.
1946–1950	,, ,,	£4.4s.0d.	14s.0d.
1951–1952	,, ,,	£5.0s.0d.	16s.8d.
1953–1957	,, ,,	£6.6s.0d.	£1.1s.0d.
1958–1962	Four Days	£5.0s.0d.	£1.5s.0d.
1963–1966	,, ,,	£5.10s.0d.	£1.7s.6d.
1967–1968	,, ,,	£6.10s.0d.	£1.12s.6d.
1969–1970	,, ,,	£7.0s.0d.	£1.15s.0d.
1971–1972	Two Days	£4.00	£2.00
1973	,, ,,	£5.00	£2.50
1974–1975	,, ,,	£6.60	£3.30
1976	,, ,,	£8.80	£4.40
1977–1978	,, ,,	£9.60	£4.80

From 1979 a price differential for all tickets was introduced.
£'s

Year	M	T	W	T	F	S	M	T	W	T	F	S	S
1979	4.60	4.60	4.60	4.60	4.60	4.60	6	6	6	6	6	6	—
1980	5	5	5	6	6	6	7	7	7	8	8	8	—
1981	6	6	6	7	7	7	9	9	9	11	11	11	—
1982	6	6	6	8	8	8	10	10	10	12	12	14	14
1983	6	6	8	8	8	8	11	11	11	14	14	16	16
1984	6	6	8	8	8	11	11	11	11	14	14	16	16
1985	7	7	9	9	9	12	12	12	12	15	15	17	17
1986	8	8	10	10	10	13	13	13	13	16	16	18	18
1987	8	8	10	10	10	13	13	14	14	18	18	20	20
1988	9	9	11	11	11	14	14	16	16	20	20	25	25
1989 {	S14	14	18	18	18	22	22	26	26	31	31	36	36
(1) {	R 9	9	11	11	11	14	14	16	16	20	20	25	25
1990 {	S15	15	19	19	19	24	24	28	28	33	33	39	39
(1) {	R10	10	12	12	12	15	15	17	17	21	21	27	27
1991 {	S16	16	20	20	20	25	27	29	29	35	38	40	40
(1)(2) {	R11	11	13	13	13	17	18	19	19	23	25	27	27
1992 {	S17	17	22	22	22	27	30	32	36	38	44	44	46
(1)(3) {	R12	12	16	16	16	20	22	24	27	28	33	33	34
1993(3)	18	18	23	23	23	28	32	34	38	40	46	46	48
1994(3)	19	19	24	24	24	29	33	35	39	41	47	47	49
1995(4)	20	20	25	25	30	30	35	35	41	41	47	47	50
1996(4)	21	21	26	26	31	31	36	36	42	42	47	47	52
1997(4)(5)	22	22	27	27	32	32	38	38	44	44	49	49	54
1998(4)	23	23	28	28	33	33	40	40	46	46	51	51	56
1999(6)	24	24	30	30	36	36	42	42	48	48	54	54	60
2000(6)	25	25	31	31	38	38	44	44	50	50	57	57	63
2001(6)(7)	26	26	33	33	40	40	46	46	53	53	60	60	66
2002(6)	27	27	35	35	42	42	48	48	56	56	63	63	69
2003	28	28	37	37	44	44	50	50	59	59	66	66	72
2004(8)	30	30	38	38	46	46	53	53	62	62	69	69	75
2005	32	32	41	41	48	48	56	56	65	65	73	73	79

2006	34	34	43	43	51	51	59	59	69	69	77	77	83
2007	36	36	45	45	54	54	62	62	72	72	80	80	87
2008	38	38	47	47	57	57	65	65	75	75	84	84	91
2009	40	40	50	50	62	62	72	72	82	82	92	92	100
2010	41	41	52	52	65	65	74	74	85	85	95	95	104
2011	43	43	54	54	68	68	78	78	90	90	100	100	110
2012	44	44	56	56	71	71	82	82	95	95	105	105	120
2013	45	45	58	58	74	74	86	86	101	101	112	112	130
2014	48	48	62	62	80	80	93	93	112	112	124	124	148
2015	50	50	65	65	84	84	98	98	119	119	133	133	160

Notes: 1. S – Standard, R – Reduced. (Seats in the back six rows.)
2. First Sunday – £10.00.
3. First Saturday – On day price reduced to £20.00.
4. First Saturday – On day price reduced to £25.00.
5. First Sunday – £15.00.
6. First Saturday – On day price reduced to £30.00.
7. Third Monday – On day price of £40.00.
8. First Sunday – On day price of £35.00.

Standing Room
(last four days)

1982–1983	£4.00 per day
1984–1986	£5.00 per day
1987	£6.00 per day
1988	£7.00 per day
1989	£8.00 per day – semi-finals, £10.00 per day – finals.

No. 1 Court (1924–1996)

Season tickets – Covered Stands

Year	Period	Price	Equivalent Daily Rate
1924–1929	Twelve Days	£2.15s.0d.	4s.7d.
1930–1939	″ ″	£3.12s.0d.	6s.0d.
1946–1950	″ ″	£5.5s.0d.	8s.9d.
1951–1952	″ ″	£6.0s.0d.	10s.0d.
1953–1962	″ ″	£7.10s.0d.	12s.6d.
1963–1966	″ ″	£9.0s.0d.	15s.0d.
1967–1968	″ ″	£10.10s.0d.	17s.6d.
1969–1970	″ ″	£12.0s.0d.	£1.0s.0d.
1971–1973	″ ″	£13.20	£1.10
1974–1975	″ ″	£22.40	£1.85
1976	″ ″	£33.00	£2.75
1977	″ ″	£36.00	£3.00
1978–1979	″ ″	£39.60	£3.30

Season tickets – West Open Stand

Year	Period	Price	Equivalent Daily Rate
1924–1932		Same price as Covered Stand	
1933–1939	Twelve Days	£2.15s.0d.	4s.7d.
1946–1950	″ ″	£3.15s.0d.	6s.3d.
1951–1952	″ ″	£4.10s.0d.	7s.6d.
1953	″ ″	£6.0s.0d.	10s.0d.
1954–1962	Six Days	£3.0s.0d.	10s.0d.
1963–1966	″ ″	£3.15s.0d.	12s.6d.
1967–1968	″ ″	£4.10s.0d.	15s.0d.

Year	Period	Price	Equivalent Daily Rate
1969–1970	,, ,,	£5.5s.0d.	17s.6d.
1971–1972	,, ,,	£6.00	£1.00
1973	Four Days	£4.00	£1.00
1974–1975	,, ,,	£6.60	£1.65
1976	,, ,,	£10.00	£2.50
1977	,, ,,	£10.80	£2.70
1978–1979	,, ,,	£12.00	£3.00

From 1980 the tickets for the Covered and West Open Stands were combined and a price differential introduced.

£'s		M	T	W	T	F	S	M	T	W	T	F	S	S
1980		4	4	4	5	5	5	6	6	6	3	3	3	—
1981		5	5	5	6	6	6	8	8	8	3	3	3	—
1982		5	5	5	7	7	7	9	9	9	4	4	4	4
1983		5	5	7	7	7	7	10	10	10	10	4	4	4
1984		5	5	7	7	7	10	10	10	10	7	4	4	4
1985		6	6	8	8	8	11	11	11	11	8	5	5	5
1986		7	7	9	9	9	12	12	12	12	9	5	5	5
1987		7	7	9	9	9	12	12	13	13	9	5	5	5
1988		8	8	10	10	10	13	13	15	15	10	6	6	6
1989	S12	12	12	14	14	14	18	18	22	22	16	9	9	9
(1)	R 8	8	8	10	10	10	13	13	15	15	6	6	6	6
1990	S13	13	13	15	15	15	19	19	24	24	17	10	10	10
(1)	R 9	9	9	11	11	11	14	14	16	16	11	7	7	7
1991	S14	14	14	16	16	16	20	22	26	26	18	11	11	11
(1)(2)	R 9	9	9	11	11	11	14	15	17	17	12	7	7	7
1992	S15	15	15	17	17	17	21	24	28	30	21	12	12	12
(1)(3)	R11	11	11	12	12	12	15	18	21	23	15	9	9	9
1993	S16	16	16	18	18	18	22	26	30	32	23	13	13	13
(1)(3)	R11	11	11	12	12	12	15	18	21	23	15	9	9	9
1994	S16	16	16	20	20	20	24	28	30	32	23	13	13	13
(1)(3)	R11	11	11	13	13	13	16	19	21	23	15	9	9	9
1995	S17	17	17	21	21	24	24	28	28	32	24	14	14	12
(1)(3)	R11	11	11	14	14	16	16	19	19	21	16	9	9	8
1996	S17	17	17	21	21	25	25	29	29	33	25	14	14	12
(1)(3)	R12	12	12	14	14	17	17	19	19	22	17	10	10	9

Notes: 1. S – Standard, R – Reduced (seats partially obscured).

2. First Sunday – 7,000 tickets (seats and standing at £10.00 each).

3. First Saturday – On day standard price reduced to £20.00.

Standing Room

£'s	M	T	W	T	F	S	M	T	W	T	F	S	S
1990	6	6	6	6	6	6	6	6	6	6	6	6	6
1991(1)	8	8	8	8	8	8	8	8	8	7	6	6	6
1992–1994	9	9	9	9	9	5	9	9	9	8	6	6	6
1995–1996	10	10	10	10	10	5	10	10	10	9	7	7	7

Note: 1. First Sunday – £10.00.

No. 1 Court (1997–2015)

£'s	M	T	W	T	F	S	M	T	W	T	F	S	S
1997(1)(2)	19	19	24	24	28	28	33	33	38	28	16	16	13
1998(1)	20	20	25	25	30	30	35	35	39	29	17	17	14
1999(3)	22	22	27	27	32	32	37	37	42	32	18	18	15
2000(3)	23	23	28	28	34	34	39	39	44	33	19	19	16

Year													
2001(3)	24	24	30	30	36	36	41	41	47	35	20	20	17
2002(3)	25	25	32	32	38	38	43	43	50	37	21	21	18
2003	26	26	34	34	40	40	45	45	53	38	22	22	19
2004(4)	28	28	36	36	42	42	48	48	56	39	25	23	21
2005	30	30	38	38	44	44	51	51	59	40	26	24	22
2006	32	32	40	40	47	47	54	54	62	42	28	26	23
2007	34	34	42	42	50	50	57	57	65	43	29	27	24
2008	36	36	44	44	53	53	60	60	68	45	30	28	25
2009	37	37	46	46	55	55	62	62	70	46	31	29	25
2010	38	38	47	47	56	56	63	63	72	47	31	29	25
2011	38	38	48	48	58	58	65	65	74	48	32	30	25
2012	39	39	49	49	60	60	67	67	71	50	33	31	26
2013	40	40	50	50	62	62	69	69	80	52	34	32	27
2014	41	41	52	52	66	66	72	72	85	54	35	33	28
2015	42	42	53	53	68	68	75	75	89	56	36	33	28

Notes 1. First Saturday – On day price reduced to £20.00.
2. First Sunday – £15.00.
3. First Saturday – On day price reduced to £25.00.
4. First Sunday – £30.00.

No. 2 Court (1923–2008)

Year	M	T	W	T	F	S	M	T	W	T	F	S	S
1923–1969 Free seating													
1970(1)	5s.0d.	5s.0d.	5s.0d.	5s.0d.	5s.0d.	5s.0d.							
1971	25p	25p	25p	25p	25p	25p							
1972	25p	25p	25p	25p	25p	25p							
1973	30p	30p	30p	30p	30p	30p							
1974	35p	35p	35p	35p	35p	35p							
1975	35p	35p	35p	35p	35p	35p							
1976	50p	50p	50p	50p	50p	50p							
1977	60p	60p	60p	60p	60p	60p							
1978	70p	70p	70p	70p	70p	70p							
1979 £'s	1	1	1	1	1	1							
1980	3.50	3.50	3.50	3.50	3.50	3.50							
1981	5	5	5	5	5	5							
1982	5	5	5	5	5	5							
1983	5	5	5	5	5	5							
1984	5	5	6	6	6	6	6	6					
1985	6	6	6	6	6	6	6	6	6				
1986	6	6	6	6	6	6	6	6	6				
1987	6	6	6	6	8	8	8	6	6				
1988	7	7	7	7	9	9	9	7	7				
1989	10	10	12	12	12	15	15	12	10				
1990	11	11	13	13	13	16	16	13	11				
1991	11	11	13	13	13	15	16	13	11				
1992(2)	12	12	14	14	14	17	18	14	12				
1993(2)	13	13	15	15	15	18	19	15	13				
1994(2)	13	13	15	15	15	18	19	15	13				
1995(2)	14	14	16	16	19	19	21	17	15				
1996(2)	14	14	17	17	20	20	22	17	16				
1997(2)	15	15	17	17	20	20	23	18	17				
1998(2)	16	16	19	19	21	21	24	19	18				
1999(3)	17	17	20	20	23	23	26	21	19				
2000(3)	18	18	21	21	24	24	27	22	20	15			
2001(3)	19	19	22	22	25	25	28	23	21	16			
2002(3)	20	20	23	23	26	26	29	24	22	17			
2003	22	22	25	25	28	28	31	25	23	18			

2004	23	23	27	27	30	30	34	26	24
2005	24	24	29	29	32	32	35	27	25
2006	25	25	30	30	35	35	38	29	26
2007	27	27	32	32	36	36	40	31	28
2008	29	29	34	34	38	38	42	33	30

Notes: 1. From 1970 to 1979 tickets were purchased from a kiosk inside the grounds (payment in addition to ground admission charge).
2. First Saturday – On day price reduced to £15.00.
3. First Saturday – On day price reduced to £20.00.

No. 2 Court (2009–2015)

£'s	M	T	W	T	F	S	M	T	W	T	F	S	S
2009	33	33	40	40	47	47	50	35	32				
2010	34	34	41	41	48	48	52	35	32				
2011	35	35	42	42	49	49	54	36	33				
2012	36	36	43	43	51	51	56	37	34				
2013	37	37	44	44	53	53	58	38	35				
2014	38	38	46	46	56	56	62	39	36				
2015	39	39	47	47	58	58	64	40	37				

No. 3 Court (1922–2008)

£'s	M	T	W	T	F	S	M	T	W	T	F	S	S
1922–1989 Free seating													
1990	9	9	11	11	11	14	6	6	6	6	6	6	6
1991–2008 Free seating													

No. 3 Court (2009)

£'s	M	T	W	T	F	S	M	T	W	T	F	S	S
2009	29	29	34	34	38	38	42						

Note: No. 3 Court was No. 2 Court, 1923–2008

No. 3 Court (2011–2015)

£'s	M	T	W	T	F	S	M	T	W	T	F	S	S
2011	35	35	42	42	49	49	54						
2012	36	36	43	43	51	51	56						
2013	37	37	44	44	53	53	58						
2014	38	38	46	46	56	56	62						
2015	39	39	47	47	58	58	64						

No. 13 Court (1980–2007)

£'s	M	T	W	T	F	S	M	T	W	T	F	S	S
1980–1989 Free seating													
1990	9	9	11	11	11	14	6	6	6	6	6	6	6
1991–2007 Free seating													

Note: No. 13 Court was No. 14 Court, 1976–1979

No. 14 Court (1980–1996, 1998–2013, 2015)

£'s	M	T	W	T	F	S	M	T	W	T	F	S	S
1980–1989 Free seating													
1990	11	11	13	13	13	16	16	13	11	6	6	6	6

1991 Free seating (except for a small number of advance sales at £10 per day)
1992 Free seating (except for a small number of advance sales at £11 per day)
1993–1996, 1998–2015 Free seating

Ground Admission

1922–1981	Access to all Courts.
1982–1989	Access to all Courts except Centre Court last four days.
1990	Access to No. 2, Nos. 4–12 and Nos. 15–17 Courts.
1991–1996	Access to Nos. 2–17 Courts.

1997	Access to Nos. 2–13, 16–19 Courts.
1998	Access to Nos. 2–13, 14, 15, 18, 19 Courts.
1999–2001	Access to Nos. 2–19 Courts.
2002	Access to Nos. 2–10, 13–19 Courts
2003–2007	Access to Nos. 2–11, 13–19 Courts
2008	Access to Nos. 2–11, 14–19 Courts
2009	Access to Nos. 3–12, 14–19 Courts
2010	Access to Nos. 5–12, 14–19 Courts
2011–2013	Access to Nos. 3–12, 14–19 Courts
2014	Access to Nos. 3–12, 16–19 Courts
2015	Access to Nos. 3–12, 14–19 Courts

| Year | Admission | | Courts with free seating |
	Day	Reduced	
1922	3s.0d		No. 3 Court
1923–1931	3s.0d.		
1932–1939	3s.0d.	After 5 p.m. 1s.6d.	
1946	5s.0d.	After 5 p.m. 2s.6d.	
1947–1952	5s.0d.	After 4 p.m. 2s.6d.	
1953	5s.0d.	After 4 p.m. 3s.0d.	
1954–1955	5s.0d.	After 4 p.m. 2s.6d.	No. 2, No. 3 Courts
1956	5s.0d.	After 5.30 p.m. 2s.6d.	
1957–1962	5s.0d.	After 5 p.m. 2s.6d.	
1963–1968	7s.6d.	After 5 p.m. 3s.6d.	
1969	9s.0d.	After 5 pm. 5s.0d.	
1970	9s.0d.	After 5 p.m. 5s.0d.	No. 3 Court
1971–1972	50p	After 5 p.m. 25p	No. 3, No. 10, No. 11 Courts
1973	55p	After 5 p.m. 30p	No. 3, No. 6, No. 7 Courts (1)
1974–1975	75p	After 5 p.m. 40p	
1976–1977	£1.00	After 5 p.m. 60p	
1978	£1.30	After 5 p.m. 70p	No. 3, No. 6, No. 7, No. 14 Courts (2)
1979	£1.50	After 5 p.m. £1.00	
1980–1981	£2.00	After 5 p.m. £1.00	
1982–1983	£3.00	After 5 p.m. £2.00	
1984–1986			
First week	£4.00	After 5 p.m. £2.00	No. 3, No. 6, No. 7, No. 13,
Second week	£3.00		No. 14 Courts
1987			
First week	£5.00	After 5 p.m. £3.00	
Second week	£4.00		
1988	£5.00	After 5 p.m. £3.00	No. 3, No. 6, No. 7, No. 13, No. 14, No. 17 Courts
1989	£6.00	After 5 p.m. £3.00	No. 3, No. 6, No. 7, No. 11, No. 13, No. 14, No. 17 Courts
1990(3)	£6.00	– –	No. 6, No. 7, No. 11, No. 17 Courts
1991(4)	£6.00	After 5 p.m. £4.00	No. 3, No. 6, No. 7, No. 11, No. 13 No. 14, No. 17 Courts
1992–1994(5)			
First week	£7.00	After 5 p.m. £5.00	
Second week	£6.00	After 5 p.m. £4.00	
1995(6)			
First week	£8.00	After 5 p.m. £6.00	No. 3, No. 6, No. 7, No. 11, No. 13
Second week	£7.00	After 5 p.m. £5.00	No. 14, No. 17 Courts
1996(6)(7)			
First week	£8.00	After 5 p.m. £6.00	
Second week	£7.00	After 5 p.m. £5.00	

Year	Admission		Courts with free seating
	Day	Reduced	
1997(6)(7)(8)			
First week	£8.00	After 5 p.m.　£6.00 ⎫	No. 3, No. 6, No. 7, No. 11, No. 13
Second week	£7.00	After 5 p.m.　£5.00 ⎬	No. 17, No. 18, No. 19 Courts
1998 (6)			
Mon–Mon	£10.00	After 5 p.m.　£7.00	
Tue–Thur	£8.00	After 5 p.m.　£6.00	No. 3, No. 6, No. 7, No. 11, No. 13,
Fri, Sat	£7.00	After 5 p.m.　£5.00	No. 14, No. 15, No. 18, No. 19 Courts
Sun	£3.00	After 5.p.m　£1.00	
1999(6)			
Mon–Mon	£10.00	After 5 p.m.　£7.00	No. 3, No. 6, No. 7, No. 11, No. 13,
Tue–Thur	£8.00	After 5 p.m.　£6.00	No. 14, No. 15, No. 16, No. 17, No. 18,
Fri, Sat	£7.00	After 5 p.m.　£5.00	No. 19 Courts
Sun	£3.00	After 5.p.m　£1.00	
2000(9)(10)			
Mon–Mon	£12.00	After 5 p.m.　£7.00	
Tue, Wed	£10.00	After 5 p.m.　£6.00	
Thu	£9.00	After 5 p.m.　£6.00	
Fri, Sat	£8.00	After 5 p.m.　£5.00	
Sun	£4.00	After 5 p.m.　£1.00	No. 3, No. 6, No. 7, No. 11, No. 13,
2001(9)(11)			No. 14, No. 15, No. 16, No. 17, No. 18,
Mon–Mon	£12.00	After 5 p.m.　£7.00	No. 19 Courts
Tue, Wed	£10.00	After 5 p.m.　£6.00	
Thu	£9.00	After 5 p.m.　£6.00	
Fri, Sat	£8.00	After 5 p.m.　£5.00	
Sun	£4.00	After 5 p.m.　£1.00	
2002(12)			
Mon–Mon	£13.00	After 5 p.m.　£8.00	
Tue, Wed	£11.00	After 5 p.m.　£7.00	No. 3, No. 6, No. 7, No. 13, No. 14,
Thu	£10.00	After 5 p.m.　£7.00	No. 15, No. 16, No. 17, No. 18,
Fri, Sat	£9.00	After 5 p.m.　£6.00	No. 19 Courts
Sun	£5.00	After 5 p.m.　£2.00	
2003			
Mon–Mon	£14.00	After 5 p.m.　£8.00	
Tue, Wed	£12.00	After 5 p.m.　£7.00	
Thu	£11.00	After 5 p.m.　£7.00	
Fri, Sat	£10.00	After 5 p.m.　£6.00	
Sun	£5.00	After 5 p.m.　£2.00	No. 3, No. 6, No. 7, No. 11, No. 13
2004(13)			No. 14, No. 15, No. 16, No. 17,
Mon–Mon	£15.00	After 5 p.m.　£9.00	No. 18, No. 19 Courts
Tue, Wed	£13.00	After 5 p.m.　£8.00	
Thu	£12.00	After 5 p.m.　£8.00	
Fri, Sat	£11.00	After 5 p.m.　£7.00	
Sun	£6.00	After 5 p.m.　£3.00	
2005			
Mon–Mon	£16.00	After 5pm　£10.00	
Tue, Wed	£14.00	After 5pm　£9.00	No. 3, No. 6, No. 7, No. 11, No. 13
Thur	£13.00	After 5pm　£9.00	No. 14–No. 19 Courts
Fri, Sat	£12.00	After 5pm　£8.00	
Sun	£7.00	After 5pm　£4.00	

Year	Admission		Courts with free seating
	Day	Reduced	
2006			
Mon–Mon	£17.00	After 5pm £11.00	No. 3, No. 6, No. 7, No. 11, No. 13
Tue, Wed	£15.00	After 5pm £10.00	No. 14–No. 19 Courts
Thur	£14.00	After 5pm £10.00	
Fri, Sat	£13.00	After 5pm £9.00	
Sun	£8.00	After 5pm £5.00	
2007			
Mon–Mon	£18.00	After 5pm £12.00	No. 3, No. 6, No. 7, No. 11, No. 13
Tue, Wed	£16.00	After 5pm £11.00	No. 14–No. 19 Courts
Thur	£15.00	After 5pm £11.00	
Fri, Sat	£14.00	After 5pm £10.00	
Sun	£8.00	After 5pm £5.00	
2008			
Mon–Mon	£20.00	After 5pm £14.00	No. 3, No. 6, No. 7, No. 11,
Tue, Wed	£17.00	After 5pm £12.00	No. 14–No. 19 Courts
Thur	£16.00	After 5pm £12.00	
Fri, Sat	£15.00	After 5pm £11.00	
Sun	£8.00	After 5pm £5.00	
2009			
Mon–Mon	£20.00	After 5pm £14.00	No. 4, No. 7, No. 8, No. 12,
Tue, Wed	£17.00	After 5pm £12.00	No. 14–No. 19 Courts
Thur	£16.00	After 5pm £12.00	
Fri, Sat	£15.00	After 5pm £11.00	
Sun	£8.00	After 5pm £5.00	
2010			
Mon–Mon	£20.00	After 5pm £14.00	No. 5, No. 12, No. 14–No. 19 Courts
Tue, Wed	£17.00	After 5pm £12.00	
Thur	£16.00	After 5pm £12.00	
Fri, Sat	£15.00	After 5pm £11.00	
Sun	£8.00	After 5pm £5.00	
2011–2013			
Mon–Mon	£20.00	After 5pm £14.00	No. 3, No. 4, No. 12, No. 14–No. 19
Tue, Wed	£17.00	After 5pm £12.00	Courts
Thur	£16.00	After 5pm £12.00	
Fri, Sat	£15.00	After 5pm £11.00	
Sun	£8.00	After 5pm £5.00	
2014			
Mon–Mon	£20.00	After 5pm £14.00	No. 3, No. 4, No. 12, No. 16–No. 19
Tue, Wed	£17.00	After 5pm £12.00	Courts
Thur	£16.00	After 5pm £12.00	
Fri, Sat	£15.00	After 5pm £11.00	
Sun	£8.00	After 5pm £5.00	
2015			
Mon–Mon	£25.00	After 5pm £18.00	No. 3, No. 4, No. 12, No. 14–No. 19
Tue–Thur	£20.00	After 5pm £14.00	Courts
Fri, Sat	£15.00	After 5pm £11.00	
Sun	£8.00	After 5pm £5.00	

Notes

1. No. 10 and No. 11 Courts became No. 6 and No. 7 Courts in 1973.
2. No. 14 Court became No. 13 Court in 1980.
3. Gates to the grounds closed when all daily tickets sold and thereafter admission only through the resale of tickets relinquished by spectators leaving the grounds. These tickets sold at £4.00 each.
4. First Sunday Admission – £5.00. After 5 p.m. – £2.00.
5. First Saturday Admission – £5.00. After 5 p.m. – £2.00.
6. First Saturday Admission – £5.00. After 5 p.m. – £3.00.
7. Second Sunday Admission – £1.00 with all proceeds to charity.
8. First Sunday Admission – £5.00.
9. First Saturday Admission – £7.00. After 5 p.m. – £4.00.
10. Third Monday Admission – £5.00.
11. Third Monday Admission – £10.00.
12. First Saturday Admission – £8.00. After 5 p.m. – £5.00.
13. First Sunday Admission – £15.00.

Championship Entries

Number of Entries

Year	Gentlemen's Singles	Gentlemen's Doubles (pairs)	Ladies' Singles	Ladies' Doubles (pairs)	Mixed Doubles (pairs)	Year	Gentlemen's Singles	Gentlemen's Doubles (pairs)	Ladies' Singles	Ladies' Doubles (pairs)	Mixed Doubles (pairs)
1877	22					1922	128	64	64	32	64
1878	35					1923	133	64	70	38	64
1879	45					1924	128	64	64	40	64
1880	61					1925	128	64	64	39	64
1881	49					1926	128	64	64	41	64
1882	29					1927	128	64	80	42	64
1883	24					1928	128	64	80	40	64
1884	29	10	13			1929	128	64	96	48	64
1885	24	11	10			1930	128	64	96	48	67
1886	24	8	9			1931 to 1936	128	64	96	48	80
1887	16	10	6			1937	128	64	97	48	80
1888	25	13	7			1938	128	64	96	48	81
1889	25	10	6			1939	128	64	96	48	80
1890	31	7	4			1946	128	64	96	48	80
1891	22	5	9			1947	128	64	96	40	81
1892	28	6	8			1948	128	64	96	40	80
1893	28	11	8			1949 to 1962	128	64	96	48	80
1894	24	11	11			1963	128	68	96	48	80
1895	18	7	9			1964 to 1972	128	64	96	48	80
1896	32	15	7			1973	128	64	96	50	80
1897	32	15	8			1974	128	64	96	48	80
1898	38	15	18			1975 1976	128	64	96	48	64
1899	38	16	18			1977	128	64	96	48	48
1900	35	15	17			1978	128	64	96	48	52
1901	37	20	31			1979	128	64	96	48	48
1902	43	21	23			1980	128	64	96	48	49
1903	43	19	28			1981 1982	128	64	96	48	48
1904	63	28	42			1983	128	64	128	56	56
1905	72	32	46			1984 to 2003	128	64	128	64	64
1906	70	29	49			2004 to 2015	128	64	128	64	48
1907	85	29	43								
1908	70	34	30								
1909	86	40	37								
1910	93	40	32								
1911	105	39	35								
1912	82	35	34								
1913	117	49	42	21	41						
1914	103	45	52	20	39						
1919	129	55	44	18	42						
1920	129	53	51	26	52						
1921	129	64	57	23	64						

The above figures include the defending champion/s, who annually "stood out", until the Challenge Round was abolished in 1922

Entry Fees

Years	Gentlemen's Singles	Gentlemen's Doubles (a pair)	Ladies' Singles	Ladies' Doubles	Mixed Doubles (each)
1877–1883	£1.1s.0d	–	–	–	
1884–1895	£1.1s.0d	£1.1s.0d	10s.6d	–	
1896–1904	£1.1s.0d	£1.1s.0d	5s.0d	–	
1905–1911	£1.1s.0d	£1.1s.0d	15s.0d	–	
1912	£1.11s.6d(1)	£2.2s.0d	15s.0d	–	
1913–1914	£1.11s.6d(1)	£2.2s.0d	£1.1s.0d	£1.1s.0d (3)	£1.1s.0d (4)
1919–1922	£2.2s.0d(2)	£3.3s.0d	£1.11s.6d	£1.11s.6d (3)	£1.11s.6d (4)
1923–1927(5)	£2.12s.0d		£1.12s.0d		
1928–1939	£1.15s.0d		£1.5s.0d		
1946–1970	£1.15s.0d		£1.5s.0d		
1971–1972	£1.75		£1.25		
1973	£2.00		£1.50		
1974–1975	£8.00		£5.00		
1976	£15.00		£10.00		
1977–1981	£12.00		£9.00		
1982–1983	£12.00		NIL		
1984	£33.00				
1985	£40.00				
1986–1987	£35.00				
1988	NIL				

(1) £2.2s.0d inclusive if also entering the Gentlemen's Doubles.
(2) £2.12s.6d inclusive if also entering the Gentlemen's Doubles.
(3) Entry free to players competing in Ladies' singles.
(4) Entry free to players competing in either Gentlemen's singles and Doubles or Ladies' singles and Doubles.
(5) From 1923 one fee for Gentlemen and Ladies, irrespective of the number of events entered.

Seeding Lists and Achievements

A simplified form of seeding was introduced in 1924 when up to four representatives of a nation were drawn in four different quarters of the draw. In 1927 full seeding was carried out and competitors were selected according to ability irrespective of nationality. Since then an unseeded player has won the Gentlemen's Singles twice, in 1985 and 2001, but never the Ladies' Singles. Thirteen unseeded players have reached the final of the Gentlemen's Singles and thirteen unseeded players have reached the final of the Ladies' Singles. Twelve unseeded pairs have won the Gentlemen's Doubles, seven unseeded pairs have won the Ladies' Doubles and 13 unseeded pairs have won the Mixed Doubles.

Seeding has been based on computer rankings from 1975.

From 2001, 32 players have been seeded in the Gentlemen's and Ladies' Singles. These are the top 32 players on the ATP Entry System Position (ESP) and the WTA Tour ranking. The former list is arranged on a surface-based system to reflect more accurately the individual player's grass court achievement as per the following formula: 1 – ESP points as at a week before The Championships: 2 – Add 100% points earned for all grass court tournaments in the past 12 months: 3 – add 75% points earned for best grass court tournament in the 12 months before that. For the Ladies, the seeding order follows the ranking list, except where in the opinion of the Committee, the grass court credentials of a particular player necessitates a change in the interest of achieving a balanced draw.

The following lists the seeded players in each event from 1927 and the seeded players who reached the concluding rounds.

The names of the Ladies are as laid down in the official programme with, where appropriate, their married names shown in brackets. Ladies listed under different names are as follows:–

Miss S. Appelmans	– Mrs. S. Haubourdin	Miss M.E. Osborne	– Mrs. W. duPont
Miss B.J. Baker	– Mrs. J.G. Fleitz	Miss S.H. Palfrey	– Mrs. M. Fabyan
Miss E.V. Bennett	– Mrs. E.O.F. Whittingstall	Miss J.S.V. Partridge	– Mrs. P. Chatrier
Miss S. Cherneva	– Mrs. S. Parkhomenko	Miss M.L. Piatek	– Mrs. P.F. Daniels
Miss T.D. Coyne	– Mrs. M.N. Long	Miss K.Y. Po	–Mrs. O.G. H-P Messerli
Miss L.A. Davenport	– Mrs. J. Leach	Miss N.A.-L. Provis	– Mrs. M.R. Bradtke
Miss C.M. Evert	– Mrs. J.M. Lloyd	Miss V. Puzejova	– Mrs. C. Sukova
Miss S. Farina	– Mrs. F. Elia	Miss J.D. Quertier	– Mrs. I.F. Rinkel
Miss E.F. Goolagong	– Mrs. R.A. Cawley	Miss S. Reynolds	– Mrs. L.E.G. Price
Miss J. Halard	– Mrs A. Decugis	Miss N.A. Richey	– Mrs. K.S. Gunter
Miss K.J. Hantze	– Mrs. J.R. Susman	Miss C.E. Rosenquest	– Mrs. E.C.S. Pratt
Miss A.S. Haydon	– Mrs. P.F. Jones	Miss M.A. Sanders	– Mrs. L.R.C. Mitchell
Miss E.L. Heine	– Mrs. J.H.K. Miller	Miss L.I. Savchenko	– Mrs. A. Neiland
Miss J. Henin	– Mrs. P.Y. Hardenne	Miss E.M. Sayers	– Mrs. P.D. Smylie
Mrs. R. Hilton	– Mrs. A.J.C. Harrison	Miss B.A.M. Schultz	– Mrs. S. McCarthy
Miss A.K. Kiyomura	– Mrs. D. Hayashi	Miss R. Schuurman	– Mrs. P. Haygarth
Miss H. Krahwinkel	– Mrs. S. Sperling	Miss A. Smashnova	– Mrs. C. Pistolesi
Mrs. P.H. Landry	– Mrs. N. Adamson	Miss M. Smith	– Mrs. B.M. Court
Miss E. Likhovtseva	– Mrs. M. Baronov	Miss J.J. Staley	– Mrs. L.A. Hoad
Miss M Maleeva	– Mrs. F. Fragniere	Miss K.E. Stammers	– Mrs. M. Menzies
Miss H. Mandlikova	– Mrs. H. Mandlikova	Miss J.A.M. Tegart	– Mrs. D.E. Dalton
Miss K.A. Melville	– Mrs. G.E. Reid	Miss S. Testud	– Mrs V. Magnelli
Miss B.J. Moffitt	– Mrs. L.W. King	Miss M.A. Vento	– Mrs. G. Kabchi
Miss C.M. Morariu	– Mrs. A. Turcinovich	Miss L.R. Turner	– Mrs. W.W. Bowrey
Miss P.E. Mudford	– Mrs. M.R. King	Miss S.A. Walsh	– Mrs. M.H. Pete
Miss J.A.B. Nicoll	– Mrs. E.W.A. Bostock	Miss W.E. White	– Mrs. S.R. Prausa
Miss H. Niessen	– Mrs. H. Masthoff	Miss H.N. Wills	– Mrs. F.S. Moody

Gentlemen's Singles Championship

1927 (8)
1–J.R. Lacoste (FRA), 2–W.T. Tilden (USA), 3–J.R. Borotra (FRA), 4–H.J. Cochet (FRA), 5–T. Harada (JPN), 6–L.B. Raymond (RSA), 7–J. Brugnon (FRA), 8–J. Kozeluh (TCH).

1928 (8)
1–H.J. Cochet (FRA), 2–J.R. Lacoste (FRA), 3–W.T. Tilden (USA), 4–F.T. Hunter (USA), 5–J.R. Borotra (FRA), 6–J.F. Hennessey (USA), 7–U.L. de Morpurgo (ITA), 8–G.L. Patterson (AUS).

1929 (8)
1–H.J. Cochet (FRA), 2–J.R. Borotra (FRA), 3–W.T. Tilden (USA), 4–F.T. Hunter (USA), 5–U.L. de Morpurgo (ITA), 6–G.M. Lott (USA), 7–B. Von Kehrling (HUN), 8–J.C. Gregory (GBR).

1930 (8)
1–H.J. Cochet (FRA), 2–W.T. Tilden (USA), 3–J.R. Borotra (FRA), 4–J.T.G.H. Doeg (USA), 5–G.M. Lott (USA), 6–H.W. Austin (GBR), 7–U.L. de Morpurgo (ITA), 8–E.F. Moon (AUS).

1931 (8)
1–J.R. Borotra (FRA), 2–H.J. Cochet (FRA), 3–F.X. Shields (USA), 4–C. Boussus (FRA), 5–F.J. Perry (GBR), 6–H.W. Austin (GBR), 7–S.B.B. Wood (USA), 8–J. Satoh (JPN).

1932 (8)
1–H.J. Cochet (FRA), 2–H.E. Vines (USA), 3–F.X. Shields (USA), 4–F.J. Perry (GBR), 5–S.B.B. Wood (USA), 6–H.W. Austin (GBR), 7–J.R. Borotra (FRA), 8–J.H. Crawford (AUS).

1933 (8)
1–H.E. Vines (USA), 2–J.H. Crawford (AUS), 3–H.J. Cochet (FRA), 4–H.W. Austin (GBR), 5–C.S. Sutter (USA), 6–F.J. Perry (GBR), 7–J. Satoh (JPN), 8–H.G.N. Lee (GBR).

1934 (8)
1–J.H. Crawford (AUS), 2–F.J. Perry (GBR), 3–G. von Cramm (GER), 4–H.W. Austin (GBR), 5–F.X. Shields (USA), 6–L.R. Stoefen (USA), 7–S.B.B. Wood (USA), 8–G. de Stefani (ITA).

1935 (8)
1–F.J. Perry (GBR), 2–G. von Cramm (GER), 3–J.H. Crawford (AUS), 4–H.W. Austin (GBR), 5–W.L. Allison (USA), 6–S.B.B. Wood (USA), 7–R. Menzel (TCH), 8–C. Boussus (FRA).

1936 (8)
1–F.J. Perry (GBR), 2–G. von Cramm (GER), 4–A.K. Quist (AUS), 4–W.L. Allison (USA), 5–J.D. Budge (USA), 6–J.H. Crawford (AUS), 7–H.W. Austin (GBR), 8–B.M. Grant (USA).

1937 (8)
1–J.D. Budge (USA), 2–G. von Cramm (GER), 3–H.E.O. Henkel (GER), 4–H.W. Austin (GBR), 5–B.M. Grant (USA), 6–R. Menzel (TCH), 7–V.B. McGrath (AUS), 8–F.A. Parker (USA).

1938 (8)
1–J.D. Budge (USA), 2–H.W. Austin (GBR), 3–R. Menzel (TCH), 4–H.E.O. Henkel (GER), 5–F. Puncec (YUG), 6–D. Mitic (YUG), 7–L. Hecht (TCH), 8–Kho Sin Kie (CHN).

1939 (8)
1–H.W. Austin (GBR), 2–R.L. Riggs (USA), 3–D. McNeill (USA), 4–F. Puncec (YUG), 5–H.E.O. Henkel (GER), 6–E.T. Cooke (USA), 7–R. Menzel (GER), 8–I.H. Tloczynski (POL).

1946 (8)
1–D.R. Pails (AUS), 2–J.A. Kramer (USA), 3–G.E. Brown (AUS), 4–F.O. Segura (ECU), 5–Y.F.M. Petra (FRA), 6–D. Mitic (YUG), 7–F. Puncec (YUG), 8–L. Bergelin (SWE).

1947 (8)
1–J.A. Kramer (USA), 2–J.E. Bromwich (AUS), 3–T.P. Brown (USA), 4–D.R. Pails (AUS), 5–G.E. Brown (AUS), 6–J. Drobny (TCH), 7–Y.F.M. Petra (FRA), 8–R. Falkenburg (USA).

1948 (8)
1–F.A. Parker (USA), 2–J.E. Bromwich (AUS), 3–G.P. Mulloy (USA), 4–T.P. Brown (USA), 5–J. Drobny (TCH), 6–J.E. Patty (USA), 7–R. Falkenburg (USA), 8–E.W. Sturgess (RSA).

1949 (8)
1–F.R. Schroeder (USA), 2–R.A. Gonzales (USA), 3–F.A. Parker (USA), 4–R. Falkenburg (USA), 5–J.E. Bromwich (AUS), 6–J. Drobny (TCH), 7–E.W. Sturgess (RSA), 8–F.A. Sedgman (AUS).

1950 (16)
1–F.A. Sedgman (AUS), 2–W.F. Talbert (USA), 3–J. Drobny (EGY), 4–E.W. Sturgess (RSA), 5–J.E. Patty (USA), 6–G.P. Mulloy (USA), 7–A.D. Larsen (USA), 8–J.E. Bromwich (AUS), 9–G.E. Brown (AUS), 10–K.B. McGregor (AUS), 11–O.W. Sidwell (AUS), 12–E.V. Seixas (USA), 13–F.T. Kovaleski (USA), 14–I.S. Dorfman (USA), 15–D.K. Bose (IND), 16–G. Cucelli (ITA)*.
*The No. 16 seed withdrew owing to injury. His position in the draw was filled by a Qualifier – A.W. Tills (NZL).

1951 (10)
1–F.A. Sedgman (AUS), 2–J. Drobny (EGY), 3–A.D. Larsen (USA), 4–J.E. Patty (USA), 5–H. Flam (USA), 6–R. Savitt (USA), 7–K.B. McGregor (AUS), 8–E.W. Sturgess (RSA), 9–G.P. Mulloy (USA), 10–L. Bergelin (SWE).

1952 (12)
1–F.A. Sedgman (AUS), 2–J. Drobny (EGY), 3–E.V. Seixas (USA), 4–R. Savitt (USA), 5–K.B. McGregor (AUS), 6–H. Flam (USA), 7–E.W. Sturgess (RSA), 8–M.G. Rose (AUS), 9–A.D. Larsen (USA), 10–G.P. Mulloy (USA), 11–H.F. Richardson (USA), 12–J.E. Patty (USA).

1953 (8)
1–K.R. Rosewall (AUS), 2–E.V. Seixas (USA), 3–M.G. Rose (AUS), 4–J. Drobny (EGY), 5–G.P. Mulloy (USA), 6–L.A. Hoad (AUS), 7–A.D. Larsen (USA), 8–E.J. Morea (ARG).

1954 (12)
1–M.A. Trabert (USA), 2–L.A. Hoad (AUS), 3–K.R. Rosewall (AUS), 4–E.V. Seixas (USA), 5–M.G. Rose (AUS), 6–A.D. Larsen (USA), 7–J.E. Patty (USA), 8–R.N. Hartwig (AUS), 9–S.V. Davidson (SWE), 10–K. Nielsen (DEN), 11–J. Drobny (EGY), 12–G.P. Mulloy (USA).

1955 (8)
1–M.A. Trabert (USA), 2–K.R. Rosewall (AUS), 3–E.V. Seixas (USA), 4–L.A. Hoad (AUS), 5–R.N. Hartwig (AUS), 6–J. Drobny (EGY), 7–J.E. Patty (USA), 8–S.V. Davidson (SWE).

1956 (8)
1–L.A. Hoad (AUS), 2–K.R. Rosewall (AUS), 3–S.V. Davidson (SWE), 4–J.E. Patty (USA), 5–J. Drobny (EGY), 6–H.F. Richardson (USA), 7–K. Nielsen (DEN), 8–E.V. Seixas (USA).

1957 (8)
1–L.A. Hoad (AUS), 2–A.J. Cooper (AUS), 3–H.F. Richardson (USA), 4–S.V. Davidson (SWE), 5–N.A. Fraser (AUS), 6–E.V. Seixas (USA), 7–H. Flam (USA), 8–M.G. Rose (AUS).

1958 (8)
1–A.J. Cooper (AUS), 2–M.J. Anderson (AUS), 3–M.G. Rose (AUS), 4–N.A. Fraser (AUS), 5–L.A. Ayala (CHI), 6–K. Nielsen (DEN), 7–S.V. Davidson (SWE), 8–B.B. Mackay (USA).

1959 (8)
1–A.R. Olmedo (USA), 2–N.A. Fraser (AUS), 3–N. Pietrangeli (ITA), 4–R.K. Wilson (GBR), 5–B.B. Mackay (USA), 6–L.A. Ayala (CHI), 7–K. Nielsen (DEN), 8–R.S. Emerson (AUS).

1960 (8)
1–N.A. Fraser (AUS), 2–B.B. Mackay (USA), 3–R.G. Laver (AUS), 4–L.A. Ayala (CHI), 5–N. Pietrangeli (ITA), 6–R.S. Emerson (AUS), 7–R. Krishnan (IND), 8–E.H. Buchholz (USA).

1961 (8)
1–N.A. Fraser (AUS), 2–R.G. Laver (AUS), 3–N. Pietrangeli (ITA), 4–R.S. Emerson (AUS), 5–M.M. Santana (ESP), 6–L.A. Ayala (CHI), 7–R. Krishnan (IND), 8–C.R. McKinley (USA).

1962 (8)
1–R.G. Laver (AUS), 2–R.S. Emerson (AUS), 3–N.A. Fraser (AUS), 4–R. Krishnan (IND), 5–C.R. McKinley (USA), 6–M.M. Santana (ESP), 7–N. Pietrangeli (ITA), 8–R.A.J. Hewitt (AUS).

1963 (8)
1–R.S. Emerson (AUS), 2–M.M. Santana (ESP), 3–K.N. Fletcher (AUS), 4–C.R. McKinley (USA), 5–M.F. Mulligan (AUS), 6–P. Darmon (FRA), 7–J.E. Lundquist (SWE), 8–M.J. Sangster (GBR).

1964 (8)
1–R.S. Emerson (AUS), 2–C.R. McKinley (USA), 3–M.M. Santana (ESP), 4–R.H. Osuna (MEX), 5–R.D. Ralston (USA), 6–F.S. Stolle (AUS), 7–N. Pietrangeli (ITA), 8–M.F. Mulligan (AUS).

1965 (8)
1–R.S. Emerson (AUS), 2–F.S. Stolle (AUS), 3–J.E. Lundquist (SWE), 4–R.D. Ralston (USA), 5–W.P. Bungert (GER), 6–J.D. Newcombe (AUS), 7–A.D. Roche (AUS), 8–R.H. Osuna (MEX).

1966 (8)
1–R.S. Emerson (AUS), 2–A.D. Roche (AUS), 3–F.S. Stolle (AUS), 4–M.M. Santana (ESP), 5–J.D. Newcombe (AUS), 6–R.D. Ralston (USA), 7–E.C. Drysdale (RSA), 8–C.E. Graebner (USA).

1967 (8)
1–M.M. Santana (ESP), 2–R.S. Emerson (AUS), 3–J.D. Newcombe (AUS), 4–A.D. Roche (AUS), 5–E.C. Drysdale (RSA), 6–K.N. Fletcher (AUS), 7–J. Leschly (DEN), 8–W.W. Bowrey (AUS).

1968 (16)
1–R.G. Laver (AUS), 2–K.R. Rosewall (AUS), 3–A. Gimeno (ESP), 4–J.D. Newcombe (AUS), 5–R.S. Emerson (AUS), 6–M.M. Santana (ESP), 7–L.A. Hoad (AUS), 8–R.A. Gonzales (USA), 9–R.D. Ralston (USA), 10–E.H. Buchholz (USA), 11–F.S. Stolle (AUS), 12–T.S. Okker (NED), 13–A.R. Ashe (USA), 14–E.C. Drysdale (RSA), 15–A.D. Roche (AUS), 16–N. Pilic (YUG).

1969 (16)
1–R.G. Laver (AUS), 2–A.D. Roche (AUS), 3–T.S. Okker (NED), 4–K.R. Rosewall (AUS), 5–A.R. Ashe (USA), 6–J.D. Newcombe (AUS), 7–C.E. Graebner (USA), 8–E.C. Drysdale (RSA), 9–R.S. Emerson (AUS), 10–A. Gimeno (ESP), 11–F.S. Stolle (AUS), 12–R.A. Gonzales (USA), 13–R.J. Moore (RSA), 14–R.A.J. Hewitt (RSA), 15–R.D. Ralston (USA), 16–S.R. Smith (USA).

1970 (16)
1–R.G. Laver (AUS), 2–J.D. Newcombe (AUS), 3–A.R. Ashe (USA), 4–A.D. Roche (AUS), 5–K.R. Rosewall (AUS), 6–Z. Franulovic (YUG), 7–S.R. Smith (USA), 8–I. Nastase (ROM), 9–C.E. Graebner (USA), 10–R.S. Emerson (AUS), 11–T.S. Okker (NED), 12–E.C. Drysdale (RSA), 13–J. Kodes (TCH), 14–A. Gimeno (ESP), 15–R.D. Ralston (USA), 16–R. Taylor (GBR).

1971 (8)
1–R.G. Laver (AUS), 2–J.D. Newcombe (AUS), 3–K.R. Rosewall (AUS), 4–S.R. Smith (USA), 5–A.R. Ashe (USA), 6–G.C. Richey (USA), 7–I. Nastase (ROM), 8–E.C. Drysdale (RSA).

1972 (8)
1–S.R. Smith (USA), 2–I. Nastase (ROM), 3–M. Orantes (ESP), 4–A. Gimeno (ESP), 5–J. Kodes (TCH), 6–P. Barthes (FRA), 7–R.A.J. Hewitt (RSA), 8–A. Metreveli (URS).

1973 (8)
1–I. Nastase (ROM), 2–J. Kodes (TCH), 3–R. Taylor (GBR), 4–A. Metreveli (URS), 5–J.S. Connors (USA), 6–B.R. Borg (SWE), 7–O.K. Davidson (AUS), 8–J. Fassbender (GER).
NOTE: The original seedings before the Boycott:–
1–S.R. Smith (USA), 2–I. Nastase (ROM), 3–J.D. Newcombe (AUS), 4–A.R. Ashe (USA), 5–K.R. Rosewall (AUS), 6–T.S. Okker (NED), 7–M.C. Riessen (USA), 8–R.S. Emerson (AUS), 9–T.W. Gorman (USA), 10–G.C. Richey (USA), 11–A. Panatta (ITA), 12–M. Orantes (ESP), 13–A. Metreveli (URS), 14–R.C. Lutz (USA), 15–J. Kodes (TCH), 16–R. Taylor (GBR).

1974 (12)
1–J.D. Newcombe (AUS), 2–I. Nastase (ROM), 3–J.S. Connors (USA), 4–S.R. Smith (USA), 5–B.R. Borg (SWE), 6–J. Kodes (TCH), 7–T.S. Okker (NED), 8–A.R. Ashe (USA), 9–K.R. Rosewall (AUS), 10–A. Metreveli (URS), 11–T.W. Gorman (USA), 12–M. Orantes (ESP).

1975 (16)
1–J.S. Connors (USA), 2–K.R. Rosewall (AUS), 3–B.R. Borg (SWE), 4–G. Vilas (ARG), 5–I. Nastase (ROM), 6–A.R. Ashe (USA), 7–S.R. Smith (USA), 8–R.C. Ramirez (MEX), 9–T.S. Okker (NED), 10–J.G. Alexander (AUS), 11–L.R. Tanner (USA), 12–J. Kodes (TCH), 13–M.C. Riessen (USA), 14–V.K. Gerulaitis (USA), 15–O. Parun (NZL), 16–A.D. Roche (AUS).

1976 (16)
1–A.R. Ashe (USA), 2–J.S. Connors (USA), 3–I. Nastase (ROM), 4–B.R. Borg (SWE), 5–A. Panatta (ITA), 6–G. Vilas (ARG), 7–L.R. Tanner (USA), 8–R.C. Ramirez (MEX), 9–T.S. Okker (NED), 10–J.D. Newcombe (AUS), 11–E.G. Dibbs (USA)*, 12–A.D. Roche (AUS), 13–J.J. Fillol (CHI), 14–B.E. Gottfried (USA), 15–J. Kodes (TCH)*, 16–S.R. Smith (USA).
*The No. 11 and 15 seeds withdrew owing to injury. Their positions in the draw were filled by Lucky Losers – J.K. Holladay (USA) and M. Holecek (STA), respectively.

1977 (16)
1–J.S. Connors (USA), 2–B.R. Borg (SWE), 3–G. Vilas (ARG), 4–L.R. Tanner (USA), 5–B.E. Gottfried (USA), 6–I. Nastase (ROM), 7–R.C. Ramirez (MEX), 8–V.K. Gerulaitis (USA), 9–R.L. Stockton (USA), 10–A. Panatta (ITA), 11–S.R. Smith (USA), 12–W.J. Fibak (POL), 13–P.C. Dent (AUS), 14–M. Cox (GBR), 15–R.C. Lutz (USA), 16–H.C. Solomon (USA).

1978 (16)
1–B.R. Borg (SWE), 2–J.S. Connors (USA), 3–V.K. Gerulaitis (USA), 4–G. Vilas (ARG), 5–B.E. Gottfried (USA), 6–L.R. Tanner (USA), 7–R.C. Ramirez (MEX), 8–A. Mayer (USA), 9–I. Nastase (ROM), 10–R.L. Stockton (USA), 11–J.P. McEnroe (USA), 12–C.J. Mottram (GBR), 13–W.J. Fibak (POL), 14–J.G. Alexander (AUS), 15–A.R. Ashe (USA), 16–J.D. Newcombe (AUS).

1979 (16)
1–B.R. Borg (SWE), 2–J.P. McEnroe (USA), 3–J.S. Connors (USA), 4–V.K. Gerulaitis (USA), 5–L.R. Tanner (USA), 6–G. Vilas (ARG), 7–A.R. Ashe (USA), 8–V. Pecci (PAR), 9–B.E. Gottfried (USA), 10–W.J. Fibak (POL), 11–J.G. Alexander (AUS), 12–J. Higueras (ESP), 13–M. Orantes (ESP), 14–J.L. Clerc (ARG), 15–T.E. Gullikson (USA), 16–C. Barazzutti (ITA).

1980 (16)
1–B.R. Borg (SWE), 2–J.P. McEnroe (USA), 3–J.S. Connors (USA), 4–V.K. Gerulaitis (USA), 5–L.R. Tanner (USA), 6–G. Mayer (USA), 7–P.B. Fleming (USA), 8–V. Pecci (PAR), 9–P. Dupre (USA), 10–I. Lendl (TCH), 11–H.C. Solomon (USA)*, 12–Y. Noah (FRA)*, 13–W.J. Fibak (POL), 14–V.C. Amaya (USA), 15–S.R. Smith (USA), 16–J.L. Clerc (ARG).

*The No. 11 and 12 seeds withdrew owing to injury. Their positions in the draw were filled by Qualifiers – K.M. Curren (RSA) and W.D. Hampson (AUS), respectively.

1981 (16)
1–B.R. Borg (SWE), 2–J.P. McEnroe (USA), 3–J.S. Connors (USA), 4–I. Lendl (TCH), 5–G. Mayer (USA)*, 6–B.D. Teacher (USA), 7–B.E. Gottfried (USA), 8–L.R. Tanner (USA), 9–J.L. Clerc (ARG), 10–G. Vilas (ARG), 11–V. Pecci (PAR), 12–P.B. McNamara (AUS), 13–Y. Noah (FRA), 14–W.J. Fibak (POL), 15–B. Taroczy (HUN), 16–V.K. Gerulaitis (USA).

*The No. 5 seed withdrew owing to injury. His position in the draw was filled by Lucky Loser – M. Estep (USA).

1982 (16)
1–J.P. McEnroe (USA), 2–J.S. Connors (USA), 3–V.K. Gerulaitis (USA), 4–A. Mayer (USA), 5–J.C. Kriek (RSA), 6–E. Mayer (USA), 7–M.A.O. Wilander (SWE), 8–P.B. McNamara (AUS), 9–A. Gomez (ECU), 10–Y. Noah (FRA)*, 11–B.D. Teacher (USA), 12–M.R. Edmondson (AUS), 13–B.E. Gottfried (USA), 14–L.R. Tanner (USA), 15–C.J. Mottram (GBR), 16–S.B. Denton (USA).

*The No. 10 seed withdrew owing to injury. His position in the draw was filled by Lucky Loser – R. Meyer (USA).

1983 (16)
1–J.S. Connors (USA), 2–J.P. McEnroe (USA), 3–I. Lendl (TCH), 4–G. Vilas (ARG), 5–M.A.O. Wilander (SWE), 6–E. Mayer (USA)*, 7–J.L. Clerc (ARG), 8–V.K. Gerulaitis (USA), 9–S.B. Denton (USA), 10–J.J. Arias (USA)*, 11–J.C. Kriek (RSA), 12–K.M. Curren (RSA), 13–B.E. Gottfried (USA), 14–W.N. Scanlon (USA), 15–H.E. Pfister (USA), 16–T.S. Mayotte (USA).

*The No. 6 and 10 seeds withdrew owing to injury. Their positions in the draw were filled by Lucky Loser – R.B. Kleege (USA) and Qualifier – S.E. Davis (USA), respectively.

1984 (16)
1–J.P. McEnroe (USA), 2–I. Lendl (TCH), 3–J.S. Connors (USA), 4–M.A.O. Wilander (SWE), 5–J.J. Arias (USA), 6–A. Gomez (ECU), 7–Y. Noah (FRA)*, 8–J.L. Clerc (ARG)*, 9–H. Sundstrom (SWE), 10–A.P. Jarryd (SWE), 11–K.M. Curren (RSA), 12–J.C. Kriek (USA), 13–T. Smid (TCH), 14–W.N. Scanlon (USA), 15–V.K. Gerulaitis (USA), 16–T.S. Mayotte (USA).

*The No. 7 and No. 8 seeds withdrew owing to injury and illness respectively. Their positions in the draw were filled by a Qualifier – P. Annacone (USA) and Lucky Loser – C. Mezzadri (SUI), respectively.

1985 (16)
1–J.P. McEnroe (USA), 2–I. Lendl (TCH), 3–J.S. Connors (USA), 4–M.A.O. Wilander (SWE), 5–A.P. Jarryd (SWE), 6–P.H. Cash (AUS), 7–K.J. Nystrom (SWE), 8–K.M. Curren (USA), 9–J.C. Kriek (USA), 10–A.D. Krickstein (USA), 11–Y. Noah (FRA), 12–M. Mecir (TCH), 13–E.T. Teltscher (USA), 14–S.B. Edberg (SWE), 15–T. Smid (TCH), 16–T.S. Mayotte (USA).

1986 (16)
1–I. Lendl (TCH), 2–M.A.O. Wilander (SWE), 3–J.S. Connors (USA), 4–B.F Becker (GER), 5–S.B. Edberg (SWE), 6–K.J. Nystrom (SWE), 7–H. Leconte (FRA), 8–A.P. Jarryd (SWE), 9–A. Gomez (ECU), 10–T.S. Mayotte (USA), 11–K.M. Curren (USA), 12–B. Gilbert (USA), 13–M. Pernfors (SWE), 14–M. Jaite (ARG), 15–G. Vilas (ARG), 16–J.C. Kriek (USA).

1987 (16)

1–B.F. Becker (GER), 2–I. Lendl (TCH), 3–M.A.O. Wilander (SWE), 4–S.B. Edberg (SWE), 5–M. Mecir (TCH), 6–Y. Noah (FRA), 7–J.S. Connors (USA), 8–A. Gomez (ECU), 9–H. Leconte (FRA), 10–T.S. Mayotte (USA), 11–P.H. Cash (AUS), 12–B. Gilbert (USA), 13–K.J. Nystrom (SWE), 14–E. Sanchez (ESP), 15–D.B. Pate (USA), 16–K.M. Curren (USA).

1988 (16)

1–I. Lendl (TCH), 2–M.A.O. Wilander (SWE), 3–S.B. Edberg (SWE), 4–P.H. Cash (AUS), 5–J.S. Connors (USA), 6–B.F. Becker (GER), 7–H. Leconte (FRA), 8–J.P. McEnroe (USA), 9–M.Mecir (TCH), 10–T.S. Mayotte (USA), 11–A.P. Jarryd (SWE), 12–J.B. Svensson (SWE), 13–E. Sanchez (ESP), 14–A. Chesnokov (URS), 15–A. Mansdorf (ISR), 16–S. Zivojinovic (YUG).

1989 (16)

1–I. Lendl (TCH), 2–S.B. Edberg (SWE), 3–B.F. Becker (GER), 4–M.A.O. Wilander (SWE), 5–J.P. McEnroe (USA), 6–J. Hlasek (SUI), 7–M. Mecir (TCH), 8–T.S. Mayotte (USA), 9–M. Chang (USA), 10–J.S. Connors (USA), 11–B. Gilbert (USA), 12–K.M. Curren (USA), 13–A.D. Krickstein (USA), 14–A.Chesnokov (URS), 15–M. Pernfors (SWE), 16–A. Mansdorf (ISR).

1990 (16)

1–I. Lendl (TCH), 2–B.F. Becker (GER), 3–S.B. Edberg (SWE), 4–J.P. McEnroe (USA), 5–A. Gomez (ECU), 6–T.S. Mayotte (USA), 7–B. Gilbert (USA), 8–A.D. Krickstein (USA)*, 9–J.S. Courier (USA), 10–J.B. Svensson (SWE), 11–G. Forget (FRA), 12–P. Sampras (USA), 13–M. Chang (USA), 14–P. Korda (TCH), 15–H. Leconte (FRA), 16–Y. Noah (FRA).

*The No. 8 seed withdrew owing to injury. His position in the draw was filled by a Qualifier – S. Matsuoka (JPN).

1991 (16)

1–S.B. Edberg (SWE), 2–B.F. Becker (GER), 3–I. Lendl (TCH), 4–J.S. Courier (USA), 5–A.K. Agassi (USA), 6–M.D. Stich (GER), 7–G. Forget (FRA), 8–P. Sampras (USA), 9–M. Chang (USA), 10–G.S. Ivanisevic (YUG), 11–E. Sanchez (ESP), 12–A. Cherkasov (URS), 13–J. Hlasek (SUI), 14–K. Novacek (TCH), 15–B. Gilbert (USA), 16–J.P. McEnroe (USA).

1992 (16)

1–J.S. Courier (USA), 2–S.B. Edberg (SWE), 3–M.D. Stich (GER), 4–B.F. Becker (GER), 5–P. Sampras (USA), 6–P. Korda (TCH), 7–M. Chang (USA), 8–G.S. Ivanisevic (CRO), 9–G. Forget (FRA), 10–I. Lendl (TCH), 11–R.P.S. Krajicek (NED), 12–A.K. Agassi (USA), 13–B. Gilbert (USA), 14–W.R. Ferreira (RSA), 15–A. Volkov (CIS), 16–D. Wheaton (USA).

1993 (16)

1–P. Sampras (USA), 2–S.B. Edberg (SWE), 3–J.S. Courier (USA), 4–B.F. Becker (GER), 5–G.S. Ivanisevic (CRO), 6–M.D. Stich (GER), 7–I. Lendl (USA), 8–A.K. Agassi (USA), 9–R.P.S. Krajicek (NED), 10–A. Medvedev (UKR), 11–P. Korda (CZE), 12–M. Chang (USA), 13–W.R. Ferreira (RSA), 14–M.O. Washington (USA), 15–K. Novacek (CZE), 16–T. Muster (AUT).

1994 (16)

1–P. Sampras (USA), 2–M.D. Stich (GER), 3–S.B. Edberg (SWE), 4–G.S. Ivanisevic (CRO), 5–J.S. Courier (USA), 6–T.C. Martin (USA), 7–B.F. Becker (GER), 8–S. Bruguera (ESP), 9–A. Medvedev (UKR), 10–M. Chang (USA), 11–P. Korda (CZE), 12–A.K. Agassi (USA), 13–C.A. Pioline (FRA), 14–M. Rosset (SUI), 15–Y. A. Kafelnikov (RUS), 16–A. Boetsch (FRA).

1995 (16)

1–A.K. Agassi (USA), 2–P. Sampras (USA), 3–B.F. Becker (GER), 4–G.S. Ivanisevic (CRO), 5–M. Chang (USA), 6–Y.A. Kafelnikov (RUS), 7–W.R. Ferreira (RSA), 8–S. Bruguera (ESP)*, 9–M.D. Stich (GER), 10–M. Rosset (SUI), 11–J.S. Courier (USA), 12–R.P.S. Krajicek (NED), 13–S.B. Edberg (SWE), 14–T.C. Martin (USA), 15–A. Medvedev (UKR), 16–G. Forget (FRA).

* The No. 8 seed withdrew owing to injury. His position in the draw was filled by the highest ranked non-seeded player – K.J.T. Enqvist (SWE).

1996 (16)
1–P. Sampras (USA), 2–B.F. Becker (GER), 3–A.K. Agassi (USA), 4–G.S. Ivanisevic (CRO), 5–Y.A. Kafelnikov (RUS), 6–M. Chang (USA), 7–T. Muster (AUT),* 8–J.S. Courier (USA), 9–K.J.T. Enqvist (SWE), 10–M.D. Stich (GER), 11–W.R. Ferreira (RSA), 12–S.B. Edberg (SWE), 13–T.C. Martin (USA), 14–M. Rosset (SUI), 15–A. Boetsch (FRA), 16–C.A. Pioline (FRA), R.P.S. Krajicek (NED).

* The No. 7 seed withdrew owing to injury. His position in the draw was filled by the highest ranked non-seeded player, R.P.S. Krajicek (NED) who was made a seed without being numbered. NOTE: Although Krajicek was shown as unseeded in the official Programme for the period of The Championships the Committee ruled that he was seeded throughout and this is reflected in the 'final' issue of the Programme.

1997 (16)
1–P. Sampras (USA), 2–G.S. Ivanisevic (CRO), 3–Y.A. Kafelnikov (RUS), 4–R.P.S. Krajicek (NED), 5–M. Chang (USA), 6–T. Muster (AUT)*, 7–M.A. Philippoussis (AUS), 8–B.F. Becker (GER), 9–M.A. Rios (CHI), 10–C. Moya (ESP), 11–G. Kuerten (BRA), 12–P. Rafter (AUS), 13–A. Medvedev (UKR), 14–T.H. Henman (GBR), 15–W.R. Ferreira (RSA), 16–P. Korda (CZE), 17–J.L. Bjorkman (SWE).

* The No. 6 seed withdrew owing to injury. His position in the draw was filled by the highest ranked non-seeded player, J.L. Bjorkman (SWE), who became the No. 17 seed.

1998 (16)
1–P. Sampras (USA), 2–M.A. Rios (CHI), 3–P. Korda (CZE), 4–G. Rusedski (GBR), 5–C. Moya (ESP), 6–P.M. Rafter (AUS), 7–Y.A. Kafelnikov (RUS), 8–C.A. Pioline (FRA), 9–R.P.S. Krajicek (NED), 10–A. Corretja (ESP), 11–J.L. Bjorkman (SWE), 12–T.H. Henman (GBR), 13–A.K. Agassi (USA), 14–G.S. Ivanisevic (CRO), 15–K. Kucera (SVK), 16–F. Mantilla (ESP).

1999 (16)
1–P. Sampras (USA), 2–P.M. Rafter (AUS), 3–Y.A. Kafelnikov (RUS), 4–A.K. Agassi (USA), 5–R.P.S. Krajicek (NED), 6–T.H. Henman (GBR), 7–M.A. Philippoussis (AUS), 8–T.C. Martin (USA), 9.–G. Rusedski (GBR), 10–G.S. Ivanisevic (CRO), 11–G. Kuerten (BRA), 12–C. Moya (ESP), 13–K. Kucera (SVK), 14–T.M. Haas (GER), 15–N. Kiefer (GER), 16–F. Mantilla (ESP).

2000 (16)
1–P. Sampras (USA), 2–A.K. Agassi (USA), 3–L.M. Norman (SWE), 4–G. Kuerten (BRA), 5–Y.A. Kafelnikov (RUS), 6–C.A. Pioline (FRA), 7–L.G. Hewitt (AUS), 8–T.H. Henman (GBR), 9–K.J.T. Enquist (SWE), 10–M.A. Philippoussis (AUS), 11–R.P.S. Krajicek (NED), 12–P.M. Rafter (AUS), 13–N. Kiefer (GER), 14–G. Rusedski (GBR), 15–M.M. Safin (RUS), 16–N.A. Lapentti (ECU).

2001 (32)
1–P. Sampras (USA), 2–A.K. Agassi (USA), 3–P.M. Rafter (AUS), 4–M.M. Safin (RUS), 5–L.G. Hewitt (AUS), 6–T.H. Henman (GBR), 7–Y.A. Kafelnikov (RUS), 8–J.C. Ferrero (ESP), 9–S.R. Grosjean (FRA), 10–K.J.T. Enquist (SWE), 11–T. Johansson (SWE), 12–J-M.C. Gambill (USA), 13–A.M.M. Clement (FRA), 14–W.R. Ferreira (RSA), 15–R. Federer (SUI), 16–V. Voltchkov (BLR), 17–T.M. Haas (GER), 18–L.M. Norman (SWE)*, 19–N. Kiefer (GER), 20–F.V. Santoro (FRA), 21–C. Moya (ESP), 22–D.Hrbaty (SVK), 23–T.C. Martin (USA), 24–N.J-C Escude (FRA), 25–A. Portas (ESP), S. Schalken (NED), 27–H. Arazi (MAR), 28–F. Squillari (ARG), 29–G. Coria (ARG), 30–N.A. Lapentti (ECU)*, 31–A. Martin (ESP), 32–G. Gaudio (ARG), 33–J.L. Bjorkman (SWE), 34–H. Levy (ISR)

* The No. 18 seed withdrew owing to injury. His position in the draw was filled by the highest ranked non-seeded player – J.L. Bjorkman (SWE) who became the No. 33 seed. The No. 30 seed withdrew owing to injury. His position in the draw was filled by the highest ranked non-seeded player – H. Levy, (ISR) who became the No. 34 seed.

2002 (32)
1–L.G. Hewitt (AUS), 2–M.M. Safin (RUS), 3–A.K. Agassi (USA), 4–T.H. Henman (GBR), 5–Y.A. Kafelnikov (RUS), 6–P. Sampras (USA), 7–R. Federer (SUI), 8–T. Johansson (SWE), 9–J.C. Ferrero (ESP), 10–G. Canas (ARG), 11–A.S. Roddick (USA), 12–J. Novak (CZE), 13–Y. El Aynaoui (MAR), 14–K.J.T. Enquist (SWE), 15–A. Pavel (ROM), 16–N.J-C. Escude (FRA), 17–R.

Schuettler (GER), 18–S. Schalken (NED), 19–J.I. Chela (ARG), 20–T. Robredo (ESP), 21–M.N. Mirnyi (BLR), 22–N.A. Lapentti (ECU), 23–G. Rusedski (GBR), 24–G. Gaudio (ARG), 25–F.V. Santoro (FRA), 26–T.C. Martin (USA), 27–X. Malisse (BEL), 28–D.P. Nalbandian (ARG), 29–J.R. Blake (USA), 30–I. Ljubicic (CRO), 31–S. Koubek (AUT), 32–J. Nieminien (FIN).

Note: From the original list the No. 5 seed, T.M. Haas (GER), withdrew for personal reasons. Seeds No. 6 to No. 32 were made seeds No. 5 to No. 31 and a new No. 32 seed added.

2003 (32)

1–L.G. Hewitt (AUS), 2–A.K. Agassi (USA), 3–J.C. Ferrero (ESP), 4–R. Federer (SUI), 5–A.S. Roddick (USA), 6–D.P. Nalbandian (ARG), 7–G. Coria (ARG), 8–S. Schalken (NED), 9–R. Schuettler (GER), 10–T.H. Henman (GBR), 11–J. Novak (CZE),12–P. Srichaphan (THA), 13–S.R. Grosjean (FRA), 14–X. Malisse (BEL), 15–A.M.M. Clement (FRA), 16–M. Youzhny (RUS), 17–G. Kuerten (BRA), 18–M.M. Safin (RUS)*, 19–F.F. Gonzales (CHI), 20–Y.A. Kafelnikov (RUS), 21–M. Verkerk (NED), 22–F. Mantilla (ESP), 23–A. Calleri (ARG), 24–A. Costa (ESP)*, 25–T. Robredo (ESP), 26–J.R. Blake (USA), 27–Y.El Aynaoui (MAR), 28–W.R. Ferreira (RSA), 29–G. Gaudio (ARG), 30–J. Nieminen (FIN), 31–V. Spadea (USA), 32–J.I. Chela (ARG), 33–N. Davydenko (RUS), 34–A. Corretja (ESP)*, 35–R. Stepanek (CZE).

* The No. 24 seed withdrew owing to injury. His position in the draw was filled by the highest ranked non-seeded player – N. Davydenko (RUS), who became the No. 33 seed. The No. 18 seed withdrew owing to injury. His position in the draw was filled by the highest ranked non-seeded player – A. Corretja (ESP), who became the No. 34 seed. The No. 34 seed withdrew owing to personal reasons, His positions in the draw was filled by the highest ranked non-seeded player, R. Stepanek (CZE), who became the No. 35 seed.

2004 (32)

1–R. Federer (SUI), 2–A.S. Roddick (USA), 3–G. Coria (ARG), 4–D.P. Nalbandian (ARG)*, 5–T.H. Henman (GBR), 6–J.C. Ferrero (ESP), 7–L.G. Hewitt (AUS), 8–R Schuettler (GER), 9–C. Moya (ESP), 10–S.R. Grosjean (FRA), 11–M.A. Philippoussis (AUS), 12–S. Schalken (NED), 13–P. Srichaphan (THA), 14–M. Fish (USA), 15–N. Massu (CHI), 16–J. Novak (CZE), 17–J.L. Bjorkman (SWE), 18–F. Lopez (ESP), 19–M.M. Safin (RUS), 20–T. Robredo (ESP), 21–J.I. Chela (ARG), 22–A. Pavel (ROM), 23–M.N. Mirnyi (BLR), 24–F.F. Gonzalez (CHI), 25–D. Hrbaty (SVK), 26–T.P. Dent (USA), 27–R.L. Ginepri (USA), 28–I. Ljubicic (CRO), 29–N. Kiefer (GER), 30–V. Spadea (USA), 31–M. Youzhny (RUS), 32–H. Arazi (MAR), 33–L. Horna (PER).

* The No. 4 seed withdrew owing to injury. His position in the draw was filled by the highest ranked non-seeded player, – L. Horna (PER), who became the No. 33 seed.

2005 (32)

1–R. Federer (SUI), 2–A.S. Roddick (USA), 3–L.G. Hewitt (AUS), 4–R. Nadal (ESP), 5–M.M. Safin (RUS), 6–T.H. Henman (GBR), 7–G.I. Canas (ARG)* , 8–N. Daveydenko (RUS), 9–S.R. Grosjean (FRA), 10–M. Ancic (CRO), 11–J. Johansson (SWE), 12–T. Johansson (SWE), 13–T. Robredo (ESP), 14–R. Stepanek (CZE), 15–G. Coria (ARG), 16–M. Puerta (ARG), 17–D. Ferrer (ESP), 18–D.P. Nalbandian (ARG), 19–T.M. Haas (GER), 20–I. Ljubicic (CRO), 21–F.F Gonzales (CHI), 22–D. Hrbaty (SVK), 23–J.C. Ferrero (ESP), 24–T.P. Dent (USA), 25–N. Kiefer (GER), 26–F. Lopez (ESP), 27–R. Gasquet (FRA), 28–J. Novak (CZE), 29–N.A. Massu (CHI), 30–R.B.C. Soderling (SWE), 31–M. Youzhny (RUS), 32–F. Volandri (ITA), 33–O.L.P.Rochus (BEL).

* The No. 7 seed withdrew. His position in the draw was filled by the highest ranked non-seeded player, – O.L.P. Rochus (BEL) , who became the No. 33 seed.

2006 (32)

1–R. Federer (SUI), 2–R. Nadal (ESP), 3–A.S. Roddick (USA), 4–D.P. Nalbandian (ARG), 5–I. Ljubicic (CRO), 6–L.G.Hewitt (AUS), 7–M. Ancic (CRO), 8–J.R.Blake (USA), 9–N.Davydenko (RUS), 10–F.F.Gonzalez (CHI), 11–T.Robredo (ESP), 12–T.Johansson (SWE), 13–T.Berdych (CZE), 14–R.Stepanek (CZE), 15–S.J.Grosjean (FRA), 16–G.Gaudio (ARG), 17–R.L.Ginepri (USA), 18–M.Baghdatis (CYP), 19–T.M.Haas (GER), 20–D.Hrbaty (SVK), 21–G.S.Monfils (FRA), 22–J.Nieminen (FIN), 23–D.Ferrer (ESP), 24–J.C.Ferrero (ESP), 25–A.K.Agassi (USA), 26–O.L.P.Rochus (BEL), 27–D.I.Tursunov (RUS), 28–F.Verdasco (ESP), 29–P.Srichhaphan (THA), 30–K.Vliegen (BEL), 31–N.A.Massu (CHI), 32–P-H.Mathieu (FRA)

Note: From the original list the No. 18 seed, N.Kiefer (GER), withdrew owing to injury. Seeds No. 19 to No. 29 were made seeds No. 18 to No. 28 and a new seed No. 29 seed added.

2007 (32)

1–R. Federer (SUI), 2–R. Nadal (ESP), 3–A.S. Roddick (USA), 4–N. Djokovic (SRB), 5–F.F. Gonzalez (CHI), 6–N. Davydenko (RUS), 7–T. Berdych (CZE), 8–A.B. Murray (GBR)*, 9–J.R. Blake (USA), 10–M. Baghdatis (CYP), 11–T. Robredo (ESP), 12–R. Gasquet (FRA), 13–T.M. Haas (GER), 14–M. Youzhny (RUS), 15–I. Ljubicic (CRO), 16–L.G. Hewitt (AUS), 17–D. Ferrer (ESP), 18–J. Nieminen (FIN), 19–J.L. Bjorkman (SWE), 20–J.C. Ferrero (ESP), 21–D.I. Tursonov (RUS), 22–G.I. Canas (ARG), 23–D.P. Nalbandian (ARG), 24–J.I. Chela (ARG), 25–C. Moya (ESP), 26–M.M. Safin (RUS), 27–P.E.H. Kohlschreiber (GER), 28–R.B.C. Soderling (SWE), 29–A. Calleri (ARG), 30–F. Volandii(ITA), 31–D. Hrbaty (SVK), 32–J. Monaco (ARG)

Note: From the original list the No. 18 seed, M.Ancic (CRO), withdrew owing to illness. Seeds No. 19 to No. 31 were made seeds No. 18 to No. 30. A new seed No. 31 was added and No. 32 seed remained. *The No. 8 seed withdrew owing to injury. His position in the draw was filled by Lucky Loser – K. Kim (USA).

2008 (32)

1–R. Federer (SUI), 2–R. Nadal (ESP), 3–N. Djokovic (SRB), 4–N. Davydenko (RUS), 5–D. Ferrer (ESP), 6–A.S. Roddick (USA), 7–D.P. Nalabandian (ARG), 8–R. Gasquet (FRA), 9–J.R. Blake (USA), 10–M. Baghdatis (CYP), 11–T. Berdych (CZE), 12–A.B. Murray (GBR), 13–S. Wawrinka (SUI), 14–P-H. Mathieu (FRA), 15–F.F. Gonzalez (CHI), 16–R. Stepanek (CZE), 17–M. Youzhny (RUS), 18–I. Karlovic (CRO), 19–N. Almagro (ESP), 20–L.G. Hewitt (AUS), 21–J.C. Ferrero (ESP), 22–F. Verdasco (ESP), 23–T. Robredo (ESP), 24–J. Nieminen (FIN), 25–D.I. Tursunov (RUS), 26–I. Ljubicic (CRO), 27–N. Kiefer (GER), 28–G. Simon (FRA), 29–A. Seppi (ITA), 30–G.S.Monfils (FRA)*, 31–F. Lopez (ESP), 32–M. Llodra (FRA)

*The No. 30 seed withdrew owing to injury. His position in the draw was filled by Lucky Loser – I. Bozoljac (SRB)

2009 (32)

1–R. Nadal (ESP)*, 2–R. Federer (SUI), 3–A.B. Murray (GBR), 4–N. Djokovic (SRB), 5–J.M. Del Potro (ARG), 6–A.S. Roddick (USA), 7–F. Verdasco (ESP), 8–G. Simon (FRA), 9–J-W. Tsonga (FRA), 10–F.F. Gonzalez (CHI), 11–M. Cilic (CRO), 12–N. Davydenko (RUS), 13–R.B.C. Soderling (SWE), 14–M.M. Safin (RUS), 15–T. Robredo (ESP), 16–D. Ferrer (ESP), 17–J.R. Blake (USA), 18–R. Schuettler (GER), 19–S. Wawrinka (SUI), 20– T. Berdych (CZE), 21–F. Lopez (ESP), 22–1. Karlovic (CRO), 23–R. Stepanek (CZE), 24–T.M. Haas (GER), 25–D.I. Tursunov (RUS), 26–J. Melzer (AUT), 27–P. Kohlschreiber (GER), 28–M. Fish (USA), 29–I. Andreev (RUS), 30–V. Troicki (SRB), 31–V. Hanescu (ROM), 32–A. Montanes (ESP), 33–N. Kiefer (GER)

Note: From the original list the No.14 seed, G.S. Monfils (FRA) withdrew owing to injury. Seeds No.15 to No.24 were made seeds No.14 to No.23. A new seed No.24 T.M. Haas (GER) was added. Seeds No.25 to 32 remained.

'Subsequently, the No.1 seed, R. Nadal (ESP) withdrew owing to injury. A new No.33 seed, N.Kiefer (GER) was added.

2010 (32)

1–R. Federer (SUI), 2–R. Nadal (ESP), 3–N. Djokovic (SRB), 4–A. B. Murray (GBR), 5– A.S. Roddick (USA), 6–R.B.C. Soderling (SWE), 7–N. Davydenko (RUS), 8–F. Verdasco (ESP), 9–D. Ferrer (ESP), 10–J-W. Tsonga (FRA), 11–M. Cilic (CRO), 12–T. Berdych (CZE), 13–M. Youzhny (RUS), 14–J.C. Ferrero (ESP), 15–L.G. Hewitt (AUS), 16–J. Melzer (AUT), 17–I. Ljubicic (CRO), 18–S. Querrey (USA), 19–N. Almagro (ESP), 20–S. Wawrinka (SUI), 21–G.S. Monfils (FRA), 22– F. Lopez (ESP), 23–J.Isner (USA), 24–M. Baghdatis (CYP), 25–T. Bellucci (BRA), 26–G. Simon (FRA), 27–E. Gulbis (LAT)*, 28–A. Montanes (ESP), 29–P. Kohlschreiber (GER), 30–T.Robredo (ESP), 31–V. Hanescu (ROM), 32–J. Benneteau (FRA), 33–P. Petzschner (GER) From the original list the No.22 seed, R. Stepanek (CZE) and No.25 seed I. Karlovic (CRO), withdrew owing to a knee and foot injury respectively. Seeds No.23 and No.24 were made seeds No.22 and No.23 and Nos. 26 to 32 were made seeds No.24 to No.30. New seeds No.31, V. Hanescu (ROM) and No.32, J. Benneteau (FRA) were added.

*The No.27 seed withdrew owing to a hamstring injury. His position in the draw was filled by the highest ranked non-seeded player, P. Petzschner (GER), who became the No.33 seed

2011 (32)

1–R. Nadal (ESP), 2–N. Djokovic (SRB), 3–R. Federer (SUI) 4–A.B. Murrary (GBR), 5– R. Soderling (SWE), 6–T. Berdych (CZE), 7–D. Ferrer (ESP), 8–A.S. Roddick (USA), 9–G. Monfils (FRA), 10–M. Fish (USA), 11–J. Melzer(AUT), 12–J-W. Tsonga (FRA), 13–V. Troicki (SRB), 14–S. Wawrinka (SUI), 15–G. Simon (FRA), 16–N. Almagro (ESP), 17–R. Gasquet (FRA), 18–M. Youzhny (RUS), 19–M. Llodra (FRA), 20–F. Mayer (GER), 21–F. Verdasco (ESP), 22–A. Dolgopolov (UKR), 23–J. Tipsarevic (SRB), 24–J.M. Del Potro (ARG), 25–J.I. Chela (ARG), 26–G. Garcia–Lopez (ESP), 27–M. Cilic (CRO), 28–D. Nalbandian (ARG), 29–N. Davydenko (RUS), 30–T. Bellucci (BRA),31–M. Raonic (CAN), 32–M. Baghdatis (CYP)

2012 (32)

1–N. Djokovic (SRB), 2–R. Federer (SUI), 3–R. Nadal (ESP), 4–A.B.Murray (GBR), 5–J-W. Tsonga (FRA), 6–T. Berdych (CZE), 7–D. Ferrer (ESP), 8–J. Tipsarevic (SRB), 9–J.M. Del Potro (ARG), 10–M. Fish (USA), 11–J. Isner (USA), 12–N. Almagro (ESP), 13–G. Simon (FRA), 14–F. Lopez (ESP), 15–J. Monaco (ARG), 16– M. Cilic (CRO), 17–F. Verdasco (ESP), 18–R. Gasquet (FRA), 19–K. Nishikori (JAP), 20–B. Tomic (AUS), 21–M. Raonic (CAN), 22–A. Dolgopolov (UKR), 23–A. Seppi (ITA), 24–M. Granollers (ESP), 25–S. Wawrinka (SUI), 26–M. Youzhny (RUS), 27–P.E.H. Kohlschreiber (GER), 28–R. Stepanek (CZE), 29–J. Benneteau (FRA), 30–A.S. Roddick (USA), 31–F. Mayer (GER), 32–K. Anderson (RSA)

2013 (32)

1–N. Djokovic (SRB), 2–A.B.Murray (GBR), 3–R. Federer (SUI), 4–D. Ferrer (ESP), 5–R. Nadal (ESP),), 6–J-W. Tsonga (FRA), 7–T. Berdych (CZE), 8–J.M. Del Potro (ARG), 9–R. Gasquet (FRA), 10–M.Cilic (CRO), 11–S. Wawrinka (SUI), 12–K. Nishikori (JAP), 13–T. Haas (GER) 14–J. Tipsarevic (SRB), 15–N. Almagro (ESP), 16–P.E.H. Kohlschreiber (GER), 17–M. Raonic (CAN), 18–J. lsner (USA), 19–G. Simon (FRA), 20–M. Youzhny (RUS), 21–S. Querry (USA) 22–J. Monaco (ARG) 23–A. Seppi (ITA), 24–J. Janowicz (POL), 25–B. Paire (FRA) 26–A. Dolgopolov (UKR) 27–K. Anderson (RSA) 28–J. Chardy (FRA) 29–G. Dimitrov (BUL) 30–F. Fognini (ITA), 31–J. Benneteau (FRA), 32–T. Robredo (ESP)

2014 (32)

2014 (32)

1–N. Djokovic (SRB), 2–R. Nadal (ESP), 3–A.B. Murray (GBR), 4–R. Federer (SUI), 5–S. Wawrinka (SUI), 6–T.Berdych (CZE), 7–D. Ferrer (ESP), 8–M. Raonic (CAN), 9–J. Isner (USA), 10–K. Nishikori (JPN), 11–G. Dimitrov (BUL), 12–E. Gulbis (LAT), 13–R. Gasquet (FRA), 14–J-W. Tsonga (FRA), 15–J. Janowicz (POL), 16–F. Fognini (ITA), 17–M. Youzhny (RUS), 18–F. Verdasco (ESP), 19–F. Lopez (ESP), 20–K. Anderson (RSA), 21–A. Dolgopolov (UKR), 22–P. Kohlschreiber (GER), 23– T. Robredo (ESP), 24–G. Monfils (FRA), 25–A. Seppi (ITA), 26–M. Cilic (CRO), 27–R. Bautista Agut (ESP), 28–G. Garcia-Lopez (ESP), 29–1. Karlovic (CRO), 30–M. Granollers (ESP), 31–V.Popisil (CAN), 32–D. Tursunov (RUS)

Note: From the original list the No.25 seed, N. Almagro (ESP) withdrew owing to injury. Seeds No.26 to No.31 were made seeds No.25 to 30. A new No.31 seed was added and No.32 seed remained.

Seeded players who reached the concluding rounds

Year	No. of Seeds	Fourth Round	Quarter-final	Semi-final	Final	Winner
1927	8	1-4, 7, 8	1-4, 7, 8	1-4	3,4	4
1928	8	1-3, 5-8	1-3, 5-7	1-3	1,2	2
1929	8	1-3, 6-8	1-3, 6, 7	1-3	1,2	1
1930	8	1-6	1-5	2-4	2	2
1931	8	1, 3-8	1, 3, 5-8	1, 3, 5, 7	3, 7	7
1932	8	2-8	2,6,8	2,6,8	2,6	2

Year	No. of Seeds	Fourth Round	Quarter-final	Semi-final	Final	Winner
1933	8	1-5, 7-8	1-3, 4, 7	1-3, 7	1, 2	2
1934	8	1-7	1, 2, 4-7	1, 2, 5, 7	1, 2	2
1935	8	1-4, 6-8	1-4, 6, 7	1-3	1, 2	1
1936	8	1-8	1-8	1, 2, 5, 7	1, 2	1
1937	8	1-5, 7, 8	1-5, 7, 8	1, 2, 4, 8	1, 2	1
1938	8	1-8	1, 2, 4, 5, 7	1, 2, 4, 5	1, 2	1
1939	8	1,2 4-6	1, 2, 4-6	2, 4-6	2, 6	2
1946	8	1-3, 5-8	1, 3, 5, 7, 8	3, 5	3, 5	5
1947	8	1-8	1, 3-8	1, 3, 4	1, 3	1
1948	8	1-4, 6-8	2-4, 6, 7	2, 3, 7	2, 7	7
1949	8	1-8	1, 3-8	1, 5-7	1, 6	1
1950	16	1-13	1-7, 12	1, 3, 5, 12	1, 5	5
1951	10	1, 3, 5-8, 10	1-3, 5-8, 10	5-8	6, 7	6
1952	12	1-8, 10, 12	1-8	1, 2, 6, 8	1, 2	1
1953	8	1-7	1-4, 6-7	2-4	2	2
1954	12	1-5, 7-12	1-5, 7, 8, 11	1, 3, 7, 11	3, 11	11
1955	8	1, 2, 4, 6-8	1, 2, 4, 6-8	1, 2, 7	1	1
1956	8	1, 2, 6, 8	1, 2, 6, 8	1, 2, 6, 8	1, 2	1
1957	8	1, 2, 4-8	1, 2, 4-8	1, 2, 4, 5	1, 2	1
1958	8	1-4, 6-8	1-4, 6-8	1, 3, 4, 6	1, 4	1
1959	8	1, 2, 4-6, 8	1, 2, 4-6, 8	1, 5, 8	1	1
1960	8	1-8	1-8	1, 3, 5, 7	1, 3	1
1961	8	1, 2, 4, 6-8	2, 4, 6-8	2, 7, 8	2, 8	2
1962	8	1-3, 6, 8	1, 3, 6, 8	1, 3	1	1
1963	8	1, 2, 4, 5, 7	1, 2, 4	2, 4	4	4
1964	8	1-4, 6, 7	1, 2, 4, 6	1, 2, 6	1, 6	1
1965	8	1, 2, 4, 6, 8	1, 2, 4, 8	1, 2, 4	1, 2	1
1966	8	1, 2, 4, 6, 7	1, 2, 4, 6, 7	4, 6, 7	4, 6	4
1967	8	2, 3, 5, 6	3, 6	3	3	3
1968	16	1, 2, 4, 5, 9-13, 15	1, 9, 10, 12, 13, 15	1, 13, 15	1, 15	1
1969	16	1-3, 5-12, 15, 16	1-3, 5-8	1, 2, 5, 6	1, 6	1
1970	16	1-5, 7-10, 14-16	2, 4, 5, 9, 10, 14, 16	2, 5, 14, 16	2, 5	2
1971	8	1-4, 6	1-4, 6	2-4	2, 4	2
1972	8	1-3, 5, 6, 8	1-3, 5, 8	1-3, 5	1, 2	1
1973	8	1-8	2-6, 8	2-4	2, 4	2
1974	12	1-4, 6, 7, 9-12	1, 3, 4, 6, 9, 10	3, 4, 9	3, 9	3
1975	16	1-4, 6, 8, 9, 11, 13, 16	1, 3, 4, 6, 8, 9, 11, 16	1, 6, 11, 16	1, 6	6
1976	16	1-4, 6-8, 12, 14, 16	2-4, 6-8	3, 4, 7, 8	3, 4	4
1977	16	1, 2, 6, 8, 9, 11-14	1, 2, 6, 8, 13	1, 2, 8	1, 2	2
1978	16	1-3, 5-9, 13, 14, 16	1-3, 5, 7-9	1-3	1, 2	1
1979	16	1-3, 5, 14,15	1, 3, 5, 15	1, 3, 5	1, 5	1
1980	16	1-7, 13	1-3, 5-7, 13	1-3	1, 2	1
1981	16	1-3, 12, 14, 16	1-3, 12	1-3	1, 2	2
1982	16	1-3, 5-7, 11, 12, 14-16	1-3, 5, 6, 11, 12	1, 2, 12	1, 2	2
1983	16	1-3, 12-14, 16	2, 3, 12, 16	2, 3, 12	2	2
1984	16	1-3, 5, 6, 11-16	1-3, 6, 13	1-3	1, 3	1
1985	16	1-3, 5, 8, 14, 16	1, 3, 5, 8	3, 5, 8	8	–
1986	16	1, 2, 4, 7, 10, 12, 13	1, 4, 7, 10	1, 4, 7	1, 4	4
1987	16	2-4, 7-9, 11, 14	2-4, 7, 9, 11	2, 4, 7, 11	2, 11	11
1988	16	1-7, 9, 10, 16	1-4, 6, 9, 10	1, 3, 6, 9	3, 6	3
1989	16	1-5, 8, 9, 13, 16	1-5, 8	1, 2, 3, 5	2, 3	3
1990	16	1-3, 7, 11, 13	1-3, 7	1-3	2, 3	3
1991	16	1, 2, 4-7, 14, 16	1, 2, 4-7	1, 2, 6	2, 6	6
1992	16	2-5, 8-10, 12, 14	2-5, 8, 9, 12	5, 8, 12	8, 12	12
1993	16	1-4, 6, 8, 9, 11, 13	1-4, 6, 8	1-4	1, 3	1
1994	16	1, 4, 6-10,12	1,4,6,7,10	1,4,6,7	1,4	1
1995	16	1-4, 6, 7, 14	1-4, 6	1-4	2, 3	2
1996	16	1, 4, 10, 13, 16, S	1, 4, 13, S	13, S	S	S
1997	16	1, 3, 4, 8, 9, 12, 14, 16	1, 8, 14	1	1	1

Year	No. of Seeds	Fourth Round	Quarter-final	Semi-final	Final	Winner
1998	16	1, 3, 6, 9, 12, 14	1, 3, 9, 12, 14	1, 9, 12, 14	1, 14	1
1999	16	1, 2, 4, 6–11, 13	1, 2, 4, 6-8, 11	1, 2, 4, 6	1, 4	1
2000	16	1, 2, 8–10, 12	1, 2, 10, 12	1, 2, 12	1, 12	1
2001	32	1-6, 10, 13, 15, 19, 23, 24	2-4, 6, 10, 15, 24	2, 3, 6	3	–
2002	32	1, 4, 18, 22, 23, 27, 28	1, 4, 18, 22, 23, 27, 28	1, 4, 27, 28	1, 28	1
2003	32	2-6, 8-10, 12, 13	4, 5, 8, 10, 13	4, 5, 13	4	4
2004	32	1, 2, 5, 7, 9, 12, 27, 30	1, 2, 5, 7, 10, 12	1, 2, 10	1, 2	1
2005	32	1-3, 9, 10, 12, 15, 18, 21, 23, 24, 26 27, 31	1-3, 9, 12, 18, 21, 26	1-3, 12	1, 2	1
2006	32	1, 2, 6, 7, 13, 14, 18, 22, 23, 27, 28	1, 2, 6, 7, 14, 18, 22	1, 2, 18	1, 2	1
2007	32	1-4, 6, 7, 10, 12-14, 16, 19, 20	1-4, 7, 10, 12, 20	1, 2, 4, 12	1, 2	1
2008	32	1, 2, 8, 10, 12, 13, 17, 20, 22, 31	1, 2, 12, 31	1, 2	1, 2	2
2009	32	2-4, 6-8, 12, 13, 19, 20, 22-24, 29	2-4, 6, 22, 24	2, 3, 6, 24	2, 6	2
2010	32	1-6, 9, 10, 12, 15, 16, 18, 32	1-4, 6, 10,12	2-4, 12	2, 12	2
2011	32	1-4, 6, 7, 10, 12, 17, 18, 19, 24	1-4, 10, 12	1, 2, 4, 12	1, 2	2
2012	32	1, 3, 4, 5, 7, 9, 10, 16, 18, 26, 27, 31	1, 3, 4, 5, 7, 26, 27, 31	1, 3, 4, 5	1, 4	1
2013	32	1, 2, 4, 7, 8, 13, 20 23, 24	1, 2, 4, 7, 8, 24	1, 2, 8, 24	1, 2	2
2014	32	1-5, 8, 10, 11, 14, 19 20, 23, 26	1, 3, 4, 5, 8, 11, 26	1, 4, 8, 11	1, 4	1

Note: S – seeded player not numbered.

Player Seeded Most Times

J.S., Connors (USA)　　　　17　　(1973–1989)

Player Seeded No. 1 Most Times

P. Sampras (USA)　　　　8　　(1993, 1994, 1996–2001)

Unseeded Semi-Finalists (52)

1928 C. Boussus (FRA)	M.F. Mulligan (AUS)	1978 T.S. Okker (NED)
1929 H.W. Austin (GBR)	1963 W.P. Bungert (GER)	1979 P. Dupre (USA)
1930 W.L. Allison (USA)	F.S. Stolle (AUS)	1980 B.E. Gottfried (USA)
1932 J. Satoh (JAP)	1964 W.P. Bungert (GER)	1981 R.J. Frawley (USA)
1935 J.D. Budge (USA)	1965 E.C. Drysdale (RSA)	1982 T.S. Mayotte (USA)
1946 T.P. Brown (USA)	1966 O.K. Davidson (AUS)	1983 C.J. Lewis (NZL)
J. Drobny (TCH)	1967 W.P. Bungert (GER)	1984 P.H . Cash (AUS)
1947 J.E. Patty (USA)	N. Pilic (YUG)	1985 B.F. Becker (GER)
1948 J. Asboth (HUN)	R. Taylor (GBR)	1986 S. Zivojinovic (YUG)
1953 K. Nielsen (DEN)	1968 C.E. Graebner (USA)	1990 G.S. Ivanisevic (YUG)
1955 K. Nielsen (DEN)	1971 T.W. Gorman (USA)	1991 D. Wheaton (USA)
1959 R.G. Laver (AUS)	1973 A. Mayer (USA)	1992 J.P. McEnroe (USA)
1961 M.J. Sangster (GBR)	1974 R.L. Stockton (USA)	1996 J.R. Stoltenberg (AUS)
1962 J.G. Fraser (AUS)	1977 J.P. McEnroe (USA)	M.O Washington (USA)

Unseeded Semi-Finalists (52) Cont.

1997 C.A. Pioline (FRA)   2001 G.S. Ivanisevic (CRO)   2008 M. Safin (RUS)
       M.D. Stich (GER)   2003 M.A. Philippoussis (AUS)   R. Schuettler (GER)
1997 T.A. Woodbridge (AUS) 2004 M. Ancic (CRO)
2000 V. Voltchkov (BLR)   2006 J.L. Bjorkman (SWE)

Unseeded Finalists (13)

1930 W.L. Allison (USA)   1963 F.S. Stolle (AUS)   1997 C.A. Pioline (FRA)
1953 K. Nielsen (DEN)   1967 W.P. Bungert (GER)   2001 G.S. Ivanisevic (CRO)
1955 K. Nielsen (DEN)   1983 C.J. Lewis (NZL)   2003 M.A. Philippoussis (AUS)
1959 R.G. Laver (AUS)   1985 B.F. Becker (GER)
1962 M.F. Mulligan (AUS)   1996 M.O. Washington (USA)

Unseeded Champions (2)

1985 B.F. Becker (GER)
2001 G.S. Ivanisevic (CRO)

Gentlemen's Doubles Championship

1927 (4)
1–J. Brugnon and H.J. Cochet (FRA), 2–J.R. Borotra and J.R. Lacoste (FRA), 3–F.T. Hunter and W.T. Tilden (USA), 4–J.H. Condon and L.B. Raymond (RSA).

1928 (4)
1–F.T. Hunter and W.T. Tilden (USA), 2–J. Brugnon and H.J. Cochet (FRA), 3–J.F. Hennessey and G.M. Lott (USA), 4–J.B. Hawkes and G.L. Patterson (AUS).

1929 (4)
1–J. Brugnon and H.J. Cochet (FRA), 2–J. Hennessey and G.M. Lott (USA), 3–F.T. Hunter and W.T. Tilden (USA), 4–I.G. Collins and J.C. Gregory (GBR).

1930 (4)
1–J.H. Doeg and G.M. Lott (USA), 2–W.L. Allison and J.W. Van Ryn (USA), 3–J. Brugnon and H.J. Cochet (FRA), 4–I.G. Collins and J.C. Gregory (GBR).

1931 (4)
1–G.M. Lott and J.W. Van Ryn (USA), 2–J. Brugnon and H.J. Cochet (FRA), 3–G.P. Hughes and F.J. Perry (GBR), 4–I.G. Collins and J.C. Gregory (GBR).

1932 (4)
1–W.L. Allison and J.W. Van Ryn (USA), 2–J.H. Crawford and H.C. Hopman (AUS), 3–G.P. Hughes and F.J. Perry (GBR), 4–J.R. Borotra and J. Brugnon (FRA).

1933 (4)
1–J.R. Borotra and J. Brugnon (FRA), 2–K. Gledhill and H.E. Vines (USA), 3–G.P. Hughes and F.J. Perry (GBR), 4–N.G. Farquharson and V.G. Kirby (RSA).

1934 (4)
1–J.R. Borotra and J. Brugnon (FRA), 2–G.M. Lott and L.R. Stoefen (USA), 3–G.P. Hughes and F.J. Perry (GBR), 4–J.H. Crawford and A.K. Quist (AUS).

1935 (4)
1–W.L. Allison and J.W. Van Ryn (USA), 2–J.H. Crawford and A.K. Quist (AUS), 3–J.R. Borotra and J. Brugnon (FRA), 4–J.D. Budge and C.G. Mako (USA).

1936 (4)
1–J.H. Crawford and A.K. Quist (AUS), 2–W.L. Allison and J.W. Van Ryn (USA), 3–J.D. Budge and C.G. Mako (USA), 4–G.P. Hughes and C.R.D. Tuckey (GBR).

1937 (4)
1–G.P. Hughes and C.R.D. Tuckey (GBR), 2–J.D. Budge and C.G. Mako (USA), 3–H.E.O. Henkel and G. von Cramm (GER), 4–J.H. Crawford and V.B. McGrath (AUS).

1938 (4)
1–J.D. Budge and C.G. Mako (USA), 2–L. Hecht and R. Menzel (TCH), 3–D. Mitic and F. Puncec (YUG), 4–H.E.O. Henkel and G.F. von Metaxa (GER).

1939 (4)
1–H.E.O. Henkel and G.F. von Metaxa (GER), 2–E.T. Cooke and R.L. Riggs (USA), 3–J.R. Borotra and J. Brugnon (FRA), 4–C.E. Hare and F.H.D. Wilde (GBR).

1946 (4)
1–G.E. Brown and D. R. Pails (AUS), 2–T.P. Brown and J.A. Kramer (USA), 3–D. Mitic and J. Pallada (YUG), 4–B.J.Y. Destremau and Y.F.M. Petra (FRA).

1947 (4)
1–R. Falkenburg and J.A. Kramer (USA), 2–J.E. Bromwich and D.R. Pails (AUS), 3–G.E. Brown and C.F. Long (AUS), 4–T.P. Brown and J.E. Patty (USA).

1948 (4)
1–R. Falkenburg and F.A. Parker (USA), 2–T.P. Brown and G.P. Mulloy (USA), 3–J.E. Bromwich and F.A. Sedgman (AUS), 4–A.J. Mottram (GBR) and E.W. Sturgess (RSA).

1949 (4)
1–G.P. Mulloy and F.R. Schroeder (USA), 2–J.E .Bromwich and F.A. Sedgman (AUS), 3–R.A. Gonzales and F.A. Parker (USA), 4–J. Drobny (TCH) and R. Falkenburg (USA).

1950 (4)
1–G.P. Mulloy and W.F. Talbert (USA), 2–J.E. Bromwich and A.K. Quist (AUS), 3–J. Drobny (EGY) and E.W. Sturgess (RSA), 4–G.E. Brown and O.W.T. Sidwell (AUS).

1951 (4)
1–K.B. McGregor and F.A. Sedgman (AUS), 2–G.P. Mulloy and R. Savitt (USA), 3–H. Flam and A.D. Larsen (USA), 4–J. Drobny (EGY) and E.W. Sturgess (RSA).

1952 (4)
1–K.B. McGregor and F.A. Sedgman (AUS), 2–G.P. Mulloy and R. Savitt (USA), 3–J. Drobny (EGY) and J.E. Patty (USA), 4–E.V. Seixas (USA) and E.W. Sturgess (RSA).

1953 (4)
1–L.A. Hoad and K.R. Rosewall (AUS), 2–G.P. Mulloy and E.V. Seixas (USA), 3–R.N. Hartwig and M.G. Rose (AUS), 4–J. Drobny (EGY) and J.E. Patty (USA).

1954 (4)
1–R.N. Hartwig and M.G. Rose (AUS), 2–E.V. Seixas and M.A. Trabert (USA), 3–L.A. Hoad and K.R. Rosewall (AUS), 4–G.P. Mulloy and J.E. Patty (USA).

1955 (4)
1–E.V. Seixas and M.A. Trabert (USA), 2–R.N. Hartwig and L.A. Hoad (AUS), 3–N.A. Fraser and K.R. Rosewall (AUS), 4–J.E. Patty and H.F. Richardson (USA).

1956 (4)
1–L.A. Hoad and K.R. Rosewall (AUS), 2–H.F. Richardson and E.V. Seixas (USA), 3–D.W. Candy (AUS) and R.M. Perry (USA), 4–L.A. Ayala (CHI) and S.V. Davidson (SWE).

1957 (4)
1–N.A. Fraser and L.A. Hoad (AUS), 2–H.F. Richardson and E.V. Seixas (USA), 3–M.J. Anderson and A.J. Cooper (AUS), 4–N. Pietrangeli and O. Sirola (ITA).

1958 (4)
1–A.J. Cooper and N.A. Fraser (AUS), 2–G.P. Mulloy and J.E. Patty (USA), 3–B.B. Mackay (USA) and M.G. Rose (AUS), 4–R.N. Howe (AUS) and A.A. Segal (RSA).

1959 (4)
1–R.S. Emerson and N.A. Fraser (AUS), 2–N. Pietrangeli and O. Sirola (ITA), 3–B.B. Mackay and A.R. Olmedo (USA), 4–R.G. Laver and R. Mark (AUS).

1960 (4)
1–R.S. Emerson and N.A. Fraser (AUS), 2–R.G. Laver and R. Mark (AUS), 3–J.L. Arilla and A. Gimeno (ESP), 4–N. Pietrangeli and O. Sirola (ITA).

1961 (4)
1–R.S. Emerson and N.A. Fraser (AUS), 2–R.G. Laver and R. Mark (AUS), 3–N. Pietrangeli and O. Sirola (ITA), 4–L.A. Ayala (CHI) and R. Krishnan (IND).

1962 (4)
1–R.S. Emerson and N.A. Fraser (AUS), 2–R.A.J. Hewitt and F.S. Stolle (AUS), 3–J.G. Fraser and R.G. Laver (AUS), 4–C.R. McKinley and R.D. Ralston (USA).

1963 (4)
1–R.A.J. Hewitt and F.S. Stolle (AUS), 2–R.S. Emerson (AUS) and M.M. Santana (ESP), 3–C.R. McKinley and R.D. Ralston (USA), 4–B. Jovanovic and N. Pilic (YUG).

1964 (4)
1–C.R. McKinley and R.D. Ralston (USA), 2–R.H. Osuna and A.R. Palafox (MEX), 3–R.A.J. Hewitt and F.S. Stolle (AUS), 4–R.S. Emerson and K.N. Fletcher (AUS).

1965 (4)
1–R.S. Emerson and F.S. Stolle (AUS), 2–J.D. Newcombe and A.D. Roche (AUS), 3–R.D. Ralston and H.F. Richardson (USA), 4–K.N. Fletcher and R.A.J. Hewitt (AUS).

1966 (4)
1–R.S. Emerson and F.S. Stolle (AUS), 2–J.D. Newcombe and A.D. Roche (AUS)*, 3–C.E. Graebner and M.C. Riessen (USA), 4–W.W. Bowrey and O.K. Davidson (AUS).
*The No. 2 seeds withdrew. Their position in the draw was filled by unseeded K.N. Fletcher and J.D. Newcombe (AUS).

1967 (4)
1–J.D. Newcombe and A.D. Roche (AUS), 2–R.A.J. Hewitt and F.D. McMillan (RSA), 3–W.W. Bowrey and O.K. Davidson (AUS), 4–R.S. Emerson and K.N. Fletcher (AUS).

1968 (8)
1–R.S. Emerson and R.G. Laver (AUS), 2–K.R. Rosewall and F.S. Stolle (AUS), 3–A. Gimeno (ESP) and R.A. Gonzales (USA), 4–J.D. Newcombe and A.D. Roche (AUS), 5–E.H. Buchholz and R.D. Ralston (USA), 6–R.A.J. Hewitt and F.D. McMillan (RSA), 7–T.S. Okker (NED) and M.C. Riessen (USA), 8–E.C. Drysdale (RSA) and R. Taylor (GBR).

1969 (8)
1–J.D. Newcombe and A.D. Roche (AUS), 2–R.S. Emerson and R.G. Laver (AUS), 3–K.R. Rosewall and F.S. Stolle (AUS), 4–R.C. Lutz and S.R. Smith (USA), 5–R.A.J. Hewitt and F.D. McMillan (RSA), 6–T.S. Okker (NED) and M.C. Riessen (USA), 7–E.C. Drysdale (RSA) and R. Taylor (GBR), 8–A.R. Ashe and C.M. Pasarell (USA).

1970 (8)
1–J.D. Newcombe and A.D. Roche (AUS), 2–T.S. Okker (NED) and M.C. Riessen (USA), 3–R.S. Emerson and R.G. Laver (AUS), 4–R.A.J. Hewitt and F.D. McMillan (RSA), 5–R.C. Lutz and S.R. Smith (USA), 6–K.R. Rosewall and F.S. Stolle (AUS), 7–E.C. Drysdale and R. Taylor (GBR), 8–W.W. Bowrey and O.K. Davidson (AUS).

1971 (4)
1–J.D. Newcombe and A.D. Roche (AUS), 2–K.R. Rosewall and F.S. Stolle (AUS), 3–R.A.J. Hewitt and F.D. McMillan (RSA), 4–I. Nastase and I. Tiriac (ROM).

1972 (4)
1–R.A.J. Hewitt and F.D. McMillan (RSA), 2–S.R. Smith and E.J. van Dillen (USA), 3–P. Barthes (FRA) and A. Gimeno (ESP), 4–J. Gisbert and M. Orantes (ESP).

1973 (4)
1–J.S. Connors (USA) and I. Nastase (ROM), 2–J.R. Cooper and N.A. Fraser (AUS), 3–R.R. Maud (RSA) and R. Taylor (GBR)*, 4–S. Likhachev and A. Metreveli (URS).
*The No. 3 seeds withdrew. Their position in the draw was filled by unseeded P.W. Curtis and R. Taylor (GBR).
NOTE: The original seedings before the Boycott were:–
1–R.C. Lutz and S.R. Smith (USA), 2–T.S. Okker (NED) and M.C. Riessen (USA), 3–E.C. Drysdale (RSA) and R. Taylor (GBR), 4–J.S. Connors (USA) and I. Nastase (ROM).

1974 (8)
1–J.S. Connors (USA) and I. Nastase (ROM), 2–R.A.J. Hewitt and F.D. McMillan (RSA), 3–R.C. Lutz and S.R. Smith (USA), 4–J.D. Newcombe and A.D. Roche (AUS), 5–A.R. Ashe and L.R. Tanner (USA), 6–O.K. Davidson and K.R. Rosewall (AUS), 7–E.C. Drysdale (RSA) and T.S. Okker (NED), 8–J.G. Alexander and P.C. Dent (AUS).

1975 (8)

1–B.E. Gottfried (USA) and R.C. Ramirez (MEX), 2–J.S. Connors (USA) and I. Nastase (ROM), 3–R.A.J. Hewitt and F.D. McMillan (RSA), 4–R.C. Lutz and S.R. Smith (USA), 5–J.G. Alexander and P.C. Dent (AUS), 6–M. Cox and R. Taylor (GBR), 7–T.S. Okker (NED) and M.C. Riessen (USA), 8–A.R. Ashe and E.J. van Dillen (USA).

1976 (8)

1–B.E. Gottfried (USA) and R.C. Ramirez (MEX), 2–J.S. Connors (USA) and I. Nastase (ROM), 3–R.A.J. Hewitt and F.D. McMillan (RSA), 4–T.S. Okker (NED) and M.C. Riessen (USA), 5–R.C. Lutz and S.R. Smith (USA), 6–V.K. Gerulaitis and A. Mayer (USA), 7–W.J. Fibak (POL) and K. Meiler (GER), 8–F.V. McNair and S.E. Stewart (USA).

1977 (8)

1–B.E. Gottfried (USA) and R.C. Ramirez (MEX), 2–R.A.J. Hewitt and F.D. McMillan (RSA), 3–R.C. Lutz and S.R. Smith (USA), 4–F.V. McNair and S.E. Stewart (USA), 5–W.J. Fibak (POL) and R.L. Stockton (USA), 6–M.C. Riessen and L.R. Tanner (USA), 7–R.L. Case and G. Masters (AUS), 8–C.M. Pasarell and E.J. van Dillen (USA).

1978 (16)

1–R.A.J. Hewitt and F.D. McMillan (RSA), 2–W.J. Fibak (POL) and T.S. Okker (NED), 3–R.C. Lutz and S.R. Smith (USA), 4–J.G. Alexander and P.C. Dent (AUS), 5–V.K. Gerulaitis and A. Mayer (USA), 6–R.L. Case and G. Masters (AUS), 7–F.V. McNair (USA) and R.C. Ramirez (MEX), 8–R.O. Ruffels and A.J. Stone (AUS), 9–M.C. Riessen and R.L. Stockton (USA), 10–J. Kodes and T. Smid (TCH)*, 11–S. Ball and K.G. Warwick (AUS), 12–C.S. Dowdeswell (SUI) and C.P. Kachel (AUS), 13–R.J. Moore (RSA) and L.R. Tanner (USA), 14–E. Mayer and H.E. Pfister (USA), 15–A. Fillol and J.J. Fillol (CHI), 16–J.D. Newcombe and A.D. Roche (AUS).

*The No. 10 seeds withdrew. Their position in the draw was filled by Lucky Losers – J.L. Durmiani (URU) and C. Motta (BRA).

1979 (16)

1–P.B. Fleming and J.P. McEnroe (USA), 2–W. Fibak (POL) and T.S. Okker (NED), 3–R.C. Lutz and S.R. Smith (USA), 4–R.A.J. Hewitt and F.D. McMillan (RSA), 5–M.C. Riessen and S.E. Stewart (USA), 6–A. Mayer and E. Mayer (USA), 7–B.E. Gottfried (USA) and R.C. Ramirez (MEX), 8–J. Kodes and T. Smid (TCH), 9–V. Pecci (PAR) and B. Taroczy (HUN), 10–M.R. Edmondson and J.M.P. Marks (AUS), 11–A.R. Ashe and R.L. Stockton (USA)*, 12–J.G. Alexander and P.C. Dent (AUS), 13–R.L. Case and G. Masters (AUS), 14–C.S. Dowdeswell and H.P. Guenthardt (SUI), 15–T.E. Gullikson and T.R. Gullikson (USA), 16–B.D. Manson and A.J. Pattison (USA).

*The No. 11 seeds withdrew. Their position in the draw was filled by Lucky Losers – V.L. Eke (AUS) and M.J. Farrell (GBR).

NOTE: The original seeding list before an error in the computer rankings was discovered was:–
1–P.B. Fleming and J.P. McEnroe (USA), 2–W.J. Fibak (POL) and T.S. Okker (NED), 3–A. Mayer and G. Mayer (USA), 4–R.C. Lutz and S.R. Smith (USA), 5–M.C. Riessen and S.E. Stewart (USA), 6–R.A.J. Hewitt and F.D. McMillan (RSA), 7–B.E. Gottfried (USA) and R.C. Ramirez (MEX), 8–J. Kodes and T. Smid (TCH), 9–R.J. Carmichael (AUS) and B.D. Teacher (USA), 10–R.L. Case and G. Masters (AUS), 11–J.G. Alexander and P.C. Dent (AUS), 12–B.D. Manson and A.J. Pattison (USA), 13–M.R. Edmondson and J.M.P. Marks (AUS), 14–V. Pecci (PAR) and B. Taroczy (HUN), 15–A.R. Ashe and R.L. Stockton (USA), 16–T.E. Gullikson and T.R. Gullikson (USA).

1980 (16)

1–P.B. Fleming and J.P. McEnroe (USA), 2–M.C. Riessen and S.E. Stewart (USA), 3–B.E. Gottfried (USA) and R.C. Ramirez (MEX), 4–R.C. Lutz and S.R. Smith (USA), 5–W.J. Fibak (POL) and T.S. Okker (NED), 6–H.P. Guenthardt (SUI) and F.D. McMillan (RSA), 7–P.M. McNamara and P.F. McNamee (AUS), 8–V.C. Amaya and H.E. Pfister (USA), 9–P. Slozil (TCH) and B. Taroczy (HUN)*, 10–A.J. Pattison and K.B. Walts (USA), 11–T.E. Gullikson and T.R. Gullikson (USA), 12–An Amritraj and V. Amritraj (IND), 13–J. Kodes and T. Smid (TCH)*, 14–C.J. Mottram (GBR) and I. Nastase (ROM), 15–J. Sadri and T.M. Wilkison (USA), 16–R.J. Frawley and G. Masters (AUS).

*The No. 9 and No. 13 seeds withdrew. Their positions in the draw were filled by Lucky Losers – C. Edwards and E. Edwards (USA) and C.M. Johnstone and G.J. Whitehouse (AUS), respectively.

1981 (16)

1–P.B. Fleming and J.P. McEnroe (USA), 2–P.B. McNamara and P.F. McNamee (AUS), 3–R.C. Lutz and S.R. Smith (USA), 4–A. Mayer and E. Mayer (USA)*, 5–H.P. Guenthardt (SUI) and B. Taroczy (HUN), 6–M.C. Riessen and S.E. Stewart (USA), 7–B.D. Manson and B.D. Teacher (USA), 8–B.E. Gottfried (USA) and R.C. Ramirez (MEX), 9–K.M. Curren (RSA) and S.B. Denton (USA), 10–V.C. Amaya and H.E. Pfister (USA)*, 11–T.E. Gullikson (USA) and B.M. Mitton (RSA), 12–F. Buehning and F. Taygan (USA), 13–P. Slozil and T. Smid (TCH), 14–A.J. Pattison and K.B. Walts (USA), 15–C. Edwards and E. Edwards (USA), 16–F.D. McMillan (RSA) and C.J. Mottram (GBR).

*The No. 4 and No. 10 seeds withdrew. Their positions in the draw were filled by Lucky Losers – R.M. Booth (GBR) and J. Windahl (SWE) and M.R.E. Appleton (GBR) and D.H. Collins (AUS), respectively.

1982 (16)

1–P.B. Fleming and J.P. McEnroe (USA), 2–S.E. Stewart and F. Taygan (USA), 3–P.B. McNamara and P.F. McNamee (AUS), 4–K.M. Curren (RSA) and S.B. Denton (USA), 5–H.P. Guenthardt (SUI) and B. Taroczy (HUN)*, 6–R.C. Lutz and S.R. Smith (USA), 7–M.R. Edmondson and K.G. Warwick (AUS), 8–P. Slozil and T. Smid (TCH), 9–V.C. Amaya and H.E. Pfister (USA), 10–A.P. Jarryd and H.K.I. Simonsson (SWE), 11–F. Buehning and P. Rennert (USA), 12–A. Mayer (USA) and F.D. McMillan (RSA), 12–B.D. Manson and B.D. Teacher (USA), 14–T.E. Gullikson and T. R. Gullikson (USA), 15–J.C. Kriek (RSA) and L. Stefanki (USA), 16–W. Fibak (POL) and J.B. Fitzgerald (AUS)*.

*The No. 5 and No. 16 seeds withdrew. Their positions in the draw were filled by Lucky Losers – J.J. Lapidus (USA) and P.D. Smylie (AUS) and M.T. Fancutt and T.C. Fancutt (AUS), respectively.

1983 (16)

1–P.B. Fleming and J.P. McEnroe (USA), 2–K.M. Curren (RSA) and S.B. Denton (USA), 3–B.E. Gottfried (USA) and P.F. McNamee (AUS), 4–M.R. Edmondson (AUS) and S.E. Stewart (USA), 5–P. Slozil and T. Smid (TCH)*, 6–A.P. Jarryd and H.K.I. Simonsson (SWE), 7–T.E. Gullikson and T.R. Gullikson (USA), 8–F. Buehning and B.D. Teacher (USA), 9–V.C. Amaya and H.E. Pfister (USA), 10–J.G. Alexander and J.B. Fitzgerald (AUS), 11–A. Mayer and F. Taygan (USA), 12–B. Dyke and R.J. Frawley (AUS), 13–A. Andrews and J. Sadri (USA), 14–L.B. Hooper and P. Rennert (USA), 15–T. Delatte (USA) and J.C. Kriek (RSA), 16–J. Gunnarson (SWE) and M. Leach (USA).

*The No. 5 seeds withdrew. Their position in the draw was filled by Qualifiers – R. Druz and T. Kruger (RSA).

1984 (16)

1–P.B. Fleming and J.P. McEnroe (USA), 2–M.R. Edmondson (AUS) and S.E. Stewart (USA), 3–T.E. Gullikson and T.R. Gullikson (USA), 4–K.M. Curren (RSA) and S.B. Denton (USA), 5–P.H. Cash and P.F. McNamee (AUS), 6–P. Slozil and T. Smid (TCH), 7–A. Mayer and F. Taygan (USA), 8–C.A. Kirmayr and C.V. Motta (BRA), 9–S.B. Edberg and A.P. Jarryd (SWE), 10–H.P. Guenthardt (SUI) and B. Taroczy (HUN), 11–B.M. Mitton (RSA) and K.B. Walts (USA), 12–J.G. Alexander and J.B. Fitzgerald (AUS), 13–A. Giammalva and S. Meister (USA), 14–B. Dyke and W. Masur (AUS), 15–C.S. Dowdeswell (GBR) and V. Winitsky (USA), 16–K.E. Flach and R.A. Seguso (USA).

1985 (16)

1–P.B. Fleming and J.P. McEnroe (USA), 2–P. Slozil and T. Smid (TCH), 3–K.E. Flach and R.A. Seguso (USA), 4–S.B. Edberg and A.P. Jarryd (SWE), 5–P.H. Cash and J.B. Fitzgerald (AUS), 6–M.R. Edmondson and K.G. Warwick (AUS), 7–K.J. Nystrom and M.A.O. Wilander (SWE), 8–H.P. Guenthardt (SUI) and B. Taroczy (HUN), 9–P.T. Annacone (USA) and C.J. Van Rensburg (RSA), 10–B. Dyke and W. Masur (AUS), 11–F. Gonzales (PAR) and M. Mitchell (USA), 12–H. Leconte and Y. Noah (FRA), 13–A.J. Giammalva and S. Giammalva (USA), 14–K.M. Curren and J.C. Kriek (USA), 15–S. Meister and E.T. Teltscher (USA), 16–P. Doohan and M.T. Fancutt (AUS).

1986 (16)

1–S.B. Edberg and A.P. Jarryd (SWE), 2–K.E. Flach and R.A. Seguso (USA), 3–J.B. Fitzgerald (AUS) and T. Smid (TCH), 4–H. Gildemeister (CHI) and A. Gomez (ECU), 5–S.E. Davis and

D.B. Pate (USA), 6–P.T. Annacone (USA) and C.J. Van Rensburg (RSA), 7–K.J. Nystrom and
M.A.O. Wilander (SWE), 8–H.P. Guenthardt (SUI) and B. Taroczy (HUN), 9–W.J. Fibak (POL)
and G. Forget (FRA), 10–S. Casal and E. Sanchez (ESP), 11–P.B. McNamara and P.F. McNamee
(AUS), 12–G.W. Donnelly and P.B. Fleming (USA), 13–M.R. Edmondson and K.G. Warwick
(AUS), 14–H. Leconte (FRA) and S.E. Stewart (USA), 15–P.H. Cash (AUS) and K.M. Curren
(USA), 16–J. Hlasek (SUI) and P. Slozil (TCH).

1987 (16)

1–G. Forget and Y. Noah (FRA), 2–P.T. Annacone (USA) and C.J. Van Rensburg (RSA), 3–A.
Gomez (ECU) and S. Zivojinovic (YUG), 4–S.B. Edberg and A.P. Jarryd (SWE), 5–K.J. Nystrom
and M.A.O. Wilander (SWE), 6–G.W. Donnelly and P.B. Fleming (USA), 7–K.E. Flach and
R.A. Seguso (USA), 8–S. Casal and E. Sanchez (ESP), 9–L.B. Hooper and M. Leach (USA), 10–
K.M. Curren and M. De Palmer (USA), 11–J.C. Steyn and D.T. Visser (RSA), 12–P. Doohan and
L. Warder (AUS), 13–S.E. Stewart (USA) and K.G. Warwick (AUS), 14–A.S. Kohlberg and
R.W.T. Van't Hof (USA), 15–S.E. Davis and D.B. Pate (USA), 16–J.B. Fitzgerald (AUS) and T.
Smid (TCH).

1988 (16)

1–K.E. Flach and R.A. Seguso (USA), 2–J.B. Fitzgerald (AUS) and A.P. Jarryd (SWE), 3–S. Casal
and E. Sanchez (ESP), 4–K.M. Curren and D.B. Pate (USA)*, 5–G. Forget (FRA) and T. Smid
(TCH), 6–R.D. Leach and J.R. Pugh (USA), 7–P.T. Annacone (USA) and C.J. Van Rensburg
(RSA), 8–K. Evernden (NZL) and J.C. Kriek (USA), 9–D.J. Cahill (AUS) and S. Zivojinovic
(YUG), 10–W. Masur and M.R. Woodforde (AUS), 11–M. Davis (USA) and B.D. Drewett
(AUS), 12–P. Aldrich and D.T. Visser (RSA), 13–K.J. Nystrom and M. Pernfors (SWE)*, 14–
A.S. Kohlberg and R.W.T. Van't Hof (USA), 15–B. Dyke (AUS) and T. Nijssen (NED), 16–M.J.
Bates (GBR) and P. Lundgren (SWE).
*The No. 4 and No. 13 seeds withdrew. Their positions in the draw were filled by Lucky Losers – B.H. Levine
(RSA) and P. Palandjian (USA) and G. Barbosa and M. Menezes (BRA), respectively.

1989 (16)

1–R.D. Leach and J.R. Pugh (USA), 2–K.E. Flach and R.A. Seguso (USA), 3–J.B. Fitzgerald
(AUS) and A.P. Jarryd (SWE), 4–J.F. Grabb and P.M. McEnroe (USA), 5–J. Hlasek (SUI) and J.P.
McEnroe (USA), 6–P.T. Annacone (USA) and C.J. Van Rensburg (RSA), 7–K.M. Curren and
D.B. Pate (USA), 8–J. Lozano (MEX) and T. Witsken (USA), 9–D.J. Cahill and M. Kratzmann
(AUS), 10–P. Aldrich and D.T. Visser (RSA), 11–S.E. Davis and T.M. Wilkison (USA), 12–P.
Doohan and L. Warder (AUS), 13–E. Jelen (GER) and M. Mortensen (DEN), 14–G.D. Connell
and G. Michibata (CAN), 15–J.S. Courier and P. Sampras (USA), 16–B.D. Drewett and W. Masur
(AUS).

1990 (16)

1–R.D. Leach and J.R. Pugh (USA), 2–P. Aldrich and D.T. Visser (RSA), 3–J.B. Fitzgerald
(AUS) and A.P. Jarryd (SWE), 4–S.E. Davis and D.B. Pate (USA), 5–P. Korda and T. Smid
(TCH), 6–G.D. Connell and G. Michibata (CAN), 7–G. Forget (FRA) and J. Hlasek (SUI), 8–
K.E. Flach and R.A. Seguso (USA), 9–D.J. Cahill and M. Kratzmann (AUS), 10–J.F. Grabb and
P.M. McEnroe (USA), 11–N.P. Broad (GBR) and G.R. Muller (RSA), 12–U. Riglewski and
M.D. Stich (GER), 13–G. Luza (ARG) and C.V. Motta (BRA), 14–M.J. Bates (GBR) and K.M.
Curren (USA), 15–G.W. Layendecker and R.A. Reneberg (USA), 16–P.J. Galbraith (USA) and D.
MacPherson (AUS).

1991 (16)

1–S.E. Davis and D.B. Pate (USA), 2–J.B. Fitzgerald (AUS) and A.P. Jarryd (SWE), 3–R.D. Leach
and J.R. Pugh (USA), 4–G.D. Connell and G. Michibata (CAN), 5–G.R. Muller and D.T. Visser
(RSA), 6–S. Casal and E. Sanchez (ESP)*, 7–P.J. Galbraith and T. Witsken (USA), 8–T.A.
Woodbridge and M.R. Woodforde (AUS), 9–U. Riglewski and M.D. Stich (GER), 10–L.B.
Jensen (USA) and L. Warder (AUS), 11–K.L. Jones (USA) and J. Lozano (MEX), 12–P.V.N.
Haarhuis and M. Koevermans (NED), 13–J.F. Grabb and P.M. McEnroe (USA), 14–N.P. Broad

(GBR) and K.M.Curren (USA), 15–W.R. Ferreira and P. Norval (RSA), 16–B. Dyke (AUS) and P. Lundgren (SWE).

From the original list the No. 8 seeds, G. Forget (FRA) and J. Hlasek (SUI) withdrew. Seeds Nos. 9 to 16 were made Nos. 8–15 and new No. 16 seeds added.

*The No. 6 seeds withdrew. Their position in the draw was filled by Lucky Losers – D. Adams (AUS) and G. Dzelde (URS).

1992 (16)

1–J.B. Fitzgerald (AUS) and A.P. Jarryd (SWE), 2–T.A. Woodbridge and M.R. Woodforde (AUS), 3–K.D. Jones and R.D. Leach (USA), 4–J.F. Grabb and R.A. Reneberg (USA), 5–S.E. Davis and D.B. Pate (USA), 6–G.D. Connell and G. Michibata (CAN), 7–T.C.J.M. Nijssen (NED) and C. Suk (TCH), 8–K.E. Flach and T. Witsken (USA), 9–M. Kratzmann and W. Masur (AUS), 10–W.R. Ferreira and P. Norval (RSA), 11–S. Devries (USA) and D.I. Macpherson (AUS), 12–L.B. Jensen (USA) and L. Warder (AUS), 13–G. Forget (FRA) and J. Hlasek (SUI), 14–J.A. Frana (ARG) and L. Lavalle (MEX), 15–K. Kinnear and S. Salumaa (USA), 16–O. Camporese (ITA) and G. Ivanisevic (CRO).

1993 (16)

1–T.A. Woodbridge and M.R. Woodforde (AUS), 2–J.B. Fitzgerald (AUS) and A.P. Jarryd (SWE), 3–P.M. McEnroe and J.A. Stark (USA), 4–M. Kratzmann and W. Masur (AUS), 5–G.D. Connell (CAN) and P.J. Galbraith (USA), 6–D.T. Visser (RSA) and L. Warder (USA), 7–J.F. Eltingh and M. Koevermans (NED), 8–S. Devries (USA) and D.I. Macpherson (AUS), 9–L.B. Jensen and M. Jensen (USA), 10–W.R. Ferreira (RSA) and M.D. Stich (GER), 11–S. Casal (ESP) and J. Hlasek (SUI), 12–K.E. Flach and R.D. Leach (USA), 13–S. Cannon and D.S. Melville (USA), 14–D.D. Adams (AUS) and A. Olhovskiy (RUS), 15–R.A. Reneberg and D. Wheaton (USA), 16–G. Michibata (CAN) and D.B. Pate (USA).

1994 (16)

1–B.H. Black (ZIM) and J.A. Stark (USA), 2–G.D. Connell (CAN) and P.J. Galbraith (USA), 3–J.F. Eltingh and P.V.N. Haarhuis (NED), 4–J. Apell and J.L. Bjorkman (SWE), 5–T.A. Woodbridge and M.R. Woodforde (AUS), 6–T.C.J.M. Nijssen (NED) and C. Suk (CZE), 7–D.D. Adams (AUS) and A. Olhovskiy (RUS), 8–H. Holm and A.P. Jarryd (SWE), 9–P.M. McEnroe and R.A. Reneberg (USA), 10–H.J. Davids (NED) and P. Norval (RSA), 11–R.D. Leach (USA) and D.T. Visser (RSA), 12–M. Damm and K. Novacek (CZE), 13–K.E. Flach (USA) and M.S. Knowles (BAH), 14–M-K.P. Goellner (GER) and Y.A. Kafelnikov (RUS), 15–B. Pearce and D. Randall (USA), 16–W.R. Ferreira (RSA) and M.D. Stich (GER).

1995 (16)

1–J.F. Eltingh and P.V.N. Haarhuis (NED), 2–T.A. Woodbridge and M.R. Woodforde (AUS), 3–G.D. Connell (CAN) and P.J. Galbraith (USA), 4–B.H. Black (ZIM) and J.A. Stark (USA), 5–J. Grabb and P.M. McEnroe (USA), 6–J.E. Palmer and R.A. Reneberg (USA), 7–J. Apell and J.L. Bjorkman (SWE), 8–C. Suk and D. Vacek (CZE), 9–T. Ho (USA) and B. Steven (NZL), 10–T. Kronemann (USA) and D.I. Macpherson (AUS), 11–M.S. Knowles (BAH) and D.M. Nestor (CAN), 12– A. Ohlovskiy (RUS) and J.M. Siemerink (NED), 13–W.A. O'Brien (USA) and S.F. Stolle (AUS), 14–M-K.P. Goellner (GER) and Y.A. Kafelnikov (RUS), 15–L.J. Bale and J-L De Jager (RSA), 16–P. Norval (RSA) and M. Oosting (NED).

1996 (16)

1–T.A. Woodbridge and M.R. Woodforde (AUS), 2–M.S. Knowles (BAH) and D.M. Nestor (CAN), 3–B.H. Black (ZIM) and G.D. Connell (CAN), 4–G Forget (FRA) and J. Hlasek (SUI), 5–P.J. Galbraith (USA) and A. Olhovskiy (RUS), 6–J.F. Eltingh and P.V.N. Haarhuis (NED), 7–S.D. Lareau (CAN) and W.A. O'Brien (USA), 8–E.R. Ferreira (RSA) and J.M. Siemerink (NED), 9–L. Pimek (BEL) and B.D. Talbot (RSA), 10–J.L. Bjorkman and L.J.N. Kulti (SWE), 11–M.A. Philippoussis and P.M. Rafter (AUS), 12–T. Carbonell and F. Roig (ESP), 13–M-K.P. Goellner (GER) and Y.A. Kafelnikov (RUS), 14–J.E. Palmer and J.A. Stark (USA), 15–J. Novak and D.Rikl (CZE), 16–H.J. Davids (NED) and C. Suk (CZE).

1997 (16)

1–T.A. Woodbridge and M.R. Woodforde (AUS), 2–J.F. Eltingh and P.V.N. Haarhuis (NED), 3–Y.A. Kafelnikov (RUS) and D. Vacek (CZE), 4–M.S. Knowles (BAH) and D.M. Nestor (CAN) 5– S.D. Lareau (CAN) and W.A. O'Brien (USA), 6–E.R. Ferreira (RSA) and P.J. Galbraith (USA), 7–M.A. Philippoussis and P.M. Rafter (AUS), 8–R.D. Leach and J.A. Stark (USA), 9–J.L. Bjorkman and L.J.N. Kulti (SWE), 10–S.F. Stolle (AUS) and C. Suk (CZE), 11–N.P. Broad (GBR) and P. Norval (RSA), 12–D.J. Johnson and F. Montana (USA), 13–M. Damn and P.Vizner (CZE), 14–L. Pimek (BEL) and B.D. Talbot (RSA), 15–G.D. Connell (CAN) and S.E. Davis (USA), 16–J.A. Eagle and A.P. Florent (AUS).

1998 (16)

1–J.F. Eltingh and P.V.N. Haarhuis (NED), 2–T.A. Woodbridge and M.R. Woodforde (AUS), 3– M.S. Bhupathi and L.A. Paes (IND), 4–E.R. Ferreira (RSA) and R.D. Leach (USA), 5– J.L. Bjorkman (SWE) and P.M. Rafter (AUS), 6–D.J. Johnson and F. Montana (USA), 7–Y.A. Kafelnikov (RUS) and D. Vacek (CZE), 8–M. Damm (CZE) and J.F. Grabb (USA), 9–P.J. Galbraith (USA) and B. Steven (NZL), 10–L.J.N. Kulti (SWE) and D.I. Macpherson (AUS), 11– M.S. Knowles (BAH) and D.M. Nestor (CAN), 12–W.H. Black (ZIM) and S.D. Lareau (CAN), 13–J.A. Eagle and A.P. Florent (AUS), 14–N.P. Broad (GBR) and P. Norval (RSA), 15–M-K.P. Goellner and D.J. Prinosil (GER), 16–S.F. Stolle (AUS) and C. Suk (CZE).

From the original list the No. 15 seeds, T. Carbonell (ESP) and L. Lobo (ARG) withdrew. Seeds No. 16 were made No. 15 and new No. 16 seeds added.

1999 (16)

1–M.S. Bhupathi and L.A. Paes (IND), 2–T.A. Woodbridge and M.R. Woodforde (AUS), 3–J.L. Bjorkman (SWE) and P.M. Rafter (AUS), 4–W.H. Black (ZIM) and S.F. Stolle (AUS), 5– O.N.H.. Delaitre and F.V. Santoro (FRA), 6–M.S. Knowles (BAH) and D.M. Nestor (CAN), 7–E. R. Ferreira (RSA) and R.D. Leach (USA), 8–P.V.N. Haarhuis (NED) and J.E. Palmer (USA), 9–S.D. Lareau (CAN) and W.A. O'Brien (USA), 10–D.D. Adams and J-L. De Jager (RSA), 11–M. Damm and C. Suk (CZE), 12–W.S. Arthurs and A.J. Kratzmann (AUS), 13–L.J.N. Kulti and M. Tillstrom (SWE), 14–D.J. Prinosil (GER) and D. Vacek (CZE), 15–P. Norval and K.R. Ullyett (RSA), 16–P.J. Galbraith and J.J. Gimelstob (USA).

2000 (16)

1–T.A. Woodbridge and M.R. Woodforde (AUS), 2–P.V.N. Haarhuis (NED) and S.F. Stolle (AUS), 3–W.A. O'Brien and J.E. Palmer (USA), 4–E.R. Ferreira (RSA) and R.D. Leach (USA), 5– J.L. Bjorkman (SWE) and B.H. Black (ZIM), 6–D.D. Adams and J-L. De Jager (RSA), 7–M. Damm (CZE) and W.R. Ferreira (RSA), 8–J. Novak and D. Rikl (CZE), 9–S.D. Lareau and D.M. Nestor (CAN), 10–M.S. Bhupathi (IND) and D.J. Prinosil (GER), 11–W.H. Black and K.R. Ullyett (ZIM), 12–L.J.N. Kulti and M. Tillstrom (SWE), 13–D.J. Johnson (USA) and P. Norval (RSA), 14–J.J. Gimelstob (USA) and M.S. Knowles (BAH), 15–J.A. Eagle and A.P. Florent (AUS), 16–T. Carbonell (ESP) and M.A. Garcia (ARG).

2001 (16)

1–J.L. Bjorkman (SWE) and T.A. Woodbridge (AUS), 2–D.M. Nestor (CAN) and S.F. Stolle (AUS), 3–J. Novak and D. Rikl (CZE), 4–D. J. Johnson and J.E. Palmer (USA), 5–E.R. Ferreira (RSA) and R.D. Leach (USA), 6–M.S. Bhupathi and L.A. Paes (IND), 7–P. Pala and P. Vizner (CZE), 8–J.A. Eagle and A.P. Florent (AUS), 9–M.R. Hill and J.G. Tarango (USA), 10–D.J. Prinosil (GER) and C. Suk (CZE), 11–M.S. Knowles (BAH) and B. MacPhie (USA), 12–W.H. Black and K.R. Ullyett (ZIM), 13–R. Federer (SUI) and W.R. Ferreira (RSA), 14–B.H. Black (ZIM) and W.A. O'Brien (USA), 15–M.C. Bryan and R.C. Bryan (USA), 16– S.M. Humphries and S.D. Lareau (CAN).

2002 (16)

1–D.J. Johnson and J.E. Palmer (USA), 2–M.S. Knowles (BAH) and D.M. Nestor (CAN), 3–M.S. Bhupathi (IND) and M.N. Mirnyi (BLR), 4–W.H. Black and K.R. Ullyett (ZIM), 5–J.L. Bjorkman (SWE) and T.A. Woodbridge (AUS), 6–M.C. Bryan and R.C. Bryan (USA), 7–M. Damm and C. Suk (CZE), 8–D.J. Prinosil (GER) and D. Rikl (CZE), 9–P.V.N. Haarhuis (NED) and Y.A. Kafelnikov (RUS), 10–J. Novak and R. Stepanek (CZE), 11–E.R. Ferreira (RSA) and

R.D. Leach (USA), 12–J.A. Eagle and S.F. Stolle (AUS), 13–M. Llodra and F.V. Santoro (FRA), 14–J.M. Boutter (FRA) and S. Schalken (NED), 15–B. MacPhie (USA) and N. Zimonjic (YUG), 16–L. Arnold and G. Etlis (ARG).

2003 (16)
1–M.S. Bhupathi (IND) and M.N. Mirnyi (BLR), 2–M.S. Knowles (BAH) and D.M. Nestor (CAN), 3–M.C. Bryan and R.C. Bryan (USA), 4–J.L. Bjorkman (SWE) and T.A. Woodbridge (AUS), 5–L.A. Paes (IND) and D. Rikl (CZE), 6–M. Llodra and F.V. Santoro (FRA), 7–W.S. Arthurs and P.J. Hanley (AUS), 8–M. Damm and C. Suk (CZE), 9–J.A. Eagle (AUS) and J.E. Palmer (USA), 10–W.H. Black and K.R. Ullyett (ZIM), 11–C.Haggard and R.Koenig (RSA), 12–F. Cermak and L. Friedl (CZE), 13–G. Etlis and M. Rodriguez (ARG), 14–P.V.N. Haarhuis (NED) and Y.A. Kafelnikov (RUS), 15–D.J. Johnson (USA) and N. Zimonjic (YUG), 16– T. Cibulec and P. Vizner (CZE).

2004 (16)
1–J.L. Bjorkman (SWE) and T.A. Woodridge (AUS), 2–M.C. Bryan and R.C. Bryan (USA) 3– M.S. Bhupathi (IND) and M.N. Mirnyi (BLR), 4–M. Llodra and F.Y. Santoro (FRA), 5–M.S. Knowles (BAH) and D.M. Nestor (CAN) 6– W.H. Black and K.R. Ullyett (ZIM), 7–W.S. Arthurs and P.J. Hanley (AUS), 8–M. Damm and C. Suk (CZE), 9–G. Etlis and M. Rodriguez (ARG), 10–J. Erlich and A. Ram (ISR), 11–L.A. Paes (IND) and D. Rikl (CZE), 12–J.E. Palmer (USA) and P. Vizner (CZE), 13–F. Cermak and L. Friedl (CZE), 14–X. Malisse and O.L.P. Rochus (BEL), 15–M. Hood and S. Prieto (ARG), 16–J. Knowle (AUT) and N. Zimonjic (SCG).

2005 (16)
1–J.L. Bjorkman (SWE) and M.N. Mirnyi (BLR), 2–M.C. Bryan and R.C. Bryan (USA) 3–M.S. Knowles (BAH) and M. Llodra (FRA), 4–W.H. Black and K.R. Ullyett (ZIM), 5–L.A. Paes (IND) and N. Zimonjic (SCG), 6–M.S. Bhupathi (IND) and T.A. Woodridge (AUS), 7–W.S. Arthurs and P.J. Hanley (AUS), 8–S.O.K Aspelin (SWE) and T. Perry (AUS), 9–F. Cermak and L. Friedl (CZE), 10–M. Damm (CZE) and M. Hood (ARG), 11–C. Suk and P. Vizner (CZE), 12–F.F. Gonzales and N.A. Massu (CHI), 13–J. Knowle and J. Melzer (AUT), 14–G.A. Etlis and M. Rodriguez (ARG), 15–J. Erlich and A. Ram (ISR), 16–Y. Allegro (SUI) and M. Kohlmann (GER).

2006 (16)
1–M.C. Bryan and R.C. Bryan (USA), 2–J.L. Bjorkman (SWE), and M.N. Mirnyi (BLR), 3–M.S. Knowles (BAH) and D.M. Nestor (CAN), 4–P.J. Hanley (AUS) and K.R. Ullyett (ZIM), 5–J. Erlich and A. Ram (ISR), 6–F.Y. Santoro (FRA) and N. Zimonjic (SCG), 7–M. Damm (CZE) and L.A. Paes (IND), 8–S.O.K. Aspelin (SWE) and T.S. Perry (AUS), 9–S.W.I. Huss (AUS) and W.A. Moodie (RSA), 10–M. Fyrstenburg and M. Matkowski (POL), 11–L. Dlouhy and P. Vizner (CZE), 12–F. Cermak and L. Friedl (CZE), 13–M.S. Bhupathi (IND) and A. Waske (GER), 14–W.H. Black (ZIM) and J.Coetzee (RSA), 15–M. Garcia and S. Prieto (ARG), 16–C. Haggard (RSA) and D. Hrbaty (SVK).

2007 (16)
1–M.C. Bryan and R.C. Bryan (USA), 2–J.L. Bjorkman (SWE), and M.N. Mirnyi (BLR), 3–M.S. Knowles (BAH) and D.M. Nestor (CAN), 4–F.Y. Santoro (FRA) and N. Zimonjic (SRB), 5–M. Damm (CZE) and L.A. Paes (IND), 6–P.J. Hanley (AUS) and K.R. Ullyett (ZIM), 7–J. Erlich and A. Ram (ISR), 8–S.O.K. Aspelin (SWE) and J. Knowle (AUT), 9–L. Dlouhy and P. Vizner (CZE), 10–A. Clement and M. Llodra (FRA), 11–M.S. Bhupathi (IND) and R. Stepanek (CZE), 12–A. Fisher (AUS) and T. Phillips (USA), 13–J. Levinsky and D. Skoch (CZE), 14–J. Coetzee (RSA) and R. Wassen (NED), 15–M. Garcia and S. Prieto (ARG), 16–M. Fyrstenberg and L. Kubot (POL).

2008 (16)
1–M.C. Bryan and R.C. Bryan (USA), 2–D.M. Nestor (CAN) and N. Zimonjic (SRB), 3–J. Erlich and A. Ram (ISR), 4–M.S. Bhupathi (IND) and M.S. Knowles (BAH), 5–S.O.K. Aspelin (SWE) and J. Knowle (AUT), 6–M. Damm and P. Vizner (CZE), 7–A. Clement and M. Llodra (FRA)*, 8–J.L. Bjorkman (SWE) and K.R. Ullyett (ZIM), 9–L. Dlouhy (CZE) and L.A. Paes (IND), 10– M. Fyrstenberg and M. Matkowski (POL), 11–J. Coetzee and W.A. Moodie (RSA), 12–M. Melo and A. Sa (BRA), 13–F. Cermak(CZE) and J. Kerr (AUS), 14–M.N. Mirnyi (BLR) and J. Murray (GBR), 15–C. Kas (GER) and R. Wassen (NED). 16–J. Benneteau and N.P.A. Mahut (FRA)

The No. 7 seeds withdrew. Their position in the draw was filled by Lucky Losers – H. Armando and J. Levine (USA)

2009 (16)

1–M.C. Bryan and R.C. Bryan (USA), 2–D.M. Nestor (CAN) and N. Zimonjic (SRB), 3–L. Dlouhy (CZE) and L.A. Paes (IND), 4–M.S. Bhupathi (IND) and M.S. Knowles (BAH), 5–B. Soares (BRA) and K.R. Ullyett (ZIM), 6–M. Fyrstenberg and M. Matkowski (POL), 7–M.N. Mirnyi (BLR) and A. Ram (ISR), 8–L. Kubot (POL) and 0. Marach (AUT), 9–W.A. Moodie (RSA) and D. Norman (BEL), 10–T. Parrott and F. Polasek (SVK), 11–M. Melo and A. Sa (BRA), 12–J. Coetzee (RSA) and J. Kerr (AUS), 13–F. Cermak (CZE) and M. Mertinak (SVK), 14–R. de Voest (RSA) and A. Fisher (AUS), 15–M. Damm (CZE) and R. Lindstedt (SWE), 16–S.W.I. Huss (AUS) and R. Hutchins (GBR)

2010 (16)

1–D.M. Nestor (CAN) and N. Zimonjic (SRB), 2–M.C. Bryan and R.C. Bryan (USA), 3–L. Dlouhy (CZE) and L.A. Paes (IND), 4–M.S. Bhupathi (IND) and M.N. Mirnyi (BLR), 5–L. Kubot (POL) and O. Marach (AUT), 6–M. Fyrstenberg and M. Matkowski (POL), 7–W.A. Moodie (RSA) and R. Norman (BEL), 8–J. Knowle (AUT) and A. Ram (ISR), 9–F. Cernak (CZE) and M. Mertinak (SVK), 10–S.O.K. Aspelin (SWE) and P.J. Hanley (AUS), 11–M. Granollers and T. Robredo (ESP), 12–J. Isner and S. Querrey (USA), 13–M. Fish (USA) and M.S. Knowles (BAH), 14–J. Benneteau and M. Llodra (FRA), 15–M. Melo and B. Soares (BRA), 16–R. Lindstedt (SWE) and H. Tecau (ROM)

2011 (16)

1–M.C. Bryan and R.C. Bryan (USA), 2–M.N. Mirnyi (BLR) and D.M. Nestor (CAN), 3–M.S. Bhupathi and L.A. Paes (IND), 4–R. Bopanna (IND) and A-U-H. Quereshi (PAK), 5–J. Metzer (AUT) and P. Petzschner (GER), 6–M. Llodra (FRA) and N.Zimonjic (SRB), 7–M. Fyrstenberg and M. Matkowski (POL), 8–R. Lindstedt (SWE) and M. Tecau (ROM), 9–E. Butorac (USA) and J-J. Rojer (AHO), 10–M.S. Knowles (BAH) and L. Kubot (POL), 11–W.A.I. Moodie (RSA) and D. Norman (BEL), 12–J.I. Chela and E. Schwank (ARG), 13–M. Melo and B. Soares (BRA), 14–M. Granollers and T. Robredo (ESP), 15–M. Lopez and D. Marrero (ESP), 16–D. Bracciaii (ITA) and F. Cernak (CZE)

2012 (16)

1–M.N. Mirnyi (BLR) and D.M. Nestor (CAN), 2–M.C. Bryan and R.C. Bryan (USA), 3–M. Fyrstenberg and M. Malkowski (POL), 4–L.A. Paes (IND) and R. Stepanek (CZE), 5–R. Lindstedt (SWE) and H. Tecau (ROM), 6–A. Peya (AUT) and N. Zimonjic (SRB), 7–M.S.Bhupathi and R. Bopanna (IND), 8–A.U.H. Qureshi (PAK), J-J. Rojer (NED), 9–M. Granollers and M. Lopez (ESP), 10–J. Melzer (AUT) and P. Petzschner (GER), 11–F. Cernak (CZE) and F. Polasek (SVK), 12–S. Gonzalez (MEX) and C. Kas (GER), 13–C. Fleming and R. Hutchins (GBR). 14–E. Butorac and J. Murray (GBR), 15–I. Dodig (CRO) and M. Melo (BRA), 16–A. Sa and B. Soares (BRA)

2013 (16)

1–M.C. Bryan and R.C. Bryan (USA), 2–M. Granollers and M. Lopez (ESP), 3–A. Peya (AUT) and B. Soares (BRA) 4– L.A. Paes (IND) and R. Stepanek (CZE) 5– A-U-H. Qureshi (PAK) and J-J. Rojer (NED), 6–R. Lindstedt (SWE) and D.M. Nestor (CAN), 7–M.N. Mirnyi (BLR) and H. Tecau (ROU), 8–M.S. Bhupathi (IND) and J. Knowle (AUT), 9–C. Fleming and J.F. Marray (GBR), 10–S. Gonzalez (MEX) and S. Lipsky (USA), 11–J. Benneteau (FRA) and N. Zimonjic (SRB), 12–1. Dodig (CRO) and M. Melo (BRA), 13–M. LLodra and N. Mahut (FRA), 14–R. Bopanna (IND) and E. Roger-Vasselin (FRA), 15–L. Kubot and M. Matkowski (POL), 16–T. Huey (PHI) and D. Inglot (GBR)

2014 (16)

1–M.C. Bryan and R.C. Bryan (USA), 2–A. Peya (AUT) and B. Soares (BRA), 3–D.M. Nestor (CAN) and N. Zimonjic (SRB), 4–J. Benneteau and E. Roger-Vasselin (FRA), 5–L. Paes (IND) and R. Stepanek (CZE), 6–M. Granollers and M. Lopez (ESP), 7–L. Kubot (POL) and R. Lindstedt (SWE), 8–R. Bopanna (IND) and A-U-H. Qureshi (PAK), 9–J. Knowle (AUT) and M. Melo (BRA), 10–T. Huey (PHI) and D. Inglot (GBR), 11–J-J. Rojer (NED) and H. Tecau (ROU), 12–M. Llodra and N.P.A. Mahut (FRA), 13–E. Butorac (USA) and R. Klaasen (RSA), 14–J. Murray (GBR) and J. Peers (AUS), 15–J. S. Cabal (COL) and M. Matkowski (POL), 16–P. Cuevas (URU) and D. Marrero (ESP)

Seeded players who reached the concluding rounds

Year	No. of Seeds	Semi-final	Final	Winner
1927	4	1, 3, 4	1, 3	3
1928	4	1-4	2, 4	2
1929	4	2-4	4	–
1930	4	1-4	1, 2	2
1931	4	1-3	1, 2	1
1932	4	1, 3, 4	3, 4	4
1933	4	1, 4	1	1
1934	4	1, 2	1, 2	2
1935	4	1-4	1, 2	2
1936	4	2, 4	4	4
1937	4	1-3	1, 2	2
1938	4	1, 4	1, 4	1
1939	4	2-4	2, 4	2
1946	4	1-3	1, 2	2
1947	4	1-3	1	1
1948	4	1-3	2, 3	3
1949	4	1, 3	1, 3	3
1950	4	2-4	2, 4	2
1951	4	1, 2, 4	1, 4	1
1952	4	1, 3, 4	1, 4	1
1953	4	1-3	1, 3	1
1954	4	1-4	1, 2	1
1955	4	1-3	2, 3	2
1956	4	1	1	1
1957	4	1, 4	1	–
1958	4	1, 3	1	–
1959	4	1, 2, 4	1, 4	1
1960	4	2	–	–
1961	4	1, 2	1	1
1962	4	1-3	2	2
1963	4	2	–	–
1964	4	2-4	3, 4	3
1965	4	2-4	2, 4	2
1966	4	3, 4	4	–
1967	4	2-4	2, 4	2
1968	8	1, 2, 4, 6	2, 4	4
1969	8	1, 2, 5, 6	1, 6	1
1970	8	1, 4, 6	1, 6	1
1971	4	–	–	–
1972	4	1, 2	1, 2	1
1973	4	1, 2	1, 2	1
1974	8	1, 3, 4, 7	3, 4	4
1975	8	–	–	–
1976	8	1, 5	1	1
1977	8	7	7	7
1978	16	1, 2, 4	1	1
1979	16	1, 4, 7	1, 7	1
1980	16	1, 4, 7	4, 7	7
1981	16	1-3	1, 3	1
1982	16	1-4	1, 3	3
1983	16	1, 2, 6, 7	1, 7	1

Year	No. of Seeds	Semi-final	Final	Winner
1984	16	1, 5, 7	1, 5	1
1985	16	1, 5, 8	5, 8	8
1986	16	6, 7, 12, 16	7, 12	7
1987	16	3, 4, 7, 8	7, 8	7
1988	16	1, 2	1, 2	1
1989	16	1-3	1, 3	3
1990	16	1, 2	1, 2	1
1991	16	1, 2, 4	2	2
1992	16	2, 4, 13	4	–
1993	16	1, 5	1,5	1
1994	16	2, 5, 14, 16	2, 5	5
1995	16	2, 11, 14	2	2
1996	16	1, 3, 8, 11	1, 3	1
1997	16	1, 2, 13	1, 2,	1
1998	16	1, 2, 5, 12	1, 2	1
1999	16	1, 5, 6, 8	1, 8	1
2000	16	1, 2, 6, 11	1, 2	1
2001	16	3, 4, 15	3, 4	4
2002	16	1, 2, 5, 6	2, 5	5
2003	16	1, 4, 5	1, 4	4
2004	16	1, 5, 7, 16	1, 16	1
2005	16	1, 2, 4	2	–
2006	16	1, 3, 6, 7	1, 6	1
2007	16	1, 4, 10	1, 10	10
2008	16	1, 2, 8, 9	2, 8	2
2009	16	1, 2, 9	1, 2	2
2010	16	7, 16	16	–
2011	16	1, 6, 8	1, 8	1
2012	16	2, 5, 10	5	–
2013	16	1, 4, 12, 14	1, 12	1
2014	16	1, 5, 12	1	–

Unseeded Champions (12)

1929	W.L. Allison and J.W. Van Ryn (USA)
1957	G.P. Mulloy and J.E. Patty (USA)
1958	S.V. Davidson and U.C.J. Schmidt (SWE)
1960	R.H. Osuna (MEX) and R.D. Ralston (USA)
1963	R.H. Osuna (MEX) and A. Palafox (MEX)
1966	K.N. Fletcher and J.D. Newcombe (AUS)
1971	R.S. Emerson and R.G. Laver (AUS)
1975	V.K. Gerulaitis and A. Mayer (USA)
1992	J.P. McEnroe (USA) and M.D. Stich (GER)
2005	S.W.I. Huss (AUS) and W.A. Moodie (RSA)
2010	J. Melzer (AUT) and P. Petzschner (GER)
2012	J.F. Marray (GBR) and F.L. Nielsen (DEN)
2014	V. Pospisil (CAN) and J.E. Sock (USA)

Ladies' Singles Championship

1927 (8)

1–Miss H.N. Wills (USA), Mrs. L.A. Godfree (GBR), 3–Miss K. Bouman (NED), 4–Miss E.M. de Alvarez (ESP), 5–Miss E.M. Ryan (USA), 6–Mrs. F.I. Mallory (USA), 7–Miss E.A.L. Heine (RSA), 8–Mrs. G.E. Peacock (RSA).

1928 (8)

1–Miss H.N. Wills (USA), 2–Miss E.M. de Alvarez (ESP), 3–Miss E.V. Bennett (GBR), 4–Miss E.M. Ryan (USA), 5–Miss K. Bouman (NED), 6–Mrs. M.R. Watson (GBR), 7–Miss C. Aussem (GER), 8–Miss H.H. Jacobs (USA).

1929 (8)

1–Miss H.N. Wills (USA), 2–Miss E.M. de Alvarez (ESP), 3–Miss B.M. Nuthall (GBR), 4–Miss E.V. Bennett (GBR), 5–Miss H.H. Jacobs (USA), 6–Miss E.A.L. Heine (RSA), 7–Mrs. R. Mathieu (FRA), 8–Miss C. Aussem (GER).

1930 (8)

1–Mrs. F.S. Moody (USA), 2–Mrs. M.R. Watson (GBR)*, 3–Miss H.H. Jacobs (USA), 4–Miss E.M. de Alvarez (ESP)*, 5–Mrs. R. Mathieu (FRA), 6–Miss C. Aussem (GER), 7–Miss P.E. Mudford (GBR), 8–Miss E.M. Ryan (USA).
*The No. 2 and No. 4 seeds both withdrew owing to illness. Their positions in the draw were not filled and opponents given walkover.

1931 (8)

1–Miss C. Aussem (GER), 2–Miss B.M. Nuthall (GBR), 3–Mrs. R. Mathieu (FRA), 4–Miss H. Krahwinkel (GER), 5–Miss E.M. de Alvarez (ESP), 6–Miss H.H. Jacobs (USA), 7–Miss P.E. Mudford (GBR), 8–Mrs. E.O.F. Whittingstall (GBR).

1932 (8)

1–Mrs. F.S. Moody (USA), 2–Mrs. R. Mathieu (ESP), 3–Miss H. Krahwinkel (GER), 4–Mrs. E.O.F. Whittingstall (GBR), 5–Miss H.H. Jacobs (USA), 6–Miss B.M. Nuthall (GBR), 7–Miss L. Payot (SUI), 8–Miss D.E. Round (GBR).

1933 (8)

1–Mrs. F.S. Moody (USA), 2–Miss D.E. Round (GBR), 3–Miss M.C. Scriven (GBR), 4–Mrs. R. Mathieu (FRA), 5–Miss H.H. Jacobs (USA), 6–Miss H. Krahwinkel (GER), 7–Miss J. Jedrzejowska (POL), 8–Miss L. Payot (SUI).

1934 (8)

1–Miss H.H. Jacobs (USA), 2–Miss D.E. Round (GBR), 3–Miss S.H. Palfrey (USA), 4–Mrs. S. Sperling (GER), 5–Miss M.C. Scriven (GBR), 6–Miss L. Payot (SUI), 7–Miss C. Aussem (GER), 8–Mrs. R. Mathieu (FRA).

1935 (8)

1–Miss D.E. Round (GBR), 2–Mrs. S. Sperling (GER), 3–Miss H.H. Jacobs (USA), 4–Mrs. F.S. Moody (USA), 5–Mrs. R. Mathieu (FRA), 6–Miss K.E. Stammers (GBR), 7–Miss M.C. Scriven (GBR), 8–Miss J.M. Hartigan (AUS).

1936 (8)

1–Miss D.E. Round (GBR), 2–Miss H.H. Jacobs (USA), 3–Mrs. M. Fabyan (USA), 4–Miss K.E. Stammers (GBR), 5–Mrs. S. Sperling (GER), 6–Mrs. R. Mathieu (FRA), 7–Miss J. Jedrzejowska (POL), 8–Miss A. M. Lizana (CHI).

1937 (8)

1–Miss H.H. Jacobs (USA), 2–Mrs. S. Sperling (GER), 3–Miss A. M. Lizana (CHI), 4–Miss J. Jedrzejowska (POL), 5–Miss A. Marble (USA), 6–Mrs. R. Mathieu (FRA), 7–Miss D.E. Round (GBR), 8–Miss K.E. Stammers (GBR).

1938 (8)
1–Mrs. F.S. Moody (USA), 2–Miss A. Marble (USA), 3–Miss J. Jedrzejowska (POL), 4–Mrs. S. Sperling (GER), 5–Mrs. R. Mathieu (FRA), 6–Miss K.E. Stammers (GBR), 7–Mrs. M. Fabyan (USA), 8–Miss M.C. Scriven (GBR).

1939 (8)
1–Miss A. Marble (USA), 2–Miss H.H. Jacobs (USA), 3–Mrs. S. Sperling (GER), 4–Mrs. R. Mathieu (FRA), 5–Miss J. Jedrzejowska (POL), 6–Miss K.E. Stammers (GBR), Miss R.M. Hardwick (GBR), 8–Mrs. M. Fabyan (USA).

1946 (8)
1–Mrs. P.M. Betz (USA), 2–Miss M.E. Osborne (USA), 3–Miss A.L. Brough (USA), 4–Mrs. M. Menzies (GBR), 5–Miss D.M. Bundy (USA), 6–Mrs. E.W.A. Bostock (GBR), 7–Miss D.J. Hart (USA), 8–Mrs. N. Laffargue (FRA).

1947 (8)
1–Mrs. M.E. Osborne (USA), 2–Miss A.L. Brough (USA), 3–Miss D.J. Hart (USA), 4–Mrs. R.B. Todd (USA), 5–Mrs. G.F. Bolton (AUS), 6–Mrs. M. Menzies (GBR), 7–Mrs. R.A. Summers (RSA), 8–Mrs. E.W.A. Bostock (GBR).

1948 (8)
1–Mrs. W. duPont (USA), 2–Miss A.L. Brough (USA), 3–Mrs. R.B. Todd (USA), 4–Miss D.J. Hart (USA), 5–Mrs. E.W.A. Bostock (GBR), 6–Mrs. R.A. Summers (RSA), 7–Mrs. P.H. Landry (FRA), 8–Miss S.J. Fry (USA).

1949 (8)
1–Miss A.L. Brough (USA), 2–Mrs. W. duPont (USA), 3–Mrs. R.B. Todd (USA), 4–Miss G.A. Moran (USA), 5–Miss S.J. Fry (USA), 6–Miss J.D. Quertier (GBR), 7–Mrs. N. Adamson (FRA), 8–Miss P.J. Curry (GBR).

1950 (8)
1–Miss A.L. Brough (USA), 2–Mrs. W. duPont (USA), 3–Miss D.J. Hart (USA), 4–Mrs. R.B. Todd (USA), 5–Miss S.J. Fry (USA), 6–Mrs. A.J.C. Harrison (GBR), 7–Miss G.A. Moran (USA), 8–Mrs. A. Bossi (ITA).

1951 (8)
1–Miss A.L. Brough (USA), 2–Mrs. W. duPont (USA), 3–Miss D.J. Hart (USA), 4–Miss S.J. Fry (USA), 5–Miss B.J. Baker (USA), 6–Mrs. R.B. Todd (USA)*, 7–Miss N.A. Chaffee (USA), 8–Mrs. J.J. Walker–Smith (GBR).
*The No. 6 seed withdrew. Her position in the draw was filled by Lucky Loser – Mrs. M.R. Couquerque (NED).

1952 (8)
1–Miss D.J. Hart (USA), 2–Miss M.C. Connolly (USA), 3–Miss S.J. Fry (USA), 4–Miss A.L. Brough (USA), 5–Mrs. R.B. Todd (USA), 6–Mrs. J.J. Walker–Smith (GBR), 7–Mrs. M.N. Long (AUS), 8–Mrs. I.F. Rinkel (GBR).

1953 (8)
1–Miss M.C. Connolly (USA), 2–Miss D.J. Hart (USA), 3–Miss S.J. Fry (USA), 4–Mrs. D.P. Knode (USA), 5–Miss F.A.M. Mortimer (GBR), 6–Miss H.M. Fletcher (GBR), 7–Mrs. P. Chatrier (GBR), 8–Mrs. N. Adamson (FRA).

1954 (8)
1–Miss M.C. Connolly (USA), 2–Miss D.J. Hart (USA), 3–Miss S.J. Fry (USA), 4–Miss A.L. Brough (USA), 5–Mrs. W. duPont (USA), 6–Miss F.A.M. Mortimer (GBR), 7–Miss H.M. Fletcher (GBR), 8–Mrs. E.C.S. Pratt (USA).

1955 (8)
1–Miss D.J. Hart (USA), 2–Miss A.L. Brough (USA), 3–Mrs. J.G. Fleitz (USA), 4–Miss F.A.M. Mortimer (GBR), 5–Mrs. D.P. Knode (USA), 6–Miss D.R. Hard (USA), 7–Miss B. Penrose (AUS), 8–Miss A. Buxton (GBR).

1956 (8)
1–Miss A.L. Brough (USA), 2–Mrs. J.G. Fleitz (USA), 3–Miss F.A.M. Mortimer (GBR), 4–Miss A. Gibson (USA), 5–Miss S.J. Fry (USA), 6–Miss A. Buxton (GBR), 7–Mrs. D.P. Knode (USA), 8–Miss S.J. Bloomer (GBR).

1957 (8)
1–Miss A. Gibson (USA), 2–Miss A.L. Brough (USA), 3–Miss S.J. Bloomer (GBR), 4–Mrs. D.P. Knode (USA), 5–Miss D.R. Hard (USA), 6–Mrs. M.N. Long (AUS), 7–Miss F.A.M. Mortimer (GBR), 8–Miss V. Puzejova (TCH).

1958 (8)
1–Miss A. Gibson (USA), 2–Miss C.C. Truman (GBR), 3–Mrs. D.P.Knode (USA), 4–Miss M.E.A. Bueno (BRA), 5–Miss S.J. Bloomer (GBR), 6–Mrs. S. Kormoczy (HUN), 7–Miss J.S. Hopps (USA), 8–Miss K.K. Fageros (USA).

1959 (8)
1–Miss C.C. Truman (GBR), 2–Miss F.A.M. Mortimer (GBR), 3–Mrs. J.G. Fleitz (USA), 4–Miss D.R. Hard (USA), 5–Miss S. Reynolds (RSA), 6–Miss M.E.A. Bueno (BRA), 7–Miss S.M. Moore (USA), 8–Miss A.S. Haydon (GBR).

1960 (8)
1–Miss M.E.A. Bueno (BRA), 2–Miss D.R. Hard (USA), 3–Miss C.C. Truman (GBR), 4–Miss A.S. Haydon (GBR), 5–Miss F.A.M. Mortimer (GBR), 6–Mrs. S. Kormoczy (HUN), 7–Miss J.P. Lehane (AUS)*, 8–Miss S. Reynolds (RSA).
*The No. 7 seed withdrew owing to injury. Her position in the draw was not filled and opponent given walkover.

1961 (8)
1–Miss S. Reynolds (RSA), 2–Miss M. Smith (AUS), 3–Miss A.S. Haydon (GBR), 4–Miss L.R. Turner (AUS), 5–Miss Y. Ramirez (MEX), 6–Miss C.C. Truman (GBR), 7–Miss F.A.M. Mortimer (GBR), 8–Miss K.J. Hantze (USA).

1962 (8)
1–Miss M. Smith (AUS), 2–Miss D.R. Hard (USA), 3–Miss M.E.A. Bueno (BRA), 4–Miss R. Schuurman (RSA), 5–Miss A.S. Haydon (GBR), 6–Miss F.A.M. Mortimer (GBR), 7–Miss L.R. Turner (AUS), 8–Mrs. J.R. Susman (USA).

1963 (8)
1–Miss M. Smith (AUS), 2–Miss L.R. Turner (AUS), 3–Mrs. P.F. Jones (GBR), 4–Miss D.R. Hard (USA), 5–Miss J.P. Lehane (AUS), 6–Mrs. C. Sukova (TCH), 7–Miss M.E.A. Bueno (BRA), 8–Miss R. Schuurman (RSA).

1964 (8)
1–Miss M. Smith (AUS), 2–Miss M.E.A. Bueno (BRA), 3–Miss B.J. Moffitt (USA), 4–Miss L.R. Turner (AUS), 5–Miss N.A. Richey (USA), 6–Mrs. P.F. Jones (GBR), 7–Miss J.P. Lehane (AUS), 8–Miss R.A. Ebbern (AUS).

1965 (8)
1–Miss M.E.A. Bueno (BRA), 2–Miss M. Smith (AUS), 3–Miss L.R. Turner (AUS), 4–Miss N.A. Richey (USA), 5–Miss B.J. Moffitt (USA), 6–Mrs. C.E. Graebner (USA), 7–Miss A.M. van Zyl (RSA)*, 8–Miss F.G. Durr (FRA).
*The No. 7 seed withdrew owing to a family bereavement. Her position in the draw was filled by Lucky Loser – Miss M. Boulle (FRA).

1966 (8)
1–Miss M. Smith (AUS), 2–Miss M.E.A. Bueno (BRA), 3–Mrs. P.F. Jones (GBR), 4–Mrs. L.W. King (USA), 5–Miss N.A. Richey (USA), 6–Miss A.M. van Zyl (RSA), 7–Miss F.G. Durr (FRA), 8–Miss N. Baylon (ARG).

1967 (8)
1–Mrs. L.W. King (USA), 2–Miss M.E.A. Bueno (BRA), 3–Mrs. P.F. Jones (GBR), 4–Miss F.G. Durr (FRA), 5–Miss N.A. Richey (USA), 6–Miss L.R. Turner (AUS), 7–Miss A.M. van Zyl (RSA), 8–Miss S.V. Wade (GBR).

1968 (8)
1–Mrs. L.W. King (USA), 2–Mrs. B.M. Court (AUS), 3–Miss N.A. Richey (USA), 4–Mrs. P.F. Jones (GBR), 5–Miss S.V. Wade (GBR), 6–Miss M.E.A. Bueno (BRA), 7–Miss J.A.M. Tegart (AUS), 8–Mrs. W.W. Bowrey (AUS).

1969 (8)
1–Mrs. B.M. Court (AUS), 2–Mrs. L.W. King (USA), 3–Miss S.V. Wade (GBR), 4–Mrs. P.F. Jones (GBR), 5–Miss N.A. Richey (USA), 6–Miss K.A. Melville (AUS), 7–Miss J.M. Heldman (USA), 8–Miss J.A.M. Tegart (AUS).

1970 (8)
1–Mrs. B.M. Court (AUS), 2–Mrs. L.W. King (USA), 3–Miss S.V. Wade (GBR), 4–Miss K.A. Melville (AUS), 5–Miss R. Casals (USA), 6–Miss J.M. Heldman (USA), 7–Miss K.M. Krantzcke (AUS), 8–Miss H. Niessen (GER).

1971 (8)
1–Mrs. B.M. Court (AUS), 2–Mrs. L.W. King (USA), 3–Miss E.F. Goolagong (AUS), 4–Miss R. Casals (USA), 5–Miss S.V. Wade (GBR), 6–Mrs. K.S. Gunter (USA), 7–Miss F.G. Durr (FRA), 8–Mrs. H. Masthoff (GER).

1972 (8)
1–Miss E.F. Goolagong (AUS), 2–Mrs. L.W. King (USA), 3–Mrs. K.S. Gunter (USA), 4–Miss C.M. Evert (USA), 5–Miss K.A. Melville (AUS), 6–Miss R. Casals (USA), 7–Miss S.V. Wade (GBR), 8–Miss F.G. Durr (FRA).

1973 (8)
1–Mrs. B.M. Court (AUS), 2–Mrs. L.W. King (USA), 3–Miss E.F. Goolagong (AUS), 4–Miss C.M. Evert (USA), 5–Miss R. Casals (USA), 6–Miss S.V. Wade (GBR), 7–Miss K.A. Melville (AUS), 8–Miss O.V. Morozova (URS).

1974 (8)
1–Mrs. L.W. King (USA), 2–Miss C.M. Evert (USA), 3–Miss E.F. Goolagong (AUS), 4–Miss R. Casals (USA), 5–Miss S.V. Wade (GBR), 6–Miss K.A. Melville (AUS), 7–Mrs. K.S. Gunter (USA)*, 8–Miss O.V. Morozova (URS).
*The No. 7 seed withdrew owing to injury. Her position in the draw was filled by Lucky Loser – Miss T. Zwaan (NED).

1975 (8)
1–Miss C.M. Evert (USA), 2–Miss M. Navratilova (TCH), 3–Mrs. L.W. King (USA), 4–Mrs. R.A. Cawley (AUS), 5–Mrs. B.M. Court (AUS), 6–Miss S.V. Wade (GBR), 7–Miss O.V. Morozova (URS), 8–Mrs. G.E. Reid (AUS).

1976 (8)
1–Miss C.M. Evert (USA), 2–Mrs. R.A. Cawley (AUS), 3–Miss S.V. Wade (GBR), 4–Miss M. Navratilova (TCH), 5–Miss O.V. Morozova (URS), 6–Miss R. Casals (USA), 7–Miss S.D. Barker (GBR), 8–Mrs. G.E. Reid (AUS).

1977 (12)
1–Miss C.M. Evert (USA), 2–Miss M. Navratilova (USA), 3–Miss S.V. Wade (GBR), 4–Miss S.D. Barker (GBR), 5–Mrs. L.W. King (USA), 6–Miss R. Casals (USA), 7–Miss B.F. Stove (NED), 8–Mrs. G.E. Reid (AUS), 9–Miss D.L. Fromholtz (AUS)*, 10–Miss M. Jausovec (YUG), 11–Miss F.G. Durr (Mrs. B.J. Browning) (FRA), 12–Miss K.A. May (USA).
*The No. 9 seed withdrew owing to illness. Her position in the draw was filled by Lucky Loser – Miss C.M. O'Neill (AUS).

1978 (16)
1–Miss C.M. Evert (USA), 2–Miss M. Navratilova (USA), 3–Mrs. R.A. Cawley (AUS), 4–Miss S.V. Wade (GBR), 5–Mrs. L.W. King (USA), 6–Miss B.F. Stove (NED), 7–Miss W.M. Turnbull (AUS), 8–Miss D.L. Fromholtz (AUS), 9–Miss T.A. Austin (USA), 10–Mrs. G.E. Reid (AUS), 11–Miss M. Kruger (RSA), 12–Miss M. Jausovec (YUG), 13–Miss V. Ruzici (ROM), 14–Miss S.D. Barker (GBR), 15–Miss R. Marsikova (TCH), 16–Miss M.A. Redondo (USA).

1979 (16)

1–Miss M. Navratilova (USA), 2–Mrs. J.M. Lloyd (USA), 3–Mrs. R.A. Cawley (AUS), 4–Miss T.A. Austin (USA), 5–Miss S.V. Wade (GBR), 6–Miss D.L. Fromholtz (AUS), 7–Mrs. L.W. King (USA), 8–Miss W.M. Turnbull (AUS), 9–Mrs. G.E. Reid (AUS), 10–Miss V. Ruzici (ROM), 11–Miss G.R. Stevens (RSA), 12–Miss S.D. Barker (GBR), 13–Miss R. Marsikova (TCH), 14–Miss K. Jordan (USA), 15–Miss B.F. Stove (NED), 16–Miss P.H. Shriver (USA).

1980 (16)

1–Miss M. Navratilova (USA), 2–Miss T.A. Austin (USA), 3–Mrs. J.M. Lloyd (USA), 4–Mrs. R.A. Cawley (AUS), 5–Mrs. L.W. King (USA), 6–Miss W.M. Turnbull (AUS), 7–Miss S.V. Wade (GBR), 8–Miss D.L. Fromholtz (AUS), 9–Miss H. Mandlikova (TCH), 10–Miss K. Jordan (USA), 11–Miss G.R. Stevens (RSA), 12–Miss V. Ruzici (ROM), 13–Miss S.D. Barker (GBR), 14–Miss A. Jaeger (USA), 15–Miss R. Marsikova (TCH), 16–Miss S. Hanika (GER).

1981 (16)

1–Mrs. J.M. Lloyd (USA), 2–Miss H. Mandlikova (TCH), 3–Miss T.A. Austin (USA), 4–Miss M. Navratilova (USA), 5–Miss A. Jaeger (USA), 6–Miss W.M. Turnbull (AUS), 7–Miss P.H. Shriver (USA), 8–Miss V. Ruzici (ROM), 9–Miss S. Hanika (GER), 10–Miss M. Jausovec (YUG), 11–Miss D.L. Fromholtz (AUS), 12–Miss K. Jordan (USA), 13–Miss B. Bunge (GER), 14–Miss B.C. Potter (USA), 15–Miss R. Marsikova (TCH), 16–Miss J.C. Russell (USA).

1982 (16)

1–Miss M. Navratilova (USA), 2–Mrs. J.M. Lloyd (USA), 3–Miss T.A. Austin (USA), 4–Miss A. Jaeger (USA), 5–Miss H. Mandlikova (TCH), 6–Miss W.M. Turnbull (AUS), 7–Miss P.H. Shriver (USA), 8–Miss M. Jausovec (YUG), 9–Miss S. Hanika (GER), 10–Miss B.C. Potter (USA), 11–Miss B. Bunge (GER), 12–Mrs. L.W. King (USA), 13–Miss A.E. Smith (USA), 14–Miss A.C. Leand (USA), 15–Miss V. Ruzici (ROM), 16–Mrs. R.A. Cawley (AUS).

1983 (16)

1–Miss M. Navratilova (USA), 2–Mrs. J.M. Lloyd (USA), 3–Miss A. Jaeger (USA), 4–Miss T.A. Austin (USA)*, 5–Miss P.H. Shriver (USA), 6–Miss B. Bunge (GER), 7–Miss W.M. Turnbull (AUS), 8–Miss H. Mandlikova (TCH), 9–Miss S. Hanika (GER), 10–Mrs. L.W. King (USA), 11–Miss B.C. Potter (USA), 12–Miss V. Ruzici (ROM), 13–Miss J.M. Durie (GBR), 14–Miss A. Temesvari (HUN), 15–Miss K.S. Rinaldi (USA), 16–Miss C.G. Kohde–Kilsch (GER).

*The No. 4 seed withdrew owing to injury. Her position in the draw was filled by Lucky Loser – Miss M. Schropp (GER).

1984 (16)

1–Miss M. Navratilova (USA), 2–Mrs. J.M. Lloyd (USA), 3–Miss H. Mandlikova (TCH), 4–Miss P.H. Shriver (USA), 5–Miss Z.L. Garrison (USA), 6–Miss K. Jordan (USA), 7–Miss M. Maleeva (BUL), 8–Miss E.K. Horvath (USA), 9–Miss W.M. Turnbull (AUS), 10–Miss J.M. Durie (GBR), 11–Miss L.J. Bonder (USA), 12–Miss C.G. Kohde–Kilsch (GER), 13–Miss B.C. Potter (USA), 14–Miss H. Sukova (TCH), 15–Miss A. Temesvari (HUN), 16–Miss C.K. Bassett (CAN).

1985 (16)

1–Mrs. J.M. Lloyd (USA) and Miss M. Navratilova (USA), 3–Miss H. Mandlikova (TCH), 4–Miss M. Maleeva (BUL), 5–Miss P.H. Shriver (USA), 6–Miss C.G. Kohde–Kilsch (GER), 7–Miss H. Sukova (TCH), 8–Miss Z.L. Garrison (USA), 9–Miss B.S. Gadusek (USA), 10–Miss K. Jordan (USA), 11–Miss S.M. Graf (GER), 12–Miss C. Lindqvist (SWE), 13–Miss C.K. Bassett (CAN), 14–Miss W.M. Turnbull (AUS), 15–Miss G.B. Sabatini (ARG), 15–Miss K.S. Rinaldi (USA).

1986 (16)

1–Miss M. Navratilova (USA), 2–Mrs. J.M. Lloyd (USA), 3–Miss H. Mandlikova (TCH), 4–Miss C.G. Kohde–Kilsch (GER), 5–Miss P.H. Shriver (USA), 6–Miss K. Rinaldi (USA), 7–Miss H. Sukova (TCH), 8–Miss M. Maleeva (BUL), 9–Miss Z.L. Garrison (USA), 10–Miss G.B. Sabatini (ARG), 11–Miss C.K. Bassett (CAN), 12–Miss S.C. Rehe (USA), 13–Miss B.C. Potter (USA)*, 14–Miss W.M. Turnbull (AUS), 15–Miss C. Lindqvist (SWE), 16–Miss K. Jordan (USA).

From the original list the No. 3 seed, Miss S.M. Graf (GER), withdrew owing to illness. Seeds No. 4 to 16 were made No. 3 to 15 and a new No. 16 was added. The No. 13 seed withdrew owing to injury. Her position in the draw was filled by Lucky Loser – Miss R. Reis (USA).

1987 (16)
1–Miss M. Navratilova (USA), 2–Miss S.M. Graf (GER), 3–Miss C.M. Evert (USA), 4–Miss H. Sukova (TCH), 5–Miss P.M. Shriver (USA), 6–Miss G.B. Sabatini (ARG), 7–Miss M. Maleeva (BUL), 8–Miss C.G. Kohde–Kilsch (GER), 9–Miss B. Bunge (GER), 10–Miss L.M. McNeil (USA), 11–Miss C. Lindquist (SWE), 12–Miss W.M. Turnbull (AUS), 13–Miss B.C. Potter (USA), 14–Miss K. Maleeva (BUL), 15–Miss R. Reggi (ITA), 16–Miss S. Hanika (GER).
Note: From the original list the No. 4 seed, Miss H. Mandlikova (TCH), withdrew owing to injury. Seeds No. 5 to 16 were made No. 4 to 15 and a new No. 16 added.

1988 (16)
1–Miss S.M. Graf (GER), 2–Miss M. Navratilova (USA), 3–Miss P.H. Shriver (USA), 4–Miss C.M. Evert (USA), 5–Miss G.B. Sabatini (ARG), 6–Miss H. Sukova (TCH), 7–Miss M. Maleeva (Mrs. F. Fragniere) (BUL), 8–Miss N.M. Zvereva (URS), 9–Miss H. Mandlikova (AUS), 10–Miss L.M. McNeil (USA), 11–Miss C.G. Kohde–Kilsch (GER)*, 12–Miss Z.L. Garrison (USA), 13–Miss L.I. Savchenko (URS), 14–Miss K. Maleeva (BUL), 15–Miss S. Hanika (GER), 16–Miss M.J. Fernandez (USA).
*The No. 11 seed withdrew owing to injury. Her position in the draw was filled by Lucky Loser – Miss S. Stafford (USA).

1989 (16)
1–Miss S.M. Graf (GER), 2–Miss M. Navratilova (USA), 3–Miss G.B. Sabatini (ARG), 4–Mrs. C.M. Evert (Mrs. A.R. Mill) (USA), 5–Miss Z.L. Garrison (USA), 6–Miss H. Sukova (TCH), 7–Miss A.I.M. Sanchez Vicario (ESP), 8–Miss P.H. Shriver (USA), 9–Miss N.M. Zvereva (URS), 10–Miss J. Novotna (TCH), 11–Miss M. Seles (YUG), 12–Miss M.J. Fernandez (USA), 13–Miss H. Kelesi (CAN), 14–Miss H. Mandlikova (AUS), 15–Miss L.M. McNeil (USA), 16–Miss S.P. Sloane (USA).

1990 (16)
1–Miss S.M. Graf (GER), 2–Miss M. Navratilova (USA), 3–Miss M. Seles (YUG), 4–Miss G.B. Sabatini (ARG), 5–Miss Z.L. Garrison (Mrs. W.L. Jackson) (USA), 6–Miss A.I.M. Sanchez Vicario (ESP), 7–Miss K. Maleeva (BUL), 8–Miss M. Maleeva (Mrs. F. Fragniere) (SUI), 9–Miss M.J. Fernandez (USA), 10–Miss H. Sukova (TCH), 11–Miss N.M. Zvereva (URS), 12–Miss J.M. Capriati (USA), 13–Miss J. Novotna (TCH), 14–Mrs. H.W. Wiesner (AUT), 15–Miss R.D. Fairbank (Mrs. R. Nideffer) (USA), 16–Miss B. Paulus (AUT).

1991 (16)
1–Miss S.M. Graf (GER), 2–Miss G.B. Sabatini (ARG), 3–Miss M. Navratilova (USA), 4–Miss A.I.M. Sanchez Vicario (ESP), 5–Miss M.J. Fernandez (USA), 6–Miss J. Novotna (TCH), 7–Miss Z.L. Garrison (Mrs. W.L. Jackson) (USA), 8–Miss K. Maleeva (BUL), 9–Miss J.M. Capriati (USA), 10–Miss H. Sukova (TCH), 11–Miss N. Tauziat (FRA), 12–Miss N.M. Zvereva (URS), 13–Miss A. Huber (GER), 14–Miss A. Frazier (USA), 15–Miss A.M. Cecchini (ITA), 16–Mrs. H.W. Wiesner (AUT).
Note: From the original seeding list the No. 1 seed Miss M. Seles (YUG) withdrew owing to injury. Seeds No. 2 to 16 were made No. 1 to 15 and a new No. 16 was added.

1992 (16)
1–Miss M. Seles (YUG), 2–Miss S.M. Graf (GER), 3–Miss G.B. Sabatini (ARG), 4–Miss M. Navratilova (USA), 5–Miss A.I.M. Sanchez Vicario (ESP), 6–Miss J.M. Capriati (USA), 7–Miss M.J. Fernandez (USA), 8–Miss I.C. Martinez (ESP), 9–Mrs. F. Maleeva–Fragniere (SUI), 10–Miss A. Huber (GER), 11–Miss J. Novotna (TCH), 12–Miss K. Maleeva (BUL), 13–Miss Z.L. Garrison (Mrs. W.L. Jackson) (USA), 14–Miss N. Tauziat (FRA), 15–Miss K. Date (JPN), 16–Mrs. H.W. Wiesner (AUT).

1993 (16)
1–Miss S.M. Graf (GER), 2–Miss M. Navratilova (USA), 3–Miss A.I.M. Sanchez Vicario (ESP), 4–Miss G.B. Sabatini, 5–Miss M.J. Fernandez (USA), 6–Miss I.C. Martinez (ESP), 7–Miss J.M. Capriati (USA), 8–Miss J. Novotna (CZE), 9–Miss A. Huber (GER), 10–Miss M. Maleeva (BUL), 11–Mrs. F. Maleeva-Fragniere (SUI), 12–Miss K. Maleeva (BUL), 13–Miss M.C. Pierce (FRA)*, 14–Miss A.J. Coetzer (RSA), 15–Miss H. Sukova (CZE), 16–Miss N. Tauziat (FRA).
*The No. 13 seed withdrew owing to illness. Her position in the draw was filled by Lucky Loser – Miss L. Field (AUS).

1994 (16)

1–Miss S.M. Graf (GER), 2–Miss A.I.M. Sanchez Vicario (ESP), 3–Miss I.C. Martinez (ESP), 4–Miss M. Navratilova (USA), 5–Miss J. Novotna (CZE), 6–Miss K. Date (JPN), 7–Miss M.C. Pierce (FRA)*, 8–Miss N.M. Zvereva (BLR), 9–Miss L.A. Davenport (USA), 10–Miss G.B. Sabatini (ARG), 11–Miss M.J. Fernandez (USA), 12–Miss A. Huber (GER), 13–Mrs. Z.L. Garrison–Jackson (USA), 14–Miss A.J. Coetzer (RSA), 15–Miss S. Hack (GER), 16–Miss M. Maleeva (BUL), 17–Miss H. Sukova (CZE).
* The No. 7 seed, withdrew, owing to personal reasons. Her position in the draw was filled by the highest ranked non-seeded player – Miss H. Sukova (CZE), who became the No. 17 seed.

1995 (16)

1–Miss S.M. Graf (GER), 2–Miss A.I.M. Sanchez Vicario (ESP), 3–Miss I.C. Martinez (ESP), 4–Miss J. Novotna (CZE), 5–Miss M.C. Pierce (FRA), 6–Miss K. Date (JPN), 7–Miss L.A. Davenport (USA), 8–Miss G.B. Sabatini (ARG), 9–Miss A. Huber (GER), 10–Miss N.M. Zvereva (BLR), 11–Miss I. Majoli (CRO), 12–Miss A. Frazier (USA), 13–Miss M.J. Fernandez (USA), 14–Miss N. Sawamatsu (JPN), 15–Mrs. S. Schultz-McCarthy (NED), 16–Miss. H. Sukova (CZE).

1996 (16)

1–Miss S.M. Graf (GER), 2–Miss M. Seles (USA), 3–Miss I.C. Martinez (ESP), 4–Miss A.I.M. Sanchez Vicario (ESP), 5–Miss A. Huber (GER), 6–Miss J. Novotna (CZE), 7–Miss C. Rubin (USA)*, 8–Miss L.A. Davenport (USA), 9–Miss M.J. Fernandez (USA), 10–Miss M. Maleeva (BUL), 11–Mrs. S. Schultz-McCarthy (NED), 12–Miss K. Date (JPN), 13–Miss M.C. Pierce (FRA), 14–Miss A.J. Coetzer (RSA), 15–Miss I. Spirlea (ROM) 16–Miss M. Hingis (SUI), 17–Miss K. Habsudova (SVK).
*The No. 7 seed withdrew owing to injury. Her position in the draw was filled by the highest ranked non-seeded player – Miss K. Habsudova (SVK), who became the No. 17 seed.

1997 (16)

1–Miss M. Hingis (SUI), 2–Miss M. Seles (USA), 3–Miss J. Novotna (CZE), 4–Miss I. Majoli (CRO), 5–Miss L.A. Davenport (USA), 6–Miss A.J. Coetzer (RSA), 7–Miss A. Huber (GER), 8–Miss A.I.M. Sanchez Vicario (ESP), 9–Miss M.C. Pierce (FRA), 10–Miss I.C. Martinez (ESP), 11–Miss M.J. Fernandez (USA), 12–Miss I. Spirlea (ROM), 13–Miss K.Y. Po (USA), 14–Mrs. S. Schultz-McCarthy (NED), 15–Miss R. Dragomir (ROM), 16–Miss B. Paulus (AUT).

1998 (16)

1–Miss M. Hingis (SUI), 2–Miss L.A. Davenport (USA), 3–Miss J. Novotna (CZE), 4–Miss S.M. Graf (GER), 5–Miss A.I.M. Sanchez Vicario (ESP), 6–Miss M. Seles (USA), 7–Miss V.E.S. Williams (USA), 8–Miss I.C. Martinez (ESP), 9–Miss A.J. Coetzer (RSA), 10–Miss I. Spirlea (ROM), 11–Miss M.C. Pierce (FRA), 12–Miss A.S. Kournikova (RUS)*, 13–Miss P. Schnyder (SUI), 14–Miss S. Testud (Mrs. V. Magnelli) (FRA), 15– Mrs. B. Van Roost (BEL), 16–Miss N. Tauziat (FRA).
* The No. 12 seed withdrew owing to injury. Her position in the draw was filled by Lucky Loser – Miss L. Osterloh (USA).

1999 (16)

1–Miss M. Hingis (SUI), 2–Miss S.M. Graf (GER), 3–Miss L.A. Davenport (USA), 4–Miss M. Seles (USA), 5–Miss J. Novotna (CZE), 6–Miss V.E.S. Williams (USA), 7–Miss A.I.M. Sanchez Vicario (ESP), 8–Miss N. Tauziat (FRA), 9–Miss M.C. Pierce (FRA), 10–Miss S.J. Williams (USA)*, 11–Mrs. A. Halard-Decugis (FRA), 12–Miss A.J. Coetzer (RSA), 13–Miss S. Testud (Mrs. V. Magnelli), (FRA), 14–Miss B. Schett (AUT), 15–Mrs. B. Van Roost (BEL), 16–Miss N.M. Zvereva (BLR), 17–Miss A.S. Kournikova (RUS).
*The No. 10 seed withdrew owing to illness. Her position in the draw was filled by the highest ranked non-seeded player – Miss A.S. Kournikova (RUS), who became the No. 17 seed.

2000 (16)

1–Miss M. Hingis (SUI), 2–Miss L.A. Davenport (USA), 3–Miss M.C. Pierce (FRA), 4–Miss I.C. Martinez (ESP), 5–Miss V.E.S. Williams (USA), 6–Miss M. Seles (USA), 7–Miss N. Tauziat (FRA), 8–Miss S.J. Williams (USA), 9–Miss A.I.M. Sanchez Vicario (ESP), 10–Miss S. Testud (Mrs. V. Magnelli) (FRA), 11–Miss A. Huber (GER), 12–Miss A.J. Coetzer (RSA), 13–Miss. A. Mauresmo (FRA), 14–Mrs. A. Halard-Decugis (FRA), 15–Miss B. Schett (AUT, 16–Mrs. B. Van Roost (BEL).

2001 (32)

1–Miss M. Hingis (SUI), 2–Miss V.E.S. Williams (USA), 3–Miss L.A. Davenport (USA), 4–Miss J.M. Capriati (USA), 5–Miss S.J. Williams (USA), 6–Miss A. Mauresmo (FRA), 7–Miss K. Clijsters (BEL), 8–Miss J. Henin (BEL), 9–Miss N. Tauziat (FRA), 10–Miss E. Dementieva (RUS), 11–Miss A.J. Coetzer (RSA), 12–Miss M. Maleeva (BUL), 13–Miss A.I.M. Sanchez Vicario (Mrs. J. Vehils) (ESP), 14–Miss J. Dokic (YUG), 15–Miss S. Testud (Mrs. V. Magnelli) (FRA), 16–Mrs. F. Farina-Elia (ITA), 17–Miss M. Shaughnessy (USA), 18– Miss A. Huber (GER), 19–Miss I.C. Martinez (ESP), 20–Miss A. Frazier (USA), 21–Miss B. Schett (AUT), 22–Miss P.L. Suarez (ARG), 23–Miss M.L. Serna (ESP), 24–Miss H. Nagyova (SUK), 25–Miss C.R. Rubin (USA), 26–Miss A. Kremer (LUX), 27–Miss A. Montolio (ESP), 28–Miss L.M. Raymond (USA), 29–Miss E. Likhovtseva (Mrs. M. Baranov) (RUS), 30–Miss P. Schnyder (SUI), 31–Miss T. Tanasugarn (THA), 32–Miss T. Panova (RUS).

2002 (32)

1–Miss V.E.S. Williams (USA), 2–Miss S.J. Williams (USA), 3–Miss J.M. Capriati (USA), 4–Miss M.Seles (USA), 5–Miss K. Clijsters (BEL), 6–Miss J. Henin (BEL), 7–Miss J. Dokic (YUG), 8– Miss S. Testud (Mrs. V. Magnelli) (FRA), 9–Miss A. Mauresmo (FRA), 10–Mrs. F. Farina-Elia (ITA), 11–Miss D. Hantuchova (SVK), 12–Miss E. Dementieva (RUS), 13–Miss M. Shaughnessy (USA), 14–Miss I. Tulyaganova (UZB), 15–Miss A. Smashnova (ISR), 16–Miss L.M. Raymond (USA), 17–Miss P. Schnyder (SUI), 18–Miss A. Myskina (RUS), 19–Miss M. Maleeva (BUL), 20–Miss T. Tanasugarn (THA), 21–Miss T. Panova (RUS), 22–Miss A. Kremer (LUX), 23–Miss I. Majoli (CRO), 24–Miss A.W. Stevenson (USA), 25–Miss N. Dechy (FRA), 26–Miss D. Bedanova (CZE), 27–Miss A. Sugiyama (JAP), 28–Miss P.L. Suarez (ARG), 29–Miss B. Schett (AUT), 30–Miss C. Fernandez (ARG), 31–Miss N. Pratt (AUS), 32–Miss A.J. Coetzer (RSA).

2003 (32)

1–Miss S.J. Williams (USA), 2–Miss K. Clijsters (BEL), 3–Mrs P.Y. Henin-Hardenne (BEL), 4–Miss V.E.S. Williams (USA), 5–Miss L.A. Davenport, (Mrs J. Leach) (USA),) 6–Miss A. Mauresmo (FRA)*, 7–Miss C.R. Rubin (USA), 8–Miss J.M. Capriati (USA), 9–Miss D. Hantuchova (SVK), 10–Miss A. Myskina (RUS), 11–Miss J. Dokic (YUG), 12–Miss M. Maleeva (BUL),   13–Miss A. Sugiyama (JAP), 14–Miss E. Danilidou (GRE), 15–Miss E. Dementieva (RUS), 16–Miss V. Zvonareva (RUS), 17–Miss A.J. Coetzer (RSA), 18–Miss I.C. Martinez (ESP), 19–Miss M. Shaughnessy (USA), 20–Miss P. Schnyder (SUI), 21–Miss E. Bovina (RUS), 22–Miss N. Dechy (FRA), 23–Miss L.M. Raymond (USA), 24–Miss M.L. Serna (ESP), 25–Mrs C. Pistolesi (ISR), 26–Miss A.W. Stevenson (USA), 27–Mrs F. Farina Elia (ITA), 28–Miss L. Granville (USA). 29–Miss N. Petrova (RUS). 30-Miss D. Chladkova (CZE), 31–Miss E. Likhovtseva (Mrs M. Baranov) (RUS), 32–Miss T. Tanasugarn (INA), 33–Miss S. Kuznetsova (RUS).

*The No. 6 seed withdrew owing to injury. Her position in the draw was filled by the highest ranked non-seeded player – Miss S. Kuznetsova (RUS), who became the No. 33 seed.

2004 (32)

1–Miss S.J. Williams (USA), 2–Miss A. Myskina (RUS), 3–Miss V.E.S. Williams (USA), 4–Miss A. Mauresmo (FRA), 5–Miss L.A. Davenport (Mrs. J. Leach) (USA),6–Miss E. Dementieva (RUS), 7–Miss J.M. Capriati (USA), 8–Miss S. Kuznetsova (RUS), 9–Miss P.L. Suarez (ARG), 10–Miss N. Petrova (RUS), 11–Miss A. Sugiyama (JPN), 12–Miss V. Zvonareva (RUS), 13–Miss M. Sharapova (RUS), 14–Mrs. F. Farina Elia (ITA), 15–Miss P. Schnyder (Mrs. R. Hofmann) (SUI), 16–Mrs. C. Smashnova-Pistolesi (ISR), 17–Miss C.R. Rubin (USA), 18–Miss F. Schiavone (ITA), 19–Miss F. Zuluaga (COL), 20–Miss E.Bovina (RUS), 21–Miss M. Maleeva (BUL), 22–Miss I.C. Martinez (ESP), 23–Miss J. Dokic (SCG), 24–Miss M.C. Pierce (FRA), 25–Miss N. Dechy (FRA), 26–Miss L.M. Raymond (USA), 27– Miss A. Molik (AUS), 28–Miss E. Loit (FRA), 29–Miss D. Safina (RUS), 30–Miss E. Daniilidou (GRE), 31–Miss A. Frazier (USA), 32–Miss M. Shaughnessy (USA).

2005 (32)

1–Miss L.A. Davenport (Mrs. J. Leach) (USA), 2–Miss M. Sharapova (RUS), 3–Miss A. Mauresmo (FRA), 4–Miss S.J. Williams (USA), 5–Miss S. Kuznetsova (RUS), 6–Miss E. Dementieva (RUS) 7–Mrs P.Y. Henin-Hardenne (BEL), 8–Miss N. Petrova (RUS), 9–Miss A. Myskina (RUS), 10–Miss P. Schnyder (Mrs R. Hoffman) (SUI), 11–Miss V. Zvonareva (RUS), 12–Miss M.C. Pierce (FRA), 13–Miss E. Likhovtseva (Mrs M. Baranov) (RUS), 14–Miss V.E.S. Williams (USA), 15–Miss K. Clijsters (BEL), 16–Miss N. Dechy (Mrs A. Maitre-Devallon) (FRA), 17–Miss J. Jankovic (SCG), 18–Miss T. Golovin (FRA), 19–Miss A. Ivanovic (SCG), 20–Miss D. Hantuchova (SVK), 21–Miss F. Schiavone (ITA), 22–Mrs. F. Farina Elia (ITA), 23– Miss A. Sugiyama (JPN), 24–Miss S. Asagoe (JPN), 25–Miss K. Sprem (CRO), 26–Miss F. Pennetta (ITA), 27–Miss N.Vaidisova (CZE), 28–Miss A. Frazier (USA), 29–Miss M. Bartoli (FRA), 30–Miss D. Safina (RUS), 31–Miss A-I. Medina Garrigues (ESP), 32–Miss V. Razzano (FRA).

2006 (32)

1–Miss A. Mauresmo (FRA), 2–Miss K. Clijsters (NED), 3–Mrs P.Y. Henin-Hardenne (BEL), 4– Miss M. Sharapova (RUS), 5–Miss S. Kuznetsova (RUS), 6–Miss V.E.S. Williams (USA), 7–Miss E. Dementieva (RUS), 8–Miss P. Schnyder (Mrs R. Hoffman) (SUI), 9–Miss A. Myskina (RUS), 10–Miss N. Vaidisova (CZE), 11–Miss F. Schiavone (ITA) 12–Miss M. Hingis (SUI), 13–Miss A.L. Groenefeld (GER), 14–Miss D. Safina (RUS), 15–Miss D. Hantuchova (SVK), 16–Miss F. Pennetta (ITA), 17–Miss M. Kirilenko (RUS), 18–Miss A. Sugiyama (JPN), 19–Miss A. Ivanovic (SCG), 20–Miss S. Peer (ISR), 21–Miss K. Srebotnik (SLO), 22–Miss N. Dechy (Mrs A. Maitre-Devallon) (FRA), 23–Miss A-I. Medina Garrigues (ESP), 24–Miss M.S. Bartoli (FRA), 25–Miss E. Likhovtseva (Mrs M. Baranov) (RUS), 26–Miss J. Jankovic (SCG), 27–Miss N. Li (CHN), 28–Miss S. Arvidsson (SWE), 29–Miss T. Golvin (FRA), 30–Miss A.Chakvetadze (RUS), 31–Miss G. Dulko (ARG), 32–Miss M. Santangelo (ITA).

Note: From the original list the No. 5 seed, Miss N.Petrova (RUS), withdrew owing to injury. Seeds No. 6 to No. 32 were made seeds No. 5 to No. 31 and a new seed No. 32 seed added.

2007 (32)

1–Miss J. Henin (BEL), 2–Miss M. Sharapova (RUS), 3–Miss J. Jankovic (SCG), 4–Miss A. Mauresmo (FRA), 5–Miss S. Kuznetsova (RUS), 6–Miss A. Ivanovic (SCG), 7–Miss S.J. Williams (USA), 8–Miss A. Chakvetadze (RUS), 9–Miss M. Hingis (SUI), 10–Miss D. Hantuchova (SVK), 11–Miss N. Petrova (RUS), 12–Miss E. Dementieva (RUS), 13–Miss D. Safina (RUS), 14–Miss N. Vaidisova (CZE), 15–Miss P. Schnyder (SUI), 16–Miss S. Peer (ISR), 17–Miss T. Golovin (FRA), 18–Miss M.S. Bartoli (FRA), 19–Miss K. Srebotnik (SLO), 20–Miss S. Bammer (AUT), 21–Miss T. Garbin (ITA), 22–Miss A-L. Medina Garrigues (ESP), 23–Miss V.E.S. Williams (USA), 24–Miss A. Bondarenko (UKR), 25–Miss L. Safarova (CZE), 26–Miss A. Sugiyama (JPN), 27–Miss S.J. Stosur (AUS), 28–Miss M. Santangelo (ITA), 29–Miss F. Schiavone (ITA), 30–Miss O. Poutchkova (BLR), 31–Miss M. Krajicek (NED), 32–Miss M. Muller (GER).

Note: From the original list the No. 18 seed, Miss N.Li (CHN), withdrew owing to a rib injury. Seeds No. 19 to No. 32 were made seeds No. 18 to No. 31 and a new seed No. 32 seed added.

2008 (32)

1–Miss A. Ivanovic (SRB), 2–Miss J. Jankovic (SRB), 3–Miss M. Sharapova (RUS), 4–Miss S. Kuznetsova (RUS), 5–Miss E. Dementieva (RUS), 6–Miss S.J. Williams (USA), 7–Miss V.E.S. Williams (USA), 8–Miss A. Chakvetadze (RUS), 9–Miss D. Safina (RUS), 10–Miss D. Hantuchova (SVK), 11–Miss M.S. Bartoli (FRA), 12–Miss P. Schnyder (SUI), 13–Miss V. Zvonareva (RUS), 14–Miss A. Radwanska (POL), 15–Miss A. Szavay (HUN), 16–Miss V. Azarenka (BLR), 17–Miss A. Cornet (FRA), 18–Miss N. Vaidisova (CZE), 19–Miss M. Kirilenko (RUS), 20–Miss F. Schiavone (ITA), 21–Miss N. Petrova (RUS), 22–Miss F. Pennetta (ITA), 23–Miss K. Srebotnik (SLO), 24–Miss S. Peer (ISR), 25–Miss L.A. Davenport (USA), 26–Miss S. Bammer (AUT), 27–Miss V. Razzano (FRA), 28–Miss A. Bondarenko (UKR), 29– Miss A. Mauresmo (FRA), 30–Miss D. Cibulkova (SVK), 31–Miss C. Wozniacki (DEN), 32– Miss S. Mirza (IND)

2009 (32)

1–Miss D. Safina (RUS), 2–Miss S.J. Williams (USA), 3–Miss V.E.S. Williams (USA), 4–Miss E. Dementieva (RUS), 5–Miss S. Kuznetsova (RUS), 6–Miss J. Jankovic (SRB), 7–Miss V. Zvonareva (RUS), 8–Miss V. Azarenka (BLR), 9–Miss C. Wozniacki (DEN), 10–Miss N. Petrova (RUS), 11–Miss A. Radwanska (POL), 12–Miss M.S. Bartoli (FRA), 13–Miss A. Ivanovic (SRB), 14–Miss D. Cibulkova (SVK), 15–Miss F. Pennetta (ITA), 16– Miss J. Zheng (CHN), 17–Miss A. Mauresmo (FRA), 18–Miss S.J. Stosur (AUS), 19–Miss N. Li (CHN), 20–Miss A.I. Medina Garrigues (ESP), 21–Miss P. Schnyder (Mrs R. Hoffman)(SUI), 22–Miss A. Cornet (FRA), 23–Miss A. Wozniak (CAN), 24–Miss M. Sharapova (RUS), 25–Miss K. Kanepi (EST), 26–Miss V. Razzano (ITA), 27–Miss A. Kleybanova (RUS), 28–Miss S.M. Cirstea (ROM), 29–Miss S. Bammer (AUT), 30–Miss A. Szavay (HUN), 31–Miss A. Pavlyuchenkova (RUS), 32–Miss A. Chakvetadze (RUS)

2010 (32)

1–Miss S.J. Williams (USA), 2–Miss V.E.S. Williams (USA), 3–Miss C. Wozniacki(DEN), 4–Miss J. Jankovic (SRB), 5–Miss F. Schiavone (ITA), 6–Miss S.J. Stosur (AUS), 7–Miss A. Radwanska (POL), 8–Miss K. Clijsters (BEL), 9–Miss N. Li (CHN), 10–Miss F. Pennetta (ITA), 11–Miss M.S. Bartoli (FRA), 12–Miss N. Petrova (RUS), 13–Miss S. Peer (ISR), 14–Miss V. Azarenka (BLR), 15–Miss Y. Wickmayer (BEL), 16–Miss M. Sharapova (RUS), 17–Miss J. Henin (BEL), 18–Miss A. Rezai (FRA), 19–Miss S. Kuznetsova (RUS), 20–Miss D. Safina (RUS)*, 21–Miss V. Zvonareva (RUS), 22–Miss M.J. Martinez Sanchez (ESP)*, 23–Miss J. Zheng (CHN), 24–Miss D. Hantuchova (SVK), 25–Miss L. Safarova (CZE), 26–Miss A. Kleybanova (RUS), 27–Miss M. Kirilenko (RUS), 28–Miss A. Bondarenko (UKR), 29–Miss A. Pavlyuchenkova (RUS), 30–Miss Y. Shvedova (KAZ), 31–Miss A. Dulgheru (ROM), 32–Miss S. Errani (ITA), 33–Miss M. Oudin (USA), 34–Miss K. Bondarenko (UKR)

*The No.22 and No.24 seeds withdrew owing to a back injury and knee injury, respectively. Their positions in the draw were filled by the highest ranked non-seeded players – Miss M. Oudin (USA) and Miss K. Bondarenko (UKR), who became the No.33 and No.34 seeds, respectively

2011 (32)

1–Miss C. Wozniacki (DEN), 2–Miss V. Zvonereva (RUS), 3–Miss N. Li (CHN), 4– Miss V. Azarenka (BLR), 5–Miss M. Sharapova (RUS), 6–Miss F. Schiavone (ITA), 7– Miss S.J. Williams (USA), 8–Miss P. Kvitoka (CZE), 9–Miss M.S. Bartoli (FRA), 10–Miss S.J. Stosur (AUS), 11–Miss A. Petkovic (GER), 12–Miss S. Kuznetsova (RUS), 13–Miss A. Radwanska (POL), 14–Miss A. Pavlyuchenkova (RUS), 15–Miss J. Jankovic (SRB), 16–Miss J. Goerges (GER), 17–Miss K. Kanepi (EST), 18–Miss A. Ivanovic (SRB), 19–Miss Y. Wickmayer (BEL), 20–Miss S. Peng (CHN), 21– Miss F. Pennetta (ITA), 22–Miss S. Peer (ISR), 23–Miss V.E.S. Williams (USA), 24– Miss D. Cibulkova (SVK), 25–Miss D. Hantuchova (SVK), 26–Miss M. Kirilenko (RUS), 27–Miss J. Gajdosova (AUS), 28–Miss E. Makarova (RUS), 29–Miss R. Vinci (ITA), 30–Miss B. Mattek–Sands (USA), 31–Miss L. Safarova (CZE), 32–Miss T. Pironkova (BUL)

Note: From the original list the No.2 seed Miss K. Clijsters (BEL) withdrew owing to a foot injury. Seeds No.3 to No.32 were made seeds No.2 to No.31 and a new No.32 seed added

2012 (32)

1–Miss M. Sharapova (RUS), 2–Miss V. Azarenka (BLR), 3–Miss A. Radwanska (POL), 4–Miss P. Kvitova (CZE), 5–Miss S. Stosur (AUS), 6–Miss S.J. Williams (USA), 7–Miss C. Wozniaki (DEN), 8–Miss A. Kerber (GER), 9–Miss M. Bartoli (FRA), 10–Miss S. Errani (ITA),11–Miss N. Li (CHN), 12–Miss V. Zvonareva (RUS), 13–Miss D. Cibulkova (SVK), 14–Miss A. Ivanovic (SRB), 15–Miss S. Lisicki (GER), 16–Miss F. Pennetta (ITA), 17–Miss M. Kirilenko (RUS), 18–Miss J. Jankovic (SRB), 19–Miss L. Safarova (CZE), 20–Miss N. Petrova (RUS), 21–Miss R. Vinci (ITA), 22–Miss J. Goerges (GER), 23–Miss P. Cetkovska (CZE), 24–Miss F. Schiavone (ITA), 25–Miss J. Zheng (CHN), 26–Miss A. Medina Garrigues (ESP), 27–Miss D. Hantuchova (SVK), 28–Miss C. McHale (USA), 29–Miss M. Niculescu (ROM), 30–Miss S. Peng (CHN), 31–Miss A. Pavlyuchenkova (RUS), 32–Miss S. Kuznetsova (RUS)

2013 (32)

1–Miss S.J. Williams (USA), 2–Miss V. Azarenka (BLR), 3–Miss M. Sharapova (RUS) 4–Miss A. Radwanska (POL), 5–Miss S. Errani (1TA), 6–Miss N. Li (CHN), 7–Miss A. Kerber (GER), 8–Miss P. Kvitova (CZE), 9–Miss C. Wozniaki (DEN), 10–Miss M. Kirilenko, 11–Miss R. Vinci (ITA), 12–Miss A. Ivanovic (SRB), 13–Miss N. Petrova (RUS), 14–Miss S. Stosur (AUS), 15–Miss M. Bartoli (ITA), 16–Miss J. Jankovic (SRB), 17–Miss S. Stephens (USA), 18–Miss D. Cibulkova (SVK), 19–Miss C. Suarez Navarro, 20–Miss K. Flipkens (BEL), 21–Miss A. Pavlyuchenkova (RUS), 22–Miss S. Cirstea (ROU), 23–Miss S. Lisicki (GER), 24–Miss S. Peng (CHN), 25–Miss E. Makarova (RUS), 26–Miss V. Lepchenko (USA), 27–Miss L. Safarova (CZE), 28–Miss T. Paszek (AUT), 29–Miss A. Comet (FRA), 30–Miss M. Barthel (GER), 31–Miss R. Oprandi (SU1), 32–Miss K. Zakopalova (CZE)

Note: From the original list the No.26 seed, Miss S. Kuznetsova (AUS), withdrew owing to injury. Seeds No.27 to 32 were made seeds No.26 to 31 and a new No.32 seed added

2014 (32)

1–Miss S.J. Williams (USA), 2–Miss N.Li (CHN), 3–Miss S. Halep (ROU), 4–Miss A. Radwanska (POL), 5–Miss M. Sharapova (RUS), 6–Miss P. Kvitova (CZE), 7– Miss J. Jankovic (SRB), 8–Miss V. Azarenka (BLR), 9–Miss A. Kerber (GER), 10– Miss D. Cibulkova (SVK), 11–Miss A. Ivanovic (SRB), 12–Miss F. Pennetta (ITA), 13–Miss E. Bouchard (CAN), 14–Miss S. Errani (ITA), 15–Miss C. Suarez Navarro (ESP), 16–Miss C. Wozniacki (DEN), 17–Miss S. Stosur (AUS), 18–Miss S. Stephens (USA), 19–Miss S. Lisicki (GER), 20–Miss A. Petkovic (GER), 21–Miss R. Vinci (ITA), 22–Miss E. Makarova (RUS), 23–Miss L. Safarova (CZE), 24– Miss K. Flipkens (BEL), 25–Miss A. Cornet (FRA), 26–Miss A. Pavlyuchenkova (RUS), 27– Miss G. Muguruza (ESP), 28–Miss S. Kuznetsova (RUS), 29–Miss S. Cirstea (ROU), 30–Miss V.E.S. Williams (USA), 31–Miss K. Koukalova (CZE), 32–Miss E. Vesnina (RUS)

Seeded players who reached the concluding rounds

Year	No. of Seeds	Fourth Round	Quarter-final	Semi-final	Final	Winner
1927	8	1-5, 8	1, 2, 4, 5, 8	1, 4, 5	1, 4	1
1928	8	1-4, 6, 7	1-4, 6, 7	1, 2, 4	1, 2	1
1929	8	1, 2, 4-6, 8	1, 5, 6	1, 5	1, 5	1
1930	8	1, 3, 5-8	1, 3, 5-8	1, 5, 6, 8	1, 8	1
1931	8	1-4, 6, 8	1-4, 6	1, 3, 4, 6	1, 4	1
1932	8	1-6, 8	1-6, 8	1, 2, 5	1, 5	1
1933	8	1-6, 8	1-6, 8	1, 2, 5, 6	1, 2	1
1934	8	1-8	1-3, 5-8	1, 2, 8	1, 2	2
1935	8	1-6, 8	1-6, 8	2-4, 8	3, 4	4
1936	8	1, 2, 4-8	1, 2, 4-8	2, 5-7	2, 5	2
1937	8	1-8	1-7	4-7	4, 7	7
1938	8	1-8	1-7	1, 2, 4	1	1
1939	8	1-8	1-8	1, 3, 6, 8	1, 6	1
1946	8	1-8	1-7	1-3, 5	1,3	1
1947	8	1-8	1-8	1-3, 7	1, 3	1
1948	8	1-8	1-5, 7, 8	1-4	2, 4	2
1949	8	1-3, 5	1-3	1-3	1, 2	1
1950	8	1-7	1-7	1-4	1, 2	1
1951	8	1-5, 7, 8	1-5, 7, 8	1, 3-5	3, 4	3
1952	8	1-8	1-8	2-5	2, 4	2
1953	8	1-6, 8	1-5	1-4	1, 2	1
1954	8	1-8	1-8	1, 2, 4, 8	1, 4	1
1955	8	1-3, 5-8	1-3, 5-8	1-3, 6	2, 3	2
1956	8	1-6, 8	1-6, 8	1, 5, 6	5, 6	5
1957	8	1-5	1, 2, 4, 5	1, 4, 5	1, 5	1
1958	8	1, 2, 4-6	1, 4-6	1, 6	1	1
1959	8	1-8	2, 4-8	4-7	4, 6	6
1960	8	1-5, 8	1-5, 8	1, 3, 4, 8	1, 8	1
1961	8	1-3, 5-8	1, 2, 5-8	1, 6, 7	6, 7	7

Year	No. of Seeds	Fourth Round	Quarter-final	Semi-final	Final	Winner
1962	8	2-8	2-5, 7, 8	3, 5, 8	8	8
1963	8	1-5, 7, 8	1, 3, 4	1	1	1
1964	8	1-6, 8	1-6, 8	1-4	1, 2	2
1965	8	1-5, 8	1-5	1, 2, 5	1, 2	2
1966	8	1, 2, 4, 6, 7	1-7	1-4	2, 4	4
1967	8	1-3, 5-8	1, 3, 6, 8	1, 3	1, 3	1
1968	8	1-4, 6-8	1-4, 6-8	1, 3, 4, 7	1, 7	1
1969	8	1-5, 7, 8	1, 2, 4, 5, 7, 8	1, 2, 4	2, 4	4
1970	8	1-8	1, 2, 5, 7, 8	1, 2, 5	1, 2	1
1971	8	1-3, 5-7	1-3, 6, 7	1-3	1, 3	3
1972	8	1-4, 6-8	1-4, 6, 7	1, 2, 4, 6	1, 2	2
1973	8	1-8	1-8	1-4	2, 4	2
1974	8	1-6, 8	1-3, 5, 6, 8	2, 5, 6, 8	2, 8	2
1975	8	1-7	1-7	1, 3-5	3, 4	3
1976	8	1-8	1-8	1-4	1, 2	1
1977	12	1-8, 12	1-8	1, 3, 4, 7	3, 7	3
1978	16	1-15	1-5, 11-13	1-4	1, 2	2
1979	16	1-11, 14, 15	1-8	1-4	1, 2	1
1980	16	1-11, 14	1-6, 11, 14	1-4	3, 4	4
1981	16	1-8, 10, 12, 14	1-4, 6-8, 10	1, 2, 4, 7	1, 2	1
1982	16	1-4, 6, 7, 9-13, 15	1-3, 10-13	1, 2, 11, 12	1, 2	1
1983	16	1, 3, 7, 8, 10-12, 15, 16	1, 3, 10, 11	1, 3, 10	1, 3	1
1984	16	1-4, 6, 7, 9,10, 12-15	1-4, 6, 7, 10	1-3, 6	1, 2	1
1985	16	1, 1, 4, 5, 7, 8, 11, 16	1, 1, 5, 7, 8, 16	1, 1, 8, 16	1, 1	1
1986	16	1-3, 7, 8, 10, 11, 15, 16	1-3, 7, 10, 15	1-3, 10	1, 3	1
1987	16	1-6, 8, 11, 15, 16	1-6, 8	1-3, 5	1, 2	1
1988	16	1-6, 8, 12-14, 16	1-4, 6, 12	1-4	1, 2	1
1989	16	1, 2, 4, 6, 7, 10-12, 14, 15	1, 2, 4, 7	1, 2, 4	1, 2	1
1990	16	1-5, 7, 10-14	1-5, 7, 11, 13	1, 2, 4, 5	2, 5	2
1991	16	1-5, 7-9, 11, 13, 14, 16	1-5, 7, 9	1, 2, 5, 9	1, 2	1
1992	16	1-4, 6, 12-14	1-4, 6, 12, 14	1-4	1, 2	2
1993	16	1-4, 6-9, 15, 16	1, 2, 4, 6-8, 15	1, 2, 6, 8	1, 8	1
1994	16	2-5, 9, 13, 14, 17	3-5, 9, 13	3, 4	3, 4	3
1995	16	1-4, 6-9, 13, 15	1-4, 6, 8, 13, 15	1-4	1, 2	1
1996	16	1, 3, 4, 6, 9, 12, 13, 16	1, 4, 6, 9, 12, 13	1, 4, 12	1, 4	1
1997	16	1, 3, 4, 8, 9, 11, 12	1, 3, 4, 8	1, 3, 8	1, 3	1
1998	16	1-3, 5-7, 10, 14-16	1-3, 5-7, 16	1, 3, 16	3, 16	3
1999	16	2, 3, 5, 6, 8, 9, 14, 15, 17	2, 3, 5, 6, 8	2, 3	2, 3	3
2000	16	1, 2, 5, 6, 8, 9, 11	1, 2, 5, 6, 8	2, 5, 8	2, 5	2
2001	32	2-5, 7-9, 12, 14, 15, 17–19, 31	2-5, 7-9, 19	2-4, 8	2, 8	2
2002	32	1-4, 6, 7, 9, 11, 12, 16, 19, 20	1-4, 6, 9, 11	1, 2, 6, 9	1, 2	2
2003	32	1-5, 8, 10, 13, 15, 16, 27, 33	1-5, 8, 27, 33	1-4	1-2	1
2004	32	1, 4, 5, 7, 9-14, 21, 31	1, 4, 5, 7, 9, 11, 13	1, 4, 5, 13	1, 13	13
2005	32	1-3, 5, 6, 8, 9, 12-16, 26	1-3, 5, 8, 9, 12, 14	1-3, 14	1, 14	14
2006	32	1-4, 7, 9, 10, 15, 16, 18, 19, 26, 27	1-4, 7, 9, 27	1-4	1-3	1
2007	32	1-7, 10, 11, 14, 15, 18, 23, 31	1, 5-7, 14, 18, 23, 31	1, 6, 18, 23	18, 23	23
2008	32	2, 4-8, 14, 15, 18, 21, 24	5-7, 14, 18, 21	5-7	6, 7	7
2009	32	1-4, 8-11, 13, 17, 26	1-4, 8-11	1-4	2, 3	2
2010	32	1-4, 7-9, 11, 16, 17, 21	1, 2, 8, 9, 21	1, 21	1, 21	1
2011	32	1, 4, 5, 7-9, 19, 20, 23, 24 ,32	4, 5, 8, 9, 24, 32	4, 5, 8	5, 8	8

Year	No. of Seeds	Fourth Round	Quarter-final	Semi-final	Final	Winner
2012	32	1-4, 6, 8, 10, 12, 14, 15, 17, 20-22, 24, 25, 28, 30	2-4, 6, 8, 15, 17	2, 3, 6, 8	3, 6	6
2013	32	1, 4, 6, 8, 11, 15, 17, 19, 20, 23	4, 6, 8, 15, 17, 20, 23	4, 15, 20, 23	15, 23	15
2014	32	3-6, 9, 13, 16, 19, 22, 23, 25	3, 6, 9, 13, 19, 22, 23	3, 6, 13, 23	6, 13	6

Player Seeded Most Times

Miss M. Navratilova (USA)   20   (1975–1994)

Players Seeded No. 1 Most Times

Miss M. Smith/Mrs. B.M. Court (AUS)   8   (1962–1964, 1966, 1969–1971, 1973)
Miss M. Navratilova (USA)   8   (1979, 1980, 1982–1987)
Miss S.M. Graf (GER)   8   (1988–1991, 1993–1996)

Unseeded Semi-Finalists (35)

1927 Miss J.C. Fry (GBR)
1928 Miss D. Akhurst (AUS)
1929 Miss E.A. Goldsack (GBR)
      Miss J.C. Ridley (GBR)
1932 Miss G.M. Heeley (GBR)
1934 Miss J.M. Hartigan (AUS)
1938 Miss H.H. Jacobs (USA)
1949 Mrs. H.P. Rihbany (USA)
1956 Miss P.E. Ward (GBR)
1957 Miss C.C. Truman (GBR)
1958 Miss A.S. Haydon (GBR)
      Miss F.A.M. Mortimer (GBR)

1961 Miss R. Schuurman (RSA)
1962 Mrs. C. Sukova (TCH)
1963 Miss B.J. Moffitt (USA)
1965 Miss C.C. Truman (GBR)
1967 Miss R. Casals (USA)
      Miss K.M. Harter (USA)
1969 Miss R. Casals (USA)
1970 Miss F.G. Durr (FRA)
1971 Mrs. D.E. Dalton (AUS)
1983 Miss Y. Vermaak (RSA)
1989 Miss C. Lindqvist (SWE)
1994 Miss B.C. Fernandez (USA)

      Miss L.M. McNeil (USA)
1996 Miss M.J. McGrath (USA)
1997 Miss A.S. Kournikova (RUS)
1998 Miss N.M. Zvereva (BLR)
1999 Miss M. Lucic (CRO)
      Miss A.W. Stevenson (USA)
2000 Miss J. Dokic (AUS)
2008 Miss J Zheng (CHN)
2010 Miss P. Kvitova (CZE)
      Miss T. Pironkova (BUL)
2011 Miss S.K. Lisicki (GER)

Unseeded Finalists (4)

1938 Miss H.H. Jacobs (USA)   1962 Mrs. C. Sukova (TCH)   1963 Miss B.J. Moffitt (USA)
1958 Miss F.A.M. Mortimer (GBR)

Unseeded Champion

None

Ladies' Doubles Championship

1927 (4)
1–Miss E.A.L. Heine and Mrs. G.E. Peacock (RSA), 2–Miss H.N. Wills and Miss E.M. Ryan (USA), 3–Mrs. L.A. Godfree and Miss B.M. Nuthall (GBR), 4–Miss E.H. Harvey and Mrs. C.G. McIlquham (GBR).

1928 (4)
1–Mrs. R. Lycett (GBR) and Miss E.M. Ryan (USA), 2–Miss E.V. Bennett and Miss E.H. Harvey (GBR), 3–Mrs. M.R. Watson and Miss M.A. Saunders (GBR), 4–Miss K. Bouman (NED) and Miss E.L. Colyer (GBR).

1929 (4)
1–Miss E.M. Ryan (USA) and Miss B.M. Nuthall (GBR), 2–Mrs. M.R. Watson and Mrs. L.R.C. Michell (GBR), 3–Mrs. B.C. Covell and Mrs. W.P. Barron (GBR), 4–Mrs. A. Neave and Miss E.A.L. Heine (RSA).

1930 (4)
1–Mrs. F.S. Moody and Miss E.M. Ryan (USA), 2–Mrs. L.A. Godfree and Mrs. M.R. Watson (GBR)*, 3–Miss E.H. Harvey and Miss J.C. Fry (GBR)*, 4–Miss E.A. Cross and Miss S.H. Palfrey (USA).
*The No. 2 and No. 3 seeds withdrew. Their position in the draw was not filled and opponents given a walkover.

1931 (4)
1–Miss B.M. Nuthall and Mrs. E.F. Whittingstall (GBR), 2–Miss C. Aussem and Miss H. Krahwinkel (GER), 3–Mrs. M. Watson and Mrs. L.R.C. Michell (GBR), 4–Miss D.E. Metaxa (FRA), and Miss J. Sigart (BEL).

1932 (4)
1–Miss B.M. Nuthall and Mrs. E.O.F. Whittingstall (GBR), 2–Miss E.M. Ryan and Miss H.H. Jacobs (USA), 3–Mrs. W.P. Barron and Mrs. M.R. King (GBR), 4–Miss D.E. Metaxa (FRA), and Miss J. Sigart (BEL).

1933 (4)
1–Miss E.M. Ryan (USA) and Mrs. R. Mathieu (FRA), 2–Miss G.M. Heeley and Miss D.E. Round (GBR), 3–Miss J. Sigart (BEL) and Miss M.C. Scriven (GBR), 4–Miss B.M. Nuthall and Mrs. E.O.F. Whittingstall (GBR).

1934 (4)
1–Miss E.M. Ryan (USA) and Mrs. R. Mathieu (FRA), 2–Miss H.H. Jacobs and Miss S.H. Palfrey (USA), 3–Miss W.A. James and Miss B.M. Nuthall (GBR), 4–Miss E.M. Dearman and Miss N.M. Lyle (GBR).

1935 (4)
1–Miss D.B. Andrus (USA) and Mrs. C.F. Henrotin (FRA), 2–Mrs. R. Mathieu (FRA) and Mrs. S. Sperling (GER), 3–Miss W.A. James and Miss K.E. Stammers (GBR), 4–Mrs. J.B. Pittman and Miss A.M. Yorke (GBR).

1936 (4)
1–Miss W.A. James and Miss K.E. Stammers (GBR), 2–Mrs. M. Fabyan and Miss H.H. Jacobs (USA), 3–Mrs. R. Mathieu (FRA) and Miss A.M. Yorke (GBR), 4–Miss J. Jedrzejowska (POL) and Miss S.D.B. Noel (GBR).

1937 (4)
1–Miss W.A. James and Miss K.E. Stammers (GBR), 2–Mrs. R. Mathieu (FRA) and Miss A.M. Yorke (GBR), 3–Miss H.H. Jacobs (USA) and Mrs. S. Sperling (GER), 4–Miss E.M. Dearman and Miss J. Ingram (GBR).

1938 (4)
1–Mrs. R. Mathieu (FRA) and Miss A.M. Yorke (GBR), 2–Mrs. M. Fabyan and Miss A. Marble (USA), 3–Miss E.M. Dearman and Miss J. Ingram (GBR), 4–Mrs. J.H.K. Miller and Miss M. Morphew (RSA).

1939 (4)
1–Miss M. Fabyan and Miss A. Marble (USA), 2–Miss H.H. Jacobs (USA) and Miss A.M. Yorke (GBR), 3–Miss J. Jedrzejowska (POL) and Mrs. R. Mathieu (FRA), 4–Miss J.A.B. Nicoll and Miss B.M. Nuthall (GBR).

1946 (4)
1–Miss A.L. Brough and Miss M.E. Osborne (USA), 2–Miss P.M. Betz and Miss D.J. Hart (USA), 3–Mrs. E.W.A. Bostock and Mrs. M. Menzies (GBR), 4–Miss D.M. Bundy and Mrs. R.B. Todd (USA).

1947 (4)
1–Miss A.L. Brough and Miss M.E. Osborne (USA), 2–Miss D.J. Hart and Mrs. R.B. Todd (USA), 3–Mrs. R. Hilton and Mrs. E.W.A. Bostock (GBR), 4–Mrs. G.F. Bolton and Mrs. H.C. Hopman (AUS).

1948 (4)
1–Miss A.L. Brough and Mrs. W. duPont (USA), 2–Miss D.J. Hart and Mrs. R.B. Todd (USA), 3–Mrs. N.W. Blair and Mrs. E.W.A. Bostock (GBR), 4–Mrs. R. Hilton and Mrs. M. Menzies (GBR).

1949 (4)
1–Miss A.L. Brough and Mrs. W. duPont (USA), 2–Miss G.A. Moran and Mrs. R.B. Todd (USA), 3–Mrs. N.W. Blair and Miss J.D. Quertier (GBR), 4–Miss J.I. Gannon and Mrs. R. Hilton (GBR).

1950 (4)
1–Miss A.L. Brough and Mrs. W. duPont (USA), 2–Miss D.J. Hart and Miss S.J. Fry (USA), 3–Miss G.A. Moran and Mrs. R.B. Todd (USA), 4–Mrs. A.J.C. Harrison and Miss K.L.A. Tuckey (GBR).

1951 (4)
1–Miss A.L. Brough and Mrs. W. duPont (USA), 2–Miss D.J. Hart and Miss S.J. Fry (USA), 3–Mrs. G.C. Davidson and Miss R.B. Todd (USA)*, 4–Miss B.J. Baker and Miss N.A. Chaffee (USA).
*The No. 3 seeds withdrew. Their position in the draw was filled by new No. 3 seeds, Mrs. G.C. Davidson and Miss C.E. Rosenquest (USA).

1952 (4)
1–Miss D.J. Hart and Miss S.J. Fry (USA), 2–Miss A.L. Brough and Miss M.C. Connolly (USA), 3–Mrs. M.N. Long (AUS) and Mrs. R.B. Todd (USA), 4–Miss J.S.V. Partridge and Mrs. I.F. Rinkel (GBR).

1953 (4)
1–Miss D.J. Hart and Miss S.J. Fry (USA), 2–Miss M.C. Connolly and Miss J. Sampson (USA), 3–Miss H.M. Fletcher and Mrs. I.F. Rinkel (GBR), 4–Mrs. G.C. Davidson and Mrs. D.P. Knode (USA).

1954 (4)
1–Miss D.J. Hart and Miss S.J. Fry (USA), 2–Miss A.L. Brough and Mrs. W. duPont (USA), 3–Miss F.A.M. Mortimer and Miss J.A. Shilcock (GBR), 4–Mrs. E.C.S. Pratt (USA) and Mrs. H. Weiss (ARG)*.
*The No. 4 seeds withdrew. Their position in the draw was filled by new No. 4 seeds, Mrs. E.C.S. Pratt (USA) and Mrs. J. Vollmer (GER).

1955 (4)
1–Mrs. G.C. Davidson and Miss D.J. Hart (USA), 2–Mrs. J.G. Fleitz and Miss D.R. Hard (USA), 3–Miss S.J. Bloomer and Miss P.E. Ward (GBR), 4–Miss F.A.M. Mortimer and Miss J.A. Shilcock (GBR).

1956 (4)
1–Miss A.L. Brough and Mrs. S.J. Fry (USA), 2–Miss F.A.M. Mortimer and Miss J.A. Shilcock (GBR), 3–Miss A. Buxton (GBR) and Miss A. Gibson (USA), 4–Mrs. J.G. Fleitz and Miss D.R. Hard (USA).

1957 (4)
1–Miss A. Gibson and Miss D.R. Hard (USA), 2–Mrs. K. Hawton and Mrs. M.N. Long (AUS), 3–Miss J.A. Shilcock and Miss P.E. Ward (GBR), 4–Miss Y. Ramirez and Miss R.M. Reyes (MEX).

1958 (4)
1–Miss M.E.A. Bueno (BRA) and Miss A. Gibson (USA), 2–Miss S.J. Bloomer and Miss C.C. Truman (GBR), 3–Mrs. K. Hawton and Mrs. M.N. Long (AUS), 4–Miss Y. Ramirez and Miss R.M. Reyes (MEX).

1959 (4)
1–Miss J.M. Arth and Miss D.R. Hard (USA), 2–Miss Y. Ramirez and Miss R.M. Reyes (MEX), 3–Mrs. J.G. Fleitz (USA) and Miss C.C. Truman (GBR), 4–Miss S. Reynolds and Miss R. Schuurman (RSA).

1960 (4)
1–Miss M.E.A. Bueno (BRA) and Miss D.R. Hard (USA), 2–Miss M.B. Hellyer (AUS) and Miss Y. Ramirez (MEX), 3–Miss K.J. Hantze and Miss J.S. Hopps (USA), 4–Miss S. Reynolds and Miss R. Schuurman (RSA).

1961 (4)
1–Miss S. Reynolds and Miss R. Schuurman (RSA), 2–Miss A.S. Haydon and Miss C.C. Truman (GBR), 3–Miss J.P. Lehane and Miss M. Smith (AUS), 4–Miss S.M. Moore (USA) and Miss L.R. Turner (AUS).

1962 (4)
1–Miss M.E.A. Bueno (BRA) and Miss D.R. Hard (USA), 2–Miss B.J. Moffitt and Mrs. J.R. Susman (USA), 3–Miss J.C. Bricka (USA) and Miss M. Smith (AUS), 4–Mrs. L.E.G. Price and Miss R. Schuurman (RSA).

1963 (4)
1–Miss R.A. Ebbern and Miss M. Smith (AUS), 2–Miss M.E.A. Bueno (BRA) and Miss D.R. Hard (USA), 3–Miss J.P. Lehane and Miss L.R. Turner (AUS), 4–Mrs. P.F. Jones (GBR) and Miss R. Schuurman (RSA).

1964 (4)
1–Miss M. Smith and Miss L.R. Turner (AUS), 2–Miss B.J. Moffitt and Mrs. J.R. Susman (USA), 3–Miss M.E.A. Bueno (BRA) and Miss R.A. Ebbern (AUS), 4–Mrs. P. Haygarth (RSA) and Mrs. P.F. Jones (GBR).

1965 (4)
1–Miss M. Smith and Miss L.R. Turner (AUS), 2–Miss M.E.A. Bueno (BRA) and Miss B.J. Moffitt (USA), 3–Mrs. C.E. Graebner and Miss N.A. Richey (USA), 4–Miss M. Schacht (AUS) and Miss A.M. van Zyl (RSA)*.

*The No. 4 seeds withdrew. Their position in the draw was filled by unseeded Miss M. Schacht (AUS) and Miss A. Dimitrieva (URS).

1966 (4)
1–Miss M. Smith and Miss J.A.M. Tegart (AUS), 2–Miss M.E.A. Bueno (BRA) and Miss N.A. Richey (USA), 3–Miss F.G. Durr and Miss J.P. Lieffrig (FRA), 4–Mrs. P.F. Jones and Miss S.V. Wade (GBR).

1967 (4)
1–Miss M.E.A. Bueno (BRA) and Miss N.A. Richey (USA), 2–Mrs. P.F. Jones and Miss S.V. Wade (GBR), 3–Miss R. Casals and Mrs. L.W. King (USA), 4–Miss J.A.M. Tegart and Miss L.R. Turner (AUS).

1968 (4)
1–Miss R. Casals and Mrs. L.W. King (USA), 2–Miss M.E.A. Bueno (BRA) and Miss N.A. Richey (USA), 3–Miss F.G. Durr (FRA) and Mrs. P.F. Jones (GBR), 4–Mrs. W.W. Bowrey and Miss J.A.M. Tegart (AUS).

1969 (4)
1–Mrs. B.M. Court and Miss J.A.M. Tegart (AUS, 2–Miss R. Casals and Mrs. L.W. King (USA), 3–Miss F.G. Durr (FRA) and Mrs. P.F. Jones (GBR), 4–Mrs. W.W. Bowrey (AUS) and Miss S.V. Wade (GBR).

1970 (4)
1–Mrs B.M. Court and Mrs. D.E. Dalton (AUS), 2–Miss R. Casals and Mrs. L.W. King (USA), 3–Miss K.M. Krantzcke and Miss K.A. Melville (AUS), 4–Miss F.G. Durr (FRA) and Miss S.V. Wade (GBR).

1971 (4)
1–Miss R. Casals and Mrs. L.W. King (USA), 2–Mrs. B.M. Court and Miss E.F. Goolagong (AUS), 3–Mrs. D.E. Dalton (AUS) and Miss S.V. Wade (GBR), 4–Mrs. J.B. Chanfreau and Miss F.G. Durr (FRA).

1972 (4)
1–Mrs. L.W. King (USA) and Miss B.F. Stove (NED), 2–Miss R. Casals (USA) and Miss S.V. Wade (GBR), 3–Mrs. D.E. Dalton (AUS) and Miss F.G. Durr (FRA), 4–Miss E.F. Goolagong (AUS) and Miss F.E. Truman (GBR).

1973 (4)
1–Miss R. Casals and Mrs. L.W. King (USA), 2–Mrs. B.M. Court and Miss L.E. Hunt (AUS), 3–Miss F.G. Durr (FRA) and Miss B.F. Stove (NED), 4–Mrs. O.V. Morozova (URS) and Miss S.V. Wade (GBR).

1974 (4)
1–Miss R. Casals and Mrs. L.W. King (USA), 2–Miss F.G. Durr (FRA) and Miss B.F. Stove (NED), 3–Miss C.M. Evert (USA) and Mrs. O.V. Morozova (URS), 4–Miss J.M. Heldman (USA) and Miss S.V. Wade (GBR).

1975 (4)
1–Mrs. R.A. Cawley (AUS) and Miss M. Michel (USA), 2–Miss R. Casals and Mrs. L.W. King (USA), 3–Miss C.M. Evert (USA) and Miss M. Navratilova (TCH), 4–Mrs. B.M. Court (AUS) and Miss S.V. Wade (GBR).

1976 (4)
1–Mrs. L.W. King (USA) and Miss B.F. Stove (NED), 2–Miss C.M. Evert (USA) and Miss M. Navratilova (TCH), 3–Mrs. O.V. Morozova (URS) and Miss S.V. Wade (GBR), 4–Mrs. R.A. Cawley (AUS) and Miss M. Michel (USA).

1977 (8)
1–Miss M. Navratilova (USA) and Miss B.F. Stove (NED), 2–Miss R. Casals and Miss C.M. Evert (USA), 3–Miss D.A. Boshoff and Miss I.S. Kloss (RSA), 4–Miss F.G. Durr (Mrs. B.J. Browning) (FRA) and Miss S.V. Wade (GBR), 5–Mrs. G.E. Reid (AUS) and Miss G.R. Stevens (RSA), 6–Miss S.D. Barker (GBR) and Miss A.K. Kiyomura (USA), 7–Miss L.J. Charles and Miss S. Mappin (GBR), 8–Mrs. L.W. King and Mrs. J.R. Susman (USA).

1978 (8)
1–Mrs. L.W. King and Miss M. Navratilova (USA), 2–Mrs. R.A. Cawley (AUS) and Miss B.F. Stove (NED), 3–Miss F.G. Durr (Mrs. B.J. Browning) (FRA) and Miss S.V. Wade (GBR), 4–Mrs. G.E. Reid and Miss W.M. Turnbull (AUS), 5–Mrs. R.L. Cawley (AUS) and Miss J.C. Russell (USA), 6–Miss S.D. Barker (GBR) and Mrs. T.E. Guerrant (USA), 7–Miss M. Jausovec (YUG) and Miss V. Ruzici (ROM), 8–Miss I.S. Kloss and Miss M. Kruger (RSA).

1979 (8)
1–Mrs. L.W. King and Miss M. Navratilova (USA), 2–Miss B.F. Stove (NED) and Miss W.M. Turnbull (AUS), 3–Miss F.G. Durr (Mrs. B.J. Browning) (FRA) and Miss S.V. Wade (GBR), 4–Miss R. Casals and Mrs. J.M. Lloyd (USA), 5–Miss D.L. Fromholtz (AUS), and Miss M. Kruger (RSA), 6–Miss M. Jausovec (YUG) and Miss V. Ruzici (ROM), 7–Miss I.S. Kloss (RSA) and Mrs. K. Stuart (USA), 8–Miss S.D. Barker (GBR) and Miss A.K. Kiyomura (USA).

1980 (8)

1–Mrs. L.W. King and Miss M. Navratilova (USA), 2–Miss R. Casals (USA) and Miss W.M.
Turnbull (AUS), 3–Miss P.H. Shriver (USA) and Miss B.F. Stove (NED), 4–Miss K. Jordan and
Miss A.E. Smith (USA), 5–Miss G.R. Stevens (RSA) and Miss S.V. Wade (GBR), 6–Mrs. J.M.
Lloyd (USA) and Miss V. Ruzici (ROM), 7–Miss S.D. Barker (GBR) and Miss A.K. Kiyomura
(USA), 8–Miss H. Mandlikova and Miss R. Tomanova (TCH).

1981 (12)

1–Miss K. Jordan and Miss A.E. Smith (USA), 2–Miss M. Navratilova and Miss P.H. Shriver
(USA), 3–Miss R. Casals (USA) and Miss W.M. Turnbull (AUS), 4–Miss S.D. Barker (GBR) and
Miss A.K. Kiyomura (USA), 5–Miss C.S. Reynolds and Miss P.G. Smith (USA), 6–Miss B.C.
Potter and Miss S.A. Walsh (USA), 7–Miss R.D. Fairbank and Miss T.J. Harford (RSA), 8–Miss
H. Mandlikova (TCH) and Miss B.F. Stove (NED)*, 9–Miss J.C. Russell (USA) and Miss V.
Ruzici (ROM), 10–Miss S. Hanika (GER) and Miss A. Jaeger (USA), 11–Mrs. J.M. Lloyd (USA)
and Miss S.V.Wade (GBR), 12–Miss M.L. Piatek and Miss W.E. White (USA).
*The No. 8 seeds withdrew. Their position in the draw was filled by Lucky Losers – Miss J.M. Mundel
and Miss S.L. Rollinson (RSA).

1982 (12)

1–Miss M. Navratilova and Miss P.H. Shriver (USA), 2–Miss K. Jordan and Miss A.E. Smith
(USA), 3–Miss R. Casals (USA) and Miss W.M. Turnbull (AUS), 4–Miss B.C. Potter and Miss
S.A. Walsh (USA), 5–Miss S.D. Barker (GBR) and Miss A.K. Kiyomura (USA), 6–Miss J.C.
Russell (USA) and Miss V. Ruzici (ROM), 7–Miss L.E. Allen (USA) and Miss M. Jausovec
(YUG), 8–Miss C.S. Reynolds and Miss P.G. Smith (USA), 9–Mrs. L.W. King (USA) and Miss
I.S. Kloss (RSA), 10–Miss R.D. Fairbank and Miss T.J. Harford (RSA), 11–Miss A. Jaeger and
Miss H.E. Nagelsen (USA), 12–Miss M.L. Piatek and Miss W.E. White (USA).

1983 (14)

1–Miss M. Navratilova and Miss P.H. Shriver (USA), 2–Miss R.D. Fairbank (RSA) and Miss C.S.
Reynolds (USA), 3–Miss J.M. Durie and Miss A.E. Hobbs (GBR), 4–Miss H. Mandlikova (TCH)
and Miss V. Ruzici (ROM), 5–Miss C.G. Kohde–Kilsch and Miss E.S. Pfaff (GER), 6–Miss R.
Casals (USA) and Miss W.M. Turnbull (AUS), 7–Miss B.C. Potter and Miss S.A. Walsh (USA),
8–Mrs. L.W. King and Mrs. J.M. Lloyd (USA), 9–Miss M. Jausovec (YUG) and Miss K. Jordan
(USA), 10–Miss A.K. Kiyomura and Miss P.G. Smith (USA), 11–Miss L. Antonoplis and Miss
B.K. Jordan (USA), 12–Miss E.M. Burgin and Miss A.A. Moulton (USA), 13–Miss B.A. Mould
(RSA) and Miss E.M. Sayers (AUS), 14–Miss C. Tanvier (FRA) and Miss A. Temesvari (HUN).

1984 (16)

1–Miss M. Navratilova and Miss P.H. Shriver (USA), 2–Miss A.E. Hobbs (GBR) and Miss W.M.
Turnbull (AUS), 3–Miss E.K. Horvath (USA) and Miss V. Ruzici (ROM), 4–Miss B.C. Potter
and Miss S.A. Walsh (USA), 5–Miss R.D. Fairbank (RSA) and Miss C.S. Reynolds (USA), 6–Miss
J.M. Durie (GBR) and Mrs. D. Hayashi (USA), 7–Miss K. Jordan and Miss A.E. Smith (USA), 8–
Miss C.G. Kohde–Kilsch (GER) and Miss H. Mandlikova (TCH), 9–Miss A.C. Leand and Miss M.L.
Piatek (USA), 10–Miss C. Jolissaint (SUI) and Miss M.A. Mesker (NED), 11–Miss L.E. Allen and
Miss A.H. White (USA), 12–Miss M. Jausovec (YUG) and Miss S.V. Wade (GBR), 13–Miss B.K.
Jordan (USA) and Miss E.M. Sayers (AUS), 14–Miss B. Bunge and Miss E.S. Pfaff (GER), 15–
Miss E.M. Burgin and Miss K.S. Rinaldi (USA)*, 16–Miss Z.L. Garrison and Miss L.M. McNeil
(USA).
*The No. 15 seeds withdrew. Their position in the draw was filled by Lucky Losers – Miss M. Kiney (USA)
and Miss R. Mentz (RSA).

1985 (16)

1–Miss M. Navratilova and Miss P.H. Shriver (USA), 2–Miss C.G. Kohde–Kilsch (GER) and
Miss H. Sukova (TCH), 3–Miss K. Jordan (USA) and Mrs. P.D. Smylie (AUS), 4–Miss H.
Mandlikova (TCH) and Miss W.M. Turnbull (AUS), 5–Miss B.C. Potter and Miss S.A. Walsh
(USA), 6–Miss S. Cherneva and Miss L.I. Savchenko (URS), 7–Miss B. Bunge and Miss E.S. Pfaff
(GER), 8–Miss R.D. Fairbank (RSA) and Miss A.E. Hobbs (GBR), 9–Miss H.E. Nagelsen and

Miss A.H. White (USA), 10–Miss J.M. Durie (GBR) and Mrs. J.M. Lloyd (USA), 11–Miss E.M. Burgin and Miss A.A. Moulton (USA), 12–Miss L. Antonoplis and Miss C.S. Reynolds (USA), 13–Miss B.C. Fernandez (PUR) and Miss J.C. Russell (USA)*, 14–Miss V. Ruzici (ROM) and Miss A. Temesvari (HUN), 15–Miss C.K. Bassett (CAN) and Miss A.C. Leand (USA), 16–Miss B.A. Mould (RSA) and Miss P.G. Smith (USA).

*The No. 13 seeds withdrew. Their position in the draw was filled by unseeded Miss C. Jolissaint (SUI) and Miss M.A. Mesker (NED).

1986 (16)
1–Miss M. Navratilova and Miss P.H. Shriver (USA), 2–Miss C.G. Kohde–Kilsch (GER) and Miss H. Sukova (TCH), 3–Miss H. Mandlikova (TCH) and Miss W.M. Turnbull (AUS), 4–Mrs. J.M. Lloyd and Miss A.H. White (USA), 5–Mrs. P.D. Smylie (AUS) and Miss C. Tanvier (FRA), 6–Miss H.E. Nagelsen (Mrs. M.H. McCormack) and Miss B.C. Potter (USA)*, 7–Miss B.C. Fernandez (PUR) and Miss R.M. White (USA), 8–Miss E.M. Burgin (USA) and Miss R.D. Fairbank (RSA), 9–Miss C.K. Bassett (CAN) and Miss A. Temesvari (HUN)*, 10–Miss K. Jordan and Miss A.A. Moulton (USA), 11–Mrs. S. Parkhomenko and Miss L.I. Savchenko (URS), 12–Miss M.A. Mesker (NED) and Miss P. Paradis (FRA)*, 13–Miss J.M. Durie and Miss A.E. Hobbs (GBR), 14–Miss L.M. McNeil (USA) and Miss C. Suire (FRA), 15–Miss Z.L. Garrison and Miss K.S. Rinaldi (USA), 16–Miss C.S. Reynolds and Miss A.E. Smith (USA).

Note: Miss S.M. Graf (GER) and Miss G.B. Sabatini (ARG) were originally seeded at No. 5.

*The No. 6, No. 9 and No. 12 seeds withdrew. Their positions in the draw were filled by Lucky Losers – Miss M. Jaggard (AUS) and Miss J.C. Kaplan (USA), unseeded Miss K. Maleeva and Miss M. Maleeva (BUL) and Lucky Losers – Miss J. Golder and Miss S. Pento (USA), respectively.

1987 (16)
1–Miss M. Navratilova and Miss P.H. Shriver (USA), 2–Miss S.M. Graf (GER) and Miss G.B. Sabatini (ARG), 3–Miss C.G. Kohde–Kilsch (GER) and Miss H. Sukova (TCH), 4–Miss E.M. Burgin (USA) and Miss R.D. Fairbank (RSA), 5–Miss H.E. Nagelsen (Mrs. M.H. McCormack) (USA) and Mrs. P.D. Smylie (AUS), 6–Mrs. S. Parkhomenko and Miss L.I. Savchenko (URS), 7–Miss L.M. McNeil and Miss R.M. White (USA), 8–Miss B. Bunge (GER) and Miss B.C. Fernandez (PUR), 9–Miss K. Jordan and Miss A.E. Smith (USA), 10–Miss M. Paz (ARG) and Miss E.S. Pfaff (GER), 11–Miss A.E. Hobbs (GBR) and Miss C.S. Reynolds (USA), 12–Miss M.L. Piatek and Miss A.H. White (USA), 13–Miss J.M. Byrne (AUS) and Miss P.A. Fendick (USA), 14–Miss C. Lindqvist (SWE) and Miss T. Scheuer–Larsen (DEN), 15–Miss E.A. Herr and Miss A.A. Moulton (USA), 16–Miss J.M. Durie (GBR) and Miss C. Tanvier (FRA).

1988 (16)
1–Miss M. Navratilova and Miss P.H. Shriver (USA), 2–Miss C.G. Kohde–Kilsch (GER) and Miss H. Sukova (TCH)*, 3–Miss S.M. Graf (GER) and Miss G.B. Sabatini (ARG), 4–Miss L.M. McNeil and Miss H.E. Nagelsen (Mrs. M.H. McCormack) (USA), 5–Miss J. Novotna (TCH) and Miss C. Suire (FRA), 6–Miss E.S. Pfaff (GER) and Mrs. P.D. Smylie (AUS), 7–Miss E.M. Burgin and Miss R.M. White (USA), 8–Miss K.M. Adams and Miss Z.L. Garrison (USA), 9–Miss R.D. Fairbank (RSA) and Miss B.C. Fernandez (PUR), 10–Miss L.G. Meskhi and Mrs. S. Parkhomenko (URS), 11–Miss L.I. Savchenko and Miss N.M. Zvereva (URS), 12–Miss H. Mandlikova (AUS) and Miss B.C. Potter (USA), 13–Mrs. C.M. Evert (USA) and Miss W.M. Turnbull (AUS), 14–Miss J.M. Durie (GBR) and Mrs. M.H. Pete (USA), 15–Miss C. Lindquist (SWE) and Miss T. Scheuer–Larsen (DEN), 16–Miss I. Demongeot and Miss N. Tauziat (FRA), 17–Miss M.M. Bollegraf (NED) and Miss N.A-L. Provis (AUS).

*The No. 2 seeds withdrew. Their position in the draw was filled by the No. 3 seeds. No. 4, 5 and 9 seeds positions reallocated and No. 17 added.

1989 (16)
1–Miss M. Navratilova and Miss P.H. Shriver (USA), 2–Miss L.I. Savchenko and Miss N.M. Zvereva (URS), 3–Miss J. Novotna and Miss H. Sukova (TCH), 4–Miss P.A. Fendick and Miss J.M. Hetherington (CAN), 5–Miss S.M. Graf (GER) and Miss G.B. Sabatini (ARG), 6–Miss B.C. Fernandez and Miss L.M. McNeil (USA), 7–Miss K.M. Adams and Miss Z.L. Garrison (USA), 8–

Mrs. P.D. Smylie and Miss W.M. Turnbull (AUS), 9–Miss E.M. Burgin (USA) and Miss R.D. Fairbank (Mrs R. Nideffer) (RSA), 10–Miss I. Demongeot and Miss N. Tauziat (FRA), 11–Miss H.E. Nagelsen (Mrs. M.H. McCormack) (USA) and Miss J.G. Thompson (AUS)*, 12–Miss M.M. Bollegraf (NED) and Miss E.S. Pfaff (GER), 13–Miss J.M. Byrne (AUS) and Miss R.M. White (USA), 14–Miss B. A.M. Schultz (NED) and Miss A. Temesvari (HUN), 15–Miss T. Scheuer–Larsen (DEN) and Miss C. Tanvier (FRA), 16–Mrs. C.M. Evert (Mrs. A.R. Mill) (USA) and Miss H. Mandlikova (AUS).

*From the original list the No. 11 seeds, Miss H.E. Nagelsen (USA) and Miss J.G. Thompson (AUS), and the No. 12 seeds, Miss J.M. Durie (GBR) and Miss M.J. Fernandez (USA), withdrew. The No. 11 seeds position in the draw was filled by Lucky Losers – Miss L.A. Eldredge (USA) and Miss L. O'Halloran (IRL). Seeds No. 13 to 16 were made No. 12 to 15 and new No. 16 seeds were added.

1990 (16)

1–Miss J. Novotna and Miss H. Sukova (TCH), 2–Miss B.C. Fernandez and Miss M. Navratilova (USA), 3–Miss L.I. Savchenko (Mrs. A. Neiland) and Miss N.M. Zvereva (URS), 4–Miss M.J. Fernandez and Miss H.E. Nagelsen (Mrs. M.H. McCormack) (USA), 5–Miss N.A-L. Provis (AUS) and Miss E. Reinach (RSA), 6–Miss K. Jordan (USA) and Mrs. P.D. Smylie (AUS), 7–Miss M. Paz and Miss A.I.M. Sanchez Vicario (ESP), 8–Miss S.M. Graf (GER) and Miss G.B. Sabatini (ARG), 9–Miss K.M. Adams and Miss L.M. McNeil (USA), 10–Miss P.A. Fendick and Miss Z.L. Garrison (Mrs. W.L. Jackson) (USA), 11–Miss E.M. Burgin and Miss R.D. Fairbank (Mrs. R. Nideffer) (USA), 12–Miss J.M. Hetherington (CAN) and Miss R.M. White (USA), 13–Miss A.E. Smith (USA) and Miss W.M. Turnbull (AUS), 14–Miss N. Medvedeva and Miss L. Meskhi (URS), 15–Mrs P.F. Daniels and Mrs. S.R. Prausa (USA), 16–Miss L.J. Gregory (RSA) and Mrs. S.W. Magers (USA).

1991 (16)

1–Miss B.C. Fernandez (PUR) and Miss J. Novotna (TCH), 2–Miss L.I. Savchenko (Mrs. A. Neiland) and Miss N.M. Zvereva (URS), 3–Miss A.I.M. Sanchez Vicario (ESP) and Miss H. Sukova (TCH), 4–Miss M.J. Fernandez and Miss Z.L. Garrison (Mrs. W.L. Jackson) (USA), 5–Miss K. Jordan and Miss L.M. McNeil (USA), 6–Miss N.A-L. Provis and Mrs. P.D. Smylie (AUS), 7–Mrs. S.W. Magers and Miss R.M. White (USA), 8–Miss M. Navratilova and Miss P.H. Shriver (USA), 9–Miss E.M. Burgin and Miss P.A. Fendick (USA), 10–Miss K.M. Adams (USA) and Miss M.M. Bollegraf (NED), 11–Miss J.M. Capriati (USA) and Miss M. Paz (ARG), 12–Miss J.M.Hetherington (CAN) and Miss K.S. Rinaldi (USA), 13–Miss C.G. Kohde–Kilsch (GER) and Miss E. Reinach (RSA), 14–Miss N. Tauziat (FRA) and Mrs. H.W. Wiesner (AUT), 15–Miss R.D. Fairbank (Mrs. R. Nideffer) (USA) and Miss B.A.M. Schultz (NED), 16–Miss L.J. Gregory (RSA) and Miss A. May (USA).

1992 (16)

1–Miss J. Novotna (TCH) and Mrs. A. Neiland (LAT), 2–Miss B.C. Fernandez (USA) and Miss N.M. Zvereva (CIS), 3–Miss A.I.M. Sanchez Vicario (ESP) and Miss H. Sukova (TCH), 4–Miss M. Navratilova and Miss P.H. Shriver (USA), 5–Miss M.J. Fernandez and Miss Z.L. Garrison (Mrs. W.L. Jackson) (USA), 6–Miss K.M. Adams (USA) and Miss M.M. Bollegraf (NED), 7–Miss L.M. McNeil (USA) and Miss R.P. Stubbs (AUS), 8–Miss J.M. Hetherington (CAN) and Miss K.S. Rinaldi (USA), 9–Miss P.A. Fendick (USA) and Miss A. Strnadova (TCH), 10–Miss S.L. Collins (USA) and Miss E. Reinach (RSA), 11–Miss N.A-L. Provis and Mrs. P.D. Smylie (AUS), 12–Miss R. McQuillan (AUS) and Miss C. Porwik (GER), 13–Miss I. Demongeot and Miss N. Tauziat (FRA), 14–Miss A. Huber and Miss C.G. Kohde–Kilsch (GER), 15–Miss K. Maleeva (BUL) and Miss B. Rittner (GER), 16–Mrs. S.W. Magers and Miss R.M. White (USA).

1993 (16)

1–Miss B.C. Fernandez (USA) and Miss N.M. Zvereva (BLS), 2–Mrs. A. Neiland (LAT) and Miss J. Novotna (CZE), 3–Miss A.I.M. Sanchez Vicario (ESP) and Miss H. Sukova (CZE), 4–Miss L.M. McNeil (USA) and Miss R.P. Stubbs (AUS), 5–Miss M.J. Fernandez and Mrs. Z.L. Garrison-Jackson(USA), 6–Miss P.H. Shriver (USA) and Mrs. P.D. Smylie (AUS), 7–Miss J.M. Capriati (USA) and Miss S.M. Graf (GER)*, 8–Miss J.M. Hetherington (CAN) and Miss K.S.

Rinaldi (USA), 9–Miss K.M. Adams (USA) and Miss M.M. Bollegraf (NED), 10–Miss A.J. Coetzer (RSA) and Miss I. Gorrochategui (ARG), 11–Miss M. Maleeva (BUL) and Mrs. F. Maleeva-Fragniere (SUI), 12–Miss P.A. Fendick and Miss M.J. McGrath (USA), 13–Miss A.M. Cecchini (ITA) and Miss P. Tarabini (ARG)*, 14–Miss E. Maniokova (RUS) and Miss L. Meskhi (GEO), 15–Miss D.A. Graham (USA) and Miss B.A.M. Schultz (NED), 16–Miss I. Demongeot (FRA) and Miss E. Reinach (RSA), 17–Miss S.L. Collins and Miss R.M. White (USA), 18–Miss M.C. Pierce (FRA) and Miss A. Strnadova (CZE)*, 19–Miss F. Labat (ARG) and Miss R. Zrubakova (SLO).

*The No. 12 seeds, Miss A.M. Cecchini (ITA) and Miss P. Tarabini (ARG), were made No. 13 seeds, and the No. 13 seeds, Miss P.A. Fendick and Miss M.J. McGrath (USA), were made No. 12 seeds. The No. 13 seeds withdrew and No. 17 seeds were added. The No. 7 seeds withdrew and No. 18 seeds were added. The No. 18 seeds withdrew and No. 19 seeds were added.

1994 (16)

1–Miss B.C. Fernandez (USA) and Miss N.M. Zvereva (BLR), 2–Miss J. Novotna (CZE) and Miss A.I.M. Sanchez Vicario, 3–Miss P.A. Fendick and Miss M.J. McGrath (USA), 4–Miss M.M. Bollegraf (NED) and Miss M. Navratilova (USA), 5–Miss P.H. Shriver (USA) and Mrs. P.D. Smylie (AUS), 6–Miss K.M. Adams (USA) and Miss H. Sukova (CZE), 7–Miss N. Medvedeva (UKR) and Mrs A. Neiland (LAT), 8–Miss A.J. Coetzer (RSA) and Miss I. Gorrochategui (ARG)*, 9–Miss L.A. Davenport and Miss L.M. Raymond (USA), 10–Miss M.J. Fernandez and Mrs Z.L. Garrison–Jackson (USA), 11–Miss L.M. McNeil (USA) and Miss R.P. Stubbs (AUS), 12–Miss J. Halard and Miss N. Tauziat (FRA), 13–Miss Y. Basuki (Mrs. H. Suharyadi) (INA) and Miss N. Miyagi (JPN), 14–Miss A.M. Cecchini and Miss P. Tarabini (ARG), 15–Miss J.M. Hetherington (CAN) and Miss S.C. Stafford (USA), 16–Miss L. Golarsa (ITA) and Miss C.M. Vis (NED).

*The No. 8 seeds withdrew. Their position in the draw was filled by Lucky Losers – Miss G.E. Coorengel (NED) and Miss A.E. Smith (GBR).

1995 (16)

1–Miss B.C. Fernandez (USA) and Miss N.M. Zvereva (BLR), 2–Miss J. Novotna (CZE) and Miss A.I.M. Sanchez Vicario (ESP), 3–Miss S.M. Graf (GER) and Miss M. Navratilova (USA)*, 4–Miss L.A. Davenport and Miss L.M. Raymond (USA), 5–Miss M.J. McGrath (USA) and Mrs A. Neiland (LAT), 6–Miss P.A.Fendick and Miss M.J. Fernandez (USA), 7–Miss M.M Bollegraf (NED) and Miss R.P. Stubbs (AUS), 8–Miss N.J. Arendt and Miss P.H. Shriver (USA), 9–Miss G.B. Sabatini (ARG) and Mrs. S. Schultz-McCarthy (NED), 10–Miss J. Halard and Miss N. Tauziat (FRA), 11–Miss I.C. Martinez (ESP) and Miss P. Tarabini (ARG), 12–Miss A.J. Coetzer (RSA) and Miss I. Gorrochategui (ARG), 13–Miss E. Reinach (RSA) and Miss I. Spirlea (ROM), 14–Miss K.M. Adams and Mrs Z.L. Garrison-Jackson (USA), 15–Miss E. Makarova and Miss E. Maniokova (RUS), 16–Miss L.M. Harvey-Wild and Miss C.R. Rubin (USA), 17–Miss K. Boogert and Mrs. N.A.M. Muns-Jagerman (NED).

*The No. 3 seeds withdrew. Their position in the draw was filled by the No. 5 seeds whose position was filled by the No. 9 seeds. The highest ranked non-seeded pair became the No. 17 seeds.

1996 (16)

1–Miss J. Novotna (CZE) and Miss A.I.M. Sanchez Vicario (ESP), 2–Miss B.C. Fernandez (USA) and Miss N.M. Zvereva (BLR), 3–Miss L.A. Davenport and Miss M.J. Fernandez (USA), 4–Miss M.J. McGrath (USA) and Mrs. A. Neiland (LAT), 5–Miss C.R. Rubin (USA) and Mrs. S. Schultz-McCarthy (NED)*, 6–Miss N.J. Arendt (USA) and Miss M.M. Bollegraf (NED), 7–Miss L.M. McNeil (USA) and Miss N. Tauziat (FRA), 8–Miss M. Hingis (SUI) and Miss H. Sukova (CZE), 9–Miss L.M. Raymond (USA) and Miss R.P. Stubbs (AUS), 10–Miss K.M. Adams (USA) and Miss M. De Swardt (RSA), 11–Miss K. Boogert (NED) and Miss I. Spirlea (ROM), 12–Miss N. Basuki (Mrs. H. Suharyadi) (INA) and Miss C.M. Vis (NED), 13–Miss I.C. Martinez (ESP) and Miss P. Tarabini (ARG), 14–Mrs. B. Dechaume-Balleret and Miss S. Testud (FRA), 15–Mrs. P.D. Smylie (AUS) and Miss L.M. Wild (USA), 16–Mrs. M.R. Bradtke and Miss R. McQuillan (AUS), 17–Miss L. Golarsa (ITA) and Miss K. Radford (AUS).

*The No. 5 seeds withdrew. Their position in the draw was filled by the No. 9 seeds, whose position was filled by the highest ranked pair who became the No. 17 seeds.

1997 (16)

1–Miss B.C. Fernandez (USA) and Miss N.M. Zvereva (BLR), 2–Miss M. Hingis (SUI) and Miss A.I.M. Sanchez Vicario (ESP), 3–Miss L.A. Davenport (USA) and Miss J. Novotna (CZE), 4–Mrs. A. Neiland (LAT), and Miss H. Sukova (CZE), 5–Miss M.J. Fernandez and Miss L.M. Raymond (USA), 6–Miss N.J. Arendt (USA) and Miss M.M. Bollegraf (NED), 7–Miss I.C. Martinez (ESP) and Miss P. Tarabini (ARG), 8–Miss N. Basuki (Mrs. H. Suharyadi) (INA) and Miss C.M. Vis (NED), 9–Miss K.M. Adams and Miss L.M. McNeil (USA), 10–Miss N. Tauziat (FRA) and Miss L.M. Wild (USA), 11–Miss N.K. Kijimuta and Miss N. Miyagi (JPN), 12– Miss S. Applemans (BEL) and Miss M.J.M.M. Oremans (NED), 13–Miss A. Fusai (FRA) and Miss R. Grande (ITA), 14–Miss A. Frazier and Miss K.Y. Po (USA), 15–Miss C.R. Rubin (USA) and Mrs. S. Schultz-McCarthy (NED), 16–Miss K. Boogert (NED) and Miss I. Spirlea (ROM).

1998 (16)

1–Miss M. Hingis (SUI) and Miss J. Novotna (CZE), 2–Miss L.A. Davenport (USA) and Miss N.M. Zvereva (BLR), 3–Miss A.I.M. Sanchez Vicario (ESP) and Miss H. Sukova (CZE), 4–Miss A. Fusai and Miss N. Tauziat (FRA), 5–Miss N. Basuki (Mrs. H. Suharyadi) (INA) and Miss C.M. Vis (NED), 6–Miss A.S. Kournikova (RUS) and Mrs. A. Neiland (LAT)*, 7–Miss L.M. Raymond (USA) and Miss R.P. Stubbs (AUS), 8–Miss K.M. Adams (USA) and Miss M.M. Bollegraf (NED), 9–Miss I.C. Martinez (ESP) and Miss P. Tarabini (ARG), 10–Miss E. Likhovtseva (RUS) and Miss A. Sugiyama (JPN), 12–Miss B. Schett (AUT) and Miss P. Schnyder (SUI), 13–Miss S. Applemans (Mrs. S. Haubourdin) (BEL) and Miss M.J.M.M. Oremans (NED), 14–Miss C. Barclay and Miss K–A. Guse (AUS), 15–Miss F. Labat (ARG) and Mrs. B. Van Roost (BEL), 16–Miss V. Ruano Pascual (ESP) and Miss P.L. Suarez (ARG), 17–Miss M. de Swardt (RSA) and Miss D.A. Graham (USA).

*The No. 6 seeds withdrew. Their position in the draw was filled by the highest ranked non–seeded pair, who became the No. 17 seeds.

1999 (16)

1–Miss J. Novotna (CZE) and Miss N.M. Zvereva (BLR), 2–Miss M. Hingis (SUI) and Miss A.S. Kournikova (RUS)*, 3–Miss A. Fusai and Miss N. Tauziat (FRA), 4–Miss S.J. Williams and Miss V.E.S. Williams (USA)*, 5–Miss E. Likhovtseva (RUS) and Miss A. Sugiyama (JAP), 6–Miss L.M. Raymond (USA) and Miss R.P. Stubbs (AUS), 7–Miss L.A. Davenport and Miss C.M. Morariu (USA), 8–Mrs. A. Neiland (LAT) and Miss A.I.M. Sanchez Vicario (ESP), 9–Miss M. de Swardt (RSA) and Miss E.V. Tatarkova (UKR), 10–Miss I. Spirlea (ROM) and Miss C.M. Vis (NED), 11–Miss I.C. Martinez (ESP) and Miss P. Tarabini (ARG), 12– Miss M.J. Fernandez and Miss M. Seles (USA), 13–Miss E.S.H. Callens (BEL) and Mrs. A. Halard-Decugis (FRA), 14–Miss V. Ruano Pascual (ESP) and Miss P.L. Suarez (ARG), 15–Miss B. Schett (AUT) and Miss P. Schnyder (SUI), 16–Miss C.C. Black (ZIM) and Miss I. Selyutina (KAZ), 17–Miss C. Cristea and Miss. R. Dragomir (ROM), 18–Miss D.A. Graham and Miss L.M. McNeil (USA).

*The No. 4 seeds withdrew. Their position in the draw was filled by the No. 5 seeds, whose position was filled by the No. 9 seeds. The highest ranked non-seeded pair became the No. 17 seeds.

The No. 2 seeds withdrew. Their position in the draw was filled by the highest ranked non-seeded pair, who became the No. 18 seeds.

2000 (16)

1–Miss L.M. Raymond (USA) and Miss R.P. Stubbs (AUS), 2–Miss L.A. Davenport and Miss C.M. Morariu (Mrs. A. Turcinovich) (USA)*, 3–Miss M. Hingis (SUI) and Miss M.C. Pierce (FRA), 4–Mrs. A. Halard-Decugis (FRA) and Miss A. Sugiyama (JAP), 5–Miss A.S. Kournikova (RUS) and Miss N.M. Zvereva (BLR), 6–Miss V. Ruano Pascual (ESP) and Miss P.L. Suarez (ARG), 7–Miss C.R. Rubin (USA) and Miss S. Testud (Mrs. V. Magnelli) (FRA), 8–Miss S.J. Williams and Miss V.E.S. Williams (USA), 9–Miss A. Fusai and Miss N. Tauziat (FRA), 10–Miss I.C. Martinez (ESP) and Miss P. Tarabini (ARG), 11–Miss N.J. Arendt (USA) and Miss M.M. Bollegraf (NED), 12–Miss I. Spirlea (ROM) and Miss C.M. Vis (NED), 13–Miss K.Y. Po (USA) and Miss A-G. Sidot (FRA), 14–Miss A. Huber (GER) and Miss B. Schett (AUT), 15–Miss L. Courtois (BEL) and Miss E. Likhovtseva (Mrs. M. Baranov) (RUS), 16–Miss T. Krizan and Miss K. Srebotnik (SLO), 17–Miss L. Horn (RSA) and Miss L. Montalvo (ARG).

*The No. 2 seeds withdrew. Their position in the draw was filled by the highest ranked non-seeded pair, who became the No. 17 seeds.

2001 (16)

1–Miss L.M. Raymond and Miss R.P. Stubbs (AUS), 2–Miss V. Ruano Pascual (ESP) and Miss P.L. Suarez (ARG), 3–Miss C.C. Black (ZIM) and Miss E. Likhovtseva (Mrs. M. Baranov) (RUS), 4–Miss S.J. Williams and Miss V.E.S. Williams (USA), 5–Mrs. K.Y. Po-Messerli (USA), and Miss N. Tauziat (FRA), 6–Miss E.S.H. Callens (BEL) and Miss M. Shaughnessy (USA), 7–Miss J. Dokic (YUG) and Miss I.C. Martinez (ESP), 8–Miss N.J. Arendt (USA) and Miss C.M. Vis (NED), 9–Miss K. Clijsters (BEL) and Miss A. Sugiyama (JPN), 10–Miss A. Fusai (FRA) and Miss R. Grande (ITA), 11–Miss N.J. Pratt (AUS) and Miss E.V. Tatarkova (UKR), 12–Miss T. Garbin (ITA) and Miss J. Husarova (SVK), 13–Miss A. Huber (GER) and Miss B Schett (AUT), 14–Miss A.J. Coetzer (RSA) and Miss L.M. McNeil (USA), 15–Miss T. Krizan and Miss K. Srebotnik (SLO), 16–Miss M. Navratilova (USA) and Miss A.I.M. Sanchez Vicario (Mrs J. Vehils) (ESP).

2002 (16)

1–Miss L.M. Raymond (USA) and Miss R.P. Stubbs (AUS), 2–Miss V. Ruano Pascual (ESP) and Miss P.L. Suarez (ARG), 3–Miss S.J. Williams and Miss V.E.S. Williams (USA), 4–Miss C.C. Black (ZIM) and Miss E. Likhovtseva (Mrs. M. Baranov) (RUS), 5–Mrs. K.Y. Po-Messerli (USA) and Miss N. Tauziat (FRA), 6–Miss S. Testud (Mrs. V. Magnelli) (FRA) and Miss R. Vinci (ITA), 7–Miss N.J. Arendt (USA) and Mrs. A. Huber (RSA), 8–Miss E. Dementieva (RUS) and Miss J. Husarova (SVK), 9–Miss R. Fujiwara and Miss A. Sugiyama (JPN), 10–Miss T. Krizan and Miss K. Srebotnik (SLO), 11–Miss J. Lee (TPE) and Miss W. Prakusya (INA), 12–Mrs F. Farina Elia (ITA) and Miss B. Schett (AUT), 13–Miss E.S.H. Callens (BEL) and Miss M. Shaughnessy (USA), 14–Miss D.Bedanova (CZE) and Miss E. Bovina (RUS), 15–Miss A.J. Coetzer (RSA) and Miss L.M. McNeil (USA), 16–Miss J.M. Capriati (USA) and Miss D. Hantuchova (SVK)

2003 (16)

1–Miss V. Ruano Pascual (ESP) and Miss P.L. Suarez (ARG), 2–Miss K. Clijsters (BEL) and Miss A. Sugiyama (JPN), 3–Miss S.J. Williams and Miss V.E.S. Williams (USA), 4–Miss L.A. Davenport (Mrs J. Leach) and Miss L.M. Raymond (USA), 5–Miss C.C. Black (ZIM) and Miss E. Likhovtseva (Mrs. M. Baranov) (RUS), 6–Miss J. Dokic (YUG) and Miss N. Petrova (RUS), 7–Miss J. Husarova (SVK) and Miss I.C. Martinez (ESP), 8–Miss S. Kuznetsova (RUS) and Miss M. Navratilova (USA), 9–Miss D. Hantuchova (SVK) and Miss C.R. Rubin (USA), 10–Mrs A. Huber (RSA) and Miss M. Maleeva (BUL), 11–Miss E. Gagliardi (SUI) and Miss M. Shaughnessy (USA), 12–Miss P. Mandula (HUN) and Miss P. Wartusch (AUT), 13–Miss N. Dechy and Miss E. Loit (FRA), 14–Miss T. Krizan and Miss K. Srebotnik (SLO), 15–Miss E. Dementieva and Miss L. Krasnoroutskaya (RUS), 16–Miss J. Lee (TPE) and Miss W. Prakusya (INA).

2004 (16)

1–Miss V. Ruano Pascual (ESP) and Miss P.L. Suarez (ARG), 2–Miss S. Kuznetsova and Miss E. Likhovtseva (Mrs. M. Baranov) (RUS), 3–Miss M. Navratilova and Miss L.M. Raymond (USA), 4– Miss N. Petrova (RUS) and Miss M. Shaughnessy (USA), 5–Mrs. A. Huber (RSA) and Miss A. Sugiyama (JPN), 6–Miss C.C. Black (ZIM) and Miss R.P. Stubbs (AUS), 7–Miss J. Husarova (SVK) and Miss I.C. Martinez (ESP), 8–Mrs. G. Vento-Kabchi (VEN) and Miss A. Widjaja (INA), 9–Miss M. Casanova (SUI) and Miss N. Pratt (AUS), 10–Miss E. Dementieva and Miss L. Krasnoroutskaya (RUS)*, 11–Miss M. Bartoli and Miss E. Loit (FRA), 12–Miss T. Li and Miss T.T. Sun (CHN), 13– Miss A. Myskina and Miss V. Zvonareva (RUS), 14–Mrs. F. Farina Elia and Miss F. Schiavone (ITA), 15–Miss E.S.H. Callens (BEL) and Miss P. Mandula (HUN), 16–Miss E.Gagliardi (SUI) and Miss R. Vinci (ITA), 17–Miss A. Molik (AUS) and Miss M.L. Serna (ESP).

*The No. 10 seeds withdrew. Their position in the draw was filled by the highest ranked non-seeded pair, who became the No. 17 seeds.

2005 (16)

1–Miss V. Ruano Pascual (ESP) and Miss P.L. Suarez (ARG)*, 2–Miss C.C. Black (ZIM) and Mrs. A. Huber (RSA), 3–Miss L.M. Raymond (USA) and Miss R.P. Stubbs (AUS), 4–Miss N. Petrova (RUS) and Miss M. Shaughnessy (USA), 5–Miss E. Likhovtseva (Mrs M. Baranov) and Miss V. Zvonareva (RUS), 6–Miss J. Husarova (SVK) and Miss I.C. Martinez (ESP), 7–Miss D. Hantuchova (SVK) and Miss A. Sugiyama (JPN), 8–Miss A-L Groenefeld (GER) and Miss M. Navratilova

(USA), 9–Miss A-I Medina Garrigues (ESP) and Miss D. Safina (RUS), 10–Miss S. Asagoe (JPN) and Miss K. Srebotnik (SLO), 11–Miss B.M. Stewart (USA) and Miss S.J. Stosur (AUS), 12–Miss L.A. Davenport (Mrs J. Leach) and Miss C.M. Morariu (USA), 13–Miss G.A. Dulko (ARG) and Mrs G.Vento-Kabchi (VEN), 14–Miss E. Daniilidou (GRE) and Miss N. Pratt (AUS), 15–Miss E. Loit (FRA) and Miss B. Strycova (CZE), 16–Miss G. Navratilova and Miss M. Pastikova (CZE), 17–Miss E.S.H. Callens (BEL) and Miss E. Gagliardi (SUI).

*The No. 1 seeds withdrew. Their position in the draw was filled by the highest non-ranked pair, who became the No. 17 seeds.

2006 (16)

1–Miss L.M. Raymond (USA) and Miss S.J. Stosur (AUS), 2–Miss C.C. Black (ZIM) and Miss R.P. Stubbs (AUS), 3–Miss D. Hantuchova (SVK) and Miss Miss A. Sugiyama (JPN), 4–Miss Z. Yan and Miss J. Zheng (CHN), 5–Miss A-L Groenefeld (GER) and Miss M. Shaughnessy (USA), 6–Miss S. Asagoe (JPN) and Miss K. Srebotnik (SLO), 7–Mrs A. Huber (RSA) and Miss M. Navratilova (USA), 8–Miss E. Dementieva (RUS) and Miss F. Pennetta (ITA), 9–Mrs T.Peschke (CZE) and Miss F. Schiavone (ITA), 10–Miss E. Daniilidou (GRE) and Miss A-I Medina Garrigues (ESP), 11–Miss E. Likhovtseva (Mrs M. Baranov) and Miss A. Myskina (RUS), 12–Miss S. Kuznetsova (RUS) and Miss A. Mauresmo (FRA), 13–Miss T. Li and Miss T-T. Sun (CHN), 14–Miss E. Loit (FRA) and Miss N.J. Pratt (AUS), 15–Miss D. Safina (RUS) and Miss R. Vinci (ITA), 16–Miss N. Dechy (Mrs A Maitre-Devallon) (FRA) and Miss G. Dulko (ARG)

2007 (16)

1–Miss L.M. Raymond (USA) and Miss S.J. Stosur (AUS), 2–Miss C.C. Black (ZIM) and Mrs A. Huber (RSA), 3–Miss Y-J. Chan and Miss C-J Chuang (TPE), 4–Miss K. Srebotnik (SLO) and Miss A. Sugiyama (JPN), 5–Mrs T. Peschke (CZE) and Miss R.P. Stubbs (AUS), 6–Miss A. Molik (AUS) and Miss M. Santangelo (ITA), 7–Miss J. Husarova (SVK) and Miss M. Shaughnessy (USA), 8–Miss A.I. Medina-Garrigues and Miss V. Ruano-Pascual (ESP), 9–Miss T. Garbin (ITA) and Miss P.L. Suarez (ARG), 10–Miss E. Likhovtseva (Mrs. M. Baranov) (RUS) and Miss T.T. Sun (CHN), 11–Miss M.E. Camerin (ITA) and Miss G. Dulko (ARG), 12–Miss M. Kirilenko and Miss Elena Vesina (RUS), 13–Miss D. Safina (RUS) and Miss R. Vinci (ITA), 14–Miss V. Dushevina (RUS) and Miss T. Perebiynis (UKR), 15–Miss V. King (USA) and Miss J. Kostanic Tosic (CRO), 16–Miss S. Mirza (IND) and Miss S. Peer (ISR).

2008 (16)

1–Miss C.C. Black (ZIM) and Mrs A. Huber (USA), 2–Miss A. Sugiyama (JPN) and Miss K. Srebotnik (SLO), 3–Miss K. Peschke (CZE) and Miss R.P. Stubbs (AUS), 4–Miss Y–J. Chan and Miss C–J. Chuang (TPE), 5–Miss A.I. Medina Garrigues (ESP) and Miss V. Ruano Pascual (ESP), 6–Miss V. Azarenka (BLR) and Miss S. Peer (ISR) 7– Miss A. Bondarenko and Miss K. Bondarenko (UKR). 8–Miss S. Peng and Miss T.I. Sun (CHN), 9–Miss Z. Yan and Miss J. Zheng (CHN), 10–Miss D. Safina (RUS) and Miss A. Szavay(HUN), 11–Miss S.J. Williams and Miss V.E.S. Williams (USA), 12–Miss S. Kuznetsova (RUS) and Miss A. Mauresmo (FRA), 13–Miss B. Mattek (USA) and Miss S. Mirza (IND), 14–Miss A. Molik (AUS) and Miss M. Santangelo (ITA), 15–Miss I. Benesova (CZE) and Miss j. Husarova (SVK), 16–Miss L.M. Raymond (USA) and Miss S.J. Stosur (AUS)

2009 (16)

1–Miss C.C. Black (ZIM) and Mrs A. Huber (USA), 2–Miss A.I. Medina Garrigues and Miss V. Ruano Pascual (ESP), 3–Miss S.J. Stosur and Miss R. Stubbs (AUS), 4–Miss S.J. Williams and Miss V.E.S. Williams (USA), 5–Miss S-W. Hsieh (TPE) and Miss S. Peng (CHN), 6–Miss D. Hantuchova (SVK) and Miss A. Sugiyama (JPN), 7–Miss V. Azarenka (BLR) and Miss E. Vesnina (RUS), 8–Miss M. Kirilenko (RUS) and Miss F. Pennetta (ITA), 9–Miss LM. Raymond (USA) and Miss V. Zvonareva (RUS), 10–Mrs B. Mattek–Sands (USA) and Miss N. Petrova (RUS), 11–Miss N. Llagostera Vives and Miss M.J. Martinez Sanchez (ESP), 12–Miss A-L. Groenefeld (GER) and Miss V. King (USA), 13–Miss Z. Yan and Miss J. Zheng (CHN), 14–Miss N. Dechy (Mrs A. Maitre-Devallon) (FRA) and Miss M. Santangelo (ITA), 15–Miss C.J. Chuang (TPE) and Miss S. Mirza (IND), 16–Miss S. Kuznetsova (RUS) and Miss A. Mauresmo (FRA)

2010 (16)

1–Miss S.J. Williams and Miss V.E.S. Williams (USA), 2–Miss N. Llagostera Vives and Miss M.J. Martinez Sanchez (ESP)*, 3–Miss N. Petrova and Miss SJ. Stosur (AUS), 4–Miss G. Dulko (ARG) and Miss F. Pennetta (ITA), 5–Mrs A. Huber and Mrs B. Mattek–Sands (USA), 6–Miss T. Peschke (CZE) and Miss K. Srebotnik (SLO), 7–Miss L.M. Raymond (USA) and Miss R.P. Stubbs (AUS), 8–Miss A. Kleybanova (RUS) and Miss F. Schiavone (ITA)*, 9–Miss Y-J. Chan (TPE) and Miss J. Zheng (CHN), 10–Miss M. Kirilenko (RUS) and Miss A. Radwanska (POL), 11–Miss C.C. Black (ZIM) and Miss D. Hantuchova (SVK), 12–Miss I. Benesova and Mrs. B. Zahlavova Strycova (CZE), 13– Miss V. Duschevina and Miss E. Makarova (RUS), 14–Miss M. Niculescu (ROM) and Miss S. Peer (ISR), 15– Miss A. Rosolska (POL) and Miss Z. Yan (CHN), 16– Miss S–W. Hsieh (TPE) and Miss A. Kudryavtseva (RUS), 17–Miss C.J. Chuang (TPE) and Miss O. Govortsova (BLR)

*The No.2 seeds withdrew. Their position in the draw was filled by the highest ranked non-seeded pair who became the No.17 seeds. The No.8 seeds withdrew. Their position in the draw was filled by Lucky Losers Miss K.C. Chang (TPE) and Miss A. Morita (JPN)

2011 (16)

1–Miss V. King (USA) and Miss Y. Shvedova (KAZ), 2–Mrs T. Peschke (CZE) and Miss K. Srebotnik (SLO), 3–Mrs A. Huber and Miss L. Raymond (USA), 4–Miss S. Mirza (IND) and Miss E. Vesnina (RUS), 5– Mrs B. Mattek–Sands and Miss M. Shaughnessy (USA), 6–Miss N. Petrova (RUS) and Miss A. Rodionova (AUS), 7– Miss A. Hlavackova and Miss L. Hradecka (CZE), 8–Miss S. Peng and Miss J. Zheng (CHN), 9–Miss J. Goerges (GER) and Miss M. Kirilenko (RUS), 10–Miss I. Benesova and Mrs B. Zahlavova Strycova (CZE), 11–Miss M.J. Martinez Sanchez and Miss A. Medina Garrigues (ESP), 12–Miss Y-J. Chan (TPE) and Miss M. Niculescu (ROM), 13–Miss D. Hantuchova (SVK) and Miss A. Radwanska (POL), 14–Miss C.C. Black (ZIM) and Miss S. Peer (ISR), 15–Miss C-J. Chuang and Miss S.W. Hsieh (TPE), 16–Miss O. Govortsova (BLR) and Miss A. Kudryavtseva (RUS)

2012 (16)

1–Mrs A. Huber and Miss L.M. Raymond (USA), 2–Miss S. Errani and Miss R. Vinci (ITA), 3– Mrs T. Peschke (CZE) and Miss K. Srebotnik (SLO), 4–Miss M. Kirilenko and Miss N. Petrova (RUS), 5–Miss E. Makarova and Miss E. Vesnina (RUS), 6–Miss A. Hlavackova and Miss L. Hradecka (CZE), 7–Miss Y. Shvedova and Miss G. Voksoboeva (KAZ), 8–Miss I. Benesova and Mrs B. Zahlavova Strycova (CZE), 9–Miss N. Llagostera Vives and Miss M.J. Martinez Sanchez (ESP), 10–Miss R. Kops-Jones and Miss A. Spears (USA), 11–MissN. Grandin (RSA) and Miss V. Uhlirova (CZE), 12–Miss A. Medina Garrigues and Miss A.P. Santonja (ESP), 13–Mrs B. Mattek-Sands (USA) and Miss S. Mirza (IND), 14–Miss G. Dulko and Miss P. Suarez (ARG), 15–Miss I-C Begu and Miss M. Niculescu (ROM), 16–Miss C-J Chuang (TPE) and Miss V. Duchevina (RUS)

2013 (16)

1–Miss S.Errani and Miss R Vinci (ITA), 2–Miss A. Hlavackova and Miss L. Hradecka (CZE), 3–Miss N. Petrova (RUS) and Miss K. Srebotnik (SLO), 4–Miss E. Makarova and Miss E. Vesnina (RUS), 5–Miss R. Kops-Jones and Miss A. Spears (USA), 6–Mrs A. Huber (USA) and Miss S. Mirza (IND), 7–Miss A-L. Groenefeld (GER) and Mrs T. Peschke (CZE), 8–Miss S-W Hsieh (TPE) and Miss S. Peng (CHN), 9–Miss A. Pavlyuchenkova (RUS) and Miss L. Safarova (CZE), 10–Miss K. Mladenovic (FRA) and Miss G. Voskoboeva (KAZ), 11– Miss C.C. Black (ZIM) and Miss M. Erakovic (NZL), 12–Miss A. Barty and Miss C. Dellacqua (AUS), 13–Miss V. King (USA) and Miss J. Zheng (CHN), 14–Miss D. Hantuchova (SVK) and Miss M. Kirilenko (RUS), 15–Miss H-C. Chan (TPE) and Miss A. Medina Garrigues (ESP), 16–Miss J. Goerges (GER) and Mrs B. Zahlavova Strycova (CZE)

2014 (16)

1–Miss S-W. Hsieh (TPE) and Miss S.Peng (CHN), 2–Miss S. Errani and Miss R. Vinci (ITA), 3–Mrs T. Peschke (CZE) and Miss K. Srebotnik (SLO), 4–Miss C. Black (ZIM) and Miss S.

Mirza (IND), 5–Miss E. Makarova (RUS) and Miss E. Vesnina (RUS), 6–Miss A. Barty and Miss
C. Dellacqua (AUS), 7–Miss R. Kops-Jones and Miss A. Spears (USA), 8–Miss S.J. Williams and
Miss V.E.S. Williams (USA), 9–Miss A. Hlavackova (CZE) and Miss J. Zheng (CHN), 10–Miss
J. Goerges and Miss A-L. Groenefeld (GER), 11–Miss A. Kudryavtseva (RUS) and Miss A.
Rodionova (AUS), 12–Miss A Medina Garrigues (ESP) and Miss Y. Shvedova (KAZ), 13–Miss
L. Hradecka (CZE) and Miss M. Krajicek (NED), 14–Miss T. Babos (HUN) and Miss K.
Mladenovic (FRA),15–Mrs L. Huber and Miss L.M. Raymond (USA), 16–Miss G. Muguruza
and Miss C. Suarez Navarro (ESP)

Seeded players who reached the concluding rounds

Year	No. of Seeds	Semi–final	Final	Winner
1927	4	1-4	1, 2	2
1928	4	1-3	2, 3	3
1929	4	1-3	2, 3	2
1930	4	1, 4	1, 4	1
1931	4	1, 4	4	–
1932	4	2, 4	2, 4	4
1933	4	1	1	1
1934	4	1	1	1
1935	4	2, 3	2, 3	3
1936	4	1, 2	1, 2	1
1937	4	2, 4	2	2
1938	4	1, 2, 4	1, 2	2
1939	4	1, 2, 4	1, 2	1
1946	4	1-4	1, 2	1
1947	4	1-3	1, 2	2
1948	4	1-3	1, 2	1
1949	4	1, 2, 4	1, 2	1
1950	4	1, 2	1, 2	1
1951	4	1-4	1, 2	2
1952	4	1-4	1, 2	1
1953	4	1-3	1, 2	1
1954	4	1-3	1, 2	2
1955	4	2-4	3, 4	4
1956	4	1-3	3	3
1957	4	1, 2, 4	1, 2	1
1958	4	1, 3, 4	1	1
1959	4	1-4	1, 3	1
1960	4	1, 3, 4	1, 4	1
1961	4	3, 4	3	–
1962	4	1-4	2, 4	2
1963	4	1, 2, 4	1, 2	2
1964	4	1-4	1, 2	1
1965	4	2, 3	2	2
1966	4	1, 2, 4	1, 2	2
1967	4	1-4	1, 3	3
1968	4	1, 3, 4	1, 3	1
1969	4	1	1	1
1970	4	2-4	2, 4	2
1971	4	1, 2, 4	1, 2	1
1972	4	1-3	1, 3	1
1973	4	1, 3	1, 3	1
1974	4	3	–	–

Year	No. of Seeds	Semi–final	Final	Winner
1975	4	2	-	–
1976	4	1, 2	1, 2	2
1977	8	1, 4, 7	1	–
1978	8	3, 4, 6, 7	4, 7	4
1979	8	1, 2, 3, 6	1, 2	1
1980	8	1, 2, 4	2, 4	4
1981	12	1, 2, 4, 7	1, 2	2
1982	12	1, 2, 3	1, 2	1
1983	14	1, 3, 6, 7	1, 6	1
1984	16	1, 4, 6, 7	1, 7	1
1985	16	1-4	1, 3	3
1986	16	1, 3, 8	1, 3	1
1987	16	3, 5-7	3, 5	3
1988	16	3, 8, 11, 13	3, 11	3
1989	16	1, 2, 3	2, 3	3
1990	16	1, 3, 6, 10	1, 6	1
1991	16	1, 2, 4, 8	1, 2	2
1992	16	1-4	1, 2	2
1993	16	1, 2, 5, 6	1, 2	1
1994	16	1, 2, 4	1, 2	1
1995	16	1, 2, 5, 9,	1, 2	2
1996	16	2, 4, 8, 15	4, 8	8
1997	16	1, 4, 6, 12	1, 6	1
1998	16	1, 2, 7, 17	1, 2	1
1999	16	1, 7, 9	7, 9	7
2000	16	1, 4, 5, 8	4, 8	8
2001	16	1, 2, 5, 9	1, 9	1
2002	16	2-4	2, 3	3
2003	16	1, 2, 4, 15	1, 2	2
2004	16	1, 3, 5, 6	5, 6	6
2005	16	2, 8, 11	2	2
2006	16	2, 4	4	4
2007	16	1, 2, 4, 6	2, 4	2
2008	16	1, 11, 16	11, 16	11
2009	16	1-4	3-4	4
2010	16	4, 5	–	–
2011	16	2, 4	2	2
2012	16	1, 6	6	–
2013	16	7, 8, 12	8, 12	8
2014	16	2, 9, 14	2, 14	2

Unseeded Champions (7)

1931	Mrs. W.P. Barron and Miss P.E. Mudford (GBR)
1961	Miss K.J. Hantze and Miss B.J. Moffitt (USA)
1974	Miss E.F. Goolagong (AUS) and Miss M. Michel (USA)
1975	Miss A.K. Kiyomura (USA) and Miss K. Sawamatsu (JAP)
1977	Mrs. R.L. Cawley (AUS) and Miss J.C. Russell (USA)
2010	Miss V. King (USA) and Miss Y.V. Shvedova (KAZ)
2012	Miss S.J. Williams and Miss V.E.S.Williams (USA)

Mixed Doubles Championship

1927 (4)
1–L.A. Godfree and Mrs. L.A. Godfree (GBR), 2–J.R. Borotra and Mrs. P.R.M. Bordes (FRA), 3–F.T. Hunter and Miss E.M. Ryan (USA), 4–W.T. Tilden and Mrs. F.I. Mallory (USA).

1928 (4)
1–H.J. Cochet (FRA) and Miss E.V. Bennett (GBR), 2–P.D.B. Spence (RSA) and Miss E.M. Ryan (USA), 3–F.T. Hunter and Miss H.N. Wills (USA), 4–C.R.O. Crole–Rees and Mrs. M.R. Watson (GBR).

1929 (4)
1–H.J. Cochet (FRA) and Miss E.V. Bennett (GBR), 2–F.T. Hunter and Miss H.N. Wills (USA), 3–J.C. Gregory (GBR) and Miss E.M. Ryan (USA), 4–J.R. Borotra (FRA) and Miss K. Bouman (NED).

1930 (4)
1–W.T. Tilden (USA) and Miss C. Aussem (GER), 2–J.H. Crawford (AUS) and Miss E.M. Ryan (USA), 3–H.J. Cochet (FRA) and Mrs. E.O.F. Whittingstall (GBR), 4–J.R. Borotra (FRA) and Miss E.M. de Alvarez (ESP)*.
*The No. 4 seeds withdrew. Their position in the draw was not filled and opponents given a walkover.

1931 (4)
1–H.J. Cochet (FRA) and Mrs. E.O.F. Whittingstall (GBR), 2–P.D.B. Spence (RSA) and Miss B.M. Nuthall (GBR), 3–V.G. Kirby (RSA) and Miss J. Sigart (BEL), 4–G.P. Hughes and Miss E.H. Harvey (GBR).

1932 (8)
1–H.E. Vines and Mrs. F.S. Moody (USA), 2–H.J. Cochet (FRA) and Mrs. E.O.F. Whittingstall (GBR), 3–J. Brugnon and Mrs. R. Mathieu (FRA), 4–E.G. Maier (ESP) and Miss E.M. Ryan (USA), 5–W.L. Allison and Miss H.H. Jacobs (USA), 6–H.C. Hopman (AUS) and Miss J. Sigart (BEL), 7–P.D.B. Spence (RSA) and Miss B.M. Nuthall (GBR), 8–G.S. Mangin and Miss S.H. Palfrey (USA).

1933 (4)
1–E.G. Maier (ESP) and Miss E.M. Ryan (USA), 2–J.R. Borotra (FRA) and Miss B.M. Nuthall (GBR), 3–G.P. Hughes (GBR) and Mrs. F.S. Moody (USA), 4–N.G. Farquharson (RSA) and Miss G.M. Heeley (GBR).

1934 (4)
1–G. von Cramm and Mrs. S. Sperling (GER), 2–G.M. Lott and Miss S.H. Palfrey (USA), 3–E. Maier (ESP) and Miss E.M. Ryan (USA), 4–J.R. Borotra (FRA) and Miss B.M. Nuthall (GBR).

1935 (4)
1–G. von Cramm and Mrs. S. Sperling (GER), 2–A. Martin Legeay and Mrs. C.F. Henrotin (FRA), 3–F.J. Perry and Miss D.E. Round (GBR), 4–W.L. Allison and Miss H.H. Jacobs (USA).

1936 (4)
1–F.J. Perry and Miss D.E. Round (GBR), 2–J.D. Budge and Mrs. M. Fabyan (USA), 3–J.R. Borotra (FRA) and Miss S.D.B. Noel (GBR), 4–C.E. Malfroy (NZL) and Mrs. S. Sperling (GER).

1937 (4)
1–J.D. Budge and Miss A. Marble (USA), 2–Y.F.M. Petra and Mrs. R. Mathieu (FRA), 3–F.H.D. Wilde and Miss M.E. Whitmarsh (GBR), 4–N.G. Farquharson (RSA) and Miss K.E. Stammers (GBR).

1938 (8)
1–J.D. Budge and Miss A. Marble (USA), 2–H.E.O. Henkel (GER) and Mrs. M. Fabyan (USA), 3–C.G. Mako (USA) and Miss J. Jedrzejowska (POL), 4–D. Mitic (YUG) and Mrs. R. Mathieu (FRA), 5–C. Boussus (FRA) and Miss N.M. Wynne (AUS), 6–J.R. Borotra (FRA) and Mrs. F.S. Moody (USA), 7–J.S. Olliff (GBR) and Mrs. J.H.K. Miller (RSA), 8–J. Brugnon (FRA) and Miss T.D. Coyne (AUS).

1939 (4)
1–E.T. Cooke and Mrs. M. Fabyan (USA), 2–R.L. Riggs and Miss A. Marble (USA), 3–C.E. Malfroy (NZL) and Miss B.M. Nuthall (GBR), 4–F. Kukuljevic (YUG) and Mrs. R. Mathieu (FRA).

1946 (4)
1–H.C. Hopman (AUS) and Miss M.E. Osborne (USA), 2–G.E. Brown (AUS) and Miss D.M. Bundy (USA), 3–T.P. Brown and Miss A.L. Brough (USA), 4–D.R. Pails (AUS) and Mrs. M. Menzies (GBR).

1947 (4)
1–J.E. Bromwich (AUS) and Miss A.L. Brough (USA), 2–T.P. Brown and Miss M.E. Osborne (USA), 3–C.F. Long and Mrs. G.F. Bolton (AUS), 4–J.E. Patty and Miss D.J. Hart (USA)*.
*The No. 4 seeds withdrew. Their position in the draw was filled by new No. 4 seeds, L. Bergelin (SWE) and Miss D.J. Hart (USA).

1948 (4)
1–J.E. Bromwich (AUS) and Miss A.L. Brough (USA), 2–T.P. Brown and Mrs. W. duPont (USA), 3–J. Drobny (TCH) and Mrs. R.B. Todd (USA), 4–F.A. Sedgman (AUS) and Miss D.J. Hart (USA).

1949 (4)
1–J.E. Bromwich (AUS) and Miss A.L. Brough (USA), 2–O.W.T. Sidwell (AUS) and Mrs. W. duPont (USA), 3–R. Falkenburg and Miss G.A. Moran (USA), 4–E.W. Sturgess and Mrs. R.A. Summers (RSA).

1950 (4)
1–E.W. Sturgess (RSA) and Miss A.L. Brough (USA), 2–W.F. Talbert and Mrs. W. duPont (USA), 3–F.A. Sedgman (AUS) and Miss D.J. Hart (USA), 4–G.E. Brown (AUS) and Mrs. R.B. Todd (USA).

1951 (4)
1–E.W. Sturgess (RSA) and Miss A.L. Brough (USA), 2–F.A. Sedgman (AUS) and Miss D.J. Hart (USA), 3–K.B. McGregor (AUS) and Mrs. W. duPont (USA), 4–S.V. Davidson (SWE) and Miss S.J. Fry (USA).

1952 (4)
1–F.A. Sedgman (AUS) and Miss D.J. Hart (USA), 2–K.B. McGregor (AUS) and Miss A.L. Brough (USA), 3–E.W. Sturgess (RSA) and Miss S.J. Fry (USA), 4–D.W. Candy (AUS) and Mrs. R.B. Todd (USA).

1953 (4)
1–E.V. Seixas and Miss D.J. Hart (USA), 2–M.G. Rose (AUS) and Miss M.C. Connolly (USA), 3–G.L. Paish and Mrs. I.F. Rinkel (GBR), 4–E.J. Morea (ARG) and Miss S.J. Fry (USA).

1954 (4)
1–E.V. Seixas and Miss D.J. Hart (USA), 2–L.A. Hoad (AUS) and Miss M.C. Connolly (USA), 3–K.R. Rosewall (AUS) and Mrs. W. duPont (USA), 4–R.N. Hartwig (AUS) and Mrs. E.C.S. Pratt (USA).

1955 (4)
1–E.V. Seixas and Miss D.J. Hart (USA), 2–E.J. Morea (ARG) and Miss A.L. Brough (USA), 3–H.F. Richardson and Miss D.R. Hard (USA), 4–L.A. Hoad and Mrs. L.A. Hoad (AUS)*.
*When the original seedings were announced, Mrs. L.A. Hoad was Miss J.J. Staley (AUS).

1956 (4)
1–E.V. Seixas and Miss S.J. Fry (USA), 2–L.A. Ayala (CHI) and Mrs. M.N. Long (AUS), 3–G.P. Mulloy and Miss A. Gibson (USA), 4–R.N. Howe (AUS) and Miss D.R. Hard (USA).

1957 (4)
1–E.V. Seixas and Miss A.L. Brough (USA), 2–N.A. Fraser (AUS) and Miss A. Gibson (USA), 3–J. Javorsky and Miss V. Puzejova (TCH), 4–M.G. Rose (AUS) and Miss D.R. Hard (USA).

1958 (4)
1–N.A. Fraser (AUS) and Mrs. W. duPont (USA), 2–K. Nielsen (DEN) and Miss A. Gibson (USA), 3–L.A. Ayala (CHI) and Mrs. M.N. Long (AUS), 4–R.N. Howe and Miss L.G. Coghlan (AUS).

1959 (4)
1–W.A. Knight (GBR) and Miss Y. Ramirez (MEX), 2–N.A. Fraser (AUS) and Miss M.E.A. Bueno (BRA), 3–R.G. Laver (AUS) and Miss D.R. Hard (USA), 4–R.N. Howe (AUS) and Miss S.M. Moore (USA).

1960 (4)
1–R.G. Laver (AUS) and Miss D.R. Hard (USA), 2–R.N. Howe (AUS) and Miss M.E.A. Bueno (BRA), 3–R.S. Emerson (AUS) and Miss A.S. Haydon (GBR), 4–R.A.J. Hewitt (AUS) and Miss J.P. Lehane (AUS).

1961 (4)
1–F.S. Stolle and Miss L.R. Turner (AUS), 2–E.J. Morea (ARG) and Miss M. Smith (AUS), 3–J. Javorsky and Mrs. C. Sukova (TCH), 4–R.N. Howe (AUS) and Miss E. Buding (GER).

1962 (4)
1–F.S. Stolle and Miss L.R. Turner (AUS), 2–R.N. Howe (AUS) and Miss M.E.A. Bueno (BRA), 3–N.A. Fraser (AUS) and Mrs. W. duPont (USA), 4–J. Javorsky and Mrs. C. Sukova (TCH).

1963 (4)
1–F.S. Stolle and Miss L.R. Turner (AUS), 2–K.N. Fletcher and Miss M. Smith (AUS), 3–R.D. Ralston (USA) and Mrs. P.F. Jones (GBR), 4–R.N. Howe (AUS) and Miss M.E.A. Bueno (BRA).

1964 (4)
1–K.N. Fletcher and Miss M. Smith (AUS), 2–F.S. Stolle and Miss L.R. Turner (AUS), 3–R.A.J. Hewitt (AUS) and Miss M.E.A. Bueno (BRA), 4–R.N. Howe (AUS) and Miss N. Baylon (ARG).

1965 (4)
1–F.S. Stolle and Miss L.R. Turner (AUS), 2–K.N. Fletcher and Miss M. Smith (AUS), 3–R.D. Ralston (USA) and Miss M.E.A. Bueno (BRA), 4–N.A. Fraser (AUS) and Miss H. Schultze (GER).

1966 (4)
1–K.N. Fletcher and Miss M. Smith (AUS), 2–A.D. Roche and Miss J.A.M. Tegart (AUS)*, 3–R.D. Ralston and Mrs. L.W. King (USA), 4–F.S. Stolle (AUS) and Miss F.G. Durr (FRA).
*The No. 2 seeds withdrew. Their position in the draw was filled by unseeded W.W. Bowrey and Miss J.A.M. Tegart (AUS).

1967 (4)
1–O.K. Davidson (AUS) and Mrs. L.W. King (USA), 2–K.N. Fletcher (AUS) and Miss M.E.A. Bueno (BRA), 3–A.D. Roche and Miss J.A.M. Tegart (AUS), 4–F.D. McMillan and Miss A.M. van Zyl (RSA).

1968 (4)
1–O.K. Davidson (AUS) and Mrs. L.W. King (USA), 2–R.A. Gonzales and Miss R. Casals (USA), 3–F.S. Stolle (AUS) and Mrs. P.F. Jones (GBR), 4–K.N. Fletcher and Mrs. B.M. Court (AUS).

1969 (4)
1–K.N. Fletcher and Mrs. B.M. Court (AUS), 2–J.D. Newcombe (AUS) and Mrs. L.W. King (USA), 3–A.D. Roche and Miss J.A.M. Tegart (AUS), 4–F.S. Stolle (AUS) and Mrs. P.F. Jones (GBR).

1970 (4)
1–M.C. Riessen (USA) and Mrs. B.M. Court (AUS), 2–R.A.J. Hewitt (RSA) and Mrs. L.W. King (USA), 3–F.D. McMillan (RSA) and Mrs. D.E. Dalton (AUS), 4–R.D. Ralston (USA) and Miss F.G. Durr (FRA).

1971 (4)
1–M.C. Riessen (USA) and Mrs. B.M. Court (AUS), 2–I. Nastase (ROM) and Miss R. Casals (USA), 3–O.K. Davidson (AUS) and Mrs. L.W. King (USA), 4–F.D. McMillan (RSA) and Mrs. D.E. Dalton (AUS).

1972 (4)
1–K.G. Warwick and Miss E.F. Goolagong (AUS), 2–I. Nastase (ROM) and Miss R. Casals (USA), 3–C.E. Graebner and Mrs. L.W. King (USA), 4–F.D. McMillan (RSA) and Mrs. D.E. Dalton (AUS).

1973 (4)
1–I. Nastase (ROM) and Miss R. Casals (USA), 2–O.K. Davidson (AUS) and Mrs. L.W. King (USA), 3–A. Metreveli and Mrs. O.V. Morozova (URS), 4–J.S. Connors and Miss C.M. Evert (USA).
Note: The original seeding list before the Boycott was:–
1–I. Nastase (ROM) and Miss R. Casals (USA), 2–M.C. Riessen (USA) and Mrs. B.M. Court (AUS), 3–O.K. Davidson (AUS) and Mrs. L.W. King (USA), 4–F.D. McMillan (RSA) and Miss S.V. Wade (GBR).

1974 (4)
1–O.K. Davidson (AUS) and Mrs. L.W. King (USA), 2–J.S. Connors and Miss C.M. Evert (USA), 3–A. Metreveli and Mrs. O.V. Morozova (URS), 4–K.G. Warwick and Miss E.F. Goolagong (AUS).

1975 (4)
1–M.C. Riessen (USA) and Mrs. B.M. Court (AUS), 2–A.D. Roche (AUS) and Mrs. L.W. King (USA), 3–J. Kodes and Miss M. Navratilova (TCH), 4–A. Metreveli and Mrs. O.V. Morozova (URS).

1976 (4)
1–A. Mayer and Mrs. L.W. King (USA), 2–F.D. McMillan (RSA) and Miss B.F. Stove (NED), 3–M.C. Riessen (USA) and Miss M. Navratilova (TCH), 4–A. Metreveli and Mrs. O.V. Morozova (URS).

1977 (4)
1–F.D. McMillan (RSA) and Miss B.F. Stove (NED), 2–P.C. Dent (AUS) and Mrs. L.W. King (USA), 3–M.C. Riessen (USA) and Miss F.G. Durr (Mrs. B.J. Browning) (FRA), 4–R.D. Ralston and Miss M. Navratilova (USA).

1978 (8)
1–F.D. McMillan (RSA) and Miss B.F. Stove (NED), 2–R.O. Ruffels (AUS) and Mrs. L.W. King (USA), 3–G. Masters (AUS) and Miss S.V. Wade (GBR), 4–A.D. Roche (AUS) and Miss F.G. Durr (Mrs. B.J. Browning) (FRA), 5–M.C. Riessen (USA) and Miss W.M. Turnbull (AUS), 6–R.L.Case (AUS) and Mrs. T.E. Guerrant (USA), 7–G.E. Reid (USA) and Mrs. G.E. Reid (AUS), 8–F.V. McNair (USA) and Miss L.E. Hunt (AUS).

1979 (8)
1–F.D. McMillan (RSA) and Miss B.F. Stove (NED), 2–R.A.J. Hewitt and Miss G.R. Stevens (RSA), 3–M.C. Riessen (USA) and Miss W.M. Turnbull (AUS), 4–J.D. Newcombe and Mrs. R.A. Cawley (AUS), 5–I. Tiriac and Miss V. Ruzici (ROM), 6–T.E. Gullikson and Miss A.E. Smith

(USA)*, 7–J.M. Lloyd (GBR) and Miss R. Casals (USA), 8–R.L. Case (AUS) and Mrs. K. Stuart (USA).
*The No. 6 seeds withdrew. Their position in the draw was filled by Qualifiers – M.R.E. Appleton (GBR) and Miss P.J. Whitecross (AUS).

1980 (8)

1–F.D. McMillan (RSA) and Miss B.F. Stove (NED), 2–R.L. Stockton and Mrs. L.W. King (USA), 3–J.D. Newcombe and Mrs. R.A. Cawley (AUS), 4–R.L. Case and Miss W.M. Turnbull (AUS), 5–V. Amritraj (IND) and Miss A.E. Smith (USA), 6–M.R. Edmondson and Miss D.L. Fromholtz (AUS), 7–C. Dowdeswell (SUI) and Miss G.R. Stevens (RSA), 8–An Amritraj (IND) and Miss R. Casals (USA).

1981 (8)

1–J.R. Austin and Miss T.A. Austin (USA), 2–F.D. McMillan (RSA) and Miss B.F. Stove (NED), 3–M.C. Riessen (USA) and Miss W.M. Turnbull (AUS), 4–I. Nastase (ROM) and Miss H. Mandlikova (TCH)*, 5–M.R. Edmondson and Miss D.L. Fromholtz (AUS), 6–S.B. Denton and Miss A.E. Smith (USA), 7–K.M. Curren and Miss T.J. Harford (RSA), 8–B.D. Teacher and Miss T.A. Holladay (USA)*.
*The No. 4 and No. 8 seeds withdrew. Their positions in the draw were filled by Lucky Losers – J. Kamiwazumi and Miss N. Sato (JPN) and M.W.C. Guntrip (GBR) and Miss H.A. Ludloff (USA), respectively.

1982 (8)

1–F.D. McMillan (RSA) and Miss B.F. Stove (NED), 2–J.R. Austin and Miss T.A. Austin (USA), 3–J.M. Lloyd (GBR) and Miss W.M. Turnbull (AUS), 4–K.M. Curren (RSA) and Miss A.E. Smith (USA), 5–S.B. Denton and Miss J.C. Russell (USA), 6–R.L. Stockton (USA) and Miss B. Bunge (GER), 7–V. Amritraj (IND) and Miss S.V. Wade (GBR), 8–O.K. Davidson (AUS) and Mrs. L.W. King (USA).

1983 (8)

1–S.B. Denton and Mrs. L.W. King (USA), 2–J.M. Lloyd (GBR) and Miss W.M. Turnbull (AUS), 3–S.E. Stewart and Miss J.C. Russell (USA), 4–F.S. Stolle (AUS) and Miss P.H. Shriver (USA), 5–J.D. Newcombe (AUS) and Miss A.C. Leand (USA), 6–T.R. Gullikson and Miss K. Jordan (USA), 7–F.D. McMillan (RSA) and Miss J.M. Durie (GBR), 8–F. Taygan and Miss B.K. Jordan (USA).

1984 (8)

1–J.M. Lloyd (GBR) and Miss W.M. Turnbull (AUS), 2–S.B. Denton and Miss K. Jordan (USA), 3–R.L. Stockton and Miss A.E. Smith (USA), 4–M.L. Estep and Miss M. Navratilova (USA), 5–K.M. Curren (RSA) and Miss A. Temesvari (HUN), 6–V. Amritraj (IND) and Mrs. L.W. King (USA)*, 7–S.E. Stewart (USA) and Miss E.M. Sayers (AUS), 8–M.C. Riessen (USA) and Miss A.E. Hobbs (GBR).
*The No. 6 seeds withdrew. Their position in the draw was filled by Lucky Losers – R.R. Grant and Miss A.L. Gulley (AUS).

1985 (8)

1–J.M. Lloyd (GBR) and Miss W.M. Turnbull (AUS), 2–P.F. McNamee (AUS) and Miss M. Navratilova (USA), 3–R.A. Seguso (USA) and Miss A.E. Hobbs (GBR), 4–P. Slozil and Miss H. Sukova (TCH), 5–S.B. Denton (USA) and Miss J.M. Durie (GBR), 6–M.R. Edmondson (AUS) and Miss K. Jordan (USA), 7–J.B. Fitzgerald and Mrs. P.D. Smylie (AUS), 8–S.E. Davis and Miss B. (H.E.) Nagelsen (USA).

1986 (16)

1–K.E. Flach and Miss K. Jordan (USA), 2–J.B. Fitzgerald and Mrs. P.D. Smylie (AUS), 3–H.P. Guenthardt (SUI) and Miss M. Navratilova (USA), 4–P.F. McNamee (AUS) and Miss H. Mandlikova (TCH), 5–S.E. Davis and Miss H.E. Nagelsen (Mrs. M.H. McCormack) (USA)*, 6–C.J. Van Rensburg and Miss R.D. Fairbank (RSA), 7–P. Slozil (TCH) and Miss C.G. Kohde–Kilsch (GER), 8–J.M. Lloyd (GBR) and Miss W.M. Turnbull (AUS), 9–E. Sanchez (ESP) and Miss B. Bunge (GER), 10–M.R. Edmondson (AUS) and Miss A.E. Hobbs (GBR), 11–S. Casal (ESP) and Miss R. Reggi (ITA), 12–G.W. Donnelly and Miss P.G. Smith (USA), 13–K.G.

Warwick and Miss J.M. Byrne (AUS), 14–S.B. Denton (USA) and Miss E.S. Pfaff (GER), 15–J. Hlasek and Miss C. Jolissaint (SUI), 16–M.J. Bates and Miss J.M. Durie (GBR).

*The No. 5 seeds withdrew. Their position in the draw was filled by Lucky Losers – H. Shirato and Miss M. Yanagi (JPN).

1987 (16)

1–K.E. Flach and Miss K. Jordan (USA), 2–P.F. McNamee (AUS) and Miss M. Navratilova (USA)*, 3–E Sanchez (ESP) and Miss P.H. Shriver (USA)*, 4–P.T. Annacone and Miss H.E. Nagelsen (Mrs. M.H. McCormack) (USA)*, 5–G. Forget and Miss C. Tanvier (FRA)*, 6–S. Zivojinovic (YUG) and Miss E.S. Pfaff (GER)*, 7–D.T. Visser and Miss R.D. Fairbank (RSA), 8–M. Kratzmann (AUS) and Miss E.M. Burgin (USA), 9–K.G. Warwick and Miss J.M. Byrne (AUS), 10–S.E. Stewart and Miss A.E. Smith (USA), 11–G.R. Muller (RSA) and Miss A.H. White (USA), 12–R.W.T. Van't Hof and Miss M.L. Piatek (USA), 13–A.S. Kohlberg and Miss P.A. Fendick (USA), 14–M. Mortensen and Miss T. Scheuer–Larsen (DEN), 15–J.B. Fitzgerald and Mrs. P.D. Smylie (AUS), 16–R.A. Seguso (USA) and Miss C.K. Bassett (CAN).

*The original No. 3 seeds, E. Sanchez (ESP) and Miss P.H. Shriver (USA) withdrew and were replaced by the new No. 3 seeds, P.B. Fleming and Miss B. (H.E.) Nagelsen (USA). The No. 2, 4, 5 and 6 seeds withdrew. Their positions in the draw were filled by Lucky Losers – D. Roberts and Miss T.A. Catlin (GBR), C. Fancutt (AUS) and Miss L. Gracie (GBR), H. Shirato and Miss M. Yanagi (JPN) and A. Olkhovsky and Miss L. Meskhi (URS), respectively.

1988 (16)

1–E. Sanchez (ESP) and Miss M. Navratilova (USA), 2–J.B. Fitzgerald and Mrs. P.D. Smylie (AUS), 3–J.R. Pugh (USA) and Miss J. Novotna (TCH), 4–P.T. Annacone and Miss H.E. Nagelsen (Mrs. M.H. McCormack) (USA), 5–C.J. Van Rensburg (RSA) and Miss H. Mandlikova (AUS), 6–D.T. Visser and Miss R.D. Fairbank (RSA), 7–M.J. Bates and Miss J.M. Durie (GBR), 8–J.F. Grabb and Miss E.M. Burgin (USA), 9–P. Slozil (TCH) and Miss S.M. Graf (GER), 10–R.D. Leach and Miss P.A. Fendick (USA), 11–D.J. Cahill and Miss N.A-L. Provis (AUS), 12–T.J.C.M. Nijssen and Miss M.M. Bollegraf (NED), 13–M. Mortensen and Miss T. Scheuer–Larsen (DEN), 14–S.E. Stewart and Miss Z.L. Garrison (USA), 15–R.W.T. Van't Hof and Mrs. P.F. Daniels (USA), 16–M. Freeman and Miss L.M. McNeil (USA).

1989 (16)

1–J.R. Pugh (USA) and Miss J. Novotna (TCH), 2–K.E. Flach and Miss J.M. Hetherington (CAN), 3–R.D. Leach and Miss H.E. Nagelsen (Mrs. M.H. McCormack) (USA), 4–R.A. Seguso and Miss L.M. McNeil (USA), 5–J.B. Fitzgerald and Mrs. P.D. Smylie (AUS), 6–S.E. Stewart and Miss Z.L. Garrison (USA), 7–P.M. McEnroe and Miss B.C. Fernandez (USA), 8–M.R. Woodforde and Miss H. Mandlikova (AUS), 9–D.T. Visser and Miss R.D. Fairbank (Mrs R. Nideffer) (RSA), 10–P. Doohan (AUS) and Miss E.M. Burgin (USA), 11–R.W.T. Van't Hof and Miss R.M. White (USA), 12–T.J.C.M. Nijssen and Miss M.M. Bollegraf (NED), 13–J. Lozano (MEX) and Miss C. Suire (FRA), 14–M. Kratzmann and Miss J.M. Byrne (AUS), 15–P. Aldrich and Miss E. Reinach (RSA), 16–M. Mortensen and Miss T. Scheuer–Larsen (DEN).

1990 (16)

1–J.R. Pugh (USA) and Miss J. Novotna (TCH), 2–P. Aldrich and Miss E. Reinach (RSA), 3–R.D. Leach and Miss Z.L. Garrison (Mrs. W.L. Jackson) (USA), 4–J.B. Fitzgerald and Mrs. P.D. Smylie (AUS), 5–T. Smid and Miss H. Sukova (TCH), 6–D.T. Visser (RSA) and Miss R.D. Fairbank (Mrs. R. Nideffer) (USA), 7–C.V. Motta (BRA) and Miss K. Jordan (USA), 8–M. Kratzmann (AUS) and Miss B.A.M. Schultz (NED), 9–D.J. Cahill (AUS), and Miss B.C. Fernandez (USA), 10–R.A. Seguso and Miss L.M. McNeil (USA), 11–P.M. McEnroe and Miss M.J. McGrath (USA), 12–K.L. Jones and Miss E.M. Burgin (USA), 13–P.T. Annacone (USA) and Miss A.I.M. Sanchez Vicario (ESP), 14–T.A. Woodbridge and Miss N.A-L. Provis (AUS), 15–M.R. Woodforde and Miss H. Mandlikova (AUS), 16–T.J.C.M. Nijssen and Miss M.M. Bollegraf (NED).

*The original seeding list did not include the names of P.M. McEnroe and Miss M.J. McGrath (USA) who, pairing at a late stage, gained entry to the event through the qualifying competition. Because of their high position on the ranking lists the decision was taken to revise the seeding list and place them at No. 11. The original No. 16 seeds, N. Pereira (VEN) and Miss N.M. Zverera (URS), were made unseeded while Nos. 11 to 15 were reallocated to Nos. 12 to 16.

1991 (16)

1–J.R. Pugh (USA) and Miss N.M. Zvereva (URS), 2–J.B. Fitzgerald and Mrs. P.D. Smylie (AUS), 3–S.E. Davis and Miss R.M. White (USA), 4–R.D. Leach and Miss Z.L. Garrison (Mrs. W.L. Jackson) (USA), 5–P.J. Galbraith and Miss P.A. Fendick (USA), 6–G. Michibata and Miss J.M. Hetherington (CAN), 7–D. Wheaton and Miss M.J. Fernandez (USA)*, 8–G.D. Connell (CAN) and Miss K.S. Rinaldi (USA), 9–T.A. Woodbridge and Miss N.A-L. Provis (AUS), 10–D.T. Visser (RSA) and Miss R.D. Fairbank (Mrs. R. Nideffer) (USA), 11–K.E. Flach and Miss K. Jordan (USA), 12–J. Lozano (MEX) and Miss A.I.M. Sanchez Vicario (ESP), 13–C. Suk and Miss H. Sukova (TCH), 14–J.F. Grabb and Miss E.M. Burgin (USA), 15–W.R. Ferreira and Miss L.J. Gregory (RSA), 16–M. Kratzmann (AUS) and Miss P.H. Shriver (USA).

*The No. 7 seeds withdrew. Their position in the draw was filled by Lucky Losers – L.J. Bale (RSA) and Miss A. Van Burren (NED).

1992 (16)

1–T.A. Woodbridge (AUS) and Miss J. Novotna (TCH), 2–A.P. Jarryd (SWE) and Miss H. Sukova (TCH), 3–C. Suk (TCH) and Mrs. A. Savchenko–Neiland (LAT), 4–R.D. Leach and Miss Z.L. Garrison (Mrs. W.L. Jackson) (USA), 5–K.L. Jones and Miss B.C. Fernandez (USA), 6–G. Michibata and Miss J.M. Hetherington (CAN), 7–M.R. Woodforde and Miss N.A-L. Provis (AUS), 8–T.J.C.M. Nijssen and Miss M.M. Bollegraf (NED), 9–J.B. Fitzgerald and Mrs. P.D. Smylie (AUS), 10–D.I. Macpherson and Miss R. McQuillan (AUS), 11–G.D. Connell (CAN) and Miss K.S. Rinaldi (USA), 12–M. Kratzmann and Miss P.H. Shriver (USA), 13–T. Witsken and Miss K.M. Adams (USA), 14–S. Devries and Miss P.A. Fendick (USA), 15–L. Warder and Miss R.P. Stubbs (AUS), 16–S.E. Davis and Miss R.M. White (USA).

1993 (16)

1–T.A. Woodbridge (AUS) and Miss A.I.M. Sanchez Vicario (ESP), 2–M. Kratzmann (AUS) and Miss N.M. Zvereva (BLS), 3–M.R. Woodforde (AUS) and Miss M. Navratilova (USA), 4–D.T. Visser (RSA) and Miss B.C. Fernandez (USA)*, 5–R.D. Leach and Mrs. Z.L. Garrison-Jackson (USA), 6–C. Suk (CZE) and Mrs. A. Neiland (LAT), 7–P.J. Galbraith and Miss K.S. Rinaldi (USA), 8–J.B. Fitzgerald and Mrs. P.D. Smylie (AUS), 9–S. Devries and Miss P.A. Fendick (USA), 10–G. Michibata and Miss J.M. Hetherington (CAN), 11–G.D. Connell (CAN) and Miss R.M. White (USA), 12–T.J.C.M. Nijssen and Miss M.M. Bollegraf (NED), 13–G.S. Van Emburgh (USA) and Miss H. Sukova (CZE), 14–L.B. Jensen and Miss M. J. McGrath (USA), 15–M. Jensen (USA) and Miss B.A.M. Schultz (NED), 16–S. Kruger and Miss A.J. Coetzer (RSA).

*The No. 4 seeds withdrew. Their position in the draw was filled by unseeded J. Donar and Miss M. Lindstrom (SWE).

1994 (16)

1–J.A. Stark and Miss P.A. Fendick (USA), 2-B.H. Black (ZIM) and Miss P.H. Shriver (USA), 3-C. Suk (CZE) and Miss B.C. Fernandez (USA), 4–T.A. Woodbridge (AUS) and Miss H. Sukova (CZE), 5–M.R. Woodforde (AUS) and Miss M.J. McGrath (USA), 6–G.D. Connell (CAN) and Miss L.A. Davenport (USA), 7–A. Olhovskiy (RUS) and Mrs. A. Neiland (LAT), 8–T.J.C.M. Nijssen and Miss M.M. Bollegraf (NED), 9–R.D. Leach and Miss L.M. Raymond (USA), 10–P.J. Galbraith and Miss D.A. Graham (USA), 11–J.B. Fitzgerald and Mrs. P.D. Smylie (AUS), 12–P. Norval (RSA) and Miss C.M. Vis (NED), 13–K.E. Flach (USA) and Miss J.A. Richardson (NZL), 14–D.D. Adams (AUS) and Miss K. Boogert (NED), 15–D.J. Cahill and Miss R.P. Stubbs (AUS)*, 16–B. Pearce (USA) and Miss K.A. Guse (AUS).

*The No. 15 seeds withdrew. Their position in the draw was filled by unseeded L. Warder and Mrs. T.J. Morton-Rodgers (AUS).

1995 (16)

1–M.R. Woodforde (AUS) and Mrs. A. Neiland (LAT), 2–G.D. Connell (CAN) and Miss L.A. Davenport (USA), 3–J.A.Stark and Miss M. Navratilova (USA), 4–C. Suk (CZE) and Miss B.C. Fernandez (USA), 5–R. Adams and Miss L.M. Raymond (USA), 6–L.J. Bale (RSA) and Miss M.J. McGrath (USA), 7–P.J. Galbraith (USA) and Miss E. Reinach (RSA), 8–A. Olhovskiy and Miss E. Maniokova (RUS), 9–S.F. Stolle (AUS) and Miss M.J. Fernandez (USA), 10–B. Steven (NZL) and

Mrs. M.R. Bradtke (AUS), 11–J.B. Fitzgerald (AUS) and Miss M.M. Bollegraf (NED), 12–R.D. Leach (USA) and Miss N.M Zvereva (BLR), 13–M. Oosting and Miss K. Boogert (NED), 14–M. Jensen (USA) and Mrs. S. Schultz-McCarthy (NED), 15–G.S. van Emburgh and Miss N.J. Arendt (USA), 16–D.I. Macpherson and Miss R. McQuillan (AUS).

1996 (16)
1–M.R. Woodforde (AUS) and Mrs. A. Neiland (LAT), 2–G.D. Connell (CAN) and Miss L.A. Davenport (USA), 3–M.S. Knowles (BAH) and Miss L.M. Raymond (USA), 4–R.D. Leach (USA) and Miss M.M. Bollegraf (NED), 5–J.A. Stark and Miss M. Navratilova (USA), 6–S.F. Stolle (AUS) and Miss M.J. Fernandez (USA)*, 7–C. Suk and Miss H. Sukova (CZE), 8–P.J. Galbraith and Miss P.H. Shriver (USA), 9–E.R. Ferreira and Miss M. de Swardt (RSA), 10–A. Olhovskiy (RUS) and Miss K. Boogert (NED), 11–L. Pimek (BEL) and Miss K.M. Adams (USA), 12–M. Keil and Miss L.M. McNeil (USA), 13–J.F. Grabb and Miss L.M. Wild (USA), 14–B.D. Talbot (RSA) and Miss C.M. Vis (NED), 15–H.P. Guenthardt (SUI) and Miss S.M. Graf (GER), 16–D. Randall (USA) and Mrs. S. Schultz-McCarthy (NED)*.
*The Nos. 6 and 16 seeds withdrew. Their positions in the draw were filled by unseeded P.T. Hand and Miss V. Lake (GBR) and J.A. Conde and Miss V. Ruano Pascual (ESP), respectively.

1997 (16)
1–G.D. Connell (CAN) and Miss L.A. Davenport (USA), 2–P.J. Galbraith and Miss L.M. Raymond (USA), 3–A. Olhovskiy (RUS) and Mrs. A. Neiland (LAT), 4–C. Suk and Miss H. Sukova (CZE), 5–R.D. Leach (USA) and Miss M.M. Bollegraf (NED), 6–S.F. Stolle (AUS) and Miss M.J. Fernandez (USA), 7–D.D. Adams (RSA) and Miss A. Fusai (FRA), 8–M.S. Knowles (BAH) and Miss A.S. Kournikova (RUS), 9–J.A. Eagle (AUS) and Miss C.M. Vis (NED), 10–D.J. Johnson and Miss L.M. Wild (USA), 11–L. Pimek and Miss S. Applemans (BEL), 12–J.F. Grabb and Miss D.A. Graham (USA), 13–L.B. Jensen and Miss K.M. Adams (USA), 14–P.A. Albano and Miss M. Paz (ARG), 15– M.S. Bhupathi (IND) and Miss R. Hiraki (JPN), 16–W.A. O'Brien and Miss C.M. Morariu (USA).

1998 (16)
1–L.A. Paes (IND) and Mrs. A. Neiland (LAT), 2–P.V.N. Haarhuis and Miss C.M. Vis (NED), 3–R.D. Leach (USA) and Miss M.M. Bollegraf (NED), 4–D.M. Nestor (CAN) and Miss N. Tauziat (FRA), 5–M.S. Bhupathi (IND) and Miss M. Lucic (CRO), 6–P.J. Galbraith (USA) and Miss L.M. Raymond (USA), 7–C. Suk and Miss H. Sukova (CZE), 8–D.D. Adams (RSA) and Miss A. Fusai (FRA), 9–D. Orsanic and Miss P. Tarabini (ARG), 10–D.I. Macpherson and Miss R. McQuillan (AUS), 11–J-L De Jager (RSA) and Miss K.M. Adams (USA), 12–N.P. Broad (GBR) and Miss M. de Swardt (RSA), 13–D. Roditi (MEX) and Miss P. L. Suarez (ARG), 14– M. Oosting (NED) and Miss S. Appelmans (Mrs. S. Haubourdin) (BEL), 15–P. Norval (RSA) and Miss C.M. Morariu (USA), 16–B. MacPhie and Miss L.A. Davenport (USA).

1999 (16)
1–L.A. Paes (IND) and Miss L.M. Raymond (USA), 2–T.A. Woodbridge (AUS) and Miss L.A. Davenport (USA), 3–J.L. Bjorkman (SWE) and Miss A.S. Kournikova (RUS), 4–M.S. Knowles (BAH) and Miss E. Likhovtseva (RUS), 5–C. Suk (CZE) and Miss C.M. Vis (NED), 6–R.D. Leach (USA) and Mrs. A. Neiland (LAT), 7–D.D. Adams and Miss M. de Swardt (RSA), 8–J.J. Gimelstob and Miss V.E.S. Williams (USA), 9–J.P. McEnroe (USA) and Miss S.M. Graf (GER), 10–W.H. Black (ZIM) and Miss C.C. Black (ZIM), 11–S.F. Stolle and Mrs. D. Kunce (AUS), 12–A.P. Florent (AUS) and Miss E.V. Tatarkova (RUS), 13–D. Rikl (CZE) and Miss K. Habsudova (SVK), 14–P. Tramacchi (AUS) and Miss A. Sugiyama (JPN), 15–M.N. Mirnyi (BLR) and Miss M.C. Pierce (FRA), 16–P. Norval (USA) and Miss K. Srebotnik (SLO).

2000 (16)
1–T.A. Woodbridge and Miss R.P. Stubbs (AUS), 2–P.V.N. Haahuis (NED) and Miss L.M. Raymond (USA), 3–E.R. Ferreira (RSA) and Miss N.J. Arendt (USA), 4–J.L. Bjorkman (SWE) and Miss A.S. Kournikova (RUS), 5–R.D. Leach (USA) and Miss A.J. Coetzer (RSA), 6–J-L De Jager (RSA) and Miss M.M. Bollegraf (NED), 7–P. Norval (RSA) and Miss K. Srebotnik (SLO), 8–D.J. Johnson and Miss K.Y. Po (USA), 9–M.R. Woodforde (AUS) and Miss K. Boogert

(NED), 10–M.S. Knowles (BAH) and Miss E. Likhovtseva (Mrs. M. Baranov) (RUS), 11–W.H. Black and Miss C.C. Black (ZIM), 12–D.D. Adams and Miss M. de Swardt (RSA), 13–L.J.N. Kulti and Miss A. Carlsson (SWE), 14–D. Orsanic (ARG) and Miss C.M. Vis (NED), 15–M.A. Garcia and Miss L. Montalvo (ARG), 16–B. MacPhie (USA) and Miss P. Tarabini (ARG).

2001 (16)

1–T.A. Woodbridge and Miss R.P. Stubbs (AUS), 2–E.R. Ferreira (RSA) and Miss A. Sugiyama (JAP), 3–S.F. Stolle (AUS) and Miss C.C. Black (ZIM), 4–M.S. Bhupathi (IND) and Miss E. Likhovtseva (Mrs. M. Baranov) (RUS), 5–D.J. Johnson and Mrs. K.Y. Po-Messerli (USA), 6–L.A. Paes (IND) and Miss L.M. Raymond (USA), 7–J.E. Palmer (USA) and Miss A.I.M. Sanchez Vicario (Mrs. J Vehils), 8–J.A. Eagle (AUS) and Miss B. Schett (AUT), 9–M.S. Knowles (BAH) and Miss N.J. Arendt (USA), 10–L. Arnold and Miss P.L. Suarez (ARG), 11–P.Pala (CZE) and Miss J. Husarova (SVK), 12–R.D. Leach (USA) and Miss A.J. Coetzer (RSA), 13–J. Novak (CZE) and Miss M.J.M.M. Oremans (NED), 14–J.G. Tarango (USA) and Miss J. Dokic (YUG), 15–D. Rikl (CZE) and Miss K. Habsudova (SVK), 16–P. Vizner (CZE) and Miss T. Garbin (ITA).

2002 (16)

1–J.E. Palmer (USA) and Miss R.P. Stubbs (AUS), 2–D.J. Johnson and Mrs. K.Y. Po-Messerli (USA), 3–M.S. Bhupathi (IND) and Miss E. Likhovtseva (Mrs M. Baranov) (RUS), 4–K.R. Ullyet (ZIM) and Miss D. Hantuchova (SVK), 5–L.A. Paes (IND) and Miss L.M. Raymond (USA), 6–M.C. Bryan (USA) and Mrs A. Huber (RSA), 7–J.L. Bjorkman (SWE) and Miss A.S. Kournikova (RUS), 8–M.S. Knowles (BAH) and Miss E. Bovina (RUS), 9–G. Etlis and Miss P.L. Suarez (ARG), 10–R.C. Bryan (USA) and Miss K. Srebotnik (SLO), 11–J.A. Eagle (AUS) and Miss B. Schett (AUT), 12–D. Rikl (CZE) and Miss T. Garbin (ITA), 13–B. MacPhie (USA) and Miss A.J. Coetzer (RSA), 14–P. Vizner (CZE) and Miss R. Vinci (ITA), 15–M. Damm and Miss K. Hrdlickova (CZE), 16–R.L. Koenig (RSA) and Miss E.S.H. Callens (BEL).

2003 (16)

1–M.S. Bhupathi (IND) and Miss P.L. Suarez (ARG), 2–M.C. Bryan and Miss L.M. Raymond (USA), 3–R.C. Bryan (USA) and Miss E. Likhovtseva (Mrs. M. Baranov) (RUS), 4–T.A. Woodbridge (AUS) and Miss S. Kuznetsova (RUS), 5–L.A. Paes (IND) and Miss M. Navratilova (USA), 6–W.H. Black and Miss C.C. Black (ZIM), 7–K.R. Ullyet (ZIM) and Miss D. Hantuchova (SVK), 8–D.J. Johnson (USA) and Miss R.P. Stubbs (AUS), 9–C. Haggard (RSA) and Mis E. Gagliardi (SUI), 10–L. Friedl (CZE) and Mrs. A. Huber (RSA), 11–C.Suk (CZE) and Miss M. Matevzic (SLO), 12–J.A. Eagle (AUS) and Miss B. Schett (AUT), 13–P. Pala (CZE) and Miss J. Husarova (SVK), 14–G. Oliver (USA) and Miss P. Mandula (HUN), 15–P.Vizner (CZE) and Miss N.J. Pratt (AUS), 16–M. Hood (ARG) and Miss T. Krizan (SLO).

2004 (16)

1–M.S. Bhupathi (IND) and Miss E. Lihkovtseva (Mrs. M Baranov) (RUS), 2–M.S. Knowles (BAH) and Miss V. Ruano Pascual (ESP), 3–M.C. Bryan and Miss L.M. Raymond (USA), 4–J.L. Bjorkman (SWE) and Miss R.P. Stubbs (AUS), 5–P.J. Hanley (AUS) and Miss A. Sugiyama (JPN). 6–W.H. Black and Miss C.C. Black (ZIM), 7–R.C. Bryan and Miss L.A. Davenport (Mrs. J. Leach) (USA), 8–T.A. Woodbridge and Miss A. Molik (AUS), 9–L.A. Paes (IND) and Miss M. Navratilova (USA), 10–C. Suk (CZE) and Miss M. Bartoli (FRA), 11–J.Erlich (ISR) and Mrs. A. Huber (RSA), 12–L. Friedl (CZE) and Miss J. Husarova (SVK), 13–M. Hood (ARG) and Mrs. G.Vento-Kabchi (VEN), 14–G. Etlis (ARG) and Miss T.T. Sun (CHN), 15–D.M. Nestor (CAN) and Miss L. Krasnoroutskaya (RUS), 16–L. Arnold (ARG) and Miss A Widjaja (INA). .

2005 (16)

1–R.C. Bryan (USA) and Miss R.P. Stubbs (AUS), 2–W.H. Black and Miss C.C. Black (ZIM), 3–J.L. Bjorkman (SWE) and Miss L.M. Raymond (USA), 4–K.R. Ullyett (ZIM) and Mrs. A. Huber (RSA), 5–M.C. Bryan and Miss M. Navratilova (USA). 6–T.A. Woodbridge and and Miss S.J. Stosur (AUS), 7–L. Friedl (CZE) and Miss J. Husarova (SVK), 8–M.S. Knowles (BAH) and Miss V.E.S. Williams (USA), 9–P. Visner (CZE) and Miss N.J. Platt (AUS), 10–N. Zimonjic (SCG) and Miss K. Srebotnik (SLO), 11–J.E. Palmer and Miss C Morariu (USA), 12–

O.L.P. Rochus and Miss K. Clijsters (BEL), 13–J. Knowle (AUT) and Miss A-L Groenefeld (GER), 14–D. Hrbaty (SVK) and Miss E. Likhovtseva (Mrs M. Baranov), 15–M. Damm and Mrs T. Peschke (CZE), 16–A. Ram (ISR) and Miss I.C. Martinez (ESP).

2006 (16)

1–J.L. Bjorkman (SWE) and Miss L.M. Raymond (USA), 2–M.N. Mirnyi (BLR) and Miss J. Zheng (CHN), 3–W.H. Black and Miss C.C. Black (ZIM), 4–L.A. Paes (IND) and Miss.S.J.Stosur (AUS), 5–D.M. Nestor (CAN) and Miss E. Likhovtseva (Mrs M. Baranov) (RUS). 6–T.S. Perry and Miss R.P. Stubbs (AUS), 7–N. Zimonjic (SCG) and Miss K. Srebotnik (SLO), 8–M.S. Knowles (BAH) and Miss M. Navratilova (USA, 9–A. Ram (ISR) and Miss V. Zvonareva (RUS), 10–M. Damm and Mrs T. Peschke (CZE), 11–M.S. Bhupathi (IND) and Miss Z. Yan (CHN), 12–L. Friedl (CZE) and Mrs A. Huber (RSA), 13–M.C. Bryan and Miss C.M. Morariu (USA), 14–J. Erlich (ISR) and Miss D. Safina (RUS), 15–K.R. Ullyett (ZIM) and Miss S. Peer (ISR), 16–F. Cermak (CZE) and Miss A-L. Groenefeld (GER)

2007 (16)

1–M.C. Bryan and Miss L.M. Raymond (USA), 2–R.C. Bryan (USA) and Miss S.J. Stosur (AUS), 3–M.S. Knowles (BAH) and Miss Z. Yan (CHN), 4– K.R. Ullyett (ZIM) and Mrs A. Huber (RSA), 5–J.L. Bjorkman (SWE) and Miss A. Molik (AUS), 6–S.O.K. Aspelin (SWE) and Miss M. Santangelo (ITA), 7–A. Ram (ISR) and Miss N. Dechy (FRA), 8–L.A. Paes (IND) and Miss M. Shaughnessy (USA), 9–M. Matkowski (POL) and Miss C.C. Black (ZIM), 10–P. Vizner and Mrs T. Peschke (CZE), 11–D.M. Nestor (CAN) and Miss E. Likhovtseva (Mrs. M. Baranov) (RUS), 12– T.S. Perry (AUS) and Miss C.J. Chuang (TPE), 13–R. Wassen (NED) and Miss Y-J. Chan (TPE), 14–J. Knowle (AUT) and Miss T. Sun (CHN), 5–J. Erlich (ISR) and Miss E. Vesnina (RUS), 16–P.J. Hanley (AUS) and Miss T. Perebiynis (UKR)

2008 (16)

1–M.C. Bryan (USA) and Miss K. Srebotnik (SLO), 2–D.M. Nestor (CAN) and Miss C.J. Chuang (TPE), 3–P. Vizner and Mrs K. Peschke (CZE), 4–P.J. Hanley (AUS) and Miss C.C. Black (ZIM), 5–K.R. Ullyett (ZIM) and Miss A. Sugiyama (JPN), 6–J. Knowle (AUT) and Miss Y–J. Chan (TPE), 7–M.S. Knowles (BAH) and Miss Z. Yan (CHN). 8–N. Zimonjic (SRB) and Miss T. Sun (CHN), 9– A. Ram (ISR) and Miss N. Dechy (FRA), 10–L.A. Paes (IND) and Miss R.P. Stubbs (AUS), 11–M.S. Bhupathi (IND) and Miss S. Mirza (IND), 12–J. Murray (GBR) and Mrs A. Huber (USA), 13– S.O.K. Aspelin (SWE) and Miss L.M. Raymond, 14–M. Damm CZE) and Miss S. Peng (CHN), 15– J. Coetzee (RSA) and Miss V. Uhlirova (CZE), 16–J. Kerr (AUS) and Miss K. Bondarenko (UKR)

2009 (16)

1–L.A. Paes (IND) and Miss C.C. Black (ZIM), 2–R.C. Bryan (USA) and Miss S.J. Stosur (AUS), 3–M. Matkowski (POL) and Miss L.M. Raymond (USA), 4– K.R. Ullyett (ZIM) and Miss S-W. Hsieh (TPE), 5–D.M. Nestor (CAN) and Miss E. Vesnina (RUS), 6–M.C. Bryan and Mrs B. Mattek-Sands (USA), 7–R. Lindstedt (SWE) and Miss R.P. Stubbs (AUS), 8–M.N. Mirnyi (BLR) and Miss N. Petrova (RUS), 9–M.S. Knowles (BAR) and Miss A.L. Groenfeld (GER), 10– N. Zimonjic (SRB) and Miss Z. Yan (CHN), 11–A. Sa (BRA) and Miss A. Sugiyama (JAP), 12– S.W.I. Huss (AUS) and Miss V. Ruano Pascual (ESP), 13–M.S. Bhupathi and Miss S. Mirza (IND), 14–M.P.D. Melo (BRA) and Miss S. Pena (CHN), 15–L. Dlouhy and Miss I. Benesova (CZE), 16–C. Kas (GER) and Miss C-J. Chuang (TPE)

2010 (16)

1–N. Zimonjic (SRB) and Miss S. Stosur (AUS), 2–L.A. Paes (IND) and Miss C.C. Black (ZIM), 3–M.S. Bhupathi (IND) and Mrs A. Huber (USA), 4–O. Marach (AUT) and Miss N. Llagostera Vives (ESP), 5–M.S. Knowles (BAH) and Miss K. Srebotnik (SLO), 6–D.M. Nestor (CAN) and Mrs B. Mattek-Sands (USA), 7–M.N. Mirnyi (BLR) and Miss A. Kleyhanova (RUS), 8–M. Fyrstenberg (POL) and Miss Z. Yan (CHN), 9–L. Dlouhy and Miss I. Benesova (CZE), 10– M.P.D. Melo (BRA) and Miss R.P. Stubbs (AUS), 11–W.A. Moodie (RSA) and Miss L.M. Raymond (USA), 12–P. Hanley (AUS) and Miss Y-J. Chan (TPE), 13–R. Lindstedt (SWE) and Miss E. Makarova (RUS), 14–M. Lopez and Miss A. Medina Garriguez (ESP)*, 15–A.Ram (ISR) and Miss E. Vesnina (RUS), 16–M. Matkowski (POL) and Miss T. Garbin (ITA).

*No.14 seeds withdrew and were replaced by an Alternate

2011 (16)

1–R.C.Bryan and Mrs A. Huber (USA), 2–M.N. Mirnyi (BLR) and Miss Y. Shvedova (KAZ), 3–N. Zimonjic (SRB) and Miss K. Srebotnik (SLO), 4–M.S. Bhupathi (IND) and Miss E. Vesnina (RUS), 5–A-U-H. Qureshi (PAK.) and Mrs T. Peschke (CZE), 6–R. Bopanna and Miss S. Mirza (IND), 7–P. Petschner (GER) and Miss B.Z. Strycova (CZE), 8–D.M. Nestor (CAN) and Miss Y-J. Chan (TPE), 9–J. Melzer (AUT) and Miss I. Benesova (CZE), 10–D. Norman (BEL) and Miss L.M. Raymond (USA), 11–M.S. Knowles (BAH) and Miss N. Petrova (RUS), 12–D. Bracciali and Miss F. Pennetta (ITA)*, 13–F. Cermak and Miss L. Hradecka (CZE), 14–L.A. Paes (IND) and Miss C.C. Black (ZIM), 15–A. Ram (ISR) and Miss M. Shaughnessy (USA), 16–D. Marrero (ESP) and Miss A. Hlavackova (CZE)
* No. 12 seeds withdrew and replaced by an Alternate

2012 (16)

1–R.C. Bryan and Mrs A. Huber (USA), 2–M.C. Bryan and Miss L.M. Raymond (USA), 3–N. Zimonjic (SRB) and Miss K. Srebotnik (SLO), 4–L.A. Paes (IND) and Miss E. Vesnina (RUS), 5–M.S. Bhupathi and Miss S. Mirza (IND), 6–D. Bracciali and Miss R. Vinci (ITA), 7–A-U-Q. Qureshi (PAK) and Miss A. Hlavackova (CZE), 8–D.M. Nestor (CAN) and Miss J. Goerges (GER), 9–M. Fyrstenberg (POL) and Miss A. Spears (USA), 10–R. Bopanna (IND) and Miss J. Zheng (CHN), 11–F. Cermak and Miss L. Hradecka (CZE) 12–J. Melzer (AUT) and Miss I. Benesova (CZE), 13–F. Fognini and Miss S. Errani (ITA), 14–D. Marrero and MissN. Llagostera Vives (ESP), 15–A. Ram (ISR) and Mrs T. Peschke (CZE), 16–A. Peya ' (AUT) and Miss A-L. Groenefeld (GER)

2013 (16)

1–B. Soares (BRA) and Miss L.M. Raymond (USA), 2–H. Tecau (ROU) and Miss S. Mirza (IND), 3–N. Zimonjic (SRB) and Miss K. Srebotnik (SLO), 4–M. Mirnyi (BLR) and Miss A. Hlavackova (CZE), 5–A. Peya (AUT) and Miss A-L. Groenefeld (GER). 6–M. Melo (BRA) and Miss L. Huber (USA), 7–R. Bopanna (IND) and Miss J. Zheng (CHN), 8–D.M. Nestor (CAN) and Miss K. Mladenovic (FRA), 9–T. Huey (PHI) and Miss R. Kops-Jones (USA), 10–A-U-Q. Qureshi (PAK), 11–M. Matkowski (POL) and Mrs T. Peschke (CZE), 12–F. Cermak (CZE) and Miss L. Hradecka (CZE) 13–S. Lipsky (USA) and Miss C. Dellacqua (AUS), 14–D. Marrero and Mrs K. Date-Kjumm (JPN), 15–L.A. Paes (IND) and Miss S. Zheng (CHN), 16–I. Dodig (CRO) and Miss M. Erakovic (NZL)

2014 (16)

1–M. Bryan (USA) and Miss K. Srebotnik (SLO), 2–R. Bryan (USA) and Mrs T. Peschke (CZE), 3–A. Peya (AUT) and Miss A. Sears (USA), 4–L. Paes (IND) and Miss C. Black (ZIM), 5–D.M Nestor (CAN) and Miss K. Mladenovic (FRA), 6–H. Tecau (ROU) and Miss S. Mirza (IND), 7 R. Bopanna (IND) and Miss A. Hlavackova (CZE), 8–J-J. Rojer (NED) and Miss A-L. Groenefeld (GER), 9–D. Marrero and Miss A. Parre-Santonja (ESP), 10–J. Murray (GBR) and Miss C. Dellacqua (AUS), 11–J-S. Cabal (COL) and Miss R. Kops-Jones (USA), 12–J. Peers and Miss A. Barty (AUS), 13–B. Soares (BRA) and Miss M. Hingis (SUI), 14–M. Mirnyi (BLR) and H-C. Chan (TPE), 15–N. Zimonjic (SRB) and Miss S. Stosur (AUS), 16–A. Qureshi (PAK) and Miss V Dushevina (RUS)

Seeded players who reached the concluding rounds

Year	No. of seeds	Semi-final	Final	Winner
1927	4	1,3	1,3	3
1928	4	2,3	2	2
1929	4	2,3	2	2
1930	4	2,3	2	2
1931	4	2	–	–
1932	8	2–4, 6	4,6	4
1933	4	2,4	4	–
1934	4	–	–	–
1935	4	1,3	3	3
1936	4	1,2,4	1,2	1
1937	4	1,2	1,2	1
1938	8	1,2	1,2	1
1939	4	1–3	2	2
1946	4	1–3	2,3	3
1947	4	1–4	1,3	1
1948	4	1–4	1,4	1
1949	4	1,2,4	1,4	4
1950	4	1,3,4	1,4	1
1951	4	1–3	2	2
1952	4	1,2,4	1	1
1953	4	1,4	1, 4	1
1954	4	1–3	1, 3	1
1955	4	1, 2, 4	1, 2	1
1956	4	1, 3, 4	1, 3	1
1957	4	2, 4	2, 4	4
1958	4	2, 4	2, 4	4
1959	4	1–3	2, 3	3
1960	4	1, 2	1, 2	1
1961	4	1–4	1, 4	1
1962	4	1–3	3	3
1963	4	1–3	2	2
1964	4	1, 2	1, 2	2
1965	4	1–3	2	2
1966	4	1, 3, 4	1, 3	1
1967	4	1, 2, 4	1, 2	1
1968	4	1, 3, 4	4	4
1969	4	1, 3, 4	3, 4	4
1970	4	3	–	–
1971	4	1–4	1, 3	3
1972	4	1–3	1, 2	2
1973	4	2, 3	2	2
1974	4	1	1	1
1975	4	1, 3, 4	1	1
1976	4	2	–	–
1977	4	1, 2, 4	1	–
1978	8	1, 2, 4	1, 2	1
1979	8	1, 2, 4	1, 2	2
1980	8	1, 4, 6	6	–
1981	8	1, 2	1, 2	2
1982	8	3, 4	3, 4	4
1983	8	1, 2, 4	1, 2	2
1984	8	1, 2, 7	1, 2	1

Year	No. of seeds	Semi-final	Final	Winner
1985	8	2, 6–8	2, 7	2
1986	16	1, 3, 9	1, 3	1
1987	16	7, 13	–	–
1988	16	2, 10, 14	14	14
1989	16	1, 3, 4, 14	1, 14	1
1990	16	1, 3, 4	3, 4	3
1991	16	1, 2, 8	1, 2	2
1992	16	3, 8	3	3
1993	16	1–3, 12	3, 12	3
1994	16	2,4,6	4	4
1995	16	1–4	3, 4	3
1996	16	1, 2, 7	1, 7	7
1997	16	1, 3, 4,	3, 4,	4
1998	16	2, 5,	5	–
1999	16	1, 3, 4, 9	1, 3	1
2000	16	8	8	8
2001	16	4, 15	–	–
2002	16	2–4, 16	3, 4	3
2003	16	5, 10	5	5
2004	16	5–8	6, 8	6
2005	16	3,4	–	–
2006	16	2, 3, 9	9	9
2007	16	5, 11	5	–
2008	16	1, 12	1	–
2009	16	1, 9, 12	1, 9	9
2010	16	2, 9–11	2, 11	2
2011	16	4, 8, 9	4, 9	9
2012	16	1–4	2, 4	2
2013	16	1, 3, 8	1, 8	8
2014	16	5, 14–16	14, 15	15

Unseeded Champions (13)

1931   G.M. Lott and Mrs L.A. Harper (USA)
1933   G. von Cramm and Miss H. Krahwinkel (GER)
1934   R. Miki (JAP) and Miss D.E. Round (GBR)
1970   I. Nastase (ROM) and Miss R. Casals (USA)
1976   A.D. Roche (AUS) and Miss F.G. Durr (FRA)
1977   R.A.J. Hewitt and Miss G.R. Stevens (RSA)
1980   J.R. Austin and Miss T.A. Austin (USA)
1987   J.M. Bates and Miss J.M. Durie (GBR)
1998   M.N. Mirnyi (BLR) and Miss S.J. Williams (USA)
2001   L. Friedl (CZE) and Miss D. Hantuchova (SVK)
2005   M.S. Bhupathi (IND) and Miss M.C. Pierce (FRA)
2007   J. Murray (GBR) and Miss J. Jankovic (SRB)
2008   R.C. Bryan (USA) and Miss S.J. Stosur (AUS)

Qualifying Competitions

Qualifying Competition

From 1919 the entries for The Championships were so numerous that it was necessary to restrict the numbers accepted. The entries fell into two categories, one consisting of the players nominated by their national associations and the other individual entries. The former were accepted without question, but the latter were subjected to a careful scrutiny by a sub-committee of five, including the Referee.

In 1925 a Qualifying competition for the five Championship events was held for the first time, during the week before, at the Roehampton Club, London. In singles the last eight survivors qualified and in the doubles, the last four pairs. In 1927 an additional Qualifying competition was held in the North of England, restricted to entries from northern counties and Scotland. In the singles the last two survivors qualified and in the doubles, the last pair.

Qualifying was not held in 1946 but both the Southern and Northern competitions were reinstated for the 1947 Championships. In 1966 the Northern competition was held for the last time and since that date qualifying has taken place in the south.

There was no qualifying for the Gentlemen's Doubles and Mixed Doubles in 1973, owing to the A.T.P. boycott, and for the Mixed Doubles in 1977, when the Ladies' Singles and Doubles were played at Eastbourne simultaneously with the Federation Cup. Qualifying for the Mixed Doubles was discontinued after 1991.

From 1925 to date all matches involving Ladies have been contested over the best of three sets. From 1925 to 1971 the Gentlemen's Singles and Doubles matches were contested throughout over the best of five sets. From 1972 to date, with the exception of 1973, 1993, 1997 and 1998 these matches were reduced to the best of three sets except in the last round, where they were contested over the best of five sets. In 1973 (A.T.P. boycott), 1993, 1997 and 1998 (rain) the best of three sets were played throughout.

Acceptance for the Qualifying competition has been by computer ranking from 1977. Seeding began in 1978.

From 1983 to 2003 the Lawn Tennis Association held Pre-Qualifying singles events, two weeks before The Championships. For further details see 'Events No Longer Held'.

Lucky Losers

Lucky losers are players who have lost in the final round of the Qualifying Competition and, if more Lucky Losers are required for substitutes, those players who have lost in the previous qualifying round. A Lucky Loser is inserted in The Championships draw as a substitution for a player who withdraws before their first round match. The procedure originated in 1937 when Lucky Losers were drawn by lot (hence the name), but from 1977-2005

Players with the highest ranking were substituted first, and so on. In 2006 and 2007, the top four highest ranked players were randomly drawn and thereafter followed the ranking. In 2008 all players were randomly drawn. From 2009 the four highest ranked players have been randomly drawn and thereafter follow the rankings, unless there are more than two vacancies, in which case the size of the random draw will be the number of vacancies plus two. Similar arrangements are made for the doubles events. Up to 1936 players withdrawing from The Championships, after the draw had been made, were not replaced.

Venues

Southern Competition

1925–1934	Roehampton Club
1935–1937	Roehampton Club (Gentlemen) / Hurlingham Club (Ladies)
1938	Roehampton Club (Gentlemen) / Richmond Cricket Club (Ladies)
1939	Roehampton Club (Gentlemen) / Bank of England Sports Club (Ladies)
1946	No competition
1947–1976	Bank of England Sports Club
1977	Bank of England Sports Club (Gentlemen) / Devonshire Park, Eastbourne (Ladies)
1978 to date*	Bank of England Sports Club

Roehampton Club, Roehampton Lane, London, SW15.
Hurlingham Club, Ranelagh Gardens, London, SW6.
Richmond Cricket Club, Kew Road, Richmond, Surrey.
Bank of England Sports Club, Priory Lane, Roehampton, London, SW15.

*1997 Due to rain during the week, the Gentlemen's Doubles second round was played indoors at the Queen's Club on the Saturday and the qualifying round played on grass at the A.E.L.T.C. on the Monday, three Ladies' qualifying round matches were played indoors at the A.E.L..T.C. on the Sunday, and the Ladies' Doubles second and qualifying rounds were played indoors at the Queen's Club on the Saturday.

*1998 Due to rain during the week, the Gentlemen's matches were not concluded until the Saturday and all the Ladies' Singles and Doubles matches were played at the Civil Service Sports Ground at Chiswick on the Friday, Saturday and Sunday.

Northern Competition

1927–1931	Chapel Allerton LTC	1956–1958	Northern LTC
1932–1934	Northern LTC	1959	Chapel Allerton and Oakwood LTC
1935	Chapel Allerton LTC	1960	Northern LTC
1936	Northern LTC	1961	Chapel Allerton and Oakwood LTC
1937	Allerton and Oakwood LTC	1962	Northern LTC
1938	Northern LTC	1963	Chapel Allerton and Oakwood LTC
1939	Allerton and Oakwood LTC	1964	Northern LTC
1946	No competition	1965	Chapel Allerton LTC
1947–1954	Northern LTC	1966	Northern LTC
1955	Chapel Allerton and Oakwood LTC		

Chapel Allerton LTC
Allerton and Oakwood LTC   } Stainbeck Lane, Leeds 7.
Chapel Allerton and Oakwood LTC
Northern LTC, Palatine Road, West Didsbury, Manchester 20.

Number of Qualifiers
Southern Competition

Years	Gentlemen's Singles	Gentlemen's Doubles (pairs)	Ladies' Singles	Ladies' Doubles (pairs)	Mixed Doubles (pairs)
1925–1966	8	4	8	4	4
1967–1970	10	4	8	4	4
1971	12	4	7	3	3
1972	16	4	7	3	3
1973	32	–	8	3	–
1974	16	8	8	3	3
1975	16	5	8	3	4
1976	16	5	8	3	3
1977	16	5	8	3	–
1978–1981	16	5	8	4	3
1982	16	5	8	4	4
1983–1991	16	5	8	4	3
1992–1993	16	5	8	4	–
1994–1999	16	3	8	2	–
2000–2014	16	4	12	4	–

Northern Competition

Years	Gentlemen's Singles	Gentlemen's Doubles (pairs)	Ladies' Singles	Ladies' Doubles (pairs)	Mixed Doubles (pairs)
1927–1966	2	1	2	1	1

Qualifiers and Lucky Losers

Gentlemen's Singles Championship

1925
Q (8) P.R.R. Hurditch (GBR), J.F. Park (GBR), N.G. Deed (GBR), L.J. Carr (GBR), U.S.E. Lindop (GBR), N.H. Latchford (GBR), F.S. Burnett (GBR), L.W. Alderson (GBR).

1926
Q (8) A.F. Yencken (GBR), J. Weakley (GBR), F. Crosbie (GBR), D.H. Williams (GBR), N. Willford (GBR), L.F. Davin (GBR), C.G. McIlquham (GBR), E Crawshay Williams (GBR).

1927
SQ (8) E. Crawshay Williams (GBR), H.G.N. Lee (GBR), G.O. Jameson (GBR), H.C. Walsh (GBR), H.G. Stoker (GBR). P.R.R. Hurditch (GBR), E.C. Penny (GBR), J.D.F. Fisher (GBR). NQ (2) C.W. Banks (GBR), G.A. Pratt (GBR).

1928
SQ (8) C.B. de Ricou (FRA), A. Zappa (ARG). J.E. Nigel Jones (GBR), V.A. Cazalet (GBR). A.D.M. Pitt (GBR), R. Dash (GBR), S.B.B. Wood (USA), E.O. Mather. (USA). NQ (2) G.O. Jameson (GBR), R. Pickersgill (GBR).

1929

SQ (8) C.S. Higgins (GBR). F.J. Perry (GBR), J.F.G. Lysaght (GBR). D.R. Fussell (GBR), A.W. Vinall (GBR), C. Colvin (GBR), H.C. Dhanda (IND), J.H. Shales (GBR).
NQ (2) H.S. Burrows (GBR), A.J. Smith (GBR).

1930

SQ (8) B.D. Helmore (GBR), A.L. Della Porta (GBR). G.H. Perkins (GBR), E.C. Metcalf (GBR). J.R. Reddall (GBR). E. Flury (GBR), R.K. Tinkler (GBR), W.G. Curtis Morgan (GBR).
NQ (2) A.J. Smith (GBR), O. Wright (GBR).

1931

SQ (8) M.V. Callendar (GBR), P.H. Partridge (GBR), B.C. Law (GBR), C.N.O. Ritchie (GBR), W. Legg (GBR), W.H. Smith (GBR), W.F. Freeman (GBR), J. Cummins (GBR).
NQ (2) E.E.R. Whitehouse (GBR), W.E. Attwell (GBR).

1932

SQ (8) C.H.E. Betts (GBR), A. Hyat (GBR), H.E. Weatherall (GBR), H.R. Price (GBR), H.D. Mackinnon (GBR), J.H. Shales (GBR), P.H. Partridge (GBR). J. Cummins (GBR).
NQ (2) A.T. England (GBR), N. Taylor (GBR).

1933

SQ (8) J.H. Shales (GBR). I.M. Bailey (GBR). A.L. Della Porla (GBR) H.C. Nunes (GBR), J.D. Morris (GBR), E.M.D. Vanderspar (GBR), H.E. Weatherall (GBR), V.A. Cazalet (GBR).
NQ (2) A.T. England ((GBR), G.L. France (GBR).

1934

SQ (8) R.M. Turnbull (GBR), M. Bhandari (IND), H.M. Culley (USA), D.R. Rutman (IND), D.B. Jarvis (GBR), R.O. Williams (GBR), G.E. Godsell (GBR), H. Billington (GBR).
NQ (2) J.B. Sturgeon (GBR), N. Taylor (GBR).

1935

SQ (8) C.H.E. Betts (GBR), L.F. Cater (GBR), E.J. Filby (GBR), H.A.Hare (GBR), L.W.J. Newman (GBR), L. Shaffi (GBR), P.H. Partridge (GBR) R.M. Turnbull (GBR).
NQ (2) J.B. Sturgeon (GBR). N. Taylor (GBR).

1936

SQ (8) J.H. Ho (CHN), H.A. Coldham (GBR), J.S. Comery (GBR), R. Morton (GBR), J.D. Anderson (GBR), L.W.J. Newman (GBR), C.F.O. Lister (GBR) H.E. Weatherall (GBR).
NQ (2) S. Stewart (GBR), G.L. France (GBR).

1937

SQ (8) S.C. Clark (GBR), J.M. Hunt (GBR), H.D. MacKinnon (GBR), M.A. Young (GBR), J.R. Reddall (GBR), D.M. Bull (GBR), M.E. Lucking (GBR), H.J. Whitney (GBR).
LL (3) H. Rothwell (GBR), J.R. Fawcus (GBR), H.F.C. Horne (GBR).
NQ (2) E.P.K. Hansom (GBR), E.A. Barlow (GBR).

1938

SQ (8) R.F. Bessemer-Clark (GBR), T.B. Henderson Brooks (GBR), S. Rinde (NOR), K. Lavarack (GBR), J. Darkins (GBR), C.J. Hovell (GBR), J. Mehta (IND), A.M. Hamburger (ROM).
LL (NIL).
NQ (2) W.T. Anderson (GBR), J.A. Moore (GBR).

1939

SQ (8) H.T. Baxter (GBR), C.L. Savara (IND), J.N. Dhamija (IND), K. Aschner (HUN), H.J. Whitney (GBR), H.E. Weatherall (GBR), J.C. Warboys (GBR), C.N.O. Ritchie (GBR).
LL (3) M.D. Maclagen (GBR), J. Charanjva (IND), M.E. Lucking (GBR).
NQ (2) B. Royds (GBR), D.H. Slack (GBR).

1946 *No Competition.*

1947
SQ (8) G.P. Jackson (GBR), J.R. Mansell (GBR), G.L. Emmett (GBR), R.G. Reeve (GBR), A.J.N. Starte (GBR), W.C. Shute (GBR), R.J. Sandys (GBR), G.D. Oakley (GBR).
LL (1) J.N. Archer (GBR).
NQ (2) W.J. Moss (GBR), J.B. Griffith (GBR).

1948
SQ (8) C.R. Fawcus (GBR), R.J.E. Mayers (KEN), Lord Ronaldshay (GBR), A.J.N. Starte (GBR), J. Morison (USA), A.L. Proctor (GBR), A.C. Dobbs (GBR), C. Jones (USA).
LL (1) T.R. Miles (GBR).
NQ (2) H.C. Bernstein (GBR), C.R.M. Clarke (GBR).

1949
SQ (8) J. Morison (USA), G.B. Leyton (GBR), D.A. Samaai (RSA), E.C. Ford (GBR), M.F. Mohtadi (IRN), W.A. Manahan (IRL), J.R. Frolik (USA), F. Wallis (GBR).
LL (NIL).
NQ (2) D.V. Connor (RSA), A. Kalman (HUN).
LL (1) A.D.L. Hunter (NZL).

1950
SQ (8) R.K. Kaley (GBR), W.J. Smith (NZL), B.E. Crouch (GBR), A.W. Tills (NZL), D. Scharenguivel (GBR), C.R. Fawcus (GBR), S. Lie (NOR), R. Haillet (FRA).
LL (3) G.I. Pettigrew (GBR), A.M. Hamburger (GBR). G.L. Ward (GBR).
NQ (2) J.G. Rutherglen (GBR). A. Kalman (HUN).

1951
SQ (8) A.E. Dehnert (NED), M. Lemasson (FRA), J. Morison (USA), H.C. Bernstein (GBR), B.E. Crouch (GBR), J.R. Mansell (GBR), J.F. Kupferburger (RSA), S. Davidson (RSA).
LL (NIL).
NQ (2) A. Kalman (HUN), W.T. Hough (GBR).

1952
SQ (8) J.W. Ager (USA), R.J.E. Mayers (KEN), S.D. Potts (USA), P.S. Eisenberg (USA), E.R. Bulmer (GBR), E. Tsai (HKG), M. Hime (GBR), B.J. Katz (SRH).
LL (NIL).
NQ (2) R.J. Lee (GBR), W.A. Knight (GBR).

1953
SQ (8) R. Krishnan (IND), R.S. Condy (IRE), S. Laslo (YUG), J. Michelmore (GBR), F.R. Kipping (GBR), I. Panajotovic (YUG), Z. Nikolich (YUG), A.L. Proctor (GBR).
LL (1) W. van Voorhees (USA).
NQ (2) D.R. Oliver (GBR), I.J. Warwick (GBR).

1954
SQ (8) F.R. Kipping (GBR), M. Hime (GBR). J.M. Ward (GBR), G.C. Pryor (AUS), P. Moys (GBR), G.L. Forbes (RSA), P. Wooldridge (GBR), W. van Voorhees (USA).
LL (NIL).
NQ (2) G.A. Cass (GBR) P. Wooller (GBR).

1955
SQ (8) H.C. Bernstein (GBR), I. Froman (RSA), C.V. Botha (RSA), G.W. Druliner (USA), H.W. Sweeney (USA), R.T. Potter (AUS), P. Scholl (GER), K. Saeed (PAK).
LL (2) J.D. Forbes (USA), A.L. Proctor (GBR).
NQ (2) J.J.F. Robinson (GBR), H.F. Walton (GBR).

1956
SQ (8) A. Ali (IND), G.E. Mudge (GBR), R. Mark (AUS). R.G. Laver (AUS), D.B. Hughes (GBR), J. Blatchford (USA), B.E. Page (RSA), K. Keretic (YUG).
LL (5) S.D. Lester (GBR), M. Pirzada (PAK), D.R. Collins (GBR), E.C. Ford (GBR), R. Goosen (RSA).
NQ (2) R.T. White (GBR), P. Wooller (GBR).

1957
SQ (8) N. Kitovitz (GBR), C. Crawford (USA), R.V. Sherman (USA), A. Bey (RHO), A.A. Charnock (RSA), C.T. Parker (NZL), E. Aguirre (CHI), D.J. Lawer (RSA).
LL (1) J.J.F. Robinson (GBR).
NQ (2) D.B. Hughes (GBR), D. Gunson (GBR).

1958
SQ (8) E.H. Buchholz (USA). O.S. Prenn (GBR), E.C. Ford (GBR). B.M. Kearney (AUS). U. Kumar (IND), G. Grant (USA), R.K. Stilwell (RHO), W. van Voorhees (USA).
LL (NIL).
NQ (2) P. Wooller (GBR) R.H. Dabbs (GBR).

1959
SQ (8) T. Lejus (URS), A.J. Clayton (GBR), A.J. Lane (AUS), C.W. Hannam (GBR), J. Mukerjea (IND), S.W. Hicks (AUS), J.M. Ward (GBR), J. Griary (USA).
LL (NIL).
NQ (2) R.W.Dixon (GBR), A.F.M. Dillon (GBR).
LL (1) T.A. Adamson (GBR).

1960
SQ (8) N. Pilic (YUG), R.F. Sanders (RSA), J.B. Hillebrand (AUS), P. Moys (GBR), J.R. McDonald (NZL), C. Holm (SWE), J.F. O'Brien (AUS), A.J. Udaykumar (IND).
LL (1) V. Presecki (YUG).
NQ (2) R. Taylor (GBR), C.R. Applewhaite (GBR).

1961
SQ (8) D. Contet (FRA), H. Elschenbroich (GER), G.J. Hughes (AUS), E.L. Scott (USA), J.E. Mandarino (BRA), I. Ingvarsson (SWE), G. Palafox (MEX), H.E. Truman (GBR).
LL (1) F.D. McMillan (RSA).
NQ (2) T.A. Adamson (GBR), R.W. Dixon (GBR).

1962
SQ (8) A.C. Kendall (AUS), W.W. Bowrey (AUS), F.D. McMillan (RSA), B.G. Knox (AUS), R.F. Sanders (RSA), H.E. Truman (GBR), M. Fujii (JPN), O.K. French (AUS).
LL (NIL).
NQ (2) R.W. Dixon (GBR), J.M. Gracie (GBR).

1963
SQ (8) J.D.C. Crump (GBR), R.J. Moore (RSA), R.J. Siska (USA), M. Pirro (ITA), R.W. Fisher (USA), W.H. Hoogs (USA), A.K. Carpenter (CAN), B.W. Geraghty (AUS).
LL (1) J.E. Baker (HAI).
NQ (2) K. Wooldridge (GBR), J.M. Gracie (GBR).

1964
SQ (8) D.A.R. Russell (JAM), T.J. Ryan (RSA), T. Hajar (NED), S.P. Misra (IND), E.A. Neely (USA), R.S. Werksman (USA), G. Battrick (GBR), M. Holecek (TCH).
LL (5) K. Andersson (SWE), G.C. Bluett (GBR), J. Saul (GBR), O. Bengtson (SWE), R.D. Senkowski (USA).
NQ (2) R.W. Dixon (GBR), C.R. Applewhaite (GBR).

1965

SQ (8) C. de Gronkel (BEL), O. Pabst (CHI), V. Zarazua (MEX), D.A.R. Russell (JAM), G.W. Stubbs (GBR), G.C. Bluett (GBR), P.J. Cramer (RSA), J.L. Moore (AUS).
LL (3) F. Bautisto (PHI), B. Holmstrom (SWE), S.R. Smith (USA).
NQ (2) C.R. Applewhaite (GBR), E.A. Beards (GBR).

1966

SQ (8) R.E. Puddicombe (CAN), J.B. Chanfreau (FRA), G.B. Primrose (AUS), O. Bengtson (SWE), G.C. Bluett (GBR), Y. Yanagi (JPN), B. Paul (FRA), R.A. Weedon (RSA).
LL (3) L.E. Lumden (JAM), I. Konishi (JPN), B.R. Butcher (RSA).
NQ (2) J.G. Clifton (GBR), E.A. Beards (GBR).

1967

Q (10) G.C. Garner (RSA), R.G. Summers (RSA), C. Iles (GBR), S. Minotra (IND), F. Tutvin (USA), R.J. Wilson (AUS), T. Akbari (IRN), O. Parun (NZL), C.D. Steele (USA), R. Mori (JPN).
LL (1) G.B. Primrose (AUS).

1968

Q (10) T.J. Ryan (RSA), D.A. Lloyd (GBR), E.A. Zuleta (ECU), J.F. Brown (AUS), P. Hombergen (BEL), J. Fassbender (GER), H. Rahim (PAK), G.C. Bluett (GBR), D.W. Schroder (RSA), S.J. Matthews (GBR).
LL (4) C. Iles (GBR), P. Castillo (COL), L.E. Lumsden (JAM), R.A. Peralta (ARG).

1969

Q (10) A.J. McDonald (AUS), R. Seegers (RSA), J.G. Paish (GBR), W.C. Higgins (USA), E.J. van Dillen (USA), J.G. Clifton (GBR), J.D. Bartlett (AUS), S. Koudelka (STA), C.D. Steele (USA), J. Krinsky (RSA).
LL (5) T. Nowicki (POL), K. Yanagi (JPN), P. Pokorny (AUT), W.B. Geraghty (AUS), E.A. Zuleta (ECU).

1970

Q (10) S.A. Warboys (GBR), R. Krog (RSA), J.G. Paish (GBR), P.M. Doerner (AUS), C.S. Dibley (AUS), R.R. Dowdeswell (RHO), P.W. Curtis (GBR), J.D. Bartlett (AUS), S. Ball (AUS), A.J. McDonald (AUS).
LL (1) E.A. Zuleta (ECU).

1971

Q (12) K. Meiler (GER), J.G. Simpson (NZL), W.N'Godrella (FRA), E di Matteo (ITA), An Amritraj (IND), J. de Mendoza (GBR), P.J. Cramer (RSA), H.J. Plotz (GER), P.M. Doerner (AUS), J. Hrebec (TCH), J.W. Feaver (GBR), G.W. Seewagen (USA).
LL (1) R.N. Howe (AUS).

1972

Q (16) A. Mayer (USA), P. Marzano (ITA), R.D. Knight (USA), W.R. Durham (AUS), P. Gerken (USA), D. Bleckinger (USA), E.L. Scott (USA), R.L. Bohrnstedt (USA), A.R. Gardiner (AUS), S.E. Stewart (USA), G.W. Seewagen (USA), W.J. Austin (USA), M. Vasquez (ARG), R. Stock (USA), M.S. Estep (USA), P.R. Hutchins (GBR).
LL (2) A. Van der Merwe (RSA), R.G. Clarke (NZL).

1973 *(See Note)*

Q (32) F. Gerbert (GER), A.J. McDonald (AUS), M. Lara (MEX), S. Ball (AUS), P. Pokorny (AUT), I. Santeiu (ROM), E.L. Scott (USA), P. Lall (IND), D.A. Parun (NZL), C. Dowdeswell (RHO), S.G. Messmer (USA), J. Hordijk (NED), J.B. Chanfreau (FRA)* J.G. Clifton (GBR), T. Sakai (JPN), J.L. Haillet (FRA), R.G. Giltinan (AUS), W. Martin (USA), J. Yuill (RSA), T. Svensson (SWE), R.W. Drysdale (GBR), K.N. Hancock (AUS), G.S. Thomson (AUS), W.L. Lloyd (AUS)*, H.J. Plotz (GER), M. Iqbal (PAK), W.R. Durham (AUS), B.M. Bertram (RSA)+, R.A. Buwalda (RSA), H. Engert (GER), G. Misra (IND), E. Russo (AUS).

LL (32 – lost in second round) S.E. Stewart (USA)+, J. Moreno (ESP), J.F. Caujolle (FRA), P.W. Curtis (GBR), P. Siviter (GBR), R.H. Stock (USA), J.D. Bartlett (AUS)*. J.P. Meyer (FRA)+, V. Zednik (TCH), P. Cornejo (BRA)*, G. Braun (AUS), D.J. Bleckinger (USA). R.A. Lewis (GBR). F.P. Waltnall (USA), P.C. Kronk (AUS), P.F. McNamee (AUS), P. Marzano (ITA), C.E. McHugo (GBR), R.J. Simpson (NZL), C. Iles (GBR), C.L. Letcher (AUS), M.J. Farrell (GBR), T.B. Karp (USA), J. Mukerjea (IND), H.W. Turnbull (AUS), R.P. Dell (USA)*, J. Hagey (USA), P. Kanderal (SUI), T. Vasquez (ARG)+, J.R. Ganzabal (ARG)*, G. Peebles (USA), D.T. Crawford (USA).
* *withdrew before main Championship draw.*
+ *withdrew after main Championship draw.*
LL (26 – lost in first round) N. Holmes (USA), J. Kuki (JPN), D. Stojovic (YUG), E.A. Zuleta (ECU), K. Pugaev (URS), C. Mukerjea (IND), E.W. Ewart (AUS), D. Joubert (RSA), S.S. Meer (PAK), K. Tanabe (JPN), R.L. Bohrnstedt (USA), K. McMillan (USA), R. Machan (HUN), R. Chavez (MEX), J.W. James (AUS), J.G. Simpson (NZL), G.W. Perkins (AUS), K. Hirai (JPN), J. Singh (IND), T. Bernasconi (FRA), S.J. Matthews (GBR), P. Joly (FRA), M.W. Collins (GBR), W.L. Brown (USA), B.M. Mitton (RSA), S.E. Myers (AUS).

NOTE: *Because of the Players' Boycott only two qualifying rounds were played. The 32 winners (3 withdrew) of the second round became Qualifiers. The 32 players (7 withdrew) defeated in the second round, together with 26 players defeated in the first round became Lucky Losers.*

1974
Q (16) J.F. Caujolle (FRA), R. Seegers (RSA), S. Krulevitz (USA), R. Thung (NED), F. Pala (TCH), P.C. Kronk (AUS), D.E. Deblicker (FRA), P. Kenderal (SUI), B.M. Mitton (RSA), J.M. Yuill (RSA), U. Pinner (GER), R.P. Dell (USA), N.A. Fraser (AUS), T. Svensson (SWE), A.C. Neely (USA), H.J. Plotz (GER).
LL (1) J.I. Muntanola (ESP).

1975
Q (16) M.R. Edmondson (AUS), B.M. Mitton (RSA). C. Mukerjea (IND), C.M. Robinson (GBR), H. Hose (VEN), J. Andrew (VEN), C. Kirmayr (BRA). G.R. Stilwell (GBR), J.G. Paish (GBR), V. Pecci (PAR), G. Battrick (GBR), A.G. Fawcett (RHO), R.J. Simpson (NZL), J.K. Holladay (USA), J.W. Blocher (USA), L. Alvarez (ARG).
LL (3) T. Svensson (SWE), T. Vazquez (ARG), J.W. James (AUS).

1976
Q (16) J. Royappa (IND), D.H. Collings (AUS), J.S. Hagey (IND), K. Hirai (JPN), J.M. Yuill (RSA), R.J. Simpson (NZL). G. Mayer (USA), T.I. Kakulia (URS), V. Borisov (URS), W. Lloyd (AUS), P.F. McNamee (AUS), C.P. Kachel (AUS), J.M.P. Marks (AUS), S.A. Warboys (GBR), M.J. Farrell (GBR), G.E. Reid (USA).
LL (3) J.K. Holladay (USA), R. Thung (NED), M. Holecek (TCH).

1977
Q (16) T. Smid (TCH), J.H. McManus (USA), G.E. Reid (USA), R.J. Simpson (NZL), H.J. Bunis (USA), C.P. Kachel (AUS), R.E. Ycaza (ECU), R. Thung (NED). S. Sorenson (IRL) J. Granat (TCH), A.R. Gardiner (AUS), J.M.P. Marks (AUS), E.T. Teltscher (USA), J.K. Holladay (USA), D. Palm (SWE), J.P. McEnroe (USA).
LL (8) S.W. Carnahan (USA), E. Montano (MEX), J.E. Mandarino (BRA), G.W. Seewagen (USA), R.J. Carmichael (AUS), W. Lofgren (USA), R.J. Chappel (RSA), R. Fisher (USA).

1978
Q (16) M.J. Farrell (GBR), J. Simbera (TCH), J.M.P. Marks (AUS), J. Royappa (IND), J.M. Bailey (USA), A. Fillol (CHI), D.H. Collings (AUS), R.J. Frawley (AUS), M.D. Wayman (GBR), F.V. McNair (USA), R.J. Carmichael (AUS), E.J. van Dillen (USA), J.C. Kriek (RSA), D. Schneider (RSA), C.P. Kachel (AUS), M.R. Edmondson (AUS).
LL (5) S. Birner (TCH), B. Manson (USA), D. Carter (AUS), D. Palm (SWE), M.H. Machette (USA).

1979

Q (16) G. Moretton (FRA), B.D. Drewett (AUS), R. Meyer (USA), R.G. Giltinan (AUS), J.A. Cortes (COL), D.P. Whyte (AUS), J.E. Norback (SWE), C.M. Pasarell (USA), U. Eriksson (SWE), C. Motta (BRA), J.B. Fitzgerald (AUS), R.C. Beven (GBR), C.L. Letcher (AUS), F. Buehning (USA), R. Fisher (USA), O. Parun (NZL).
LL (3) J.M. Yuill (RSA), N.R. Phillips (AUS). A. Fillol (CHI).

1980

Q (16) J.G. Paish (GBR), C.P. Kachel (AUS), O. Parun (NZL), M.N. Doyle (USA), S. Sorensen (IRL), G. Hardie (USA), I. El Shafei (EGY), C.M. Johnstone (AUS), J.B. Fitzgerald (AUS), S.E. Davis (USA), K.M. Curren (RSA), P. Doohan (AUS), R. Krishnan (IND), J.M. Yuill (RSA), W.D. Hampson (AUS), E. Edwards (USA).
LL (6) S. Menon (IND), S. Ball (AUS), V. Winitsky (USA), D. Schneider (ISR), L. Palin (FIN). J.R. Austin (USA).

1981

Q (16) T.C. Fancutt (AUS), D.H. Collings (AUS), W.R. Pascoe (AUS), G. Moretton (FRA), C.A. Miller (AUS), G.S. Holroyd (USA), S. McCain (USA), E.J. van Dillen (USA), C.J. Wittus (USA), M. Davis (USA), M.A.O. Wilander (SWE), J. Bailey (USA), C.M. Dunk (USA), S. Menon (IND), C.L. Letcher (AUS), J. Windahl (SWE).
LL (8) C.M. Johnstone (AUS), A. Fillol (CHI), K.J. Nystrom (SWE), M. Estep (USA), S. Denton (USA), H. Leconte (FRA), S.E. Davis (USA), U. Marten (GER).

1982

Q (16) V. Amritraj (IND), E. Edwards (USA), D. Schneider (ISR), R. Evett (USA), P. Doohan (AUS), S. Menon (IND), H. Sundstrom (SWE), S. Ball (AUS), L. Stefanki (USA), C. Dowdeswell (SUI), C.M. Dunk (USA), C.J. Wittus (USA), D. Dowlen (USA), M.T. Fancutt (AUS), D. Gitlin (USA), S.W.van der Merwe (RSA).
LL (4) O.B. Pirow (RSA), M.P. Myburg (RSA), G.J. Whitecross (AUS), R. Meyer (USA).

1983

Q (16) R.J. Frawley (AUS), M. Leach (USA), J. Sadri (USA), B.M. Mitton (RSA), P.B. Fleming (USA), S.E. Davis (USA), J. Turpin (USA), T.E. Gullikson (USA), T.C. Fancutt (AUS), J. Hlasek (SUI), C.R.O. Viljoen (RSA), D.T. Visser (RSA), B. Dyke (AUS), W.D. Hampson (AUS), A. Andrews (USA), E. Korita (USA).
LL (4) S. Menon (IND), M. Brunnberg (USA), J.C. McCurdy (AUS), R.B. Kleege (USA).

1984

Q (16) B. Manson (USA), C.J. Wittus (USA), S.E. Stewart (USA). B.F. Becker (GER), R.J. Simpson (NZL), T. Cain (USA), K.E. Flach (USA), G. Forget (FRA), C.A. Miller (AUS), C. Kirmayr (BRA), E. Edwards (RSA), C.H. Cox (USA), P.T. Annacone (USA), C. Van Rensburg (RSA), J. Turpin (USA), M. Kratzmann (AUS).
LL (3) M. Schapers (NED), C. Mezzadri (SUI), S. Perkiss (ISR).

1985

Q (16) A. Maurer (GER), A. Giammalva (USA), B. Moir (USA), C. Steyn (RSA), G. Muller (RSA), R. Saad (ARG), C.M. Dunk (USA), R. Acuna (CHI), C.A. Miller (AUS), K. Evernden (NZL), R.A. Seguso (USA), M.W. Anger (USA), D.G.C. Mustard (NZL), C.H. Cox (USA), R. Van't Hof (USA), T. Champion (FRA).
LL (NIL).

1986

Q (16) B. Pearce (USA), B. Custer (AUS), A. Zverev (URS), C. Hooper (USA), C.J. Van Rensburg (RSA), K.E. Flach (USA), M. Flur (USA), C. Saceanu (GER), M. Bauer (USA), S. Glickstein (ISR), B.H. Levine (RSA), P. Chamberlin (USA), M. Robertson (RSA), K. Moir (RSA), J. Lapidus (USA), M. Kratzmann (AUS).
LL (1) W. Scanlon (USA).

1987

Q (16) L. Shiras (USA), M. Flur (USA), G. Muller (RSA), S. Youl (AUS), M. Bauer (USA), L. Scott (USA), M.R. Woodforde (AUS), T. Mmoh (NIG), L. Stefanki (USA), A. Volkov (URS), D. Tyson (AUS), K.E. Flach (USA), R. Saad (ARG), A. Olkhovsky (URS), R.A. Reneberg (USA), C. Saceanu (ROM).
LL (NIL).

1988

Q (16) D. Nargiso (ITA), G.S. Ivanisevic (YUG), B.N. Moir (RSA), H. Moraing (GER), G. Layendecker (USA), T. Svantesson (SWE), T.A. Woodbridge (AUS), W. Scanlon (USA), A. Olkhovsky (URS), G. Fichardt (RSA), J.R. Stoltenberg (AUS), H.P. Van Boeckel (NED) S. Barr (AUS), R. Acuna (CHI), C.A. Limberger (AUS), G. Michibata (CAN).
LL (2) M. Laurendeau (CAN), N. Odizor (NIG).

1989

Q (16) B. Garnett (USA), R. Bathman (SWE), S. Giammalva (USA), J. Rive (USA), Z. Ali (IND), S. Warner (USA), B. Shelton (USA), K.L. Jones (USA), N.A. Fulwood (GBR), P. Baur (GER), M. Laurendeau (CAN), H. Holm (SWE), M. Robertson (RSA), W. Scanlon (USA), G. Holmes (USA), T.A. Woodbridge (AUS).
LL (1) M.W. Anger (USA).

1990

Q (16) G. Raoux (FRA), M. Robertson (RSA). R. Bathman (SWE). S. Matsuoka (JPN), H. Holm (SWE), R.D. Leach (USA), D. Dier (GER), N.P. Broad (GBR), V. Amritraj (IND), A. Lesch (FRG), D.T. Visser (RSA), W.R. Ferreira (RSA), D. Poliakov (URS), R. Kok (NED), K.E. Flach (USA), L.E. Herrera (MEX).
LL (3) C. Costa (ESP), T.A. Woodbridge (AUS), B. Dyke (AUS).

1991

Q (16) M. Kratzmann (AUS), S.F. Stolle (AUS), M. Keil (USA), D. Marcelino (BRA), G. Pozzi (ITA), B. Dyke (AUS), A. Boetsch (FRA), J.A. Frana (ARG), F. Roese (BRA), J.C. Kriek (USA), G. Michibata (CAN), R. Vogel (TCH), S. Zivojinovic (YUG), G. Layendecker (USA), D. Orsanic (ARG), H. Holm (SWE).
LL (5) M. Laurendeau (CAN), N. Kroon (SWE), D. Nargiso (ITA), M. Ruah (VEN), A. Olhovskiy (URS).

1992

Q (16) K. Kinnear (USA), A. Olhovskiy (CIS), J.A. Stark (USA), G. Raoux (FRA), R.D. Leach (USA), J.B. Fitzgerald (AUS), N. Kroon (SWE), C. Saceanu (GER), S.E. Davis (USA), J.-L.De Jager (RSA), M.S. Knowles (BAH), D. Randall (USA), B. Stankovic (TCH), H. Holm (SWE), G. Doyle (AUS), S. Bryan (USA).
LL (4) F. Roese (BRA), C.A. Limberger (AUS), G. Stafford (RSA), M. Ondruska (RSA).

1993

Q (16) P. Kilderry (AUS), D. Nainkin (RSA), L.P.A. Tieleman (ITA), T. Nelson (USA), S. Youl (AUS), P.M Rafter (AUS), M. Keil (USA), G. Doyle (AUS), S. Bryan (USA), F. Wibier (NED), B. Devening (USA), D. Randall (USA), P. Moraing (GER), S.D. Lareau (CAN), B. Joelson (USA), G. Rusedski (CAN).
LL (NIL).

1994

Q (16) J. Canter (USA), J.F. Altur (ESP), L.P.A. Tieleman (ITA), M. Tebbutt (AUS), G.D. Connell (CAN), C. Saceanu (GER), S. Youl (AUS), E.R. Ferreira (RSA), D. Witt (USA), M.S. Knowles (BAH), J.B. Fitzgerald (AUS), S.D. Lareau (CAN), K. Thorne (USA), A. Mronz (GER), A. Thoms (GER), B. Shelton (USA).
LL (1) D. Flach (USA).

1995

Q (16) A. Painter (AUS), L. Burgsmuller (GER), J. Morgan (AUS), P. Tramacchi (AUS), K.E. Flach (USA), N. Borwick (AUS), P. Baur (GER), D. Nargiso (ITA), L. Gloria (USA), C. Bergstrom (SWE), W. Masur (AUS), D.M. Nestor (CAN), A. Chang (CAN), M.S. Knowles (BAH), S.F. Stolle (AUS), A. Thoms (GER).

LL (6) E. Alvarez (ESP), L. Barthez (FRA), D. Norman (BEL), S. Simian (FRA), E. Erlich (ISR), S. Draper (AUS).

1996

Q (16) J.F. Grabb (USA), S.A.C. Huet (FRA), T. Kempers (NED), D.M. Nestor (CAN), D. Flach (USA), N. Godwin (RSA), J.E. Palmer (USA), P. Bouteyre (FRA), A. Ilie (AUS), W. A. O'Brien (USA)*, D. Nargiso (ITA), P. Tramacchi (AUS), J. Renzenbrink (GER), L. Manta (SUI), T. Champion (FRA), M. Navarra (ITA).

* withdrew

LL (4) A.P. Jarryd (SWE), L.A. Paes (IND), D. Nainkin (RSA), A. Chang (CAN).

1997

Q (16) P.H. Cash (AUS), H.J. Davids (NED), M.S. Bhupathi (IND), J. Van Lottum (NED), M. Tebbutt (AUS), Q. Burrieza (ESP), J. Salzenstein (USA), P. Baur (GER), W. McGuire (USA), C. Van Garsse (BEL), A. Clement (FRA), T. Larkham (AUS), D. Rikl (CZE), S. Duran (ESP), R. Gilbert (FRA), L.E. Herrera (MEX).

LL (4) N. Perieira (VEN), S.A.C. Huet (FRA), B. Ellwood (AUS), S. Bryan (USA).

1998

Q (16) W.A. O'Brien (USA), S.C. Grosjean (FRA), V. Voltchkov (BLR), M.S. Bhupathi (IND), D. Nainkin (RSA), T. Ketola (FIN), M.S. Knowles (BAH), M. Draper (AUS), W. McGuire (USA), D. Dilucia (USA), S. Pescosolido (ITA), B. MacPhie (USA), D. Bracciali (ITA), I. Heuberger (SUI), N. Godwin (RSA), A. Radulescu (GER).

LL (1) C. Van Garsse (BEL).

1999

Q (16) W.S. Arthurs (AUS), C. Caratti (ITA), J. Delgado (GBR), A. Hernandez (MEX), L. Manta (SUI), N. Marques (POR), A. Parmar (GBR), R.A. Reneberg (USA), A.R. Sa (BRA), D.E. Sapsford (GBR), P. Srichaphan (THA), G. Stafford (RSA), S.F. Stolle (AUS), M. Tillstrom (SWE), C.M. Vinck (GER), N. Zimonjic (YUG).

LL (1) M. Kohlmann (GER).

2000

Q (16) V. Voltchkov (BLR), S.A.C. Huet (FRA), I. Gaudi (ITA), O.L.P. Rochus (BEL), W.A. O'Brien (USA), M. Russell (USA), D.J. Prinosil (GER), N. Godwin (RSA), P. Kilderry (AUS), H. Levy (ISR), M. Llodra (FRA), D. Petrovic (AUS), J. Melzer (AUT), C.M. Vinck (GER), J. Bower (RSA), T. Dent (USA).

LL (6) F. Jonsson (SWE), C.B. Saulnier (FRA), S.D. Lareau (CAN), W.H. Black (ZIM), M. Kohlmann (GER), W. Eschauer (AUT).

2001

Q (16) L. Milligan (GBR), T.A. Woodbridge (AUS), J.S. Knowles (BAH), R.C. Bryan (USA), N. Godwin (RSA), A. Derepasko (RUS), I. Heuberger (SUI), F. Jonsson (SWE), D.M. Nestor (CAN), C. Mamiit (USA), Y. Yoon (KOR), M. Llodra (FRA), S. Draper (AUS), T. Dent (AUS), L.A. Paes (IND), S.A.C. Huet (FRA).

LL (5) A.R. Sa (BRA), P. Srichaphan (THA), J. Vacek (CZE), W.H. Black (ZIM), M. Fish (USA).

2002

Q(16) C. Saulnier (FRA), J. Melzer (AUT), C. Caratti (ITA), H-T. Lee (KOR), N. Thomann (FRA), K. Beck (SVK), J-B. Guzman (ARG), S. Draper (AUS), J. Brasington (USA), K. Economidis (GRE), J-F. Bachelot (FRA), A. Waske (GER), M. Ancic (CRO), J. Bower (RSA), R. Stepanek (CZE), G. Carraz (FRA).

LL (4) J. Morrison (USA), B.P. Vahaly (USA), G. Bastl (SUI), D. Golovanov (RUS).

2003

Q(16) K. Economidis (GRE), I. Karlovic (CRO), D. Norman (BEL), W. Moodie (RSA), P. Luxa (CZE), F. Verdasco (ESP), C. Saulnier (FRA), F. Niemeyer (CAN), P. Baccanello (AUS), M. Llodra (FRA), R. Soderling (SWE), T. Larkham (AUS), I. Heuberger (SUI), T. Suzuki (JPN), G. Elseneer (BEL), M. Mertinak (SVK).

LL (4) T. Zib (CZE), V. Hanescu (ROM), R. Kendrick (USA), I. Kunitsyn (RUS).

2004

Q(16) J. Delgado (GBR), A. Sa (BRA), I. Navarro Pastor (ESP), R. Gasquet (FRA), R. Delgado (PAR), G. Weiner (USA), J.Hernych (CZE), C.P. Rochus (E), A. Falla (COL), I. Heuberger (SUI), D. Bracciali (ITA), Y-T. Wang (TPE), O. Patience (FRA), J. Knowle (AUT), A. Ram (ISR), J. Tipsarevic (SCG).

LL (5) J. Benneteau (FRA), D. Sanguinetti (ITA), A. Peya (AUT), P. Starace (ITA), S. Pescosolido (ITA).

2005

Q(16) A. Seppi (ITA), A.M.M. Clement (FRA), G.E. Bastl (SUI), J. Delgado (GBR), J.A. Morrison (USA), A. Dupuis (FRA), D. Udomchoke (THA), G. Elseneer (BEL), R. Karanusic (CRO), D. Norman (BEL), A. Garcia (CHI), Y-H Lu (TPE), N. Okun (ISR), T. Ketola (FIN), N. Djokovic (SCG), T. Summerer (GER)

LL (3) J.J. Gimelstob (USA), P.H. Goldstein (USA), Bracciali (ITA).

2006

Q(16) K. Kim (USA), I. Labadze (GEO), R. Karanusic (CRO), M. Granollers-Pujol (ESP), M. Berrer (GER), F.Dancevic (CAN), A. Falla (COL), S. Stadler (GER), A. Peya (AUT), K. Pless (DEN), J. Goodall (GBR), S. Galvani (ITA), W.S. Arthurs (AUS), B. Dorsch (GER), R. Kendrick (USA), B. Becker (GER).

LL (1) J-C. Faurel (FRA)

2007

Q(16) Y-T. Wang (TPE), N.P.A. Mahut (FRA), E. Roger-Vasselin (FRA), A-U-H. Qureshi (PAK), B. Reynolds (USA), B. Ulihrach (CZE), S. Warburg (USA), Z. Fleishman (USA), L. Childs (GBR), A. Falla (COL), G. Muller (GER), R. De Voest (RSA), W. Arthurs (AUS), M Zverev (GER), F. Vicente (ESP), T. Zib (CZE).

LL (2) F. Dancevic (CAN), K. Kim (USA)

2008

Q(16) K. Kim (USA), P. Petzschner (GER), S. Stakhovsky (UKR), A. Peyer (AUT), P. Snobel, (CZE), S. Stadler (GER), C. Eaton (GBR), I. Van Der Merwe (RSA), C. Rochus (BEL), F. Gil (POR), E. Roger-Vasselin (FRA), J. Levine (USA),D. Olejniczak (POL), J. Hernych (CZE), S. Galvani (ITA), A. Beck (GER)

LL (2) I. Bozoljac (SRB), T. Kamke (GER)

2009

Q(16) R. Ram (USA), S. Greul (GER), X. Malisse (BEL), R. Karanusic (CRO), L. Lacko (SVK), A. Peya (AUT), A. Falla (COL), E. Roger-Vassselin (FRA), G. Zemlja (SLO), S. Gonzalez (MEX), T. Dent (USA), R. Ghedin (ITA), A. Mannarino (FRA), L. Gregorc (SLO), M. Yani (USA), J. Levine (USA)

LL (4) P. Cuevas (URU), T. Alves (BRA), K. Beck (SVK), D. Lidomchoke (THA)

2010

Q (16) T. Dent (USA), M. Fischer (AUT), I. Bozoljac (SRB), C. Ball (AUS), R. De Voest (RSA), I. Dodig (CRO), G. Alcaide (ESP), B. Tomic (AUS), T. Kamke (GER), J. Huta-Galling (NED), M. Ilhan (TUR), R. Kendrick (USA), N.P.A. Mahut (FRA), B. Evans (USA), J. Witten (USA), R. Berbanks (LTU).

LL (7) J. Levine (USA), R. Sweeting (USA), S.Ventura (ESP), R. Delgado (PAR), J. Reister (GER), S. Koubek (AUT), G. Soeda (JPN).

2011

Q(16) I. Sijsling (NED), L. Kubot (POL), B. Tomic (AUS), M. Matosevic (AUS), A. Beck (GER), K. Beck (SVK). R. De Voest (RSA), M. Fischer (AUT), F. Cipolla (ITA), F. Dancevic (CAN), C. Niland (IRL), E. Roger-Vasselin (FRA), K. De Schepper (FRA), C. Stebe (GER), R. Bemelmans (BEL), L. Lacko (SVK) .

LL (5) M. Gicquel (FRA), S. Bolelli (ITA), G. Zemila (SUI), R.Harrison (USA), G. Soedal (JPN)

2012

Q(16) J. Zopp (EST), A. Menendez-Maceiras (ESP), G. Rufin (FRA), M. Russell (USA), J. Levine (USA), F. Serra (FRA), R. Sweeting (USA). D. Brown (GER), S. Bolelli (ITA), J. Wang (TPE), B. Baker (USA), K. De Schepper (FRA), R. Bemelmans (BEL), I. Cervantes (ESP), J. Janowicz (POL), A. Kuznetsov (RUS).

LL (1) W. Odesnik (USA).

2013

Q(16) S. Roberts (FRA), B. Knittel (GER), J. Reister (GER), W. Odesnik (USA), D. Brown (GER), D. Kudla (USA), J. Struff (GER), M. Reid (AUS), Y-T. Wang (TPE), J. Duckworth (AUS), M. Przysiezny (POL), B. Reynolds (USA), G. Soeda (JPN), A. Kuznetzov (USA), M. Gicquel (FRA), T. Gabashvili (RUS).

LL (1) O. Rochus (BEL).

2014

Q(16) L. Saville (AUS), J. Duckworth (AUS), A. Kuznetsov (USA), G. Muller (LUX), A. Pavic (CRO), K. Kravchuk (RUS), M. Ilhan (TUR), Y. Sugita (JPN), D. Kudla (USA), J. Wang (TPE), P. Herbert (FRA), T. Puetz (GER), S. Groth (AUS), T. Ito (JPN), J. Hernych (CZE), R. Harrison (USA).

LL (4) A. Bedene (SLO), S. Bolelli (ITA), M. Jaziri (TUN), F. Danevic (CAN)

Gentlemen's Doubles Championship

1925
Q (4) L.J. Carr and L. Darby (GBR), W.E.T. Cole and R.C. Wackett (GBR), L.W. Alderson and E.H. Carr (GBR), W. Irwin and W.M. Swinden (GBR).

1926
Q (4) J. Pennycuick and D. Powell (GBR), C.P. Dixon and F. Wallers (GBR), L.R.C. Mitchell and J.E. Pogson Smith (GBR), H.S. Owen and F.T. Stowe (GBR).

1927
SQ (4) G.F. Mathieson and J.B. Pittman (GBR), F.T. Stowe and E.U. Williams (GBR), C.H. Campbell and F. Crawshay Williams (GBR), W.T. Tucker and D.H. Williams (GBR).
NQ (1) A.T. Hollins and A.M. Wedd (GBR).

1928
SQ (4) I.H. Wheatcroft and E.U. Williams (GBR), L.C.R. Mitchell and A.W. Vinall (GBR), A.C. Belgrave and E.C. Penny (GBR), E.R. Avory and C.S. Higgins (GBR).
NQ (1) C.W. Banks and R. Pickersgill (GBR).

1929
SQ (4) K.C. Gander Dower and I.C. Maddock (GBR), J.H. van Alen and W. van Alen (USA), F.J. Perry and F.H.D. Wilde (GBR), G.A. Barber and C.H. Watson (GBR).
NQ (1) M.H.B. Eddowes and E.T. Hollins (GBR).

1930
SQ (4) C.A. Magrane and B.O. Porter (GBR), R. Deterding and J.R. Reddall (GBR), H.F. David and C.K. Horne (GBR), G.A. Barber and C.H. Watson (GBR).
NQ (1) L.P. Antrobus and O. Wright (GBR).

1931
SQ (4) G.R. Ashton and I.H. Wheatcroft (GBR), H.H.S. Hillier and D.H. Williams (GBR), A.L. Della Porta and H.G. Gunn (GBR), L.W. Alderson and G.F. Mathieson (GBR).
NQ (1) J.D. Burrows and H.S. Burrows (GBR).

1932
SQ (4) A.C. Crossley and R. Stone (GBR), M.A.V. Russell and P.V.V. Sherwood (GBR), H.D. Mackinnon and P.S. Young (GBR), W.F. Freeman and D.P. Van Meurs (GBR).
NQ (1) N. Taylor and O. Wright (GBR).

1933
SQ (4) M. Benavitch (GBR) and F.C. De Saram (CEY), M.A.V. Russell and P.V.V. Sherwood (GBR), W.F. Freeman and D.P. Van Meurs (GBR), F.R.L. Crawford and J.M. Hunt (GBR).
NQ (1) H. Aldred and E.A.G. Caroe (GBR).

1934
SQ (4) J.C. Hudson and A.G.C. King (GBR), J.B. Gilbert and H.S. Lewis-Barclay (GBR), E. Higgs and R.M. Turnbull (GBR), J.D.F. Fisher and R.G. MacInnes (GBR).
NQ (1) N. Taylor and J.B. Sturgeon (GBR).

1935
SQ (4) N. de Manby and R.C. Wackett (GBR), A.L. Della Porta and L.J. Walter (GBR), T.B. Henderson-Brooks and R. Morton (GBR), H.D. Mackinnon and P.S. Young (GBR).
NQ (1) E.C.B. Farmer and E.P.K. Hansom (GBR).

1936

SQ (4) A.G.C. King and W.R. Latham (GBR). C.J. Hovell and J.N. Wright (GBR), C.F.O. Lister and N. Taylor (GBR), C.F. Nicholls and D.H. Williams (GBR).
NQ (1) L.P. Antrobus and S. Stewart (GBR).

1937

SQ (4) D.M. Bull and C.F. Duncan (GBR), S.C. Clark and W.L. Grossmith (GBR), R.F. Bessemer Clark and H.A. Coldham (GBR), C.R. Fawcus and J.R. Fawcus (GBR).
LL (NIL).
NQ (1) W.T. Anderson and T.C. Braithwaite (GBR).

1938

SQ (4) J.K. Hamilton and F.D. Leyland (GBR), M.E. Lucking and J.D. Morris (GBR), T.B. Henderson-Brooks and G.I. Pettigrew (GBR), A.L. Della Porta and L.J. Walter (GBR).
LL (NIL).
NQ (1) W.T. Anderson and T.C. Braithwaite (GBR).

1939

SQ (4) A.L. Della Porta and L.J. Walter (GBR), H.T. Baxter and B.E. Whiteman (GBR), C.F. Hall and F.G. Hill (GBR), K. Aschner (HUN) and C.L. Savara (IND).
LL (NIL).
NQ (1) J.R. Briggs and B.W. Finnigan (GBR).

1946 *No Competition.*

1947

SQ (4) S.C. Clark and B.E. Whiteman (GBR), N.D. Cox and A.L. Della Porta (GBR), J. Clynton-Reed and J.W. Spence (GBR), B.G. Neal and R.C. Thorn (GBR).
LL (NIL).
NQ (1) J.B. Griffith and J.A. Moore (GBR).

1948

SQ (4) A.L. Proctor and J.A. White (GBR), L.E. Cater and F. Wallis (GBR), J. Clynton-Reed and M.D. Maclagan (GBR), C. Jones and J.M. Stas (USA).
LL (NIL).
NQ (1) W.T. Anderson and D.C. Argyle (GBR).

1949

SQ (4) J.A.T. Horn (GBR) and A.W. Tills (NZL), A. Dawes and T.G.N. Rowland (GBR), F.D. Leyland (GBR) and J. Morison (USA), A.L. Della Porta and H. Watkins (GBR).
LL (NIL).
NQ (1) J.A. Moore and J.R. Statham (GBR).

1950

SQ (4) A. Dawes and T.G.N. Rowland (GBR), D. Scharenguivel and A.J.N. Starte (GBR), A.L. Proctor and J.A. White (GBR), R.C.F. Nichols and H.J. Whitney (GBR).
LL (NIL).
NQ (1) J.B. Fulton and J.G. Rutherglen (GBR).

1951

SQ (4) A. Dawes and J.S. Ross (GBR), J.F. Kupferburger and O.G. Williams (RSA), P. Chatrier and M. Lemasson (FRA), C.J. Grindley and N.E. Hooper (GBR).
LL (NIL).
NQ (1) W.T. Anderson and A.T. England (GBR).

1952
SQ (4) P.S. Eisenberg and R.C. Sorlien (USA), C.J. Hovell and H.F. Walton (GBR), K.H. Ip and E. Tsai (HGK), H.C. Bernstein and D.J. Paton (GBR).
LL (NIL).
NQ (1) W.A. Knight and R.J. Lee (GBR).

1953
SQ (4) E.R. Bulmer and R.K. Kaley (GBR), G.L. Ward and J.M. Ward (GBR), S.C. Clark and C.J. Hovell (GBR), B.E. Crouch and G.K. Piercy (GBR).
LL (NIL).
NQ (1) J.H. Brown (GBR) and E. Tsai (HKG).

1954
SQ (4) A.J. Clayton (GBR) and I.G. Coghill (AUS), C.W. Hannam and I.J. Warwick (GBR), S.D. Lester and R.C. Thorn (GBR), J.K. Draper and I.C. King (GBR).
LL (1) D.C. Hamilton and G.B. Robinson (GBR).
NQ (1) R.G. Harris and J.B. Wilson (GBR).

1955
SQ (4) C.W. Hannam (GBR) and R.T. Potter (AUS), R. Huber and P. Scholl (GER), R.K. Kaley and F. Wallis (GBR), J.K. Drinkall and M. Hime (GBR).
LL (2) B.F. Hutchins and G.D. Owen (GBR), N. Dale and J. Melhuish ((JBR).
NQ (1) A. Kalman and D.E. Wright (GBR).

1956
SQ (4) W.S. Farrer and I.L. Phillips (RSA), B.F. Hutchins and G.D. Owen (GBR), L.V. Surville (AUS) and H.W. Sweeney (USA), J.B.G. Collar and H.E. Truman (GBR).
LL (1) E.R. Bulmer and J.M. Ward (GBR).
NQ (1) R.H. Hack and A. Kalman (GBR).

1957
SQ (4) W.T. Anderson and H.F. Walton (GBR), A.A. Charnock (RSA) and I.C. King (GBR), P. Moys and J.M. Ward (GBR), G.N. Bassett and R.V. Sherman (USA).
LL (NIL).
NQ (1) F.S. Field and R.M. Powell (GBK).

1958
SQ (4) D. Achondo and P. Rodriguez (CHI), T.A. Freiberg and D.W. Junta (USA), K.B.G. Collar and D.R. Collins (GBR), M.P. Hann and I.J. Warwick (GBR).
LL (NIL).
NQ (1) J.W.E. Sharp and J.M. Watson (GBR).

1959
SQ (4) H.C. Bernstein and G.A. Cass (GBR), A.J. Lane and B.J. Phillips Moore (AUS), S.W. Hicks and N. Nette (AUS), D. Achondo and J. Tort (CHI).
LL (NIL).
NQ (1) R.W. Dixon and F.S. Field (GBR).

1960
SQ (4) G.D. Oakley and H.E. Truman (GBR), L.P. Coni and F.S. Field (GBR), A.E.G. Bailey and D.A. Samaai (RSA), J. Mukerjea and A.J. Udaykumar (IND).
LL (NIL).
NQ (1) T.A. Adamson and C.R. Applewhaite (GBR).

1961
SQ (4) G.L. Ward and I.J. Warwick (GBR), G.D. Oakley and H.E. Truman (GBR), H. Elschenbroich (GER) and A.J. Lane (AUS), P. Moys and J.M. Ward (GBR).
LL (NIL).
NQ (1) T.A. Adamson and C.R. Applewhaite (GBR).

1962
SQ (4) F.D. McMillan and A.F. Rawstorne (RSA), M. Fujii and O. Ishiguro (JAP), W.W. Bowrey and B.G. Knox (AUS), B.W. Geraghty (AUS) and R. Taylor (GBR).
LL (NIL).
NQ (1) D. Gunson and G.W. Stubbs (GBR).

1963
SQ (4) P.H. Hutchins and G.M. Price (GBR). J.E. Baker (HAI) and K. Carpenter (CAN). A. Ochoa (MEX) and A.F. Rawstone (RSA), G.C. Bluett and C. Iles (GBR).
LL (NIL).
NQ (1) R.W. Dixon and K. Wooldridge (GBR).

1964
SQ (4) J.A. Stephens and B.R. Tobin (AUS), P.S. Cornejo and P.H. Rodriguez (CHI), K. Andersson and O. Bengtson (SWE), E. Blanke and D. Herdy (AUT).
LL (1) J.G. Keller (AUS) and R.A. Weeden (RSA).
NQ (1) E.A. Beards and R.W. Dixon (GBR).

1965
SQ (4) G.J. Baulch and J.L. Moore (AUS), J.R. Pinto Bravo (CHI) and V. Zarazua (MEX), B.L. Higgins (AUS) and J. Saul (RSA), S.R. Smith and S.J. Sidball (USA).
LL (NIL).
NQ (1) E.A. Beards and R.W. Dixon (GBR).

1966
SQ (4) G.L. Ward and I.J. Warwick (GBR), T.D. Phillips (GBR) and R.A. Weedon (RSA), T.J. Ryan and R.G. Summers (RSA), Z. Franulovic and Z. Mincek (YUG).
LL (NIL).
NQ (1) E.A. Beards and R.W. Dixon (GBR).

1967
Q (4) T. Nowicki and M. Rybarczyk (POL), G.C. Bluett (GBR) and R.J. Wilson (AUS), J.A. Pickens and W.A. Tym (USA), J.F. Brown (AUS) and L. Olander (SWE).
LL (NIL).

1968
Q (4) T.J. Ryan and R.G. Summers (RSA), W.G. Birt and G.C. Garner (RSA), F. Tutvin (CAN) and J.G. Bartlett (AUS), I. Wantanabe and K. Wantanabe (JPN).
LL (1) J.A. Dewitts (USA) and L. Olander (SWE).

1969
Q (4) S.J. Matthews and J.G. Paish (GBR), J.F. Brown and I.G. Fletcher (AUS), L.E. Lumsden and D.A.R. Russell (JAM), T.A. Mozur and C.D. Steele (USA).
LL (NIL).

1970
Q (4) T. Lejus and L. Palman (URS), R.L. Case and A.R. Gardiner (AUS), R.R. Dowdeswell and D. Irvine (RHO), M.M. Baleson (RSA) and A.G. Fawcett (RHO).
LL (NIL).

1971
Q (4) P.J. Cramer (RSA) and P.M. Doerner (AUS), D.A.R. Russell (JAM), and S.A. Warboys (GBR), J.D. Bartlett and G.W. Perkins (AUS), B.M. Bertram and W.T. Freer (RSA).
LL (NIL)

1972

Q (4) A.G. Fawcett (RHO) and J. Yuill (RSA), J.G. Simpson (NZL) and S.E. Stewart (USA), M. Machette (USA) and R.C. Ramirez (MEX), D.H. Irvine (RHO) and G.W. Perkins (AUS).
LL (2) A.R. Dawson and W.L. Lloyd (AUS), W.J. Austin and A. Mayer (USA).

1973 *No Competition.*

1974

Q (8) R. Krog and D.W. Schroder (RSA), T. Bernasconi and J.L. Haillet (FRA), B. Prajoux (CHI) and H.J. Plotz (GER), J. Andrew (VEN) and S. Krulevitz (USA), C.S. Dowdeswell (RHO) and J.M. Yuill (RSA), R.F. Keldie (AUS) and R. Seegers (RSA), C.S. Faulk and J.P. Fort (USA), J.G. Clifton and J.R. Smith (GBR).
LL (NIL).

1975

Q (5) J.P. Fort and A.C. Neely (USA), J.R. Smith (GBR) and L.C. Turville (USA), K. Hirai and T. Sakai (JPN), D. Joubert and B.M. Mitton (RSA), M.R. Edmondson and S.R. Wright (AUS).
LL (2) P.M. Doerner and J.W. James (AUS), J.B. Chanfreau (FRA) and V. Pecci (PAR).

1976

Q (5) P.R. Langsford (NZL) and J. Soares (BRA), P.B. Fleming and B.D. Teacher (USA), M.J. Farrell and S.A. Warboys (GBR), G. Mayer and E.L. Scott (USA), J.B. Chanfreau (FRA) and W. Redondo (USA).
LL (4) M.P. Myburg and R.C.W. Van't Hof (RSA), B.D. Drewett and P.B. McNamara (AUS), R. Chavez and E. Montana (BRA), P.G. Campbell (AUS) and L. Parker (USA).

1977

Q (5) D.N. Collings and G.P. Hutchinson (AUS), R.J. Keighery and W. Maher (AUS), J.L. Clerc (ARG) and R.E. Ycaza (ECU), R.J. Frawley and G.S. Thompson (AUS), S.W. Carnahan (USA) and M.D. Wayman (GBR).
LL (7) E.W. Ewert and J.C. Trickey (AUS), As. Amritraj (IND) and A.R. Gardiner (AUS), P.R. Langsford (NZL) and L. Palin (FIN), P.G. Campbell (AUS) and J.K. Holladay (USA). M.R.E. Appleton and J.M. Dier (GBR), U. Marten and R. Probst (GER), H.J. Bunis and G.W. Seewagen (USA).

1978

Q (5) R.J. Kelly and G.S. Thomson (AUS), D.H. Collings and K.W. Hancock (AUS), R.C. Giltinan and J.C. Trickey (AUS), B.D. Drewett and W. Maher (AUS), S. Birner and J. Simbera (TCH).
LL (5) J.L. Dumiani (URU) and C. Motta (BRA), J.B. Chanfreau (FRA) and S.E. Myers (AUS), V.L. Elke and N. Callaghan (AUS), P.B. McNamara and T. Rocavert (AUS), M.T Fancutt and W.D. Hampson (AUS).

1979

Q (5) T. Graham (USA) and R.O. Ruffels (AUS). M.D. Andrews and D. Sherbeck (USA), J.B. Fitzgerald and W.R. Pascoe (AUS), S. Nisho and S. Sakamoto (JPN), W.D. Hampton and R.J. Kelly (AUS).
LL (2) V.L. Eke (AUS) and M.J. Farrell (GBR), C. Aguilar and P. Pearson (USA).

1980

Q (5) J.B. Fitzgerald and C.A. Miller (AUS), M.N. Doyle (USA) and S. Sorensen (IRL), J. Gunnarsson and S. Svensson (SWE), K. Cain (USA) and H. Ismail (ZIM), M.R.E. Appleton and J.G. Paish (GBR).
LL (5) A.R. Gardiner and B.C. Guan (AUS), P.C. Dellavedova and P. Doohan (AUS), E. Edwards and C. Edwards (USA), C.M. Johnstone and G.J. Whitecross (AUS), A. Gattiker and C. Gattiker (ARG).

1981

Q (5) T. Graham and B. Nichols (USA), C.R.O. Viljoen and D.T. Visser (RSA), M.W. Anger and S.E. Davis (USA), R.J. Chappell and S.W. Van Der Merwe (RSA), M.T. Fancutt and T.C. Fancutt (AUS).

LL (5) M.R.E. Appleton (GBR) and D.H. Collings (AUS), R.M. Booth (GBR) and J. Windahl (SWE), B. Moir and M. Robertson (RSA), C.F. Aguillar and J. Edwards (USA). S. McCain and S. Meister (USA).

1982

Q (5) T. Bennett (USA) and N.G.H. Mohtadi (CAN), J.C. McCurdy and G.J. Whitecross (AUS), E.W. Davies and M.W.C. Guntrip (GBR), B. Dyke (USA) and P. Johnston (AUS), F. Sauer and S.W. Van Der Merwe (RSA).

LL (5) J.J. Lapidus (USA) and P.D. Smylie (AUS), C.A. Louw and B.N. Moir (RSA), M.T. Fancutt and T.C. Fancutt (AUS), D.G.C. Mustard (NZL) and W.R. Pascoe (AUS), T.R. Crowley and A. Scheinman (USA).

1983

Q (5) R. Druz and T. Kruger (USA), S.B. Edberg (SWE) and B.H. Levine (USA), C.S. Dowdeswell and R.W. Drysdale (GBR), C.H. Cox (USA) and J. Hlasek (SUI), C. Bradnam and D.A. Lloyd (GBR).

LL (2) M.P. Myburg and C. Van Rensburg (RSA), S. Giammalva (USA) and H. Sundstrom (SWE).

1984

Q (5) T. Cain and P. McEnroe (USA), A. Kohlberg and R. Meyer (USA), S. Menon (IND) and G. Michibata (CAN), M.N. Doyle (IRL) and A. Maurer (GER), D.G.C. Mustard and R.J. Simpson (NZL).

LL (4) A. Mansdorf and S. Perkiss (ISR), P. Doohan and M.T. Fancutt (AUS), P. Annacone and M. Depalmer (USA), R. Nelson (USA) and H. Shirato (JPN).

1985

Q (5) D. Campos (BRA) and R. Harmon (USA), M. Kratzmann and S. Youl (AUS), D.J. Cahill (AUS) and B.P. Derlin (NZL), M. Freeman and J. Turpin (USA), K. Evernden (NZL) and M. Robertson (RSA).

LL (NIL).

1986

Q (5) A. Chesnokov (URS) and K. Jones (USA), R.D. Leach and B. Pearce (USA), M. Bauer (USA) and R. Saad (ARG), P. Chamberlin and J. Klaparda (USA), A. Jordan (COL) and J.R. Pugh (USA).

LL (NIL).

1987

Q (5) An. Amritraj (IND) and J.A. Frana (ARG), R.J. Simpson (NZL) and L. Stefanki (USA), P. Aldrich and W.B. Green (RFA), C.H. Cox (USA) and M.T. Fancutt (AUS), G. Bloom and A. Mansdorf (ISR).

LL (1) R. Barlow (AUS) and H. Rittersbacher (GER).

1988

Q (5) M. Basham (AUS) and L.B. Jensen (USA), T. Champion and E. Winogradsky (FRA), S. Medem (GER) and O. Rahnasto (FlN), S. Devries and R. Matuszewski (USA), N.P. Broad and S. Kruger (RSA).

LL (5) A. Brice and J.M. Goodall (GBR), H. Moraing and P. Moraing (GER), G. Barbosa and M. Menezes (BRA), Z. Ali and M. Ferreira (IND), B.H. Levine (RSA) and L. Palandjian (USA).

1989

Q (5) J. Daher and F. Roese (BRA), L.J. Bale (AUS) and M. Nastase (ROM), B. Page and S. Warner (USA), Z. Ali (IND) and J. Canter (USA), G. Raoux and E. Winogradsky (FRA).

LL (NIL).

1990
Q (5) W.R. Ferreira and P. Norval (RSA), P.T. Hand and C. Wilkinson (GBR), P. Baur and C. Saceanu (GER), A. Boetsch and G. Raoux (FRA), G. Pfitzner (AUS) and T. Theine (GER).
LL (2) R. Bergh and H. Holm (SWE), R. Deppe and B. Talbot (RSA).

1991
Q (5) H. Holm and P. Nyborg (SWE), B. Haygarth and B. Talbot (RSA), B.H. Black (ZlM) and T.J. Middleton (USA), M. Laurendeau (CAN) and F. Roese (BRA), N. Borwick and A.P. Kratzmann (AUS).
LL (1) D.D. Adams (AUS) and G. Dzelde (URS).

1992
Q (5) H. Holm and P. Nyborg (SWE), M. Bauer and B. Joleson (USA), A. Boetsch and G. Raoux (FRA), J-L. De Jager and M. Ondruska (RSA), D. Eisenman (USA) and M.S. Knowles (BAH).
LL (NIL)

1993
Q (5) L.A. Paes (IND) and L.P.A. Tieleman (ITA), A. Radulescu (GER) and M. Stadling (SWE), L.J. Bale (RSA) and A. Kratzmann (AUS), D. Dilucia and B. MacPhie (USA), J-I. Garat (ARG) and S. Noszaly (HUN).
LL (NIL).

1994
Q (3) N. Noteboom and F. Wibier (NED), J.A. Eagle (AUS) and L. Rehmann (GER), G. Doyle and P. Kilderry (AUS).
LL (2) W.S. Arthurs and B. Larkham (AUS), K. Kempers (NED) and M. Tebbutt (AUS).

1995
Q (3) J. Delgado and G. Henderson (GBR), D. Flach and M. Joyce (USA), S. Draper and P. Tramacchi (AUS).
LL (1) G. Doyle and T. Larkham (AUS).

1996
Q (3) A. Kitinov (MKD) and G. Manal (AUT), M. Ardinghi and N. Bruno (ITA), D. DiLucia and S.M. Humphries (USA).
LL (NIL).

1997
Q (3) B. Ellwood and P. Tramacchi (AUS), R. Koenig (RSA) and A. Rueb (USA), D. Dilucia (USA) and R. Smith (BAH).
LL (3) B. Behrens (USA) and C. Haggard (RSA), R. Lavergne and S. Simian (FRA), H. Holm and M. Holm (SWE).

1998
Q (3) J. Holmes and A. Painter (USA), R.S. Matheson and N. Weal (GBR), P. Luxa and D. Skoch (CZE).
LL (NIL).

1999
Q (3) A. Ferreira (BRA) and G. Motomura (JPN), B. Kokavec (CAN) and G. Trifu (ROM), M. Navarra and S. Pescosolido (ITA).
LL (1) A. Hadad (ISR) and D. Roberts (RSA).

2000
Q (4) J. Blake and K. Kim (USA), S. Pescosolido and V. Santopadre (ITA), N. Behr (ISR) and S. Iwabuchi (JPN), J. Robichaud (CAN) and M. Sell (USA).
LL (NIL).

2001
Q (4) B. Hawk (USA) and G. Silcock (AUS), J. Erlich and A. Ram (ISR), K. Kim and G. Weiner (USA), J. Blake (USA) and M. Merklein (BAH).
LL (NIL).

2002
Q(4) K. Beck (SVK) and J. Levinsky (CZE), A. Waske (GER) and L. Zovko (CRO), A. Hadad (ISR) and A-U-H. Qureshi (PAK), R. Kendrick (USA) and R. Wassen (NED).
LL (1) D. Petrovic (AUS) and D. Skoch (CZE).

2003
Q(4) S.W.I. Huss (AUS) and L. Landsberg (SWE), T. Perry (AUS) and T. Shimada (JPN), M. Chiudinelli (SUI) and L. Zovko (CRO), J. Erlich and A. Ram (ISR).
LL (2) A. Hadad (ISR) and A-U-H Qureshi (PAK), S.D. Draper and P. Luczak (AUS).

2004
Q(4) S.W.I. Huss (AUS) and R. Lindstedt (SWE), G. Kisgyorgy (HUN) and L. Kubot (POL), R. DeVoest (RSA) and N. Healey (AUS), D. Bracciali and G. Galimberti (ITA)
LL (3) D. Bowen and T. Phillips (USA), D. Ayala and B. Vahaly (USA), K. Carlsen (DEN) and T. Ketola (FIN).

2005
Q(4) T. Ketola (FIN) and F. Niemeyer (CAN), R.A. Delgado (PAR) and A.R. Sa (BRA), R. Lindstedt (SWE) and A. Peya (AUT), S.W.I. Huss (AUS) and W.A. Moodie (RSA)*,
LL (2) L. Dlouhy and D. Skoch (CZE), R. Hutchins and M. Lee (GBR).
*Won Championship.

2006
Q(4) I. Labadze (GEO) and D. Vermic (SCG), N. Bamford and J. May (GBR), R. Delgado (PAR) and A. Sa (BRA), K. Kim and C. Mamit (USA).
LL (3) F. Niemeyer (CAN) and G. Weiner (USA), Sau. Raitiwatana and Sou. Ratiwatana (THA), Z. Fleishman (USA) and R. Smeets (AUS), T. Caki and P Snobel (CZE).

2007
Q(4) S. Lipsky and D. Martin (USA), H. Levy (ISR) and R. Ram (USA), I Bozoljac (SRB) and D. Norman (BEL), A. Zuznetsov (USA) and M. Zverev (GER).
LL (3) L. Burgsmuller (GER) and O. Teveshshuk (LKR), S. Ratiwatana and S. Ratiwatana (THA), K. Kim and R. Smeets (USA).

2008
Q(4) P.Pala (CZE) and I. Zelenay (SVK), F. Gil (POR) and D. Norman (BEL), KJ. Hippensteel and T. Phillips (USA), A. Delic and B. Evans (USA)
LL (3) H. Armando and J. Levine (USA), J. Brunstrom (SWE) and A. Feeney (AUS), M. Elgin and A. Kudryavtsev (RUS).

2009
Q(4) C. Eaton and A. Slabinsky (GBR), K. Anderson (RSA) and S. Devvarman (IND), P. Amritraj (IND) and A-V-H. Qureshi (PAK), S. Gonzalez (MEX) and T. Rettenmaier (USA).
LL (6) D. Martin (USA) and J-C. Scherrer (SUI), A. Motti (ITA) and J. Siranni (AUS), R. Junaid (AUS) and P. Marx (GER), K. Beck (SVK) and J. Levinsky (CZE) S. Ratiwatana and S. Ratiwatana (THA), C. Guccione (AUS) and F. Moser (GER).

2010
Q(4) R. Bozoljac (SRB) and H. Mankad (IND), S. Devvarman (IND) and T.C. Huey (PHI), R. de Voest (RSA) and M. Zverev (GER), J. Levine and R. Sweeting (USA).
LL (2) S. Ratiwatana and S. Ratiwatana (THA), T. Bednarek and M. Kowalczyk (POL).

2011

Q(4) R. Harrison and T. Rettenmaier (USA), K. Beck (SVK) and D. Skoch (CZE), D. Rice and S. Thornley (GBR), T-C. Huey (PHI) and I. Van der Merwe (USA).
LL (5) A. Motti (ITA) and S. Robert (FRA), San. Rathwatana and Son. Rathwatana (THA). L. Friedl (CZE) and D. Martin (USA), L. Lacko (SVK) and L. Rosol (CZE), F. Cipola and P. Lorenzi (ITA).

2012

Q(4) A. Begemann (GER) and I. Zelenay (SVK), M. Bachinger and T. Kamke (GER), R. Reynolds (USA) and I. Van Der Merwe (RSA), L. Burton and G. Morgan (GBR).
LL (1) Sa Ratiwatana and So Ratiwatana (THA).

2013

Q(4) J. Levine and V. Pospisil (CAN), S. Groth and C. Guccione (AUS), D. Meffert (GER) and P. Oswald (AUT), P. Raja and D. Shara (IND).
LL (3) D. Kudia and T. Smyczek (USA), D. Brown (GER) and R. Junaid (AUS), S. Johnson (USA) and A. Siljestrom (SWE).

2014

Q (4) M. Demoliner (BRA) and P. Raja (IND), A. Siljestrom (SWE) and I. Zelenay (SVK), R. Harrison and K. King (USA), A. Bolt and A. Whittington (AUS).

Ladies' Singles Championship

1925
Q (8) Miss I.A. Maltby (GBR), Miss S.K. Johnson (GBR), Miss B.C. Brown (GBR), Miss V. Southam (GBR), Miss E.A. Goldsack (GBR), Miss E.V. Bennett (GBR), Miss C. Beckingham (GBR), Miss M. Cambridge (GBR).

1926
Q (8) Miss E. Morle (GBR), Miss M.V. Chamberlain (GBR), Mrs. Crawshaw Williams (GBR), Miss E.D. Holman (GBR), Mrs. H.G. Broadbridge (GBR), Miss P. Dransfield (GBR), Mrs. M.B. Reckitt (GBR), Miss M.E. Dix (GBR).

1927
SQ (8) Miss D. Busby (GBR), Miss M.P. Davies (GBR), Miss H.L. Eddis (GBR), Miss B. Feltham (GBR), Miss N. Trentham (GBR), Miss S.K. Johnson (GBR), Miss E. Hemmant (GBR), Mrs. M.L. Morison (GBR).
NQ (2) Miss E.C. Connell (GBR), Mrs. W.M.C. Bower (GBR).

1928
SQ (8) Miss V. Marshall (GBR), Miss N. Trentham (GBR), Miss P.E. Mudford (GBR), Miss B.C. Brown (GBR), Miss B. Feltham (GBR), Miss D.E. Round (GBR), Miss D. Busby (GBR), Miss H. Evelyn Jones (GBR).
NQ (2) Miss K.T. Anningson (GBR), Miss D.E. Anderson (GBR).

1929
SQ (8) Miss V.H. Montgomery (GBR), Miss V. Marshall (GBR), Miss A. Mellows (GBR), Miss G. Harry (GBR), Miss S.K. Johnson (GBR), Miss G.M. Thompson (GBR), Miss H. Bourne (GBR), Miss B.E. Boas (GBR).
NQ (2) Mrs. D. Munro (GBR), Miss E. Goldsworth (GBR).

1930
SQ (8) Mrs. E.S. Law (GBR), Mrs. I.D. Brumwell (GBR), Miss D.V. Eastley (GBR), Miss G. Vaughton (GBR), Mrs. H.G. Broadbridge (GBR), Mrs. M. Stork (GBR), Mrs. P.M. Ryland (GBR), Miss L. Johnstone (GBR).
NQ (2) Miss M.G. Hargreaves (GBR), Miss W.A. James (GBR).

1931
SQ (8) Mrs. A.T. Price (GBR), Miss E. Perry (GBR), Mrs. H.A. Lewis (GBR), Mrs. V. Barr (GBR), Mrs. G. Lucas (GBR), Miss K.E. Stammers (GBR), Miss S.K. Hewitt (GBR), Miss J. Couchman (GBR).
NQ (2) Mrs. J.G. Stephens (GBR), Miss M.E. Rudd (GBR).

1932
SQ (8) Miss B. Holly (GBR). Mrs. H.G. Broadbridge (GBR), Miss G. Southwell (GBK), Miss B.E. Boas (GBR), Mrs. P. Thomas (GBR), Miss D.H. Crichton (GBR), Mrs. M. Stork (GBR), Mrs. W.J. Dyson (GBR).
NQ (2) Miss M.G. Hargreaves (GBR), Miss B.G. Beazley (GBK).

1933
SQ (8) Mrs. M.M. Moss (GBR), Miss S.G. Chuter (GBR), Miss D.H. Crichton (GBR), Miss A.A. Wright (GBR), Miss M. Johnstone (GBR), Miss B. Soames (GBR), Miss D.M.S. White (GBR), Miss K.E. Robertson (GBR).
NQ (2) Miss B.G. Beazley (GBR), Miss B.I.E. Drew (GBR).

1934
SQ (8) Miss B.E. Frye (GBR)*, Miss E.N.S. Dicken (GBR), Miss M. Burgess-Smith (GBR), Miss J.E. Cunningham (GBR), Miss A.A. Wright (GBR), Miss G.A. Clark-Jervoise (GBR), Mrs. R.M. Turnbull (GBR), Miss P.L.F. Thomson (GBR).
* *withdrew*
NQ (2) Miss R.J. Smith (GBR), Miss M.G. Hargreaves (GBR).

1935

SQ (8) Miss J. Dawbarn (GBR), Miss P.L.F. Thomson (GBR), Miss P.J. Owen (GBR), Miss P.M. Weekes (GBR), Miss S. Mavrogordato (GBR), Miss L. St. John Maule (GBR), Miss S. Travers (GBR), Miss M.E. Lumb (GBR).
NQ (2) Miss R.J. Smith (GBR), Miss B.I.E. Drew (GBR).

1936

SQ (8) Miss A. Page (USA), Mrs. E.W. Luxton (GBR), Mrs. K.A.T. Bowden (GBR), Mrs. M. Cable (GBR), Miss P.J. Owen (GBR), Mrs. D. Trentham (GBR), Miss L. Green (GBR), Mrs. H.G. Broadbridge (GBR).
NQ (2) Miss D.A. Huntbach (GBR), Mrs. R.V. Fontes (GBR).

1937

SQ (8) Miss M.G. Norman (GBR), Mrs. M.B. Lewis (GBR), Miss A. Samuelson (SWE), Mrs. H.S. Uber (GBR), Miss C.G. Hoahing (GBR), Miss P.C. Grover (GBR), Miss K. Keith-Steele (GBR), Mrs. O. Haycraft (GBR).
LL (1) Miss A.P. Cardinall (GBR).
NQ (2) Miss E.A. Middleton (GBR), Mrs. E.H. Fenwick (GBR).

1938

SQ (8) Mrs. W.D. Porter (GBR), Miss J.M. Lacy (GBR), Miss F.B. Cooke (GBR), Miss P.L.F. Thomson (GBR), Miss E.E. Curtis (GBR), Miss G.M. Southwell (GBR), Miss M. Trouncer (GBR), Miss M. Cootes (USA).
LL (NIL).
NQ (2) Miss E.A. Middleton (GBR), Miss N.K. Maingay (GBR).

1939

SQ (8) Miss M.F. Brace (GBR), Mrs. L. Herbst (BOM), Mrs. M.B. Lewis (GBR), Mrs. P.R. Goodwyn (IRL), Miss J.P. Curry (GBR), Miss S. Mavrogordato (GBR), Miss O.V. Cooper (GBR), Miss B. Rodway (GBR).
LL (NIL).
NQ (2) Miss E.A. Middleton (GBR), Miss N. Liebert (GBR).

1946 *No Competition.*

1947

SQ (8) Miss P. Rodgers (GBR), Mrs. E.E. Pool (GBR), Miss G.E. Woodgate (GBR), Mrs. M.B. Lewis (GBR), Miss L. Churcher (GBR), Mrs. B.E. Walton (GBR), Miss K.L.A. Tuckey (GBR), Miss H.S. Morgan (GBR).
LL (NIL).
NQ (2) Miss P. Cowney (GBR), Miss N. Liebert (GBR).

1948

SQ (8) Miss E.M. Percival (GBR), Mrs. J.B. Parker (GBR), Mrs. T.S. Wallace (GBR), Mrs. M.B. Lewis (GBR), Mrs. E.E. Pool (GBR), Mrs. P.J. Kerr (GBR), Mrs. M. Wavish (GBR), Miss E.M.S. Andrews (GBR).
LL (NIL).
NQ (2) Miss P. Fisher (GBR), Mrs. H.E.F. Behr (GBR).

1949

SQ (8) Miss A.R.N. Feiron (GBR), Miss E.M. Stephens (GBR), Mrs. J.B. Parker (GBR), Mrs. J.M. Beswick (GBR), Miss E.M. Sutton (GBR), Mrs. L.F. Byrne (GBR), Mrs J.A. Quelch (GBR), Miss M. Buxton-Knight (EGY).
LL (2) Miss A.V. Mothersole (GBR), Miss Z.J. Lusty (GBR).
NQ (2) Miss N.C. Potts (GBR), Miss R. Walsh (GBR).

1950

SQ (8) Miss J.M. Trower (GBR), Mrs. A.T.P. Luxton (GBR), Mrs. J.M. Beswick (GBR), Mrs. J.M. Wagstaff (GBR), Mrs. B.W. Knott (GBR), Mrs. G.M. Worrall (GBR), Mrs. P.M. Johns (GBR), Mrs. A. Varin (FRA).
LL (NIL).
NQ (2) Miss N. Liebert (GBR), Mrs. H.R. Phillips (GBR).

1951

SQ (8) Miss A.L. Morgan (GBR), Miss E.G. Attwood (NZL), Miss S. Schmitt (FRA), Mrs. R.L. Scott (GBR), Miss J. Ross-Dilley (GBR), Mrs. R.A. Gilbert (GBR), Mrs. G.R. Lines (GBR), Miss P.A. Lewis (GBR).
LL (3) Mrs. J.A. Starling (GBR), Miss M.S. White (GBR), Miss M.R. Couquerque (NED).
NQ (2) Miss M.P. Harrison (GBR), Miss F. Walthew (GBR).

1952

SQ (8) Mrs. R.B.R. Wilson (GBR), Mrs. P.J. Kerr (GBR), Miss E.M. Watson (GBR), Miss M. Harris (GBR), Miss A.M. Carlisle (GBR), Mrs. B. Abbas (EGY), Mrs. J.M. Beswick (GBR), Miss S. Speight (GBR).
LL (2) Miss A. Buxton (GBR), Miss S.I. Odling (GBR).
NQ (2) Miss F. Walthew (GBR), Miss J.A. MacLeod (GBR).

1953

SQ (8) Mrs. A.C. Brighton (GBR), Mrs. H.L.K. Brock (GBR), Miss J.E. Bowyer (RHO), Miss D. Herbst (GBR), Miss D. Midgley (GBR), Miss K. Fageros (USA), Miss J.S. Reid (USA), Miss S.G. Mackay (GBR).
LL (NIL).
NQ (2) Miss R.H. Bentley (GBR), Miss N. Liebert (GBR).

1954

SQ (8) Miss M. Bonstrom (SWE), Miss J. Knight (GBR), Miss R. Davar (IND), Miss M.E. Govett (GBR), Miss J.M. Boundy (GBR), Mrs. J.A. Collier (GBR), Miss E.E. Ruffin (AUS), Mrs. J.A. Quelch (GBR).
LL (2) Miss Z.J. Lusty (GBR), Miss A.I. Bilse (RSA).
NQ (2) Miss K.M. Stott (GBR), Miss G.C.F. Rhodes (GBR).

1955

SQ (8) Mrs. J.A. Quelch (GBR), Miss M. Craig-Smith (GBR), Miss A.M. Gibb (GBR). Miss S.F. Pool (GBR), Miss S.M. Griffen (GBR), Mrs. V.E.A. Morris (GBR), Miss N.A. Schuurman (RSA), Miss S. Speight (GBR).
LL (2) Miss A.M. Price (GBR), Miss F. Lemal (FRA).
NQ (2) Mrs. J. Kemsey-Bourne (GBR). Miss J.A. MacLeod (GBR).

1956

SQ (8) Miss H.L.K. Brock (GBR). Miss K. Newcombe (AUS), Miss C. Monnot (FRA), Miss J. Rook (GBR), Miss E. Becroft (NZL), Miss P.J.A. Wheeler (GBR), Miss F. de la Courtie (FRA), Miss S.G. Waddington (RSA).
LL (NIL).
NQ (2) Miss H. Moorley (GBR), Miss J. Godfrey (GBR).

1957

SQ (8) Miss M.O. Bouchet (FRA), Mrs. P.C. Bramley (GBR), Mrs. G.E. Marshall (KEN), Miss S.M. Cox (GBR), Miss B.M. Horton (GBR), Mrs. J.M. Wagstaff (GBR), Miss P.A. Ingram (GBR), Miss M.E. Morgan (GBR).
LL (NIL).
NQ (2) Miss J.A. Fulton (GBR), Mrs. B.S. Worrall (GBR).

1958
SQ (8) Miss M. Grace (GBR), Miss S.M. Hannah (GBR), Miss C.M. Leather (GBR). Mrs. I.J. Warwick (GBR), Mrs. V.A. Roberts (GBR), Mrs. J.M. Wagstaff (GBR), Mrs. R.B.R. Wilson (GBR), Miss J.M. Young (GBR).
LL (NIL).
NQ (2) Mrs. P. Rushton (GBR), Miss P.C. Drew (GBR).

1959
SQ (8) Miss U. Hulkrantz (SWE), Miss E.T. Court (AUS), Mrs. J.W. Cawthorn (GBR), Miss D. Thomas (AUS), Miss J.N. Trewby (GBR), Mrs. C.T. Clark (GBR), Mrs. R.B.R. Wilson (GBR), Mrs. A.C. Brighton (GBR).
LL (2) Mrs. H.L.K. Brock (GBR), Mrs. E. Launert (GER).
NQ (2) Mrs. G.E. Marshall (KEN), Miss L.M. Grundy (GBR).

1960
SQ (8) Mrs. P.C. Bramley (GBR), Mrs. H.G. Macintosh (GBR), Miss C. Hernandez-Coronado (ESP), Mrs. I.J. Warwick (GBR), Miss J. Knight (GBR), Miss P.M. Burrell (GBR), Miss F.E. Walton (GBR), Miss J.E. Kemp (GBR).
LL (1) Mrs. C.F.O. Lister (GBR).
NQ (2) Miss L.M. Grundy (GBR), Mrs. D.K. Illingworth (GBR).

1961
SQ (8) Miss E. Dodge (CAN), Miss J. Bourgnon (SUI), Miss J.E. Scoble (GBR), Mrs. J.M. Wagstaff (GBR), Miss J.M. Tee (GBR), Miss D.S. Butt (CAN), Miss V.S. White (GBR), Miss H.J.M. Durose (GBR).
LL (NIL).
NQ (2) Miss E.M. O'Neill (IRL), Miss G.M. Houlihan (IRL).

1962
SQ (8) Miss R. Ostermann (GER), Miss M.L. Gerson (RSA), Miss M. Grace (GBR), Miss A. McAlpine (GBR), Mrs. J.M. Wagstaff (GBR), Miss S.V. Wade (GBR), Miss P.A. Belton (NZL), Miss J. Knight (GBR).
LL (NIL).
NQ (2) Mrs. M.C. Cheadle (GBR), Miss E.M. O'Neill (IRL).

1963
SQ (8) Mrs. K. Bartholdson (SWE), Miss D.C. Tuckey (GBR), Miss M.B.H. McAnally (GBR), Miss J.M. Tee (GBR), Miss H.W. Allen (GBR), Miss J.M. Barnes (AUS), Miss U. Sandulf (SWE), Miss M.M. Lee (GBR).
LL (NIL).
NQ (2) Miss S.J. Holdsworth (GBR), Miss J.A. Fulton (GBR).

1964
SQ (8) Miss P.R. McClenaughan (AUS), Miss D.C. Tuckey (GBR), Miss H. Schildknecht (GER), Miss B.F. Stove (NED), Miss H.N. Plaisted (AUS) Miss A.L. Owen (GBR), Miss M. Fourie (RSA), Miss F.E. Walton (GBR).
LL (2) Miss A.J. Stroud (GBR), Mrs. P.J. Kerr (AUS).
NQ (2) Miss G.M. Houlihan (IRL), Miss M.R. O'Donnell (GBR).

1965
SQ (8) Mrs. W.A. Tym (USA), Miss E.M. Spruyt (NED), Mrs. D.K. Illingworth (GBR), Miss H.C. Sherriff (AUS), Miss A. Rigby (GBR), Miss E. Krocke (NED), Mrs. J.L. Deloford (GBR), Miss F.V.M. MacLennan (GBR).
LL (1) Miss M. Boulle (FRA).
NQ (2) Miss S.M. Tutt (GBR), Miss M.R. O'Donnell (GBR).

1966

SQ (8) Miss A.E. Jansen-Venneboer (NED), Miss L.M. Bellamy (AUS), Miss A.L. Suurbeck (NED), Mrs. C. Rouchon (FRA), Miss C.M. Spinoza (FRA), Mrs. W.T. Reed (USA), Miss S.S. Behlmer (USA), Miss T.M. van Haren (AUS).
LL (NIL).
NQ (2) Miss J.C.L. Poynder (GBR), Miss S.J. Holdsworth (GBR).

1967

Q (8) Miss M.O. Harris (AUS), Miss V.A. Coombs (GBR), Mrs. W.A. Tym (USA), Miss M.M. Henreid (USA), Miss A. Bakker (NED), Mrs. E.C.S. Pratt (USA), Miss K. Seelbach (GER), Miss R. Islanova (URS).
LL (2) Miss A.T. Mackay (AUS), Miss M.J. Aubet (ESP).

1968

Q (8) Miss M.O. Harris (AUS), Miss K. Sawamatsu (JPN), Miss R.C. Giscarfe (ARG), Miss N.E. Netter (USA), Miss K.S. Schediwy (GER), Miss H.J. Amos (AUS), Mrs. L.A. Hoad (AUS), Miss M.J. Aschner (USA).
LL (1) Miss W.V. Hall (GBR).

1969

Q (8) Miss E.M. Ernest (GBR), Miss J.K. Anthony (USA), Miss J.M. Wilshere (RSA), Miss W.V. Hall (GBR), Miss L. Liem (INA), Miss P.A. Teeguarden (USA), Miss M.B.E. Kaligis (INA), Miss J.M. Boundy (GBR).
LL (1) Miss T. Zwaan (NED).

1970

Q (8) Miss C. Murakami (JPN), Miss S.J. Alexander (AUS), Miss J.A. Fayter (GBR), Miss F. Luff (AUS), Miss J.E. O'Hara (CAN), Miss S.H. Walsham (AUS), Miss M.J. Pryde (NZL), Miss S.J. Holdsworth (GBR).
LL (1) Miss M.E. Greenwood (GBR).

1971

Q (7) Miss B. Vest (USA), Miss G.L. Coles (GBR), Miss V. Lancaster (AUS), Miss A.T. Colman (AUS), Miss D.H. Botha (RSA), Miss S.J. Hudson-Beck (RHO), Miss P.A. Reese (USA).
LL (NIL).

1972

Q (7) Miss J.K. Anthony (USA), Miss K. Blake (USA), Miss D.J. Riste (GBR), Miss M. Gurdal (BEL), Miss S. Mappin (GBR), Miss W. Appleby (USA), Miss T.E. O'Shaughnessy (USA).
LL (NIL).

1973

Q (8) Miss C.S. Colman (GBR), Miss M.B.K. Wikstedt (SWE), Miss M. Michel (USA), Miss K.D. Latham (USA), Miss J.L. Tindle (CAN), Miss V.A. Berner (CAN), Miss A.M. Coe (GBR), Miss T.A. Fretz (USA).
LL (1) Miss J. Dixon (USA).

1974

Q (8) Miss C.F. Matison (AUS), Miss P.L. Bostrom (USA), Miss A.H.G. Anliot (SWE), Miss S. Greer (USA), Miss R.J. Tenney (USA), Miss C.M. O'Neill (AUS), Miss N.F. Gregory (AUS), Miss M. Jausovec (YUG).
LL (2) Miss E. Appel (NED), Miss T. Zwaan (NED).

1975

Q (8) Miss H. Eisterlehner (GER), Miss K.A. May (USA), Miss J.L. Dimond (AUS), Miss N. Sato (JPN), Miss R. Stark (USA), Miss P.A. Reese (USA), Miss L.A. Rupert (USA), Miss L.M. Tenney (USA).
LL (2) Miss C. Molesworth (GBR), Miss J.B. Haas (USA).

1976
Q (8) Miss M.B.K. Wikstedt (SWE), Miss P.L. Bostrom (USA), Miss C.F. Matison (AUS), Miss M. McLean (AUS), Miss C. Molesworth (GBR), Miss A. Spex (CUB), Mrs. H.E. Lancaster-Kerr (AUS), Miss C.A. Martinez (USA).
LL (3) Miss S.E. Saliba (AUS), Miss A.P. Cooper (GBR), Miss C.J. Newton (NZL).

1977
Q (8) Miss A. Spex (USA), Mrs. H. Sparre-Viragh (DEN), Miss R.S. Fox (USA), Mrs. E. Peled (ISR), Miss C.F. Matison (AUS), Miss N.U. Bohm (SWE), Miss E.M. Dignam (USA), Miss A.E. Smith (USA).
LL (3) Miss C.M. O'Neill (AUS), Miss R.C. Giscarfe (ARG), Miss S.H. Hagey (USA).

1978
Q (8) Miss I.S. Kloss (RSA), Miss M. Pinterova (TCH), Miss J.D. Chaloner (NZL), Mrs. E. Peled (ISR), Miss W. Barlow (CAN), Miss M. Gurdal (BEL), Miss M.L. Blackwood (CAN), Miss P.G. Smith (USA).
LL (1) Miss H.A. Ludloff (USA).

1979
Q (8) Miss M.L. Blackwood (CAN), Miss T.J. Harford (RSA), Miss A. Whitemore (USA), Miss L.J. Charles (GBR), Miss M. Pakker (NED), Miss M.A. Mesker (NED), Miss D. Morrison (USA), Miss S.P.M. Simmonds (ITA).
LL (NIL).

1980
Q (8) Miss J. Walker (AUS), Miss P.J. Whytcross (AUS), Miss N.F. Gregory (AUS), Miss L.K. Forood (USA), Miss L. Antonoplis (USA), Miss M.L. Blackwood (CAN), Miss S.E. Saliba (AUS), Miss A. Buchanan (USA).
LL (NIL).

1981
Q (8) Miss M.A. Mesker (NED), Miss C. Pasquale (SUI), Miss E.M. Gordon (RSA), Miss C.M. O'Neill (AUS), Miss C. Jolissaint (SUI), Miss E.M. Little (AUS), Miss M.B.K Wikstedt (SWE), Miss G. Langela (BRA).
LL (1) Miss J.M. Mundel (RSA).

1982
Q (8) Miss E.M. Gordon (RSA), Miss B.J. Remilton (AUS), Miss T.J. Harford (RSA), Miss K.A. Steinmetz (USA), Miss R.L. Blount (USA), Miss M. Maleeva (BUL), Miss E.M. Sayers (AUS), Miss S.L. Rollinson (RSA).
LL (NIL).

1983
Q (8) Miss E. Minter (AUS), Miss L.A. Spain (USA), Miss J. Golder (USA), Miss N.F. Gregory (AUS), Miss S.K. Rimes (USA), Miss E. Ekblom (SWE), Miss B. Randall (AUS), Miss D. Freeman (AUS).
LL (4) Miss M. Schropp (GER), Miss M. Schillig (USA), Miss B.J. Remilton (AUS), Miss L.A. Bernstein (USA).

1984
Q (8) Miss S. Cherneva (URS), Miss C. Karlsson (SWE), Miss L.I. Savchenko (URS), Miss K.A. Steinmetz (USA), Miss C.S. Reynolds (USA), Miss K. Kinney (USA), Miss E. Eliseenko (URS), Miss H. Pelletier (CAN).
LL (NIL).

1985

Q (8) Miss B.J. Jordan (USA), Miss M. Van Nostrand (USA), Miss E. Reinach (RSA), Miss J.M. Byrne (AUS), Miss P.A. Fendick (USA), Miss Hu Na (CHN), Miss A. Betzner (GER), Miss E. Ekblom (SWE).
LL (2) Miss L. Pichova (TCH), Miss K. Kinney (USA).

1986

Q (8) Miss D.S. Van Rensburg (RSA), Miss J. Novotna (TCH), Miss A.M. Fernandez (USA), Miss G. Rush (USA), Miss D.L. Farrell (USA), Miss J.A. Richardson (NZL), Miss K.A. Steinmetz (USA), Miss K.D. McDaniel (USA).
LL (4) Miss J.V. Forman (USA), Miss P. Barg (USA), Miss R. Bryant (AUS), Miss R. Reis (USA).

1987

Q (8) Miss B.J. Cordwell (NZL), Miss L. Golarsa (ITA), Miss K. Okamoto (JPN), Miss M. Jaggard (AUS), Miss K.T. Schimper (RSA), Miss N. Medvedeva (URS), Miss I. Kuczynska (POL), Miss G. Miro (BRA).
LL (1) Miss A. M. Fernandez (USA).

1988

Q (8) Miss L. Field (AUS), Miss S.L. Collins (USA). Miss P. Barg (USA). Miss J.-A. Faull (AUS) Miss K. Okamoto (JPN), Miss R. Reis (USA), Miss L. Gregory (RSA), Miss K.F. Hunter (GBR).
LL (3) Miss K. Quentrec (FRA), Miss L. O'Neill (AUS), Miss S. Stafford (USA).

1989

Q (8) Miss S. Amiach (FRA), Miss M. Jaggard (AUS), Miss T.J. Morton (AUS), Miss J. Smoller (USA), Miss K. Date (JPN), Miss C. Bakkum (NED), Miss S.L. Collins (USA), Miss K. Radford (AUS).
LL (3) Miss G. Miro (BRA), Miss D. Graham (USA), Miss C. Suire (FRA).

1990

Q (8) Miss E. Brioukhovets (URS), Miss R.P. Stubbs (AUS), Miss R. Field (RSA), Miss K.M. Adams (USA), Miss E.S. Pfaff (GER), Miss H.A. Ludloff (USA), Miss A. Devries (BEL), Miss K. Kschwendt (LUX).
LL (4) Miss J.J. Santrock (USA), Mrs. R. Baranski (POL), Miss A. Ivan (USA), Miss P. Etchemendy (FRA).

1991

Q (8) Miss N.A.M. Jagerman (NED), Miss M.J.M.M. Oremans (NED), Miss P. Kamstra (NED), Miss E. S.H. Callens (BEL), Miss C. Suire (FRA), Miss I. Demongeot (FRA), Miss K.L. Radford (AUS), Miss R.P. Stubbs (AUS).
LL (5) Miss C.N. Toleafoa (NZL), Miss J.-A. Faull (AUS), Miss N.J. Pratt (AUS), Miss J.M. Hetherington (CAN), Miss K. Date (JPN).

1992

Q (8) Miss C. Tessi (ARG), Miss C.D. Wegink (NED), Miss J.J. Santrock (USA), Miss L. Field (AUS), Miss A. Devries (BEL), Miss M.J.M.M. Oremans (NED) Miss R. Hiraki (JPN), Miss K. Kschwendt (GER).
LL (2) Miss J.-A. Faull (AUS), Miss T.R. Whittington (USA).

1993

Q (8) Miss K. Sharpe (AUS), Miss M.J. McGrath (USA), Miss T.A. Price (RSA), Miss C. MacGregor (USA), Miss L. Golarsa (ITA), Miss D.S. Van Rensburg (RSA), Miss A. Sugiyama (JPN), Miss C.D. Wegink (NED).
LL (3) Miss M. Kochta (GER), Miss J.M. Byrne (AUS), Miss L. Field (AUS).

1994

Q (8) Mrs. P.D. Smylie (AUS), Mrs. B. Dechaume-Balleret (FRA), Miss L. Field (AUS), Miss K.M. Adams (USA), Miss N. Miyagi (JPN), Miss M. Paz (ARG), Miss I. Demongeot (FRA), Miss N. Feber (BEL).
LL (4) Miss C.D. Wegink (NED), Miss A. Sugiyama (JPN), Miss A. Strnadova (CZE), Miss T.A. Price (RSA).

1995

Q (8) Miss R.P. Stubbs (AUS), Miss L. Lee (USA), Miss M. Schnell (AUT), Miss C. Porwik (GER), Miss K.M. Adams (USA), Miss P. Kamstra (NED), Miss G. Pizzichini (ITA), Miss A.M.H. Wainwright (GBR).
LL (1) Miss A.M. Vento (VEN).

1996

Q (8) Miss M. Paz (ARG), Miss A. Ellwood (AUS), Miss K.-A. Guse (AUS), Miss A.L. Kremer (LUX), Miss M. Drake (CAN), Miss L. Golarsa (ITA), Miss A. Cocheteux (FRA), Miss C. Cristea (ROM).
LL (2) Miss L. Perfetti (ITA), Miss A. Olsza (POL).

1997

Q (8) Miss A.L. Kremer (LUX), Miss L. Golarsa (ITA), Miss M.A. Vento (VEN), Miss N.J. Pratt (AUS), Miss N. Feber (BEL), Miss K.M. Cross (GBR), Miss H. Inoue (JPN), Miss M. Schnitzer (GER).
LL (1) Miss N. Miyagi (JPN).

1998

Q (8) Miss C.C. Black (ZIM), Miss S. Talaja (CRO), Miss R. Bobkova (CZE), Miss S. De Beer (RSA), Miss M. Schnitzer (GER), Miss R.P. Stubbs (AUS), Miss H. Inoue (JPN).
LL (2) Miss K. Miller (USA), Miss L. Osterloh (USA).

1999

Q (8) Miss K. Clijsters (BEL), Miss E.R. De Lone (USA), Miss J. Dokic (AUS), Miss A. Foldenyi (HUN), Miss S. Noorlander (NED), Miss N. Petrova (RUS), Miss A.W. Stevenson (USA), Miss L.M. Wild (USA).
LL (1) Miss E. Dementieva (RUS).

2000

Q (12) Miss Y. Yoshida (JPN), Miss M. Grzybowska (POL), Miss R. De Los Rios (Mrs. G. Neffa) (PAR), Miss G. Casoni (ITA), Miss L. Krasnoroutskaya (RUS), Miss G. Arn (GER), Miss S. Agagoe (JPN), Miss Y. Basting (NED), Miss D. Bedanova (CZE), Miss M. Schnell (AUT), Miss M. Washington (USA), Miss A. Rippner (USA).
LL (NIL).

2001

Q (12) Miss S. Foretz (FRA), Miss Ad. Serra-Zanetti (ITA), Miss W. Prakusya (INA), Miss E. Daniilidou (GRE), Miss A. Barna (GER), Miss K.M. Cross (GBR), Miss C. Fernandez (ARG), Miss M. Drake (CAN), Miss M. Schnitzer (GER), Miss K. Boogert (NED), Miss B. Schwartz (AUT), Miss M. Matevzic (SLO).
LL (1) Miss J. Lee (TPE).

2002

Q(12) Miss A. Fusai (FRA), Miss T. Perebiynis (UKR), Miss R. Vinci (ITA), Miss Z. Ondraskova (CZE), Miss E.V. Tatarkova (UKR), Miss M. Casanova (SUI), Miss M.A. Sanchez Lorenzo (ESP), Miss E.S.H. Callens (BEL), Miss I. Benesova (CZE), Miss An Serra Zanetti (ITA), Mrs. M.A. Vento-Kabchi (VEN), Miss L. Granville (USA).
LL (NIL).

2003

Q(12) Miss M. Sucha (SVK), Miss S. Hrozenska (SVK), Miss C. Gullickson (USA), Miss J. Lee (TPE), Miss M. Sequera (VEN), Miss B. Bielik (USA), Miss A. Kapros, (HUN), Miss S.J. Sfar (TUN), Miss L. Osterloh (USA), Miss E. Fislova (SVK), Miss M. Drake (CAN), Miss B. Strycova (CZE).

LL (2) Miss A. Parra (ESP), Miss S. Noorlander (NED).

2004

Q(12) Miss N. Llagostera Vives (ESP), Miss A. Widjaja (INA), Miss T. Panova (RUS), Miss T.T. Sun (CHN), Miss M. Washington (USA), Miss E. Birnerova (CZE), Miss V. Razzano (FRA), Miss J. Hopkins (USA), Miss S. Foretz (FRA), Miss Y. Beygelzimer (UKR), Miss E. Gallovits (ROM), Miss C. Wheeler (AUS).

LL (NIL).

2005

Q(12) Miss Bohmova (CZE), Miss S. Ardvisson (SWE), Miss A. Harkleroad (Mrs A. Bogolomov) (USA), Miss E.S.H. Callens (BEL), Miss J. Jackson (USA), Miss M. Tu (USA), Miss S. Obata (JPN), Miss M. Santangelo (ITA), Miss S. Klaschka (GER), Miss K. Bondarenko (UKR), Miss J. Vakulenko (UKR), Miss P. Poutchek (BLR).

LL (3) Miss E. Birnerova (CZE), Miss S. Beltrame (FRA), Miss M. Czink (HUN).

2006

Q(12) Miss R. Oprandi (ITA), Miss N. J. Pratt (AUS), Mrs. E. Bremond (FRA), Miss T. Tanasugarn (THA), Miss C. Fernandez (ARG), Miss K. Barrois (GER), Miss Y-J. Chan (TPE), Miss V. Bardina (RUS), Miss I. Abramovic (CRO), Miss M. Tu (USA), Miss Y. Shvedova (RUS), Miss K. Flipkens (BEL)

LL (1) Miss J. Vakulenko (UKR).

2007

Q(12) Miss A. Szavay (HUN), Miss K. Brandi (PUR), Miss C. Dell'Acqua (AUS), Miss N. Ozegovic (CRO), Miss J. Cravero (ARG), Miss A. Morita (JPN), Miss O. Govortsova (BLR), Miss S-W. Hseih (TPE), Miss T. Perebiynis (UKR), Miss H. Sromova (CZE), Z. Yan (CHN), B. Strycova (CZE).

LL (1) Miss A. Cornet (FRA).

2008

Q(12) Miss M. Rybarikova (SVK), Miss Z. Ondraskova (CZE), Miss M. Johansson (FRA), Miss R. Fujiwara (JPN),Miss B. Zahlovova Strycova (CZE), Miss A. Pavlyuchenkova (RUS), Miss S. Bremond (FRA) Miss M E Camerin (ITA), Miss V. Kutuzova (UKR), Miss S. Foretz (FRA), Miss M J Martinez Sanchez (ESP), Miss E. Hrdinova (CZE).

2009

Q(12) Miss V. Kutuzova (UKR), Mrs K. Zakopalova (CZE), Miss T. Malek (GER), Miss A. Nakamura (JPN), Miss A. Parra Santonia (ESP), Miss S. Karatancheva (KAZ), Miss R. Kulikova (RUS), Miss M. Oudin (USA), Miss A. Brianti (ITA), Miss N. Silva (POR), Miss V. Manasieva (RUS), Miss A. Sevastova (LAT).

LL (1) K. Kucova (SVK).

2010

Q(12) Miss K. Kanepi (EST), Miss N. Llagostera Vives (ESP), Miss R.S. Oprandi (ITA), Mrs B. Mattek-Sands (USA), Miss S. Perry (USA), Miss A. Yakimora (JPN), Miss G. Arn (HUN), Miss M. Lucic (CRO), Miss K. Nara (JPN), Miss M. Niculescu (ROM), Miss A. Hlavackova (CZE), Miss E. Daniilidou (GRE).

LL (2) Miss A. Pivovatova (RUS), Miss S. Dubois (CAN).

2011

Q(12) Miss K. Chang (TPE), Miss M. Erakovic (NZL), Miss C. Giorgi (ITA), Miss I. Falconi (USA), Miss T. Tanasugarn (THA), Miss L. Tsurenko (UKR), Miss V. Diatchenko (RUS),Miss M. Doi (JPN), Miss K. Pliskova (CZE), Miss M. Barthel (GER), Miss A. Glatch (USA), Miss A. Wozniak (CAN).
LL (2) S. Dubois (CZE), S.F. Gacon (FRA).

2012

Q(12) Miss M. Czink (HUN), Miss A. Beck (GER), Miss M.A. Camerin (ITA), Miss K. Mladenovic (FRA), Miss S. Zaniewska (POL), Miss V. Dolonc (SRB), Miss J. Cepelova (SVK), Miss K. Pliskova (CZE), Miss C. Giorgi (ITA), Miss C. Vandeweghe (USA), Miss L. Lucic (CRO).
LL (1) M.Doi (JPN).

2013

Q(12) Miss C. Wiitthoeft (GER), Miss G. Voskoboeva (KAZ), Miss C. Garcia (FRA), Miss P. Cetkovska (CZE), Miss A. Tomljanvic (CRO), Miss M. Camerin (ITA), Miss Y. Meusburger (AUT), Miss V. Razzano (FRA), Miss E. Bimerova (CZE), Mrs B. Zahlavova Strycova (CZE), Miss M. Duque-Marino (COL), Miss M. Larcher de Brito (POL).
LL (2) Miss A. Schmiedlova (SVK), Miss V. King (USA).

2014

Q (12) Miss A. Kudryavtseva (RUS), Miss T. Smitkova (CZE), Miss T. Bacsinszky (SUI), Miss M. Larcher de Brito (POR), Miss A. Wozniak (CAN), Miss L. Tsurenko (UKR), Miss P. Kania (POL), Miss A. Konjuh (CRO), Miss V. Duval (USA), Miss T. Paszek (AUT), Miss A. Kontaveit (EST), Miss A. Mitu (ROU).
LL (NIL).

Ladies' Doubles Championship

1925
Q (4) Mrs. E.H. Burgess-Smith and Miss C. Hardie (GBR), Mrs. Hollick and Mrs. C. Marriot (GBR), Miss E. Phayre and Miss M. Phayre (GBR), Mrs. J. Barrett and Miss J.E. Brown (GBR).

1926
Q (4) Miss E. Norman and Mrs. M.B. Reckett (GBR), Miss M. Cambridge and Mrs. D.K. Craddock (GBR), Mrs. Jackson Feildon and Miss N. Welch (GBR), Miss L. Bull and Mrs. A. Rodocanachi (GBR).

1927
SQ (4) Miss S.K. Johnson and Miss E.F. Rose (GBR), Miss M.P. Davies and Miss M.P. Gordon (GBR), Mrs. E.H. Burgess-Smith and Miss C. Kalber (GBR), Miss B.C. Brown and Miss D. Busby (GBR).
NQ (1) Mrs. C.P. Brocklesby and Mrs. J.H. King (GBR).

1928
SQ (4) Mrs. H.V. Edwards and Miss E.Z. Stokes (GBR), Mrs. W.D. List and Mrs. P. Bouverie (GBR), Mrs. F.M. Strawson and Miss E. Hemmant (GBR), Mrs. R.R.W. Jackson and Miss S. Stokes (GBR).
NQ (1) Mrs. M. Bower and Miss M.F. Harland (GBR).

1929
SQ (4) Miss E.Z. Stokes and Miss S. Stokes (GBR), Miss K. Lewis and Mrs. H.S. Uber (GBR), Miss D. Bourne and Miss H. Bourne (GBR), Mrs. M. Stork and Miss M.A. Thomas (GBR).
NQ (1) Miss D. Anderson and Miss W.M.C. Bower (GBR).

1930
SQ (4) Miss G.K. Osborne and Mrs. B.C. Windle (GBR) Miss D.M. Furnivall and Miss L. Philip (GBR), Miss E.Z. Stokes and Miss S. Stokes (GBR). Miss L. Johnstone and Miss M. Johnstone (GBR).
NQ (1) Mrs. L.P. Antrobus and Miss F. James (GBR).

1931
SQ (4) Miss M. Elton and Miss M.E. Nonweiler (GBR), Mrs. G.N. Macready and Mrs. I.H. Wheatcroft (GBR), Miss R.M. Hardwick and Miss S.K. Hewitt (GBR), Mrs. G. Lucas and Miss D.V. Eastley (GBR).
NQ (1) Mrs. J.G. Stephens and Miss J. Lawson (GBR).

1932
SQ (4) Mrs. H.W. Backhouse and Miss L. Philip (GBR), Mrs. G. Hawkins and Miss D. Busby (GBR), Miss A.M. Knapp and Miss D.M.S White (GBR), Mrs. J. Pennycuick and Miss M. Johnstone (GBR).
NQ (1) Mrs. J.S. Kirk and Miss M. Wynne (GBR).

1933
SQ (4) Miss B.E. Boas and Miss P.J.E. Cargill (GBR), Mrs. B.V. Bouch and Miss V. King (GBR), Miss G.A. Clarke-Jervoise and Miss J. Couchman (GBR), Mrs. M.M. Moss and Miss D.H. Crichton (GBR).
NQ (1) Miss B.I.E. Drew and Miss M.G. Hargreaves (GBR).

1934
SQ (4) Miss P.C. Grover and Miss P.M. Weekes (GBR), Miss T.R. Jarvis and Miss A.A. Wright (GBR), Miss J. Marshall and Miss J. Morfey (GBR), Miss D. Kitson and Miss J. McAlpine (GBR).
NQ (1) Miss B.G. Beazley and Miss B.I.E. Drew (GBR).

1935
SQ (4) Mrs. R.A. Chamberlain and Mrs. L.G. Owen (GBR), Miss B. Batt and Miss M. Burgess-Smith (GBR), Miss F.S. Ford and Miss P.J. Owen (GBR), Miss C. Tyrrell and Miss P.M. Weekes (GBR).
NQ (1) Mrs. R.V. Fontes and Miss R.J. Smith (GBR).

1936

SQ (4) Mrs. J. Pennyciuck and Mrs. D. Trentham (GBR), Miss P.C. Grover and Miss G.K. Osborne (GBR), Lady Rowallan and Mrs. N.B. Black (GBR), Mrs. G.L. Baker and Mrs. E.A. Kemp (GBR).
NQ (1) Miss M. Parr and Miss W. Sargeant (GBR).

1937

SQ (4) Miss M.M. Bray and Miss A.P. Cardinall (GBR), Mrs. G.A. Myers and Miss A.Y. Richardson (GBR), Miss J. Goss and Mrs. A.L. Semmence (GBR), Miss B.M. Smith and Miss M. Trouncer (GBR).
LL (NIL).
NQ (1) Miss F.M. Burton and Miss E.A. Middleton (GBR).

1938

SQ (4) Miss C. Douglas and Miss B.M. Turner (GBR), Miss M. MacTier and Mrs. A.H. Mellows (GBR), Miss B.E. Lumb and Miss M.E. Lumb (GBR), Miss M.M. Bray and Mrs. A.P. Cardinall (GBR).
LL (NIL).
NQ (1) Miss B.G. Beazley and Mrs. J.E. Tew (GBR).

1939

SQ (4) Mrs. C.Z. Morse and Miss M.E. Parker (GBR), Mrs. P.R. Goodwyn and Mrs. C.F. Myerscough (GBR), Mrs. A.T. Kenyon and Miss S. Stoney (GBR), Mrs. R.D. McKelvie and Miss A.J. Wenyon (GBR).
LL (NIL).
NQ (1) Miss M. Law and Miss B. Watson (GBR).

1946 *No Competition.*

1947

SQ (4) Mrs. J. David and Miss P.C. Grover (GBR), Mrs. D.R. Bocquet and Mrs. E.E. Pool (GBR), Mrs. D.L. Coutts and Mrs. J.J. Walker-Smith (GBR), Miss L. Churcher and Miss K.L. A. Tuckey (GBR).
LL (NIL).
NQ (1) Mrs. J.S. James and Miss N. Liebert (GBR).

1948

SQ (4) Miss O.V. Cooper and Miss M.E. Parker (GBR), Miss J. Coles and Miss K.L.A. Tuckey (GBR), Miss V.M. Miles and Miss J.R.M. Morgan (GBR), Mrs. R.M. Dowdeswell (KEN) and Mrs. G.R. Lines (GBR).
LL (NIL).
NQ (1) Mrs. K.F. Knight and Miss N. Liebert (GBR).

1949

SQ (4) Miss A. Ross-Diley and Miss J. Ross-Diley (GBR), Mrs. F.G. Downing and Mrs. F.M. Frost (GBR), Miss A.M. Carlisle and Mrs. P.M. Johns (GBR), Mrs. P. Knight and Mrs. E.M. Sutton (GBR).
LL (NIL).
NQ (1) Mrs. J.B. Fulton and Miss N. Liebert (GBR).

1950

SQ (4) Mrs. P.L.B. Gardner and Miss J.R.M. Morgan (GBR), Miss A.G. Bates and Miss K.M. Ernest (GBR), Mrs. P. Knight and Miss E.M. Sutton (GBR), Mrs. D.R. Bocquet and Mrs. R.L. Scott (GBR).
LL (NIL).
NQ (1) Miss M.M. Eyre and Mrs. H.R. Phillips (GBR).

1951

SQ (4) Miss A. Ross-Diley and Miss J. Ross-Diley (GBR), Miss D.M. Spiers and Mrs. J.A. White (GBR), Mrs. M.B. Lewis and Mrs. R.L. Scott (GBR), Miss L.M. Cornell and Miss E.M. Watson (GBR).

LL (NIL).

NQ (1) Mrs. J.B. Fulton and Mrs. C.G. Moeller (GBR).

1952

SQ (4) Miss B.M. Goodman and Mrs. B.W. Knott (GBR), Miss J.I. Coles and Mrs. P.G. Wavish (GBR), Miss M. Grace and Mrs. J.M.E. Wallace (GBR), Mrs. B. Abbas (EGY) and Miss D. Spiers (GBR).

LL (NIL).

NQ (1) Miss J.A. MacLeod and Mrs. J.W. Mercer (GBR).

1953

SQ (4) Mrs. R.H. Chapman and Miss V. Uber (GBR), Miss S.C. Collett and Mrs. J. Maltby (GBR), Mrs. M.B. Lewis and Mrs. W.J. Nickles (GBR), Miss J. Knight and Miss E.M. Stephens (GBR).

LL (NIL).

NQ (1) Miss R.M. Bennett and Miss J.M. Petchell (GBR).

1954

SQ (4) Miss B. de Chambure and Miss C. Monnot (FRA), Miss K. Neville-Smith and Miss E.E. Ruffin (AUS), Miss S. Kamo (JPN) and Miss A. Soisbault (FRA), Miss J. Knight and Mrs. T.S. Wallace (GBR).

LL (1) Miss M.E. Govett and Mrs. N.A. Watkins (GBR).

NQ (1) Miss N. Liebert and Miss G.C.F. Rhodes (GBR).

1955

SQ (4) Miss S.M. Colebrooke and Mrs. J.A. White (GBR) Miss J.R.M. Morgan and Miss S. Speight (GBR), Mrs. V.E.A. Morris and Mrs. J.M. Wagstaff (GBR) Mrs. H.L.K. Brock and Miss P.M. Titchener (GB).

LL (NIL).

NQ (1) Mrs. J.B. Fulton and Mrs. F.B. Webb (GBR).

1956

SQ (4) Mrs. R.A. Gilbert and Miss S.E. Waters (GBR), Miss G. Evans (GBR) and Miss E. Van Tonder (RSA), Miss S. Reynolds and Miss S.G. Waddington (RSA), Mrs. J.A. White and Mrs. R.B.R. Wilson (GBR).

LL (NIL).

NQ (1) Miss P. Edwards and Miss H. Moorley (GBR).

1957

SQ (4) Miss M.G. Fry and Mrs. R.L. Scott (GBR) Mrs. H.L.K. Brock and Mrs. L.L. Glover (GBR). Mrs. G.E. Marshall (KEN) and Mrs. W.A.L. Michell (GBR) Mrs. J.M. Wagstaff and Mrs. R.B.R. Wilson (GBR).

LL (NIL).

NQ (1) Miss P.C. Drew and Miss M.M. Gell (GBR).

1958

SQ (4) Mrs. B.H. Chamberlain and Miss J. Knight (GBR), Miss H.J.K. Durose (GBR) and Miss P.M. Nettleton (NZL), Miss C.L. Levy (GBR) and Miss D. McCamley (AUS), Mrs. I.J. Warwick and Miss S.E. Waters (GBR).

LL (NIL).

NQ (1) Mrs. G.E. Marshall (KEN) and Miss R.M. Thackray (GBR).

1959

SQ (4) Mrs. D. Silk and Miss C. Webb (GBR), Mrs. G.J. Clissett and Miss E.E. Lester (GBR), Mrs. J.M. Wagstaff and Mrs. R.B.R. Wilson (GBR), Miss H.S. Clarke and Miss V.R. Cox (GBR).
LL (NIL).
NQ (1) Miss L.M. Bishop and Mrs. F.A. Devitt (GBR).

1960

SQ (4) Miss J.M. Chamberlain and Mrs. H.G. Macintosh (GBR), Mrs. P.C. Bramley and Mrs. A.C. Brighton (GBR), Mrs. P. Rushton and Miss J.M. Tee (GBR), Mrs. P.L.B. Gardner and Miss M. Grace.
LL (NIL).
NQ (1) Miss L.M. Grundy and Miss J.A. Thomson (GBR).

1961

SQ (4) Miss J. MacIntosh and Miss J.A. Watts (GBR), Miss M. Bove and Mrs. N.B. de Somoza (ARG), Mrs. P.C. Bramley and Mrs. A.C. Brighton (GBR), Mrs. C.T. Clark and Mrs. P.J. Hustwit (GBR).
LL (NIL).
NQ (1) Miss C. Lyon and Miss J.M. Wilson (GBR).

1962

SQ (4) Miss S.H. Clarke and Miss J.M. Young (GBR), Miss P.A. Belton and Miss J. Davidson (NZL), Mrs. P. Rushton and Miss J.M. Tee (GBR), Miss H. Ross and Mrs. A.R. Thiele (AUS).
LL (NIL).
NQ (1) Mrs. M.C. Cheadle and Miss M.R. O'Donnell (GBR).

1963

SQ (4) Miss H.W. Allen and Miss M.B.H. McAnally (GBR). Miss J. Albert and Miss S.S. Behlmar (USA), Miss J.M. Barnes (AUS) and Miss J.M. Stroud (GBR), Miss S.M.E. Porter and Miss S. Worsfield (GBR).
LL (NIL).
NQ (1) Miss J.A. Haskew and Miss J.C.L. Poynder (GBR).

1964

SQ (4) Mrs. C.T. Clark and Miss J.A. Fulton (GBR), Miss M.M. Lee and Miss A.L. Owen (GBR), Miss J. Knight and Mrs. J.M. Wagstaff (GBR), Miss M.O. Harris and Miss F.M.E. Toyne (AUS).
LL (NIL).
NQ (1) Mrs. P. Rushton and Mrs. J.R. White (GBR).

1965

SQ (4) Mrs. D.K. Illingworth and Mrs. P. Rushton (GBR), Miss P. Reyes and Miss E. Subirats (MEX), Miss M.E. Roche (RSA) and Miss A.J. Stroud (GBR). Miss V.H. Dennis and Miss M.O. Harris (AUS).
LL (NIL).
NQ (1) Mrs. D.A. Craven and Miss M.R. O'Donnell (GBR).

1966

SQ (4) Miss S. Percivall and Mrs. J.M. Wagstaff (GBR), Miss E.E. Andersson and Miss M.V.A.M. Pegel (SWE), Miss L.M. Bellamy and Miss D.A. Whitely (AUS), Miss G. Chapman and Miss W.V. Hall (GBR).
LL (NIL).
NQ (1) Miss S.L. Cullen-Smith and Miss E.M. Tew (GBR).

1967

Q (4) Miss M.O. Harris (AUS) and Miss S.J. Holdsworth (GBR), Miss E.M. Ernest and Miss S. Mappin (GBR), Miss J. Knight and Mrs. D.H. Roberts (GBR), Miss A. Rigby and Miss S.M. Tutt (GBR).
LL (NIL).

1968

Q (4) Miss V. Caceres (PER) and Miss R.C. Giscafre (ARG), Miss J. Knight and Mrs. D.H. Roberts (GBR), Miss J. Sawamatsu and Miss K. Sawamatsu (JPN), Mrs. C.W. Brasher (GBR) and Mrs. B.L. Mattes (USA).
LL (NIL).

1969

Q (4) Miss M.B.E. Kaligis and Miss L. Liem (INA), Miss G.C. Dove and Miss J.M. Wilshere (RSA), Miss R. Bailey and Miss J.V. Davenport (USA), Miss J.E. O'Hara and Miss J.L. Tindle (CAN).
LL (NIL).

1970

Q (4) Miss H.J. Kayser and Miss H. Sheedy (AUS), Miss S.J. Alexander and Miss S.H. Walsham (AUS), Miss A. Avis and Miss F. Luff (AUS), Miss W.V. Hall (GBR) and Miss B.S. Walsh (AUS).
LL (1) Miss R.R. Legg and Miss M.J. Pryde (NZL).

1971

Q (3) Miss P.A. Hardgrave and Miss D.J. Riste (GBR), Miss J.L. Harris (AUS) and Miss A.M. Martin (CAN), Miss L.J. Charles and Miss W.G. Slaughter (GBR).
LL (NIL).

1972

Q (3) Miss J.J. Helliar (GBR) and Miss S. Hole (AUS), Miss S.A. Stap and Miss L.M. Tenney (USA), Miss L.D. Blachford (GBR) and Mrs. H.T. Barnville (IRL).
LL (NIL).

1973

Q (3) Miss C.F. Matison and Miss M.J. Tesch (AUS), Miss V.A. Berner (CAN) and Mrs. R.N. Faulkner (AUS), Miss M. Christenson and Miss J. Dixon (USA).
LL (NIL).

1974

Q (3) Miss D.R. Evers and Miss N.F. Gregory (AUS), Miss S.L. Barman and Miss M. Christenson (USA), Miss M. Jausovec (YUG) and Miss R.J. Tenney (USA).
LL (1) Miss J.S. Hudson-Beck (RHO) and Miss S.H. Minford (IRL).

1975

Q (3) Miss J. Walker and Miss K. Walker (AUS), Miss F. Mihai (ROM) and Miss N. Sato (JPN), Miss J.L. Diamond (AUS) and Miss P.J. Moor (GBR).
LL (NIL).

1976

Q (3) Miss J.R. Morton and Miss J.L. Wilton (AUS), Miss D.R. Evers and Mrs. C.E. Zeeman (AUS), Miss C.M. O'Neill and Miss J. Walker (AUS).
LL (1) Miss D.A. Jevans (GBR) and Miss C.F. Matison (AUS).

1977

Q (3) Miss C.F. Matison and Miss P.J. Whytcross (AUS), Miss S.E. Saliba and Miss M.T. Sawyer (AUS), Miss G.B. Samuel and Miss L.J. Whitfield (RSA).
LL (3) Miss R. Khan and Miss N.W. Weigel (USA), Miss P.J. Moor (GBR) and Miss J.B. Preyer (USA), Miss E.M. Dignam and Miss C.E. Lane (USA).

1978

Q (4) Miss J. Nachand and Miss N. Yeargin (USA), Miss G.B. Samuel (RSA) and Miss C.V. Thomas (USA), Miss L.J. Harrison (AUS) and Miss N.W. Weigel (USA), Miss N.F. Gregory (AUS) and Mrs. M. Pinterova (TCH).
LL (1) Miss S.E. Saliba and Miss M.T. Sawyer (AUS).

1979

Q (4) Miss R.C. Giscafre (ARG) and Miss J.S. Stratton (USA), Miss K.A. Hallam (AUS) and Miss J.B. Preyer (USA), Miss K.Y. Sands and Miss A. Whitmore (USA), Miss W.S. Gilchrist (AUS) and Miss B.M. Perry (NZL).

LL (2) Miss A.M. Coe and Miss C. Molesworth (GBR), Miss S.P.M. Simmonds (ITA) and Miss N.W. Weigel (USA).

1980

Q (4) Miss L. Antonoplis (USA) and Miss D.R. Evers (AUS), Miss P.S. Medrado and Miss C.C. Monteiro (BRA), Miss D. Freeman and Miss S.E. Saliba (AUS), Miss N. Sato (JPN) and Miss S. Urroz (CHI).

LL (1) Miss B.A. Mould and Miss R. Uys (RSA).

1981

Q (4) Miss E.M. Burgin and Miss H.A. Ludloff (USA), Miss K.L. Gulley and Miss K.M. Pratt (AUS), Miss R. Du Toit (RSA) and Miss B.J. Remilton (AUS), Miss D.K. Chesterton (AUS) and Miss D.K.A. Taylor (GBR).

LL (2) Miss B. Blaney (USA) and Miss C.M. O'Neill (AUS), Miss J.M. Mundel and Miss S.L. Rollinson (RSA).

1982

Q (4) Miss E.M. Gordon and Miss B.A. Mould (RSA), Miss E.M. Burgin and Miss A.A. Moulton (USA), Miss N.F. Gregory (AUS) and Miss K.A. Steinmetz (USA), Miss J.A. Mundel and Miss S.L. Rollinson (RSA).

LL (1) Miss A.B. Henricksson (USA) and Miss P.J. Whytcross (AUS).

1983

Q (4) Miss S. Cherneva and Miss L.I. Savchenko (URS), Miss C.J. Drury and Miss E.D. Lightbody (GBR), Miss B. Randell and Miss K. Staunton (AUS), Miss R. Mentz and Miss M. Reinach (RSA).

LL (3) Miss A.L. Minter and Miss E. Minter (AUS), Miss P. Brailsford and Miss R. Lewis (GBR), Miss N.F. Gregory (AUS) and Mrs. H.A. Mochizuki (USA).

1984

Q (4) Miss E. Eliseenko and Miss N. Reva (URS), Miss M. Quinlan and Miss M. Van Nostrand (USA), Miss K.B. Cummings and Miss R.M. White (USA), Miss C. Copeland and Mrs. H.A. Mochizuki (USA).

LL (2) Miss C. Anderholm (SWE) and Miss M. Yangi (JPN), Miss K. Kinney (USA) and Miss R. Mentz (RSA).

1985

Q (4) Miss R.L. Blount and Miss D.L. Farrell (USA) Miss A.M. Fernandez (USA) and Miss H. Na (CHN), Miss B.J. Cordwell and Miss J.A. Richardson (NZL). Miss K. McDaniel and Miss W.E. White (USA).

LL (NIL).

1986

Q (4) Miss K. Deed and Miss N.A. Provis (AUS), Miss G. Miro (BRA) and Miss P. Tarabini (ARG), Miss B.S. Gerken (USA) and Miss D.S. Van Rensburg (RSA), Mrs. G.R. Dingwall (AUS) and Mrs. H.J. Short (USA).

LL (3) Miss J. Golder and Miss S. Pendo (USA), Miss M. Jaggard (AUS) and Miss J.C. Kaplan (USA), Miss C. MacGregor and Miss C.B. MacGregor (USA).

1987

Q (4) Miss K. Okamoto and Miss N. Sato (JPN), Miss M. Javer and Miss N. Sodupe (USA), Miss L. Meskhi and Miss L.M. Zvereva (URS), Miss M.M. Bollegraf (NED) and Miss M. Lindstrom (SWE).

LL (1) Miss K.T. Schimper (RSA) and Miss M. Yanagi (JPN).

1988

Q (4) Miss Y. Koizumi (JPN) and Miss K.A. Steinmetz (USA), Miss A. Dechaume and Miss E. Derly (FRA), Miss J-A Faull and Miss R. McQuillan (AUS), Miss L. Field (AUS) and Miss E. Krapl (SUI).
LL (2) Miss L. O'Neill (AUS) and Miss J. Smoller (USA), Miss A. Grossman (USA) and Miss M. Yanagi (JPN).

1989

Q (4) Miss R. Hiraki (JPN) and Miss A. Van Buuren (NED), Miss P. Hy (HGK) and Miss M. McGrath (USA), Miss M. Kidowaki and Miss A. Nishiya (JPN), Miss K.L. McDonald and Miss K. Radford (AUS).
LL (2) Miss A.M. Fernandez (USA) and Miss T. Zambrzycki (BRA), Miss L.A. Eldredge (USA) and Miss L. O'Halloran (IRL).

1990

Q (4) Miss N.J. Pratt and Miss K. Sharpe (AUS), Miss K.L. McDonald and Miss T.J. Morton (AUS), Miss I. Driehuis and Miss C.M. Viz (NED), Miss K-A. Guse and Miss J. Hodder (AUS).
LL (2) Miss A. Devries (BEL) and Miss K. Godridge (AUS), Miss L. Antonoplis (USA) and Miss M. Strandlund (SWE).

1991

Q (4) Miss B. Griffiths and Miss J. Wood (GBR), Miss R. Hiraki and Miss A. Nishiya (JPN), Miss C. Benjamin and Miss T.R. Whittington (USA), Miss J. Halard (FRA) and Miss A. Huber (GER).
LL (3) Miss L. Novelo (MEX) and Miss B. Somerville (USA), Miss K. Date and Miss E. Iida (JPN), Miss J. Limmer and Miss A. Woolcock (AUS).

1992

Q (4) Miss J. Hodder and Miss K. Sharpe (AUS), Miss C. Bakkum (NED) and Miss M. Strandlund (SWE), Miss A. Kijimuta and Miss N. Sawamatsu (JPN), Miss D.J. Jones (AUS) and Miss T.A. Price (RSA).
LL (NIL).

1993

Q (4) Miss J.M. Bryne and Miss N.J. Pratt (AUS), Miss T.A. Price and Miss D.A. Van Rensburg (RSA), Miss K.L. MacDonald and Miss K Sharpe (AUS), Miss K.L. Godridge and Miss J. Limmer (AUS).
LL (4) Miss E. Bond and Miss C. Taylor (GBR), Miss H. Sprung (AUT) and Miss D. Thomas (AUS), Mrs. N. Egorova and Mrs. S. Parkhomento (URS), Miss C. Benjamin (USA) and Miss T.J. Morton (AUS).

1994

Q (2) Miss K. Quentrec and Miss S. Testud (FRA), Miss M. Lindstrom and Miss M. Strandlund (SWE).
LL (2) Miss N.J. Pratt (AUS) and Miss J. Steven (USA), Miss G.E. Coorengel (NED) and Miss A.E. Smith (GBR).

1995

Q (2) Miss K. Godridge and Miss K. Sharpe (AUS). Miss Y. Basting and Miss P. Kamstra (NED).
LL (1) Miss K. Kruger (RSA) and Mrs. P. Schwarz-Ritter (AUT).

1996

Q (2) Miss I. Demongeot and Miss C. Dhenin (FRA), Miss J.M. Pullin and Miss L.A. Woodroffe (GBR).
LL (2) Miss D.I. Jones (AUS) and Miss T.A. Price (RSA), Miss J. Lutrova (RUS) and Miss T. Tanasugarn (THA).

1997

Q (2) Miss E. Brioukhovets and Miss E.V. Tatarkova (UKR), Miss V. Lake (GBR) and Miss L. Pleming (AUS)
LL (1) Miss J. Lutrova (RUS) and Miss J. Wood (GBR).

1998

Q (2) Miss C.C. Black (ZIM) and Miss I. Selyutina (KAZ), Miss M. Drake (CAN) and Miss L. Osterloh (USA).
LL (1) Miss A. Rippner (USA) and Miss J. Steck (RSA).

1999

Q (2) Miss J. Abe (GER) and Miss N. Petrova (RUS), Miss J. Dokic (AUS) and Miss T. Pisnik (SLO).
LL (2) Miss S. Reeves and Miss M. Washington (USA), Miss A. Jidkova (RUS) and Miss L. Schaerer (PAR).

2000

Q (4) Miss S. Asagoe (JPN) and Miss S. Reeves (USA), Miss A. Bachmann (GER) and Miss E. Dyrberg (DEN) Miss H. Crook and Miss V.E. Davies (GBR), Miss S. Sfar (TUN) and Miss J. Woehr (GER).
LL (2) Miss J. Hopkins (USA) and Miss P. Rampre (SLO), Miss C. Dhenin (FRA) and Miss R. Kolbovic (CAN).

2001

Q (4) Miss E. Martincova (CZE) and Miss T. Perebiynis (UKR), Miss M. Matevzic (SLO) and Miss D. Zaric (YUG), Miss A. Augustus and Miss J. Embry (USA), Miss D. Buth (Mrs S. Spirak) (USA) and Miss N. Grandin (RSA).
LL (NIL)

2002

Q (4) Miss R. Kolbovic (CAN) and Miss M. Sequera (VEN), Miss A. Jidkova (RUS) and Miss B. Stewart (AUS), Miss G. Dulko (ARG) and Miss S. Kuznetsova (RUS), Miss A. Hawkins and Miss J. O'Donoghue (GBR).
LL (1) Miss L. Nemeckova (CZE) and Miss A. Vanc (ROM).

2003

Q (4) Miss B. Stewart and Miss C. Wheeler (AUS), Miss J. Craybas (USA) and Miss V. Webb (CAN), Miss N. Sewell and Miss S. Stone (AUS), Miss F. Schiavone and Miss Ad. Serra Zanetti (ITA).
LL (NIL)

2004

Q (4) Miss L. Baker (NZL) and Miss N. Sewell (AUS), Miss M-R. Jeon (KOR) and Miss Y. Yoshida (JPN), Miss L. Bacheva (BUL) and Miss E. Birnerova (CZE), Miss E. Dominkovic (AUS) and Miss A. Rodionova (RUS).
LL (3) Miss B. Schwartz (AUT) and Miss J. Woehr (GER), Miss A. Augustus (USA) and Miss N. Grandin (RSA), Miss C. Curran (IRL) and Miss J. O'Donoghue (GBR).

2005

Q (4) Miss E Dominikovic (AUS) and Miss A. Nakamura (JPN), Miss A. Bondarenko (UKR) and Miss A. Rodionova (RUS), Miss R. Fujiwara and Miss S. Obata (JPN), Miss T. Poutchek and Miss A. Yakimova (BLR).
LL (3) Miss J. Fedak (UKR) and Miss L. Osterloh (USA), Miss E. Krauth (ARG) and Miss M-E. Pelletier (CAN), Miss E.K. Gallovits (ROM), and Miss A.J. Haynes (USA).

2006

Q (4) Miss J. Fedak and Miss T. Perebiynis (UKR), Miss L. Hradecka and Miss H. Sromova (CZE), Miss S, Cohen Aloro (FRA) and Miss M. Martinez Sanchez (ESP), Miss L. Osterloh and Miss A.Rolle (USA).
LL (3) Miss M. Czink (HUN) and Miss V. King (USA), Miss C-W. Chart and Miss S-W Hsieh (TPE), Miss M. Diaz-Oliva (ARG) and Miss N. Grandin (RSA).

2007

Q (4) Miss S-W. Hsieh (TPE) and Miss A. Kudryavtseva (RUS), Miss J. Ditty and Miss R. Kops-Jones (USA), Miss S. Foretz (FRA) and Miss S. Sfar (TUN), Miss S. Arvidsson (SWE) and Miss L. Osterloh (Uitzpatrick and Miss E. Webley-Smith (GBR), Miss A. Hlavackova (CZE) and Miss S. Kloesel (GER), Miss H. Sromova and Mrs K. Zakopalova (CZE).

2008

Q (4) Miss A. Hlavackova (CZE) and Miss 0. Savchuk (UKR), Miss M. Kirilenko (RUS) and Miss F. Pennetta (ITA), Miss R. Kops-Jones and Miss A. Spears (USA), Miss J. Cravero and Miss B. Jozami (ARG).
LL (3) Miss C.A. Fusano and Miss A. Haynes (USA), Miss A. Morita and Miss J. Namigata (JPN), Miss A. Smith and Miss G. Stoop (GBR).

2009

Q (4) Miss V. Fedak (UKR) and Miss M. Jugic-Salkic (BIH), Miss R. Fujiwara and Miss A. Nakamura (JPN), Miss T. Malek and Miss A. Petkovic (GER), Miss E. Gallovits (ROM) and Miss K. Marosi (HUN).
LL (NIL).

2010

Q (4) Miss E. Daniilidou (GRE) and Miss J. Woehr (GER), Miss M. Koryltseva (UKR) and Miss D. Kustova (BLR), Miss J. Craybas (USA) and Miss M. Erakovic (NZL), Miss K. Kanepi (EST) and Miss S. Zhang (CHN).
LL (2) Miss K-C Chang (TPE) and Miss A. Morita (JPN), Miss K. Marosi (HUN) and Miss K.Woerle (GER).

2011

Q (4) Miss V. Dolonts (RUS) and Miss K. Marosi (HUN), Miss S. Aoyama and Miss R. Fujiwara (JPN), Miss U. Radwanska (POL) and Miss A. Rodionova (RUS), Miss L. Lee-Waters and Miss M. Moulton-Levy (USA).
LL (3) Miss N. Lertcheewakarn (THA) and Miss J. Moore (USA), Miss M. Erakovc (NZL) and Miss T. Tanasugarn (THA), Miss S. Lefevre (FRA) and Miss E. Rodina (RUS).

2012

Q (4) Miss D. Jurak (CRO) and Miss K. Marosi (HUN), Miss M.Lucic (CRO) and Miss V. Savinykh (RUS), Miss L. Lee-Waters and Miss M. Moulton-Levy (USA), Miss V. Dolonc (SBR) and Miss O. Savchak (UKR)
LL (NIL)

2013

Q (4) Miss S. Foretz Gacon (FRA) and Miss E. Hrdinova (CZE), Miss M.Irigoyen and Miss P. Ormaechea (ARG), Miss R. Olaru (ROM) and Miss O. Savchuk (UKR), Miss V. Solovyeva (RUS) and Miss M. Zanevska (UKR).

2014

Q (4) Miss L. Kichenok and Miss N. Kichenok (UKR), Miss J. Gajdosova and Miss A. Rodionova (AUS), Miss P. Parmentier and Miss L. Thorpe (FRA), Miss V. Dolonc (SRB) and Miss D. Seguel (CHI).
LL (1) Miss Y. Beygelzimer (UKR) and Miss K. Jans-Ignacik (POL).

Mixed Doubles Championship

1925
Q (4) J.G. Hogan and Miss I. Maltby (GBR), J.H. Wheatcroft and Miss C. Hardie (GBR), N. Jones and Miss B.G. Morrison (GBR), W.T. Tucker and Miss L. Bull (GBR).

1926
Q (4) J. Pennycuick and Miss E. Morle (GBR), F.S. Burnett and Mrs. C.M.B. Marriott (GBR), M. Whitmore and Mrs. P.H. Wilkin (GBR), V. Burr and Mrs. C.O. Tuckey (GBR).

1927
SQ (4) F.S. Burnett and Mrs. C.M.B. Marriott (GBR), A.D. Stocks and Mrs. A.D. Stocks (GBR), E.A. Dearman and Miss E.M. Dearman (GBR), N.H. Latchford and Miss M.P. Davies (GBR).
NQ (1) E.T. Hollins and Miss E.G. Newton (GBR).

1928
SQ (4) H.G. Mackintosh and Mrs. R.E. Haylock (GBR), B.R. Lawrence and Mrs. Shepherd Wellesley (GBR), A.M.D. Pitt and Mrs. P. Bouverie (GBR), J.W. Olmsted and Miss V. Marshall (GBR).
NQ (1) A.S. Drew and Miss B.E. Drew (GBR).

1929
SQ (4) A. Brown and Miss C. Tyrell (GBR), N.H. Latchford and Mrs. H.G. Broadbridge (GBR), J.D.F. Fisher and Mrs. H.S. Uber (GBR), G.R. Sherwell and Mrs. R.E. Haylock (GBR).
NQ (1) E.T. Hollins and Miss B.E. Drew (GBR).

1930
SQ (4) J. Pennycuick and Miss L. Johnstone (GBR), L.J. Hill and Miss M.K. Phayre (GBR), G.H. Perkins and Mrs. W. Tucker (GBR), W.A.H. Duff and Mrs. F.M. Strawson (GBR).
NQ (1) H.S. Burrows and Miss D.E. Anderson (GBR).

1931
SQ (4) I.H. Wheatcroft and Mrs. I.H. Wheatcroft (GBR) L.H.A. Hankey and Miss O.L. Webb (GBR), D.A. Hodges and Mrs. G.N. Macready (GBR), D.H. Williams and Mrs. W.J. Dyson (GBR).
NQ (1) H.S. Burrows and Miss J. Lawson (GBR).

1932
SQ (4) J.E. Giesen and Miss M.E. Dix (GBR). C.N.O. Ritchie and Miss G. Harry (GBR), D.A. Hodges and Mrs. M. Stork (GBR), H.R. Price and Mrs. G. Lucas (GBR).
NQ (1) O. Wright and Miss J. McAlpine (GBR).

1933
SQ (4) N.H. Latchford and Mrs. S.K. Edwards (GBR), A.S.C. Hulton and Mrs. G. Hawkins (GBR), H. Billington and Miss A.M. Knapp (GBR), R.G. De Quetteville and Mrs. H.W. Backhouse (GBR).
NQ (1) J.H. Booth and Miss M. Wynne (GBR).

1934
SQ (4) R.M. Turnbull and Mrs. R.M. Turnbull (GBR), G.E. Bean and Miss C. Tyrrell (GBR), R.C. Wackett and Miss P.M. Weekes (GBR), B.R. Lawrence and Mrs. B.R. Lawrence (GBR).
NQ (1) G.A. Pratt and Miss J. Strettell (GBR).

1935
SQ (4) C.R. Fawcus and Miss M.E. Lumb (GBR), G.E. Bean and Miss C. Tyrrell (GBR), W. Filmer-Sankey and Miss A.A. Wright (GBR), W.A.R. Collins and Lady Rowallan (GBR).
NQ (1) J.B. Sturgeon and Miss M. Burrows (GBR).

1936
SQ (4) C.M. Jones and Miss P.J. Owen (GBR), R.A. Shayes and Miss I. Cater (GBR). M.E. Lucking and Miss G.K. Osborne (GBR), S.H. Hawkins and Miss T. Kingsbury (GBR).
NQ (1) N. Melland and Miss D.A. Huntback (GBR).

1937
SQ (4) L.E. King and Miss M.G. Norman (GBR), C.H.E. Betts and Miss Y.J. Allnatt (GBR), J.N. Wright and Mrs. P. Knight (GBR), W.F. Freeman and Mrs. W.F. Freeman (GBR).
LL (NIL).
NQ (1) G.L. France and Miss M. Parr (GBR).

1938
SQ (4) H.A. Hare and Miss N.B. Brown (GBR), W.P.W. Anderson and Mrs. W.T. Cooke (GBR), G.I. Pettigrew and Miss S. Mavrogordato (GBR), M.E. Lucking and Miss G.K. Osborne (GBR).
LL (NIL).
NQ (1) T.C. Braithwaite and Miss D.M. Davison (GBR).

1939
SQ (4) R.C. Nicol and Miss A.J. Wenyon (GBR), H.J. Whitney and Miss P.M. Seaton (GBR), B. Butters and Miss M.F. Brace (GBR), G.E. Bean and Mrs. H.S. Huber (GBR).
LL (NIL).
NQ (1) J.B. Fulton and Mrs. J.B. Fulton (GBR).

1946 No Competition.

1947
SQ (4) J. Michelmore and Miss E.M. Stephens (GBR). A.L. Della Porta and Miss P. Rodgers (GBR), J.C. Warboys and Miss R.F. Woodgate (GBR), D.H. Slack and Miss G.E. Woodgate (GBR).
LL (NIL).
NQ (1) R.V. Fontes and Mrs. R.V. Fontes (GBR).

1948
SW (4) A.L. Della Porta and Mrs. P. Knight (GBR), E. Urlwin-Smith and Mrs. E. Urlwin-Smith (GBR), Hon. C.N.O. Ritchie and Miss B.N. Knapp (GBR), R.C. Thorn and Miss V.S. White (GBR).
LL (NIL).
NQ (1) J.B. Fulton and Mrs. J.B. Fulton (GBR).

1949
SQ (4) W.C. Shute and Miss A.L. Morgan (GBR), J.M. Lloyd and Mrs. J. David (GBR), D.A. Samaai (RSA) and Miss M. Buxton-Knight (EGY), L.E. Cater and Mrs. A.C. Brighton (GBR).
LL (NIL).
NQ (1) P.E. Hare and Mrs. H.R. Phillips (GBR).

1950
SQ (4) W.T. Anderson and Miss J.S.V. Partridge (GBR), L.E. Cater and Mrs. A.C. Brighton (GBR), R. Guise and Mrs. D.R. Bocquet (GBR), J.M. Lloyd and Mrs. J. David (GBR).
LL (NIL).
NQ (1) J.R. Statham and Miss H.M. Fletcher (GBR).

1951
SQ (4) D.J. Paton and Mrs. J.M.E. Wallace (GBR), S.D. Lester and Mrs. G. Preston (GBR), W.C. Shute and Mrs. J.A. Collier (GBR), J. Morison and Miss R.F. Woodgate (GBR).
LL (NIL).
NQ (1) D.H. Shaw and Miss M.P. Harrison (GBR).

1952
SQ (4) L.E. Cater and Mrs. A.C. Brighton (GBR), D. Brown and Mrs. J.A. White (GBR), W.C. Shute and Mrs. J.A. Collier (GBR), R.B.R. Wilson and Mrs. R.B.R. Wilson (GBR).
LL (NIL).
NQ (1) R.J. Lee and Miss N.T. Seacy (GBR).

1953
SQ (4) D.L.M. Black (RHO) and Miss D. Midgley (GBR), T.L. Tan (INA) and Miss M. Reeves (RSA), J.A. White and Miss A.M. Carlisle (GBR), W.A. Knight and Miss J. Knight (GBR).
LL (NIL).
NQ (1) R.H. Hack and Mrs. K.F. Knight (GBR).

1954
SQ (4) G.L. Forbes and Miss J. Scott (RSA), M. Hime (GBR) and Miss E.G. Attwood (NZL), P. Moys and Miss J.M. Boundy (GBR), G.L. Talbot (RSA) and Miss K. Neville-Smith (AUS).
LL (1) E.C. Ford and Mrs. E.C. Ford (GBR).
NQ (1) B.A. Haughton (IRL) and Miss N. Liebert (GBR).

1955
SQ (4) C.V. Botha and Miss H. Pascoe (RSA), M. Lasry and Miss B. de Chambure (FRA), A.D. Marshall (AUS) and Miss P.M. Titchener (GBR), R.T. Potter and Miss E.E. Ruffin (AUS).
LL (1) P.V.V. Sherwood (GBR) and Mrs. E. Watermeyer (RSA).
NQ (1) F.B. Webb and Mrs. F.B. Webb (GBR).

1956
SQ (4) R.G.M. Guiney (RSA) and Miss M.O. Bouchet (FRA), J. Blatchford (USA) and Miss D. Midgley (GBR), S. Khoury (LEB) and Mrs. P.C. Bramley (GBR), R.B.R. Wilson and Mrs. R.B.R. Wilson (GBR).
LL (NIL).
NQ (1) R.T. White and Miss P.C. Drew (GBR).

1957
SQ (4) D.R. Collins and Mrs. F.J. Tomlin (GBR), B.F. Hutchins and Mrs. R.A. Chamberlain (GBR), E.A. Crump and Mrs. N.R. Allport (GBR), R.K. Stilwell (RHO) and Miss J.M. Chamberlain (GBR).
LL (1) K.B.G. Collar and Miss Z.J. Lusty (GBR).
NQ (1) R.M. Powell and Miss E.B. Lawrenson (GBR).

1958
SQ (4) W.T. Anderson and Miss J. Knight (GBR), I.J. Warwick and Mrs. I.J. Warwick (GBR), P.F. Hearnden (AUS) and Mrs. R.B.R. Wilson (GBR), G. Stewart (AUS) and Miss H.J.M. Durose (GBR).
LL (NIL).
NQ (1) G.R. Smith and Mrs. J. Kemsey-Bourne (GBR).

1959
SQ (4) S. Khoury (LEB) and Mrs. P.C. Bramley (GBR), N. Nette and Miss E.T. Court (AUS), A. Ali (IND) and Miss C.M. Leather (GBR), G. Sanders (GER) and Mrs. J.W. Cawthorn (GBR).
LL (NIL).
NQ (1) C.R. Applewhaite and Mrs. R.D. Armstrong (GBR).

1960
SQ (4) M. Cox and Miss F.E. Walton (GBR), D.B. Hughes and Miss P.M. Burrell (GBR), J.R. McDonald (NZL) and Miss J.M. Tee (GBR), C.G. Judge and Miss C. Webb (GBR).
LL (NIL).
NQ (1) J.C. Upton and Mrs. D.K. Illingworth (GBR).

1961

SQ (4) I.S. Crookenden (NZL) and Miss F.E. Walton (GBR), N.T. Holland (AUS) and Miss C.A. Rosser (GBR), W. Schneiders (GER) and Mrs. P.L.B. Gardner (GBR), G.K. Pares (AUS) and Miss D.S. Butt (CAN).
LL (NIL).
NQ (1) J.C. Upton and Mrs. D.K. Illingworth (GBR).

1962

SQ (4) A.C. Kendall and Mrs. J.P. Young (AUS), F.S. Salomon (RHO) and Mrs. J.H. Edrich (USA), J.D.C. Crump and Miss A.P. Anderson (GBR), W.W. Bowrey (AUS) and Miss D.C. Tuckey (GBR).
LL (NIL).
NQ (1) R.W. Dixon and Miss C. Lyon (GBR).

1963

SQ (4) A.J. Hagan and Miss C.M. Callanan (RSA). A.K. Carpenter (CAN) and Miss M.B.H. McAnally (GBR), M.A. Otway (NZL) and Miss J.M. Trewby (GBR), J. Keller and Miss D.D. Howe (AUS).
LL (NIL).
NQ (1) R.W. Dixon and Miss C. Lyon (GBR).

1964

SQ (4) R.D. Ambrose and Miss S.M.E. Porter (GBR), N.J. Perry (USA) and Miss V.A. Berner (CAN), T.J. Ryan and Miss P.M. Walkden (RSA), M. Price and Miss P.A. Spencer (GBR).
LL (NIL).
NQ (1) R.W. Dixon and Miss C. Lyon (GBR).

1965

SQ (4) C.E. McHugo and Miss W.V. Hall (GBR), G.M. Price and Miss V.M. Rees (GBR), V. Zarazua and Miss E. Subirats (MEX), J.R. Pinto Bravo (CHI) and Miss E.M. Spruyt (NED).
LL (1) J.C. Fletcher and Mrs. C.T. Clark (GBR).
NQ (1) G.W. Stubbs and Miss M.R. O'Donnell (GBR).

1966

SQ (4) R. Venkatesan (IND) and Miss A.E. Jansen Venneboer (NED), J.L. Decker and Miss M.O. Harris (AUS), R. Hernando and Miss S.S. Behlmar (USA), G. Grisillo (AUS) and Miss K.S. Schediwy (GER).
LL (NIL).
NQ (1) J.C. Harrison and Miss E.M. Tew (GBR).

1967

Q (4) J.A. Pickens and Miss W.A. Overton (USA), B.A. Cheney and Miss M.M. Henried (USA), K. Hiskins (AUS) and Miss E.M. Ernest (GBR), N. Fleury and Miss A. Bakker (NED).
LL (NIL).

1968

Q (4) J. Subirats and Miss E. Subirats (MEX), M.M. Baleson (RSA) and Miss H.W. Allen (GBR), B. White (AUS) and Miss M.M. Lee (GBR), L.A. Ayala and Mrs. L.A. Ayala (CHI).
LL (NIL).

1969

Q (4) H. Nerell and Miss M. Strandberg (SWE), S.J. Matthews and Miss E.M. Ernest (GBR), B.M. Bertram and Miss A.L. van Deventer (RSA), P. Pokorny (AUT) and Miss H.J. Amos (AUS).
LL (1) B. Anstey (RSA) and Miss S. Okin (GBR).

1970
Q (4) M. Iqbal (PAK) and Miss J.A. Fayter (GBR), R.N. Hawkes and Miss M.J. Pryde (NZL), A.L. Jones and Miss D.J. Riste (GBR), A.G. Fawcett amd Miss L.J. McDonald (RSA).
LL (1) R.B. Perry (USA) and Miss K. Sawamatsu (JPN).

1971
Q (3) L.W. Collins and Miss W. Appleby (USA), An. Amritraj and Mrs. N.A. Mankad (IND), A.G. Hammond and Miss S. Hole (AUS).
LL (1) P.J. Cramer and Miss S. von Brandis (RSA).

1972
Q (3) H.W. Turnbull and Miss W.M. Turnbull (AUS), E.W. Ewert (AUS) and Miss M.B.K. Wikstedt (SWE), D.B. McCormick (CAN) and Miss P. Cody (USA).
LL (NIL).

1973 *No Competition.*

1974
Q (3) S. Tidball and Miss M. Christenson (USA). J.C. Trickey (AUS) and Miss A.K. Schwickert (USA), E.D. McCabe and Miss D.R. Evers (AUS).
LL (NIL).

1975
Q (4) A.G. Fawcett (RHO) and Miss P.A. Reece (USA), B.M. Mitton and Mrs. C. Vlotman (RSA), T.J. Little and Miss P.J. Whytcross (AUS), N.M. Callaghan and Miss J. Walker (AUS).
LL (1) E.W. Ewert (AUS) and Miss M.B.K. Wikstedt (SWE).

1976
Q (3) P.F. McNamee and Miss K.D. Ruddell (AUS), A.M. Jarrett and Miss D.A. Jevans (GBR), J.P. Geraghty and Miss L. Antonoplis (USA).
LL (3) Y. Tezuka and Miss N. Sato (JPN), M.P. Myberg (RSA) and Miss K.A. Hallam (AUS), S.A. Warboys (GBR) and Miss D.R. Evers (AUS).

1977 *No Competition.*

1978
Q (3) S.S. Vuille and Miss H.A. Ludloff (USA), R. Verdieck and Miss S. Acker (USA), G. Grisillo (RSA) and Miss R.L. Blount (USA).
LL (6) K.W. Hancock and Mrs. J.G. Paish (AUS), W. Maher and Miss L.J. Harrison (AUS), A.H. Lloyd and Mrs. R. Lewis (GBR), N.A. Rayner and Miss C. Harrison (GBR), S.W. Carnahan and Miss D. Desfor (USA), V.R. Van Patten and Miss S.H. Hagey (USA).

1979
Q (3) D. Sherbeck and Miss J.S. Stratton (USA), T. Koch (BRA) and Miss R.C. Giscafre (ARG), M.R.E. Appleton (GBR) and Miss P.J. Whytcross (AUS).
LL (2) J. Whiteford and Miss J. Plackett (GBR), C.S. Wells and Miss D.S. Parker (GBR).

1980
Q (3) S.W. Van Der Merwe and Miss Y. Vermaak (RSA), J. Kamiwazumi and Miss N. Sato (JPN), C.L. Letcher and Miss C.A. Griffiths (AUS).
LL (NIL).

1981
Q (3) T.C. Fancutt and Miss S.E. Saliba (AUS), D.H. Collings and Miss K.L. Gulley (AUS), S.R. Simon and Miss L. Antonoplis (USA).
LL (3) J. Kamiwazumi and Miss N. Sato (JPN), D.T. Visser and Miss S.L. Rollinson (RSA), M.W.C. Guntrip (GBR) and Miss H.A. Ludloff (USA).

1982
Q (4) J. Turpin and Miss K.A. Steinmetz (USA), M.H. Bates and Miss B.J. Remilton (AUS), E.H. Fromm and Miss E.M. Burgin (USA), M.W.C. Guntrip (GBR) and Miss H.A. Ludloff (USA). LL (NIL).

1983
Q (3) P. Doohan and Miss C.M. O'Neill (AUS), J.M. Dier and Miss B. Randall (AUS), J. Turpin (GBR) and Miss K.A. Steinmetz (USA).
LL (5) C. Van Rensburg and Miss M. Reinach (RSA), M.D. Wayman (GBR) and Miss N.F. Gregory (AUS), A. Cortes (COL) and Miss N. Sato (JPN). G.R. Dingwall and Miss A.M. Tobin (AUS), B.H. Levine and Miss S.A. McInerney (USA).

1984
Q (3) B. Dyke (AUS) and Miss H. Strachonova (TCH), C.A. Miller and Miss B.J. Remilton (AUS), M. Kratzmann and Miss J.M. Byrne (AUS).
LL (4) R.R. Grant and Miss A.L. Gulley (AUS), P. Doohan and Miss N.A. Leipus (AUS), G. Whitecross (AUS) and Miss J.M. Hetherington (CAN), R.J. Simpson and Miss B.M. Perry (NZL).

1985
Q (3) E. Fernandez (PUR) and Miss B.M. Perry (NZL), G. Michibata (CAN) and Miss P. Hy (HGK), D. Campos (BRA) and Miss M. Van Nostrand (USA).
LL (2) M. Kratzmann and Miss J.M. Byrne (AUS), R. Meyer and Miss L. Howell (USA).

1986
Q (3) A. Jordan (COL) and Mrs. G.R. Dingwall (AUS), M. Tidman (SWE) and Miss L. Field (AUS), B. Custer and Miss N.A-L. Provis (AUS)*.
* *withdrew.*
LL (4) G. Luza (ITA) and Miss G. Miro (BKA), G. Niebur and Miss H.A. Crowe (USA), D. MacPherson and Miss L. O'Neill (AUS), H. Shirato and Miss M. Yanagi (JPN).

1987
Q (3) T.A. Woodbridge (AUS) and Miss P. Moreno (PHI), J. Letts and Miss L. Antonoplis (USA), A. Maasdorp (RSA) and Mrs. H.A. Mochizuki (USA).
LL (5) A. Olkhovskiy and Miss L. Meskhi (URS), C. Fancutt (AUS) and Miss L. Gracie (GBR), H. Shirato and Miss M. Yanagi (JPN), D. Roberts and Miss T.A. Catlin (GBR), K. Hutter and Miss S. Norris (AUS).

1988
Q (3) C.D. Miller and Miss J. Smoller (USA). R. Smith (BAH) and Miss K. Foxworth (USA), S. Barr (AUS) and Miss S.L. Collins (USA).
LL (4) G. Layendecker and Miss S. Stafford (USA), P. Hoysted and Miss T. Morton (AUS), M.T. Walker and Miss J.M. Tacon (GBR), S. Kruger (RSA) and Miss M. Van Nostrand (USA).

1989
Q (3) S. Furlong and Miss K. Radford (AUS), C. Banducci (ITA) and Miss H.A. Ludloff (USA), B.H. Levine (RSA) and Miss M.J. McGrath (USA).
LL (8) P. Palandjian and Miss J.E. Thomas (USA), B. Talbot (RSA) and Miss D.L. Faber (USA), P. Wright (IRL) and Miss L. Antonoplis (USA), C. Honey (RSA) and Miss A. Van Buuren (NED), L.E. Herrera (MEX) and Miss C. Tessi (ARG), N. Borwick (AUS) and Miss P. Moreno (HKG), L. Scott (USA) and Miss T. Zambrzycki (BRA), G. Pfitzner and Miss H. Sprung (AUT).

1990
Q (3) P.M. McEnroe and Miss M.J. McGrath (USA), B.P. Derlin and Miss J.A. Richardson (NZL), B. Garnett (USA) and Miss K.L. Radford (AUS).
LL (4) P. Norval and Miss M. De Swardt (RSA), K. Kinnear (USA) and Miss R. Field (RSA), G. Michibata (CAN) and Miss A. Huber (GER), L.J. Bale (RSA) and Miss J. Thomas (USA).

1991
Q (3) S.F. Stolle (AUS) and Miss N. Van Lottum (FRA), E. Amend and Miss H.A. Ludloff (USA), A.J. Kratzmann and Miss K-A Guse (AUS).
LL (3) J. Morgan and Miss D.J. Jones (AUS), M.R. Woodforde (AUS) and Miss A. Frazier (USA), L.J. Bale (RSA) and Miss A. Van Buuren (NED).
Qualifying discontinued.

Alternates
Subsequent replacements for withdrawals from the main draw have been taken from a list of Alternatives. This is a list of pairs whose combined doubles rankings are insufficient to gain them direct acceptance or not selected as Wild Cards.

1992
A (Nil)

1993
A (2) J. Donar and Miss M. Lindstrom (SWE), T.J. Middleton and Miss A.B. Henricksson (USA).

1994
A (1) L. Warder and Mrs. T.J. Morton-Rodgers (AUS).

1995
A (2) K.E. Flack and Miss L. Poruri (USA), M. Ondruska (RSA) and Miss L. Pleming (AUS).

1996
A (2) J.A. Conde and Miss V. Ruano Pascual (ESP), P.T. Hand and Miss V. Lake (GBR).

1997
A (2) D. Randall (USA) and Miss D. Jones (AUS), P.T. Hand and Miss V. Lake (GBR).

1998
A (1) T.C.J.M. Nijssen (NED) and Miss Y. Basuki (INA).

1999
A (2) D. DiLucia and Miss M. Shaughnessy (USA), J. Coetzee (RSA) and Miss E. Melicharova (CZE).

2000
A (2) P. Tramacchi and Miss B. Stewart (AUS), E. Ran (ISR) and Miss K. Marosi-Aracama (HUN).

2001
A (3) A. Schneiter (ITA) and Miss R. Hiraki (JAP), M. Sprengelmeyer and Miss L. Osterloh (USA), A. Fisher (AUS) and Miss K. Grant (USA).

2002
A (2) J. Kerr (AUS) and Miss A. Van Exel (NED), T. Perry and Miss A. Augustus (USA).

2003
A (3) J. Auckland and Miss S. Borwell (GBR), L. Childs and Miss E. Baltacha (GBR), M. Lee and Miss J. O'Donoghue (GBR).

2004
A (3) D. Hrbaty and Miss H. Nagyova (SVK), M. Matkowski (POL) and Miss M. Washington (USA), J.Coetzee (RSA) and Miss T. Krizan (SLO).

2005
A (3) R. Koenig (RSA) and Miss S. Talaja (CRO), B. MacPhie and Miss A. Spears (USA), G. Etlis (ARG) and Miss L. McShea (AUS).

2006
A (1) L. Diouhy and Miss E. Birnerova (CZE).

2007
A (2) V. Spadea and Miss V. King (USA), M. Melo (BRA) and Miss T. Paszek (AUT).

2008
A (1) S. Ratiwatana (THA) and Miss A. Kleybanova (RUS).

2009
A (Nil).

2010
A (2) I. Zelenay (SVK) and Miss A. Rosolska (POL), Miss L. Friedl and Miss L. Hradecka (CZE).

2011
A (3) R Wassen (NED) and Miss A. Rosolska (POL), C. Barlocq (ARG) and Miss M. Kondratieva (RUS), M. Damm and Miss R. Voracova (CZE).

2012
A (4) J. Brunstrom (SWE) and Miss A. Klepac (SLO), J. Erlich and Miss S. Peer (ISR), J. Cerretani (USA) and Miss P. Martic (CRO), A. Fisher (AUS) and Miss M. Barthel (GER).

2013
A (1) J. Levinsky (CZE) and L.Dekmeijerc (LAT).

2014
A (2) J.H. Galung (NED) and Miss A. Klepac (SLO), M. Venus (NZL) and Miss A. Rosolska (POL).

The following Qualifiers have made the most progress in The Championships:-

Gentlemen's Singles	*Ladies' Singles*
Quarter-final	**Quarter-final**
1984 P.T. Annacone (USA)	1984 Miss C. Karlsson (SWE)
1985 R. Acuna (CHI)	1985 Miss M. van Norstand (USA)
2011 B. Tomic (AUS)	1999 Miss J. Dokic (AUS)
	2006 Mrs. E. Bremond (FRA)
	2010 Miss K. Kanepi (EST)
Semi-final	**Semi-final**
1977 J.P. McEnroe (USA)	1999 Miss A.W. Stevenson (USA)
2000 V. Voltchkov (BLR)	

Gentlemen's Doubles	*Ladies' Doubles*
Champions	**Semi-Final**
2005 S.W.I. Huss (AUS) and	2006 Miss Y. Fedak and
W.A. Moodie (RSA)	Miss T. Perebiynis (UKR)

The following Lucky Losers have made the most progress in The Championships:-

Gentlemen's Singles	*Ladies' Singles*
Fourth Round	**Third Round (1)**
1973 B.M. Mitton (RSA)	1955 Miss F. Lemal (FRA)
J. Mukerjea (IND)	1959 Mrs. E. Launert (GER)
1983 J.C. McCurdy (AUS)	1974 Miss T. Zwaan (NED)
1995 D. Norman (BEL)	

Note (1) all three players were given a first round bye and hence won only one match. Over the years many players have won one match to reach the second round.

Qualifying Records

Most Games in a Match

Gentlemen's Singles	— 95 S. Warner (USA) bt M.W. Anger (USA) 7-5 1-6 7-6(7-2) 3-6 28-26 (1989-Third Round) 5hrs-22mins
Gentlemen's Doubles	— 76 A. Hadad (ISR) and A.U.H. Qureshi (PAK) bt I. Hirigoyen (ARG) and D. Sistermans (NED) 6-7(3-6) 6-3 6-7(5-7) 7-6(7-3) 15-13 (2002-Second Round) (3hrs-55mins)
Ladies' Singles	— 48 Miss B.J. Coldwell (NZL) bt Miss J.M. Hetherington (CAN) 5-7 7-5 13-11 (1985-First Round)
Ladies' Doubles	— 52 Miss P. Cranfield and Miss K.E. Robinson (GBR) bt Miss B. Baynes and Miss E.M. Roe (GBR) 6-8 10-8 11-9 (1933-First Round)
Mixed Doubles	— 50 L.H.A. Hankey and Miss O.L. Webb (GBR) bt M. W. Whitmore and Miss E.Z. Stokes (GBR) 8-10 9-7 9-7 (1931-Second Round)
	— 50 G.L. Talbot (RSA) and Miss K. Neville-Smith (AUS) bt E.J. Filby and Miss S.M. Colebrooke (GBR) 4-6 7-5 15-13 (1954-First Round)

Most Games in a Set

Gentlemen's Singles	— 54 S. Warner (USA) bt M.W. Anger (USA) 7-5 1-6 7-6 (7-2) 3-6 28-26 (1989-Third Round)
Gentlemen's Doubles	— 44 R. Matuszewski and T. Nelson (USA) bt T.J. Middleton (USA) and A.Thoms (GER) 6-4 4-6 23-21 (1995-First Round)
Ladies' Singles	— 30 Mrs. W.A. Tym (USA) bt Miss A.L. van Deventer (RSA) 16-14 6-3 (1967-Second Round)
Ladies' Doubles	— 40 Miss M.M. Lee and Miss J.C.L. Poynder (GBR) bt Miss J.M Boundy and Mrs. R.B.R. Wilson (GBR) 21-19 6-3 (1968-Second Round)
Mixed Doubles	— 34 L.J. Hill and Mrs. M.K. Phayre (GBR) bt A.W. Vinall and Miss B. Feltham (GBR) 18-16 6-2 (1930-Second Round)
	— 34 J.D. Page and Miss K. Smith (GBR) bt W.H. Entwhistle and Miss G.J. Gilder (GBR) 6-3 18-16 (1931-Second Round)

Most Points in Tie-break

Gentlemen's Singles	— 40 M. Llodra (FRA) bt R. Fromberg (Aus) 6-3 6-7 (19-21) 8-6 (2001-First Round)
Gentlemen's Doubles	— 34 An. Armritraj (IND) and J. Frana (ARG) bt N. Aerts and F.Roese (BRA) 7-6 (18-16) 7-5 (1987-Second Round)
Ladies' Singles	— 22 Miss A. Betzner (GER) bt Miss C. Caverzasio (ITA) 7-6 (12-10) 6-4 (1988-First Round)
	— 22 Miss L. Gregory (RSA) bt Miss L. O'Neill (AUS) 6-7 (10-12) 6-0 6-4 (1988-Third Round)
	— 22 Miss F. Perfetti (ITA) bt Miss C. Barclay (AUS) 7-6 (12-10) 6-2 (1996-First Round)
	— 22 Miss Miss E. Dominikovic (AUS) bt Miss L. Nemeckova (CZE) 6-7 (10-12) 6-2 6-1 (2000-First Round)
Ladies' Doubles	— 20 Mrs. D. Parker and Miss J. Plackett (GBR) bt Miss M.R. Collins and Miss S.J. Leach (GBR) 7-6 (11-9) 6-4 (1984-First Round)
	— 20 Miss C. Copeland (USA) and Miss B.M. Perry (NZL) bt Miss D. Castillejo (PHI) and Miss M. Dewouters (BEL) 6-2 7-6 (11-9) (1985-First Round)
Mixed Doubles	— 26 L. Scott (USA) and Miss J. Zambryzcki (BRA) bt P. Wright and Miss L. Antonoplis (USA) 6-2 7-6 (14-12) (1989-Second Round)

The following players won through the three Competitions (1925–1991) in the same year: Gentleman (6): R.M. Turnbull (GBR), 1955 –R.T. Potter (AUS), 1962 –W.W. Bowrey (AUS), 1963 –A.K. Carpenter (CAN), 1975 –B.M. Mitton (RSA), 1981 –T.C. Fancutt (AUS). Ladies (7): 1927 –Miss M.P. Davies (GBR), 1930 –Miss M. Johnstone (GBR), 1958 –Mrs. I.J. Warwick (GBR), 1963 –Miss M.B.H. McAnally (GBR), 1982 –Miss K.A. Steinmetz (USA), 1983 –Miss B. Randall (AUS), 1989 – Miss K. Radford (AUS).

The following players competed in the Singles Competitions, previous to becoming Champions: Gentleman: 1928 –S.B.B. Wood (USA), 1929 –F.J. Perry (GBR), 1956 –R.G. Laver (AUS), 1984 –B.F. Becker (GER), 1988 –G.S. Ivanisevic (YUG), N.A. Fraser (AUS), 1974 and Pat Cash (AUS), 1997, played in the Singles Competition after becoming Champion]. Ladies: 1928 –Miss D.E. Round (GBR), 1962 –Miss S.V. Wade (GBR), 1986 – Miss J. Novotna (TCH).

In the Gentlemen's Singles Competition the only occasion a 6-0 6-0 6-0 occurred was when T.A. Woodbridge (AUS) beat J. Ortegren (SWE) in the qualifying round in 2001.

G. Muller (RSA) served 51 aces against P.Lundgren (SWE) in the first round match of the Qualifying Singles in 1993.

Wild Cards

Wild Cards are players without high enough world ranking to go straight into the draw but are specially nominated by the Committee, usually because of past performances at Wimbledon or to increase British interest. Wild Cards have been allocated to The Championship draws from 1977 and to the Qualifying competitions from 1981.

From 2003, a number of the Gentlemen's and Ladies' singles Wild Cards, allocated to the Championship draw, were decided by play-off competitions, held two weeks before The Championships. In 2003 a restricted draw for the events took place, but from 2004 to 2006 a 24-draw for both singles events comprised of 20 direct acceptances dependent on World Ranking, and four Wild Cards decided by LTA. The winner of each event was guaranteed a place in The Championship draw. Prize money was awarded. These events were only open to British players. The procedure was abandoned after 2006 and reverted to the system of Wild Cards being allocated directly by the Committee.

Since 1981 Wild Cards have been allocated to the Qualifying Competitions. From 2007 a number of Gentlemen's and Ladies' Singles Wild Cards allocated to the Qualifying draws has been decided by play-off competitions, held two weeks before The Championships.

Play-off Competitions for The Championship Singles Draw.

Years	Venue	Gentlemen's Singles		Ladies' Singles	
		Entries	Wild Cards	Entries	Wild Cards
2003	Raynes Park	8	3	4	1
2004	Raynes Park	24	3	24	2
2005	Raynes Park	24	1	24	3
2006	Raynes Park	24	3	24	1

Prize Money

Years	Winners	Runners-up	Third place	Fourth place
2003	Nil	Nil	Nil	Nil
2004	£1,000	£750	£500	£250
2005	£1,000	£750	£500	£250
2006	£1,000	£750	£500	£250

Play-off Competitions for the Qualifying Singles Draw.

Years	Venue	Gentlemen's Singles		Ladies' Singles	
		Entries	Wild Cards	Entries	Wild Cards
2007	Raynes Park	32	4	16	4
2008	Aorangi Park	16	2	16	2
2009	Aorangi Park	16	3	16	2
2010	Aorangi Park	16	2	16	4
2011	Aorangi Park	16	2	16	2

Years	Venue	Gentlemen's Singles		Ladies' Singles	
		Entries	Wild Cards	Entries	Wild Cards
2012	Aorangi Park	16	2	16	2
2013	Aorangi Park	16	2	16	2
2014	Aorangi Park	16	2	16	2
2015	Aorangi Park	16	2	16	2

Prize Money

2007	Semi-finalists	£625
2008–2015		Nil

Gentlemen's Singles Championship

1977
(8) P. Dominguez (FRA), R.W Drysdale (GBR), A.M. Jarrett (GBR), A.H. Lloyd (GBR), D.A. Lloyd (GBR), R.D. Ralston (USA), J.R. Smith (GBR), M.D. Wayman (GBR).

1978
(8) C.E. Bradnam (GBR), J.W. Feaver (GBR), R.A.J. Hewitt (RSA), A.M. Jarrett (GBR), D.A. Lloyd (GBR), J.G. Paish (GBR), J.R. Smith (GBR), F.S. Stolle (AUS).

1979
(8) R.W. Drysdale (GBR), I. El Shafei (UAR), J.W. Feaver (GBR), A.M. Jarrett (GBR), R.A. Lewis (GBR), D.A. Lloyd (GBR), J.R. Smith (GBR), R. Taylor (GBR).

1980
(8) E.C. Drysdale (RSA), R.W. Drysdale (GBR), J.W Feaver (GBR), A.M. Jarrett (GBR), R.A. Lewis (GBR), J.M.Lloyd (GBR), J.R. Smith (GBR), R. Taylor (GBR).

1981
(8) J.G. Alexander (AUS), M. Cox (GBR), R.W. Drysdale (GBR), J.W. Feaver (GBR), A.M. Jarrett (GBR), J. Kodes (TCH), R.A. Lewis (GBR), J.M. Lloyd (GBR).

1982
(8) M.J. Bates (GBR), N. Brown (GBR), J.W. Feaver (GBR), P.B. Fleming (USA), A. Gomez (ECU), A.M. Jarrett (GBR), J.M. Lloyd (GBR), J.R. Smith (GBR).

1983
(8) V. Amritraj (IND), S.M. Bale (GBR), M.J. Bates (GBR), C.E. Bradnam (GBR), A.M. Jarrett (GBR), R.A. Lewis (GBR), J.M. Lloyd (GBR), J.R. Smith (GBR).

1984
(8) S.M. Bale (GBR), M.J. Bates (GBR), J.W. Feaver (GBR), N.A. Fulwood (GBR), R.A. Lewis (GBR), S.M. Shaw (GBR), J.R. Smith (GBR), R.L. Stockton (USA).

1985
(8) L. Alfred (GBR), S.M. Bale (GBR), M.J. Bates (GBR), S.B. Denton (USA), C. Dowdeswell (GBR), J.M. Goodall (GBR), N.A. Fulwood (GBR), P.B. McNamara (AUS).

1986
(8) S.M. Bale (GBR), S. Botfield (GBR), P.H. Cash (AUS), A.N. Castle (GBR), C. Dowdeswell (GBR), N.A. Fulwood (GBR), S.M. Shaw (GBR), M.T. Walker (GBR).

1987
(8) V. Amritraj (IND), C.B. Bailey (GBR), S.M. Bale (GBR), M.J. Bates (GBR), S. Botfield (GBR), A.N. Castle (GBR), N.A. Fulwood (GBR), S.M. Shaw (GBR).

1988
(8) C.B. Bailey (GBR), S. Botfield (GBR), D.C. Felgate (GBR), N.A. Fulwood (GBR), J.M. Goodall (GBR), M.R.J. Petchey (GBR), S.M. Shaw (GBR), R.A.W. Whichello (GBR).

1989
(8) C.B. Bailey (GBR), M.J. Bates (GBR), S. Botfield (GBR), N. Brown (GBR), A.N. Castle (GBR), K.E. Flach (USA), M.R.J. Petchey (GBR), J.M. Turner (GBR).

1990
(8) C.B. Bailey (GBR), N. Brown (GBR), P.H. Cash (AUS), A.N. Castle (GBR), M.R.J. Petchey (GBR), D.E. Sapsford (GBR), J.M. Turner (GBR), M.R. Woodforde (AUS).

1991
(8) M.J. Bates (GBR), N. Brown (GBR), A.N. Castle (GBR), J.S. Connors (USA), M.R.J. Petchey (GBR), J.R. Pugh (USA), D.E. Sapsford (GBR), C. Wilkinson (GBR).

1992
(8) C.B. Bailey (GBR), P.H. Cash (AUS), A.N. Castle (GBR), A.L. Foster (GBR), H. Leconte (FRA), A.L. Richardson (GBR), M.R.J. Petchey (GBR), C. Wilkinson (GBR).

1993
(8) C.B. Bailey (GBR), S.C.S. Cole (GBR), J.B. Fitzgerald (AUS), A.L. Foster (GBR), R.S. Matheson (GBR), C.M. Maclagan (GBR), M.R.J. Petchey (GBR), C. Wilkinson (GBR).

1994
(8) C.B. Bailey (GBR), B.A. Cowan (GBR), A.L. Foster (GBR), N. Gould (GBR), T.H. Henman (GBR), C.M. Maclagan (GBR), T. Muster (AUT), C. Wilkinson (GBR).

1995
(8) P.H. Cash (AUS), B.A. Cowan (GBR), G. Henderson (GBR), T.H. Henman (GBR), R.S. Matheson (GBR), C.M. Maclagan (GBR), D.E. Sapsford (GBR), C. Wilkinson (GBR).

1996
(8) M.J. Bates (GBR), C. Beecher (GBR), A.L. Foster (GBR), N. Gould (GBR), L. Milligan (GBR), M.R.J. Petchey (GBR), D.E. Sapsford (GBR), C. Wilkinson (GBR).

1997
(8) J. Delgado (GBR), M. Lee (GBR), L. Milligan (GBR), M.R.J. Petchey (GBR), A.L. Richardson (GBR), D.E. Sapsford (GBR), N. Weal (GBR)*, C. Wilkinson (GBR).
*Replaced F. Dewulf (BEL), who was accepted into the main Championship draw.

1998
(8) B.A. Cowan (GBR), M. Lee (GBR), M.R.J. Petchey (GBR), A.L. Richardson (GBR), M. Safin (RUS), D.E. Sapsford (GBR), D. Wheaton (USA), C. Wilkinson (GBR).

1999
(8) B.A. Cowan (GBR), R. Federer (SUI), M. Filippini (URU), M. Lee (GBR), C.M. Maclagan (GBR) L. Milligan (GBR), T. Spinks (GBR), C. Wilkinson (GBR).

2000
(8) M.S. Bhupathi (IND), B.A. Cowan (GBR), J. Delgado (GBR), M. Lee (GBR), C.M. MacLagan (GBR), A. Parmar (GBR), T.A. Woodbridge (AUS), M.R. Woodforde (AUS).

2001
(8) L. Childs (GBR), B.A. Cowan (GBR), J Delgado (GBR), M. Hilton (GBR), G.S. Ivanisevic (CRO), M. Lee (GBR), A. Parmar (GBR), K. Pless (DEN).

2002
(8) J. Auckland (GBR),* A. Bogdanovic (GBR), B.A. Cowan (GBR), J. Delgado (GBR), A. Mackin (GBR), P-H. Mathieu (FRA), A. Parmar (GBR), M.A. Philippoussis (AUS). *Withdrew – injury.

2003
(8) L. Childs (GBR)+, A. Mackin (GBR), A. Parmar (GBR), A. Bogdanovic (GBR), R. Bloomfield (GBR)+, M. Lee (GBR), M. Hilton (GBR), J. Delgado (GBR)+. + via play-off competition.

2004
(8) A. Bogdanovic (GBR), R. Bloomfield (GBR)+, L. Childs (GBR), M.A. Hilton+ (GBR), J. Marray (GBR), A. Parmar (GBR)+, T. Reid (AUS), G. Rusedski (GBR). *+via play-off competition..*

2005
(8) J.R. Blake (USA), A. Bogdanovic (GBR)+, J. Goodall (GBR), A.R. Mackin (GBR), J. Marray (GBR), A. Murray (GBR), M.A. Phillippoussis (AUS), D. Sherwood (GBR). *+via play-off competition.*

2006
(8) J. Baker (GBR), R. Bloomfield (GBR), R Bogdanovic (GBR), J. Delgado (GBR)+, M. Lee (GBR)+, A.R. Macklin (GBR)+, A. Pavel (ROM), M.A. Phillippousis (AUS). *+via play-off competition.*

2007
(8) J. Baker (GBR), R. Bloomfield (GBR), R Bogdanovic (GBR), T. de Bakker (NED), M. Cilic (CRO), J. Goodall (GBR), J. Marray (GBR), J-W. Tsonga (FRA).

2008
(4) J. Baker (GBR), A. Bogdanovic (GBR), J. Cardy (FRA), X. Malisse (BEL).

2009
(7) A. Bogdanovic (GBR), D. Dimitrov (BUL), D. Evans (GBR), J.C. Ferrero (ESP), J. Goodall (GBR), N.P.A. Mahut (FRA), J. Ward (GBR).

2010
(5) J. Baker (GBR), T. Gabashvili (RUS), N. Kiefer (GER), A. Kuznetsov (RUS), K. Nishikori (JAP).

2011
(7) A. Clement (FRA), D. Cox (GBR), D. Evans (GBR), A. Falla (COL), G. Muller (LUX), D. Sela (ISR), J. Ward (GBR).

2012
(8) J. Baker (GBR), D. Goffin (BEL), O. Golding (GBR), J. Goodall (GBR), T. Haas (GER), L.G. Hewitt (AUS), J. Ward (GBR), G. Zemlja (SLO).

2013
(5) M. Ebden (AUS), K. Edmund (GBR), S. Johnson (USA), N. Mahut (FRA), J. Ward (GBR).

2014
(8) M. Baghdatis (CYP), D. Cox (GBR), K. Edmund (GBR), D. Evans (GBR), N. Kyrgios (AUS), D. Smethurst (GBR), J. Vesely (CZE), J. Ward (GBR).

Gentlemen's Doubles Championship

1981
(5) R.C. Beven and J.M. Dier (GBR), R.W. Drysdale and R.A. Lewis (GBR), T.R. Gullikson and R.D. Ralston (USA)*, A.H. Lloyd and J.M. Lloyd (GBR), J.D. Newcombe and A.D. Roche (AUS). *Withdrew.

1982
(5) M.J. Bates and N. Brown (GBR), C. Dowdeswell (ZIM) and R.W. Drysdale (GBR), J.D. Newcombe and A.D. Roche (AUS), T.S. Okker (NED) and M.C. Riessen (USA), T. Whitehead and J.M. Dier (GBR).

1983
(5) V. Amritraj (IND) and R.L. Tanner (USA), M.J. Bates and J.M. Dier (GBR), N. Brown and S.M. Shaw (GBR), A.M. Jarrett and C.J. Mottram (GBR), J.D. Newcombe and A.D. Roche (AUS).

1984
(5) S.M. Bale and R.A. Lewis (GBR), M.J. Bates and J.M. Dier (GBR), C.E. Bradnam and S.M. Shaw (GBR), J.W. Feaver and J.R. Smith (GBR), M. Kratzmann and S. Youl (AUS).

1985
(5) S.M. Bale and R.A. Lewis (GBR), M.J. Bates and J.W. Feaver (GBR), C. Dowdeswell and S.M. Shaw (GBR), D.C. Felgate and N. Brown (GBR), P.B. McNamara and P.F. McNamee (AUS).

1986
(4) M.J. Bates and N.A. Fulwood (GBR), N. Brown and J.R. Smith (GBR), A.N. Castle and J.M. Turner (GBR), J.M. Goodall and R.A.W. Whichello (GBR).

1987
(5) M.J. Bates and A.N. Castle (GBR), S. Botfield and M.T. Walker (GBR), D.C. Felgate and J.M. Goodall (GBR), T.E. Gullikson and T.R. Gullikson (USA), J.M. Lloyd and S.M. Shaw (GBR).

1988
(5) C.B. Bailey and M.R.J. Petchey (GBR), D.C. Felgate and N.A. Fulwood (GBR), H.P. Guenthardt (SUI) and B. Taroczy (HUN), J.M. Lloyd and S.M. Shaw (GBR), A. Olkhovsky and A. Volkov (URS).

1989
(5) V. Amritraj (IND) and C.B. Bailey (GBR), S. Botfield and J.M. Turner (GBR), N. Brown and N.A. Fulwood (GBR), D.C. Felgate and J.M. Goodall (GBR), J.M. Lloyd and S.M. Shaw (GBR).

1990
(5) C.B. Bailey and D.P. Ison (GBR), S. Botfield and J.M. Turner (GBR), N.A. Fulwood (GBR) and P. Lundgren (SWE), J.M. Goodall and U. Nganga (GBR), M.R.J. Petchey and D.E. Sapsford (GBR).

1991
(5) S. Botfield and J.M. Turner (GBR), N.A. Fulwood and D.E. Sapsford (GBR), P.T. Hand and C. Wilkinson (GBR), D.P. Ison and M.R.J. Petchey (GBR), G.S. Ivanisevic (YUG) and J.P. McEnroe (USA).

1992
(6) C.B. Bailey and C. Wilkinson (GBR), M.J. Bates (GBR) and C.J. Van Rensburg (RSA), N. Brown and A.L. Richardson (GBR), A.N. Castle and C.M. Maclagan (GBR), A.L. Foster and D.E. Sapsford (GBR), D.P. Ison and M.R.J. Petchey (GBR).

1993
(5) C.B. Bailey and T.H. Henman (GBR), S.C.S. Cole and C.M. Maclagan (GBR), A.L. Foster and M.R.J. Petchey (GBR), P.T. Hand and C. Wilkinson (GBR), R.S. Matheson and A.L. Richardson (GBR).

1994
(5) C.B. Bailey (GBR) and G. Rusedski (CAN), B.A. Cowan and A.L. Richardson (GBR), P.T. Hand and C. Wilkinson (GBR), T.H. Henman and M.R.J. Petchey (GBR), A.L. Foster and C.M. Maclagan (GBR).

1995
(6) M.J. Bates and T.H. Henman (GBR), B.A. Cowan and A.L. Richardson (GBR), K.E. Flach and R.A. Seguso (USA), A.L. Foster and D.E. Sapsford (GBR), P.T. Hand and R.S. Matheson (GBR), M.R.J. Petchey and C. Wilkinson (GBR).

1996
(5) M.R.J. Petchey and D.E. Sapsford (GBR), A.L. Foster and P.T. Hand (GBR), M.J. Bates and C. Wilkinson (GBR), J. Delgado and L. Milligan (GBR), R.S. Matheson and T. Spinks (GBR).

1997
(5) M.R.J. Petchey and A.L. Richardson (GBR), D.E. Sapsford and C. Wilkinson (GBR), J. Delgado and A.L. Foster (GBR), M. Lee and J.M. Trotman (GBR), B.A. Cowan and N. Weal (GBR), J. Siemerink (NED) and J.R. Stoltenberg (AUS).

1998
(5) B.A. Cowan and T. Spinks (GBR), J. Delgado and A.L. Foster (GBR), N. Gould and M.R.J. Petchey (GBR), C.M. Maclagan and A.L. Richardson (GBR), L. Milligan and A. Parmar (GBR).

1999
(6) L. Childs and S. Dickson (GBR), B.A. Cowan (GBR) and W. Whitehouse (RSA), C.M. Maclagan and A. Parmar (GBR), D.E. Sapsford and C. Wilkinson (GBR), D. Sherwood and T. Spinks (GBR), R. Federer (SUI) and L.G. Hewitt (AUS).

2000
(5) N.P. Broad and A. Parmar (GBR), B.A. Cowan and K. Spencer (GBR), J. Davidson and O. Freelove (GBR), J. Delgado and M. Lee (GBR), M. Hilton and J. Nelson (GBR).

2001
(7) L. Childs and J. Nelson (GBR), B.A. Cowan and J. Delgado (GBR), A. Clement and N. Escude (FRA), O. Freelove and K. Spencer (GBR), M. Lee and A. Parmar (GBR) M.N. Mirnyi and V. Voltchkov (BLR), M. Rosset (SUI) and M.M. Safin (RUS).

2002
(7) J. Auckland and R. Hutchins (GBR),* L. Childs and M. Hilton (GBR), B.A. Cowan and J. Delgado (GBR), J.C. Ferrero and T. Robredo (ESP), M. Lee and A. Parmar (GBR), J. Marray and D. Sherwood (GBR), L. Milligan and K. Spencer (GBR).
*Withdrew.

2003
(7) R. Bloomfield and M.A. Hilton (GBR), A. Lopez-Moron and F. Mantilla (ESP), J. Auckland and L. Childs (GBR), J. Delgado and A. Parmar (GBR), J. Marray and D. Sherwood (GBR), G. Lapentti and N.A. Lapentti (ECU), M. Lee and M. Maclagan (GBR).

2004
(6) J. Auckland and L. Childs (GBR), A. Banks and A. Bogdanovic (GBR), J. Delgado and A. Parmar (GBR), I. Flanagan and M. Lee (GBR), M.A. Hilton and J. Marray (GBR), D. Kiernan and D. Sherwood (GBR).

2005
(6) J. Auckland and D. Kiernan (GBR), A.M. Banks and A.R. Mackin (GBR), R. Barker and
W. Barker (GBR), A. Bogdanovic and J. Goodall (GBR), J. Delgado and A. Parmar (GBR),
M.A. Hilton and J. Marray (GBR), A. Murray and D. Sherwood (GBR).

2006
(5) J. Auckland and J. Delgado (GBR), L. Childs (GBR) and A Pavel (ROM)*, C. Fleming and
J. Murray (GBR), J. Goodall and R. Hutchins (GBR), M. Lee and J. Marray (GBR).
* *withdrew*

2007
(5) J. Baker and A. Bogdanovic (GBR), N. Bamford and J. May (GBR), R. Bloomfield and J.
Marray (GBR), L. Childs and J. Delgado (GBR), J. Goodall and R. Hutchins (GBR).

2008
(5) J. Auckland and J. Delgado (GBR), N. Bamford and J. Goodall (GBR), R. Bloomfield and
K. Skupski (GBR), A. Bogdanovic and J. Marray (GBR), C. Eaton and A. Slabinsky (GBR).

2009
(5) J. Auckland and J. Goodall (GBR), A. Bogdanovic and J. Ward (GBR), J. Delgado and J.
Marray (GBR), C. Fleming and K. Skupski (GBR), M. Llodra and N.P.A. Mahut (FRA).

2010
(4) A. Bogdanovic and A. Slabinsky (GBR), J. Delgado and J. Goodall (GBR), C. Eaton and D.
Inglot (GBR), J. Marray and J. Murray (GBR).

2011
(3) D. Cox and J. Ward (GBR), C. Eaton and J. Goodall (GBR), L. Hewitt (AUS) and P. Moser
(GER).
Note: J. Delgado and J. Marray (GBR) and C. Fleming and R. Hutchins (GBR) were originally selected as
wild cards.

2012
(5) L. Broady and O. Golding (GBR), J. Delgado and K. Skupski (GBR), J.Goodall and J. Ward
(GBR), C. Guccione and L.G. Hewitt (AUS), J.F. Marray (GBR) and F.L. Nielsen (DEN).

2013
(3) J. Baker and K. Edmund (GBR), L. Hewitt (AUS) and M. Knowles (BAH), D. Rice and S.
Thornley (GBR).

2014
(5) E. Corrie and D. Smethurst (GBR), J. Delgado (GBR) and G. Muller (LUX), K. Edmund
(GBR) and S. Stakhovsky (UKR), D. Evans and J. Ward (GBR), C. Fleming and R. Hutchins
(GBR).

Ladies' Singles Championship

1977
(6) Miss J.M. Durie (GBR), Miss A.E. Hobbs (GBR), Miss S.E. Saliba (AUS), Mrs. J.R. Susman (USA), Miss B.R. Thompson (GBR), Mrs. K.Wooldridge (GBR).

1978
(6) Mrs. W.W. Bowrey (AUS), Miss J.M. Durie (GBR), Miss J.A. Fayter (GBR), Miss A.E. Hobbs (GBR), Miss L.J. Mottram (GBR), Mrs. K. Wooldridge (GBR).

1979
(6) Miss M. Carillo (USA), Miss G.L. Coles (GBR), Miss A.P. Cooper (GBR), Miss J.M. Durie (GBR), Miss D.A. Jevans (GBR), Miss B.R. Thompson (GBR).

1980
(6) Miss K.J. Brasher (GBR), Miss L.J. Charles (GBR), Miss A.P. Cooper (GBR), Miss L. Geeves (GBR), Miss D.A. Jevans (GBR), Miss S.L. Rollinson (RSA).

1981
(6) Miss K.J. Brasher (GBR), Miss R. Casals (USA), Miss L.J. Charles (GBR), Miss G.L. Coles (GBR), Miss A.P. Cooper (GBR), Miss D.A. Jevans (GBR).

1982
(6) Miss K.J. Brasher (GBR), Miss A.N. Croft (GBR), Miss Z.L. Garrison (USA), Miss E.S. Jones (GBR), Miss E.D. Lightbody (GBR), Miss S.A. Walpole (GBR).

1983
(8) Miss K.J. Brasher (GBR), Miss A.J. Brown (GBR), Miss A.N. Croft (GBR), Miss C.J. Drury (GBR), Miss R.L. Einy (GBR), Miss S.L. Gomer (GBR), Miss R. Mentz (RSA), Miss J.A. Salmon (GBR).

1984
(8) Miss K.J. Brasher (GBR), Miss R.L. Einy (GBR), Miss S.L. Gomer (GBR), Miss J. Louis (GBR), Miss S.T. Mair (GBR), Miss S.E. Reeves (GBR), Miss J.A. Salmon (GBR), Miss S.A. Walpole (GBR).

1985
(8) Miss K.J. Brasher (GBR), Miss R.L. Einy (GBR), Miss J. Louis (GBR), Miss S.E. Reeves (GBR), Miss J.A. Salmon (GBR), Miss A.E. Smith (USA), Miss J.M. Tacon (GBR), Miss C.J. Wood (GBR).

1986
(8) Miss B.A. Borneo (GBR), Miss G.L. Coles (GBR), Miss A.L. Grunfeld (GBR), Miss J. Louis (GBR), Miss D. Parnell (GBR), Miss S.E. Reeves (GBR), Miss J.A. Salmon (GBR), Miss J.M. Tacon (GBR).

1987
(8) Miss T.A. Catlin (GBR), Miss L.C. Gould (GBR), Miss A.L. Grunfeld (GBR), Miss V. Lake (GBR), Miss J. Louis (GBR), Miss J.A. Salmon (GBR), Miss C.J. Wood (GBR), Miss J.V. Wood (GBR).

1988
(8) Miss T.A. Catlin (GBR), Miss L.C. Gould (GBR), Miss A.L. Grunfeld (GBR), Miss V. Lake (GBR), Miss S.J. Loosemore (GBR), Miss J.A. Salmon (GBR), Miss A. Simpkin (GBR), Miss C.J. Wood (GBR).

1989
(8) Miss A.L. Grunfeld (GBR), Miss A.E. Hobbs (GBR), Miss V. Lake (GBR), Miss J.A. Salmon (GBR), Miss A. Simpkin (GBR), Miss S.L. Smith (GBR), Miss W.M. Turnbull (AUS), Miss C.J. Wood (GBR).

1990
(8) Miss B.A. Borneo (GBR), Miss J.M. Durie (GBR), Miss S.L. Gomer (GBR), Miss K. Jordan (USA), Miss J.A. Salmon (GBR), Miss A. Simpkin (GBR), Miss S.L. Smith (GBR), Miss C.J. Wood (GBR).

1991
(8) Miss S.L. Bentley (GBR), Miss B.A. Borneo (GBR), Miss B. Griffiths (GBR), Miss A.L. Grunfeld (GBR), Miss V.S. Humphreys-Davies (GBR), Miss K.D. Hand (GBR), Miss S.J. Loosemore (GBR), Miss J.A. Salmon (GBR).

1992
(8) Miss S.L. Bentley (GBR), Miss A.L. Grunfeld (GBR), Miss C. Hall (GBR), Miss V.S. Humphreys-Davies (GBR), Miss V. Lake (GBR), Miss S.J. Loosemore (GBR), Miss S-A. Siddall (GBR), Miss C.J. Wood (GBR).

1993
(8) Miss K.M. Cross (GBR), Miss A.L. Grunfeld (GBR), Miss C. Hall (GBR), Miss M. Javer (GBR), Miss S-A. Siddall (GBR), Miss A.M.H. Wainwright (GBR), Miss C.J. Wood (GBR), Miss L.A. Woodroffe (GBR).

1994
(8) Miss K.M. Cross (GBR), Miss J.M. Durie (GBR), Miss M. Javer (GBR), Miss J.M. Pullin (GBR), Miss S-A. Siddall (GBR), Miss C. Taylor (GBR), Miss A.M.H. Wainwright (GBR), Miss J. Ward (GBR).

1995
(8) Miss K.M. Cross (GBR), Miss J.M. Durie (GBR), Miss E.E. Jelfs (GBR), Miss M. Miller (GBR), Mrs. R. Nideffer (RSA), Miss J.M. Pullin (GBR), Miss S-A. Siddall (GBR), Miss C.J. Wood (GBR).

1996
(8) Miss M. Miller (GBR), Mrs. K.S. Rinaldi Stunkel (USA), Miss S.L. Smith (GBR), Miss P.H. Shriver (USA), Miss C. Taylor (GBR), Miss R. Viollett (GBR), Miss J. Ward (GBR), Miss C.J. Wood (GBR).

1997
(8) Miss L.A. Ahl (GBR), Miss G. (B.C.) Fernandez (USA), Miss J.M. Pullin (GBR), Miss S-A. Siddall (GBR), Miss S.L. Smith (GBR), Miss C. Taylor (GBR), Miss C.J Wood (GBR), Miss L.A. Woodroffe (GBR).

1998
(8) Miss J.M. Capriati (USA), Miss K.M. Cross (GBR), Miss L. Latimer (GBR), Miss L.M. McNeil (USA), Miss J.M. Pullin (GBR), Miss S.L. Smith (GBR), Miss J. Ward (GBR), Miss L.A. Woodroffe (GBR).

1999
(8) Miss L.A. Ahl (GBR), Miss K.M. Cross (GBR), Miss L. Latimer (GBR), Miss J.M. Pullin (GBR), Miss B. Schwartz (AUT), Miss A. Tordoff (GBR)*, Miss. J. Ward (GBR), Miss L.A. Woodroffe (GBR).
*Replaced Miss J.M. Capriati (USA).

2000

(8) Miss L.A. Ahl (GBR), Miss H. Collin (GBR), Miss K.M. Cross (GBR), Miss L. Latimer (GBR), Miss J.M. Pullin (GBR), Miss S.L. Smith (GBR), Miss J. Ward (GBR), Miss L.A. Woodroffe (GBR).

2001

(8) Miss L.A. Ahl (GBR), Miss E. Baltacha (GBR), Miss H. Collin (GBR), Miss A.V. Keothavong (GBR), Miss L. Latimer (GBR), Miss J.M. Pullin (GBR), Miss A.W. Stevenson (USA), Miss L.A. Woodroffe (GBR).

2002

(6) Miss L.A. Ahl (GBR), Miss E. Baltacha (GBR), Miss H. Collin (GBR), Miss A.V. Keothavong (GBR), Miss J. O'Donoghue (GBR), Miss J.M. Pullin (GBR), Miss R. Viollet (GBR), Miss N.M. Zvereva (BLR).

2003

(8) Miss J.M. Pullin (GBR)+, Miss C. Morariu (Mrs A. Turcinovich (USA), Miss J. O'Donoghue (GBR), Miss E. Baltacha (GBR), Miss M. Sharapova (RUS), Miss S. Stosur (AUS), Miss A.V. Keothavong (GBR), Miss L.A. Ahl (GBR).
+ via play-off competition.

2004

(8) Miss E. Baltacha (GBR), Miss A. Janes (GBR), Miss A.V. Keothavong (GBR), Miss M. Navratilova (USA), Miss K. O'Brien (GBR)+, Miss J. O'Donaghue (GBR), Miss P. Schnyder (Mrs. R. Hofmann) (SUI), Miss E. Webley-Smith (GBR)+.
+*via play-off competition.*

2005

(8) Miss E. Baltacha (GBR), Miss C.C. Black (ZIM), Miss S. Borwell (GBR)*+, Miss A. Janes (GBR), Miss A.V. Keothavong (GBR), Miss R. Llewellyn (GBR)+, Miss K. O'Brien (GBR), Miss J. O'Donohue (GBR)+.
* *replaced Miss M. Krajicek (NED).*
+*via play-off competition.*

2006

(8) Miss C.C. Black (ZIM)*, Miss S. Borwell (GBR), Miss N. Cavaday (GBR)+, Miss A.V. Keothavong (GBR), Miss A. Molik (AUS), Miss K. O'Brien (GBR), Miss M. South (GBR), Miss A. Radwanska (POL).
* *replaced Miss V. Azarenka (BLR).*
+*via play-off competition.*

2007

(8) Miss E. Baltacha (GBR), Miss N. Cavaday (GBR), Miss A.V. Keothavong (GBR), Miss V. Kutuzova (UKR), Miss K. O'Brien (GBR), Miss A. Pavlyuchenkova (RUS), Miss M. South (GBR), Miss C. Wozniacki (DEN).

2008

(8) Miss E. Baltacha (GBR), Miss N. Cavaday (GBR), Miss K. O'Brien (GBR), Miss U. Radwanska (POL), Miss M. South (GBR), Miss C. Suarez Navarro (ESP), Miss S. Stosur (AUS), Miss J. Zheng (CHN).

2009

(5) Miss E. Baltacha (GBR), Mrs K. Date-Krumm (JPN), Miss A. Glatch (USA), Miss M. Larcher de Brito (POR), Miss K. O'Brien (GBR), Miss L.M. Robson (GBR), Miss M. South (GBR), Miss G. Stoop (GBR).

2010
(7) Miss N. Lertcheewakarn (THA), Miss K. O'Brien (GBR), Miss A. Riske (USA), Miss L.M.D. Robson (GBR), Miss C.C. Scheepers (RSA), Miss M. South (GBR), Miss H. Watson (GBR).

2011
(7) Miss N. Broady (GBR), Miss E. Daniilidou (GER), Miss S. Lisicki (GER), Miss K. O'Brien (GBR), Miss L.M.D. Robson (GBR), Miss H. Watson (GBR), Miss E. Webley-Smith (GBR).

2012
(7) Miss A. Barty (AUS), Miss N. Broady (GBR), Miss J. Konta (GBR), Miss M. Oudin (USA), Miss V. Razzano (FRA), Miss L.M.D. Robson (GBR), Miss Y. Shvedova (KAZ), (Miss H. Watson (GBR) was originally in the list)

2013
(8) Miss E. Baltacha (GBR), Miss L. Hradecka (CZE), Miss A. Keothavong (GBR), Miss J. Konta (GBR), Miss T. Moore (GBR), Miss S. Murray (GBR), Miss A. Petkovic (GER), Miss A. Riske (USA).

2014
(8) Miss N. Broady (GBR), Miss J. Gajdosova (AUS), Miss T. Moore (GBR), Miss S. Murray (GBR), Miss K. Pliskova (CZE), Miss S. Soler-Espinosa (ESP), Miss T. Townsend (USA), Miss V. Zvonareva (RUS).

Ladies' Doubles Championship

1982
(2) Miss D. Jevans and Miss E. Jones (GBR), Miss S.L. Gomer and Miss J.A. Salmon (GBR).

1983
(2) Miss A.J. Brown and Miss R.L. Einy (GBR), Miss S.L. Gomer and Miss J.A. Salmon (GBR).

1984
(2) Miss L.C. Gracie and Miss E.S. Jones (GBR), Mrs. J.M. Lloyd (USA) and Miss C. Tanvier (FRA).

1985
(4) Miss B.A. Borneo and Miss J.M. Tacon (GBR), Miss R.L. Einy and Miss L.C. Gracie (GBR), Miss S.L. Gomer and Miss J.A. Salmon (GBR), Miss S.M. Graf (GER) and Miss A.E. Smith (USA).

1986
(4) Miss B.A. Borneo and Miss V. Lake (GBR), Miss A.J. Brown and Miss J.M. Tacon (GBR), Miss L.C. Gracie and Miss J.A. Salmon (GBR), Miss J. Louis and Miss J.V. Wood (GBR).

1987
(5) Miss C.L. Billingham and Miss K.F. Hunter (GBR), Miss B.A. Borneo and Miss J.A. Salmon (GBR), Miss B.J. Cordwell (NZL) and Miss A.L. Minter (AUS), Miss S.L. Gomer (GBR) and Miss M. Jaggard (AUS), Miss V. Lake and Miss C.J. Wood (GBR).

1988
(4) Miss S. Godman and Miss A.M. Niepel (GBR), Miss S.L. Gomer and Miss J.A. Salmon (GBR), Miss V. Lake and Miss C.J. Wood (GBR), Miss A. Simpkin and Miss J.M. Tacon (GBR).

1989
(4) Miss B.A. Borneo and Miss C.J. Wood (GBR), Miss S.L. Gomer and Miss J.A. Salmon (GBR), Miss A.L. Grunfeld and Miss J. Louis (GBR), Miss J. Holden and Miss C. Pollard (GBR).

1990
(4) Miss B.A. Borneo and Miss C.J. Wood (GBR), Miss S.L. Gomer and Miss J.A. Salmon (GBR), Miss M. Javer and Miss A.H. White (GBR), Miss S.J. Loosemore and Miss A. Simpkin (GBR).

1991
(4) Miss S.L. Gomer and Miss V. Lake (GBR), Miss A.L. Grunfeld and Miss S.J. Loosemore (GBR), Miss K.D. Hand and Miss J.A. Salmon (GBR), Miss M. Javer and Miss S.L. Smith (GBR).

1992
(4) Mrs. R.D. Fairbank-Nideffer (RSA) and Miss B. (H.E.) Nagelsen (USA), Miss A.L. Grunfeld and Miss J.A. Salmon (GBR), Miss C. Hall and Miss S-A. Siddall (GBR), Miss M. Javer and Miss V. Lake (GBR).

1993
(3) Miss A.L. Grunfeld and Miss J.A. Salmon (GBR), Miss V. Lake and Miss C.J. Wood (GBR), Miss J.M. Pullin and Miss L.A. Woodroffe (GBR).

1994
(4) Miss J.M. Durie (GBR) and Miss L. Field (AUS), Miss J.M. Pullin and Miss L.A. Woodroffe (GBR), Miss S-A. Siddall and Miss A.M.H. Wainwright (GBR), Miss C. Taylor and Miss J. Ward (GBR).

1995
(3) Miss E.L. Bond and Miss J. Moore (GBR), Miss J.M. Pullin and Miss L.A. Woodroffe (GBR), Miss S-A. Siddall and Miss A.M.H. Wainwright (GBR).

1996
(4) Miss H.E. (B) Nagelsen and Miss M. Seles (USA), Miss V. Lake and Miss S.L. Smith (GBR), Miss S-A. Siddall and Miss A.M.H. Wainright (GBR), Miss H. Crook and Miss V.E. Davies (GBR).

1997
(4) Miss J.M. Pullin and Miss L.A. Woodroffe (GBR), Miss S-A. Siddall and Miss A.M.H. Wainwright (GBR), Miss C. Taylor and Miss J.Ward (GBR), Miss O. Barabanschikova (BLR) and Miss S.L. Smith (GBR).

1998
(4) Miss L.A. Ahl and Miss A.M.H. Wainwright (GBR), Miss H. Crook and Miss V.E. Davies (GBR), Miss K.M. Cross and Miss L. Latimer (GBR), Miss S.L. Smith and Miss J. Ward (GBR).

1999
(4) Miss H. Crook and Miss V.E. Davies (GBR), Miss K.M. Cross and Miss J. Ward (GBR), Miss J.M. Pullin and Miss L.A. Woodroffe (GBR), Miss S. De Beer (RSA) and Miss S.L. Smith (GBR).

2000
(4) Miss M. de Swardt (RSA) and Miss M. Navratilova (USA), Miss L. Latimer and Miss S.L. Smith (GBR), Miss J.M. Pullin and Miss L.A. Woodroffe (GBR), Miss S.J. Williams and Miss V.E.S. Williams (USA)*.
*Won Championship

2001
(4) Miss L.A. Ahl and Miss H. Collin (GBR), Miss E. Baltacha and Miss N. Trinder (GBR), Miss H. Crook and Miss V.E. Davies (GBR), Miss J. Hopkins (USA) and Miss L. Latimer (GBR).

2002
(6) Miss L.A. Ahl and Miss E. Baltacha (GBR), Miss H. Crook and Miss V.E. Davies (GBR), Miss M. Irvin and Miss A.W. Stevenson (USA), Miss A.V. Keothavong and Miss R. Viollet (GBR), Miss J.M. Pullin and Miss L.A. Woodroffe (GBR), Miss S.J. Williams and Miss V.E.S. Williams (USA).*
*Won Championship

2003
(6) Miss A. Janes and Miss A.V. Keothavong (GBR), Miss S.J. Williams and Miss V.E.S. Williams (USA), Miss L.A. Ahl (GBR) and Miss S.J. Sfar (TUN), Miss E. Baltacha and Miss J.M. Pullin (GBR), Miss H. Crook and Miss A. Hawkins (GBR), Miss S. Borwell and Miss J. O'Donoghue (GBR).

2004
(6) Miss E. Baltacha and Miss A. Janes (GBR), Miss S. Borwell and Miss E. Webley-Smith (GBR), Miss H. Collin and Miss A.V. Keothavong (GBR), Miss H.Crook and Miss A.Hawkins (GBR), Miss A.Medina Garrigues and Miss A.I.M. Sanchez-Vicario (Mrs. J. Vehils) (ESP), Miss T. Golovin and Miss M. Pierce (FRA).

2005
(6) Miss E. Baltacha and Miss J. O'Donoghue (GBR), Miss S. Borwell and Miss E. Webley-Smith (GBR), Miss C.S. Curran (GBR) and Miss N. Grandin (RSA), Miss A.Hawkins (GBR) and Miss R. Llewellyn (GBR), Miss A. Janes and Miss A.V. Keothavong (GBR), Miss K. O'Brien and Miss M. South (GBR).

2006
(5) Miss S. Borwell and Miss J. O'Donahue (GBR), C.S. Curran (GBR) and Miss J. Jackson (USA), Mrs A. Keen and Miss A.V. Keothavong (GBR), Miss R. Llewellyn and Miss K. Paterson (GBR), Miss K. O'Brien and Miss M. South (GBR).

2007
(5) Miss E. Baltacha and Miss N. Cavaday (GBR), Miss S. Borwell and Miss J. Curtis (GBR), Miss C.S. Curran and Miss A.V. Keothavong (GBR), Miss K. Paterson and Miss M. South (GBR), Miss S.J. Williams and Miss V.E.S. Williams (USA)*.
*replaced Miss A. Elliot and Miss K. O'Brien (GBR).

2008
(5) Miss E. Baltacha and Miss N. Cavaday (GBR), Miss S. Borwell and Miss J.Rae (GBR), Miss A. Elliott and Miss K. O'Brien (GBR), Miss A.V. Keothavong and Miss M. South (GBR), Miss A. Fitzpatrick and Miss A. Hawkins (GBR).

2009
(5) Miss E. Baltacha and Miss A. Elliott (GBR), Miss N. Cavaday and Miss K. O'Brien (GBR), Miss J. Curtis and Miss A. Smith (GBR), Miss J. Rae and Miss M. South (GBR), Miss L.M.D. Robson and Miss G. Stoop (GBR).

2010
(5) Miss N. Broady and Miss K. O'Brien (GBR), Miss N. Cavaday and Miss A. Smith (GBR), Miss A. Keothavong and Miss M. South (GBR), Miss S. Peers (AUS) and Miss L.M.D. Robson (GBR), Miss J. Rae and Miss H. Watson (GBR).

2011
(3) Miss N. Broady and Miss E. Webley-Smith (GBR), Miss A. Keothavong and Miss L.M.D. Robson (GBR), Miss J. Rae and Miss H. Watson (GBR).

2012
(3) Miss N. Broady and Miss J. Konta (GBR), Miss T. Moore and Miss M. South (GBR), Miss L.M.D. Robson and Miss H. Watson (GBR).

2013
(5) Miss A. Keothavong amd Miss J. Konta (GBR), Miss T. Moore and Miss M. South (GBR), Miss S. Murray and Miss J. Windley (GBR), Miss S. Peer (ISR) and Miss Z. Yan (CHN), Miss N. Slater and Miss L. Whybourn (GBR).

2014
(4) Miss N. Broady (GBR) and Miss E. Daniilidou (GRE), Miss M. Hingis (SUI) and Miss V. Zvonareva (RUS), Miss J. Konta and Miss T. Moore (GBR), Miss J. Rae and Miss A. Smith (GBR).

Mixed Doubles Championship

1982–1985 (no cards allocated)

1986
(7) O.K. Davidson (AUS) and Miss A.N. Croft (GBR), J.W. Feaver and Miss S.V. Wade (GBR), R.A.J. Hewitt (RSA) and Miss M. Werdel (USA), R.A. Lewis and Miss S.L. Gomer (GBR), F.D. McMillan (RSA) and Miss B.F. Stove (NED), J.D. Newcombe and Miss J.G. Thompson (AUS), R.D. Ralston (USA) and Miss C.K. Bassett (CAN).

1987
(4) O.K. Davidson (AUS) and Miss A.N. Croft (GBR), J.W. Feaver and Miss S.V. Wade (GBR), R.D. Ralston and Miss M.J. Fernandez (USA), J.A. Southcombe and Miss S.L. Gomer (GBR).

1988
(6) C.B. Bailey and Miss T.A. Catlin (GBR), K.E. Flach (USA) and Mrs. R.A. Seguso (CAN), N.A. Fulwood and Miss J.A. Salmon (GBR), J.M. Lloyd (GBR) and Miss W.M. Turnbull (AUS), S.M. Shaw (GBR) and Miss C. Lindquist (SWE), P. Slozil (TCH) and Miss S.M. Graf (GER).

1989
(5) D.C. Felgate and Miss C.J. Wood (GBR), N.A. Fulwood and Miss J.A. Salmon (GBR), J.M. Goodall and Miss V. Lake (GBR), J.M. Lloyd (GBR) and Miss W.M. Turnbull (AUS), S.E. Stewart and Miss Z.L. Garrison (USA).

1990
(4) D.P. Ison and Miss A. Simpkin (GBR), N.A. Fulwood and Miss J.A. Salmon (GBR), M.R.J. Petchey and Miss S.J. Loosemore (GBR), S.E. Stewart (USA) and Miss S.L. Smith (GBR).

1991
(5) N.A. Fulwood and Miss S.L. Gomer (GBR), T.S. Mayotte and Miss B.C. Fernandez (USA), M.R.J. Petchey and Miss S.J. Loosemore (GBR), R.A. Seguso (USA) and Mrs. R.A. Bassett-Seguso (CAN), C.J. Van Rensburg and Miss E. Reinach (RSA).

1992
(S) P.T. Annacone and Miss E.M. Burgin (USA), J.A. Frana and Miss G.B. Sabatini (ARG), H.P. Guenthardt (SUI) and Miss S.M. Graf (GER), M.R.J. Petchey and Miss S.J. Loosemore (GBR), C. Wilkinson and Miss S.L. Gomer (GBR).

1993
(5) C.B. Bailey and Miss M. Javer (GBR), A.L. Foster and Miss A.L. Grunfeld (GBR), C.M. Maclagan and Miss A.M.H. Wainwright (GBR), M.R.J. Petchey and Miss C.J. Wood (GBR), C. Wilkinson and Miss J.A. Salmon (GBR).

1994
(5) C.B. Bailey (GBR) and Miss A.I.M. Sanchez Vicario (ESP), A.L. Foster and Miss C. Taylor (GBR), P.T. Hand and Miss V. Lake (GBR), A. Medvedev (UKR) and Miss A. Huber (GER), M.J.R. Petchey and Miss C.J. Wood (GBR).

1995
(5) M.J. Bates and Miss J.M. Durie (GBR), P.T. Hand and Miss V. Lake (GBR), M.R.J. Petchey and Miss C.J. Wood (GBR), D.E. Sapsford and Miss S-A. Siddall (GBR), C. Wilkinson and Miss A.M.H. Wainwright (GBR).

1996
(5) M.J. Bates (GBR) and Mrs. M.R. Bradtke (AUS), P.H. Cash (AUS) and Miss M. Pierce (FRA), D.E. Sapsford and Miss S-A, Siddall (GBR), H.P. Guenthardt (SUI) and Miss S.M. Graf (GER), J.A. Stark and Miss M. Navratilova (USA).

1997
(5) C.J. Van Rensburg (RSA) and Miss V.E.S. Williams (USA), M.R.J. Petchey and Miss C.J. Wood (GBR), C. Wilkinson and Miss S.L. Smith (GBR), T.M. Haas (GER) and Miss I. Majoli (CRO), D.E. Sapsford and Miss S-A. Siddall (GBR).

1998
(5) W.H. Black and Miss C.C. Black (ZIM), J. Delgado and Miss E.E. Jelfs (GBR), L. Milligan and Miss J. Moore (GBR), D.E. Sapsford and Miss J.M. Pullin (GBR), C. Wilkinson and Miss L.A. Woodroffe (GBR).

1999
(5) B.A. Cowan and Miss J.M. Pullin (GBR), J.P. McEnroe (USA) and Miss S.M. Graf (GER), C.M. Maclagan and Miss K.M. Cross (GBR), D.E. Sapsford and Miss L.A. Woodroffe (GBR), C. Wilkinson and Miss S.L. Smith (GBR).

2000
(5) M.S. Bhupathi (IND) and Miss M. Navratilova (USA), B.A. Cowan and Miss J.M. Pullin (GBR), J. Coetzee (RSA) and Miss L. Latimer (GBR), X. Malisse (BEL) and Miss J.M. Capriati (USA), K. Spencer and Miss S.L. Smith (GBR).

2001
(5) S. Capriati and Miss J.M. Capriati (USA), B.A. Cowan and Miss J.M. Pullin (GBR), J. Davidson and Miss V.E. Davies (GBR), J. Nelson and Miss H. Crook (GBR), K. Spencer and Miss L.A. Woodroffe (GBR)

2002
(5) L. Childs and Miss E. Baltacha (GBR), B.A. Cowan and Miss V.E. Davies (GBR), N.A. Lapentti (ECU) and Miss I. Majoli (CRO), D. Sherwood and Miss L.A. Ahl (GBR), K. Spencer and Miss L.A. Woodroffe (GBR).

2003
(5) A. Parmar and Miss A.V. Keothavong (GBR), O. Freelove and Miss H. Crook (GBR), D. Sherwood and Miss A.L. Ahl (GBR), C.M. MacLagen and Miss A. Janes (GBR), A. Bogdanovic (GBR) and Miss M. Sharapova (RUS)*.
* withdrew

2004
(5) J.Marray and Miss A. Janes (GBR), J. Palmer (USA), and Miss A.I.M Sanchez-Vicario (Mrs. J. Vehils) (ESP), A Parmer and Miss J.O Donoghue (GBR), A. Ram (ISR) and Miss A. Rodionova (RUS), D. Sherwood and Miss A.V. Keothavong (GBR).

2005
(5) A. Parmar and Miss J.O Donoghue (GBR), R. Barker and Miss C.S. Curran (GBR), A. Murray (GBR) and Miss S. Peer (ISR), J. Delgado and Miss A. Janes (GBR), D. Sherwood and Miss E. Baltacha (GBR).

2006
(5) J. Auckland and Miss C.S. Curran (GBR), A. Murray (GBR) and Miss K. Flipkens (BEL), W.S. Arthurs and Miss.A. Molik (AUS), C. Suk and Miss H.Sukova (CZE), P.J. Hanley (AUS) and Miss T. Perebiynis (UKR).

2007
(5) J. Auckland and Miss C.S. Curran (GBR), R. Bloomfield and Miss S. Borwell (GBR), A. Bogdanovic and Miss M. South (GBR), L. Childs and Miss K. O'Brien (GBR), J. Delgado and Miss A. Keothavong (GBR).

2008
(5) J. Auckland and Miss E. Baltacha (GBR), R. Bloomfield and Miss S. Borwell (GBR), J. Delgado and Miss K. O'Brien (GBR), A. Bogdanovic and Miss M. South (GBR), R. Hutchins and Miss A.K. Keothavong (GBR).

2009
(5) C. Fleming and Miss S. Borwell (GBR), K.S. Kupski and Miss K. O'Brien (GBR), A. Bogdanovic and Miss M. South (GBR), J. Auckland and Miss E. Baltacha (GBR), J. Goodall and Miss N. Cavaday (GBR).

2010
(5) C. Fleming and Miss S. Borwell (GBR), R.C. Bryan and Miss L.A. Davenport (Mrs J. Leach) (USA), J. Murray and Miss L.M.D. Robson (GBR), J. Marray and Miss A. Smith (GBR), R. Hutchins and Miss A. Keothavong (GBR).

2011
(5) J.F. Marray and Miss A. Keothavong (GBR), R. Hutchins and Miss H. Watson (GBR) J. Delgado and Miss M. South (GBR), C. Fleming and Miss J. Rae (GBR), K. Skupski and E. Baltacha (GBR).

2012
(4) J.F. Marray and Miss A. Keothavong (GBR), D. Inglot and Miss L.M. Robson (GBR), K. Skupski and Miss M. South (GBR), R. Hutchins and Miss H. Watson (GBR).

2013
(5) K. Edmund (GBR) and Miss E. Bouchard (CAN), J. Delgado and Miss T. Moore (GBR), J. Blake (USA) and Miss D. Vekic (CRO), D. Ingot and Miss J. Konta (GBR), M. Knowles (BAH) and Miss S. Lisicki (GER).

2014
(4) J. Ward and Miss A. Smith (GBR), C. Fleming and Miss J. Rae (GBR), N. Skupski and Miss N. Broady (GBR), R. Hutchins and Miss H. Watson (GBR).

Gentlemen's Singles Qualifying

1981
(9) M.R.E. Appleton (GBR), R.M. Booth (GBR), F.S. Farrell (GBR), D.C. Felgate (GBR), M.W.C. Guntrip (GBR), F. McNair (USA), S. Matthews (GBR), T. Robson (GBR), S.M. Shaw (GBR).

1982
(8) M. Brunning (USA), P. Doohan (AUS), M.W.C. Guntrip (GBR), C. Haworth (GBR), P.S. Heath (GBR), B. Mills (GBR), R.W. Scott (GBR), N. Sears (GBR).

1983–1990
Details not available

1991
(9) S.C.S. Cole (GBR), A.L. Foster (GBR), D.P. Ison (GBR), J. Kriek (USA), C.M. MacLagan (GBR), L. Matthews (GBR), A.L. Richardson (GBR), P.C. Robinson (GBR), A. Rouse (GBR).

1992
(9) C. Beecher (GBR), P.T. Hand (GBR), T.H. Henman (GBR), D. Kirk (GBR), R.D. Leach (USA), C.M. MacLagan (GBR), L. Matthews (GBR), U. Nganga (GBR), M. Schofield (GBR).

1993
(8) C. Beecher (GBR), J. Delgado (GBR), P.T. Hand (GBR), T.H. Henman (GBR), M. Kratzmann (AUS), J.J. Hunter (GBR), L. Matthews (GBR), D.E. Sapsford (GBR).

1994
(9) G.D. Connell (CAN), J. Delgado (GBR), J.B. Fitzgerald (AUS), P.T. Hand (GBR), L. Milligan (GBR), A.L. Richardson (GBR), C. Saceanu (GER), G. Saffrey (GBR), M. Wyeth (GBR).

1995
(7) J. Delgado (GBR), J.B. Fitzgerald (AUS), P.T. Hand (GBR), M. Lee (GBR), P. Martin (GBR), A.L. Richardson (GBR), D. Williams (GBR).

1996
(9) T. Hand (GBR), W. Herbert (GBR), M. Lee (GBR), M. Mirnyi (BER), A. Parmar (GBR), S.T. Pender (GBR), T. Spinks (GBR), N. Weal (GBR), M. Wyeth (GBR).

1997
(9) C. Bennett (GBR), P.H. Cash (AUS), B.A. Cowan (GBR), P.T. Hand (GBR), D. Lobb (GBR), P. Maggs (GBR), T. Spinks (GBR), C. Wall (GBR), D. Ward (GBR).

1998
(9) A. Foster (GBR), J. Fox (GBR), B. Haran (GBR), M.S. Knowles (BAH), D. Lobb (GBR), R. Matheson (GBR), A. Olhovskiy (RUS), T. Spinks (GBR), N. Weal (GBR).

1999
(9) J. Davidson (GBR), S. Dickson (GBR), P. Hand (GBR), R. Hanger (GBR), A. Reichel (USA), D. Sapsford (GBR), D. Sherwood (GBR), J. Thomas (GBR), N. Weal (GBR).

2000
(9) C. Bennett (GBR), L. Childs, (GBR), N. Gould (GBR), M. Hilton (GBR), J. Melzer (AUT), L. Milligan (GBR), J. Nelson (GBR), T. Spinks (GBR), N. Zimonjic (YUG).

2001
(9) A. Banks (GBR), J. Davidson (GBR), S. Dickson (GBR), R. Hanger (GBR), M.S. Knowles (BAH), L. Milligan (GBR), J. Nelson (GBR), J. Smith (GBR), N. Weal (GBR).

2002
(9) A. Banks (GBR), L. Childs (GBR), S. Dickson (GBR), J. Fox (GBR), M. Hilton (GBR), J. Layne (GBR), J. Marray (GBR), L. Milligan (GBR), D.M. Nestor (CAN).

2003
(9) J. Auckland (GBR), W.H. Black (ZIM), T. Burn (GBR), I. Flanagan (GBR), M.S. Knowles (BAH), C. Lewis (GBR), D.M. Nestor (CAN), T. Reid (AUS), D. Sanger (GBR).

2004
(9) A. Banks (GBR), J. Benneteau (FRA), R.C. Bryan (USA), J. Delgado (GBR), A. Falla (COL), I. Flanagan (GBR), C. Lewis (GBR), F. Mergea (ROM), A. Ram (ISR).

2005
(9) J. Auckland (GBR), N. Bamford (GBR), A. Banks (GBR), L. Childs (GBR), J. Knowle (AUT), A. Parmar (GBR), M. Smith (GBR), K. Vliegen (BEL), N. Zimonjic (SCG).

2006
(9) J. Auckland (GBR), K. Carlsen (DEN), J. Chardy (FRA), L. Childs (GBR), C. Fleming (GBR), J. Goodall (GBR), J. Marray (GBR), W. Whitehouse (RSA), N. Zimonjic (SCG).

2007
(9) N. Bamford (GBR)+, D. Brewer (GBR), L. Childs (GBR), C. Eaton (GBR), R. Irwin (GBR)+, J. May (GBR)+, T. Rushby (GBR)+, J. Ward (GBR), N. Zimonjic (SRB).
+ via play-off competition

2008
(7) R. Bloomfield (GBR), D. Cox (GBR)+, C. Eaton (GBR), J. Marray (GBR)+, M. Phillips (GBR), E. Seator (GBR), K. Skupski (GBR).
+ via play-off competition

2009
(7) R. Bloomfield (GBR), D. Cox (GBR), T. Dent (USA), C. Eaton (GBR), J. Milton (GBR)+, A. Slabinsky (GBR), D. Smethurst (GBR)+, B. Tomic (AUS), M. Wills (GBR)+
+ via play-off competition

2010
(9) D. Cox (GBR)+, C. Eaton (GBR), D. Evans (GBR)+, J. Goodall (GBR), J. Milton (GBR), M. Phillips (GBR), D. Rice (GBR), D. Smethurst (GBR), A. Ward (GBR), J. Ward (GBR)*
* withdrew
+ via play-off competition

2011
(9) A. Baker (GBR), A. Bogdanovic (GBR), L. Broady (GBR), M. Fucsovics (HUN), O Golding (GBR), J. Milton (GBR), G. Morgan (GBR), D. Smethurst (GBR)+, A. Ward (GBR)+
+ via play-off competition

2012
(9) L. Bambridge (GBR). R. Bloomfield (GBR), L. Broady (GBR), E. Corrie (GBR), C. Eaton (GBR)+, K. Edmund (GBR), A. Fitzpatrick (GBR), G. Morgan (GBR), D. Rice (GBR)+
+ via play-off competition

2013
(9) J. Baker (GBR), A. Bogdanovic (GBR), L. Burton (GBR)+, E. Corrie (GBR), D. Evans (GBR), J. Goodall (GBR), F. Peliwo (CAN), D. Rice (GBR)+, J. Ward-Hibbert (GBR).
+ via play-off competition

2014
(9) E. Corrie (GBR), S. Darcis (BEL), O. Golding (GBR), B.Klein (GBR)+, J. Milton (GBR)+,
D. Rice (GBR), A. Ward (GBR), J. Ward Hibbert (GBR), M. Willis (GBR).
+ via play-off competition

Gentlemen's Doubles Qualifying

1981
Details not available

1982
(3) G. Hardie (USA) and D. Tarr (RSA), P.A. Heath and S.M. Shaw (GBR), A.H. Lloyd and D.A. Lloyd (GBR).

1983–1985
Details not available

1986
(3) M.W.C. Guntrip and J. Whiteford (GBR), S. Heron and C. Peet (GBR), C.B. Bailey and L. Matthews (GBR).

1987–1990
Details not available

1991
(3) C.B. Bailey and U. Nganga (GBR), J. Haycock and J.J. Hunter (GBR), C. Beecher and A.L. Foster (GBR).

1992
(2) N. Adams and D. Collins (GBR), C. Beecher and M. Schofield (GBR).

1993
(2) N. Kroon and P. Lundgren (SWE), L. Paes (IND) and L. Tieleman (ITA).

1994
(2) R.S. Matheson and D. E. Sapsford (GBR), C. Beecher and J. Delgado (GBR).

1995
(1) C. Wall and D. Ward (GBR).

1996
(2) G. Saffrey and M. Wyeth (GBR), T. Hand and K. Spencer (GBR).

1997
(2) C. Beecher and T. Spinks (GBR), P.T. Hand and C.M. MacLagan (GBR).

1998
(2) J. Fox and J. Trotman (GBR), R. Matheson and N. Weal (GBR).

1999
(1) N. Gould and J. Layne (GBR).

2000
1 S. Dickson and T. Sninks.

2001
(Nil)

2002
(1) O. Freelove and J. Smith (GBR)

2003
(1) O. Freelove and C. Lewis (GBR).

2004
(Nil)

2005
(1) R. Hutchins and M. Lee (GBR).

2006
(1) N. Bamford and J. May (GBR).

2007
(2) I. Flanagan and T. Rushby (GBR), R. Irwin and J. May (GBR).

2008
(2) N. Pauffley and M. Willis (GBR), E. Seator and D. Smethurst (GBR).

2009
(2) C. Eaton and A. Slabinsky (GBR), D. Smethurst (GBR) and M. Willis (GBR).

2010
(2) R. Bloomfield and M. Willis (GBR), J. Milton and A. Ward (GBR).

2011
(2) K. Beck (SVK) and D. Skoch (CZE), D. Rice and S. Thornley (GBR).

2012
(2) L. Burton and G. Morgan (GBR), D. Rice and S. Thornley (GBR).

2013
(2) L. Burton and D. Evans (GBR), E. Corrie and N. Skupski (GBR).

2014
(2) L. Burton and M. Willis (GBR), D. Rice and S. Thornley (GBR).

Ladies' Singles Qualifying

1981–1990
Details not available

1991
(8) Miss C.L. Billingham (GBR), Miss N. Giles (GBR), Miss C. Hall (GBR), Miss C. Hunt (GBR), Miss T. Ignatieva (URS), Miss V. Lake (GBR), Miss S-A. Siddall (GBR), Miss J. Wood (GBR).

1992
(7) Miss C.L. Billingham (GBR), Miss B. Griffiths (GBR), Miss C.J. Herbert (GBR), Miss B. Nagelsen (USA), Miss J.M. Pullin (GBR), Miss J.A. Salmon (GBR), Miss A.M.H. Wainwright (GBR).

1993
(8) Miss L.A. Ahl (GBR), Miss C.J. Billingham (GBR), Miss E.L. Bond (GBR), Miss E.E. Jelfs (GBR), Miss V. Lake (GBR), Miss B. Nagelsen (USA), Miss J.A. Salmon (GBR), Miss A.E. Smith (GBR).

1994
(8) Miss L.A. Ahl (GBR), Miss M. de Swardt (RSA), Miss C.J. Herbert (GBR), Miss M.L. Mair (GBR), Miss Z. Mellis (GBR), Miss J. Moore (USA), Miss A.E. Smith (GBR), Miss L.A. Woodroffe (GBR).

1995
(8) Miss L.A. Ahl (GBR), Miss K.D. Hand (GBR), Miss M.L. Mair (GBR), Miss C. Porwick (GER), Miss C. Taylor (GBR), Miss A.M.H. Wainwright (GBR), Miss J. Ward (GBR), Miss K.V. Warne-Holland (GBR).

1996
(8) Miss L.A. Ahl (GBR), Miss E.L. Bond (GBR), Miss K.M. Cross (GBR), Miss D.A. Graham (USA), Miss J.M. Pullin (GBR), Miss S-A. Siddall (GBR), Miss A.M.H. Wainwright (GBR), Miss J. Wood (GBR).

1997
(8) Miss H. Crook (GBR), Miss K.M. Cross (GBR), Miss A. Janes (GBR), Miss E.E. Jelfs (GBR), Miss L. Latimer (GBR), Miss A. Tordoff (GBR), Miss K.V. Warne-Holland (GBR), Miss A.M.H. Wainwright (GBR).

1998
(8) Miss L.A. Ahl (GBR), Miss H. Collin (GBR), Miss L. Herbert (GBR), Miss A. Janes (GBR), Miss C. Lyte GBR), Miss J. Moore (GBR), Miss A. Tordoff (GBR), Miss K.V. Warne-Holland (GBR).

1999
(8) Miss H. Collin (GBR), Miss H. Crook (GBR), Miss V. Davies (GBR), Miss L. Herbert (GBR), Miss E.E. Jelfs (GBR), Miss H. Matthews (GBR), Miss N. Payne (GBR). Miss K.V. Warne-Holland (GBR).

2000
(8) Miss E. Baltacha (GBR), Miss A. Barnes (GBR), Miss V. Davies (GBR), Miss H. Farr (GBR), Miss A.V. Keothavong (GBR), Miss J. O'Donoghue (GBR), Miss A. Tordoff (GBR), Miss K. Vymetal (GBR).

2001
(8) Miss A. Barnes (GBR), Miss H. Crook (GBR), Miss K.M. Cross (GBR), Miss C. Grier
(GBR), Miss A. Janes (GBR), Miss J. O'Donoghue (GBR), Miss R. Viollet (GBR), Miss J.
Ward (GBR).

2002
(8) Miss Barabanchikova (BLR), Miss A. Barnes (GBR), Miss H. Crook (GBR), Miss C. Grier
(GBR), Miss A. Janes (GBR), Miss M. South (GBR), Miss E. Webley-Smith (GBR), Miss L.
Woodroffe (GBR).

2003
(8) Miss S. Borwell (GBR), Miss H. Crook (GBR), Miss C. Dellacqua (AUS), Miss V.
Douchevina (RUS), Miss C. Grier (GBR), Miss C. Gullickson (USA), Miss A. Hawkins (GBR),
Miss E. Webley-Smith (GBR).

2004
(8) Miss H. Bagshaw (GBR), Miss C. Coombs (GBR), Miss K. Flipkens (BEL) Miss H. Fritche
(GBR), Miss C. Grier (GBR), Miss A. Mackenzie (GBR), Miss B. Schwartz (AUS), Miss M.
South (GBR).

2005
(8) Miss K. Bondarenko (UKR), Miss H. Collin (GBR), Miss J. Curtis (GBR), Miss C.
Gullikson (USA), Miss A. Hawkins (GBR), Miss K. Paterson (GBR), Miss M. South (GBR),
Miss E. Webley-Smith (GBR).

2006
(8) Miss I. Abramovic (GRO), Miss S. Coles (GBR), Miss J. Dokic (AUS), Mrs. A. Keen
(GBR), Miss J. O'Donoghue (GBR), Miss K. Paterson (GBR), Miss G. Stoop (GBR), Miss C.
Wozniacki (DEN).

2007
(8) Miss J. Bone (GBR), Miss S. Borwell (GBR), Miss A. Fitzpatrick (GBR)+, Miss R.
Llewellyn (GBR)+, Miss K. Paterson (GBR)+, Miss T. Perebiynis (UKR), Miss M Rybarikova
(SVK), Miss E. Webley-Smith (GBR)+
+ via play-off competition

2008
(8) Miss S. Borwell (GBR), Miss N. Broady (GBR), Miss A. Elliott (GBR), Miss A. Fitzpatrick
(GBR), Miss T. Moore (GBR), Miss A. Smith (GBR)+, Miss G. Stoop (GBR), Miss E. Thomas
(GBR)+
+ via play-off competition

2009
(8) Miss N. Broady (GBR), Miss N. Cavaday (GBR), Miss J. Curtis (GBR), Miss A. Elliott
(GBR)+, Miss O. Rogowska (AUS), Miss N. Lertcheewakarn (THA), Miss E. Thomas
(GBR)+, Miss E. Webley-Smith (GBR)
+ via play-off competition

2010
(8) Miss N. Broady (GBR), Miss L. Brown (GBR)+, Miss M. Erakovic (NZL), Miss T. Paszek
(AUT), Miss J. Rae (GBR)+, Miss A. Smith (GBR), Miss E. Webley-Smith (GBR)+, Miss L.
Whybourn (GBR)+
+ via play-off competition

2011

(8) Miss C. Dellacqua (AUS), Miss A. Fitzpatrick (GBR), Miss T. Moore (GBR), Miss S. Murray (GBR)+, Miss K. Pliskova (CZE), Miss M. South (GBR), Miss F. Stevenson (GBR)+, Miss J. Windley (GBR)

+ via play-off competition

2012

(8) Miss K. Dunne (GBR)+, Miss A. Fitzpatrick (GBR)+, Miss T. Moore (GBR), Miss S. Murray (GBR), Miss M. South (GBR), Miss E. Webley-Smith (GBR), Miss L. Whybourn(GBR), Miss J. Windley (GBR).

+via play-off competition

2013

(8) Miss N. Broady (GBR), Miss A. Carreras (GBR), Miss K. Dunne, (GBR), Miss A. Smith (GBR)+, Miss M. South (GBR)+, Miss E. Webley-Smith (GBR) Miss L. Whybourn (GBR), Miss J. Windley (GBR).

+via play-off competition

2014

(7) Miss K. Boulter (GBR), Miss F. Christie (GBR), Miss K. Dunne (GBR), Miss G. Taylor (GBR)+, Miss E. Webley-Smith (GBR)+, Miss L. Whybourn (GBR), Miss J. Windley (GBR).

+via play-off competition

Ladies' Doubles Qualifying

1990
Details not available

1991
(2) Miss A. Gray and Miss J.M. Pullin (GBR), Miss G.L. Coles and Miss D. Parnell (GBR).

1992
(2) Miss K.D. Hand and Miss C.J. Herbert (GBR), Miss L. Ahl and Miss C. Hunt (GBR).

1993
(1) Miss T. Crosson and Miss Wyatt (GBR).

1994
(1) Miss L.A. Ahl and Miss J. Moore (USA).

1995
(1) Miss K.D. Hand and Miss C. Taylor (GBR).

1996
(1) Miss J. Choudhury and Miss L. Latimer (GBR).

1997
(Nil)

1998
(1) Miss H. Collin and Miss A. Tordoff (GBR).

1999
(1) Miss E.E. Jelfs and Miss K.V. Warne-Holland (GBR).

2000
(1) Miss K.M. Cross and Miss J. Ward (GBR).

2001
(Nil)

2002
Miss A. Hawkins and Miss J. O'Donoghue (GBR).

2003
(Nil)

2004
(1) Miss C. Curran and Miss J. O'Donoghue (GBR).

2005
(1) Miss H. Collin and Miss K. Paterson (GBR).

2006
(1) Miss N. Khan and Miss C. Peterzan (GBR).

2007
(1) Miss A. Fitzpatrick and Miss E. Webley-Smith (GBR).

2008
(2) Miss J. Curtis and Miss E. Thomas (GBR), Miss A. Smith and Miss G. Stoop (GBR).

2009
(2) Miss N. Broady and Miss E. Thomas (GBR), Miss A. Fitzpatrick and Miss E. Webley-Smith (GBR).

2010
(2) Miss E. Webley-Smith and Miss L. Whyborne (GBR), Miss A. Fitzpatrick and Miss J. Windley (GBR).

2011
(2) Miss N. Lertcheewakarn (THA) and Miss J. Moore (AUS), Miss N. Bratchikova and Miss V. Savinykh (RUS).

2012
(2) Miss S. Murray and Miss E. Webley-Smith (GBR), Miss A. Fitzpatrick and Miss J. Windley (GBR).

2013
(2) Miss N. Broady and Miss A. Smith (GBR), Miss A. Fitzpatrick and Miss E. Webley-Smith (GBR).

2014
(2) Miss S. Murray (GBR) and Miss J. Windley (GBR), Miss K. Boulter (GBR) and Miss K. Dunne (GBR).

Mixed Doubles Qualifying

1990
Details not available

1991
(1) P.T. Hand and Miss K.D. Hand (GBR)

1992 to date
No competition

The following Wild Cards have made the most progress in The Championships:-

Gentlemen's Singles
Champion
2001   G.S. Ivanisevic (CRO)

Ladies' Singles
Fourth round
1982   Miss Z.L. Garrison (USA)
1985   Miss A.E. Smith (USA)
1998   Miss S.L. Smith (GBR)
2003   Miss M. Sharapova (RUS)

Semi-final
2008   Miss J. Zheng (CHN)
2011   Miss S. Lisickl (GER)

Gentlemen's Doubles
Semi-final
1985   P.B. McNamara and
          P.F. McNamee (AUS)
Champions
2012   J.F. Marray (GBR)
          F.L. Nielsen (DEN)

Ladies' Doubles
Champions
2000   Miss S.J. Williams and
          Miss V.E.S. Williams (USA)
2002   Miss S.J. Williams and
          Miss V.E.S. Williams (USA)

Mixed Doubles
Semi-final
1991   C.J. Van Rensburg and
          Miss E. Reinach (RSA)
1999   J.P. McEnroe (USA) and
          Miss S.M. Graf (GER)

Championship Trophies

Gentlemen's Singles Championship

The Field Cup, 1877–1883

The original Gentlemen's Singles trophy, won by the first Wimbledon Champion, S.W. Gore, in 1877, was the Field Cup. This Challenge Cup was presented to The All England Croquet and Lawn Tennis Club, especially for the event, by "The Field" newspaper. Mr. J.H. Walsh, who was the Honorary Secretary of the Club and the editor of "The Field", persuaded his Proprietors to support the new venture by providing the 25 guineas Cup.

The Cup, which is made of sterling silver, stands $14^1/_2$ inches high, with a base diameter of 6 inches and a rim diameter of $7^1/_2$ inches. The hallmark, beneath the rim, indicates a date of 1877. The Cup has two handles and a raised foot. Decoration consists of two crossed tennis rackets and three tennis balls at the front, below which lies the following inscription:

The All England Lawn Tennis
Challenge Cup
Presented by the Proprietors of The
Field
For competition by Amateurs
Wimbledon
July, 1877

The reverse of the Cup is engraved with the dates and names of the Champions from 1877 to 1883, the last being W. Renshaw, who having won the Cup three times in succession was permitted under the regulations to take possession.

The Cup, which is owned by the Renshaw family, is on permanent display in The Wimbledon Lawn Tennis Museum.

Challenge Cup (AELTC), 1884–1886

After the 1883 Championship The All England Lawn Tennis Club purchased a new 50 guineas Challenge Cup to replace the trophy retired by W. Renshaw. Regulations stated that the Cup would be held for one year but if won by the same player in three successive years would become his property, just as was stipulated with The Field Cup.

W. Renshaw won this second Challenge Cup in three successive years, 1884–1886, and consequently retired the trophy.

Details and whereabouts of the trophy are unknown.

Challenge Cup (AELTC), 1887 to date

Faced with the problem of providing a new Challenge Cup, The All England Lawn Tennis Club spent 100 guineas from the profits of the 1886 Championships to purchase a trophy. The Club was not prepared to risk losing a third Cup to a future three-times Champion so the decision was taken that the new trophy would "never become the property of the winner".

The Cup, which is made of silver gilt, stands 18 inches high and has a diameter of $7^1/_2$ inches. The hallmark indicates a date of 1883. The Cup has a classical style with two handles and a raised foot. The lid is formed with a pineapple on the top and there is a head wearing a winged helmet beneath each handle. There are two decorative borders with floral work and ovolo mouldings on the bowl of the Cup and on the handles.

The inscription on the Cup reads:

The All England
Lawn Tennis Club
Single Handed
Championship
of the World

Around the bowl are engraved the dates and names of the Champions. Although H.F. Lawford was the first Champion to win the Cup in 1887 the decision was taken to engrave all the Champions' names from 1877. In 2009, there being no space left to engrave the names of the champions, a black plinth with an ornamented silver band was designed to accompany the Cup.

From 1949 to 2006 all Champions received a miniature replica of the Cup (height $8^1/_2$ inches). From 2007 all Champions have received a three-quarter size replica of the Cup bearing the names of all past Champions (height 13½ inches).

The Renshaw Cup, 1905–1989

The Renshaw Cup, a prize rather than a trophy, was won outright annually. This elegant Cup was originally presented to The All England Lawn Tennis Club in 1905 by the surviving members of the family of Ernest and William Renshaw, who contributed so much to lawn tennis in the 1880s, as First Prize to the winner of the All Comers' Singles. However, from 1922, when the challenge round was abolished, until 1989 the Cup was presented to the Champion.

Originally the Cup stood 10 inches high with a base diameter of $4^1/_2$ inches and the bowl diameter, rim to rim, of 7 inches. From 1953 the practice of presenting a "full size" Cup ceased and instead the Champion received a miniature replica (height 5 inches).

The Cup was originally a registered design, manufactured by Messrs. Elkington and Co. Ltd. of Birmingham, in sterling silver, with a value of £20. The design consists of an octagonal base, supporting a round plinth on which stands a winged, mercurial figure with arms stretched upwards to support the bowl of the Cup. The first winner in 1905 was N.E. Brookes of Australia.

Several examples of this Trophy may be seen on display in The Wimbledon Lawn Tennis Museum.

The President's Cup, 1908–1994

The 1907 Championships were particularly memorable because The All England Lawn Tennis Club was honoured by the presence of Their Royal Highnesses The Prince and Princess of Wales. As a result of this visit Prince George, later King George V, became President of the Club and expressed a wish to present a "perpetual Challenge Cup" to be competed for annually at The Championships. The Committee decided that the trophy should be held for the year by the winner of the All Comers' Singles.

The Cup stands 17 inches high and is 7½ inches in diameter. This magnificent silver trophy has a lid or cover and a raised foot.

The inscription on the Cup reads:

> Presented by George, Prince of Wales,
> to the All England Lawn Tennis Club
> to be held for the year by the Winner
> of the All Comers' Singles Championship of the World.

The wording of this inscription is rather ambiguous. From 1908 to 1921, the last year of the challenge round, the winner of the All Comers' Singles did not become Champion of the World – only if he defeated the defending Champion. When the challenge round was abolished in 1922 the defending Champion had to "play through" and there was no longer an All Comers' Singles. From then to 1994 the Champion became the holder of the President's Cup and the Challenge Cup (AELTC). After 1994 the President's Cup was retired.

The dates and names of the winners of the All Comers' Singles, from A.W. Gore in 1908 to 1921 and the dates and names of the Champions, 1922–1994 are engraved on the bowl of the Cup.

From 1949 to 1994 all Champions received a miniature replica of the Cup (height 9 inches).

Gentlemen's Doubles Championship

Gentlemen's Pairs Trophy, 1884 to date

In 1884, seven years after the inauguration of the Gentlemen's Singles Championship, The All England Lawn Tennis Club added a Gentlemen's Doubles Championship to the programme. Earlier in that year the Oxford University Lawn Tennis Club had decided owing to lack of support to discontinue their championship, which had been instituted in 1879, and offered to transfer the Challenge Cup to The All England Lawn Tennis Club. The Committee was pleased to accept the offer and agreed that the inscription on the trophy should be altered as little as possible (see page 437).

The 60 guineas Challenge Cup, which is made of sterling silver, stands 9 inches high and has a diameter of 11 inches. The Cup has a wide open bowl and stands on a raised foot. There are two handles, decorated with acanthus leaves. The front bears the emblem of the Oxford University Lawn Tennis Club and the following inscription:

All England Lawn Tennis Club
Challenge Cup
For Pairs

Presented in 1884   By the Oxford University
To the A.E.L.T.C.   Lawn Tennis Club.

By Whom it was instituted as a
Challenge Cup Open to All England

On either side of the inscription are crossed rackets.

On the reverse of the bowl is a delightful scene, executed in repoussé work, showing a "four handed" match in progress, as it would have looked c1884.

The trophy stands upon a round black plinth, encircled by a silver band, on which are engraved the dates and names of all winners from 1879.

Gentlemen's Doubles Trophy, 1937 *to date*

The Gentlemen's Doubles Trophy was introduced as a companion to the Gentlemen's Pairs Trophy in 1937. The All England Lawn Tennis Club presented the Cup to Sir Herbert Wilberforce upon his resignation from the Chairmanship of the Club and he in turn gave the Trophy back to the Club to be held as a pair to the Oxford University Cup.

The trophy, made of sterling silver by Messrs. Elkington and Co. Ltd. of Birmingham, 1936, is identical with the Pairs Trophy except for the motif and inscription on the front of the bowl. Instead of the Oxford University Lawn Tennis Club emblem, the trophy bears the crossed rackets in a circle of the Club and the inscription reads:

The Gentlemen's Doubles Championship.
This Challenge Cup was presented in 1937 by the Members of
The All England Lawn Tennis Club
To Sir Herbert Wilberforce on his resigning the Chairmanship
of the Club and was given by him to the Club to be held as
a companion of the Oxford University Cup.

The trophy stands upon a round black plinth, encircled by a silver band on which are engraved the dates and names of all winners from 1879.

From 1949 to 2011 both Champions received a miniature replica of the trophy (height $4\frac{1}{2}$ inches). From 2012 both Champions received a three-quarter size trophy.

Ladies' Singles Championship

The Ladies' Singles Plate, 1886 to date

The Ladies' Singles Trophy is a silver salver, sometimes referred to as the "Rosewater Dish" or "Venus Rosewater Dish" which was first won by the Champion when the challenge round was introduced in 1886.

The 50 guineas trophy was made in 1864 by Messrs. Elkington and Co. Ltd. of Birmingham and is a copy of an electrotype, obtained by Casper Enderlein, from a pewter original in the Louvre.

The salver, which is made of sterling silver, partly gilded, is $18^{3}/_{4}$ inches in diameter. There is a central boss surrounded by four reserves, with eight on the spreading rim. The remainder of the surface is decorated with gilt renaissance strapwork and foliate motifs in relief against a rigid silver ground.

The theme of the decoration is mythological. The central boss has a figure of Temperance, seated on a chest with a lamp in her right hand and a jug in her left, with various attributes such as a sickle, fork and caduceus around her. The four reserves on the boss of the dish each contain a classical god, together with attribute Venus, Jupiter, Mercury and Water Goddess, representing the four elements. The reserves around the rim show Minerva presiding over the seven Liberal Arts: Astrology, Geometry, Arithmetic, Music, Rhetoric, Dialectic and Grammar, each with relevant attribute. The rim of the salver has an ovolo moulding.

The trophy bears no inscription other than the engraving showing the dates and names of all the Champions. Although Miss B. Bingley was the first Champion to win the trophy in 1886, the name of Miss M. Watson, the Champion of 1884 and 1885, has been added. Dates and names from 1884 to 1957 are to be found around the inside of the bowl and from 1958 to date around the outside of the bowl.

From 1949 to 2006 all Champions have received a miniature replica of the trophy (diameter 8 inches). From 2007 all Champions have received a three-quarter size replica of the trophy, bearing the names of all past Champions (diameter 14 inches).

Over the years the Club have received many enquiries from people who possess salvers made to a design identical to that of the Ladies' Singles Plate. Some have been made in silver and others in copper or tin. Since these salvers are "electrotypes" created by electric deposition of copper on a mould, it is reasonable to assume that Elkingtons made many. However, only one salver has been used since 1886 as the trophy for the Ladies' Singles Championship. There is no truth in the story that Queen Victoria donated the trophy to the Club.

Ladies' Doubles Championship

Challenge Trophies (LTA), 1913–1939

Following the creation of the International Lawn Tennis Federation in 1913, the Lawn Tennis Association accepted, on behalf of the British Isles, the "World Championships on Grass". The All England Lawn Tennis Club agreed to merge these Championships with the three existing Championships and to extend the programme to include Ladies' Doubles and Mixed Doubles Championships.

The LTA decided to present two silver Challenge Trophies to the winners of each new event. With the outbreak of the Second World War in 1939 the LTA withdrew the trophies for safe keeping but in 1941 the trophies were lost when the building where they were lodged was destroyed by enemy action.

Details of the trophies are unknown.

The Challenge Cup (D of K), 1949 to date

The Ladies' Doubles Championship Trophy is an elegant silver Challenge Cup, presented to The All England Lawn Tennis Club by H.R.H. The Duchess of Kent in 1949.

The Cup, which is made of sterling silver, stands 17 inches high, with a base diameter of $4^1/_2$ inches and a bowl diameter, rim to rim, of 6 inches. The hallmark indicates a date of 1913.

The Cup, with two handles and a lid, is engraved with the following inscriptions:

Front:

Duchess of Kent
Challenge Cup
1949

Reverse:

Presented by
Her Royal Highness the Duchess of Kent
To The
All England Lawn Tennis Club
To be held for the Year
by the winners of
The Ladies' Doubles Championship

The trophy stands upon a round black plinth encircled by two silver bands on which are engraved the dates and names of the winners from 1949.

The Challenge Cup (AELTC), 2001

The Ladies' Doubles Championship Trophy was presented in 2001 by The All England Lawn Tennis Club as a companion to the Challenge Cup, donated by H.R.H. The Duchess of Kent in 1949. The introduction of a second trophy allowed the champions to receive one each at the presentation ceremony, instead of sharing as previously.

The Cup, made of sterling silver by Wakely & Wheeler of London is identical in design and size to the companion, except for the engraving on the front and reverse sides which are inscribed as follows:

Front:

Duchess of Kent
Challenge Cup

Reverse:

This Challenge Cup was presented
by the
All England Lawn Tennis Club

in 2001
as a companion to the
Challenge Cup
donated by
H.R.H. The Duchess of Kent in 1949
To be held for the Year
by the winners of
The Ladies' Doubles Championship

The trophy stands on a round black plinth encircled by two silver bands on which are engraved the dates and names of the winners from 1949.

From 1949 to 2011 both champions received a miniature replica of a Challenge Cup (height 8½ inches). From 2012 both Champions received a three-quarter size cup

Mixed Doubles Championship

Challenge Trophies (LTA), 1913–1939

See "Ladies' Doubles Championship – Challenge Trophies (LTA), 1913–1939" on page 296.

The Challenge Cup (S.H. Smith), 1949 to date

The Mixed Doubles Championship Trophy was presented to The All England Lawn Tennis Club by the family of the late S.H. Smith, who was Wimbledon Doubles Champion in 1902 and 1906. Originally S.H. Smith retired the Cup after winning the singles three times in succession at the Northern Championships in 1904.

The Cup, made by Barnard & Sons with Robert Dubock of London, is made of sterling silver and stands 17 inches high, with a base diameter of $5^1/_2$ inches and a bowl diameter, rim to rim, of $6^1/_4$ inches. The hallmark indicates a date of 1901. The Cup, which has a raised foot, two handles and a lid, is engraved with the following inscriptions:

Front:

All England
Lawn Tennis Club
Mixed Doubles Championship
Challenge Cup

Reverse:

Presented
by the family of the late
S.H. Smith
to
The All England Lawn Tennis Club
to be held for the year by
the winners of
the Mixed Doubles Championship

The trophy stands upon a round black plinth, enclosed by two silver bands on which are engraved the dates and names of the winners from 1949.

The Challenge Cup (AELTC), 2001

The Mixed Doubles Championship Trophy was presented in 2001 by the All England Lawn Tennis Club as a companion to the Challenge Cup, donated by the family of the late S.H. Smith in 1949. The introduction of a second trophy allowed the champions to receive one each at the presentation ceremony, instead of sharing as previously.

The Cup, made of sterling silver by Wakely & Wheeler of London, is identical in design and size to the companion, except for the engraving on the front and reverse sides, which are inscribed as follows:

Front:

All England
Lawn Tennis Club
Mixed Doubles Championship
Challenge Cup

Reverse:

This Challenge Cup
was presented by
The All England Lawn Tennis Club
in 2001
as a companion to the
Challenge Cup
presented by the family of the late
S.H. Smith in 1949
To be held for the year by
the winners of
The Mixed Doubles Championship

The trophy stands on a round black plinth encircled by two silver bands on which are engraved the dates and names of the winners from 1949.

From 1949 to 2011 both champions received a miniature replica of a Challenge Cup (height 8½ inches). From 2012 both Champions received a three-quarter size cup.

Silver Salvers

From 1987 the runners-up of the five Championship events have received a silver salver, on which is engraved a view of the Clubhouse and Centre Court building. The diameter of the salvers are: Singles, 1987–1997 – 10 inches, 1998 to date – 14 inches. Doubles, 1987 to date – 8 inches.

Originally the engraving showed one Clubhouse balcony, but from 2002 the design was changed to incorporate two new side balconies.

Engraving

Immediately the winners and runners-up of the events at the Championships are known, the replica trophies and salvers are engraved, enabling the players to leave with them in their possession.

Presentation of Trophies

The practice of presenting the Trophy to the Singles Champions on the Centre Court originated in 1949, when on Friday 1st July, H.R.H. The Duchess of Kent, President of The All England Lawn Tennis Club, consented to go down onto the Centre Court for the ceremony and so "give the photographers a break". Ted Schroeder of the United States was the recipient.

On the following day the Duchess of Kent presented the Ladies' Singles trophy to Louise Brough in the Royal Box but later in the afternoon she went on Court to present the Ladies' Doubles Trophy (which she had just donated to the Club) to Louise Brough and Margaret duPont. From 1946 to 1948 the trophies were presented in the Royal Box. Previously, the trophies were not presented in private or public, but occasionally the champions and runners-up were summoned to the Royal Box to receive the Royal congratulations.

From 1950 to 1953 there was no set pattern and the Gentlemen's and Ladies' Singles trophy was presented either in the Royal Box or on Court.

In 1954 both singles champions received their trophy on Court and this has been the practice ever since. Quite often in the fifties and early sixties the winners of the doubles events received their trophies on Court but since then, with the exception of 1973 (Gentlemen's Doubles) and 2000 (Ladies' Doubles), the ceremonies have always taken place in the Royal Box.

Traditionally the presenter of the singles trophies has been escorted on to the Centre Court by the Chairman and Secretary/Chief Executive of the AELTC and the President of the LTA. There have been very few exceptions. From the mid-seventies until recent years, the custom was for both the Duke and Duchess of Kent to go on Court, irrespective of which one of them was making the presentation.

From 1946 to 1967 the Gentlemen's Singles champion was presented with the President's Cup but from 1968 to date the AELTC Challenge Cup has been preferred, as the delicate gold colouring of the trophy shows to better advantage on colour television.

The following lists show the names of the presenter and the location of the presentation of the trophies from 1946.

Gentlemen's Singles Championship

Year	Champion	Presenter	Location
1946	Y.F.M. Petra	Mr C.R. Attlee	Royal Box
1947	J.A. Kramer	H.M. King George VI	Royal Box
1948	R. Falkenburg	H.R.H. Duchess of Kent	Royal Box
1949	F.R. Schroeder	H.R.H. Duchess of Kent	On Court
1950	J.E. Patty	H.R.H. Princess Alice	Royal Box
1951	R. Savitt	H.R.H. Duchess of Kent	Royal Box
1952	F.A. Sedgman	H.R.H. Duchess of Kent	On Court
1953	E.V. Seixas	H.R.H. Duchess of Kent	On Court

Presentation on Centre Court		
Year	Champion	Presenter
1954	J. Drobny	H.R.H. Duchess of Kent
1955	M.A. Trabert	H.R.H. Duchess of Kent
1956	L.A. Hoad	H.R.H. Duchess of Kent
1957	L.A. Hoad	H.R.H. Prince Philip
1958	A.J. Cooper	H.R.H. Duchess of Kent
1959	A.R. Olmedo	H.R.H. Duchess of Kent
1960	N.A. Fraser	H.R.H. Prince Philip
1961	R.G. Laver	H.R.H. Princess Marina, Duchess of Kent
1962	R.G. Laver	H.M. Queen Elizabeth II
1963	C.R. McKinley	H.R.H. Princess Marina, Duchess of Kent
1964	R.S. Emerson	H.R.H. Princess Marina, Duchess of Kent
1965	R.S. Emerson	H.R.H. Princess Marina, Duchess of Kent
1966	M. Santana	H.R.H. Princess Marina, Duchess of Kent
1967	J.D. Newcombe	H.R.H. Princess Marina, Duchess of Kent
1968	R.G. Laver	H.R.H. Princess Marina, Duchess of Kent
1969	R.G. Laver	H.R.H. Duke of Kent
1970	J.D. Newcombe	H.R.H. Princess Margaret
1971	J.D. Newcombe	H.R.H. Duke of Kent
1972	S.R. Smith	H.R.H. Duke of Kent
1973	J. Kodes	H.R.H. Duke of Kent
1974	J.S. Connors	H.R.H. Duke of Kent
1975	A.R. Ashe	H.R.H. Duke of Kent
1976	B.R. Borg	H.R.H. Duke of Kent
1977	B.R. Borg	H.R.H. Duke of Kent
1978	B.R. Borg	H.R.H. Duke of Kent
1979	B.R. Borg	H.R.H. Duchess of Kent
1980	B.R. Borg	H.R.H. Duke of Kent
1981	J.P. McEnroe	H.R.H. Duke of Kent
1982	J.S. Connors	H.R.H. Duke of Kent
1983	J.P. McEnroe	H.R.H. Duke of Kent
1984	J.P. McEnroe	H.R.H. Duke of Kent
1985	B.F. Becker	H.R.H. Duke of Kent
1986	B.F. Becker	J.R. Borotra, accompanied by the Duke and Duchess of Kent
1987	P.H. Cash	H.R.H. Duke of Kent
1988	S.B. Edberg	H.R.H. Duke of Kent
1989	B.F. Becker	H.R.H. Duke of Kent
1990	S.B. Edberg	H.R.H. Duke of Kent
1991	M.D. Stich	H.R.H. Duke of Kent
1992	A.K. Agassi	H.R.H. Duke of Kent
1993	P. Sampras	H.R.H. Duke of Kent
1994	P. Sampras	H.R.H. Duke of Kent
1995	P. Sampras	H.R.H. Duke of Kent
1996	R.P.S. Krajicek	H.R.H. Duke of Kent
1997	P. Sampras	H.R.H. Duke of Kent
1998	P. Sampras	H.R.H. Duke of Kent
1999	P. Sampras	H.R.H. Duke of Kent
2000	P. Sampras	H.R.H. Duke of Kent
2001	G.S. Ivanisevic	H.R.H. Duke of Kent
2002	L.G. Hewitt	H.R.H. Duke of Kent
2003	R. Federer	H.R.H. Duke of Kent
2004	R. Federer	H.R.H. Duke of Kent
2005	R. Federer	H.R.H. Duke of Kent

Year	Champion	Presenter
2006	R. Federer	H.R.H. Duke of Kent
2007	R. Federer	H.R.H. Duke of Kent
2008	R. Nadal	H.R.H. Duke of Kent
2009	R. Federer	H.R.H. Duke of Kent
2010	R. Nadal	H.R.H. Duke of Kent
2011	N. Djokovic	H.R.H. Duke of Kent
2012	R. Federer	H.R.H. Duke of Kent
2013	A.B. Murray	H.R.H. Duke of Kent
2014	N. Djokovic	H.R.H. Duke of Kent

Gentlemen's Doubles Championship

Year	Champions	Presenter	Location (1)
1946	Brown/Kramer		CCRB
1947	Falkenburg/Kramer	H.R.H. Duchess of Kent	CCRB
1948	Bromwich/Sedgman	H.M. Queen Mary	CCRB
1949	Gonzales/Parker	H.R.H. Duchess of Kent	CCRB
1950	Bromwich/Quist	H.R.H. Duchess of Kent	CCOC
1951	McGregor/Sedgman	H.R.H. Duchess of Kent	CCRB
1952	McGregor/Sedgman	H.R.H. Duchess of Kent	CCRB
1953	Hoad/Rosewall	H.R.H. Duchess of Kent	CCRB
1954	Hartwig/Rose	H.R.H. Duchess of Kent	CCRB
1955	Hartwig/Hoad	H.R.H. Duchess of Kent	CCRB
1956	Hoad/Rosewall	H.R.H. Duchess of Kent	CCRB
1957	Mulloy/Patty	H.M. Queen Elizabeth	CCOC
1958	Davidson/Schmidt	H.R.H. Duchess of Kent	CCRB
1959	Emerson/Fraser	H.R.H. Duchess of Kent	CCRB
1960	Osuna/Ralston	H.R.H. Duchess of Kent	CCRB
1961	Emerson/Fraser	H.R.H. Princess Alice	CCRB
1962	Hewitt/Stolle	H.R.H. Princess Marina, Duchess of Kent	CCRB
1963	Osuna/Palafox	H.R.H. Princess Marina, Duchess of Kent	CCRB
1964	Hewitt/Stolle	H.R.H. Princess Marina, Duchess of Kent	CCRB
1965	Newcombe/Roche	H.R.H. Princess Marina, Duchess of Kent	CCRB
1966	Fletcher/Newcombe	H.R.H. Princess Marina, Duchess of Kent	CCRB
1967	Hewitt/McMlillan	H.R.H. Princess Marina, Duchess of Kent	CCRB
1968	Newcombe/Roche	H.R.H. Princess Marina, Duchess of Kent	CCRB
1969	Newcombe/Roche	H.R.H. Duke of Kent	CCRB
1970	Newcornbe/Roche	H.R.H. Princess Margaret	CCRB
1971	Emerson/Laver	H.R.H. Princess Alexandra	CCRB
1972	Hewitt/McMillan	H.R.H. Duke of Kent	CCRB
1973	Connors/Nastase	H.R.H. Duke of Kent	CCOC (3)
1974	Newcombe/Roche	H.R.H. Duke of Kent	CCRB
1975	Gerulaitis/Mayer	H.R.H. Duke of Kent	CCRB
1976	Gottfried/Ramirez	H.R.H. Duke of Kent	CCRB
1977	Case/Masters	H.R.H. Duke of Kent	CCRB
1978	Hewitt/McMillan	H.R.H. Duchess of Kent	CCRB
1979	Fleming/McEnroe	H.R.H. Duke of Kent	CCRB
1980	McNamara/McNamee	H.R.H. Duchess of Kent	No. 1 OC
1981	Fleming/McEnroe	H.R.H. Duke of Kent	CCRB
1982	McNamara/McNamee	H.R.H. Duke of Kent	CCRB
1983	Fleming/McEnroe	H.R.H. Duke of Kent	CCRB
1984	Fleming/McEnroe	H.R.H. Duke of Kent	CCRB

Notes on page 329

Year	Champions	Presenter	Location (1)
1985	Guenthardt/Taroczy	H.R.H. Duke of Kent	CCRB
1986	Nystrom/Wilander	H.R.H. Duke of Kent	CCRB (4)
1987	Flach/Seguso	H.R.H. Duke of Kent	CCRB
1988	Flach/Seguso	H.R.H. Duke of Kent	No. 1 OC (4)
1989	Fitzgerald/Jarryd	H.R.H. Duke of Kent	No. 1 OC
1990	Leach/Pugh	H.R.H. Duke of Kent	CCRB
1991	Fitzgerald/Jarryd	H.R.H. Duke of Kent	CCRB
1992	McEnroe/Stich	Mr. J.A.H. Curry	No. 1 OC
1993	Woodbridge/Woodforde	H.R.H. Duchess of Kent	CCRB
1994	Woodbridge/Woodforde	H.R.H. Duke of Kent	CCRB
1995	Woodbridge/Woodforde	H.R.H. Duke of Kent	CCRB
1996	Woodbridge/Woodforde	H.R.H. Duke of Kent	CCRB
1997	Woodbridge/Woodforde	H.R.H. Duke of Kent	CCRB
1998	Eltingh/Haarhuis	H.R.H. Duke of Kent	CCRB
1999	Bhupathi/Paes	Mr. M.P. Hann	No. 1 OC(5)
2000	Woodbridge/Woodforde	H.R.H. Duke of Kent	CCRB
2001	Johnson/Palmer	Mr. M.P. Hann	No. 1 OC(5)
2002	Bjorkman/Woodbridge	Mr. M.P. Hann	No. 1 OC(5)
2003	Bjorkman/Woodbridge	H.R.H. Duke of Kent	CCRB
2004	Bjorkman/Woodbridge	Mr. M.P. Hann	No. 1 OC(5)
2005	Huss/Moodie	Mr. R. Taylor	No. 1 OC(5)
2006	Bryan / Bryan	H.R.H Duke of Kent	CCRB
2007	Clement / Llodra	Mr. R. Taylor	No. 1 OC
2008	Nestor / Zimonjic	H.R.H Duke of Kent	CCR
2009	Nestor/Zimonjic	H.R.H. Duke of Kent	CCRB
2010	Melzer/Petzschner	H.R.H. Duke of Kent	CCRB
2011	Bryan/Bryan	H.R.H Duke of Kent	CCRB
2012	Marray/Nielsen	H.R.H Duke of Kent	CCRB
2013	Bryan/Bryan	H.R.H Duke of Kent	CCRB
2014	Pospisil/Sock	H.R.H Duke of Kent	CCRB

Notes on page 329

Ladies' Singles Championship

Year	Champion	Presenter	Location
1946	Miss P.M. Betz	H.M. Queen Mary	Royal Box
1947	Miss M.E. Osborne	H.R.H. Duchess of Kent	Royal Box
1948	Miss A.L. Brough	H.M. Queen Mary	Royal Box
1949	Miss A.L. Brough	H.R.H. Duchess of Kent	Royal Box
1950	Miss A.L. Brough	H.M. Queen Mary	Royal Box
1951	Miss D.J. Hart	H.R.H. Duchess of Kent	On Court
1952	Miss M.C. Connolly	H.R.H. Duchess of Kent	On Court
1953	Miss M.C. Connolly	H.R.H. Duchess of Kent	Royal Box

Presentation on Centre Court	
Year / Champion	Presenter

Year	Champion	Presenter
1954	Miss M.C. Connolly	H.R.H. Duchess of Kent
1955	Miss A.L. Brough	H.R.H. Duchess of Kent
1956	Miss S.J. Fry	H.R.H. Duchess of Kent
1957	Miss A. Gibson	H.M. Queen Elizabeth II
1958	Miss A. Gibson	H.R.H. Duchess of Kent
1959	Miss M.E.A. Bueno	H.R.H. Duchess of Kent

Year	Champion	Presenter
1960	Miss M.E.A. Bueno	H.R.H. Duchess of Kent
1961	Miss F.A.M. Mortimer	H.R.H. Princess Alice
1962	Mrs. J.R. Susman	H.R.H. Princess Marina, Duchess of Kent
1963	Miss M. Smith	H.R.H. Princess Marina, Duchess of Kent
1964	Miss M.E.A. Bueno	H.R.H. Princess Marina, Duchess of Kent
1965	Miss M. Smith	H.R.H. Princess Marina, Duchess of Kent
1966	Mrs. L.W. King	H.R.H. Princess Marina, Duchess of Kent
1967	Mrs. L.W. King	H.R.H. Princess Marina, Duchess of Kent
1968	Mrs. L.W. Kin	H.R.H. Princess Marina, Duchess of Kent
1969	Mrs. P.F. Jones	H.R.H. Princess Anne
1970	Mrs. B.M. Court	H.R.H. Princess Margaret
1971	Miss E.F. Goolagong	H.R.H. Princess Alexandra
1972	Mrs. L.W. King	H.R.H. Duke of Kent
1973	Mrs. L.W. King	H.R.H. Duke of Kent
1974	Miss C.M. Evert	H.R.H. Duke of Kent
1975	Mrs. L.W. King	H.R.H. Duke of Kent
1976	Miss C.M. Evert	H.R.H. Duchess of Kent
1977	Miss S.V. Wade	H.M. Queen Elizabeth II
1978	Miss M. Navratilova	H.R.H. Duchess of Kent
1979	Miss M. Navratilova	H.R.H. Duchess of Kent
1980	Mrs. R.A. Cawley	H.R.H. Duchess of Kent
1981	Mrs. J.M. Lloyd	H.R.H. Duchess of Kent
1982	Miss M. Navratilova	H.R.H. Duchess of Kent
1983	Miss M. Navratilova	H.R.H. Duke of Kent
1984	Miss M. Navratilova	H.R.H. Duchess of Kent
1985	Miss M. Navratilova	H.R.H. Duchess of Kent
1986	Miss M. Navratilova	Mrs. K. Godfree, accompanied by the Duke and Duchess of Kent
1987	Miss M. Navratilova	H.R.H. Duchess of Kent
1988	Miss S.M. Graf	H.R.H. Duchess of Kent
1989	Miss S.M. Graf	H.R.H. Duchess of Kent
1990	Miss M. Navratilova	H.R.H. Duchess of Kent
1991	Miss S.M. Graf	H.R.H. Duchess of Kent
1992	Miss S.M. Graf	H.R.H. Duchess of Kent
1993	Miss S.M. Graf	H.R.H. Duchess of Kent
1994	Miss I.C. Martinez	H.R.H. Duchess of Kent
1995	Miss S.M. Graf	H.R.H. Duchess of Kent
1996	Miss S.M. Graf	H.R.H. Duchess of Kent
1997	Miss M. Hingis	H.R.H. Duchess of Kent
1998	Miss J. Novotna	H.R.H. Duchess of Kent
1999	Miss L.A. Davenport	H.R.H. Duchess of Kent
2000	Miss V.E.S. Williams	H.R.H. Duchess of Kent
2001	Miss V.E.S. Williams	H.R.H. Duchess of Kent
2002	Miss S.J. Williams	H.R.H. Princess Alexandra
2003	Miss S.J. Williams	H.R.H. Duke of Kent
2004	Miss M. Sharapova	H.R.H. Duke of Kent
2005	Miss V.E.S. Williams	H.R.H. Duke of Kent
2006	Miss A. Mauresmo	H.R.H. Duke of Kent
2007	Miss V.E.S. Williams	H.R.H. Duke of Kent
2008	Miss V.E.S. Williams	H.R.H. Duke of Kent
2009	Miss S.J. Williams	H.R.H. Duke of Kent
2010	Miss S.J. Williams	H.R.H. Duke of Kent
2011	Miss P. Kvitova	H.R.H. Duke of Kent
2012	Miss S.J. Williams	H.R.H. Duke of Kent
2013	Miss M.S. Bartoli	H.R.H. Duke of Kent
2014	Miss P. Kvitova	H.R.H. Duke of Kent

Ladies' Doubles Championship

Year	Champions	Presenter	Location (1)
1946	Brough/Osborne		CCRB
1947	Hart/Todd	H.R.H. Duchess of Kent	CCRB
1948	Brough/Dupont	H.R.H. Duchess of Kent	CCRB
1949	Brough/Dupont	H.R.H. Duchess of Kent	CCOC
1950	Brough/Dupont	H.M. Queen Mary	CCRB
1951	Fry/Hart	H.R.H. Duchess of Kent	CCOC
1952	Fry/Hart	H.R.H. Duchess of Kent	CCOC
1953	Fry/Hart	H.R.H. Duchess of Kent	CCOC
1954	Brough/Dupont	H.R.H. Duchess of Kent	CCOC
1955	Mortimer/Shilcock	H.R.H. Duchess of Kent	CCOC
1956	Buxton/Gibson	H.R.H. Duchess of Kent	CCOC
1957	Gibson/Hard	H.R.H. Duchess of Kent	CCOC
1958	Bueno/Gibson	H.R.H. Duchess of Kent	CCOC
1959	Arth/Hard	H.R.H. Duchess of Kent	CCOC
1960	Bueno/Hard	H.R.H. Duchess of Kent	CCOC
1961	Hantze/Moffitt	Mr. H.F. David	CCRB
1962	Moffitt/Susman	H.R.H. Princess Marina, Duchess of Kent	CCOC
1963	Bueno/Hard	H.R.H. Princess Marina, Duchess of Kent	CCOC
1964	Smith/Turner	H.R.H. Princess Marina, Duchess of Kent	CCRB
1965	Bueno/Moffitt	H.R.H. Princess Marina, Duchess of Kent	CCOC
1966	Bueno/Richey	H.R.H. Princess Marina, Duchess of Kent	CCRB
1967	Casals/King	H.R.H. Princess Marina, Duchess of Kent	CCRB
1968	Casals/King	H.R.H. Princess Marina, Duchess of Kent	CCRB
1969	Court/Tegart	H.R.H. Princess Marina, Duchess of Kent	CCRB
1970	Casals/King	H.R.H. Princess Margaret	CCRB
1971	Casais/King	H.R.H. Princess Alexandra.	CCRB
1972	King/Stove	H.R.H. Duke of Kent	No. 1 OC
1973	Casals/King	H.R.H. Duke of Kent	CCRB
1974	Goolagong/Michel	H.R.H. Duchess of Kent	CCRB
1975	Kiyomura/Sawamatsu	H.R.H. Duchess of Kent	CCRB
1976	Evert/Navratilova	H.R.H. Duke of Kent	CCRB
1977	Cawley/Russell	H.R.H. Duke of Kent	CCRB
1978	Reid/Turnbull	H.R.H. Duchess of Kent	CCRB
1979	King/Navratilova	H.R.H. Duchess of Kent	CCRB
1980	Jordan/Smith	H.R.H. Duchess of Kent	CCRB
1981	Navratilova/Shriver	H.R.H. Duchess of Kent	CCRB
1982	Navratilova/Shriver	H.R.H. Duchess of Kent	CCRB
1983	Navratilova/Shriver	H.R.H. Duchess of Kent	CCRB
1984	Navratilova/Shriver	H.R.H. Duchess of Kent	CCRB
1985	Jordan/Smylie	H.R.H. Duchess of Kent	CCRB
1986	Navratilova/Shriver	H.R.H. Duke of Kent	CCRB (3)
1987	Kohde-Kilsch/Sukova	H.R.H. Duchess of Kent	CCRB
1988	Graf/Sabatini	H.R.H. Duke of Kent	No. 2 OC
1989	Novotna/Sukova	H.R.H. Duchess of Kent	No. 1 OC
1990	Novotna/Sukova	H.R.H. Duchess of Kent	CCRB
1991	Savchenko/Zvereva	H.R.H. Duchess of Kent	CCRB
1992	Fernandez/Zvereva	H.R.H. Duchess of Kent	No. 1 OC
1993	Fernandez/Zvereva	H.R.H. Duchess of Kent	CCRB
1994	Fernandez/Zvereva	H.R.H. Duke of Kent	CCRB
1995	Novotna/Sanchez Vicario	H.R.H. Duchess of Kent	CCRB
1996	Hingis/Sukova	Mr. J.A.H. Curry	CCRB

Notes on page 329

Year	Champions	Presenter	Location (1)
1997	Fernandez/Zvereva	H.R.H. Duke of Kent	No. 1 OC
1998	Hingis/Novotna	H.R.H. Duchess of Kent	CCRB
1999	Davenport/Morariu	Mrs. P.F. Jones	No. 1 OC(5)
2000	Williams/Williams	Mr. T.D. Phillips	CCOC
2001	Raymond/Stubbs	H.R.H. Duke of Kent	CCRB
2002	Williams/Williams	H.R.H. Duke of Kent	CCRB
2003	Clijsters/Sugiyama	H.R.H. Duke of Kent	CCRB
2004	Black/Stubbs	Mrs. P.F. Jones	No. 2 OC(5)
2005	Black/Huber	H.R.H. Duke of Kent	CCRB
2006	Yan/Zheng	H.R.H. Duke of Kent	CCRB
2007	Black/Huber	Miss S.V. Wade	No. 1 OC
2008	Williams/Williams	H.R.H. Duke of Kent	CCRB
2009	Williams/Williams	Mrs P.F. Jones	CCRB
2010	King/Shvedova	H.R.H. Duke of Kent	CCRB
2011	Peschke/Srebotnik	H.R.H. Duke of Kent	CCRB
2012	Williams/Williams	H.R.H. Duke of Kent	CCRB
2013	Hsieh/Peng	H.R.H. Duke of Kent	CCRB
2014	Errani/Vinci	H.R.H. Duke of Kent	CCRB

Mixed Doubles Championship

Year	Champions	Presenter	Location (1)
1946	Brown/Brough		CCRB
1947	Bromwich/Brough	H.R.H. Duchess of Kent	CCRB
1948	Bromwich/Brough	H.R.H. Duchess of Kent	CCRB
1949	Sturgess/Summers	Mrs. C.R. Atlee	CCRB
1950	Sturgess/Brough	H.M. Queen Mary	CCRB
1951	Sedgman/Hart	H.R.H. Duchess of Kent	CCRB
1952	Sedgman/Hart	H.R.H. Duchess of Kent	CCRB
1953	Seixas/Hart	H.R.H. Duchess of Kent	CCOC
1954	Seixas/Hart	H.R.H. Duchess of Kent	CCOC
1955	Seixas/Hart	Mr. A.H. Riseley	CCOC
1956	Seixas/Fry	H.R.H. Duchess of Kent	CCOC
1957	Rose/Hard	H.R.H. Duchess of Kent	CCOC
1958	Howe/Coghlan	H.R.H. Duchess of Kent	CCRB
1959	Laver/Hard		CC
1960	Laver/Hard		CC
1961	Stolle/Turner		CCRB (3)
1962	Fraser/Dupont		CC
1963	Fletcher/Smith	H.R.H. Princess Marina, Duchess of Kent	CCRB
1964	Stolle/Turner	H.R.H. Princess Marina, Duchess of Kent	CCRB
1965	Fletcher/Smith	H.R.H. Princess Marina, Duchess of Kent	CCRB
1966	Fletcher/Smith	H.R.H. Princess Marina, Duchess of Kent	CCRB
1967	Davidson/King		CCRB
1968	Fletcher/Court	H.R.H. Princess Marina, Duchess of Kent	CCRB
1969	Stolle/Jones	Mr. H.F. David	CCRB
1970	Nastase/Casals		CCRB
1971	Davidson/King	H.R.H. Princess Alexandra	CCRB
1972	Nastase/Casals	H.R.H. Duke of Kent	CCRB
1973	Davidson/King	H.R.H. Duke of Kent	CCRB
1974	Davidson/King	H.R.H. Duke of Kent	CCRB
1975	Riessen/Court	H.R.H. Duke of Kent	CCRB

Year	Champion	Presenter	Location (1)
1976	Roche/Durr	H.R.H. Duchess of Kent	CCRB
1977	Hewitt/Stevens		CCRB
1978	McMillan/Stove	H.R.H. Duke of Kent	CCRB
1979	Hewitt/Stevens	H.R.H. Duke of Kent	CCRB
1980	Austin/Austin	H.R.H. Duchess of Kent	CCRB
1981	McMillan/Stove	H.R.H. Duchess of Kent	CCRB
1982	Curren/Smith	H.R.H. Duke of Kent	No. 3 OC
1983	Lloyd/Turnbull	H.R.H. Duke of Kent	CCRB
1984	Lloyd/Turnbull	H.R.H. Duchess of Kent	CCRB
1985	McNamee/Navratilova	H.R.H. Duchess of Kent	CCRB
1986	Flach/Jordan	H.R.H. Duke of Kent	CCRB
1987	Bates/Durie	H.R.H. Duke of Kent	CCRB
1988	Stewart/Garrison	Mr. R.E.H. Hadingham	No. 1 OC
1989	Pugh/Novotna	H.R.H. Duchess of Kent	No. 1 OC
1990	Leach/Garrison	H.R.H. Duke of Kent	CCRB
1991	Fitzgerald/Smylie	H.R.H. Duke of Kent	CCRB
1992	Suk/Neiland	Mr. J.A.H. Curry	No. 1 OC
1993	Woodforde/Navratilova	H.R.H. Duke of Kent	CCRB
1994	Woodbridge/Sukova	H.R.H. Duke of Kent	CCRB
1995	Stark/Navratilova	H.R.H. Duke of Kent	CCRB
1996	Suk/Sukova	Mr. J.A.H. Curry	CCRB
1997	Suk/Sukova	H.R.H. Duke of Kent	No. 1 OC
1998	Mirnyi/S. Williams	H.R.H. Duke of Kent	CCRB(3)
1999	Paes/Raymond	H.R.H. Duke of Kent	CCRB
2000	Johnson/Po	Mrs. P.F. Jones	No. 1 OC(5)
2001	Friedl/Hantuchova	Mr. M.P. Hann	No. 1 OC(5)
2002	Bhupathi/Likhovtseva	Mr. T.D. Phillips	CCRB
2003	Paes/Navratilova	H.R.H. Duke of Kent	CCRB
2004	Black/Black	H.R.H. Duke of Kent	CCRB
2005	Bhupathi/Pierce	H.R.H. Duke of Kent	CCRB
2006	Ram/Zvonareva	Mrs P.F. Jones	CCRB
2007	Murray/Jankovic	H.R.H. Duke of Kent	CCRB
2008	R.C. Bryan/Stosur	Mrs P.F. Jones	No. 1 OC
2009	Knowles/Groenefeld	Mrs P.F. Jones	CCRB
2010	Paes/Black	H.R.H. Duke of Kent	CCRB
2011	Melzer/Benesova	H.R.H. Duke of Kent	CCRB
2012	M.C. Bryan/Raymond	H.R.H. Duke of Kent	CCRB
2013	Nestor/Mladenovic	H.R.H. Duke of Kent	CCRB
2014	Zimonjic/Stosur	H.R.H Duke of Kent	CCRB

Notes   1. CCRB – Centre Court Royal Box. CCOC – Centre Court on Court. No. 1 OC – No. 1 on Court.
        No. 2 OC – No. 2 On Court. No. 3 OC – No. 3 On Court.
        2. The Duchess of Kent (1946–1960) became Princess Marina, Duchess of Kent (1961–1968). The
        Duchess of Kent (Katharine) (1961 to date).
        3. Final played on No. 1 Court.
        4. Final started on Centre Court and concluded on No. 1 Court.
        5. The Champions were presented with their trophies a second time in the Centre Court Royal Box
        by the Duke of Kent.

Prizes

Gentlemen's Singles Championship

1877	Champion	Challenge Cup (Field)
		Gold Prize – value 12 guineas
	Runner-up	Silver Prize – value 7 guineas
	Semi-finalist (1)	Third prize – value 3 guineas

1878	Champion	Challenge Cup (Field)
	All Comers' Singles	
	Winner	Gold Prize – value 19 guineas
	Runner-up	Silver Prize – value unknown
	Semi-finalist (1)	Third Prize – value 4 guineas
	Fourth and Fifth places	– saved their stakes

1879	Champion	Challenge Cup (Field)
	All Comers' Singles	
	Winner	Gold Prize – value 25 guineas
	Runner-up	Silver Prize – value 12 guineas
	Semi-finalist (1)	Third Prize – value 5 guineas
	Fourth, Fifth and Sixth places	– saved their stakes

1880	Champion	Challenge Cup (Field)
	All Comers' Singles	
	Winner	Gold prize – value 30 guineas
	Runner-up	Silver Prize – value 14 guineas
	Semi-finalists (2)	Third prize – value 6 guineas
	Fifth, Sixth, Seventh and	
	Eighth places	– saved their stakes

1881	Champion	Challenge Cup (Field)
	All Comers' Singles	
	Winner	Gold Prize – value 25 guineas
	Runner-up	Silver Prize – value 12 guineas
	Semi-finalist (1)	Third Prize – value 8 guineas
	Fourth, Fifth and Sixth places	– saved their stakes

1882	Champion	Challenge Cup (Field)
	All Comers' Singles	
	Winner	Gold Prize – 25 guineas
	Runner-up	Silver Prize – 12 guineas
	Semi-finalists (2)	Third Prize – 3 guineas

1883	Champion	Challenge Cup (Field)
	All Comers' Singles	
	Winner	Gold Prize – value 30 guineas
	Runner-up	Silver Prize – value 15 guineas
	Semi-finalist (1)	Third Prize – value 5 guineas

1884–1886	Champion	Challenge Cup (AELTC)
	All Comers' Singles	
	Winner	Gold Prize – value 30 guineas
	Runner-up	Silver prize – value 15 guineas
	Semi-finalists (2)	Third Prize – value 5 guineas

1887–1894	Champion	Challenge Cup (AELTC)
		Gold Medal
	All Comers' Singles	
	Winner	First Prize – value 30 guineas
	Runner-up	Second Prize – value 15 guineas
	Semi-finalists (2)	Third Prize – value 5 guineas

1895	Champion	Challenge Cup (AELTC)
		Gold Medal
	All Comers' Singles	
	Winner	First Prize – value £30
	Runner-up	Second Prize – value £15
	Semi-finalists (2)	Third Prize – value £5

1896–1898	Champion	Challenge Cup (AELTC)
		Gold Medal
	All Comers' Singles	
	Winner	First Prize – value £20
	Runner-up	Second Prize – value £10
	Semi-finalists (2)	Third Prize – value £5

1899–1903	Champion	Challenge Cup (AELTC)
		Gold Medal
	All Comers' Singles	
	Winner	First Prize – value unknown
	Runner-up	Second prize – value unknown
	Semi-finalists (2)	Third Prize – value unknown

1904	Champion	Challenge Cup (AELTC)
		Gold Medal
	All Comers' Singles	
	Winner	First prize – value £18
	Runner-up	Second Prize – value £9
	Semi-finalists (2)	Third Prize – value £5

1905–1907	Champion	Challenge Cup (AELTC)
		Gold Medal
	All Comers' Singles	
	Winner	First Prize – Renshaw Cup
	Runner-up	Second Prize – value £10
	Semi-finalists (2)	Third Prize – value £5
	Quarter-finalists (4)	Fourth Prize – value £2.10s.

1908–1910	Champion	Challenge Cup (AELTC)
		Gold Medal
		Memento to value of £20 (provided he was not the winner of the All Comers' Singles)

	All Comers' Singles	
	Winner	Challenge Cup (President's)
		First Prize – Renshaw Cup
	Runner-up	Second prize – value £10
	Semi-finalists (2)	Third Prize – value £5
1911	Champion	Challenge Cup (AELTC)
		Gold Medal
		Memento to value of £20 (provided he was not the winner of the All Comers' Singles)
	All Comers' Singles	
	Winner	Challenge Cup (President's)
		First Prize – Renshaw Cup
	Runner-up	Second prize – value £10
	Semi-finalists (2)	Third prize – value £5
	Quarter-finalists (4)	Third Prize – value £2.10s.
1912	Champion	Challenge Cup (AELTC)
		Gold Medal
		Memento to value of £20 (provided he was not the winner of the All Comers' Singles)
	All Comers' Singles	
	Winner	Challenge Cup (President's)
		First Prize – Renshaw Cup
	Runner-up	Second Prize – value £10
	Semi-finalists (2)	Third Prize – value £5
1913–1914 1919–1921	Champion	Challenge Cup (AELTC)
		Gold Medal
		Gold Medal (LTA)
		Memento to value of £20 (provided he was not the winner of the All Comers' Singles)
	All Comers' Singles	
	Winner	Challenge Cup (President's)
		First Prize – Renshaw Cup
	Runner-up	Second Prize – value £10
	Semi-finalists (2)	Third Prize – value £5
1922–1923	Champion	Challenge Cup (AELTC)
		Challenge Cup (President's)
		First Prize – Renshaw Cup
		Gold Medal
		Gold Medal (LTA)
	Runner-up	Second Prize – value £10
	Semi-finalists (2)	Third Prize – value £5
1924–1939	Champion	Challenge Cup (AELTC)
		Challenge Cup (President's)
		First Prize – Renshaw Cup
		Gold Medal
	Runner-up	Second Prize – value £10
	Semi-finalists (2)	Third Prize – value £5

1946–1948	Champion	Challenge Cup (AELTC)
		Challenge Cup (President's)
		First Prize – Renshaw Cup
		Bronze Medal
	Runner-up	Second Prize – value £10
	Semi-finalists (2)	Third Prize – value £5
1949–1951	Champion	Challenge Cup (AELTC)
		Challenge Cup (President's)
		Miniature replicas of both Challenge Cups
		First Prize – Renshaw Cup
	Runner-up	Second Prize – value £10
		Silver Medal
	Semi-finalists (2)	Third Prize – value £5
		Bronze Medal
1952	Champion	Challenge Cup (AELTC)
		Challenge Cup (President's)
		Miniature replicas of both Challenge Cups
		First Prize – Renshaw Cup
	Runner-up	Second Prize – value £15
		Silver Medal
	Semi-finalists (2)	Third Prize – value £8
		Bronze Medal
1953–1964	Champion	Challenge Cup (AELTC)
		Challenge Cup (President's)
		Miniature replicas of both Challenge Cups
		First Prize – Miniature Renshaw Cup
	Runner-up	Second Prize – value £15
		Silver Medal
	Semi-finalists (2)	Third Prize – value £8
		Bronze Medal
1965–1967	Champion	Challenge Cup (AELTC)
		Challenge Cup (President's)
		Miniature replicas of both Challenge Cups
		First Prize – Miniature Renshaw Cup
	Runner-up	Second Prize – value £30
		Silver Medal
	Semi-finalists (2)	Third Prize – value £16
		Bronze Medal

Prize Money

1968–1969

Players competing for prize money

	Champion	Challenge Cup (AELTC)
		Challenge Cup (President's)
		Miniature replicas of both Challenge Cups
		First Prize – Miniature Renshaw Cup
	Runner-up	Silver Medal
	Semi-finalists (2)	Bronze Medal

Players not competing for prize money

	Champion	Challenge Cup (AELTC)
		Challenge Cup (President's)
		Miniature replicas of both Challenge Cups
		First Prize – Miniature Renshaw Cup
	Runner-up	Prize – value £30
		Silver Medal
	Semi-finalists (2)	Prize – value £16
		Bronze Medal

1970–1986	Champion	Challenge Cup (AELTC)
		Challenge Cup (President's)
		Miniature replicas of both Challenge Cups
		First Prize – Miniature Renshaw Cup
	Runner-up	Silver Medal
	Semi-finalists (2)	Bronze Medal

Note: In 1977 the Champion also received a Silver Salver marking the occasion of H.M. The Queen's Silver Jubilee and the Centenary of The Championships.

1987–1989	Champion	Challenge Cup (AELTC)
		Challenge Cup (President's)
		Miniature replicas of both Challenge Cups
		First Prize – Miniature Renshaw Cup
	Runner-up	Personal prize (Silver Salver)
		Silver Medal
	Semi-finalists (2)	Bronze Medal

1990	Champion	Challenge Cup (AELTC)
		Challenge Cup (President's)
		Miniature replicas of both Challenge Cups
	Runner-up	Personal prize (Silver Salver)
		Silver Medal
	Semi-finalists (2)	Bronze Medal

1991–1994	Champion	Challenge Cup (AELTC)
		Challenge Cup (President's)
		Miniature replicas of both Challenge Cups
	Runner-up	Silver Salver
	Semi-finalists (2)	Bronze Medal

1995–2006	Champion	Challenge Cup (AELTC)
		Miniature replica of Challenge Cup
	Runner-up	Silver Salver
	Semi-finalists (2)	Bronze Medal

2007–2015	Champion	Challenge Cup (AELTC)
		Three-quarter size Challenge Cup
	Runner-up	Silver Salver
	Semi-finalists (2)	Bronze Medal

Gentlemen's Doubles Championship

1884	Champions (2)	Challenge Cup (OULTC)
		First Prize – Silver Cup value £10
	Runners-up (2)	Second Prize – Silver Cup value £5
	Semi-finalists (4)	Third Prize – Silver Cup value £5
1885	Champions (2)	Challenge Cup (OULTC)
		First Prize – Silver Cup value £10
	Runners-up (2)	Second Prize – Silver Cup value £5
1886–1888	Champions (2)	Challenge Cup (OULTC)
	All Comers' Doubles	
	Winners (2)	First Prize – Silver Cup value £10
	Runners-up (2)	Second Prize – Silver Cup value £5
1889–1894	Champions (2)	Challenge Cup (OULTC)
	All Comers' Doubles	
	Winners (2)	First Prize – Silver Cup value 10 guineas
	Runners-up (2)	Second Prize – Silver Cup value 5 guineas
1895–1898	Champions (2)	Challenge Cup (OULTC)
		Gold Medal
	All Comers' Doubles	
	Winners (2)	First Prize – Silver Cup value £10
	Runners-up (2)	Second Prize – Silver Cup value £5
1899–1903	Champions (2)	Challenge Cup (OULTC)
		Gold Medal
	All Comers' Doubles	
	Winners (2)	First Prize – value unknown
	Runners-up (2)	Second Prize – value unknown
1904	Champions (2)	Challenge Cup (OULTC)
		Gold Medal
	All Comers' Doubles	
	Winners (2)	First prize – Silver Cup value £8
	Runners-up (2)	Second Prize – Silver Cup value £4
1905–1907	Champions (2)	Challenge Cup (OULTC)
		Gold Medal
	All Comers' Doubles	
	Winners (2)	First Prize – Silver Cup value £8
	Runners-up (2)	Second Prize – Silver Cup value £4
	Semi-finalists (4)	Third Prize – value £2
1908–1911	Champions (2)	Challenge Cup (OULTC)
		Gold Medal
		Memento to value £10 (provided they were
		not the winners of the All Comers' Doubles)
	All Comers' Doubles	
	Winners (2)	First Prize – Silver Cup value £10
	Runners-up (2)	Second Prize – Silver Cup value £5
	Semi-finalists (4)	Third Prize – value £2.10s.

1912	Champions (2)	Challenge Cup (OULTC) Gold Medal Memento to value £10 (provided they were not the winners of the All Comers' Doubles)
	All Comers' Doubles	
	Winners (2)	First Prize – Silver Cup value £10
	Runners-up (2)	Second Prize – Silver Cup value £5
1913–1914 1919–1921	Champions (2)	Challenge Cup (OULTC) Gold Medal Gold Medal (LTA) Memento to value £10 (provided they were not the winners of the All Comers' Doubles)
	All Comers' Doubles	
	Winners (2)	First Prize – value £10
	Runners-up (2)	Second Prize – Silver Cup value £5
1922–1923	Champions (2)	Challenge Cup (OULTC) First Prize – Silver Cup value £10 Gold Medal (LTA) Gold Medal
	Runners-up (2)	Second Prize – Silver Cup value £5
1924–1932	Champions (2)	Challenge Cup (OULTC) First Prize – Silver Cup value £10 Gold Medal
	Runners-up (2)	Second Prize – Silver Cup value £5
1933–1934	Champions (2)	Challenge Cup (OULTC) First Prize – Silver Cup value £10 Gold Medal
	Runners-up (2)	Second prize – Silver Cup value £5
	Semi-finalists (4)	Third Prize – value £2.10s.
1935–1936	Champions (2)	Challenge Cup (OULTC) First Prize – value £10 Gold Medal
	Runners-up (2)	Second Prize – value £5
	Semi-finalists (4)	Third Prize – value £2.10s.
1937–1939	Champions (2)	Challenge Cup (OULTC) Challenge Cup (H. Wilberforce) First Prize – value £10 Gold Medal
	Runners-up (2)	Second Prize – value £5
	Semi-finalists (4)	Third Prize – value £2.10s.

1946–1948	Champions (2)	Challenge Cup (OULTC)
		Challenge Cup (H. Wilberforce)
		First Prize – value £10
		Bronze Medal
	Runners-up (2)	Second Prize – value £5
	Semi-finalists (4)	Third Prize – value £2.10s.

1949–1951	Champions (2)	Challenge Cup (OULTC)
		Challenge Cup (H. Wilberforce)
		Miniature replica of Challenge Cup
		First Prize – value £10
	Runners-up (2)	Second Prize – value £5
		Silver Medal
	Semi-finalists (4)	Third Prize – value £2.10s.
		Bronze Medal

1952–1964	Champions (2)	Challenge Cup (OULTC)
		Challenge Cup (H. Wilberforce)
		Miniature replica of Challenge Cup
		First Prize – value £10
	Runners-up (2)	Second Prize – value £8
		Silver Medal
	Semi-finalists (4)	Third Prize – value £5
		Bronze Medal

1965–1967	Champions (2)	Challenge Cup (OULTC)
		Challenge Cup (H. Wilberforce)
		Miniature replica of Challenge Cup
		First Prize – value £20
	Runners-up (2)	Second Prize – value £16
		Silver Medal
	Semi-finalists (4)	Third Prize – value £10
		Bronze Medal

Prize Money

1968–1969

Players competing for prize money

	Champions (2)	Challenge Cup (OULTC)
		Challenge Cup (H. Wilberforce)
		Miniature replica of Challenge Cup
	Runners-up (2)	Silver Medal
	Semi-finalists (4)	Bronze Medal

Players not competing for prize money

	Champions (2)	Challenge Cup (OULTC)
		Challenge Cup (H. Wilberforce)
		Miniature replica of Challenge Cup
		Prize – value £20
	Runners-up (2)	Prize – value £16
		Silver Medal
	Semi-finalists (4)	Prize – value £10
		Bronze Medal

1970–1986	Champions (2)	Challenge Cup (OULTC)
		Challenge Cup (H. Wilberforce)
		Miniature replica of Challenge Cup
	Runners-up (2)	Silver Medal
	Semi-finalists (4)	Bronze Medal
1987–1990	Champions (2)	Challenge Cup (OULTC)
		Challenge Cup (H. Wilberforce)
		Miniature replica of Challenge Cup
	Runners-up (2)	Personal prize (Silver Salver)
		Silver Medal
	Semi-finalists (4)	Bronze Medal
1991–2011	Champions (2)	Challenge Cup (OULTC)
		Challenge Cup (H. Wilberforce)
		Miniature replica of Challenge Cup
	Runners-up (2)	Silver Salver
	Semi-finalists (4)	Bronze Medal
2012–2015	Champions (2)	Challenge Cup (OULTC)
		Challenge Cup (H. Wilberforce)
		Three-quarter size Challenge Cup
	Runners-up (2)	Silver Salver
	Semi-finalists (4)	Bronze Medal

Ladies' Singles Championship

1884	Champion	First Prize – value 20 guineas
		(silver flower basket)
	Runner-up	Second Prize – value 10 guineas (silver and
		glass hand mirror and silver backed brush)
1885	Champion	First Prize – 20 guineas
	Runner-up	Second Prize – value 10 guineas
1886–1895	Champion	Challenge Trophy (AELTC)
		Bracelet – value 5 guineas
	All Comers' Singles	
	Winner	First prize – value 20 guineas
	Runner-up	Second Prize – value 10 guineas
1896–1897	Champion	Challenge Trophy (AELTC)
		Bracelet – value 5 guineas
	All Comers' Singles	
	Winner	First Prize – value £10
	Runner-up	Second Prize – value £5
1898	Champion	Challenge Trophy (AELTC)
		Bracelet – value 5 guineas
	All Comers' Singles	
	Winner	First Prize – value £10
	Runner-up	Second Prize – value £5
	Semi-finalists (2)	Third Prize – value £1

1899–1903	Champion	Challenge Trophy (AELTC)
		Bracelet – value 5 guineas
	All Comers' Singles	
	Winner	First Prize – value unknown
	Runner-up	Second Prize – value unknown
	Semi-finalists (2)	Third Prize – value unknown

1904	Champion	Challenge Trophy (AELTC)
		Bracelet – value 5 guineas
	All Comers' Singles	
	Winner	First Prize – value £8
	Runner-up	Second Prize – value £4
	Semi-finalists (2)	Third Prize – value £1

1905–1906	Champion	Challenge Trophy (AELTC)
		Bracelet – value 5 guineas
	All Comers' Singles	
	Winner	First prize – value £8
	Runner-up	Second Prize – value £4
	Semi-finalists (2)	Third Prize – value £2
	Quarter-finalists (4)	Fourth Prize – value £1

1907	Champion	Challenge Trophy (AELTC)
		Bracelet – value 5 guineas
	All Comers' Singles	
	Winner	First Prize – value £8
	Runner-up	Second Prize – value £4
	Semi-finalists (2)	Third Prize – value £1

1908–1912	Champion	Challenge Trophy (AELTC)
		Bracelet – value 5 guineas
		Memento to value £10 (provided she was not the winner of the All Comers' Singles)
	All Comers' Singles	
	Winner	First Prize – value £10
	Runner-up	Second Prize – value £5
	Semi-finalists (2)	Third Prize – value £2.10s.

1913–1914 1919–1921	Champion	Challenge Trophy (AELTC)
		Bracelet – value 5 guineas
		Gold Medal (LTA)
		Memento to value £10 (provided she was not the winner of the All Comers' Singles)
	All Comers' Singles	
	Winner	First Prize – value £10
	Runner-up	Second Prize – value £5
	Semi-finalists (2)	Third Prize – value £2.10s.

1922–1923	Champion	Challenge Trophy (AELTC)
		First Prize – value £10
		Bracelet – value 5 guineas
		Gold Medal (LTA)
	Runner-up	Second Prize – value £5
	Semi-finalists (2)	Third Prize – value £2.10s.

1924–1932	Champion	Challenge Trophy (AELTC)
		First Prize – value £10
		Bracelet – value 5 guineas
		Gold Medal
	Runner-up	Second Prize – value £5
	Semi-finalists (2)	Third Prize – value £2.10s.

1933–1939	Champion	Challenge Trophy (AELTC)
		First Prize – value £15
		Gold Medal
	Runner-up	Second prize – value £7.10s.
	Semi-finalists (2)	Third Prize – value £3.15s.

1946–1948	Champion	Challenge Trophy (AELTC)
		First Prize – value £15
		Bronze Medal
	Runner-up	Second Prize – value £7.10s.
	Semi-finalists (2)	Third prize – value £3.15s.

1949–1951	Champion	Challenge Trophy (AELTC)
		Miniature replica of Challenge Trophy
		First Prize – value £15
	Runner-up	Second Prize – value £7.10s.
		Silver Medal
	Semi-finalists (2)	Third Prize – value £3.15s.
		Bronze Medal

1952–1964	Champion	Challenge Trophy (AELTC)
		Miniature replica of Challenge Trophy
		First prize – value £15
	Runner-up	Second Prize – value £10
		Silver Medal
	Semi-finalists (2)	Third Prize – value £5
		Bronze Medal

1965–1967	Champion	Challenge Trophy (AELTC)
		Miniature replica of Challenge Trophy
		First Prize – value £30
	Runner-up	Second Prize – value £20
		Silver Medal
	Semi-finalists (2)	Third Prize – value £10
		Bronze Medal

Prize Money

1968–1969

Players competing for prize money

Champion	Challenge Trophy (AELTC)
	Miniature replica of Challenge Trophy
Runner-up	Silver Medal
Semi-finalists (2)	Bronze Medal

Players not competing for prize money

Champion	Challenge Trophy (AELTC)
	Miniature replica of Challenge Trophy
	Prize – value £30
Runner-up	Prize – value £20
	Silver Medal
Semi-finalists (2)	Prize – value £10
	Bronze Medal

1970–1986	Champion	Challenge Trophy (AELTC)
		Miniature replica of Challenge Trophy
	Runner-up	Silver Medal
	Semi-finalists (2)	Bronze Medal

Note: In 1977 the Champion also received a Silver Salver marking the occasion of H.M. The Queen's Silver Jubilee and the Centenary of The Championships.

1987–1990	Champion	Challenge Trophy (AELTC)
		Miniature replica of Challenge Trophy
	Runner-up	Personal prize (Silver Salver)
		Silver Medal
	Semi-finalists (2)	Bronze Medal

1991–2006	Champion	Challenge Trophy (AELTC)
		Miniature replica of Challenge Trophy
	Runner-up	Silver Salver
	Semi-finalists (2)	Bronze Medal

2007–2015	Champion	Challenge Trophy (AELTC)
		Three-quarter size Challenge Trophy
	Runner-up	Silver Salver
	Semi-finalists (2)	Bronze Medal

Ladies' Doubles Championship

1913–1914	Champions (2)	Challenge Trophies (LTA)
1919–1921		First Prize – value £10
		Gold Medal (LTA)
	Runners-up (2)	Second Prize – value £5

| 1922–1923 | Champions (2) | Challenge Trophies (LTA)
First Prize – Silver Cup value £10
Gold Medal (LTA) |
| | Runners-up (2) | Second Prize – Silver Cup value £5 |

| 1924–1932 | Champions (2) | Challenge Trophies (LTA)
First Prize – Silver Cup value £10
Gold Medal |
| | Runners-up (2) | Second Prize – Silver Cup value £5 |

1933–1934	Champions (2)	Challenge Trophies (LTA) First Prize – Silver Cup value £10 Gold Medal
	Runners-up (2)	Second Prize – Silver Cup value £5
	Semi-finalists (4)	Third Prize – value £2.10s.

1935–1939	Champions (2)	Challenge Trophies (LTA) First Prize – value £10 Gold Medal
	Runners-up (2)	Second Prize – value £5
	Semi-finalists (4)	Third Prize – value £2.10s.

1946–1948	Champions (2)	First Prize – value £10 Bronze Medal
	Runners-up (2)	Second Prize – value £5
	Semi-finalists (4)	Third Prize – value £2.10s.

1949–1951	Champions (2)	Challenge Cup (D of K) Miniature replica of Challenge Cup First Prize – value £10
	Runners-up (2)	Second Prize – value £5 Silver Medal
	Semi-finalists (4)	Third Prize – value £2.10s. Bronze Medal

1952–1964	Champions (2)	Challenge Cup (D of K) Miniature replica of Challenge Cup First Prize – value £10
	Runners-up (2)	Second Prize – value £8 Silver Medal
	Semi-finalists (4)	Third Prize – value £5 Bronze Medal

1965–1967	Champions (2)	Challenge Cup (D of K) Miniature replica of Challenge Cup First Prize – value £20
	Runners-up (2)	Second Prize – value £16 Silver Medal
	Semi-finalists (4)	Third Prize – value £10 Bronze Medal

Prize Money

1968–1969

Players competing for prize money

	Champions (2)	Challenge Cup (D of K)
		Miniature replica of Challenge Cup
	Runners-up (2)	Silver Medal
	Semi-finalists (4)	Bronze Medal

Players not competing for prize money

	Champions (2)	Challenge Cup (D of K)
		Miniature replica of Challenge Cup
		Prize – value £20
	Runners-up (2)	Prize – value £16
		Silver Medal
	Semi-finalists (4)	Prize – value £10
		Bronze Medal

1970–1986	Champions (2)	Challenge cup (D of K)
		Miniature replica of Challenge Cup
	Runners-up (2)	Silver Medal
	Semi-finalists (4)	Bronze Medal
1987–1990	Champions (2)	Challenge Cup (D of K)
		Miniature replica of Challenge Cup
	Runners-up (2)	Personal prize (Silver Salver)
		Silver Medal
	Semi-finalists (4)	Bronze Medal
1991–2000	Champions (2)	Challenge Cup (D of K)
		Miniature replica of Challenge Cup
	Runners-up (2)	Silver Salver
	Semi-finalists (4)	Bronze Medal
2001–2011	Champions (2)	Challenge Cup (D of K)
		Challenge Cup (AELTC)
		Miniature replica of Challenge Cup
	Runners-up (2)	Silver Salver
	Semi-finalists (4)	Bronze Medal
2012–2015	Champions (2)	Challenge Cup (D of K)
		Challenge Cup (AELTC)
		Three-quarter size Challenge Cup
	Runners-up (2)	Silver Salver
	Semi-finalists (4)	Bronze Medal

Mixed Doubles Championship

1913–1914	Champions (2)	Challenge Trophies (LTA)
1919–1921		First Prize – value £10
		Gold Medal (LTA)
	Runners-up (2)	Second Prize – value £5

| 1922–1923 | Champions (2) | Challenge Trophies (LTA)
First Prize – Silver Cup value £10
Gold Medal (LTA) |
| | Runners-up (2) | Second Prize – Silver Cup value £5 |

| 1924–1932 | Champions (2) | Challenge Trophies (LTA)
First Prize – Silver Cup value £10
Gold Medal |
| | Runners-up (2) | Second Prize – Silver Cup value £5 |

1933–1934	Champions (2)	Challenge Trophies (LTA) First Prize – Silver Cup value £10 Gold Medal
	Runners-up (2)	Second Prize – Silver Cup value £5
	Semi-finalists (4)	Third Prize – value £2.10s.

1935–1939	Champions (2)	Challenge Trophies (LTA) First Prize – value £10 Gold Medal
	Runners-up (2)	Second Prize – value £5
	Semi-finalists (4)	Third Prize – value £2.10s.

1946–1948	Champions (2)	First Prize – value £10 Bronze Medal
	Runners-up (2)	Second Prize – value £5
	Semi-finalists (4)	Third Prize – value £2.10s.

1949–1951	Champions (2)	Challenge Cup (S.H. Smith) Miniature replica of Challenge Cup First Prize – value £10
	Runners-up (2)	Second Prize – value £5 Silver Medal
	Semi-finalists (4)	Third Prize – value £2.10s. Bronze Medal

1952–1964	Champions (2)	Challenge Cup (S.H. Smith) Miniature replica of Challenge Cup First Prize – value £10
	Runners-up (2)	Second Prize – value £8 Silver Medal
	Semi-finalists (4)	Third Prize – value £5 Bronze Medal

1965–1967	Champions (2)	Challenge Cup (S.H. Smith) Miniature replica of Challenge Cup First Prize – value £20
	Runners-up (2)	Second Prize – value £16 Silver Medal
	Semi-finalists (4)	Third Prize – value £10 Bronze Medal

Prize Money

1968–1969

Players competing for prize money

Champions (2)	Challenge Cup (S.H. Smith)
	Miniature replica of Challenge Cup
Runners-up (2)	Silver Medal
Semi-finalists (4)	Bronze Medal

Players not competing for prize money

Champions (2)	Challenge Cup (S.H. Smith)
	Miniature replica of Challenge Cup
	Prize – value £20
Runners-up (2)	Prize – value £16
	Silver Medal
Semi-finalists (4)	Prize – value £10
	Bronze Medal

1970–1986	Champions (2)	Challenge Cup (S.H. Smith)
		Miniature replica of Challenge Cup
	Runners-up (2)	Silver Medal
	Semi-finalists (4)	Bronze Medal
1987–1990	Champions (2)	Challenge Cup (S.H. Smith)
		Miniature replica of Challenge Cup
	Runners-up (2)	Personal prize (Silver Salver)
		Silver Medal
	Semi-finalists (4)	Bronze Medal
1991–2000	Champions (2)	Challenge Cup (S.H. Smith)
		Miniature replica of Challenge Cup
	Runners-up (2)	Silver Salver
	Semi-finalists (4)	Bronze Medal
2001–2011	Champions (2)	Challenge Cup (S.H. Smith)
		Challenge Cup (AELTC)
		Miniature replica of Challenge Cup
	Runners-up (2)	Silver Salver
	Semi-finalists (4)	Bronze Medal
2012–2015	Champions (2)	Challenge Cup (S.H. Smith)
		Challenge Cup (AELTC)
		Three-quarter Size Challenge Cup
	Runners-up (2)	Silver Salver
	Semi-finalists (4)	Bronze Medal

From 2012 the diameter of all silver and bronze medals was increased from 38mm to 50mm. They are presented in a box with new Wimbledon logo.

Prize Money

Summary

Year	Gentlemen's Singles Champion	Gentlemen's Doubles Champions (pair)	Ladies' Singles Champion	Ladies' Doubles Champions (pair)	Mixed Doubles Champions (pair)	Total for Meeting
	£	£	£	£	£	£
1968	2,000	800	750	500	450	26,150
1969	3,000	1,000	1,500	600	500	33,370
1970	3,000	1,000	1,500	600	500	41,650
1971	3,750	750	1,800	450	375	37,790
1972	5,000	1,000	3,000	600	500	50,330
1973	5,000	1,000	3,000	600	500	52,400
1974	10,000	2,000	7,000	1,200	1,000	97,100
1975	10,000	2,000	7,000	1,200	1,000	114,875
1976	12,500	3,000	10,000	2,400	2,000	157,740
1977	15,000	6,000	13,500	5,200	3,000	222,540
1978	19,000	7,500	17,100	6,500	4,000	279,023
1979	20,000	8,000	18,000	6,930	4,200	277,066
1980	20,000	8,400	18,000	7,276	4,420	293,464
1981	21,600	9,070	19,400	7,854	4,770	322,136
1982	41,667	16,666	37,500	14,450	6,750	593,366
1983	66,600	26,628	60,000	23,100	12,000	978,211
1984	100,000	40,000	90,000	34,700	18,000	1,461,896
1985	130,000	47,500	117,000	41,100	23,400	1,934,760
1986	140,000	48,500	126,000	42,060	25,200	2,119,780
1987	155,000	53,730	139,500	46,500	27,900	2,470,020
1988	165,000	57,200	148,500	49,500	29,700	2,612,126
1989	190,000	65,870	171,000	56,970	34,200	3,133,749
1990	230,000	94,230	207,000	81,510	40,000	3,819,730
1991	240,000	98,330	216,000	85,060	41,720	4,010,970
1992	265,000	108,570	240,000	93,920	46,070	4,416,820
1993	305,000	124,960	275,000	108,100	53,020	5,048,450
1994	345,000	141,350	310,000	122,200	60,000	5,682,170
1995	365,000	149,540	328,000	129,300	63,500	6,025,550
1996	392,500	160,810	353,000	139,040	68,280	6,465,910
1997	415,000	170,030	373,500	147,010	72,200	6,884,952
1998	435,000	178,220	391,500	154,160	75,700	7,207,590
1999	455,000	186,420	409,500	167,770	79,180	7,595,330
2000	477,500	195,630	430,000	176,070	83,100	8,056,480
2001	500,000	205,000	462,500	189,620	87,000	8,525,280
2002	525,000	210,000	486,000	194,250	88,500	8,825,320
2003	575,000	210,000	535,000	194,250	88,500	9,373,990
2004	602,500	215,000	560,500	200,000	90,000	9,707,280
2005	630,000	218,500	600,000	203,250	90,000	10,085,510
2006	655,000	220,690	625,000	205,280	90,000	10,378,710
2007	700,000	222,900	700,000	222,900	90,000	11,282,710
2008	750,000	230,000	750,000	230,000	92,000	11,812,000
2009	850,000	230,000	850,000	230,000	92,000	12,550,000
2010	1,000,000	240,000	1,000,000	240,000	92,000	13,725,000
2011	1,100,000	250,000	1,100,000	250,000	92,000	14,600,000
2012	1,150,000	260,000	1,150,000	260,000	92,000	16,060,000
2013	1,600,000	300,000	1,600,000	300,000	92,000	22,560,000
2014	1,760,000	325,000	1,760,000	325,000	96,000	25,000,000
2015	1,880,000	340,000	1,880,000	340,000	100,000	26,750,000

In 1971 travel allowances amounting to one third of the prize money were paid automatically to the organization under whose authority the competitor entered. This sum totalled £12,680.

From 1975 to 1989 the total prize money for the meeting includes Bonus Pools.

From 1987 the total prize money includes daily payments towards accommodation and travel as follows:–

1987 – £50, 1988 – £55, 1989 – £75, 1990 – £80, 1991 – £90, 1992 – £100, 1993 – £105, 1994 – £110, 1995 – £120, 1996 – £130, 1997 – £135 (Qualifiers £68); 1998 – £140 (Qualifiers £70); 1999 – £150 (Qualifiers £75); 2000 – £155 (Qualifiers £80); 2001–2005 – £165 (Qualifiers £85); 2006–2011 – £170 (Qualifiers £85), 2012–2015 – £200 (Qualifiers £100)

In addition the following annual contributions have been made:–

Pre and post-Wimbledon grass court tournaments: 1983 – £135,000, 1984 – £162,000, 1985–1988 – £300,000, 1989–1991 – £400,000, 1992 – £500,000, 1993 – £550,000, 1994 – £600,000, 1995–2015 – £1,000,000.

I.T.F. worldwide development: 1985–1988 – £100,000, 1989 – £125,000.

Gentlemen's Singles Championship
£s

Year	Champion	Runner-up	Semi-Finalists	Quarter-Finalists	Losers Fourth Round	Losers Third Round	Losers Second Round	Losers First Round
1968	2,000	1,300	750	400	150	100	75	50
1969	3,000	1,500	800	450	175	125	80	50
1970	3,000	1,500	800	450	220	165	125	100
1971	3,750	2,250	750	415	225	150	95	75
1972	5,000	3,000	1,000	550	300	200	125	100
1973	5,000	3,000	1,000	550	300	200	125	100
1974	10,000	6,000	2,000	1,000	600	300	200	150
1975	10,000	6,000	2,000	1,000	600	300	200	150
1976	12,500	7,000	3,000	1,500	1,100	550	300	150
1977	15,000	8,000	4,000	2,000	1,200	600	350	200
1978	19,000	9,600	4,800	2,400	1,440	720	350	200
1979	20,000	10,000	5,000	2,500	1,500	760	440	265
1980	20,000	10,000	5,000	2,500	1,600	850	500	300
1981	21,600	10,800	5,400	2,700	1,730	920	540	325
1982	41,667	20,833	10,417	5,278	3,056	1,667	972	556
1983	66,600	33,300	16,650	8,430	4,880	2,662	1,553	888
1984	100,000	50,000	25,000	12,500	6,850	3,850	2,200	1,300
1985	130,000	65,000	32,500	16,500	8,680	4,864	2,865	1,750
1986	140,000	70,000	35,000	17,725	9,330	5,225	3,080	1,880
1987	155,000	77,500	38,750	19,635	10,335	5,785	3,410	2,080
1988	165,000	82,500	41,250	20,900	11,000	6,160	3,630	2,215
1989	190,000	95,000	47,500	24,065	12,665	7,095	4,180	2,550
1990	230,000	115,000	57,500	29,900	16,100	9,310	5,635	3,450
1991	240,000	120,000	60,000	31,200	16,800	9,715	5,880	3,600
1992	265,000	132,500	66,250	34,450	18,550	10,730	6,490	3,975
1993	305,000	152,500	76,250	39,650	21,350	12,350	7,470	4,575
1994	345,000	172,500	86,250	44,850	24,150	13,970	8,450	5,175
1995	365,000	182,500	91,250	47,450	25,550	14,780	8,940	5,475
1996	392,500	196,250	98,125	51,025	27,475	15,900	9,615	5,885
1997	415,000	207,500	103,750	53,925	29,050	16,810	10,165	6,225
1998	435,000	217,500	108,750	56,550	30,450	17,610	10,660	6,530
1999	455,000	227,500	113,750	59,150	31,850	18,420	11,150	6,830
2000	477,500	238,750	119,380	62,080	33,420	19,330	11,700	7,160
2001	500,000	250,000	125,000	65,000	35,000	20,250	12,250	7,500

Year	Champion	Runner-up	Semi-Finalists	Quarter-Finalists	Losers Fourth Round	Losers Third Round	Losers Second Round	Losers First Round
2002	525,000	262,500	131,250	68,250	36,750	21,260	12,860	7,880
2003	575,000	287,500	143,750	74,750	40,250	23,280	14,090	8,630
2004	602,500	301,250	150,630	78,330	42,170	24,390	14,760	9,040
2005	630.000	315,000	157,500	81,900	44,100	25,510	15,440	9,450
2006	655,000	327,500	163,750	85,150	45,850	26,520	16,050	9,830
2007	700,000	350,000	175,000	88,550	47,250	27,050	16,325	10,000
2008	750,000	375,000	187,500	93,750	50,000	28,125	17,000	10,250
2009	850,000	425,000	212,500	106,250	53,250	29,250	17,750	10,750
2010	1,000,000	500,000	250,000	125,000	62,500	31,250	18,750	11,250
2011	1,100,000	550,000	275,000	137,500	68,750	34,375	20,125	11,500
2012	1,150,000	575,000	287,500	145,000	75,000	38,875	23,125	14,500
2013	1,600,000	800,000	400,000	205,000	105,000	63,000	38,000	23,500
2014	1,760,000	880,000	440,000	226,000	117,000	71,000	43,000	27,000
2015	1,880,000	940,000	470,000	241,000	127,000	77,000	47,000	29,000

Qualifying Competition
£s

Year	Losers of Third Round	Losers of Second Round	Losers of First Round
1984	650	—	—
1985	875	—	—
1986	1,250	625	315
1987	1,385	695	345
1988	1,475	740	370
1989	1,700	850	425
1990	2,300	1,150	575
1991	2,400	1,200	600
1992	2,650	1,325	660
1993	3,050	1,525	760
1994	3,450	1,725	860
1995	3,650	1,825	910
1996	3,925	1,960	980
1997	3,952	1,976	988
1998	4,140	2,070	1,035
1999	4,330	2,170	1,080
2000	4,550	2,270	1,140
2001	4,760	2,380	1,190
2002	5,000	2,500	1,250
2003	5,480	2,740	1,370
2004	5,740	2,870	1,435
2005	6,000	3,000	1,500
2006	6,240	3,120	1,560
2007	6,300	3,150	1,575
2008	6,500	3,250	1,625
2009	6,700	3,350	1,675
2010	7,000	3,500	1,750
2011	7,000	3,500	1,750
2012	8,500	4,250	2,125
2013	12,000	6,000	3,000
2014	13,500	6,750	3,375
2015	14,500	7,250	3,625

Gentlemen's Doubles Championship
£s (per pair)

Year	Champions	Runners-up	Semi-Finalists	Quarter-Finalists	Losers Third Round	Losers Second Round	Losers First Round
1968	800	500	350	180	—	—	—
1969	1,000	600	400	200	—	—	—
1970	1,000	600	400	200	—	—	—
1971	750	450	300	150	—	—	—
1972	1,000	600	400	200	—	—	—
1973	1,000	600	400	200	—	—	—
1974	2,000	1,200	800	400	—	—	—
1975	2,000	1,200	800	400	200	—	—
1976	3,000	1,500	1,000	500	250	—	—
1977	6,000	3,000	2,000	1,000	500	150	—
1978	7,500	3,600	2,000	1,000	500	160	75
1979	8,000	4,000	2,000	1,000	520	170	80
1980	8,400	4,200	2,100	1,050	570	190	90
1981	9,070	4,540	2,270	1,140	620	200	100
1982	16,666	8,834	4,166	1,666	834	278	140
1983	26,628	13,314	6,656	2,664	1,330	444	222
1984	40,000	20,000	10,000	4,000	2,000	1,000	584
1985	47,500	23,750	11,880	5,450	2,810	1,490	870
1986	48,500	24,250	12,130	6,160	3,180	1,680	980
1987	53,730	26,870	13,430	6,820	3,510	1,860	1,090
1988	57,200	28,600	14,300	7,260	3,740	1,980	1,160
1989	65,870	32,930	16,470	8,360	4,310	2,280	1,330
1990	94,230	47,110	24,180	12,560	6,680	3,630	2,130
1991	98,330	49,160	25,230	13,100	6,980	3,790	2,220
1992	108,570	54,280	27,860	14,460	7,710	4,190	2,450
1993	124,960	62,480	32,060	16,640	8,870	4,810	2,820
1994	141,350	70,670	36,260	18,820	10,040	5,440	3,190
1995	149,540	74,770	38,360	19,910	10,620	5,760	3,370
1996	160,810	80,400	41,250	21,420	11,420	6,200	3,620
1997	170,030	85,010	43,620	22,650	12,070	6,550	3,830
1998	178,220	89,100	45,730	23,740	12,650	6,870	4,020
1999	186,420	93,200	47,830	24,830	13,230	7,180	4,210
2000	195,630	97,810	50,200	26,060	13,890	7,540	4,420
2001	205,000	102,500	52,500	27,250	14,500	7,900	4,650
2002	210,000	105,000	53,780	27,910	14,850	8,090	4,760
2003	210,000	105,000	53,780	27,910	14,850	8,090	4,760
2004	215,000	107,500	55,100	28,600	15,200	8,300	4,870
2005	218,500	109,250	56,000	29,100	15,450	8,440	4,950
2006	220,690	110,340	56,560	29,390	15,600	8,520	5,000
2007	222,900	111,440	57,130	29,680	15,760	8,610	5,050
2008	230,000	115,000	57,500	30,000	16,000	9,000	5,250
2009	230,000	115,000	57,500	30,000	16,000	9,000	5,250
2010	240,000	120,000	60,000	30,000	16,000	9,000	5,250
2011	250,000	125,000	62,500	31,250	16,000	9,000	5,250
2012	260,000	130,000	65,000	32,500	16,650	9,350	5,450
2013	300,000	150,000	75,000	37,500	20,000	12,000	7,750
2014	325,000	163,000	81,500	41,000	21,500	13,000	8,500
2015	340,000	170,000	85,000	43,000	22,500	13,750	9,000

Ladies' Singles Championship
£s

Year	Champion	Runner-up	Semi-Finalists	Quarter-Finalists	Losers Fourth Round	Losers Third Round	Losers Second Round	Losers First Round
1968	750	450	300	150	90	50	35	25
1969	1,500	750	350	200	125	90	70	50
1970	1,500	750	400	225	150	125	100	75
1971	1,800	1,000	450	265	150	115	75	55
1972	2,400	1,330	600	350	200	150	100	75
1973	3,000	2,000	700	400	250	150	100	75
1974	7,000	4,000	1,500	750	500	250	175	150
1975	7,000	4,200	1,500	750	500	250	175	150
1976	10,000	5,600	2,400	1,200	600	300	200	150
1977	13,500	7,000	3,500	1,600	925	460	270	150
1978	17,100	8,400	4,200	1,920	1,100	552	324	188
1979	18,000	8,750	4,375	2,000	1,160	585	340	200
1980	18,000	8,750	4,375	2,000	1,245	660	390	230
1981	19,440	9,450	4,725	2,160	1,345	715	420	250
1982	37,500	18,875	9,125	4,222	2,445	1,300	755	428
1983	60,000	30,000	14,585	7,123	3,904	2,048	1,196	684
1984	90,000	45,000	21,900	10,704	5,866	3,080	1,796	1,027
1985	117,000	58,500	28,500	13,954	6,950	3,750	2,210	1,350
1986	126,000	63,000	30,700	15,025	7,485	4,040	2,380	1,450
1987	139,500	69,750	33,900	16,690	8,270	4,485	2,645	1,610
1988	148,500	74,250	36,090	17,765	8,800	4,775	2,815	1,715
1989	171,000	85,500	41,560	20,455	10,135	5,500	3,240	1,975
1990	207,000	103,500	50,315	25,415	12,880	7,215	4,370	2,675
1991	216,000	108,000	52,500	26,520	13,440	7,530	4,560	2,790
1992	240,000	120,000	57,970	29,280	14,840	8,315	5,035	3,080
1993	275,000	137,500	66,720	33,700	17,080	9,570	5,790	3,545
1994	310,000	155,000	74,000	38,000	20,000	10,800	6,550	4,010
1995	328,000	164,000	78,000	40,200	21,160	11,430	6,930	4,250
1996	353,000	176,500	83,900	43,230	22,750	12,300	7,450	4,570
1997	373,500	186,750	88,350	45,825	24,000	13,025	7,880	4,825
1998	391,500	195,750	92,440	48,070	25,120	13,650	8,260	5,060
1999	409,500	204,750	96,690	50,280	26,280	14,270	8,640	5,290
2000	430,000	215,000	101,470	52,760	28,410	15,460	9,360	5,730
2001	462,500	231,250	112,500	56,875	29,750	16,200	9,800	6,000
2002	486,000	243,000	118,125	59,720	31,240	17,000	10,290	6,300
2003	535,000	267,500	129,350	65,400	34,200	18,620	11,270	6,900
2004	560,500	280,250	135,560	68,540	35,850	19,510	11,810	7,230
2005	600,000	300,000	145,690	73,710	37,480	20,400	12,350	7,560
2006	625,000	312,500	151,500	76,650	38,970	21,210	12,840	7,860
2007	700,000	350,000	175,000	88,550	47,250	27,050	16,325	10,000
2008	750,000	375,000	187,500	93,750	50,000	28,125	17,000	10,250
2009	850,000	425,000	212,500	106,250	53,250	29,250	17,750	10,750
2010	1,000,000	500,000	250,000	125,000	62,500	31,250	18,750	11,250
2011	1,100,000	550,000	275,000	137,500	68,750	34,375	20,125	11,500
2012	1,150,000	575,000	287,500	145,000	75,000	38,875	23,125	14,500
2013	1,600,000	800,000	400,000	205,000	105,000	63,000	38,000	23,500
2014	1,760,000	880,000	440,000	226,000	117,000	71,000	43,000	27,000
2015	1,880,000	940,000	470,000	241,000	127,000	77,000	47,000	29,000

From 1968 to 1982, byes who lost in the Second Round counted as First Round losers.

Qualifying Competition
£s

Year	Losers of Third Round	Losers of Second Round	Losers of First Round
1984	514	—	—
1985	675	—	—
1986	970	485	245
1987	1,080	540	270
1988	1,145	570	285
1989	1,315	660	330
1990	1,785	890	445
1991	1,860	930	465
1992	2,050	1,030	515
1993	2,360	1,185	595
1994	2,670	1,340	675
1995	2,825	1,415	715
1996	3,035	1,520	770
1997	3,064	1,532	766
1998	3,210	1,605	805
1999	3,360	1,680	840
2000	3,640	1,820	910
2001	3,810	1,910	950
2002	4,000	2,000	1,000
2003	4,380	2,190	1,100
2004	4,600	2,300	1,150
2005	4,800	2,400	1,200
2006	4,990	2,495	1,250
2007	6,300	3,150	1,575
2008	6,500	3,250	1,625
2009	6,700	3,350	1,675
2010	7,000	3,500	1,750
2011	7,000	3,500	1,750
2012	8,500	4,250	2,125
2013	12,000	6,000	3,000
2014	13,500	6,750	3,375
2015	14,500	7,250	3,625

Ladies' Doubles Championship
£s (per pair)

Year	Champions	Runners-up	Semi-Finalists	Quarter-Finalists	Losers Third Round	Losers Second Round	Losers First Round
1968	500	300	150	100	—	—	—
1969	600	400	200	100	—	—	—
1970	600	400	200	100	—	—	—
1971	450	300	150	75	—	—	—
1972	600	400	200	100	—	—	—
1973	600	400	200	100	—	—	—
1974	1,200	700	350	200	—	—	—
1975	1,200	700	400	200	100	—	—
1976	2,400	1,200	500	250	125	—	—
1977	5,200	2,600	1,600	800	350	100	—
1978	6,500	3,120	1,600	800	350	110	50
1979	6,930	3,464	1,600	800	364	116	54
1980	7,276	3,638	1,680	840	400	130	62

Year	Champions	Runners-up	Semi-Finalists	Quarter-Finalists	Losers Third Round	Losers Second Round	Losers First Round
1981	7,854	3,932	1,816	912	434	140	70
1982	14,450	7,226	3,332	1,332	620	200	100
1983	23,100	11,550	5,324	2,130	974	320	160
1984	34,700	17,350	8,000	3,200	1,460	480	240
1985	41,100	20,550	9,500	4,360	2,100	1,100	640
1986	42,060	21,030	9,700	4,930	2,390	1,250	720
1987	46,500	23,250	10,740	5,460	2,630	1,400	800
1988	49,500	24,750	11,430	5,810	2,800	1,490	850
1989	56,970	28,490	13,170	6,690	3,230	1,710	960
1990	81,510	40,750	19,350	10,050	5,010	2,720	1,540
1991	85,060	45,520	20,190	10,480	5,230	2,840	1,610
1992	93,920	46,950	22,290	11,570	5,780	3,130	1,780
1993	108,100	54,050	25,650	13,310	6,650	3,610	2,050
1994	122,200	61,100	29,000	15,100	7,520	4,080	2,320
1995	129,300	64,650	30,700	16,000	7,950	4,320	2,450
1996	139,040	69,300	33,010	17,220	8,560	4,660	2,630
1997	147,010	73,270	34,900	18,210	9,050	4,930	2,780
1998	154,160	77,070	36,580	18,990	9,490	5,150	2,920
1999	167,770	83,880	40,660	21,110	10,920	5,570	3,260
2000	176,070	88,030	42,670	22,150	11,800	6,030	3,530
2001	189,620	94,810	47,250	23,840	12,330	6,320	3,720
2002	194,250	97,130	48,400	24,430	12,630	6,470	3,810
2003	194,250	97,130	48,400	24,430	12,630	6,470	3,810
2004	200,000	100,000	50,000	25,000	12,850	6,600	3,860
2005	203,250	101,630	50,800	25,400	13,100	6,700	3,920
2006	205,280	102,650	51,310	25,650	13,230	6,770	3,960
2007	222,900	111,440	57,130	29,680	15,760	8,610	5,050
2008	230,000	115,000	57,500	30,000	16,000	9,000	5,250
2009	230,000	115,000	57,500	30,000	16,000	9,000	5,250
2010	240,000	120,000	60,000	30,000	16,000	9,000	5,250
2011	250,000	125,000	62,500	31,250	16,000	9,000	5,250
2012	260,000	130,000	65,000	32,500	16,650	9,350	5,450
2013	300,000	150,000	75,000	37,500	20,000	12,000	7,750
2014	325,000	163,000	81,500	41,000	21,500	13,000	8,500
2015	340,000	170,000	85,000	43,000	22,500	13,750	9,000

From 1978 to 1983, byes who lost in the Second Round counted as First Round losers.

Mixed Doubles Championship
£s (per pair)

Year	Champions	Runners-up	Semi-Finalists	Quarter-Finalists	Losers Third Round	Losers Second Round	Losers First Round
1968	450	300	150	100	—	—	—
1969	500	350	175	100	—	—	—
1970	500	350	175	100	—	—	—
1971	375	265	130	75	—	—	—
1972	500	350	175	100	—	—	—
1973	500	350	175	100	—	—	—
1974	1,000	500	300	150	—	—	—
1975	1,000	500	300	200	100	—	—
1976	2,000	1,000	300	200	100	—	—
1977	3,000	1,500	700	400	200	—	—
1978	4,000	2,000	840	480	240	—	—

Year	Champions	Runners-up	Semi-Finalists	Quarter-Finalists	Losers Third Round	Losers Second Round	Losers First Round
1979	4,200	2,100	1,000	500	250	—	—
1980	4,420	2,210	1,050	520	260	—	—
1981	4,770	2,390	1,140	560	280	—	—
1982	6,750	3,400	1,700	800	400	—	—
1983	12,000	6,000	3,000	1,400	700	350	150
1984	18,000	9,000	4,500	2,100	1,050	526	226
1985	23,400	11,700	5,850	2,730	1,370	680	300
1986	25,200	12,600	6,300	2,930	1,470	730	330
1987	27,900	13,950	6,980	3,240	1,620	810	370
1988	29,700	14,850	7,430	3,450	1,720	860	390
1989	34,200	17,100	8,550	3,930	1,970	980	440
1990	40,000	20,000	10,000	4,600	2,300	1,150	520
1991	41,720	20,860	10,430	4,800	2,400	1,200	540
1992	46,070	23,030	11,520	5,300	2,650	1,320	600
1993	53,020	26,510	13,260	6,100	3,050	1,520	690
1994	60,000	30,000	15,000	6,900	3,450	1,720	780
1995	63,500	31,750	15,870	7,300	3,650	1,810	830
1996	68,280	34,140	17,080	7,860	3,920	1,950	890
1997	72,200	36,100	18,060	8,310	4,150	2,060	940
1998	75,700	37,850	18,920	8,700	4,350	2,160	990
1999	79,180	39,590	19,790	9,100	4,550	2,280	1,030
2000	83,100	41,540	20,770	9,550	4,780	2,390	1,080
2001	87,000	43,500	21,750	10,000	5,000	2,500	1,130
2002	88,500	44,250	22,130	10,170	5,090	2,550	1,150
2003	88,500	44,250	22,130	10,170	5,090	2,550	1,150
2004	90,000	45,000	22,500	10,300	5,180	2,600	1,180
2005	90,000	45,000	22,500	10,300	5,180	2,600	1,180
2006	90,000	45,000	22,500	10,300	5,180	2,600	1,180
2007	90,000	45,000	22,500	10,300	5,180	2,600	1,180
2008	92,000	46,000	23,000	10,500	5,200	2,600	1,300
2009	92,000	46,000	23,000	10,500	5,200	2,600	1,300
2010	92,000	46,000	23,000	10,500	5,200	2,600	1,300
2011	92,000	46,000	23,000	10,500	5,200	2,600	1,300
2012	92,000	46,000	23,000	10,500	5,200	2,600	1,300
2013	92,000	46,000	23,000	10,500	5,200	2,600	1,300
2014	96,000	48,000	24,000	11,500	5,600	2,800	1,400
2015	100,000	50,000	25,000	12,000	6,000	3,000	1,500

In 1983, byes who lost in the Second Round counted as First Round losers.

Leading Winners
Gentlemen

Name	Singles £	Doubles £	Mixed £	Total £
R. Federer (SUI) 1999–2014	6,804,870	26,895	–	6,831,763
N. Djokovic (SRB) 2005–2014	4,557,110	4,260	–	4,561,370
A.B. Murray (GBR) 2005–2014	3,303,610	2,475	1,890	3,307,975
R. Nadal (ESP) 2003, 2005–2008, 2010–2014	3,179,845	4,220		3,184,065
P. Sampras (USA) 1989–2002	2,942,715	2,155	–	2,944,870
A.S. Roddick (USA) 2001–2012	1,494,330	2,325	–	1,496,655
L.G. Hewitt (AUS) 1999–2014	1,296,815	29,565	20,770	1,347,150
G.S. Ivanisevic (YUG/CRO) 1988–2001, 2004	1,316,480	10,775	–	1,327,255
B.F. Becker (GER) 1984–1997, 1999	1,265,885	1,037	–	1,266,922
T.A. Woodbridge (AUS) 1987–2005	214,375	884,435	82,135	1,180,945
T. Berdych (CZE) 2004–2014	1,109,575	4,220		1,113,795
J.L. Bjorkman (SWE) 1993–2008	481,140	503,470	69,510	1,054,390
A.K. Agassi (USA) 1987, 1991–1996, 1998–2003, 2006	1,021,385	–	–	1,021,385
R.C. Bryan (USA) 1999–2014	12,250	794,960	127,190	933,900
J-W. Tsonga (FRA) 2007, 2009–2014	919,000	–	–	919,000
M.C. Bryan (USA) 1999–2014	–	794,460	115,080	909,540
T.H. Henman (GBR) 1993–2007	832,130	5,815	–	837,945
P. M. Rafter (AUS) 1993–2001	715,750	77,185	–	792,935
M.R. Woodforde (AUS) 1986–2000	146,585	558,375	60,325	765,285
S.B. Edberg (SWE) 1983–1996	744,113	9,721	–	753,834
D. Ferrer (ESP) 2003–2014	682,190	12,415	–	694,605
D.M. Nestor (CAN) 1994–2004, 2006–2014	83,380	499,790	107,640	690,810
R.P.S. Krajicek (NED) 1991–2000, 2002	681,115	1,895	–	683,010
J. Melzer (AUT) 2000, 2002–2006, 2008–2014	417,260	213,105	48,000	678,365
M.A. Philippoussis (AUS) 1994–2000, 2002–2006	591,530	41,905	–	633,435
J.M. Del Potro (ARG) 2007–2009, 2011–2013	594,825	5,145	–	599,970
N. Zimonjic (YUG/CRO) 1999–2014	18,420	486,175	94,470	599,065
M.D. Stich(GER) 1989–1997	467,835	80,440	–	548,275
T.M. Haas (GER) 1997–2009, 2011–2013	542,630	–	–	542,630
G. Dmitrov (BUL) 2009, 2011–2014	532,000	10,500	–	542,500
M. Raonic (CAN) 2011–2014	521,250	–	–	521,250
D.P. Nalbandian (ARG) 2002–2003, 2005–2008, 2011, 2012	497,345	6,545	–	503,890

Ladies

Name	Singles £	Doubles £	Mixed £	Total £
Miss S.J. Williams (USA) 1998, 2000–2005, 2007–2014	5,201,945	584,905	37,850	5,824,700
Miss V.E.S. Williams (USA) 1997–2012, 2014	4,293,445	584,905	39,570	4,917,920
Miss P. Kvitova (CZE) 2008–2014	3,481,000	7875	–	3,488,875
Miss M. Sharapova (RUS) 2003–2014	2,357,690	–	–	2,357,690
Miss M.S. Bartoli (FRA) 2003–2013	2,282,100	25,670	1,950	2,309,720
Miss S.M. Graf (GER) 1984, 1985 1987–1996, 1998, 1999	2,086,791	35,680	12,800	2,135,271

Name	Singles £	Doubles £	Mixed £	Total £
Miss M. Navratilova (TCH/USA) 1973–1996, 2000–2006	1,304,020	231,812	141,170	1,677,002
Miss S. Lisicki (GER) 2008–2014	1,562,500	75,425	1,300	1,639,225
Miss L.A. Davenport (Mrs J. Leach) (USA) 1993–2001, 2003–2005, 2008, 2010	1,387,090	174,475	49,670	1,610,235
Miss A. Radwanska (POL) 2006–2014	1,440,645	35,830	590	1,477,065
Miss J. Novotna (TCH/CZE) 1986–1999	986,220	353,425	25,180	1,364,825
Miss A. Mauresmo (FRA) 1998, 2000–2002, 2004–2009	1,183,185	71,260	–	1,254,445
Miss J. Henin/Mrs P-Y. Hardenne (BEL) 2000–2003, 2005–2007, 2010	1,042,015	6,165	–	1,048,180
Miss V. Zvonareva (RUS) 2002–2006, 2008–2012, 2014	791,050	149,390	47,600	988,040
Miss E. Bouchard (CAN), 2013, 2014	943,000	14,250	650	957,900
Miss V. Azarenka (BLR) 2006–2014	844,035	29,920	3,190	877,145
Miss A.I.M. Sanchez Vicario (Mrs. J. Vehils) (ESP) 1987–2001, 2004	618,860	176,990	11,060	806,910
Miss K. Clijsters (BEL) 1999–2003,2005, 2006, 2010, 2012	621,135	147,545	31,170	799,850
Miss L.M. Raymond (USA) 1993–2014	239,950	377,135	172,400	789,485
Miss M. Hingis (SUI) 1995–2001, 2006, 2007, 2014	605,250	165,130	10,880	781,260
Miss N.M. Zvereva (URS/CIS/BLR) 1987–2000, 2002	259,980	447,105	21,045	728,130
Miss I.C. Martinez (ESP) 1992–2005	652,935	56,975	2,590	712,500
Miss C.C. Black (ZIM) 1998–2011, 2014	94,710	464,410	152,910	712,030
Miss A. Sugiyama (JPN) 1993–2009	329,335	336,880	28,925	695,140
Miss E. Dementieva (RUS) 1999–2009	641,070	37,035	–	678,105
Miss N. Petrova (RUS 2003–2005, 2007–2013, 1999–2001	532,555	98,960	9,700	641,215
Miss A. Kerber (GER) 2007, 2008, 2010–2014	614,500	13,350	650	628,500
Miss L. Safarova (CZE) 2005, 2007–2014	579,485	45,440	–	624,925
Miss S. Stosur (AUS) 2003–2014	232,980	271,915	119,390	624,285
Miss N. Tauziat (FRA) 1985–2002	474,485	72,610	2,175	549,270
Miss S. Kuznetsova (RUS) 2002–2012, 2014	429,975	107,500	5,085	542,560
Miss K. Flipkens (BEL) 2006–2014	526,860	12,875	590	540,325
Mrs L. Huber (RSA/USA) 2001–2014	–	439,435	96,850	536,285
Miss H. Sukova (TCH/CZE) 1982–1998, 2006	201,672	228,097	105,820	535,589
Miss S. Halep (ROM) 2011–2014	512,625	9225	–	521,850

Medals presented by The LTA

In 1913 the newly created International Lawn Tennis Federation awarded
The Lawn Tennis Association, on behalf of the British Isles, the World's
Championships on Grass, for services rendered to the game over the years.
The All England Lawn Tennis Club agreed to merge these Championships
with the three existing Championships and extend the programme to include
Ladies' Doubles and Mixed Doubles events.

The LTA decided to present a medal to players reaching the concluding
rounds of the five events and after several months of obtaining suitable
designs selected the work of Frank Ramson, a London sculptor. Initially the
execution of the work was carried out by Messrs. Fattorini and Sons, medallists
of Bradford and London, who produced the die and the finished medal, which
is 1.5 inches diameter.

The obverse side of the medal is intended to be a symbolical interpretation
of the World's Lawn Tennis Championships on Grass. The kneeling figure
represents Merit, bearing a figure of Victory in the left hand, while the right
hand is in the act of plucking a laurel wreath from the globe. Lawn Tennis is
indicated by the net and the open air by the sun in the background. The oak
leaves in the foreground stand for strength and endurance. Around the figure
are the words WORLD'S LAWN TENNIS CHAMPIONSHIPS ON GRASS.
On the reverse side is engraved the year, event and name/s of the recipient/s,
around which is a foliate design.

The medal was presented in 1913, 1914 and from 1919 to 1923, after which
the title World's Championship on Grass ceased to exist. From 1924 the
design of the medal on the obverse side was altered by the deletion of the
words 'WORLD'S CHAMPIONSHIPS ON GRASS and on the reverse side
by the replacement of the foliate design with the words THE LAWN
TENNIS CHAMPIONSHIPS.

From 1913 to 1921, gold, silver and bronze medals were presented, but
from 1922, when the Challenge Round was abolished, gold medals were
presented to the champions and silver medals to the runners-up. The whole
practice ceased after 1939.

Anniversary Celebrations

1926 Jubilee Championships

On Monday, 21st June, at 3 p.m., 34 surviving champions of the Gentlemen's Singles and Doubles and Ladies' Singles paraded on the Centre Court and each received a silver commemorative medal (1) from H.M. King George V and Queen Mary.

Order of Presentation:
1. P.F. Hadow (S1878); 2. J.T. Hartley (S1879, 1880, D1882) (2); 3. W.J. Hamilton (S1890); 4. W. Baddeley (S1891, 1892, 1895, D1891, 1894-1896); 5. J. Pim (S1893, 1894, D1890, 1893); 6. F.O. Stoker (D1890, 1893); 7. A.W. Gore (S1901, 1908, 1909, D1909); 8. R.T. Richardson (D1882) (2); 9. C.E. Welldon (D1883) (2); 10. H.W.W. Wilberforce (D1887); 11. P. Bowes-Lyon (D1887); 12. H. Baddeley (D1891, 1894-1896); 13. E.W. Lewis (D1892); 14. S.H. Smith (D1902, 1906); 15. F.L. Riseley (D1902, 1906); 16. M.J.G. Ritchie (D1908, 1910); 17. H.R. Barrett (D1909, 1912, 1913); 18. C.P. Dixon (D1912, 1913); 19. M.O. Decugis (D1911); 20. A.H. Gobert (D1911); 21. R. Lycett (D1921–1923); 22. M. Woosnam (D1921); 23. L. A. Godfree (D1923); 24. V. Richards (D1924); 25. J.R. Borotra (S1924, D1925); 26. Miss M.E. Watson (S1884, 1885); 27. Miss B. Bingley/Mrs. G.W. Hillyard (S1886, 1889, 1894, 1897, 1899, 1900); 28. Miss C. Dod (S1887, 1888, 1891-1893); 29. Miss C.R. Cooper/Mrs. A. Sterry (S1895, 1896, 1898, 1901, 1908); 30. Miss D.K. Douglass/Mrs. R.L. Chambers (S1903, 1904, 1906, 1910, 1911, 1913, 1914); 31. Miss P.D.H. Boothby (Mrs. A.C. Geen) (S1909); 32. Mrs. D.T.R. Larcombe (S1912); 33. Miss S.R.F. Lenglen (S1919–1923, 1925); 34. Miss K.McKane (Mrs. L.A. Godfree) (S1924).

The following champions, who were not present, received their medal later:– N.E. Brookes (S1907, 1914, D1907, 1914), G.L. Patterson (S1919, 1922), W.T. Tilden (S1920, 1921), W.M. Johnston (S1923), P.O. Wood (D1919), R.V. Thomas (D1919), C.S. Garland (D1920), R.N. Williams (D1920), J.O. Anderson (D1922), F.T. Hunter (D1924), J.R. Lacoste (S1925, D1925), Miss M.G. Sutton, (S1905, 1907).

Notes:
(1) The silver commemorative medal, two inches in diameter, has the Gentlemen's Singles Challenge Cup (AELTC) featured as the centrepiece on the obverse side. Around the Cup are the words JUBILEE LAWN TENNIS CHAMPIONSHIPS. On the reverse side are the words WIMBLEDON 1877–1926 and a decorative panel which contains the engraved name of the recipient.
(2) Winners of the Oxford University Doubles Championship.

Each competitor received a bronze commemorative medal having the same design as the silver medal.

1961 75th Championships

On Wednesday, 28th June, 38 past champions were entertained to luncheon by the Club in the Members' Enclosure:

J.R. Borotra (S1924, 1926, D1925, 1932, 1933, M1925), J. Brugnon (D1926, 1928, 1932, 1933), H.J. Cochet (S1927, 1929, D1926, 1928), M.O. Decugis (D1911), J. Drobny (S1954), R.S. Emerson (D1959), N.A. Fraser (S1960, D1959), L.A. Godfree (D1923, M1926), R.N. Howe (M1958), G.P. Hughes (D1936), J.A. Kramer (S1947, D1946, 1947), R.G. Laver (M1959, 1960), G.P. Mulloy (D1957), J.E. Patty (S1950, D1957), F.J. Perry (S1934–1936, M1935, 1936), R.D. Ralston (D1960), U.C.J. Schmidt (D1958), M.A. Trabert (S1955), C.R.D. Tuckey (D1936), G. von Cramm (M1933), M. Woosnam (D1921), Miss P.D.H. Boothby (Mrs. A.C. Geen) (S1909, D1913), Miss A. Buxton (Mrs. D. Silk) (D1956), Miss C.R. Cooper/Mrs. A. Sterry (S1895, 1896, 1898, 1901, 1908), Miss W.A. James (Mrs. S.H. Hammersley) (D1935, 1936), Miss K. McKane/Mrs. L.A. Godfree (S1924, 1926, M1924, 1926), Mrs. R. Mathieu (D1933, 1934, 1937), Mrs. E.G. Parton (Mrs. T.M. Mavrogordato) (1), Miss D.E. Metaxa (Mrs. P.D. Howard) (D1932), Miss F.A. M. Mortimer (D1955), Miss P.E. Mudford (Mrs. M.R. King) (D1931), Miss D.E. Round (Mrs. D.L. Little) (S1934, 1937, M1934–1936), Miss E.M. Ryan (D1914, 1919–1923, 1925–1927, 1930, 1933, 1934, M1919, 1921, 1923, 1927, 1928, 1930, 1932), Miss J.A. Shilcock (Mrs. J.K. Spann) (D1955), Miss K.E. Stammers (Mrs. M. Menzies) (D1935, 1936), Mrs. R.A. Summers (M1949), Mrs. C.O. Tuckey (D1913), Mrs. M.R. Watson (Mrs. W.L. Blakstad) (D1928, 1929).

Note:

(1) Winner of the 1911 non-championship Mixed Doubles Event.

All competitors, umpires and past champions received an engraved commemorative silver pencil.

1977 Centenary Championships

On Monday, 20th June, at 2 p.m., 41 out of 52 surviving singles champions paraded on the Centre Court and each received a silver commemorative medal (1) from T. R. H. The Duke and Duchess of Kent.

Order of presentation:

1. Miss K. McKane/Mrs. L.A. Godfree (1924, 1926); 2. J.R. Borotra (1924, 1926); 3. J.R. Lacoste (1925, 1928); 4. H.J. Cochet (1927, 1929); 5. B.R. Borg (1976) (2); 6. S.B.B. Wood (1931); 7. H.E. Vines (1932); 8. Miss D.E. Round (Mrs. D.L. Little) (1934, 1937); 9. F.J. Perry (1934–1936); 10. J.D. Budge (1937, 1938); 11. Miss A. Marble (1939); 12. R.L. Riggs (1939); 13. Y.F.M. Petra (1946); 14. Miss M.E. Osborne (Mrs. W. duPont) (1947); 15. J. A. Kramer (1947); 16. Miss A.L. Brough (Mrs. A.T. Clapp) (1948–1950, 1955); 17. R. Falkenburg (1948); 18. J.E. Patty (1950); 19. Miss D.J. Hart (1951); 20. R. Savitt (1951); 21. F.A. Sedgman (1952); 22. E.V. Seixas (1953); 23. J. Drobny (1954); 24. M.A. Trabert (1955); 25. Miss S.J. Fry (Mrs. K.E. Irvin) (1956); 26. L.A. Hoad (1956, 1957); A.J. Cooper (1958); 28. Miss M.E.A.

Bueno (1959, 1960, 1964); 29. N.A. Fraser (1960); 30. Miss F.A.M. Mortimer (Mrs. J.E. Barrett) (1961); 31. R.G. Laver (1961, 1962, 1968, 1969); 32. Mrs. J.R. Susman (1962); 33. Mrs. L.W. King (1966–1968, 1972, 1973, 1975); 34. M. Santana (1966); 35. J.D. Newcombe (1967, 1970, 1971); 36. Mrs. P.F. Jones (1969); 37. Miss E.F. Goolagong (Mrs. R.A. Cawley) (1971); 38. S.R. Smith (1972); 39. J. Kodes (1973); 40. A.R. Ashe (1975); 41. Miss C.M. Evert (1974, 1976). Miss E. M. Ryan and J. Brugnon, who represented all the doubles winners, then followed and each received a silver commemorative medal.

The following champions, who were not present, received their medal later: Miss H.N. Wills/Mrs. F.S. Moody (1927–1930, 1932, 1933, 1935, 1938); Miss H.H. Jacobs (1936); Miss P.M. Betz (Mrs. R.R. Addie) (1946); Miss A. Gibson (Mrs. W.A. Darben) (1957, 1958); Miss M. Smith/Mrs. B.M. Court (1963, 1965, 1970); J.H. Crawford (1933); F.R. Schroeder (1949): A. Olmedo (1959); C.R. McKinley (1963); R.S. Emerson (1964, 1965); J.S. Connors (1974).

Notes:

(1) The silver commemorative medal, 1⅞ inches in diameter, has a contemporary gentleman and lady tennis player featured on the obverse side. Around the figures are the words WIMBLEDON CENTENARY YEAR and the date 1977. On the reverse side a gentleman and a lady tennis player are featured in older style costume, together with the date 1877. The medal is centrally mounted in a shallow silver dish, 3¼ inches in diameter, with the inscription 1877 WIMBLEDON 1977 and the recipient's name and date/s of their Championship/s engraved around the inside of the bowl.

(2) Allowed out of turn owing to being committed to play the opening match on the Court.

On Friday, 1st July, H.M. The Queen, accompanied by H.R.H. The Duke of Edinburgh, honoured The Championships with her presence. After watching the Ladies' Singles final, she presented the trophy to the winner, Miss Virginia Wade, on the Centre Court. The whole of the gate money that day was donated to The Queen's Silver Jubilee Fund.

A Queen's Silver Jubilee Salver was given to the winner of the Gentlemen's and Ladies' Singles. Each competitor and certain officials received a gold-plated pen and pencil set, while the members of the Committee of Management and some senior officials were given the silver commemorative medal/dish. A specially designed Spode commemorative plate was produced. As part of the celebrations the Wimbledon Lawn Tennis Museum and the Kenneth Ritchie Wimbledon Library were opened in May by H.R.H. The Duke of Kent.

1984 Ladies' Centenary Championships

On Monday, 2nd July, at 1.50 p.m. (1) 17 out of 20 surviving Ladies' Singles champions paraded on the Centre Court and each received a commemorative Vase (2) from T.R.H. The Duke and Duchess of Kent.

Order of presentation:

1. Miss M. Navratilova (1978, 1979, 1982, 1983); 2. Miss S.V. Wade (1977); 3. Miss C.M. Evert/Mrs. J.M. Lloyd (1974, 1976, 1981); 4. Miss E.F. Goolagong/Mrs. R.A. Cawley (1971, 1980); 5. Mrs. P.F. Jones (1969); 6. Mrs. L.W. King (1966–1968, 1972, 1973, 1975); 7. Miss M. Smith/Mrs. B.M.

Court (1963, 1965, 1970); 8. Miss F.A.M. Mortimer (Mrs. J.E. Barrett) (1961); 9. Miss M.E.A. Bueno (1959, 1960, 1964); 10. Miss A. Gibson (Mrs. S. Llewellyn) (1957, 1958); 11. Miss S.J. Fry (Mrs. K.E. Irvin) (1956); 12. Miss D.J. Hart (1951); 13. Miss A.L. Brough (Mrs. A.T. Clapp) (1948–1950, 1955); 14. Miss M.E. Osborne (Mrs. W. duPont) (1947); 15. Miss P.M. Betz (Mrs. R.R. Addie) (1946); 16. Miss A. Marble (1939); 17. Miss K. McKane/Mrs. L.A. Godfree (1924, 1926).

The following champions, who were not present, received their Vase later:

Miss H. N. Wills/Mrs. F. S. Moody (1927–1930, 1932, 1933, 1935, 1938); Miss H. H. Jacobs (1936); Mrs. J. R. Susman (1962).

Notes:

(1) Because of rain the ceremony was delayed until 2.18 p.m.

(2) The Vase, a specially commissioned piece of Waterford Crystal, is $10^{1}/_{2}$ inches high with a raised foot and a scalloped rim, 4 inches in diameter. On the body an opaque area is engraved with a shield, within which are the words LADIES CENTENARY, 1884–1984, and, in a circle bordering crossed rackets, THE CHAMPIONSHIPS WIMBLEDON. Also engraved are the name of the Champion and the date/s of her championship/s.

Of the 23 vases produced, 20 were presented to the champions. H.R.H. The Duke of Kent and Mr. R.E.H. Hadingham, President and Chairman of The All England Lawn Tennis Club, were each given one, while the remaining item is held on display in the Clubhouse.

1986 100th Championships

The occasion was marked in a variety of ways, including the formation of the Last 8 Club, a Dinner Party held in the Members' Enclosure on Thursday, 3rd July, for invited guests who had made significant contributions to The Championships in the past, and the design of a special logo.

A specially designed Royal Doulton commemorative plate, bearing the special logo, was available for presentation purposes. All competitors received a 100th Championship shirt.

1993 100th Ladies' Championships

A number of commemorative events were held to celebrate the occasion. The surviving 19 Ladies' Singles champions were each presented with a special gold bracelet (1), while all lady competitors received a gold bracelet (2) and a commemorative shirt.

Banners and drapes were hung on the Members' Balcony and Debenture Holders' Lounge and in Aorangi Park a large flower-bed display depicted a specially commissioned 100th Ladies' Championships logo.

Notes:

(1) The bracelet, designed by Garrard & Co., is a 9 carat gold lady's identity bracelet in curb link pattern with central bar, engraved on one side with the words THE 100TH LADIES CHAMPIONSHIPS and on the reverse side the recipient's name. Of the 20 items produced 19 were presented to the champions while the remaining item is held by the Wimbledon Lawn Tennis Museum. The champions attending The Championships were given their bracelets, while the remainder received theirs later.

(2) The bracelet, designed by Garrard & Co., is a 9 carat gold belcher pattern bracelet with a logo charm, featuring cross rackets around which are the words THE 100TH LADIES CHAMPIONSHIPS, WIMBLEDON. On the reverse side of the charm is the date 1993.

2000 Millennium Championships

On Saturday 1st July, 64 Singles Champions, Doubles Champions four or more times and Singles finalists at least twice were presented with a commemorative Waterford Crystal Plate (1) on the Centre Court, by H.R.H. The Duchess of Gloucester, Honorary President of the LTA accompanied by Mr. T.D. Phillips and Mr. C.J. Gorringe, Chairman and Chief Executive of the AELTC and Mr. J.M. Gracie, President of the LTA.

Positioned in the north west corner of the Court was the Band of the Royal Scots Guards, resplendent in their bright red tunics. At 1 p.m. the main ceremony took place when, following an introduction by the Master of Ceremonies, Mr. J.E. Barrett, 59 of the players walked on Court to the music of 'Purple and Green' and sat on chairs provided at the south end. Following 'God Save the Queen', the players, one by one were directed to the centre of the Court to receive a 'token' plate(2) from the Duchess of Gloucester.

Following presentation each player walked to the north end of the court and at the conclusion of the ceremony, group photographs were taken.

The order of presentation was:

1. A.K. Agassi (USA) (S 1982) (3) 2. K.B. McGregor (AUS) (GSD 1951) 3. R.A.J. Hewitt (AUS/RSA) (D 1962, 1964, 1967, 1972, 1978) 4. K.N. Fletcher (AUS) (D 1966, M 1963, 1965, 1966, 1968) 5. A.D. Roche (AUS) (D 1965, 1968–1970, 1974) 6. Miss R. Casals (USA) (D 1967, 1968, 1970, 1971, 1973) 7. O.K. Davidson (AUS) (M 1967, 1971, 1973, 1974) 8. F.D. McMillan (RSA) (D 1967, 1972, 1978, M 1978, 1981) 9. P.B. Fleming (USA) (D 1979, 1981, 1983, 1984) 10. Miss P.H. Shriver (USA) (D 1981–1984, 1986) 11. Miss H. Sukova (TCH) (D 1987, 1989, 1990, 1996) 12. Miss N.M. Zvereva (URS/CIS/BLR) (D 1991–1994, 1997) 13. Miss B.C. Fernandez (USA) (D 1992–1994,1997) 14. H.W. Austin (GBR) (SF 1932, 1938)15. K. Nielsen (DEN) (SF 1953, 1955) 16. K.R. Rosewall (AUS) (SF 1954, 1956, 1970, 1974) 17. Miss D.R. Hard (USA) (D 1957, 1959, 1960, 1963) 18. F.S. Stolle (AUS) (D 1962, 1964, M 1961, 1964, 1969) 19. Miss H. Mandlikova (TCH) (SF 1981, 1986) 20. G.S. Ivanisevic (CRO) (SF 1992, 1994, 1998) 21. S.B.B. Wood (USA) (S 1931) 22. Miss P.M. Betz (Mrs. R.R. Addie) (USA) (S 1946) 23. R. Falkenburg (USA) (S 1948) 24. F.R. Schroeder (USA) (S 1949) 25. J.E. Patty (USA) (S 1950) 26. R. Savitt (USA) (S 1951) 27. F.A. Sedgman (AUS) (S 1952) 28. E.V. Seixas (USA) (S 1953) 29. J. Drobny (EGY) (S 1954) 30. M.A. Trabert (USA) (S 1955) 31. Miss S.J. Fry (Mrs. K.E. Irvin) (USA) (S 1956) 32. A.J. Cooper (AUS) (S 1958) 33. Miss M.E.A. Bueno (BRA) (S 1959, 1960, 1964) 34. A.R. Olmedo (USA) (S 1959) 35. N.A. Fraser (AUS) (S 1960) 36. Miss F.A.M. Mortimer (Mrs. J.E. Barrett) (GBR) (S 1961) 37. R.G. Laver (AUS) (S 1961, 1962, 1968, 1969) 38. Miss M. Smith/Mrs. B.M. Court (AUS) (S 1963, 1965, 1970) 39. R.S. Emerson (AUS) (S 1964, 1965) 40. Miss B.J. Moffitt/Mrs. L.W. King (USA) (S 1966–1968, 1972, 1973, 1975) 41. M. Santana (ESP) (S 1966) 42. J.D. Newcombe (AUS) (S 1967, 1970, 1971) 43. Mrs. P.F. Jones (GBR) (S 1969) 44. Miss E.F. Goolagong/Mrs. R.A. Cawley (AUS) (S 1971, 1980) 45. S.R. Smith (USA) (S

1972) 46. J. Kodes (TCH) (S 1973) 47. Miss C.M. Evert/Mrs. J.M. Lloyd
(Mrs. A.R. Mill) (USA) (S 1974, 1976, 1981) 48. B.R.Borg (SWE) (S 1976–
1980) 49. Miss S.V. Wade (GBR) (S 1977) 50. Miss M. Navratilova (USA) (S
1978, 1979, 1982–1987, 1990) 51. J.P. McEnroe (USA) (S 1981, 1983,
1984) 52. B.F. Becker (GER) (S 1985, 1986, 1989) 53. P.H. Cash (AUS) (S
1987) 54. Miss S.M. Graf (GER) (S 1988, 1989, 1991–1993, 1995, 1996)
55. S.B. Edberg (SWE) (S 1988, 1990) 56. M.D. Stich (GER) (S 1991) 57.
Miss I.C. Martinez (ESP) (S 1994) 58. Miss J. Novotna (CZE) (S 1998) 59.
Miss L.A. Davenport (USA) (S 1999).

Later in the afternoon, between the second and third match, five more
Champions (4) were presented with their Plate in the Royal Box, by the
Duchess of Gloucester.

The order of presentation was:

60.   T.A. Woodbridge (AUS) (D 1993–1997) 61. M.R. Woodforde
(AUS) (D 1993–1997) 62. Miss A.I.M. Sanchez-Vicario (ESP) (SF 1995,
1996) 63. Miss M. Hingis (SUI) (S 1997) 64. P. Sampras (USA) (S 1993–
1995, 1997–1999).

The following ten players, who were not present, received their Plate later:
Miss A.L. Brough (Mrs. A.T, Clapp) (USA) (S 1948–1950, 1955), Miss
M.E. Osborne (Mrs. W. duPont) (USA) (S 1947), Miss D.J. Hart (USA) (S
1951), Miss A. Gibson (Mrs. S. Llewellyn) (USA) (S 1957,1958), Mrs. J.R.
Susman (USA) (S 1962), J.S. Connors (USA) (S 1974,1982), R.P.S. Krajicek
(NED) (S 1996), J.A. Kramer (USA) (S 1947), I. Lendl (TCH) (SF
1986,1987), I. Nastase (ROM) (SF 1972,1976).

Notes.

(1) The commemorative Waterford Crystal Plate, 10½ inches in diameter has a ½ inch raised
rim around the plate. The design is broken up into distinct patterns representing three types
of tennis formats: cross-cuts – Singles, X-cuts – Doubles, Olive – Mixed.

In the centre of the Plate, within a 3½ inches diameter circle, is the Championship logo of
cross rackets, surrounded by the words THE MILLENNIUM CHAMPIONSHIPS
WIMBLEDON. The recipient's name and championship event/s are engraved, above and
below the circle.

Of the 80 Plates produced, 74 were presented to the Champions. H.R.H. The Duchess of
Gloucester, The AELTC and the Wimbledon Lawn Tennis Museum were each given one,
leaving three items in reserve.

(2) Inclement weather, just prior to the ceremony, prevented individual Plates being
presented on Court but these were given later.

(3) Allowed out of turn owing to being committed to play later.

(4) These players were unable to attend the main ceremony, owing to being committed by
their playing schedule.

(5) S – Singles Champions, D – Doubles Champions, M – Mixed Doubles Champions, SF –
Singles Finalists, GSD – Grand Slam Doubles Champion.

2011 125ᵗʰ Championships

To commemorate the occasion each competitor was given a souvenir. The
gentlemen received a 'Links of London' black leather washbag, embossed
with the 125ᵗʰ Championships logo, while the ladies were given a 'Links of
London' silver bracelet, incorporating the 125ᵗʰ Championship logo.

Royalty

British royalty has been associated with The Championships since 1907 when the Prince of Wales, accompanied by Princess Mary, visited the Worple Road ground on Saturday, 29th June. Arriving by motor car at about 3.15p.m., they were met by the Committee at the entrance to the ground and escorted to the Committee Box, which had temporarily been fitted out as a Royal Box. They stayed until a thunderstorm put an end to the day's play, having watched the last of W.V. Eaves v L.H. Escombe, Miss M.G. Sutton v Miss A.M. Morton and part of a doubles contest.

Before leaving the ground the Prince accepted an offer of the Presidency of the Club and declared his intention of donating to the Club a challenge trophy. The Prince remained President until his accession to the throne as King George V in 1910. He then became Patron of the Club, a position subsequently maintained by succeeding monarchs.

King George V and Queen Mary were avid spectators at The Championships, being present each year from 1919 to 1934, with the exception of 1927 and 1929. Queen Mary continued this association and from 1935 to 1951 missed only the meeting of 1936.

When in 1922 King George V, accompanied by Queen Mary, opened the Church Road ground, the Prince of Wales (later King Edward VIII and Duke of Windsor) and Prince Albert (later Duke of York and King George VI) were present. In 1926, on the occasion of The Jubilee Championships, the latter competed in the Gentlemen's Doubles event in partnership with L. Greig (later Sir Louis Greig, Chairman of The All England Lawn Tennis Club), but they were well beaten in the first round by H.R. Barrett and A.W. Gore. In 1947 King George VI and Queen Elizabeth were present to watch the Gentlemen's Singles final.

Queen Elizabeth II visited The Championships on Saturday, 6th July, 1957, Friday, 6th July, 1962 and during her Silver Jubilee year, on Friday, 1st July, 1977, on the occasion of The Championship's Centenary. Her Majesty's latest visit was on Thursday, 24th June, 2010. Prince Philip, Duke of Edinburgh, attended in 1949, 1953, 1954, 1957, 1960 and 1977. The Prince of Wales was present in 1970 and 2012 accompanied by the Duchess of Cornwall.

In 1929 Prince George became President of the Club and so began the long association of the Kent family. When he died in 1942 his widow, the Duchess of Kent (later Princess Marina) succeeded in the post and up to her death in 1968 attended 23 successive years, many of them most days.

Happily the tradition continues with the present Duke of Kent, who succeeded his mother in 1969. He attends frequently each year and presents the trophies. Other members of the Royal family are regular visitors.

The very first royal visit to Wimbledon was on Monday, 15th July, 1895, when the Crown Princess Stephanie of Austria, accompanied by Prince Batthyany Strattmann, witnessed the Gentlemen's Doubles Challenge Round.

Programmes

The programme at the first Championship in 1877 was printed on thin card, folded into two, to give a page size of 6 x 4 inches. On the front page appeared the words "All England Croquet and Lawn Tennis Club", followed by the date, "List of Players" and "Price Sixpence". The rear page was devoted to showing the layout of the 12 courts, relative to the Pavilion.

Inside appeared the full draw of the "Lawn Tennis Championship" (Gentlemen's Singles only), together with a list of prizes and a statement that "The official score will be posted on the Notice Board in the pavilion after each tie". The programme was kept up to date, with the name of the winner of each match being printed overnight, a practice which has continued to the present time.

The programme had a similar appearance until the early 1890's, when very thin cards, 6x4 inches, were provided. Printed on both sides were the draws of one, two or three events. These cards, easy to slip into the pocket, cost threepence and gave much information, such as a plan of the grounds, a timetable for trains between Wimbledon and Waterloo, a list of the Committee of Management members, times of play and the match scores.

As the number of events and competitors increased the programme was enlarged accordingly. From 1899 to 1904 the card was folded into two, to give a page size of 8 x 5 inches. The court layout and times of play were not detailed and from 1902 the train times were deleted. The more commercial aspects of the production were apparent when the first advertisement was shown in 1903, offering a book for sale.

From 1905 the card was folded into three and by 1914 the page size had risen to 13 x 5 inches. The 1909 edition re-introduced the layout of the courts and the day's schedule of matches.

After the First World War in 1919, the programme was expanded again to consist of eight pages of paper, 12½ x 10 inches, folded into two. The manner of presentation of the draws and other information laid the foundation of the present day programme. In 1924 the programme was produced in a stapled book form to include a cover. The size of this page remained around 12 x 10 inches and for the first time a list of previous winners of the events was included.

During the Twenties and Thirties the programme remained substantially unchanged. There was a rotation of colour used for the front cover board and as the advertisements grew so did the number of pages.

The 1946 programme had a touch of austerity but a year later the first photographs appeared with an aerial view of the Centre Court on the front cover, which was printed green throughout the fortnight, with a page inside showing various pictures from the previous year's Championships.

In 1948 the front cover was printed in a different colour each day of the week and these were repeated during the second week. A photograph of a player appeared daily as an integral part of the front cover. Inside each day was a different article written by Brigadier J.G. Smyth, V.C., M.C., together with a selection of photographic illustrations. Also evident for the first time were full page four-colour advertisements. In 1949 an alphabetical "List of Competitors" was given. For the next twenty years or so the programme's format changed little, although occasionally in the late Fifties and Sixties a colour photograph appeared on the front cover of the final programme. New ground was broken in 1977 when the Centenary programme provided player biographies, accompanied by colour photographs. Since that date the programme has expanded to provide many more articles and other information. In 1985 the Qualifying singles results and the previous year's Championship singles draws were included for the first time.

In 2002, there was a break with tradition when for the first time the competitors' forenames, instead of initials, were shown in the opening round of the Gentlemen's and Ladies' Singles events. Thereafter, in these two draws, initials were retained, together with the ladies' titles, Mrs or Miss. However, in 2009 all five Championship draws showed forenames throughout, while the ladies' titles were dropped.

From 2010 the pages of the Programme were perfect bound and in 2015 advertising in the Programme was limited to official suppliers only.

Price of programmes

1877 – c 1889	6d.	1984 – 1985	£1.70
c 1890 – 1898	3d. (per card)	1986 – 1987	£2.00
1899 – 1914	6d.	1988 – 1989	£2.50
1919 – 1939 }	1s.0d.	1990 – 1991	£3.00
1946 – 1947 }		1992 – 1993	£3.50
1948 – 1951	2s.0d.	1994 – 1995	£4.00
1952 – 1965	2s.6d.	1996 – 1997	£4.50
1966 – 1968	3s.0d.	1998 – 2000	£5.00
1969 – 1970	3s.6d.	2001 – 2002	£5.50
1971 – 1972	20p	2003 – 2004	£6.00
1973 – 1974	25p	2005 – 2006	£6.50
1975 – 1976	50p	2007 – 2009	£7.00
1977	75p	2010 – 2015	£8.00
1978 – 1980	£1.00		
1981 – 1983	£1.50		

Note: Special programmes were printed for Sunday 30th June, 1991, priced £1.00 Sunday 29th June, 1997, priced £1.50 and Sunday 27th June, 2004, priced £2.00.

Referees and Assistant Referees

Referees

Year	Name	Date of Birth/ Death	Place of Birth/ Death
1877–1885	Henry JONES	b. 2 Nov 1831 d. 10 Feb. 1899	London Hyde Park, Middlesex
1886	Julian MARSHALL	b. 24 Jun 1836 d. 21 Nov 1903	Headingley, Leeds, Yorkshire Hampstead, Middlesex
1887–1889	Samuel Alfred Einem HICKSON	b. 13 May 1857 d. 13 May 1939	Highgate, London Withersfield, Suffolk
1890–1905	Bonham Carter EVELEGH	b. 1843 d. 7 Mar 1910	Portsmouth, Hampshire Wimbledon Common, Surrey
1906–1914	Harry Stanley SCRIVENER	b. 1 Oct 1865 d.17 Aug 1937	London Wimbledon, Surrey
1919–1936	Francis Russell BURROW	b. 30 Jan 1866 d. 16 Dec 1945	Malvern, Worcesterhsire Highgate, London
1937–1939	Douglas Hamilton PRICE	b. 25 Jan 1893 d. 7 Dec 1942	Lambeth, London Fulham, London
1946–1950	Capt. Albyn Kemble TROWER	b. 11 Mar 1892 d. 14 Oct 1950	Kensington, London Holton, Oxfordshire
1951–1962	Col. Walter John LEGG O.B.E.	b. 30 Jan 1894 d. 22 May 1970	Birmingham Horsham, Sussex
1963–1975	Capt. Michael Bradford GIBSON	b. 20 Mar 1929 d. 29 Aug 1993	Manchester Warnham, Sussex
1976–1982	Frederick William HOYLES	b. 1 Oct 1923 d. 25 Mar 2004	Spalding, Lincolnshire Wisbech, Cambridgeshire
1983–2005	Alan Ronald MILLS C.B.E.	b. 6 Nov 1935	Stretford, Manchester
2006–	Andrew Michael JARRETT	b. 9 Jan 1958	Belper, Derbyshire

Assistant Referees

1910–1911	C. Marriott	1977–2002	T.D. Gathercole
1912–1914 1919–1920	} D.T.R. Larcombe	1977–1982 1981–2006	A.R. Mills P.J.A. Mornard
1921–1929	E.U. Story	1983–2002	Mrs. J.M. Sexton
1930–1936	D.H. Price	2001–2005	A.M. Jarrett
1937–1939	Capt. A.D.C. Macaulay	2002–2011, 2013–	Miss C.J. Wood
1939	Capt. A.K. Trower	2006–2007	M.J. Morrisey
1946–1950	Col. W.J. Legg O.B.E.	2006–	Miss D. Parnell
1962	Capt. M.B. Gibson	2007–	G.C.W. Armstrong
1963–1976	See note.	2012	Miss P. Whitecross

Note: From 1963 to 1976 there was no officially appointed Assistant Referee. During this
period the following people assisted the Referee at various times: T.R. Kirkpatrick,
B.J. Austin, M. Seaton, F.W. Hoyles, J.R. Cochrane, Mrs. B.M. Seal and T.D.
Gathercole.

Umpires of the Finals and Semi-finals

Year	Gentlemen's Singles Semi-Final	Gentlemen's Singles Final	Gentlemen's Doubles Semi-Final	Gentlemen's Doubles Final	Ladies' Singles Semi-Final	Ladies' Singles Final	Ladies' Doubles Semi-Final	Ladies' Doubles Final	Mixed Doubles Semi-Final	Mixed Doubles Final
1927	H.T. Parry	E. Timmis		C. Nolan Hyem		G.W. Hillyard		A. Sharp		G. Allardyce
1932		C.W. Bruton		F.R. Chippendale		G.W. Hillyard		H.J. Chivers		R. Powell
1935		H.T. Kitchener		C.W. Bruton		N.J. Chivers		L.R. Finn		H.A. Furber
1948		F.R. Weatherley		C.J. Johnson		T.P. Harris		P. Adorian		F.R. Weatherley
1949		H.A. LeBair		L.R. Carr		A.D. Chisholm		P.F.L. Burges		E.G. Hughes
1950		L.R. Carr		G. Hastings		F.R. Weatherley		C.J. Johnson		J. A. Watson
1951	H.E.G. Salkilld	C.J. Passfield	E.G. Hughes	T.P. Harris	L.R. Carr	C.J. Johnson	R. Powell	C.G. French	C. Chesterman	C. Chesterman
	R.P. Petherick		W.J. Air		P. Adorian		A.A. Mather		C. Chesterman	
1952	L.R. Carr	T.P. Harris	H.E.G. Salkilld	C.J. Johnson	C.J. Passfield	W.J. Air	J.A. Watson	A.A. Mather	R. Powell	
	A.D. Cooper		R.P. Petherick		T.A. Heron		E.G. Hughes		G.H. Agnew	
1953	T.P. Harris	C.J. Johnson	P. Adorian	F.R. Weatherley	E.G. Hughes	C.J. Passfield	T.A. Heron	H.E.G. Salkilld	G.E. Butt	L.R. Carr
	A.D. Cooper		R.P. Petherick		W.J. Air		R. Powell		A.G. Stackwood	
1954	W.J. Air	P. Adorian	L.R. Carr	H.E.G.Salkilld	R.H.H. Osborne	G.H. Agnew	E.G. Brown	G.E. Butt	L. Holloway	A.G. Stackwood
	C. Chesterman		T.P. Harris		H.A. Snydercombe		K.P. Hedge		T.A. Heron	
1955	R. Bint	H.E.G. Salkilld	R.P. Petherick	G.H. Agnew	E.G. Brown	G.E. Butt	R.H. Osborne	A.G. Stackwood	P.A.L. Hodges	A.D. Cooper
	L. Holloway		L.R. Carr		K.P. Hedge		H.A. Syndercombe		R.F. Chatham	
1956	G.H. Agnew	R.D. Warnock	A.D. Cooper	G.E. Butt	R.F. Chatham	R.P. Petherick	J.G. Rae	R. Bint	R. Williams	L. Holloway
	C. Chesterman		A.G. Stackwood		H.A. Syndercombe		P.A.L. Hodge		K.P. Hedge	
1957	C.J. Johnson	A.D. Cooper	C.J. Passfield	G.H. Agnew	T.A. Heron	A.G. Stackwood	E.G. Brown	R.F. Chatham	C. Chesterman	K.P. Hedge
	R.H.H. Osborne		H.A. Syndercombe		E.G. Hughes		R.P. Petherick		J.G. Rae	
1958	T.P. Harris	G.H. Agnew	L.R. Carr	R.H.H. Osborne	G.E. Butt	R.F. Chatham	T.A. Heron	K.P. Hedge	I.S. Hine	H.A. Syndercombe
	R.P. Petherick		J.G. Rae		C. Chesterman		D.F.J. Byrne		A.G. Stackwood	
1959	H.E.G. Salkilld	G.E. Butt	D.F.J. Byrne	R.F. Chatham	C.J. Passfield	K.P. Hedge	C.J. Johnson	C. Chesterman	R.H.H. Osborne	R.P. Petherick
	H.A. Syndercombe		I.S. Hine		P.A.L. Hodges		A.L. Kittle		E.G. Hughes	
1960	T.P. Harris	R.P. Petherick	C. Chesterman	H.A. Syndercombe	D.V. Dutton	D.F.J. Byrne	H.E. Duncombe	J.G. Rae	J.H.W. Evans	P.A.L. Hodges
	H. Targett		E.B. Auger		K.P. Hedge		A.G. Stackwood		A.L. Kittle	
1961	A.D. Cooper	R.F. Chatham	A.G. Stackwood	P.A.L. Hodges	H.E.G. Salkilld	R.H.H. Osborne	J.H.W. Evans	H.A. Syndercombe	E.B. Auger	C. Chesterman
	C.J. Passfield		K.P. Hedge		C.J. Johnson		E.G. Hughes		D.F.J. Byrne	

Year	Gentlemen's Singles Semi-Final	Gentlemen's Singles Final	Gentlemen's Doubles Semi-Final	Gentlemen's Doubles Final	Ladies' Singles Semi-Final	Ladies' Singles Final	Ladies' Doubles Semi-Final	Ladies' Doubles Final	Mixed Doubles Semi-Final	Mixed Doubles Final
1962	T.P. Harris	H.A. Syndercombe	G.H. Agnew	J.G. Rae	E.B. Auger	H. Targett	D.F.J. Byrne	R.H.H. Osborne	C. Chesterman	J.H.W. Evans
	P.A.L. Hodges		R.G. Emmett		A.E. Knight		A.L. Kittle		A.G. Stackwood	
1963	C. Chesterman	R.H.H. Osborne	A.L. Kittle	H. Targett	E.G. Hughes	E.B. Auger	K.P. Hedge	L.E MacCallum	H.E. Duncombe	R.G. Emmett
	H.E.G. Salkilld		A.E. Knight		A. Scott		A.G. Stackwood		W. Telfer	
1964	R.G. Emmett	K.P. Hedge	C. Chesterman	D.F.J. Byrne	G.H. Agnew	P.A.L. Hodges	E.B. Auger	A.L. Kittle	A.E. Knight	J.G. Rae
	R. Williams		T.P. Harris		H. Targett		W. Telfer		A. Scott	
1965	A.E. Knight	P.A.L. Hodges	E.G. Hughes	C. Chesterman	L.E. MacCallum	A.L. Kittle	H.E. Duncombe	H. Targett	E.B. Auger	D.F.J. Byrne
	J.G. Rae		H.E.G. Salkilld		W. Telfer		A. Scott		R.G. Emmett	
1966	H.A. Syndercombe	D.F.J. Byrne	H. Targett	E.B. Auger	J.G. Rae	R.G. Emmett	L.E. MacCallum	R.O Williams	G.W. Armstrong	A.E. Knight
	G.H. Agnew		W. Telfer		L. Holloway		H.G. Collins		W.S. Carroll	
1967	L.E. MacCallum	J.G. Rae	H.G. Collins	R.G. Emmett	G.W. Armstrong	A.E. Knight	W.S. Carroll	E.B. Auger	W.A. Breeze	W. Telfer
	H. Targett		R.H.H. Osborne		H.E.G. Salkilld		L. Holloway		C.J. Collett	
1968	E.B. Auger	H. Targett	G.H. Agnew	L.E. MacCallum	R.G. Emmett	W. Telfer	W.A. Breeze	J.H.W. Evans	L. Holloway	G.W. Armstrong
	K.P. Hedge		H.A. Syndercombe		A.E. Knight		C.J. Collett		J. Timberlake	
1969	G.W. Armstrong	R.G. Emmett	E.B. Auger	A.E. Knight	J.H.W. Evans	L.E. MacCallum	G.M. Culpan	C.J. Collett	C.G.P. Alderson	W.A. Breeze
	W. Telfer		A.G. Stackwood		J.G. Salkilld		F.A. Gibson		J.G. Harbord	
1970	G.H. Agnew	E.B. Auger	L.E. MacCallum	G.W. Armstrong	D.F.J. Byrne	C.J. Collett	A.E. Knight	W.A. Breeze	J.G. Harbord	G.M. Culpan
	H.A. Syndercombe		F.R. Bowron		C.G.P. Alderson		L.P. Lockie		G.W. Hole	
1971	J.G. Rae	A.E. Knight	G.W. Armstrong	F.R. Bowron	G.M. Culpan	G.W. Hole	C.G.P. Alderson	L.P. Lockie	H.G. Collins	J.G. Harbord
	J.G. Salkilld		Y.N. Makar		C.J. Collett		A.G. Stackwood		L.E. MacCallum	
1972	F.R. Bowron	L.E. MacCallum	G.M. Culpan	Y.N. Makar	W.A. Breeze	G.W. Armstrong	J.G. Harbord	C.G.P. Alderson	D.C.T. Humphries	C.J. Collett
	D.F.J. Byrne		L.P. Lockie		P. Harffey		G.W. Hole		H. Targett	
1973	R.G. Emmett	C.J. Collett	C.G.P. Alderson	W.A. Breeze	G.M. Culpan	F.R. Bowron	G.W. Armstrong	G.W. Hole	A.G. Stackwood	L.P. Lockie
	Y.N. Makar		J.G. Harbord		H.A. Syndercombe		P. Harffey		C.H. Hall	
1974	G.W. Armstrong	F.R. Bowron	G.D. King	P. Harffey	E.B. Auger	Y.N. Makar	D.F.J. Byrne	J.G. Harbord	G.W. Hole	C.G.P. Alderson
	W.A. Breeze		H. Targett		C.F. Horn		J.H.W. Evans		H.G. Collins	
1975	R.P. Jenkins	G.W. Armstrong	W.A. Breeze	G.W. Hole	E.O. James	G.D. King	C.G.P. Alderson	H.G. Collins	P. Harffey	C.F. Horn
	A.E. Knight		R.G. Emmett		H.A. Syndercombe		F. Ashton		F.W. Rumble	
1976	C.F. Horn	W.A. Breeze	E.B. Auger	F. Ashton	J.J. Shales	C.G.P. Alderson	D.C. Howie	Y.N. Makar	J.G. Harbord	P. Harffey
	E.O. James		R.P. Jenkins		H. Targett		H.G. Collins		G.D. King	
1977	C.G.P. Alderson	G.W. Hole	D.C. Howie	C.F. Horn	F. Ashton	H.G. Collins	J.G. Rae	E.O. James	R. Hughes	R.P. Jenkins
	J.J. Shales		A.E. Knight		Y.N. Makar		H.A. Syndercombe		W.J. Pickup	

Year	Gentlemen's Singles		Gentlemen's Doubles		Ladies' Singles		Ladies' Doubles		Mixed Doubles	
	Semi-Final	Final	Semi-Final	Final	Semi-Final	Final	Semi-Final	Final	Semi-Final	Final
1978	H.G. Collins P. Harffey	Y.N. Makar	E.O. James W.J. Pickup	D.C. Howie	J.G. Harbord R.P. Jenkins	J.J. Shales	E.B. Auger B.J. Wise	R.G. Hughes	C.J. Grenside C.F. Horn	F. Ashton
1979	D.C. Howie J.M. Huntington	C.G.P. Alderson	J. Kinton P.J. Smyth	J.G. Harbord	A.E. Knight A.E. Seymour	P. Harffey	A.J. Arnot V. Sampson	W.J. Pickup	G.W. Armstrong H.A. Syndercombe	E.O. James
1980	J. Kinton P.J. Smyth	P. Harffey	A.J. Arnot J.M. Huntington	J.J. Shales	D. Johnson W.J. Pickup	D.C. Howie	E.O. James R.P. Jenkins	C.J. Grenside	C.D.H. Aris J.R. Palmer	R.G. Hughes
1981	G.H. Grime J.J. Shales	R.P. Jenkins	G.W. Armstrong J.R. Grime	P.B. Webster	C.J. Grenside W. Macdonald	W.J. Pickup	D. Johnson E.O. James	J.M. Huntington	D.C. Howie D.J. Mercer	P.J. Smyth
1982	D.J. Mercer P.B. Webster	R.P. Jenkins	W. Macdonald J.M. Huntington	D.C. Howie	Miss C.S. McTavish C.G.P. Alderson	G.H. Grime	Mrs. J.R. Jones Mrs. J.R. Jones	J.J. Shales	S.J. Winyard M.R. Cox	D. Johnson
1983	M.J. Lugg S.J. Winyard	J.M. Huntington	R.P. Jenkins G.H. Grime	D.J. Mercer	Mrs. G. Clark D.C. Howie	P.B. Webster	E.O. James J.D. Parry	M.R. Cox	C.G.P. Alderson W. Macdonald	J.J. Shales
1984	J.M. Huntington J.J. Shales	D.J. Mercer	J.D. Parry R.P. Jenkins	M.J. Lugg	G.H. Grime D. Johnson	Mrs. G. Clark	S.J. Winyard B.L.J. Maddock	W. MacDonald	M.R. Cox Mrs. J.R. Jones	D.C. Howie
1985	M.J. Lugg S.J. Winyard	D.C. Howie	G.H. Grime J.M. Huntington	J.J. Shales	R.J. Lumb R.B. Smith	M.R. Cox	J.D. Parry J.A. Hodges	D. Johnson	J.D. Bryson G.C.W. Armstrong	W. MacDonald
1986	D.C. Howie J.J. Shales	G.H. Grime	G.C.W. Armstrong R.J. Lumb	J.M. Huntington	J.D. Bryson R.G. Kaufman	S.J. Winyard	B.L.J. Maddock J.E. Relf	R.B. Smith	J.A. Hodges W. Macdonald	J.D. Parry
1987	K.M. Slye G.C.W. Armstrong	S.J. Winyard	R.J. Lumb J.D. Bryson	R. Kaufman	R.B. Smith Miss J. Tabor	J.D. Parry	J.M. Huntington D.C. Howie	J.J. Shales	J.E. Relf G.H. Grime	B.L.J. Maddock
1988	S.H. Gangji R.G. Kaufman	G.C.W. Armstrong	J.J. Shales R. Ings	J.D. Parry	J.G. Frame R.J. Lumb	J.M. Huntington	J.D. Bryson J.A. Hodges	J.E. Relf	S.H. Gangji Mrs. P.A. Wilson	Mrs. J.R. Jones
1989	R. Ings P.S. Pereira	J.D. Parry	J.J. Shales R.G. Kaufman	G.H. Grime	Mrs. J. Vormbaum S.J. Winyard	G.C.W. Armstrong	B.E. Mardling S.H. Gangji	Miss J.V. Tabor	E.L. Watts J.G. Frame	J.D. Bryson
1990	R.G. Kaufman S.J. Winyard	J.J. Shales	D. Loconto S.H. Gangji	J.D. Bryson	Mrs. F. McDowell Miss J.V. Tabor	J.G. Frame	K.A.M. Craven Miss M. van Noortwijk	G.H. Grime	M.A. Wright B.E. Mardling	E.L. Watts
1991	W. McKewen D. Littlefield	J.D. Bryson	J.G. Frame D.F. Crymble	S.H. Gangji	S.J. Winyard J.D. Parry	Miss J.V. Tabor	Mrs. F. McDowell Mrs. S.J. Watts	E.L. Watts	R. Berndes I.M. Greig	K.A.M. Craven
1992	B. Rebeuh J. Snyder	J.G. Frame	K.A.M. Craven Mrs. F. McDowell	G.C.W. Armstrong	J.J. Shales E.L. Watts	S.H. Gangji	Miss J.V. Tabor R. Berndes	Mrs. S.J. Watts	M.J. Morrissey A.M. Wynne	G.H. Grime

Year	Gentlemen's Singles		Gentlemen's Doubles		Ladies' Singles		Ladies' Doubles		Mixed Doubles	
	Semi-Final	Final	Semi-Final	Final	Semi-Final	Final	Semi-Final	Final	Semi-Final	Final
1993	G.C.W. Armstrong / W.O. McKewen	S.H. Gangji	J.D. Bryson / K.A.M. Craven	M.J. Morrissey	J.J. Shales / Miss J.V. Tabor	E.L. Watts	G.H. Grime / A.M. Wynne	J.D. Parry	Mrs. F. McDowell / R.T. Lumb	R. Berndes
1994	B. Rebeuh / J.J. Shales	M.J. Morrissey	G.C.W. Armstrong / D.F. Crymble	E.L. Watts	W. McKewen / Miss J.V. Tabor	K.A.M. Craven	R. Berndes / Miss D. Ring	S.H. Gangji	A.M. Wynne / J.D. Bryson	J.G. Frame
1995	M.J. Morrissey / G.C.W. Armstrong	K.A.M. Craven	W. McKewen / E.L. Watts	J.G. Frame	Miss D. Butler / A. Egli	Miss J.V. Tabor	A.M. Wynne / G.H. Grime	J.J. Shales	R. Berndes / L. McArthur	J.D. Parry
1996	W.O. McKewen / B. Rebeuh	J.G. Frame	J. Dias / J.D. Parry	K.A.M. Craven	Mrs. G. Harvey / E.L. Watts	M.J. Morrissey	G.H. Grime / Miss D. Butler	G.C.W. Armstrong	A.M. Wynne / Miss F.J. Edwards	J.J. Shales
1997	A. Egli / W.O. McKewen	G.C.W. Armstrong	K.A.M. Craven / J.G. Frame	M.J. Morrissey	Mrs. G. Harvey / Miss D. Butler	J.J. Shales	A. Little / J.D. Parry	Miss F.J. Edwards	G.H. Grime / E.L. Watts	A.M. Wynne
1998	K.A.M. Craven / J. Dias	M.J. Morrissey	A. Egli / J. Moreno	A.M. Wynne	J.J. Shales / Miss F.J. Edwards	Mrs. G. Harvey	J.D. Parry / Miss H.R. Hunter	J.G. Frame	N. Calvert / A. Little	E.L. Watts
1999	M.J. Morrissey / B. Rebeuh	J.G. Frame	L.E.M. Graff / A.M. Wynne	K.A.M. Craven	J. Dias / A. Egli	Miss F.J. Edwards	Miss A.D. Lang / J.J. Shales	Mrs. G. Harvey	J.D. Parry / E.L. Watts	Miss H.R. Hunter
2000	L. Graff / W.O. McKewen	M.J. Morrissey	J.D. Parry / J.J. Shales	J. Dias	Mrs. G. Harvey / Miss H.R. Hunter	G.C.W. Armstrong	E.L. Watts / Miss F.J. Edwards	K.A.M. Craven	A. Wilson / A.M. Wynne	Miss A.D. Lang
2001	A. Egli / M.J. Morrissey	J. Dias	K.A.M. Craven / J. Moreno	G.C.W. Armstrong	Miss A.D. Lang / Mrs. A. Lasserre-Ullrich	Mrs. G. Harvey	A.M. Wynne / Miss L. Ceccarelli	J.D. Parry	J.J. Shales / E.L. Watts	Miss F.J. Edwards
2002	E. Molina / P. Maria	M.J. Morrissey	J.J. Shales / K.A.M. Craven	A. Egli	Miss L. Ceccarelli / Miss A.D. Lang	Mrs G. Harvey	Miss F.J. Edwards / J.D. Parry	Miss S. De Jenken	E.L. Watts / J. McMahon	A.J. Wilson
2003	E. Molina / A. Egli	G.C.W. Armstrong	E.L. Watts / J. Moreno	K.A.M. Craven	Miss F.J. Edwards / Miss S. De Jenken	M.J. Morrissey	A.J. Wilson / Miss C. Olausson	Miss A.D. Lang	J.J. Shales / R. Simkins	J.D. Parry
2004	W.O. McKewen / A. Egli	M.J. Morrissey	E. Molina / J. Moreno	G.C.W. Armstrong	Miss C. Olausson / Miss S De Jenken	Miss A.D. Lang	Miss M. Alvas / Miss L. Welch	K.A.M. Craven	Miss F.J. Edwards / J.D. Parry	J.J. Shales
2005	P. Maria / E. Molina	W.O. McKewen	J.J. Shales / D. Steiner	A. Egli	Miss A.D. Lang / Miss C. Olausson	G.C.W. Armstrong	Miss F.J. Edwards / Miss S. De Jenken	C.J.B. Ramos	A.J. Wilson / J. Crowson	K.A.M. Craven
2006	A. Egli / Miss S. DeJenken	G.C.W. Armstrong	P. Maria / F. Murphy	E. Molina	Miss L. Welch / C.J.B. Ramos	Miss A.D. Lang	Miss C. Olausson / Miss M. Alves	Miss F.J. Edwards	Miss L. Grant / K.A.M. Craven	J.B. Keothavong
2007	E. Molina / A. Egli	C.J.B. Ramos	P. Maria / A. Aref	L.E.M. Graff	Miss M. Alves / Miss S. De Jenken	Miss A.D. Lang	J.B. Keothavong / K.A.M. Craven	Miss F.J. Edwards	D. Zammit / Miss L. Grant	J.P.M. Crowson
2008	L.E.M. Graff / J. Garner	P.G.F. Maria	F. Murphy / J.B. Keothavong	E. Molina	Miss E. Asderaki / Miss M. Alves	C.J.B Ramos	Miss L. Welch / Miss F.J. Edwards	Miss A.D Lang	K.A.M. Craven / J.P.M. Crowson	Miss L. Grant

Year	Gentlemen's Singles		Gentlemen's Doubles		Ladies' Singles		Ladies' Doubles		Mixed Doubles	
	Semi-Final	Final	Semi-Final	Final	Semi-Final	Final	Semi-Final	Final	Semi-Final	Final
2009	P. Maria / E. Molina	L.E.M. Graff	C. Bernardes / M. Lahgani	C.J.B Ramos	Miss M. Alves / Miss E. Asderaki	Miss A.D. Lang	Miss L Engzell / Miss L. Welsh	J.B. Keothavong	R. Haigh / A. Kalebi	J. Garner
2010	C.J.B. Ramos / C. Bernardes	J Garner	M. El Jennati / C. Mourier	J. Keothavong	Miss A.D. Lang / Miss E. Asderaki	Miss M. Alves	K.A.M. Craven / Miss F.J. Edwards	Miss L. Engzell	R. Haigh / B. Anderson	Miss L. Grant
2011	M. Lahyani / C.J.B. Ramos	C. Bernardes	L.E.M. Graff / J.B. Keothavong	E. Molina	Miss L. Engzell / Miss K. Cramer	Miss A.D. Lang	Miss F.J. Edwards / B. Anderson	Miss L. Grant	M. Porsz / Miss K. Thomson	R. Haigh
2012	J.B. Keothavong / C.J.B. Ramos	E. Molina	S. Ullrich / Miss M. Alves	Miss E. Asderaki	Miss A.D. Lang / Miss M. Alves	L.E.M. Graff	Miss F. J. Edwards / Miss L. Grant	B. Anderson	Miss K. Thomson / J. Brace	M. Lahyani
2013	J. Garner / J.B. Keothavong	M. Lahyani	F. Murphy / A. Nili	M. El Jennati	Miss M. Cicak / Miss A. Hughes	Miss E. Asderaki	B. Anderson / R. Haigh	Miss F. J. Edwards	G. Jones / J. Brace	Miss K. Thomson
2014	A. Nili / P. Maria	J. Keothavong	J. Blom / M. Messina	D. Dumusois	K. Nouni / Miss A. Hughes	Miss M. Cicak	Miss K.Thompson / A. Gabos	R. Haigh	Miss L. Grant / Miss F.J. Edwards	B. Anderson

Also:

Gentlemen's Singles Finals: 1882 – A. Schacht, 1883 – A. Schacht, 1887 – J.A.E. Hickson, 1888 – H. Chipp, 1900 – H. Chipp, 1904 – F.H. Pearce, 1913 – H.T. Schmidt, 1921 – H.T. Parry, 1925 – F.H. Pearce, 1927 – Mr. Timmis, 1933 – H. Wager, 1934 – H. Wager, 1936 – L.W.S. Newman, 1937 – C.N. Hyem, 1946 – C.J. Passfield, 1947 – E.G. Hughes.

Ladies' Singles Finals: 1900 – C.O. Gillibanks, 1905, 1907 – H.T. Parry, 1919-1932 – G.W. Hillyard, 1933 – F.R. Chippendale, 1934 – H.J. Chivers, 1937 – C.W. Bruton.

The umpire of the first match at the Church Road ground on 26th June, 1922 (Centre Court) was Mr E. Timmis.

Miss J.V. Tabor – Mrs. G. Harvey

Opening Matches of Meeting

From 1934 the opening match of the Meeting has traditionally been played on the first Monday on the Centre Court by the Gentlemen's Singles Champion from the previous year or, in his absence, by the Runner-up.

Likewise, the Ladies' Singles Champion or Runner-up from the previous year has normally opened play on the Centre Court on the first Tuesday, which for many years was known as 'Ladies' Day'. In 1983 the Ladies' Singles draw was increased from 96 to 128 and for the first time ladies' matches were played on the opening day of the Meeting. However, the Champion or Runner-up from the previous year has continued to open the play on the first Tuesday.

Exceptions to the foregoing are noted in the following tables:-

Gentlemen's Singles Championship

Year	Champion or Runner up	Note	Opening Matches
1934	C		J.H. Crawford (AUS) v I. Tloczynski (POL)
1935	C		F.J. Perry (GBR) v M. Rainville (CAN)
1936	C		F.J. Perry (GBR) v G.D. Stratford (USA)
1937	–	(1)	H.W. Austin (GBR) v G.L. Rogers (GBR)
1938	C		J.D. Budge (USA) v K.C. Gandar Dower (GBR)
1939	–	(1)	R. Menzel (GER) v E.C. Peters (GBR)
1946	–	(2)	D. Scharenguivel (CEY) v D.W. Butler (GBR)
1947	C		Y.F.M Petra (FRA) v D.W Butler (GBR)
1948	R	(3)	T.P. Brown (USA) v D.W. Butler (GBR)
1949	C		R. Falkenburg (USA) v D. Mitic (YUG)
1950	R	(3)	J. Drobny (EGY) v C. Grandet (FRA)
1951	C		J.E. Patty (USA) v D.A. Lurie (RSA)
1952	C		R. Savitt (USA) v N. Kumar (IND)
1953	R	(3)	J. Drobny (EGY) v B. Destremau (FRA)
1954	C		E.V. Seixas (USA) v G.A. Cass (GBR)
1955	C		J. Drobny (EGY) v R. Buser (SUI)
1956	R	(3)	K. Nielsen (DEN) v R. Mark (AUS)
1957	C		L.A. Hoad (AUS) v P. Darmon (FRA)
1958	R	(3)	A.J. Cooper (AUS) v G.D. Owen (GBR)
1959	R	(3)	N.A Fraser (AUS) v P. Darmon (FRA)
1960	R	(3)	R.G. Laver (AUS) v G.L. Ward (GBR)
1961	R	(4)	R.G. Laver (AUS) v T. Lejus (URS)
1962	C		R.G. Laver (AUS) v N. Kumar (IND)
1963	R	(3)	M.F. Mulligan (AUS) v M. Belkhodja (TUN)
1964	C		C.R. McKinley (USA) v T.J. Ryan (USA)
1965	C		R.S. Emerson (AUS) v I. Pimentel (VEN)
1966	C		R.S. Emerson (AUS) v H. Fauquier (CAN)
1967	C		M.M. Santana (ESP) v C.M. Pasarell (USA)
1968	C		J.D. Newcombe (AUS) v O.K. Davidson (AUS)
1969	C	(5)	R.G. Laver (AUS) v N. Pietrangeli (ITA)
1970	C		R.G. Laver (AUS) v G.L. Seewagen (USA)
1971	C		J.D. Newcombe (AUS) v R.A.J. Hewitt (RSA)
1972	R	(3)	S.R. Smith (USA) v H.J. Plotz (GER)

Year	Champion or Runner up	Note	Opening Matches
1973	R	(3)	I. Nastase (ROM) v H.J. Plotz (GER)
1974	C		J. Kodes (TCH) v S.E. Stewart (USA)
1975	C		J.S. Connors (USA) v J.M. Lloyd (GBR)
1976	C		A.R. Ashe (USA) v F. Taygan (USA)
1977	C		B.R. Borg (SWE) v A. Zugarelli (ITA)
1978	C		B.R. Borg (SWE) v V.C. Amaya (USA)
1979	C		B.R. Borg (SWE) v T.W. Gorman (USA)
1980	C		B.R. Borg (SWE) v I. El Shafei (EGY)
1981	C		B.R. Borg (SWE) v P. Rennert (USA)
1982	C		J.P. McEnroe (USA) v V.A.W. Winitsky (USA)
1983	C		J.S. Connors (USA) v E. Edwards (USA)
1984	C		J.P. McEnroe (USA) v P.F. McNamee (AUS)
1985	C		J.P. McEnroe (USA) v P.B. McNamara (AUS)
1986	C		B.F. Becker (GER) v E. Bengoechea (ARG)
1987	C	(5)	B.F. Becker (GER) v K. Novacek (TCH)
1988	C		P.H. Cash (AUS) v T.A. Woodbridge (AUS)
1989	C		S.B. Edberg (SWE) v C. Pridham (CAN)
1990	C		B.F. Becker (GER) v L.E. Herrera (MEX)
1991	C	(6)	S.B. Edberg (SWE) v M. Rosset (SUI)
1992	C		M.D. Stich (GER) v S. Pescosolido (ITA)
1993	C		A.K. Agassi (USA) v B. Karbacher (GER)
1994	C		P. Sampras (USA) v J.E. Palmer (USA)
1995	C		P. Sampras (USA) v K. Braasch (GER)
1996	C		P. Sampras (USA) v R.A. Reneberg (USA)
1997	C		R.P.S. Krajicek (NED) v M. Craca (GER)
1998	C		P. Sampras (USA) v D. Hrbaty (SVK)
1999	C		P. Sampras (USA) v S. Draper (AUS)
2000	C		P. Sampras (USA) v J. Vanek (CZE)
2001	C		P. Sampras (USA) v F.J. Clavet (ESP)
2002	–	(2)	H. Levy (ISR) v A.K. Agassi (USA)
2003	C		L.G. Hewitt (AUS) v I. Karlovic (CRO)
2004	C		R. Federer (SUI) v A. Bogdanovic (GBR)
2005	C		R. Federer (SUI) v P.H. Mathieu (FRA)
2006	C		R. Federer (SUI) v R. Gasquet (FRA)
2007	C		R. Federer (SUI) v T. Gabashvili (RUS)
2008	C		R. Federer (SUI) v D. Hrbaty (SVK)
2009	R	(3)	R. Federer (SUI) v Y-H Lu (TPE)
2010	C		R. Federer (SUI) v A. Falla (COL)
2011	C		R. Nadal (ESP) v M. Russell (USA)
2012	C		N. Djokovic (SRB) v J.C. Ferrero (ESP)
2013	C		R. Federer (SUI) v V. Hanescu (ROU)
2014	C		A.B. Murray (GBR) v D. Goffin (BEL)

C – Champion from previous year. R – Runner-up from previous year.

Notes:
(1) Champion did not compete. Runner-up competed, but did not open programme.
(2) Champion and Runner-up did not compete.
(3) Champion did not compete.
(4) The Champion, N.A. Fraser, played on No. 1 Court and the Runner-up opened the programme on Centre Court.
(5) Match played on Tuesday as rain washed out play on Monday.
(6) Match played on Tuesday as rain washed out play on Monday. The Champion played the second match on court following the opening ladies' match.

Ladies' Singles Championship

Year	Champion or Runner up	Note	Opening Matches
1946	–	(1)	Mrs. R.B. Todd (USA) v Miss V.S. Dace (GBR)
1947	–	(1)	Mrs. E.W.A. Bostock (GBR) v Miss S. Kormoczy (HUN)
1948	R	(2)(3)	Miss D.J. Hart (USA) v Miss J.I. Gannon (GBR)
1949	C	(3)	Miss A.L. Brough (USA) v Miss E.A. Middleton (GBR)
1950	–	(3)(4)	Miss D.J. Hart (USA) v Miss K.L.A. Tuckey (GBR)
1951	C		Miss A.L. Brough (USA) v Mrs. R.L. Scott (GBR)
1952	C		Miss D.J. Hart (USA) v Miss S.I. Odling (GBR)
1953	C		Miss M.C. Connolly (USA) v Miss D. Kilian (RSA)
1954	C		Miss M.C. Connolly (USA) v Miss J. Scott (RSA)
1955	–	(1)	Miss D.J. Hart (USA) v Mrs. H.C. Hopman (AUS)
1956	C		Miss A.L. Brough (USA) v Miss J.R. Forbes (RSA)
1957	–	(5)	Miss S.J. Bloomer (GBR) v Miss P.E. Ward (GBR)
1958	C		Miss A. Gibson (USA) v Miss M.B. Hellyer (AUS)
1959	R	(6)	Miss F.A.M. Mortimer (GBR) v Mrs. M.T. Weiss (ESP)
1960	C		Miss M.E.A. Bueno (BRA) v Miss C. Mercelis (BEL)
1961	–	(1)(3)	Miss C.C. Truman (GBR) v Miss M.B. Hellyer (AUS)
1962	C		Miss F.A.M. Mortimer (GBR) v Miss M. Grace (GBR)
1963	R	(3)(6)	Mrs C. Sukova (TCH) v Miss J.T. Albert (USA)
1964	C		Miss M. Smith (AUS) v Miss A.M. van Zyl (RSA)
1965	C		Miss M.E.A. Bueno (BRA) v Miss W.M. Shaw (GBR)
1966	C		Miss M. Smith (AUS) v Miss D.E. Starkie (GBR)
1967	C		Mrs. L.W. King (USA) v Miss I.A.R.F. Lofdahl (SWE)
1968	C		Mrs. L.W. King (USA) v Miss J.M. Bartkowicz (USA)
1969	C	(7)	Mrs. L.W. King (USA) v Mrs. V. Vukovich (RSA)
1970	–	(1)(8)	Miss W.M. Shaw (GBR) v Miss K. Harris (AUS)
1971	C		Mrs. B.M. Court (AUS) v Mrs. J.D.G. Robinson (AUS)
1972	C		Miss E.F. Goolagong (AUS) v Miss M.J. Pryde (NZL)
1973	C		Mrs. L.W. King (USA) v Miss L. Bassi (ITA)
1974	C		Mrs. L.W. King (USA) v Miss K.A. May (USA)
1975	C	(3)	Miss C.M. Evert (USA) v Miss C.M. O'Neil (AUS)
1976	R	(6)	Mrs. R.A. Cawley (AUS) v Mrs. E. Vessies-Appel (NED)
1977	C		Miss C.M. Evert (USA) v Miss R. Gerulaitis (USA)
1978	C		Miss S.V. Wade (GBR) v Miss E. Ekblom (SWE)
1979	C		Miss M. Navratilova (USA) v Miss T.J. Harford (RSA)
1980	C		Miss M. Navratilova (USA) v Miss I.S. Kloss (RSA)
1981	R	(6)	Mrs. J.M. Lloyd (USA) v Miss C.M. O'Neil (AUS)
1982	C		Mrs. J.M. Lloyd (USA) v Miss B.S. Gerken (USA)
1983	C		Miss M. Navratilova (USA) v Miss B.A. Mould (RSA)
1984	C		Miss M. Navratilova (USA) v Miss M. Louie (USA)
1985	C		Miss M. Navratilova (USA) v Miss L. Bonder (USA)
1986	C		Miss M. Navratilova (USA) v Mrs. G.R. Dingwall (AUS)
1987	C	(7)	Miss M. Navratilova (USA) v Miss C. Porwik (GER)
1988	C		Miss M. Navratilova (USA) v Miss S. Goles (YUG)
1989	C		Miss S.M. Graf (GER) v Miss J.A. Salmon (GBR)
1990	C		Miss S.M. Graf (GER) v Miss C. Porwik (GER)
1991	C		Miss M. Navratilova (USA) v Miss E. Reinach (RSA)
1992	C		Miss S.M. Graf (GER) v Miss N. van Lottum (FRA)
1993	C		Miss S.M. Graf (GER) v Miss K. Sharpe (AUS)
1994	C		Miss S.M. Graf (GER) v Miss L.M. McNeil (USA)
1995	C		Miss I.C. Martinez (ESP) v Miss A. Carlsson (SWE)

Year	Champion or Runner up	Note	Opening Matches
1996	C		Miss S.M. Graf (GER) v Miss L. Richterova (CZE)
1997	R	(6)	Miss A.I.M. Sanchez Vicario (ESP) v Miss C.J. Wood (GBR)
1998	C		Miss M. Hingis (SUI) v Miss L.M. Raymond (USA)
1999	C		Miss J. Novotna (CZE) v Miss S-T. Wang (TPE)
2000	C		Miss L.A. Davenport (USA) v Miss C.M. Morariu (Mrs. A. Turcinovich)
2001	C		Miss V.E.S. Williams (USA) v Miss S. Asagoe (JPN)
2002	C		Miss V.E.S. Williams (USA) v Miss J. O'Donoghue (GBR)
2003	C		Miss S.J. Williams (USA) v Miss J. Craybas (USA)
2004	C		Miss S.J. Williams (USA) v Miss J. Zheng (CHN)
2005	C		Miss M. Sharapova (RUS) v Miss N. Llagostera Vives (ESP)
2006	C	(9)	Miss V.E.S. Williams (USA) v Miss B. Mattek (USA)
2007	C	(9)	Miss A. Mauresmo (FRA) v Miss J. Jackson (USA)
2008	C		Miss V.E.S. Williams (USA) v Miss N. Cavaday (GBR)
2009	C		Miss V.E.S. Williams (USA) v Miss S. Voegele (SUI)
2010	C		Miss S.J. Williams (USA) v Miss M. Larcher De Brito (POR)
2011	C		Miss S.J. Williams (USA) v Miss A. Rezai (FRA)
2012	C		Miss P. Kvitova (CZE) v Miss A. Pavlyuchenkova (RUS)
2013	C		Miss S.J. Williams (USA) v Miss M. Minella (LUX)
2014	R		Miss S. Lisicki (GER) v Miss J. Glushko (ISR)

C – Champion from previous year. R – Runner-up from previous year.

Notes:
(1) Champion did not compete. Runner-up competed, but did not open the programme.
(2) Champion competed, but did not open the programme.
(3) Second match on court.
(4) Champion and Runner-up competed, but did not open the programme.
(5) Champion and Runner-up did not compete.
(6) Champion did not compete.
(7) Match played on Wednesday as play was washed out on Monday.
(8) Third match on court.
(9) Match played on Wednesday as rain restricted play on the Monday to 45minutes.

Singles Champions not defending title

Gentlemen's Singles Championship

Year	Champion	Reason
1879	P.F. Hadow	Did not travel from Ceylon
1887	W.C. Renshaw	Injured – tennis elbow
1891	W.J. Hamilton	Illness – blood poisoning
1895	J. Pim	Retired from game
1907	H.L. Doherty	Semi-retired
1908	N.E. Brookes	Did not travel from Australia
1922	W.T. Tilden	Did not travel from USA
1923	G.L. Patterson	Did not travel from Australia
1924	W.M. Johnston	Did not travel from USA
1926	J.R. Lacoste	Illness – chest ailment
1929	J.R. Lacoste	Pressure of business
1931	W.T. Tilden	Turned professional
1937	F.J. Perry	Turned professional
1939	J.D. Budge	Turned professional
1946	R.L. Riggs	Turned professional
1948	J.A. Kramer	Turned professional
1950	F.R. Schroeder	Restricted play due to business commitments
1953	F.A. Sedgman	Turned professional
1956	M.A. Trabert	Turned professional
1958	L.A. Hoad	Turned professional
1959	A.J. Cooper	Turned professional
1960	A.R. Olmedo	Turned professional
1963	R.G. Laver	Turned professional
1972	J.D. Newcombe	ITF ban on WCT professionals
1973	S.R. Smith	ATP boycott
2002	G.S. Ivanisevic	Recovering from operation on left shoulder
2009	R. Nadal	Injured – tendinitis of the knees.

Ladies' Singles Championship

Year	Champion	Reason
1889	Miss C. Dod	Bored with Tennis
1890	Mrs. G.W. Hillyard	Expecting first child
1891	Miss H.G.B. Rice	Retired from game
1894	Miss C. Dod	Retired from game
1895	Mrs. G.W. Hillyard	Expecting second child
1898	Mrs. G.W. Hillyard	Below form
1903	Miss M.E. Robb	Retired from game
1908	Miss M.G. Sutton	Did not travel from USA
1909	Mrs. A. Sterry	Illness
1912	Mrs. R.L. Chambers	Not match fit following birth of second child
1913	Mrs. D.T.R. Larcombe	Injured – struck by ball the day before Challenge Round.
1931	Mrs. F.S. Moody	Resting from overseas tours
1932	Miss C. Aussem	Illness – appendicitis operation

Year	Champion	Reason
1934	Mrs. F.S. Moody	Unfit following long illness
1936	Mrs. F.S. Moody	Resting from overseas tour
1938	Miss D.E. Round	Semi-retired after marriage
1939	Mrs. F.S. Moody	Retired from game
1946	Miss A. Marble	Turned professional
1947	Miss P.M. Betz	Turned professional
1955	Miss M.C. Connolly	Injured – broken leg
1957	Miss S.J. Fry	Retired from game following marriage
1959	Miss A. Gibson	Turned professional
1961	Miss M.E.A. Bueno	Illness- jaundice
1963	Mrs. J.R. Susman	Expecting first child
1970	Mrs. P.F. Jones	Retired from game
1976	Mrs. L.W.King	Retired from singles play
1981	Mrs. R.A. Cawley	Rested following birth of second child
1997	Miss S.M. Graf	Injured – knee
2014	Miss. M.S. Bartoli	Retired from game

Left-Handed Champions, Runners-Up and Semi-finalists

Gentlemen
Champions

N.E. Brookes	(AUS)	S 1907, 1914, D 1907, 1914
J.B. Gilbert	(GBR)	M 1924
J. Drobny	(EGY)	S 1954
M.G. Rose	(AUS)	D 1954, M 1957
N.A. Fraser	(AUS)	S 1960, D 1959, 1961, M 1962
R.G. Laver	(AUS)	S 1961, 1962, 1968, 1969
		D 1971, M 1959,1960
A.D. Roche	(AUS)	D 1965, 1968–1970, 1974,
		M 1976
O.K. Davidson	(AUS)	M 1967, 1971, 1973, 1974

J.S. Connors	(USA)	S 1974, 1982, D 1973
J.P. McEnroe	(USA)	S 1981, 1983, 1984
		D 1979, 1981, 1983,
		1984, 1992
R.D. Leach	(USA)	D 1990, M 1990
M.R. Woodforde	(AUS)	D 1993–1997, 2000,
		M 1993
D.J. Johnson	(USA)	D 2001, M 2000
G. Ivanisevic	(CRO)	S 2001
R.C. Bryan	(USA)	D 2006, 2011, M 2008
M. Llodra	(FRA)	D 2007
R. Nadal	(ESP)	S 2008, 2010
D.M. Nestor	(CAN)	D 2008, 2009, M 2013
J. Melzer	(AUT)	D 2010

Runners-up

D.F. Davis	(USA)	D 1901
B.C. Wright	(USA)	D 1907
R.J. Casey	(USA)	D 1925
J.B. Hawkes	(AUS)	D 1928
J.T.G.H. Doeg	(USA)	D 1930
C.E. Hare	(GBR)	D 1936, 1939
G.R. von Metaxa	(GER)	D 1938
N. Pilic	(YUG)	D 1962
M.J. Farrell	(GBR)	M 1974
R.O. Ruffels	(AUS)	M 1978

L.R. Tanner	(USA)	S 1979
T.R. Gullikson	(USA)	D 1983
M. Kratzmann	(AUS)	M 1989
D.T. Visser	(RSA)	D 1990
J.A. Frana	(ARG)	D 1991
L. Lavalle	(MEX)	D 1991
G.D. Connell	(CAN)	D 1993, 1994, 1996
P.J. Galbraith	(USA)	D 1993, 1994
D. Rikl	(CZE)	D 2001
J. Knowle	(AUT)	D 2004

Semi-finalists

J. Washer	(BEL)	M 1923
L.B. Raymond	(RSA)	S 1924, D 1924, 1927, M 1927
C. Boussus	(FRA)	S 1928, D 1932
V.G. Kirby	(RSA)	D 1933
F. Kukuljevic	(YUG)	D 1938
J. Pallada	(YUG)	D 1938, 1946
A.D. Larsen	(USA)	D 1956
T.T. Fancutt	(RSA)	M 1956
W.A. Knight	(GBR)	M 1958, 1959
T. Ulrich	(DEN)	D 1959
A.A. Segal	(RSA)	D 1963
I.S. Crookenden	(NZL)	D 1964
M. Cox	(GBR)	D 1966, 1977
R. Taylor	(GBR)	S 1967, 1970, 1973

T. Koch	(BRA)	D 1971
M. Orantes	(ESP)	D 1972
J.G. Paish	(GBR)	D 1973
T.M. Wilkison	(USA)	D 1979
H. Leconte	(FRA)	S 1986
A. Gomez	(ECU)	D 1987
A.S. Kohlberg	(USA)	M 1987
G.R. Muller	(RSA)	D 1988, 1993
G. Forget	(FRA)	D 1992
E.R. Ferreira	(RSA)	D 1996
J.M. Siemerink	(NED)	D 1996
W.S. Arthurs	(AUS)	D 2004
D. Norman	(BEL)	D 2009

Ladies
Champions

Mrs. L.A. Harper	(USA)	M 1931
Miss K.E. Stammers	(GBR)	D 1935, 1936
Mrs. P.F. Jones	(GBR)	S 1969, M 1969

Miss M. Navratilova	(USA)	S 1978, 1979,
		1982–1987, 1990, D
		1976, 1979, 1981–1984,
		1986, M 1985, 1993,
		1995, 2003.
Miss P. Kvitova	(CZE)	S2011, 2014
Miss I. Benesova	(CZE)	M2011

Runners-up

Mrs J.G. Fleitz*	(USA)	S1955, D1959
Miss D.G. Seeney	(AUS)	D 1956
Miss D.L. Fromholtz	(AUS)	M 1980
Miss M. Seles	(YUG)	S 1992

Miss N.J. Arendt	(USA)	D 1997
Miss E.V. Tatarkova	(UKR)	D 1999
Miss C. Dellacqua	(AUS)	D 2013

*Ambidextrous

Semi-finalists

Miss M.C. Scriven	(GBR)	D	1934
Miss H.M. Fletcher	(GBR)	D	1953
Mrs. W. Brewer	(BER)	D	1954
Mrs. L.A. Hoad	(AUS)	D	1955
Miss J.C. Bricka	(USA)	D	1962, M 1964
Miss A.V. Dmitrieva	(URS)	D	1963
Miss G.J. Groenman	(NED)	M	1964

Miss I.S. Kloss	(RSA)	D	1976
Miss B.C. Potter	(USA)	D	1983, 1984
Miss E.S. Burgin	(USA)	D	1986
Miss S. Applemans	(BEL)	D	1997
Miss I. Benesova	(CZE)	M	2010
Miss A. Kerber	(GER)	D	2012
Miss L. Safarova	(CZE)	S	2014

Double-Handed Champions, Runners-Up and Semi-finalists

Gentlemen

Champions

			Note
J.E. Bromwich	(AUS)	D 1948, 1950, M 1947, 1948	4
R.N. Howe	(AUS)	M 1958	1
F.D. McMillan	(RSA)	D 1967, 1972, 1978, M 1978, 1981	5
J.S. Connors	(USA)	S 1974, 1982, D 1973	2
B.R. Borg	(SWE)	S 1976–1980	1
P.F. McNamee	(AUS)	D 1980, 1982, M 1985	1
K.J. Nystrom	(SWE)	D 1986	1
M.A.O. Wilander	(SWE)	D 1986	1
K.E. Flach	(USA)	D 1987, 1988, M 1986	1
A.P. Jarryd	(SWE)	D 1989, 1991	1
J.R. Pugh	(USA)	D 1990, M 1989	5
R.D. Leach	(USA)	D 1990, M 1990	2
A.K. Agassi	(USA)	S 1992	1
M.R. Woodforde	(AUS)	D 1993–1997, 2000, M 1993	1
J.A. Stark	(USA)	M 1995	1
P.V.N. Haarhuis	(NED)	D 1998	1
M.S. Bhupathi	(IND)	D 1999, M2002, 2005	1
G.S. Ivanisevic	(CRO)	S 2001	2
L.G. Hewitt	(AUS)	S 2002	1
J.L. Bjorkman	(SWE)	D 2002, 2003, 2004	1
W.H. Black	(ZIM)	M 2004	1
A. Clement	(FRA)	D 2007	1
R. Nadal	(ESP)	S 2008, 2010	2
D.M. Nestor	(CAN)	D 2008, 2009, M 2013	2
J. Melzer	(AUT)	D 2010	1
P. Petzschner	(GER)	D 2010	1
N. Djokovic	(SRB)	S 2011, 2014	1
F.L. Nielsen	(DEN)	D 2012	1
A.B Murray	(GBR)	S 2013	1
V. Pospisil	(CAN)	D 2014	1
J.E. Sock	(USA)	D 2014	1

Runners-up

G.E. Brown	(AUS)	S 1946, D 1946, 1950, M 1946, 1950	4
J.C. Barclay	(FRA)	D 1963	1
R.A. Reneberg	(USA)	D 1992	1
J.S. Courier	(USA)	S 1993	1
D.S. Melville	(USA)	D 1995	1
M.O. Washington	(USA)	S 1996	1
B.H. Black	(ZIM)	D 1996	5

D. Rikl	(CZE)	D 2001	2
D.P. Nalbandian	(ARG)	S 2002	1
A.S. Roddick	(USA)	S 2004, 2005, 2009	1
J. Knowle	(AUT)	D 2004	6
F.V. Santoro	(FRA)	D 2006	5
T. Berdych	(CZE)	S 2010	1
H.V. Tecau	(ROM)	D 2010, 2011, 2012	1
R. Lindstedt	(SWE)	D 2010, 2011, 2012	1
I. Dodig	(CRO)	D 2013	1
M.P.D. Melo	(BRA)	D 2013	1

Semi-finalists

F. Segura-Cano	(ECU)	D 1946	3
E.C. Drysdale	(RSA)	S 1965, D 1974, 1977	1
H-J. Pohmann	(GER)	D 1975	1
E. Mayer	(USA)	D 1980	5
M. Mecir	(TCH)	S 1988	3
Y.A. Kafelnikov	(RUS)	D 1994, 1995	1
D. Wheaton	(USA)	S 1991	1
W.R. Ferreira	(RSA)	D 1991, 1994	1
T.C. Martin	(USA)	S 1994, 1996	1
L.J.N. Kulti	(SWE)	D 2000	1
M. Tillstrom	(SWE)	D 2000	1
N.A. Lapentti	(ECU)	M 2000	1
V. Voltchkov	(BLR)	S 2000, D 2001	1
X. Malisse	(BEL)	S 2002	1
S.R. Grosjean	(FRA)	S 2003, 2004	1
J.S.H. Kerr	(AUS)	M 2003	1
M. Ancic	(CRO)	S 2004	1
T. Johansson	(SWE)	S 2005	1
M. Baghdatis	(CYP)	S 2006	1
A.R. Sa	(BRA)	D 2007	1
I. Andreev	(RUS)	M 2008	1
M. Safin	(RUS)	S 2008	1
L Dlouhy	(CZE)	D 2008, M 2010	1
R. Schuettler	(GER)	S 2008	1
M. Fish	(USA)	D 2009	1
D. Norman	(BEL)	D 2009, 2010	
J.I. Chela	(ARG)	D 2010	1
E.J. Schwank	(ARG)	D 2010	1
C. Kas	(GER)	D 2011	1
J-W. Tsonga	(FRA)	S 2011, 2012	1
J. Janowicz	(POL)	S 2013	1
J.M. Del Potro	(ARG)	S 2013	1
E.D. Roger-Vasselin	(FRA)	D 2013	1
R. Stepanek	(CZE)	D 2013, 2014	1
J-J Rojer	(NED)	M 2013	1
M. Raonic	(CAN)	S 2014	1
G. Dimitrov	(BUL)	S 2014	1

Ladies
Champions

Miss C.M. Evert/			
Mrs. J.M. Lloyd	(USA)	S 1974, 1976, 1981, D 1976	1
Miss T.A. Austin	(USA)	M 1980	1
Miss N.M. Zvereva	(URS/CIS/	D 1991–1994,1997	1
	BLR)		

Miss A.I.M. Sanchez Vicario	(ESP)	D 1995	1
Miss M. Hingis	(SUI)	S 1997, D 1996, 1998	1
Miss S.J. Williams	(USA)	S 2002, 2003, 2009, 2010, 2012, D 2000,	1
		2002, 2008, 2009, 2012, M 1998	
Miss L.A. Davenport	(USA)	S 1999, D 1999	1
Miss V.E.S. Williams	(USA)	S 2000, 2001, 2005, 2007, 2008	1
		D 2000, 2002, 2008, 2009, 2012	
Miss K.Y. Po	(USA)	M 2000	1
Miss D. Hantuchova	(SVK)	M 2001	1
Miss E. Likhovtseva (Mrs M. Baranov)	(RUS)	M 2002	1
Miss K. Clijsters	(BEL)	D 2003	1
Miss A. Sugiyama	(JPN)	D 2003	1
Miss C.C. Black	(ZIM)	D 2004, 2005, 2007, M 2004, 2010	1
Miss M. Sharapova	(RUS)	S 2004	1
Mrs A. Huber	(RSA, USA)	D 2005, 2007	1
Miss M.C. Pierce	(FRA)	M 2005	1
Miss Z. Yan	(CHN)	D 2006	5
Miss J.Zheng	(CHN)	D 2006	1
Miss V. Zvonareva	(RUS)	M 2006	1
Miss J. Jankovic	(SRB)	M 2007	1
Miss S.J. Stosur	(AUS)	M 2008, 2014	1
Miss A-L Groenefeld	(GER)	M 2009	1
Miss V. King	(USA)	D 2010	1
Miss Y.V. Shvedova	(KAZ)	D 2010	1
Miss P. Kvitova	(CZE)	S 2011, 2014	2
Miss K. Srebotnik	(SLO)	D 2011	1
Miss I Benesova	(CZE)	M 2011	2
Mrs T. Peschke	(CZE)	D 2011	1
Miss K. Mladenovic	(FRA)	M 2013	1
Miss S-W Hsieh	(TPE)	D 2013	5
Miss S. Peng	(CHN)	D 2013	5
Miss M.S. Bartoli	(FRA)	S 2013	5

Runners-up

Miss J.P. Lehane	(AUS)	D 1961	1
Miss A. Jaeger	(USA)	S 1983	1
Miss N.A-L. Provis	(AUS)	M 1987	1
Miss M. Seles	(YUG)	S 1992	6
Miss M.J. McGrath	(USA)	D 1996	1
Miss M.M. Bollegraf	(NED)	D 1997, M 1993	1
Miss M. Lucic	(CRO)	M 1998	1
Miss E.V. Tatarkova	(UKR)	D 1999	2
Miss A.S. Kournikova	(RUS)	M 1999	1
Mrs. A. Decugis	(FRA)	D 2000	1
Miss P.L. Suarez	(ARG)	D 2002, 2003, 2006	1
Miss A. Rodionova	(RUS)	M 2003	1
Miss S. Kuznetsova	(RUS)	D 2005	1
Miss T. Perebiynis	(UKR)	D 2005	1
Miss E.S. Vesnina	(RUS)	D 2010, M 2011, 2012	1
Miss S. Lisicki	(GER)	S 2013, D 2011	1
Miss A. Radwanska	(POL)	S 2012	1
Miss L. Hradecka	(CZE)	D 2012	5
Miss A. Barty	(AUS)	D 2013	1
Miss C. Dellacqua	(AUS)	D 2013	2
Miss E.C.M.. Bouchard	(CAN)	S 2014	1
Miss T. Babos	(HUN)	D 2014	1

Semi-finalists

Miss A. Temesvari	(HUN)	M 1983	1

Miss K.S. Rinaldi	(USA)	S 1985, M 1991	1
Miss E.S. Burgin	(USA)	D 1986	2
Miss J.M. Hetherington	(CAN)	D 1986	1
Mrs. A. Parkhomenko	(URS)	D 1987	1
Miss K.M. Adams	(USA)	D 1988	1
Miss E. Reinach	(RSA)	D 1989, M 1986, 1991	1
Miss J.M. Capriati	(USA)	S 1991, 2001	1
Miss M.J. Fernandez	(USA)	S 1991, D 1991, 1993	1
Miss K. Date	(JPN)	S 1996	1
Miss L. Golarsa	(ITA)	M 1996	1
Miss S. Applemans	(BEL)	D 1997	2
Miss D.A. Graham	(USA)	D 1998	1
Miss J. Dokic	(AUS)	S 2000	1
Miss A. Huber	(GER)	M 2000	1
Miss B. Schett	(AUT)	M 2000	1
Miss K. Habsudova	(SVK)	M 2001	1
Miss C.R. Rubin	(USA)	D 2002	1
Miss E.S.H. Callens	(BEL)	M 2002	1
Miss E. Dementieva	(RUS)	S 2008, 2009, D 2003	1
Miss L. Krasnoroutskaya	(RUS)	D 2003	1
Miss M. Sequera	(VEN)	M 2003	1
Miss B. M. Stewart	(AUS)	D 2005	1
Miss Y. Fedak	(UKR)	D 2006	1
Miss A. Ivanovic	(SRB)	S 2007	1
Miss M. Santangelo	(ITA)	D 2007	1
Miss N. Dechy	(FRA)	D 2008	1
Miss M. Kirilenko	(RUS)	M 2008	1
Miss M. Safina	(RUS)	S 2009	1
Miss A.I Medina Garrigues	(ESP)	D 2009, M 2009	1
Miss T. Pironkova	(BUL)	S 2010	1
Miss G.A. Dulko	(ARG)	D 2010	1
Miss F. Pennetta	(ITA)	D 2010, 2012	1
Mrs B.L. Sands	(USA)	D 2010	1
Miss M. Erakovic	(NZL)	D 2011	1
Miss T. Tanasugarn	(THA)	D 2011	1
Miss Y-J. Chan	(TPE)	M 2011	1
Miss A. Kerber	(GER)	S 2012	2
Miss V. Azarenka	(RUS)	S 2012	1
Miss K. Flipkens	(BEL)	S 2013	1
Miss S. Aoyama	(JPN)	D 2013	5
Miss C. Scheepers	(RSA)	D 2013	1
Miss V. Dushevina	(RUS)	M 2013, 2014	1
Miss S. Halep	(ROM)	S 2014	1
Miss L. Safarova	(CZE)	S 2014	2
Miss A. Petkovic	(CZE)	D 2014	1
Miss A. Hlavackova	(CZE)	D 2014	1
Miss M. Rybarikova	(SVK)	D 2014	1
Miss J. Zheng	(CHN)	D 2014	1
Miss H-C Chan	(TPE)	M 2014	1

Note

1. Right-handed – Double-handed backhand
2. Left-handed – Double-handed backhand
3. Right-handed – Double-handed forehand, right-handed backhand
4. Right-handed – Double-handed forehand, left-handed backhand
5. Right-handed – Double-handed forehand and double-handed backhand
6. Left-handed – Double-handed forehand and double-handed backhand

Rackets used by the Singles Champions, Doubles Champions and Runners-Up

Gentlemen's Singles Championship

Year	Champion	Manufacturer of racket	Runner-Up	Manufacturer of racket
1877	S.W. Gore	Ayres	W.C. Marshall	
1878	P.F. Hadow		S.W. Gore	Ayres
1879	J.T. Hartley		V.T. St. Leger Goold	
1880	J.T. Hartley		H.F. Lawford	Tate
1881	W.C. Renshaw	Tate	J.T. Hartley	
1882	W.C. Renshaw	Tate	J.E. Renshaw	Tate
1883	W.C. Renshaw	Tate	J.E. Renshaw	Tate
1884	W.C. Renshaw	Tate	H.F. Lawford	Tate
1885	W.C. Renshaw	Tate	H.F. Lawford	Tate
1886	W.C. Renshaw	Tate	H.F. Lawford	Tate
1887	H.F. Lawford	Tate	J.E. Renshaw	Tate
1888	J.E. Renshaw	Tate	H.F. Lawford	Tate
1889	W.C. Renshaw	Tate	J.E. Renshaw	Tate
1890	W.J. Hamilton	Slazenger	W.C. Renshaw	Tate
1891	W. Baddeley		J. Pim	Slazenger
1892	W. Baddeley		J. Pim	Slazenger
1893	J. Pim	Slazenger	W. Baddeley	
1894	J. Pim	Slazenger	W. Baddeley	
1895	W. Baddeley		W.V. Eaves	Slazenger
1896	H.S. Mahony	Slazenger	W. Baddeley	
1897	R.F. Doherty	Slazenger	H.S. Mahony	Slazenger
1898	R.F. Doherty	Slazenger	H.L. Doherty	Slazenger
1899	R.F. Doherty	Slazenger	A.W. Gore	Slazenger
1900	R.F. Doherty	Slazenger	S.H. Smith	
1901	A.W. Gore	Slazenger	R.F. Doherty	Slazenger
1902	H.L. Doherty	Slazenger	A.W. Gore	Slazenger
1903	H.L. Doherty	Slazenger	F.L. Riseley	Slazenger
1904	H.L. Doherty	Slazenger	F.L. Riseley	Slazenger
1905	H.L. Doherty	Slazenger	N.E. Brookes	
1906	H.L. Doherty	Slazenger	F.L. Riseley	Slazenger
1907	N.E. Brookes	Ayres	A.W. Gore	Slazenger
1908	A.W. Gore	Slazenger	H.R. Barrett	Slazenger
1909	A.W. Gore	Slazenger	M.J.G. Ritchie	Williams
1910	A.F. Wilding	Ayres	A.W. Gore	Slazenger
1911	A.F. Wilding	Ayres	H.R. Barrett	Slazenger
1912	A.F. Wilding	Ayres	A.W. Gore	Slazenger
1913	A.F. Wilding	Ayres	M.E. McLoughlin	Wright & Ditson
1914	N.E. Brookes	Ayres	A.F. Wilding	Ayres
1919	G.L. Patterson	Slazenger	N.E. Brookes	

Year	Champion	Manufacturer of racket	Runner-Up	Manufacturer of racket
1920	W.T. Tilden	Bancroft	G.L. Patterson	Slazenger
1921	W.T. Tilden	Bancroft	B.I.C. Norton	Slazenger
1922	G.L. Patterson	Bancroft	R. Lycett	
1923	W.M. Johnston	Mass	F.T. Hunter	
1924	J.R. Borotra	Williams	J.R. Lacoste	Darsonval
1925	J.R. Lacoste	Darsonval	J.R. Borotra	Williams
1926	J.R. Borotra	Williams	H.O. Kinsey	
1927	H.J. Cochet	Cochet Sport	J.R. Borotra	Williams
1928	J.R. Lacoste	Darsonval	H.J. Cochet	Cochet Sport
1929	H.J. Cochet	Cochet Sport	J.R. Borotra	Williams
1930	W.T. Tilden	Spalding	W.L. Allison	Spalding
1931	S.B.B. Wood	Spalding	F.X. Shields	Spalding
1932	H.E. Vines	Bancroft	H.W. Austin	Slazenger
1933	J.H. Crawford	Alexander	H.E. Vines	Spalding
1934	F.J. Perry	Slazenger	J.H. Crawford	Alexander
1935	F.J. Perry	Slazenger	G. von Cramm	Dunlop
1936	F.J. Perry	Slazenger	G. von Cramm	Dunlop
1937	J.D. Budge	Wilson	G. von Cramm	Dunlop
1938	J.D. Budge	Wilson	H.W. Austin	Hazell
1939	R.L. Riggs	Wilson	E.T. Cooke	Wilson
1946	Y.F.M. Petra	Bocla	G.E. Brown	Slazenger
1947	J.A. Kramer	Wilson	T.P. Brown	Wilson
1948	R. Falkenburg	Wilson	J.E. Bromwich	Slazenger
1949	F.R. Schroeder	Wilson	J. Drobny	Dunlop
1950	J.E. Patty	Wilson	F.A. Sedgman	Oliver
1951	R. Savitt	Spalding	K.B. McGregor	Slazenger
1952	F.A. Sedgman	Oliver	J. Drobny	Dunlop
1953	E.V. Seixas	Wilson	K. Nielsen	Slazenger
1954	J. Drobny	Dunlop	K.R. Rosewall	Slazenger
1955	M.A. Trabert	Wilson	K. Nielsen	Slazenger
1956	L.A. Hoad	Dunlop	K.R. Rosewall	Slazenger
1957	L.A. Hoad	Dunlop	A.J. Cooper	Spalding
1958	A.J. Cooper	Spalding	N.A. Fraser	Slazenger
1959	A.R. Olmedo	Wilson	R.G. Laver	Dunlop
1960	N.A. Fraser	Slazenger	R.G. Laver	Dunlop
1961	R.G. Laver	Dunlop	C.R. McKinley	Wilson
1962	R.G. Laver	Dunlop	M.F. Mulligan	Dunlop
1963	C.R. McKinley	Wilson	F.S. Stolle	Dunlop
1964	R.S. Emerson	Slazenger	F.S. Stolle	Dunlop
1965	R.S. Emerson	Slazenger	F.S. Stolle	Dunlop
1966	M.M. Santana	Slazenger	R.D. Ralston	Spalding
1967	J.D. Newcombe	Slazenger	W.P. Bungert	Dunlop
1968	R.G. Laver	Dunlop	A.D. Roche	Dunlop
1969	R.G. Laver	Dunlop	J.D. Newcombe	Slazenger
1970	J.D. Newcombe	Slazenger	K.R. Rosewall	Slazenger
1971	J.D. Newcombe	Slazenger	S.R. Smith	Wilson
1972	S.R. Smith	Wilson	I. Nastase	Dunlop
1973	J. Kodes	Wilson	A. Metreveli	Dunlop
1974	J.S. Connors	Wilson	K.R. Rosewall	Seamco
1975	A.R. Ashe	Head	J.S. Connors	Wilson
1976	B.R. Borg	Donnay	I. Nastase	Wilson

Year	Champion	Manufacturer of racket	Runner-Up	Manufacturer of racket
1977	B.R. Borg	Donnay	J.S. Connors	Wilson
1978	B.R. Borg	Donnay	J.S. Connors	Wilson
1979	B.R. Borg	Donnay	L.R. Tanner	P.D.P.
1980	B.R. Borg	Donnay	J.P. McEnroe	Wilson
1981	J.P. McEnroe	Dunlop	B.R. Borg	Donnay
1982	J.S. Connors	Wilson	J.P. McEnroe	Dunlop
1983	J.P. McEnroe	Dunlop	C.J. Lewis	Prince
1984	J.P. McEnroe	Dunlop	J.S. Connors	Wilson
1985	B.F. Becker	Puma	K.M. Curren	Kneissl
1986	B.F. Becker	Puma	I. Lendl	Adidas
1987	P.H. Cash	Prince	I. Lendl	Adidas
1988	S.B. Edberg	Wilson	B.F. Becker	Puma
1989	B.F. Becker	Estusa	S.B. Edberg	Wilson
1990	S.B. Edberg	Wilson	B.F. Becker	Estusa
1991	M.D. Stich	Fischer	B.F. Becker	Estusa
1992	A.K. Agassi	Donnay	G. Ivanisevic	Head
1993	P. Sampras	Wilson	J.S. Courier	Wilson
1994	P. Sampras	Wilson	G. Ivanisevic	Head
1995	P. Sampras	Wilson	B.F. Becker	Estusa
1996	R.P.S. Krajicek	Yonex	M.O. Washington	Yonex
1997	P. Sampras	Wilson	C.A. Pioline	Head
1998	P. Sampras	Wilson	G. Ivanisevic	Head
1999	P. Sampras	Wilson	A.K. Agassi	Head
2000	P. Sampras	Wilson	P.M. Rafter	Prince
2001	G.S. Ivanisevic	Head	P.M. Rafter	Prince
2002	L.G. Hewitt	Yonex	D.P. Nalbandian	Prince
2003	R. Federer	Wilson	M.A. Philippoussis	Dunlop
2004	R. Federer	Wilson	A.S. Roddick	Babolat
2005	R. Federer	Wilson	A.S. Roddick	Babolat
2006	R. Federer	Wilson	R. Nadal	Babolat
2007	R. Federer	Wilson	R. Nadal	Babolat
2008	R. Nadal	Babolat	R. Federer	Wilson
2009	R. Federer	Wilson	A.S. Roddick	Babolat
2010	R. Nadal	Babolat	T. Berdych	Head
2011	N. Djokovic	Head	R. Nadal	Babolat
2012	R. Federer	Wilson	A.B. Murray	Head
2013	A.B. Murray	Head	N. Djokovic	Head
2014	N. Djokovic	Head	R. Federer	Wilson

Ladies' Singles Championship

Year	Champion	Manufacturer of racket	Runner-Up	Manufacturer of racket
1884	Miss M.E.E. Watson		Miss L.M. Watson	
1885	Miss M.E.E. Watson		Miss B. Bingley	
1886	Miss B. Bingley		Miss M.E.E. Watson	
1887	Miss C. Dod		Miss B. Bingley	
1888	Miss C. Dod		Mrs. G.W. Hillyard	
1889	Mrs. G.W. Hillyard		Miss H.G.B. Rice	
1890	Miss H.G.B. Rice		Miss M. Jacks	
1891	Miss C. Dod		Mrs. G.W. Hillyard	
1892	Miss C. Dod		Mrs. G.W. Hillyard	
1893	Miss C. Dod		Mrs. G.W. Hillyard	

Year	Champion	Manufacturer of racket	Runner-Up	Manufacturer of racket
1894	Mrs. G.W. Hillyard		Miss E.L. Austin	
1895	Miss C.R. Cooper		Miss H. Jackson	
1896	Miss C.R. Cooper		Mrs. W.H. Pickering	
1897	Mrs. G.W. Hillyard	Tate	Miss C.R. Cooper	
1898	Miss C.R. Cooper	Slazenger	Miss M.L. Martin	
1899	Mrs. G.W. Hillyard	Tate	Miss C.R. Cooper	
1900	Mrs. G.W. Hillyard	Tate	Miss C.R. Cooper	
1901	Mrs. A. Sterry		Mrs. G.W. Hillyard	
1902	Miss M.E. Robb		Mrs. A. Sterry	
1903	Miss D.K. Douglass	Slazenger	Miss E.W. Thomson	
1904	Miss D.K. Douglass	Slazenger	Mrs. A. Sterry	
1905	Miss M.G. Sutton	Wright & Ditson	Miss D.K. Douglass	Slazenger
1906	Miss D.K. Douglass	Slazenger	Miss M.G. Sutton	Wright & Ditson
1907	Miss M.G. Sutton	Wright & Ditson	Mrs. R.L. Chambers	Slazenger
1908	Mrs. A. Sterry	Davis	Miss A.M. Morton	Gardner
1909	Miss P.D.H. Boothby		Miss A.M. Morton	Gardner
1910	Mrs. R.L. Chambers	Slazenger	Miss P.D.H. Boothby	
1911	Mrs. R.L. Chambers	Slazenger	Miss P.D.H. Boothby	
1912	Mrs. D.T.R. Larcombe	Slazenger	Mrs. A. Sterry	
1913	Mrs. R.L. Chambers	Slazenger	Mrs. R.J. McNair	Slazenger
1914	Mrs. R.L. Chambers	Slazenger	Mrs. D.T.R. Larcombe	
1919	Miss S.R.F. Lenglen	Williams	Mrs. R.L. Chambers	Slazenger
1920	Miss S.R.F. Lenglen	Williams	Mrs. R.L. Chambers	Slazenger
1921	Miss S.R.F. Lenglen	Williams	Miss E.M. Ryan	
1922	Miss S.R.F. Lenglen	Williams	Mrs. F.I. Mallory	
1923	Miss S.R.F. Lenglen	Williams	Miss K. McKane	Slazenger
1924	Miss K. McKane	Slazenger	Miss H.N. Wills	Bancroft
1925	Miss S.R.F. Lenglen	Williams	Miss J.C. Fry	Ayres
1926	Mrs. L.A. Godfree	Slazenger	Miss E.M.de Alvarez	Slazenger
1927	Miss H.N. Wills	Spalding	Miss E.M. de Alvarez	Slazenger
1928	Miss H.N. Wills	Spalding	Miss E.M. de Alvarez	Slazenger
1929	Miss H.N. Wills	Spalding	Miss H.H. Jacobs	
1930	Mrs. F.S. Moody	Spalding	Miss E.M. Ryan	
1931	Miss C. Aussem	Spalding	Miss H. Krahwinkel	Dunlop
1932	Mrs. F.S. Moody	Spalding	Miss H.H. Jacobs	Dunlop
1933	Mrs. F.S. Moody	Spalding	Miss D.E. Round	Slazenger
1934	Miss D.E. Round	Slazenger	Miss H.H. Jacobs	Dunlop
1935	Mrs. F.S. Moody	Spalding	Miss H.H. Jacobs	Dunlop
1936	Miss H.H. Jacobs	Dunlop	Mrs. S. Sperling	Dunlop
1937	Miss D.E. Round	Slazenger	Miss J. Jedrzejowska	Slazenger
1938	Mrs. F.S. Moody	Wright & Ditson	Miss H.H. Jacobs	Dunlop
1939	Miss A. Marble	Wilson	Miss K.E. Stammers	Dunlop
1946	Miss P.M. Betz	Wilson	Miss A.L. Brough	Spalding
1947	Miss M.E. Osborne	Spalding	Miss D.J. Hart	Wilson
1948	Miss A.L. Brough	Spalding	Miss D.J. Hart	Wilson
1949	Miss A.L. Brough	Spalding	Mrs. W. duPont	Spalding
1950	Miss A.L. Brough	Spalding	Mrs. W. duPont	Spalding
1951	Miss D.J. Hart	Wilson	Miss S.J. Fry	Wilson
1952	Miss M.C. Connolly	Wilson	Miss A.L. Brough	Wright & Ditson
1953	Miss M.C. Connolly	Wilson	Miss D.J. Hart	Wilson
1954	Miss M.C. Connolly	Wilson	Miss A.L. Brough	Spalding

Year	Champion	Manufacturer of racket	Runner-Up	Manufacturer of racket
1955	Miss A.L. Brough	Spalding	Mrs. J.G. Fleitz	Spalding
1956	Miss S.J. Fry	Spalding	Miss A. Buxton	Slazenger
1957	Miss A. Gibson	Slazenger	Miss D.R. Hard	Spalding
1958	Miss A. Gibson	Lee	Miss F.A.M. Mortimer	Dunlop
1959	Miss M.E.A. Bueno	Wilson	Miss D.R. Hard	Spalding
1960	Miss M.E.A. Bueno	Wilson	Miss S. Reynolds	Dunlop
1961	Miss F.A.M.Mortimer	Dunlop	Miss C.C. Truman	Slazenger
1962	Mrs. J.R. Susman	Wilson	Mrs. C. Sukova	Dunlop
1963	Miss M. Smith	Spalding	Miss B.J. Moffitt	Wilson
1964	Miss M.E.A. Bueno	Wilson	Miss M. Smith	Slazenger
1965	Miss M. Smith	Slazenger	Miss M.E.A. Bueno	Wilson
1966	Mrs. L.W. King	Wilson	Miss M.E.A. Bueno	Wilson
1967	Mrs. L.W. King	Wilson	Mrs. P.F. Jones	Dunlop
1968	Mrs. L.W. King	Wilson	Miss J.A.M. Tegart	Slazenger
1969	Mrs. P.F. Jones	Wilson	Mrs. L.W. King	Wilson
1970	Mrs. B.M. Court	Chemold	Mrs. L.W. King	Wilson
1971	Miss E.F. Goolagong	Dunlop	Mrs. B.M. Court	Chemold
1972	Mrs. L.W. King	Wilson	Miss E.F. Goolagong	Dunlop
1973	Mrs. L.W. King	Wilson	Miss C.M. Evert	Wilson
1974	Miss C.M. Evert	Wilson	Miss O.V. Morozova	Wilson
1975	Mrs. L.W. King	Bancroft	Mrs. R.A. Cawley	Dunlop
1976	Miss C.M. Evert	Wilson	Mrs. R.A. Cawley	Dunlop
1977	Miss S.V. Wade	Dunlop	Miss B.F. Stove	Slazenger
1978	Miss M. Navratilova	Bancroft	Miss C.M. Evert	Wilson
1979	Miss M. Navratilova	Bancroft	Mrs. J.M. Lloyd	Wilson
1980	Mrs. R.A. Cawley	Dunlop	Mrs. J.M. Lloyd	Wilson
1981	Mrs. J.M. Lloyd	Wilson	Miss H. Mandlikova	Wilson
1982	Miss M. Navratilova	Yonex	Mrs. J.M. Lloyd	Wilson
1983	Miss M. Navratilova	Yonex	Miss A. Jaeger	Wilson
1984	Miss M. Navratilova	Yonex	Mrs. J.M. Lloyd	Wilson
1985	Miss M. Navratilova	Yonex	Mrs. J.M. Lloyd	Wilson
1986	Miss M. Navratilova	Yonex	Miss H. Mandlikova	Wilson
1987	Miss M. Navratilova	Yonex	Miss S.M. Graf	Dunlop
1988	Miss S.M. Graf	Dunlop	Miss M. Navratilova	Dunlop
1989	Miss S.M. Graf	Dunlop	Miss M. Navratilova	Yonex
1990	Miss M. Navratilova	Yonex	Miss Z.L. Garrison	Wilson
1991	Miss S.M. Graf	Dunlop	Miss G.B. Sabatini	Prince
1992	Miss S.M. Graf	Dunlop	Miss M. Seles	Yonex
1993	Miss S.M. Graf	Dunlop	Miss J. Novotna	Prince
1994	Miss I.C. Martinez	Donnay	Miss M. Navratilova	Yonex
1995	Miss S.M. Graf	Wilson	Miss A.I.M. Sanchez Vicario	Dunlop
1996	Miss S.M. Graf	Wilson	Miss A.I.M. Sanchez Vicario	Yonex
1997	Miss M. Hingis	Yonex	Miss J. Novotna	Prince
1998	Miss J. Novotna	Prince	Miss N. Tauziat	Pro-Kennex
1999	Miss L.A. Davenport	Wilson	Miss S.M. Graf	Wilson
2000	Miss V.E.S. Williams	Wilson	Miss L.A. Davenport	Wilson
2001	Miss V.E.S. Williams	Wilson	Miss J. Henin	Wilson
2002	Miss S.J. Williams	Wilson	Miss V.E.S. Williams	Wilson
2003	Miss S.J. Williams	Wilson	Miss V.E.S. Williams	Wilson
2004	Miss M. Sharapova	Prince	Miss S.J. Williams	Wilson
2005	Miss V.E.S. Williams	Wilson	Miss L.A. Davenport	Wilson
2006	Miss A. Mauresmo	Dunlop	Mrs P.Y. Hardenne	Wilson

Year	Champion	Manufacturer of racket	Runner-Up	Manufacturer of racket
2007	Miss V.E.S. Williams	Wilson	Miss M.S. Bartoli	Prince
2008	Miss V.E.S. Williams	Wilson	Miss S.J. Williams	Wilson
2009	Miss S.J. Williams	Wilson	Miss V.E.S. Williams	Wilson
2010	Miss S.J. Williams	Wilson	Miss V. Zvonareva	Prince
2011	Miss P. Kvitova	Wilson	Miss M. Sharapova	Head
2012	Miss S.J. Williams	Wilson	Miss A. Radwanska	Babolat
2013	Miss M.S. Bartoli	Prince	Miss S.K. Lisicki	Yonex
2014	Miss P. Kvitova	Wilson	Miss E.C.M. Bouchard	Babolat

Gentlemen's Doubles Championship

Year	Champion	Manufacturer of racket	Champion	Manufacturer of racket
1946	T.P. Brown	Wilson	J.A. Kramer	Wilson
1947	R. Falkenburg	Wilson	J.A. Kramer	Wilson
1948	J.E. Bromwich	Slazenger	F.A. Sedgman	Oliver
1949	R.A. Gonzales	Spalding	F.A. Parker	Spalding
1950	J.E. Bromwich	Slazenger	A.K. Quist	Dunlop
1951	K.B. McGregor	Slazenger	F.A. Sedgman	Oliver
1952	K.B. McGregor	Slazenger	F.A. Sedgman	Oliver
1953	L.A. Hoad	Dunlop	K.R. Rosewall	Slazenger
1954	R.N. Hartwig	Spalding	M.G. Rose	Slazenger
1955	R.N. Hartwig	Spalding	L.A. Hoad	Dunlop
1956	L.A. Hoad	Dunlop	K.R. Rosewall	Slazenger
1957	G.P. Mulloy	Spalding	J.E. Patty	Dunlop
1958	S.V. Davidson	Dunlop	U.C.J. Schmidt	Dunlop
1959	R. S. Emerson	Dunlop	N.A. Fraser	Slazenger
1960	R.H. Osuna	Wilson	R.D. Ralston	Wilson
1961	R.S. Emerson	Slazenger	N.A. Fraser	Slazenger
1962	R.A.J. Hewitt	Dunlop	F.S. Stolle	Dunlop
1963	R.H. Osuna	Wilson	A. Palafox	Dunlop
1964	R.A.J. Hewitt	Dunlop	F.S. Stolle	Dunlop
1965	J.D. Newcombe	Slazenger	A.D. Roche	Dunlop
1966	K.N. Fletcher	Slazenger	J.D. Newcombe	Slazenger
1967	R.A.J. Hewitt	Dunlop	F.D. McMillan	Dunlop
1968	J.D. Newcombe	Slazenger	A.D. Roche	Dunlop
1969	J.D. Newcombe	Slazenger	A.D. Roche	Dunlop
1970	J.D. Newcombe	Slazenger	A.D. Roche	Chemold
1971	R. S. Emerson	Chemold	R.G. Laver	Chemold
1972	R.A.J. Hewitt	Dunlop	F.D. McMillan	Dunlop
1973	J. S. Connors	Wilson	I. Nastase	Dunlop
1974	J.D. Newcombe	Slazenger	A.D. Roche	Yonex
1975	V. Gerulaitis	Wilson	A. Mayer	Snauwaert
1976	B.E. Gottfried	Wilson	R.C. Ramirez	Wilson
1977	R.L. Case	Adidas	G. Masters	Adidas
1978	R.A.J. Hewitt	Fischer	F.D. McMillan	Fischer
1979	P.B. Fleming	Yonex	J.P. McEnroe	Wilson
1980	P.B. McNamara	Adidas	P.F. NcNamee	Prince
1981	P.B. Fleming	Prince	J.P. McEnroe	Dunlop
1982	P.B. McNamara	Prince	P.F. NcNamee	Prince
1983	P.B. Fleming	Dunlop	J.P. McEnroe	Dunlop
1984	P.B. Fleming	Dunlop	J.P. McEnroe	Dunlop
1985	H.P. Guenthardt	Kneissl	B. Taroczy	Dunlop

Year	Champion	Manufacturer of racket	Champion	Manufacturer of racket
1986	K.J. Nystrom	Wimbledon	M.A.O. Wilander	Rossignol
1987	K.E. Flach	Wimbledon	R.A. Seguso,	Pro Kennex
1988	K.E. Flach	Wimbledon	R.A. Seguso	Pro Kennex
1989	J.B. Fitzgerald	Puma	A.P. Jarryd	Spalding
1990	R.D. Leach	Wilson	J.R. Pugh	Wilson
1991	J.B. Fitzgerald	Estusa	A.P. Jarryd	Fischer
1992	J.P. McEnroe	Dunlop	M.D. Stich	Fischer
1993	T.A. Woodbridge	Wilson	M.R. Woodforde	Snauwaert
1994	T.A. Woodbridge	Wilson	M.R. Woodforde	Snauwaert
1995	T.A. Woodbridge	Wilson	M.R. Woodforde	Wilson
1996	T.A. Woodbridge	Wilson	M.R. Woodforde	Wilson
1997	T.A. Woodbridge	Wilson	M.R. Woodforde	Wilson
1998	J.F. Eltingh	Prince	P.V.N. Haarhuis	Estusa
1999	M.S. Bhupathi	Wilson	L.A. Paes	Prince
2000	T.A. Woodbridge	Wilson	M.R. Woodforde	Wilson
2001	D.J. Johnson	Head	J.E. Palmer	Babolat
2002	J.L. Bjorkman	Wilson	T.A. Woodbridge	Wilson
2003	J.L. Bjorkman	Wilson	T.A. Woodbridge	Wilson
2004	J.L. Bjorkman	Wilson	T.A. Woodbridge	Wilson
2005	S.W.I. Huss	Wilson	W.A. Moodie	Technifibre
2006	M.C. Bryan	Wilson	R.C. Bryan	Wilson
2007	A. Clement	Head	M. Llodra	Wilson
2008	D.M. Nestor	Wilson	N. Zimonjic	Head
2009	D.M. Nestor	Wilson	N. Zimonjic	Head
2010	J. Melzer	Dunlop	P. Petzschner	Wilson
2011	M.C. Bryan	Prince	R.C. Bryan	Prince
2012	J.F. Marray	Dunlop	F.L. Nielsen	Prince
2013	M.C. Bryan	Prince	R.C. Bryan	Prince
2014	V. Pospisil	Wilson	J.E. Sock	Babolat

Gentlemen's Doubles Championship

Year	Runner up	Manufacturer of racket	Runner up	Manufacturer of racket
1946	G.E. Brown	Slazenger	D.R. Pails	Spalding
1947	A.J. Mottram	Dunlop	O.W.T. Sidwell	Slazenger
1948	T.P. Brown	Wilson	G.P. Mulloy	Spalding
1949	G.P. Mulloy	Spalding	F.R. Schroeder	Wilson
1950	G.E. Brown	Slazenger	O.W.T. Sidwell	Slazenger
1951	J. Drobny	Dunlop	E.W. Sturgess	Spalding
1952	E.V. Seixas	Wilson	E.W. Sturgess	Dunlop
1953	R.N. Hartwig	Spalding	M.G. Rose	Slazenger
1954	E.V. Seixas	Wilson	M.A. Trabert	Wilson
1955	N.A. Fraser	Slazenger	K.R. Rosewall	Slazenger
1956	N. Pietrangeli	Dunlop	O. Sirola	Slazenger
1957	N.A. Fraser	Slazenger	L.A. Hoad	Dunlop
1958	A.J. Cooper	Spalding	N.A. Fraser	Slazenger
1959	R.G. Laver	Dunlop	R. Mark	Dunlop
1960	M.G. Davies	Slazenger	R.K. Wilson	Dunlop
1961	R.A.J. Hewitt	Dunlop	F.S. Stolle	Dunlop
1962	B. Jovanovic	Dunlop	N. Pilic	Dunlop
1963	J.C. Barclay	Dunlop	P. Darmon	Dunlop

Year	Runner-up	Manufacturer of racket	Runner-up	Manufacturer of racket
1964	R.S. Emerson	Slazenger	K.N. Fletcher	Slazenger
1965	K.N. Fletcher	Slazenger	R.A.J. Hewitt	Dunlop
1966	W.W. Bowrey	Dunlop	O.K. Davidson	Spalding
1967	R.S. Emerson	Slazenger	K.N. Fletcher	Slazenger
1968	K.R. Rosewall	Slazenger	F.S. Stolle	Spalding
1969	T.S. Okker	Dunlop	M.C. Riessen	Wilson
1970	K.R. Rosewall	Slazenger	F.S. Stolle	Dunlop
1971	A.R. Ashe	Head	R.D. Ralston	Wilson
1972	S.R. Smith	Wilson	E.J. Van Dillen	Spalding
1973	J.R. Cooper	Slazenger	N.A. Fraser	Slazenger
1974	R.C. Lutz	Head	S.R. Smith	Wilson
1975	C. Dowdeswell	Slazenger	A.J. Stone	Fischer
1976	R.L. Case	Adidas	G. Masters	Adidas
1977	J.G. Alexander	Slazenger	P.C. Dent	Dunlop
1978	P.B. Fleming	Yonex	J.P. McEnroe	Wilson
1979	B.E. Gottfried	Wilson	R.C. Ramirez	Wilson
1980	R.C. Lutz	Yamaha	S.R. Smith	Fischer
1981	R.C. Lutz	Yamaha	S.R. Smith	Fischer
1982	P.B. Fleming	Prince	J.P. McEnroe	Dunlop
1983	T.E. Gullikson	Head	T.R. Gullikson	Head
1984	P.H. Cash	Slazenger	P.F. McNamee	Prince
1985	P.H. Cash	Prince	J.B. Fitzgerald	Pro-Kennex
1986	G.W. Donnelly	Dunlop	P.B. Fleming	Dunlop
1987	S. Casal	Head	E. Sanchez	Head
1988	J.B. Fitzgerald	Wimbledon	A.P. Jarryd	Spalding
1989	R.D. Leach	Wilson	J.R. Pugh	Wilson
1990	P. Aldrich	Wilson	D.T. Visser	Wilson
1991	J.A. Frana	Snauwert	L. Lavalle	Snauwert
1992	J.F. Grabb	Wilson	R. Reneberg	Prince
1993	G.D. Connell	Prince	P.J. Galbraith	Wilson
1994	G.D. Connell	Prince	P.J. Galbraith	Wilson
1995	R.D. Leach	Wilson	D.S. Melville	Yonex
1996	B.H. Black	Prince	G.D. Connell	Prince
1997	J.F. Eltingh	Prince	P.V.N. Haarhuis	Pro-Kennex
1998	T.A. Woodbridge	Yonex	M.R. Woodforde	Yonex
1999	P.V.N. Haarhuis	Estusa	J.E. Palmer	Head
2000	P.V.N. Haarhuis	Estusa	S.F. Stolle	Prince
2001	J. Novak	Volkl	D. Rikl	Babolat
2002	M.S. Knowles	Head	D.M. Nestor	Wilson
2003	M.S. Bhupathi	Babolat	M.N. Mirnyi	Wilson
2004	J. Knowle	Head	N. Zimonjic	Head
2005	M.C. Bryan	Wilson	R.C. Bryan	Wilson
2006	F.V. Santoro	Head	N. Zimonjic	Head
2007	M.C. Bryan	Wilson	R.C. Bryan	Wilson
2008	J.L. Bjorkman	Wilson	K.R. Ullyett	Wilson
2009	M.C. Bryan	Prince	R.C. Bryan	Prince
2010	R. Lindstedt	Wilson	H.V. Tecau	Wilson
2011	R. Lindstedt	Wilson	H.V. Tecau	Wilson
2012	R. Lindstedt	Wilson	H.V. Tecau	Wilson
2013	I. Dodig	Head	M.P.D. Melo	Babolat
2014	M.C. Bryan	Prince	R.C. Bryan	Prince

Ladies' Doubles Championship

Year	Champion	Manufacturer of racket	Champion	Manufacturer of racket
1946	Miss A.L. Brough	Spalding	Miss M.E. Osborne	Spalding
1947	Miss D.J. Hart	Wilson	Mrs. R.B. Todd	Wilson
1948	Miss A.L. Brough	Spalding	Mrs. W. duPont	Spalding
1949	Miss A.L. Brough	Spalding	Mrs. W. duPont	Spalding
1950	Miss A.L. Brough	Spalding	Mrs. W. duPont	Spalding
1951	Miss S.J. Fry	Wilson	Miss D.J. Hart	Wilson
1952	Miss S.J. Fry	Wilson	Miss D.J. Hart	Wilson
1953	Miss S.J. Fry	Wilson	Miss D.J. Hart	Wilson
1954	Miss A.L. Brough	Spalding	Mrs. W. duPont	Spalding
1955	Miss F.A.M. Mortimer	Dunlop	Miss J.A. Shilcock	Slazenger
1956	Miss A. Buxton	Slazenger	Miss A. Gibson	Slazenger
1957	Miss A. Gibson	Slazenger	Miss D.R. Hard	Spalding
1958	Miss M.E.A. Bueno	Wilson	Miss A. Gibson	Lee
1959	Miss J.M. Arth	Wilson	Miss D.R. Hard	Spalding
1960	Miss M.E.A. Bueno	Wilson	Miss D.R. Hard	Spalding
1961	Mrs. K.J. Hantze	Wilson	Miss B.J. Moffitt	Wilson
1962	Miss B.J. Moffitt	Wilson	Mrs. J.R. Susman	Wilson
1963	Miss M.E.A. Bueno	Wilson	Miss D.R. Hard	Wilson
1964	Miss M. Smith	Slazenger	Miss L.R. Turner	Slazenger
1965	Miss M.E.A. Bueno	Wilson	Miss B.J. Moffitt	Wilson
1966	Miss M.E.A. Bueno	Wilson	Miss N.A. Richey	Bancroft
1967	Miss R. Casals	Wilson	Mrs. L.W. King	Wilson
1968	Miss R. Casals	Wilson	Mrs. L.W. King	Wilson
1969	Mrs. B.M. Court	Slazenger	Miss J.A.M. Tegart	Slazenger
1970	Miss R. Casals	Wilson	Mrs. L.W. King	Wilson
1971	Miss R. Casals	Spalding	Mrs. L.W. King	Wilson
1972	Mrs. L.W King	Wilson	Miss B.F. Stove	Slazenger
1973	Miss R. Casals	Spalding	Mrs. L.W. King	Wilson
1974	Miss E.F. Goolagong	Dunlop	Miss M. Michel	Dunlop
1975	Miss A.K. Kiyomura	Wilson	Miss K. Sawamatsu	Kawasaki
1976	Miss C.M. Evert	Wilson	Miss M. Navratilova	Spalding
1977	Mrs. R.L. Cawley	Spalding	Miss J.C. Russell	Bancroft
1978	Mrs. G.E. Reid	Adidas	Miss W.M. Turnbull	Yonex
1979	Mrs. L.W. King	Bancroft	Miss M. Navratilova	Bancroft
1980	Miss K. Jordan	Wilson	Miss A.E. Smith	Adidas
1981	Miss M. Navratilova	Bancroft	Miss P.H. Shriver	Prince
1982	Miss M. Navratilova	Yonex	Miss P.H. Shriver	Prince
1983	Miss M. Navratilova	Yonex	Miss P.H. Shriver	Prince
1984	Miss M. Navratilova	Yonex	Miss P.H. Shriver	Prince
1985	Miss K. Jordan	Pro Kennex	Mrs. P.D. Smylie	Head
1986	Miss M. Navratilova	Yonex	Miss P.H. Shriver	Yonex
1987	Miss C. Kohde-Kilsch	Wilson	Miss H. Sukova	Kneissl
1988	Miss S.M. Graf	Dunlop	Miss G.B. Sabatini	Prince
1989	Miss J. Novotna	Volkl	Miss H. Sukova	Puma
1990	Miss J. Novotna	Volkl	Miss H. Sukova	Puma
1991	Miss L. Savchenko	Rossignol	Miss N.M. Zvereva	Yonex
1992	Miss B.C. Fernandez	Yonex	Miss N.M. Zvereva	Yonex
1993	Miss B.C. Fernandez	Yonex	Miss N.M. Zvereva	Yonex
1994	Miss B.C. Fernandez	Yonex	Miss N.M. Zvereva	Yonex
1995	Miss J. Novotna	Prince	Miss A. Sanchez Vicario	Dunlop
1996	Miss M. Hingis	Yonex	Miss H. Sukova	Mizuno

Year	Champion	Manufacturer of racket	Champion	Manufacturer of racket
1997	Miss B.C. Fernandez	Yonex	Miss N.M. Zvereva	Yonex
1998	Miss M. Hingis	Yonex	Miss J. Novotna	Prince
1999	Miss L.A. Davenport	Wilson	Miss C.M. Morariu	Yonex
2000	Miss S.J. Williams	Wilson	Miss V.E.S. Williams	Wilson
2001	Miss L.M. Raymond	Prince	Miss R.P. Stubbs	Prince
2002	Miss S.J. Williams	Wilson	Miss V.E.S. Williams	Wilson
2003	Miss K. Clijsters	Babolat	Miss A. Sugiyama	Prince
2004	Miss C.C. Black	Babolat	Miss R.P. Stubbs	Prince
2005	Miss C.C. Black	Babolat	Mrs A. Huber	Prince
2006	Miss Z. Yan	Yonex	Miss J. Zheng	Wilson
2007	Miss C.C. Black	Babalot	Mrs A. Huber	Prince
2008	Miss S.J. Williams	Wilson	Miss V.E.S. Williams	Wilson
2009	Miss S.J. Williams	Wilson	Miss V.E.S. Williams	Wilson
2010	Miss V. King	Babloat	Miss Y.V. Shvedova	Head
2011	Mrs. T. Peschke	Prince	Miss K. Srebotnik	Prince
2012	Miss S.J. Williams	Wilson	Miss V.E.S. Williams	Wilson
2013	Miss S-W.Hsieh	Yonex	Miss S. Peng	Babolat
2014	Miss S. Errani	Babolat	Miss R. Vinci	Head

Ladies' Doubles Championship

Year	Runner up	Manufacturer of racket	Runner up	Manufacturer of racket
1946	Miss P.M. Betz	Wilson	Miss D.J. Hart	Wilson
1947	Miss A.L. Brough	Spalding	Miss M.E. Osborne	Spalding
1948	Miss D.J. Hart	Wilson	Mrs. R.B. Todd	Wilson
1949	Miss G.A. Moran	Spalding	Mrs. R.B. Todd	Wilson
1950	Miss S.J. Fry	Wilson	Miss D.J. Hart	Wilson
1951	Miss A.L. Brough	Spalding	Mrs. W. DuPont	Spalding
1952	Miss A.L. Brough	Wright & Ditson	Miss M.C. Connolly	Wilson
1953	Miss M.C. Connolly	Wilson	Miss J.A. Sampson	Wilson
1954	Miss S.J. Fry	Wilson	Miss D.J. Hart	Wilson
1955	Miss S.J. Bloomer	Slazenger	Miss P.E. Ward	Slazenger
1956	Miss E.F. Muller	Slazenger	Miss D.G. Seeney	Dunlop
1957	Mrs. K.E. Hawton	Slazenger	Mrs. M.N. Long	Slazenger
1958	Mrs. W. DuPont	Spalding	Miss M. Varner	Spalding
1959	Mrs. J.G. Fleitz	Spalding	Miss C.C. Truman	Slazenger
1960	Miss S. Reynolds	Dunlop	Miss R. Schuurman	Dunlop
1961	Miss J.P. Lehane	Slazenger	Miss M. Smith	Spalding
1962	Mrs. L.E.G. Price	Dunlop	Miss R. Schuurman	Dunlop
1963	Miss R.A. Ebbern	Spalding	Miss M. Smith	Spalding
1964	Miss B.J. Moffitt	Wilson	Mrs. J.R. Susman	Wilson
1965	Miss F.G. Durr	Dunlop	Miss J.P. Lieffrig	Gauthier
1966	Miss M. Smith	Slazenger	Miss J.A.M. Tegart	Slazenger
1967	Miss M.E.A. Bueno	Wilson	Miss N.A. Richey	Bancroft
1968	Miss F. G. Durr	Slazenger	Mrs. P.F. Jones	Wilson
1969	Miss P.S.A. Hogan	Wilson	Miss M. Michel	Dunlop
1970	Miss F. G. Durr	Slazenger	Miss S.V. Wade	Dunlop
1971	Mrs. B.M. Court	Chemold	Miss E.F. Goolagong	Dunlop
1972	Mrs. D.E. Dalton	Wilson	Miss F.G. Durr	Slazenger
1973	Miss F.G. Durr	Head	Miss B.F. Stove	Slazenger

Year	Runner up	Manufacturer of racket	Runner up	Manufacturer of racket
1974	Miss H.F. Gourlay	Spalding	Miss K.M. Krantzcke	Wilson
1975	Miss F.G. Durr	Wilson	Miss B.F. Stove	Slazenger
1976	Mrs. L.W. King	Wilson	Miss B.F. Stove	Slazenger
1977	Miss M. Navratilova	Bancroft	Miss B.F. Stove	Slazenger
1978	Miss M. Jausovec	Wilson	Miss V. Ruzici	Dunlop
1979	Miss B.F. Stove	Slazenger	Miss W.M. Turnbull	Yonex
1980	Miss R. Casals	Spalding	Miss W.M. Turnbull	Yonex
1981	Miss K. Jordan	Wilson	Miss A.E. Smith	Adidas
1982	Miss K. Jordan	Wilson	Miss A.E. Smith	Adidas
1983	Miss R. Casals	Spalding	Miss W.M. Turnbull	Yonex
1984	Miss K. Jordan	Wilson	Miss A.E. Smith	Adidas
1985	Miss M. Navratilova	Yonex	Miss P.H. Shriver	Prince
1986	Miss H. Mandlikova	Wilson	Miss W.M. Turnbull	Yonex
1987	Miss H.E. Nagelsen	Pro-Kennex	Mrs. P.D. Smylie	Head
1988	Miss L.I. Savchenko	Slazenger	Miss N.M. Zvereva	Yonex
1989	Miss L.I. Savchenko	Slazenger	Miss N.M. Zvereva	Yonex
1990	Miss K. Jordan	Pro-Kennex	Mrs. P.D. Smylie	Head
1991	Miss B.C. Fernandez	Yonex	Miss J. Novotna	Volkl
1992	Miss J. Novotna	Volkl	Mrs. A. Neiland	Rossignol
1993	Miss J. Novotna	Prince	Mrs. A. Neiland	Prince
1994	Miss J. Novotna	Prince	Miss A.I.M. Sanchez Vicario	Slazenger
1995	Miss B.C. Fernandez	Yonex	Miss N.M. Zvereva	Yonex
1996	Miss M.J. McGrath	Yonex	Mrs. A. Neiland	Prince
1997	Miss N.J. Arendt	Prince	Miss M.M. Bollegraf	Prince
1998	Miss L.A. Davenport	Wilson	Miss N.M. Zvereva	Yonex
1999	Miss M. deSwardt	Prince	Miss E.V Tatarkova	Prince
2000	Mrs. A. Halard-Decugis	Major	Miss A. Sugiyama	Prince
2001	Miss K. Clijsters	Babolat	Miss A. Sugiyama	Prince
2002	Miss V. Ruano-Pascual	Yonex	Miss P.L. Suarez	Prince
2003	Miss V. Ruano-Pascual	Fischer	Miss P.L. Suarez	Prince
2004	Mrs. A. Huber	Prince	Mrs. A. Sugiyama	Prince
2005	Miss S. Kuznetsova	Head	Miss A. Mauresmo	Dunlop
2006	Miss V. Ruano-Pascual	Fischer	Miss P.L. Suarez	Prince
2007	Miss K. Srebotnik	Babolat	Miss A. Sugiyama	Prince
2008	Miss L.M. Raymond	Prince	Miss S.J. Stosur	Prince
2009	Miss S. Stosur	Babolat	Miss R. Stubbs	Babolat
2010	Miss E.S. Vesnina	Babolat	Miss Y.Zvonareva	Prince
2011	Miss S. Lisicki	Wilson	Miss S, Stosur	Babolat
2012	Miss A. Hlavackova	Yonex	Miss L. Hradecka	Wilson
2013	Miss A. Barty	Head	Miss C. Dellacqua	Head
2014	Miss T. Babos	Head	Miss K. Mladenovic	Wilson

Mixed Doubles Championship

Year	Champion	Manufacturer of racket	Champion	Manufacturer of racket
1946	T.P. Brown	Wilson	Miss A.L. Brough	Spalding
1947	J.E. Bromwich	Slazenger	Miss A.L. Brough	Spalding
1948	J.E. Bromwich	Slazenger	Miss A.L. Brough	Spalding
1949	E.W. Sturgess	Dunlop	Miss R.A. Summers	Slazenger
1950	E.W. Sturgess	Dunlop	Miss A.L. Brough	Spalding

Year	Champion	Manufacturer of racket	Champion	Manufacturer of racket
1951	F.A. Sedgman	Oliver	Miss D.J. Hart	Wilson
1952	F.A. Sedgman	Oliver	Miss D.J. Hart	Wilson
1953	E.V. Seixas	Wilson	Miss D.J. Hart	Wilson
1954	E.V. Seixas	Wilson	Miss D.J. Hart	Wilson
1955	E.V. Seixas	Wilson	Miss D.J. Hart	Wilson
1956	E.V. Seixas	Wilson	Miss S.J. Fry	Wilson
1957	M.G. Rose	Slazenger	Miss D.R. Hard	Spalding
1958	R.N. Howe	Slazenger	Miss L.G. Coghlan	Dunlop
1959	R.G. Laver	Dunlop	Miss D.R. Hard	Spalding
1960	R.G. Laver	Dunlop	Miss D.R. Hard	Spalding
1961	F.S. Stolle	Dunlop	Miss L.R. Turner	Slazenger
1962	N.A. Fraser	Slazenger	Mrs. W. duPont	Spalding
1963	K.N. Fletcher	Slazenger	Miss M. Smith	Spalding
1964	F.S. Stolle	Dunlop	Miss L.R. Turner	Slazenger
1965	K.N. Fletcher	Slazenger	Miss M. Smith	Slazenger
1966	K.N. Fletcher	Slazenger	Miss M. Smith	Slazenger
1967	O.K. Davidson	Spalding	Mrs. L.W. King	Wilson
1968	K.N. Fletcher	Slazenger	Mrs. B.M. Court	Slazenger
1969	F.S. Stolle	Spalding	Mrs. P.F. Jones	Wilson
1970	I. Nastase	Dunlop	Miss R. Casals	Wilson
1971	O.K. Davidson	Chemold	Mrs. L.W. King	Wilson
1972	I. Nastase	Dunlop	Miss R. Casals	Spalding
1973	O.K. Davidson	Dunlop	Mrs. L.W. King	Wilson
1974	O.K. Davidson	Dunlop	Mrs. L.W. King	Wilson
1975	M.C. Riessen	Dunlop	Mrs. B.M. Court	Yamaha
1976	A.D. Roche	Yonex	Miss F.G. Durr	Head
1977	R.A.J. Hewitt	Fischer	Miss G.R. Stevens	Wilson
1978	F.D. McMillan	Fischer	Miss B.F. Stove	Snauwert
1979	R.A.J. Hewitt	Fischer	Miss G.R. Stevens	Adidas
1980	J.R. Austin	Adidas	Miss T.A. Austin	Spalding
1981	F.D. McMillan	Fischer	Miss B.F. Stove	Slazenger
1982	K.M. Curren	Wilson	Miss A.E. Smith	Spalding
1983	J.M. Lloyd	Wilson	Miss W.M. Turnbull	Yonex
1984	J.M. Lloyd	Wilson	Miss W.M. Turnbull	Yonex
1985	P.F. McNamee	Prince	Miss M. Navratilova	Yonex
1986	K.E. Flach	Wimbledon	Miss K. Jordan	Pro Kennex
1987	M.J. Bates	Wilson	Miss J.M. Durie	Fischer
1988	S.E. Stewart	Wimbledon	Miss Z.L. Garrison	Wilson
1989	J.R. Pugh	Wilson	Miss J. Novotna	Volkl
1990	R.D. Leach	Wilson	Miss Z.L. Garrison	Wilson
1991	J.B. Fitzgerald	Estusa	Mrs. P.D. Smylie	Prince
1992	C. Suk	Volkl	Mrs. A. Neiland	Rossignol
1993	M.R. Woodforde	Snauwert	Miss M. Navratilova	Yonex
1994	T.A. Woodbridge	Wilson	Miss H. Sukova	Mizuno
1995	J. Stark	Head	Miss M. Navratilova	Yonex
1996	C. Suk	Volkl	Miss H. Sukova	Mizuno
1997	C. Suk	Volkl	Miss H. Sukova	Mizuno
1998	M. Mirnyi	Wilson	Miss S.J. Williams	Wilson
1999	L.A. Paes	Prince	Miss L.M. Raymond	Prince
2000	D.J. Johnson	Head	Miss K.Y. Po	Prince
2001	L. Friedl	Wilson	Miss D. Hantuchova	Babolat
2002	M.S. Bhupathi	Wilson	Miss E. Likhovtseva	Wilson

Year	Champion	Manufacturer of racket	Champion	Manufacturer of racket
2003	L.A. Paes	Babolat	Miss M. Navratilova	Prince
2004	W.H. Black	Babolat	Miss C.C. Black	Babolat
2005	M.S. Bhupathi	Wilson	Miss M.C. Pierce	Yonex
2006	A. Ram	Wilson	Miss V. Zvonerena	Prince
2007	J. Murray	Dunlop	Miss J. Jankovic	Prince
2008	R.C. Bryan	Prince	Miss S.J. Stosur	Prince
2009	M.S. Knowles	Head	Miss A-L Groenefeld	Fischer
2010	L.A. Paes	Babolat	Miss C.C. Black	Babolat
2011	J. Melzer	Dunlop	Miss I. Benesova	Wilson
2012	M.C. Bryan	Prince	Miss L.M. Raymond	Prince
2013	D. Nestor	Wilson	Miss K. Mladenovic	Wilson
2014	N. Zimonjic	Head	Miss S. Stosur	Babolat

Mixed Doubles Championship

Year	Runner up	Manufacturer of racket	Runner up	Manufacturer of racket
1946	G.E. Brown	Slazenger	Miss D.M. Bundy	Spalding
1947	C.F. Long	Spalding	Mrs. G.F. Bolton	Spalding
1948	F.A. Sedgman	Oliver	Miss D.J. Hart	Wilson
1949	J.E. Bromwich	Slazenger	Miss A.L. Brough	Spalding
1950	G.E. Brown	Slazenger	Mrs. R.B. Todd	Wilson
1951	M.G. Rose	Slazenger	Mrs. G.F. Bolton	Spalding
1952	E.J. Morea	Wilson	Mrs. M.N. Long	Slazenger
1953	E.J. Morea	Wilson	Miss S.J. Frey	Wilson
1954	K.R. Rosewall	Slazenger	Mrs. W. DuPont	Spalding
1955	E.J. Morea	Wilson	Miss A.L. Brough	Spalding
1956	G.P. Mulloy	Spalding	Miss A. Gibson	Slazenger
1957	N.A. Fraser	Slazenger	Miss A. Gibson	Slazenger
1958	K. Nielsen	Slazenger	Miss A. Gibson	Lee
1959	N.A. Fraser	Slazenger	Miss M.E.A. Bueno	Wilson
1960	R.N. Howe	Slazenger	Miss M.E.A. Bueno	Wilson
1961	R.N. Howe	Slazenger	Miss E. Buding	Dunlop
1962	R.D. Ralston	Wilson	Miss A.S. Haydon	Dunlop
1963	R.A.J. Hewitt	Dunlop	Miss D.R. Hard	Wilson
1964	K.N. Fletcher	Slazenger	Miss M. Smith	Slazenger
1965	A.D. Roche	Dunlop	Miss J.A.M. Tegart	Slazenger
1966	R.D. Ralston	Spalding	Mrs. L.W. King	Wilson
1967	K.N. Fletcher	Slazenger	Miss M.E.A. Bueno	Wilson
1968	A. Metreveli	Dunlop	Miss O.V. Morozova	Slazenger
1969	A.D. Roche	Dunlop	Miss J.A.M. Tegart	Slazenger
1970	A. Metreveli	Dunlop	Miss O.V. Morozova	Wilson
1971	M.C. Riessen	Dunlop	Mrs. B.M. Court	Chemold
1972	K.G. Warwick	Dunlop	Miss E.F. Goolagong	Dunlop
1973	R.C. Ramirez	Wilson	Miss J.S. Newberry	Wilson
1974	M.J. Farrell	Dunlop	Miss L.J. Charles	Dunlop
1975	A.J. Stone	Fischer	Miss B.F. Stove	Slazenger
1976	R.L. Stockton	Wilson	Miss R. Casals	Spalding
1977	F.D. McMillan	Fischer	Miss B.F. Stove	Slazenger
1978	R.O. Ruffels	Yonex	Mrs. L.W. King	Bancroft
1979	F.D. McMillan	Fischer	Miss B.F. Stove	Slazenger
1980	M.R. Edmondson	Fila	Miss D.L. Fromholtz	Yonex
1981	J.R. Austin	Adidas	Miss T.A. Austin	Spalding

Year	Runner up	Manufacturer of racket	Runner up	Manufacturer of racket
1982	J.M. Lloyd	Wilson	Miss W.M. Turnbull	Yonex
1983	S.B. Denton	Pro-Kennex	Mrs. L.W. King	Yonex
1984	S.B. Denton	Pro-Kennex	Miss K. Jordan	Wilson
1985	J.B. Fitzgerald	Pro-Kennex	Mrs. P.D. Smylie	Head
1986	H.P. Guenthardt	Kneissl	Miss M. Navratilova	Yonex
1987	D.A. Cahill	Prince	Miss N.A. Provis	Wilson
1988	K.I. Jones	Head	Mrs. S.W. Magers	Prince
1989	M. Kratzmann	Prince	Miss J.M. Byrne	Snauwert
1990	J.B. Fitzgerald	Puma	Mrs. P.D. Smylie	Head
1991	J.R. Pugh	Wilson	Miss N.M. Zvereva	Yonex
1992	J.F. Eltingh	Prince	Miss M.J.M.M. Oremans	Wilson
1993	T.J.C.M. Nijssen	Wilson	Miss M.M. Bollegraf	Prince
1994	T.J. Middleton	Spalding	Miss L.M. McNeill	Prince
1995	C. Suk	Volkl	Miss B.C. Fernandez	Yonex
1996	M.R. Woodforde	Wilson	Mrs. A. Neiland	Prince
1997	A. Olhovskiy	Volkl	Mrs. A. Neiland	Prince
1998	M.S. Bhupathi	Wilson	Miss M. Lucic	Prince
1999	J.L. Bjorkman	Wilson	Miss A.S. Kournikova	Yonex
2000	L.G. Hewitt	Yonex	Miss K. Clijsters	Babolat
2001	M.C. Bryan	Wilson	Mrs. A. Huber	Prince
2002	K.R. Ullyett	Wilson	Miss D. Hantuchova	Babolat
2003	A. Ram	Wilson	Miss A. Rodionova	Wilson
2004	T.A. Woodbridge	Wilson	Miss A. Molik	Dunlop
2005	P.J. Hanley	Wilson	Miss T. Perebiynis	Wilson
2006	R.C. Bryan	Wilson	Miss V.E.S. Williams	Wilson
2007	J.L. Bjorkman	Wilson	Miss A. Molik	Dunlop
2008	M.C. Bryan	Prince	Miss K.Srebotnik	Prince
2009	L.A. Paes	Babolat	Miss C.C Black	Babolat
2010	W.A. Moodie	Head	Miss L.M. Raymond	Prince
2011	M. Bhupathi	Wilson	Miss E. Vesnina	Babolat
2012	L.A. Paes	Babolat	Miss E. Vesnina	Babolat
2013	B.F. Soares	Wilson	Miss L.M. Raymond	Wilson
2014	M.N. Mirnyi	Wilson	Miss H-C Chan	Wilson

Players who have played 100 or more Championship Matches

Gentlemen

NAME, COUNTRY, YEAR	TOTAL	SINGLES		DOUBLES		MIXED	
		Won	Lost	Won	Lost	Won	Lost
J.R. Borotra (FRA) 1922–1939, 1948–1964	223	55	10	59	31	40	28
R.A.J. Hewitt (AUS/RSA) 1959–1972, 1974–1979, 1983, 1986	185	34	19	68	15	33	16
J. Brugnon (FRA) 1920, 1922–1939, 1948	180	37	19	69	16	23	16
F.D. McMillan (RSA) 1961–1972, 1974–1986	173	9	17	53	19	57	18
N.A. Fraser (AUS) 1954–1962, 1965, 1972–1977	164	38	13	50	13	37	13
R.S. Emerson (AUS) 1954, 1956, 1957, 1959–1971	160	60	14	60	12	10	4
T.A. Woodbridge (AUS) 1987–2005	158	18	13	73	8	32	14
A.W. Gore (BRI/GBR) 1888–1922, 1924–1927	155	64	26	33	27	2	3
F.S. Stolle (AUS) 1960–1966, 1968–1971, 1978–1980, 1983	149	31	12	40	10	46	10
J.D. Newcombe (AUS) 1961–1971, 1974, 1976–1986	146	45	11	52	14	14	10
M.J.G. Ritchie (BRI/GBR) 1897–1912, 1914, 1919–1924, 1926	143	62	24	37	20	0	0
A.D. Roche (AUS) 1963–1971, 1974–1976, 1978, 1981–1983, 1985	140	32	13	42	10	33	10
M.C. Riessen (USA) 1961, 1964–1971, 1974–1982, 1984, 1985	138	25	16	36	18	31	12
J.P. McEnroe (USA) 1977–1985, 1988–1992, 1999	136	59	11	51	6	7	2
R.D. Ralston (USA) 1960–1966. 1968–1971, 1974, 1977–1984, 1986, 1987	135	29	13	35	14	31	13
R.N. Howe (AUS) 1954–1971	133	18	17	23	17	43	15
M.R. Woodforde (AUS) 1986–2000	133	18	15	59	8	24	9
J.L. Bjorkman (SWE) 1993–2008	129	28	15	49	12	18	7
G.P. Mulloy (USA) 1948–1963, 1965–1970, 1973	128	31	18	37	18	13	11
H.R. Barrett (BRI/GBR) 1898–1902, 1907–1914, 1919–1924, 1926, 1927	125	39	14	43	18	6	5
J.B. Fitzgerald (AUS) 1979–1995	125	17	15	34	14	33	12

NAME, COUNTRY, YEAR	TOTAL	SINGLES		DOUBLES		MIXED	
		Won	Lost	Won	Lost	Won	Lost
G.L. Paish (GBR)	124	11	17	25	19	33	19
1946–1964							
S.R. Smith (USA)	124	45	17	40	17	3	2
1965–1972, 1974–1983							
L.A. Paes (IND)	122	1	5	41	19	41	15
1993, 1994, 1996–1999, 2001–2014							
J.S. Connors (USA)	123	84	18	12	4	4	1
1972–1989, 1991, 1992							
R.C. Bryan (USA)	123	1	1	63	13	33	12
1999–2014							
R. Lycett (BRI/GBR)	122	24	10	39	8	34	7
1919–1929							
D.M. Nestor (CAN)	124	6	7	57	18	25	11
1994–2004, 2006–2014							
R.K. Wilson (GBR)	120	42	19	28	20	4	7
1952–1977							
K.N. Fletcher (AUS)	120	21	10	33	10	40	6
1959, 1961–1969, 1971–1973							
O.K. Davidson (AUS)	120	18	11	23	13	40	15
1962, 1963, 1965–1971, 1973, 1974,							
1979, 1980, 1982–1987							
T.M. Mavrogordato (BRI/GBR)	119	37	21	22	20	10	9
1904–1914, 1919–1928							
H.J. Cochet (FRA)	119	43	8	33	6	21	8
1922, 1925–1933							
J.E. Patty (USA)	119	44	14	39	12	8	2
1946–1961							
T.S. Okker (NED)	118	40	16	29	16	8	9
1964–1971, 1974–1982							
R.G. Laver (AUS)	117	50	7	33	10	15	2
1956, 1958–1962, 1968–1971, 1977							
J. Drobny (TCH/BOM/EGY/GBR)	116	50	16	26	8	11	5
1938, 1939, 1946–1960, 1971							
K.R. Rosewall (AUS)	115	47	11	41	8	6	2
1952–1956, 1968–1971, 1974, 1975							
G.P. Hughes (GBR)	114	22	12	40	13	16	11
1926–1939							
R. Taylor (GBR)	114	28	20	24	16	14	12
1959–1971, 1973–1980							
H.W. Austin (GBR)	113	56	13	14	5	16	9
1926–1939							
M.S. Knowles (BAH)	112	4	5	47	22	20	14
1992–2013							
R.D. Leach (USA)	111	0	2	40	19	33	17
1986–2005							
M.C. Bryan (USA)	111	0	0	63	13	22	13
1999–2014							
A.A. Segal (RSA)	107	24	17	25	19	10	12
1951, 1954–1972							
A. Metreveli (URS)	107	32	13	12	13	27	10
1963–1976							
E.V. Seixas (USA)	103	31	8	24	11	26	3
1950, 1952–1957, 1967, 1969, 1972, 1973							
L.A. Hoad (AUS)	102	32	7	36	8	15	4
1952–1957, 1968, 1970, 1972, 1974, 1976							

NAME, COUNTRY, YEAR	TOTAL	SINGLES		DOUBLES		MIXED	
		Won	Lost	Won	Lost	Won	Lost
N. Pietrangeli (ITA) 1954–1970, 1972–1974	102	29	18	30	17	4	4
E.C. Drysdale (RSA) 1962–1971, 1974, 1976, 1977, 1979, 1980	101	28	15	32	15	7	4
I. Nastase (ROM) 1966, 1967, 1969–1978, 1980–1982	101	35	15	23	9	17	2

45 PLAYERS

Note: Walkovers, won or lost, are not included

Ladies

NAME, COUNTRY, YEAR	TOTAL	SINGLES		DOUBLES		MIXED	
		Won	Lost	Won	Lost	Won	Lost
Miss M. Navratilova (TCH/USA) 1973–1996, 2000– 2006	325	120	14	100	21	55	15
Miss B.J. Moffitt/Mrs. L.W. King (USA) 1961–1980, 1982, 1983	265	95	15	74	12	55	14
Miss E.M. Ryan (USA) 1912–1914, 1919–1930, 1932–1934	218	47	15	73	4	70	9
Miss S.V. Wade (GBR) 1962–1987	212	64	23	53	24	24	24
Miss R. Casals (USA) 1966–1977, 1979–1985, 1988, 1989	193	48	18	57	15	40	15
Miss C.M. Evert/Mrs. J.M. Lloyd (Mrs. A.R. Mill) (USA) 1972–1989	174	96	15	37	15	7	4
Miss L.M. Raymond (USA) 1993–2014	168	24	14	57	20	37	16
Miss F.G. Durr (Mrs B.J. Browning) (FRA) 1963–1979	164	35	17	51	17	29	15
Miss B.F. Stove (NED) 1964–1967, 1969–1986	164	27	17	42	16	45	17
Miss M. Smith/Mrs. B.M. Court (AUS) 1961–1966, 1968–1971, 1973, 1975	161	51	9	41	9	47	4
Miss A.S. Haydon/Mrs. P.F. Jones (GBR) 1956–1969, 1977	157	57	13	33	15	29	10
Miss L.I. Savchenko/Mrs. A. Neiland (URS/LAT) 1983–2000	157	20	16	61	16	33	11
Miss A.L. Brough (USA) 1946–1952, 1954–1957	155	56	7	39	4	44	5
Miss H. Sukova (TCH/CZE) 1982–1998, 2006	155	39	17	53	12	25	9
Miss W.M. Turnbull (AUS) 1972–1990	153	29	18	44	16	33	13
Miss P.H. Shriver (USA) 1978–1989, 1991–1997	150	40	16	64	13	12	5
Miss K. McKane/Mrs. L.A. Godfree (BRI/GBR) 1919–1927, 1930–1934	146	38	11	33	12	40	12
Miss D.J. Hart (USA) 1946–1948, 1950–1955, 1968	145	43	8	36	6	47	5

NAME, COUNTRY, YEAR	TOTAL	SINGLES		DOUBLES		MIXED	
		Won	Lost	Won	Lost	Won	Lost
Miss J. Novotna (TCH/CZE) 1986–1999	144	50	13	56	8	14	3
Miss V.E.S Williams (USA) 1997–2012, 2014	144	73	12	39	3	12	5
Mrs. R. Mathieu (FRA) 1926, 1927, 1929–1939, 1946, 1947	142	46	14	35	12	21	14
Miss J.A.M. Tegart/Mrs. D.E. Dalton (AUS) 1962–1972, 1975, 1977, 1978, 1984, 1985	141	32	12	37	12	32	16
Miss N.M. Zvereva (URS/CIS/BLR) 1987–2000, 2002	141	31	15	66	10	13	6
Miss L.M. McNeill (USA) 1984–2002	138	26	15	36	18	28	15
Miss M.E.A. Bueno (BRA) 1958–1960, 1962–1968, 1976, 1977, 1980	137	50	9	37	4	29	8
Miss S.J. Williams (USA) 1998, 2000–2005, 2007–2013	130	72	10	39	3	6	0
Miss E.H. Harvey (BRI/GBR) 1920, 1922–1939, 1946–1948	129	15	18	34	21	21	20
Miss E.M. Sayers/Mrs. P.D. Smylie (AUS) 1981–1994, 1996, 1997	127	15	13	38	14	36	11
Miss A.I.M. Sanchez Vicario (Mrs. J. Vehils) (ESP) 1987–2001, 2004	126	41	15	39	15	8	8
Miss B.M. Nuthall (GBR) 1926–1934, 1936–1939, 1946	125	27	13	28	14	29	14
Miss M.E. Osborne/Mrs. W. du Pont (USA) 1946–1951, 1954, 1958, 1962	125	34	8	38	4	33	8
Miss L.A. Davenport (Mrs J. Leach) (USA) 1993–2001, 2003–2005, 2008, 2010	124	49	11	25	7	24	8
Miss K.E. Stammers/Mrs. M. Menzies (GBR) 1931–1939, 1946–1949	122	32	11	34	10	23	12
Miss Z.L. Garrison/Mrs. W.L. Jackson (USA) 1982–1986, 1988–1995	122	38	13	29	12	22	8
Miss R.P. Stubbs (AUS) 1990–1996, 1998–2011	119	2	7	54	19	19	18
Miss K.A. Melville/Mrs. G.E. Reid (AUS) 1966–1979	116	38	14	32	9	13	10
Miss D.K. Douglass/Mrs. R.L. Chambers (BRI/GBR) 1900–1908, 1910, 1911, 1913, 1914, 1919–1927	115	32	8	29	11	24	11
Miss P.H. Carr/Mrs. C.R. Satterthwaite (BRI/GBR) 1911–1914, 1919–1925, 1927–1935	114	33	19	16	15	15	16
Miss R.D. Fairbank/Mrs. R. Nideffer (RSA/USA) 1980–1993, 1995–1997	114	25	15	26	16	20	12
Miss E.F. Goolagong/Mrs. R.A. Cawley (AUS) 1970–1976, 1978–1980, 1982, 1983	113	49	9	21	7	19	8

NAME, COUNTRY, YEAR	TOTAL	SINGLES		DOUBLES		MIXED	
		Won	Lost	Won	Lost	Won	Lost
Miss J.M. Durie (GBR) 1977–1988, 1990–1995	113	18	18	19	17	28	13
Miss B.C. Fernandez (USA) 1984–1997	113	21	13	53	9	12	5
Miss C.C. Black (ZIM) 1998–2011, 2013, 2014	113	7	9	43	13	27	14
Miss W.A. James/Mrs. S.H. Hammersley (GBR) 1930–1939, 1946, 1949–1955	112	21	13	30	14	18	16
Miss W.G. Ramsey/Mrs. A.E. Beamish (BRI/GBR) 1910–1914, 1919–1933	111	23	18	24	17	16	13
Miss F.A.M. Mortimer/Mrs. J.E. Barrett (GBR) 1950–1968	111	36	11	35	18	5	6
Miss A. Sugiyama (JPN) 1993–2009	111	25	17	36	15	11	7
Miss S.M. Graf (GER) 1984, 1985, 1987–1996, 1998, 1999	110	74	7	14	6	7	2
Miss L. Horn/Mrs A. Huber (RSA/USA) 1995, 1997–2014	110	0	0	50	17	26	17
Miss D.A. Shepherd/Mrs. W.P. Barron (BRI/GBR) 1920, 1921, 1923, 1924, 1926, 1928, 1929, 1931–1935, 1937–1939	109	16	12	26	14	27	14
Miss H.H. Jacobs (USA) 1928–1939	109	55	11	18	8	10	7
Miss D.E. Round/Mrs. D.L. Little (GBR) 1928–1939	107	35	9	19	10	27	7
Miss C.C. Truman/Mrs. G.T. Janes (GBR) 1957–1963, 1965, 1967–1969, 1971, 1973, 1974	107	34	14	16	13	16	14
Miss P.E. Mudford/Mrs M.R. King (GBR) 1928–1939, 1947, 1949, 1950, 1953	107	27	16	28	11	13	12
Miss K. Jordan (USA) 1979–1987, 1990, 1991	106	21	10	39	9	21	6
Miss N. Tauziat (FRA) 1985–2002	106	40	16	29	18	2	1
Miss L.R. Turner/Mrs. W.W. Bowrey (AUS) 1961–1965, 1967–1969, 1971, 1978	103	29	10	21	9	27	7
Miss S.J. Fry (USA) 1948–1954, 1956	102	34	7	31	4	21	5
Miss E. Likhovtseva 1999–2007	102	23	14	23	13	19	10
Miss H.E. Nagelsen/Mrs. M.H. McCormack (USA) 1974–1996	101	14	18	19	19	19	12
Miss D.R. Hard (USA) 1955–1957, 1959, 1960, 1962, 1963	100	29	7	27	2	31	4

54 PLAYERS

Note: Walkovers, won or lost, are not included.

Players who have played 50 or more Championship Singles Matches

Gentlemen

NAME, COUNTRY, YEAR	TOTAL	Won	Lost
J.S. Connors (USA) (1982–1989, 1991, 1992)	102	84	18
A.W. Gore (BRI) (1888–1894, 1896–1914, 1919–1922)	90	64	26
M.J.G. Ritchie (BRI/GBR) (1897–1912, 1914, 1919–1924, 1926)	86	62	24
B.F. Becker (GER) (1984–1997, 1999)	83	71	12
R.S. Emerson (AUS) (1956, 1957, 1959–1971)	74	60	14
R. Federer (SUI) (1999–2014)	82	73	9
P. Sampras (USA) (1989–2002)	70	63	7
J.P. McEnroe (USA) (1977–1985, 1988–1992)	70	59	11
W.H. Austin (GBR) (1926, 1928–1939)	69	56	13
J. Drobny (TCH/BOM/EGY/GBR) (1938, 1939, 1946–1960)	66	50	16
J.R. Borotra (FRA) (1922–1932, 1935)	65	55	10
G.S. Ivanisevic (YUG/CRO) (1988–2002, 2004)	63	49	14
S.R. Smith (USA) (1965–1972, 1974–1983)	62	45	17
I. Lendl (TCH) (1979–1981, 1983–1995)	62	48	14
R.K. Wilson (GBR) (1952–1970)	61	42	19
S.B. Edberg (SWE) (1983–1996)	61	49	12
A.K. Agassi (USA) (1987, 1991–1996. 1998–2003)	59	46	13
K.R. Rosewall (AUS) (1952–1956, 1968–1971, 1974, 1975)	58	47	11
J.E. Patty (USA) (1946–1960)	58	44	14

Ladies

NAME, COUNTRY, YEAR	TOTAL	Won	Lost
Miss M. Navratilova (TCH/USA) (1973–1994, 2004)	134	120	14
Miss C.M. Evert/Mrs J.M. Lloyd (USA) (1972–1989)	111	96	15
Miss B.J. Moffitt/Mrs L.A. King (USA) (1961–1975, 1977–1980, 1982, 1983)	110	95	15
Miss S.V. Wade (GBR) (1962–1985)	87	64	23
Miss V.E.S. Williams (USA) (1997–2013)	86	74	12
Miss S.M. Graf (GER) (1984, 1985, 1987–1996, 1998, 1999)	81	74	7
Miss S.J. Williams (USA) (1998, 2000–2005, 2007–2012)	75	61	8
Miss A.S. Haydon/Mrs P.F. Jones (GBR) (1956–1969)	70	57	13
Miss H.H. Jacobs (USA) (1928–1929)	66	55	11
Miss B. Bingley/Mrs G.W. Hillyard (BRI) (1884–1889, 1891–1894, 1897, 1899–1902, 1904–1910, 1912, 1913)	66	48	18
Miss R. Casals (USA) (1966–1977, 1979–1984)	66	48	18
Miss J. Novotna (TCH/CZE) (1986–1999)	63	50	13
Miss L.A. Brough (USA) (1946–1952)	63	56	7
Miss E.M. Ryan (USA) (1912–1914, 1919–1930, 1932)	62	47	15
Mrs R. Mathieu (FRA) (1926, 1927, 1929–1939, 1946)	60	46	14
Miss L.A. Davenport/Mrs J. Leach (USA) (1993–2001, 2003–2005, 2008)	60	49	11
Miss M. Smith/Mrs B.M. Court (AUS) (1961–1966, 1968–1971, 1973, 1975)	60	51	9
Miss M.E.A. Bueno (BRA) (1958–1960, 1962–1968, 1976, 1977)	59	50	9

NAME, COUNTRY, YEAR	TOTAL	Won	Lost	NAME, COUNTRY, YEAR	TOTAL	Won	Lost
T. M. Mavrogordato (BRI/GBR) (1904–1914, 1919–1928)	58	37	21	Miss E. Goolagong/Mrs R. Cawley (AUS) (1970–1976, 1978–1980, 1982)	58	49	9
R.G. Laver (AUS) (1956, 1958–1962, 1968–1971, 1977)	57	50	7	Miss N. Tauziat (FRA) (1986–2007)	56	40	16
T.H. Henman (GBR) (1994–2007)	57	43	14	Miss H. Sukova (TCH/CZE) (1982–1998)	56	39	17
T.S. Okker (NED) (1964–1971, 1974–1981)	56	40	16	Miss C.R. Cooper/Mrs A. Sterry (BRI) 1893–1902, 1904, 1906–1908. 1912–1914, 1919)	56	43	13
J.D. Newcombe (AUS) (1969–1971, 1974, 1976, 1978)	56	45	11	Miss P.M. Shriver (USA) (1978–1989, 1991–1992, 1994–1996)	56	40	16
J. Brugnon (FRA) 1920, 1922–1939	56	37	19	Miss A. Sanchez Vicario (ESP) (1987–2001)	56	41	15
L.G. Hewitt (AUS) (1999–2014)	56	41	15	Miss H.N. Wills/Mrs F.S. Moody (USA) (1924, 1927–1930, 1932–1933, 1935, 1938)	56	55	1
B.R. Borg (SWE) (1973–1981)	55	51	4	Miss G.S. Sabatini (ARG) (1985–1995)	53	42	11
R.J. Hewitt (AUS) (1959–1972, 1974–1978)	53	34	19	Miss P.H. Satterthwaite (BRI/GBR) (1911–1914, 1919–1925, 1927–1934)	52	33	19
H.R. Barrett (BRI) (1898–1902, 1908–1914, 1919, 1921)	53	39	14	Miss K.A. Melville/Mrs G.E.Reid (AUS) (1966–1979)	52	38	14
A.S. Roddick (USA) (2001–2012)	53	41	12	Miss F. Durr (FRA) (1963–1979)	52	35	17
N.A. Fraser (AUS) (1954–1962, 1965, 1972–1975	51	38	13	Miss I.C. Martinez (ESP) (1992–2005)	51	38	13
H.J. Cochet (FRA) (1922, 1925–1933)	51	43	8	Miss M. Sharapova (RUS) (2003–2014)	52	41	11
S.H. Smith (BRI) (1893, 1897–1906)	50	39	11	Miss D.J. Hart (USA) (1946–1948, 1950–1955)	51	43	8
I. Nastase (ROM) (1966–1967, 1969–1978, 1980–1982	50	35	15	Miss Z.L. Garrison (USA) (1982–1986, 1988–1995)	51	38	13

The Champions

GENTLEMEN

Name	Date of Birth	Place of Birth	Date of Death	Place of Death	Event and year
AGASSI, Andre Kirk	29 Apr 1970	Las Vegas, Nevada, USA			S 1992
ALLISON, Wilmer Lawson	8 Dec 1904	San Antonio, Texas, USA	20 Apr 1977	Austin, Texas, USA	D 1929, 1930
ANDERSON, James Outram	17 Sep 1895	Enfield, N.S.W., Australia	22 Dec 1973	Sydney, N.S.W., Australia	D 1922
ASHE, Arthur Robert	10 Jul 1943	Richmond, Virginia, USA	6 Feb 1993	New York, New York, USA	S 1975
AUSTIN, John Reed	31 Jul 1957	Los Angeles, California, USA			M 1980
BADDELEY, Herbert	11 Jan 1872	Bromley, Kent, England	20 Jul 1931	Cannes, France	D 1891, 1894, 1895, 1896
BADDELEY, Wilfred	11 Jan 1872	Bromley, Kent, England	24 Jan 1929	Mentone, France	S 1891, 1892, 1895, D 1891, 1894, 1895, 1896
BARLOW, Harry Sibthorpe	5 Apr 1860	Hammersmith, Middlesex, England	16 Jul 1917	Kennington, London, England	D 1892
BARRETT, Herbert Roper	24 Nov 1873	Upton, Essex, England	27 Jul 1943	Horsham, Sussex, England	D 1909, 1912, 1913
BATES, Michael Jeremy	19 Jun 1962	Solihull, Birmingham, England			M 1987
BECKER, Boris Franz	22 Nov 1967	Leimen, West Germany			S 1985, 1986, 1989
BHUPATHI, Mahesh Shrinivas	7 Jun 1974	Madras, India			D 1999, M 2002, 2005
BJORKMAN, Jonas Lars	23 Mar 1972	Vaxjo, Sweden			D 2002, 2003, 2004
BLACK, Wayne Hamilton	14 Nov 1973	Harare, Zimbabwe			M 2004
BORG, Bjorn Rune	6 Jun 1956	Stockholm, Sweden			S 1976, 1977, 1978, 1979, 1980
BOROTRA, Jean Robert	13 Aug 1898	Arbonne, Basses-Pyrenees, France	17 Jul 1994	Arbonne, Basses-Pyrenees, France	S 1924, 1926, D 1925, 1932, 1933, M 1925
BOWES-LYON, Hon. Patrick	5 Mar 1863	Belgravia, Middlesex, England	5 Oct 1946	Westerham, Kent, England	D 1887
BROMWICH, John Edward	14 Nov 1918	Sydney, N.S.W., Australia	21 Oct 1999	Geelong, Victoria, Australia	D 1948, 1950, M 1947, 1948
BROOKES, Norman Everard	14 Nov 1877	Melbourne, Victoria, Australia	28 Sep 1968	Melbourne, Victoria, Australia	S 1907, 1914, D 1907, 1914
BROWN, Thomas Pollock	26 Sep 1922	Washington, D.C., USA	27 Oct 2011	Castro Valley, California, USA	D 1946, M 1946
BRUGNON, Jacques	11 May 1895	Paris, France	20 Mar 1978	Paris, France	D 1926, 1928, 1932, 1933
BRYAN, Michael Carl	29 Apr 1978	Camarillo California, USA			D 2006, 2011, 2013, M 2012
BRYAN, Robert Charles	29 Apr 1978	Camarillo California, USA			D 2006, 2011, 2013, M 2008
BUDGE, John Donald	13 Jun 1915	Oakland, California, USA	20 Jan 2000	Scranton, Pennsylvania, USA	S 1937, 1938, D 1937, 1938, M 1937, 1938
CASE, Ross Llewellyn	1 Nov 1951	Toowoomba, Queensland, Australia			D 1977
CLEMENT, Arnaud Marcel Maurice	17 Dec 1977	Aix-en-Provence, France			D 2007
CASH, Patrick Hart	27 May 1965	Melbourne, Victoria, Australia			S 1987
COCHET, Henri Jean	14 Dec 1901	Villeurbanne, Nr Lyon, France	1 Apr 1987	Paris, France	S 1927, 1929, D 1926, 1928

Name	Date of Birth	Place of Birth	Date of Death	Place of Death	Event and year
CONNORS, James Scott	2 Sep 1952	East St. Louis, Illinois, USA			S 1974, 1982, D 1973
COOKE, Elwood Thomas	5 Jul 1913	Ogden, Utah, USA			D 1939
COOPER, Ashley John	15 Sep 1936	Melbourne, Victoria, Australia			S 1958
CRAWFORD, John Herbert	22 Mar 1908	Albury, N.S.W., Australia			S 1933, D 1935, M 1930
CRISP, Hope	6 Feb 1884	Highgate, Middlesex, England			M1913
CURREN, Kevin Melvyn	2 Mar 1958	Durban, Natal, South Africa			M 1982
DAVIDSON, Owen Keir	4 Oct 1943	Melbourne, Victoria, Australia			M 1967, 1971, 1973, 1974
DAVIDSON, Sven Viktor	13 Jul 1928	Boras, Sweden	28 May 2008	Arcadia, California, USA	D 1958
DECUGIS, Maxime Omer	24 Sep 1882	Paris, France	6 Sep 1978	Biot, France	D 1911
DIXON, Charles Percy	7 Feb 1873	Grantham, Lincolnshire, England	29 Apr 1939	West Norwood, London, England	D 1912, 1913
DJOKOVIC, Novak	22 May 1987	Belgrade, Yugoslavia			S 2011, 2014
DOHERTY, Hugh Laurence	8 Oct 1875	Wimbledon, Surrey, England	21 Aug 1919	Broadstairs, Kent, England	S 1902, 1903, 1904, 1905, 1906 D 1897, 1898, 1899, 1900, 1901, 1903, 1904, 1905
DOHERTY, Reginald Frank	14 Oct 1872	Wimbledon, Surrey, England	29 Dec 1910	Kensington, London, England	S 1897, 1898, 1899, 1900 D 1897, 1898, 1899, 1900, 1901, 1903, 1904, 1905
DROBNY, Jaroslav	12 Oct 1921	Prague, Czechoslovakia	13 Sep 2001	Tooting, London, England	S 1954
EDBERG, Stefan Bengt	19 Jan 1966	Vastervik, Sweden			S 1988, 1990
ELTINGH, Jacco Folkert	29 Aug 1970	Heerde, The Netherlands			D 1998
EMERSON, Roy Stanley	3 Nov 1936	Blackbutt, Queensland, Australia			S 1964, 1965, D 1959, 1961, 1971
FALKENBURG, Robert	29 Jan 1926	New York, New York, USA			S 1948, D 1947
FEDERER, Roger	8 Aug 1981	Basle, Switzerland			S 2003, 2004, 2005, 2006, 2007, 2009, 2012
FITZGERALD, John Basil	28 Dec 1960	Cummins, S.A., Australia			D 1989, 1991, M 1991
FLACH, Kenneth Eliot	24 May 1963	St. Louis, Missouri, USA			D 1987, 1988, M 1986
FLEMING, Peter Blair	21 Jan 1955	Chatham, New Jersey, USA			D 1979, 1981, 1983, 1984
FLETCHER, Kenneth Norman	15 Jun 1940	Brisbane, Queensland, Australia	11 Feb 2006	Brisbane, Queensland, Australia	D 1966, M 1963, 1965, 1966, 1968
FRASER, Neale Andrew	3 Oct 1933	Melbourne, Victoria, Australia			S 1960, D 1959, 1961, M 1962
FRIEDL, Leos	1 Jan 1977	Jindrichov Hrade, Czechoslovakia			M 2001
GARLAND, Charles Stedman	29 Oct 1898	Pittsburgh, Pennsylvania, USA	28 Jan 1971	Baltimore, Maryland, USA	D 1920
GERULAITIS, Vitas Kevin	26 Jul 1954	New York, New York, USA	18 Sep 1994	Southampton, New York, USA	D 1975
GILBERT, John Brian	17 Jul 1887	Barnes, Surrey, England	28 Jun 1974	Roehampton, London, England	M 1924
GOBERT, Andre Henri	30 Sep 1890	Paris, France	6 Dec 1951	Paris, France	D 1911
GODFREE, Leslie Allison	27 Apr 1885	Brighton, Sussex, England	17 Nov 1971	East Sheen, London, England	D 1923, M 1926
GONZALES, Richard Alonzo (Pancho†)	9 May 1928	Los Angeles, California, USA	3 Jul 1995	Las Vegas, Nevada, USA	D 1949
GORE, Arthur William Charles (Wentworth†)	2 Jan 1868	Lyndhurst, Hampshire, England	1 Dec 1928	Kensington, London, England	S 1901, 1908, 1909, D 1909

Name	Date of Birth	Place of Birth	Date of Death	Place of Death	Event and year
GORE, Spencer William	10 Mar 1850	Wimbledon, Surrey, England	19 Apr 1906	Ramsgate, Kent, England	S 1877
GOTTFRIED, Brian Edward	27 Jan 1952	Baltimore, Maryland, USA			D 1976
GUENTHARDT, Heinz Peter	8 Feb 1959	Zurich, Switzerland			D 1985
HAARHUIS, Paul Vincent Nicholas	19 Feb 1966	Eindhoven, The Netherlands			D 1998
HADOW, Patrick Francis	24 Jan 1855	Regents Park, Middlesex, England	29 Jun 1946	Bridgwater, Somerset, England	S 1878
HAMILTON, Willoby (Willoughby James†)	9 Dec 1864	Monasterevan, Co. Kildare, Ireland	27 Sep 1943	Dundrum, Dublin, Ireland	S 1890
HARTLEY, John Thorneycroft	9 Jan 1849	Wolverhampton, Staffordshire, England	21 Aug 1935	Knaresborough, Yorkshire, England	S 1879, 1880
HARTWIG, Rex Noel	2 Sep 1929	Culcain, N.S.W., Australia			D 1954, 1955
HEWITT, Lleyton Glynn	24 Feb 1981	Adelaide, S.A. Australia			S 2002
HEWITT, Robert Anthony John	12 Jan 1940	Sydney, N.S.W., Australia			D 1962, 1964, 1967, 1972 1978, M 1977, 1979
HOAD, Lewis Alan	23 Nov 1934	Glebe, N.S.W., Australia	3 July 1994	Fuengirola, Spain	S 1956, 1957, D 1953, 1955, 1956
HOWE, Robert Neville	3 Aug 1925	Sydney, N.S.W., Australia	30 Nov 2004	Santa Ana, California, USA	M 1958
HUGHES, George Patrick	21 Dec 1902	Sutton Coldfield, Warwickshire, England	8 May 1997	Chertsey, Surrey, England	D 1936
HUNTER, Francis Townsend	28 Jun 1894	New York, New York, USA	2 Dec 1981	Palm Beach, Florida, USA	D 1924, 1927, M 1927, 1929
HUSS, Stephen Walter Ivar	10 Dec 1975	Bendigo, NSW, Australia			D 2005
IVANISEVIC, Goran Simun	13 Sep 1971	Split, Yugoslavia			S 2001
JARRYD, Anders Pierre	13 Jul 1961	Lidkoping, Sweden			D 1989, 1991
JOHNSON, Donald James	9 Sep 1968	Bethlehem, Pennsylvania, USA			D 2001, M2000
JOHNSTON, William (M.†)	2 Nov 1894	San Francisco, California, USA	1 May 1946	San Francisco, California, USA	S 1923
KNOWLES, Mark Samuel	4 Sep 1971	Nassau, Bahamas			M 2009
KODES, Jan	1 Mar 1946	Prague, Czechoslovakia			S 1973
KRAJICEK, Richard Peter Stanislav	6 Dec 1971	Rotterdam, Netherlands			S 1996
KRAMER, John Albert	1 Aug 1921	Las Vegas, Nevada, USA	12 Sep 2009	Los Angeles, California, USA	S 1947, D 1946, 1947
LACOSTE, Jean Rene	2 Jul 1904	Paris, France	12 Oct 1996	St. Jean de Luz, France	S 1925, 1928, D 1925
LAVER, Rodney George	9 Aug 1938	Rockhampton, Queensland, Australia			S 1961, 1962, 1968, 1969, D 1971, M 1959, 1960
LAWFORD, Herbert Fortescue	15 May 1851	Bayswater, Middlesex, England	20 Apr 1925	Dess, Aberdeenshire, Scotland	S 1887
LEACH, Ricard David	28 Dec 1964	Arcadia, California, USA			D 1990, M 1990
LEWIS, Ernest Wool	5 Apr 1867	Hammersmith, Middlesex, England	19 Apr 1930	Plymouth, Devon, England	S 1892
LLODRA, Michael	18 May 1980	Paris, France			D2007
LLOYD, John Michael	27 Aug 1954	Leigh-on-Sea, Essex, England			M 1983, 1984
LOTT, George Martin	16 Oct 1906	Springfield, Illinois, USA	2 Dec 1991	Chicago, Illinois, USA	D 1931, 1934, M 1931

Name	Date of Birth	Place of Birth	Date of Death	Place of Death	Event and year
LYCETT, Randolph	27 Aug 1886	Birmingham, England	9 Feb 1935	Jersey, Channel Islands	D 1921, 1922, 1923, M 1919, 1921, 1923
McENROE, John Patrick	16 Feb 1959	Wiesbaden, West Germany			S 1981, 1983, 1984, D 1979, 1981, 1983, 1984, 1992
McGREGOR, Kenneth Bruce	2 June 1929	Adelaide, S.A. Australia	1 Dec 2007	Adelaide, S A, Australia	D 1951, 1952
McKINLEY, Charles Robert	5 Jan 1941	St. Louis, Missouri, USA	11 Aug 1986	Dallas, Texas, USA	S 1963
McMILLAN, Frew Donald	20 May 1942	Springs, Transvaal, South Africa			D 1967, 1972, 1978, M 1978, 1981
McNAMARA, Peter Bernard	5 Jul 1955	Melbourne, Victoria, Australia			D 1980, 1982
McNAMEE, Paul Francis	12 Nov 1954	Melbourne, Victoria, Australia			D 1980, 1982, M 1985
MAHONY, Harold Segerson	13 Feb 1867	Edinburgh, Scotland	27 Jun 1905	Caragh Hill, Nr. Killorglin, Co. Kerry, Ireland	S 1896
MAIER, Enrique Gerardo	31 Dec 1910	Barcelona, Spain	22 Aug 1981	Madrid, Spain	M 1932
MAKO, Constantine Eugene	24 Jan 1916	Budapest, Hungary	14 Jun 2013	Los Angeles, California, USA	D 1937, 1938
MARRAY, Jonathan Francis	10 Mar 1981	Liverpool, England			D 2012
MASTERS, Geoffrey	19 Sep 1950	Brisbane, Queensland, Australia			D 1977
MAYER, Alexander	5 Apr 1952	New York, New York, USA			D 1975
MELZER, Jurgen	22 Mar 1981	Vienno, Austria			D 2010, M 2011
MIKI, Tatsuyoshi (Ryuki†)	11 Feb 1904	Takamatsu, Japan	9 Jan 1967	Tokyo, Japan	M 1934
MIRNYI, Maxim Nikolaevich	6 July 1977	Minsk, U.S.S.R.			M1998
MOODIE, Wesley Arthur	14 Feb 1979	Durban, Natal, South Africa			D 2005
MULLOY, Gardnar Putnam	22 Nov 1913	Washington, D.C., USA			D 1957
MURRAY, Andrew Barron	15 May 1987	Glasgow, Scotland			S 2013
MURRAY, Jamie Robert	13 Feb 1986	Glasgow, Scotland			M 2007
NADAL, Rafael	3 June 1986	Manacor, Mallorca			S 2008, 2010
NASTASE, Ilie	19 Jul 1946	Bucharest, Romania			D 1973, M 1970, 1972
NESTOR, Daniel Mark	4 Sep 1972	Belgrade, Yugoslavia			D 2008, 2009, M 2013
NEWCOMBE, John David	23 May 1944	Sydney, N.S.W., Australia			S 1967, 1970, 1971, D 1965, 1966, 1968, 1969, 1970, 1974
NIELSEN, Frederik Loechte	27 Aug 1983	Kyngby, Denmark			D 2012
NYSTROM, Karl Joakim	20 Feb 1963	Skellefrea, Sweden			D 1986
O'HARA WOOD, Hector	30 Apr 1891	Melbourne, Victoria, Australia	3 Dec 1961	Melbourne, Victoria, Australia	D 1919, M1922
OLMEDO, Alejandro Rodriguez	24 Mar 1936	Arequipa, Peru			S 1959
OSUNA, Rafael Herrera	15 Sep 1938	Mexico City, Mexico	4 Jun 1969	Nr. Monterrey, Mexico	D 1960, 1963
PAES, Leander Adrian	17 Jun 1973	Calcutta, India			D 1999, M 1999, 2003, 2010
PALAFOX, Antonio	28 Apr 1936	Guadalajara, Mexico			D 1963
PALMER, Jared Eiseley	2 July 1971	New York, New York, USA			D 2001
PARKE, James Cecil	26 Jul 1881	Clones, Co. Monaghan, Ireland	27 Feb 1946	Llandudno, North Wales	M 1914
PARKER, Frank Andrew	31 Jan 1916	Milwaukee, Wisconsin, USA	24 Jul 1997	San Diego, California, USA	D 1949

Name	Date of Birth	Place of Birth	Date of Death	Place of Death	Event and year
PATTERSON, Gerald Leighton	17 Dec 1895	Melbourne, Victoria, Australia	13 Jun 1967	Melbourne, Victoria, Australia	S 1919, 1922, M 1920
PATTY, Jesse Edward (Budge†)	11 Feb 1924	Fort Smith, Arkansas, USA			S 1950, D 1957
PERRY, Frederick John	18 May 1909	Stockport, Cheshire, England	2 Feb 1995	Melbourne, Victoria, Australia	S 1934, 1935, 1936, M 1935, 1936
PETRA, Yvon Francois Marie	8 Mar 1916	Cholon, Indo China	12 Sep 1984	Paris, France	S 1946
PETZSCHNER, Philipp	24 Mar 1984	Bayreuth, West Germany			D 2010
PIM, Joshua	20 May 1869	Bray, Co. Wicklow, Ireland	15 Apr 1942	Dublin, Ireland	S 1893, 1894, D 1890, 1893
POSPISIL, Vasek	23 Jun 1990	Vernon, British Colombia, Canada			D 2014
PUGH, James Robert	5 Feb 1964	Burbank, California, USA			D 1990, M 1989
QUIST, Adrian Karl	23 Jan 1913	Medindie, S.A. Australia	17 Nov 1991	Sydney, N.S.W., Australia	D 1935, 1950
RALSTON, Richard Dennis	27 Jul 1942	Bakersfield, California, USA			D 1960
RAM Andres (Andy†)	10 Apr 1980	Montevideo, Uruguay			M2006
RAMIREZ, Raul Carlos	20 Jun 1953	Ensenado, Mexico			D 1976
RENSHAW, James Ernest	3 Jan 1861	Leamington, Warwickshire, England	2 Sep 1899	Waltham St. Lawrence, Twyford, Berkshire, England	S 1888, D 1884, 1885, 1886, 1888, 1889
RENSHAW, William Charles	3 Jan 1861	Leamington, Warwickshire, England	12 Aug 1904	Swanage, Dorset, England	S 1881, 1882, 1883, 1884, 1885, 1886, 1889, D 1884, 1885, 1886, 1888, 1889
RICHARDS, Vincent	20 Mar 1903	New York, New York, USA	28 Sep 1959	New York, New York, USA	D 1924
RIESSEN, Martin Claire	4 Dec 1941	Hinsdale, Illinois, USA			M 1975
RIGGS, Robert Larimore	25 Feb 1918	Los Angeles, California, USA	25 Oct 1995	Luecadia, California, USA	S 1939, D 1939, M 1939
RISELEY, Frank Lorymer	6 Jul 1877	Clifton, Bristol, England	6 Feb 1959	Torquay, Devon, England	D 1902, 1906
RITCHIE, Major Josiah George	18 Oct 1870	Westminster, Middlesex, England	28 Feb 1955	Ashford, Middlesex, England	D 1908, 1910
ROCHE, Anthony Dalton	17 May 1945	Wagga Wagga, N.S.W., Australia			D 1965, 1968, 1969, 1970, 1974, M 1976
ROSE, Mervyn Gordon	23 Jan 1930	Coffs Harbour, N.S.W., Australia			D 1954, M 1957
ROSEWALL, Kenneth Robert	2 Nov 1934	Sydney, N.S.W., Australia			D 1953, 1956
SAMPRAS, Pete	12 Aug 1971	Washington, D.C., USA			S 1993, 1994, 1995, 1997, 1998, 1999, 2000
SANTANA, Manuel Martinez	10 May 1938	Madrid, Spain			S 1966
SAVITT, Richard	4 Mar 1927	Bayonne, New Jersey, USA			S 1951
SCHMIDT, Ulf Christian Johan	12 Jul 1934	Nacka, Stockholm, Sweden			D 1958
SCHROEDER, Frederick Rudolph (Ted†)	20 Jul 1921	Newark, New Jersey, USA	26 May 2006	La Jolla, California, USA	S 1949
SEDGMAN, Francis Arthur (Frank†)	29 Oct 1927	Mount Albert, Victoria, Australia			S 1952, D 1948, 1951, 1952, M 1951, 1952
SEGUSO, Robert Arthur	1 May 1963	Minneapolis, Minnesota, USA			D 1987, 1988
SEIXAS, Elias Victor	30 Aug 1923	Philadelphia, Pennsylvania, USA			S 1953, M 1953, 1954, 1955, 1956
SMITH, Stanley Roger	14 Dec 1946	Pasadena, California, USA			S 1972

Name	Date of Birth	Place of Birth	Date of Death	Place of Death	Event and year
SMITH, Sidney Howard	3 Feb 1872	Stroud, Gloucestershire, England	27 Mar 1947	Stroud, Gloucestershire, England	D 1902, 1906
SOCK, Jack Edward	24 Sep 1992	Lincoln, Nebraska, USA			D 2014
SPENCE, Patrick Dennis Benham	11 Feb 1898	Queenstown, Cape Province, South Africa	21 Nov 1983	Johannesburg, Transvaal, South Africa	M 1928
STARK, Jonathan Alan	3 Apr 1971	Medford, Oregon, USA			M 1995
STEWART, Sherwood Earl	6 Jun 1946	Goose Creek, Texas, USA			M 1988
STICH, Michael Detlef	18 Oct 1968	Pinneberg, West Germany			S 1991, D 1992
STOEFEN, Lester Rollo	30 Mar 1911	Des Moines, Iowa, USA	8 Feb 1970	La Jolla, California, USA	D 1934
STOKER, Frank Owen	29 May 1867	Dublin, Ireland	8 Jan 1939	Dublin, Co. Dublin, Ireland	D 1890, 1893
STOLLE, Frederick Sidney	8 Oct 1938	Hornsby, N.S.W., Australia			D 1962, 1964, M 1961, 1964, 1969
STURGESS, Eric William	10 May 1920	Johannesburg, Transvaal, South Africa	14 Jan 2004	Johannesburg, Transvaal, South Africa	M 1949, 1950
SUK, Cyril	29 Jan 1967	Prague, Czechoslovakia			M 1992, 1996, 1997
TAROCZY, Balazs	9 May 1954	Budapest, Hungary			D 1985
THOMAS, Ronald Victor	7 Aug 1888	Hammond, S.A., Adelaide, Australia	30 Dec 1936	Kensington Park, S.A. Australia	D 1919
TILDEN, William Tatem	10 Feb 1893	Germantown, Pennsylvania, USA	5 Jun 1953	Los Angeles, California, USA	S 1920, 1921, 1930, D 1927
TRABERT, Marion Anthony	16 Aug 1930	Cincinnati, Ohio, USA			S 1955
TUCKEY, Charles Raymond	15 Jun 1910	Godalming, Surrey, England	15 Oct 2005	Banbury, Oxfordshire, England	D 1936
VAN RYN, John William Davys	30 Jun 1905	Newport News, Virginia, USA	7 Aug 1999	Palm Beach, Florida, USA	D 1929, 1930, 1931
VINES, Henry Ellsworth	28 Sep 1911	Los Angeles, California, USA	17 Mar 1994	La Quinta, California, USA	S 1932
von CRAMM, Gottfried Alexander Maximilian Walter Kurt	7 Jul 1909	Nettlingen, nr. Hanover, Germany	9 Nov 1976	Nr. Cairo, Egypt	M 1933
WILANDER, Mats Arne Olof	22 Aug 1964	Vaxjo, Sweden			D 1986
WILBERFORCE, Herbert William Wrangham	8 Feb 1864	Munich, Germany	28 Mar 1941	Kensington, London, England	D 1887
WILDING, Anthony Frederick	31 Oct 1883	Apawa Nr. Christchurch, New Zealand	9 May 1915	Neuve Chapelle, France	S 1910, 1911, 1912, 1913, D 1907, 1908, 1910, 1914
WILLIAMS, Richard Norris	29 Jan 1891	Geneva, Switzerland	2 Jun 1968	Bryn Mawr, Pennsylvania, USA	D 1920
WOOD, Sidney Burr Beardslee	1 Nov 1911	Black Rock, Connecticut, USA	10 Jan 2009	Palm Beach, Florida, USA	S 1931
WOODBRIDGE, Todd Andrew	2 Apr 1971	Sydney, N.S.W., Australia			D 1993, 1994, 1995, 1996, 1997 2000, 2002, 2003, 2004, M 1994
WOODFORDE, Mark Raymond	23 Sep 1965	Adelaide, S.A., Australia			D 1993, 1994, 1995, 1996, 1997 2000, M 1993
WOOSNAM, Maxwell	6 Sep 1892	Liverpool, England	14 Jul 1965	Westminster, London, England	D 1921
ZIMONJIC, Nenad	4 Jan 1976	Belgrade, Yugoslavia			D 2008, 2009, M 2014

† forenames generally used
A total of 178 Champions, 64 singles

Champions who were also Runners-up

Name	Event and year	Name	Event and year	Name	Event and year
AGASSI A.K.	S 1999	ELTINGH J.F.	D 1997, M 1992	McKINLEY C.R.	S 1961
ALLISON W.L.	S 1930, D 1935	EMERSON R.S.	D 1964, 1967	McMILLAN F.D.	M 1977, 1979
ASHE A.R.	D 1971	FEDERER R.	S 2008, 2014	McNAMEE P.F.	D 1984
AUSTIN J.R.	M 1981	FITZGERALD J.B.	D 1985, 1988, M 1985, 1990	MAHONY H.S.	S 1897
BADDELEY H.	D 1892, 1897	FLEMING P.B.	D 1978, 1982, 1986	MASTERS G.	D 1976
BADDELEY W.	S 1893, 1894, 1896, D 1892, 1897	FLETCHER K.N.	D 1964, 1965, 1967, M 1964, 1967	MIRNYI M.N.	D 2003, M 2014
BARLOW H.S.	D 1893, 1894	FRASER N.A.	S 1958, D 1955, 1957, 1958, 1973, M 1957, 1959	MOODIE W.A.	M 2010
BECKER B.F.	S 1988, 1990, 1991, 1995			MULLOY G.P.	D 1948, 1949, M 1956
BHUPATHI M.S.	M 1998, D 2003, M 2011	GOBERT A.H.	D 1912	MURRAY, A.B.	S 2012
BJORKMAN J.L.	D 2008, M 1999	GODFREE L.A.	M 1924, 1927	NADAL R.	S 2006, 2007, 2011
BORG B.R.	S 1981	GORE A.W.	S 1899, 1902, 1907, 1910, 1912, D 1908, 1910	NASTASE I.	S 1972, 1976
BOROTRA J.R.	S 1925, 1927, 1929, D 1934	GORE S.W.	S 1878	NEWCOMBE J.D.	S 1969
BOWES-LYON P.	D 1888	GOTTFRIED B.E.	D 1979	NESTOR D.M.	D 200
BROMWICH J.E.	S 1948, M 1949	GUENTHARDT H.P.	M 1986	PAES L.A.	M 2009
BROOKES N.E.	S 1905, 1919	HAARHUIS P.V.N.	D 1997, 1999, 2000	PALMER J.E.	D 1999
BROWN T.P.	S 1947, D 1948	HARTLEY J.T.	S 1881	PARKE J.C.	D 1920, M 1913
BRUGNON J.	D 1927, 1951, 1934	HARTWIG R.N.	D 1953	PATTERSON G.L.	S 1920, D 1922, 1928
BRYAN M.C	D 2005, 2009, 2014, M 2001, 2008	HEWITT L.G.	M 2000	PERRY F.J.	D 1932
		HEWITT R.A.J.	D 1961, 1965, M 1963	PETRA Y.F.M.	M 1937
BRYAN R.C.	D 2005, 2009, 2014, M 2006	HOAD L.A.	D 1957	PIM J.	S 1891, 1892, D 1891
BUDGE J.D.	M 1936	HOWE R.N.	M 1960, 1961	PUGH J.R.	D 1989, M 1991
CASE R.L.	D 1976	HUGHES G.P.	D 1932, 1937	RALSTON R.D.	S 1966, D 1971, M 1962, 1966
CASH P.H.	D 1984, 1985	HUNTER F.T.	S 1923	RAM A	M 2003
COCHET H.J.	S 1928, D 1927, 1931	IVANISEVIC G.	S 1992, 1994, 1998	RAMIREZ R.C.	D 1979, M 1973
CONNORS J.S.	S 1975, 1977, 1978, 1984	JARRYD A.P.	D 1988	RENSHAW J.E.	S 1882, 1883, 1887, 1889
COOKE E.T.	S 1939	KNOWLES M.S.	D 2002	RENSHAW W.C.	S 1890
COOPER A.J.	S 1957, D 1958	LACOSTE J.R.	S 1924	RICHARDS V.	D 1926
CRAWFORD J.H.	S 1934, M 1928	LAVER R.G.	S 1959, 1960, D 1959	RIESSEN M.C.	D 1969, M 1971
CURREN K.M.	S 1985	LAWFORD H.F.	S 1880, 1884, 1885, 1886, 1888	RISELEY F.L.	S 1903, 1904, 1906, D 1903, 1904, 1905
DAVIDSON O.K.	D 1966	LEACH R.D.	D 1989, 1995	RITCHIE M.J.G.	S 1909, D 1911
DECUGIS M.O.	D 1912	LEWIS E.W.	S 1884, 1889, 1890, 1893, 1895	ROCHE A.D.	S 1968, M 1965, 1969
DIXON C.P.	D 1914	LLOYD J.M.	M 1982	ROSE M.G.	D 1953, M 1951
DJOKOVIC N.	S 2013	LOTT G.M.	D 1930	ROSEWALL K.R.	S 1954, 1956, 1970, 1974, D 1955, 1968, 1970, M 1954
DOHERTY H.L.	S 1898, D 1902, 1906	LYCETT R.	S 1922, D 1919, M 1920, 1922	SCHROEDER F.R.	D 1949
DOHERTY R.F.	S 1901, D 1896, 1902, 1906	McENROE J.P.	S 1980, 1982, D 1978, 1982	SEDGMAN F.A.	S 1950, M 1948
DROBNY J.	S 1949, 1952, D 1951	McGREGOR K.B.	S 1951		
EDBERG S.B.	S 1989				

Name	Event and year
SEIXAS E.V.	D 1952, 1954
SMITH S.H.	S 1900, D 1903, 1904, 1905
SMITH S.R.	S 1971, D 1972, 1974, 1980, 1981
STOKER F.O.	D 1891
STOLLE F.S.	S 1963, 1964, 1965, D 1961, 1968, 1970
STURGESS E.W.	D 1951, 1952

Name	Event and year
SUK C.	M 1995
TRABERT M.A.	D 1954
TUCKEY C.R.D.	D 1937
VAN RYN J.W.	D 1935
VINES H.E.	S 1933
Von CRAMM G.A.	S 1935, 1936, 1937
WILBERFORCE H.W.W.	D 1888

Name	Event and year
WILDING A.F.	S 1914, D 1911, M 1914
WILLIAMS R.N.	D 1924
WOOD P.O.	D 1922
WOODBRIDGE T.A.	D 1998, M2004
WOODFORDE M.R.	D 1998, M 1996
WOOSNAM M.	M 1921
ZIMONJIC N.	D2004, 2006

LADIES

Name	Date of Birth	Place of Birth	Date of Death	Place of Death	Event and year
ARTH, Jeanne Marie	21 Jul 1935	St. Paul, Minnesota, USA			D1959
AUSSEM, Cacilia Edith (Cilly†) (della Corte Brae, Countess F.M.)	4 Jan 1909	Cologne, Germany	22 Mar 1963	Portofino, Genoa, Italy	S 1931
AUSTIN, Tracy Ann (Holt, Mrs. S.K.)	12 Dec 1962	Los Angeles, California, USA			M 1980
BARRON, Mrs. W.P. (Shepherd, Dorothy Cunliffe)	24 Nov 1897	Beighton, Norfolk, England			D 1931
BARTOLI, Marion Sophie	2 Oct 1984	Le Puy en Velay, France			S 2013
BINGLEY, Blanche / HILLYARD, Mrs. G.W.	3 Nov 1863	Greenford, Middlesex, England	6 Aug 1946	Pulborough, Sussex, England	S 1886, 1889, 1894, 1897, 1899, 1900
BENESOVA, Iveta	1 Feb 1983	Most, Czechoslovakia			M 2011
BETZ, Pauline May (Addie, Mrs. R.R.)	6 Aug 1919	Dayton, Ohio, USA	31 May 2011	Potomac, Maryland, USA	S 1946
BLACK, Cara Cavell (Stephens, Mrs B.)	17 Feb 1979	Harare, Zimbabwe			D 2004, 2005, 2007, M 2004, 2010
BOOTHBY, Penelope Dora Harvey (Geen, Mrs. A.C.)	2 Aug 1881	Finchley, Middlesex, England	22 Feb 1970	Hammersmith, London, England	S 1909, D 1913
BROUGH, Althea Louise (Clapp, Mrs. A.T.)	11 Mar 1923	Oklahoma City, Oklahoma, USA	3 Feb 2014	Vista, California, USA	S 1948, 1949, 1950, 1955, D 1946, 1948, 1949, 1950, 1954, M 1946, 1947, 1948, 1950
BROWNE, Mary Kendall (Kenneth-Smith, Mrs. K.)	3 Jun 1891	Santa Monica, California, USA	19 Aug 1971	Laguna Hills, California, USA	D 1926
BUENO, Maria Esther Andion	11 Oct 1939	Sao Paulo, Brazil			S 1959, 1960, 1964, D 1958, 1960, 1963, 1965, 1966
BUXTON, Angela (Silk, Mrs. D.)	16 Aug 1934	Liverpool, England			D 1956

Name	Date of Birth	Place of Birth	Date of Death	Place of Death	Event and year
CASALS, Rosemary	16 Sep 1948	San Francisco, California, USA			D 1967, 1968, 1970, 1971, 1973, M 1970, 1972
CAWLEY, Mrs. R.A. – see GOOLAGONG					
CAWLEY, Mrs. R.L. (Gourlay, Helen Florence) (Cape, Mrs. W.T.)	23 Dec 1946	Launceston, Tasmania, Australia			D 1977
CHAMBERS, MRS. R.L. – SEE DOUGLASS					
CLIJSTERS, Kim (Lynch, Mrs B)	8 Jun 1983	Bilzen, Belgium			D 2003
COGHLAN, Lorraine Georgina (Robinson, Mrs. J.D.G.) (Green, Mrs. G.S.)	23 Sep 1937	Warrnambool, Victoria, Australia			M 1958
CONNOLLY, Maureen Catherine (Brinker, Mrs. N.)	17 Sep 1934	San Diego, California, USA	21 Jun 1969	Dallas, Texas, USA	S 1952, 1953, 1954
COOPER, Charlotte Reinagle } STERRY, Mrs. A.	22 Sep 1870	Ealing, Middlesex, England	10 Oct 1966	Helensburgh, Scotland	S 1895, 1896, 1898, 1901, 1908
COURT, Mrs. B.M. – see SMITH					
DAVENPORT, Lindsay Ann (Leach, Mrs. J.)	8 Jun 1976	Palos Verdes, California, USA			S 1999, D 1999
DOD, Charlotte (Lottie†)	24 Sep 1871	Bebington, Cheshire, England	27 Jun 1960	Sway, Hampshire, England	S 1887, 1888, 1891, 1892, 1893
DOUGLASS, Dorothea Katherine CHAMBERS, Mrs. R.L. } duPONT, Mrs. W. – see OSBORNE	3 Sep 1878	Ealing, Middlesex, England	7 Jan 1960	Kensington, London, England	S 1903, 1904, 1906, 1910 1911, 1913, 1914
DURIE, Joanna Mary	27 Jul 1960	Bristol, England			M 1987
DURR, Francoise Germaine (Browning, Mrs. B.J.)	25 Dec 1942	Algiers, Algeria			M 1976
ERRANI, Sara	29 Apr 1987	Bologna, Italy			D 2014
EVERT, Christine Marie } LLOYD, Mrs. J.M. (Mill, Mrs. A.R.) (Norman, Mrs G.J.)	21 Dec 1954	Fort Lauderdale, Florida, USA			S 1974, 1976, 1981, D 1976
FABYAN, Mrs. M. (Palfrey, Sarah Hammond) (Cooke, Mrs. E.T.) (Danzig, Mrs. J.A.)	18 Sep 1912	Sharon, Massachusetts, USA	27 Feb 1996	New York, New York, USA	D 1938, 1939

Name	Date of Birth	Place of Birth	Date of Death	Place of Death	Event and year
FERNANDEZ, Beatriz Cristina (Gigi†)	22 Feb 1964	San Juan, Puerto Rico			D 1992, 1993, 1994, 1997
FRY, Shirley June (Irvin, Mrs. K.E.)	30 Jun 1927	Akron, Ohio, USA			S 1956, D 1951, 1952, 1953 M 1956
GARRISON, Zina Lynna (Jackson, Mrs. W.L.)	16 Nov 1963	Houston, Texas, USA			M 1988, 1990
GIBSON, Althea (Darben, Mrs. W.A.) (Llewellyn, Mrs. S.)	25 Aug 1927	Silver, South Carolina, USA	28 Sep 2003	East Orange, New Jersey, USA	S 1957, 1958, D 1956, 1957, 1958
GODFREE, Mrs. L.A. – see McKANE					
GOOLAGONG, Evonne Fay } CAWLEY, Mrs. R.A.	31 Jul 1951	Griffith, N.S.W., Australia			S 1971, 1980, D 1974
GRAF, Stefanie Maria (Steffi†) (Agassi, Mrs A.K.)	14 Jun 1969	Neckarau, Mannheim, West Germany			S1988, 1989, 1991, 1992, 1993, 1995, 1996, D 1988
GROENEFELD Anna-Lena	4 Jun 1985	Nordhorn, West Germany			M2009
HANTUCHOVA, Daniela	23 Apr 1983	Bratislava, Czechoslovakia			M 2001
HANTZE, Karen Janice } SUSMAN, Mrs. J.R.	11 Dec 1942	San Diego, California, USA			S 1962, D 1961, 1962
HARD, Darlene Ruth (Waggoner, Mrs. R.H.)	6 Jan 1936	Los Angeles, California, USA			D 1957, 1959, 1960, 1963, M 1957, 1959, 1960
HARPER, Mrs. L.A. (McCune, Anna Virginia)	2 Jul 1902	Santa Barbara, California, USA			M 1931
HART, Doris Jane	20 Jun 1925	St. Louis, Missouri, USA	14 Jun 1999	Moraga, California, USA	S 1951, D 1947, 1951, 1952, 1953 M 1951, 1952, 1953, 1954, 1955
HILLYARD, Mrs. G.W. – see BINGLEY					
HINGIS, Martina (Hutin, Mrs T)	30 Sep 1980	Kosice, Czechoslovakia			S 1997, D 1996, 1998
HUBER Mrs A. (Horn, Leizel)	21 Aug 1976	Durban, Natal, South Africa			D 2005, 2007
HSIEH, Su-Wei	4 Jan 1986	Kaohsiung, Taiwan			D 2013
JACOBS, Helen Hull	6 Aug 1908	Globe, Arizona, USA	2 Jun 1997	Easthampton, New York. USA	S 1936
JAMES, Winifred Alice (Freda†) (Hammersley, Mrs. S.H.)	13 Jan 1911	Nottingham, England	27 Dec 1988	Warwick, Warwickshire, England	D 1935, 1936
JANKOVIC, Jelena	28 Feb 1985	Belgrade, Yugoslavia			M2007
JONES, Mrs. P.F. (Haydon, Adrianne Shirley) (Ann†)	17 Oct 1938	Birmingham, England			S 1969, M 1969
JORDAN, Kathryn	3 Dec 1959	Bryn Mawr, Pennsylvania, USA			D 1980, 1985, M 1986

Name	Date of Birth	Place of Birth	Date of Death	Place of Death	Event and year
KING, Mrs. L.W. – see Moffitt					
KING, Vania	3 Feb 1989	Monterey Park, California, USA			D 2010
KIYOMURA, Ann Kazuyo (Hayashi, Mrs. D.)	22 Aug 1955	San Mateo, California, USA			D 1975
KOHDE-KILSCH, Claudia Gertrud	11 Dec 1963	Saarbrucken, West Germany			D 1987
KRAHWINKEL, Hilde (Lehmann, Mrs. R.F.) (Sperling, Mrs. S.)	26 Mar 1908	Essen, Germany	7 Mar 1981	Halsingborg, Sweden	M 1933
KVITOVA, Petra	8 Mar 1990	Bilovec, Czechoslovakia			S 2011, 2014
LARCOMBE, Mrs. D.T.R. (Thomson, Ethel Warneford)	8 Jun 1879	Islington, Middlesex, England	10 Aug 1965	Budleigh Salterton, Devon, England	S 1912, M 1914
LENGLEN, Suzanne Rachel Flore	24 May 1899	Paris, France	4 Jul 1938	Paris, France	S 1919, 1920, 1921, 1922, 1923 1925, D 1919, 1920, 1921, 1922 1923, 1925, M 1920, 1922, 1925 M 2002
LIKHOVTSEVA, Elena Alexandrova (Baronov, Mrs. M.)	8 Sep 1975	Alma Ata, Kazakhstan			
LLOYD, Mrs. J.M. – see EVERT					
McKANE, Kathleen (Kitty†) } GODFREE, Mrs. L.A.	7 May 1896	Bayswater, London, England	19 Jun 1992	Barnes, London, England	S 1924, 1926, M 1924, 1926
McNAIR, Mrs. R.J. (Slocock, Winifred Margaret)	9 Aug 1877	Donnington, nr. Newbury, Berkshire, England	28 Mar 1954	Kensington, London, England	D 1913
MARBLE, Alice	28 Sep 1913	Plumas County, California, USA	13 Dec 1990	Palm Springs, California, USA	S 1939, D 1938, 1939, M 1937, 1938, 1939
MARTINEZ, Inmaculada Concepcion (Conchita†)	16 Apr 1972	Monzon, Nr Huesca, Spain			S 1994
MATHIEU, Mrs. R. (Passemard, Simone)	31 Jan 1908	Neuilly-sur-Seine, France	7 Jan 1980	Paris, France	D 1933, 1934, 1937
MAURESMO, Amelie	5 Jul 1979	St.Germaine en Laye, France			S 2006
METAXA, Doris Emily (Howard, Mrs. P.D.)	12 Jun 1911	Marseilles, France			D 1932
MICHEL, Margaret MICHELL, Mrs. L.R.C. – see SAUNDERS	2 Feb 1949	Santa Monica, California, USA			D 1974
MLADENOVIC, Kristina	14 May 1993	Saint Pol sur Mer, France			M 2013
MOFFITT, Billie Jean } KING, Mrs. L.W.	22 Nov 1943	Long Beach, California, USA			S 1966, 1967, 1968, 1972 1973, 1975, D 1961, 1962, 1965, 1967, 1968, 1970, 1971, 1972, 1973, 1979, M 1967, 1971, 1973, 1974

Name	Date of Birth	Place of Birth	Date of Death	Place of Death	Event and year
MOODY, Mrs. F.S. – see WILLS					
MORARIU, Corina Maria (Turcinovich, Mrs. A.)	26 Jan 1978	Detroit, Michigan, USA			D 1999
MORTIMER, Florence Angela Margaret (Barrett, Mrs. J.E.)	21 Apr 1932	Plymouth, Devon, England			S 1961, D 1955
MORTON, Agnes Mary (Agatha†) (Stewart, Lady H.H.)	6 Mar 1872	Halstead, Essex, England	5 Apr 1952	Kensington, London, England	D 1914
MUDFORD, Phyllis Evelyn (King, Mrs. M.R.)	23 Aug 1905	Wallington, Surrey, England	27 Jan 2006	Reigate, Surrey, England	D 1931
NAVRATILOVA, Martina	18 Oct 1956	Prague, Czechoslovakia			S 1978, 1979, 1982, 1983, 1984, 1985, 1986, 1987, 1990 D 1976, 1979, 1981, 1982, 1983, 1984, 1986, M 1985, 1993, 1995, 2003
NOVOTNA, Jana	2 Oct 1968	Brno, Czechoslovakia			S 1998, D 1989, 1990, 1995, 1998, M 1989
OSBORNE, Margaret Evelyn duPONT, Mrs. W.	4 Mar 1918	Joseph, Oregon, USA			S 1947, D 1946, 1948, 1949, 1950, 1954, M 1962
PENG, Shuai	8 Jan 1986	Hunan, China			D 2013
PESCHKE, Mrs T. (Hrdlickova, Kveta)	9 Jul 1975	Bilovec, Czechoslovakia			D 2011
PIERCE, Mary, Caroline	15 Jan 1975	Montreal, Quebec, Canada			M 2005
PO, Kimberly Yasuko (Messerli, Mrs. O.G. H-P)	20 Oct 1971	Los Angeles, California, USA			M2000
RAYMOND, Lisa Mary	10 Aug 1973	Norristown, Pennsylvania, USA			D 2001, M 1999, 2012
REID, Mrs. G.E. (Melville, Kerry Anne)	7 Aug 1947	Sydney, N.S.W., Australia			D 1978
RICE, Helena Bertha Grace (Lena†)	21 Jun 1866	New Inn, nr. Cahir, Tipperary, Ireland	21 Jun 1907	New Inn, nr. Cahir, Tipperary, Ireland	S 1890
RICHEY, Nancy Ann (Gunter, Mrs. K.S.)	23 Aug 1942	San Angelo, Texas, USA			D 1966
ROBB, Muriel Evelyn	13 May 1878	Newcastle, Northumberland, England	12 Feb 1907	Newcastle, Northumberland, England	S 1902
ROUND, Dorothy Edith Little, Mrs. D.L.)	13 Jul 1909	Dudley, Worcestershire, England	12 Nov 1982	Kidderminster, England	S 1934, 1937, M 1934, 1935 1936
RUSSELL, JoAnne Carleton (Longdon, Mrs. G.)	30 Oct 1954	Miami, Florida, USA			D 1977

Name	Date of Birth	Place of Birth	Date of Death	Place of Death	Event and year
RYAN, Elizabeth Montague	5 Feb 1892	Anaheim, Los Angeles, California, USA	6 Jul 1979	Wimbledon, London, England	D 1914, 1919, 1920, 1921, 1922, 1923, 1925, 1926, 1927, 1930, 1933, 1934, M 1919, 1921, 1923, 1927, 1928, 1930, 1932
SABATINI, Gabriela Beatriz	16 May 1970	Buenos Aires, Argentina			D 1988
SANCHEZ VICARIO, Aranzazu Isabel Maria (Aranxa†) (Vehils Mrs. J.)	18 Dec 1971	Barcelona, Spain			D 1995
SAUNDERS, Margaret Amy (Peggy*) MICHELL, Mrs. L.R.C.	28 Jan 1905	Chiswick, Middlesex, England	19 Jun 1941	Harrow, Middlesex, England	D 1928, 1929
SAVCHENKO, Larisa Ivanovna (Neiland, Mrs. A)	21 Jul 1966	Lvov, Ukraine, U.S.S.R.			D 1991, M 1992
SAWAMATSU, Kazuko (Yoshida, Mrs. M.)	5 Jan 1951	Nishinomiya, Japan			D 1975
SHARAPOVA, Maria	19 Apr 1987	Nyagan, USSR			S 2004
SHILCOCK, Jacqueline Anne (Spann, Mrs. J.K.)	13 Jun 1932	Hartford, Sussex, England			D 1955
SHRIVER, Pamela Howard (Shapiro, Mrs. J.) (Lazenby, Mrs. G.R.)	4 Jul 1962	Baltimore, Maryland, USA			D 1981, 1982, 1983, 1984, 1986
SHVEDOVA, Yaroslava Vyacheslavonna	12 Sep 1987	Moscow, USSR			D 2010
SIGART, Josane (de Meulemeester, Mrs. J.)	7 Jan 1909	Brussels, Belgium	20 Aug 1999	Brussels, Belgium	D 1932
SMYLIE, Mrs. P.D. (Sayers, Elizabeth Marie)	11 Apr 1963	Perth, W.A. Australia			D 1985, M 1991
SMITH, Anne Elizabeth	1 Jul 1959	Dallas, Texas, USA			D 1980, M 1982
SMITH, Margaret COURT, Mrs. B.M.	16 Jul 1942	Albury, N.S.W., Australia			S 1963, 1965, 1970, D 1964, 1969, M 1963, 1965, 1966, 1968, 1975
SREBOTNIK, Katarine	12 May 1981	Sloverj Gradee, Yugoslavia			D 2011
STAMMERS, Katherine Esther (Menzies, Mrs. M.) (Bullitt, Mrs. T.W.)	3 Apr 1914	St Albans, Hertfordshire, England	23 Dec 2005	Louisville, Kentucky, USA	D 1935, 1936
STERRY, Mrs. A. – see COOPER					

Name	Date of Birth	Place of Birth	Date of Death	Place of Death	Event and year
STEVENS, Greer Ruth (Leo-Smith, Mrs. K.)	15 Feb 1957	Pietermaritzburg, Natal, South Africa			M 1977, 1979
STOSUR, Samantha Jane	30 Mar 1984	Brisbane, Queensland, Australia			M 2008, 2014
STOVE, Betty Flippina	24 Jun 1945	Rotterdam, Netherlands			D 1972, M 1978, 1981
STUBBS, Rennae Patricia	26 Mar 1971	Sydney, N.S.W., Australia			D 2001, 2004
SUGIYAMA, Ai	5 July 1975	Tokyo, Japan			D 2003
SUKOVA, Helena	23 Feb 1965	Prague, Czechoslovakia			D 1987, 1989, 1990, 1996, M 1994, 1996, 1997
SUMMERS, Mrs. R.A. (Piercey, Sheila Audrey)	18 Mar 1919	Johannesburg, Transvaal, South Africa	14 Aug 2005	Johannesburg, Transvaal, South Africa	M 1949
SUSMAN, Mrs J.R. – see HANTZE					
SUTTON, May Godfray (Bundy, Mrs. T.C.)	25 Sep 1886	Plymouth, Devon, England	4 Oct 1975	Santa Monica, California, USA	S 1905, 1907
TEGART, Judith Anne Marshall (Dalton, Mrs. D.E.)	12 Dec 1937	Melbourne, Victoria, Australia			D 1969
TODD, Mrs. R.B.	22 Jul 1922	San Francisco, California, USA			D 1947
TUCKEY, Mrs. C.O. (Canning, Mary Patricia) (Daniell, Agnes Katherine Raymond)	8 Jul 1877	Marylebone, Middlesex, England	13 May 1972	Winchester, Hampshire, England	M 1913
TURNBULL, Wendy May	26 Nov 1952	Brisbane, Queensland, Australia			D 1978, M 1983, 1984
TURNER, Lesley Rosemary (Bowrey, Mrs. W.W.)	16 Aug 1942	Sydney, N.S.W., Australia			D 1964, M 1961, 1964
VINCI, Roberta	18 Feb 1983	Taranto, Italy			D 2014
WADE, Sarah Virginia	10 Jul 1945	Bournemouth, Hampshire, England			S 1977
WATSON, Mrs. M.R. (Holcroft, Phoebe Catherine) (Blakstad, Mrs. W.L.)	7 Oct 1898	St. Leonards-on-Sea, Sussex, England			D 1928, 1929
WATSON, Maud Edith Eleanor	9 Oct 1864	Harrow, Middlesex, England	5 Jun 1946	Charmouth, Dorset, England	S 1884, 1885
WIGHTMAN, Mrs. G.W. (Hotchkiss, Hazel Virginia)	20 Dec 1886	Healdburg, California, USA	5 Dec 1974	Chestnut Hill, Massachusetts, USA	D 1924
WILLIAMS, Serena Jamika	26 Sept 1981	Saginaw, Michigan, USA			S 2002, 2003, 2009, 2010, 2012, D 2000, 2002, 2008, 2009, 2012, M 1998
WILLIAMS, Venus Ebony Starr	17 Jun 1980	Lynwood, California, USA			S 2000, 2001, 2005, 2007, 2008, D 2000, 2002, 2008, 2009, 2012
WILLS, Helen Newington MOODY, Mrs. F.S. (Roark, Mrs. A.)	6 Oct 1905	Centerville, Alameda County, California, USA	1 Jan 1998	Carmel, California, USA	S 1927, 1928, 1929, 1930, 1932, 1933, 1935, 1938, D 1924, 1927, 1930, M 1929
YAN, Zi	12 Nov 1984	Cheng Du, Si Chuan, China			D 2006

Name	Date of Birth	Place of Birth	Date of Death	Place of Death	Event and year
YORKE, Adeline Maud (Billie†)	19 Dec 1910	Rawalpindi, Punjab, India	9 Dec 2000	La Jolla, California, USA	D 1937
ZHENG, Jie (Zhang Mrs Y.)	5 July 1983	Cheng Du, Si Chuan, China			D 2006
ZVEREVA, Natasha Maratovna	16 Apr 1971	Minsk, U.S.S.R.			D 1991, 1992, 1993, 1994, 1997
ZVONAREVA, Vera	7 Sept 1984	Moscow, USSR			M 2006

† forenames generally used.   A total of 119 Champions, 44 singles

Champions who were also Runners-up

Name	Event and year	Name	Event and year	Name	Event and year
AUSTIN T.A.	M 1981	SUSMAN J.R.	S 1957, 1959, M 1963	RYAN E.M.	S 1921, 1930, D 1932, M 1920, 1922, 1925
BARRON W.P.	D 1929, M 1923, 1924, 1934	HARD D.R.	S 1947, 1948, 1953, D 1946, 1948, 1950, 1954, M 1948	SABATINI G.B.	S 1991
BARTOLI M.S.	S 2007	HART D.J.	D 2004, M 2001	SANCHEZ VICARIO A.	S 1995 1996, D 1994
BINGLEY B./ HILLYARD G.W.	S 1885, 1887, 1888, 1891, 1892, 1893, 1901	HUBER A.	S 1929, 1932, 1934, 1935, 1938, D 1932, 1936, 1939	SAVCHENKO L.I./ NEILAND A.	D 1988, 1989, 1992, 1993, 1996, M 1996, 1997
BETZ P.M.	D 1946	JACOBS H.H.	D 1933	SHRIVER P.H.	D 1985
BLACK C.C.	2009	JAMES W.A.	S 1967, D 1968, M 1962	SIGART J.	D 1931, M 1932
BOOTHBY P.D.H.	S 1910, 1911	JONES P.F.	D 1981, 1982, 1984, 1990 M 1984	SMYLIE P.D.	D 1987, 1990, M 1985, 1990
BROUGH A.L.	S 1946, 1952, 1954, D 1947, 1951, 1952, M 1949, 1955	JORDAN K.	S 1931, 1936, D 1935, M 1930	SMITH A.E.	D 1981, 1982, 1984
BROWNE M.K.	M 1926	KRAHWINKEL H.	S 1903, 1914, D 1914, 1919, 1920, M 1913	SMITH M/ COURT B.M.	S 1964, 1971, D 1961, 1963, 1966, 1971, M 1964, 1971
BUENO M.E.A.	S 1965, 1966, D 1967, M 1959, 1960, 1967	LARCOMBE D.T.R.	S 1923, D 1922, 1924, 1926, M 1927	SHARAPOVA M.	S 2011
BUXTON A.	S 1956	MCKANE K/ GODFREE L.A.	S 1913	SREBOTNIK K.	D 2007, M 2008
CASALS R.	D 1980, 1983, M 1976	MCNAIR R.J.	D 1935, 1938, M 1937	STAMMERS K.E.	S 1939
CAWLEY R.L.	D 1974	MATHIEU R.	D 2005	STOSUR S.J.	D 2008, 2009
CLIJSTERS K.	D2001, M 2000	MAURESMO. A	D 1931	STOVE B.F.	S 1977, D 1973, 1975, 1976, 1977, 1979, M 1975, 1977, 1979
CONNOLLY M.C.	D 1952, 1953	METAXA D.E.	D 1969	STUBBS R.P.	D 2009
COOPER C.R/ STERRY A.	S 1897, 1899, 1900, 1902, 1904, 1912, D 1913	MICHEL M.	D 2014	SUGIYAMA A	D2000, 2001, 2004
DAVENPORT L.A.	S 2000, 2005 D 1998	MLADENOVIC, K	S 1963, 1969, 1970, D 1964, 1976, M 1966, 1978, 1983	SUTTON M.G.	S 1906
DOUGLASS D.K/ CHAMBERS R.L.	S 1905, 1907, 1919, 1920 D 1913, 1919, 1920, M 1919	MOFFITT B.J./ KING L.W.	S 1958	TEGART J.A.M./ DALTON D.E.	S 1968, D 1966, 1972, M 1965, 1969
DURR F.G.	D 1965, 1968, 1970, 1972, 1973, 1975	MORTIMER F.A.M.	S 1908, 1909	TODD R.B.	D 1948, 1949, M 1950
EVERT C.M/ LLOYD J.M.	S 1973, 1978, 1979, 1980, 1982, 1984, 1985	MORTON A.M.	D 1937	TURNBULL W.M.	D 1979, 1980, 1983, 1986, M 1982
FABYAN M.	D 1930, 1936, M 1936, 1938	MUDFORD P.E.	S 1988, 1989, 1994, D 1977, 1985, M 1986	WADE S.V.	D 1970
FERNANDEZ B.C.	D 1991, 1995, M 1995,	NAVRATILOVA M.	S 1993, 1997 D 1991, 1992, 1993, 1994	WATSON M.E.	S 1886
FRY S.J.	S 1951, D 1950, 1954, M 1953	NOVOTNA J.	S 1949, 1950, D 1947, 1951, 1958, M 1954	WILLIAMS S.J.	S 2004, 2008
GARRISON Z.L.	S 1990	OSBORNE M.E/ DUPONT W.	D 2008, M 2010, 2013	WILLIAMS V.E.S.	S 2002, 2003, 2009, M 2006
GIBSON A.	M 1956, 1957, 1958	RAYMOND L.M.	S 1889	WILLS H.N/ MOODY F.S.	S 1924
GOOLAGONG E.F/ CAWLEY R.A.	S 1972, 1975, 1976 D 1971, M 1972	RICE H.B.G.	D 1967	YORKE A.M.	D 1933, 1938, 1939
GRAF S.M.	S 1987, 1999	RICHEY N.A.	S 1933	ZVEREVA N.M.	D 1988, 1989, 1995, 1998 M 1991
HANTUCHOVA D.	M 2002	ROUND D.E.		ZVONAREVA V.	S 2010, D 2010
HANTZE K.J/	D 1964				

Lady Champions – marriages

Maiden name	Married to	Date of marriage	Place of marriage
Aussem	Brae, Count Fermo Merdari Della Corte	11 March 1936	Berg, Starnberger See, Germany
Austin	Holt, Scott Kelly	17 April, 1993	Beverly Hills, California, USA
Bingley	Hillyard, George Whiteside	13 July 1887	Greenford, Middlesex, England
Benesova	Melzer, Jurgen	14 September 2012	Laxenburg, Austria
Betz	Addie, Robert Richard	2 February 1949	Los Angeles, California, USA
Black	Stephens, Brett	2 December 2006	Spurwing Island, Lake Kariba, Zimbabwe
Boothby	Geen, Arthur Cecil	9 April 1914	London, England
Brough	Clapp, Alan Townsend	9 August 1958	Santa Barbara, California, USA
Browne	Kenneth-Smith, Kenneth	June 1958	Honolulu, Hawaii
Buxton	Silk, Donald	8 February 1959	Marylebone, London, England
Canning	Todd, Richard Bradburn	25 December 1941	Berkeley, California, USA
Clijsters	Lynch, Brian	13 July, 2007	Bree, Belgium
Coghlan	Robinson, John Douglas Gair	19 December 1959	Caulfield, Victoria, Australia
	Green, Gordon Stanley	10 September 1990	Melbourne, Victoria, Australia
Connolly	Brinker, Norman	11 June 1955	San Diego, California, USA
Cooper	Sterry, Alfred	12 January 1901	Surbiton, Surrey, England
Daniell	Tuckey, Charles Orpen	17 April 1906	Ilfracombe, Devon, England
Davenport	Leach, Jonathan	25 April 2003	Kona, Hawaii, USA
Douglass	Chambers, Robert Lambert	6 April 1907	Ealing, Middlesex, England
Durr	Browning, Boyd James	31 December 1975	Dallas, Texas, USA
Evert	Lloyd, John Michael	17 April 1979	Fr. Lauderdale, Florida, USA
	Mill, Andy Ray	30 Jul 1988	Miami, Florida, USA
	Norman, Gegory John	28 July 2008	Paradise Island, Barbados
Fry	Irvin, Karl Eugene	16 February 1957	Sydney, N.S.W., Australia
Garrison	Jackson, Willard Lee	23 September 1989	Houston, Texas, USA
Gibson	Darben, William A.	17 October 1965	Las Vegas, Nevada, USA
	Llewellyn, Sydney	11 April 1983	Elkton, Maryland, USA
Goolagong	Cawley, Roger Anson	19 June 1975	Canterbury, Kent, England
Gourlay	Cawley, Richard Leon	22 January 1977	Launceston, Tasmania, Australia
	Cape, William Timothy	26 October 1986	Canberra, ACT, Australia
Graf	Agassi, Andre Kirk	22 October 2001	Las Vegas, Nevada, USA
Hantze	Susman, James Rodney	21 September 1961	San Antonio, Texas, USA
Hard	Waggoner, Richard Harold	20 August 1980	Woodland Hills, California, USA

Maiden name	Married to	Date of marriage	Place of marriage
Haydon	Jones, Philip Frank	30 August 1962	Hampstead, London, England
Hingis	Hutin, Thibault	10 December, 2010	Paris, France
Holcroft	Watson, Michael Ramsey	7 April 1925	Hartley Wintney, Hampshire, England
	Blakstad, William Launtson	28 July 1933	Birmingham, England
Horn	Huber, Anthony	19 February, 2000	Durban, Natal, South Africa
Hotchkiss	Wightman, George William	24 February 1912	Berkeley, California, USA
Hrdlickova	Peschke, Torsten	5 May 2003	Berlin, Germany
Kiyomura	Hayashi, David	21 January 1984	Mountain View, California, USA
Kohde-Kilsch	Lehmann, Ralf Friedhelm	24 November 2000	Saarbrucken, Germany
Krahwinkel	Sperling, Svend	28 December 1933	Essen, Germany
Likhovtseva	Baranov, Michael	21 September, 1999	Las Vegas, Nevada, USA
McCune	Harper, Lawrence Averell	7 July 1925	Pacific Grove, California, USA
McKane	Godfree, Leslie Allison	18 January 1926	Kimberley, O.F.S., South Africa
Melville	Reid, Grover Eugene	27 April 1975	Greenville, South Carolina, USA
Metaxa	Howard, Peter Dunsmore	17 December 1932	Marseilles, France
Moffitt	King, Larry William	17 September 1965	Long Beach, California, USA
Morariu	Turcinovich, Andrew	29 November 1999	Boca Raton, Florida, USA
Mortimer	Barrett, John Edward	3 April 1967	Wimbledon, London, England
Morton	Stewart, Sir Hugh Houghton Bt	1 August 1925	Paddington, London, England
Mudford	King, Maurice Richard	30 April 1932	Reigate, Surrey, England
Osborne	duPont, William	26 November 1947	Wilmington, Delaware, USA
Palfrey	Fabyan, Marshall	6 October 1934	Boston, Massachusetts, USA
	Cooke, Ellwood Thomas	2 October 1940	New York, New York, USA
	Danzig, Jerry Allison	27 April 1951	New York, New York, USA
Passemard	Mathieu, Rene	14 October 1925	St. Cloud, nr. Paris, France
Piercey	Summers, Ronald Alexander	8 July 1943	Johannesburg, Transvaal, South Africa
Po	Messerli, Oliver George Hans-Peter	4 May 2001	Rancho Palos Verdes, California, USA
Richey	Gunter, Kenneth S.	15 December 1970	San Angelo, Texas, USA
Round	Little, Douglas Leigh	2 September 1937	Dudley, Worcestershire, England
Russell	Longdon, George	22 September 1990	Baltimore, Maryland, USA
Saunders	Michell, Lewis Robert Collorryan	12 July 1928	Kensington, London, England
Savchenko	Neiland, Alexsandr	21 December 1989	Moscow, U.S.S.R.
Sawamatsu	Yoshida, Munehiro	14 February 1976	Tokyo, Japan
Sayers	Smylie, Peter David	10 November 1984	Perth, Western Australia, Australia

Maiden name	Married to	Date of marriage	Place of marriage
Sanchez Vicario	Vehils, Joan	21 July 2000	Cerdanyola, Barcelona, Spain
	Santacana, Jose	12 September 2008	Girona, Spain
Shepherd	Barron, Wilfred Philip	23 September 1921	Bombay, India
Shilcock	Spann, John Keith	6 August 1960	Chichester, Sussex, England
Shriver	Shapiro, Joe	5 December, 1998	La Quinta, California, USA
	Lazenby, George Robert	12 June, 2002	Pacific Palisades, California, USA
Sigart	de Meulemeester, John	7 October 1933	Brussels, Belgium
Slocock	McNair, Roderick James	24 April 1908	Caversham, Berkshire, England
Smith	Court, Barry Michael	28 October 1967	Perth, Western Australia, Australia
Stammers	Menzies, Michael	24 January 1940	Westminster, London, England
	Bullitt, Thomas Walker	27 September 1975	Philadelphia, Pennsylvania, USA
Stevens	Leo-Smith, Kevin	14 February 1981	Pietermaritzburg, Natal, South Africa
Sutton	Bundy, Thomas Clarke	11 October 1912	Los Angeles, California, USA
Tegart	Dalton, David Edmund	18 November 1969	Melbourne, Victoria, Australia
Thomson	Larcombe, Dudley Thomas Reynolds	15 October, 1906	Budleigh Salterton, Devon, England
Turner	Bowrey, William Walter	23 February 1968	Woollahra, Sydney, N.S.W., Australia
Wills	Moody, Frederick Shander	23 December 1929	Berkeley, California, USA
	Roark, Aidan	28 October 1939	Las Vegas, Nevada, USA
Yan	Lee, Shing Kan	23 December 2009	Wuzhou, China
Zheng	Zhang Yu	2006	

The Runners-up

GENTLEMEN

Name	Date of Birth	Place of Birth	Date of Death	Place of Death	Event and year
ALDRICH, Pieter	7 Sep 1965	Johannesburg, Transvaal South Africa			D 1990
ALEXANDER, John Gillient	4 Jul 1951	Sydney, N.S.W., Australia			D 1977
AUSTIN, Henry Wilfred (Bunny†)	26 Aug 1906	Norwood, London, England	26 Aug 2000	Coulsdon, Surrey, England	S 1932, 1938, M 1934
BARCLAY, Jean Claude	30 Dec 1942	Paris, France			D 1963
BERDYCH, Tomas	17 Sept 1985	Valasske Mezirici, Czechoslovakia			S 2010
BLACK, Byron Hamish	6 Oct 1969	Harare, Zimbabwe			D 1996
BOWREY, William Walter	25 Dec 1943	Sydney, N.S.W., Australia			D 1966
BROWN, Geoffrey Edmund	7 Apr 1924	Murrurundi, N.S.W., Australia	20 Jun 2001	Euroa, Victoria, Australia	S 1946, D 1946, 1950, M 1946, 1950
BUNGERT, Wilhelm Paul	1 Apr 1939	Mannheim, Germany			S 1967
CAHILL, Darren John	2 Oct 1965	Adelaide, S.A., Australia			M 1987
CASAL, Sergio	8 Sep 1962	Barcelona, Spain			D 1987
CASEY, Raymond John	15 Feb 1900	San Francisco, California, USA	2 Jan 1982	Palo Alto, California, USA	D 1925
COLLINS, Ian Glen	23 Apr 1903	Glasgow, Scotland	20 Mar 1975	Glasgow, Scotland	D 1929, M 1929, 1931
CONNELL, Grant Douglas	17 Nov 1965	Regina, Saskatchewan, Canada			D 1993, 1994, 1996
COOPER, John Richard	4 Nov 1946	Alexandra, Victoria, Australia			D 1973
COURIER, James Spencer	17 Aug 1970	Sanford, Florida, USA			S 1993
DARMON, Pierre	14 Jan 1934	Tunis, Tunisia			D 1963
DAVIES, Michael Grenfell	9 Jan 1936	Swansea, Wales			D 1960
DAVIS, Dwight Filley	5 Jul 1879	St. Louis, Missouri, USA	28 Nov 1945	Washington D.C., USA	D 1901
de GOMAR, Count Manuel	21 Sep 1897	Madrid, Spain	21 Feb 1935	Madrid, Spain	D 1923
de MORPURGO, Baron Umberto Luigi	12 Jan 1896	Paris, France	26 Feb 1961	Geneva, Switzerland	M 1925
DEANE, Lewis Seymour	12 Mar 1882	Meerut, United Provinces, India	18 Dec 1934	Delhi, India	M 1923
DENT, Philip Clive	14 Feb 1950	Sydney, N.S.W., Australia			D 1977
DENTON, Steve Branch	5 Sep 1956	Kingsville, Texas, USA			M 1983, 1984
DODIG, Ivan	2 Jan 1985	Medjugorje, Bosnia-Herzegovina			D 2013
DOEG, John Thomas Godfray Hope	7 Dec 1908	Guaymas, Sonora County, Mexico	27 Apr 1978	Redding, California, USA	D 1930
DONNELY, Gary Wayne	3 Jun 1962	Phoenix, Arizona, USA			D 1986
DOWDESWELL, Colin	12 May 1955	London, England			D 1975
EAVES, Wilberforce Vaughan	10 Dec 1867	Melbourne, Victoria, Australia	12 Feb 1920	London, England	S 1895, D 1895

Name	Date of Birth	Place of Birth	Date of Death	Place of Death	Event and year
EDMONDSON, Mark Ronald	28 Jun 1954	Gosford, N.S.W., Australia			M 1980
FARQUHARSON, Norman Gordon	18 Jul 1907	Johannesburg, Transvaal, South Africa	11 Aug 1992	Durban, Natal, South Africa	M 1933
FARRELL, Mark Joseph	6 May 1953	Liverpool, England			M 1974
FARRER, Claude Erskine	15 Sep 1864	Regents Park, Middlesex, England	16 Feb 1890	Cannes, France	D 1885, 1886
FLAQUER, Eduardo	4 Sep 1894	Barcelona, Spain	18 Aug 1951	San Sebastian, Spain	D 1923
FRANA, Javier Alberto	25 Dec 1966	Rafaela, Argentina			D 1991
GALBRAITH, Patrick James	16 Apr 1967	Tacoma, Washington, USA			D 1993, 1994
GRABB, James Franklin	14 Apri 1964	Tucson, Arizona, USA			D 1992
GREGORY, John Colin	28 Jul 1903	Beverley, Yorkshire, England	10 Jan 1959	Wimbledon, London, England	D 1929
GULLIKSON, Thomas Robert	8 Sep 1951	La Crosse, Wisconsin, USA			D 1983
GULLIKSON, Timothy Ernest	8 Sep 1951	La Crosse, Wisconsin, USA	3 May 1996	Wheaton, Illinois, USA	D 1983
HANLEY, Paul Jason	12 Nov 1977	Melbourne, Victoria, Australia			M 2005
HARE, Charles Edgar	16 Jul 1915	Wembley, London, England	18 Nov 1996	Salisbury, Wiltshire, England	D 1936, 1939
HAWKES, John Bailey	7 Jun 1899	Geelong, Victoria, Australia	31 Mar 1990	Geelong, Victoria, Australia	D 1928
HENKEL, Heinrich Ernst Otto (Henner†)	9 Oct 1915	Posen, Germany	13 Jan, 1943	Rossok, Nr Voronezh, U.S.S.R.	D 1938, M 1938
HENNESSEY, John Francis	27 Oct 1900	Indianapolis, Indiana, USA	18 Aug 1981	Stuart, Florida, USA	D 1925
HILLYARD, George Whiteside	6 Feb 1864	Hanwell, Middlesex, England	24 Mar 1943	Pulborough, Sussex, England	D 1889, 1890
HOBART, Clarence	27 Jun 1870	Waltham, Massachusetts, USA	2 Aug 1930	Asheville, North Carolina, USA	D 1898, 1899
HOPMAN, Henry Christian	12 Aug 1906	Sydney, N.S.W., Australia	27 Dec 1985	Largo, Florida, USA	M 1932, 1935
JONES, Kelly Lee	31 May 1964	Fort Gordon, California, USA			M 1988
JOVANOVIC, Boro	21 Oct 1939	Zagreb, Yugoslavia			D 1962
KINSEY, Howard Oreon	3 Dec 1899	St. Louis, Missouri, USA	26 Jul 1966	San Francisco, California, USA	S 1926, D 1926, M 1926
KLEINSCHROTH, Heinrich	15 Mar 1890	Kitzingen, Germany	10 Jan 1979	Munich, West Germany	D 1913
KNOWLE, Julian	29 Apr 1974	Lauterach, Austria			D 2004
KRATZMANN, Mark	17 May 1966	Murgon, Queensland, Australia			M 1989
LAVALLE, Leonardo	14 Jul 1967	Mexico City, Mexico			D 1991
LENDL, Ivan	7 Mar 1960	Ostrava, Czechoslovakia			S 1986, 1987
LEWIS, Christopher John (Chris†)	9 Mar 1957	Auckland, New Zealand			S 1983
LINDSTEDT, Robert Jan	19 Mar, 1977	Sunbyberg, Sweden			D 2010, 2011, 2012
LONG, Colin Foster	23 Mar 1918	Melbourne, Victoria, Australia	8 Nov 2009	East Malvern, Victoria, Australia	M 1947
LUTZ, Robert Charles	29 Aug 1947	Lancaster, Pennsylvania, USA			D 1974, 1980, 1981
McLOUGHLIN, Maurice Evans	18 Nov 1890	Carson City, Nevada, USA	10 Dec 1957	Hermosa Beach, California, USA	S 1913
MARK, Robert	28 Nov 1937	Albury, N.S.W., Australia	21 Jul 2006	East Malvern, Victoria, Australia	D 1959
MARSHALL, William Cecil	29 Apr 1849	Mayfair, Middlesex, England	24 Jan 1921	Hindhead, Surrey, England	S 1877
MELO, Marcelo Pinheiro Davide	23 Sep 1983	Belo Horizonte, Brazil			D 2013
MELVILLE, Donald Scott	4 Aug 1966	Fort Ord, California, USA			D1995

Name	Date of Birth	Place of Birth	Date of Death	Place of Death	Event and year
METREVELI, Alexander Irakleivich	2 Nov 1944	Tbilisi, Georgia, U.S.S.R.			S 1973, M 1968, 1970
MIDDLETON, Todd Jason	2 May 1968	Auburn, New York, USA			M 1994
MOREA, Enrique Jorge	11 Apr 1924	Buenos Aires, Argentina			M 1952, 1953, 1955
MOTTRAM, Anthony John	8 Jun 1920	Coventry, Warwickshire, England			D 1947
MULLIGAN, Martin Frederick	18 Oct 1940	Sydney, N.S.W., Australia			S 1962
NALBANDIAN, David Pablo	1 Jan 1982	Urquillo, Cordoba, Argentina			S 2002
NIELSEN, Kurt	19 Nov 1930	Copenhagen, Denmark			S 1953, 1955, M 1958
NIJSSEN, Thomas Jozef Cornelis Marie	10 Oct 1964	Maastricht, The Netherlands	11 June 2011	Lyngby, Denmark	M 1993
NISBET, Harold Adair	22 Jun 1873	Kilburn, London, England	12 Mar 1937	London, England	D 1896, 1898, 1899, 1900
NORTON, Brian Ivan Cobham	10 Oct 1899	Cape Province, South Africa	16 Jul 1956	Agnew, California, USA	S 1921
NOVAK, Jiri	22 Mar 1975	Zlin, Czechoslovakia			D 2001
NUNOI, Ryosuki	18 Jan 1909	Kobe, Japan	21 Jul 1945	Burma	D 1933
OKKER, Tom Samuel	22 Feb 1944	Amsterdam, Netherlands			D 1969
OLHOVSKIY, Andrei	15 Apr 1966	Moscow, USSR			M1997
PAILS, Dennis Robert (Dinny)	4 Mar 1921	Nottingham, England			D 1946
PHILIPPOUSSIS, Mark Anthony	7 Nov 1976	Melbourne, Victoria, Australia	22 Nov 1986	Sydney, N.S.W., Australia	S2003
PIETRANGELI, Nicola	11 Sep 1933	Tunis, Tunisia			D 1956
PILIC, Nikola	27 Aug 1939	Split, Yugoslavia			D 1962
PIOLINE, Cedric Adrien	15 Jun 1969	Neuilly/Seine, Paris, France			S 1997
PREBBLE, Albert Davis	22 Oct 1873	Islington, Middlesex, England	27 Aug 1946	Eastbourne, Sussex, England	M 1919
PRENN, Daniel Dan	7 Sep 1904	Vilna, Russia	3 Sep 1991	Dorking, Surrey, England	M 1930
RAFTER, Patrick Michael	28 Dec 1972	Mount Isa, Queensland, Australia			S 2000, 2001
RAHE, Friedrich Wilhelm	16 Apr 1888	Rostock, Germany	16 Feb 1949	Rostock, Germany	D 1913
RENEBERG, Richard Arlen	5 Oct 1965	Phoenix, Arizona, USA			D 1992
RIKL, David	27 Feb 1971	Brandys, Czechoslovakia			D 2001
RODDICK, Andrew Stephen	30 Aug 1982	Omaha, Nebraska, USA			S 2004, 2005, 2009
RUFFELS, Raymond Owen	23 Mar 1946	Sydney, N.S.W., Australia			M 1978
SANCHEZ, Emilio	29 May 1965	Madrid, Spain			D 1987
SATOH, Jiro	5 Jan 1908	Gunma Prefecture, Japan	5 Apr 1934	At sea off Singapore	D 1933
SANTORO, Fabrice Vetea	9 Dec 1972	Tahiti, French Polynesia			D2006
SHIELDS, Francis Xavier	18 Nov 1909	New York, New York, USA	19 Aug 1975	New York, New York, USA	S 1931
SIDWELL, Oswald William Thomas	16 Apr 1920	Goulburn, N.S.W., Australia			D 1947, 1950
SIROLA, Orlando	30 Apr 1928	Fiume, Italy	13 Nov 1995	Bologna, Italy	D 1956
SOARES, Bruno Fraga	27 Feb 1982	Belo Horizonte, Brazil			M 2013
STOLLE, Sandon Frederick	13 Jul 1970	Sydney, NSW, Australia			D 2000
STANLEY, Arthur John	26 Jun 1863	London, England	16 Jul 1935	London, England	D 1885, 1886

Name	Date of Birth	Place of Birth	Date of Death	Place of Death	Event and year
STOCKTON, Richard LeClede	18 Feb 1951	New York, New York, USA			M 1976
STONE, Allan James	14 Oct 1945	Launceston, Tasmania, Australia			D 1975, M 1975
TANNER, Leonard Roscoe	15 Oct 1951	Chattanooga, Tennessee, USA			S 1979
TECAU, Horia Vlad	19 Jan 1985	Brasov, Romania			D 2010, 2011, 2012
ULLYETT, Kevin Robert	23 May 1972	Harare, Zimbabwe			D 2008, M 2002
van DILLEN, Erik Jacobus	21 Feb 1951	San Mateo, California, USA			D 1972
VISSER, Daniel Theron	26 Jul 1961	Rustenburg, Transvaal, South Africa			D 1990
von METAXA, Georg Felix	7 Oct 1914	Vienna, Austria	12 Dec 1944	Arnoldsweiler, Nr. Duren, Germany	D 1938
WARD, Holcombe	23 Nov 1878	New York, New York, USA	23 Jan 1967	Red Bank, New Jersey, USA	D 1901
WARWICK, Kimberley Grant	8 Apr 1952	Sydney, N.S.W., Australia			M 1972
WASHBURN, Watson McLean	13 Jun 1894	New York, New York, USA	2 Dec 1973	New York, New York, USA	D 1924
WASHINGTON, MaliVai Onyeaka	20 Jun 1969	Glen Cove, Washington, USA			S 1996
WILDE, Frank Herbert David	19 Mar 1911	Wimbledon, Surrey, England	6 Feb 1982	Eastergate, West Sussex, England	D 1936, 1939, M 1939
WILLIAMS, Edward Lake (Teddy)	1 Jul 1866	Bushey, Hertfordshire, England		Johannesburg, Transvaal, South Africa	D 1884
WILSON, Robert Keith	22 Nov 1935	Hendon, Middlesex, England			D 1960

† forenames generally used
114 players

LADIES

Name	Date of Birth	Place of Birth	Date of Death	Place of Death	Event and year
AKHURST, Daphne Jessie (Cozens, Mrs. R.S.)	22 Apr 1903	Ashfield, N.S.W., Australia	10 Jan 1933	Sydney, N.S.W., Australia	M 1928
ALVAREZ de, Elia Maria (Lili†) (Valdene, Countess J. de G.)	9 May 1905	Rome, Italy	8 Jul 1998	Madrid, Spain	S 1926, 1927, 1928
ANDRUS, Dorothy Bourne (Burke, Mrs. W.A.) (Voorhees, Mrs. C.E.)	14 Jun 1908	New York, New York, USA	29 Sep 1989	Sarasota, Florida, USA	D 1934
ARENDT, Nicole Jacquline	26 Aug 1969	Somerville, New Jersey, USA			D1997
AUSTIN, Joan Winifred (Lycett, Mrs. R.) (Chiesman, Mrs. F.R.) (Jepson, Mrs. D.S.) (Baker, Mrs. D.A.)	23 Jan 1903	London, England	2 April 1998	Horley, Surrey, England	D 1923

Name	Date of Birth	Place of Birth	Date of Death	Place of Death	Event and year
BABOS, Tímea	10 May 1993	Sopron, Hungary			D 2014
BARTY, Ashleigh	24 Apr 1996	Ipswich, Queensland, Australia			D 2013
BEAMISH, Mrs. A.E. (Ramsey, Winifred Geraldine)	23 Jun 1885	London, England	10 May 1972	London, England	D 1921
BENNETT, Eileen Viviyen (Fearnley Whittingstall, Mrs. E.O.) (Marsh, Mrs. M.M.) (Akroyd, Mrs. G.) (Forslind, Mrs. C.V.)	16 Jul 1907	Paddington, London, England	6 Nov 1979	Middleton Tyas, nr. Richmond, Yorkshire, England	D 1928
BLOOMER, Shirley Juliet (Brasher, Mrs. C.W.)	13 Jun 1934	Grimsby, Lincolnshire, England			D 1955
BOLLEGRAF, Manon Maria	10 Apr 1964	den Bosch, The Netherlands	9 Dec 2001	North Balwyn, Nr Melbourne, Victoria Australia	D 1997, M 1993
BOLTON, Mrs. G.F. (Wynne, Nancye Meredith)	10 Jun 1917	Melbourne, Victoria, Australia			M 1947, 1951
BOUCHARD, Eugenie Caitlin Murphy	25 Feb 1944	Montreal, Canada			S 2014
BRIDGE, Mrs. A.V. (Lidderdale, Kathleen Eleanora)	6 Sep 1894	Henley-on-Thames, Oxfordshire, England	29 Jan 1973	Cheltenham, Gloucestershire, England	D 1925
BROQUEDIS, Marie Marguerite (Billout, Mrs. J.) (Bordes, Mrs. P.R.M.)	17 Apr 1893	Pau, France	23 Apr 1983	Orleans, France	M 1914
BROWN, Nina Borein (Hamilton, Mrs. E.R.)	21 Jan 1915	London, England			M 1939
BUDING, Edda (Duechting, Mrs.)	13 Nov 1936	Lovrin, Romania			M 1961
BUNDY, Dorothy May (Cheney, Mrs. A.C.)	1 Sep 1916	Los Angeles, California, USA	23 Nov 2014	Escondido, California, USA	M 1946
BYRNE, Jennifer Margaret	25 Feb 1967	Perth, Western Australia, Australia			M 1989
CHAN, Hao-Ching	19 Sep 1993	Taipei, Chinese Taipei			M 2014
CHARLES, Lesley Joan	15 Jul 1952	Worcester, England			M 1974
COLYER, Evelyn Lucy (Munro, Mrs. H.A.)	16 Aug 1902	Streatham, London, England	4 Nov 1930	Assam, India	D 1923, 1926
COVELL, Mrs. B.C. – see Howkins					
CROSS, Edith Ann (Jensen, Mrs. C.E.)	2 Aug 1907	San Francisco, California, USA	15 Jul 1983	Burlingame, California, USA	D 1930

Name	Date of Birth	Place of Birth	Date of Death	Place of Death	Event and year
de SWARDT, Mariaan	18 Mar 1971	Johannesburg, South Africa			D 1999
DECUGIS, Mrs. A. (Halard, Julie)	10 Dec 1970	Versailles, France			D 2000
DELLACQUA, Casey	11 Feb 1985	Perth, Western Australia, Australia			D 2013
EBBERN, Robyn Ann (Vincenzi, Mrs. E.J.)	2 Jul 1944	Brisbane, Queensland, Australia			D 1963
FLEITZ, Mrs. J.G. (Baker, Beverly Joyce) (Beckett, Mrs. S.)	13 Apr 1930	Providence, Rhode Island, USA			S 1955, D 1959
FROMHOLTZ, Dianne Lee (Balestrat, Mrs. C.M.)	10 Aug 1956	Albury, N.S.W., Australia			M 1980
FRY, Joan Cradock (Lakeman, Mrs. T.A.)	6 May 1906	Horsham, Sussex, England	29 Sep 1985	Birmingham, England	S 1925, M 1929
HANNAM, Mrs. F.J. (Boucher, Edith Margaret)	28 Nov 1878	Bristol, England	16 Jan 1951	Bristol, England	D 1914
HARVEY, Ermyntrude Hilda	9 Jun 1895	London, England	4 Oct 1973	Woking, Surrey, England	D 1928
HAWTON, Mrs. K.E. (Bevis, Mary Renetta)	4 Sep 1924	Sydney, N.S.W., Australia	16 Jan 1981	Sydney, N.S.W., Australia	D 1957
HEELEY, Gertrude Mary (Cartwright, Mrs. D.F.) (Bosomworth, Mrs. C.R.)	30 Mar 1911	Birmingham, England	14 Aug 2002	Cape Town, Cape Province, South Africa	M 1933
HEINE, Esther Annie Laurie (Bobbie*) (Miller, Mrs. J.H.K.) (Davie, Mrs. W.R.)	5 Dec 1909	Estcourt, Natal, South Africa			D 1927
HENIN, Justine } HARDENNE, Mrs P-Y (Jung, Sylvia)	1 Jun 1982	Liège, Belgium			S 2001, 2006
HENROTIN, Mrs. C.F. (Lafaurie, Mrs. R.) (Welton, Mrs.)	10 Jul 1904	Le Havre, France	15 Dec 1970	Lake Placid, New York, USA	D 1934
HLAVACKOVA, Andrea	10 Aug 1986	Pizen, Czechoslovakia			D 2012
HOGAN, Patti St. Anne (Fordyce, Mrs. I.M.)	21 Dec 1949	San Diego, California, USA			D 1969
HOPMAN, Mrs. H.C. (Hall, Eleanor Mary) (Nell†)	19 Mar 1909	Sydney, N.S.W., Australia	10 Jan 1968	Melbourne, Victoria, Australia	M 1935
HOWKINS, Phyllis Lindrea } COVELL, Mrs. B.C.	22 May 1895	Windlesham, Surrey, England	28 Oct 1982	Hoyle, West Sussex, England	D 1924, 1929, M 1921
HRADECKA, Lucie	21 May 1985	Prague, Czechoslovakia			D 2012
JAEGER, Andrea	4 Jun 1965	Chicago, Illinois, USA			S 1983

Name	Date of Birth	Place of Birth	Date of Death	Place of Death	Event and year
JAUSOVEC, Mima	20 Jul 1956	Maribor, Yugoslavia			D 1978
JEDRZEJOWSKA, Jadwiga (Gallert, Mrs. A.)	15 Oct 1912	Krakow, Austria (Poland)	28 Feb 1980	Katowice, Poland	S 1937
KOURNIKOVA, Anna Sergeevna	7 Jun 1981	Moscow, USSR			M 1999
KRANTZCKE, Karen Mary	1 Feb 1947	Brisbane, Queensland, Australia	11 Apr 1977	Tallahassee, Florida, USA	D 1974
KUZNETSOVA, Svetlana	27 Jun 1985	St. Petersburg, USSR			D 2005
LEHANE, Janice Patricia (O'Neill, Mrs. J.J.)	9 Jul 1941	Grenfell, N.S.W., Australia			D 1961
LIEFFRIG, Jeanine Pierrette	12 Sep 1938	Paris, France			D 1965
LISICKI, Sabine Katharina	29 Sep 1989	Troisdorf, West Germany			S 2013, D 2011
LONG, Mrs. M.N. (Coyne, Thelma Dorothy)	14 Oct 1918	Sydney, N.S.W., Australia	14 Apr 2015	Sydney, NSW, Australia	D 1957, M 1952
LUCIC, Mirjana (Baroni Mrs. D.)	9 Mar 1982	Dortmund, West Germany			M 1998
MAGERS, Mrs. S.W. (Rush, Gretchen Anne)	7 Feb 1964	Pittsburgh, Pennsylvania, USA			M 1988
McGRATH, Meredith Jane	28 Apr 1971	Midland, Michigan, USA			D 1996
McILQUHAM, Mrs. C.G. (Hart, Mary Melinda)	10 Sep 1901	Bamburgh, Northumberland, England			D 1925
McNEIL, Lori Michelle	18 Dec 1963	San Diego, California, USA			M 1994
MALLORY, Mrs. F. I. (Bjurstedt, Anna Margrethe) (Molla†)	6 Mar 1884	Oslo, Norway			S 1922
MANDLIKOVA, Hana (Sadlek, Mrs. J.)	19 Feb 1962	Prague, Czechoslovakia			S 1981, 1986, D 1986
MOLIK, Alicia Helena (Sullivan, Mrs. T.)	27 Jan 1981	Adelaide, SA, Australia			M 2004, 2007
MORAN, Gertrude Augusta (Corbally, Mrs. T.J.) (Hand, Mrs. E.J.) (Simpson, Mrs. F.M.)	8 Sep 1923	Santa Monica, California, USA	16 Jan 2013	Los Angeles, California, USA	D 1949
MOROZOVA, Olga Vasilevna (Rubanov, Mrs. V.B.)	22 Feb 1949	Moscow, U.S.S.R.			S 1974, M 1968, 1970
MULLER, Esme Fay (Robinson, Mrs. A.A.) (Colthorpe, Mrs. R.W.)	4 Nov 1933	Laidley, Queensland, Australia			D 1956

Name	Date of Birth	Place of Birth	Date of Death	Place of Death	Event and year
NAGELSEN, Helen Elizabeth (Betsy†) (McCormack, Mrs. M.H.)	23 Oct 1956	St. Petersburg, Florida, USA			D 1987
NEWBERRY, Janet Scott (Wright, Mrs. F.I.) (Howe, Mrs. R.E.)	6 Aug 1953	Los Angeles, California, USA			M 1973
OREMANS, Maria Johanna Martina Miriam (Vermeer, Mrs. C.)	9 Sep 1972	Berlicum, The Netherlands			M 1992
PEACOCK, Mrs. G.E. (Bowder, Irene Evelyn)	29 Jul 1892	Ferozepore, Bengal, India	13 Jun 1978	Johannesburg, Transvaal, South Africa	D 1921, 1927
PEREBIYNIS, Tatiana (Zadorozhnly, Mrs D.)	15 Dec 1982	Kharkov, USSR			M 2005
PICKERING, Mrs. W.H. (Simpson, Alice Mabel)	1860	Ledsham, Yorkshire, England	18 Feb 1939	Doncaster, Yorkshire, England	S 1896
PITTMAN, Mrs. J.B. (Goldsack, Elsie Alice) (Rowbottom, Mrs. G.F.) (Furlonge, Lady G.W.)	21 Jan 1904	Brockley, London, England	28 Mar 1975	London, England	D 1937
PRICE, Mrs L.E.G. – see Reynolds					
PROVIS, Nicole Anne-Louise (Bradtke, Mrs. M.R.)	22 Sep 1969	Melbourne, Victoria, Australia			M 1987
REYNOLDS, Sandra PRICE, Mrs. L.E.G. }	4 Mar 1939	Bloemfontein, O.F.S., South Africa			S 1960, D 1960, 1962
RADWANSKA, Agnieszka Roma	6 Mar 1989	Krakow, Poland			S 2012
RIDLEY, Joan Cowell (O'Meara, Mrs. D.J.P.)	11 Jul 1903	Ipswich, Suffolk, England	Oct 1983	Bury St. Edmunds, Suffolk, England	M 1931
RODIONOVA, Anastassia	12 May 1982	Tambov, USSR			M2003
RUANO PASCUAL, Virginia	21 Sep 1973	Madrid, Spain			D 2002, 2003, 2006
RUZICI, Virginia	31 Jan 1955	Cimpia-Turzii, Romania			D 1978
SAMPSON, Julia Anne (Haywood, Mrs. D.A.)	2 Feb 1934	Los Angeles, California, USA	27 Dec 2011	Newport Beach, California, USA	D 1953
SCHUURMAN, Renee (Haygarth, Mrs. P.) (Osborne, Mrs. R.)	22 Oct 1939	Durban, Natal, South Africa	30 May 2001	Howick, Natal, South Africa	D 1960, 1962

Name	Date of Birth	Place of Birth	Date of Death	Place of Death	Event and year
SEENEY, Daphne Grace (Fancutt, Mrs. T.T.)	2 Feb 1933	Monto, Queensland, Australia			D 1956
SELES, Monica	2 Dec 1973	Novi Sad, Yugoslavia			S 1992
STOCKS, Mrs. A.D. (McKane, Margaret)	26 Apr 1895	London, England	1 Jan 1985	Littlestone, Kent, England	D 1922
SUAREZ, Paola Lorena	23 Jun 1976	Pergamino, Argentina			D 2002, 2003, 2006
SUKOVA, Mrs. C. (Puzejova, Vera)	13 Jun 1931	Uherske Hradiste, Czechoslovakia	13 May 1982	Prague, Czechoslovakia	S 1962
TATARKOVA, Elena Valeriyvna	22 Aug 1976	Dushanbe, Tadijkistan			D 1999
TAUZIAT, Nathalie (Feltham, Mrs T)	17 Oct 1967	Bangui, Central African Republic			S 1998
TRUMAN, Christine Clara (Janes, Mrs. G.T.)	16 Jan 1941	Loughton, Essex, England			S 1961, D 1959
VARNER, Margaret (Bloss, Mrs. W.G.)	4 Oct 1927	El Paso, Texas, USA			D 1958
VESNINA, Elana Sergeevna	1 Aug 1986	Lvov, USSR			D 2010, M 2011, 2012
WARD, Patricia Evelyn (Hales, Mrs. R.)	27 Feb 1929	London, England	22 Jun 1985	Brighton, Sussex, England	D 1955
WATSON, Lilian Mary	17 Sep 1857	Harrow, Middlesex, England	27 May 1918	Berkswell, Warwickshire, England	S 1884

† forenames generally used.
85 Players

Lady Runners-up – marriages

Maiden name	Married to	Date of marriage	Place of marriage
Akhurst	Cozens, Royston Stuckley	26 February 1930	Sydney, N.S.W., Australia
Alvarez	Valdene, Count Jean de Galliard	14 November 1935	Madrid, Spain
Andrus	Burke, Walter Anthony	30 November 1931	Stamford, Connecticut, USA
	Voorhees, Charles Edmund	14 June 1941	New York, New York, USA
Austin	Greville, Turketil George Pearson	18 September 1899	Kensington, London, England
Austin	Lycett, Randolph	12 February 1925	Westminster, London, England
	Chiesman, Frederick Royden	18 September 1936	Croydon, Surrey, England
	Jepson, Derek Schofield	22 December 1948	Reigate, Surrey, England
Baker	Baker, Donald Alex	1 March 1973	Reigate, Surrey, England
	Beckett, Scott	28 September 1949	Las Vegas, Nevada, USA
	Fleitz, John Griffen	6 October 1951	Santa Monica, California, USA
Bennett	Fearnley Whittingstall, Edmund Owen	19 November 1929	Westminster, London, England
	Marsh, Marcus Maskell	28 September 1936	Chelsea, London, England
	Akroyd, Geoffrey	6 May 1947	Westminster, London, England
	Forslind, Carl V.	6 June 1957	London, England
Bevis	Hawton, Keith Ernest	16 October 1949	Sydney, N.S.W., Australia
Bjurstedt	Mallory, Franklin Isaac	3 September 1919	New York, New York, USA
Bloomer	Brasher, Christopher William	28 April 1959	Chelsea, London, England
Boucher	Hannam, Francis John	5 May 1909	Nailsea, Somerset, England
Bowder	Peacock, Gerald Eustace	14 November 1917	Rawalpindi, Bengal, India
Broquedis	Billout, Marcel	16 August 1917	Champeaux, Seine et Marne, France
	Bordes, Pierre Raymond Marie	2 November 1925	La Ferré-Imbault, Loir et Cher, France
Brown	Hamilton, Everett Rubicam	23 August 1941	Northport Point, Michigan, USA
Buding	Duechting	August 1969	
Bundy	Cheney, Arthur Charles	17 October, 1946	Santa Monica, California, USA
Colyer	Munro, Hamish A.	13 February 1930	Streatham, London, England
Coyne	Long, Maurie Newton	30 January 1941	Sydney, N.S.W., Australia
Cross	Jenson, Carroll Ernest	9 September 1933	San Francisco, California, USA
Ebbern	Vincenzi, Edward John	6 April 1968	Brisbane, Queensland, Australia
Fromholtz	Balestrat, Claude Maurice	26 December 1982	Dural, Sydney, N.S.W., Australia
Fry	Lakeman, Thomas Ashley	12 November 1930	Kensington, London, England
Goldsack	Pitrman, John Bernard	4 January 1930	Marylebone, London, England
	Rowbottom, Gordon Fardel	5 February 1942	Westminster, London, England
	Furlonge, Sir Geoffrey Warren	21 June 1952	Chelsea, London, England
Halard	Decugis, Arnaud	22 September 1995	Neuilly/Seine, Paris, France

Maiden name	Married to	Date of marriage	Place of marriage
Hall	Hopman, Henry Christian	19 March 1934	Sydney, N.S.W., Australia
Hart	McIlquaham, Clinton Gilbert	5 April 1923	Bamburgh, Northumberland, England
Heeley	Cartwright, David Frederick	3 December 1938	Boldmere, Sutton Coldfield, England
	Bosomworth, Claude Richard	9 April 1969	Wynberg, Cape Town, South Africa
Heine	Miller, James Henry Knipe	6 April 1931	Winterton, Natal, South Africa
	Davie, William Ritchie	19 September 1948	Durban, Natal, South Africa
Henin	Hardenne, Pierre-Yves	16 November, 2002	Marloie, Namur, Belgium
Hogan	Fordyce, Ian McLennan	29 December 1976	Chelsea, London, England
Howkins	Covell, Beverley Carthew	23 September 1921	Bombay, India
Jedrzejowska	Gallert, Alfred	1947	Katowice, Poland
Jung	Lafaurie, Raoul	June 1922	
	Henrotin, Charles Fernand	March 1930	
	Welton, Sernane		
Lehane	O'Neill, James John	19 February 1966	Grenfell, N.S.W., Australia
Lidderdale	Bridge, Allman Vizer	20 October 1924	Prestbury, Gloucestershire, England
Lucic	Baroni, Daniele	15 November, 2011	Sarasota, Florida, USA
Mandlikova	Sadlek, Jan	25 July 1986	Prague, Czechoslovakia
McKane	Stocks, (later Sir) Andrew Denys	15 February 1922	Kensington, London, England
Molik	Sullivan, Timothy	February, 2011	Yarra Valley, Victoria, Australia
Moran	Corbally, Thomas James	6 August 1956	Staten Island, New York, USA
	Hand, Edward James	28 January 1957	Las Vegas, Nevada, USA
	Simpson, Frank Milhaus	22 July 1962	Lahaina, Maui, Hawaii
Morozova	Rubenov, Victor Borisovich	23 February 1971	Moscow, U.S.S.R.
Muller	Robinson, Arden Arthur	27 February 1960	Brisbane, Queensland, Australia
	Colthorpe, Robert William	27 February 1971	Brisbane, Queensland, Australia
	McCormack, Mark Hume	1 March 1986	Asheville, North Carolina, USA
Nagelsen	Wright, Francis Irvin	28 July 1981	Greenwich, Washington, New York, USA
Newberry	Howe, Ralph Elliot	12 August, 1997	St. Petersburg, Florida, USA
Oremans	Vermeer Christ	20 December 2003	Berlicom, The Netherlands
Perebiyas	Zadorozhnly	15 October, 2005	Kharkov, Ukraine
Provis	Bradtke, Mark Robert	27 February 1994	Melbourne, Victoria, Australia
Puzejova	Suk, Cyril	5 May 1961	Prague, Czechoslovakia
Ramsey	Beamish, Alfred Ernest	30 September 1911	Marylebone, London, England
Reynolds	Price, Lowell Eldred Grant	28 October 1961	Bloemfontein, O.F.S., South Africa
Ridley	O'Meara, Daniel Joseph Patrick	3 October 1935	Bury St. Edmonds, Suffolk, England
Rush	Magers, Stephen Walter	19 December 1986	San Antonio, Texas, USA
Sampson	Hayward, Daniel Abbott	4 October 1958	Pasadena, California, USA

Maiden name	Married to	Date of marriage	Place of marriage
Schuurman	Haygarth, Peter	29 May 1964	Durban, Natal, South Africa
	Osborne, Robin	1977	–
Seeney	Fancutt, Trevor Thomas	14 April 1957	Yeoville, Johannesburg, Transvaal, South Africa
Simpson	Pickering, William Henry	28 July 1885	Tow Law, Durham, England
Tatarkova	Feltham, Timothy	14 September 2007	Surbiton, Surrey, England
Tauziat	Palaurena, Ramuncho	16 July, 2005	Biarritz, France
Truman	Janes, Gerald Thomas	1 December 1967	Loughton, Essex, England
Ward	Hales, Robert	28 November 1959	Hove, Sussex, England
Wynne	Bolton, George Frederick	6 July 1940	Melbourne, Victoria, Australia
Varner	Bloss, William Gerald	22 July 1969	Ruidoso, New Mexico, USA

The Semi-finalists

GENTLEMEN

Name	Date of Birth	Place of Birth	Date of Death	Place of Death	Event and Year
ADAMS, David Dixey	5 Jan 1970	Durban, Natal, South Africa			D 2000
AITKEN, Harold Issidro Tower	9 April 1877	Lima, Peru	27 Jul 1939	Esher, Surrey, England	M 1914
AMRITRAJ, Anand	20 Mar 1952	Madras, India			D 1976
AMRITRAJ, Vijay	14 Dec 1953	Madras, India			D 1976
ANCIC, Mario	30 Mar 1984	Split, Yugoslavia			S 2004
ANDREEV, Igor	14 Jul 1983	Moscow, USSR			M 2008
ANNACONE, Paul Thomas	20 Mar 1963	Southampton, N.Y., USA			D 1986
ARTHURS, Wayne Sean	18 Mar 1971	Adelaide, SA Australia			D 2004
ASBOTH, Jozsef	18 Sep 1917	Szombathely, Hungary	11 Sep 1986	Munich, West Germany	S 1948
AYALA, Luis Alberto	18 Sep 1932	Santiago, Chile			M 1957
BAGHDATIS, Marcos	17 Jun 1985	Limassol, Cyprus			S 2006
BECKER, Roger	6 Feb 1934	South Norwood, Surrey, England			D 1957
BERGELIN, Lennart	10 Jun 1925	Alingsas, Sweden	4 Nov 2008	Stockholm, Sweden	M 1947
BERGER, R. Arthur					M 1926
BERGH, Rikard Hakan	14 Jun 1966	Karlskoga, Sweden			D 1993
BLAKE, James Riley	29 Dec 1979	Yonkers, New York, USA			D 2009
BOPANNA, Rohan	4 Mar 1980	Bangalore, India			D 2013
BOUSSUS, Jacques Christian	5 Mar 1908	Hyeres, France	12 Aug 2003	Neuilly, Hauts-de-Seine, France	S 1928, D1932
BRICHANT, Jacques	28 Mar 1930	Mont-sur-Marchienne, Belgium	9 May 2011		S 1953
BROAD, Neil Peter	20 Nov 1966	Cape Town, Cape Province, South Africa			M 1997
CANDY, Donald William	31 Mar 1929	Adelaide, SA Australia			M 1952
CANER, George Colket	5 Jul 1894	St. Davids, Pennsylvania, USA	23 June 1984	Manchester, Massachusetts, USA	D 1922
CARMICHAEL, Robert John	4 Jul 1940	Melbourne, Victoria, Australia	18 Nov 2003	Melbourne, Victoria, Australia	D 1977
CONDON, John Joseph (Jack)	9 Sep 1903	Johannesburg, Transvaal, South Africa	1 Jan 1967	Champagne Castle, Escourt, Natal, South Africa	D 1927
CONTRERAS, Francisco	16 Jun 1934	Mexico City, Mexico			M 1958
CORNEJO SECKEL, Patricio	6 Jun 1944	Santiago, Chile			D 1972
COX, Mark	5 Jul 1943	Leicester, England			D 1966, 1977
CRAMER, Patrick John	21 Mar 1947	Brakpan, Transvaal, South Africa	16 April, 2003	South Africa	M 1972
CREALY, Richard Douglas	18 Sep 1944	Sydney, NSW, Australia			D 1975

Name	Date of Birth	Place of Birth	Date of Death	Place of Death	Event and Year
CROLE-REES, Gordon Rhind Oak	17 Nov 1883	Southend, Essex, England	9 Jun 1954	Chichester, Sussex, England	M 1928, 1930
CHELA, Juan Ignacio	30 Aug 1979	Buenos Aires, Argentina			D 2010
CROOKENDEN, Ian Sinclair	10 Dec 1943	Lower Hutt, Wellington, New Zealand			D 1964
CURTIS, Peter William	29 Aug 1945	Woking, Surrey, England			D 1967
DAMM, Martin	1 Aug 1972	Liberec, Czechoslovakia			D 1997, 2006
DAVIS, Scott Eirik	27 Aug 1962	Santa Monica, California, USA			M 1985
DE-JAGER, John-Laffnie	17 Mar 1973	Johannesburg, Transvaal, South Africa			D 2000
DEL POTRO, Juan Martin	23 Sep 1988	Tandil, Argentina			S 2013
DELAITRE, Olivier Nicolas Herve	1 Jun 1967	Metz, France			D 1999
DIMITROV, Grigor	16 May 1961	Mascover, Bulgaria			S 2014
DLOUHY, Lukas	9 Apr 1987	Pisek, Czechoslovakia			D 2008, M 2010
DOOHAN, Peter	2 May 1961	Newcastle, NSW, Australia			D 1984, 1988
DRYSDALE, Eric Clifford	26 May 1941	Nelspruit, Transvaal, South Africa			S 1965, D 1974, 1977
DUPRE, Patrick	16 Sep 1954	Liege, Belgium			S 1979
EAGLE, Joshua Andrew	10 May 1973	Toowoomba, Queensland, Australia			M 2000
ERLICH, Dario Jonathan	5 Apr 1977	Buenos Aires, Argentina			D2003
EDWARDS, Henry (Eddie+)	3 Jul 1956	Pretoria, Transvaal, South Africa			D 1988
FANCUTT, Michael Thomas	20 Feb 1961	Brisbane, Queensland, Australia			D 1984
FANCUTT, Trevor Thomas	14 Jul 1934	Kokstad, Natal, South Africa			M 1956
FASSBENDER, Jurgen	21 May 1948	Wesseling, West Germany			D 1973, 1975
FERREIRA, Ellis Russell	19 Feb 1970	Pretoria, Transvaal, South Africa			D 1996
FERREIRA, Wayne Richard	15 Sep 1971	Johannesburg, Transvaal, South Africa			D 1991, 1994
FIBAK, Wojciech-Jan	30 Aug 1952	Poznan, Poland			D 1978
FILLOL, Jaime Jose	3 Jun 1946	Santiago, Chile			D 1972
FISH, Mardy	9 Dec 1981	Edina, Minnesota, USA			D 2009
FLAM, Herbert	7 Nov 1928	New York, N.Y., USA	25 Nov 1980	Los Angeles, California, USA	S 1951 1952
FORBES, Gordon Lovell	21 Feb 1934	Burgersdorp, Cape Province, South Africa			D 1963
FORGET, Guy	4 Jan 1965	Casablanca, Morocco			D 1992
FRASER, John Gavan	1 Aug 1935	Melbourne, Victoria, Australia			S 1962, D 1962
FRAWLEY, Rodney John	8 Sep 1952	Brisbane, Queensland, Australia			S 1981
FROEHLING, Frank Arthur	19 May 1942	San Diego, California, USA			M 1964
FYZEE, Ali Hassan	9 Oct 1879	Bombay, India			D 1923
GASQUET, Richard	18 Jun 1986	Beziers, France			S 2007
GERRARD, Lewis Albert	5 Apr 1938	Auckland, New Zealand			D 1964
GIAMMALVA, Anthony John	21 Apr 1958	Houston, Texas, USA			M 1984

Name	Date of Birth	Place of Birth	Date of Death	Place of Death	Event and Year
GIMELSTOB, Justin Jeremy	26 Jan 1977	Livingston, New Jersey, USA			M 1998
GIMENO, Andres	3 Aug 1937	Barcelona, Spain			S 1970
GOELLNER, Marc-Kevin Peter	22 Sep 1970	Rio de Janeiro, Brazil			D 1994, 1995
GOMEZ, Andres	27 Feb 1960	Guayaquil, Ecuador			D 1987
GORMAN, Thomas Warner	19 Jan 1946	Seatle, Washington, USA			S 1971
GRAEBNER, Clark Edward	4 Nov 1943	Cleveland, Ohio, USA			S 1968, D 1965, 1966, 1971,
					M 1972
GREEN, Cecil John Tindell	3 Jul 1889	Sunderland, Durham, England	15 Mar 1941	Sunderland, Durham, England	M 1922
GREIG, Donald McNeil	31 Jan 1897	Battersea, London, England	15 Sep 1959	Teddington, Middlesex, England	M 1927
GROSJEAN, Sebastien Rene	29 May 1978	Marseille, France			S 2003, 2004
HAAS, Thomas Mario	3 Apr 1978	Hamburg, West Germany			S 2009
HARPER, Jack Edwin	8 Apr 1914	St. Kilda, Victoria, Australia	17 Jan 2005	Melbourne, Victoria, Australia	D 1948
HECHT, Ladislav	31 Aug 1910	Zilina, Czechoslovakia	27 May 2004	New York, New York, USA	D 1937
HENMAN, Timothy Henry	6 Sep 1974	Oxford, England			S 1998, 1999, 2001, 2002
HLASEK, Jakob	12 Nov 1964	Prague, Czechoslovakia			D 1986, 1992
IRVINE, Douglas (Hank+)	1 Sep 1943	Bulawayo, Rhodesia			M 1970
JANOWICZ, Jerzy	13 Nov 1990	Lodz, Poland			S 2013
JAVORSKY, Jiri	9 Feb 1932	Prague, Czechoslovakia			M 1960, 1961
JOHANSSON, Thomas Karl	24 Mar 1975	Linkoping, Sweden			S 2005
JOHNSTONE, Chris. Mark	12 Oct 1960	Perth, W.A. Australia			M 1982
KAFELNIKOV, Yevgeny Alexandrovich	18 Feb 1974	Sochi, USSR			D 1994, 1995
KAS, Christopher	13 Jun 1980	Trostburg, West Germany			D 2011
KERR, Jordan Spencer Hastings	26 Oct 1979	Adelaide, SA, Australia			M 2003
KIDSON, Norman Studholme Brownrigg	20 Feb 1885	Double Bay, NSW Australia	29 Sep 1954	Dublin, Ireland	M 1913
KINGSLEY, Charles Herbert	6 Mar 1899	Moulmein, Burma			M 1933
KIRBY, Vernon Gordon (Bob+)	22 Jun 1911	Durban, Natal, South Africa			D 1933
KNIGHT, William Arthur	12 Nov 1935	Northampton, England			M 1958, 1959
KOCH, Thomaz	11 May 1945	Porto Alegre, Brazil			D 1971
KOENIG, Robert Louis	5 Jul 1971	Durban, Natal, South Africa			M 2002
KOHLBERG, Andrew Scott	17 Aug 1959	New York, N.Y., USA			M 1987
KRISHNAN, Ramanathan	11 Apr 1937	Madras, India			S 1960, 1961
KRUGER, Stefan	3 Aug 1966	Cape Town, Cape Province, South Africa			D 1990
KUHNEN, Patrick Kurt	11 Feb 1966	Putrlingen, West Germany			D 1993
KUKULJEVIC, Franjo	1909	Zagreb, Yugoslavia	2000	Johannesburg, Transvaal, South Africa	D 1938

Name	Date of Birth	Place of Birth	Date of Death	Place of Death	Event and Year
KULTI, Lars Johan Nicklas	22 Apr 1971	Kungsanen, Stockholm, Sweden			D 2000
LAMB, Ernest Talbot Thomas	5 Sep 1881	Stamford Hill, London, England	12 Sep 1962	Southgate, London, England	M 1924
LAPENTTI, Nicolas Alexander	13 Aug 1976	Guayaquil, Ecuador			M 2000
LAREAU, Sebastien Dennis	27 Apr 1973	Montreal, Quebec, Canada			D 1998
LARSEN, Arthur David (Art+)	17 Apr 1925	Haywood, California, USA	7 Dec 2012	San Leandro, California, USA	D 1956
LECONTE, Henri	4 Jul 1963	Lillers, France			S 1986
LEE, Harold GeorgeNewcombe	15 Jun 1907	Teddington, Middlesex, England	14 Apr 1998	Frome, Somerset, England	M 1934
LEEDS, Laurence Cary	16 Apr 1957	New York, N.Y., USA	30 Jan 2003	Miami, Florida, USA	M 1981
LEGENSTEIN, Ladislav	19 Nov 1926	Cakovec, Yugoslavia			D 1959
LLOYD, David Alan	3 Jan 1948	Leigh-on-Sea, Essex, England			D 1973
MAHUT, Nicholas Pierre Armand	21 Jan 1982	Angers, France			D 2014
MACKAY, Barry Bruce	31 Aug 1935	Cincinnati, Ohio, USA	15 Jun 2012	San Francisco, California, USA	S 1959, D 1958
MALFROY, Camille Enright	21 Jan 1909	Hokitaka, Westland, New Zealand	8 May 1966	Taupo, New Zealand	M 1936, 1939
MALISSE, Xavier	19 Jul 1980	Kortrijk, Belgium			S 2002
MARTIN, Todd Christopher	8 Jul 1970	Lansing, Michigan, USA			S 1994, 1996
MATHEY, Dean	23 Nov 1890	Brooklyn, N.Y., USA	16 Apr 1972	Princeton, New Jersey, USA	D 1922
MAVROGORDATO, Theodore Michel	31 Jul 1883	London, England	24 Aug 1941	Limpsfield, Surrey, England	M 1913
MAYER, Eugene	11 Apr 1956	New York, NY, USA			D 1980
MAYOTTE, Timothy Spence	3 Aug 1960	Springfield, Massachusetts, USA			S 1982
MECIR, Miloslav	19 May 1964	Bojnice, Czechoslovakia			S 1988
MEILER, Karl	30 Apr 1949	Erlangen, Bayern, West Germany	17 Apr 2014	Munich, Germany	D 1973
MENZEL, Roderich Ferdinand Ortomar	13 Apr 1907	Reichenberg, Bohemia	18 Oct 1987	Munich, West Germany	D 1937
MERLIN, Andre	15 Nov 1911	Brazzaville, Congo	5 Sep 1960	Paris, France	D 1932
MICHIBATA, Glenn	13 Jun 1962	Toronto, Ontario, Canada			D 1991
MILLS, Alan Ronald	6 Nov 1935	Stretford, Manchester, England			D 1966
MITIC, Dragutin	16 Sep 1917	Zagreb, Yugoslavia			D 1946
MULLER, Gary Robert	27 Dec 1964	Durban, Natal, South Africa			D 1988,1993
NELSON, Todd	18 Mar 1961	The Dalles, Oregon, USA			M 1990
NORMAN, Dick	1 Mar 1971	Waregam, Belgium			D 2009, 2010, 2011
NORVAL, Pieter	7 Apr 1970	Bellville, Cape Town, South Africa			D 1991
NOURNEY, Wilhelm Orto Eberhard	23 Apr 1904	Cologne, Germany	31 July 1936	Brunshaupten, Nr. Rostock, Germany	D 1933
OLLIFF, John Sheldon	1 Dec 1908	London, England	29 Jun 1951	Chiswick, Middlesex, England	D 1939, M 1934
ORANTES, Manuel	6 Feb 1949	Granada, Spain			S 1972
OTWAY, Mark Anthony	9 Oct 1931	Auckland, New Zealand			M 1954
PAISH, John Geoffrey	25 Mar 1948	Croydon, Surrey, England			D 1973

Name	Date of Birth	Place of Birth	Date of Death	Place of Death	Event and Year
PALLADA, Josip	5 Feb 1912	Zagreb, Yugoslavia	3 May 1994	Zagreb, Yugoslavia	D 1938, 1946
PEYA, Alexander	27 Jun 1980	Vienna, Austria			D 2011
POHMANN, Hans-Jurgen	23 May 1947	Cologne, West Germany			D 1975
PUNCEC, Franjo A.	25 Nov 1913	Charkovitz, Yugoslavia	5 Jan 1985	Johannesburg, Transvaal, South Africa	S 1938, 1939
QURESHI, Alsam-ul-Haq	17 Mar 1980	Lahore, Pakistan			M 2014
RAONIC, Milos	27 Dec 1990	Podgorica, Montenegro			S 2014
RAYMOND, Louis Bosman	28 Jun 1895	Pretoria, Transvaal, South Africa	30 Jan 1962	Johannesburg, Transvaal, South Africa	S 1924, D1924, 1927 M 1927
RICHARDSON, Hamilton Farrar	24 Aug 1933	Baton Rouge, Louisiana, USA	5 Nov 2006		S 1956, D 1951, 1965
ROBERTSON, Michael	2 Jul 1963	Johannesburg, Transvaal, South Africa			M 1986
ROGER-VASSELIN, Edouard Christophe	28 Nov 1983	Gennevillers, France			D 2013
ROJER, Jean-Julien	25 Aug 1981	Curaçao			M 2013
RUSSELL, Alejo Domingo	1 Sep 1916	Cordoba, Argentina			M 1938
SA, Andre Rezende	6 May 1977	Belo Horizonte, Brazil			D 2007
SADRI, John	19 Sep 1956	Charlotte, North Carolina, USA			D 1979
SAFIN, Marat	27 Jan 1980	Moscow, USSR			S 2008
SANGSTER, Michael John	11 Sep 1940	Kingskerswell, Devon, England	30 Apr 1985	Torquay, Devon, England	S 1961
SCHUETTLER, Rainer	25 Apr 1976	Korbach, West Germany			S 2008
SCHWANK, Eduardo Jonatan	23 Apr 1986	Rosario, Argentina			D 2010
SEGAL, Alan Abraham	23 Oct 1930	Johannesburg, Transvaal, South Africa			D 1963
SEGURA-CANO, Francisco Olegario	20 Jun 1921	Guayaquil, Ecuador			D 1946
SHAYES, Ronald Alfred	12 Sep 1912	Croydon, Surrey, England	17 Dec 1940	Rhodesia	D 1939, M 1938
SHELTON, Bryan Cleveland	12 Dec 1965	Huntsville, Alabama, USA			M 1992
SIEMERINK, Johannes Martinus	14 Apr 1970	Rijnsburg, The Netherlands			D 1996
SIMONSSON, Hans Kent Ingvar	1 May 1962	Hyltebruk, Sweden			D 1983
SLOZIL, Pavel	29 Dec 1955	Opara, Czechoslovakia			D 1986
STEPANEK, Radek	27 Nov 1978	Karvina, Czechoslovakia			D 2013, 2104
STILWELL, Graham Rodney	5 Nov 1945	Denham, Buckinghamshire, England			D 1967
STOLTENBERG, Jason Robert	4 Apr 1970	Narrabri, NSW, Australia			S 1996
STRODE, Charles Darlington	5 Sep 1957	El Cajon, California, USA			M 1982, 1983
TALBOT, Byron Derek	15 Sep 1964	Johannesburg, Transvaal, South Africa			D 1993
TAYGAN, Ferdi	5 Dec 1956	Worcester, Massachusetts, USA			D 1982, 1984
TAYLOR, Roger	14 Oct 1941	Sheffield, Yorkshire, England			S 1967, 1970, 1973
TEACHER, Brian David	23 Dec 1954	San Diego, California, USA			D 1977

Name	Date of Birth	Place of Birth	Date of Death	Place of Death	Event and Year
TILLSTROM, Mikael	5 Mar 1972	Jonkoping, Sweden			D 2000
TIRIAC, Ion	9 May 1939	Brasov, Romania			D 1970
TSONGA, Jo–Wilfried Evrard	17 Apr 1985	Le Mans, France			S 2011, 2012
ULRICH, Torben	4 Oct 1932	Copenhagen, Denmark			D 1959
VAN LENNEP, Christiaan	3 Jan 1887	Hilversum, The Netherlands			D 1926
VAN EMBURGH, Gregory Scott	10 May 1966	New York, N.Y., USA			D 1990
VAN RENSBURG, Christo Jensen	23 Oct 1962	Uitenhage, Cape Province, South Africa	5 Dec 1955	Territet, Switzerland	D 1986 M 1991, 1996
VON KEHRLING, Bela	25 Jan 1891	Budapest, Hungary	26 Apr 1937	Budapest, Hungary	D 1925, 1926
VIZNER, Pavel	15 Jul 1970	Prague, Czechoslovakia			D 1997
VOLTCHKOV, Vladimir	7 Apr 1978	Minsk, USSR			S 2000
WASHER, Jean	22 Aug 1894	Brussels, Belgium	23 Mar 1972	Geneva, Switzerland	M 1923
Name	Date of Birth	Place of Birth	Date of Death	Place of Death	Event and Year
WASHER, Philippe	6 Aug 1924	Brussels, Belgium			D 1953
WHEATLEY, John David Patrick	1 Jan 1899	O.F.S., South Africa	5 Nov 1967	Kensington, London, England	M 1925
WHEATON, David	2 Jun 1969	Minneapolis, Minnesota, USA			S 1991
WILKISON, Timothy McLane	21 Nov 1959	Shelby, North Carolina, USA			D 1979
WORTHINGTON, George Allan	10 Oct 1928	Marrickville, Sydney, N.S.W., Australia	8 Dec 1964	Westminster, London, England	D 1955, M 1949, 1950, 1953
ZIVOJINOVIC, Slobodan	23 July 1963	Belgrade, Yugoslavia			S 1986, D 1987

+ forenames generally used

171 players

LADIES

Name	Date of Birth	Place of Birth	Date of Death	Place of Death	Event and Year
ACKER, Sherry L.	16 Jun 1959	Kalamazoo, Michigan, USA			M 1981
ADAMS, Katrina Michelle	5 Aug 1968	Chicago, Illinois, USA			D 1988
ADDISON, Marion Lilian	21 Dec 1885	New Glenieg, Adelaide, SA Australia	27 Nov 1982	Kew, Melbourne Victoria, Australia	M 1919
ARMSTRONG, Mrs. B.R. (Bell, Theodora Mary) (Dora+)	25 Feb 1876	Kingston upon Thames, Surrey, England	6 Dec 1962	Wivelsfield, East Sussex, England	D 1913, 1920
ANTHONY, Julie Kathleen (Butera, Mrs. R.)	13 Jan 1948	Los Angeles, California, USA			D 1974
AOYAMA, Shuko	19 Dec 1987	Kabagawa, Japan			D 2013
APPELMANS, Sabine (Haubourdin, Mrs. S.)	22 Apr 1972	Aalst, Belgium			D 1997
AZARENKA, Victoria Fiodorovna	31 Jul 1989	Minsk, USSR			S 2011, 2012

Name	Date of Birth	Place of Birth	Date of Death	Place of Death	Event and Year
BARKER, Susan Dorothy (Tankard, Mrs. L.P.)	19 Apr 1956	Paignton, Devon, England			S 1977, D1978, 1981
BLAIR, Mrs.N.W. (Molly+) (Lincoln, Winifred Mary)	4 Jul 1918	Goodmayes, Essex, England	2 Feb 2004	Ledbury, Herefordshire, England	D 1947, 1948
BONICELLI, Fiorella M (Duxin, Mrs. P.)	21 Dec 1951	Lima, Peru			D 1973
BOSHOFF, Delina Ann (Linky+) (Mortlock, Mrs.)	12 Nov 1956	Port Elizabeth, Eastern Province, South Africa			D 1976
BOSTOCK, Mrs. E.W.A. - see NICOLL					
BOYD, Esna Flora (Robertson, Mrs. A.)	21 Sep 1900	Melbourne, Victoria, Australia	13 Nov 1966	Dunfermline, Fife, Scotland	D 1928
BREMOND, Mrs E Severine, Aurelie Beltrame)	14 Aug 1979	Montpelier, France			M 2007
BREWER, Mrs. W. (Nicolls, Heather Mary Hope) (Segal, Mrs. A.A.)	25 Jul 1931	Southport, Lancashire, England			D 1954
BRICKA, Justina A (Horwitz, Mrs. C.R.)	14 Feb 1943	St. Louis, Missouri, USA			D 1962, M 1964
BUCK, Mrs. R.A. (Midge+) (Gladman, Marjorie Kathleen) (Van Ryn, Mrs. J.W.)	23 Jun 1909	Vancouver, British Columbia, Canada	9 Nov 1999	Peterborough, New Hampshire, USA	D 1950
BUNGE, Bettina	13 Jun 1963	Adliswil, Switzerland			S 1982, D 1982, M 1981, 1986
BURGIN, Elise Marie	5 Mar 1962	Baltimore, Maryland, USA			D 1986
BURKE, Judith Frances (Tinnock, Mrs. W.J.)	21 Feb 1931	Takaka, Nelson, New Zealand			M 1954
CALLENS, Els Sidonia Hendrika	20 Aug 1970	Antwerp, Belgium			M 2002
CAPRIATI, Jennifer Marie	29 Mar 1976	New York, N.Y., USA			S 1991, 2001
CHAFFEE, Nancy Ann (Kiner, Mrs. R.) (Whitaker, Mrs. J.)	6 Mar 1929	Ventura, California, USA	11 Aug 2002	Coronado, California, USA	D 1950, 1951
CHAN, Jung-Jan	17 Aug 1989	Taipei, Chinese Taipei	M 2011		
CHANFREAU, Mrs. J.B. (Sherriff, Gail Vivian) (Lovera, Mrs. J.J.) (Benedetti, Mrs J-P)	3 Apr 1945	Sydney, N.S.W., Australia			D 1971, 1975
CLARKE, Edith R.					D 1925, 1926

Name	Date of Birth	Place of Birth	Date of Death	Place of Death	Event and Year
CRADDOCK, Mrs A.C. (Covell, Doris Kate)	26 Feb 1885	Brixton, Surrey, England	5 Mar 1963	Winchester, Hampshire, England	D 1921
CURTIS, Mrs. P.W. (Eisel, Mary Ann Clark) (Beattie, Mrs. D.)	25 Nov 1946	St. Louis, Missouri, USA			D 1969, 1971
DATE, Kimiko (Krumm, Mrs. M.)	28 Sep 1970	Kyoto, Japan			S 1996
DAVIDSON, Mrs. G.C. - see SCOFIELD					
DEARMAN, Evelyn Mary (Cleverly, Mrs.R.H.)	8 Sep 1908	Putney, Surrey, England	2 Dec 1993	Eastbourne, Sussex, England	M 1937
DECHY, Nathalie (Maitre-Devallon, Mrs. A.)	21 Feb 1979	Abimes, Guadeloupe			D 2008
DEMENTIEVA, Elena Vyachesiavn(Afinogenov, Mrs. M.)	15 Oct 1981	Moscow, USSR			S 2008, 2009, D 2003
DMITRIEVA, Anna Vladimirovna (Tolstoy, Mrs. M.) (Chukovsky, Mrs. D.)	10 Dec 1940	Moscow, USSR			D 1963
DOKIC, Jelena	12 Apr 1983	Belgrade, Yugoslavia			S 2000
DULKO, Gisela Alejandra (Gago, Mrs. F.)	30 Jan 1985	Buenos Aires, Argentina			D 2010
DUSHEVINA, Vera Yevgenyvna	6 Oct 1986	Moscow, USSR			M 2013, 2014
ERAKOVIC, Marina	6 Mar 1988	Split, Yugoslavia			D 2011
FAIRBANK, Rosalyn Doris (Nideffer, Mrs. R.)	2 Nov 1960	Durban, Natal, South Africa			D 1981, 1986, M 1987
FEDAK, Yuliana	8 June 1983	Novaya, Kakhouka, Ukraine, USSR			D 2006
FEILDEN, Mrs. H.J. (Bannister, Naomi Victoria Juliet)	4 Feb 1897	Cork, Cork, Ireland			D 1926
FELTHAM, Mary Hilda Beatrice (Russell, Mrs. M.A.V.)	9 May 1907	Sutton, Surrey, England	11 Jun 1984	Bournemouth, Dorset, England	D 1930
FENDICK, Patricia Ann (Patty+) (McCain, Mrs. S.L.)	31 Mar 1965	Sacramento, California, USA	13 Sep 1997	Ewhurst, Surrey, England	D 1986, 1990, M 1987, 1988
FERNANDEZ DE SOTO, Marie Isabel	18 Sep 1950	Cali, Colombia			D 1973
FERNANDEZ, Maria Jose (Mary Joe+) (Godsick, Mrs. A.)	19 Aug 1971	Dominican Republic			S 1991, D 1991, 1993

Name	Date of Birth	Place of Birth	Date of Death	Place of Death	Event and Year
FLETCHER, Helen Margaret (Barker, Mrs. M.)	24 Aug 1931	Heanor, Derbyshire, England			D 1953
FLIPKENS, Kirsten	10 Jan 1986	Gell, Belgium			S 2103
GANNON, Joyce Irene }	21 Mar 1928	Enfield, Middlesex, England			D 1949, 1950
MOTTRAM, Mrs. A.J. }					
GOLARSA, Laura	27 Nov 1967	Milan, Italy			M 1996
GOSS, Eleanor A (Lanning, Mrs. C.E.)	18 Nov 1895	New York, N.Y., USA	6 Nov 1982	Salisbury, Connecticut, USA	D 1924
GRAHAM, Deborah Anne (Shaffer, Mrs. W.C.)	25 Aug 1970	Walnut Creek, California, USA			D 1998
GRAEBNER, Mrs. C.E. (Caldwell, Carole Ann)	24 Jun 1943	Pittsburgh, Pennsylvania, USA	19 Nov 2008	New York, New York, USA	D 1965
GROENMAN, Gertrude Johanna (Trudy+) (Walhof, Mrs. C.G.) (Hoolboom, Mrs. M.A.)	15 Jan 1944	Groningen, The Netherlands			M 1964
GUERRANT, Mrs. T.E. - see SCHALLAU					
HABSUDOVA, Karina (Cilekova, Mrs. M.)	2 Aug 1973	Bratislava, Czechoslovakia			M 2001
HALEP, Simona	27 Sep 1991	Constanta, Romania			S 2014
HALL, Mrs. A.A.					D 1919
HARFORD, Tanya Jane (Gemmell, Mrs. D.)	28 Nov 1958	Capetown, Cape Province, South Africa			D 1981
HARTER, Kathleen Marie (Kathy+) (Marcus, Mrs. M.P.) (Shubin, Mrs. S.A.)	27 Oct 1946	Los Angeles, California, USA			S 1967
HARTIGAN, Joan Marcia (Bathurst, Mrs. R.H.)	6 Jun 1912	Sydney, NSW, Australia	31 Aug 2000	Sydney, NSW, Australia	S 1934, 1935
HAYLOCK, Mrs. R.E. (McAlpin, Elsa Maude)	27 Oct 1901	Leicester, Leicestershire, England	20 Aug 1980	Leicester, Leicestershire, England	D 1935
HELLYER, Margaret Batten (Burston, Mrs. K.J.)	29 Jul 1937	Sydney, NSW, Australia			M 1957
HETHERINGTON, Jill Margaret (Hultquist, Mrs. R.A.)	27 Oct 1964	Brampton, Ontario, Canada			D 1986

Name	Date of Birth	Place of Birth	Date of Death	Place of Death	Event and Year
HILTON, Mrs. R (Clements, Betty Evelyn) (Harrison, Mrs. A.J.C.) (Smart, Mrs. L.R.)	12 Feb 1920	Birmingham, England			D 1947, 1949
HOAD, Mrs. L.A. (Staley, Jennifer Jane)	3 Mar 1934	Melborne, Victoria, Australia			D 1955
HOBBS, Anne Elizabeth C	21 Aug 1959	Nottingham, Nottinghamshire, England			D 1983
HOGARTH, Harriet Gilroy (Calder, Mrs. A.H.)	4 Dec 1892		24 Dec 1973		D 1920
HOLMAN, Edith Dorothy	18 Jul 1883	Hendon, Middlesex, England	15 Jun 1968	Willesden, Brent, London, England	D 1919, 1922
HOPPS, Janet Stephanie (Adkisson, Mrs. W.C.D.)	4 Aug 1934	Berkeley, California, USA			D 1960
HUBBELL, Katharine Mary	29 Apr 1921	Boston, Massachusetts, USA			D 1954
HUBER, Anke	4 Dec 1974	Bruchsal, West Germany			M 2000
HUNT, Margaret Lilian (Price, Mrs A.R.)	25 Apr 1942	Vryheid, Natal, South Africa			D 1961
HUTCHINGS, Lynnette Margaret (Nette, Mrs. N.)	26 May 1942	Johannesburg, Transvaal, South Africa			D 1961
INGRAM, Joan Mary	28 Feb 1910	Harrow, Middlesex, England	4 Feb 1981	Westminster, London, England	D 1936, 1937, M 1934
IVANOVIC, Ana	6 Nov 1987	Belgrade, Yugoslavia			S 2007
JESSUP, Mrs. J.B. (Zinderstein, Marion Hall) (MacLure, Mrs. H.G.)	3 May 1896	Allentown, Pennsylvania, USA	14 Aug 1980	Wilmington, Delaware, USA	D 1924
KERBER, Angelique	18 Jan 1988	Bremen, West Germany			S 2012
KIRILENKO, Maria	25 Jan 1987	Moscow, USSR			M 2008
KIRK, Mrs. J.S. (Armstrong, Ruth Marjorie) (Barnett, Mrs S.A.)	7 Jan 1904	Bedford Park, Bedforshire, England	7 Aug 1978	Sutton Coldfield, Birmingham, England	D 1935
KLOSS, Ilana Sheryl	22 Mar 1956	Johannesburg, Transvaal, South Africa			D 1976
KNODE, Mrs. D.P. (Head, Alice Dorothy)	4 Jul 1925	Richmond, California, USA			S 1953, 1957
KORMOCZY SZEKELY, Zsuzsu (Susie+) (Branny, Mrs. E.) (Gero, Mrs. A.)	25 Aug 1924	Budapest, Hungary	16 Sep 2006	Budapest, Hungary	S 1958

Name	Date of Birth	Place of Birth	Date of Death	Place of Death	Event and Year
KRASNOROUTSKAYA, Lina	29 Apr 1984	Obninsk, USSR			D 2003
LEISK, Mrs. J.L.	6 Dec 1881	Sunderland, Durham, England	26 May 1947	Aylesbury, Buckinghamshire, England	D 1922
(Aitchison, Frances Helen)					
LINDQVIST, Catarina	13 Jun 1963	Kristinehamn, Sweden			S 1989
(Ryan, Mrs. J.W.)					
LLOYD, Mrs. J.A.G.	21 Feb 1944	London, England			D 1968
(Blakelock, Robina Averil)					
(Primrose, Mrs. G.B.)					
McCARTHY, Mrs. S.	28 Dec 1970	Haarlem, The Netherlands			D 1995
(Schultz, Brenda Anna Marie)					
MACLENNAN, Frances	20 Dec 1943	Glasgow, Scotland			D 1968
Veronica Margaret					
(Taylor, Mrs. R.)					
MANSER, Olive Braikenridge	19 Mar 1885	Tunbridge Wells, Kent, England	27 Dec 1965	St. Georges di Didonne, Charente Maritime, France	D 1913, 1920
MAPPIN, Susan	7 Nov 1947	Sheffield, Yorkshire, England			D 1976, 1977
MEDINA, GARRIGUES,	31 July 1982	Torrent, Valencia, Spain			D 2009
Ana Isabel					
MIRZA, Sania	15 Nov 1986	Mumbai, India			D 2011
(Malik, Mrs. S.)					
MORPHEW, Margaret (Peggy+)	3 Aug 1916	Clansthal, Natal, South Africa	6 Sep 1997	Howick, Natal, South Africa	D 1938
MOORE, Sally Marie	8 Jun 1940	Long Beach, California, USA			S 1959, D 1961
(Huss. Mrs. M.A.)					
MOTTRAM, Mrs. A.J.					
– see GANNON					
NICOLL, Jean Addie Bisset ⎫	14 Dec 1922	Leytonstone, Essex, England	2 Apr 1965	Ipswich, Suffolk, England	D 1939, 1946, 1947, 1948
BOSTOCK, Mrs. E.W. A ⎬					
NUTHALL, Betty May	23 May 1911	Surbiton, Surrey, England	8 Nov 1983	New York, N.Y., USA	D 1927, 1929, 1931, 1939 M 1933, 1939
(Shoemaker, Mrs. F.C.)					
O'NEILL, Mrs. E.A.	2 Sep 1867	Lytham, Lancaster, England	3 Jun 1934	Cannes, France	M 1913
(Fisher, Madeline Agnes)					
PARKHOMENKO, Mrs. A.	8 Oct 1962	Moscow, USSR			D 1987
(Cherneva, Svetlana Germanovna)					
PARTON, Mrs. E.G.	22 Jul 1881	Hampstead, Middlesex, England	12 Aug 1962	Oxted, Surrey, England	D 1913, 1919, M 1913
(Squire, Mabel Bramwell)					
(Mavrogordato, Mrs. T.M.)					

Name	Date of Birth	Place of Birth	Date of Death	Place of Death	Event and Year
PARTRIDGE, Joan Susan Vernon (Chatrier, Mrs. P.) (Crosnier, Mrs. J.R.)	12 Sep 1930	Albrighton, Nr. Shifnal, Shropshire, England	4 Dec 1999	Paris, France	D 1952
PAYOT, Lolette (Dodille, Mrs. R.)	17 Apr 1911	Lausanne, Switzerland	23 Feb 1988	Lausanne, Switzerland	D 1932, 1934
PENNETTA, Flavia Lizzy	25 Feb 1982	Brindisi, Italy			D 2010, 2012
PENROSE, Beryl Ethel Jean (Collier, Mrs. J.A.F.)	22 Dec 1930	Rockdale, Sydney, N.S.W. Australia			M 1955
PETKOVIC, Andrea	9 Sep 1987	Tuzla, Yugoslavia			D 2014
PINCKNEY, Violet Millicent	11 Mar 1871	Salisbury, Wiltshire, England	13 Mar 1955	Southampton, Hampshire, England	D 1914
PIRONKOVA, Tsvetana, Kirilova	13 Sep 1987	Plovdiv, Bulgaria			S 2010
POTTER, Barbara Cummings	22 Oct 1961	Waterbury, Connecticut, USA			D 1983, 1984
PRATT, Mrs. E.C.S. (Rosenquest, Charlotte Elizabeth (Betty+)	15 Apr 1925	Virginia, Minnesota, USA			S 1954, D 1951
PRETORIUS, Mrs Q.C. – see WALKDEN					
RADFORD, Kristine Louise (Kunce, Mrs. D.)	3 Mar 1970	Sydney, N.S.W., Australia			D 1994
RAMIREZ, Yolanda (Ochoa, Mrs. A.)	1 Mar 1935	Mexico City, Mexico			D 1957, 1958, 1959, M 1959
REINACH, Elna (Carstens, Mrs. P.A.)	2 Dec 1968	Pretoria, Transvaal, South Africa			D 1989, M 1986, 1991
REYNOLDS, Candy Sue	24 Mar 1955	Wichita, Kansas, USA			D 1980
REYES, Rosa Maria Delgado (Darmon, Mrs. P.)	23 Mar 1939	Mexico City, Mexico			D 1957, 1958, 1959, M 1958
RIHBANY, Mrs. E.H. (Pedersen, Helen A.) (McLaughlin, Mrs W.)	16 Jul 1916	Stamford, Connecticut, USA	5 Jul 1998	Barnstable, Massachusetts, USA	S 1949, D 1948, 1949
RINALDI, Kathleen Suzanne (Stunkel, Mrs. B)	24 Mar 1967	Stuart, Florida, USA			S 1985 M 1991
RINKEL, Mrs. I.F. (Quertier, Jean D.)	12 Nov 1925	Beckenham, Kent, England			D 1952, 1953
ROSE, Eleanor Florence	17 Feb 1880	Malton, Yorkshire, England	5 Oct 1971	Eastbourne, Sussex, England	D 1923
RUBIN, Chanda Renee	18 Feb 1976	Lafayette, Louisiana, USA			D 2002
RYBARIKOVA, Magdalena	4 Oct 1988	Piestany, Yugoslavia			D 2014
SAFAROVA, Lucie	4 Feb 1987	Brno, Czechoslovakia			S 2014

Name	Date of Birth	Place of Birth	Date of Death	Place of Death	Event and Year
SAFINA, Dinara Mikhailovna	27 Apr 1986	Moscow, USSR			S 2009
SANTANGELO, Mara	28 Jun 1981	Latina, Italy			D 2007
SAUNDERS, Jean Dorothy	30 July 1914	Calgary, Alberta, Canada			M 1938
SANDS, Mrs J (Mattek, Bethanie Lynn)	23 Mar 1985	Rochester, USA			M 2010
SCHALLAU, Ramona Anne GUERRANT, Mrs. T.E.	28 Nov 1948	Marengo, Iowa, USA			D 1974, 1978
SCHEEPERS, Chanelle (Anderson, Mrs R.)	13 Mar 1984	Harrismith, OFS, South Africa			D 2013
SCHETT, Barbara (Eagle, Mrs J.)	10 Mar 1976	Innsbruck, Austria			M 2000
SCHIAVONE, Francesca	23 Jun 1980	Milan, Italy			D 2012
SCHULTZE, Helga (Hoesl, Mrs. E.) Thaw, Mrs. D.M.)	2 Feb 1940	Berlin, Germany			D 1965
SCOFIELD, Barbara Van Alen DAVIDSON, Mrs. G.C.	24 Jun 1926	San Francisco, California, USA			D 1948, 1951
SEQUERA, Milagros (Huss Mrs S.)	30 Sep 1980	San Felipe, Yaracuy, Venezuela			M 2003
SCRIVEN, Margaret Croft (Peggy+) (Vivian, Mrs. F.H.)	17 Aug 1912	Chapel Allerton, Leeds, Yorkshire, England	25 Jan 2001	Haslemere, Surrey, England	D 1934
SHAW, Winifred Mason (Wooldridge, Mrs. K.)	18 Jan 1947	Glasgow, Scotland	30 Mar 1992	Woking, Surrey, England	D 1972
SMITH, Paula G.	10 Jan 1957	Boulder, Colorado, USA			D 1980
STEVENSON, Alexandra Winfield	15 Dec 1980	San Diego, California, USA			S 1999
STEWART, Bryanne Maree (Crabb, Mrs. J.)	9 Dec 1979	Sydney, NSW, Australia			D 2005
STRAWSON, Mrs. F.M. (Reid-Thomas, Edith Joan) (Hughes, Mrs. R.P.)	31 Aug 1903	Hampstead, Middlesex, England	8 Nov 1993	Tamworth, Staffordshire, England	M 1926
TANASUGARN, Tamarine	24 May 1977	Los Angeles, California, USA			D 2011
TEMESVÁRI, Andrea (Trunkos, Mrs. A.)	26 Apr 1966	Budapest, Hungary			M 1983
THOMAS, Muriel Alice (Viscontai, Mrs. C.)	1 May 1905	Santa Cruz, Tenerife, Canary Islands	19 Nov 1979	Carshalton, Sutton, London, England	D 1932, 1934

Name	Date of Birth	Place of Birth	Date of Death	Place of Death	Event and Year
VAN ZYL, Annette M. (Du Plooy, Mrs. J.L.)	25 Sep 1943	Pretoria, Transvaal, South Africa			M 1966, 1967
VERMAAK, Yvonne	18 Dec 1956	Port Elizabeth, Eastern Province, South Africa			S 1983
VIS, Caroline Michelle	4 Mar 1970	Vlaardingen, The Netherlands			M 1998
VLASTO, Julie Penelope (Serpieri, Mrs. J.)	8 Aug 1903	Marseille, France	2 Feb 1985	Lausanne, Switzerland	S 1926
WALKDEN, Patricia Molly (PRETORIUS, Mrs. Q.C.) }	12 Feb 1946	Bulawayo, Rhodesia			D 1970 M 1972
WALSH, Sharon Ann (Pete, Mrs. M.H.) (Arnold, Mrs. S.N.)	24 Feb 1952	San Francisco, California, USA			D 1983, 1984, M 1984
WELCH, Nora					D 1926
WHITE, Robin Maureen	10 Dec 1963	San Diego California, USA			D 1987
WHITMARSH, Mary Eileen (Halford, Mrs. W.C.J.)	14 Dec 1915	Hong Kong, South China			M 1936
WILLIAMS, Mrs. G.M. (Barclay, Joyce Stewart) (Hume, Mrs. I.) (Englefield, Mrs. A.D.) (Sacerdote, Mrs. G.) (Bennett, Mrs. R.D.)	22 Jul 1944	Dundee, Scotland			D 1972
WILD, Linda Marie (formerly Harvey-Wild) (Secord, Mrs. B.F.)	11 Feb 1971	Arlington Heights, Illinois, USA			D 1996
YOULE, Mrs. J.S. (Spofforth, Vera Ethel)	6 Nov 1891	Hampstead, London, England	30 Mar 1977	Egham, Surrey, England	D 1923, M 1922
YOUNG, Janet Anne (Langford, Mrs. J.)	22 Nov 1951	Melbourne, Victoria, Australia			D 1973
ZIEGENFUSS, Valerie Jean (Bradshaw, Mrs. D.)	29 Jun 1949	San Diego, California, USA			D 1969, 1971

+ forenames generally used
144 players

Lady Semi-finalists – marriages

Maiden name	Married to	Date of marriage	Place of marriage
Aitchison	Leisk, John Laurence	5 September 1914	Sutton, Surrey, England
Anthony	Butera, Richard	28 December 1976	
Appelmans	Haubourdin, Serge	20 September 1997	Erembodegem, Belgium
Armstrong	Kirk, John Symons	15 April 1926	Peterborough, Northampton, England
Bannister	Barnett, Sydney Alfred	14 August 1946	Birmingham, England
	Feilden, Harold Jackson	4 February 1920	Holborn, Middlesex, England
Barclay	Williams, Gerald Martin	21 March 1964	Kirkcaldy, Fife, Scotland
	Hume, Ian	12 September 1973	Glasgow, Scotland
	Englefield, Anthony Devereux	2 September 1988	Reigate, Surrey, England
	Sacerdote, Giacomo	13 April 1994	Merton, London, England
Barker	Bennett, Reginald Donald	20 November 1998	Sutton, London, England
Bell	Tankard, Lance Paul	14 October 1988	Esher, Surrey, England
Beltrame	Armstrong, Blosse Richard	30 April 1903	Surbiton, Surrey, England
Blakelock	Bremond, Eric	10 September, 2005	
	Lloyd, John Arthur Geoffrey	6 October 1962	Knightsbridge, Middlesex, England
Bonicelli	Primrose, Graham Burton	14 December 1970	Chelsea, Westminster, London, England
Boshoff	Duxin, Philippe	19 August 1978	Boulogne, Paris, France
	Mortlock,		
Boyd	Robertson, Angus	11 March 1929	Edinburgh, Scotland
Bricka	Horwitz, Charles Richard	11 March 1966	St Louis, Missouri, USA
Burke	Tinnock, William James	16 May 1955	Pukekura Park, New Plymouth, New Zealand
Caldwell	Graebner, Clark Edward	10 July 1964	Cleveland Heights, Ohio, USA
Chaffee	Kiner, Ralph	14 October 1951	Santa Barbara, California, USA
	Whitaker, John	4 April 1991	Rancho Mirage, California, USA
Chernieva	Parkhomenko, Alexander	1 September 1984	Moscow, USSR
Clements	Hilton, Raymond	2 September 1942	Erdington, Birmingham, England
	Harrison, Andrew James Christopher	19 June 1950	Erdington, Birmingham, England
	Smart, Lesley Raymond	19 September 1973	Stratford-upon-Avon, Warwickshire, England
Covell	Craddock, Albert Chase	23 February 1909	Tulse Hill, London, England
Date	Krumm, Michael	1 December 2001	Tokyo, Japan
Dearman	Cleverly, Ralf Harry	4 April 1944	Westminster, London, England
Dechy	Maitre-Devallon, Antoine	18 September 2004	Luberon, France
Dementieva	Afinogenov, Maxim	16 July 2011	Moscow, Russia
Dmitrieva	Tolstoy, Michael	14 July 1964	Moscow, USSR
	Chukovsky, Dmitry	5 December 1965	Moscow, USSR

Maiden name	Married to	Date of marriage	Place of marriage
Dulko	Gago, Fernando	27 July 2011	Buenos Aires, Argentina
Eisel	Curtis, Peter William	17 April 1969	St. Louis, Missouri, USA
	Beattie, Donald	12 May 1972	St. Louis, Missouri, USA
Fairbank	Nideffer, Robert	6 May 1989	Durban, Natal, South Africa
Feltham	Russell, Malcolm Alwyn Valentine	22 July 1933	Sutton, Surrey, England
Fendick	McCain, Scott Lawrence	20 December 1997	Sacramento, California, USA
Fernandez	Godsick, Anthony	8 April 2000	Miami, Florida, USA
Fisher	O'Neill, Edward Armstrong	9 October 1890	Lytham, Lancaster, England
Fletcher	Barker, Michael	13 November 1954	Heanor, Derbyshire, England
Gannon	Mottram, Anthony John	10 September 1949	Zurich, Switzerland
Gladman	Van Ryn, John William	22 October 1930	Santa Monica, California, USA
	Buck, Richard Albin	4 March 1947	Chula Vista, California, USA
Goss	Lanning, Charles Edward	11 January 1934	Kew Garden, New York, USA
Graham	Shaffer, Wilbur Clinton	3 August 2002	
Groenman	Walhof, Christiaan Gerrit	12 December 1969	Groningen, The Netherlands
	Hoolboom, Marinus Anton	7 September 1987	The Hague, The Netherlands
Habsudova	Cilek Milan	24 October 2003	Bratislava, Slovakia
Harford	Gemmell, David	4 February 1989	Johannesburg, Transvaal, South Africa
Harter	Marcus, Michael Phillips	27 June 1980	Maui, Hawaii
	Shubin, Steven Allen	19 June 1995	Westlake, California, USA
Hartigan	Bathhurst, Hugh Boxon	14 April 1947	Sydney, N.S.W., Australia
Head	Knode, Donald P	16 October 1952	Spanish Tangier, Morocco
Hellyer	Burston, Kenneth John	17 May 1963	Sydney, N.S.W., Australia
Hetherington	Richard Alan	23 September 2000	Seattle, Washington, USA
Hogarth	Calder, Archibald Hunter	25 April 1922	
Hopps	Adkisson, William Charles Duncan	5 May 1962	Seattle, Washington, USA
Hrdlickova	Peschke, Torsten	5 May 2003	Berlin, Germany
Hunt	Price, Anthony Robin	24 October 1964	Pretoria, Transvaal, South Africa
	Barnard, Johannes	17 December 1976	Pretoria, Transvaal, South Africa
Hutchings	Nette, Neville	30 September 1961	Johannesburg, Transvaal, South Africa
Kormoczy	Branny, Eugen	15 December 1946	Budapest, Hungary
	Gero, Alexander	11 November 1958	Budapest, Hungary
Lincoln	Blair, Norman William	27 July 1946	Putney, London, England
Lindqvist	Ryan, James William	16 July 1988	Malmo, Sweden
MacLennan	Taylor, Roger	14 February 1969	Glasgow, Scotland
McAlpin	Haylock, Robert Edward	14 April 1924	Sheringham, Norfolk, England
Mattek	Sands, Justin	29 November 2008	Edwater Beach, Naples Florida, USA

Maiden name	Married to	Date of marriage	Place of marriage
Mirza	Malik, Shoaib	12 April 2010	Hyderabad, India
Moore	Huss, Marvin Attress	31 October 1976	Aspen, Colorado, USA
Nicholls	Brewer, William Jefferson	June 1952	Bermuda
	Segal, Alan Abraham	7 September 1957	Westminster, London, England
Nicoll	Bostock, Edward William Augustus	30 January 1943	Westminster, London, England
Nuthall	Shoemaker, Franklin Comly	29 May 1954	New York, N.Y., USA
Partridge	Chatrier, Philippe	23 April 1953	Wolverhampton, Staffordshire, England
	Crosnier, Jean Roger	25 October 1973	Paris, France
Payot	Dodille, Robert	1937	Paris, France
Pedersen	Rihbany, Edward Herbert	4 January 1941	Brookline, Massachusetts, USA
	McLaughlin, William	1966	
Penrose	Collier, James Arthur Frances	30 March 1957	Sydney, N.S.W., Australia
Quertier	Rinkel, Ivo Ferdinand	28 February 1952	Roehampton, London, England
Radford	Kunce, Damian Michael	30 November 1996	Gordon, Sydney, NSW Australia
Ramirez	Ochoa, Alfonso	29 August 1962	Mexico City, Mexico
Reid-Thomas	Strawson, Frank Merlin	17 September 1925	Westminster, London, England
	Hughes, Richard Pierce	4 November 1954	Kensington, London, England
Reinach	Carstens, Pieter Andries	27 January 1996	George, Cape Province, South Africa
Reyes	Darmon, Pierre	28 January 1960	Mexico City, Mexico
Rinaldi	Stunkel, Brad	11 December 1993	Amelia Island, Florida, USA
Rosenquest	Pratt, Edward Carrol Seymour	13 October 1951	South Orange, New Jersey, USA
Saunders	Poynder, John Seymour	11 April 1944	Harrogate, Yorkshire, England
Schett	Eagle, Joshua	7 July 2007	Innsbruck, Austria
Schallau	Guerrant, Terry	25 October 1975	Fort Worth, Texas, USA
Scheepers	Anderson, Roger	10 November 2012	South Africa
Schultz	McCarthy, Sean	8 April 1995	Heemstede, The Netherlands
Schultze	Hoesl, Ernst	16 July 1968	Munich, West Germany
	Thaw, David Martin	15 December 1988	Munich, West Germany
Scofield	Davidson, Gordon Chambers	16 April 1951	Spanish Tangier, Morocco
Scriven	Vivian, Frank Harvey	28 November 1940	Bramley, Surrey, England
Sequera	Huss, Stephen	29 December 2009	Dandenong Ranges, Australia
Shaw	Wooldridge, Keith	2 October 1972	Williamwood, Glasgow, Scotland
Sherriff	Chanfreau, Jean Baptiste	17 December 1968	Sydney, N.S.W., Australia
	Lovera, Jean Joseph	12 February 1976	Champagnier, Isere, France
	Benedetti, Jean-Philippe	29 September 2005	Ville-di-Pietrabugno, Corsica, France
Spofforth	Youle, James Stewart	26 January 1918	Walton-on-Thames, Surrey, England

Maiden name	Married to	Date of marriage	Place of marriage
Squire	Parton, Ernest George	15 May 1906	West Hampstead, Middlesex, England
	Mavrogordato, Theodore Michel	19 July 1924	Bayswater, London, England
Staley	Hoad, Lewis Alan	18 June 1955	Wimbledon, London, England
Stewart	Crabb, Jaymon	November 2008	
Temesvari	Trunkos, Andras	17 May 1988	Miami, Florida, USA
	Viscontai, Csongor	7 October 2000	Budapest, Hungary
Van Zyl	Du Plooy, Jan L	20 April 1968	Pretoria, Transvaal, South Africa
Vlasto	Serpieri, Johnny	17 February 1927	Athens, Greece
Walkden	Pretorius, Quentin Christopher	3 September 1971	Bulawayo, Southern Rhodesia
Walsh	Pete, Michael Henry	20 April 1985	Sausalito, California, USA
	Arnold, Steven Nixon	7 July 2007	Colorado Spring, Colorado, USA
Wild	Secord, Brian Frederick	11 October 2003	Chicago, Illinois, USA
Whitmarsh	Halford, Wilfrid Charles Julian	26 July 1940	Westminster, London, England
Young	Langford, Struan Newton	28 February 1982	Toorak, Victoria, Australia
Ziegenfuss	Bradshaw, Dale	28 July 1979	San Diego, California, USA
Zinderstein	Jessup, John Butler	11 June 1921	Longwood, Massachusetts, USA
	MacLure, Henry Goldsborough	1974	

All Comers' Runners-up

GENTLEMEN

Name	Date of Birth	Place of Birth	Date of Death	Place of Death	Event and Year
ALLEN, Charles Gladstone	28 Dec 1868	Colmworth, Bedfordshire, England	21 Dec 1924	Prestbury, Nr. Cheltenham, Gloucestershire, England	D 1896
ALLEN, Edward Roy	28 Dec 1868	Colmworth, Bedfordshire, England	4 Nov 1931	Prestbury, Nr. Cheltenham, Gloucestershire, England	D 1896
ALONSO, Manuel	12 Nov 1895	San Sebastian, Spain	11 Oct 1984	Madrid, Spain	S 1921
BAILEY, Walter George	18 Dec 1869	Fulham, Middlesex, England	1 Jan 1910	Birmingham, England	D 1895
BEAMISH, Alfred Ernest	6 Aug 1879	Richmond, Surrey, England	28 Feb 1944	Nairn, Highland, Scotland	D 1912, 1913
Name	Date of Birth	Place of Birth	Date of Death	Place of Death	Event and Year
BEHR, Karl Howell	30 May 1885	Brooklyn, New York, USA	15 Oct 1949	New York, New York, USA	D 1907
CARIDIA, George Aristides	20 Aug 1868	Calcutta, Bengal, India	21 Apr 1937	Marylebone, London, England	D 1904
CAZALET, Clement Haughton Langston	16 July 1879	Paddington, London, England	23 Mar 1950	Harrow, Middlesex, England	D 1897, 1902, 1906
CRISPE, James Herbert	10 Dec 1860	City of London, England	10 Nov 1942	Pangbourne, Berkshire, England	D 1887
DOUST, Stanley Norwood	29 Mar 1879	Sydney, N.S.W., Australia	13 Dec 1961	London, England	S 1913 D 1909
DUNLOP, Alfred Wallace	12 Jan 1875	Christchurch, New Zealand	7 Apr 1933	Australia	D 1905
ERSKINE, Lestocq Robert	6 Sep 1857	Edinburgh, Midlothian, Scotland	29 May 1916	Llandridrod Wells, Wales	S 1878
FROITZHEIM, Otto	2 Apr 1884	Strasburg, Germany	20 Oct 1962	Wiesbaden, West Germany	S 1914
GOOLD, Vere Thomas St. Leger	2 Oct 1853	Waterford, Waterford, Ireland	8 Sep 1909	Devils Island, French Guiana	S 1879
GRINSTEAD, Charles Walder	1 Dec 1860	East Teignmouth, Devon, England	16 Mar 1930	Nikenbah, Queensland, Australia	S 1884
HARDY, Samuel Percy	23 Nov 1876	Oakland, California, USA	25 Jan 1953	Stamford, Connecticut, USA	D 1911
HEATH, Wilfrid Rodney	15 Jun 1884	Melbourne, Victoria, Australia	26 Oct 1936	Melbourne, Victoria, Australia	D 1919
KINGSCOTE, Algernon Robert Fitzhardinge	3 Dec 1888	Bangalore, India	21 Dec 1964	Woking, Surrey, England	S 1919 D 1920
LOWE, Arthur Holden	29 Jan 1886	Edgbaston, Warwickshire, England	22 Oct 1958	Kensington, London, England	D 1914, 1921
LOWE, Francis Gordon	21 Jun 1884	Edgbaston, Warwickshire, England	17 May 1972	Kensington, London, England	D 1914, 1921
MARTIN, Charles Henry	16 Jan 1870	Madras, India	21 Sep 1937	Wilkie, Saskatchewan, Canada	D 1894
MEERS, Ernest George	25 Feb 1849	Kingsnorth, Ashford, Kent, England	20 Aug 1928	York, Yorkshire, England	D 1888
MEWBURN, George Richmond	14 Feb 1865	Hexham, Northumberland, England	5 Jan 1941	St. Ives, Cornwall, England	D 1889
PARKER, Harry Alabaster.	6 May 1873	Christchurch, New Zealand	14 May 1961	Balgowlah, Sydney, NSW, Australia	D 1909

Name	Date of Birth	Place of Birth	Date of Death	Place of Death	Event and Year
POWELL, Kenneth	8 Apr 1885	Hampstead, Middlesex, England	18 Feb 1915	Flanders, Belgium	D 1910
POWELL, Robert Branks	2 Apr 1881	Victoria, British Columbia, Canada	28 Apr 1917	Vimy, Pas de Calais, France	D 1910
RICHARDSON, Richard Taswell	9 Aug 1852	Broughton, Nr. Stockbridge, Southampton, England	16 May 1930	Capenhurst, Nr. Chester, England	S 1881, 1882
SHIMIDZU, Zenzo	25 Mar 1891	Tokyo, Japan	12 Apr 1977	Amagaski City, Hyogo, Japan	S 1920
SIMOND, Charles Francois	28 Dec 1873	London, England	12 Mar 1957	Kensington, London, England	D 1895
SIMOND, George Mieville	23 Jan 1867	London, England	8 Apr 1941	Bretagne, Monaco	D 1901, 1906
SMITH, Ernest William Barratt	14 Aug 1857	Berkeley Sq, Mayfair, Middlesex, England	5 May 1925	Steyning, West Sussex, England	D1887
STEWART, Donald Charles	12 Dec 1859	Kensington, Middlesex, England	13 Sep 1885	Lower Sheringham, Norfolk, England	S 1883
WRIGHT, Beals Coleman	19 Dec 1879	Boston, Massachusetts, USA	23 Aug 1961	Alton, Illinois, USA	D 1907
WOODHOUSE, Orway Edward	21 Oct 1855	Bloomsbury, Middlesex, England	21 Sep 1887	Brighton, Sussex, England	S 1880
ZIFFO, Andrew	11 Aug 1868	Kensington, Middlesex, England	28 May 1955	Paddington, London, England	D 1888

35 players

LADIES

Name	Date of Birth	Place of Birth	Date of Death	Place of Death	Event and Year
AUSTIN, Edith Lucy (Greville, Mrs. T.G.P.)	15 Dec 1867	Broughton, Flintshire, Wales	27 Jul 1953	Kensington, London, England	S 1894, 1896
COLE, Mrs. C.J. (Coleridge, Edith Mary Hutchinson)	10 Sep 1862	Stuttgart, Germany	22 Oct 1945	Hove, Sussex, England	S 1887
DURLACHER, Mrs. N.J. (Dyas, Ruth)	22 Jul 1876	Dublin, Ireland	21 Sept 1946	Stoke Poges, Buckinghamshire, England	S 1899
HOWES					S1888
JACKS, M.					S 1890
JACKSON, Helen (Atkins, Mrs. G.J.M.)	19 Dec 1867	Hexham, Northumberland, England	28 May 1940	Lichfield, Stafford, England	S 1895
JOHNSON, Emily Frances Godschall (Edith+)	31 Jan 1874	East Molesey, Surrey, England	9 Feb 1950	Bolney, Sussex, England	S 1910
MARTIN, Mary Louisa	3 Sep 1865	Newtowngore, Leitrim, Ireland	24 Oct 1941	Portrush, Antrim, Northern Ireland	S 1898, 1900, 1901
SATTERTHWAITE, Mrs. C.R. (Carr, Phyllis Helen)	26 Jan 1886	Kensington, Middlesex, England	20 Jan 1962	Kensington, London, England	S 1919, 1921

Name	Date of Birth	Place of Birth	Date of Death	Place of Death	Event and Year
SHACKLE, Edith Maud (Reid-Thomas, Mrs. G.)	4 Aug 1870	Hayes, Middlesex, England	16 Feb 1962	Epsom, Surrey, England	S 1892, 1893
TABOR, Agneta Maud	10 May 1862	Cheam, Surrey, England			S 1886
WILSON, Constance Mary (Luard, Mrs. J.F.)	2 Sep 1881	Walton, Surrey, England	17 Dec 1955	Eastbourne, Sussex, England	S 1905, 1907

12 players

Ladies' All Comers' Runners-up – marriages

Maiden name	Married to	Date of marriage	Place of marriage
Austin	Greville, Turketil George Pearson	18 September 1899	Kensington, London, England
Carr	Satterthwaite, Clement Richard	13 April 1912	Chiswick, Middlesex, England
Coleridge	Cole, Charles John	16 April 1884	Hove, Sussex, England
Dyas	Durlacher, Neville John	17 December 1898	Killiney, Dublin, Ireland
Jackson	Atkins, George James Murray	10 April 1902	Hexham, Northumberland, England
Shackle	Reid-Thomas, Gwyn	20 June 1899	Hayes, Middlesex, England
Tabor	Shaw, Henry Hawley	3 January, 1893	Pembury, Kent, England
Wilson	Luard, John Frank	21 September 1907	Hove, Sussex, England

Records and Statistics

Countries whose representatives first played at The Championships up to 1914

Gentlemen

1884	U.S.A	J. Dwight, R.D. Sears, A.L. Rives
1901	New Zealand	H.A. Parker
1902	Belgium	P. de Borman, W. Lemaine
1905	Australia	N.E. Brookes, A.W. Dunlop, B. Murphy
1905	Denmark	E. Larson, T. Hillerup
1905	South Africa	H.A. Kitson
1906	Germany	R.E. Lalberer, L. Kalenkampf, R. Schomburgk
1907	Austria	R. Zinzl, C. van Wessley
1907	Canada	R.B. Powel
1908	France	M. Germot
1908	India	Sirdar Nihal Singh
1909	Argentina	E. Knight, H.B. Knight
1910	Netherlands	B.J. Pfleiderer, R.A. Pfleiderer
1911	Italy	C. de Martino
1913	Switzerland	A.C. Simon

Ladies

1900	U.S.A	Miss M. Jones
1907	Austria	Miss M. Klima, Miss W. Klima
1907	Canada	Miss V. Summerhayes
1909	Norway	Miss M. Bjurstedt
1910	Denmark	Miss C. Castenschiold
1912	Belgium	Miss J. Liebrechts
1912	France	Mrs M. Decugis
1913	Germany	Mrs M. Rieck

Countries whose representatives first won a Championship title

Gentlemen

1877	British Isles	S.W. Gore (S)
1907	Australia	N.E. Brookes (S, D)
1907	New Zealand	A.F. Wilding (D)
1911	France	M.O. Decugis (D)
		A.H. Gobert (D)
1920	USA	W.T. Tilden (S)
1923	Gt.Britain	R. Lycett (D, M)
1932	Spain	E.G. Maier (M)
1933	Germany	G. Von Cramm
1934	Japan	R. Miki (M)
1949	South Africa	E.W. Sturgess (M)
1954	Egypt	J. Drobny (S)
1958	Sweden	E.V. Davidson (D)
		U.C.J. Schmidt (D)
1960	Mexico	R.H. Osuna (D)
1970	Romania	I. Nastase (M)
1973	Czechoslovakia	J. Kodes (S)
1985	Switzerland	M.P. Guenthardt (D)
	Hungary	B. Tarczoy (D)
1996	Netherlands	R.P.S. Krajicek (S)
1998	Belarus	M.N. Mirnyi (M)
1999	India	L.A. Paes (M)

2001	Croatia	G.S. Ivanisevic (S)
2004	Zimbabwe	W.H. Black (M)
2006	Israel	A. Ram (M)
2008	Serbia	N. Zimonjic (D)
	Canada	D.M. Nestor (D)
2010	Austria	J. Melzer (D)
2012	Denmark	F.L. Nielsen (D)

Ladies

1884	British Isles	Miss M.E.E.Watson (S)
1905	USA	Miss M.G. Sutton (S)
1919	France	Miss S.R.F. Lenglen (S)
1924	Gt. Britain	Miss K. McKane (S)
1930	Germany	Miss C. Aussem (S)
1932	Belgium	Miss J. Sigart (D)
1949	South Africa	Mrs R.A. Summers (M)
1958	Brazil	Miss M.E.A. Bueno (D)
1958	Australia	Miss L.G. Coghlan (M)
1972	Netherlands	Miss B.F. Stove (D)
1975	Japan	Miss K. Sawarmatsu (D)
1976	Czechoslovakia	Miss M. Navratilova (D)
1988	Argentina	Miss G. Sabatini (D)
1991	Russia	Miss L.I. Savchenko (D)
		Miss N.M. Zvereva (D)
1992	Latvia	Mrs A. Neiland (D)
	CIS	Miss N.M. Zvereva (D)
1993	Belarus	Miss N.M. Zvereva (D)
1994	Czech Republic	Miss H. Sukova (M)
1994	Spain	Miss I.C. Martinez (S)
1996	Switzerland	Miss M. Hingis (S)
2001	Slovakia	Miss D. Hantuchova (M)
2004	Zimbabwe	Miss C.C. Black (D, M)
2006	China	Miss Z. Yan (D)
		Miss J. Zheng (D)
2007	Serbia	Miss J. Jankovic (M)
2010	Kazakhstan	Miss Y.V. Shvedova (D)

Countries whose representatives have won the Singles Championships

Gentlemen – 128

Australia	21	France	7	Serbia	1
British Isles	32	Germany	4	Spain	3
Croatia	1	Gt. Britain	5	Sweden	7
Czechoslovakia	1	Netherlands	1	Switzerland	7
Egypt	1	New Zealand	4	United States	33

Ladies – 121

Australia	5	France	8	Spain	1
Brazil	3	Germany	8	Switzerland	1
British Isles	29	Gt. Britain	7	United States	55
Czech Republic	3				

Winners of most Gentlemen's Singles Championships

7	W.C. Renshaw	(BRI)	1881–1886, 1889
7	P. Sampras	(USA)	1993–1995, 1997–2000
7	R. Federer	(SUI)	2003–2007, 2009, 2012
5	H.L. Doherty	(BRI)	1902–1906
5	B.R. Borg	(SWE)	1976–1980
4	R.F. Doherty	(BRI)	1897–1900
4	A.F. Wilding	(NZL)	1910–1913
4	R.G. Laver	(AUS)	1961, 1962, 1968, 1969
3	W. Baddeley	(BRI)	1891, 1892, 1895
3	A.W. Gore	(BRI)	1901, 1908, 1909
3	W.T. Tilden	(USA)	1920, 1921, 1930
3	F.J. Perry	(GBR)	1934–1936
3	J.D. Newcombe	(AUS)	1967, 1970, 1971
3	J.P. McEnroe	(USA)	1981, 1983, 1984
3	B.F. Becker	(GER)	1985, 1986, 1989

Winners of most Gentlemen's Doubles Championships

9	T.A. Woodbridge	(AUS)	1993–1997, 2000, 2002–2004
8	H.L. Doherty	(BRI)	1897–1901, 1903–1905
8	R.F. Doherty	(BRI)	

Winners of most Ladies' Singles Championships

9	Miss M. Navratilova	(USA)	1978, 1979, 1982–1987, 1990
8	Miss H.N. Wills/		
	Mrs F.S. Moody	(USA)	1927–1930, 1932, 1933, 1935, 1938
7	Miss D.K. Douglass/	(BRI)	1903, 1904, 1906, 1910, 1911,
	Mrs. R.L. Chambers		1913, 1914
7	Miss S.M. Graf	(GER)	1988, 1989, 1991–1993, 1995, 1996
6	Miss B. Bingley/		
	Mrs. G.W. Hillyard	(BRI)	1886, 1889, 1894, 1897, 1899, 1900
6	Miss S.R.F. Lenglen	(FRA)	1919–1923, 1925
6	Mrs. L.W. King	(USA)	1966–1968, 1972, 1973, 1975
5	Miss C. Dod	(BRI)	1887, 1888, 1891–1893
5	Miss C.R. Cooper/		
	Mrs. A. Sterry	(BRI)	1895, 1896, 1898, 1901, 1908
5	Miss V.E.S. Williams	(USA)	2000, 2001, 2005, 2007, 2008
5	Miss S.J. Williams	(USA)	2002, 2003, 2009, 2010, 2012
4	Miss A.L. Brough	(USA)	1948–1950, 1955
3	Miss M.E.A. Bueno	(BRA)	1959, 1960, 1964
3	Miss M.C. Connolly	(USA)	1952–1954
3	Miss M. Smith/		
	Mrs. B.M. Court	(AUS)	1963, 1965, 1970
3	Miss C.M. Evert/		
	Mrs. J.M. Lloyd	(USA)	1974, 1976, 1981

Winner of most Ladies' Doubles Championships

12	Miss E.M. Ryan	(USA)	1914, 1919–1923, 1925–1927, 1930, 1933, 1934

Winners of most Mixed Doubles Championships – Gentlemen

4	O.K. Davidson	(AUS)	1967, 1971, 1973, 1974
4	K.N. Fletcher	(AUS)	1963, 1965, 1966, 1968
4	E.V. Seixas	(USA)	1953–1956

Winner of most Mixed Doubles Championships – Ladies

7	Miss E.M. Ryan	(USA)	1919, 1921, 1923, 1927, 1928, 1930, 1932

Winner of most Singles, Doubles and Mixed Doubles Championships – Gentlemen

13	H.L. Doherty	(BRI)	5 singles, 8 doubles, 1897–1906

Winner of most Singles, Doubles and Mixed Doubles Championships – Ladies

20	Miss B.J. Moffitt/	(USA)	6 singles, 10 doubles, 4 mixed,
	Mrs. L.W. King		1961–1979
20	Miss M. Navratilova	(TCH/USA)	9 singles, 7 doubles, 4 mixed, 1976–2003
19	Miss E.M. Ryan	(USA)	12 doubles, 7 mixed, 1914–1934

Winners of Singles, Doubles and Mixed Doubles Championships in one year – Gentlemen

1937	J.D. Budge	(USA)
1938	J.D. Budge	(USA)
1939	R.L. Riggs	(USA)
1952	F.A. Sedgman	(AUS)

Winners of Singles, Doubles and Mixed Doubles Championships in one year – Ladies

1920	Miss S.R.F. Lenglen	(FRA)
1922	Miss S.R.F. Lenglen	(FRA)
1925	Miss S.R.F. Lenglen	(FRA)
1939	Miss A. Marble	(USA)
1948	Miss A.L. Brough	(USA)
1950	Miss A.L. Brough	(USA)
1951	Miss D.J. Hart	(USA)
1967	Mrs. L.W. King	(USA)
1973	Mrs. L.W. King	(USA)

Runners-up of Singles, Doubles and Mixed Doubles Championships in one year – Gentlemen

1926	H.O. Kinsey	(USA)
1946	G.E. Brown*	(AUS)

* *G.E. Brown never lost a set in the three events until the finals.*

Runners-up of Singles, Doubles and Mixed Doubles Championships in one year – Ladies

1948	Miss D.J. Hart	(USA)
1971	Mrs. B.M. Court	(AUS)
1977	Miss B.F. Stove	(NED)

Winners of Gentlemen's Singles Championship without loss of a set

(Since abolition of Challenge Round in 1922)

			Sets	Games
1938	J.D. Budge	(USA)	21-0	129-48
1955	M.A. Trabert	(USA)	21-0	131-60
1963	C.R. McKinley	(USA)	21-0	140-82
1976	B.R. Borg	(SWE)	21-0	133-70

Note: In 1947 J.A. Kramer (USA) lost one set but conceded less games than those listed above – Sets 21-1, Games 130-37.

Winners of Gentlemen's Doubles Championship without loss of a set

(Since abolition of Challenge Round in 1922)

		Sets	Games
1947	R. Falkenburg and J.A. Kramer (USA)	18-0	115-59
1967	R.A.J. Hewitt and F.D. McMillan (RSA)	18-0	120-61

Winners of Ladies' Singles Championship without loss of a set

(Since abolition of Challenge Round in 1922)

			Sets	Games
1922	Miss S.R.F. Lenglen	(FRA)	12-0	75-20
1923	Miss S.R.F. Lenglen	(FRA)	12-0	72-11
1925	Miss S.R.F. Lenglen	(FRA)	10-0	60-5
1928	Miss H.N. Wills	(USA)	12-0	72-18
1929	Miss H.N. Wills	(USA)	12-0	72-16
1930	Mrs. F.S. Moody	(USA)	12-0	72-19
1932	Mrs. F.S. Moody	(USA)	12-0	72-13
1938	Mrs. F.S. Moody	(USA)	12-0	81-47
1939	Miss A. Marble	(USA)	12-0	72-21
1946	Miss P.M. Betz	(USA)	12-0	72-20
1947	Miss M.E. Osborne	(USA)	12-0	73-31
1951	Miss D.J. Hart	(USA)	14-0	86-34
1953	Miss M.C. Connolly	(USA)	12-0	75-19
1954	Miss M.C. Connolly	(USA)	12-0	73-19
1955	Miss A.L. Brough	(USA)	12-0	77-28
1957	Miss A. Gibson	(USA)	12-0	72-30
1962	Mrs. J.R. Susman	(USA)	14-0	93-55
1965	Miss M. Smith	(AUS)	12-0	73-21
1967	Mrs. L.W. King	(USA)	10-0	63-28
1981	Mrs. J.M. Lloyd	(USA)	14-0	85-26
1983	Miss M. Navratilova	(USA)	14-0	85-25
1984	Miss M. Navratilova	(USA)	13-0	80-35
1986	Miss M. Navratilova	(USA)	14-0	85-34
1990	Miss M. Navratilova	(USA)	14-0	84-29
1999	Miss L.A. Davenport	(USA)	14-0	86-37
2002	Miss S.J. Williams	(USA)	14-0	87-43
2008	Miss V.E.S. Williams	(USA)	14-0	89-50
2010	Miss S.J. Williams	(USA)	14-0	88-41
2013	Miss M.S. Bartoli	(FRA)	14-0	88-48

Winners of Ladies' Doubles Championship without loss of a set

(Since abolition of Challenge Round in 1922)

		Sets	Games
1922	Miss S.R.F. Lenglen (FRA) and Miss E.M. Ryan (USA)	10-0	61-14
1923	Miss S.R.F. Lenglen (FRA) and Miss E.M. Ryan (USA)	10-0	60-11
1924	Mrs. G.W. Wightman and Miss H.N. Wills (USA)	8-0	50-28
1925	Miss S.R.F. Lenglen (FRA) and Miss E.M. Ryan (USA)	12-0	72-16
1927	Miss E.M. Ryan and Miss H.N. Wills (USA)	12-0	72-26
1949	Miss A.L. Brough and Mrs. W. DuPont (USA)	10-0	63-23
1951	Miss S.J. Fry and Miss D.J. Hart (USA)	10-0	67-23
1952	Miss S.J. Fry and Miss D.J. Hart (USA)	10-0	63-23
1953	Miss S.J. Fry and Miss D.J. Hart (USA)	8-0	48-4
1957	Miss A. Gibson and Miss D.R. Hard (USA)	10-0	62-23
1958	Miss M.E.A. Bueno (BRA) and Miss A. Gibson (USA)	10-0	61-24
1961	Miss K.J. Hantze and Miss B.J. Moffitt (USA)	10-0	63-26
1963	Miss M.E.A. Bueno (BRA) and Miss D.R. Hard (USA)	10-0	68-32
1964	Miss M. Smith and Miss L.R. Turner (AUS)	10-0	61-18
1965	Miss M.E.A. Bueno (BRA) and Miss B.J. Moffitt (USA)	10-0	61-23
1969	Mrs. B.M. Court and Miss J.A.M. Tegart (AUS)	10-0	63-28
1970	Miss R. Casals and Mrs. L.W. King (USA)	10-0	62-28
1986	Miss M. Navratilova and Miss P.H. Shriver (USA)	10-0	61-29

1999	Miss L.A. Davenport and Miss C.M. Morariu (USA)	12-0	75-38
2001	Miss L.M. Raymond (USA) and Miss R.P. Stubbs (AUS)	12-0	74-31
2005	Miss C.C. Black (ZIM) and Mrs A. Huber (RSA)	12-0	73-22
2008	Miss S.J. Williams and V.E.S. Williams (USA)	12-0	72-29
2009	Miss S.J. Williams and V.E.S. Williams (USA)	12-0	74-31

Winners of Mixed Doubles Championship without loss of a set
(Since abolition of Challenge Round in 1922)

		Sets	Games
1922	P.O. Wood (AUS) and Miss S.R.F. Lenglen (FRA)	12-0	72-25
1923	R. Lycett (GBR) and Miss E.M. Ryan (USA)	12-0	79-50
1926	L.A. Godfree and Mrs. L.A. Godfree (GBR)	12-0	73-30
1927	F.T. Hunter and Miss E.M. Ryan (USA)	12-0	78-37
1933	G. von Cramm and Miss H. Krahwinkel (GER)	12-0	78-43
1938	J.D. Budge and Miss A. Marble (USA)	12-0	74-30
1953	E.V. Seixas and Miss D.J. Hart (USA)	12-0	77-33
1963	K.N. Fletcher and Miss M. Smith (AUS)	12-0	81-43
1972	I. Nastase (ROM) and Miss R. Casals (USA)	12-0	76-38
2005	M.S. Bhupathi (IND) and Miss M.C. Pierce (FRA)	12-0	75-41
2011	J. Melzer (AUT) and Miss I. Benesova (CZE)	8-0	48-27

Winners of Gentlemen's Singles Championship losing most sets

1949	F.R. Schroeder (USA)	8
1985	B.F. Becker (GER)	8

The record for the event is 10, lost by runner-up, J.R. Borotra (FRA), in 1927.

Winners of Gentlemen's Doubles Championship losing most sets

1963	R.H. Osuna and A. Palafox (MEX)	8
1977	R.L. Case and G. Masters (AUS)	8

The record for the event is 12, lost by runners-up, P.H. Cash and P.F. McNamee (AUS), in 1984.

Winner of Ladies' Singles Championship losing most sets

1994	Miss I.C. Martinez (ESP)	4

Winners of Ladies' Doubles Championship losing most sets

1980	Miss K. Jordan and Miss A.E. Smith (USA)	4

Winners of Mixed Doubles Championship losing most sets

1981	F.D. McMillan (RSA) and Miss B.F. Stove (NED)	5

Singles Champions at first attempt

Gentlemen			Ladies		
1877	S.W. Gore	(BRI)	1884	Miss M.E.E. Watson	(BRI)
1878	P.F. Hadow	(BRI)*	1887	Miss C. Dod	(BRI)*
1879	J.T. Hartley	(BRI)	1905	Miss M.G. Sutton	(USA)

1919	G.L. Patterson	(AUS)
1920	W.T. Tilden	(USA)
1932	H.E. Vines	(USA)
1939	R.L. Riggs	(USA)*
1949	F.R. Schroeder	(USA)*
1951	R. Savitt	(USA)

1919	Miss S.R.F. Lenglen	(FRA)*
1946	Miss P.M. Betz	(USA)*
1952	Miss M.C. Connolly	(USA)*

* *These Champions were unbeaten in singles at any time. P.F. Hadow and Miss P.M. Betz never lost a set.*

Elimination of Holder or No. 1 Seed in opening match of Gentlemen's Singles Championship

| 1967 | M.M. Santana | (ESP) | Holder and No. 1 seed: lost in first round to C.M. Pasarell (USA) 10-8 6-3 2-6 8-6 |
| 2003 | L.G. Hewitt | (AUS) | Holder and No. 1 seed: lost in first round to I. Karlovic (CRO) 1-6 7-6 (7-5) 6-3 6-4 |

Elimination of Holder or No. 1 Seed in opening match of Ladies' Singles Championship

1962	Miss M. Smith	(AUS)	No. 1 seed: lost in second round (first round bye) to Miss B.J. Moffitt (USA) 1-6 6-3 7-5
1994	Miss S.M. Graf	(GER)	Holder and No. 1 seed: lost in first round to Miss L.M. McNeil (USA) 7-5 7-6 (7-5)
1999	Miss M. Hingis	(SUI)	No. 1 seed: lost in first round to Miss J. Dokic (AUS) 6-2 6-0.
2001	Miss M. Hingis	(SUI)	No. 1 seed: lost in first round to Miss V. Ruano Pascual (ESP) 6-4 6-2

The Youngest Champions

Gentlemen's Singles	– B.F. Becker	(GER)	17 years, 227 days (1985)
	– W. Baddeley	(BRI)	19 years, 174 days (1891)
	– S.B.B. Wood	(USA)	19 years, 245 days (1931)
	– B.R. Borg	(SWE)	20 years, 22 days (1976)
	– H.E. Vines	(USA)	20 years, 278 days (1932)
Gentlemen's Doubles	– R.D. Ralston	(USA)	17 years, 341 days (1960)
Ladies' Singles	– Miss C. Dod	(BRI)	15 years, 285 days (1887)
	– Miss M. Hingis	(SUI)	16 years, 278 days (1997)
	– Miss M. Sharapova	(RUS)	17 years, 75 days (2004)
	– Miss M.C. Connolly	(USA)	17 years, 292 days (1952)
	– Miss M.G. Sutton	(USA)	18 years, 286 days (1905)
	– Miss S.M. Graf	(GER)	19 years, 18 days (1988)
Ladies' Doubles	– Miss M. Hingis	(SUI)	15 years, 282 days (1996)
Mixed Doubles	– R.G. Laver	(AUS)	20 years, 328 days (1959)
	– Miss S.J. Williams	(USA)	16 years, 282 days (1998)

The Oldest Champions

Gentlemen's Singles	– A.W. Gore	(BRI)	41 years, 182 days (1909)
Gentlemen's Doubles	– G.P. Mulloy	(USA)	43 years, 226 days (1957)
Ladies' Singles	– Mrs. A. Sterry	(BRI)	37 years, 282 days (1908)
Ladies' Doubles	– Miss E.M. Ryan	(USA)	42 years, 152 days (1934)
Mixed Doubles	– S.E. Stewart	(USA)	42 years, 28 days (1988)
	– Miss M. Navratilova	(USA)	46 years, 261 days (2003)

Note: The oldest players to win the Singles Championships for the first time were H.F. Lawford (BRI), 1887, 36 years, 53 days and Mrs. D.T.R. Larcombe (BRI), 1912, 33 years, 30 days.

The Youngest Competitors

Gentlemen's Singles	– S.B.B. Wood	(USA)	15 years, 231 days (1927)
Gentlemen's Doubles	– S.B.B. Wood	(USA)	15 years, 234 days (1927)
Ladies' Singles	– Miss J.M. Capriati	(USA)	14 years, 90 days (1990)
	– Miss K.S. Rinaldi	(USA)	14 years, 91 days (1981)
Ladies' Doubles	– Miss J.M. Capriati	(USA)	14 years, 92 days (1990)
	– Miss K.S. Rinaldi	(USA)	14 years, 93 days (1981)

The Oldest Competitors

Gentlemen's Singles	– M.J.G. Ritchie	(GBR)	55 years, 247 days (1926)
Gentlemen's Doubles	– J.R. Borotra	(FRA)	65 years, 317 days (1964)
Ladies' Singles	– Mrs. A.E. O'Neill	(GBR)	54 years, 304 days (1922)
Ladies' Doubles	– Mrs. C.O. Tuckey	(GBR)	54 years, 352 days (1932)
Mixed Doubles	– J. R. Borotra	(FRA)	64 years, 320 days (1963)
	– Mrs. A.E. O'Neill	(GBR)	55 years, 304 days (1923)

The Youngest Seeds

| Gentlemen's Singles | – B.R. Borg | (SWE) | 17 years, 19 days (1973) |
| Ladies' Singles | – Miss J.M. Capriati | (USA) | 14 years, 89 days (1990) |

The Oldest Seeds

| Gentlemen's Singles | – R.A. Gonzales | (USA) | 41 years, 45 days (1969) |
| Ladies' Singles | – Mrs. L.W. King | (USA) | 39 years, 210 days (1983) |

Ambidextrous Players (Single-handed) – Gentlemen

H. Chipp (BRI) 1882, 1884, 1886, 1888, 1891.
G. de Stefani (ITA) 1928, 1933–1935, 1937, 1939.
R.W. Higgin (GBR) 1938, 1939.
P. Hutka (TCH) 1979.
L.B. Jensen (USA)* 1988–1998.
*Served left or right-handed

Ambidextrous Players (Single-handed) – Ladies

Miss E.M. Shackle (BRI) 1886, 1887, 1891-1893, 1895.
Miss B.J. Baker/Mrs. J.G. Fleitz (USA) 1951, 1955, 1956, 1959.
Miss M. Jansen/Mrs. N. Schaar (NED) 1968–1975.
Miss L. Liem/Mrs. R.M. Sugiarto (IND) 1969–1973, 1975.
Miss E. Koulikovskaya (RUS)* 1999, 2003, 2004
*Served left-handed

Champions who won from match point down

1889 Gentlemen's Singles – All Comers' Final
W.C. Renshaw (BRI) beat H.S. Barlow (BRI) 3-6 5-7 8-6 10-8 8-6, after being six match points down in the fourth set, two at 2-5, two at 3-5 and two at 6-7.

1889 Ladies' Singles – All Comers' Final
Mrs. G.W. Hillyard (BRI) beat Miss H.G.B. Rice (BRI) 4-6 8-6 6-4, after being three match points down in the second set at 3-5.

1895 Gentlemen's Singles – All Comers' Final
W. Baddeley (BRI) beat W.V. Eaves (BRI) 4-6 2-6 8-6 6-2 6-3, after being one match point down in the third set at 5-6.

1901 Gentlemen's Singles – All Comers' Quarter-final
A.W. Gore (BRI) beat G.W. Hillyard (BRI) 6-1 2-6 4-6 8-6 6-2, after being two match points down in the fourth set at 4-5.

1919 Ladies' Singles – Challenge Round
Miss S.R.F. Lenglen (FRA) beat Mrs. R.L. Chambers (BRI) 10-8 4-6 9-7, after being two match points down in the third set at 5-6.

1921 Gentlemen's Singles – Challenge Round
W.T. Tilden (USA) beat B.I.C. Norton (RSA) 4-6 2-6 6-1 6-0 7-5, after being two match points down in the fifth set at 4-5.

1926 Ladies' Doubles – Second Round
Miss M.K. Browne and Miss E.M. Ryan (USA) beat Miss S.R.F. Lenglen and Miss D. Vlasto (FRA) 3-6 9-7 6-2, after being three match points down in the second set at 6-7.

1927 Gentlemen's Singles – Final
H.J. Cochet (FRA) beat J.R. Borotra (FRA) 4-6 4-6 6-3 6-4 7-5, after being six match points down in the fifth set, one at 2-5 and five at 3-5.

1927 Gentlemen's Doubles – Final
F.T. Hunter and W.T. Tilden (USA) beat J. Brugnon and H.J. Cochet (FRA) 1-6 4-6 8-6 6-3 6-4, after being two match points down in the third set at 4-5.

1932 Ladies' Doubles – First Round
Miss D.E. Metaxa (FRA) and Miss J. Sigart (BEL) beat Miss G.M. Heeley and Miss W.A. James (GBR) 2-6 6-4 7-5, after being three match points down in the third set at 2-5.

1935 Ladies' Singles – Final
Mrs. F.S. Moody (USA) beat Miss H.H. Jacobs (USA) 6-3 3-6 7-5, after being one match point down in the third set at 3-5.

1935 Gentlemen's Doubles – Final
J.H. Crawford and A.K. Quist (AUS) beat W.L. Allison and J. Van Ryn (USA) 6-3 5-7 6-2 5-7 7-5, after being one match point down in the fifth set at 4-5.

1947 Ladies' Doubles – Final
Miss D.J. Hart and Mrs. R.B. Todd (USA) beat Miss A.L. Brough and Miss M.E. Osborne (USA) 3-6 6-4 7-5, after being three match points down in the third set at 3-5.

1948 Gentlemen's Singles – Final
R. Falkenburg (USA) beat J.E. Bromwich (AUS) 7-5 0-6 6-2 3-6 7-5, after being three match points down in the fifth set at 3-5.

1949 Gentlemen's Singles – Quarter final
F.R. Schroeder (USA) beat F.A. Sedgman (AUS) 3-6 6-8 6-3 6-2 9-7, after being two match points down in the fifth set, one at 4-5 and one at 5-6.

1954 Ladies' Doubles – Final
Miss A.L. Brough and Mrs. W. duPont (USA) beat Miss S.J. Fry and Miss D.J. Hart (USA) 4-6 9-7 6-3, after being two match points down in the second set at 3-5.

1960 Gentlemen's Singles – Quarter-final
N.A. Fraser (AUS) beat E.H. Buchholz (USA) 4-6 6-3 4-6 15-15 ret'd, after being five match points down in the fourth set, one at 4-5, two at 5-6 and two at 13-14.

1960 Mixed Doubles – Final
R.G. Laver (AUS) and Miss D.R. Hard (USA) beat R.N. Howe (AUS) and Miss M.E.A. Bueno (BRA) 13-11 3-6 8-6, after being three match points down in the third set at 4-5.

1976 Mixed Doubles – Final
A.D. Roche (AUS) and Miss F. Durr (FRA) beat R.L. Stockton and Miss R. Casals (USA) 6-3 2-6 7-5, after being one match point down in the third set at 4-5.

1978 Ladies' Doubles – Final
Mrs. G.A. Reid and Miss W.M. Turnbull (AUS) beat Miss M. Jausovec (YUG) and Miss V. Ruzici (ROM) 4-6 9-8 (12-10) 6-3, after being two match points down in the second set tie break.

1980 Mixed Doubles – Final
J.R. Austin and Miss T.A. Austin (USA) beat M.R. Edmondson and Miss D.L. Fromholtz (AUS) 4-6 7-6 (8-6) 6-3, after being three match points down in the second set, one at 4-5 and two in the tie break.

1985 Mixed Doubles – Semi-final
P.F. McNamee (AUS) and Miss M. Navratilova (USA) beat S.E. Davis and Miss B. (H.E.) Nagelsen (USA) 6-7 (4-7) 7-5 23-21, after being two match points down, one in the second set at 4-5 and one in the third set at 6-7.

1986 Gentlemen's Doubles – Quarter-final
J.K. Nystrom and M.A.O. Wilander (SWE) beat K.E. Flach and R.A. Seguso (USA) 3-6 4-6 7-6 (8-6) 6-4 11-9, after being six match points down, four in the third set, three at 4-5 and one in the tie-break and two in the fifth set at 4-5.

1988 Ladies' Doubles – Final
Miss S.M. Graf (GER) and Miss G.B. Sabatini (ARG) beat Miss L.I. Savchenko and Miss N.M. Zvereva (URS) 6-3 1-6 12-10, after being two match points down in the third set at 4-5.

1989 Gentlemen's Doubles – First Round
J.B. Fitzgerald (AUS) and A.P. Jarryd (SWE) beat M.W. Anger and M. Davis (USA) 6-7 (3-7) 6-4 6-4 4-6 18-16, after being one match point down in the fifth set at 10-11.

1989 Mixed Doubles – Quarter-final
J.R. Pugh (USA) and Miss J. Novotna (TCH) beat D. Wheaton and Miss M.J. Fernandez (USA) 2-6 6-4 9-7, after being one match point down in the third set at 6-7.

1991 Mixed Doubles – Semi-final
J.B. Fitzgerald and Mrs. P.D. Smylie (AUS) beat C.J. Van Rensburg and Miss E. Reinach (RSA) 7-5 3-6 7-5, after being one match point down in the third set at 4-5.

1992 Gentlemen's Doubles – Final
J.P. McEnroe (USA) and M.D. Stich (GER) beat J.F. Grabb and R.A. Reneberg (USA) 5-7 7-6 (7-5) 3-6 7-6 (7-5) 19-17, after being two match points down in the fifth set at 6-7.

1992 Ladies' Doubles – Semi-final
Miss B.C. Fernandez (USA) and Miss N.M. Zvereva (CIS) beat Miss A.I.M. Sanchez Vicario (ESP) and Miss H. Sukova (TCH) 6-1 6-7 (2-7) 7-5, after being one match point down in the third set at 4-5.

1996 Mixed Doubles – Second Round
C. Suk and Miss H. Sukova (CZE) beat P. Tramacchi and Miss R.P. Stubbs (AUS) 5-7 7-6 (7-3) 6-2, after being one match point down in the second set at 4-5.

2001 Gentlemen's Doubles – Quarter Final
D.J. Johnson and J.E. Palmer (USA) beat J.M. Balcells (ESP) and S. Schalken (NED) 3-6 6-7 (5-7) 7-6 (7-5) 7-6 (8-6) 6-4, after being four match points down in the fourth set at 5-6.

2004 Mixed Doubles – Third Round

W.H. Black and Miss C.C. Black beat L.A. Paes (IND) and Miss M. Navratilova (USA) 7-6(9-7) 6-7(5-7) 13-11, after being two match points down in the third set at 4-5.

2004 Mixed Doubles – Final

W.H. Black and Miss C.C. Black (ZIM) beat T.A. Woodbridge and Miss A. Molik (AUS) 3-6 7-6(10-8) 6-4, after being six match points down in the second set tie-break.

2005 Ladies' Singles – Final

Miss V.E.S. Williams (USA) beat Miss L.A. Davenport (Mrs J. Leach)(USA) 4-6 7-6 (7-4) 9-7, after being one match point down in the third set at 4-5.

2009 Ladies' Singles – Semi-final

Miss S.J. Williams (USA) beat Miss E. Dementieva (RUS) 6-7 (4-7) 7-5 8-6, after being one match point down in the third set at 4-5.

2014 Ladies' Doubles – Second Round

Miss S. Errani and Miss R. Vinci (ITA) beat Miss L. Kichenok and Miss N. Kichenok (UKR), 5-7 7-6 (12-10) 6-1, after being five match points down in the second set tie-break.

The Longest Match in the History of Lawn Tennis

THE LAWN TENNIS CHAMPIONSHIPS
WIMBLEDON
Tuesday, Wednesday, Thursday
22nd, 23rd, 24th June 2010

RECORD TIME AND NUMBER OF GAMES

NO.18 COURT

J.R. Isner (USA) bt N.P.A. Mahut (FRA) 6-4 3-6 6-7 (7-9) 7-6 (7-3) 70-68

Total time – 11 hrs 5 mins

1st set – 32 mins, 2nd set – 30 mins
3rd set – 48 mins, 4th set – 1 hr 5 mins
5th set – 8 hrs 10 mins

Number of games – 183

Aces served: Isner – 113, Mahut – 103
(fastest service – Isner 143 mph)

168 consecutive service games without a break
Isner won on 5th match point

Warm sunny weather

Umpire: Mohamed Lahyani

John Robert Isner, born Greensboro, USA, 26th April 1985

Nicolas P.A. Mahut, born Angers, France, 21st January 1982

A plaque commemorating the event was
installed at the south end of No. 18 Court
in 2011

Most Games in a Match

Gentlemen's Singles
— 183 J.R. Isner (USA) bt N.P.A. Mahut (FRA) 6-4 3-6 6-7 (7-9) 7-6 (7-3) 70-68 (2010 – First Round) (11 hrs-5 mins)
— 112 R.A. Gonzales (USA) bt C.M. Pasarell (USA) 22-24 1-6 16-14 6-3 11-9 (1969 – First Round) (5 hrs-12 mins)
— 93 J. Drobny (EGY) bt J.E. Patty (USA) 8-6 16-18 3-6 8-6 12-10 (1953 – Third Round) (4 hrs-20 mins)
— 90 R. Holmberg (USA) bt M.C. Reissen (USA) 14-16 11-13 6-4 6-2 10-8 (1964 – Second Round) (3 hrs-55 mins)
— 89 P. Barthes (FRA) bt M.J. Franks (USA) 12-10 7-9 15-17 6-3 6-4 (1964 – Third Round) (3 hrs-50mins)
— 89 G.C. Richey (USA) bt A.D. Roche (AUS) 3-6 3-6 19-17 14-12 6-3 (1967 – Second Round) (3 hrs-45 mins)
— 87 R.G Laver (AUS) bt B.B. McKay (USA) 11-13 11-9 10-8 7-9 6-3 (1959 – Semi-Final) (3 hrs-45 mins)
— 87 S.R. Smith (USA) bt A.J. Stone (AUS) 20-22 6-4 9-7 4-6 6-3 (1969 – First Round)
— 84 W.W. Bowrey (AUS) bt P.S. Cornejo (CHI) 6-8 6-4 16-18 7-5 8-6 (1970 – First Round)
— 83 D.W. Candy (AUS) bt W.A. Knight (GBR) 7-5 5-7 13-15 6-3 12-10 (1958 – First Round) (3hrs-18 mins)
— 83 M.A. Philippoussis (AUS) bt. S. Schalken (NED) 4-6 6-3 6-7 (7-9) 7-6 (7-4) 20-18 (2000 – Third Round) (5hrs-5 mins.) (longest singles match in a day)
[Most games in a match in three straight sets – 76. R. Taylor (GBR) bt. J.F. Shepherd (AUS) 9-7 13-11 19-17 (1962 – Second Round – 3 hrs-19 mins.)]

Gentlemen's Doubles
— 102 M.P.D. Melo and A.R. Sa (BRA) bt P.J. Hanley (AUS) and K.R. Ullyett (ZIM) 5-7 7-6(7-4) 4-6 7-6(9-7) 28-26 (2007 – Second Round) (5hrs-58 mins.)
— 98 E.L. Scott (USA) and N. Pilic (YUG) bt G.C. Richey (USA) and T. Ulrich (DEN) 19-21 12-10 6-4 4-6 9-7 (1966 – First Round)
— 94 J.E. Patty and M.A. Trabert (USA) bt K.B. McGregor and F.A. Sedgman (AUS) 6-4 31-29 7-9 6-2 (1950 – Quarter-final) (4 hrs-5 mins)
— 94 A.R. Olmedo (PER) and F.O. Segura (ECU) bt G.L. Forbes and A.A. Segal (RSA) 32-30 5-7 6-4 6-4 (1968 – Second Round)
— 87 H.P. Guenthardt (SUI) and B. Taroczy (HUN) bt P.T. Annacone (USA) and C.J. van Rensburg (RSA) 6-4 2-6 6-4 6-7 (4-7) 24-22 (1985 – Quarter-Final) (5 hrs- 5 mins)
— 87 M.S. Knowles (BAH) and D.M.Nestor (CAN) bt. S.O.K. Aspelin (SWE) and T.S. Perry (AUS) 5-7 6-3 6-7 (5-7) 6-3 23-21 (2006 – Quarter-final) (6hrs 9 mins)
— 86 H. Denker and H.E.O. Henkel (GER) bt L. de Borman and A. Lacroix (BEL) 16-14 7-5 4-6 5-7 12-10 (1934 – First Round)
— 86 R.H. Osuna (MEX) and R.D. Ralston (USA) bt R.G. Laver and R. Mark (USA) 4-6 10-8 15-13 4-6 11-9 (1960 – Semi-Final) (3 hrs-30 mins)
— 86 J. Kodes and J. Kukal (TCH) bt P. Darmon and J.L. Rouyer (FRA) 4-6 5-7 20-18 6-4 9-7 (1969 – First Round)
— 84 B.B. Mackay (USA) and M.G. Rose (AUS) bt W.A. Knight and J.A. Pickard (GBR) 13-11 6-4 26-24 (1958 – Second Round) (3 hrs-15 mins)
— 83 J.L. Arilla and M.M. Santana (ESP) bt H.J. Plotz and B. Weinmann (GER) 6-4 6-3 21-23 11-9 (1967 – First Round)

— 83 R.C. Lutz and S.R. Smith (USA) bt T.W. Addison and R.F. Keldie (AUS) 16-14 16-18 6-3 6-4 (1969 – First Round)

— 83 S. Baranyi and P. Szoke (HUN) bt S. Ball and G. Masters (AUS) 9-8 ( ) 7-9 9-7 5-7 12-10 (1971 – First Round)

— 83 J.P. McEnroe (USA) and M.D. Stich (GER) bt J.F. Grabb and R.A. Reneberg (USA) 5-7 7-6 (7-5) 3-6 7-6 (7-5) 17-15 (1992 – Final) (5 hrs-1 min)

— 81 R.H. Osuna (MEX) and R.D. Ralston (USA) bt G.D. Oakley and H.E. Truman (GBR) 6-3 6-4 9-11 5-7 16-14 (1960 – First Round)

— 81 R.C. Lutz and S.R. Smith (USA) bt B.E. Fairlie and O. Parun (NZL) 8-6 11-9 3-6 20-18 (1969 – Third Round)

— 81 R.R. Maud (RSA) and Z. Franulovic (YUG) bt B.E. Fairlie (NZL) and I. El Shafei (EGY) 4-6 6-3 6-4 7-9 19-17 (1971-First Round)

— 80 J. Leschly and J. Ulrich (DEN) bt A. Metreveli and S. Likhachev (URS) 9-11 6-4 8-10 12-10 6-4 (1967 – First Round)

Ladies' Singles   — 58 Miss C.R. Rubin (USA) bt Mrs. P. Hy-Boulais (CAN) 7-6 (7-4) 6-7 (5-7) 17-15 (1995 – Second Round) (3hrs- 45 mins)

— 54 Miss A. Weiwers (FRA) bt Mrs. O. Anderson (USA) 8-10 14-12 6-4 (1948 – Second Round)

— 53 Miss J. Goerges (GER) bt Miss K. Srebotnik (SLO) 4-6 7-6 (8-6) 16-14 (2008 – First Round) (3hrs 41 mins)

— 52 Miss H. Schultze (GER) bt Miss J.P. Lieffrig (FRA) 4-6 11-9 12-10 (1966 – First Round) (2 hrs-45 mins)

Ladies' Doubles   — 50 Miss M. Hingis (SUI) and Miss A.I.M. Sanchez Vicario (ESP) bt Miss C.R. Rubin (USA) and Mrs. S. Schultz-McCarthy (NED) 7-6 (14-12) 6-7 (6-8) 13-11 (1997 – Third Round). (3hrs-9mins.)

— 49 Miss L. Horn (RSA) and Miss K. Srebotnik (SLO) bt Miss K. Boogert (NED) and Miss A-G. Sidot (FRA) 6-4 1-6 17-15 (1999 – Quarter-final) (3hrs-5 mins)

— 49 Mrs. G. Vento-Kabchi (VEN) and Miss A. Widjaja (INA) bt. Miss W. Prakusya (INA) and Miss T. Tanasugarn (THA) 6-4 3-6 16-14 (2004–Second Round) (3hrs-27 mins)

— 48 Mrs. I. Wheatcroft and Miss P.G. Brazier (GBR) bt Miss M.E. Nonweiler and Miss B. Soames (GBR) 11-9 5-7 9-7 (1933 – First Round)

— 48 Miss S. Cherneva and Miss L.I. Savchenko (URS) bt Mrs. J.M. Lloyd (USA) and Miss C. Tanvier (FRA) 3-6 7-6 14-12 (1984 – Third Round)

Mixed Doubles   — 77 M. Schapers and Miss B.A.M. Schultz (NED) bt T.J.C.M. Nijssen (NED) and Miss A. Temesvari (HUN) 6-3 5-7 29-27 (1991 – First Round) (4 hrs-14 mins)

— 69 P.F. McNamee (AUS) and Miss M. Navratilova (USA) bt S.E. Davis and Miss H.E. Nagelsen (USA) 6-7 (4-7) 7-5 23-21 (1985 – Semi-Final) (3 hrs-21 mins)

Most Games in a Set

Gentlemen's Singles   — 138 J.R. Isner (USA) bt N.P.A. Mahut (FRA) 6-4 3-6 6-7 (7-9) 7-6 (7-3) 70-68 (2010 – First Round) (8 hrs-11 mins)

— 46 N. Pietrangeli (ITA) bt N. Pilic (YUG) 24-22 6-2 6-4 (1962 – Second Round)

— 46 R.A. Gonzales (USA) bt C.M. Pasarell (USA) 22-24 1-6 16-14 6-3 11-9 (1969 – First Round)

— 42 A.A. Segal (RSA) bt A.D. Marshall (AUS) 6-2 6-2 22-20 (1956 – Third Round)

— 42 J-L Arilla (ESP) bt P. Rodriguez (CHI) 20-22 4-6 6-2 6-2 6-2 (1966 – First Round)

— 42 S.R. Smith (USA) bt A.J. Stone (AUS) 20-22 6-4 9-7 4-6 6-3 (1969 – First Round)

— 42 J. Leschly (DEN) bt J.L. Rouyer (FRA) 6-4 22-20 6-4 (1969 – Second Round)

— 38 D. Sturdza (SUI) bt. J.E. Baker (HAI) 20-18 6-3 6-4 (1963 – First Round)

— 38 M.A. Philippoussis (AUS) bt. S. Schalken (NED) 4-6 6-3 6-7 (7-9) 7-6 (7-4) 20-18 (2000 – Third Round (2 hrs-20 mins.) (Most games – singles fifth set)

Gentlemen's Doubles

— 62 A.R. Olmedo (PER) and F.O. Segura (ECU) bt G.L. Forbes and A.A. Segal (RSA) 32–30 5-7 6-4 6-4 (1968 – Second Round)

— 60 J.E. Patty and M.A. Trabert (USA) bt K.B. McGregor and F.A. Sedgman (AUS) 6-4 31-29 7-9 6-2 (1950 – Quarter-final) (2 hrs-35 mins)

— 58 W.W. Bowrey and O.K. Davidson (AUS) bt M. Cox and R. Taylor (GBR) 6-1 6-2 30-28 (1967 – Third Round)

— 54 M.P.D. Melo and A.R. Sa (BRA) bt P.J. Hanley (AUS) and K.R. Ullyett (ZIM) 5-7 7-6(7-4) 4-6 7-6(9-7) 28-26 (2007 – Second Round) (3 hrs 5 mins.)

— 50 B.B. Mackay (USA) and M.G. Rose (AUS) bt W.A. Knight and J.A. Pickard (GBR) 13-11 6-4 26-24 (1958 – Second Round)

— 48 D. Contet and F. Jauffret (FRA) bt J.G. Alexander and P.C. Dent (AUS) 9-7 25-23 7-5 (1969 – Second Round)

— 46 H.P. Guenthardt (SUI) and B. Taroczy (HUN) bt P.T. Annacone (USA) and C. van Rensberg (RSA) 6-4 2-6 6-4 6-7(4-7) 24-22 (1985 – Quarter-Final) (2hrs-41 mins)

— 44 J.L. Arilla and M. Santana (ESP) bt H.J. Plotz and B. Weinmann (GER) 6-4 6-3 21-23 11-9 (1967-First Round)

— 44 C.E. Graebner and J. Osborne (USA) bt V. Korotkov and A. Volkov (URS) 23-21 7-5 6-2 (1968 – First Round)

— 44 M.S.Knowles (BAH) and D.M. Nestor (CAN) bt. S.O.K. Aspelin (SWE) and T.S.Perry (AUS) 5-7 6-3 6-7(5-7) 6-3 23-21 (2006 – Quarter-final) (3hrs 13mins)

— 42 J.D. Newcombe and A.D. Roche (AUS) bt A.R. Ashe and W.E. Bond (USA) 6-2 2-6 20-22 6-3 6-4 (1964 – Second Round)

— 40 C.J. Hovell and P.V.V. Sherwood (GBR) bt T. Abe (JPN) and K.C. Gandar Dower (GBR) 10-8 21-19 6-0 (1938 – Second Round)

— 40 O. Sirola and N. Pietrangel(ITA) bt W.A. Knight and J.A. Pickard (GBR) 6-4 2-6 6-4 19-21 6-1 (1959 – Third Round)

— 40 N. Pilic (YUG) and E.L. Scott (USA) bt G.C. Richey (USA) and T. Ulrich (DEN) 19-21 12-10 6-4 4-6 9-7 (1966 – First Round)

Ladies' Singles

— 32 Miss C.R. Rubin (USA) bt Mrs. P. Hy Boulais (CAN) 7-6 (7-4) 6-7 (5-7) 17-15 (1995 – Second Round) (2hrs 3 mins)

— 30 Miss J. Goerges (GER) bt Miss K. Srebotnik (SLO) 4-6 7-6 (8-6) 16-14 (2008 – First Round) (2 hrs 17 mins)

— 26 Mrs. A.E. Beamish (BRI) bt Mrs. A.G. Wilkinson (BRI) 7-5 14-12 (1919 – Third Round)

— 26 Mrs. M. Hazel (GBR) bt Mrs. C.R. Satterthwaite (GBR) 12-14 6-2 6-3 (1925 – Third Round)

— 26 Miss A. Weiwers (FRA) bt Mrs. O. Anderson (USA) 8-10 14-12 6-4 (1948 – Second Round)

— 26 Mrs. B.M. Court (AUS) bt Mrs. L.W. King (USA) 14-12 11-9 (1970 – Final) (1 hr-28 mins)

— 26 Miss J.N. Connor (NZL) bt Miss F. Guedy (BEL) 6-3 2-6 14-12 (1975 – First Round)

	— 26 Miss N.J. Arendt (USA) bt Miss I. Demongeot (FRA) 2-6 6-3 14-12 (1993 – First Round) (1 hr-50 mins)
Ladies' Doubles	— 32 Miss L. Horn (RSA) and Miss K. Srebotnik (SLO) bt Miss K. Boogert (NED) and Miss A-G. Sidot (FRA) 6-4 1-6 17-15 (1999 – Quarter-final) (1 hr-59 mins)
	— 30 Miss M.W. Haughton and Mrs. R.R.W. Jackson (BRI) bt Mrs.R.C. Middleton and Miss P.H. Dransfield (BRI) 6-3 2-6 16-14 (1921– First Round)
	— 30 Mrs. G. Vento-Kabchi (VEN) and Miss A. Widjaja (INA) bt. Miss W. Prakusya (INA) and Miss T. Tanasugarn (THA) 6-4 3-6 16-14 (2004 – Second Round) (2hrs 8mins)
Mixed Doubles	— 56 M. Schapers and Miss B.A.M. Schultz (NED) bt T.J.C.M. Nijssen (NED) and Miss A. Temesvari (HUN) 6-3 5-7 29-27 (1991 – First Round) (3 hrs-7 mins).
	— 44 P.F. McNamee (AUS) and Miss M. Navratilova (USA) bt. S.E. Davis and Miss H.E. Nagelsen (USA) 6-7 (4-7) 7-5 23-21 (1985 – Semi–final) (2 hrs-10 mins)

Most Games in a Final

Gentlemen's Singles	— 77 R. Federer (SUI) bt A.S. Roddick (USA) 5-7 7-6 (8-6) 7-6 (7-5) 3-6 16-14 (2009) (4hrs-18mins)
	— 62 R. Nadal (ESP) bt R. Federer (SUI) 6-4 6-4 6-7 (5-7) 6-7 (8-10) 9-7 (2008) (4 hrs-48 mins)
	— 58 J. Drobny (EGY) bt K.R. Rosewall (AUS) 13-11 4-6 6-2 9-7 (1954) (2 hrs-37 mins)
Gentlemen's Doubles	— 83 J.P. McEnroe (USA) and M.D. Stich (GER) bt J.F. Grabb and R.A. Reneberg (USA) 5-7 7-6 (7-5) 3-6 7-6 (7-5) 19-17 (1992) (5 hrs-1 min)
Ladies' Singles	— 46 Mrs. B.M. Court (AUS) bt Mrs. L.W. King (USA) 14-12 11-9 (1970) (2 hrs-28 mins). Note: in 1902 Miss M.E. Robb (BRI) bt Mrs. A. Sterry (BRI) 7-5 6-1 after abandoning the match started the day before, due to rain, with the score at 4-6, 13-11. The total games played were 53.
Ladies' Doubles	— 38 Mrs. R. Mathieu (FRA) and Miss E.M. Ryan (USA) bt Miss W.A. James and Miss A.M. Yorke (GBR) 6-2 9-11 6-4 (1933)
	— 38 Miss R. Casals and Mrs. L.W. King (USA) bt Miss M.E.A. Bueno (BRA) and Miss N.A. Richey (USA) 9-11 6-4 6-2 (1967)
	— 38 Miss S.M. Graf (GER) and Miss G.B. Sabatini (ARG) bt Miss L.I. Savchenko and Miss N.M. Zvereva (URS) 6-3 1-6 12-10 (1988) (2 hrs-49 mins)
Mixed Doubles	— 48 E.W. Sturgess and Mrs R.A. Summers (RSA) bt J.E. Bromwich (AUS) and Miss A.L. Brough (USA) 9-7 9-11 7-5 (1949)

Most Games in a Set in a Final

Gentlemen's Singles	— 30 R. Federer (SUI) bt A.S. Roddick (USA) 5-7 7-6 (8-6) 7-6 (7-5) 3-6 16-14 (2009) (95mins)
	— 24 J. Drobny (EGY) bt K.R. Rosewall (AUS) 13-11 4-6 6-2 9-7 (1954) (59 mins)
	— 24 A.J. Cooper (AUS) bt N.A. Fraser (AUS) 3-6 6-3 6-4 13-11 (1958)
Gentlemen's Doubles	— 36 J.P. McEnroe (USA) and M.D. Stich (GER) bt J.F. Grabb and R.A. Reneberg (USA) 5-7 7-6 (7-5) 3-6 7-6 (7-5) 19-17 (1992) (2 hrs-12 mins)
Ladies' Singles	— 26 Mrs. B.M. Court (AUS) bt Mrs. L.W. King (USA) 14-12 11-9 (1970)
Ladies' Doubles	— 24 Miss S.J. Fry and Miss D.J. Hart (USA) bt Miss A.L. Brough and Mrs. W. duPont (USA) 6-3 13-11 (1951)

| Mixed Doubles | — 28 O.K. Davidson (AUS) and Mrs. L.W. King (USA) bt M.C. Riessen (USA) and Mrs. B.M. Court (AUS) 3-6 6-2 15-13 (1971) |

Most Games in a Semi-final

Gentlemen's Singles	— 87 R.G. Laver (AUS) bt B.B. McKay (USA) 11-13 11-9 10-8 7-9 6-3 (1959) (3 hrs-45 mins)
Gentlemen's Doubles	— 86 R.H. Osuna (MEX) and R.D. Ralston (USA) bt R.G. Laver and R. Mark (AUS) 4-6 10-8 15-13 4-6 11-9 (1960) (3hrs-5mins)
Ladies' Singles	— 41 Miss M.E.A. Bueno (BRA) bt Mrs. P.F. Jones (GBR) 6-3 9-11 7-5 (1966) (1 hr-50 mins)
Ladies' Doubles	— 42 Miss H.H. Jacobs (USA) and Miss A.M. Yorke (GBR) bt Miss J. Nicoll and Miss B.M. Nuthall (GBR) 5-7 6-4 11-9 (1939)
Mixed Doubles	— 69 P.F. McNamee (AUS) and Miss M. Navratilova (USA) bt S.E. Davis and Miss H.E. Nagelsen (USA) 6-7 (4-7) 7-5 23-21 (1985) (3 hrs-21 mins)

Most Games in a Set in a Semi-final

Gentlemen's Singles	— 36 N.A. Fraser (AUS) bt K. Nielsen (DEN) 6-4 6-4 17-19 6-4 (1958) (1 hr-43 mins)
Gentlemen's Doubles	— 30 R.N. Hartwig and M.G. Rose (AUS) bt G.P. Mulloy and E.V. Seixas (USA) 14-16 6-3 6-3 6-4 (1953)
Ladies' Singles	— 22 Mrs. P.F. Jones (GBR) bt Mrs. B.M. Court (AUS) 10-12 6-3 6-2 (1969) (1 hr-6 mins)
	— 22 Mrs. F.S. Moody (USA) bt Mrs. S. Sperling (DEN) 12-10 6-4 (1938) (1 hr-15 mins)
Ladies' Doubles	— 22 Mrs D.B. Andrus (USA) and Miss S. Henrotin (FRA) bt Mrs. L.A. Godfree and Miss M.C. Scriven (GBR) 6-3 12- 10 (1934)
Mixed Doubles	— 44 P.F. McNamee (AUS) and Miss M. Navratilova (USA) bt S.E. Davis and Miss H.E. Nagelsen (USA) 6-7 (4-7) 7-5 23-21 (1985) (2 hrs-10 mins)

Least Games in a Final

Gentlemen's Singles	— 20 W.C. Renshaw (BRI) bt J.T. Hartley (BRI) 6-0 6-1 6-1 (1881)
	— 20 F.J. Perry (GBR) bt G. von Cramm (GER) 6-1 6-1 6-0 (1936)
Gentlemen's Doubles	— 22 M.J.G. Ritchie (BRI) and A .F. Wilding (NZL) bt A.W. Gore and H.R. Barrett (BRI) 6-1 6-1 6-2 (1910)
Ladies' Singles	— 12 Mrs. R.L. Chambers (BRI) bt Miss P.D.H. Boothby (BRI) 6-0 6-0 (1911) (24 mins.)
Ladies' Doubles	— 12 Miss S.J. Fry and Miss D.J. Hart (USA) bt Miss M.C. Connolly and Miss J.A. Sampson (USA) 6-0 6-0 (1953)
Mixed Doubles	— 12 R. Lycett (BRI) and Miss E.M. Ryan (USA) bt A.D. Prebble and Mrs. R.L. Chambers (BRI) 6-0 6-0 (1919)

Least Games in a Semi-final

Gentlemen's Singles	— 22 R. Federer (SUI) bt J.L. Bjorkman (SWE) 6-2 6-0 6-2 (2006) (1 hr 17 mins)
Gentlemen's Doubles	— 24 R.L. Case and G. Masters (AUS) bt M. Cox (GBR) and E.C. Drysdale (RSA) 6-1 6-4 6-1 (1977)
Ladies' Singles	— 12 Miss S.R.F. Lenglen (FRA) bt Mrs A.E. Beamish (GBR) 6-0 6-0 (1923)
	— 12 Miss S.R.F. Lenglen (FRA) bt Miss K. McKane (GBR) 6-0 6-0 (1925) (30 mins)
	— 12 Miss A.Marble (USA) bt Mrs S.Sperling (GER) 6-0 6-0 (1939) (19 mins)

Ladies' Doubles	— 12 Miss S.J. Fry and Miss D.J. Hart (USA) bt Miss H.M. Fletcher and Mrs I.M. Rinkel (GBR) 6-0 6-0 (1953)
Mixed Doubles	— 13 A.D. Prebble and Mrs R.L. Chambers (BRI) bt M.O. Decugis (FRA) and Miss L.M. Addison (BRI) (1919)

Longest Matches

Gentlemen's Singles	— 11 hrs 5 mins J.R. Isner (USA) bt N.P.A. Mahut (FRA) 6-4 3-6 6-7 (7-9) 7-6 (7-3) 70-68 (2010 – First Round) Played over three days.
	— 5 hrs 31 mins M. Cilic (CRO) bt S. Querrey (USA) 7-6 (8-6), 6-4 6-7 (2-7) 6-7 (3-7) 17-15 (2012 – Third Round) Played in one day.
	— 5 hrs 28 mins G. Holmes (USA) bt. T. Witsken (USA) 5-7 6-4 7-6 (7-5) 4-6 14-12 (1989-Second Round) Played over three days.
	— 5 hrs 12 mins R.A. Gonzales (USA) bt. C.M. Pasarell (USA) 22-24 1-6 16-14 6-3 11-9 (1969-First Round) Played over two days.
	— 5 hrs 12 mins R. Schuettler (GER) bt A.M.M. Clement (FRA) 6-3 5-7 7-6 (8-6) 6-7 (7-9) 8-6 (2008 – Quarter-final). Played over two days
	— 5 hrs 5 mins M.A. Philippoussis (AUS) bt. S. Schalken (NED) 4-6 6-3 6-7 (7-9) 7-6 (7-4) 20-18 (2000-Third Round) Played in one day.
Gentlemen's Doubles	— 6 hrs 9 mins M. Knowles (BAH) and D.M. Nestor (CAN) bt. S.O.K. Aspelin (SWE) and T.S. Perry (AUS) 5-7 6-3 6-7 (5-7) 6-3 23-21 (2006 – Quarter-final) Played over two days.
	— 5 hrs 58 mins M. Merlo and A. Sa (BRA) bt P.J. Handley (AUS) and K.R. Ullyet (ZIM) 5-7 7-6 (7-4) 4-6 7-6 (9-7) 28-26 (2007 – Second Round) Played over four days. Longest fifth set at The Championships.
	— 5 hrs 5 mins H.P. Guenthardt (SUI) and B. Taroczy (HUN) bt. P.T. Annacone (USA) and C.J. van Rensburg (RSA) 6-4 2-6 6-4 6-7 (4-7) 24-22 (1985-Quarter-final) Played in one day.
	— 5 hrs 1 min J.P. McEnroe (USA) and M.D. Stich (GER) bt. J.F. Grabb and R.A. Renberg (USA) 5-7 7-6 (7-5) 3-6 7-6 (7-5) 17-15 (1992-Final) Played over two days.
Ladies' Singles	— 3 hrs 45 mins Miss C.C. Rubin (USA) bt. Mrs. P. Hy-Boulais (CAN) 7-6 (7-4) 6-7 (5-7) 17-15 (1995-Second Round) Played in one day.
	— 3 hrs 43 mins Miss T. Paszek (AUT) bt Miss F. Schiavone (ITA) 3-6 6-4 11-9 (2011 – Third Round)
	— 3 hrs 41 mins Miss J. Goerges (GER) bt Miss K. Srebotnik (SLO) 4-6 7-6 (8-6) 16-14 (2008) – First Round)
	— 3 hrs 24 mins Miss A. Ivanovic (SRB) bt Miss N. Dechy (FRA) 6-7 (2-7) 7-6 (7-3) 10-8 (2008 – Second Round) Played in one day.
Ladies' Doubles	— 3 hrs 27mins Mrs. G. Vento-Kabchi (VEN) and Miss A. Widjaja (INA) bt. Miss W. Prakusya (INA) and Miss T. Tanasugarn (THA) 6-4 3-6 16-14 (2004 – Second Round) Played in one day.
	— 3 hrs 9 mins Miss M. Hingis (SUI) and Miss A.I.M. Sanchez Vicario (ESP) bt. Miss C.R. Rubin (USA) and Mrs. S. Schultz-McCarthy (NED) 7-6 (14-12) 6-7 (6-8) 13-11 (1997-Third Round) Played over two days.
	— 3 hrs 5 mins Miss L. Horn (RSA) and Miss K. Srebotnik (SLO) bt. Miss K. Boogert (NED) and Miss A-G. Sidot (FRA) 6-4 1-6 17-15 (1999-Quarter-final) Played in one day.
Mixed Doubles	— 4 hrs 14 mins M. Schapers and Miss B.A.M. Schultz (NED) bt. T.C.M. Nijssen (NED) and Miss A. Temesvari (HUN) 6-3 5-7 29-27 (1991-First Round) Played in one day.

Longest Finals

Gentlemen's Singles	— 4 hrs. 48 mins R. Nadal (ESP) bt R. Federer (SUI) 6-4 6-4 6-7 (5-7) 6-7 (8-10) 9-7 (2008) (Concluded at 9.16pm)
	— 4 hrs. 18 mins R. Federer (SUI) bt A.S. Roddick (USA) 5-7 7-6 (8-6) 7-6 (7-5) 3-6 16-14 (2009)

	— 4 hrs. 16 mins J.Connors (USA) bt J.P. McEnroe (USA) 3-6 6-3 6-7 (2-7) 7-6 (7-5) 6-4 (1982)
Gentlemen's Doubles	— 5 hrs. 1 min. J.P. McEnroe (USA) and M.D. Stich (GER) bt J.F. Grabb and R.A. Reneberg (USA) 5-7 7-6 (7-5) 3-6 7-6 (7-5) 19-17 (1992)
Ladies' Singles	— 2 hrs. 46 mins. Miss. V.E.S Williams (USA) bt Miss L.A. Davenport (Mrs J. Leach) 4-6 7-6 (7-4) 9-7 (2005)
Ladies' Doubles	— 2hrs. 49 mins. Miss S.M. Graf (GER) and Miss G.B. Sabatini (ARG) bt Miss L.I. Savchenko and Miss N.M. Zvereva (URS) 6-3 1-6 12-10 (1988)

Longest Semi-finals

Gentlemen's Singles	— 4 hrs 44 mins N. Djokovic (SRB) beat J.M. Del Potro (ARG) 7-5 4-6 7-6 (7-2) 7-7 (6-8) 6-3 (2013)
	— 4 hrs 1 min B.F.Becker (GER) beat I. Lendl (TCH) 7-5 6-7 (2-7) 2-5 6-4 6-3 (1989)
Gentlemen's Doubles	— 3 hrs 33 mins P.V.N. Haarhuis (NED) and J.E. Palmer (USA) beat M.S. Knowles (BAH) and D.M. Nestor (CAN) 3-6 7-5 7-6 (7-4) 4-6 8-6 (1999) Ladies' Singles
Ladies' Singles	— 2 hrs 50 mins Miss S.J. Williams (USA) beat Miss E. Dementieva (RUS) 6-7 (4-7) 7-5 8-6 (2009)
Ladies' Doubles	— 2 hrs 38 mins Miss M.J. McGrath (USA) and Mrs A. Neiland (LAT) beat Miss B.C. Fernandez (USA) and Miss N.M. Zvereva (BLR) 6-4 3-6 11-9 (1996)
Mixed Doubles	— 3 hrs 21 mins P.F. McNamee (AUS) and Miss M. Navratilova (USA) beat S.E. Davis and Miss H.E. Nagelsen (USA) 6-7 (4-7) 7-5 23-21 (1985)

Shortest Finals

Gentlemen's Singles	— 37 mins W.C. Renshaw (BRI) bt J.T. Hartley (BRI) 6-0 6-1 6-1 (1881)
	— 40 mins F.J. Perry (GBR) bt G. von Cramm (GER) 6-1 6-1 6-0 (1936)
Ladies' Singles	— 23 mins. Miss S.R.F. Lenglen (FRA) bt Mrs. F.I. Mallory (USA) 6-2 6-0 (1922)
	— 24 mins. Mrs. R.L. Chambers (BRI) bt Miss P.D.H. Boothby (BRI) 6-0 6-0 (1911)
	— 25 mins. Miss S.R.F. Lenglen (FRA) bt Miss J.C. Fry (GBR) 6-2 6-0 (1925)

Shortest Semi-finals

Gentlemen's Singles	— 40 mins H.E. Vines (USA) beat J.H. Crawford (AUS) 6-2 6-1 6-3 (1932)
Gentlemen's Doubles	— 1 hr 24 mins P.B. Fleming and J.P. McEnroe (USA) beat T.S. Okker (NED) and D.L. Stockton (USA) 6-3 6-2 6-4 (1981)
Ladies' Singles	— 19 mins Miss A. Marble (USA) beat Mrs S. Sperling (GER) 6-0 6-0 (1939)
Ladies' Doubles	— 46 mins Miss B.C. Fernandez (USA) and Miss N.M. Zvereva (BLR) beat Miss S. Appelmans and Miss M.J.M.M. Oremans (NED) 6-1 6-2 (1997)
Mixed Doubles	— 52 mins J.M. Lloyd (GBR) and Miss W.M. Turnbull (AUS) beat C.M. Johnstone and Miss P.J. Whytcross (AUS) 6-4 6-0 (1982)

Most Games in a Championship

Gentlemen's Singles	— 322 (182-140) A.J. Cooper (AUS) 1958
Gentlemen's Doubles	— 313 (165-148) P.H. Cash and P.F. McNamee (AUS) 1984
Ladies' Singles	— 173 (104-69) Miss I.C. Martinez (ESP) 1994
Ladies' Doubles	— 174 (93-81) Miss H.E. Nagelsen (USA) and Mrs. P.D. Smylie (AUS) 1987

Mixed Doubles   — 184 (108-76) P.F. McNamee (AUS) and Miss M. Navratilova
                         (USA) 1985

Most Games in the Singles, Doubles and Mixed Doubles Championships

Gentlemen   — 368 R.G. Laver (AUS) 1959
                         (Singles: 166-117, Doubles: 141-96, Mixed: 79-39)
Ladies   — 436 Miss M. Navratilova (USA) 1985
                         (Singles: 91-50, Doubles: 78-33, Mixed: 108-76)

Most Matches Won Consecutively

Gentlemen's Singles   — 41 B.R. Borg (SWE) 1976–1981
Gentlemen's Doubles   — 35 T.A. Woodbridge and M.R. Woodforde (AUS) 1993–1998
Ladies' Singles   — 50 Miss H.N. Wills/Mrs. F.S. Moody (USA) 1927–1930, 1932,
                         1933, 1935, 1938
Ladies' Doubles   — 29 Miss N.M. Zvereva (URS/CIS/BLR) 1991–1995
Mixed Doubles   — 25 E.V. Seixas (USA) 1953–1957
                         — 32 Miss D.J.Hart (USA) 1951–1955, 1968

Most Points in a Tie-break

Gentlemen's Singles   — 38 B.R. Borg (SWE) bt P.J. Lall (IND) 6-3 6-4 9-8 (20-18)
                         (1973 – First Round)
                         — 36 J.R. Isner (USA) bt J. Nieminen (FIN) 7-6 (19-17) 7-6 (7-3)
                         7-5 (2014 – Second Round)
Gentlemen's Doubles   — 50 J. Gunnarson (SWE) and M. Mortensen (DEN) bt J. Frawley
                         (AUS) and V. Pecci (PAR) 6-3 6-4 3-6 7-6 (26-24) (1985 – First
                         Round)
Ladies' Singles   — 28 Miss S.V. Wade (GBR) bt Miss J.M. Durie (GBR) 3-6 7-6
                         (15-13) 6-2 (1982 – First Round)
Ladies Doubles   — 26 Miss M. Hingis (SUI) and Miss A.I.M. Sanchez Vicario
                         (ESP) bt Miss C.R. Rubin (USA) and Mrs. S. Schultz-McCarthy
                         (NED) 7-6 (14-12) 6-7 (6-8) 13-11 (1997 – Third Round).
                         — 26 Miss M. Sequera (VEN) and Miss M. Washington (USA) bt.
                         Miss E. Gagliardi (SUI) and Miss M. Shaughnessy (USA) 7-6 (14-
                         12) 6-7 (7-0) 6-2 (2003 – Second Round)
Mixed Doubles   — 32 L. Friedl (CZE) and Mrs. A. Huber (RSA) bt. M. Damm
                         (CZE) and Miss B. Rittner (GER) 7-6 (17-15) 6-0 (2003 – Second
                         Round)

Most Points in a Tie-break in a Final

Gentlemen's Singles   — 34 B.R. Borg (SWE) bt J.P. McEnroe (USA) 1-6 7-5 6-3 6-7
                         (16-18) 8-6 (1980)
Gentlemen's Doubles   — 26 D.M. Nestor (CAN) and N. Zimonjic (SRB) bt J.L. Bjorkman
                         and K.R. Ullyett (ZIM) 7-6 (14-12) 6-7 (3-7) 6-3 6-3 (2008)
Ladies' Singles   — 14 Miss S.M. Graf (GER) bt Miss J. Novotna (CZE) 7-6 (8-6)
                         1-6 6-4 (1993)
Ladies' Doubles   — 18 Mrs. G.E. Reid and Miss W.M. Turnbull (AUS) bt Miss M.
                         Jausovec (YUG) and Miss V. Ruzici (ROM) 4-6 9-8 (10-8) 6-3
                         (1978)
Mixed Doubles   — 22 M.J. Bates and Miss J.M. Durie (GBR) bt D.J. Cahill and
                         Miss N.A-L. Provis (AUS) 7-6 (12-10) 6-3 (1987)

Most Points in a Tie-break in a Semi-Final

Gentlemen's Singles   — 18 I. Lendl (TCH) bt. S.B. Edberg (SWE) 3-6 6-4 7-6 (10-8) 6-4
                         (1987)

	— 18 B.F. Becker (GER) bt I. Lendl (TCH) 6-4 6-3 6-7 (8-10) 6-4 (1988)
Gentlemen's Doubles	— 26 K.E. Flach and R.A. Seguso (USA) bt E. Edwards and G.R. Miller (RSA) 6-4 6-4 7-6 (14-12) (1988)
	— 26 R.D. Leach and D.S. Melville (USA) bt. M-K.P. Goellner (GER) and Y.A. Kafelnikov (RUS) 3-6 7-6 (14-12) 6-7 (2-7) 7-6 (7-3) 6-3 (1995)
Ladies' Singles	— 14 Miss M. Navratilova (USA) bt. Miss B.C. Fernandez (USA) 6-4 7-6 (8-6) (1994)
	— 14 Miss P. Kvitova (CZE) bt Miss E.C.M. Bouchard (CAN) 7-6 (8-6) 6-1 (2014)
Ladies' Doubles	— 16 Miss B.C. Fernandez (USA) and Miss N.M. Zvereva (BLR) bt Miss M.J. McGrath (USA) and Mrs. A. Neiland (LAT) 7-6 (7-5) 6-7 (7-9) 6-2 (1995)
	— 16 Miss C.C. Black (ZIM) and Miss R.P. Stubbs (AUS) bt. Miss V. Ruano Pascual (ESP) and Miss P.L. Suarez (ARG) 7-6 (9-7) 4-6 6-4 (2004)
Mixed Doubles	— 22 S.E. Stewart and Miss Z.L. Garrison (USA) bt. J.B. Fitzgerald and Mrs. P.D. Smylie (AUS) 6-4 6-7 (10-12) 6-3 (1988)
	— 22 R.D. Leach and Miss Z.L. Garrison (USA) bt. J.R. Pugh (USA) and Miss J. Novotna (TCH) 7-6 (12-10) 7-6 (7-4) (1990)

Most Tie-break Sets in a Match

Gentlemen's Singles	The maximum of four sets has been achieved four times:
	1991 – First Round. J.F. Eltingh (NED) bt. R. Vogel (TCH) 7-6 (7-2) 6-7 (6-8) 7-6 (7-5) 6-7 (7-9) 6-3
	1999 – First Round. W.S. Arthurs (AUS) bt V. Santopadre (ITA) 7-6 (9-7) 6-7 (5-7) 7-6 (12-10) 7-6 (7-4) (No service breaks)
	2002 – Third Round. W.S. Arthurs (AUS) bt. T.P. Dent (USA) 7-6 (7-2) 7-6 (7-3) 6-7 (4-7) 7-6 (7-5) (No service breaks)
	2002 – Fourth Round. R.P.S. Krajicek (NED) bt. M.A. Philippoussis (AUS) 6-7 (2-7) 7-6 (7-4) 6-7 (1-7) 7-6 (7-5) 6-4
Gentlemen's Doubles	The maximum of 4 sets has been achieved eight times.
Ladies' Singles	The maximum of 2 sets has been achieved 50 times.
Ladies' Doubles	The maximum of 2 sets has been achieved 35 times.
Mixed Doubles	The maximum of 2 sets has been achieved 52 times.

Family Doubles

Champions

Brothers	— J.E. Renshaw and W.C. Renshaw (BRI) 1884–1886, 1888, 1889
	— H. Baddeley and W. Baddeley (BRI) 1891, 1894–1896
	— H.L. Doherty and R.F. Doherty (BRI) 1897–1901, 1903–1905
	— M.C. Bryan and R.C.Bryan (USA) 2006, 2011, 2013
Sisters	— Miss S.J. Williams and Miss V.E.S. Williams (USA) 2000, 2002, 2008, 2009, 2012
Brother and Sister	— J.R. Austin and Miss T.A. Austin (USA) 1980
	— C. Suk and Miss H. Sukova (CZE) 1996, 1997
	— W.H. Black and Miss C.C. Black (ZIM) 2004
Husband and Wife	— L.A. Godfree and Mrs. L.A. Godfree (GBR) 1926

Runners-up

Brothers	— H. Baddeley and W. Baddeley (BRI) 1892, 1897
	— H.L. Doherty and R.F. Doherty (BRI) 1902, 1906
	— T.E. Gullikson and T.R. Gullikson (USA) 1983
	— M.C. Bryan and R.C.Bryan (USA) 2005, 2007, 2009

Sisters	— Miss K.McKane and Mrs. A.D. Stocks (BRI) 1922
Brother and Sister	— J.R. Austin and Miss T.A. Austin (USA) 1981
Husband and Wife	— L.A. Godfree and Mrs. L.A. Godfree (GBR) 1927
	— H.C. Hopman and Mrs. H.C. Hopman (AUS) 1935

Champions who wore headgear in a Singles Final

N.E. Brookes	(AUS)	1914	Tweed Cap
G.L. Patterson	(AUS)	1922	White Headband
J.R. Borotra	(FRA)	1924, 1926	French Beret
J.R. Lacoste	(FRA)	1925, 1928	White Cap
H.E. Vines	(USA)	1932	White Cap
Y.F.M. Petra	(FRA)	1946	White Baseball Cap
B.R. Borg	(SWE)	1976-1980	Thin 'FILA' Headband
J.P. McEnroe	(USA)	1981	Broad Red Headband
P.H. Cash	(AUS)	1987	Black and White Check Headband
A.K. Agassi	(USA)	1992	White 'NIKE' Baseball Cap
R. Federer	(SUI)	2003-2007, 2009, 2012	White 'NIKE' Bandana
R. Nadal	(ESP)	2008, 2010	White 'NIKE' Bandana
N. Djokovic	(SRB)	2011	White 'TACCHINI' Cap
Miss M.E.A. Watson	(BRI)	1884	Straw Hat
Miss C. Dod	(BRI)	1887	White Cap
Miss S.R.F. Lenglen	(FRA)	1919	Cloche Hat
	(FRA)	1920-23, 1925	Bandeau
Miss K. McKane	(GBR)	1924, 1926	Bandeau
Miss H.N. Wills/	(USA)	1927-1938	Eye Shade
Mrs. F.S. Moody			
Miss C. Aussem	(GER)	1931	Eye Shade
Miss A. Marble	(USA)	1939	White Jockey Cap
Miss P.M. Betz	(USA)	1946	Thin Alice Band
Miss A.L. Brough	(USA)	1948, 1950	Alice Band
Miss M.C. Connolly	(USA)	1952-1954	Ribbon Alice Band
Miss M. Smith	(AUS)	1963	Broad Alice Band
Miss M. Navratilova	(USA)	1990	Thin Purple Ribbon Headband
Miss S.M. Graf	(GER)	1991, 1993	Thin Printed Headband
		1995, 1996	Thin Paisley Headband
Miss I.C. Martinez	(ESP)	1994	Broad Navy Blue Printed Headband
Miss M. Hingis	(SUI)	1997	Broad 'TACCHINI' Headband, Orange and Green Bordered
Miss J. Novotna	(CZE)	1998	Broad white 'PRINCE' Headband
Miss S.J. Williams	(USA)	2002	Tiara
		2009, 2010, 2012	White 'NIKE' Headband
Miss V.E.S Williams	(USA)	2005, 2007	White 'REEBOK' Eye Shade
		2008	White 'ELEVEN' Eye Shade
Miss P. Kvitova	(CZE)	2011, 2014	White 'NIKE' Headband

Champions who wore glasses in a final

J. Drobny	(EGY)	S 1954
C.S. Garland	(USA)	D1920
F.A. Parker	(USA)	D 1949
G.P. Mulloy	(USA)	D 1957
Miss B.J. Moffitt/	(USA)	S 1966–1968, 1972, 1973, 1975, D 1961, 1962, 1965, 1967
Mrs. L.W. King		1968, 1970–1973, 1979, M 1967, 1971, 1973, 1974
Miss K. Sawamatsu	(JPN)	D 1975
Miss M. Navratilova	(USA)	S 1985–1987, 1990, D 1986, M 1985, 1993, 1995, 2003

Runners-up who wore glasses in a final

H.O. Kinsey	(USA)	S 1926, D 1926, M 1926
J. Drobny	(TCH/EGY)	S 1949, 1952, D 1951
J.C. Barclay	(FRA)	D 1963
A.R. Ashe	(USA)	D 1971
C.F. Long	(AUS)	M 1947
G.P. Mulloy	(USA)	M 1956
Miss B.J. Moffitt/	(USA)	S 1963, 1969, 1970, D 1964, 1976, M 1966, 1978, 1983
Mrs. L.W. King		
Miss J.P. Lieffrig	(FRA)	D 1965
Miss F. Durr	(FRA)	D 1965, 1968, 1970
Miss M. Navratilova	(USA)	S 1988, 1989, 1994, D 1985, M 1986

Other items

Championships

J.R. Borotra (FRA) played in a record 35 Championships over a period of 43 years (Singles: 12 – 1922–1932, 1935, Doubles only: 23 – 1933, 1934, 1936–39, 1948–1964).

A.W. Gore (BRI) played in 34 Championships over a period of 40 years (Singles: 30 – 1888–1894, 1896–1914, 1919–1922, Doubles only: 4 – 1924–1927).

Miss M. Navratilova (TCH/USA) played in 31 Championships (24 consecutive) (Singles: 23 – 1973–1994, 2004. Doubles only: 8, 1995, 1996, 2000–2003, 2005, 2006).

Miss S.V. Wade (GBR) played in a record 26 Championships (consecutive) (Singles: 24 – 1962–1985, Doubles only: 2 – 1986, 1987).

R.K. Wilson (GBR) played in 25 consecutive Championships (Singles 1952-1970, Doubles only 1971–1977.

Miss B. Bingley/Mrs. G.W. Hillyard (BRI) played in 24 Championships over a period of 30 years (Singles: 24 – 1884–1889, 1891–1894, 1897, 1899–1902, 1904–1910, 1912, 1913).

R.N. Howe (AUS) played in the three Championships events for 16 consecutive years, 1954-1969.

Service

Mrs. H. Billington (GBR), 1946–1956, was the last player to regularly serve underarm.

Miss M.H. de Amorim (BRA) lost to Mrs. L.B.E. Thung (NED) 6-3 4-6 6-1 in the second round of the Ladies' Singles in 1957, after serving 17 consecutive double faults at the beginning of the match.

Miss L. Anderson (GBR) lost to Mrs. F.H. Vivian (GBR) 1-6 1-6 in the first round of the Ladies' Singles in 1946, after serving 11 consecutive double faults.

P. Sampras (USA) won 118 consecutive service games in singles from his 3rd round match (second set) in 2000 to his 2nd round match (fourth set) in 2001.

During the course of winning his seven Singles finals, P. Sampras (USA lost his service only four times out of 131 – twice against J.S. Courier (USA), 1993 and twice against G.S. Ivanisevic (CRO).

In 1999 W.S. Arthurs (AUS) won 111 consecutive service games in singles – 38 qualifying and 73 reaching the 4th round.

H.Redl (AUT), 1947–1956, played with only one arm. He lost his left arm on active service during the Second World War but was allowed to serve using the racket to throw up the ball.

Speed of Service

The fastest recorded services are: Gentlemen – 148 mph – T. Dent (USA), 2010; Ladies – 129 mph – Miss V.E.S.. Williams (USA), 2008 (Recorded on Centre and Nos, 1, 2, 3 and 18 Courts)

Aces

The maximum number of aces served by a player in a Gentlemen's Singles match is 113 by J.R. Isner versus N. Mahut during the first round in 2010. Mahut served 103 aces, making the combined total for the match at 216. R. Federer (SUI) served 50 aces against A.S. Roddick in the 2009 final. G.S. Ivanisevic (CRO) served a record 212 aces during his seven matches in the Gentlemen's Singles in 2001. Miss S.J. Williams served a record 102 aces during her seven matches in the Ladies' Singles in 2012. On Thursday 5th July 2012 she served 24 aces against Miss V. Azarenka in the semi-final of the Ladies Singles.

Whitewash

There have been 16 occasions when a player has been beaten 6-0 6-0 6-0 in the Gentlemen's Singles: 1878 – 1st round A.S. Tabor (BRI) bt C. Wallis (BRI), A.C. Brown (BRI) bt F.M. Ashley (BRI); 1899 – 2nd round H.R. Barrett (BRI) bt C.G. Allen; 1905 – 3rd round T.M. Mavrogordato (BRI) bt H.P. Gaskell (BRI); 1910 – 4th round A.F. Wilding (NZL) bt R.J. McNair (BRI); 1911 – 1st round A.W. Gore (BRI) bt A. Popp (GER); 1913 – 1st round F.G. Lowe (BRI) bt H.B. Bland (BRI); 1914 – 2nd round N.E. Brookes (AUS) bt L.F. Davin (BRI); 1923 – 2nd round A.H. Fyzee (IND) bt R.R. Boyd (GBR); 1926 – 1st round V. Richards (USA) bt A.F. Yencken (GBR); 1937 – 1st round J. Yamagishi (JAP) bt E.P.K. Hanson (GBR); 1939 – 1st round J. Pallada (YUG) bt J. Warboys (GBR); 1946 – 2nd round L. Bergelin (SWE) bt M.E. Lucking (GBR); 1947 – 1st round T. Johannson (SWE) bt B. Royds (GBR) and 2nd round bt P. Geelhand (BEL); 1987 – 1st round S.B. Edberg (SWE) bt S. Eriksson (SWE).

There have been 125 occasions when a player has been beaten 6-0 6-0 in the Ladies' Singles. 48 have occurred in the 1st Round, 42 in the 2nd Round, 19 in the 3rd Round, eight in the 4th Round: 1925 – Miss S.R.F. Lenglen (FRA) bt Mrs. A.E. Beamish (GBR), 1928 – Miss M. Watson (GBR) bt Mrs. H. Edgington (GBR), 1930 – Miss P.E. Mudford (GBR) bt Mrs. H.S. Uber (GBR), 1950 – Miss A.L. Brough (USA) bt Miss E.M.S. Andrews (GBR), 1954 Miss M.C. Connolly (USA) bt Miss A. Buxton (GBR), 1960 – Miss M.E.A. Bueno (BRA) bt Miss M.B. Hellyer (AUS), 1981 – Mrs. J.M. Lloyd (USA) bt Miss C. Pasquale (SUI), 1987 – Miss H. Sukova (TCH) bt Miss R. Reggi (ITA), four in the quarter-final; 1891 – Miss C. Dod (BRI) bt Mrs. Parsons (BRI), 1901 – Mrs. A. Sterry (BRI) bt Miss M.E. Robb (BRI), 1923 – Miss E. Ryan (USA) bt Miss E.F. Rose (GBR), 1981 – Miss H. Mandlikova (TCH) bt Miss W.M. Turnbull (AUS), three in the semi-final: 1923 – Miss S.R.F. Lenglen (FRA) bt Mrs. A.E. Beamish (GBR), 1925 – Miss S.R.F. Lenglen (FRA) bt Miss K. McKane (GBR), 1939 – Miss A. Marble (USA) bt Mrs. S. Sperling (DEN) and one in the Challenge Round: Mrs. R.L. Chambers (BRI) bt Miss P.D.H. Boothby (BRI) 1911. (In 1953 Miss D.J. Hart (USA) won two matches, 6-0 6-0 – second round – bt Miss J.R.M. Morgan (GBR) and – third round – bt Miss T. Zehden (GER).

In 1953 Miss S.J. Fry and Miss D.J. Hart (USA) won the Ladies' Doubles Championship with the loss of only 4 games: a bye into the third round, followed by 6-0 6-0, 6-2 6-2, 6-0 6-0, 6-0 6-0 victories.

The following players have won a match 6-0 6-0 in the Ladies' Singles and Doubles in the same year:- 1923 – Miss S.R.F. Lenglen (FRA), 1946 – Miss M.E. Osborne (USA), 1950 – Miss A.L. Brough (USA), 1953 – Miss D.J. Hart (USA), 1956 – Miss A.L. Brough (USA), 1964 – Mrs. P.F. Jones (GBR).

In 1999 Miss M. Weingartner (GER) was beaten 6-0 6-0 in two events. She lost in the second round of the Ladies' Singles to Miss M. Seles (USA) and in the first round of the Ladies' Doubles in partnership with Miss M.F. Lander (ARG), to Miss L.A. Davenport and Miss C.M. Morariu (USA).

Brothers

There have been eleven occasions when brothers have met in the Gentlemen's Singles – 1882 – W.C. Renshaw (BRI) bt J.E. Renshaw (BRI) 6-1 2-6 4-6 6-2 6-2; 1883 – W.C. Renshaw (BRI) bt J.E. Renshaw (BRI) 2-6 6-3 6-3 4-6 6-3; 1889 – W.C. Renshaw (BRI) bt J.E. Renshaw (BRI) 6-4 6-1 3-6 6-0; 1884 – W. Milne (BRI) bt O. Milne (BRI) 9-7 8-6 1-6 6-3; 1885 – W. Milne bt O. Milne 8-6 2-6 6-3 7-5; 1898 – R.F. Doherty (BRI) bt H.L. Doherty (BRI) 6-3 6-3 2-6 5-7 6- 1; 1909 – F.G. Lowe (BRI) bt A.H. Lowe (BRI) 3-6 6-2 6-3 6-2; 1911 – F.G. Lowe (BRI) bt A.H. Lowe (BRI) 5-7 7-5 6-4 retd; 1912 – F.G. Lowe (BRI) bt A.H. Lowe (BRI) 2-6 6-2 6-1 6-3; 1988 – E. Sanchez (ESP) bt J. Sanchez (ESP) 6-3 6-3 6-4; 2002 – C.P. Rochus bt O.L.P. Rochus (BEL) 6-2 3-6 7-6 (8-6) 6-0.

Sisters

There have been seven occasions when sisters have met in the Ladies' Singles – 1884 Final – Miss M.E.E. Watson (BRI) bt L.M. Watson (BRI) 6-8 6-3 6-3; 1966 second round – Miss G.V. Sherriff (AUS) bt Miss H.C. Sherriff (AUS) 8-10 6-3 6-3: 2000 Semi-final – Miss V.E.S. Williams (USA) bt Miss S.J. Williams (USA) 6-2 7-6 (7-3); 2002 Final – Miss S.J. Williams (USA) bt Miss V.E.S. Williams (USA) 7-6 (7-4) 6-3. 2003 Final – Miss S.J. Williams (USA) bt. Miss V.E.S. Williams (USA) 4-6 6-4 6-2, 2008 Final – Miss V.E.S. Williams (USA) bt Miss S.J. Williams 7-5 6-4. 2009 Final – Miss S.J. Williams (USA) bt Miss V.E.S. Williams 7-6 (7-3) 6-2.

Family

The only mother and son pair to compete in the Mixed Doubles is Mrs. C.O. Tuckey and C.R.D. Tuckey (GBR), 1931, 1932. The only father and daughter pairs to compete in the Mixed Doubles are W.A. Ingram and Miss A.M. Ingram/Mrs. P.H. Bouverie (GBR), 1921–1927, 1929–1933, and A.S. Drew and Miss B.E. Drew (GBR), 1928.

For the first time in 1977 three brothers competed in the Gentlemen's Singles – A.H. Lloyd (GBR), D.A. Lloyd (GBR) and J.M. Lloyd (GBR). For the first time in 1990 and subsequently in 1992 and 1993, three sisters competed in the Ladies' Singles – Miss K. Maleeva (BUL), Miss M. Maleeva (BUL) and Mrs. M. Maleeva-Fragniere (SUI). In 1993 all three sisters were seeded.

The 1968 Mixed Doubles event had 13 married couples competing.

Four mothers have won the Ladies' Singles: Mrs. G.W. Hillyard (BRI) – 1894, 1897, 1899, 1900; Mrs. A Sterry (BRI) – 1908; Mrs. R. L. Chambers (BRI) – 1910, 1911, 1913, 1914; Mrs. R.A. Cawley (AUS) – 1980.

Height

The shortest gentleman player was F.H. Ampon (PHI), 1948–1953, who stood 4 feet 11 inches, whilst the tallest gentlemen was I. Karlovic (CRO), 2003–2009, 2011, 2012, 2014 who stood 6 feet 11 inches. Other tall players were J. Isner (USA) 2008, 2010–2014 who stood 6 feet 10 inches tall, M. Srejber (TCH) – 1986–1990 and D. Norman (BEL) – 1995 who were 6 feet 8 inches. The shortest lady player was Miss C.G. Hoahing (GBR) – 1937–1938, 1946–1961, who stood 4 feet 9$^1/_2$ inches and the tallest were Miss L.A. Davenport (USA) – 1993–2001, 2003-2005, 2008 and Miss E. Bovina (RUS) – 2001–2004 who were 6 feet 2$^1/_2$ inches. In 2000 A. Popp (GER) and M. Rosset (SUI) faced each other in the 4th round of the Gentlemen's Singles – both were 6 feet 7 inches tall. The 2000 Ladies' Singles final was contested by two exceptionally tall players – Miss L.A. Davenport and Miss V.E.S. Williams (USA) who were 6 feet 2$^1/_2$ inches and 6 feet 1 inch respectively.

Miscellaneous

J. Drobny is unique in having competed at The Championships representing four different countries:- Czechoslovakia 1938, 1946–1949; Bohemia Moravia 1939; Egypt 1950–1959; Great Britain 1960, 1971.

Seven players have been seeded No. 1 in all three events: H.J. Cochet (FRA) 1929; J.D. Budge (USA) 1938; F.A. Sedgman (AUS) 1952; Miss A.L. Brough (USA) 1949–1951; Miss D.J. Hart (USA) 1952, 1955; Miss M. Smith/Mrs B .M. Court (AUS) 1964, 1966, 1969, 1970; Mrs. L.W. King (USA) 1968, 1974. Only on three occasions have the selections been justified: Budge 1938, Sedgman 1952, Miss Brough 1950.

Players immediately winning the Singles Championship on the Centre Court, have scaled the terraces to the Players' Match Seats Box to embrace their kin or supporters: 1987 – P.H. Cash (AUS), 1990 – Miss.M. Navratilova (USA), 1993, 1995 – Miss S.M. Graf (GER), 1998 – Miss J. Novotna (CZE), 2000 – Miss V.E.S. Williams (USA), 2000 – P. Sampras (USA) (West Stand), 2001 – G.S. Ivanisevic (CR0), 2002 – L.G. Hewitt (AUS), 2004 –Miss M. Sharapova (RUS), 2006 Miss A. Mauresmo (FRA), 2008 – R. Nadal (ESP), 2013 – Miss M.S. Bartoli (FRA), 2013 – A.B. Murray (GBR), 2014 – N. Djokovic (SRB), 2014 – Miss P. Kvitova (CZE).

The champion of 1927 H.J. Cochet (FRA) won the title after being two sets to love down in his quarter-final (F.T. Hunter (USA) 3-6 3-6 6-2 6-2 6-3), semi-final (W.T. Tilden (USA) 2-6 4-6 7-5 6-4 6-3) and final match (J.R. Borotra (FRA) 4-6 4-6 6-3 6-4 7-5).

In 1995 C. Brandi (ITA) and M. Ondruska (RSA) beat T. Ho (USA) and B. Steven (NZL) in the second round of the Gentlemen's Doubles 0-0 0-15 retired. On the very first point of the match Steven served and Ho, trying to intercept the return, injured his back and was forced to retire.

In 2001 G. Kuerten (BRA) was the first player ranked at No. 1 in the world not to compete at The Championships since ATP lists started in 1973.

In 2014 no United States player reached the last 16 of the Gentlemen's Singles since 1911.

Miss H. Schultze (GER) beat Miss J.P. Lieffrig (FRA) 4-6 11-9 12-10 in the first round of the Ladies' Singles in 1966 after saving 11 match points.

N. Kyrgios (AUS) beat R. Gasquet (FRA) 3-6 6-7 (4-7) 6-4 7-5 10-8 in the second round of the Gentlemen's Singles in 2014 after saving 9 match points.

Miss A. Pavlyuchenkova and Miss L. Safarova (CZE) beat Miss C. Black (ZIM) and Miss S.

Mirza (IND) 2-6 7-6 (9-7) 6-4 in the second round of the Ladies' Singles in 2014 after saving 9 match points.

On Saturday 2nd July, 1949 Miss A.L. Brough (USA) played 117 games on the Centre Court contesting three finals. She was on court for 5 hrs 20 mins.

On Monday 8th July, 1996, Miss L. Neiland (LAT) played four consecutive matches on the Centre Court, lasting a total of 6 hours 25 minutes.

On Saturday, 30th June 2012, Miss Y. Shvedova (KAZ) playing Miss S. Errani (ITA) in the third round of the Ladies' Singles, won the first set without conceding a point (24)

On Tuesdsay, 26th June 2012, a first round Ladies' Singles between Miss S. Errani (ITA) and Miss C. Vandeweghe (USA) was abandoned for the day due to rain, with the former leading 6-1 5-3 and advantage. On resumption the following afternoon, Miss Vandeweghe double-faulted to bring the match to a conclusion in two minutes.

Latest evening play on Centre Court
(Before installation of roof – 2009)

9.35pm Tuesday 30th June 1981. Third Round, Miss S.D. Barker (GBR) and Miss A.K. Kiyomura (USA) v Miss J.C. Russell (USA) and Miss V. Ruzici (ROM), 4-6 7-6 ( ) 5-5, halted due to bad light.

9.28pm Tuesday 30th June 2008. Fourth Round, A.B. Murray (GBR) bt R. Gasquet (FRA) 5-7 3-6 7-6 (7-3) 6-2 6-4

(With roof closed)

11.02pm Saturday 30th June 2012. Third Round, A.B. Murray (GBR) bt M. Baghdatis (CYP) 7-6 3-6 7-5 6-1

10.58pm Monday 21st June 2010. First Round, N. Djokovic (SRB) bt O. Rochus (BEL) 4-6 6-2 3-6 6-4 6-2

10.51pm Saturday 7th July, 2012. Final, Miss S.J. Williams and Miss V.E.S.Williams (USA) bt Miss A. Hlavacko and Miss L. Hradecka (CZE) 7-5 6-4 10.39pm Monday 29th June 2009. Fourth Round, A.B. Murray (GBR) bt S. Wawrinka (SUI) 2-6 6-3 6-3 5-7 6-3

10.03pm Thursday 28th June 2012. Second Round, L. Rosol (CZE) bt R. Nadal (ESP) 6-7 (9-11) 6-4 6-4 2-6 6-4

Latest evening play outside the Centre Court

9.41pm Mon 24th June 1974 No. 10 Court. First Round, B.E. Gottfried bt R. Moore (RSA) 6-3 4-6 7-5 2-6 10-8

9.39pm Friday 27th June 2014 No.3 Court (transferred from No.1 Court). Third Round, M. Cilic (CRO) bt T. Berdych (CZE) 7-6 (7-5) 6-4 7-6 (8-6).

(These times are very late but there is no way of determining whether they are records. The author can recall a finish at 9.50pm but cannot provide the details).

Other Facts and Figures

ATP World Tour Finals

The Grand Slams, The International Tennis Federation and the ATP created a Gentlemen's season finale known as the Tennis Masters Cup in 2000. This jointly -owned event replaced both the Gentlemen's Grand Slam Cup and the ATP Tour World Championship. Starting in 2009 the season finale, named the ATP World Tour Finals is held each year in London at the 02 Arena in November. The format of the event is an eight man singles round-robin, plus doubles. The best players in the annual ATP Champions Race, including Grand Slam Winners in the top 20, are eligible to compete.

Throughout their association with the Men's Year End event, the Grand Slams have continued to add to their remarkable and unique contribution to the international development of the sport. In the ten years of the Grand Slam Cup, the nine years of the Tennis Masters Cup and the first five years of the ATP World Tour Finals, the Grand Slams have delivered more than $42 million to the Grand Slam Development Fund, which is administered by the ITF for the benefit of the game worldwide.

Ball Boys and Girls

In the twenties and thirties, the ball boys were provided by the Shaftesbury Homes. From 1946 they have been provided by volunteers from institutions and schools as follows:

1946–1966	Dr. Barnardo's Homes
1967–1968	Shaftesbury Homes
1969–1986	The Wandsworth School Southfields
1969–1989	The Nork Park Secondary School
1969–1989	Westmeads High Shool, Morden
1969–2002	Eastfields High School, Mitcham
1969–2006	Tamworth Manor High School, Mitcham
1969–current	Raynes Park High School, Raynes Park
1969–current	Rutlish High School, Merton
1969–current	Wimbledon College, Wimbledon
1977–2002	Rowan High School, Streatham
1977–current	Ricards Lodge High School, Wimbledon
1977–current	Ursuline High School, Wimbledon
1987–1991	The John Archer School, Wandsworth
1990–current	The Beacon School, Banstead
1998–current	Sunbury Manor School, Sunbury
1998–current	Holy Cross Convent School, New Malden
1999–current	Wimbledon High School, Wimbledon
2000–current	Bishopsford Community School, Merton (Watermeads, Garth)
2001–current	Overton Grange School, Sutton
2001–current	Wilson's School, Wallington
2003–current	Sutton Grammar School, Sutton
2003–2006	Mitcham Vale School (Eastfield and Rowan)
2003	Richard Challoner School, New Malden
2004–current	Graveney School, Tooting
2005	Southfields Community School, Southfields
2006–current	John Fisher School, Purley
2006–current	Southborough, Kingston

2007–current	Hall School Wimbledon
2007–2008, 2010–current	Harris Academy, Merton
2007–current	Sutton High School, Sutton
2009–current	Teddington School, Teddington
2009–current	Tiffin School, Kingston
2010–current	Glyn School, Surrey
2010–current	Saint Cecilias's School, Wandsworth
2010–current	Surbiton High School, Kingston
2010–current	and from the Wimbledon Junior Tennis Initiative
2011–current	Greycourt School, Richmond
2011–current	Sacred Heart High School, Hammersmith
2011–current	Tolworth Girls' School, Surbiton
2012–current	Tiffin Girls' School, Kingston
2013–current	Burntwood School, Wandsworth
2013–current	Putney High School, Wandsworth

Selection

Participating schools (and WJTI) make the initial nominations of the ball boys/girls. No particular weight and height is required.

Schools/WJTI are asked to send candidates who meet the following requirements: Have completed the first 8 modules of the online training programme, registered their details online and applied to be considered as a prospective ball boy/girl.

Are generally in Year 9 or 10

Have no exams during The Championships

Are able to give priority to training during the training period

Are physically fit

Have a good knowledge of the laws of tennis

Are available to start training at 4 pm

Understand that absence for **any** reason (including illness and injury) lasting two weeks or longer may result in failure to qualify for further training

Are available for middle Sunday if required

Are sure that work experience/school trips will not result in missed sessions.

Qualification for Full Training

To qualify for full training students must:

Pass a written test on the rules and scoring of tennis at Wimbledon

Attend a court session

Be able to carry out instructions & drills

Be able to complete a circuit and then stand still for three minutes

Show good speed in shuttle runs

Pass tests of hand eye co-ordination

Training

Wimbledon training is directed by Sarah Goldson, currently teaching at Queen Mary's College, Basingstoke.

Final total of approximately 250 from around 700 applicants. Approximately 160 are selected from about 540 year 9 and 10 applicants and approximately 90 are chosen from about 180 ballboys/girls from previous years. Approximately ratio of boys/girls is 50/50. Average age being 15 years. Training is once a week before and after Easter from February onwards at the AELTC. Each prospective ball boy/girl will train once a fortnight and also attend four brief court training sessions at the Covered Courts before Easter.

After the Easter break all training takes place at Wimbledon (mainly on the Covered Courts) and lasts until mid June apart from school holidays.

Weekly training sessions last about two to two and a half hours with up to 60 children per session. Four sessions per week.

Training sessions involve general fitness & movement exercises, circuits, ball skills (rolling, feeding, receiving, work on knowledge of the game), scoring (e.g. knowing from the score at which end should the balls be), and set pieces (marching, start and end of game, tie break, ball change, suspended play etc.) Throughout training each candidate is constantly assessed.

Wimbledon ballboys/girls are not involved in the Qualifying Competition.
The Championships

During The Championships, five teams of six, selected by Sarah Goldson are responsible for the Centre and No. 1 Courts. Six teams of six rotate around the other show courts. The remainder in teams of six rotate around the other courts. The usual routine is one hour on and one hour off. The ball boys/girls usually arrive at 10 am and leave as soon as possible after the last court is closed.

The number of ball boys/girls has grown steadily over the years from the late thirties, when 46 were employed. In 1995 the figure noticeably increased from 138 to 182 to allow a full allocation of six to a court and in 2007 the number reached 250.

Ball girls were first introduced in 1977, and mixed teams in 1980. In 1986 ball girls were used on the Centre Court for the first time. In 1984 ball boys/girls were initially provided for the Qualifying Competition.

The ball boys have dressed as follows:- 1922-1931 – grey shirt, dark short trousers and dark stockings. 1932-1954 – greyshirt and dark long trousers. 1955-1957 – shirt in Club colours and long dark trousers. 1958-1995 – shirt in Club colours and shorts. 1996-2005 – purple shirt and green shorts. In 2006 a different uniform was introduced, designed by Polo Ralph Lauren. For The Championships in 2011 a new uniform was introduced featuring the 125th logo. Up to 1939 hats were occasionally worn and in recent years caps have featured.

Books on The Championships

The books listed below, published in Great Britain, are completely devoted to The Championships but there have been many others published which partly cover the subject.

1914 *The Lawn Tennis Championship Souvenir*
1925 *Wimbledon Lawn Tennis Illustrated,* Lillywhites, London. *Last Eights at Wimbledon, 1877–1925 (Reprints 1926, 1929, 1931),* F.R. Burrow, Lawn Tennis & Badminton, London.
1926 *Fifty Years of Wimbledon,* A. Wallis Myers, The Field, London.
1931 *Wimbledon Championship Souvenir,* Various Contributors.
1934 *Wimbledon Who's Who,* Dunlop Rubber Co., London.
1947 *Wimbledon Story,* Norah Gordon Cleather, Sporting Handbooks, London.
1949 *The Romance of Wimbledon,* John Olliff, Hutchinson, London.
1957 *The Centre Court Story,* Maurice Brady, W. Foulsham, London.
1965 *Behind the Scenes at Wimbledon,* Duncan Macaulay, Collins, London.
1972 *Wonderful Wimbledon,* Alastair Revie, Pelham Books, London.
1973 *Wimbledon The Hidden Drama,* Gwen Robyns, David & Charles, Newton Abbot.

1977 *100 Years of Wimbledon* Lance Tingay, Guinness Superlatives, London. *The Changing Face of Wimbledon 1877–1977 (Reprints 1986, 1987, 1989),* Alan Little, Wimbledon Lawn Tennis Museum, London. *100 Years of the Wimbledon Tennis Championships,* James Medlycott, Hamlyn, London. *Wimbledon, 1877–1977,* Max Robertson, Arthur Baker, London.

1981 *Wimbledon – Centre Court of the Game,* Max Robertson, B.B.C., London. *Rothman's Wimbledon on Camera,* Geoff Peters, Rothmans Publications, London. *The Book of Wimbledon,* Ronald Atkin, Heinemann/Quixote Press, London.

1982 *Classic Moments of Wimbledon,* Charles Landon, Moorland Publishing, London.

1984 *Wimbledon Ladies – A Centenary Record, 1884–1984*, Alan Little and Lance Tingay, Wimbledon Lawn Tennis Museum, London.

1986 *The Field Story of Wimbledon,* Jeremy Alexander, Associated Magazine, London. *Wimbledon – 100 Years of Men's Singles,* Malcolm Rowley, Sidgwick & Jackson, London. *Wimbledon Men – A Hundred Championships, 1877–1986. The Singles,* Alan Little and Lance Tingay, Wimbledon Lawn Tennis Museum, London. *100 Wimbledon Championships A Celebration,* John Barrett, Collins Willow, London.

1987 *Wimbledon Centre Court of the Game. Final Verdict,* Max Robertson, B.B.C., London.

1991 *The Lawns of Wimbledon (The Construction and Maintenance of Grass Courts),* Jim Thorn, All England Lawn Tennis Club, London.

1997 *The Ballad of Worple Road, A poetic History of the Early Wimbledon Championships*, Max Roberson, Queen Anne Press, London.

2001 *Wimbledon – The Official History of The Championships,* John Barrett, Collins Willow, London. (Second Edition)

2002 *Wimbledon 1922 – The New Ground and Centre Court,* Alan Little, Wimbledon Lawn Tennis Museum, London.

2002 *Wimbledon 1922–2002 – The Changing Face of Church Road,* Alan Little, Wimbledon Lawn Tennis Museum, London.

2003 *Wimbledon 1869–1921 – The Changing Face of Worple Road*, Alan Little, Wimbledon Lawn Tennis Museum, London.

2003 *Wimbledon – Serving Through Time. A Handbook from the Wimbledon Lawn Tennis Museum,* John Barrett, Wimbledon Lawn Tennis Museum, London.

2005 *Wimbledon Ladies' Singles Champions 1884–2004,* John Barrett and Alan Little, Wimbledon Lawn Tennis Museum, London.

2005 *Wimbledon 1922. The New Ground and Centre Court,* Alan Little, Wimbledon Lawn Tennis Museum, London. (Second Edition).

2005 *Wimbledon 1922–2005. The Changing Face of Church Road,* Alan Little, Wimbledon Lawn Tennis Museum, London. (Second Edition).

2006 *Wimbledon Gentlemen's Singles Champions 1877–2005,* John Barrett and Alan Little, Wimbledon Lawn Tennis Museum, London.

2009 *Centre Court: The Jewel in Wimbledon's Crown,* John Barrett and Ian Hewitt, Vision Sports Publishing, Kingston-on-Thames.

2009 *Wimbledon 1922–2009 – The Changing Face of Church Road*, Alan Little, Wimbledon Lawn Tennis Museum, London. (Third Edition).

2009 *Holding Court*, Christopher Gorringe with Jo Russell, Century, London.
2010 *Anyone for Tennis?* The Telegraph Book of Wimbledon, Martin Smith (Editor), Aurum Press, London.
   The Wimbledon Miscellany, Spencer Vignes, History Press, Stroud *Centre Court: The Jewel in Wimbledon's Crown*, John Barrett and Ian Hewitt, Vision Sports Publishing, Kingston-on-Thames (Second Edition).
2011 *Wimbledon – Visions of The Championships*, Ian Hewitt and Bob Martin, Visions Sports Publishing, Kingston-on-Thames.
2012 *Wimbledon Gentlemen's Singles Champions 1877–2011*, John Barrett and Alan Little, Wimbledon Lawn Tennis Museum, London.
   Wimbledon Ladies' Singles Champions 1884–2011, John Barrett and Alan Little, Wimbledon Lawn Tennis Museum, London
   Wimbledon 1922–2011. The Changing Face of Church Road, Alan Little, Wimbledon Lawn Tennis Museum, London (Fourth Edition).
2013 *Wimbledon. The Official History*, John Barrett, Vision Sports Publishing, Kingston-on-Thames. (Third Edition).
   The Olympic Tennis Event at Wimbledon, 2012, Alan Little, Wimbledon Lawn Tennis Museum, London.
2014 *Wimbledon. The Official History*, John Barrett. Vision Sports Publishing, Kingston-on-Thames (Fourth Edition).
   Wimbledon 1922–2014. The Changing Face of Church Road, Alan Little, Wimbledon Lawn Tennis Museum, London (Fifth Edition).
2015 *Wimbledon Lawn Tennis Museum Souvenir Handbook,* Wimbledon Lawn Tennis Museum, London.

Annuals

The Championships Wimbledon 1983–2003 John Parsons; 2004–2013, Neil Harman, 2014, Paul Newman, Various Publishers. *The Wimbledon Compendium 1991–2015.* Alan Little, All England Lawn Tennis Club, London. *This is Wimbledon, The Official Guide to the Championships, 1981–2013.* Alan Little, All England Lawn Tennis Club, London. 2014 – All England Lawn Tennis Club, London.

Broadcast Centre

This is the nineteenth year for the world's leading broadcasters to use the purpose-built, 5,000 sq. metre, Broadcast Centre which was opened for the 1997 Championships. It continues to provide a range of facilities unmatched by any other sporting organisation in a permanent installation.

Television Host Broadcaster

The BBC acts as host broadcaster to more than thirty other international networks, in what has become the largest annual outside broadcast operation in the world. In 2014, more than 2,500 sports accreditations were processed for broadcasting personnel covering The Championships.

So extensive is the BBC's commitment to Wimbledon that their coverage of nine courts effectively amounts to nine separate outside broadcast operations, each with a minimum of three cameras (up to 21 on Centre Court), a slow motion facility, a director with support staff, engineering and audio control, and a graphics organisation.

Design

The top floor of the Centre, overlooking No. 14 – No. 17 Courts and No. 18 and No. 19 Courts provides studio space for 12 networks. The proximity of studios to No. 18 Court offer television a more intimate atmosphere and a feeling of being more closely involved with play.

Production Areas

The two lower floors are dedicated to technical, production and editing rooms, much of the building digging deep into the hillside that used to overlook Aorangi Park.

TOC

At the heart of the Broadcast Centre sits TOC, the technical operations centre. TOC receives the vision and audio signals from the nine show courts, together with several extra camera feeds and distributes them to all broadcasters. The Club and the BBC continue to work closely together to develop innovative ways to improve coverage of the tournament.

Television Distribution

All 15 Mixed Court Feeds, together with a number of unilateral feeds, are sent from Wimbledon to IMG at Stockley Park, the BBC at Broadcasting House, and a number of other locations using dual / diverse fibre optic circuits.

Satellite connectivity is also used to augment the fibre optic circuits.

CCTV

For those members of staff and the media needing to follow the progress of play on all courts, the Club's closed circuit television network includes coverage of every Championship court. In addition to interviews, a continuous breakdown of match statistics is also available on this network, almost making it unnecessary for broadcasting and media personnel to be near a court to keep in touch with the progress of a particular match.

Catering

Feeding the broadcasters throughout the day and much of the night is an essential requirement and the restaurant is sited at the lowest level of the Broadcast Centre, taking up an extended underground area between No. 14 and No. 19 Courts. This has a seating capacity of 300, and the design has allowed for a number of tables to be located in the open air on either side of the restaurant and also on the roof during fine weather.

Project Team

The Broadcast Centre was designed by Building Design Partnership in consultation with the Club and the broadcasters and built by Try Construction Ltd.

Car parking

There are eight official car parks situated adjacent to the Club. No. 1, 2 and 3 are to the west, with entrances in Somerset Road. No. 1 has an additional entrance in Marryat Road. No. 4 is to the north, with an entrance in Somerset Road. No. 5 (Wimbledon Club), and Nos. 6 and 8 (Wimbledon Park Golf Club) are to the east, with entrances in Church Road and also for No. 6 in

Home Park, No. 10 (Wimbledon Park, operated by the London Borough of Merton), is to the north-east, with an entrance in Wimbledon Park Road.

Car Park Nos. 1, 2, 3, 5 and 8 are predominently reserved parking. Nos. 4 (coaches and motor cycles only), 6 and 10 are largely unreserved.

There is a Park and Ride service in operation at Morden Park. Car parking is £15.00 per car, with no charge for the bus ride.

Catering

Wimbledon is the largest single annual sporting catering operation carried out in Europe. All the catering for Wimbledon is in the hands of Facilities Management Catering Limited.

Around 1,800 FMC staff are required to operate the catering outlets and the quantity of food and drink served by them during the Fortnight is enormous. Typical examples are: 12,000 kilos of poached and smoked salmon; 28,000 kilos of English strawberries; 32,000 portions of fish and chips; 6,000 stone-baked pizzas; 190,000 sandwiches; 135,000 ice creams; 350,000 cups of tea and coffee; 250,000 bottles of water; 30,000 litres of milk; 7,000 litres of dairy cream; a combined total of 150,000 bath buns, scones, pastries and doughnuts; 230,000 glasses of Pimm's; 100,000 pints of draught beer and lager and 28,000 bottles of champagne. In addition, over 207,000 lunches are served, as well as 30,000 meals for FMC's own staff.

Strawberries and cream at Wimbledon has changed very little over the years. To ensure utmost freshness, Kent Grade 1 strawberries are picked the day before and arrive at Wimbledon at 5.30 a.m. prior to being inspected and hulled.

Catering at the Church Road ground: 1922–1935 Messrs. Ring and Brymer, 1936–1962 J. Lyons & Co. Ltd., 1963–1991 Town & County Catering Co. Ltd., 1992–1998 Town & County Catering, 1999– Facilities Management Catering Ltd.

Chair Umpires and Line Umpires

There are 360 officials at The Championships working as Chair Umpires, Line Umpires, Review Officials and management staff. These officials cover over 650 matches played during the fortnight.

There are approximately 240 British officials, all LTA Licensed Officials and members of the Association of British Tennis Officials (ABTO) and approximately 120 overseas officials from all over the world, including the team of six ITF/Grand Slam Chair Umpires that officiates at all four Grand Slams, and one full time ATP Chair Umpire.

Around 48 Chair Umpires are assigned each day, the other officials working as Line Umpires and Review Officials. Chair Umpires normally umpire two matches a day, although not necessarily on the same court. Line Umpires work in teams, two teams being assigned to each court. The teams work on a timed rotation, 60 minutes on, 60 minutes off, with nine Line Umpires per team on Centre Court and Nos 1, 2, 3, 12 and 18 Courts, and seven Line Umpires per team on other courts.

Chair Umpires use computers to score the match, each point scored being displayed automatically on scoreboards around the grounds and on the Club's website. Net cord machines are used by the Chair Umpire on all courts, and the Hawk-Eye electronic system is used on Centre, No 1, 2, 3, 12 and 18 Courts to allow line calls to be reviewed.

LTA Officiating staff are responsible for selecting the officials and all administrative arrangements of officials both before and during The Championships. They work closely with Jenny Higgs the Chief Umpire who is responsible for the overall management and assignment of Chair and Line Umpires during The Championships using a custom-made computer system and assisted by a small management team.

Chair and Line Umpires wear the Ralph Lauren designed uniform introduced in 2006.

Chairman's Guests

From 1986 the Chairman of the Committee of Management has invited to The Championships special guests from the membership of the Last 8 Club as follows:

1986   G.P. Hughes, F.J. Perry, .C.R.D. Tuckey, Miss E.M. de Alvarez, Mrs. T.W. Bullitt (Miss K.E. Stammers), Mrs. L.A. Godfree (Miss K. McKane), Mrs. S.H. Hammersley (Miss W.A. James).

1987   R.G. Laver, Mrs. F.H. Vivian (Miss M.C. Scriven), Mrs. M.R. King (Miss P.E. Mudford).

1988   J.D. Budge, H.W. Austin, Miss A. Marble, Mrs. B.M. Court (Miss M. Smith).

1989   J.A. Kramer, T.P. Brown, Mrs. A.T. Clapp (Miss A.L. Brough), Mrs. W. duPont (Miss M.E. Osborne), Mrs. R.R. Addie (Miss P.M. Betz).

1990   F.R. Schroeder, Mrs. R.B. Todd.

1991   F.A. Sedgman, K.B. McGregor, Mrs. K.E. Irvin (Miss S.J. Fry).

1992   J. Drobny, J.E. Patty, E.W. Sturgess, Mrs. J.G. Fleitz (Miss B.J. Baker).

1993   Mrs. J.E. Barrett (Miss F.A.M. Mortimer), Miss M.E.A. Bueno, Mrs. B.M. Court (Miss M. Smith), Mrs. L.E.G. Price (Miss S. Reynolds), Mrs. P. Haygarth (Miss R. Schuurman).

1994   R.G. Laver, F.J. Perry, Mrs. A. Buxton.

1995   F.A. Parker, S.B.B. Wood, Mrs. B.J. Browning (Miss F. Durr), Mrs. G.T. Janes (Miss C.C. Truman).

1996   K. Nielsen, E.V. Seixas, Mrs J. K. Spann (Miss J.A. Shilcock).

1997   Special guests were invited for the opening ceremony on the New No. 1 Court.

1998   J.D. Budge, A.J. Cooper, Miss D.R. Hard.

1999   R.N. Hartwig, A.R. Olmedo, F.R. Schroeder, Miss M.E.A. Bueno.

2001   No guests.

2000   Millennium guests.

2002   K.R. Rosewall, F.A. Sedgman.

2003   N.A. Fraser.

2004   No guests.

2005   M.A. Trabert, Mrs L.W. King (Miss B.J. Mofitt).

2006   M. Santana, Mrs B.M. Court (Miss M. Smith).

2007   J.A. Kramer, Miss S.V. Wade.

2008   A.J. Cooper, Mrs L.W. King (Miss B.J. Mofitt).
2009   R.G. Laver, Miss M.E.A. Bueno.
2010   J.E. Patty, N.A. Fraser, Mrs A.T. Clapp (Miss A.L. Brough), Mrs R.A.
       Cawley (Miss E.F. Goolagong).
2011   J.D. Newcombe, Mrs. J.E. Barrett (Miss F.A.M. Mortimer).
2012   A.K. Agassi, R.G. Laver, F.A. Sedgman, Mrs A.K. Agassi (Miss S.M. Graf).
2013   J. Kodes, E.V. Seixas, Mrs B.M. Court (Miss M. Smith) Mrs L.W. King
       (Miss B.J. Mofitt).
2014   R.S. Emerson, K.R. Rosewall, Miss M.E.A. Bueno.
2015   B.F. Becker, B.R. Borg, S.B. Edberg, Miss M. Navratilova.

Champions' Dinner and LTA Ball

The customary Champions' Dinner, held annually at the Savoy Hotel (1977–2007), the Hotel Intercontinental, Park Lane (2008-2013), Royal Opera House, Covent Garden (2014) on the final evening of The Championships when the function replaced the traditional staging of the LTA Ball. At the Dinner, which is hosted by the Committee of Management, the gathering of many international players and officials and others prominent in the game toast the newly crowned singles champions. The Champions' Dinner in 1986 commemorated the 100th Championships.

In 1977 the LTA Ball moved to the first Saturday in order to stage The Championships Centenary Ball, which was held at the Hilton Hotel. The function has remained fixed to that evening ever since, initially taking place at the Hilton Hotel, before being held at the Grosvenor House, 1987-2003, the Lancaster Gate Hotel, 2004-2005, the Hurlingham Club, 2006-2012, the Boiler House, Battersea Power Station, 2013 and the Hurlingham Club in 2014.

The history of the LTA Ball stretches back to 1935, at the Dorchester Hotel. This function superseded the annual Banquet or Dinner held for many years at the close of The Championships, at various hotels, including the Savoy and Piccadilly. The LTA felt that the new venture was in keeping with changing times and that guests preferred an evening of dancing (with supper) rather than the formal dignity of a banquet. The following year the venue was changed to the Grosvenor House and this was maintained up to 1976 (during the austerity years, 1946–1950, the functions were styled Buffet Dances).

Coin Tossing Ceremony

In 2000 an innovation was introduced whereby two youngsters performed a coin tossing ceremony prior to the Gentlemen's and Ladies' Singles Finals. They were nominated on behalf of charities chosen by distinguished people associated with the game. The practice has continued to date.

	Event	Nominator	Charities	Coin Tossers
2000	Gentlemen's Singles	Tim Henman	Sargent Cancer Care For Children	Raju Tital (12)
	Ladies' Singles	Duchess of Kent	Future Hope, Calcutta	Anthony Mills (17)

	Event	Nominator	Charities	Coin Tossers
2001	Gentlemen's Singles	Duke of Kent	The Scout Association	Michael Brown (16)
	Ladies' Singles	J.A.H. Curry	Action for Kids	Kyle Weaver (15)
2002	Gentlemen's Singles	ACM Sir Brian Burnett	Barnado's	Robert Bowden (12)
	Ladies' Singles	Duchess of Gloucester	National Asthma Campaign	Shauna Godin (6)
2003	Gentlemen's Singles	R.E.H. Hadingham	SPARKS	Scott Blanche (10)
	Ladies' Singles	Angela Mortimer	The Stroke Association	Emma Buggins (9)
2004	Gentlemen's Singles	Roger Taylor	CRY (Cardiac Risk in the Young)	Laura John (14)
	Ladies' Singles	Ann Jones	Birmingham Children's Hospital Charity	Emily Bailes (5)
2005	Gentlemen's Singles	–	–	Peter Norfolk, Paralympic Gold Medalist
	Ladies' Singles	Virginia Wade	Community Links	Laila Shenair (10)
2006	Gentlemen's Singles	Christopher Gorringe	Cancer Research UK	William Caines (7)
	Ladies' Singles	Christine Janes	Torch Trophy Trust	Kate Ward (24)
2007	Gentlemen's Singles	Barry Weatherill	The Guide Dogs for the Blind Association	Sidney Tambin (16)
	Ladies' Singles	Duke of Kent	Royal Masonic Trust for Girls and Boys	Georgina Brown (14)
2008	Gentlemen's Singles	John Barrett	British Lung Foundation	Blair Manns (13)
	Ladies Singles	AELTC	Dan Maskell Tennis Trust	Jordanne Whiley (16)
2009	Gentlemen's Singles	Peter Moys	Get Kids Going Foundation	James Doherty (14)
	Ladies' Singles	Duchess of Gloucester	CRY	Peter Norfolk and Lila Simpson (11)
2010	Gentlemen's Singles	–	Barnado's	Hannah Clinton (14)
	Ladies' Singles	–	UK Youth	Hana Pierce (9)
2011	Gentlemen's Singles	–	Me Too and Co.	George Griffiths (12)
	Ladies' Singles	–	Muscular Dystrophy Campaign	Chloe Ball-Hopkins (15)
2012	Gentlemen's Singles	–	Make-A-Wish	Elijah Ortiz-Herrera (11)
	Ladies' Singles	–	Sparks	Archie Baker (13)

	Event	Nominator	Charities	Coin Tossers
2013	Gentlemen's Singles	–	Smile Train	Pinki Sonkar (11)
	Ladies' Singles	–	East Anglia's Children's Hospices	Sophie Snowling (14)
2014	Gentlemen's Singles	Andy Murray	Action for Children, Scotland	Nathan Baltimore (12)
	Ladies' Singles	Marion Barkli	European Association for the advancement of research in Leukodystrophies	Medina Djouada (15)

Competitors' Dress and Shoes

Since 1963 Wimbledon Championship Entry Conditions laid down that except for a cardigan, pullover or headwear, competitors must be dressed predominantly in white throughout. In 1995 this Condition was clarified to mean 'almost entirely white'. Any competitor who appears on court dressed in a manner deemed unsuitable by the Committee will be liable to be defaulted.

No shoes, other than those with rubber soles, without heels, ribs, studs or coverings, shall be worn by competitors except with the express permission of the Referee.

Court Covers

All courts have been provided with covers from 1971. Provision was first made as follows:-

Centre Court	1922	No. 6 Court	1951
No. 1 Court (old)	1924	Nos. 7-9 Courts	1955
No. 2 Court (old)	1928	Nos. 10-14 Courts	1971
Nos.3 and 4 Courts	1935	Nos. 15-17 Courts	1980
No. 5 Court	1936	Nos. 1, 18 and 19 Courts	1997

Courts Named After Wimbledon Champions

Anthony Wilding – Christchurch Tennis Courts, Wilding Park, Christchurch, New Zealand. **Suzanne Lenglen** – 1. Suzanne Lenglen Court, Stade Roland Garros, Paris, France – 2. Court at Maretz-sur-Metz, France. **Pancho Gonzales** – Mission Hills Country Club Courts, Rancho Mirage, California, USA. **Victor Seixas** – Victor Seixas Court, Harbor Point Racquet and Beach Club, California, USA. **Tony Trabert** – Cincinnati Tennis Club, Cincinatti, Ohio, USA. **Roy Emerson** Arena, Tennis Club Gstaad, Gstaad, Switzerland. **Rafael Osuna** – Centro Deportivo Chapultepec Stadium, Mexico City, Mexico. **Rod Laver** – 1 Rod Laver Court, Park Avenue Tennis Club, Rockhampton, Queensland, Australia – 2 Rod Laver Arena, Melbourne Park, Melbourne, Victoria, Australia. **Billie Jean King** – Billie Jean Moffit King Tennis Centre, Long Beach Tennis Club, California USA. **Margaret Court** – Margaret Court Arena, Melbourne Park, Victoria, Australia. **Arthur Ashe** – Arthur Ashe Stadium, Flushing Meadows, New York, USA. **Boris Becker** –

Boris Becker Halle, Tennis Club Blau-Weiss, Leimen, Baden Wurttemberg, Germany. **Steffi Graf** – Steffi Graf Stadion, Rot-Weiss Tennis Club, Berlin, Germany. **Roger Federer** – Roger Federer Centre Court, T.C. Old Boys, Basle, Switzerland.

Crowd Management

The Association of Wimbledon Honorary Stewards is responsible for crowd management and acts as 'host' to the public, directing, advising and giving help and guidance to visitors. The members marshal the queue, inside and outside the grounds, and supervise the seating of spectators with the assistance of volunteer Service Stewards, including military personnel on leave, and a contingent provided by the London Fire Brigade.

The presence of Honorary Stewards at Wimbledon originated in 1927, but it was not until June, 1950 that the Association was formed. The present membership is approximately 185.

Service personnel were first used in 1946 and members of the London Fire Brigade in 1965.

Digital

Since 1995, information about the Club and The Championships has been available to users on the Internet originally at www.wimbledon.org.

The Internet site contains information about the Club and the history of Wimbledon. During The Championships it contains a wealth of information including current point-by-point scores, statistics, news, photos and videos. The site also carried live Radio Wimbledon giving computer users around the world the opportunity to listen to live commentary on matches and to receive the latest news. Also included is the Wimbledon shop where visitors are able to make an electronic purchase from the limited range of Championships merchandise.

In 2000 mobile phone users from around the world were able to register with the website, allowing them to receive match results for their favourite players and news during The Championships.

An added service in 2000 and extended for 2001 was the WAP service. This allowed users to browse key pages of the website from their mobile phones, including the order of play and point by point scores.

In 2006, mobile phone users were able to receive updates via their service providers. In some cases this included live video of matches.

New in 2006 was the ability to watch live match play on www.wimbledon.org. Prior to 2006 users had been able to watch archive material and match highlights. In 2006 via a subscription service in most parts of the world, users could access multiple live matches on up to nine show courts. This service was repeated in 2007 and 2008. From 2009, a new m.wimbledon.org site provided an optimised experience for fans looking at the world wide web from their mobile phone. IBM also developed the first Grand Slam iPhone 'app' including point-by-point scores, video, news, schedules and results. There were 890,000 iphone downloads and 640,000 Android downloads during The Championships 2012, bringing the Wimbledon experience to new global audience. Social networking sites such as Facebook and Twitter also grew in popularity, bringing users an alternative view of The Championships.

From 2009, the Club worked with our broadcast partners around the world to provide access to live play as well as highlights and archive material on our website. In 2011, coinciding with the 125th Anniversary of The Championships the website launched as www. wimbledon.com. In 2012 the website relaunched with a completely new design; in addition to scores, schedules and player data, the site makes use of some iconic photography about the grounds and The Championships. From 2012 the year-round and Championships websites were combined into a single site, hosted in the IBM Cloud. The website also hosted the live@Wimbledon service, including analysis and interviews, plus a limited view of some live tennis action, as well as the radio commentaries previously distributed as Radio Wimbledon.

New for 2013 was an iPad app which offered unique views of the grounds, as well as up-to-date information about scores and results. The iPad received 370,000 downloads in its first year.

In 2014, The AELTC re-launched mobile apps for iPhone and Android, completing the platform portfolio with a personalised experience based on being 'the next best thing to being here.' Beautifully designed, the app allowed the user to tailor the scores, draws and results according to their favourite player, country and/or event. The apps were widely acclaimed, and, together with the website, reached a digital audience of over 17 million. In 2015, the AELTC will present a re-designed Wimbledon.com.

Gardens

Each year the gardeners strive to bring the landscaping of the AELTC to an ever higher standard. With the planting traditions in previous years brought to the Club by an external contractor the AELTC now have an in house Gardening team who will now deliver and seek evermore imaginative ways to enhance and compliment the tennis site with thoughtful landscaping designs, flowering plants and planting *schemes*.

The Gardening team will be selecting and planting a wide variety of shrubs, perennials and colourful annuals into many individual planting displays throughout the site. Traditional colour schemes cascade from window boxes and hanging baskets. Hedges and topiary are clipped with precision and a sea of purples, whites, blues and greens will be there to welcome each and every visitor. The AELTC will source wherever possible from local and British growers and suppliers to create the Wimbledon look "an English garden".

Hospitality Facilities

Hospitality facilities are provided in Marquees at the South Apex of the grounds and in Suites in Centre Court and No. 1 Court Stadiums.

Information Service

The Official Information Technology Supplier, IBM, develops and provides IT services for the All England Lawn Tennis Club and The Championships.

Designed to offer a comprehensive source of data on every aspect of the Championships, the multimedia Wimbledon Information Services (WIS), a web browser based Intranet, provides access to live scores and statistics, order of play and results, player biographies with Grand Slam and Tour results as well as other tour information. WIS is updated in real time and is used to provide up-to-date and accurate information to broadcasters and the press. WIS is also available to players, public and officials.

The information is collected from a variety of IT systems and databases. One of the most important is the court-side statistics entry system, operated on all courts by tennis experts using a laptop computer, which records details of each point scored during the tournament. As well as being used for WIS, IBM use this data to produce the score and statistical TV graphics for the host broadcaster (BBC) which are seen around the world.

As well as up-to-date information on the current Championships, WIS gives access to comprehensive statistical information on The Championships since 1992 and Historical results dating back to the first Championships in 1877.

International Box

The International Box, situated in the North Open Stand of the Centre Court, has some 85 seats reserved for representatives of international lawn tennis associations.

Last 8 Club

The Last 8 Club, inaugurated in 1986 as part of the 100th Championship celebrations, recognises the contribution made to lawn tennis by players who have reached the quarter-finals of the Singles, the semi-finals of the Gentlemen's and Ladies' Doubles or the final of the Mixed Doubles of The Championships. (Prior to 2001 the qualification for the Mixed Doubles was semi-finalist.) A hospitality facility for Last 8 Members is situated in a private suite adjacent to Gate 5.

Approximately 630 players are eligible for membership of the Last 8 Club. In 2014 174 attended The Championships.

Lest We Forget and Not Forgotten Associations' Seats

On Centre Court for the first 11 days and on No. 1 Court for the first five days of each week, 16 seats per day are allocated between the Lest We Forget and Not Forgotten Associations, whose members include Chelsea Pensioners as well as service personnel involved in more recent conflicts.

Live @ Wimbledon

The AELTC's official radio and online television channel, based in the Broadcast Centre, distributed on www.wimbledon.com and the official apps for iPhone, Android and iPad. Live @ Wimbledon offers live coverage of play, match reports and analysis, interviews, colour features, and other bits and pieces from around the Grounds. Live @ Wimbledon TV, which launched in 2012, is available to audiences in the UK, USA, South America (excl Brazil), Asia (excl China), Australia, New Zealand and Russia, and has

a studio on the Broadcast Centre roof. Live @ Wimbledon radio, which first
went on air in 1992, is available worldwide online on Wimbledon.com and
the apps. There are also three FM services which operate within a radius of
four miles of the Grounds. The main service is on 87.7FM, Centre Court
commentary is on 96.3FM, and No. 1 Court commentary is on 97.8FM.

Military and other Bands

Military Bands The first military band to entertain the public at Wimbledon
occurred on the opening day of the Jubilee Championships in 1926, when the
Band of the Royal Military School at Kneller Hall played in the precincts of the
Centre Court, prior to the presentations of medals to ex-champions by King
George V and Queen Mary.

From 1964 a military band has been engaged to entertain in the precincts of
the Centre Court prior to play on both Final days (1964–1981 – Friday and
Saturday, 1982 to date – Saturday and Sunday). Exceptionally in 1977,
Centenary Year, the band played on five days on the Centre Court. From 1988
the band has also played in Aorangi Park for a period before moving to the
Centre Court. In 1996 the band performed for the whole period in Aorangi
Park due to bad weather causing an early start on the Centre Court. In 1997 on
the first Monday the band also played on the picnic terrace in Aorangi Park
before attending the opening of the No. 1 Court. In 2000 the Band of the Scots
Guards played on the Centre Court on the first Saturday for the occasion of the
Millennium Parade of Champions.

1926	Band of the Royal Military School of Music at Kneller Hall.	1985	Central Band of the Royal Air Force.
1964	Band of the Welsh Guards.	1986	Band of the Life Guards.
1965	Band of the Welsh Guards.	1987	Band of the Royal Artillery.
1966	Band of the Welsh Guards.	1988	Band of the Royal Engineers.
1967	Central Band of the Royal Air Force.	1989	Band of the Royal Marines.
1968	Band of the Royal Marines (Plymouth Group).	1990	Band of the Royal Corp of Signals.
1969	Band of the Grenadier Guards.	1991	Central Band of the Royal Air Force.
1970	Central Band of the Royal Air Force.	1992	Band of the Welsh Guards.
1971	Staff Band of the Royal Military Academy, Sandhurst.	1993	Staff Band of the Adjutant General's Corp. (Ladies)
1972	Band of the 2nd Royal Greenjackets.	1994	Band of the Blues and Royals.
1973	Band of the Royal Marines (Naval Air Command).	1995	Regimental Band Coldstream Guards.
1974	Central Band of the Royal Air Force.	1996	Band of the Life Guards
1975	Central Band of the Royal Air Force.	1997	Central Band of the Royal Air Force.
1976	Band of the Royal Military Academy, Sandhurst.	1998	Band of the Royal Marines, Plymouth.
1977	Band of the Welsh Guards.	1999	Band of The Adjutant General's Corp.
1978	Band of the Royal Marines (Royal Marines School of Music).	2000	Royal Artillery Band
1979	Band of the Honourable Artillery Company.	2001	Band of the Welsh Guards
		2002	Band of the Irish Guards
1980	Band of the Welsh Guards.	2003	Band of the Scots Guards
1981	Central Band of the Royal Air Force.	2004	Central Band of The Royal Air Force
1982	Band of the First Battalion of the Queen's Regiment.	2005	Band of the Royal Marines, Plymouth
1983	Band of Royal Marines.	2006	Central Band of The Royal British Legion.
1984	Staff Band of the Women's Royal Army Corp.	2007 Legion	Central Band of the Royal British
		2008	Band of The Honourable Artillery Company
		2009	Central Band of the Royal Air Force
		2010	Central Band of the Royal British Legion

2011	Central Band of the Royal British Legion		2014	Central Band of the Royal British Legion
2012	Central Band of the Royal British Legion		2015	Central Band of the Royal British Legion
2013	Central Band of the Royal British Legion			

Youth Bands A local youth band has entertained the public, prior to play on the second Thursday and Friday. (1988–1996 – Aorangi Park, 1997–2000 – Aorangi Park and Tea Lawn, 2001–2010 – Tea Lawn).

1988–1991	Merton Schools Concert Band.	1996–2015	Merton Youth Concert Band and Jazz Orchestra
1992	Stoneleigh Youth Orchestra.		
1993–1995	Merton Youth Concert Band.	2014–2015	Wandsworth Pops Orchestra

Jazz Bands A Jazz band has entertained the public prior to play on the first Saturday. 1992–1994 – in the precincts of the Centre Court, 1995–1996 – outside the grounds and then in Aorangi Park and 1997 – outside the grounds and then on the Tea Lawn. From 1998 various bands have played on the Tea Lawn on all days, with evening sessions from 2003.

1992–1993	Ray Terry Jazz Band.	1998–2015	Red Hot & Blue Orchestra and other combinations.
1994–1997	Red Hot & Blue Orchestra.		

Order of Play and Results Boards

The first Order of Play board at the Church Road ground was erected in 1923, above the entrance to the tunnel between No. 2 and No. 3 Courts. Access to the players' names was via an iron ladder fixed to the wall of No. 3 Court.

In 1948 Results Boards were installed on the walls either side of the tunnel, but in 1964 a huge combined Order of Play and Results board, stretching above the entrance to the tunnel, replaced the previous structures. This was in turn demolished in 1990 to make way for a new building to house the Control Room. However, a Matches on Court board attached to the wall of No. 2 Court was made available but this was removed in 2001.

When Aorangi Park was commissioned in 1982, a structure in the middle of the ground displayed the order of play, the score of each match, game by game, and the final result of each match. After 1985 this structure was rebuilt as the Octagon to provide public services.

However, in 1985 a large manually operated scoreboard was established on the Debentures Holders' wall facing No. 15 to No. 17 Courts, showing the full draw of each of the five Championship events, which are updated as soon as the matches are completed. An Order of Play board was added in 1987.

In 1994 an electronic scoreboard was installed overlooking the south concourse, opposite the Members' Enclosure (now Café Pergola), which displays in turn current scores of matches on court. In 1997 two similar electronic scoreboards were installed at the entrance to the North-East and South-East Halls of the new No. 1 Court Stadium and in 2001 a further electronic scoreboard was installed on the north wall of the Press Centre.

In 1997 a large manually operated scoreboard was installed in the new Championship Entrance area, showing the full draw of each of the five

Championship events, which are updated as soon as the matches are completed, and the order of play for all courts.

A Match Information Display was positioned on the north wall of No. 2 Court in 2001 and 2002 but moved to the south-west wall of the Centre Court in 2003. This electronic display shows the latest point by point scores for the matches on all 18 courts. Before play starts, the full order of play is shown.

In 2003 an Electronic Match board, displaying point by point information, using flip dot technology, was installed between the south ends of No. 11 and No. 13 Courts. In 2007, both the Match Information and Electronic Match Boards were replaced by full colour video boards showing the same information. In 2008 there was no room to locate the board in the south part of the grounds so this was positioned above the bandstand on the Tea Lawn. From 2009, the Match Information Boards was repositioned on the northern wall of the Café Pergola, facing the Tea Lawn and at the south west corner of the Centre Court. They showed the order of play, point by point scores and player profiles, depending on the time of day.

In 2010, a third Electronic Match Information Display was located at the north east area of the ground, facing out from No. 1 Court towards Aorangi Pavilion. This provided the same information as the two boards at the southern end of the ground.

In 2014, nine Electronic Information Display Boards were installed to provide messages, order of play and score information to the public. Six boards are attached to the Centre Court, one to the Millennium Building and two to No. 1 Court. The new EID boads are in exactly the same places as the old 'flip dot' ones, which were installed in 1981.

Players exhibited at Madame Tussauds in London

Champions: W.T. Tilden (USA) 1921, 1924, Miss S.R.F. Lenglen (FRA) 1921–1934, Mrs. F.S. Moody (USA) 1930–1950, F.J. Perry (GBR) 1933–1948, Miss D.E. Round (GBR) 1934–1948, J.D. Budge (USA) 1938–1957, Miss A.L. Brough (USA) 1950–1959, Miss M.C. Connolly (USA) 1952, J. Drobny (TCH/BOM/EGY/GBR) 1955–1958, Miss M.E.A. Bueno (BRA) 1961–1968, R.G. Laver (AUS) 1963–1974, Miss M. Smith (AUS) 1963–1967, Miss S.V. Wade (GBR) 1978–1979, B.R. Borg (SWE) 1979–1984, J.P. McEnroe (USA) 1981, 1990, Miss M. Navratilova (TCH/USA) 1985–2002, B.F. Becker (GER) 1987–1998, 2007–, Miss M. Hingis (SWI) 1998–2003 R. Nadal (ESP) 2012– (Note: Mrs. P.F. Jones (GBR) waxed but not exhibited)

Runners-up: H.W. Austin (GBR) 1934–1947, Miss C.C. Truman (GBR) 1959–1968, I Nastase (ROM) 1975–1979.

Semi-finalists: Miss B.M. Nuthall (GBR) 1931–1937, T.H. Henman (GBR) 1999–2003.

Dates indicate years exhibited.

Players' Waiting Rooms

An official is responsible for ensuring that players are ready and waiting to go on the Centre and No. 1 Courts at the appropriate time. He also ensures that they are wearing the correct clothing as stated in the rules, both with regard to colour and advertising. The players are assembled in the Players' Waiting Room, which is underneath the Royal Box on the Centre Court, until called.

Over the entrance to the Centre Court, through which the players pass, is the following inscription from Rudyard Kipling's poem 'If':

> "If you can meet with triumph and disaster
> And treat those two impostors just the same."

The original board bearing the inscription was presented to the Club by Lord Curzon and first placed in the autumn of 1923, but this was replaced by a new board and inscription, just prior to the 1995 Championships. This second board was replaced when the Clubhouse was completely refurbished in 2002. The original is on display in The Wimbledon Lawn Tennis Museum.

There is also a Players' Waiting Room, situated in the south end of the No. 1 and No. 2 Court Stadiums.

Post Office Services

The Post Office first provided a range of services to spectators in 1939, when a mobile Post Office was positioned for the fortnight just inside the grounds at the Church Road entrance. On resumption of The Championships, after the Second World War in 1946, no services were offered. However, the following year the mobile Post Office returned but was stationed in the North Hall of the Centre Court.

From 1948 to 1978, the mobile Post Office was on duty at the Church Road entrance, but reverted to the North Hall site from 1979 to 1981. When Aorangi Park was brought within the perimeter of the grounds in 1982 restricted services were provided in "tented" accommodation until they moved to the Octagon from 1986 to 1994. From 1995 to 2003 services were provided in or adjacent to the No. 1 Court Stadium. From 2004 full Post Office services ceased but stamps etc. were obtainable from the newsagents.

Postage Stamps Featuring Wimbledon

The only postage stamp produced by the British Post Office featuring Wimbledon was issued on 2nd August, 1994. This was one of a set of five on the theme of "Summertime", which depicted traditional British events around the country. The 25p multi–coloured stamp, entitled "Wimbledon", shows a view overlooking an outside court with marquees and St. Mary's Church steeple in the background. (1835)

The following foreign postage stamps **featuring Wimbledon** have been issued:-

Australia, 24th January, 2003. Two multi-coloured stamps of four, featuring Australian Legends. 50c–Rod Laver, MBE, Tennis Player and 50c–Margaret Court, MBE, Tennis Player, holding their Wimbledon trophies. (2270,2268)

Brazil 15th December, 1960. One Airmail 6,00 cr brown stamp of Maria Bueno. World Champion of Women's Tennis, Wimbledon, 1959–60. (1041).

Croatia 31st August, 2001. One of six stamps, yellow and gold on white, K.250, of Goran Ivanisevic holding Championship Cup at Wimbledon, 2001. (652)

Dominica 9th February, 1998. Four multi-coloured stamps of eight in a miniature sheet. Famous People and Events. Two stamps of Boris Becker, $1.00 each, one portrait and one in action. Youngest Wimbledon Champion, 1985. Two stamps of Arthur Ashe $1.00 each, one portrait and one in action and holding the Wimbledon Cup.

Gambia 2nd January, 1990. Set of 20 multi-coloured stamps of Wimbledon Champions (all with Wimbledon logos). 20b – John Newcombe; 20b – Mrs. G.W. Hillyard; 50b – Roy Emerson; 50b – Dorothy Chambers; 75b Donald Budge; 75b – Suzanne Lenglen; D1 – Laurence Doherty; D1 – Helen Wills Moody; D1.25 – Bjorn Borg; D1.25 – Maureen Connolly; D4 – Jean Borotra; D4 Maria Bueno; D5 – Anthony Wilding; D5 – Louise Brough; D7 Fred Perry; D7 – Margaret Court; D10 – Bill Tilden; D10 – Billie Jean King; D12 – Rod Laver; D12 – Martina Navratilova. Also two miniature sheets; D15 – Rod Laver (different); D15 – Martina Navratilova (different). (969-89).

Guinea-Bissau 30th December, 1986. Two of a set of 16 multi-coloured stamps, forming a vertical composite design. Anniversaries and Events. 15p – Boris Becker – Wimbledon Men's Singles Champion 1986 (head and arms); 15p – Boris Becker (body). (1987–8).

Hungary 15th June, 1965. One of a set of nine stamps on the History of Tennis. A Ifo. 50 + 50f, brown on green stamp showing the 'Field Cup', Wimbledon, 1877. (2087).

Monaco 29th June, 1977. One fl.40 grey, green and brown stamp. Centenary of the Wimbledon Lawn Tennis Championships, 1877–1977, showing the Centre Court and the first Championships. (1324).

Niue 14th October, 1988. One of four multi-coloured stamps of Steffi Graf. $1.05, overprinted 'Wimbledon 2 July 88 – US Open 10 Sept 1988'. (672).

Paraguay 17th September, 1986. One multi-coloured stamp. GS2. Boris Becker serving. Boris Becker Wimbledon Winner 1985-1986. Federal Republic of Germany. Wimbledon logo of crossed rackets.

Paraguay October 1986. One multi-coloured stamp in a miniature sheet. Tribute to world-wide tennis players. Gs 25. Martina Navratilova (1978, 79, 82–86) and Boris Becker (1985, 6) holding their Wimbledon trophies. ( )

Romania 22nd August, 1988. Two multi-coloured stamps of four, forming a horizontal composite design, in a miniature sheet. Grand Slam Tennis Championships, Wimbledon Centre Court and ladies' singles match. 3L each. (5195).

St. Vincent 22nd June, 1987. Five of a set of eight multi-coloured stamps of players in action at Wimbledon. 40c – Hana Mandlikova; 80c – Ivan Lendl; $1.50 – John McEnroe; $1.75 – Martina Navratilova holding Wimbledon Trophy; $2.00 – Boris Becker holding Wimbledon Cup. Also miniature sheet: $2.25 – Boris Becker holding Wimbledon Cup; Martina Navratilova holding Trophy. (1057,59,62-65).

St. Vincent Grenadines 29th July, 1988. Set of eight multi-coloured stamps of International players in action at Wimbledon. 15c – Pam Shriver; 50c – Kevin Curren; 75c – Wendy Turnbull; $1.00 – Evonne Cawley; $ 1.50 – Ilie Nastase;

$2.00 – Billie Jean King; $3.00 – Bjorn Borg; $3.50 – Virginia Wade holding trophy. Also miniature sheet: $2.25 – Stefan Edberg with Wimbledon Cup; $2.25 – Steffi Graf with Wimbledon Trophy. (582-90).

Sierra Leone 4th September, 1987. Set of eight multi-coloured stamps of Wimbledon Tennis Champions. Le2 – Evonne Goolagong; Le5 – Martina Navratilova; Le10 – Jimmy Connors; Le15 – Bjorn Borg; Le30 – Boris Becker; Le40 – John McEnroe; Le50 – Chris Evert Lloyd; Le75 – Virginia Wade. Also two miniature sheets – Le100 – Boris Becker (different); Le10 – Steffi Graf. (1068-76).

Uruguay 19th November, 1997. One multi-coloured stamp of four in a miniature sheet. International Coin and Stamp Exhibition, Shanghai 97'. $3.50. Martina Hingis – World Champion, Wimbledon, 1997. (MS 2413).

Australia 24th January, 2003 Two multi-coloured stamps. Australia Legends. Rod Laver with Wimbledon trophy and in action. 50c (2266, 2267)

Switzerland 10th April, 2007. One multi-coloured stamp of Roger Federer holding Championship Cup SFr 1.(1727)

Great Britain 8th August, 2013. Set of four multi-coloured stamps of Andy Murray, winning the Wimbledon Singles Championship in 2013. Two 1st class stamps and two at £1.28 (2664).

(Stanley Gibbons catalogue number in brackets).

Presentations

Thursday 2nd July, 1953: To J. Drobny and J.E. Patty. During the afternoon in the Clubhouse, The Duchess of Kent, on behalf of the Committee of Management, presented J. Drobny (EGY) and J.E. Patty (USA) each with a silver cigarette case to commemorate their 4 hours 15 minutes singles match, played on Thursday 25th June. The inscription read "Presented to Mr. J. Drobny (Mr. J.E. Patty) on behalf of the Committee of The Championships at Wimbledon as a memento of one of the most outstanding matches in the history of Lawn Tennis in which Drobny beat Patty 8-6 16-18 3-6 8-6 12-10, 93 games in all".

Wednesday, 27th June 1979: To British teams. Just before play commenced on the Centre Court at 2pm 1978 the British Davis Cup and Wightman Cup teams were presented with the BBC Sportsview Team of the Year Award (a mounted minature T.V. camera). The ceremony had been delayed from the previous December. The teams were:- M. Cox, P.R. Hutchins, R.A. Lewis, D.A. Lloyd, J.M. Lloyd, C.J. Mottram, R. Taylor, R. Becker (trainer), J. Matthews (physiotherapist), Miss S.D. Barker, Miss A.E. Hobbs, Miss S. Mappin, Miss M. Tyler, Miss S.V. Wade.

Sunday, 8th July 1984: To Commander Charles D. Lane. Immediately after the Gentlemen's singles final, The Duchess of Kent, accompanied by The Duke of Kent, made a special presentation on the Centre Court of a commemorative clock to Commander Charles D. Lane, who was retiring after directing the ball boys/girls operation at Wimbledon for 18 years.

Monday. 22nd June 1992: To Dan Maskell. In the Royal Box, just before play commenced at 2pm, The Duchess of Kent accompanied by The Duke of Kent, presented a silver salver to Dan Maskell, on behalf of the A.E.L.T.C. and the L.T.A., to mark his retirement from broadcasting. The salver was engraved with a picture of the front of the A.E.L.T.C. and important dates in his tennis life.

Monday 20th June, 1994: To The Duke and Duchess of Kent and R.G. Laver. In the Royal Box, just before play commenced at 2pm, Mr. J.A.H. Curry presented a minature Gentlemen' Singles Trophy to the Duke of Kent to mark his 25th year as President of The Club. Mr. Curry also presented the Duchess of Kent with a miniature Ladies' Singles Trophy. The Duke of Kent then presented a Waterford Crystal Vase to R.G. Laver (AUS) to mark the 25th anniversary of his second Grand Slam in 1969.

Friday, 1st July, 1994: To F.J. Perry. During the evening Cocktail Party of the All England Lawn Tennis Club, held in the Members' Enclosure, Mr. J.A.H. Curry presented F.J. Perry (GBR) with a Waterford Crystal Vase to mark his first singles victory in The Championships of 1934.

Tuesday, 1st July, 1997: To S.B. Edberg. In the Royal Box, at approximately 1.35pm, The Duke of Kent presented a Waterford Crystal Vase to S.B. Edberg in recognition of his special role at Wimbledon over the years.

Tuesday, 30th June, 1998: To J.D. Budge. In the Royal Box, at approximately 4pm. The Duke of Kent presented a Waterford Crytstal Vase to J.D. Budge to mark the 60th anniversary of his Grand Slam in 1938

Saturday, 29th June, 2002: To Robert Brooke. Just after 1pm John Barrett introduced to the spectators on the Centre Court, Mr. Robert Brooke, Chairman of Dunlop Slazenger, who was presented with a piece of Waterford Crystal by Mr. Tim Phillips, the Chairman of the Club, in the Royal Box, to mark the 100th anniversary between Slazenger and the AELTC.

Sunday, 3rd July, 2005: To A.R. Mills and C.J. Gorringe. Immediately after the Gentlemen's Singles final on the Centre Court, the Duke of Kent presented A.R. Mills (Referee) and C.J. Gorringe (Assistant Secretary/Secretary/Chief Executive) with a Waterford Crystal Vase in recognition of their retirement after 23 and 33 years service to The Championships, respectively.

Saturday, 1st July, 2006: Mrs S. Agassi (Graf), Miss M. Bueno, Mrs M. Court (Smith), Mrs B.J. King (Moffit) and Miss M. Navratilova. In the Royal Box, just before play commenced, these great champions, who between them had won 28 singles and 38 doubles titles, were introduced to the crowd and each presented with a Waterford Crystal Lismore Bowl by The Duchess of Gloucester, Honorary President of the LTA.

Press, Radio and Photographers

In the past 10 years the average number of writers and international radio reporters attending The Championships has been around 725, drawn from 45 countries. Of these, 168 have full access to the Centre Court Press Box and a further 220 or so have limited access. The remainder have full or day Rover passes which allow them to use the reserved press accommodation on the remaining Show Courts and a variety of facilities, including a 24 hour Media restaurant situated under No. 14 Court, purpose-built for the 2015 Championships. On any given day the average number of press attending is 450 to 500.

The British press corps totals between 330–375, the figure often dependent on other major sporting events taking place at the same time as The Championships. For example, in the year 2010, when the football World Cup coincided with The Championships, 333 British journalists were accredited; in 2008 when the football European Cup was being staged at the same time as Wimbledon, 317 British press were accredited.

Most National newspapers and press agencies have up to 14 journalists attending – sport, features and news – and journalists from provincial publications attend, particularly if a British player is local to them. The next country with the largest representation is the United States which averages 48 correspondents every year, followed by France, Italy, Japan, Germany and Switzerland who all have between 20–39 representatives amongst the press. Countries who have between 10–19 press include Australia, India, Russian Federation, The Netherlands, Poland, Spain, Belgium and increasingly, China.

The number of press attending The Championships from a foreign country is usually reflected by the number of players from that particular country competing. In the year 2014, 538 journalists were accredited from 43 countries while 200 photographers' passes were issued from 108 international publications or agencies.

Since the year 2000 the press and photographers have been provided with brand new facilities in the Millennium Building. The international written press and radio reporters are housed on three floors with the Press Interview Rooms on the Ground Floor and the Press café on the top floor – with grand views overlooking Nos 14–19 Courts. Photographers are relocated in a new, state of the art facility under No. 14 Court.

There are three writing rooms, one on each floor, with enough desks for 350 journalists – an increase on the 315 in the old Press Office. Each desk is fully equipped with closed circuit television incorporating 33 channels as well as all Championships information and latest results from each court as they become available. Those members of the press who do not have a desk assigned to them are able to follow the event in a monitor room close to the writing rooms. Throughout the 13 days of The Championships, press attend a succession of post match interviews with the players in the Main Interview Room and all these interviews are relayed live to the writing rooms for those who are unable to attend the interview in person. Thus, senior tennis writers are provided with all the Wimbledon action without having to leave their writing rooms – a facility which is often necessary when deadlines are approaching.

The Press and Photographers are looked after by a Media team employed by the Club specifically for that purpose. Work on accreditation and administration of the Press and Photography facilities begins in January each year. Information during the 13 days of The Championships is also supplied to the Press by staff from the ladies' and men's tour organisations and IBM.

The Committee of Management maintains a close link with the press throughout the year and members of the Commercial and Media Sub-Committee accompany players for the post match interviews – one of the traditions which makes Wimbledon unique amongst the Grand Slam events.

Referee's Systems

The Referee's Office systems support all aspects of the operation from the entry of competitors, the draws, the scheduling of matches, recording results and the payment of prize money.

The daily Order of Play was prepared using the "Womble" board which allowed the Referee to plan matches on up to 20 courts, checking to ensure that there are no clashes for competitors in several events. In 2010, the Womble Board was replaced by a new panoramic HD video wall display in the Referee's Office, which allows several of the Referee's team to schedule matches for different events simultaneously.

The Chair Umpire uses a scorepad system, introduced in 2001, which allows them to score a match directly from the chair, thus providing real-time scores to the rest of the systems. In 2014, a new, larger tablet-style PDA was used by umpires at Qualifying and at the main site.

Linked to the Order of Play is an Umpire's system. This helps in the allocation of the officials for each court during The Championships.

By using a wireless network, the Referee's Systems which are in use at the Qualifying competition were expanded, to feed live scores to the Club and the Wimbledon website.

In 2013, the wireless connections were replaced by ethernet cables which were felt to provide a more reliable feed of up-to-date scores from Qualifying.

Resale of Tickets

Spectators leaving before the end of play are invited to return their tickets for resale at a nominal sum, with the proceeds going to charity. Approximately 1.5 million pounds has been raised to date.

HSBC, the official banking partner of The Championships has kindly agreed to donate to charity a sum equal to the total amount raised by the ticket resale since 2008. Tickets have been resold within the Grounds, apart from 1990 when tickets were sold to those queueing outside the Grounds.

Year	Charge £'s	Sum to Charity	Year	Charge £'s	Sum to Charity
1954–1964	1s 0d	350/year approx.	1979		2,340
1964–1970	2s 0d	800/year approx.	1980	30p	2,232
1971–1974	10p	850/year approx.	1981		2,845
1975	20p	1,087	1982		3,984
1976		1,499	1983	50p	4.731
1977	30p	1,802	1984		5,583
1978		1,511	1985		5,403

Year	Charge £'s	Sum to Charity	Year	Charge £'s	Sum to Charity
1986		8,034	2001	£5.00	60,192
1987	£1.00	9,522	2002	before 5pm	70,316
1988		9,910	2003	£3.00	71,488
1989	£1.00	10,487	2004	after 5pm	53,344
1990	£4.00	18,011	2005		81,117
1991		19,579	2006		81,615
1992	£4.00 before 5pm	22,791	2007	£5.00	82,557
1993	£2.00 after 5pm	27,872	2008		111,164
1994		29,515	2009		123,009
1995		30,285	2010		108,386
1996	£5.00	39,791	2011	£5.00 CC Second Week £10.00	125,242
1997	before 5pm £3.00	40,912	2012		167,000
1998	after 5pm	45.995	2013	£5.00 CC £10.00	152,115
1999		55,898	2014		157,581
2000		63,029			

Charities

1954–1986	National Playing Fields Association.
1987–1991	NPFA and SPARKS (the Sportsman's Charity).
1992	NPFA, SPARKS and National Wheelchair Tennis Association.
1993	Arthur Ashe Foundation for the Defeat of Aids (majority) and NWTA.
1994–1995	NPFA, SPARKS and NWTA.
1996–1998	NPFA, SPARKS and 'Tennis for People with Disabilities'.
1999–2000	NPFA, SPARKS, Dan Maskell Fund – 'Tennis for People with Disabilities', St. John Ambulance and the WRVS.
2001	NPFA, SPARKS, Dan Maskell Fund – 'Tennis for People with Disabilities', Merton MENCAP.
2002–2003	NPFA, SPARKS, Dan Maskell Fund – 'Tennis for people with Disabilities', Local Merton charities.
2004	NPFA, SPARKS, Dan Maskell Tennis Foundation, Local charities.
2005	SPARKS, Dan Maskell Tennis Trust, Queen Elizabeth's Foundation, Local charities.
2006	SPARKS, Dan Maskell Tennis Trust, Queen Elizabeth's Foundation, ClearVision Project, London's Air Ambulance, Local charities.
2007–2010	SPARKS, Dan Maskell Tennis Trust, Local charities.
2011–2013	A variety of charities including the Services and Local charities.
2014–2015	The entire proceeds donated via the Wimbledon Foundation to charity, including local charities and the services.

Royal Box

There has been a Royal Box at the south end of the Centre Court since the opening of the grounds in 1922. In 2002 the Royal Box was rebuilt as part of the work carried out on the Clubhouse and south end of the Centre Court. At the old grounds at Worple Road a Royal Box did not exist but when royalty attended the Committee Box was suitably converted for the occasion.

The Royal Box, which seats 75 people, is used for the entertainment of guests from the Royal Family, the tennis world, including supporters of British tennis and other walks of life. Invitations come from the Chairman of the Club and the Committee of Management, taking into account suggestions from the Committee Members of the Club, The Lawn Tennis Association and other sources. Guests are invited to lunch, tea and drinks at the end of the day, which take place within the Clubhouse. Dress is smart, lounge suits/jacket and tie etc. Ladies are asked not to wear hats as they tend to obscure the vision of those seated behind them.

The Queen honoured the Club with her presence in 1957, 1962, 1977 and 2010 and other members of the Royal Family are regular attendees.

Scoreboards

Centre Court, No. 1 Court, No. 2 Court and No. 3 Court

When the Centre Court at Church Road was opened in 1922 there were two manually operated scoreboards, one at each side of the court, in line with the net and at the front of the standing area behind the open seating. The scoreboards showed the names of the players, the server and the score in sets and games.

In 1924 when the No. 1 Court was brought into commission a large manually operated, V-shaped, double scoreboard was positioned in line with the net, high above the standing area on the west side of the court. By having two faces to the scoreboard all spectators were able to see the score, irrespective of their seating position.

The scoreboards at the sides of the Centre Court were abandoned in 1928 and new manual items installed in the north-west and south-east corners of the court (same position as present). As before, these scoreboards showed the names of the players, the server and the score in sets and games.

However, these scoreboards were short lived, for the following year, in 1929, they were replaced by two electric scoreboards, designed and manufactured by Automatic Totalisator Ltd. of Ealing, which in addition to recording sets and games, showed points. Also, a third scoreboard was fixed above the Referee's Office, to the left of the entrance to the South-West Hall, allowing those unable to gain admittance to the Centre Court to follow the matches. The control board for the scoreboards was a desk-like structure, positioned immediately behind the Umpire's chair, operated by a man who was seated throughout the match.

Spectators and players were so delighted with the scoreboards that the All England Lawn Tennis Club requested the manufacturer to install on the Centre Court not only enlarged scoreboards, which in addition recorded the full details of previous sets, but also to provide similar scoreboards on the No. 1 Court, one in the north-west corner, high above the spectators in the open stand, and the other on the wall of the Centre Court overlooking the court. A third to pair with the Centre Court scoreboard over the Referee's Office was also provided. By the 1930 Championships, all the scoreboards were in position with suitable concrete boxes for the scoreboards built to house the apparatus. The necessity to have the operator on court was removed when a telephone line was connected from the umpire to the operator and his control board suitably positioned out of sight. In 1963 the scoreboard in the north-west corner of the No. 1 Court was repositioned at ground level. In 1979 the Centre Court and No. 1 Court scoreboards were fitted with digital clocks, which also indicated the length of each match.

In 1950 a minor limitation of the scoreboards was seen when those on No. 1 Court failed to register beyond 19 all in the 31–29 second set of the Gentlemen's

Doubles match between J.E. Patty and M.A. Trabert (USA) and K.B. McGregor and F.A. Sedgman (AUS).

When the No. 1 Court Complex was rebuilt for the 1981 Championships, the scoreboards were replaced with electronic versions, allowing the player's names to be more readily changed. With the Referee's Office demolished, the scoreboards referring to the Centre Court and No. 1 Court, overlooking the main concourse, were replaced by electronic repeater scoreboards installed above the Members' balcony at the main entrance to the Clubhouse. These were renewed in 2001. Another pair of repeater scoreboards were erected on the wall near the Museum entrance, overlooking the Tea Lawn extension. In 1982 the Centre Court was also fitted with electronic scoreboards, while a third was added to the south-west corner of the No. 1 Court for the convenience of the spectators in the North stand.

With the demise of the old No. 1 Court in 1997, the electronic scoreboards were repositioned. The older boards (first used in 1981) replaced those on the Museum walls and the Museum boards were relocated to the new No. 1 Court. One was positioned in the north-west corner of the court, the other in the south-east corner while a new board was installed at the entrance to the South-West Hall. In 2001 two further electronic repeater scoreboards for the Centre Court and No. 1 Court were installed on the wall of the Centre Court West Building. In 2002 the Centre Court scoreboards were renewed.

These electronic scoreboards were designed for high visibility in any ambient lighting conditions and for ease of use. The display modules used are 5 x 7 dot matrix modules, utilising electromagnetic "flip-dot" technology for high reliability and low power consumption. The dots are coloured flat black on one side and fluorescent yellow on the other. To display characters a pattern of dots are "flipped" over so that the character is displayed as a highly visible fluorescent yellow character on a flat black background. This gives maximum contrast and ensures visibility even in poor light.

Each scoreboard is fitted with heaters and fans to ensure that internal condensation is prevented, thus helping to maintain the reliability and longevity of the electronic and display components. Total power consumption of each scoreboard is about 100 watts.

In 2006, the scoreboards were linked to the umpire's scorepad and updated automatically at the end of each rally. Scores from other courts are also displayed, at the change of ends.

Prior to play safety and information messages are displayed on the scoreboards. Player profiles are shown as each match starts.

Back-up computers are available in each control room and these are used to test the boards before play starts each day.

In case of a mains power failure a back-up supply ensures scoring will continue for at least 90 minutes.

In 2007, large video boards were installed on Centre and No. 1 Courts to allow the Player challenge replays, provided by the Hawk-Eye system, to be seen by the spectators. In 2008, the main scoreboards were replaced by new video boards, which combined the scores and Hawk-Eye replays in one location. These boards allowed the Club to show video and selected BBC TV output as appropriate.

From 2009, video boards were installed on the new No. 2 Court. From 2010 all three courts continued to show the scoreboard, Hawk-Eye replays, BBC output and other video material as required and these facilities were extended to the new No. 3 Court in 2011. In 2013, higher resolution video blocks were introduced on all four Show Courts for scoreboards and speed of serve indicators. When it rains and play continues on Centre Court, the match may be shown on the screens on the other courts.

Outside Courts

The first scoreboards were free-standing and were located on the grass at the east side of each court in line with the net. They showed sets and games, using number plates.

In 1928 a permanent scoreboard was installed on No. 2 Court above the seating on the east side of the court. However, this was abandoned in 1934 when a new double-sided V-shaped scoreboard for use on No. 2 and No. 3 Courts was mounted high at the south end of the newly built combined stand between the two courts. On this site in 1955 was erected a small concrete building, to which was fitted a new combined scoreboard for the No. 2 and No. 3 Courts. There was access to behind the scoreboard and also, via an iron spiral staircase, to a balcony overlooking No. 11 Court (now No. 7 Court).

New scoreboards were provided for other outside Courts in 1931. Either side of the player's name were reels, containing large figures, which were revolved by hand. Sets were shown on the left and games on the right. In 1955 these scoreboards were renewed and the opportunity was taken to modify the layout to have players' names at the top.

The current much larger manual scoreboards were provided over the seasons 1988 and 1989. Together with the modified scoreboard for No. 2 and No. 3 Courts, these showed points for the first time.

When No. 18 and No. 19 Courts were brought into use in 1997, the former was provided with electronic scoreboards and the latter manual scoreboards similar to other courts.

In 2010, No. 14–17 Courts trialled the use of video scoreboards. These were smaller than on the Centre Court as they did not show Hawk-Eye replays. Following the success of the trial, the use of electronic scoreboards was extended across the other outside courts in 2011. In 2013 electronic scoreboards were used on all courts at the Qualifying tournament.

Scoreboard Operators and Data Collectors

From 1994, two teams operated the scoreboards, one covering the show courts (Centre Court and Nos. 1, 2, 3, 13 and 14 Courts) and the other the remainder of the courts. For the first time ladies were allocated to operate the electronic scoreboards on the Centre Court and No. 1 Court.

Previously three teams had been responsible, one exclusively for the Centre Court and No. 1 Court (traditionally manned by male only members of the Oxford and Cambridge University tennis teams), one for Nos. 2, 3 13 and 14 Courts and one for the other courts.

Prior to 1989, all the manual scoreboards (those other than the Centre Court and No. 1 Court) were operated by the ball boys/girls as part of their duty. From 1989 to 1995 a scoreboard operator was allocated to each of these courts to carry out that function and in addition to operate an "electronic box" which conveyed the score, point by point, to the central computer. From 1996 to 1998 the data collection function on each court was performed by a dedicated team of students.

From 1999 the manual scoreboards were operated by the Court Attendants who were responsible for the dressing of the court and the court covering under the supervision of the Head Groundsman. Data collection remained the responsibility of a dedicated team of students.

From 2006 the scoreboards on Centre and No. 1 Courts were linked to the Chair Umpire's electronic scorecard which automatically updated the score. From 2009 the boards on the new No. 2 Court were updated in a similar manner, as were the scoreboards on the new No. 3 Court in 2011.

Number of Scoreboard operators

	Electronic	Manual
1964 – 1979	6	10
1980 – 1983	7	10
1984 – 1985	7	13

Number of Scoreboard operators

	Electronic	Manual
1986 – 1988	7	14
1989	6	33
1990 – 1995	6	35

Number of Scoreboard operators and Data Collectors

1996	81
1997	72
1998	70

Electronic Scoreboard Operators and Data Collectors

| 1999–2008 | 46 |

Data Collectors and Radar Operators

| 2009–2014 | 44 |

Seat Cushions

The facility for spectators to hire seat cushions was first provided by The Soft Seats Company in 1924. The following year The British Cushion Supply Company took over and they continued the service up to 2008, apart from 1936–1938, when The London Cushion Supply Company controlled the business. The provision of the new wider padded seats in the Centre Court and No. 2 Court render the seat cushions virtually unneccesary. Souvenir cushions have been on sale since 1992.

Daily Hire Charge

1924–1925 – 3d	1948–1966 – 1s 0d	1971–1974 – 10p
1926–1939 – 6d	1967–1968 – 1s 6d	1975 – 15p
1946–1947 – 6d	1969–1970 – 2s 0d	1976–1978 – 20p

1979	– 25p	1990–1991 – 60p	2000–2001 – £1.50
1980–1982	– 30p	1992–1993 – 70p	2002–2003 – £1.70
1983–1984	– 35p	1994–1995 – £1.00	2004–2006 – £2.00
1985–1986	– 40p	1996–1997 – £1.20	2007 – £2.50
1987–1989	– 50p	1998–1999 – £1.40	2008 – £3.00

Purchase

1992–1993	£3.50	1999–2000	£6.00	2011–2014	£8.00
1994–1995	£4.00	2001–2007	£5.50	2015–	£10.00
1996–1998	£5.00	2008–2010	£7.00		

A special souvenir cushions was on sale in 2010, priced £15.00.

Speed of Service

A radar gun measuring the 'speed of service' was first used on the Centre Court in 1991 and later on the new No. 1 Court in 1997. Both locations did not provide a visual indication. However, in 1999 spectators on both courts were able immediately to see the speed of players' service when displayed in units installed at ground level at both ends of each court. This facility was extended to No. 2 and No. 18 Courts in 2001 and No. 3 and No. 12 Courts in 2003. From 2008 the boards on Centre and No. 1 Court were video boards and this was extended to the No. 2 Court in 2009 and the new No. 3 Court in 2011. This allows the Club to show additional statistical service information at change of ends.

Staff

An approximate list of officials and staff engaged for the duration of The Championships is as follows:–

Ball Boys and Girls 250

House Keeping (night) 163

Ball distributors 9

Lift Operators 30

Buildings and Services Personnel 84

Massage Therapists 8

Catering staff 1,800

Physiotherapists 9

Court attendants 176

Podiatrists 2

Court officials 327

Practice Courts 6

Dressing room attendants 22

Press Staff 22

Data collectors 44

Referee's Office 16

Groundsmen/Women 32

Service Stewards 602

Honorary Stewards 185

Transport service drivers 320

House Keeping (day) 181

Qualifying Staff at Bank of England ground 160

Television

Play was televised for the first time in 1937, when matches were transmitted by the BBC from the Centre Court for up to half an hour each day of the meeting. Two cameras were used, one at the south-east corner of the court, giving close-up views and the other in a fixed position at the other end of the court, providing a general view of the scene. The cameras were connected by cable to a unit in the car park which transmitted by radio to Alexandra Palace. On the opening day, viewers saw 25 minutes of the match between "Bunny" Austin and George Lyttleton Rogers. The commentator was F.H. Grisewood, who during the Fortnight was assisted by Capt. H.B.T. Wakelam and Col. R.H. Brand. Soon after The Championships, the BBC returned to Wimbledon to televise the Davis Cup Inter-Zone Final and Challenge Round, again for a short period each day.

In 1938 and 1939 a third camera was used to televise The Championships. After the Second World War in 1946, television covered the annual Wightman Cup tie in mid-June and then The Championships, but not before the first Saturday. An interview took place for the first time on the final Saturday, when the new champions, Yvon Petra and Pauline Betz, were interviewed by Alice Marble, the 1939 champion.

Eurovision came in 1954 and in 1956 Independent Television started to compete with the BBC, but withdrew after 1968, realising that double coverage was not commercially viable. The very first colour television transmission in this country took place on the first Saturday in 1967 when BBC2 showed a four and a half hour programme from the Centre Court, commencing at 2pm. The first match was Cliff Drysdale (RSA) versus Roger Taylor (GBR). Transmissions in colour were also made each afternoon of the following week, plus a 30 minute highlights programme each evening. In August that year a professional tournament produced by the BBC to mark the introduction of colour television, was held on Centre Court. The pattern was set for all future Championships.

The BBC acts as host broadcaster for The Championships, simultaneously producing coverage from up to nine courts, including Centre and No. 1 Court.

More than a 1,000 hours are made available to the All England Club and distributed around the world – to nearly 200 television territories in 2014.

Because of the growing overlap of terrestrial, cable and satellite broadcasters' transmissions footprints, it is impossible to calculate exact figures of the number of people who follow Wimbledon each year; but it is safe to say that it is seen by more people throughout the world than any other tennis tournament. This audience continues to grow as a result of the Club's agreements with a wide range of television stations.

In the United Kingdom the BBC transmitted 150 hours of coverage on BBC 1 and BBC 2 including a daily highlights programme in the evening, and many more hours on their digital interactive service, and on-line.

For the BBC and more than 40 foreign television companies producing Wimbledon coverage on site, 2015 is the 19th year for them to use the new Broadcast Centre. This building, occupying three floors on its own site west of No. 14 and 18 Courts is the largest and best equipped permanent outside broadcast facility in the world. After decades of working from vehicles, marquees and a variety of temporary cabins and studios, leading broadcasters are now using purpose-built accommodation.

Owing to the various time differences around the world, it is inevitable that somewhere a Wimbledon programme, either live or recorded, is being broadcast 24 hours a day throughout the Fortnight. Consequently, the Centre is one of the busiest locations in the grounds, remaining open from breakfast time through to the early hours of the following morning.

Television Screen

A 142 sq ft television screen is provided for spectator viewing at the Aorangi Terrace. There are seats for 214 people in addition to the informal terrace viewing area.

Tennis Balls

About 54,250 tennis balls are used on a average during The Championships. New balls are supplied after seven games (to allow for the preliminary warm-up) and then after every nine games. Yellow balls were used for the first time in 1986. Subject to availability balls are sold daily from a kiosk positioned near No. 14 Court. The proceeds are donated to the schools' tennis programme delivered by the Tennis Foundation.

'This is Wimbledon' and other booklets

The present day booklet 'This is Wimbledon', the official guide to The Championships, has its roots reaching back to 1954 when the Club published for the first time a 12 page booklet containing facts and figures on the Club and The Championships entitled 'Can You Help Me ?' This gave a list of 70 questions and answers on a variety of subjects which were basically compiled to assist journalists reporting at Wimbledon. Surprisingly the introduction stated that the production was "intended as only a rough guide and no guarantee was given to its accuracy".

In the sixties the booklet cover was green and showed an aerial photograph of the Club. This was on sale to the public, priced 1s 0d. By the seventies the size was slightly larger and the title changed to 'Know Your Wimbledon', while the question and answer format was dropped in favour of different sections dealing with a variety of aspects of the organisation etc.

The last issue of 'Know Your Wimbledon' was in 1980, priced 50p, and thereafter 'This is Wimbledon', with the inclusion of photographs, colour from 1990, has been updated and available each year.

Other booklets published annually by the Club, mainly for internal use, are:- Media Guide – 1976 to date, Competitors' Guide – 1982 to date, Junior Competitors' Guide – 1984 to date, Broadcast Centre Guide – 1997–1999.

Tickets

There has always been a considerable demand for tickets, especially since the advent of large-scale air travel and the consequent increase in the number of foreign visitors to Wimbledon, and equitable distribution is inevitably a subject which causes much debate both within the Club and outside. However, only the Debenture Holders, Members of the Club and Council Members of The Lawn Tennis Association obtain them as a matter of right.

Special allocations are made to British Tennis Membership and overseas Lawn Tennis Associations for distribution to their affiliated clubs, etc. and to other organisations with special claims. A set number of tickets for the Centre Court, No. 1 Court and No. 2 Court are allocated to schools affiliated to The Lawn Tennis Association.

A substantial proportion of the total number of tickets is retained for issue to the general public either in advance, via an annual public ballot, online on the day before play or at the turnstiles on the day of play.

The systems for issuing tickets are reviewed annually.

Cancellation of Play Due to Rain

Details of the Raincheck policy introduced in 2001 are as follows and apply to all 13 scheduled days of The Championships, including the final Sunday.

i.   If there is less than one hour's play because of rain on the court for which tickets have been bought, the *original purchasers* of the tickets for that court on that day will be refunded with the amount which they paid for those tickets – the maximum refund payable will be the face value of the tickets for the day concerned.

ii.   Purchasers of Grounds Passes at the turnstiles (except those purchased after 5 pm) will be eligible for a full refund if, due to rain, the average amount of play on those courts accessible with a Grounds Pass and for which play was originally scheduled is less than one hour.

iii.   If there is more than one hour's play, but less than two hours' play, refunds will be limited to half the amount paid.

iv.   The Referee's decision on how much play has taken place will be final.

v.   Only the *original purchasers* are eligible for refunds under this policy. Refunds will be paid out automatically for tickets bought in advance, but tickets bought at the turnstiles (prior to 5 pm only) should be returned without delay to: The Ticket Office, AELTC 'Raincheck', PO Box 98, London SW19 5AE.

vi.   In view of the numbers that could be involved, *please do not call the at the AELTC's Ticket Office or telephone the AELTC.*

vii.   Tickets purchased at the Ticket Resale kiosk are not covered by this policy as the monies are passed to charity.

viii. Separate terms and conditions apply a) to Debenture Holders as notified by The All England Lawn Tennis Ground plc and b) to any extra days of play.

Important note:

Refunds are calculated as defined above and using the Referee's record of how much play has taken place on any given day. It is this official figure which determines whether or not customers are entitled to refunds, rather than the amount of play which an individual spectator may have seen.

Transport Service

From 1972 various companies have provided cars and drivers to transport the competitors, officials and press as follows:-

1972–1978 British Leyland	1989–1994 Rover
1979–1981 Austin Morris	1995–2014 Hertz (UK) Ltd.
1982–1988 Austin Rover Group	2015 Jaguar Land Rover Ltd.

In 2014 the car fleet consisted of 139 Ford Galaxies and 25 'S' Max and two luggage vans, plus two executive coaches. Over 290 drivers and 42 controllers made 17,125 journeys, carried approximately 34,876 passengers and covered more than 225,000 miles. Operations are conducted by specialist Courtesy Car Company – Corniche Events Ltd, under the management of AELTC's Transport Manager, Andy Quelch.

Wheelchair Spaces

On Centre Court there are 20 wheelchair spaces in the upper level, five spaces in the north east corner at courtside and three spaces at the southern end of the courts with 28 seats for guests. There are 40 spaces on the No. 1 Court together with seats for guests. On No. 2 Court, 20 spaces and 20 seats for guests are available at the south end. On No. 3 Court 10 spaces are available. There are also unreserved areas for a small number of wheelchairs by the side of all outside courts and a designated area on the Aorangi Terrace.

Wimbledon Posters

From the early 1920s, posters were issued by London Transport to advertise The Championships (also Davis Cup and Wightman Cup ties) on stations in London. The more recent posters were colourful and contained much information, such as directions and ticket prices. However, in 1995 use of the poster on the London Underground was discontinued as the advent of websites and local radio providing relevant information dispensed with the need for this form of advertising.

In the early 1980's the All England Lawn Tennis Club undertook the design of the posters with London Transport arranging the distribution. Because the posters have become very popular with the public, the Club decided to produce annually, for sale, a similar poster, but with reduced information. Since 1986, a poster has been on sale to the public and a 2015 version is available priced £7.00, from the Wimbledon Shops.

The poster for 2015, created by Yulia Brodskaya, provides a reminder of the new date of The Championships, which is a week later than previously. The Russian artist working in the UK creates beautiful 'paper graphics' by rolling, cutting and folding paper.

Centre Court Retractable Roof

How it works

Type of folding fabric concertina, which allows the roof to be folded into a very compressed area when not in use.

Fabric (Tenara) is a special waterproof structural material that is very strong, highly flexible and at 40% translucent is not transparent for players/spectators but will let in natural light. Around 5,200 square metres of fabric used.

Key element of the design allows natural light to reach the grass – brought about by re-contouring the fixed roof.

An airflow system removes condensation from within the bowl to provide good court surface conditions conducive to the playing of tennis when the roof is closed.

Roof is divided into two sections, with a total of nine bays of tensioned fabric – four bays in one section and five in the other. Each of the nine bays of tensioned fabric is clamped on either side to prismatic steel trusses. There are 10 trusses spanning approximately 77 metres across the court. Ends of each truss are supported by a set of bogies that move along parallel tracks positioned at either side within the new 'fixed' roof.

In preparation for closing the roof, one section is parked in its folded state at the north end of the court while the other is parked at the south end. The coordinated electro mechanical movement moves the trusses apart and, at the same time, unfolds and stretches out the fabric between the trusses over the court until the two sections meet in an overlapping seam above the middle of the court.

The arch shape to the tops of the trusses helps the structure to withstand their own dead weight and loading from elements such as snow and wind when the roof is stretched and closed over the court. The roof has been designed to close in a maximum of 10 minutes. If the roof is being closed for rain, court covers will protect the grass in the usual way while closure is in progress. After the roof has been closed, play can resume after a period of around 30 minutes, depending on climatic conditions.

Roof by numbers

8	Litres per second of fresh air per person pumped into the bowl to manage the environment
9	Chiller units required to cool the air
10	Minutes (maximum) that the roof takes to close
10	Trusses holding up the roof
16	Metres – height of the roof above the court surface
30	Minutes – maximum time expected before play can start/continue after the roof is closedand the internal environment is controlled and stabilised
43	Miles per hour – wind speed up to which the roof can be deployed/retracted

77	Metres – the span of the moving roof trusses (width of football pitch = 68m)
70	Tonnes – weight of each of the 10 trusses without extra parts
100	Tonnes – weight of each of the 10 trusses with all extras – eg motors, locking arms --
100	Percent of the roofs fabric which is recyclable
214	MM per second – maximum speed of truss deployment
1,200	Extra seats installed in 2008
3,000	Tonnes – combined weight (both fixed and moving) of the roof
5,200	Square metres, area of retractable roof when fully deployed
7,500	Wimbledon umbrellas, needed to cover the same area as the retractable roof
15,000	Maximum spectator capacity
143,000	Litres per second – total amount of conditioned air that the air-management system supplies to the bowl
290million	Tennis balls – number that could fit in the Centre Court with the roof closed

Roof Award

In July 2009 the Centre Court roof won an Award at the Annual Structural Steel Design Awards, which celebrate high standards of structural and architectural design attainable in the use of steel. The judges commented: "The 1000 tonne retractable roof uses structural steel to its full advantages, with skilful marriage of heavy precision engineering and state-of-the-art technology, to achieve the all-weather operations so long desired."

Centre Court Invasions

1949 Tuesday 21st June. The duel between A.C. van Swol (NED) and R. Abdesselam (FRA) was held up for a short period when a squirrel appeared on Court. The players relaxed while the ball boys chased it away.

1957 Saturday 6th July. During the Gentlemen's Doubles final, Mrs Helen Jarvis of Croydon invaded the Court, shouting and waving a banner in her campaign for a new world banking system. The message on the banner began with the words "God Save our Queen". the intruder was escorted from the Court by the Referee and a policeman. The Queen watched the incident from the Royal Box.

1973 Tuesday 3rd June. At the conclusion of the R. Taylor (GBR) v B.R. Borg (SWE) match, schoolgirls ran on to the court and asked Borg for his autograph. Police cleared the Court and groundstaff straightened the turf and made sure there were no heel marks.

1974 Monday 24th June. After the I. Nastase (ROM) v J. Hrebec (CZE) match a girl ran on to the court. She was restrained by a policeman, but before being escorted away, Nastase gave her his autograph.

1976 Saturday 26th June. People advertising a pop concert ran on to the Court during the match between J.S. Connors (USA) and S.R. Smith (USA). Connors was given a rose.

1981 Tueday 30th June. The contest between Miss S.D. Barker (GBR) and Miss A.K. Kiyomura (USA) and Miss J.C. Russell (USA) and Miss V. Ruzici (ROM) was halted at 9.35 pm due to bad light with score at 5-all in the final set. Amid boos and jeers, cushions, programmes and other objects were thrown on to the Court.

1982 Friday 26th June. During the second set of the match between Miss P.H. Shriver (USA) and Miss K.S. Rinaldi (USA) a swarm of bees descended on the Court. Miss Shriver swatted them with her racket but one stung Miss Rinaldi on the arm. Miss Shriver gallantly crossed over and removed the sting.

1989 Friday 7th July. During the Gentleman's semi-final, two sparrows disturbed the play between S.B. Edberg (SWE) and J.P. McEnroe (USA).

1990 Wednesday to Friday 4th–6th July. Play was disturbed by a pied wagtail in the following matches – B.F. Becker (GER) v B. Gilbert (USA) (Quarter-final), Miss S.M. Graf (GER) v Miss Z.L. Garrison (USA) (Semi-final) and I. Lendl (TCH) v S.B. Edberg (SWE) (Semi-final).

1991 Sunday 7th July. At the start of the second set of the final between B.F. Becker (GER) and M.D. Stich (GER) a protester claiming to be the American President and brandishing a picture of his daughter disturbed play for a short period. He was quickly removed.

1996 Sunday 7th July. Immediately before the Gentlemen's Singles final between R.P.S. Krajicek (NED) and M.O. Washington (USA), a female streaker ran across the Court.

1998 Monday 22nd June. A mouse interrupted play between Y.A. Kafelnikov (RUS) and M.A. Philippoussis (AUS).

1999 Thursday 24th June. During the second set of the singles match between B.F. Becker and N. Kiefer, both of Germany, a group of pigeons twice interrupted play, disturbing Becker's service and his opponent's concentration.

1999 Saturday 3rd July. During the second set of the singles semi-final match between P. Sampras (USA) and T.H. Henman (GBR), a pigeon interrupted play for a short period, causing the latter to lose his concentration while serving.

2002 Thursday 27th June. Just prior to the T.H. Henman (GBR) v S. Draper (AUS) match, two pranksters, dressed in whites and carrying rackets, climbed over the barrier and began knocking a ball to and fro over the net. The presence of security guards forced the pair to leave the court for the nearest exit.

2002 Sunday 7th July. During the Gentlemen's Singles final between L.G. Hewitt (AUS) and D.P. Nalbandian (ARG), a male streaker invaded the court.

2006 Thursday 29th June. During the singles matches between J. Benneteau (FRA) and A. Murray (GBR) a group of pigeons interrupted play.

2006 Tuesday 4th July. During the second set of the match between Miss E. Dementieva (RUS) and Miss M. Sharapova (RUS) a male streaker invaded the court.

2006 Wednesday 5th July. During the first set of the match between M. Ancic (CRO) and R. Federer (SUI), two protesters from the Real Fathers for Justice group, carrying tennis rackets, managed to hit a ball over the net before being escorted away.

Junior Championships

Originally in 1947 the Committee of Management invited 18 junior champions from ten European countries to watch the second week's play during The Championships.

In the mornings Dan Maskell, the Club professional, organised an American tournament for the boys and girls on the hard courts. The boy's event was won by 16 year-old Kurt Nielsen of Denmark. His prize was a small silver cup, donated by Maskell, which was presented by the newly crowned Wimbledon Champion, Jack Kramer. The girls' winner was Miss Genevieve Domken of Belgium who received a prize, donated by Dr. J.C. Gregory.

The juniors were invited again in 1948 and, as in the previous year, competitions took place on the hard courts during the mornings.

In 1949 the two events were held in public on the outside grass courts during the afternoons of the second week under normal knock-out conditions. This practice has continued ever since, with both events raised to Championship status in 1975. Seeding began in 1977.

For the first time in 1998 a Qualifying competition for the Boys' and Girls' Singles, for up to 48 in each event, was held at the Bank of England Sports Club during the first week of The Championships.

Trophies

Boys' Singles Championship Cup

The Cup was donated to the All England Lawn Tennis Club in 1970 by the family of A.W. Gore, the Wimbledon Champion in 1901, 1908 and 1909. The Cup was originally won by Gore when he became the All Comers' Singles winner in 1901.

The inscription on the Cup reads:-
Front side

> A E L T C
> All Comers' Singles
> Wimbledon, 1901
> 1st Prize
> Won by A.W. Gore

Also engraved are the dates and names of the Champions from 1877 to 1901. In 1976 the A.E.L.T.C. presented the Cup for perpetual competition for the Boys' Singles Championship and added the following inscription to the reverse side:

> Presented to the A E L T & C C
> by members of the Gore Family in 1970
> This Cup was subsequently presented by the
> Club Committee for the
> Boys' Singles Championship

The dates and names of the winners are engraved on the Cup from 1975, when the event became a Championship.

Girls' Singles Championship Cup

The Cup was donated to the All England Lawn Tennis Club in 1945 by the family of Miss Bertha Steedman, who was a prominent player before the turn of the century. The Cup was originally one of a pair won by Miss Steedman who, in partnership with Miss Blanche Hillyard, retired the trophy after winning the All England Ladies' Doubles Championship three times in succession at the Buxton tournament in 1895.

The inscription on the Cup reads:-

Front side

Buxton
Open
Lawn Tennis Tournament
Ladies' Doubles
All England Championship

Reverse side:

Challenge
Cup
Presented
by the Directors
of the Buxton
Garden Company
Limited

Around the base of the Cup are the following inscriptions, which were added in 1998:

THE GIRLS' SINGLES CHAMPIONSHIP

Presented to the A.E.L.T.C. by the Steedman family, 1945

In 1976 the A.E.L.T.C. presented the Cup for perpetual competition for the Girls' Singles Championship. The dates and names of the winners are engraved on the Cup from 1975, when the event became a Championship.

(There are no dates or names which refer to Buxton engraved on the Cup)

Boys' and Girls' Doubles Championship Cups

Both Cups were presented by the A.E.L.T.C. in 1985. The dates and names of the winners are engraved on the Cups from 1985, although the Championships were instituted in 1982. (The Cups were not listed in the Wimbledon Programme until 1986.)

Number of Entries

Year	Boys' Singles	Boys' Doubles (pairs)	Girls' Singles	Girls' Doubles (pairs)	Year	Boys' Singles	Boys' Doubles (pairs)	Girls' Singles	Girls' Doubles (pairs)
1947	10		8		1982	64	16	48	16
1948	12		12		1983	64	16	48	16
1949	18		7		1984	64	16	48	16
1950	18		10		1985	64	16	48	16
1951	22		12		1986	64	32	64	29
1952	17		12		1987	64	16	64	16
1953	16		13		1988	64	32	64	28
1954	19		12		1989	64	32	64	32
1955	15		12		1990	64	32	64	30
1956	20		12		1991	64	16	64	16
1957	23		17		1992	64	32	64	32
1958	22		13		1993	64	31	64	32
1959	23		12		1994	64	32	64	32
1960	23		15		1995	64	32	64	32
1961	19		18		1996	64	16(1)	64	16(1)
1962	25		18		1997	64	16(1)	64	16(1)
1963	27		14		1998	64	16(1)	64	16(1)
1964	26		17		1999	64	32	64	32
1965	18		15		2000	64	27	64	32
1966	23		18		2001	64	32	64	32
1967	27		19		2002	64	32	64	32
1968	26		25		2003	64	16	64	16
1969	27		24		2004	64	32	64	32
1970	30		23		2005	64	32	64	32
1971	27		21		2006	64	32	64	32
1972	29		19		2007	64	32	64	32
1973	30		27		2008	64	32	64	32
1974	34		25		2009	64	32	64	32
1975	48		33		2010	64	32	64	32
1976	48		32		2011	64	32	64	32
1977	49		34		2012	64	32	64	32
1978	48		40		2013	64	32	64	32
1979	48		40		2014	64	32	64	32
1980	48		40		2015	64	32	64	32
1981	64		48						

1) *Reduced from 32 pairs owing to bad weather*

Boys' Singles Championship*

Trophies and Prizes

1947	Winner	Small Cup (D. Maskell)
1948–74	Winner	Miniature Cup
1975	Champion	Miniature Cup
	Runner-up	Silver Pencil

1976–1987	Champion	Silver Cup (AELTC/A.W. Gore)
		Miniature Cup
	Runner-up	Silver Pencil
1988–2007	Champion	Silver Cup (AELTC/A.W. Gore)
		Miniature Cup
	Runner-up	Memento (Carriage clock)
2008–2011	Champion	Silver Cup (AELTC/A.W. Gore)
		Silver Cup (¾ size)
	Runner-up	Silver Salver (6 inches)
2012–2015	Champion	Silver Cup (AELTC/A.W. Gore)
		Three-quarter size Silver Cup
	Runner-up	Silver Salver (6 inches)

1947–1974 – Invitation Event

Prize Money
Nil

Finals and Scores

Year	No. of Seeds	Winner	Seeding Position	Runner-up	Seeding Position	Score
1947		K. Nielsen (DEN)		S.V. Davidson (SWE)		8-6 6-1 9-7
1948		S.O. Stockenberg (SWE)		D. Vad (HUN)		6-0 6-8 5-7 6-4 6-2
1949		S.O. Stockenberg (SWE)		J.A.T. Horn (GBR)		6-2 6-1
1950		J.A.T. Horn (GBR)		K. Mobarek (EGY)		6-0 6-2
1951		J. Kupferburger (RSA)		K. Mobarek (EGY)		8-6 6-4
1952		R.K. Wilson (GBR)		T.T. Fancutt (RSA)		6-3 6-3
1953		W.A. Knight (GBR)		R. Krishnan (IND)		7-5 6-4
1954		R. Krishnan (IND)		A.J. Cooper (AUS)		6-2 7-5
1955		M.P. Hann (GBR)		J.E. Lundquist (SWE)		6-0 11-9
1956		R.E. Holmberg (USA)		R.G. Laver (AUS)		6-1 6-1
1957		J.I. Tattersall (GBR)		I. Ribeiro (BRA)		6-2 6-1
1958		E.H. Buchholz (USA)		P.J. Lall (IND)		6-1 6-3
1959		T. Lejus (URS)		R.W. Barnes (BRA)		6-2 6-4
1960		A.R. Mandelstam (RSA)		J. Mukerjea (IND)		1-6 8-6 6-4
1961		C.E. Graebner (USA)		E. Blanke (AUT)		6-3 9-7
1962		S.J. Matthews (GBR)		A. Metreveli (URS)		10-8 3-6 6-4
1963		N. Kalogeropoulos (GRE)		I. El Shafei (EGY)		6-4 6-3
1964		I. El Shafei (EGY)		V. Korotkov (URS)		6-2 6-3
1965		V. Korotkov (URS)		G. Goven (FRA)		6-2 3-6 6-3
1966		V. Korotkov (URS)		B.E. Fairlie (NZL)		6-3 11-9
1967		M. Orantes (ESP)		M.S. Estep (USA)		6-2 6-0
1968		J.G. Alexander (AUS)		J. Thamin (FRA)		6-1 6-2
1969		B.M. Bertram (RSA)		J.G. Alexander (AUS)		7-5 5-7 6-4
1970		B.M. Bertram (RSA)		F. Gebert (GER)		6-0 6-3
1971		R.I. Kreiss (USA)		S.A. Warboys (GBR)		2-6 6-4 6-3
1972		B.R. Borg (SWE)		C.J. Mottram (GBR)		6-3 4-6 7-5
1973		W.W. Martin (USA)		C.S. Dowdeswell (RHO)		6-2 6-4
1974		W.W. Martin (USA)		Ash. Amritraj (IND)		6-2 6-1
1975		C.J. Lewis (NZL)		R. Ycaza (ECU)		6-1 6-4
1976		H.P. Guenthardt (SUI)		P. Elter (GER)		6-4 7-5
1977	8	V.A.W. Winitsky (USA)	U	T.E. Teltscher (USA)	3	6-1 1-6 8-6
1978	8	I. Lendl (TCH)	1	J. Turpin (USA)	U	6-3 6-4

Year	No. of Seeds	Winner	Seeding Position	Runner-up	Seeding Position	Score
1979	8	R. Krishnan (IND)	1	D. Siegler (USA)	2	6-0 6-2
1980	8	T. Tulasne (FRA)	3	H.D. Beutel (GER)	U	6-4 3-6 6-4
1981	8	M.W. Anger (USA)	7	P.H. Cash (AUS)	6	7-6 (7-3) 7-5
1982	8	P.H. Cash (AUS)	1	H. Sundstrom (SWE)	2	6-4 6-7 (5-7) 6-3
1983	8	S.B. Edberg (SWE)	1	J. Frawley (AUS)	2	6-3 7-6 (7-5)
1984	16	M. Kratzmann (AUS)	2	S. Kruger (RSA)	U	6-4 4-6 6-3
1985	16	L. Lavalle (MEX)	1	E. Velez (MEX)	U	6-4 6-4
1986	16	E. Velez (MEX)	4	J. Sanchez (ESP)	3	6-3 7-5
1987	16	D. Nargiso (ITA)	4	J.R. Stoltenberg (AUS)	6	7-6 (8-6) 6-4
1988	16	N. Pereira (VEN)	6	G. Raoux (FRA)	13	7-6 (7-4) 6-2
1989	16	L.J.N. Kulti (SWE)	1	T.A. Woodbridge (AUS)	2	6-4 6-3
1990	16	L.A. Paes (IND)	11	M. Ondruska (RSA)	2	7-5 2-6 6-4
1991	16	K.J.T. Enqvist (SWE)	2	M. Joyce (USA)	U	6-4 6-3
1992	16	D. Skoch (TCH)	10	B. Dunn (USA)	4	6-4 6-3
1993	16	R. Sabau (ROM)	9	J. Szymanski (VEN)	7	6-1 6-3
1994	16	S.M. Humphries (USA)	11	M.A. Philippoussis (AUS)	3	7-6 (7-5) 3-6 6-4
1995	16	O. Mutis (U)	U	N. Kiefer (GER)	1	6-2 6-2
1996	16	V. Voltchkov (BLR)	6	I. Ljubicic (CRO)	U	3-6 6-2 6-3
1997	16	W. Whitehouse (RSA)	5	D. Elsner (GER)	1	6-3 7-6 (8-6)
1998	16	R. Federer (SUI)	5	I. Labadze (GEO)	7	6-4 6-4
1999	16	J. Melzer (AUT)	U	K. Pless (DEN)	1	7-6 (9-7) 6-3
2000	16	N.P.A. Mahut (FRA)	1	M. Ancic (CRO)	4	3-6 6-3 7-5
2001	16	R. Valent (SUI)	10	G. Muller (LUX)	2	3-6 7-5 6-3
2002	16	T.C. Reid (AUS)	5	L. Quahab (ALG)	7	7-6 (7-5) 6-4
2003	16	F. Mergea (ROM)	6	C. Guccione (AUS)	8	6-2 7-6 (7-3)
2004	16	G. Monfils (FRA)	1	M. Kasiri (GBR)	U	7-5 7-6 (8-6)
2005	16	J. Chardy (FRA)	U	R. Haase (NED)	14	6-4 6-3
2006	16	T. De Bakker (NED)	1	M. Gawron (POL)	U	6-2 7-6 (7-4)
2007	16	D. Young (USA)	3	V. Ignatic (BLR)	1	7-5 6-1
2008	16	G. Dimitrov (BUL)	9	H. Kontinen (FIN)	U	7-5 6-3
2009	16	A. Kuznetsov (RUS)	U	J. Cox (USA)	U	4-6 6-2 6-2
2010	16	M.Fucsovics (HUN)	13	B. Mitchell (USA)	U	6-4 6-4
2011	16	L. Saville (AUS)	16	L. Broady (GBR)	15	2-6 6-4 6-2
2012	16	F. Peliwo (CAN)	4	L. Saville (AUS)	1	7-5 6-4
2013	16	G. Quinzi (ITA)	6	H. Chung (KOR)	U	7-5 7-6 (7-2)
2014	16	N. Rubin (USA)	U	S. Kozlov (USA)	6	6-4 4-6 6-3

Name	Date of Birth	Place of Birth	Note
ALEXANDER, John Gillient	4 Jul 1951	Sydney, N.S.W., Australia	1
ANGER, Matthew	20 Jun 1963	Walnut Creek, California, USA	1
BERTRAM, Byron Maxwell	29 Oct 1952	Johannesburg, Transvaal, S.A.	1
BORG, Bjorn Rune	6 Jun 1956	Stockholm, Sweden	3
BUCHHOLZ, Earl Henry	16 Sep 1940	St. Louis, Missouri, USA	1
CASH, Patrick Hart	27 May 1965	Melbourne, Victoria, Australia	1
CHARDY, Jeremy	12 Feb 1987	Pau, France	3
DE BAKKER, Thiemo	19 Sept 1988	The Hague, Netherlands	1
DIMITROV, Grigor	16 May 1991	Haskova, Bulgaria	1
EDBERG, Stefan Bengt	19 Jan 1966	Vastervik, Sweden	1
EL SHAFEI, Ismail Adly Abdel Hamid	15 Nov 1947	Cairo, Egypt	2
ENQVIST, Karl Johan Thomas	13 Mar 1974	Farsta, Stockholm, Sweden	3
FEDERER, Roger	8 Aug 1981	Basle, Switzerland	1
FUCSOVICS, Marton	8 Feb 1992	Nyireghala, Hungary	2
GRAEBNER, Clark Edward	4 Nov 1943	Cleveland, Ohio, USA	1

Name	Date of Birth	Place of Birth	Note
GUENTHARDT, Heinz Peter	8 Feb 1959	Zurich, Switzerland	1
HANN, Michael Preston	24 Aug 1937	Sheffield, England	1
HOLMBERG, Ronald Edward	27 Jan 1938	Brooklyn, New York, USA	1
HORN, John Alfred Thomas	6 Nov 1931	Plaistow, London, England	1
HUMPHRIES, Scott Marshall	26 May 1976	Greeley, Colorado, USA	1
KALOGEROPOULOS, Nicholas	18 Feb 1945	Costa Rica	1
KNIGHT, William Arthur	12 Nov 1935	Northampton, Northants, Eng.	2
KOROTKOV, Vladimir	23 Apr 1948	Moscow, U.S.S.R.	1
KRATZMANN, Mark	17 May 1966	Murgon, Queensland, Australia	2
KREISS, Robert Irwin	30 Apr 1953	Los Angeles, California, USA	1
KRISHNAN, Ramanathan	11 Apr 1937	Madras, India	1
KRISHNAN, Ramesh	5 Jun 1961	Madras, India	1
KULTI, Lars Johan Nicklas	22 Apr 1971	Kungsanen, Stockholm, Sweden	3
KUZNETSOV, Andrey	22 Feb 1991	Tula, Russia	3
KUPFERBUGER, Johann	2 Oct 1933	Pretoria, Transvaal, South Africa	1
LAVALLE, Leonardo	14 Jul 1967	Mexico City, Mexico	2
LEJUS, Toomas	28 Aug 1941	Tallinn, U.S.S.R.	1
LENDL, Ivan	7 Mar 1960	Ostrava, Czechoslovakia	1
LEWIS, Christopher John	9 Mar 1957	Auckland, New Zealand	1
MAHUT, Nicolas Pierre Armand	21 Jan 1982	Angers, France	1
MANDELSTAM, Rodney	8 Apr 1942	Boksburg, Transvaal, S.A.	1
MARTIN, William Ward	25 Dec 1956	Evanston, Illinois, USA	3
MATTHEWS, Stanley John	29 Nov 1945	Stoke, Staffordshire, England	1
MELZER, Jurgen	22 May 1981	Vienna, Austria	4
MERGEA, Florin	26 Jan 1985	Craiova, Romania	1
MONFILS, Gael	1 Sept 1986	Paris, France	3
MUTIS, Olivier	2 Feb 1978	Russange, France	3
NARGISO, Diego	15 Mar 1970	Naples, Italy	2
NIELSEN, Kurt	19 Nov 1930	Copenhagen, Denmark	1
ORANTES, Manuel	5 Feb 1949	Granada, Spain	2
PAES, Leander Adrian	16 Jun 1973	Calcutta, India	1
PELIWO, Filip	30 Jan 1994	Vancouver, Canada	3
PEREIRA, Nicolas	29 Sep 1970	Salto, Uruguay	1
QUINZI, Gianluigi	1 Feb 1996	Cittadella, Italy	4
REID, Todd Charles	3 Jun 1984	Sydney, NSW, Australia	3
RUBIN, Noah	21 Feb 1966	New York, New York, USA	
SABAU, Razvan	18 Jun 1977	Bucharest, Romania	1
SAVILLE, Luke	1 Feb 1994	Berri, SA Australia	3
SKOCH, David	6 Nov 1976	Prague, Czechoslovakia	3
STOCKENBERG, Staffan Oscar	14 Sep 1931	Orebro, Sweden	1
TATTERSALL, James Irvine	27 Mar 1940	Gloucester, England	1
TULASNE, Thierry	12 Jul 1963	Aix-Les-Bains, France	1
VALENT, Roman	8 Jul 1983	Zurich, Switzerland	3
VELEZ, Eduardo	20 Apr 1969	Monterrey, Mexico	3
VOLTCHKOV, Vladimir	7 Apr 1978	Minsk, U.S.S.R.	1
WHITEHOUSE, Westley	13 Mar 1979	Empangeni, S.A.	4
WILSON, Robert Keith	22 Nov 1935	Hendon, Middlesex, England	1
WINITSKY, Van Alan	2 Mar 1959	Miami, Florida, U.S.A.	2
YOUNG, Donald	23 Jul 1989	Chicago, U.S.A.	4

1. Right-handed   3. Right-handed, two handed backhand
2. Left-handed   4. Left-handed, two handed backhand

Boys' Doubles Championship
Trophies and Prizes

1982–1984	Champions (2)	Miniature Cup
	Runners-up (2)	Silver pencil
1985–1987	Champions (2)	Silver Cup (AELTC)
		Miniature Cup
	Runners-up (2)	Silver pencil
1988–2007	Champions (2)	Silver Cup (AELTC)
		Miniature Cup
	Runners-up (2)	Memento (Carriage clock)
2008–2011	Champions (2)	Silver Cup (AELTC)
		Silver Cup (½ size)
	Runners-up (2)	Silver Salver (6 inches)
2012–2015	Champions (2)	Silver Cup (AELTC)
		Three-quarter size Silver Cup
	Runners-up (2)	Silver Salver (6 inches)

Prize Money
Nil

Finals and Scores

Year	No. of Seeds	Winners	Seeding Position	Runners-up	Seeding Position	Score
1982	4	P.H. Cash and J. Frawley (AUS)	3	R.D. Leach and J.J. Ross (USA)	1	6-3 6-4
1983	4	M. Kratzmann and S. Youl (AUS)	4	M. Nastase (ROM) and O. Rahnasto (FIN)	3	6-4 6-4
1984	4	R. Brown and R.V. Weiss (USA)	U	M. Kratzmann (AUS) and J. Svensson (SWE)	1	1-6 6-4 11-9
1985	4	A. Moreno (MEX) and J. Yzaga (PER)	U	P. Korda and C. Suk (TCH)	2	7-6 (7-3) 6-4
1986	8	T. Carbonell (ESP) and P. Korda (TCH)	U	S. Barr (AUS) and H. Karrasch (CAN)	U	6-1 6-1
1987	4	J.R. Stoltenberg and T.A. Woodbridge (AUS)	3	D. Nargiso and E. Rossi (ITA)	1	6-3 7-6 (7-2)
1988	8	J.R. Stoltenberg and T.A. Woodbridge (AUS)	1	D. Rikl and T. Zdrazila (TCH)	5	6-4 1-6 7-5
1989	8	J.E. Palmer and J.A. Stark (USA)	2	J-L. De Jager and W.R. Ferreira (RSA)	4	7-6 (7-4) 7-6 (7-2)
1990	8	S. Lareau and S. Leblanc (CAN)	1	C. Marsh and M. Ondruska (RSA)	5	7-6 (7-5) 4-6 6-3
1991	4	K. Alami (MAR) and G. Rusedski (CAN)	4	J-L. De Jager (RSA) and A. Medvedev (URS)	3	1-6 7-6 (7-4) 6-4
1992	8	S. Baldas and S. Draper (AUS)	3	M.S. Bhupathi and N. Kirtane (IND)	U	6-1 4-6 9-7
1993	8	S. Downs and J. Greenhalgh (NZL)	1	N. Godwin and G. Williams (RSA)	2	6-7 (6-8) 7-6 (7-4) 7-5
1994	8	B. Ellwood and M.A. Philippoussis (AUS)	1	V. Platenik (SVK) and R. Schlachter (BRA)	7	6-2 6-4
1995	8	M. Lee and J.M. Trotman (GBR)	U	A. Hernandez (MEX) and M. Puerta (ARG)	2	7-6 (7-2) 6-4
1996	4	D. Bracciali (ITA) and J. Robichaud (CAN)	1	D. Roberts and W. Whitehouse (RSA)	2	6-2 6-4
1997	4	L. Horna (PER) and N. Massu (CHI)	1	J. Van de Westhuizen and W. Whitehouse (RSA)	2	6-4 6-2

1998	4	R. Federer (SUI) and O.L.P. Rochus (BEL)	U	M. Llodra (FRA) and A. Ram (ISR)	4	6-4 6-4
1999	8	G. Coria and D. Nalbandian (ARG)	1	T. Enev (BUL) and J. Nieminem (FIN)	U	7-5 6-4
2000	8	D. Coene and K. Vliegen (BEL)	7	A. Banks and B. Riby (GBR)	U	6-3 1-6 6-3
2001	8	F. Dancevic (CAN) and G. Lapentti (ECU)	8	B. Echagaray and S. Gonzales (MEX)	1	6-1 6-4
2002	8	F. Mergea and H. Tecau (ROM)	U	B. Baker and R. Ram (USA)	U	6-4 4-6 6-4
2003	4	F. Mergea and H. Tecau (ROM)	1	A. Feeney and C. Guccione (AUS)	U	7-6 (7-4) 7-5
2004	8	B. Evans and S. Oudsema (USA)	2	R. Haase (NED) and V. Troicki (SCG)	U	6-4 6-4
2005	8	J. Levine and M. Shabaz (USA)	U	S. Groth (AUS) and A. Kennaugh (GBR)	U	6-4 6-1
2006	8	K. Damico and N. Schnugg (USA)	U	M. Klizan and A. Martin (SVK)	2	7-6 (9-7) 6-2
2007	8	D. Lopez and M. Trevisan (ITA)	7	R. Jebavy (CZE) M. Klizan (SVK)	U	7-6 (7-5) 4-6 (10-8)
2008	8	C-P. Hsieh and T-H. Yang (TPE)	U	M. Reid and B. Tomic (AUS)	3	6-4 2-6 12-10
2009	8	P-H Herbert (FRA) and K. Krawietz (GER)	U	J. Obry and A. Puget (FRA)	U	6-7 (3-7) 6-2 12-10
2010	8	L. Broady and T. Farquharson (GBR)	U	L. Burton and G. Morgan	U	7-6 (7-4) 6-4
2011	8	G. Morgan (GER) and M. Pavic (CRO)	2	O. Golding (GBR) and J. Vesely (CZE)	1	3-6 6-4 7-5
2012	8	A. Harris and N. Kyrgios (AUS)	4	M. Donati and P. Licciardi (ITA)	U	6-2 6-4
2013	8	T. Kokkinakis and N. Kyrgios (AUS)	U	E. Couacaud (FRA) and S. Napolitano (ITA)	U	6-2 6-3
2014	8	O Lutz and M. Zormann (BRA)	3	S. Kozlov (USA) and A. Rublev (RUS)	1	6-4 3-6 8-6

Girls' Singles Championship

Trophies and Prizes

1947	Winner	Paper Knife
1948–1974	Winner	Miniature Cup
1975	Champion	Miniature Cup
	Runner-up	Silver Pencil
1976–1987	Champion	Silver Cup (AELTC/Miss B. Steedman) Miniature Cup
	Runner-up	Silver Pencil
1988–2007	Champion	Silver Cup (AELTC/Miss B. Steedman) Miniature Cup
	Runner-up	Memento (Carriage clock)
2008–2011	Champion	Silver Cup (AELTC/Miss B. Steedman) Silver Cup (¾ size)
	Runner-up	Silver Salver (6 inches)
2012–2015	Champion	Silver Cup (AELTC/Miss B. Steedman) Three-quarter size Silver Cup
	Runner-up	Silver Salver (6 inches)

1947–1974 – Invitation Event

Prize Money

Nil

Finals and Scores

Year	No. of Seeds	Winner	Seeding Position	Runner-up	Seeding Position	Score
1947		Miss G. Domken (BEL)		Miss B. Wallen (SWE)		6-1 6-4
1948		Miss O. Miskova (TCH)		Miss V. Rigollet (SUI)		6-4 6-2
1949		Miss C. Mercelis (BEL)		Miss J.S.V. Partridge (GBR)		6-4 6-2
1950		Miss L.M. Cornell (GBR)		Miss A. Winter (NOR)		6-2 6-4
1951		Miss L.M. Cornell (GBR)		Miss S. Lazzarino (ITA)		6-3 6-4
1952		Miss F.J.I. ten Bosch (NED)		Miss R. Davar (IND)		5-7 6-1 7-5
1953		Miss D. Kilian (RSA)		Miss V.A. Pitt (GBR)		6-4 4-6 6-1
1954		Miss V.A. Pitt (GBR)		Miss C. Monnot (FRA)		5-7 6-3 6-2
1955		Miss S.M. Armstrong (GBR)		Miss B. de Chambure (FRA)		6-2 6-4
1956		Miss A.S. Haydon (GBR)		Miss I. Buding (GER)		6-3 6-4
1957		Miss M.G. Arnold (USA)		Miss E. Reyes (MEX)		8-6 6-2
1958		Miss S.M. Moore (USA)		Miss A. Dmitrieva (URS)		6-2 6-4
1959		Miss J. Cross (RSA)		Miss D. Schuster (AUT)		6-1 6-1
1960		Miss K.J. Hantze (USA)		Miss L.M. Hutchings (RSA)		6-4 6-4
1961		Miss G. Baksheeva (URS)		Miss K.D. Chabot (USA)		6-4 8-6
1962		Miss G. Baksheeva (URS)		Miss E.P. Terry (NZL)		6-4 6-2
1963		Miss D.M. Salfati (FRA)		Miss K. Dening (AUS)		6-4 6-1
1964		Miss J.M. Bartkowicz (USA)		Miss E. Subirats (MEX)		6-3 6-1
1965		Miss O.V. Morozova (URS)		Miss R. Giscafre (ARG)		6-3 6-3
1966		Miss B. Lindstrom (FIN)		Miss J.A. Congdon (GBR)		7-5 6-3
1967		Miss J.H. Salome (NED)		Miss E.M. Strandberg (SWE)		6-4 6-2
1968		Miss K.S. Pigeon (USA)		Miss L.E. Hunt (AUS)		6-4 6-3
1969		Miss K. Sawamatsu (JPN)		Miss B.I. Kirk (RSA)		6-1 1-6 7-5
1970		Miss S.A. Walsh (USA)		Miss M.V. Kroshina (URS)		8-6 6-4
1971		Miss M.V. Kroshina (URS)		Miss S.H. Minford (GBR)		6-4 6-4
1972		Miss I.S. Kloss (RSA)		Miss G.L. Coles (GBR)		6-4 4-6 6-4
1973		Miss A.K. Kiyomura (USA)		Miss M. Navratilova (TCH)		6-4 7-5
1974		Miss M. Jausovec (YUG)		Miss M. Simionescu (ROM)		7-5 6-4
1975		Miss N.Y. Chmyreva (URS)		Miss R. Marsikova (TCH)		6-4 6-3
1976		Miss N.Y. Chmyreva (URS)		Miss M. Kruger (RSA)		6-3 2-6 6-1
1977	8	Miss L. Antonoplis (USA)	U	Miss Mareen Louie (USA)	3	7-5 6-1
1978	8	Miss T.A. Austin (USA)	1	Miss H. Mandlikova (TCH)	2	6-0 3-6 6-4
1979	8	Miss M.L. Piatek (USA)	3	Miss A.A. Moulton (USA)	5	6-1 6-3
1980	8	Miss D. Freeman (AUS)	U	Miss S.J. Leo (AUS)	5	7-6 ( ) 7-5
1981	8	Miss Z.L. Garrison (USA)	8	Miss R.R. Uys (RSA)	U	6-4 3-6 6-0
1982	8	Miss C. Tanvier (FRA)	2	Miss H. Sukova (TCH)	1	6-2 7-5
1983	8	Miss P. Paradis (FRA)	U	Miss P. Hy (HKG)	5	6-2 6-1
1984	8	Miss A.N. Croft (GBR)	3	Miss E. Reinach (RSA)	U	3-6 6-3 6-2
1985	8	Miss A. Holikova (TCH)	3	Miss J.M. Byrne (AUS)	7	7-5 6-1
1986	16	Miss N.M. Zvereva (URS)	U	Miss L. Meskhi (URS)	U	2-6 6-2 9-7
1987	16	Miss N.M. Zvereva (URS)	1	Miss J. Halard (FRA)	U	6-4 6-4
1988	16	Miss B.A.M. Schultz (NED)	1	Miss E. Derly (FRA)	7	7-6 (7-5) 6-1
1989	16	Miss A. Strnadova (TCH)	U	Miss M.J. McGrath (USA)	6	6-2 6-3
1990	16	Miss A. Strnadova (TCH)	7	Miss K. Sharpe (AUS)	6	6-2 6-4
1991	16	Miss B. Rittner (GER)	1	Miss E. Makarova (URS)	U	6-7 (6-8) 6-2 6-3
1992	16	Miss C.R. Rubin (USA)	2	Miss L. Courtois (BEL)	U	6-2 7-5
1993	16	Miss N. Feber (BEL)	1	Miss R. Grande (ITA)	7	7-6 (7-3) 1-6 6-2
1994	16	Miss M. Hingis (SUI)	8	Miss M-R Jeon (KOR)	5	7-5 6-4
1995	16	Miss A. Olsza (POL)	9	Miss T. Tanasugarn (THA)	5	7-5 7-6 (8-6)
1996	16	Miss A. Mauresmo (FRA)	10	Miss M.L. Serna (ESP)	U	4-6 6-3 6-4
1997	16	Miss C.C. Black (ZIM)	3	Miss A. Rippner (USA)	6	6-3 7-5

1998	16	Miss K. Srebotnik (SLO)	7	Miss K. Clijsters (BEL)	U	7-6 (7-3) 6-3
1999	16	Miss I. Tulyaganova (UZB)	4	Miss L. Krasnoroutskaya (RUS)	7	7-6 (7-3) 6-4
2000	16	Miss M.E. Salerni (ARG)	4	Miss T. Perebiynis (UKR)	2	6-4 7-5
2001	16	Miss A. Widjaja (INA)	8	Miss D. Safina (RUS)	15	6-4 0-6 7-5
2002	16	Miss V. Douchevina (RUS)	8	Miss M. Sharapova ((RUS)	7	4-6 6-1 6-2
2003	16	Miss K. Flipkens (BEL)	U	Miss A. Tchakvetadze (RUS)U	6-4 3-6 6-3
2004	16	Miss K. Bondarenko (UKR)	6	Miss A. Ivanovic (SCG)	3	6-4 6-7 (2-7) 6-2
2005	16	Miss A.R. Radwanska (POL)	U	Miss T. Paszek (AUT)	U	6-3 6-4
2006	16	Miss C. Wozniacki (DEN)	4	Miss M. Rybarikova (SVK)	6	6-2 7-6 (7-4)
2007	16	Miss U. Radwanska (POL)	6	Miss M. Brengle (USA)	7	2-6 6-3 6-0
2008	16	Miss L.M.D Robson (GBR)	U	Miss N. Lertcheewakarn (THA)	3	6-3 3-6 6-1
2009	16	Miss N. Lertcheewakarn (THA)	4	Miss K. Mladenovic (FRA)	1	3-6 6-3 6-1
2010	16	Miss K. Pliskova (CZE)	9	Miss S. Ishizu (JPN)	10	6-3 4-6 6-4
2011	16	Miss A. Barty (AUS)	12	Miss I. Khromacheva (RUS)	3	7-5 7-6 (7-3)
2012	16	Miss E.C.M. Bouchard (CAN)	5	Miss E. Svitolina (UKR)	3	6-2 6-2
2013	16	Miss B. Bencic (SUI)	1	Miss T. Townsend (USA)	5	4-6 6-1 6-4
2014	16	Miss J. Ostapenko (LAT)	U	Miss K. Schmiedlova (SVK)	8	2-6 6-3 6-0

Name	Date of Birth	Place of Birth	Note
ANTONOPLIS, Lea	20 Jan 1959	West Covina, California, USA	1
ARMSTRONG, Sheila	14 Jul 1939	Manchester, England	1
ARNOLD, Miriam	27 Feb 1939	Hollywood, California, USA	1
AUSTIN, Tracy Ann	12 Dec 1962	Los Angeles, California, USA	3
BAKSHEEVA, Galina	12 Jul 1945	Kiev, U.S.S.R.	1
BARTKOWICZ, Jane Marie (Peaches)	16 Apr 1949	Hamtramck, Michigan, USA	3
BARTY, Ashleigh	24 Apr 1996	Ipswich, Queensland, Australia	3
BENCIC, Belinda	10 Mar 1997	Flawil, Switzerland	3
BLACK, Cara Cavell	17 Feb 1979	Harare, Zimbabwe	3
BONDARENKO, Kateryna	8 Aug 1986	Krejery Rig, Ukraine, USSR	3
BOUCHARD, Eugenie Caitlin Murphy	25 Feb 1994	Montreal, Canada	3
CHMYREVA, Natasha	28 May 1958	Moscow, U.S.S.R.	1
CORNELL, Lorna Muriel	3 Jan 1933	London, England	1
CROFT, Annabel Nicola	12 Jul 1966	London, England	1
CROSS, Joan	9 Mar 1941	Port Elizabeth, Eastern Province, S.A.	1
DOMKEN, Genevieve	4 Sep 1927	Heusy-Verviers, Belgium	1
DOUCHEVINA, Vera	6 Oct 1986	Moscow, USSR	3
FEBER, Nancy	5 Feb 1976	Antwerp, Belgium	4
FLIPKENS, Kirsten	10 Jan 1986	Geel, Belgium	3
FREEMAN, Debbie	5 Jun 1962	Sydney, N.S.W., Australia	1
GARRISON, Zina Lynna	16 Nov 1963	Houston, Texas, USA	1
HANTZE, Karen Janice	11 Dec 1942	San Diego, California, USA	1
HAYDON, Adrianne Shirley	17 Oct 1938	Birmingham, England	2
HINGIS, Martina	30 Sep 1980	Kosice, Czechoslovakia	3
HOLIKOVA, Andrea	15 Jan 1968	Prague, Czechoslovakia	4
JAUSOVEC, Mima	20 Jul 1956	Maribor, Yugoslavia	1
KILIAN, Dora	5 Mar 1935	Barkley East, Cape Province, S.A.	1
KIYOMURA, Ann Kazuyo	22 Aug 1955	San Mateo, California, USA	1
KLOSS, Ilana Sheral	22 Mar 1956	Johannesburg, Transvaal, S.A.	2
KROSHINA, Marina	18 Apr 1953	Alma Ata, U.S.S.R.	1
LERTCHEEWAKARN Noppawan	18 Nov 1991	Chiang Mai, Thailand	3
LINDSTROM, Birgitta Maria	14 Jan 1948	Helsinki, Finland	1
MAURESMO, Amelie	5 Jul 1979	St. Germain en Laye, France	1
MERCELIS, Christiane	5 Oct 1931	Brussels, Belgium	1
MISKOVA, Olga	8 Apr 1929	Prague, Czechoslovakia	1

Name	Date of Birth	Place of Birth	Note
MOORE, Sally Maria	8 Jun 1940	Long Beach, California, USA	1
MOROZOVA, Olga Vasilevna	22 Feb 1949	Moscow, U.S.S.R.	1
OLSZA, Aleksandra	8 Dec 1977	Katowice, Poland	3
OSTAPENKO, Jelena	8 Jan 1997	Riga, Latvia	3
PARADIS, Pascale	24 Apr 1966	Troyes, France	1
PIATEK, Mary Lou	6 Aug 1961	Whiting, Indiana, USA	3
PIGEON, Kristine Sue	15 Aug 1950	San Mateo, California, USA	2
PITT, Valerie Anne	6 Jun 1936	Birmingham, England	1
PLISKOVA, Kristyna	21 Mar 1992	Louny, Czech Republic	4
RADWANSKA, Agnieszka Roma	6 Mar 1989	Krakow, Poland	3
RADWANSKA, Urszula	7 Dec 1990	Ahaus, Germany	3
RITTNER, Barbara	25 Apr 1973	Krefeld, Germany	3
ROBSON, Laura Margaret Dwyer	21 Jan 1994	Melbourne, Victoria, Austarlia	4
RUBIN, Chanda Renee	18 Feb 1976	Lafayette, Louisiana, USA	3
SALERNI, Maria Emilia	14 May 1983	Rafaela, Argentina	3
SALFATI, Monique	18 May 1945	Cannes, France	1
SALOME, Judith Henriette	10 Feb 1949	Amsterdam, The Netherlands	2
SAWAMATSU, Kazuko	5 Jan 1951	Nishinomiya, Japan	1
SCHULTZ, Brenda Anna Maria	28 Dec 1970	Haarlem, The Netherlands	1
SREBOTNIK, Katarina	12 Mar 1981	Slovenj Gradec, Yugoslavia	3
STRNADOVA, Andrea	28 May 1972	Prague, Czechoslovakia	3
TANVIER, Catherine	28 May 1965	Toulouse, France	3
ten BOSCH, Fenny Johanna Ina	12 Aug 1935	Voorburg, The Netherlands	1
TULYAGANOVA, Iroda	7 Jan 1982	Tashkent, Uzbekistan	3
WIDJAJA, Angelique	12 Dec 1984	Bandung, Indonesia	3
WALSH, Sharon Ann	24 Feb 1952	San Francisco, California, USA	1
WOZNIACKI, Caroline	11 Jul 1990	Odense, Denmark	1
ZVEREVA, Natalia Maratovna	16 Apr 1971	Minsk, U.S.S.R.	3

1. Right-handed   3. Right-handed, two handed backhand
2. Left-handed   4. Left-handed, two handed backhand

Girls' Doubles Championship

Trophies and Prizes

1982–1984	Champions (2)	Miniature Cup
	Runners-up (2)	Silver Pencil
1985–1987	Champions (2)	Silver Cup (AELTC)
		Miniature Cup
	Runners-up (2)	Silver Pencil
1988–2007	Champions (2)	Silver Cup (AELTC)
		Miniature Cup
	Runners-up (2)	Memento (Carriage clock)
2008–2011	Champions (2)	Silver Cup (AELTC)
		Silver Cup (½ size)
	Runners-up (2)	Silver Salver (6 inches)
2012–2015	Champions (2)	Silver Cup (AELTC)
		Three-quarter size Silver Cup
	Runners-up (2)	Silver Salver (6 inches)

Prize Money

Nil

Finals and Scores

Year	No. of Seeds	Winners	Seeding Position	Runners-up	Seeding Position	Score
1982	4	Miss P. Barg and Miss E.A. Herr (USA)	2	Miss B.S. Gerken and Miss G.A. Rush (USA)	3	6-1 6-4
1983	4	Miss P.A. Fendick (USA) and Miss P. Hy (HKG)	2	Miss C. Anderholm and Miss H. Olsson (SWE)	U	6-1 7-5
1984	4	Miss C. Kuhlman and Miss S.C. Rehe (USA)	U	Miss V. Milvidskaya and Miss L.I. Savchenko (URS)	1	6-3 5-7 6-4
1985	4	Miss L. Field and Miss J.G. Thompson (AUS)	4	Miss E. Reinach (RSA) and Miss J.A. Richardson (NZL)	2	6-1 6-1
1986	8	Miss M. Jaggard and Miss L. O'Neill (AUS)	8	Miss L. Meskhi and Miss N.M. Zvereva (URS)	6	7-6 (7-3) 6-7 (4-7) 6-4
1987	4	Miss N. Medvedeva and Miss N.M. Zvereva (URS)	4	Miss I.S. Kim (KOR) and Miss P.M. Moreno (HKG)	U	6-2 5-7 6-0
1988	8	Miss J.A. Faull and Miss R. McQuillan (AUS)	2	Miss A. Dechaume and Miss E. Derly (FRA)	1	4-6 6-2 6-3
1989	8	Miss J.M. Capriati and Miss M.J. McGrath (USA)	2	Miss A. Strnadova and Miss E. Sviglerova (TCH)	3	6-4 6-2
1990	8	Miss K. Habsudova and Miss A. Strnadova (TCH)	3	Miss N.J. Pratt and Miss K. Sharpe (AUS)	2	6-3 6-2
1991	4	Miss C. Barclay (AUS) and Miss L. Zaltz (ISR)	4	Miss J. Limmer and Miss A. Woolcock (AUS)	2	6-4 6-4
1992	8	Miss M. Avotins and Miss L. McShea AUS)	4	Miss P. Nelson and Miss J. Steven (USA)	7	2-6 6-4 6-3
1993	8	Miss L. Courtois and Miss N. Feber (BEL)	1	Miss H. Mochizuki and Miss Y. Yoshida (JPN)	5	6-3 6-4
1994	8	Miss E. De Villiers (RSA) and Miss E.E. Jelfs (GBR)	6	Miss C.M. Morariu (USA) and Miss L. Varmuzova (SMR)	2	6-3 6-4
1995	8	Miss C.C. Black (ZIM) and A. Olsza (POL)	3	Miss T. Musgrave and Miss J. Richardson (AUS)	4	6-0 7-6 (7-5)
1996	4	Miss O. Barabanschikova (BLR) and Miss A. Mauresmo (FRA)	U	Miss L. Osterloh and Miss S. Reeves (USA)	3	5-7 6-3 6-1
1997	4	Miss C.C. Black (ZIM) and Miss I. Selyutina (KAZ)	1	Miss M. Matevzic and Miss K. Srebotnik (SLO)	2	3-6 7-5 6-3
1998	4	Miss E. Dyrberg (DEN) and Miss J. Kostanic (CRO)	U	Miss P. Rampre (SLO) and Miss I. Tulyaganova (UZB)	U	6-2 7-6 (7-5)
1999	4	Miss D. Bedanova (CZE) and Miss M.E. Salerni (ARG)	2	Miss T. Perebiynis (UKR) and Miss I. Tulyaganova (UZB)	7	6-1 2-6 6-2
2000	8	Miss I. Gaspar (ROM) and Miss T. Perebiynis (UKR)	2	Miss D. Bedanova (CZE) and Miss M.E. Salerni (ARG)	1	7-6 (7-2) 6-3
2001	8	Miss G. Dulko (ARG) and Miss A. Harkleroad (USA)	3	Miss C. Horiatopoulos (AUS) and Miss B. Mattek (USA)	U	6-3 6-1
2002	8	Miss E. Clijsters (BEL) and Miss B. Strycova (CZE)	1	Miss A. Baker (USA) and Miss A-L. Groenfeld (GER)	2	6-4 5-7 8-6
2003	4	Miss A. Kleybanova (RUS) and Miss S. Mirza (IND)	U	Miss K. Bohmova (CZE) and Miss M. Krajicek (NED)	U	2-6 6-3 6-2
2004	8	Miss V.A. Azarenka and Miss V. Havartsova (BLR)	3	Miss M. Erakovic (NZL) and Miss M. Niculescu (ROM)	4	6-4 3-6 6-4
2005	8	Miss V.A. Azarenka (BLR) and Miss A. Szavay (HUN)	1	Miss M. Erakovic (NZL) and Miss M. Niculescu (ROM)	2	6-7 (5-7) 6-2 6-0
2006	8	Miss A. Klebanova and Miss A. Pavlyuchenkova (RUS)	2	Miss K. Antoniychuk (UKR) and Miss A. Dulgheru (ROM)	1	6-1 6-2

2007	8	Miss A. Pavlyuchenkova (RUS) 1 and Miss U. Radwanska (POL)	Miss M. Doi and Miss K. Nara (JPN)	U	6-4 2-6 (10-7)
2008	8	Miss P. Hercog (SLO) 6 and Miss J. Moore (AUS)	Miss I Holland and Miss S Peers (AUS)	U	6-3 1-6 6-2
2009	8	Miss N. Lertcheewakarn (THA) U and Miss S. Peers (AUS)	Miss K. Mladenovic (FRA) and Miss S. Njiric (CRO)	2	6-1 6-1
2010	8	Miss T. Babos (HUN) 4 and Miss S. Stephens (USA)	Miss I. Khromacheva (RUS) and Miss E. Svitolina (UKR)	1	6-7 (7-9) 6-2 6-2
2011	8	Miss E. Bouchard (CAN) 2 and Miss G. Min (USA)	Miss D. Schuurs (NED) and Miss H.C. Tang (CHN)	U	5-7 6-2 7-5
2012	8	Miss E. Bouchard (CAN) 1 and Miss T. Townsend (USA)	Miss B. Bencic (SUI) and Miss A. Konjuh (CRO)	U	6-4 6-3
2013	8	Miss B. Krejcikova Miss K. Siniakova (CZE)	Miss A. Kalinina (UKR) and Miss I Shymanovich (BLR)	8	6-3 6-1
2014	8	Miss T. Grende (INA) U and Miss Qui Yu Ye (CHN)	Miss M. Bouzkova (CZER) and Miss D. Galfi (HUN)	U	6-2 7-6 (5-5)

The following juniors were invited to Wimbledon in 1947 and competed in the first tournament: Boys: (10) Erwin Balestra (SUI), Jaromir Becka (CZE), Sven Davidson (SWE), Lennart Huguson (SWE), Petrus Sebastianus Lathouwers (NED), R. Mortlett (BEL), Kurt Nielsen (DEN), Francis Nys (FRA), Arthur Gordon Roberts (GBR), Jan Fredrik Ruud (NOR) Girls: (8) Miss Maria Akrivou (GRE), Miss Genevieve Domken (Mrs. A. Dubois) (BEL), Miss Evelyne Fery (Mrs. Scherrer) (SUI), Miss Lilli Henriksen (DEN), Miss Dora Holter-Soerensen (Mrs. Berggrau) (NOR), Miss Dien Johanna Vorenkamp (Mrs. Heuteman) (NED), Miss Helen Voultzos (Mrs. Ralli) (GRE), Miss Birgit Wallen (Mrs. Bjorklund) (SWE). Miss Patricia Rodgers (GBR) was present but did not compete.

Kurt Nielsen donated the Cup he won in 1947 to The Wimbledon Lawn Tennis Museum in 1979.

Junior Records

The Youngest Champions

Boys' Singles 1992	D.S. Koch (TCH)	15 years 242 days
Girls' Singles 1994	Miss M. Hingis (SUI)	13 years 276 days

Most Games in Match

Boys' Singles	— 75 R.Henry (AUS) bt C. Morel (FRA) 7-5 6-7 (3-7) 26-24 (2002 Second Round) (4hrs-15mins)
Boys' Doubles	— 60 A. Chesnokov and A. Olkovskiy (URS) bt A.G. Fichart (RSA) and M. Rodriguez (CHI) 5-7 6-4 20-18 (1983 First Round)
Girls' Singles	— 49 Miss A. Glatch (USA) bt Miss A. Kudryavtseva (RUS) 5-7 7-6 (7-3) 13-11 (2005-First Round)
Girls' Doubles	— 47 Miss V. Humphreys-Davies and Miss S.J. Loosemore (GBR) bt Miss V. Martinek and Miss M Zivec (GER) 6-7 (4-7) 6-4 13-11 (1988 First Round)

Most Games in a Set

Boys' Singles	— 50 R. Henry (AUS) by C. Morel (FRA) 7-6 6-7 (3-7) 26-24 (2002 Second Round) (2hrs 40 mins)
Boys' Doubles	— 38 A. Chesnokov and A. Olhovskiy (URS) bt A.G. Fichart (RSA) and M. Rodriguez (CHI) 5-7 6-4 20-18 (1983 First Round)

Girls' Singles	— 26 Miss S. Thunig (GER) bt Miss M. Kozelvhova (TCH) 6-2 14-12 (1968 First Round)
Girls' Doubles	— 24 Miss V. Humphreys-Davies and Miss S.J. Loosemore (GBR) bt Miss V. Martinek and Miss M. Zivec (GER) 6-7 (4-7) 6-4 13-11 (1988 First Round)
	— 24 Miss Y. Schnack and Miss K. Tsang (USA) by Miss W.H. Hsu (TPE) and Miss S.N. Sun (CHN) 4-6 6-4 13-11 (2004 First Round (1 hr 50 mins)

Most Points in a Tie-Break

Boys' Singles	— 36 M. Kasiri (GBR) bt R. Arevalo Gonzales (ESA) 6-0 7-6 (19-17) (2004 First Round)
Boys' Doubles	— 26 A. Brizzi (ITA) and J. Zimmermann (USA) bt A. Falla Ramirez and C. Salamanca (COL) 6-7 (12-14) 7-6 (7-5) 6-4 (2001 First Round)
Girls' Singles	— 32 Miss I. Selyutina (KAZ) bt Miss S. Rizzi (FRA) 7-6 (17-15) 6-1 (1997 Third Round)
Girls' Doubles	— 22 Miss Z. Reyes and Miss M. Torres (MEX) bt Miss C. Maes (BEL) and Miss T. Nemeth (HUN) 6-2 7-6 (12-10) (2000 First Round)

Junior Champions who have subsequently become Champions: Singles – B.R. Borg (SWE) 1972; P.H. Cash (AUS) 1982; S.B. Edberg (SWE) 1983; R. Federer (SUI) 1998; Miss A.S. Haydon (Mrs P.F. Jones) (GBR) 1956; Miss K.J. Hantze (Mrs J.R. Susman) (USA) 1960; Miss M. Hingis (SUI) 1994, Miss A. Mauresmo (FRA) 1996. Doubles – T.A. Woodbridge (AUS) 1987, 1988; J.E. Palmer (USA) 1989; Miss N.M. Zvereva (URS) 1987; Miss C.C. Black (ZIM) 1995.

Miscellaneous

In 1977, 2005 and 2014 both singles championships were unseeded.
In 2014 the winner of the Boys' Singles, N. Rubin (USA) was a qualifier.

Competitors – Longest names: -Boys-Trongcharoenchaikul, W (THA), 2013

-Girls-Barabanschikova, Olga (BLR), 1999

-Krasnoroutskaya, Lina (RUS), 1996

Qualifying Competition

A qualifying competition for the Boys' and Girls' Singles was held for the first time in 1998, during the Thursday and Friday of the first week of The Championships.

Year	Venue	No. of Entries		No. of Qualifiers	
		Boys	Girls	Boys	Girls
1998	Roehampton*	40	32	8	8
1999	Roehampton	32	25	8	8
2000	Roehampton**	31	32	8	8
2001–2015	Roehampton	32	32	8	8

Venue: Bank of England Sports Ground, Priory Lane, Roehampton, London, SW15.

*1998 Due to rain during the week, matches were played indoors with the boys at Esporta Club at Croydon and the girls at The David Lloyd Club, Raynes Park.
**2000 Due to rain on the Friday, matches were played indoors at the Sutton Junior Tennis Centre, Sutton.

Qualifiers and Lucky Losers

Boys' Singles

1998

Q (8) S. Aickele (GER), T. Higgins (GBR), D. Kiernan (GBR), P. King (USA), N. McDonald (RSA), L. Magdincev (MKD), L. Pampoulov (AUT), A. Park (USA).
LL (2) A. Kedryuk (KAZ), M. Ziwar (EGY).

1999

Q (8) S. Berke (USA), D. Britzen (GER), A. Bogomolov (USA), J. Froberg (SWE), U. Kiendl (GER), A. Kracman (SLO), Y. Miyazaki (JPN), L. Pampoulov (AUT).
LL (2) R. Becker (GER), R. Russell (JAM).
Note: R. Russell should have been shown as a Lucky Loser in the 'final' Wimbledon Programme.

2000

Q (8) A. Balzekas (LTU), R. Bloomfield (GBR), D. Khumalo (ZIM), R. Klaasen (RSA), G. Lapentti (ECU), C. Lewis (GBR), H. Mivzdeh (USA), L. Radovanovich (NZL).
LL (3) G.C. Capuccio (VEN), P. Harboe (CHI), R. Russell (JAM).

2001

Q (8) P. Amritraj (IND), B. Baker (USA), R. Durek (AUS), H. Heyl (RSA), J. Kanev (BUL), P. Petzschnev (GER), S. Sipaeya (IND), K. Skupski (GBR).

2002

Q (8) A. Skrypo (BLR), F. Mergea (ROM), A. Ruiz (MEX), R. Durek (AUS), C. Evans (GBR), A. Sitak (RUS), T. Gabashvili (RUS), D. Brown (JAM).
LL (1) A. Juska (LAT).

2003

Q (8) A. Kuznetsov (USA), R. Hutchins (GBR), R. Smeets (AUS), P.Steinberger (GER), D. Zivkovic (USA), D. Muller (GER), M. Lowe (GBR), K. Kravschuck (RUS).

2004

Q (8) K. Anderson (RSA), J. Chardy (FRA), T.Fujii (JPN), M. Fischer (AUT), R. Herold (GER), M. Kryvonos (USA), G. Ouellette (USA), J. Paukku (FIN).
LL (1) P.Oswald (AUT).

2005

Q (8) C. Hodl (AUT), M. Karpol (CRO), B. Koniecko (USA), J. Kosler, (CZE), P. Nicholls (AUS), K. Nishikori (JPN), P. Polansky (CAN), J. Strydom (NAM),
LL (2) A. Fattar (MAR), E. Masso (ARG).

2006

Q (8) G. Elias (POR), J-R. Velasco (BOL), J. Xu (CHN), J-P. Smith (AUS), M. Gawron (POL), R. Urzua (CHI), D. Sessagesimi (SUI), E. Rodriguez (COL) LL (NIL).

2007

Q (8) N. Angus (GBR), V. Dimov (BUL), A. Karatchenia (BLR), D. Kieftakos (GER), A. Martin (SVK), M. Szmigiel (POL), Ty. D. Trombetta (USA), M. Verryth (AUS).

2008

Q (8) D. Britton (USA), E. Crepaldi (ITA), H. Ehara (JPN), F. Krajinovic (SRB), P. Lang (AUT), D. Propoggia (AUS), M. Raonic (CAN), B. Rola (SLO)
LL (2) N. Moser (AUT), M. Ndimande (ZIM).

2009
Q (8) A. Bega (ITA), L. Broady (GBR), J. Cox (USA), K. Krawietz (GER), E. Molina (ITA), D. Thomson (GBR), J.R. van Overbeek (USA), A. Vasilevski (BLR).

2010
Q (8) S. Lavie (NZL), L. Burton (GBR), D. Webb (USA), B. Mitchell (AUS), M. Gecchinato (ITA), F. Corie (ARG), G. Barrere (FRA), M. Libietis (LAT).

2011
Q (8) R. Kern (GER), H. Ndayishimiye (BDI), O. Roca Batalla (ESP), E. Couacaud (ARG), D. Novikov (USA), N. Kyrgios (AUS), D. Novak (AUT), A. Alvarez Llamas (ESP).

2012
Q (8) S. Vinti (ITA), M. Marterer (GER), E. Ymer (SWE), T-S Kwiatkowski (USA), H. Ndayishimiye (BDI), P.T. Bague (ESP), S. Kozlov (USA), M. Routa (CZE).

2013
Q (8) J. Andrijic (AUS), J. Cash (GBR), J.I. Galleguillos (CHI), J. Haerteis (GER), J. Malik (GBR), J. O'Mara (GBR), W. Trongcharoenchaikul (THA), D. Windahl (SWE).

2014
Q (8) N. Rubin (USA), S-C. Hong (KOR), S-F. Soendergaard (DEN), M. Berrettini (ITA), A. Santillan (AUS), J. Arconada (ARG), R. Matos (BRA), A. Pellegrino (ITA)

Girls' Singles
1998
Q (8) R. Kern (GER), H. Ndayishimiye (BDI), O. Roca Batalla (ESP), E. Couacaud (ARG), D Novikov (USA), N. Kyrigios (AUS), D. Novak (AUT), A. Alvarez Llamas (ESP)

1999
Q (8) Miss R. Barnes (GBR), Miss L. Barnikow (USA), Miss N. Culum (SLO), Miss A. Nikolaeva (BLR), Miss J. Scaringe (USA), Miss S. Stosur (AUS), Miss N. Rencken (RSA), Miss C. Wallace (GBR). LL (1) Miss R. Uda (JPN).

2000
Q (8) Miss M. Adamczak (AUS), Miss B. Berecz (HUN), Miss M. Bradley (USA), Miss C. Grier (GBR), Miss J. Hewitt (AUS), Miss R. Llewellyn (GBR), Miss A. Nakamura (JPN), Miss J. Pandzic (CRO).
LL (2) Miss L. Van Den Knapp (NED), Miss N. Kriz (AUS).

2001
Q (8) Miss N. Brattchikova (RUS), Miss D. Casanova (SUI), Miss E. Laine (FIN), Miss L. Lopez (MEX), Miss K. O'Brien (GBR), Miss S. Peng (CHN), Miss N. Pitts (USA), Miss L. Smolenakova (SUK).

2002
Q (8) Miss E. Laine (FIN), Miss Y. Sema (JPN), Miss A. Barnes (GBR), Miss S. Tanaka (JPN), Miss T. Terblanche (RSA), Miss I. Kuryanovich (BLR), Miss R. Rankin (GBR), Miss T. Welford (AUS).
LL (3) Miss M. Tavares (BRA), Miss D. Ivanov (AUS), Miss M. Vialiamovskaia (RUS).

2003
Q (8) Miss S. Ferguson (AUS), Miss S. Dubois (CAN), Miss M. Falcon (USA), Miss A. Tchakvetadze (RUS), Miss M. Kawatoko (JPN), Miss M. Andersson (SWE), Miss A. Gonzales Penas (ARG), Miss V. Havartsova (BLR).

2004
Q (8) Miss K. Baker (GBR), Miss E. Kosminskaya (RUS), Miss E. Kirianova (RUS), Miss E Kobak (USA), Miss T. Mircic (SCG), Miss I. Pavlovic (FRA), Miss Y. Sema (JPN), Miss A-M. Zubori (FRA).
LL (2) Miss N. Thijssen (NED, Miss C. Wozniaki (DEN).

2005
Q (8) Miss E. Barry (NZL), Miss M. Gaverova (RUS), Miss M. Gloria (CAN), Miss S. Lisicki (GER), Miss S. McDowell (AUS), Miss U. Radwanska (POL), Miss A. Revzina (RUS), Miss A. Vermoezen (BEL).
LL (3) Miss C. Dentoni (ITA), Miss A-C. Duarte (BRA), Miss E. Nze (USA).

2006
Q (8) Miss T. Calderwood (AUS), Miss L. Litvak (USA), Miss K. Tuohimaa (FIN), Miss A. Berkova (CZE), Miss J. Bone (GBR), Miss M. Klaffner (AUT), Miss K. Kramperova (CZE), Miss A. Pivarova (RUS).

2007
Q (8) Miss A. Bai (AUS), Miss J. Boserup (USA), Miss K Frilling (USA), Miss J. Gavenko (RUS), Miss J. Jackson (GBR), Miss M. Mosolova (RUS), Miss S. Peers (AUS), Miss S. Roma (SWE).
LL (1) Miss D. Ripoll (GER).

2008
Q (8) Miss B. Borecka (CZE), Miss T. Calderwood (AUS), Miss G. Dabrowski (CAN), Miss S. Ishizu (JPN), Miss K. Narattana (THA), Miss R. Tabakova (SVK), Miss M. Trevisan (ITA).
LL (1) Miss A. Guarachi (USA).

2009
Q (8) Miss E. Bouchard (CAN), Miss M. Ejdesgaard (DEN), Miss L. Kurnkhum (THA), Miss A-S. Mestach (BEL), Miss A. Omae (JPN), Miss S. Peers (USA), Miss I. Stoica (ROM), Miss S. Vickery (USA).
LL (1) Miss A. van der Meer (NED).

2010
Q (8) Miss N. Beazant (USA), Miss S. Sharipova (UZB), Miss A. Sasnovich (BLR), Miss L. Butkovska (SVK), Miss K. Hardebeck (USA), Miss N. Abduraimova (UZB), Miss S. Shumilina (RUS), Miss C. De Bernadi (FRA).

2011
Q (8) Miss M. Katsitadze (RUS), Miss K. Lennert (GER), Miss C. Harrison (USA), Miss T. Smitkova (CZE), Miss R. Seaborne (GBR), Miss M. Bianco (SUI), Miss B. Haddad Maia (BRA), Miss S. Wagner (GER).

2012
Q (8) Miss V. Lushkova (UKR), Miss S. Sanders (AUS), Miss B. Haas (AUT), Miss E. Silva (GBR). Miss C. Harrison (USA), Miss A. Komardina (RUS), Miss N. Abduraimova (UZB), Miss I. Soylu (TUR).

2013
Q (8) Miss M. Adachi (JPN), Miss L. Cabera (AUS), Miss D. Chiesa (ITA), Miss J. Fett (CRO), Miss P. Horn (GBR), Miss D. Ivanova (USA), Miss G. Minnen (BEL), Miss K. Okamura (JPN).

2014
Q (8) Miss I. Soylu (TUR), Miss K. Sebov (CAN), Miss D. Galfi (HUN), Miss A. Brogan (GBR), Miss M. Gordon (USA), Miss Y. Ogando (PUR), Miss J. Mikulskyte (LTU), Miss H. Hutchinson(GBR)

Other Events

Gentlemen's Invitation Doubles

Trophies and Prizes

2007–	Winners (2)	Silver Cup (AELTC)
		Miniature silver salver
	Runners-up (2)	Silver Medal
2008–2011	Winners (2)	Silver Cup (AELTC)
		Silver Cup (4 inches)
	Runners-up (2)	Silver Medal
2012–2015	Winners (2)	Silver Cup (AELTC)
		Silver Cup Three-quarter size
	Runners-up (2)	Silver Medal

Prize Money (Pair) £'s

Year	Winners	Runners-up	Group Second Place	Group Third Place	Group Fourth Place
2007	16,500	13,500	10,000	9,000	8,000
2008	17,000	14,000	10,500	9,500	9,000
2009	17,000	14,000	10,500	9,500	9,000
2010	17,500	14,500	11,500	10,500	9,500
2011	17,500	14,500	11,500	10,500	9,500
2012	19,000	16,000	13,000	12,000	11,000
2013	20,000	17,000	14,000	13,000	12,000
2014	21,000	18,000	15,000	14,000	13,000
2015	22,000	19,000	16,000	15,000	14,000

Finals and Scores

Year	No. of Seeds	Winners	Seeding Position	Runners-up	Seeding Position	Score
2007	–	J.F. Eltingh and P.V.N. Haahuis (NED)	–	M.R.J. Petchey and C. Wilkinson (GBR)	–	6-2 6-2
2008	–	D.J. Johnson and J.E. Palmer (USA)	–	J.F. Eltingh and P.V.N. Haarhuis (NED)	–	W.O.
2009	–	J.F Eltingh and P.V.N. Haarhuis (NED)	–	D.J. Johnson and J.E. Palmer (USA)	–	7-6 (7-2) 6-4
2010	–	D.J. Johnson and J.E. Palmer (USA)	–	W. Ferreira (RSA) and Y Kafelnikov (RUS)	–	6-3 6-2
2011	–	J. Eltingh and P.V.N. Haarhuis (NED)	–	J.L. Bjorkman (SWE) and T.A. Woodbridge (AUS)	–	3-6 6-3 (13-11)
2012	–	G. Rusedski (GBR) and F. Santoro (FRA)	–	T. Enqvist (SWE) and M. Philippoussis (AUS)	–	6-7 (3-7) 6-4 (11-9)
2013	–	T. Enquist (SWE) and M. Philippoussis (AUS)	–	G. Rusedski (GBR) and F. Santoro (FRA)	–	7-6 (8-6) 6-3
2014	–	T. Enquist (SWE) and M. Philippoussis (AUS)	–	J. Eltingh and P. Haarhuis (NED)	–	3-6 6-3 10-8

2007–2015 – 8 pairs round robin

Gentlemen's Senior Invitation Doubles
Trophies and Prizes

2007–	Winners (2)	Silver Cup (AELTC)
		Miniature silver salver
	Runners-up (2)	Silver Medal
2008–2015	Winners (2)	Silver Cup (AELTC)
		Silver Cup half size
	Runners-up (2)	Silver Medal

Prize Money (Pair) £'s

Year	Winners	Runners-up	Group Second Place	Group Third Place	Group Fourth Place
2007	16,500	13,500	10,000	9,000	8,000
2008	17,000	14,000	10,500	9,500	9,000
2009	17,000	14,000	10,500	9,500	9,000
2010	17,500	14,500	11,500	10,500	9,500
2011	17,500	14,500	11,500	10,500	8,500
2012	19,000	16,000	13,000	12,000	11,000
2013	20,000	17,000	14,000	13,000	12,000
2014	21,000	18,000	15,000	14,000	13,000
2015	22,000	19,000	16,000	15,000	14,000

Finals and Scores

Year	No. of Seeds	Winners	Seeding Position	Runners-up	Seeding Position	Score
2007	–	M.J. Bates (GBR) and A.P. Jarryd (SWE)	–	K.M. Curren and J.C. Kriek (USA)	–	6-3 6-3
2008	–	K.E. Flach and R.A. Seguso (USA)	–	M.J. Bates (GBR) and A.P. Jarryd (SWE)	–	7-6 (7-1) 6-7 (5-7) (10-7)
2009	–	M.J. Bates (GBR) and A.P. Jarryd (SWE)	–	M. Bahrami (IRI) and H.Leconte (FRA)	–	6-4 7-6 (7-4)
2010	–	P.H. Cash and M.R. Woodforde (AUS)	–	M.J. Bates (GBR) A.P. Jarryd (SWE)	–	6-2 7-6 7-5
2011	–	P.H. Cash and M.R. Woodforde (AUS)	–	M.J. Bates (GBR) A.P. Jarryd(SWE)	–	6-3 5-7 (10-5)
2012	–	P.H. Cash and M.R. Woodforde (AUS)	–	M.J. Bates (GBR) A.P. Jarryd (SWE)	–	6-3 6-4
2013	–	P.H. Cash and M.R. Woodforde (AUS)	–	M.J. Bates (GBR) A.P. Jarryd (SWE)	–	6-3 6-3
2014	–	G. Forget and C. Pioline (FRA)	–	R. Leach (USA) and M.R. Woodforde (AUS)	–	6-4 6-3

2007–2015 – 8 pairs round robin

Ladies' Invitation Doubles
Trophies and Prizes

2007–	Winners (2)	Silver Cup (AELTC) Miniature silver salver
	Runners-up (2)	Silver Medal
2008–2011	Winners (2)	Silver Cup (AELTC) Silver Cup (4 inches)
	Runners-up (2)	Silver Medal
2012–2014	Winners (2)	Silver Cup (AELTC) Silver Cup three-quarter size
	Runners-up (2)	Silver Medal

Prize Money (Pair) £'s

Year	Winners	Runners-up	Group Second Place	Group Third Place	Group Fourth Place
2007	16,500	13,500	10,000	9,000	8,000
2008	17,000	14,000	10,500	9,500	9,000
2009	17,000	14,000	10,500	9,500	9,000
2010	17,500	14,500	11,500	10,500	9,500
2011	17,500	14,500	11,500	10,500	8,500
2012	19,000	16,000	13,000	12,000	11,000
2013	20,000	17,000	14,000	13,000	12,000
2014	21,000	18,000	15,000	14,000	13,000
2015	22,000	19,000	16,000	15,000	14,000

Finals and Scores

Year	No. of Seeds	Winners	Seeding Position	Runners-up	Seeding Position	Score
2007	–	Miss J. Novotna and Miss H. Sukova (CZE)	–	Miss I. Kloss and Mrs R. Nideffer (RSA)	–	6-3 6-3
2008	–	Miss J. Novotna (CZE) and Miss K. Rinaldi (USA)	–	Miss M. Navratilova (USA) and Mis H. Sukova (CZE)	–	5-7 6-3 (10-5)
2009	–	Miss M. Navratilova (USA) and Miss H. Sukova (CZE)	–	Miss I. Kloss and Mrs R. Nideffer (ESA)	–	6-3 6-2
2010	–	Miss M. Navratilova (USA) and Mis J Novotna (CZE)	–	Miss T. Austin and Mrs K. Stunkel (USA)	–	7-5 6-0
2011	–	Miss L.A. Davenport (USA) and Miss M. Hingis (SWI)	–	Miss M. Navratilova (USA) Miss J. Novotna (CZE)	–	6-4 6-4
2012	–	Miss L.A. Davenport (USA) and Miss M. Hingis (SUI)	–	Miss M. Navratilova (USA) and Miss J. Novotna (CZE)	–	6-3 6-2
2013	–	Miss L.A. Davenport (USA) and Miss M. Hingis (SUI)	–	Miss J. Novotna (CZE) and Miss B. Schett (AUT)	–	6-2 6-2
2014	–	Miss J. Novotna (CZE) and Miss B. Schett (AUT)	–	Miss M. Navratilova (USA) and Miss S. Sfar (TUN)	–	6-0 7-6 (7-1)

2007–2015 – 8 pairs round robin

Wheelchair Gentlemen's Doubles

Trophies and Prizes

2005–2015	Winners (2)	Cup (AELTC)
		Silver salver (8 inches)
	Runners-up (2)	Silver Medal

Prize Money (Pair) £'s

Year	Winners	Runners-up	Third Place	Fourth Place
2005	2,600	1,800	1,000	600
2006	2,600	1,800	1,000	600
2007	6,000	3,200	1,800	1,000
2008	6,750	3,750	2,250	1,250
2009	6,750	3,750	2,250	1,250
2010	7,000	4,000	2,500	1,500
2011	7,000	4,000	2,500	1,500
2012	8,000	4,500	2,750	1,750
2013	8,500	5,000	3,250	2,250
2014	12,000	6,000	4,000	3,000
2015	15,000	7,750	5,250	4,000

Finals and Scores

Year	No. of Seeds	Winners	Seeding Position	Runners-up	Seeding Position	Score
2005	2	M. Jeremiasz (FRA) and J. Mistry (GBR)	1	D. Hall (AUS) and M. Legner (AUT)	2	4-6 6-3 7-6 (7-3)
2006	2	S. Kunieda and S. Saida (JPN)	1	M. Jeremiasz (FRA) and J. Mistry (GBR)	U	7-5 6-2
2007	2	R. Ammerlaan and R. Vink (NED)	2	S. Kunieda and S. Saida (JPN)	1	4-6 7-5 6-2
2008	2	R. Ammerlaan and R. Vink (NED)	1	S. Houdel and N. Peifer (FRA)	2	6-7 (6-8) 6-1 6-3
2009	2	S. Houdet and M. Jeremiasz (FRA)	S	R. Ammerlaan (NED) and S. Kunieda (JPN)	U	1-6 6-4 7-6 (7-3)
2010	2	R. Ammerlaan (NED) and S. Olsson (SWE)	U	S. Houdet (FRA)) and S. Kunieda (JPN)	1	6-4 7-6 (7-4)
2011	–	M. Scheffers and R. Vink (NED)	1	S. Houdet and M. Jeremiasz (FRA)	U	7-5 6-2
2012	2	T. Egberink (NED) and H. Jeremiasz (FRA)	U	R. Ammeriaan and R. Vink (NED)	1	6-4 6-2
2013	2	S. Houdet (FRA) and S. Kunieda (JPN)	1	F. Cattaneo (FRA) and R. Vink (NED)	2	6-4 6-2
2014	2	S. Houdet (FRA) and S. Kunieda (JAP)	1	M. Scheffers and R. Vink (NED)	2	2-6 6-2 7-5

2005–2015 – 4 pairs

Wheelchair Ladies' Doubles

Trophies and Prizes

2009–2015	Winners (2)	Cup (AELTC)
		Silver salver (8 inches)
	Runners-up (2)	Silver Medal

Prize Money (Pair) £'s

Year	Winners	Runners-up	Third Place	Fourth Place
2009	6,750	3,750	2,250	1,250
2010	7,000	4,000	2,500	1,500
2011	7,000	4,000	2,500	1,500
2012	8,000	4,500	2,750	1,750
2013	8,500	5,000	3,250	2,250
2014	12,000	6,000	4,000	3,000
2015	15,000	7,750	5,520	4,000

Finals and Scores

Year	No. of Seeds	Winners	Seeding Position	Runners-up	Seeding Position	Score
2009	2	Miss K. Homan and Miss E. Vergeer (NED)	S	Miss D. Di Toro (AUS) and Miss L. Shuker (GBR)	U	6-1 6-3
2010	2	Miss E. Vergeer and Miss S. Walraven (NED)	1	Miss D. Di Toro (AUS) and Miss L. Shuker (GBR)	U	6-2 6-3
2011	2	Miss E. Vergeer and Miss S. Walraven (NED)	1	Miss J. Griffioen and Miss A. Van Koot (NED)	2	6-4 3-6 7-5
2012	2	Miss J. Griffioen and Miss A. Vankoot (NED)	U	Miss l. Shuker (GBR) and Miss J. Whiley		6-1 6-2
2013	2	Miss J. Griffioen and Miss A. Van Koot (NED)	1	Miss Y. Kamiji (JPN) and Miss J. Whiley (GBR)	–	6-4 7-6 (8-6)
2014	2	Miss Ykamiji (JAP) and Miss J. Whiley (GBR)	1	Miss J. Griffoen and Miss A. Van Koot (NED)	2	5-7 6-0 6-3

2009–2015 – 4 pairs

From 2012 the diameter of all silver medals was increased from 38mm to 50mm. They are presented in a box with new Wimbledon logo.

Events No Longer Held

The All England Plate (1896–1981)

Trophies and prizes

1896–1906	Winner Runner-up	First prize – value £5 Second prize – value £3
1907–1911	Winner Runner-up Semi-finalists (2)	First prize – value £5 Second prize – value £3 Third prize – value £1.10s.
1912–1914 1919–1939 1946–1955	Winner Runner-up	First prize – value £5 Second prize – value £3
1956	Winner Runner-up	Silver Salver (H.M. Yeatman) First prize – value £5 Second prize – value £3
1957–1964	Winner Runner-up	Silver Salver (H.M. Yeatman) Miniature replica of trophy First prize – value £5 Second prize – value £3
1965–1969	Winner Runner-up	Silver Salver (H.M. Yeatman) Miniature replica of trophy First prize – value £10 Second prize – value £6
1970–1974	Winner Runner-up	Silver Salver (H.M. Yeatman) Miniature replica of trophy First prize – value £30 Second prize – value £15

Prize Money

1975–1981	Winner	Silver Salver (H.M. Yeatman) Miniature replica of trophy

Prize Money £'s

Year	Winner	Runner-up	Semi-Finalists	Quarter-Finalists	Losers Third Round	Losers Second Round	Losers First Round
1975	500	300	200	150	100	75	50
1976	750	500	300	200	100	75	50
1977	900	600	400	200	100	75	50
1978	1,080	720	480	240	120	90	60
1979	1,100	750	500	250	125	95	65
1980	1,155	785	525	265	132	100	68
1981	1,250	850	570	280	140	105	70

In 1981, byes who lost in the Second Round counted as First Round Losers.

Finals and scores

Qualification

From 1896 to 1974. Players beaten in the first and second rounds of the Gentlemen's Singles Championship.

From 1975 to 1981. Players beaten in the first, second and third rounds of the Gentlemen's Singles Championship and players taking part only in the Doubles events.

Year	Winner	Runner-up	Score
1896	A.W. Gore (BRI)	H.L. Doherty (BRI)	1-6 6-2 7-5
1897	H. Baddeley (BRI)	A.E. Crawley (BRI)	6-1 6-3 5-7 6-2
1898	G.W. Hillyard (BRI)	A.C. Pearson (BRI)	6-3 8-6
1899	W.V. Eaves (BRI)	G.W. Hillyard (BRI)	w.o.
1900	G. Greville (BRI)	E.D. Black (BRI)	6-2 4-6 6-3
1901	P.G. Pearson (BRI)	H.W. Davies (BRI)	6-1 4-6 6-2 7-5
1902	B. Hillyard (BRI)	C.R.D. Pritchett (BRI)	8-6 6-1
1903	A.W. Gore (BRI)	C. Hobart (USA)	7-5 6-3
1904	G. Greville (BRI)	B. Hillyard (BRI)	6-3 6-0
1905	W.V. Eaves (BRI)	B. Murphy (AUS)	6-3 6-2
1906	G.W. Hillyard (BRI)	T.M. Mavrogordato (BRI)	6-2 6-4
1907	A.F. Wilding (NZL)	C. von Wessely (AUT)	6-3 6-4
1908	O. Kreuzer (GER)	V.R. Gauntlett (RSA)	6-3 6-4
1909	R.B. Powell (CAN)	H.A. Parker (NZL)	3-6 6-3 6-1
1910	A.H. Gobert (FRA)	P.M. Davson (BRI)	6-4 6-4
1911	A.H. Lowe (BRI)	J.C. Parke (BRI)	6-0 8-6
1912	F.M. Pearson (BRI)	F.E. Barritt (AUS)	6-0 10-8
1913	F.G. Lowe (BRI)	F.F. Roe (BRI)	8-10 6-3 6-3
1914	C.P. Dixon (BRI)	R.W.F. Harding (BRI)	6-1 6-2
1919	F.L.R. Crawford (BRI)	M. Woosnam (BRI)	6-3 5-7 7-5
1920	F.G. Lowe (BRI)	C.P. Dixon (BRI)	1-6 8-6 6-3
1921	J.B. Gilbert (BRI)	F.M.B. Fisher (NZL)	7-5 4-6 6-0
1922	B.I.C. Norton (RSA)	R.C. Wertheim (AUS)	6-2 6-2
1923	J. Washer (BEL)	M.J.G. Ritchie (GBR)	6-3 6-4
1924	J.J. Condon (RSA)	J.M. Hillyard (GBR)	7-5 6-2
1925	B. von Kehrling (HUN)	R. George (FRA)	6-3 6-4
1926	J.B. Gilbert (GBR)	F.L.R. Crawford (GBR)	10-8 6-2
1927	A. Gentien (FRA)	O.G.N. Turnbull (GBR)	1-6 6-2 6-0
1928	M. Sleem (IND)	J.B. Gilbert (GBR)	6-3 6-3

1929	E.G. Chandler (USA)	W.H. Powell (GBR)	6-4 6-1
1930	E. du Plaix (FRA)	C.E. Malfroy (NZL)	6-1 8-6
1931	V.G. Kirby (RSA)	G.E.L. Rogers (IRL)	2-6 6-3 6-3
1932	H.J. Cochet (FRA)	T. Kuwabara (JPN)	6-2 6-4
1933	F.H.D. Wilde (GBR)	J.D.P. Wheatley (GBR)	6-2 6-4
1934	H.W. Artens (AUT)	C.R.D. Tuckey (GBR)	5-7 7-5 6-1
1935	J. Yamagishi (JPN)	J. Lesueur (FRA)	6-2 6-2
1936	D.N. Jones (USA)	I.G. Collins (GBR)	6-0 6-2
1937	W.R. Sabin (USA)	N.G. Farquharson (RSA)	2-6 6-0 6-3
1938	D.W. Butler (GBR)	O. Szigeti (HUN)	6-1 8-10 6-3
1939	W.D. McNeill (USA)	J. van den Eynde (BEL)	8-6 6-2
1946	R. Abdesselam (FRA)	C. Spychala (POL)	7-5 6-3
1947	E.W. Sturgess (RSA)	A.J. Mottram (GBR)	6-3 6-3
1948	F.H. Ampon (PHI)	H. Weiss (ARG)	11-9 6-4
1949	E.H. Cochell (USA)	G.P. Jackson (IRL)	4-6 6-3 6-1
1950	G.L. Paish (GBR)	J. Brichant (BEL)	6-4 6-4
1951	N.M. Cockburn (RSA)	K.H. Ip (HKG)	7-5 5-7 10-8
1952	L.A. Ayala (CHI)	N. Kumar (IND)	8-6 6-2
1953	G.L. Paish (GBR)	J.W. Ager (USA)	4-6 6-0 7-5
1954	H.W. Stewart (USA)	A. Vieira (BRA)	8-6 6-4
1955	N.A. Fraser (AUS)	R.N. Howe (AUS)	6-2 7-5
1956	H.W. Stewart (USA)	G.P. Mulloy (USA)	4-6 6-4 6-4
1957	G.L. Forbes (RSA)	A.A. Segal (RSA)	10-8 11-13 6-3
1958	P. Remy (FRA)	J.N. Grinda (FRA)	6-3 11-9
1959	J. Javorsky (TCH)	M. Fox (USA)	6-3 6-2
1960	T. Ulrich (DEN)	O. Sirola (ITA)	6-4 7-5
1961	J. Ulrich (DEN)	N. Kumar (IND)	6-4 10-12 6-3
1962	J.A. Douglas (USA)	A.A. Segal (RSA)	3-6 6-2 6-3
1963	E.L. Scott (USA)	I.S. Crookenden (NZL)	w.o.
1964	R.K. Wilson (GBR)	W.W. Bowrey (AUS)	6-4 6-3
1965	O.K. Davidson (AUS)	T.S. Okker (NED)	6-3 8-6
1966	R. Taylor (GBR)	R.N. Howe (AUS)	6-4 2-6 7-5
1967	J.H. McManus (USA)	E.L. Scott (USA)	6-3 6-2
1968	G. Battrick (GBR)	H.S. FitzGibbon (USA)	6-4 3-6 7-5
1969	T. Koch (BRA)	R.O. Ruffels (AUS)	6-1 6-3
1970	R.R. Maud (RSA)	R.R. Barth (USA)	6-4 6-3
1971	R.D. Crealy (AUS)	P.S. Cornejo (CHI)	6-3 6-4
1972	K.G. Warwick (AUS)	*	w.o.
1973	J.G. Clifton (GBR)	S.G. Messmer (USA)	6-4 4-6 6-1
1974	T.I. Kakulia (URS)	P.C. Kronk (AUS)	6-3 7-5
1975	T. Koch (BRA)	V.K. Gerulaitis (USA)	6-3 6-2
1976	B.E. Fairlie (NZL)	R. Taylor (GBR)	4-6 6-3 6-4
1977	M.C. Riessen (USA)	G.E. Reid (USA)	6-4 5-7 9-7
1978	D.H. Collings (AUS)	T.W. Wilkison (USA)	3-6 9-8 (9-7) 6-4
1979	P.C. Kronk (AUS)	M.R. Edmondson (AUS)	6-7 ( ) 6-2 6-4
1980	S. Glickstein (ISR)	P. Dominguez (FRA)	6-3 7-6 (7-2)
1981	D.J. Carter (AUS)	C.M. Johnstone (AUS)	6-3 6-4

*Both players retired at semi-final stage.

The All England Ladies' Plate (1933–1989)

Trophies and prizes

1933–1939	Winner	First prize – value £5
1946–1956	Runner-up	Second prize – value £3

1957–1964	Winner	Silver Cup (A.H. Riseley)
		Miniature replica of cup
		First prize – value £5
	Runner-up	Second prize – value £3

1965–1969	Winner	Silver Cup (A.H. Riseley)
		Miniature replica of cup
		First prize – value £10
	Runner-up	Second prize – value £6

1970–1974	Winner	Silver Cup (A.H. Riseley)
		Miniature replica of cup
		First prize – value £30
	Runner-up	Second prize – value £15

Prize Money

1975–1989	Winner	Silver Cup (A.H. Riseley)
		Miniature replica of cup

Prize Money £'s

Year	Winner	Runner-up	Semi-Finalists	Quarter-Finalists	Losers Third Round	Losers Second Round	Losers First Round
1975	350	225	150	100	-	75	50
1976	350	225	150	100	87.5	75	50
1977	720	480	320	160	80	40	25
1978	864	576	384	192	99	48	30
1979	880	600	400	200	100	52	33
1980	925	628	420	212	105	55	35
1981	1,000	680	456	224	110	60	40
1982	1,300	880	600	300	145	80	50
1983	1,700	1,100	750	375	180	100	70
1984	2,550	1,650	1,125	563	270	150	105
1985	3,315	2,145	1,465	730	350	195	140
1986	3,570	2,310	1,574	785	375	210	150
1987	3,950	2,560	1,740	870	415	235	165
1988	4,205	2,725	1,850	925	440	250	175
1989	4,845	3,150	2,130	1,065	510	290	200

From 1975 to 1989, byes who lost in the Second Round counted as First Round Losers.

Finals and scores

Qualification

From 1933 to 1974. Players beaten in the first and second rounds of the Ladies' Singles Championship.

From 1975 to 1982. Players beaten in the first, second and third rounds of the Ladies' Singles Championship and also players taking part in only the Doubles events.

From 1983 to 1989. Players beaten in the first and second rounds of the Ladies' Singles Championship and also players taking part only in the Doubles events.

Year	Winner	Runner-up	Score
1933	Miss C. Rosambert (FRA)	Miss J. Goldschmidt (FRA)	6-4 6-1
1934	Miss L. Valerio (ITA)	Miss J. Saunders (GBR)	7-5 6-3
1935	Miss L. Valerio (ITA)	Miss A.E.L. McOstrich (GBR)	6-1 1-6 6-0
1936	Miss F.S. Ford (GBR)	Miss J.M. Riddell (GBR)	6-4 6-4
1937	Miss W.A. James (GBR)	Miss M.E. Lumb (GBR)	6-0 7-5
1938	Miss D. Stevenson (AUS)	Miss J.M. Hartigan (AUS)	6-4 6-4
1939	Mrs. R.D. McKelvie (GBR)	Miss A. Weiwers (LUX)	6-4 4-6 6-2
1946	Miss J. Jedrzejowska (POL)	Miss P.A. O'Connell (GBR)	6-4 7-5
1947	Miss J. Jedrzejowska (POL)	Mrs. N.W. Blair (GBR)	6-2 7-5
1948	Mrs. H. Weiss (ARG)	Miss E.M. Wilford (GBR)	6-1 5-7 7-5
1949	Mrs. A. Bossi (ITA)	Miss B. Gulbrandsson (SWE)	6-0 7-5
1950	Miss K.L.A. Tuckey (GBR)	Miss B. Rosenquest (USA)	6-4 6-1
1951	Mrs. F.J. Bartlett (RSA)	Miss G.E. Woodgate (GBR)	3-6 6-1 6-2
1952	Mrs. B. Abbas (EGY)	Miss C.G. Hoahing (GBR)	0-6 6-4 6-3
1953	Miss M.P. Harrison (GBR)	Miss E.F. Lombard (IRL)	1-6 6-3 6-3
1954	Miss R. Walsh (GBR)	Miss P.A. Hird (GBR)	6-2 7-5
1955	Miss E.F. Muller (AUS)	Miss L.L. Felix (USA)	6-4 6-4
1956	Mrs. T.D. Long (AUS)	Miss I. Buding (GER)	6-3 6-4
1957	Miss M.B. Hellyer (AUS)	Miss R. Schuurman (RSA)	6-4 6-4
1958	Miss S. Reynolds (RSA)	Miss M.B. Hellyer (AUS)	6-2 6-2
1959	Mrs. C.W. Brasher (GBR)	Mrs. M. Sladek (CAN)	3-6 6-3 7-5
1960	Miss D.M. Catt (GBR)	Mrs. J.W. Cawthorn (GBR)	6-3 6-2
1961	Miss R.H. Bentley (GBR)	Miss A. Dimitrieva (URS)	6-4 3-6 6-3
1962	Miss M.L. Gerson (RSA)	Miss M.B. Hellyer (AUS)	6-2 6-1
1963	Miss F.G. Durr (FRA)	Miss A. Dimitrieva (URS)	6-1 6-3
1964	Mrs. C. Sukova (TCH)	Miss J.C. Bricka (USA)	0-6 6-2 6-2
1965	Miss A. Dimitrieva (URS)	Miss F.E. Truman (GBR)	6-2 6-1
1966	Miss P.M. Walkden (RSA)	Mrs. J.A.G. Lloyd (GBR)	6-4 6-0
1967	Miss P.S.A. Hogan (USA)	Miss G.V. Sherriff (AUS)	6-2 9-7
1968	Miss S.V. Wade (GBR)	Miss K.M. Harter (USA)	6-2 12-10
1969	Miss B.A. Grubb (USA)	Miss L.A. Rossouw (RSA)	6-3 4-6 6-4
1970	Miss E.F. Goolagong (AUS)	Miss L. Liem (INA)	6-2 6-1
1971	Miss M.R. Wainwright (GBR)	Miss B.F. Stove (NED)	6-4 0-6 6-2
1972	Miss K.M. Krantzcke (AUS)	Miss S.A. Walsh (USA)	6-1 6-4
1973	Miss H.F. Gourlay (AUS)	Miss V.A. Burton (GBR)	6-1 4-6 6-1
1974	Miss M.V. Kroshina (URS)	Miss L.J. Beaven (GBR)	6-3 8-6
1975	Miss D.L. Fromholtz (AUS)	Miss V.A. Burton (GBR)	6-4 6-2
1976	Miss M.B.K. Wikstedt (SWE)	Miss A. Bruning (USA)	4-6 6-3 6-3
1977	Miss Y. Vermaak (RSA)	Miss S. Mappin (GBR)	6-2 7-5
1978	Miss T.E. Guerrant (USA)	Miss H. Strachanova (TCH)	6-2 8-6
1979	Miss S.D. Barker (GBR)	Miss S.P.M. Simmonds (ITA)	7-6 ( ) 6-0
1980	Miss R.D. Fairbank (RSA)	Miss S.A. Walsh (USA)	6-4 6-2
1981	Miss S.E. Saliba (AUS)	Miss P.S. Casale (USA)	6-3 6-3

1982	Miss C.C. Monteiro (BRA)	Miss R.L. Blount (USA)	6-3 2-6 6-2
1983	Miss A.J. Brown (GBR)	Miss A.M. Tobin (AUS)	3-6 6-3 6-4
1984	Miss M.L. Brown (USA)	Miss R.M. White (USA)	6-2 7-5
1985	Miss E. Reinach (RSA)	Miss T.A. Holladay (USA)	6-4 6-2
1986	Miss P.H. Shriver (USA)	Miss S.C. Rehe (USA)	4-6 7-6 (7-1) 6-0
1987	Miss S.L. Gomer (GBR)	Miss K.A. Gompert (USA)	6-3 6-4
1988	Mrs. S.W. Magers (USA)	Miss S.L. Gomer (GBR)	6-1 retd.
1989	Miss W.E. White (USA)	Miss E. Reinach (RSA)	6-3 6-4

Ladies' Doubles (1899–1907)
(Non-Championship)

Trophies and prizes

| 1899–1907 | Winners (2) | First prize – value £5 |
| | Runners-up (2) | Second prize – value £2.10s. |

Finals and scores

Year	Winners	Runners-up	Score
1899	Mrs. G.W. Hillyard and Miss B. Steedman (BRI)	Mrs. N.J. Dulacher and Mrs. W.H. Pickering (BRI)	6-4 2-6 6-4
1900	Mrs. W.H. Pickering and Miss M.E. Robb (BRI)	Mrs. G.W. Hillyard and Miss L.M. Martin (BRI)	2-6 6-4 6-4
1901	Mrs. G.W. Hillyard and Mrs. A. Sterry (BRI)	Countess Schulenburg (GER) and Mrs. W.H. Pickering (BRI)	6-3 6-0
1902	Miss A.M. Morton and Mrs. A. Sterry (BRI)	Miss H. Lane and Miss C.M. Wilson (BRI)	w.o.
1903	Miss D.K. Douglass and Mrs. W.H. Pickering (BRI)	Miss H. Lane and Miss C.M. Wilson (BRI)	6-2 6-1
1904	Miss W.A. Longhurst and Miss E.W. Thomson (BRI)	Miss D.K. Douglass and Mrs. A. Sterry (BRI)	6-4 3-6 7-5
1905	Miss W.A. Longhurst and Miss E.W. Thomson (BRI)	Miss A.M. Morton (BRI) and Miss M.G. Sutton (USA)	6-3 6-3
1906	Mrs. G.W. Hillyard (BRI) and Miss M.G. Sutton (USA)	Miss A.M. Morton and Mrs. A. Sterry (BRI)	10-8 6-4
1907	Mrs. R.L. Chambers and Miss C.M. Wilson (BRI)	Miss A.M. Morton and Mrs. A. Sterry (BRI)	7-9 6-3 6-2

Mixed Doubles (1900–1912)
(Non-Championship)

Trophies and prizes

| 1900–1912 | Winners (2) | First prize – value £5 |
| | Runners-up (2) | Second prize – value £2.10s. |

Finals and scores

Year	Winners	Runners-up	Score
1900	H.A. Nisbet and Mrs. W.H. Pickering (BRI)	H.R. Barrett and Miss E.J. Bromfield (BRI)	8-6 6-3
1901	H.L. Doherty and Mrs. A. Sterry (BRI)	W.V. Eaves and Mrs. N.J. Durlacher (BRI)	6-2 6-3
1902	H.L. Doherty and Mrs. A. Sterry (BRI)	C.H.L. Cazalet and Miss M.E. Robb (BRI)	6-4 6-3
1903	S.H. Smith and Miss E.W. Thomson (BRI)	C. Hobart (USA) and Miss E.J. Bromfield (BRI)	6-2 6-3
1904	S.H. Smith and Miss E.W. Thomson (BRI)	W.V. Eaves and Mrs. R.J. Winch (BRI)	7-5 12-10
1905	A.W. Gore and Miss C.M. Wilson (BRI)	A.F. Wilding (NZL) and Miss E.W. Thomson (BRI)	8-6 6-4
1906	A.F. Wilding (NZL) and Miss D.K. Douglass (BRI)	A.W. Gore and Miss E.W. Thomson (BRI)	4-6 6-2 6-3
1907	B.C. Wright and Miss M.G. Sutton (USA)	A.D. Prebble and Miss P.D.H. Boothby (BRI)	6-1 6-3
1908	A.F. Wilding (NZL) and Mrs. R.L. Chambers (BRI)	H.R. Barrett and Mrs. A. Sterry (BRI)	6-4 6-3
1909	H.R. Barrett and Miss A.M. Morton (BRI)	A.D. Prebble and Miss P.D.H. Boothby (BRI)	6-2 7-5
1910	S.N. Doust (AUS) and Mrs. R.L. Chambers (BRI)	R.B. Powell (CAN) and Mrs. A. Sterry (BRI)	6-2 7-5
1911	T.M. Mavrogordato and Mrs. E.G. Parton (BRI)	S.N. Doust (AUS) and Mrs. R.L. Chambers (BRI)	6-2 6-4
1912	J.C. Parke and Mrs. D.T.R. Larcombe (BRI)	A.D. Prebble and Miss P.D.H. Boothby (BRI)	6-4 6-2

Gentlemen's Doubles-Veterans (1964–1977, 1980).

Trophies and prizes

1964	Winners (2)	First prize – value £10
	Runners-up (2)	Second prize – value £5
1965	Winners (2)	First prize – value £20
	Runners-up (2)	Second prize – value £10
1966–1969	Winners (2)	Silver Cup (A.R.F. Kingscote) Memento
	Runners-up (2)	First prize – value £20 Second prize – value £10
1970–1976	Winners (2)	Silver Cup (A.R.F. Kingscote) Memento
	Runners-up (2)	Silver Medal
1977	Nil	

1980	Winners (2)	Silver Cup (A.R.F. Kingscote)
		Memento
	Runners-up (2)	Silver Medal

Prize Money (pair)

1964–1976, 1980 Nil
1977   Winners – £1,500; Runners-up – £800; Third – £500; Fourth – £300: Group;
                second place – £225; third place – £150; fourth place – £100.

Finals and scores

Year	Winners	Runners-up	Score
1964	B.J.Y. Destremau (FRA) and W.F. Talbert (USA)	G.R. McCall and A.V. Martini (USA)	7-5 6-3
1965	G.P. Mulloy and W.F. Talbert (USA)	G.R. McCall and A.V. Martini (USA)	6-3 6-1
1966	G.P. Mulloy and W.F. Talbert (USA)	R.J. Freedman and R.V. Sherman (USA)	6-8 6-2 6-3
1967	J. Drobny (GBR) and A.V. Martini (USA)	R.J. Freedman and R.V. Sherman (USA)	6-2 6-4
1968	J. Drobny (GBR) and A.V. Martini (USA)	S. Match and G.P. Mulloy (USA)	6-2 7-5
1969	J. Drobny (GBR) and E.V. Seixas (USA)	E.G. Slack and R.C. Sorlien (USA)	9-7 8-6
1970	J. Drobny (GBR) and R.L. Riggs (USA)	G.R. McCall and F. Segura (USA)	6-2 6-2
1971	G.P. Mulloy and A. Vincent (USA)	L.S. Clark and E.V. Seixas (USA)	6-3 6-2
1972	L.S. Clark and E.V. Seixas (USA)	G.P. Mulloy and A. Vincent (USA)	6-3 9-8 ( )
1973	J.D. Budge (USA) and F.A. Sedgman (AUS)	L. Bergelin (SWE) J. Drobny (GBR)	4-6 6-3 6-4
1974	R. Dunas and G.P. Mulloy (USA)	H.K. Richards and R.C. Sorlien (USA)	6-3 6-2
1975	L. Bergelin (SWE) and J.E. Patty (USA)	J.D. Budge and G.P. Mulloy (USA)	6-3 6-3
1976	L. Bergelin (SWE) and J.E. Patty (USA)	H.K. Richards and R.C. Sorlien (USA)	6-1 4-6 6-1
1977	S.V. Davidson (SWE) and T. Ulrich (DEN)	R.N. Hartwig (AUS) and E.V. Seixas (USA)	8-6 6-4
1980	R. Becker and R.K. Wilson (GBR)	A.A. Segal and O.G. Williams (RSA)	6-2 6-2

Grand Masters' Singles (1978)

Trophies and prizes

1978	Winner	Challenge Cup (AELTC)
		Memento
	Runner-up	Silver Medal

Prize Money

1978	Winner – £1,600; Runner-up – £1,000; Semi-finalists – £700; Losers Second Round – £500; Losers First Round – £400.

Final and score

Year	Winner	Runner-up	Score
1978	S.V. Davidson (SWE)	N.A. Fraser (AUS)	6-4 3-6 8-6

Grand Masters' Doubles (1978–1979)

Trophies and prizes

1978	Winners (2)	Silver Cup (A.R.F. Kingscote)
		Memento
	Runners-up (2)	Silver Medal
1979	Winners (2)	Silver Cup (A.R.F. Kingscote)
		Memento
	Runners-up (2)	Silver Medal

Prize Money (pair)

1978	Winners – £1,600; Runners-up – £1,100; Semi-finalists – £500; Losers first round – £400.
1979	Nil

Finals and scores

Year	Winners	Runners-up	Score
1978	R.N. Hartwig and F.A. Sedgman (AUS)	R.A. Gonzales and W.R. Reed (USA)	6-0 6-1
1979	R.N. Hartwig and F.A. Sedgman (AUS)	N.A. Fraser (AUS) and R.A. Gonzales (USA)	6-3 3-6 6-4

35 and Over Gentlemen's Invitation Singles (1982–1991)

Trophies and Prizes

1982–1991	Winner	Cup (AELTC)
		Miniature silver salver
	Runner-up	Silver Medal

Prize Money £'s

Year	Winner	Runner-up	Semi-Finalists	Quarter-Finalists	Losers Third Round
1982	2,500	2,000	1,250	750	500
1983	5,000	4,000	2,500	1,500	1,000
1984	7,500	6,000	3,750	2,250	1,500
1985	10,000	8,000	5,000	3,000	2,000
1986	10,750	8,600	5,380	3,230	2,150
1987	11,300	9,050	5,650	3,400	2,250
1988	12,000	9,635	6,015	3,620	2,395
1989	12,930	10,345	6,465	3,880	2,585
1990	15,000	12,000	7,500	4,500	3,000
1991	15,000	12,000	7,500	3,000	2,000

Finals and Scores

Year	Winner	Runner-up	Score
1982	J.D. Newcombe (AUS)	F.D. McMillan (RSA)	6-4 7-6 ( )
1983	C.S. Dibley (AUS)	R.J. Moore (RSA)	6-2 6-2
1984	S.R. Smith (USA)	C.S. Dibley (AUS)	7-6 (7-5) 6-3
1985	S.R. Smith (USA)	J.J. Fillol (CHI)	4-6 7-6 (7-3) 7-6 (7-5)
1986	J.J. Fillol (CHI)	A.D. Roche (AUS)	6-3 6-2
1987	T.R. Gullikson (USA)	R. C. Lutz (USA)	6-3 7-6 (7-3)
1988	T.R. Gullikson (USA)	T.E. Gullikson (USA)	6-2 7-6 (13-11)
1989	T.R. Gullikson (USA)	T.E. Gullikson (USA)	7-5 6-3
1990	T.R. Gullikson (USA)	T.E. Gullikson (USA)	4-6 6-2 7-6 (7-2)
1991	T.E. Gullikson (USA)	J.M. Lloyd (GBR)	7-6 (9-7) 3-6 6-2

Pre-Qualifying Competition (1983–2003)

From 1983 to 2003 The Lawn Tennis Association held Wimbledon Pre-Qualifying singles events two weeks before The Championships with entries restricted to British players: ie those qualified to represent Great Britain under rule 35 of the "Rules of the L.T.A.".

In the early years the number of players accepted in the Competition varied from year to year. From 1993 to 1998 the entry was restricted to 48 gentlemen and 32 ladies.

In 2004 the events were discontinued and amalgamated with the LTA Wild Card Play-off competitions.

The matches were played outside the All England Lawn Tennis Club.

Number of Entries and Qualifiers

Years	Venue	Gentlemen's Singles		Ladies' Singles	
		Entries	No. of Qualifiers	Entries	No. of Qualifiers
1983	Surbiton				
1984	Surbiton	84	6	50	6
1985	Surbiton	99	6	30	6
1986	Surbiton	108	6	47	6
1987	Richmond		6	46	6
1988	Richmond	72	6	35	6
1989	Richmond		6		6
1990	Richmond	48	6	37	6
1991	Richmond	48	4	34	4
1992	Chiswick	48	6	32	4
1993	Chiswick	48	4	33	4
1994	Chiswick	44	4	32	4
1995	Surbiton	48	4	36	4
1996	Surbiton	39	4	32	4
1997	Chiswick	48	4	32	4
1998	Chiswick	48	4	29	4
1999	Chiswick	48	4	22	3
2000	Chiswick	48	4	24	3
2001	Chiswick	48	4	29	4
2002	Chiswick	48	4	32	4
2003	Chiswick	48	4	24	3

Venues: Surbiton LTC, Berrylands, Surbiton, Surrey.
Richmond Cricket Club, Old Deer Park, Kew Road, Richmond, Surrey.
Civil Service Sports Ground, Dukes Meadows, Chiswick, London, W4 2SH.

Qualifiers

Gentlemen's Singles

1983
Details not available

1984
(6) A. Alfred, C. Clarke, D.C. Felgate, J.M. Goodall, S.A. King, P.L. Reekie.

1985
(6) M.T. Blincow, S. Botfield, D.C. Felgate, P.E. Hughesman, H.S. McGuiness, P.L. Reekie.

1986
(6) L. Alfred, M.R.E. Appleton, S. Botfield*, D.C. Felgate, J.M. Goodall, M.T. Walker*
direct into the main Championship draw as Wild Cards

1987
Details not available

1988
(6) P.T. Hand, S. Heron, J.J. Hunter, L. Matthews, A. Rouse, C. Wilkinson.

1989
Details not available

1990
(6) A.L. Foster, P.T. Hand, R.S. Matheson, A. Rouse, N. Russell, C. Wilkinson..

1991
(4) S.C.S Cole, L. Matthews, P.C. Robinson, A. Rouse.

1992
(6) C. Beecher, P.T. Hand, T.H. Henman, D. Kirk, U. Nganga, M. Schofield.

1993
(4) N.P. Broad, C. Beecher, G. Henderson, D.E. Sapsford.

1994
(4) C. Beecher, P.T. Hand, G. Henderson, D.E. Sapsford.

1995
(4) N. Gould*, P.T. Hand, P. Martin, D. Williams.
*Withdrew

1996
(4) P.T. Hand, W. Herbert, N. Weal, M. Wyeth.

1997
(4) C. Bennett, B.A. Cowan, P.T. Hand, P. Maggs.

1998
(4) J. Delgado, R. Matheson, T. Spinks, N. Weal.

1999
(4) J. Davidson, P.T. Hand, D.E. Sapsford, N. Weal.
(Sapsford went on to win through the Qualifying competition and reach the third round of The Championships.)

2000
(4) C. Bennett, L. Childs, N. Gould, J. Nelson.

2001
(4) J. Davidson, R. Hanger, J. Smith, N. Weal.

2002
(4) A. Banks, S. Dickson, J. Fox, J. Layne.

2003
(4) D. Sanger (GBR), C. Lewis (GBR), I. Flanagan (GBR), T. Burn (GBR).

Ladies' Singles
1983
Details not available

1984
(6) Miss C.H. Berry, Miss B.A. Borneo, Miss L. Geeves, Miss L.C. Gracie, Miss E.D. Lightbody, Miss D. Parnell.

1985
(6) Miss B.A. Borneo, Miss L. Geeves, Miss L.C. Gracie, Miss J. Griffiths, Miss V. Lake, Miss S.T. Mair.

1986
(6) Miss B.A. Borneo*, Miss G.L. Coles*, Miss A.L. Grunfeld*, Miss J. Louis*, Miss D. Parnell*, Miss J.M. Tacon.*
direct into main Championship draw as Wild Cards

1987
(6) Miss T.A. Catlin*, Miss G.L. Coles, Miss L.C. Gould*, Miss A.L. Grunfeld*, Miss J. Louis*, Miss J.V. Wood.*
direct into main Championship draw as Wild Cards

1988
(6) Miss B.A. Borneo, Miss A.L. Grunfeld*, Miss K.F. Hunter, Miss S.L. Smith, Miss S.L. Sullivan, Miss J.M. Tacon.
direct into main Championship draw as Wild Card

1989
Details not available

1990
(6) Miss C.L. Billingham, Miss T.A. Catlin, Miss S. Gulati, Miss K.D. Hand, Miss A.S. Hill, Miss K. Rickett.

1991
(4) Miss C.L. Billingham, Miss N. Giles, Miss V. Lake, Miss J. Wood.

1992
(4) Miss B. Griffith, Miss C.J. Herbert, Miss J.A. Salmon, Miss T. Wainwright.

1993
(4) Miss L.A. Ahl, Miss C.L. Billingham, Miss E.L. Bond, Miss A.E. Smith.

1994
(4) Miss C.J. Herbert, Miss Z. Mellis, Miss A.E. Smith, Miss L.A. Woodroffe.

1995
(4) Miss K.D. Hand, Miss M.L. Mair, Miss A.M.H. Wainwright, Miss J. Ward.

1996
(4) Miss L.A. Ahl, Miss J.M.Pullin, Miss S-A. Siddall, Miss J. Wood.

1997
(4) Miss H. Crook, Miss A. Janes, Miss E.E. Jelfs, Miss K.V. Warne-Holland.

1998
(4) Miss L. Herbert, Miss C. Lyte, Miss J. Moore, Miss K.V. Warne-Holland.

1999
(3) Miss L. Herbert, Miss E.E. Jelfs, Miss K.V. Warne-Holland.

2000
(3) Miss E. Baltacha, Miss V.E. Davies, Miss J. O'Donoghue.

2001
(4) Miss A. Barnes, Miss K.M. Cross, Miss A. Janes, Miss J. Ward.

2002
(4) Miss H. Crook, Miss C. Grier, Miss A. Janes, Miss M. South.

2003
(3) Miss H. Crook, Miss A. Janes, Miss A. Hawkins (GBR).

35 and Over Gentlemen's Invitation Doubles (1983–2006)
Trophies and Prizes

1983–2006	Winners (2)	Silver Cup (AELTC)
		Miniature silver salver
	Runners-up (2)	Silver Medal

Prize Money (Pair) £'s

Year	Winners	Runners-up	Semi-Finalists	Quarter-Finalists	Losers First Round
1983	4,000	3,000	2,000	—	1,000
1984	6,500	4,500	3,000	—	1,500
1985	8,000	6,000	4,000	—	2,000
1986	8,620	6,460	4,300	—	2,150
1987	9,050	6,780	4,520	—	2,260
1988	9,630	7,220	4,810	—	2,400
1989	10,343	7,760	5,170	—	2,590
1990	12,000	9,000	6,000	—	3,000
1991	12,000	9,000	6,000	4,500	3,000

Year	Winners	Runners-up	Semi-Finalists	Group Second Place	Group Third Place	Group Fourth Place
1992	14,000	10,000	7,000	5,500	4,500	3,500
1993	15,000	11,000	8,000	6,000	4,700	3,500
1994	12,000	9,500	7,500	6,000	5,500	5,000
1995	12,700	10,050	7,900	6,350	5,800	5,300
1996	13,250	10,500	8,250	6,600	6,050	5,530
1997	14,000	11,000	8,650	6,950	6,350	5,800
1998	14,500	11,400	9,000	7,200	6,600	6,000
1999	15,000	11,780	9,300	7,470	6,810	6,150
2000	15,500	12,170	9,610	7,720	7,040	6,360
2001	16,000	12,560	9,920	7,970	7,260	6,560
2002	16,000	12,560	9,920	7,970	7,260	6,560
2003	16,000	12,560	9,920	7,970	7,260	6,560
2004	16,250	12,760	10,080	8,090	7,380	6,660
2005	16,250	12,760	10,080	8,090	7,380	6,660
2006	16,250	12,760	10,080	8,090	7,380	6,660

Finals and Scores

Year	No. of Seeds	Winners	Seeding Position	Runners-up	Seeding Position	Score
1983	4	S.E. Stewart (USA) and F.S. Stolle (AUS)	1	O.K. Davidson (AUS) and E.C. Drysdale (RSA)	4	7-6 (7-5) 6-2
1984	4	M.C. Riessen and S.E. Stewart (USA)	2	C.S. Dibley (AUS) and J. Fillol (CHI)	U	6-3 3-6 11-9

Year	No. of Seeds	Winners	Seeding Position	Runners-up	Seeding Position	Score
1985	4	C.S. Dibley (AUS) and J. Fillol (CHI)	2	M.C. Riessen and S.E. Stewart (USA)	1	6-3 7-5
1986	4	M.C. Riessen and S.E. Stewart (USA)	1	C.S. Dibley (AUS) and J. Fillol (CHI)	2	6-3 6-4
1987	4	T.E. Gullikson and T.R. Gullikson (USA)	1	M.C. Riessen and S.E. Stewart (USA)	2	7-6 (11-9) 6-4
1988	4	R.A. J. Hewitt and F.D. McMillan (RSA)	U	K.R. Rosewall and F.S. Stolle (AUS)	U	6-4 7-5
1989	4	An. Amritraj and V. Amritraj (IND)	U	R.C. Lutz and R.L. Stockton (USA)	U	6-3 6-2
1990	4	P.B. McNamara and P.F. McNamee (AUS)	2	T.E. Gullikson and T.R. Gullikson (USA)	1	6-7 (2-7) 7-6 (7-2) 13-11
1991	4	P.B. Fleming and S.R. Smith (USA)	U	P.B. McNamara and P.F. McNamee (AUS)	1	7-6 (7-4) 7-6 (7-4)
1992	4	P.B. Fleming and S.R. Smith (USA)	S	M.R. Edmondson and K.G. Warwick (AUS)	U	6-7 (5-7) 7-6 (7-5) 6-4
1993	4	P.B. Fleming and H.E. Pfister (USA)	S	P.B. McNamara and P.F. McNamee (AUS)	S	6-4 3-6 6-1
1994	4	H.P. Guenthardt (SUI) and B. Taroczy (HUN)	U	A.M. Jarrett and J.R. Smith (GBR)	U	6-7 (2-7) 6-3 6-2
1995	4	P.B. McNamara (AUS) and L. Shiras (USA)	S	M. Bahrami (IRN) and J. Higueras (ESP)	U	7-6 (12-10) 7-5
1996	4	W. Fibak (POL) and T. Wilkison (USA)	U	P. Slozil and T. Smid (CZE)	U	6-2 5-7 6-1
1997	4	M.J. Bates (GBR) and R. Krishnan (IND)	S	K.M. Curren and J.C. Kriek (USA)	U	6-4 6-4
1998	4	G. Mayer and T. Wilkison (USA)	U	G.W. Donnelly (USA) and D.T. Visser (RSA)	S	6-4 7-5
1999	4	K.E. Flach and R.A. Seguso (USA)	U	P.B. McNamara and P.F. McNamee (AUS)	U	6-3 3-6 9-7
2000	4		Divided			
		K.E. Flach and R.A. Seguso (USA)	S	M.J. Bates and N.A. Fulwood (GBR)	U	
2001	4	J.B. Fitzgerald and W. Masur (AUS)	S	S. Casal and E. Sanchez (ESP)	U	7-6 (6-2) 6-0
2002	4	S.E. Davis and D.B. Pate (USA)	U	M.J. Bates and N.A. Fulwood (GBR)	U	6-3 7-6 (7-3)
2003	4	M.J. Bates and N.A. Fulwood (GBR)	S	G.W. Donnelly and L.B. Jensen (USA)	U	6-2 6-4
2004	4	T.J. Middleton and D. Wheaton (USA)	U	C.A. Pioline (FRA) and R.A. Seguso (USA)	S	4-6 6-1 6-1
2005	4	E. R. Ferreira (RSA) and P.V.N. Haarhuis (NED)	S	T.J. Middleton and D.Wheaton(USA)	S	6-3 6-4
2006	4	T.A. Woodbridge and M.R. Woodforde (USA)	S	T.J. Middleton and D. Wheaton (USA)	U	6-3 7-6 (7-3)

1983–1990 –8 pairs, 1991 – 12 pairs, 1992–2006 – 16 pairs round robin.

45 and Over Gentlemen's Invitation Doubles (1992–2006)
Trophies and Prizes

1992–2006	Winners (2)	Silver Cup (AELTC)
		Miniature silver salver
	Runners-up (2)	Silver Medal

Prize Money (Pair) £'s

Year	Winners	Runners-up	Semi-Finalists	Losers Third Round	Losers Second Round	Losers First Round
1992	11,000	9,000	6,000	–	–	3,000
1993	12,000	9,000	6,500	–	4,500	3,000
1994	9,500	7,500	6,000	–	5,000	4,500
1995	10,100	7,900	6,350	–	5,300	4,750
1996	10,500	8,250	6,650	–	5,500	5,000
1997	11,000	8,750	7,000	–	5,750	5,000
1998	11,400	9,000	7,200	–	6,000	5,200
1999	11,780	9,300	7,470	–	6,150	5,370
2000	12,170	9,610	7,720	–	6,360	5,550
2001	12,560	9,920	7,970	6,560	5,730*	5,000
2002	12,560	9,920	7,970	–	6,560	5,730
2003	12,560	9,920	7,970	–	6,560	5,730
2004	12,760	10,080	8,090	–	6,660	5,820
2005	12,760	10,080	8,090	–	6,660	5,820

*Byes losing in the Second Round count as First Round Losers.

Year	Winners	Runners-up	Semi-Finalists	Group Second place	Group third place
2006	13,000	10,250	8.250	6,750	6,000

Finals and Scores

Year	No. of Seeds	Winners	Seeding Position	Runners-up	Seeding Position	Score
1992	4	M.C. Riessen and S.E. Stewart (USA)	1	J.D. Newcombe and A.D. Roche (AUS)	2	3-6 6-3 6-3
1993	3	M.C. Riessen and S.E. Stewart (USA)	1	J.D. Newcombe and A.D. Roche (AUS)	2	7-5 7-6 (7-3)
1994	4	J.D. Newcombe and A.D. Roche (AUS)	2	K.R. Rosewall and F.S. Stolle (AUS)	4	6-1 6-2
1995	4	J.D. Newcombe and A.D. Roche (AUS)	1	O.K. Davidson (AUS) and E.C. Drysdale (RSA)	3	6-4 7-5
1996	4	J.G Alexander and P.C. Dent (AUS)	U	M.C. Riessen and S.E. Stewart (USA)	3	7-6 (7-3) 6-2
1997	4	J.Fillol (CHI) and R.L. Stockton (USA)	U	O.K. Davidson (AUS) and E.C. Drysdale (RSA)	U	6-1 6-2
1998	4	M.C. Riessen and S.E. Stewart (USA)	4	B.E. Gottfried and T.R. Gullikson (USA)	U	W.O.
1999	4	B.E. Gottfried and T.R. Gullikson (USA)	2	R.L. Case and G. Masters (AUS)	U	6-1 7-6 (7-0)
2000	4	P.B. Fleming and A. Mayer (USA)	U	A. Amritraj and V. Amritraj (IND)	U	6-2 6-4
2001	4	P.B. McNamara and P.F. McNamee (AUS)	2	C. Dowdeswell and C.J. Mottram (GBR)	U	6-4 6-3
2002	4	C. Dowdeswell and C.J. Mottram (GBR)	2	P.B. Fleming and A. Mayer (USA)	3	7-5 6-4
2003	4	K.M. Curren and J.C. Kriek (USA)	U	C. Dowdeswell and C.J. Mottram (GBR)	1	6-3 6-0
2004	4	K.M. Curren and J.C. Kriek (USA)	1	H.P. Guenthardt (SUI) and B. Taroczy (HUN)	3	4-6 6-1 6-4

| 2005 | 4 | K.M. Curren and J.C. Kriek (USA) | 1 | P.B. McNamara and P.F. McNamee (AUS) | U | 6-4 3-6 7-6 (7-4) |
| 2006 | 4 | K.M. Curren and J.C. Kriek (USA) | S | P.B. McNamara and P.F. McNamara (AUS) | S | 7-5 6-7 (8-10) 7-6 (11-9) |

1992 – 8 pairs, 1993–1996 – 12 pairs, 1997–2000 – 16 pairs, 2001 – 20 pairs, 2002-2005 – 16 pairs.
2006 – 12 pairs round robin.

35 and Over Ladies' Invitation Doubles (1990-2006)
Trophies and Prizes

| 1990–2006 | Winners (2) | Silver Cup (AELTC) Miniature silver cup |
| | Runners-up (2) | Silver Medal |

Prize Money (Pair) £'s

Year	Winners	Runners-up	Semi-Finalists	Losers First Round
1990	9,600	7,200	4,800	2,400
1991	9,600	7,200	4,800	2,400
1992	10,000	8,000	5,000	2,500
1993	10,500	7,500	5,000	2,750
1994	8,500	6,500	5,000	4,000
1995	9,000	6,900	5,300	4,200

Year	Winners	Runners-up	Group Second Place	Group Third Place	Group Fourth Place
1996	9,400	7,200	5,500	5,000	–
1997	10,000	7,500	5,750	5,250	4,500
1998	10,400	7,800	6,000	5,450	4,650
1999	10,700	8,030	6,150	5,630	4,800
2000	11,050	8,290	6,360	5,810	4,960
2001	11,410	8,560	6,560	6,000	5,120
2002	11,410	8,560	6,560	6,000	5,120
2003	11,410	8,560	6,560	6,000	5,120
2004	11,590	8,690	6,660	6,090	5,200
2005	11,590	8,690	6,660	6,090	5,200
2006	11,590	8,690	6,660	6,090	5,200

Playback

Year	Winners	Runners-up	Losers First Round
1993	1,000	750	500
1994	1,000	750	500
1995	1,050	800	550

Finals and Scores

Year	No. of Seeds	Winners	Seeding Position	Runners-up	Seeding Position	Score
1990	4	Miss W.M. Turnbull (AUS) and Miss S.V. Wade (GBR)	1	Miss R. Casals and Mrs. M.H. Pete (USA)	2	6-2 6-4
1991	4	Miss W.M. Turnbull (AUS) and Miss S.V. Wade (GBR)	1	Miss R. Casals and Mrs. M.H. Pete (USA)	2	6-3 6-4
1992	4	Miss W.M. Turnbull (AUS) and Miss S.V. Wade (GBR)	1	Miss R. Casals and Miss S.A. Walsh (USA)	2	3-6 6-3 7-5
1993	4	Miss H.E.. Nagelsen and Miss J.C. Russell (USA)	2	Miss W.M. Turnbull (AUS) and Miss S.V. Wade (GBR)	1	3-6 6-3 6-3
1994	4	Miss W.M. Turnbull (AUS) and Miss S.V. Wade (GBR)	2	Miss H.E. Nagelsen and Miss J.C. Russell (USA)	1	6-1 3-6 13-11
1995	4	Miss W.M. Turnbull (AUS) and Miss S.V. Wade (GBR)	1	Miss H.E. Nagelsen and Miss J.C. Russell (USA)	2	6-3 7-6 (7-5)
1996	2	Miss J.M. Durie (GBR) and Miss A.E. Smith (USA)	U	Miss M. Jausovec (SLO) and Miss Y. Vermaak (RSA)	U	6-3 6-2
1997	2	Miss J.M. Durie (GBR) and Miss A.E. Smith (USA)	S	Miss W.M. Turnbull (AUS) and Miss S.V. Wade (GBR)	U	6-2 6-1
1998	2	Miss P.H. Shriver (USA) and Mrs. P.D. Smylie (AUS)	S	Miss J.M. Durie (GBR) and Miss A.E. Smith (USA)	S	3-6 6-4 6-3
1999	2	Mrs. P.D. Smylie and Miss W.M. Turnbull (AUS)	S	Mrs. S.W. Magers (USA) and Miss B.F. Stove (NED)	U	7-5 6-3
2000	2	Mrs. R. Nideffer and Miss Y. Vermaak (RSA)	U	Mrs. S.W. Magers (USA) and Miss S.V. Wade (GBR)	U	6-4 6-2
2001	2	Miss I.S. Kloss and Mrs. R. Nideffer (RSA)	U	Miss J.M. Durie (GBR) and Miss M. Jausovec (SLO)	U	6-4 5-7 6-3
2002	2	Miss M. Jausovec (SLO) and Mrs. S.W. Magers (USA)	U	Mrs R. Nideffer (RSA) and Miss H.Sukova (CZE)	S	6-3 6-3
2003	2	Miss I.S. Kloss (RSA) and Miss K.S. Rinaldi (Mrs. B. Stunkel) (USA)	U	Miss J.M. Durie (GBR) and Mrs. S.W. Magers (USA)	U	6-4 4-6 7-5
2004	2	Miss M. Jausovec (SLO) and Miss J. Novotna (CZE)	U	Miss J.M. Durie (GBR) and Miss H. Sukova (CZE)	U	1-6 7-5 6-1
2005	2	Miss T.A. Austin (USA) and Miss J. Novotna (CZE)	S	Miss K. Adams (USA) and Mrs R. Nideffer (USA)	U	6-2 6-4
2006	2	Mrs R. Nideffer (USA) and Miss J. Novotna (CZE)	S	Miss T.A. Austin (USA) and Miss N. Tauziat (FRA)	S	6-4 6-3

1990–1992 – 8 pairs, 1993–1995 – 8 pairs with play back, 1996 – 6 pairs round robin, 1997–2006 – 8 pairs round robin.

Other Major Events Staged at Wimbledon

Davis Cup

Worple Road

1904   Final Round. Belgium beat France 3-2 on 27–29 June (Centre Court).

      Challenge Round. British Isles beat Belgium 5-0 on 2, 4 and 5 July (Centre Court).

1905   Challenge Round. British Isles beat USA 5-0 on 21, 22 and 24 July (Centre Court).

1906   Challenge Round. British Isles beat USA 5-0 on 15, 16 and 18 June (Centre Court).

1907   First Round. Australasia beat USA 3-2 on 13, 15 and 16 July (Centre Court).

      Challenge Round. Australasia beat British Isles 3-2 on 20, 22 and 23 July (Centre Court).

1913   Final Round. USA beat Canada 3-0 on 18 and 19 July (Centre Court)).

      Challenge Round. USA beat British Isles 3-2 on 25, 26 and 28 July (Centre Court).

1914   Second Round. British Isles beat France 4-1 on 11, 13 and 14 July (Centre Court).

1920   Second Round. USA beat British Isles 5-0 on 16, 17 and 19 July (Centre Court).

Church Road

1933   European Zone Final Round. Great Britain beat Australia 3-2 on 13–15 July (Centre Court).

1934   Inter-Zone Final Round. USA beat Australia 3-2 on 21, 23–25 July (Centre Court).

      Challenge Round. Great Britain beat USA 4-1 on 28, 30 and 31 July (Centre Court).

1935   Inter-Zone Final Round. USA beat Germany 4-1 on 20, 22–24 July (No. 1 Court).

      Challenge Round. Great Britain beat USA 5-0 on 27, 29 and 30 July (Centre Court).

1936   Inter-Zone Final Round. Australia beat Germany 4-1 on 18, 20 and 21 July (No. 1 Court).

      Challenge Round. Great Britain beat Australia 3-2 on 25, 27 and 28 July (Centre Court).

1937   Inter-Zone Final Round. USA beat Germany 3-2 on 17, 19 and 20 July (Centre Court).

      Challenge Round. USA beat Great Britain 4-1 on 24, 26 and 27 July (Centre Court).

1939   European Zone Third Round. Great Britain beat France 3-2 on 25–27 May (No. 1 Court).

1949   European Zone Second Round. Czechoslovakia beat Great Britain 4-1 on 14, 16 and 17 May (No. 1 Court).

1951   European Zone Second Round. Great Britain beat France 3-2 on 19, 21 and 22 May (No. 1 Court).

1960   European Zone Semi-Final Round. Italy beat Great Britain 4-1 on 14–16 July (No. 1 Court).

1963   European Zone Final Round. Great Britain beat Sweden 3-2 on 1–3 and 5 August (No. 1. Court).

1969   Inter-Zone Semi-Final Round. Great Britain beat Brazil 3-2 on 31 July, 1–3 August (No. 1 Court).

      Inter-Zone Final Round. Romania beat Great Britain 3-2 on 14–16 August (No. 1 Court).

1976   European Zone B Final Round. Italy beat Great Britain 4-1 on 5–7 August (No. 1 Court).

1986   Non-Zonal Competition Quarter-Final Round. Australia beat Great Britain 4-1 on 18–20 July (No. 1 Court).

1996   Euro/African Zone Group II. Great Britain beat Egypt 5-0 on 20-22 September (No. 1 Court).

2000   World Group Qualifying Round – Ecuador beat Great Britain 3-2 on 14–16 July (No. 1 Court).

2007 World Group Qualifying Round – Great Britain beat Croatia 4-1 on 21–23 September (No. 1 Court).

2008 World Group Qualifying Round – Austria beat Great Britain 3-2 on 19–21 September (No. 1 Court)

Wightman Cup

1924 Great Britain beat USA 6-1 on 18, 19 June (Centre Court).
1926 USA beat Great Britain 4-3 on 17, 18 June (Centre Court).
1928 Great Britain beat USA 4-3 on 15, 16 June (Centre Court).
1930 Great Britain beat USA 4-3 on 13, 14 June (Centre Court).
1932 USA beat Great Britain 4-3 on 10, 11 June (Centre Court).
1934 USA beat Great Britain 5-2 on 15, 16 June (Centre Court).
1936 USA beat Great Britain 4-3 on 12, 13 June (Centre Court).
1938 USA beat Great Britain 5-2 on 10, 11 June (Centre Court).
1946 USA beat Great Britain 7-0 on 14, 15 June (No. 1 Court).
1948 USA beat Great Britain 6-1 on 11, 12 June (No. 1 Court).
1950 USA beat Great Britain 7-0 on 16, 17 June (No. 1 Court).
1952 USA beat Great Britain 7-0 on 13, 14 June (No. 1 Court).
1954 USA beat Great Britain 6-0 on 11, 12 June (No. 1 Court).
1956 USA beat Great Britain 5-2 on 15, 16 June (No. 1 Court).
1958 Great Britain beat USA 4-3 on 13, 14 June (No. 1 Court).
1960 Great Britain beat USA 4-3 on 10, 11 June (No. 1 Court).
1962 USA beat Great Britain 4-3 on 15, 16 June (No. 1 Court).
1964 USA beat Great Britain 5-2 on 12–14 June (No. 1 Court).
1966 USA beat Great Britain 4-3 on 10, 11 June (No. 1 Court).
1968 Great Britain beat USA 4-3 on 14, 15 June (No. 1 Court).
1970 USA beat Great Britain 4-3 on 12, 13 June (No. 1 Court).
1972 USA beat Great Britain 5-2 on 16, 17 June (No. 1 Court).

Olympic Games

1908 6–11 July – Worple Road
Gentlemen's Singles – Final: M.J.G. Ritchie (BRI) beat O. Froitzheim (GER) 7-5 6-3 6-4.
Gold Medal – M.J.G. Ritchie (BRI)
Silver Medal – O. Froitzheim (GER)
Bronze Medal – W.V. Eaves (BRI)

Gentlemen's Doubles – Final: G.W. Hillyard and R.F. Doherty (BRI) beat M.J.G. Ritchie and J.C. Parke (BRI) 9-7 7-5 9-7
Gold Medal – G.W. Hillyard and R.F. Doherty (BRI)
Silver Medal – M.J.G. Ritchie and J.C. Parke (BRI)
Bronze Medal – C.H.L. Cazalet and C.P. Dixon (BRI)

Ladies' Singles – Final: Mrs. R.L. Chambers (BRI) beat Miss P.D.H. Boothby (BRI) 6-1 7-5
Gold Medal – Mrs. R.L. Chambers (BRI)
Silver Medal – Miss P.D.H. Boothby (BRI)
Bronze Medal – Mrs. R.J. Winch (BRI)

2012 28 July–5 August – Church Road
Gentlemen's Singles – Final: A.B. Murray (GBR) beat R. Federer 6-2 6-1 6-4
Gold Medal – A.B. Murray (GBR)
Silver Medal – R. Federer (SUI)
Bronze Medal – J-M. del Potro (ARG)

Gentlemen's Doubles – Final: R.C. Bryan & M.C. Bryan (USA) beat M. Llodra & J-W. Tsonga (FRA) 6-4 7-6 (7-2)
Gold Medal – R.C. Bryan and M.C. Bryan (USA)
Silver Medal – M. Llodra and J-W. Tsonga (FRA)
Bronze Medal – J. Benneteau and R. Gasquet (FRA)

Womens' Singles – Final: Miss S.J. Williams (USA) beat Miss M. Sharapova (RUS) 6-0 6-1
Gold Medal – Miss S.J. Williams (USA)
Silver Medal – Miss M. Sharapova (RUS)
Bronze Medal – Miss V. Azarenka (BLR)

Women' Doubles – Final: Miss S.J. Williams and Miss V.E.S. Williams (USA) beat Miss A. Hlavackova and Miss L. Hradecka (CZE) 6-4 6-4
Gold Medal – Miss S.J. Williams and Miss V.E.S. Williams (USA)
Silver Medal – Miss A. Hlavackova and Miss L. Hradecka (CZE)
Bronze Medal – Miss M. Kirilenko and Miss N. Petrova (RUS)

Mixed Doubles – Final: M.N. Mirnyi and Miss V. Azarenka (BLR) beat A.B. Murray and Miss L.M. Robson (GBR) 2-6 6-3 (10-8)
Gold Medal – M.N. Mirnyi and Miss V. Azarenka (BLR)
Silver Medal – A.B. Murray and Miss L.M. Robson (GBR)
Bronze Medal – M.C. Bryan and Miss L.M. Raymond (USA)

Wimbledon World Professional Championships

1967   25, 26 and 28 August (Centre Court)
Gentlemen's Singles – Final: R.G. Laver (AUS) beat K.R. Rosewall (AUS) 6-2 6-2 12-10
Gentlemen's Doubles – Final: A. Gimeno (ESP) and R.A. Gonzales (USA) beat R.G. Laver and F.S. Stolle (AUS) 6-4 14-12.

The Management of The Championships

Committee of Management

The Lawn Tennis Championship Meeting is under the joint management of The All England Tennis and Croquet Club through its wholly owned subsidiary, The All England Lawn Tennis Club (Championships) Limited ('AELTC') and the Lawn Tennis Association through its wholly owned subsidiary, LTA Operations Limited.

A Committee of Management consisting of the AELTC board (twelve members) and seven nominees of LTA Operations Limited form sub-committees for all major aspects of the meeting, e.g. commercial, catering, finance, ground, tennis and tickets. The AELTC provides the staff back-up.

Committee for 2015: AELTC – P.G.H. Brook (Chairman), N.A. Basing, R.M. Gradon, T.H. Henman OBE, I.L. Hewitt, Mrs A.W.L. Innes, Mrs. A.S. Jones, CBE, S.A. Jones, LVO, G.M. Newton, R.T. Stoakes, K.F. Weatherley, LTA Operation Limited – Mrs C.M. Sabin (President), R.A. Baker, R.L. Battersby, P.W. Bretherton, M.F. Corrie, D.J. Gregson, S.G. Smith.

Various Agreements and Arrangements between The All England Lawn Tennis and Croquet Club and The Lawn Tennis Association

1907

The Club gave effect to an LTA ruling and accepted, for the first time, two LTA delegates on to its Committee of Management of The Lawn Tennis Championships at Wimbledon.

1913

Following the inaugural meeting of The International Lawn Tennis Federation, where the LTA accepted the "World's Championships on Grass Courts" on behalf of the British Isles, an arrangement was made with the Club to combine such Championships with the Club's three existing Championships and upgrade the Ladies' Doubles and Mixed Doubles events to Championship status.

1914

In a memorandum of understanding the two parties confirmed the arrangements for staging the five Championship events at the Club. LTA representation on the Committee was increased to four and the LTA was allocated a share in the profits for the first time, although for a period the LTA waived its share to allow for heavy expenditure on ground improvements.

1920

A company was formed (The All England Lawn Tennis Ground Ltd.) with the object of the Club purchasing and equipping a new ground at Wimbledon Park, (Church Road) and with a view to raising capital by the issue of debentures and entering into a formal Agreement which would lock together the interests of the Club and the LTA.

1922

The parties formalised their arrangements by executing an Agreement for a term of 25 years; generally its provisions were preoccupied with the redemption of debentures and ensuring LTA use of the ground for competitions, matches and the training of players; a joint Committee was constituted (four members each) for the purpose of controlling extraordinary expenditure. Following an International Lawn Tennis Federation decision to abolish the title of the "World's Championships on Grass Courts", a Supplementary Agreement in 1923 altered the title to "Official Lawn Tennis Championships recognised by The International Lawn Tennis Federation"; a further Supplementary Agreement in 1928 contained minor financial changes.

1934

A new Agreement between the Club and the LTA was negotiated to remain in force until at least 1972; it set up (inter alia) a Joint Committee of Management of The Championships for the purpose of controlling and managing The Championships (twelve Club and six LTA nominees), payment to the LTA of all the Surplus arising therefrom, the provision and maintenance of Special Reserve Funds and the transfer by the Club to the LTA of one half of its share holding in the Ground Company. A Supplementary Agreement in 1950 dealt entirely with financial matters which arose in the course of previous arrangements. In 1966 the Principal Agreement was updated by the amendment of a few specific minor provisions to meet changing conditions; the number of LTA's nominees to the Joint Committee of Management was increased to seven and the Agreement extended to at least 1999.

1993

The 1934 Agreement was varied by a Deed of Variation to give effect to changes appropriate to the circumstances in the 1990s and beyond: it expires on 31 July 2013. Generally the Deed of Variation regulates the relationship between the Club and the LTA, perpetuates the principle that the surplus derived from The Championships goes to British tennis and recognises the part played by the Club in staging The Championships.

2009

On 14th May 2009 the Club, the LTA and the Ground Company agreed arrangements for the continuation of their relationship in respect of The Championships for at least a further 40 years from 1st August 2013. Under a revised long term agreement effective from that date the Club will receive 10% and the LTA 90% of the surplus generated by The Championships and the Ground Company will continue to receive a facility fee out of the income of The Championships before determination of the distributable surplus.

On 1st August 2013, the Club became again the 100% owner of the Ground Company as a result of the Club and the Ground Company itself buying the LTA's shares in the Ground Company.

2011

In 2011, formal reorganisations took place whereby (i) the Club was converted into a company limited by guarantee as The All England Lawn Tennis & Croquet Club Limited, (ii) The All England Lawn Tennis Club (Championships) Limited (AELTC) was formed as a wholly-owned subsidiary and acquired all assets and liabilities and rights and obligations of the Club relating to The Championships and (iii) the Lawn Tennis Association also incorporated and formed two new companies, Lawn Tennis Association Limited and LTA Operations Limited. The 2009 Agreement between the Club and the LTA was revised to reflect the new incorporated entities.

Consequent upon these reorganisations, The Championships have been controlled, managed and promoted by AELTC under the supervision of the Committee of Management comprising 12 AELTC members and 7 nominees of LTA Operations Limited.

Finance

Championship Surplus

From 1877 to 1912, The Championships were promoted and managed by The All England Lawn Tennis Club and all profits remained in their control.

In 1913, the Club amalgamated their three Championships with the five World Championships awarded by The Lawn Tennis Association and, in return, agreed to pay the LTA a percentage of the gate receipts. In practice, the LTA waived their right to this income for the years 1913 and 1914 to allow the Club to expand further the Worple Road Centre Court facilities. The LTA also took no money in 1919 but in 1920 and 1921 received a very small percentage of the gross receipts from admission and seats.

In 1920 a company was formed (The All England Lawn Tennis Ground Ltd.) with the object of the Club purchasing and equipping a new ground at Wimbledon (present site) and with a view to raising capital by the issue of debentures and entering into a formal Agreement which would lock together the interests of the Club and The Lawn Tennis Association. The interlocking of the finances of The Championships between the Club, The Lawn Tennis Association and the Ground Company stems from an Agreement made in 1922, whereby the surplus from The Championships was shared between the Club and the LTA after paying the running expenses of the Club and deducting a preferential sum towards the redemption of debentures.

A revised Agreement made in 1934 provided, *inter alia*, for joint arrangements for managing The Championships instituted by the Club, mutual obligations in the event of a Championships financial deficiency and/or insufficiency, the transfer by the Club to the LTA of one half of its share-holding in the Ground Company and the payment to the LTA of all the surplus arising from The Championships after meeting expenses incurred in running and administering the Club and the expenses of running The Championships (other than capital expenditure).

The 1934 Agreement was varied by a Deed of Variation in 1993 to give effect to changes appropriate to the circumstances in the 1990s and beyond: it will expire on 31st July, 2013. The Deed of Variation perpetuates the financial principles set out in the earlier Agreement, recognises the part played by the Club in staging The Championships and incorporates The All England Lawn Tennis Club (Wimbledon) Limited. as the fourth party to the Agreement – a company formed for the purpose of exploiting commercially any trademarks, trade names etc. for the financial benefit of The Championships.

The funds generated by The Championships, less tax, are used by the LTA to develop tennis in Great Britain. The sum paid in 1981 exceeded the million pound mark, for the first time, and this figure has substantially increased over the years.

Year	Surplus	Year	Surplus	Year	Surplus
1877	(1)	1895	–£33	1913	£3,518
1878	(1)	1896	£142	1914	£5,741
1879	£116	1897	£132	1919	£6,769
1880	£306	1898	£70	1920	£6,430
1881	£541	1899	£200	1921	£5,679
1882	£344	1900	£311	1922	£7,009
1883	£426	1901	£735	1923	£8,121
1884	£614	1902	£548	1924	£16,742
1885	£797	1903	£780	1925	£17,165
1886	£535	1904	£1,291	1926	£17,372
1887	£276	1905	£2,104	1927	£18,676
1888	£530	1906	£2,263	1928	£13,973
1889	£436	1907	£1,268	1929	£16,160
1890	£321	1908	£1,165	1930	£27,224
1891	£256	1909	£1,103	1931	£18,408
1892	£318	1910	£1,760	1932	£22,936
1893	£270	1911	£2,401	1933	£25,380
1894	£218	1912	£2,292		

Note: 1. No details available.

Year	Surplus	Year	Surplus
1934	£24,413	1972	£64,993
1935	£24,349	1973	£58,048
1936	£25,571	1974	£87,478
1937	£27,367	1975	£121,422
1938	£24,217	1976	£184,516
1939	£23,705	1977	£501,616
1946	£25,100	1978	£515,976
1947	£21,881	1979	£306,737
1948	£30,101	1980	£420,810
1949	£35,803	1981	£1,068,952
1950	£30,875	1982	£1,530,585
1951	£41,088	1983	£2,751,154
1952	£35,227	1984	£4,252,193
1953	£69,417	1985	£5,373,444
1954	£60,445	1986	£6,200,848
1955	£61,983	1987	£7,154,990
1956	£59,416	1988	£7,670,657
1957	£50,233	1989	£9,202,486
1958	£51,458	1990	£9,620,856
1959	£50,964	1991	£11,990,761
1960	£51,926	1992	£14,282,940
1961	£48,521	1993	£16,419,974
1962	£46,607	1994	£27,876,306
1963	£58,310	1995	£27,932,657
1964	£57,712	1996	£29,125,964
1965	£55,270	1997	£31,002,000
1966	£49,041	1998	£33,078,748
1967	£60,054	1999	£30,222,804
1968	£37,310	2000	£31,136,610
1969	£73,685	2001	£32,044,906
1970	£57,245	2002	£25,626,034
1971	£66,973	2003	£25,869,917

Year	Surplus	Year	Surplus
2004	£26,840,761	2010	£31,002,330
2005	£27,035,130	2011	£35,173,814
2006	£25,544,765	2012	£37,753,390
2007	£25,001,737	2013	£35,107,812
2008	£25,666,827	2014	£32,040,186
2009	£29,170,015		

Note: From 1934 to 1955 a diminishing proportion of the surplus was allocated to The All England Lawn Tennis Ground Ltd.

Debentures

Every five years, Centre Court Debentures are sold. It is from this source that The All England Lawn Tennis Ground plc (1), wholly owned from 1 August 2013 by The All England Lawn Tennis & Croquet Club Limited, derives most of its funds to meet capital expenditure.

The original Debentures were issued in 1920. During the years immediately prior to the First World War, the Club considerably expanded the facilities at the Worple Road ground to meet the growing demand of the public, by increasing the capacity of the Centre Court and purchasing adjacent houses and gardens. Even so, when the tournament resumed after the War, in 1919, the grounds still could not cope with the greater than ever crowds and, as further expansion was not possible, the Club sought new premises.

In June, 1920, the Club formed the 'Ground' Company primarily with the object of acquiring 13½ acres of freehold land at Wimbledon Park, Surrey (the present site of the Club), and to develop the grounds for the purpose of staging The Lawn Tennis Championships and other competitions.

To fund the capital required, the 'Ground' Company raised £75,000 by the issue of 'A' and 'B' Debentures at £50 each. The 'A' Debentures carried an interest rate of 7½% per annum, redeemable in or before August, 1947, and also conferred on the holder the right to purchase one seat in the Centre Court Stand for each day of the Championship meetings up to and including 1947, at the prices current at such meetings. The 'B' Debentures carried no interest but conferred upon the holder the right, without payment, to one seat in the Centre Court Stand for a similar period. The Debenture issue was oversubscribed and increased to £100,000. Because of the Second World War, the Debentures were extended by six years until the end of the 1953 Championships.

In 1948, existing holders were offered the opportunity of extending their rights until the 1959 Championships with a new issue of 2,100 Debentures at £50 each. Money was required to effect repairs to the Club's premises, including bomb damage, none having been carried out for nine years, and to improve the Centre Court and catering facilities.

So the process has continued and, apart from one year only, 1960, Debentures have been issued every five years. The three issues of 2,100 Debentures for 1986–1990, 1991–1995 and 1996–2000 realised approximately £11 million, £35 million and £35 million, respectively. Arising from the extension of the west side of the Centre Court, an additional 200 Debentures, making a total of 2,300, were offered for 2001–2005. These realised £46 million. In April 2004 the Company announced a new issue of 2006-2010 series of Centre Court Debentures, which once again realised £46 million. Following the increase in capacity, resulting from the completion of the Centre Court redevelopment in 2008, a further 200 debentures, making a total of 2,500 were offered for 2011–2015. These realised £60 million. In April 2014, the Company announced the 2016–2020 series of Centre Court Debentures which raised £105 million.

Since the late 1970s, income from Debentures has funded many major works programmes to provide expanded and improved facilities for the players, spectators, officials and media, such as: 1979 – Raising of the Centre Court roof and the construction of a new Debenture Holders' Lounge on the north side of the Centre Court, 1980 – Members' Enclosure made a permanent building, 1981 – No. 1 Court Competitors' Complex rebuilt, 1985 – East Side Centre Court Building constructed, 1986 – new two-storey Pavilion in Aorangi Park, 1989 – three new covered courts, 1991 – Centre Court North Building extended to provide greater accommodation for Debenture Holders and offices, 1992 – Replacement of Centre Court roof. The proceeds of the last three issues were used to help finance the Long Term Plan for The Championships. The proceeds of the 2011–2015 Centre Court series were used to fund the increase in the seating capacity to approx. 15,000 with wider and more comfortable seats, the construction of a retractable roof and improved catering facilities.

In recent years, further funding has been provided by the issue of Debentures for the new No. 1 Court. The issue of 1,000 Debentures for 1997–2001 realised £8 million, 834 Debentures for 2002–2006 realised £7 million, and 850 Debentures the issue for 2007–2011 realised £8.9 million. In 2011 the new issue of 1,000 debentures for 2012–2016 No. 1 Court realised £11.2 million.

Notes

1.   The status prior to 24th January, 1996 was a private limited company.

The All England Lawn Tennis and Croquet Club

Membership of the Club

Membership of the club consists of five categories: (a) Full Members, (b) Life Members, (c) Honorary Members, (d) Temporary Members, (e) Junior Temporary Members. Members under headings (a), (b) and (c) are limited to 500 in number. Honorary Members include past singles champions, other eminent Lawn Tennis players, benefactors of the club or Championships, and other persons who have rendered special service to Lawn Tennis. Temporary Members are elected from year to year and generally are active players who make regular use of the Club and play in Club matches during their period of membership.

Club Title

The Club was founded on the 23rd July, 1868 as 'The All England Croquet Club'. The Club title has been changed as follows:- 14th April, 1877 – 'The All England Croquet and Lawn Tennis Club'. 4th December, 1882 – 'The All England Lawn Tennis Club'. 2nd December, 1899 – 'The All England Lawn Tennis and Croquet Club'.

Club Colours

The present Club Colours, dark green and purple, were introduced in 1909, following the discovery that the previous colours of the Club were almost identical with those of the Royal Marines, which were blue, yellow, red and green. The decision as to why dark green and purple were chosen is not stated in the Club's records.

Club Grounds

The Club grounds consist of 17 grass courts (including the Centre Court and No. 1 Court), six American Clay courts and five indoor courts, two Greenset Velvelux and three Greenset Trophy. In Aorangi Park, there are 22 grass courts for practice before and during The Championships, and two green acrylic courts. The total area, including the Club's car parks, covers over 42 acres.

Grass Courts

see 'Layout of Championship Courts', page 153.

Hard Courts

Years	En-Tout-Cas/ Red Shale	Cont. Clay	Artificial Grass	American HAR/TRU	Soft B	Total
1922–1965	9					9
1966–1979	8					8
1980–1989	9 (1-9)					9
1990–1993	5 (1-5)	3 (6-8)	1 (9)			9
1994–2001	5 (1-5)	3 (6-8)		1 (9)		9
2002–2004	5 (1-5)	3 (6-8)		1 (9)	1 (10)	10
2005–2006	5 (1-5)	1 (6)		3 (7-9)	1 (10)	10
2007	3 (1, 2, 10)	1 (6)		6 (3-5, 7-9)		10
2008–2009	1 (1)	1 (6)		5 (3-5, 7-8)		7
2010–2015				8 (1-8)		8

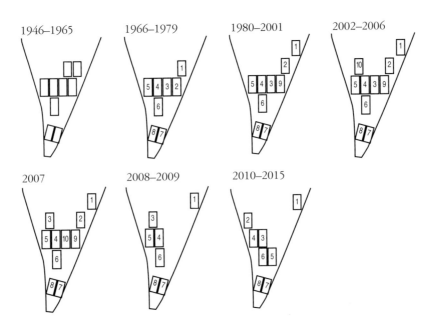

1946–1965   1966–1979   1980–2001   2002–2006

2007   2008–2009   2010–2015

Covered Courts

Years	En-Tout-Cas	Red Velvet	Supreme	Greenset Velvelux Carpet	Greenset Trophy	Total
1956(1)–1982	2					2
1983–1988		2				2
1989–1992		2	3			5
1993–2000			3	2		5
2001			2	2	1	5
2002–2015				2	3	5

(1) Courts not covered until 1958.

Acrylic Courts

Years	Aorangi Park
1991–2015	2

Staff

The permanent members of the AELTC's staff consist of Chief Executive (R.A. Lewis), Championships Director (Ms.S. Clarke), Finance Director (R.G. Atkinson), Commercial Director (M.J. Desmond), I.T. Director (T.J. Wilson), Estate Director (R.C.G. Deatker), Club Director (M.W.C. Guntrip) and 75 other administrative (including IT) staff.

There are 20 permanent members of the ground staff (including four based at Raynes Park sports ground) six horticultural staff and 35 staff in the Facilities Management team. The dressing rooms have a staff of six. Eleven staff work for the Estate Development team.

The Museum has 12 permanent staff positions and three long-term contract staff. The Wimbledon Foundation has four staff positions.

A number of temporary and contract staff support the AELTC.

Use of Courts

Apart from the grass courts, the courts are used all year round by the Club members and LTA sponsored players. The grass courts are in play from May to September (except the Centre Court and other show courts which are used only for The Championships). The courts are lent to a number of clubs and organisations, mainly of a national character, for the staging of various events.

Aorangi Park

The area north of the Centre Court became known as Aorangi Park after the Club purchased the 11 acres from John Barker Ltd. of Kensington in 1967 and subsequently granted a lease to the New Zealand Sports and Social Club. (Aorangi, meaning "Cloud in the Sky", is the Maori name for Mount Cook.)

Each year during The Championships a small part of the land was set aside for car parking. In 1977 the Tea Lawn was extended into Aorangi Park and a year later the boundary of the original ground (North Road) was also extended northwards to line up with the Tea Lawn, so as to allow the construction of the new Debenture Holders' Lounge and four grass courts. These courts were commissioned in 1980 and numbered 14–17. Two years later Aorangi Park was repossessed and brought within the perimeter of the grounds.

Sport was first played on the ground by the Argyle Athletic Association in 1906. The ground was used by John Barker Ltd when the Club took adjacent residence in 1922.

In the past few years Aorangi Park has been the scene of much activity with the construction of the new No. 1 Court Stadium, Broadcast Centre, two grass courts and a tunnel under the hill connecting Church Road with Somerset Road as part of the Club's Long Term Plan.

Landmarks

From 1931 until early in 2006 the wrought-iron Doherty Memorial Gates were situated at the main Church Road entrance to the ground. These were presented by the Rev. William Doherty in memory of his two younger brothers Laurie and Reggie, who dominated the game at the turn of the 20th century. The gates were moved to the southern end of the ground to allow new wider gates to be erected at the main entrance.

The steel roller, situated opposite the Museum building, played a significant part in Wimbledon's history for over 80 years. Bought from Cottis and Sons of Epping in 1899, it was first used at the Club's Worple Road ground, where it was pulled by a horse. In 1922, when the Club moved to the present ground at Church Road, the roller came too and for two years did service on the Centre Court before moving to the No. 1 Court. The roller was taken out of service in 1986.

In 2007, the Water Tower, which had stood since 1922, was demolished as part of the Long Term Plan south of the Centre Court. Originally the Tower was connected by pipeline to the Wimbledon Park lake, east of the ground, but was seldom used due to technical difficulties. The ground floor was used as an incinerator. Initial designs of the Tower to incorporate a clock on each face were abandoned.

The Fred Perry statue was unveiled in 1984 to commemorate the 50th Anniversary of the first of his three victories in the Gentlemen's Singles Championship. The sculptor was David Wynne. Until March 2005 the statue was situated at the south concourse entrance to the Tea Lawn, when it was relocated to a site near the entrance to Café Pergola to allow future work to be carried out in connection with the modernization of the east side of the Centre Court. With the building works completed in March, 2010 the statue was relocated to the north-east corner of Centre Court, opposite the Museum entrance to the ground. The gates at the Somerset Road entrance to the ground were dedicated to Fred Perry, in 1984.

The weather-vane, situated on the roof of the Café Pergola, was presented to the Club by Sir Brian Burnett, to mark his retirement as Chairman, 1974–1983.

Five head and shoulder sculptures of the British Ladies' Singles Champions who won their titles at Church Road, Kathleen McKane/Godfree, Dorothy Round, Angela Mortimer, Ann Jones and Virginia Wade, are positioned at the entrance to the Clubhouse. They were unveiled by the players/relatives in April 2004. The sculptor was Ian Rank-Broadley.

The two cottages, No. 133 and No. 135 Somerset Road, located at the southern end of the grounds next to the west boundary wall, were the only existing structures from when the Club purchased the land for the present ground in 1921 and, were the oldest landmarks. Built before the First World War as farm cottages, the buildings have been used by the Club over the years to accommodate various staff but were demolished in 2009.

In Remembrance

In the ground floor corridor of the Clubhouse is a plaque commemorating Club members who were killed serving in the Two Great World Wars. 1914–1918 Major I.D. Bloggs, D.S.O, Royal Engineers; 2nd Lieutenant F.W. Goldberg, Queen's Royal West Surrey; Lance Corporal I.L. Hampton, London Rifle Brigade, Captain A.M. Hendriks, Royal Fusiliers; 2nd Lieutenant H.S. Kenion, Lancashire Fusiliers; Private K. Powell, HAC Infantry; Lieutenant R.B. Powell, Canadian Pioneer Battalion; Major A.J. Ross, D.S.O. Royal Flying Corp; Captain A.F. Wilding, Royal Marines; Private F.J. Woods, Royal Fusiliers. 1939–1945 Air Commodore H.R.H Duke of Kent K.G, Royal Air Force (President of the Club); Major V.A. Cazalet, M.C., M.P., Royal Artillery; Captain W.R. Findlay, Royal East Kent Regt., K.C. Gandar Dower, War Correspondent.

Merchandising

The Wimbledon Merchandising programme was started by The All England Lawn Tennis Club in 1979 and has three objectives: to increase awareness of Wimbledon throughout the world; to enhance further the image of The Championships and to provide additional funds for the development of lawn tennis.

The All England Tennis Club has 17 licensees worldwide. The principal products licensed are tennis and casual wear, footwear, tennis rackets and bags, towels and tennis balls. In addition the Club licenses a range of luxury products such as fine leather goods, sunglasses and jewellery. The trademarks of the Wimbledon Crossed Rackets and Flying "W" are registered in some 42 countries. Wimbledon merchandise is available at www.wimbledon.com/shop.

Retail facilities within the grounds have been expanded in recent years with Wimbledon Shops located within the buildings of Centre Court, No. 1 Court and the Museum. In addition there are a number of kiosks situated around the grounds for spectators to purchase souvenir items.

The All England Club's Junior Initiatives

In May 2001, the Club launched a series of junior initiatives, using the draw of the Wimbledon name to inspire children to play tennis.

There are three tenets to this scheme. The first is the Wimbledon Junior Tennis Initiative. WJTI, as it has become known as over the years, is the Club's community tennis programme. It is run by Dan Bloxham, the AELTC Head Coach and his team of 15 coaches. At Easter 2013 Dan and his team had made 750 visits to state schools in Merton and Wandsworth. These visits have offered over 165,000 children a lively and constructive experience of tennis WJTI style!

Up to four children from each school visit can be selected to join the WJTI and attend the weekend coaching sessions which are held at the Club for 47 weeks a year.

Around 4000 children have joined the WJTI and receive free coaching throughout their junior tennis career. During the course of a weekend up to 300 children will play tennis with Dan and the team. As the Initiative has developed the children who first started playing tennis with the WJTI have offered their help with the younger players and the eldest are now taking coaching exams and forming a significant part of the coaching team.

The WJTI Squad continues to offer the players with the greatest potential the opportunity to fully develop their game. The Squad trains for 49 weeks a year and compete with success at all levels and age groups from eight and under to 18 and under. In 2014 the WJTI has three teams in the AEGON Team Tennis Competition, three of which are in the Premier Division for the first time. Strength and conditioning sessions are offered to the stronger Squad players, with four players receiving individual tennis lessons at a performance level, two of whom are national standard, six are regional and two are county standard. In 2014 players from the Programme enjoyed being a part of the Club's Road to Wimbledon event at both club and regional levels.

Elizabeth Nyenwe, formerly a player and coach with the Programme, is due to graduate this year from Bethune-Cookman University in Florida with a degree in Business Management and Sport. Another member of the Programme, Leah Gonzales-Edwards, represented Great Britain at 10 and under level.

A combined AELTC/WJTI team have competed in matches against Real Club, Barcelona, Fitzwilliam Lawn Tennis Club, Dublin, St George's Lawn Tennis Club, Weybridge and llkley Lawn Tennis and Squash Club. The WJTI Squad 'perform' on No. 14 Court on the middle Saturday and final Sunday of The Championships, where Dan shows how to grow a player with WJTI players from 4 years and upwards. Players from the Programme competed in the Road to Wimbledon at Club and Regional level.

In addition, the WJTI continues to support the local community with pop up tennis at the Wimbledon Village Fair, developing Merton teachers in their delivery of tennis at the annual Merton Teachers Evening and with teacher training sessions for NQTs.

The second segment of the Club's support for juniors is the HSBC Road to Wimbledon 14 & under Challenge which first began in 2002 where every year some 700 clubs, schools and parks organise their own Road to Wimbledon with the winners and often the runners up qualifying for the 44 County Finals.

The boys and girls county finals winners then have gone through to play in the National Finals at Wimbledon each year in mid-August.

In 2014 there were several new initiatives for the HSBC Road to Wimbledon as it continued to expand and be successful.

Firstly in the UK a new regional event was introduced for the more highly rated players at 7 regional venues around the UK culminating in the National Finals joining the players who had qualified via their clubs and county finals.

Also the Club decided to expand the event into Asia with a Pilot scheme run in India consisting of two qualifying events and a junior Masters in Delhi whereby the last two boys and girls were invited to the UK National Finals as wild cards into the regional track of the finals.

This resulted in success for the Indian player Siddhant Banthia who won the boys singles with all the Indian players making a great impression both off and on court and adding impetus and interest to the finals. The success of the Pilot scheme has resulted in the Road to Wimbledon being expanded in India in 2015 with 4 qualifying events and a Masters with again the two boys and two girls Masters Finalists coming over the HSBC Road to Wimbledon National Finals.

Also in India HSBC Ambassador Tim Henman and Dan Bloxham joined Tournament Director Paul Hutchins in a series of clinics, coach education and parents meetings to offer advice and experience during the successful India events.

Tim and Dan as usual are involved at the UK Finals as well as on the middle Saturday of the Championships with a tennis clinic for prize winners and juniors of the WJTI.

The LTA, county offices and a large number of volunteers and parents contribute to the HSBC Road to Wimbledon in the UK with the Club being appreciative of all the support for this Nationwide Club junior initiative.

All information on the UK and Indian activities can be found on www.hsbcroadtowimbledon.com

The third element is Wimbledon Lawn Tennis Museum's Learning programme. Since starting in 2001, the Learning programme, formerly known as the Education department, has seen over 53,000 students pass through its doors. In the past year over 6,800 students have participated in Learning sessions, which include curriculum based workshops and tours for 5–18 year olds, as well as lectures for undergraduate and postgraduate students. The primary school programme supports the National Curriculum subject areas of History, Geography, Art and Design and Literacy. The secondary school programme has been developed to meet the needs of students studying for GCSE, BTEC and A-Level courses in Business Studies, Geography and Physical Education. Bespoke packages have been designed for Universities – both national and international - on the themes of marketing and sport management. All tours and workshops ensure a unique and engaging experience for every student.

Another part of the Learning programme is the Community Art Project, launched in 2011 to celebrate the 125th Championships. The project involved 125 people, drawn from local schools, art groups and a tennis club, turning 125 wooden rackets into unique pieces of art that celebrated The Championships. For the 2012 Championships, visual artist Sally Booth worked with two local schools on images depicting life behind the scenes at Wimbledon. Expanding on this theme, the 2013 Community Art Project was called 'Quite Revealing', a series of behind the scenes interviews and films on the Wimbledon website. In 2014, designer maker Maggie Ruddy created...the 'Hippopotennis' a life size hippo suspended in a pyramid and appearing to float in a lake of water hyacinth made from tennis balls. This represented the volume and mass of the 54, 250 tennis balls used during the Championships. The 2015 project will use sound effects created by local students under the watchful eye of Foley artist Louise Brown to create an installation that 'Sounds like Wimbledon'.

Croquet

The All England Croquet Club was founded in July, 1868 but being without a ground the first Club Croquet Championships were held at Crystal Palace in 1869. Late that year the Worple Road ground was secured and formally opened in 1870 with the staging of the second Championships.

In 1875 lawn tennis was first played at the Club and when in 1877 the inaugural Lawn Tennis Championship was held the title of the Club was amended to the 'All England Croquet and Lawn Tennis Club'. Gradually interest in croquet declined and by the end of 1882 participation had ceased and 'Croquet' was removed from the Club's title.

During 1896 the croquet players were invited to return. In 1899 the Club Championship was reinstated and 'Croquet' was restored to the Club's title. However, the upsurge in interest did not last long and after the 1904 Championship the game faded again, but the Club retained the title of 'All England Lawn Tennis and Croquet Club'.

Croquet was not provided for when the Club moved to the present Church Road ground, and was first played on 7th September, 1953 when exhibition matches were staged by the Croquet Association to mark the Coronation Year.

From 1st June 1957 to 2nd September 2007 the croquet lawn was situated at the southern end of the grounds, alongside the Church Road boundary fence. This was not full size and competitive play was restricted to Club tournaments. The Club Croquet Championship was reintroduced together with a Handicap singles event in 1960 and in recent years a golf croquet event was started. In the autumn of 2007 the Club 's Long Term Plan necessitated other use for the area and a new lawns was created in the Southlands College ground which was opened on 19th April 2008 by Professor Bernard Neal, President of the Croquet Association.

Professor Neal, was the Club champion 38 times between 1963 and 2005. The 2014 champion was Jonathan Smith. David Godfree acted as Hon. Secretary for the Croquet section from 1975 to 2014. This position is now taken by Michael Hann.

Wimbledon Foundation

The Wimbledon Foundation, established in 2013, is the charity of The All England Lawn Tennis Club. The Foundation builds on the success of an extensive programme of community and charitable activities over a number of years – including the WJTI, Road To Wimbledon, Learning, Ticket Resale Scheme and other community support.

The mission of the Wimbledon Foundation is to change people's lives using the resources and heritage of the All England Club and The Championships. Through its programmes the Foundation aims to:
- make a real contribution to meeting social needs in the London Boroughs of Merton and Wandsworth
- use the power of sport, particularly tennis, to advance young people's education and development
- encourage and support charities and community activities relating to The Championships.

A key focus over the last year has been support of the local community. In 2014, the Wimbledon Foundation Community Fund was launched which over twelve months will distribute £100,000 in grants to charities and community organisations tackling social problems in Merton and Wandsworth. In March 2015, the Wimbledon Foundation launched a Health & Wellbeing Fund awarding grants to projects in Merton and Wandsworth that support better mental health, improve healthy living, bring families and communities together and make neighbourhoods safer.

Wimbledon Lawn Tennis Museum

The original Wimbledon Lawn Tennis Museum was opened by H.R.H. The Duke of Kent in 1977 as part of the Centenary celebrations. The construction of the Centre Court East Side Building in 1984/5 led to the design of a completely new Museum, in which more of the expanding collection could be seen.

In 1993 H.R.H. The Duke of Kent consented to become Patron and during 1994 visited the Museum.

The announcement in 2002 of the Club's plans for a roof on Centre Court and the redevelopment of the East Side necessitated the removal of the Museum and all its associated activities. A new Museum, designed by Mather & Company and housed in the Museum Building was opened on 12th April 2006 by H.R.H. The Duke of Kent.

The Museum contains historic galleries, themed galleries devoted to tennis equipment and tennis fashions, zones focussing on tennis today and life on the circuit. The Museum employs new technology with a variety of interactive displays, touchscreens and audioguides in ten languages. Highlights include the 'ghost' of John McEnroe who appears in the Gentlemen's Dressing Room

In September 2009, Centre Court 360, a glass viewing platform together with interactive displays, was installed for the first time. Open to all Museum visitors, outside of The Championships, it is accessed through the Wingfield Cafe.

During 2014 the exhibition On the Riviera: Tennis in the South of France 1874–1939 was installed in the Museum Gallery. Following the publication of the book The Golden Days of Tennis on the French Riviera 1874–1939 by the Museum's Honorary Librarian, Alan Little, the exhibition was extended and refreshed in the light of his research and the emergence of new exhibits. A new enlarged gallery for the Championship trophies was opened in April 2014. This offers 360 degree views of the Singles trophies and a film. Also included is a touchscreen where visitors can view images of every winner of every Championship event since 1877 and two weights, enabling visitors to feel the weight of the Singles trophies.

A new exhibition was opened in 2015: Powerful Posters: Tennis and Advertising, 1893–2015 shows spectacular posters from the Museum's collection and explores how tennis has been used to advertise a surprising array of products.

Tours of the Grounds

Tours were introduced for private groups in the spring of 2000, and proved very popular. They became available to the general public in late summer 2001 and the following year the tours were awarded a Gold Award as Best New Tourist Attraction from Visit London.

In the early years tours ran only in the summer, but demand was such that in 2006 they were offered year-round, with the exception of the period during and around The Championships. There are now four tours a day in the winter rising to nine tours a day in the summer.

In 2011 Spanish language tours were introduced in the summer period and these are well-established.

The tours are led by professionally qualified London Blue Badge Guides, which guarantees a consistently high quality experience for the approximately 60,000 visitors who take the tours each year. The linguistic skills of the guides also mean that the tours can be provided for pre-booked groups in 19 languages. Individual visitors can join one of the public tours. Tours include the Aorangi Terrace, No. 1 Court, the Broadcast Centre, Press Interview Room and Centre Court, as well as the Museum.

The Wimbledon Shop sells a wide range of Wimbledon leisurewear, gifts, souvenirs and DVDs. Museum publications, highlighting the history of Wimbledon and aspects of the collections, are available from the Shop.

The Museum is open during The Championships from 9.30am – 8pm (or close of play if earlier). Throughout the year, the Museum is open daily from 10am – 5.30pm (April – September) and 10am – 5pm (October to March) with the exception of the following days:

Closed the Sunday immediately prior to The Championships, the Monday immediately after The Championships (unless there is play) and the Tuesday after The Championships

Christmas Eve, Christmas Day, Boxing Day and New Year's Day

Further details of opening times and tour bookings are obtainable on 020 8946 6131, museum@aeltc.com or www.wimbledon.com/museum

The Wingfield Cafe is available to visitors for refreshments throughout the year, excluding The Championships.

Kenneth Ritchie Wimbledon Library

The Kenneth Ritchie Wimbledon Library, which is part of Wimbledon Lawn Tennis Museum, contains an outstanding collection of British and foreign lawn tennis books, annuals, periodicals, programmes, newspaper cuttings, video cassettes etc., which is available to the public for study and research. Items originate from nearly 90 countries. Facilities are available for photocopying and the screening of video cassettes. A 2015 Catalogue, listing all items held by the Library, is available from the Wimbledon Shop.

The Library is situated in the Museum Building, with the entrance at the north end, at level -1.

Normally the Library is open Monday to Friday, 10.30am to 1pm, 2pm to 5pm, but is closed to the public during The Championships. Admission is by appointment and readers should apply to Audrey Snell, Assistant Librarian by post, telephone (020 8879 5609) or e-mail (asne@aeltc.com).

Patrons
1910–1936   H.M. King George V
1936   H.M. King Edward VIII
1936–1952   H.M. King George VI
1952–   H.M. Queen Elizabeth II

Presidents
1907–1910   H.R.H. The Prince of Wales K.G., K.T., K.P., G.C.S.I., G.C.M.G., G.C.I.E., G.C.V.O., I.S.O.
1911–1912   A.W. Gore
1912–1915   The Lord Desborough K.C.V.O.
1915–1921   H. Wilson Fox M.P.
1921–1929   H.W.W. Wilberforce
1929–1934   H.R.H. The Prince George K.G., G.C.M.G.,G.C.V.O.
1934–1942   H.R.H. The Duke of Kent K.G., K.T., G.C.M.G., G.C.V.O., P.C.
1944–1961   H.R.H. The Duchess of Kent C.I., G.C.V.O., G.B.E.
1961–1968   H.R.H. Princess Marina, Duchess of Kent C.I., G.C.V.O., G.B.E.
1969–   H.R.H. The Duke of Kent K.G., G.C.M.G., G.C.V.O., A.D.C.

Vice-Presidents

1911–1919	H.L. Doherty
1911–1923	R.B. Hough
1911–1915	D. Jones
1911–1921	H.W.W. Wilberforce
1937–1941	Sir Herbert Wilberforce
1914–1921	W.H. Collins
1915–1945	The Rt. Hon. Lord Desborough, K.G., G.C.V.O.
1928	A.W. Gore
1932–1941	The Rt. Hon. Viscount d'Abernon, P.C., G.C.B., G.C.M.O.
1934–1944	Sir Samuel Hoare, Bt., G.C.S.I., G.B.E., C.M.G., M.P.
1944–1959	The Rt. Hon. Viscount Templewood, G.C.S.I, G.B.E., C.M.G.
1945–1946	Hon. P. Bowes-Lyon
1947–1951	The Rt. Hon. Viscount Jowitt
1951–1957	The Rt. Hon. Earl Jowitt
1953–1972	Lady Greig
1955–1961	A.H. Riseley, O.B.E.
1957–2004	His Grace The Duke of Devonshire, K.G., P.C., M.C.
1965–1967	His Honour Judge C.D. Aarvold, O.B.E., T.D.
1968–1991	Sir Carl D. Aarvold, O.B.E., T.D.
1975	The Rt. Hon. Lord Ritchie of Dundee, P.C.
1975–1985	E.C. Peters
1976–1986	E.C. Simond
1976–1986	R.K. Tinkler
1977–1982	Lt. Col. A.D.C. Macaulay, O.B.E.
1977–1989	The Marquis of Zetland
1980–1981	R.B. Sterry
1980–1995	E.R. Avory
1982–2012	Air Vice-Marshal E.L. Frith, C.B., R.A.F. (Ret'd.)
1982–2001	R.A.A. Holt
1983–2011	Air Chief Marshal Sir Brian K. Burnett, G.C.B., D.F.C., A.F.C., R.A.F. (Ret'd.)
1989–1992	Mrs. K. Godfree
1989–2005	R.E.H. Hadingham, C.B.E., M.C., T.D.
1991–2012	The Rt. Hon. Lord Carr of Hadley, P.C.
1991–	P. Jackson, C.B.E.
1994–1997	B.F. Hutchins
1996–	Professor B.G. Neal
1999–	J.A.H. Curry C.B.E.
2002–	B.N.A. Weatherill C.B.E.
2004–	J.E. Barrett M.B.E.
2004–	M.P. Hann
2006–	Sir Ronald Hampel
2010–	T.D. Phillips C.B.E.
2012–	J.S. Dunningham O.B.E.

Chairmen

Up to 1929 there was no permanently elected Chairman – the chair was normally taken at Committee meetings by the President.

1929–1936	Sir Herbert Wilberforce
1937–1953	Group Captain Sir Louis Greig K.B.E., C.V.O., D.L.
1953–1955	A.H. Riseley O.B.E.
1955–1959	Dr. J.C. Gregory
1959–1974	H.F. David C.B.E.
1974–1983	Air Chief Marshal Sir Brian K. Burnett G.C.B., D.F.C., A.F.C., R.A.F. (Ret'd.)
1983–1989	R.E.H. Hadingham C.B.E., M.C., T.D.
1989–1999	J.A.H. Curry C.B.E.
1999–2010	T.D. Phillips C.B.E.
2010–	P.G.H. Brook

Vice-Chairmen

1946–1953	A.H. Riseley O.B.E.		1974–1980	R.A.A. Holt
1953–1955	Dr. J.C. Gregory		1999	T.D. Phillips
1959–1974	R.B. Sterry		2009–2010	P.G.H. Brook

Secretaries/Chief Executives

On 1st January, 1983 the Secretary became the Chief Executive.

1868–1869	W.J. Whitmore		1871	H. Jones
1869	E.B. Mitchell		1871–1879	J.H. Walsh
1869–1871	S.H.C. Maddock		1880–1888	J. Marshall
1888–1891	H.W.W. Wilberforce		1979–2005	C.J. Gorringe C.B.E.
1891–1898	A. Chitty		2005–2012	I.R. Ritchie
1899–1906	A. Palmer		2012–	R.A. Lewis C.B.E.
1907–1925*	Commander G.W. Hillyard			
1925–1939	Major D.T.R. Larcombe			
1939–1945	Miss N.G. Cleather (Acting)			
1946–1963	Lt. Col. A.D.C. Macaulay O.B.E.			
1963–1979	Major A.D. Mills			

*From November 1914 to May 1919, C.A. Caridia was Acting Hon. Secretary while the Secretary was on active service.

Assistant Secretaries

1927–1928	E.R. Clarke		1963–1974	A.B. Cooper
1928–1929	W.S. Hutchings		1974–1979	C.J. Gorringe
1939	Miss N.G. Cleather		1979–1983	A.R.M. Grier
1948–1963	Maj. A.D. Mills			

Championship Secretary

1983–1985	A.R.M. Grier

Championship Director

1985–2013	A.R.M. Grier
2013–	Ms. S. Clarke

Hon Treasurers

1868–1869	S.H.C. Maddock
1869–1875	J.H. Walsh
1875–1882	Rev. D.I. Heath
1882–1886	F.W. Oliver

1886–1898	A.J. Chitty
1899–1909	A. Palmer
1910–1937	C.A. Caridia

From 1937 to 1980 the post of Treasurer was combined with that of the Secretary.

Financial Controller
1981–1985 J.A. Hughes

Finance Director
1985–2007 J.A. Hughes
2007– R.G. Atkinson

Marketing Director
1985–2011 R.E. McCowen

Commercial Director
2010– M.J. Desmond

T.V. Marketing Director
1989–2002 I.F. Edwards

Director of Television
2002–2009 J. Rowlinson

Information Technology Director
1995–2010 J.C. Lucas
2010– T.J. Wilson

Estate Director
2014– R.C.G. Deatker

Club Secretary
1983–1984 J.D.C. Crump
1984–2005 R.D. Ambrose
2005–2015 M.W.C. Guntrip

Club Director
2015– M.W.C. Guntrip

Head Groundsmen

1888–1907	Thomas Coleman
1907–1938	William Coleman
1938–1967	Edwin Fuller
1967–1976	Bob Twynam

1976–1982	Jack Yardley
1982–1991	Jim Thorn
1991–2012	Eddie Seaward M.B.E.
2012–	Neil Stubley

Wimbledon Lawn Tennis Museum

Patron
1993– H.R.H. The Duke of Kent K.G., G.C.M.G., G.C.V.O., A.D.C.

Chairmen
1977–1985 E.R. Avory
1985–1997 B.F. Hutchins
1997–2000 Prof. B.G. Neal
2000–2004 R.J. Presley O.B.E.
2004–2011 Sir Ronald Hampel
2011– T.D. Phillips C.B.E

Curators
1977–1985 A.B. Cooper
1985–1999 Miss V.A. Warren
1999–2014 Miss H.E. Godfrey M.B.E.
2014– Ms A.K. Renton

Hon. Librarian
1977– J.A. Little M.B.E.

All England Lawn Tennis Ground Company plc
Chairmen

1920–1921	H. Wilson Fox, M.P.
1922–1928	A.W. Gore
1928–1941	T.M. Mavrogordato
1941–1942	Mr Justice Langton
1942–1955	A.H. Riseley, O.B.E.
1955–1959	Dr J.C. Gregory
1959–1962	H. Garton Ash
1962–1981	A. Sterry
1981–1986	Air Chief Marshal Sir Brian Burnett, G.C.B., D.F.C., A.F.C., RAF. (Ret'd)
1986–1990	R.E.H. Hadingham, C.B.E., M.C., T.D.
1990–2011	J.A.H Curry, C.B.E
2012–	P.G.H. Brook

Wimbledon into the 21st Century

Long Term Plan, 1993–2011

In March 1993 The Committee of Management of The Championships unveiled its Long Term Plan to take Wimbledon into the 21st century. The plan represene the most ambitious facility improvement programme undertaken since The All England Lawn Tennis Club's move to Church Road in 1922. It was designed to protect the long term future of The Championships by improving the quality of the event for all involved – players, spectators, media, officials and neighbours. The overall objective of the plan was to upgrade all facilities to maintain The Championships position as the world's premier tennis tournament and, importantly, to achieve this within the existing grounds, without acquiring additional land or moving location.

The Plan

Good circulation was the key to the plan. Untangling the existing maze of routes was achieved by driving two broad pathways north and south, linked by concourses into a ladder pattern. A new No. 1 Court, seating 11,000 spectators is sited to the northern edge of the layout and a new No. 2 Court is ultimately planned at the extreme south. Spectator seats will then be evenly spread over the grounds rather than concentrated in the middle.

Secondly, the site was arranged to work like a theatre with a "front and back of house". The re-developed Wimbledon will concentrate visitor access on the east side, and "back stage" access to the west. The character of Wimbledon was conserved and enhanced by re-establishing Centre Court as the focal point; a "country house" in its garden and parkland setting. The considerable amount of new building required is being blended into the landscape as "outbuildings".

The new No. 1 Court was an updating of the proven design of Centre Court. It is circular in plan provides good sightlines, lighting, ventilation and acoustics for players and spectators alike. The essence of the new No. 1 Court is its openness and informality. To maintain its status as younger brother to Centre Court, the new stadium is counter sunk into the hillside; it is surrounded by terraces of restaurants, hospitality, retail and service spaces.

Timing

Stage 1

The initial stage of the development comprised the construction of the new No. 1 Court Stadium, offering a multitude of facilities, a new, largely, underground Broadcast Centre, a road tunnel linking Somerset Road with Church Road, two new No. 18 and No. 19 Courts, cut into the hillside to give flexibility for other courts to be moved, and a new Championships Entrance Building in Church Road.

Work on the construction commenced on 25th July, 1994 and was completed just prior to the 1997 Championships, ceasing work twice to enable The Championships to take place in 1995 and 1996.

Stage 2

This stage of the development comprised the construction of the following: A new Facilities Building, on the site of the old No. 1 Court, to provide dining and rest areas for competitors, Members, press and photographers, officials, stewards and ball boys/girls, together with press writing and interview rooms. The extension of the West Stand of the Centre Court to provide 750 additional spectator seats, commentary boxes, competitors' changing facilities and public toilets. The re-siting of No. 14, No. 15, No. 16 and No. 17 Courts to improve crowd circulation during The Championships. Landscaping to include competitors' and Members' lawns, a new access road from Somerset Road serving competitors and press entrances and a brick/railing boundary along Somerset Road. Completion of St. Mary's Walk between the Centre Court West Stand extension and the Facilities Building was also planned.

Preliminary work, including demolition, commenced after the 1996 Championships. The main construction began in the spring of 1997 and was completed by the 2000 Championships.

Stage 2c

This stage of the development comprised the construction of a new Museum Building, housing office accommodation for Club Staff, the Wimbledon Lawn Tennis Museum and Library, Barclays Bank, Ticket Office and incorporating the Turnstile Entrance to the ground at Gate 3 commenced immediately after the 2003 Championships. This was fitted out and occupied by the end of 2005, and the new Museum opened in April of 2006. This left the Centre Court East Side empty and allowed the development of innovative plans for the Centre Court of the future, including raising the capacity from 13,800 to 15,000, better facilities for the public and Debenture Holders, and a retractable roof over the Court.

The Centre Court programme was completed for the 2009 Championships.

Stage 3

The next phase of the modernisation programme was to complete the planned work at the southern end of the grounds.

This consisted of the construction of a new 2,000 seat No.3 Court (old No.2), a new No.4 Court (old No.3) the provision of a single storey facilities building (maintenance equipment and storage), a two storey office and workplace accommodation for groundstaff and a single storey maintenance workshop linked to a new lavatory block. Also, three new HAR TRU hard courts are to be laid down and the Somerset Road boundary wall completed.

The above plan will secure a five metre plus walkway between the two new grass courts, which will greatly improve the overall circulation within the grounds. Conceptually there will therefore be a wide walkway either side of the grounds, so improving comfort and safety for all.

The programme commenced in July 2009 and was completed in May 2011. In the first year, the foundations and the build of the basic structures of the new buildings took place. The two new grass courts were constructed and soil put down. The three hard courts were ready for play just after the 2010 Championships.

During the second year of construction the fitting out of the above buildings was completed and new No. 3 and No. 4 Courts came into play for the 2011 Championships.

In addition to the above works, in the second year the Club commissioned the design and construction of two new balcony terraces a the south-west and south-east corners of No 1 Court for the Debenture Holders; which were delivered in time for the 2011 Championships.

Another scheme to build a Junior Tennis Centre below the Aorangi Park Courts No. 1 and No. 2, in front of the Pavilion, has been shelved indefinitely at present.

Construction

1994–1995

Firstly the stability of the hill in Aorangi Park was maintained before excavations for the new No. 1 Court could commence. A technique known as "soil nailing" was employed. A soil nail is a small diameter pile, inserted into the ground at a shallow angle. When a number of these piles are inserted on a grid, soil friction is increased and slippage becomes less likely. To eliminate any chance of soil movement, over 700 soil nails were placed.

The site was then reduced in level to allow piling rigs to operate. Initially four piling rigs formed over 1,000 piles over the site of the new No. 1 Court, both Compression piles to support the structure and Tension piles to "hold the building down", or more correctly to reduce the effects of ground heave once the mass of heavy clay was excavated from Aorangi Park.

Contiguous piles were formed to act as retaining walls to the new No. 1 Court and as tunnel walls for the service tunnel linking Church Road with Somerset Road. Contiguous piles are piles which are formed so close to each other that they create a wall in the ground allowing the earth on one side of the wall to be removed. In total over 2,000 piles were formed, enough when joined end to end to stretch from The All England Lawn Tennis Club to St. Paul's Cathedral and back!

Excavations resulted in over 100,000 cubic metres of clay being removed from site. The concrete frame structure for the new No. 1 Court was commenced early in 1995. Only the first two floor levels were constructed then thus allowing the extensive flat slab areas to be used as a platform for marquees and various other public facilities for the 1995 Championships.

Over 26,000 cubic metres of concrete were placed during the first year requiring over 3,000 tonnes of reinforcing steel. Four tower cranes were erected.

1995–1996

After the 1995 Championships an additional crane was erected. All piling was completed together with the major portion of the remaining excavation, with the exception of the area immediately in front of the Aorangi Park Pavilion which was programmed to be carried out after the 1996 Championships. The playing area of the new No. 1 Court was turfed in the Autumn of 1995 and the substructure to the two new outside Courts No. 18 and No. 19 put in place prior to 1996 Championships.

The reinforced concrete structure to the new No. 1 Court and tunnel was completed at the beginning of the year and that to the Broadcast Centre was completed up to existing adjacent ground level for the 1996 Championships. The precast concrete terracing was also in place and the external cladding to the new Stadium was well advanced. Internal blockwork partitioning was completed and finishings, and mechanical and electrical services' installations were well advanced. Likewise the roof steelwork and roof cladding.

Certain areas of the new Stadium were open to the public for the 1996 Championships. These areas were temporarily fitted out and adjacent public toilets completed and fully fitted.

1996–1997

The third year of the project concluded Stage 1 of the Plan, whereby the No. 1 Court Stadium and Broadcast Centre were fully functional and all areas in use for the 1997 Championships. The tunnel linking Somerset Road with Church Road was completed and the hillside landscaped with plantings and water feature, incorporating the Picnic Area. In addition to the No. 1 Court, No. 18 and No. 19 Courts were available for use. Also completed were the underground Players' set-down area at the Aorangi Park Pavilion entrance, the main Championships Entrance Building adjacent to Gate 3 and the new boundary brick/railing wall along part of Church Road.

Stage 2 of the project, on the new Facilities Building and Centre Court extension, was commenced soon after the 1996 Championships. The North Stand and part of the West Stand of the old No. 1 Court were demolished and the playing surface removed, leaving the facilities within the remaining Stands, including part of the West Stand, in use during the 1997 Championships. No. 14 and No. 15 Courts were completely removed to construct an underground Royal and Buggy route to link the new No. 1 Court with the Centre Court complex. The courts were reconstructed adjacent to their original positions to improve pedestrian circulation, re-turfed and ready for use at the 1998 Championships.

1997–1998

Demolition and piling, which had commenced prior to the 1997 Championships, was completed by October. Only the South Stand, which was programmed for demolition after the 1999 Championships, remained. The bulk excavation and carting away progressed during this time and this was finished by the end of 1997. In the meantime, two tower cranes, one at the North end and one at the South end of the site were erected. The Lodge was demolished in August 1997.

The next major work undertaken was the erection of the reinforced concrete frame which was completed shortly after Easter. The precast concrete terrace to support this stadium seating in the Centre Court West Stand extension was put in place together with the steel roof structure over. A substantial amount of internal blockwork partitioning and some external cladding was carried out. Installation of engineering services commenced and many large items of plant were installed.

The site was enclosed by hoarding and left safe for The Championships. Part of the reinforced concrete structure of the Officials' Building sited at the north end of the construction site was used to provide public toilet facilities. No. 14 and No. 15 Courts were in use but No. 16 and No. 17 Courts, although finished and grassed, were not in play.

1998–1999

Construction work continued apace after the 1988 Championships and all buildings were wind and weatherproof shortly after Christmas. Work also commenced, ahead of programme, on that part of the existing South Stand of the old No. 1 Court adjacent to the Centre Court complex. Consequently, this gave the Club earlier access than originally planned to certain areas of the new building, which was of particular benefit to those officials who will require early access to prepare for the 2000 Championships.

By the 1999 Championships the internal finishings and fitting out were well advanced together with installation of joinery, flooring and suspended ceilings. Most of the mechanical and electrical services, including the network of systems required for The Championships to operate efficiently, were in place. Drainage work was complete and external works, where appropriate, were also finished.

The tower crane at the north end of the site was removed at Easter leaving one remaining crane to service works at the southern end of the site.

Visitors to the Championships saw in use approximately 700 additional stadium seats provided by the new extension on the West side of the Centre Court, together with public toilets installed under the stand. Also back in use were the Nos. 16 and 17 Courts. The construction site was enclosed by hoarding for safety reasons for the duration of The Championships.

1999–2000

After the 1999 Championships the remaining section of the South Stand of the old No. 1 Court was demolished and in its place the Southern 'finger' of the new Facilities Building was erected and completed at the same time as the remainder of the Facilities Building and the Centre Court extension.

Furniture, furnishings and equipment were installed within the final weeks and all areas were fully functional and ready for the 2000 Championships. The new facilities available were accommodated within three separate buildings, namely the Centre Court West Stand extension, the new Millennium (Facilities) Building and the Officials' Pavilion, linked by high level bridges.

The Centre Court West Stand extension comprised:
    Level 1 Ladies' North and South No 2 Changing Rooms; Public Toilets
        2 Ladies' and Gentlemen's No 1 Changing Rooms; Public Toilets; Press areas; Radio Wimbledon and First Aid rooms

   3 Gentlemen's North and South No 2 Changing Rooms and bridge to Millennium Building

   4 Commentary positions overlooking Centre Court and Southern Courts.

The Millennium Building comprised:

  Level 1 Members' Entrance and Reception; Officials' Buttery; Ball-Girls/Boys Changing, Rest and Canteen facilities; Competitors' Courtyard, Mini Gymnasium, Doctors' Surgery and Drugs' Testing Rooms; Plant areas and extension of Royal and Buggy Routes

    2 Members' Garden and Self-Service Restaurant; Press Entrance and Reception, Writing and Interview Rooms; Photographers' facilities and Press Courtyard

    3 Competitors' Main Entrance and Garden; Members' Private Party Dining and Lido areas; Press and Photographers' rooms

    4 Competitors' Dining, Lounge and Lido areas; Press Writing rooms and Dining facilities

    5 Plant areas

The Officials' Pavilion comprised:

  Level 1 Lower Referees, Umpires and Ball Boys/Girls Offices.

    2 Referees' Offices, Meeting Room and bridge to Millennium Building

    3 Press Restaurant and bridge to Millennium Building

2000–2001

During this period the Clubhouse was closed while exploration and enabling works were carried out in readiness for the refurbishment planned for after the 2001 Championships (Stage 2B). Besides the complete removal of the Boston Ivy, the entire face of the building required grit blasting and the cutting out of defective concrete. There was also a need to undertake internal investigation to the condition of the floors and rake beams within the Club's rooms as well as the installation of a new main drain down the road in front of the Clubhouse. During the closure of the Clubhouse, the Members' facilities and Club offices were transferred to the Millennium Building.

2001–2002

The complete refurbishment of the Clubhouse was carried out, with the rearrangement of the Main Entrance Hall to incorporate twin dog-leg staircases up to the Members' dining and lounge facilities and linking to new entrances/exits to the Royal Box. Also included was a designated corridor to the Millennium building. The Members' Balcony was renewed and extended with bridge links to new balconies on each side. Other facilities such as a Games Room, Boardroom and function rooms were provided. Extensive alterations were also carried out in the Centre Court where improvements were made to the Royal Box, commentary boxes and the terraces to the southern stands. During the closure of the Clubhouse, the Members' facilities and Club Offices were transferred to the Millennium Building.

In Car Park 4, two grassed terraces (each capable of containing two practice courts) and a gardener's complex was constructed, all of which is enclosed within security fencing and hedging, Initially the lower terrace will have two courts and the top terrace, temporary Championship facilities.

The first part of Stage 3 commenced at the southern end of the grounds, with No. 11 and No. 12 Courts and the gardeners' quarters being demolished. In their place a single Court No. 11 (grass) was constructed to replace the courts, using foundation laid pallets (to speed the process of consolidation). Alongside to the west an experiment SoftB clay court was laid, Shale courts 4 and 5 were moved 3 metres in a southerly direction.

2002–2003

Work was carried out to construct six new practice grass courts and attendant facilities on the Southlands College triangular area between Bathgate and Queensmere Roads.

The terracing within the bowl of the Centre Court from the south-west corner to the north-east corner, rows A–H, was completely replaced with a lighter weight concrete with new steel reinforcement within.

2003–2004

Immediately after the 2003 Meeting, the Championship Entrance Building (turnstiles) including Barclays Bank, adjacent to Gate 3 and the Wimbledon Lawn Tennis Museum Shop, on the Tea Lawn Extension, were completely demolished. The clearing of the site made way for the construction of a new building (Museum Building) containing Club Offices, Turnstile Entrance, Wimbledon Lawn Tennis Museum and Library, Ticket Office and Bank scheduled for occupation by December 2005.

2004–2005

After the 2004 Championships work continued on the construction of the Museum Building.

In the Autumn, four new major projects were undertaken: The diversion of services to the North Road, Tea Lawn and South Road and the installation of new subterranean services for both the Centre Court and the Championship Entrance Building were carried out. Work on the replacement of the terracing in the bowl of the Centre Court continued with a further 12 rows (H-T) being renewed, clockwise from the south-west corner to the north-east corner. The existing panel and post walling between Gate 9 and Gate 11, at the southern end of the grounds, was replaced with a new solid brick wall, similar to that provided in Somerset Road. At the same time two existing Continental Clay courts (No. 7 and 8) were excavated and relaid with a HAR-Tru type surface. The grass in Car Parks 2 and 3 was removed and a firm Fibresand surfacing laid down. A new durable grass surface was introduced, enabling the car parks to be used all the year, irrespective of the weather.

2005–2006

After the 2005 Championships until the end of the year, a programme was carried out to evacuate the Centre Court East Side to allow the development of the Centre Court. The Café Centre Court was closed and catering facilities transferred to part of the Renshaw Restaurant in the No. 1 Court Stadium. Also, Museum accomodation for the Education and Playing for Success groups was relocated to Suites G, H and J in the same building.

At the end of October, the Wimbledon Lawn Tennis Museum and Library closed and all objects etc. stored in the basement, level 2 of the Museum Building in preparation for the opening of the Museum. At the same time a new Wimbledon shop, situated on the ground floor at the south end of the building was opened. Also a temporary Visitor Centre was made available to the public in part of the Renshaw Restaurant.

At the beginning of December, Club Staff moved into the first floor offices of the Museum Building, with the ticket office personnel occupying the ground floor at the north end. The staff restaurant was closed and catering transferred to the restaurant in the Broadcast Centre. In April the Wimbledon Lawn Tennis Museum and Library were opened. Further enabling works were commenced to facilitate the Centre Court development project. This comprised asbestos survey works, ground irrigation works, piling and foundation works, diversion of existing electrical data and telephone services, water services and drainage. Subsequent to the evacuation of the East Side of Centre Court, strip out and demolition works, commenced inside the existing building.

2006–2007

Following the 2006 Championships, all areas of the Centre Court and Tea Lawn were vacated in preparation for a rapid construction start. The whole of the Stadium became a restricted area. The Members' Clubhouse facilities were moved to the Millennium Building, while accomodation for the Ladies' Dressing Room was relocated to the covered courts and the Gentlemen's Dressing Room to the No. 2 Court Building.

Between July and September the roof was completely removed, the North Stand accomodation for the old Museum Offices and Library was demolished and a large section of the East Stand removed. The North Debenture Holders' accomodation was stripped out ready for refurbishment.

The new structural steelwork for the North and West Stand extensions commenced early in September and was followed by the installation of new precast concrete terraces and prefabricated commentary boxes. Groundwork, foundations and reinforced concrete works for the new East Stand recommenced in mid September and the new structural steel and concrete frame started erection in November.

At the start of 2007, construction activity resumed on all fronts of the Centre Court. On the west side, the relocation of the plantrooms was completed in January, the exterior cladding over St. Mary's Walk finished in February and the scaffold struck in March. On the north side, work on the internal blockwork walls and first fix mechanical and electrical services commenced. Exterior cladding was completed in March and the scaffold came down in April. The old Debenture areas at first floor level were turned into temporary rainshelter areas for The Championships and new permanent public toilets were completed at ground floor level., along with permanent accommodation for Radio

Wimbledon staff restroom, 'Cyclops' storage, and an ATM enclosure. On the south side, structural repairs were completed to the parapets above the Clubhouse roof.

On the east side, the structural steelwork recommenced and was completed by early March. The new precast concrete terraces and new poured concrete floor slabs followed sequentially and then the new commentary boxes were installed at the top concourse level. Elements of exterior cladding, new masonry walls and first fix mechanical and electrical commenced, in tandem with all the necessary temporary works, to achieve a temporary 'Long Bar' facility for The Championships, with all the attendant back-of-house areas for catering, cleaning and waste removal.

The scaffold and protection to the Clubhouse was removed in the Spring and prepared for reoccupation by early June.

In Car Park 2, substantial steelwork elements for the new fixed roof were fabricated between late February and early May and left there in storage ready for a rapid start after The Championships, when the sections will be hauled across Somerset Road and through Gate 13 ready for hoisting into position.

Finally, and in tandem with the above, a series of enabling works were carried out around southern grass No. 3, No. 4 and No. 5 Courts in preparation for future Stage 3 works: timing was driven by the necessity to be clear of the South Road, as this was the 'launch pad' for the new roof steelwork erection.

2007–2008

In a repeat of the previous year, but with even more urgency, following the completion of the Championships 2007 all areas of the Centre Court and Tea Lawn were vacated for a rapid construction start. Workers were back on site on the Monday, a mobile crane followed on Tuesday and within two weeks all four tower cranes for Centre Court were back in operation.

Inside the bowl a temporary working platform, at roof height, was erected over the terraces and significant amounts of engineered temporary structural steelwork were installed to provide support for the incoming fixed roof truss sections. In July, Somerset Road was closed off for a period of six weeks and a temporary haul road constructed to facilitate the transportation of the ten separate truss sections (the heaviest of which weighed in at over 100 tonnes) from Car Park 2 to the lifting positions in the South Road in front of the Clubhouse. Lifting of the truss sections (by a 1000 tonne capacity crane specially brought in for the task) commenced in mid August, and by the end of November the erection and welding of the main trusses had been completed, enabling successful "de-jacking" of the structures and the removal of the temporary supports to commence. This process was immediately followed, in sequence, by the erection of secondary roof steelwork, installation of the metal roof decking and gutters, and commencement of the mechanical and electrical systems within the roof voids (these systems would not be required to be operational until the following year for the moving roof). The rails for the moving roof were installed and then, in late April, two of the ten moving roof trusses (each over 70 metres long) were craned into position up on the roof and "parked" at the North end.

In parallel with the above bowl/roof works, the interior spaces of the Centre Court East and North Buildings (constructed in the previous year but left void for the 2007 Championships) were finished and fitted out to a high level of specification to create the new Public and Debenture Restaurant and bar facilities with associated kitchens, stores and toilet facilities, the new retail shop and first aid facility. To finish the spaces off with a distinctive "Wimbledon feel" a separate design commission was awarded to theme each of the major spaces, including fitting out showcases with Museum exhibits in the North Building Restaurant.

The Centre Court facilities comprised:

East Building	Ground floor	Tea Lawn (Public self-service buffet)
	First floor	Wingfield Restaurant (Public Waitress Service)
	Second floor	Terrace Restaurant (Debentures' Self-service during The Championships, Museum Cafe and Staff Canteen for other weeks of the year, after 2009)
	Third floor	Champagne Gallery (Debentures' Bar and Lounge) and eight suites
	Fourth floor	The Roof Top (Bar area)

At the south end of the building, a new public toilet facility and Wimbledon Shop was provided.

North Building	First Floor	The Courtside Restaurant (Debentures' waitress service and Champagne Bar)

For the bowl, any existing seats that had been removed for construction operations for the 2008 Championships were refitted, together with 800 of the new specification wider, padded seats to bring the Centre Court up to the new capacity of 15,000.

In Car Park 2 meanwhile, once the steelwork had been moved out, the completion of the infrastructure works (underground pipework, cables, valve pits, and the like) for the future Championships chiller plant area was commenced and completed by May 2008. In addition, a start was made on the future electrical substation building (to be completed in the following year) which would house the electrical supplies and equipment to feed the chillers. Offsite, the AELTC commissioned a further new additional electricity supply, which was installed between December 2007 and May 2008 and comprised a pair of underground High Voltage cables being brought to the site all the way from New Malden.

Alongside all the Centre Court and Car Park 2 works, the construction of new No 2 Court and the completion of the new court surounds to grass courts Nos 7 to 10 started in earnest. Demolition of the Water Tower, maintenance workshops and toilet block in July was followed by the removal of the Croquet

Lawn in early September. The piling and groundworks for the new No 2 Court commenced in August and by May 2008 the new structure for the 4,000 seater Court was essentially complete.

2008–2009

Construction works on Centre Court began immediately following The Championships and all four tower cranes were back up and operational within two weeks. Critical activities were the removal of the seats from the bowl of Centre Court to facilitate the re-erection of the temporary working platform at roof level and the commencement of the fabrication process of the next three roof trusses in front of the Clubhouse. These three trusses (each weighing in excess of 70 tonnes) and the ten end-arm units (each weighing 16 tonnes) were lifted up during the first week of September. This completed the heavy lifting for the five Northern trusses and fabric installation commenced on these trusses early in October. The next three (Southern) trusses were lifted at the end of October and the final two in December.

The mock-up site near Rotherham was decommissioned and the site restored to its original condition, with all testing of the mechanical and electrical systems and controls for the moving trusses having been successfully completed.

Construction works on the new substation building behind the Covered Courts was completed. Delivery of the high voltage switchgear took place in October. This building will deliver power to the moving roof and to the nine large chiller units that supply the chilled water to Centre Court roof for cooling (and thus dehumidifying) the air supply for the bowl when the roof is closed. The new additional high voltage supply to the site, brought in from New Malden, was installed to provide additional power needed to the site's existing network.

Completion of the fitting out of the basement areas of new No. 2 Court continued and the construction of the adjacent first aid and toilet facilities.

The first consignment of the new wider padded seats for Centre Court and No. 2 Court, manufactured in Australia, arrived at Wimbledon early in December. There was phased delivery of all the new seats, with the containers being stored in Car Park 3. The installation of the seats was completed by April.

During early spring, the installation of the Centre Court roof was completed, enabling the testing and commissioning process to be carried out. On Sunday 17th May the new roof and management systems were tested during exhibition matches being played before a capacity crowd of 15,000 people.

The installation of the roof brought the complete modernization programme for the Centre Court Stadium to an end.

The Centre Court seats were re-numbered to a 3 digit system.

The new No. 2 Court and adjacent facilities were available for use. The introduction of this court necessitated re-numbering of the southern courts, with No. 2–No. 11 becoming No. 3–No. 12

Gate Houses 4 and 5, plus the ticket collection and accreditation offices were built and the permanent boundary wall in Church Road between Gate 5 and Gate 8 was in place.

2009–2010

The completion of The Championships saw the commencement of a two-year construction programme to complete the Masterplan Stage 3 works. Old No. 2 Court and the grandstand overlooking old No. 3 Court were demolished along with the Groundsman's Cottage and the remaining sections of old-style boundary wall fencing on Somerset Road. The construction site was essentially in two separate areas, north and south.

On the North site, the new 2000 seater bowl for (new) No. 3 Court and the concrete substructure for (new) No. 4 Court were constructed, but would not be ready for play until the 2011 Championships. Immediately to the south a new Facilities Building was constructed and completed. This building houses stores and workshops essential to the successful running of The Championships at the southern end of the Grounds.

2010–2011

Between the 2010–2011 Championships all the facilities under construction at the southern end of the site were completed; this comprised the construction and fitting out of the new Groundsman's accommodation and workshops, and the new public and marquee guest toilets; the completion of the fitting out to new No. 3 Court, including bowl rim planting and glazed balustrading; and the new seating to No. 3 and No. 4 Courts. At the same time the last remaining section of old boundary wall on Church Road between Gates 5 and 6 was demolished and rebuilt in the new brick panel design. In addition, two new balcony terraces with canopied covers were constructed at the south-west and south-east corners of No. 1 Court to provide additional restaurant and bar facilities for the No. 1 Court Debenture Holders'.

With the No. 3 and No. 4 Courts brought into play the 2011 Championships saw the completion of the original Long Term Plan.

————————————

Wimbledon Master Plan

In late 2011, the Club began a planning process for further development of the grounds over the next decade or so. The objective of this process was to create a Wimbledon Master Plan designed to ensure that the grounds and buildings would continue to provide The Championships with the best possible facilities and environment and, therefore, help to ensure that The Championships would continue to be widely regarded as being the world's premier tennis tournament.

The Wimbledon Master Plan sets out a vision for the future and was presented to Members, the media, neighbours and other interested parties in April 2013. This is designed to meet the expectations and needs of all constituencies including players, spectators, Members, media, staff and contractors and it is expected to provide a blueprint for construction and development work for many years to come.

Programme

The key components of the vision outlined in the Wimbledon Master Plan are: the comprehensive redevelopment of No.1 Court including the installation of a new fixed and retractable roof, expected to be completed by 2019; the construction of new covered courts and new clay courts on the grounds to the west of Somerset Road; a thorough refurbishment of the Millennium Building to provide expanded and improved facilities for players, Members and the press; a major redevelopment of the area to the north of No. 1 Court including new Championships courts; a removal of the clay courts and a reorganisation of The Championships courts at the southern end of the grounds to improve spectator circulation and viewing opportunities; the creation of new accommodation underground for staff and support operations; the refurbishment of the Clubhouse and a commitment to do all this following the aesthetic of 'tennis in an English garden'.

2013–2014

In August 2013 construction began to create new basement space under No. 14 and 15 Courts, to provide accommodation for the ballboys and girls, photographers and an expanded 24 hour restaurant for the Media, ready for the 2015 Championships. Also, construction started to create a tunnel under Somerset Road, directly linking the main grounds to the proposed new covered courts and new clay court area. The refurbishment of the Clubhouse began in September and was officially opened on 3rd April.

2014–2015

The re-introduction of No. 14 and No. 15 Courts brought the total number of courts available during The Championships up to the normal number of 19. Basement accommodation was provided for Ball Boys and Girls, Photographers and an expanded 24-hour Media Restaurant. Consequently, as a result, the space freed up in the Millennium Building was used to provide much needed stretching areas, medical facilities, massage space and ice baths, as well as a larger lounge for the players.

The tunnel under Somerset Road was completed, but not opened.

The Aorangi Pavilion has been turned into a dedicated player facility. Improvements include locker rooms doubled in size, a new restaurant, a lift to make the building accessible on both levels, new creche facilities, separate toilets for guests and a new warm-up space at the rear.

In Aorangi Park a long-term temporary building has been constructed and will accommodate the Service Stewards, LSS Cleaners and G4S Security Staff during The Championships. Outside The Championships this area will be used for house staff working on the No. 1 Court project.

The project to install new wrought iron railings along Church Road was completed.

Miscellany

Open Tennis

The expansion of air travel in the fifties resulted in a great increase in the number of foreign players at Wimbledon and other tournaments throughout the world, but with this surge came an epidemic of what had become known as "shamateurism" – the receiving by amateur players of financial assistance in excess of amounts permitted by the International Tennis Federation.

The need for reform was evident. The initiative came from The All England Lawn Tennis Club, led by the then Chairman, Herman David, who in late 1959 put forward a proposal to The Lawn Tennis Association that The Championships be made open to all players. In July 1960 the ITF rejected this move and several years followed in which argument persisted at all levels of the game. In 1964 the Club tried to persuade the LTA unilaterally to declare The Championships "open" but support was not forthcoming.

In August 1967 an invitation tournament for men (sponsored by the BBC to mark the introduction of colour television) was held on the Centre Court, with eight players taking part – all professionals. Most of these players had won honours at Wimbledon in their amateur days but had forfeited the right to play there on turning professional. The segregation of the two categories was soon to come to an end.

In December that year the Annual General Meeting of the LTA voted overwhelmingly to admit players of all categories to Wimbledon and other tournaments in Britain. At a special meeting held in Paris on 30th March, 1968, the ITF, faced with a *fait accompli*, yielded and allowed each nation to determine its own legislation regarding amateur and professional players. Three months later the first Open Wimbledon, offering £26,150 in prize money, was staged. A new era had begun.

Oxford University Doubles Championship, 1879–1883

When early in 1884 The All England Lawn Tennis Club decided to add a Gentlemen's Doubles Championship to their programme the Oxford University Lawn Tennis Club offered to transfer their 60 guinea Challenge Cup to the new event. The Committee were pleased to accept and agreed that the inscription on the trophy should be altered as little as possible.

The O.U.L.T.C. had instituted a gentlemen's doubles event for the "Oxford University Challenge Cup for Pairs" in 1879 when, at the new Norham Gardens, 14 *club* pairs contested the matches, each over the best of *seven* sets.

The following year 12 pairs competed, but in 1881 and 1882, when eight pairs participated, the matches were reduced to the best of five sets. In 1883 the number of entries dwindled to six, but due to withdrawals only three matches were played to settle the issue. Interest in the event had considerably waned, with the leading players expressing the opinion they could not justify spending several days just playing doubles. Consequently the University discontinued the tournament.

Apart from the transference of the trophy there is no connection between the Oxford event and The Championship at Wimbledon, although for sentimental reasons the surviving champions from Oxford were presented with a commemorative medal at the Jubilee Championships in 1926. Also, the Wimbledon Programme traditionally lists the champions and runners-up from Oxford.

All England Championships

Sometimes the title "All England Championships" is incorrectly given to the events at Wimbledon, because of the promotion of the properly named "The Lawn Tennis Championships" by the All England Lawn Tennis Club.

However, long before the Ladies' Doubles and Mixed Doubles Championships were inaugurated at Wimbledon in 1913, All England Championship titles existed elsewhere. The All England Ladies' Doubles Championship was held annually from 1884 to 1953 in conjunction with the Derbyshire Championships at Buxton and the All England Mixed Doubles Championship was held annually from 1888 to 1938 in association with the Northern Championships, staged alternately at Liverpool and Manchester.

The Ladies' Doubles event from 1899 to 1907 and the Mixed Doubles event from 1900 to 1912, held at Wimbledon, both had non-Championship status and were used mainly to augment the programme.

Junior Championships

The Junior Wimbledon Championships have been staged on grass during the second week of The Championships from 1947 to date, originally as an invitational event, but from 1975 upgraded to Championship status. Quite often this event is confused with the Junior Championships of Great Britain (under 18), which was staged on the hard courts of The All England Lawn Tennis Club from 1924 to 1939 and 1946 to 1990 (early September up to 1981 and April thereafter). From 1970 the event was generally known as the British Junior Hard Court Championships. The tournament was staged under the management of the Lawn Tennis Association.

The former event is quite often referred to as "Junior Wimbledon" which is acceptable, but to refer to the latter event by the same title is confusing and incorrect.

Challenge Round

From 1878 to 1921 the holder of the Gentlemen's Singles title did not compete until the Challenge Round, when he met the winner of the All Comers' Singles to decide The Championship. When the holder did not defend his title the winner of the All Comers' Singles automatically became champion. The same system applied to the Ladies' Singles and Gentlemen's Doubles from 1886 to 1921, but not the Ladies' Doubles and Mixed Doubles, which both commenced in 1913.

In 1912 the United States LTA abolished the Challenge Round system in the Gentlemen's Singles at the American Championships held in the autumn.

During the following winter The All England Lawn Tennis Club conducted a poll amongst the leading players of the day, which showed that 68 were in favour of playing through and 48 retaining the Challenge Round. The Committee decided that the majority was not sufficient to justify a change.

However, another poll carried out in 1921 showed that the numbers were 91 in favour and 27 to the contrary. The margin was considered large enough to bring about an alteration and with the consent of the holders, the new system was introduced for the 1922 Championships.

The author wishes to acknowledge the assistance of Audrey Snell, Assistant Librarian at the Wimbledon Lawn Tennis Museum, for her work with the typing and proof-reading.

Printed by Remous Ltd., Milborne Port, Sherborne, Dorset

Index

THE CHAMPIONSHIPS
WIMBLEDON

TO THE QUEUE
TO CAR PARK 10
TO SOUTHFIELDS

COMPETITORS'
PRACTICE
COURTS

CHURCH ROAD

CAR PARK 4

FANZONE
PRACTICE COURT VIEWING

ST MARY'S
GATE

CAR PARK 8

LARGE SCREEN TV
AORANGI TERRACE
TICKET RESALE
ACCESS TO AORANGI FOOD COURT
AORANGI CAFÉ

BRITISH TENNIS
MEMBERSHIP SUITE

ST MARY'S
WALK

No.1
COURT

CONSERVATORY KITCHEN
FOOD VILLAGE

LOWER LEVEL:
PHARMACY
NEWSAGENT

ROSE ARBOUR
THE AA
TO
WIMBLEDON
COMMON

SOMERSET RD

MATCH STATISTICS
OFFICIAL BANKING PARTNER

HSBC BANK
AELTC OFFICES

BROADCAST
CENTRE

NEWSTEAD WAY

14   15   16   17

NORTH CONCOURSE

NON-TICKET HOLDERS'
ENTRANCE (VIA THE QUEUE)

MUSEUM (VIA WIMBLEDON SHOP)

PRESS CENTRE

CAR PARK 3

COMPETITORS' COMPLEX

LIFT

ST MARY'S WALK

FRED
PERRY
STATUE

LEVEL 5

CENTRE
COURT

LIFT

TAXIS TO SOUTHFIELDS
(NORTH)

WINGFIELD RESTAURANT

LONG BAR & LAWN BUFFET

TEA LAWN

TICKET COLLECTION OFFICE

MEMBERS' ENCLOSURE

LOST PROPERTY

TAXIS TO WIMBLEDON (SOUTH)

No.3

SOUTH CONCOURSE

4   5   6   7

8   9   10   11

MEETING TREE

LAST 8 CLUB

CAR PARK 5

CAFÉ PERGOLA

THE BASELINE

CAR PARK 6

ST MARY'S WALK

12

No.2

CAR PARK 1

PARK & RIDE
VICTORIA,
MARBLE ARCH
& ST PANCRAS

MARRYAT ROAD

PLAY TENNIS

WIMBLEDON

THE BAKERY

COURT BUFFET

PRIVATE MARQUEES

11a

11   8,9

CHURCH ROAD

SOMERSET ROAD

TO WIMBLEDON
AND VILLAGE

NORTH

YARDS   50   100

AS AT JANUARY 2015

KEY

UNRESERVED SEATING		FIRST AID	
TOILETS FOR THOSE IN THE QUEUE		INFORMATION	
NON-TICKET HOLDERS' ENTRANCE VIA THE TURNSTILES		LEFT LUGGAGE	
TICKET HOLDERS' ENTRANCES		MUSEUM	
PRIVATE AND CONTRACTORS' ENTRANCES		PRIVATE MARQUEES	
DEBENTURE ENTRANCE		RECOMMENDED ROUTES FOR WHEELCHAIR USERS	
DEBENTURE FACILITIES		REFRESHMENTS	
ATM		STEPS	
BANDSTAND		TAXI STAND	
DESIGNATED WHEELCHAIR VIEWING – AORANGI TERRACE		TELEPHONE	
		THE WIMBLEDON SHOP	
DRINKING FOUNTAIN		TOILETS	
		USED TENNIS BALL KIOSK	